NATURAL SCIENCES IN AMERICA

NATURAL SCIENCES IN AMERICA

Advisory Editor
KEIR B. STERLING

Editorial Board
EDWIN H. COLBERT
EDWARD GRUSON
ERNST MAYR
RICHARD G. VAN GELDER

BIRDS OF THE NORTHWEST

By ELLIOTT COUES

ARNO PRESS
A New York Times Company
New York, N. Y. • 1974

Reprint Edition 1974 by Arno Press Inc.

Reprinted from a copy in the State Historical
  Society of Wisconsin Library

NATURAL SCIENCES IN AMERICA
ISBN for complete set: 0-405-05700-8
See last pages of this volume for titles.

Manufactured in the United States of America

————◆————

Library of Congress Cataloging in Publication Data

Coues, Elliott, 1842-1899.
    Birds of the Northwest.

    (Natural sciences in America)
    Reprint of the 1874 ed. published by the U. S. Govt.
Print. Off., Washington, which was issued as Miscellaneous publications.no. 3 of the U. S. Geological Survey
of the Territories.
    1. Birds--United States. I. Title. II. Series.
III. Series: United States. Geological and Geographical Survey of the Territories. Miscellaneous publications, no. 3.
QL682.C68 1974   598.2'978   73-17815
ISBN 0-405-05731-8

DEPARTMENT OF THE INTERIOR.

UNITED STATES GEOLOGICAL SURVEY OF THE TERRITORIES.

F. V. HAYDEN, U. S. GEOLOGIST-IN-CHARGE.

MISCELLANEOUS PUBLICATIONS—No. 3.

BIRDS OF THE NORTHWEST:

A HAND-BOOK

OF

THE ORNITHOLOGY

OF THE

REGION DRAINED BY THE MISSOURI RIVER AND ITS TRIBUTARIES.

By ELLIOTT COUES,

CAPTAIN AND ASSISTANT SURGEON U. S. ARMY.

WASHINGTON:

GOVERNMENT PRINTING OFFICE.

1874.

TABLE OF CONTENTS.

INTRODUCTORY.

[*Dr. Coues to Dr. Hayden.*]

FORT RANDALL, DAKOTA, *May* 13, 1873.

SIR : Herewith I transmit, in compliance with your request, for pub-lication under the auspices of the Geological Survey of the Territories, a Work on the Ornithology of the Missouri Region, on which, as you are aware, I have been long engaged, its completion having been delayed by various circumstances needless to detail. In this connection, how-ever, I may refer to the circumstances under which the work originated, in explanation of its present plan and scope. This is a matter with which you are yourself already familiar, but one which may be presented to answer the purposes of a preface which would otherwise be required.

The basis of the present volume is mainly an unpublished report which I prepared at Washington, in the year 1862, upon the ornitholo-gical collections made by yourself and Mr. G. H. Trook as Naturalists of the Expedition under Captain (now General) W. F. Raynolds, United States Engineers. The specimens submitted to me for elaboration were subjected to careful examination, and found to represent a decided ad-vance in the knowledge then possessed of the geographical distribution of the species in the region under consideration. The interest attaching to this series of specimens, as an element in the history of Western Or-nithology, renders it advisable, in my judgment, to preserve throughout the present volume the "List of Specimens" which were formally tab-ulated* for the original report.

In 1867, while stationed at Columbia, South Carolina, I desired to recall my MSS. in order to retouch them according to the steady advance of our knowledge of the subject during the intervening five years. On this occasion it seemed advisable to extend the article to embrace the ornithological results which you had obtained as Naturalist of the previ-ous Explorations, conducted in 1856–'57 in the region of the Upper Missouri, Yellowstone, and Platte Rivers, by Lieutenant (now General) G. K. Warren, United States Engineers. Such addition would not only

---

* In these tables, the *first* column gives the number which the specimen bears on the register of the National Museum at Washington ; the *second*, the "original" or collect-or's number ; *third*, the locality ; *fourth*, sex ; *fifth* and *sixth*, date of collection, and by whom collected ; *seventh, eighth, ninth*, measurements (upon collector's authority) of, respectively, total length, extent of wings, and length of wing from carpus to apex of longest primary. To economize space, these several headings have been omitted from the text, with explanation in this place, which will prevent misunderstanding.

present, in connected form, your labors in the field of ornithology, but would illustrate more clearly the ornithological characteristics of the region in question, by affording the means of comparing and contrasting the distribution of species in the several special areas. The specimens collected on these Expeditions having been incorporated by Prof. S. F. Baird* in his general Report upon the Ornithology of the various Pacific Railroad Explorations, in 1858, and having been made the subject of a Report, with field-notes, by yourself,† in 1861, are not tabulated in the present volume, but will be found catalogued by the National Museum number, with indication of locality where obtained.

At a second interval of five years, namely, in 1872, you intimated to me your desire to publish a treatise on the Ornithology of the Western Territories you had then explored, suggesting that the still unpublished report I had long since made to you might be available in substance for this purpose, in connection with an elaboration I was desired to make of the material collected under your direction in various parts of the West, during 1870‡ and 1872,§ by Mr. J. Stevenson, Mr. H. D. Smith, and Mr. C. H. Merriam. Without instituting comparisons between these collections, all of which proved to be of interest and importance, I know that I simply express your own convictions in alluding to the unflagging energy, zeal, and perseverance which have marked Mr. Stevenson's course during his long and continuous association with you in developing the Zoology of the West. Having examined the collections for my own information, and being then stationed, as I am now, in the region under consideration, where I could supplement your results by my own personal observations, I willingly undertook the task. The copy now furnished you for publication by the Survey is the result. It is believed to be fairly abreast of the present state of the science; and the hope is indulged that, during its passage through the press, opportunity may offer of bringing it up to the very date of issue, by incorporation of the latest published items bearing on the subject in hand.

---

* Reports of Explorations and Surveys to ascertain the most practicable and economical Route for a Railroad from the Mississippi River to the Pacific Ocean. Made under direction of the Secretary of War, in 1853–'56, according to acts of Congress of March 3, 1853, May 31, 1854, and August 5, 1854. Vol. IX. Birds: By Spencer F. Baird, Assistant Secretary Smithsonian Institution, with the co-operation of John Cassin and George N. Lawrence. Washington, D. C., 1858. [Quoted in the present volume as "Bd., B. N. A."]

† On the Geology and Natural History of the Upper Missouri, being the substance of a Report made to Lieutenant G. K. Warren, T. E., U. S. A. By Dr. F. V. Hayden, Surgeon and Geologist of the Expedition to the Upper Missouri and Yellowstone, under command of Lieut. Warren.—Transactions of the American Philosophical Society, Vol. XII, Art. i, pt. iii, Chap. xvi, pp. 151–176. 4to. Philadelphia, 1862. [Quoted in the present volume as "Hayd. Rep."]

‡ A List of Mammals and Birds collected in Wyoming Territory by Mr. H. D. Smith and Mr. James Stevenson, during the Expedition of 1870. < Rep. U. S. Geol. Surv. Ter. 1870, pp. 461–466. 8vo. Washington, 1871.

§ Report on Mammals and Birds of the Expedition [of 1872]. By C. H. Merriam. < Sixth Ann. Rep. U. S. Geol. Surv. Ter. 1872, pp. 661–715. 8vo. Washington, 1873.

The scope and plan of the proposed work having been left entirely to my discretion, you may reasonably desire to be informed in advance of its character. To bring the work within the compass of a single volume, and, particularly, to give it a distinctive character apart from the several North American Ornithologies published or in progress,* it seemed necessary to restrict its scope to some particular portion of the West. The Missouri Region, in its broadest sense, as embracing the whole water-shed of that great river and its tributaries, was selected in illustration of the "Birds of the Northwest"—both as affording a practically convenient limitation, and as being the scene of most of your ornithological field-work, as well as of some of my own. All the species at present known to inhabit this region (representing a large majority of the birds of North America) are given; and I have not hesitated, moreover, to introduce certain others, some notice of which seemed desirable to complete an account of particular groups. Three families, namely, *Laridæ*, *Colymbidæ*, and *Podicipidæ*, which have been with me the subjects of special study, are treated monographically, as far as the North American genera and species are concerned.

The birds of the Missouri Region, like most others of North America, having been repeatedly and sufficiently described, text of this technical kind has been omitted as a rule to make room for fresher matter of more general interest. In some cases, however, I describe particular plumages not yet well known, while throughout the monographs above mentioned, descriptions both of external features and anatomical characters will be found in detail. For other descriptions I must refer to general treatises.

The matter of geographical distribution receives the special consideration which its importance warrants. Correct indication of *habitat* is one of the most essential items in the history of a species. The distribution of the species, their residence or migration, and their abundance or scarcity, are worked out, not only within the region indicated, but throughout the general area they inhabit.

The study of these important points having necessarily involved a protracted examination of the general ornithological literature bearing upon this subject, one result of such investigation has been the collation of very extensive synonymatic lists. Nothing like this amount of bibliographical matter has before been presented in any work upon American Ornithology. The synonymy, as simply such, is believed to be very nearly complete, while the many thousand additional references furnish an extensive index to the literature of the subject. The labor of such compilation does not appear upon the surface, and is only mentioned in the sincere hope that, once accomplished, the weary drudgery of future workers in the same vein may be materially lightened. The quotations have been personally made or verified, in all cases in which this was

---

* The allusion is here to the magnificent general work, in course of preparation by Baird, Brewer, and Ridgway.

reasonably practicable, though many others have been taken at second hand, upon the simple principle that even such are better than none at all. Synonyms and references for which I am unwilling to become responsible, are placed between quotation marks; I answer for the rest, being satisfied of their general accuracy, though no one is more fully aware than I am of the typographical difficulties in the way of printing numerous references in which figures are concerned.

It must not be hastily inferred that these synonymatic lists have no other value than that which attaches to them as bibliographical indices or mere references to the published records. They not only serve as a guide to research, and as vouchers for facts of geographical distribution, but they also have a direct bearing upon the important matter of nomenclature, fixity and precision of which are nowhere more desirable than in the natural sciences, where names become in a great measure the exponents of biological generalizations. A preliminary step required for the establishment of nomenclature upon a firm and enduring basis, is searching scrutiny of the literature of the subject, not only in order to sift out synonyms and to pin down names to the species they represent, but also to ascertain which one, of the number which have been affixed to most species, has the priority which entitles it to recognition and adoption according to the established usages of naturalists. This is a matter which repays the uninviting labor bestowed upon a task otherwise one of little profit and no attractions. The subject has formed a part of my desk-work for several years, and I may congratulate myself that some of the results reached are at length brought to light under very favorable auspices.

With this matter of nomenclature questions of classification are inseparably connected in existing methods of zoological notation. As you need .not be informed, no leading ornithologists are as yet agreed in detail upon a system of classification; nor is there any probability that such agreement will soon be brought about. That we are, however, gradually approaching this desirable consummation, is shown by the very general acceptance of many groups established of late years upon investigation of structural characters which were long in receiving the attention their importance demanded, as well as in an equally general admission of a certain sequence of these groups. The questions which remain open have less concern with the definition of groups, excepting some of those among *Passeres*, than with their value in the taxonomic scale. It has become evident that certain old "orders" of birds cannot endure in the light of recent discoveries; and that the *Raptores*, which long headed the system, must give way to the more highly-organized *Oscines*. It is most probable, according to present indications, that those remarkable extinct forms, the *Archæopteryx* and *Ichthyornis*, represent one primary group of *Aves* (*Saururæ*); that the struthious birds constitute another (*Ratitæ*); and that all remaining birds compose a third (*Carinatæ*). These divisions may be rated either as subclasses or as orders; to consider them as of only ordinal grade, would probably be to correlate them most nearly with the recognized orders in other classes of Vertebrates. Upon such basis the *Carinatæ* are susceptible of division into a large number—some fifteen or more—of groups of approximately equivalent value, to be rated as suborders or superfamilies.

I merely touch upon this subject in the present connection to prevent any misunderstanding of my views which might result from the presence on my pages of groups conventionally denominated "Orders" and "Suborders." A work of this character being no occasion for the discussion of taxonomic questions, or the remodeling of a system of classification, I preferred to retain without change a scheme, the main features of which have met with general approval. The classification adopted in the present volume is that presented in my late work,* while the nomenclature is identical, excepting in a few isolated instances where change was absolutely required, with that of the same work and of my forthcoming List.† This uniformity seemed me more desirable for present purposes than the good that might result from changes that, nevertheless, may hereafter become necessary.

In the general text of the volume it has been my aim to be brief, or even silent, in the cases of the best known Eastern birds, in order to devote more space to the history of species upon which less has already been written. Most of the biographical matter rests upon my personal observations; but where these are deficient or wanting, the experiences of others are freely collated if desired. In few instances is the complete history of a species presented; to do this systematically and satisfactorily for all the birds given in the work, would require more time than I have had to bestow, and several volumes instead of one. In preparing simply a "Hand-book," I have been controlled by circumstances which have not been favorable to unity of plan, and I present it rather as a contribution of material for future elaboration, than as in itself a completed and final result.

At risk of unduly protracting this communication, I wish to indicate some of the leading ornithological features of the region under consideration, and to present briefly certain general conclusions.

The Missouri water-shed represents the greater portion of the North American Middle Faunal Province as defined by Professor Baird. Belonging distinctively here, it nevertheless extends to the border of the Western Province, along the main divide of the mountains, and the other direction largely overlaps the boundary of the Eastern Province, as practically indicated rather by the irregular limits of continuous

---

* Key to North American Birds: Containing a concise account of every species of living and fossil bird at present known from the continent north of the Mexican and United States boundary. Illustrated with 6 steel plates and upward of 250 wood-cuts. Imp. 8vo. pp. 361. Salem: Naturalists' Agency. 1872.

† Field Ornithology: Comprising a Manual of Instruction for Procuring, Preparing, and Preserving Birds, and a Check-list of North American Birds. 8vo. pp. i–iv, 1–116 and 1–137. Salem: Naturalists' Agency. [In press.]

arboreal vegetation than by any meridian of longitude.   It includes Nebraska, the greater portion of Dakota, Montana, Wyoming, Colorado, Kansas and Missouri, portions of Iowa and Minnesota, together with a small area in the British Provinces near the head-waters of the Sas-katchewan, where the *Coteau de Missouri*, running obliquely northwest-ward, crosses the parallel of 49° N.   Much of the western portions is mountainous, as in Montana, Wyoming and Colorado, the easternmost ele-vations of any note being the Black Hills, lying across the boundary of Wyoming and Dakota.   Extensive areas are cut up into *Mauvaises Terres*, or "Bad Lands."   Most of the region, however, is the great elevated central plateau of the continent, of low mean annual rain-fall, and con-sequently treeless, or nearly so, and more or less sterile, supporting for the most part a comparatively meagre or stunted vegetation.   Trees are in effect restricted to the mountainous tracts and to a slender precarious fringe along most of the larger streams.

It results from these physical conditions that the Avi-fauna proper of the region is not rich.   Notwithstanding the great extent of country, there is no single species absolutely confined to it.   There are, however, several abundant and generally diffused species which may be held by this circumstance to be characteristic.   Such are *Eremophila leucolæma* (in the breeding season), *Neocorys spraguei*, *Centronyx bairdii*, *Coturni-culus lecontii*, *Zonotrichia harrisi*, *Calamospiza bicolor*, *Plectrophanes ornatus* and *P. maccownii*, *Falco richardsoni*, *Pediœcetes columbianus*, and some others less distinctively of the same category.   The great number of species treated in the present volume is due to accessions from both of the contiguous Faunal Provinces above mentioned, as well as of those species of general diffusion over the continent, as most *Raptores*, *Limi-colæ*, and *Lamellirostres*.   It results from the extensive overlapping of the Missouri Region upon the Eastern Province, that in effect nearly all the birds of Eastern North America are represented fairly within this area, the exceptions being chiefly the marine Atlantic species, and a few others peculiar to the South Atlantic and Gulf States.   The low position of Saint Louis in the Mississippi Valley, which affords a ready approach from the south, renders it probable that some of these last named, not yet known to proceed so far north, may finally be found within Missouri limits.

In discussing the western limits of eastern species, it is not easy to overestimate the effect of the larger streams, and especially of the great artery itself—the Missouri—in prolonging au eastern bird-fauna *in streaks* to or toward the Rocky Mountains.   These streams, with a general east-and-west course, and with their usual fringe of trees, often the only timber of various large areas, form attractive highways of mi-gration, as it were, along which avenues birds push on beyond their general limit.   From this it results that the boundary line of the Middle and Eastern Provinces in these latitudes is a zigzag of interdigitations.

The general *facies* of the birds of this region may be summed in a word. They are characterized by a *pallor* of plumage, the direct result of the low annual rain-fall, in accordance with now generally recognized laws which have been ably elucidated by Allen, Baird, and others.

There only remains the grateful duty of recording here an acknowledgment of favors received in the preparation of this work. My pleasure might have been increased by mention of various other names, had not the circumstances under which the book has been written deprived me in great measure of the desired and freely offered cooperation of several kind friends. I am particularly indebted to Mr. T. M. Trippe, of Colorado, for a valuable paper on the birds of that Territory, which I have incorporated with my pages. My thanks are likewise due to Mr. J. A. Allen for various interesting communications based upon his original observations in different parts of the West; to Mr. J. Stevenson, to whose collections I have frequent occasion to allude; and to Mr. T. G. Gentry and Dr. J. M. Wheaton. In the labor of compiling synonymy I have been materially assisted by some manuscript records of quotations which Professor Baird very kindly placed at my service.

I cannot close this communication without an expression of the obligation under which other ornithologists beside myself rest to you for the very material services you have rendered to Ornithology—both by your successful personal labors and by your able direction of other means at your command—services the more commendable in the fact that they have been gratuitously rendered apart from your own special lines of scientific inquiry. I do not hesitate to say that no one, not an ornithologist, has contributed more to the advance of our knowledge of the birds of the West.

I am, Sir, &c.,

ELLIOTT COUES.

Dr. F. V. HAYDEN,
    U. S. Geologist, &c., &c., &c.,
        In charge Geological Survey of the Territories,
            Washington, D. C.

ORDER PASSERES: PERCHERS.

SUBORDER OSCINES: SINGING BIRDS.

Family TURDIDÆ : Thrushes.

Subfamily TURDINÆ: *Typical Thrushes.*

TURDUS MIGRATORIUS, Linn.

Robin.

Turdus migratorius, LINN., Syst. Nat. i, 1766, 292.—FORST., Phil. Trans. lxii, 1772, 382.—
VIEILL., Ois. Am. Sept. ii, 1807, 5, pls. 60, 61.—WILS., Am. Orn. i, 1808, 35, pl. 2,
f. 2.—BP., Syn. 1828, 75.—NUTT., Man. i, 1832, 338.—AUD., Orn. Biog. ii, 1832,
190; v, 1839, 442; pl. 131.—AUD., Syn. 1839, 89.—AUD., B. Am. iii, 1841, 14, pl.
142.—BD., B. N. A. 1858, 218.—COOP. & SUCK., Nat. Hist. Wash. Ter. 1860,
172.—HAYD., Rep. 1862, 159.—BD., Rev. 1864, 28.—COOP., B. Cal. i, 1870, 7.—
MAYN., B. Fla. 1872, 2.—COUES, Key N. A. Birds, 1872, 71, fig. 13.—And of
authors generally.
Merula migratoria, SWS. & RICH., Fn. Bor.-Am. ii, 1831, 176.
Turdus canadensis, BRISS., Orn. ii, 1760, 225.
Turdus confinis, BD., Rev. 1864, 29. (Var., Cape St. Lucas.)

Hab.—Continent of North America, and portions of Mexico. West Indies, rarely.
Accidental in Europe. (*Gould*, pl. 74; *Naum.*, pl. 362.)

List of specimens.

| 19191 | 173 | Pumpkin Butte. | .... | .... | F. V. Hayden. | 9.50 | 16.00 | 5.00 |
| 19192 | .... | Wind River.... | ♂ | May 28, 1860 | ...... do ..... | 10.25 | 17.00 | 5.75 |

Lieutenant Warren's Expedition.—4705, Blackbird Hill; 5281, Fort Pierre; 5282, Yellowstone River.
Later Expeditions.—54324, 60935-38, 61161, Wyoming (*Schmidt & Stevenson*); 61650,
62275-77, Utah, Idaho, and Wyoming (*Merriam*).

Occurs in suitable localities throughout the Missouri region; breeds;
resident, but most abundant in spring and autumn, during the migrations.

TURDUS NÆVIUS, Gm.

Varied Thrush; Oregon Robin.

Turdus nævius, GM., Syst. Nat. i, 1788, 817.—VIEILL., Ois. Am. Sept. ii, 1807, 10.—AUD.,
Orn. Biog. iv, 1838, 489; v, 1839, 284; pls. 369, 433.—AUD., Syn. 1839, 89.—AUD.,
B. Am. iii, 1841, 22, pl. 143.—CAB., Journ. Bost. Soc. iii, 1848, 17 (New Jersey,
not Boston, Mass.).—BP., Consp. 1850, 271.—LAWR., Ann. Lyc. N. Y. v, 1852,
221 (New York).—SCL., P. Z. S. 1857, 4; 1859, 331.—NEWB., P. R. R. Rep.
vi, 1857, 81.—BD., B. N. A. 1858, 219.—HEERM., P. R. R. Rep. x, 1859, part vi,
45.—BD., Zool. Ives's Expd. 1860, 5 (Colorado Valley).—COOP. & SUCK., N. H.
Wash. Ter. 1860, 172.—BD., Rev. Am. Birds, 1864, 32.—ALLEN, Pr. Ess. Inst. v,
1864, 82 (New Jersey).—LORD, Pr. Roy. Art. Inst. Woolwich, iv, 1864, 114.—
LAWR., Ann. Lyc. N. Y. viii, 1866, 281 (New York).—COUES, Pr. Phila. Acad.
1866, 68 (Colorado Valley).—COUES, Pr. Ess. Inst. v, 1868, 312.—ALLEN, Am.
Nat. iii, 1869, 572 (Ipswich, Mass., Dec., 1864).—COOP., Am. Nat. iii, 1869, 31
(Cœur d'Alene Mts., Montana).—TURN., B. E. Pa. 1869, 41 (New Jersey).—
DALL & BANN., Trans. Chic. Acad. i, 1869, 276 (Alaska).—MAYN., Guide, 1870,
89 (Ipswich, Mass.).—COOP., B. Cal. i, 1870, 10.—COUES, Key, 1872, 72.

Orpheus meruloides, Sw. & Rich., F. B. A. ii, 1831, 187, pl. 38 (Fort Franklin, lat. 65¼°).
" *Mimus meruloides*, Bp."
" *Ixoreus nævius*, Bp."
Hesperocichla nævia, Bd.

Hab.—Rocky Mountains to the Pacific, from the Yukon to the Colorado. Winters in California, Oregon, and Washington. Mackenzie's River. Montana (*Cooper*). Accidental in New Jersey (*Cabot*), near New York City (*Lawrence*), and at Ipswich, Mass. (*Coues, fide Allen*).

Although this species, which was not obtained by either expedition, is essentially a west-coast bird, it is known to occur further eastward, and that not only in the exceptional instances above quoted; for Dr. Cooper found it "common" near the summit of the Cœur d'Alène Mountains in September, frequenting dark coniferous regions, as in its usual Pacific habitat. Mr. Dall found it nesting on the Nulato River, May 22. "The nest was built in the midst of a large bunch of rubbish in a clump of willow, about two feet from the ground, and close to the river bank. Eggs bluish, speckled with brown." The eggs, in this instance, were only two, but probably the full complement had not been laid; they usually number four or five, and measure about 1.10 by 0.80 inches.

TURDUS MUSTELINUS, Gm.

Wood Thrush.

Turdus mustelinus, Gm., S. N. i, 1788, 817.—Lath., Ind. Orn. ii, 1790, 331.—Vieill., Ois. Am. Sept. ii, 1807, 6, pl. 62.—Bp., Syn. 1828, 75.—Nutt., i, 1832, 343.—Aud., Orn. Biog. i, 1832, 372; v, 1839, 446; pl. 73.—Aud., Syn. 1839, 90.—Aud., B. Am. iii, 1841, 24, pl. 144.—Scl., P. Z. S. 1856, 294; 1859, 325.—Bd., B. N. A. 1858, 212.— Hayd., Rep. 158.—Bd., Rev. 1864, 13.—McIlwraith, Pr. Ess. Inst. v, 1866, 84 (Hamilton, C. W.).—Sumich., Mem. Bost. Soc. i, 1869, 543 (Vera Cruz, transient).—Allen, Bull. M. C. Z. 1872, 124, 173 (Kansas).—Coues, Key, 1872, 72.
Merula mustelina, Rich., List, 1837, p. —.
Turdus melodus, Wils., Am. Orn. i, 1808, 35, pl. 2, f. 1.
Turdus densus, Bp., Comptes Rendus, xxviii, 1853, 2.
Hylocichla mustelina, Bd.

Hab.—Eastern United States, north to New England and Canada West; not recorded from Maine; west to Dakota; south to Central America in winter. Breeds throughout its United States range. Winters on the Gulf coast (*Audubon*). Occasional in the West Indies (Cuba, *D'Orbigny*, La Sagra's Cuba, Ois. 1840, 49). Bermuda.
Not obtained by Captain Raynolds' Expedition.
Lieutenant Warren's Expedition.—4650, Fort Pierre, Dakota.

This distinctively eastern species ascends the Missouri as far at least as Fort Pierre, and is reported by Dr. Hayden as being quite numerous along the wooded river bottoms. Mr. Allen found it "exceedingly abundant" in Eastern Kansas, but not beyond.

As is well known, the nest of this species is saddled on the bough of a bush, shrub, or low tree, and has mud in its composition; other material, outside, is grass and leaves, the lining being usually fibrous rootlets. The eggs are four or five in number, pale greenish-blue, rarely, if ever, speckled; they measure 0.95 by 0.65 inches.

TURDUS PALLASI, Cab.

Hermit Thrush.

a. *pallasi*.

Turdus pallasi, Cab., Wieg. Arch. i, 1847, 205; Mus. Hein. i, 1850, 5; J. f. O. 1855, 470 (Cuba).—Bd., B. N. A. 1858, 212.—Scl., P. Z. S. 1859, 325; Cat. 1862, 2.—Coues & Prent., Smiths. Rep. for 1861 (1862), 404 (D. C., migr.).—Verr., Pr. Ess. Inst. iii, 1862, 146 (Maine, abundant in summer).—Boardm., Pr. Bost. Soc. ix,

1862, 124 (Maine, breeding).—VERR., *ibid.* 137 (Anticosti).—ALLEN, Pr. Ess. Inst. iv, 1864, 56 (Massachusetts, migratory).—LAWR., Ann. Lyc. N. Y. viii, 1866, 281.—McILWRAITH, Pr. Ess. Inst. v, 1866, 84 (Canada West, migratory).— COUES, *ibid.* vi, 1868, 266.—COUES, Pr. Bost. Soc. xii, 1868, 106 (South Carolina, common in winter, October to March).- TURN., B. E. Pa. 1869, 14 (chiefly migratory, some wintering).—RIDGW., Pr. Phila. Acad. 1869, 128.—ALLEN, Mem. Bost. Soc. i, 1868, 514 (Illinois).—MAYN., Guide; 1870, 89 (Southern New England, until November).—MAYN., Pr. Bost. Soc. xiv, 1871 (breeding, Maine and New Hampshire).—ALLEN, Bull. M. C. Z. ii, 1871, 254 (Florida, in winter); iii, 1872, 173 (Kansas and Colorado).—MAYN., B. Fla. 1872, 8.—COUES, Key, 1872, 72.—SNOW, 13 B. Kas. 1873, 4.

Turdus solitarius, WILS., Am. Orn. v, 1812, 95 (not of Linnæus; not the plate 43, f. 2, which is *swainsoni*).—BP., Comp. List, 1838, 17.—AUD., Syn. 1839, 91.—AUD., B. Am. iii, 1841, 29, pl. 146.—BREWER, Pr. Bost. Soc. 1844, 191.—BP., Consp. Av. i, 1850, 270.—WOODH., Sitgr. Rep. 1853, 72 (Texas and New Mexico).—PUTN., Pr. Ess. Inst. i, 1856, 209 (Massachusetts, occasional in winter).—SCL., P. Z. S. 1857, 212.—TRIPPE, Pr. Ess. Inst. vi, 1871 (Minnesota, migratory).

Merula solitaria, SWS. & RICH., F. B. A. ii, 1831, 184, pl. "35," by error for 37.—VIEILL., Ois. A. S. ii, 1807, 7, pl. 63 (in part).—BREWER, Pr. Bost. Soc. 1844, 191.

Turdus minor, BP., Journ. Phila. Acad. iv, 1824, 33.—BP., Syn. 1828, 75.—NUTT., Man. i, 1832, 346.—AUD., Orn. Biog. i, 1832, 303, pl. 58; v, 1839, 445.—GIRAUD, B. L. Isl. 1844, 90.—(?) REINH., Birds Greenland, 6 (" *T. minor,* Gm.")

" *Turdus guttatus,* CAB., Fn. Peru. 1844, 6, 147" (*fide* Baird).

b. *nanus.*

Turdus nanus, AUD., Orn. Biog. v, 1839, 201, pl. 419 (name *T. minor* on plate).—AUD., B. Am. iii, 1841, 32, pl. 147.—GAMB., Pr. A. N. S. i, 1843, 262; 1844, 14; 1846, 113; Journ. 1847, 41.—BD., B. N. A. 1858, 213.—SCL., P. Z. S. 1859; Cat. 1862, 2.— HEERM., P. R. R. Rep. x, 1859, part vi, 45.—BD., Rev. 1864, 15.—COUES, Pr. Phila. Acad. 1866, 65.—RIDGW., Pr. Phila. Acad. 1869, 129.—DALL & BANN., Trans. Chic. Acad. i, 1869, 275.—COOP., B. Cal. i, 1870, 4.

Turdus pallasi var. *nanus,* COUES, Key, 1872, 72.

"(?) *Turdus aonalaschka,* GM.—(? ?) *Muscicapa guttata,* PALL." (Baird).

c. *aubonii.*

Merula silens, SWS., Philos. Mag. i, 1827, 647; *nec T. silens,* V.—SWS., F. B. A. ii, 1831, 186.— BD., B. N. A. 1858, 213, 922 (Fort Bridger).—SCL., P. Z. S. 1858, 325 (La Parada); 1859, 325 (Oaxaca); Cat. 1862, 2.

Turdus aubonii, BD., Rev. 1864, 16.—RIDGW., Pr. Phila. Acad. 1869, 129.—SUMICH,, Mem. Bost. Soc. i, 1869, 542 (Vera Cruz, alpine region, resident).—STEVENSON, U. S. Geol. Surv. Ter. 1870, 463.—MERRIAM, *ibid.* 1872.

Turdus pallasi var. *aubonii,* COUES, Key, 1872, 72.

Hab.—The typical form ranges over the whole Eastern Province of North America; and it appears that specimens from the Middle and Western Provinces also are frequently indistinguishable. Also, Greenland, if Reinhardt's quotation belongs to this species. Breeds from New England northward; winters abundantly in the Southern, and occasionally in the Middle (*Turnbull*) States. Var. *nanus* chiefly from the regions west of the Rocky Mountains, but also accredited to Pennsylvania. Var. *aubonii* is only quoted from the Southern Rocky Mountain region, and thence southward on the table-lands of Mexico, where it is stated to be resident.

This species was not noticed by either of the earlier expeditions.

Later Expeditions.—var. *aubonii,* 60675, Uintah Mountains; 59852, Middle Park, Col. (*Schmidt & Stevenson*).

There is unquestionably but a single species of Hermit Thrush in North America. It is impossible to draw any dividing line between the so-called species, and, in fact, it is sufficiently difficult to predicate varietal distinction.

The Hermit Thrush is, upon the whole, a more northerly bird than any of its allies; not that the Olive-backed Thrush may not proceed as far north in summer, but the Hermit Thrush migrates earlier in the spring, lingers northward later in the fall, and winters further north. I have found no Central American quotations. At Washington, D. C., for instance, an intermediate point, the Hermit Thrush arrives in the van of the other three species, some time in March, becomes at once abundant, and is seen through the following month; it does not come back until

October, and remains until November. I never found it wintering in Maryland or Virginia, but it certainly does so in the Carolinas; and Dr. Turnbull says a few linger through that season in the Middle States. Mr. Maynard states that he has found it in Northern New Hampshire when the snow was on the ground, in Maine as late as November 6, and in Massachusetts until quite late in the same month. The same writer speaks of its breeding in Massachusetts, citing a nest and eggs taken at North Beverly in June, 1868; this is, I believe, the southernmost breeding-record. The nest is built in bushes, and the eggs are plain greenish-blue; they measure 0.90 by 0.62 inches.

Mr. Allen informs me by letter that "the Hermit Thrush is more or less common in the breeding season in the mountains of Colorado, from about 8,000 feet up to timber line. Several pairs were observed at our camp near Fairplay, but it was more common near the timber line in the vicinity of Mount Lincoln than we found it elsewhere. Several broods of young, scarcely able to fly, were seen at the last-named locality about July 25. The old birds were shy, and difficult to approach."

TURDUS SWAINSONI, Cab.

Olive-backed Thrush.

a. *swainsoni.*

Turdus minor, GM., Syst. Nat. i, 1788, 809 (in part; mixed with *fuscescens*).—VIEILL., O. A. S. ii, 1807, 7, pl. 63 (in part; mixed with *pallasi*).—BP., Comp. List, 1838, 17; Consp. i, 1850, 271.
Turdus solitarius, WILS., Am. Orn. v, 1812, pl. 13, f. 2 (not the text on p. 95).—COUES, Pr. Bost. Soc. xii, 1868, 106 (*lapsu* for "*swainsoni*").
Merula wilsoni, SWS. & RICH., F. B. A. ii, 1831, 182 (excl. syn. "*mustelinus,* Wils.")
Turdus olivaceus, GIRAUD, B. L. I. 1844, 92 (*nec* Linnæus).
Merula olivacea, BREWER, Pr. Bost. Soc. i, 1844, 191.
Turdus swainsoni, CAB., "Fn. Peru. 188; v. Homeyer's Reise, ii, 149¿;" Mus. Hein. i, 1850, 5 (Siberia).—"(?) SCL. & SALV., Ibis, 1859, 6 (Guatemala)."—SCL., P. Z. S. 1858, 451 (Ecuador); 1859, 326; Cat. 1862, 2.—BD., B. N. A. 1858, 216.—GUNDLACH, J. f. O. 1861, 324 (Cuba).—COUES & PRENT., Smiths. Rep. 1861 (1862), 405 (Washington, D. C., migratory).—HAYD., Rep. 1862, 158.—VERR., Pr. Ess. Inst. iii, 1862, 146 (Maine, in summer).—VERR., Pr. Bost. Soc. ix, 1862, 137 (Anticosti, very common).—BOARDM., *ibid.* 124 (Calais, Me., breeding).—BD., Rev. 1864, 19.—ALLEN, Pr. Ess. Inst. iv, 1864, 56 (Massachusetts, migratory).— MCILWRAITH, *ibid.* v, 1866, 84 (Hamilton, migratory).—COUES, *ibid.* v, 1868, 266 (New England, breeding northerly; migratory elsewhere).—TRIPPE, *ibid.* 1871, 115 (Minnesota, migratory).—LAWR., Ann. Lyc. ix, 1868, 91 (Costa Rica).— ALLEN, Mem. Bost. Soc. i, 1868, 514 (Illinois).—ALLEN, Bull. M. C. Z. ii, 1871, 251 (Florida, in winter).—ALLEN, Bull. M. C. Z. iii, 1872, 173 (Kansas).—DALL & BANN., Tr. Chic. Acad. i, 1869, 275 (Alaska).—TURN., B. E. Pa. 1869, 14 (says it winters; doubtful).—RIDGW., Pr. Phila. Acad. 1869, 128.—MAYN., Guide, 1870, 90 (Massachusetts, migratory).—MAYN., Pr. Bost. Soc. xiv, 1871 (breeding in Maine and New Hampshire).—COOP., B. Cal. i, 1871, 6.—MAYN., B. Fla. 1872, 6.—COUES, Key, 1872, 72.—SNOW B. Kas. 1873, 4.
Turdus minimus, LAFRES., R. Z. 1848, 5.—SCL., P. Z. S. 1854, 111.—BRYANT, Pr. Bost. Soc. vii, 1860, 226 (Bogota).—LAWR., Ann. Lyc. N. Y., viii, May, 1863 (Panama).—
"*Turdus nanus,*" SAMUELS, Am. Nat. ii, 1868, 218 (error).

b. *aliciæ.*

Turdus aliciæ, BD., B. N. A. 1858, 217, pl. 81, f. 2.—COUES, Pr. Phila. Acad. 1861, 217 (Labrador).—COUES & PRENT., Smiths. Rep. for 1861, 405 (Washington, D. C., migratory, common).—HAYD., Rep. 1862, 159.—BD., Rev. 1864, 21.—COUES, Pr. Ess. Inst. v, 1868, 267 (New England).—DALL & BANN., Trans. Chic. Acad. i, 1869, 275 (Alaska).—RIDGW., Pr. Phil. Acad. 1869, 128.—LAWR., Ann. Lyc. ix, 1868, 91 (Costa Rica).
Turdus swainsoni var. *aliciæ,* COUES, Key, 1872, 73.

c. *ustulatus.*

Turdus ustulatus, NUTT., i, 1840, 2d ed., 400 ("*cestulatus*").—BD., B. N. A. 1858, 215, pl. 81, f. 1.—COOP. & SUCK., Nat. Hist. Wash. Ter. 1860, 171.—BD., Rev. 1864, 18.—

TURDUS SWAINSONI, OLIVE-BACKED THRUSH. 5

RIDGW., Pr. Phila. Acad. 1869, 129.—DALL & BANN., Tr. Chic. Acad. i, 1869, 275.—COOP., B. Cal. i, 1871, 5.—LAWR., Pr. Bost. Soc. June, 1871 (Tres Marias). *Turdus swainsoni* var. *ustulatus*, COUES, Key, 1872, 73.

Hab.—The typical form ranges over nearly the whole of North America; north to the Arctic Ocean, northwest to Behring's Straits, west to the Columbia, south to Central America, New Granada, and Ecuador. Cuba. Greenland, Europe, and Siberia (acci dental). Not observed in Southwestern United States. Breeds from Maine and New Hampshire northward (? from New York, *Gregg*, Pr. Elmira Acad. 1870). Winters from Florida southward. Var. *aliciæ* has a nearly coincident range, but on the whole appears somewhat more northerly; south to Costa Rica (*v. Frantzius*). Var. *ustulatus* inhabits the Pacific coast, from Sitka to Mexico (Tres Marias Islands, *Grayson*).

List of specimens.

| 19193 | 27 | Wind River.. | ♀ | May 28, 1860 | F. V. Hayden.. | 6.50 | 11.50 | 4.00 |

Lieutenant Warren's Expedition.—4707, mouth of the Missouri River; 4710, "Nebraska;" 8818, Black Hills. Var. *aliciæ:* 4708, Upper Missouri; 4711, Jacques River; 4709, 4712, Vermilion River.

Late information has greatly extended the known range of this species, and in time the above-mentioned exception of its apparent non-occurrence in the Southwestern United States will probably be done away with.

As Mr. Allen has repeatedly contended, the characteristics formerly supposed to be specifically distinctive of *T. aliciæ* have proved inconstant and not always tangible. I am now nearly satisfied of the propriety of treating it as a variety, though I entertained the contrary opinion for some years. The evidence best favoring the supposition of its validity lies in the fact that, while occupying substantially the same range as typical *swainsoni*, it generally shows some slight peculiarities; these, however, apparently shade into those of *swainsoni*. The fact of intergradation may be proved, however we may account for the discrepancies observed in most cases. I think the solution of the problem may be looked for in the probability that *aliciæ* as a rule consists of more northerly-born individuals; this would bring the case under some known rules, that might account for its peculiarities of larger size and darker color.

The relationships of var. *ustulatus* were long supposed to be with *fuscescens*, which is by no means the case. The clew to its true interpretation was found in the discovery that the eggs are speckled as in *swainsoni*, not plain as in *fuscescens*. Attention was first called to this and other evidences of relationship by Mr. Ridgway in the paper above quoted. He then, however, treated *ustulatus* as specifically distinct. Nothing appears to contradict the view I have adopted, and published as above, that *ustulatus* is a geographical variety, the features of which depend upon the moisture of the heavily wooded coast region it inhabits.

All the forms of this species nest alike in bushes, and lay speckled eggs, usually four, measuring about 0.92 by 0.62 inches. The Olive-backed Thrush is a very abundant bird in the Eastern United States during the migrations in April and October. It has not been observed to breed south of Maine and New Hampshire, nor is the evidence satisfactory that it winters north of Florida. As will be seen by the above quotations, it penetrates very far southward in winter.

TURDUS FUSCESCENS, Steph.

Wilson's Thrush; Tawny Thrush; Veery.

Turdus mustelinus, WILS., Am. Orn., v, 1812, 98, pl. 43 (*nec* GM., *nec auctt.*)
Turdus fuscescens, STEPH., Shaw's Gen. Zool. x, 1817, 182.—CAB., J. f. O. 1855, 470 (Cuba).—BD., B. N. A. 1858, 214.—SCL., P. Z. S. 1859, 326; Cat. 1862, 2.—COUES &

PRENT., Smiths. Rep. 1861, 404 (Washington, D. C., migratory).—HAYD.,
Rep. 1862, 158.—VERR., Pr. Ess. Inst. iii, 1862, 146 (Maine, breeds).—BD., Rev
1864, 17.—ALLEN, Pr. Ess. Inst. iv, 1864, 56 (Massachusetts, breeds).—LAWR.,
Ann. Lyc. N. H. N. Y. viii, 1866, 281 (New York).—MCILWRAITH, Pr. Ess.
Inst. v, 1866, 84 (Hamilton, Canada West, breeds).—COUES, Pr. Ess. Inst. v,
1868, 266.—COUES, Pr. Bost. Soc. 1868, xii, 106 (South Carolina, chiefly migra-
tory, some probably wintering).—ALLEN, Mem. Bost. Soc. i, 1868, 493 (Iowa,
July), 514.—TURN., B. E. Pa. 1869, 14 ("plentiful from April to October, a few
remaining during winter").—RIDGW., Pr. Phila. Acad. 1869, 127.—MAYN.,
Guide, 1870, 90 (Massachusetts, abundant in summer).—MAYN., Pr. Bost.
Soc. xiv, 1871 (Maine and New Hampshire, summer).—ALLEN, Bull. M. C. Z. ii,
1871, 256 (Florida, wintering); iii, 1872, 155, 173 (mountains of Colorado).—
MAYN., B. Fla. 1872, 10.—COUES, Key, 1872, 73.
Turdus silens, VIEILL., Enc. Met. ii, 1823, 647 (= *mustelinus,* WILS.; not *silens,* SWS.)
Turdus wilsoni, BP., Obs. Wils. 1825, 34, No. 73; Syn. 1828, 75, No. 100; Consp. i, 1850,
271.—NUTT., Man. i, 1832, 349.—AUD., Orn. Biog. ii, 1834, 362; v, 1839, 446, pl.
166.—AUD., Syn. 1839, 90.—AUD., B. Am. iii, 1841, 27, pl. 145.—GIRAUD, B. L. I.
1844, 89.—CAB., "Fn. Peru. 1844-'46, 205."—PUTN., Pr. Ess. Inst. i, 1856, 209
(Massachusetts, breeding).—TRIPPE, *ibid.,* vi, 1871, 115 (Minnesota, breeding).
Merula wilsoni, BREWER, Pr. Bost. Soc. 1844, 191.
"*Turdus minor,* D'ORBIGNY, La Sagra's Cuba, Ois. 1840, 47, pl. 5 (Cuba)."
Merula minor, SWS. & RICH., F. B. A. ii, 1831, 179, pl. 36.

Hab.—Eastern North America. North to Hudson's Bay and the Saskatchewan. West
to the Rocky Mountains (Colorado, *Allen;* Fort Bridger, *Baird*). South to Panama.
Cuba. Breeds from Southern New England (from Pennsylvania, *Turnbull*), and Iowa
northward. Winters from Florida and Gulf States (? from South Carolina, *Coues;*
from Pennsylvania, *Turnbull*) southward. Not seen in Alaska.
Not obtained by Captain Raynolds' Expedition.
Lieutenant Warren's Expedition.—4713, mouth of Vermilion River.
Later Expeditions.—60676, Green River (*Schmidt & Stevenson*).

This is an Eastern species, but not exclusively so, although its range
is much more limited, both to the northward and westward, than that
of either *swainsoni* or *pallasi.* Dr. Hayden reports it from the Lower
Missouri; it has not been observed higher up than the locality above
given. Prof. Baird gives a Fort Bridger record. Mr. Allen met with
it at several points in Colorado between Denver and the Park, especially along the North Fork of the South Platte. It occurs in winter
as far south as Panama, and in Cuba. It does not appear to run into
varieties like the more extensively dispersed *pallasi* and *swainsoni,* but
is as constant as *mustelinus,* that, like it, is restricted in range. These
facts seem mutually explanatory.

The nest of this species is built on or close to the ground, and the
eggs are unmarked.

'A Veery's nest, which I found near Pembina, Dakota, on the Red
River of the North, was placed on a little heap of decaying leaves caught
at the foot of a bush; resting on these, it was settled firmly in the crotch
formed by several stems diverging at once from the root. The base of
the nest was quite damp, but the floor was sufficiently thick to keep the
interior dry. The nest was built of various slender weed-stems, grass-
stalks, and fibrous strips of bark, compactly woven and mixed with
dried leaves; the latter formed the lining of the base inside. The cavity
is rather small, considering the bulkiness of the whole nest, measuring
only about two inches and a half across by less than two in depth. The
whole is as large as an infant's head, and of irregular contour, fitting the
crotch in which it was placed, and bearing deep impress of the ascending
stems of the bush. This nest contained four eggs, fresh (June 9); they
measured, on an average, 0.86 by 0.66, and were pale greenish-blue, without spots. The female, scared from her nest by my approach, flew silently
off to a little distance, where she rested to observe my actions. The
bird breeds very abundantly in the heavy shrubbery along the river,
and is one of the sweetest songsters of that region. When its clear

bell-like notes, resonant, distinct, yet soft and of undescribable sadness, fall upon the ear as we press through the tangled undergrowth beneath the shade of stately trees, we pause involuntarily to listen to music that for the moment makes us forget the terrible torture of body and vexation of spirit that we endure continually from the innumerable hosts of the scourge—musquitoes.

The *Merula minor* of Swainson is certainly this species; every point of the diagnosis, as well as the plate, points to *fuscescens*. *M. wilsoni* of the same author is *swainsoni*. *M. solitaria* of the same work is *pallasi*, the plate erroneously marked "35" for 37. I make these determinations, which differ somewhat from those of Professor Baird, who assigns the plates otherwise. In my copy of the Fauna, plate "35" (37), the tawny of the rump and other points of coloration are certainly little like those of *swainsoni*.

Mr. Allen has erroneously included *T. ustulatus* among the synonyms of *fuscescens* in his Memoirs on Iowan and Floridan Birds, above cited; but I am happy to be able to state that he now endorses the view presented in the "Key." He also informs me that Wilson's Thrush, which was met with in considerable numbers at several points between Denver and South Park, chiefly frequented the dense thickets near the streams, and were hence difficult to observe or procure, although easily recognized by their song. None were met with in or about South Park, or above an altitude of about 9,000 feet.

Subfamily MIMINÆ : *Mocking Thrushes.*

OREOSCOPTES MONTANUS, (Towns.) Bd.

Mountain Mockingbird.

Orpheus montanus, TOWNS., Journ. Acad. Phila. 1837, 192.—AUD., Syn. 1839, 89.—AUD., B. Am. ii, 1841, 194, pl. 139.
Turdus montanus, AUD., Orn. Biog. iv, 1838, 437, pl. 369, f. 1.
Mimus montanus, BP., List, 1838, 17.—BP., Consp. Av. i, 1850, 276.
Oreoscoptes montanus, BD., B. N. A. 1858, 347 ; Rev. 1864, 42.—SCL., P. Z. S. 1859, 340 ; Cat, 1862, 8.—HAYD., Rep. 1862, 163.—COOP., Pr. Cal. Acad. 1870, 75 (Colorado River) ; B. Cal. i, 1870, 13.—STEV., U. S. Geol. Surv. Ter. 1870, 464 (Wyoming).— MERRIAM, *ibid.* 1872, 670, 705 (Utah).—ALLEN, Bull. M. C. Z. iii, 1872, 174 (western edge of the Colorado Plains).—HOLD., Pr. Bost. Soc. 1872, 194 (Black Hills).—COUES, Key, 1872, 74.

Hab.—United States, from the Rocky Mountains to the Pacific; south to Mexico and Cape St. Lucas; east to Fort Laramie and the Black Hills.

This species bears no slight resemblance to the *young* of the common Mockingbird, which is, like it, spotted below, and for which it might be mistaken upon superficial examination. It is, however, much more heavily and sharply marked with triangular spots on nearly all the under parts, and differs, besides, in its generic characters. The bill is slenderer and comparatively longer; the wings are relatively much longer and more pointed, equaling or exceeding the tail, which is little rounded, the outer feathers being only about ¼ inch shorter than the middle ones. Length about 8.00; wing 4.00; tail rather more; tarsus 1.15; bill, 0.65.

List of specimens.

| 19226 | 21 | Rattlesnake Hills. | .... | May 16, 1860 | F. V. Hayden. | 8.25 | 13.00 | 3.75 |
| 19347 | .... | Willow Springs .. | ♂ | May 14, 1860 | G. H. Trook.. | ...... | ...... | ...... |

Lieutenant Warren's Expedition.—8821, Black Hills.
Later Expeditions.—60447, 60711-19, various Wyoming localities; 61651-2, Salt Lake, Utah.

Dr. Hayden's specimen, from the Black Hills, and Dr. Cooper's, from Fort Laramie, probably indicate the extreme eastern range of the species. Mr. Holden's notice is corroborative; he found them rare in the Black Hills, only five or six specimens being observed in the course of his collecting. "They remain concealed during the middle of the day in some low thicket, and on the approach of evening the males mount some high point and sing till after dusk."

Of the nidification of the Mountain Mockingbird I remain ignorant. A set of four eggs in the Smithsonian collection, from Wyoming, offers the following characters: Size, 1.03 by 0.70, 1.00 by 0.70, 0.99 by 0.68, 0.94 by 0.69. Color rather light greenish-blue, boldly, sharply, and rather heavily spotted all over with burnt umber. A single egg of another set from the same locality is more minutely speckled and dotted in diffuse pattern, approaching some styles of Mockingbird's eggs. Mr. Merriam took a nest containing four fresh eggs, June 10, 1872, at Salt Lake, Utah.

MIMUS POLYGLOTTUS, (L.) Boie.

Mockingbird.

Turdus polyglottus, L., S. N. i, 1766, 293.—WILS., Am. Orn. ii, 1810, 14, pl. 10, f. 1.—BP., Syn. 1828, 74.—AUD., Orn. Biog. i, 1831, 108; v, 1839, 438; pl. 21.—NUTT., Man. i, 1832, 320.
Mimus polyglottus, BOIE, Isis, 1826, 972.—BP., Comp. List, 1838, 17; Consp. i, 1850, 276.— WOODH., Sitgr. Rep. 1853, 72.—SCL., P. Z. S. 1856, 212; 1859, 340; Cat. 1862, 8.— BD., B. N. A. 1858, 344; Rev. i, 1864, 48.—KENN., P. R. R. Rep. x, 1859, pt. iv, 25.—HEERM., *ibid.* pt. vi, 44.—WHEAT., Ohio Agr. Rep. 1860, No. 118 (Ohio, formerly common).—COUES & PRENT., Smiths. Rep. 1861, 410 (rare).—ALLEN, Pr. Ess. Inst. iv, 1864, 67 (Massachusetts, northern limit).—LAWR., Ann. Lyc. N. Y. viii, 1866, 282 (Long Island, occasional).—COUES, Pr. Phila. Acad. 1866, 65 (Arizona).—COUES, Pr. Bost. Soc. xii, 1868, 107 (South Carolina, resident).— ALLEN, Mem. Bost. Soc. i, 1868, 523 (Indiana).—SUMICH., *ibid.* i, 1869, 543 (Vera Cruz, Gulf shore up to plateau; breeding at Orizaba).—TURN., B. E. Pa. 1869, 15 (rare, stated to have wintered).—MAYN., Guide, 1870, 92 (Massachusetts); B. Fla. 1872, 16.—COOP., B. Cal. i, 1870, 21.—LAWR., Pr. Bost. Soc. June, 1871 (Tres Marias).—ALLEN, Bull. M. C. Z. ii, 1871, 259 (Florida, in winter); iii, 1872, 134 (Middle Kansas, common, breeding).—COUES, Key, 1872, 74, fig. 16.
Orpheus polyglottus, SWS., Zool. Journ. iii, 1827, 167.—AUD., Syn. 1839, 87.—AUD., B. Am. ii, 1841, 187, pl. 137.
Orpheus leucopterus, VIG., Zool. Beechey's Voy. 1839, p. —.
Orpheus polygothus, PUTN., Pr. Ess. Inst. i, 1856, 224 (error).
Mimus caudatus, BD., B. N. A. 1858, 345 ("*canadatus*," error).—COOP., Pr. Cal. Acad. 1870, 75.

Hab.—United States, from Atlantic to Pacific; north regularly to the Middle States, rarely to Massachusetts, beyond which no record. Ohio, Indiana, Illinois, Kansas; New Mexico, Arizona, and Southern California; Tres Marias Islands. Resident from the Carolinas southward, and in Mexico. Several insular races in various West Indian Islands. Breeds throughout its range.

The Mockingbird was not noticed by either expedition, but has lately been ascertained to breed in Kansas, where Mr. Allen found it common, in June, along Big Creek. It probably does not proceed further northward in the Missouri region.

The Mockingbird's eggs measure nearly or quite an inch long by three-fourths wide, and are gray, irregularly speckled and blotched with brown and lavender, chiefly about the larger end, but often over the whole surface. Two or three broods are reared in the South.

MIMUS CAROLINENSIS, (Linn.) Gray.

Catbird.

Muscicapa carolinensis, LINN., Syst. Nat. i, 1766, 328.
Turdus carolinensis, LICHT., Verzeichn. 1823, 38.
Orpheus carolinensis, AUD., B. Am. ii, 1841, 195, pl. 140.
Mimus carolinensis, GRAY.—BD., B. N. A. 1858, 346.—HAYD., Rep. 1862, 163.—COOP., Am. Nat. iii, 1869, 73 (common across Rocky Mountains to Cœur d'Aleñe Mission); 295

(Fort Union, breeding).—COUES, Key, 1872, 74.—ALLEN, Bull. M. C. Z. iii, 1872, 174 (Kansas, Colorado, Utah).—MAYN., B. Fla. 1872, 19.—And of most late authors.
Galeoscoptes carolinensis, CAB.—BD., Rev. 1864, 54.—SUMICH., Mem. Bost. Soc. i, 1869, 544 (Vera Cruz, transient).—SCL., P. Z. S. 1870, 836 (Honduras).—STEV., U. S. Geol. Surv. 1870, 464.—MERR., *ibid.* 1872, 670.
Felivox carolinensis, BP., Comp. Rend. xxviii, 1853, p. —
Turdus felivox, VIEILL., Ois. Am. Sept. ii, 1807, 10, pl. 67.—BP., Journ. Phila. Acad. iv, 1825, 30; Syn. 1828, 75.—NUTT., i, 1832, 332.—AUD., Orn. Biog. ii, 171; v, 440; pl. 128.
Orpheus felivox, SW. & RICH., F. B. A. ii, 1831, 192.—AUD., Syn. 1839, 88.—AUD., B. Am. ii, pl. 140.
Mimus felivox, BP., Comp. List, 1838, 18; Consp. Av. i, 1850, 276.
Turdus lividus, WILS., Am. Orn. ii, 1810, 90, pl. 14, f. 3.

Hab.—United States, north to Red River and Saskatchewan (latitude 54°, *Richardson*); west to the Columbia, to Utah, Wyoming and Colorado; south to Panama. Mexico. Cuba. Resident in the Southern States. Breeds throughout its North American range. Not obtained by Captain Raynolds' Expedition.
Lieutenant Warren's Expedition.—4704, White River; 5285, 5286, Fort Lookout.
Later Expeditions.—59853, Berthoud's Pass. Colorado; 60443, La Bonté Creek, Wyoming; 60720, Fort Bridger; 61653, Ogden, Utah.

The known range of this familiar species has been greatly extended of late. It was taken in Washington Territory by the Northwest Boundary Survey Commission; in Kansas, Colorado, and Utah by Mr. Allen's expedition from the Museum of Comparative Zoology, and in Wyoming by Mr. Stevenson. Dr. Hayden remarks its abundance from the mouth of the Missouri to the mountains.

Eggs pure dark-green, unmarked, 0.92 by 0.68 in size, four or five in number. Nest in bushes, bulky and inartistic, made of bark-strips, weed-stalks, leaves, and rootlets.

HARPORHYNCHUS RUFUS, (Linn.) Cab.

Sandy Mockingbird; Thrasher.

Turdus rufus, LINN., Syst. Nat. i, 1766, 293.—VIEILL., Ois. Am. Sept. ii, 1807, 4, pl. 59.—WILS., Am. Orn. ii, 1810, 83, pl. 14.—BP., Syn. 1828, 75.—AUD., Orn. Biog. ii, 1834, 102; v, 1839, 441; pl. 116.
Orpheus rufus, SWS. & RICH., F. B. A. ii, 1831, 189.—NUTT., Man. i, 1832, 328.—AUD., B. Am. iii, 1841, 9, pl. 141.—TRIPPE, Pr. Ess. Inst. vi, 1871, 116 (Minnesota).
Mimus rufus, GRAY, Genera of Birds.—BP., Comp. List, 1838, 18.
Toxostoma rufum, CAB., Weigm. Archiv. 1847, 207.
Harporhynchus rufus, CAB., Mus. Hein. 1851, 82.—BD., B. N. A. 1858, 353.—HAYD., Rep. 1862, 163.—BD., Rev. 1864, 44.—COOP., Am. Nat. iii, 1869, 296 (Upper Missouri, breeding).—COUES, Key, 1872, 75.—ALLEN, Bull. M. C. Z. iii, 1872, 173.—MAYN., B. Fla. 1872, 21.—And of most late authors.
Harporhynchus rufus var. *longicauda*, BD., B. N. A. 1858, 353, in text.—STEV., U. S. Geol. Surv. 1872, 464.

Hab.—Eastern United States; north to Red River; west through Nebraska, Dakota, and Colorado. From the Rio Grande southward replaced by a longer-billed, darker-colored race (*H. longirostris*). Winters in Southern United States. Breeds throughout its range. (No West Indian or Central American quotations.)

List of specimens.

| 19346 | .... | Sage Creek .. | ♂ | June 13, 1860 | G. H. Trook ... | 11.00 | 13.50 | 4.38 |

This specimen represents the subvariety *rufus longicauda*. So, also, does No. 60442, expedition of 1870, Bitter Cottonwood Creek, Wyoming.
Lieutenant Warren's Expedition.—4553, Missouri River; 5283, 5284, Fort Lookout; 4703, Running Water; 8819, 8820, Loup Fork.

These specimens are of the ordinary form, and probably represent nearly the western limit of the typical species. I have seen it at Fort Randall. The following interesting biographical note is communicated by Mr. Allen:

"The Brown Thrush is an abundant species in Eastern and Middle Kansas, and is also of frequent occurrence in the foot-hills at the eastern base of the Rocky Mountains, in Colorado, up to about 7,500 feet. We found its nests, containing full sets of eggs, at Leavenworth during the first week of May. Here the nests were built in low bushes, the soil being clayey and damp; but at Topeka, toward the end of May, we found nests on the ground, the soil being dry and sandy. At Fort Hays its nests were usually placed in trees, sixteen to twenty feet from the ground, to avoid the contingency of floods. The trees here grew principally along the bed of Big Creek; and the stream being subject in summer to sudden freshets, the scattered undergrowth, as well as the lower branches of the trees, are thus often submerged, so that any nests built on or near the ground would be liable to be destroyed by the rise of the stream. The driftal *débris* adhering to the trees serves to mark the 'high-water' line, and we rarely found a bird's nest below this limit. These birds, that usually breed near the ground, in bushes or on the lower branches of trees, thus modified their habits to suit the exigencies of the locality."

The Thrasher's nest is rather bulky and flattish, composed of small sticks, weed-stalks, strips of bark, and rootlets. The eggs, four or five in number, are an inch or rather more in length, by three-fourths in breadth, pale greenish-olive, finely speckled and dotted with reddish-brown, generally all over the surface, though tending to aggregate about the larger end, around which they sometimes form a perfect wreath.

Family CINCLIDÆ : Dippers ; Water Ouzels.

CINCLUS MEXICANUS, Sw.

American Dipper ; Water Ouzel.

Cinclus pallasii, Bp., Am. Orn. ii, 1828, 173, pl. 16, f. 1 (not of authors).
Cinclus mexicanus, Sw., Phil. Mag. i, 1827, 368.—Bd., Rev. 1864, 60.—Coop., B. Cal. i, 1870, 25.—Sumich., Mem. Bost. Soc. i, 1869, 544 (alpine region of Vera Cruz).—Coues, Key, 1872, 77.—Allen, Bull. M. C. Z. iii, 1872, 174 (mountains of Colorado, up to timber-line; Ogden, Utah).—Merr., U. S. Geol. Surv. Ter. 1872, 671 (Montana).—Dall, Pr. Cal. Acad. 1873 (Unalaska, resident).
Hydrobata mexicana, Bd., B. N. A. 1858, 229.—Coop. & Suck., Nat. Hist. Wash. Ter. 1860, 175.—Coop., Am. Nat. iii, 1869, 32 (Montana).—Dall & Bann., Trans. Chic. Acad. i, 1869, 277.—Hold., Pr. Bost. Soc. xv, 1872, 194 (Black Hills).
Cinclus americanus, Sw. & Rich., F. B. A. ii, 1831, 173.—Nutt., Man. i, 1832, 569.—Aud., B. Am. ii, 1841, 182, pl. 137.—Newb., P. R. R. Rep. vi, 1857, 80.—Heerm., P. R. R. Rep. x, 1859, pt. vi, 44.
Cinclus unicolor, Bp., Comp. and Geog. List, 1838, 18.
Cinclus mortoni, Towns., Narr. 1839, 337.
Cinclus townsendii, "Aud." Id., *ibid.* 340.

Hab.—Clear mountain-streams of Western North America, from the region of the Yukon into Mexico.

List of specimens.

19195	229	Deer Creek ..	♀	Jan. 5, 1860	G. H. Trook ...	7.50	11.50	3.75
19196	231	..... do	....	Jan. 6, 1860	...... do	7.50	11.50	3.75
19198	248	..... do	♀	Dec. 10, 1859	...... do	7.50	11.75	3.50
19199	232	..... do	....	....	...... do	7.75	11.50	3.25
19201	231	..... do	....	Jan. 4, 1860	...... do	....	....	....
19197	227	..... do	....	..... do	F. V. Hayden..	7.00	13.00	3.75
19200	230	..... do	♀	Jan. 5, 1860	J. Stevenson...	8.00	12.50	4.00

Later Expeditions.—62341-2, Mystic Lake, Montana (*Merriam*).

This interesting bird was not obtained by Lieutenant Warren's Expedition, and the fine *suite* above recorded represent about its easternmost extension as far as known. The conditions of its existence appear to be only met in *clear* streams. This restricts it practically to mountainous regions, where little or no alluvium is suspended in the water. The aquatic habits of birds of this family are unique among the Oscines; their general economy—ability to progress under water and procure food with the aid of the wings, by a sort of subaquatic flying and scrambling—is well known, and the perfect adaptation of form and plumage requires no comment. Their food consists of aquatic insects of all sorts. The nidification has only recently been elucidated. One of the most perfect and beautiful samples of bird-architecture I ever saw was a nest of this species Dr. Hayden showed me after one of his late trips. It is an elegant ball of soft green moss, as large as a man's head, roofed over, with a small round hole in one side. Dr. Cooper speaks of a similar structure: "It was built under the shelving roots of an immense *arbor-vitæ* tree that had floated over and rested, in a slanting position, against a mill-dam. The floor was made of small twigs, and bare; the sides and roof arching over it like an oven, and formed of moss projecting above so as to shelter the opening. This was large enough to admit the hand, and the inside was very capacious. It contained half-fledged young [July 5]. The old birds were familiar and fearless, being accustomed to the noise of the mill, and the society of the men, who were much interested by their curious habits. They had already raised a brood in the same nest that summer." The nest appears to be variously situated, but always in a nook or crevice near the water.

Mr. Merriam's report, above cited, contains an account of another nest, which was discovered by the artist of the expedition, Mr. W. H. Holmes, about half a mile from Mystic Lake, Montana: "The bird was observed to fly directly through the falling water, disappearing from view. Suspecting that a nest must be there, we returned the following day, when, with the assistance of Mr. Holmes, I secured the nest, containing three young, and shortly after shot both the old birds. The nest was made of moss, measuring nearly a foot in diameter and six inches in depth. It was built upon the edge of a narrow shelf of rock, and so near the fall that the outside was constantly wet with spray, while the interior was dry and warm. The birds entered it by a small lateral opening in the lower half of the nest, the top being built up against a projecting rock." —(*W. B. Platt.*)

Other extracts from the observations of naturalists will illustrate the natural history of the species. Dr. George Suckley writes: "One curious fact I noticed regarding this bird is, that I frequently saw it *singly* or *in pairs*, but never *more than two together*. In fact, they seem to prefer solitude, and eschew all sociable communion or the slightest attempt at gregarious life, except the indispensable union of a pair for the purpose of procreation. I never saw this bird on or near still water. They prefer and delight in wild mountain-streams, where, among cascades, eddies, and swift currents, they lead their curious lives." Mr. George Gibbs speaks of the Dipper as common on Salmon River, a rapid, brawling stream, and continues: "As I sat at my cradle on the bank, a pair of them * * * used to play in the water near me, sometimes alighting at the head of a rapid, allowing themselves to be swept under, and then rising below. They dive with great celerity, and at times beat the water with their wings, throwing the spray over themselves. Their whistle was sweet and rather sad, but they seemed very happy and busy notwithstanding, and in nowise afraid of the harsh rattle of the miner's cradle."

Dr. Newberry gives the following note: "This singular little bird I found only in the rapid and shallow streams in the Cascade Mountains. It was always flitting along in the bed of the stream, from time to time plunging into the water and disappearing, but soon re-appearing across or up or down the stream, skipping from stone to stone, jerking its tail and turning its body, with much the manners of the wrens, occasionally uttering a short and sharp chirp." Mr. W. H. Dall's notice is one of the most northern records. He says, like Dr. Suckley, that the bird "is essentially solitary. Several specimens were obtained in January, February, and March, always near some open, unfrozen spot, on some small stream, such as the Nulato River. * * * The Indians told me, and my own observation confirmed it, that this bird, when disturbed, will dive into the water even in mid-winter; and as it is never found but near open water, I suspect it obtains its food from thence. I noticed that the bill and legs of some of the specimens were light ochre-yellow, and others dark slate-color." The former were probably young birds.

"The American Ouzel (*Cinclus mexicanus*) is doubtless a frequent inhabitant of nearly all the mountain-streams of Colorado. We met with it near Colorado City, on the Fontaine-qui-bout, even fairly out on the plains, and in the mountains up to the remotest sources of the South Platte, within a few hundred feet of the timber-line. Remarkable alike for the melody of its song and its singular habits, it is one of the most interesting members of the avian fauna of our continent. It prefers the swiftest mountain-torrents, above the roar of which its melodious notes can at times be scarcely heard. At such localities, as is well known, it seeks its food at the bottom of the stream, easily withstanding the swiftest current. Along Ogden River, Utah, a powerful mountain torrent, we found it more common in September and October than we had seen it at any other point; here, in the course of an hour, we easily obtained a dozen specimens."—(*Allen, in epist.*)

The Dipper's egg is pure white in color, and of rather elongate, pointed shape. Two specimens in Dr. Hayden's collection, taken by Mr. Stevenson near Berthoud's Pass, measure 1.05 by 0.70, and 1.04 by 0.69, respectively. They formed part of a set of three.

We have been favored with the following interesting communication from Mr. J. Stevenson, of Dr. Hayden's party:

"While the camp of the United States Geological Survey of the Territories, to which I was attached, was located near Berthoud's Pass, in the Rocky Mountains, I collected the nest, eggs, and mother-bird of the Water Ouzel, which had constructed its little house near the margin of a small stream, but a little distance from our camp. Having some leisure time, I interested myself in watching and noting some of the actions of this little bird. It was not very timid, having built its nest not far from a saw-mill in which several persons were employed, and who were daily witnesses of the movements of the bird; indeed, one of these men seemed deeply grieved when he learned that I had killed the bird and taken its nest, for it had been his custom to approach the spot daily, and watch with interest the curious manœuvres of this little animal. After my attention was called to it I took pains to spend an hour or so each day for several days, watching its actions. The nest was built on a slab, about four feet from the water's edge, and was composed of green moss, the inside being lined with fine dry grass; it was oval-shaped, being about six inches high and about thirty in circumference at the base. The outside or walls of the nest were composed of green moss, most ingeniously interwoven, so that its growth in this manner might add to the strength of the nest and the protection of the bird, its eggs, and young. One of the first things that attracted my attention was its manner of diving down into the water and then darting back and perching itself on the summit of its mound-like dwelling, where it would shake the water from its feathers and distribute it over the nest, apparently for the purpose of keeping the moss moist and in a growing condition, thereby increasing its strength and dimensions. The entrance to its little house was also carefully arranged; the archway was quite perfect, and the moss around it was so directed in its growth as not to obstruct the entrance, which was situated on one side, near the bottom of the nest. The operation of sprinkling the nest was repeated daily. An examination of the nest, which is in the museum of the Smithsonian Institution, together with the preceding facts, would induce one to believe that the performances of this little bird were for the purpose of keeping the outer lining of its nest green and growing, that it might keep its miniature dwelling in repair, while rearing its family, without the aid of a bricklayer, plasterer, or carpenter, showing that among the feathered tribe there are mechanics as well as musicians."

A model piece of bird-biography is the account given by Audubon, from the pen of William Macgillivray, who writes fascinatingly, as well as instructively, of the European Dipper, with the habits of which ours accords in all essentials. An excellent and thoroughly reliable monograph of the family has been published by Mr. Osbert Salvin in the Ibis, 1867, pp. 109–122, pl. 2 ; also pp. 382, 383.

Family SAXICOLIDÆ : Stone Chats.

Chiefly an Old World group, closely allied to if really separable from the *Turdidæ*, represented in North America by stragglers of the typical genus *Saxicola*, and by the characteristic American genus *Sialia*.

SIALIA SIALIS, (Linn.) Hald.

Eastern Bluebird.

Motacilla sialis, LINN., Syst. Nat. i, 1766, 336.
Sylvia sialis, LATH., Ind. Orn. ii, 1790, 522.—VIEILL., Ois. Am. Sept. ii, 1807, 40, pls. 101,
    102, 103.—WILS., Am. Orn. i, 1808, 56, pl. 3.
Saxicola sialis, BP., Syn. 1828, 39.
Ampelis sialis, NUTT., Man. i, 1832, 444.
Sialia sialis, HALD., Trego's Geog. of Pa. 1843, 77 ; Am. Nat. 1869, iii, 159—BD., B. N. A.
    1858, 222 ; Rev. 1864, 62.—HAYD., Rep. 1862, 159.—COOP., Am. Nat. iii, 1869, 32
    (Milk River and Fort Laramie).—COUES, Key, 1872, 76.—ALLEN, Bull. M.
    C. Z. iii, 1872, 174 (to Fort Hays, Kans.).—HOLD., Pr. Bost. Soc. xv, 1872, 194
    (Fountain, Col.).—MAYN., B. Fla. 1872, 23.—And of most late authors.
Sialia wilsoni, SW., Zool. Journ. iii, 1827, 173.—AUD., B. Am. ii, 1841, 171, pl. 134.
Erythaca (Sialia) wilsoni, SW. & RICH., F. B. A. ii, 1831, 210 (to latitude 48° north).
(?) *Sialia azurea*, SW., Phil. Mag. i. 1827, 369.—BD., Rev. 1864, 62 (var. (?) from Mexico
    and Central America).—SUMICH., Mem. Bost. Soc. i, 1869, 544 (Vera Cruz).

Hab.—Eastern faunal area of temperate North America ; north to 48° ; west to Western Kansas (to Colorado, *Holden*) and Lower Missouri region. Bermuda. Cuba.

Not obtained by Captain Raynolds' Expedition, which passed beyond its known western range, nor by either of the later expeditions.

Lieutenant Warren's Expedition.—4723, Bald Island ; 5288, 5290, Fort Lookout ; 5289, mouth of Powder River ; 4722, Nebraska ; 4658, White River ; 8884, Platte River ; 8880, Loup Fork ; 8882, near Loup Fork.

Specimens of the Eastern Bluebird are occasionally found with part of the reddish-brown of the throat replaced by rich blue, thus showing an approach to the characters of *S. mexicana*.

SIALIA MEXICANA, Sw.

Western Bluebird.

Sialia mexicana, Sw., F. B. A. ii, 1831, 202.—Bp., List, 1838, 16.—Bd., B. N. A. 1858, 223; Rev. 1864, 63.—Kenn., P. R. R. Rep. x, 1859, pt. iv, 23.—Heerm., *ibid.* pt. vi, 43.—Coop. & Suck., N. H. Wash. Ter. 1860, 173.—Scl., P. Z. S. 1859, 362 (Xalapa); 1856, 293 (Cordova).—Coues. Pr. Phila. Acad. 1866, 66 (Arizona).—Coop., B. Cal. 1870, 28.—Sumich., Mem. Bost. Soc. i, 1869, 544 (Vera Cruz, alpine).—Coop., Am. Nat. iii, 1869, 32 (Montana).—Coop., Pr. Cal. Acad. 1870, 75 (Colorado River).—Aiken, Pr. Bost. Soc. xv, 1872, 194 (Eastern Colorado).—Allen, Bull. M. C. Z. iii, 1872, 174 (Denver, Colorado).—Coues, Key, 1872, 76.
Sialia occidentalis, Towns., Journ. Phila. Acad. 1837, 188.—Aud., B. Am. ii, 1841, 176, pl. 135.—Nutt., Man. i, 2d ed. 1840, 513.—Woodh., Sitgr. Rep. 1853, 68 (New Mexico).—Newb., P. R. R. Rep. vi, 1857, 80.
Sylvia occidentalis, Aud., Orn. Biog, v, 1839, 41, pl. 393.
Sialia cæruleicollis, Vig., Zool. Beechey's Voy. 1839, 18, pl. 3.

Hab.—United States, from the eastern foot-hills of the Rocky Mountains to the Pacific. Mexico.
Not procured by any of the Expeditions.

The Western Bluebird apparently inhabits only a limited area in the southwestern part of the Missouri region. Mr. Ridgway informs me of its occurrence in Iowa, but this must be highly exceptional. It has not been observed by any of Dr. Hayden's parties in regions where *S. arctica* is abundant, nor have I seen it myself anywhere along the Missouri. Mr. Allen and Mr. Aiken both report it from Eastern Colorado, where it is abundant, as it is also along the Pacific slopes to a higher latitude than it has been observed to reach in the interior. I found it resident and abundant in the mountainous portions of Arizona. Since, according to Mr. Ridgway, it is apparently absent from the Great Basin, it would seem to have two divaricating lines of migration, one carrying it far along the Pacific slopes, and the other taking it not so far along the main chain of the Rocky Mountains. In both cases it chooses wooded as well as mountainous regions. In its habits it is the counterpart of its familiar Eastern relative.

SIALIA ARCTICA, Sw.

Rocky Mountain Bluebird.

Erythaca (Sialia) arctica, Sw., F. B. A. ii, 1831, 209, pl. 39.—Rich., List, 1837.
Sialia arctica, Nutt., Man. ii, 1834, 573; 2d ed. i, 1840, 514.—Bp., List, 1838, 16.—Aud., Syn. 1839, 84; B. Am. ii, 1841, 178, pl. 136.—McCall, Pr. Phila. Acad. 1851, 215.—Woodh., Sitgr. Rep. 1853, 68.—Bd., B. N. A. 1858, 224; Rev. 1864, 64; P. R. R. Rep. x, 1859, pt. iii, 13, pl. 35.—Kenn., *ibid.* pt. iv, 24.—Heerm., *ibid.* pt. vi, 44.—Hayd., Rep. 1862, 159.—Coues, Pr. Phila. Acad. 1866, 66—Coop., Am. Nat. iii, 1869, 32; Pr. Cal. Acad. 1870, 75; B. Cal. 1870, 29.—Stev., U. S. Geol. Surv. Ter. 1870, 463.—Merr., *ibid.* 1872, 671.—Allen, Bull. M. C. Z. iii, 1872, 174.—Aiken, Pr. Bost. Soc. xv, 1872, 194.—Coues, Key, 1872, 76.
Sylvia arctica, Aud., Orn. Biog. v, 1839, 38, pl. 393.
Sialia macroptera, Bd., Stansbury's Rep. 1852, 314.

Hab.—Eastern foot-hills of the Rocky Mountains to the Pacific, chiefly in mountainous regions. North to 64½°; south to Mexico. Less common on the Pacific slopes, where *S. mexicana* prevails.

List of specimens.

| 19194 | 79 | Snake River... | ♂ | June 15, 1860 | F. V. Hayden. | 7.00 | 13.50 | 4.50 |
| 19339 | .... | Bighorn River. | .... | June 6, 1860 | G. H. Trook.. | 7.00 | 12.50 | 4.50 |

Lieutenant Warren's Expedition.—8883–90, Black Hills.
Later Expeditions.—60434, Bitter Cottonwood Creek; 60682–6, Fort Bridger, Sweetwater, and Uintah Mountains; 60939–47, Green River, &c.; 61164, Wyoming (*Schmidt and Stevenson*). 62330–2, Idaho and Wyoming (*Merriam*).

The original specimen of this beautiful species came from Fort Franklin, Great Bear Lake, as described and figured in the Fauna Boreali-Americana. Dr. Richardson observes that it is merely a summer visitor to the Fur Countries. At the other extreme of its range, about the Mexican border, which, so far as known, it does not pass, it is observed only in winter. In the mountainous portions of Arizona I found it rather uncommon, and only late in the autumn, or in winter; I do not think it breeds in the vicinity of Fort Whipple, though probably it does so in the higher mountains not far distant. Dr. Cooper noticed its occurrence in numbers about San Diego, in the severe winter of 1861-'62; they remained until February, and suddenly disappeared. "They were at that time," he continues, "sitting perched on the low weeds and bushes about the plains, often quite a flock together, and some constantly hovering like blue butterflies over the grass, at a height often of fifty feet, on the watch for insects." This accords perfectly with my own observations. The same naturalist found the birds numerous, with lately fledged young, about Lake Tahoe and the summits of the Sierra Nevada, at an elevation of over 6,000 feet. Colonel McCall speaks of their breeding as far south as Santa Fé, New Mexico, in boxes provided for them, just like our Eastern species. Mr. Holden found it using old woodpecker holes, and, in one instance, four eggs were deposited in an old car-wheel. The habits of all the species of *Sialia* are essentially similar, however differently they may be carried out in detail according to circumstances. The eggs of all are alike, pale blue in color, and cannot be distinguished with any certainty. Those of the present species measure 0.90 to 0.95 in length by about 0.70 in breadth, being thus rather larger than those of *S. sialis*, which average about 0.85 by 0.68.

Dr. Hayden procured specimens on all the expeditions, finding the species common near the mountains; "at Laramie Peak, and thence to the Black Hills, it was one of the most abundant birds noticed."

Family SYLVIIDÆ: Sylvias.

An extensive and highly characteristic Old-World family, sparingly represented in the New. A typical Sylvine has been lately ascertained to inhabit this country (*Phyllopneuste borealis*, BLAS.; see TRISTRAM, Ibis, 1871, 231; COUES, Key, 77; *P. kennicottii*, BD., Trans. Chic. Acad. i, 313, pl. 30, f. 2, Alaska). The exclusively American genus *Polioptila* and the widely dispersed genus *Regulus* are each made with most authors, the type of a subfamily.

Subfamily REGULINÆ: Kinglets.

REGULUS CALENDULA, (Linn.) Licht.

Ruby-crowned Kinglet.

Calendula pennsylvanica, BRISS., Orn. iii, 584.
Motacilla calendula, LINN., Syst. Nat. i, 1766, 337.—GM., Syst. Nat. i, 1788, 994.
Sylvia calendula, LATH., Ind. Orn. ii, 1790, 549.—WILS., Am. Orn. i, 1808, 83, pl. 5, fig. 3.
Regulus calendula, LICHT., Verzeichn. 1823.—NUTT., Man. i, 1832, 415.—BP., Syn. 1828, 91; List, 1838, 19.—AUD., Orn. Biog. ii, 546, pl. 195; Syn. 1839, 83; B. Am. ii, 1841, 168, pl. 133.—WOODH., Sitgr. Rep. 1853, 67.—SCL., P. Z. S. 1857, 202; 1858, 300; 1859, 362; 1860, 172 (various Mexican localities).—BD., B. N. A. 1858, 226; Rev. 1864, 66.—KENN., P. R. R. Rep. x, 1859, pt. iv, 24.—HEERM., *ibid.* pt. vi, 43.—COOP. & SUCK., N. H. Wash. Ter. 1860, 174.—HAYD., Rep. 1862, 159.—COUES & PRENT., Smiths. Rep. 1861, 405.—WHEAT., Ohio Agric. Rep. 1860.—DRESS., Ibis, 1865, 476.—COUES, Pr. Phila. Acad. 1866, 66.—COOP., Am. Nat. iii, 1869, 32; Pr.

Cal. Acad. 1870, 75 ; B. Cal. 1870, 33.—DALL & BANN., Tr. Chic. Acad. i, 1869,
276.—STEV., U. S. Geol. Surv. Ter. 1870, 463.—MERR., *ibid.* 1872, 672.—MAYN.,
B. Fla. 1872, 27.—ALLEN, Bull. M. C. Z. iii, 1872, 174.—AIKEN, Pr. Bost. Soc.
xv, 1872, 195.—TRIPPE, *ibid.* 234.—COUES, Key, 1872, 78.—SNOW, B. Kans. 1873,
4.—And of authors generally.
Reguloides calendula, BP., Consp. Av. i, 1850, 292.
Phyllobasileus calendula, CAB., Mus. Hein. 1851, 33.
Regulus rubineus, VIEILL., Ois. Am. Sept. ii, 1807, 49, pls. 104, 105.
Ruby-crowned Wren, EDW., Birds, pl. 254, f. 2.—PENN., Arct. Zool. ii, No. 320.—LATH.,
Syn. iv, 511.

Hab.—The whole of North America. South through Mexico to Central America.
Greenland (REINH., Ibis, iii, 5). Accidental in Europe (GOULD, P. Z. S. 1858, 290 ;
BREE, B. Eur. ii, 109 ; HARTING, Br. B. i, 1872, 107).
Not obtained by Captain Raynolds' Expedition.
Lieutenant Warren's Expedition.—4683–85, mouth of Big Sioux River.
Later Expeditions.—60696-7, Green River and Little Sandy ; 60948-57, Green River
and Henry's Fork (*Schmidt* and *Stevenson*). 62333-4, Wyoming (*Merriam*).

The range of this species proves much more extensive than was formerly supposed, as shown by the above quotations. I have traced it
along the Atlantic coast from Labrador to South Carolina, found it
abundant in Arizona, and observed it during the migrations in Eastern
Dakota. Alaska has lately been added to the list of quotations, as well
as various places in Mexico and thence to Guatemala. Mr. Allen states
that it is a common summer resident of the mountains of Colorado, from
9,000 feet up to timber line, and that he obtained young in the vicinity
of Mount Lincoln toward the end of July. It appears to breed mainly
in mountainous regions or in high latitudes. A nest is said to have been
recently discovered in Western New York ; it was built in the fork of a
tree, and contained young. But in most parts of the United States the
bird is a migrant only, passing through in large numbers, in company
with *R. satrapa*, titmice, and various warblers ; frequenting orchards,
thickets and copses, more rarely high, open woods. It is incessant in
motion, hopping nimbly in search of the minute insects and larvæ which
form its food, uttering its weak chirps. It winters abundantly all along
our southern border, whence it retires in March, reaching the Middle
districts by the end of that month. Some linger well into May, and
come into full song before they leave. Their vocal powers are remarkable for such small birds ; the song is a clear and pleasing warble. In
the fall, when they appear in still greater number than in the spring,
many linger in the Middle districts until the second week in November.

There has been some discussion respecting a supposed sexual difference in the scarlet crest of this species. But the fact is that both sexes
possess this ornament ; and that neither gains it for at least one year is
proved by the circumstance that in the spring migrations a number of
individuals are found with the head perfectly plain. The sexes are never
positively distinguishable by outward characters. In this respect the
species differs from *R. satrapa*, the female of which lacks the scarlet
central patch in the yellow of the crown.

REGULUS SATRAPA, Licht.

Golden-crested Kinglet.

Regulus satrapa, LICHT., Verzeichn. 1823, No. 410.—BP., List, 1838, 19.—AUD., Syn. 1839,
82 ; B. Am. ii, 1841, 165, pl. 132.—WOODH., Sitgr. Rep. 1853, 67 (New Mexico).—
SCL., P. Z. S. 1857, 212 (Orizaba).—BD., B. N. A. 1858, 227 ; Rev. 1864, 65.—
COOP. & SUCK., N. H. Wash. Ter. 1860, 174.—BAED., J. f. O. iv, 33, pl. 1, fig. 8
(egg. Labrador).—COUES & PRENT., Smiths. Rep. 1861, 405 (Washington, D. C.,
wintering).—LORD, Pr. Roy. Art. Inst. 1864, 114 (Vancouver).—DRESS., Ibis,
1865, 476 (Texas).—COUES, Pr. Phil. Acad. 1866, 66 (Arizona).—DALL & BANN.,

Tr. Chic. Acad. i, 1869, 277 (Alaska).—Coop., Am. Nat. iii, 1869, 32 (Montana);
B. Cal. i, 1870, 32.—Aiken, Pr. Bost. Soc. xv, 1872, 195 (Eastern Colorado).—
Trippe, *ibid.* 234 (Iowa).—Allen, Bull. M. C. Z. ii, 1871, 260 (Florida).—Mayn.,
B. Fla. 1872, 25.—Coues, Key, 1872, 78, fig. 19.—Snow, B. Kans. 1873, 4.—And
of authors generally.
Regulus satrapa var. *olivascens*, Bd., Rev. 1864, 65 (in text).
Sylvia regulus, Wils., Am. Orn. i, 1808, 126, pl. 8, f. 2.
Regulus cristatus, Vieill., Ois. Am. Sept. ii, 1807, 50, pl. 106.—Bp. Syn. 1828, 91.—Nutt.,
Man. i, 1832, 420.—Aud., Orn. Biog. ii, 1834, 476, pl. 183.
Regulus tricolor, Nutt., Man. i, 1832, 420.
(?) *Regulus cuvieri*, Aud., Orn. Biog. i, 1832, 288, pl. 55; Syn. 1839, 82; B. Am. ii, 1841,
163, pl. 131.—Nutt., Man. i, 1832, 416.—Bp., List, 1838, 19.

Hab.—North America at large. Mexico.
Not observed by any of the Expeditions.

With a range somewhat corresponding to that of *R. calendula*, and
nearly as extensive, this species is rather more northerly. Thus, it
winters abundantly in the Middle States, and even as far north as Massachusetts, on the Atlantic side; while on the Pacific it occurs at the
same season at least as high as Washington Territory. Its winter range
extends to our southern borders, and into Mexico, but not, so far as we
now know, to Central America. Similarly, nothing is known with certainty of its breeding anywhere in the United States, though it probably will be found to do so in mountainous regions toward our northern
border. It has been found nesting in Newfoundland by Audubon, and
in Labrador, according to Baedecker, who notices the egg, as above;
but I have never myself seen an authentic specimen.

At a very early age the crown is perfectly plain, but it soon shows the
golden of both sexes, and subsequently the flame-color of the male.
There appears to be little probability that *R. cuvieri* will be established
as a species, and nothing to show that the true *R. cristatus* of Europe
occurs in this country, though it is so given by Nuttall.

Subfamily POLIOPTILINÆ : *Gnat-catchers.*

POLIOPTILA CŒRULEA, (Linn.) Scl.

Blue-gray Gnat-catcher.

Motacilla cærulea, Linn., Syst. Nat. i, 1766, 43.—Gm., Syst. Nat. i, 1788, 992.
Sylvia cærulea, Lath., Ind. Orn. ii, 1790, 540.—Vieill., Ois. Am. Sept. ii, 1807, 30, pl. 88.—
Bp., Syn. 1828, 85.
Muscicapa cærulea, Wils., Am. Orn. ii, 1810, 164, pl. 18, f. 3.—Nutt., Man. i, 1832, 297.—
Aud., Orn. Biog. i, 1831, 431, pl. 84.
Culicivora cærulea, Bp., List, 1838, 24.—Aud., Syn. 1839, 46; B. Am. i, 1840, 244, pl. 70.—
Giraud, B. L. I. 1844, 46.—Bp., C. Av. i, 1850, 316.—Cab., J. f. O. 1855, 471 (Cuba).
Sylvania cærulea, Nutt., Man. i, 2d ed. 1840, 337.
Polioptila cærulea, Scl., Pr. Z. S. 1855, 11.—Bd., B. N. A. 1858, 380; Rev. 1864, 74.—
Heerm., P. R. R. Rep. x, pt. vi, 1859, 39.—Hayd., Rep. 1862, 164.—Coues &
Prent., Smiths. Rep. 1861, 411.—Dress., Ibis, 1865, 231.—Coues, Pr. Phila.
Acad. 1866, 66.—Allen, Pr. Ess. Inst. iv, 1864, 83.—Coues, *ibid.* v, 1868, 268.—
Lawr., Ann. Lyc. N. Y. viii, 1866, 283.—Turn., B. E. Pa. 1869, 21.—Lawr., Ann.
Lyc. N. Y. ix, 1869, 199 (Yucatan).—Coop., Pr. Cal. Acad. 1870, 75; B. Cal. 1870,
35.—Allen, Bull. M. C. Z. ii, 1871, 261; iii, 1872, 124.—Scott, Pr. Bost. Soc. xv,
1872.—Trippe, *ibid.* 236 (Iowa).—Mayn., B. Fla. 1872, 28.—Coues, Key, 1872,
78.—Snow, B. Kans. 1873, 6.
Motacilla cana, Gm., Syst. Nat. i, 1788, 973.
Sylvia cana, Lath., Ind. Orn. ii, 1790, 543.
Culicivora mexicana, Bp., Consp. Av. i, 1850, 316 (♀ ; not of Cassin).
Polioptila mexicana, Scl., Pr. Z. S. 1859, 363, 373.

Hab.—United States from Atlantic to Pacific ; north to Southern New England,
and on the Pacific side to 42°. Mexico, and south to Guatemala. Cuba. Bahamas.
Winters along the Southern United States border (Florida, Colorado Valley, &c.).
Not obtained by Captain Raynolds' Expedition, nor by any of the later ones.
Lieutenant Warren's Expedition.—4682, Bald Island.

There is a variance in the accounts of the northern limit of this species. Audubon says that he "saw it on the border-line of Upper Canada, along the shores of Lake Erie." The Rev. W. B. O. Peabody's Report (p. 297) gives it, on Dr. Brewer's authority, as found in Massachusetts, and as far north as the Canada line. Mr. Allen states it has been found "in New York north of the latitude of Boston, as well as in Nova Scotia and in Connecticut." I do not know who is responsible for this Nova Scotia quotation, and cannot verify it; the others are doubtless authentic. Its natural limit appears to be the Connecticut Valley and corresponding latitudes, but it is rare or casual north of the Middle States. Mr. Trippe enumerates it among the birds of Iowa, but did not find it in Minnesota. Dr. D. W. Prentiss and I found it very common about Washington, D. C.; it comes there early in April, just before the trees are leafy, and stays well through September. Mr. Allen records it among the winter birds of Florida; Audubon, among the summer birds of Louisiana, arriving in March. Dr. Hayden found one specimen, as above noted. Mr. Allen notes it from Florida in winter, and from Eastern Kansas in May. I found it rarely in Arizona; it reaches Fort Whipple (latitude about 35°) in April. Dr. Cooper states that it winters in the Colorado Valley, and that it has been taken as far north as Yreka, Cal. (near 42°), in May. Southward it extends through Mexico to Guatemala (the so-called *P. mexicana*). Our other two species, *P. melanura* and *P. plumbea*, are not known to come anywhere near the Missouri region, being restricted to the Southwestern United States. Both occur in Arizona.

Although familiar with this elegant little bird, I never recognized its song, nor was I aware of its vocal powers until recently, when my attention was attracted by Mr. Maynard's agreeable description: "I was walking in a narrow path through a hummock, which lies back of the old fort at Miami, Florida, and had paused to observe a female of this species, when I heard a low warbling which sounded like the distant song of some bird I had never heard before. I listened attentively, but could make nothing of it, and advanced a few paces when I heard it more plainly. This time it appeared to come from above me, and looking upward I saw a male Gnat-catcher hopping nimbly from limb to limb on some small trees which skirted the woods. Although he was but a short distance away, I was obliged to watch the motion of his little throat before I became convinced that this music came from him. It was even so, and nothing could be more appropriate to the delicate marking and size of the tiny, fairy-like bird, than the silvery warble which filled the air with sweet continuous melody. I was completely surprised, for I never imagined that any bird was capable of producing notes so soft and low, yet each one given with such distinctness that the ear could catch every part of the wondrous and complicated song. I watched him for some time, but he never ceased singing save when he sprang into the air to catch some passing insect. The female seemed to enjoy the musical efforts that were accomplished for her benefit, for she drew gradually nearer, until she alighted upon the same tree with her mate. At this moment she took alarm and flew a short distance, followed by her mate. As I walked away I could hear the murmur of the love-song till it became indistinguishable from the gentle rustling of the leaves around." Mr. Maynard gives the following description of a nest of the Blue-gray Gnat-catcher, taken May 23d, in South Carolina: "It is composed of fine stalks of some delicate plants, which are mixed with thistle-down, and woven together with cob-webs. The whole is formed into a neat structure, and smoothly covered with gray lichens which are also kept in place with the fine silk of spider-webs, after the manner of the Wood Pewee or the Hummingbird. It is lined with thistle-down and lichens. The interior is somewhat purse-shaped, for the mouth is contracted. The nest strikingly reminds one of that of a Humming-bird, only it is much larger, being, in fact, very large for the species to which it belongs; yet its beautiful finish does credit to its delicate archi-tect. Eggs from four to six in number, short oval in form, pure white in color, spotted and blotched irregularly with reddish, brown umber and lilac. Dimensions from 0.46 by 0.60 to 0.43 by 0.56." The egg varies greatly in amount of speckling, which, however, is generally pretty evenly distributed. Blown specimens frequently offer a faint bluish cast. Two specimens I measured were 0.60 by 0.47 and 0.58 by 0.48, respectively.

Family PARIDÆ : Titmice.

LOPHOPHANES BICOLOR, (Linn.) Bp.

Tufted Titmouse.

Parus bicolor, LINN., Syst. Nat. i, 1766, 340.—GM., Syst. Nat. i, 1788, 1005.—LATH., Ind. Orn. ii, 1790, 567.—WILS., Am. Orn. i, 1808, 137, pl. 8, f. 5.—BP., Journ. Phila. Acad. iv, 1825, 225; Syn. 1828, 100; List, 1838, 20.—AUD., Orn. Biog. i, 1831, 199; v, 1839, 472; pl. 39; Syn. 1839, 78; B. Am. ii, 1841, 143, pl. 125.—NUTT., Man. i, 1832, 236.—LINSLEY, Am. Journ. Sci. xliv, 1843, 255 (Connecticut).—GIRAUD, B. L. I. 1844, 78.
Lophophanes bicolor, BP., Consp. Av. i, 1850, 228.—CASS., Ill. i, 1853, 18.—WOODH., Sitgr. Rep. 1853, 68.—MAXIM., J. f. O. 1858, 117.—BD., B. N. A. 1858, 384; Rev. 1864, 73.—COUES & PRENT., Smiths. Rep. 1861, 411.—HAYD., Rep. 1862, 174.—ALLEN, Pr. Ess. Inst. iv, 1864, 83.—COUES, *ibid.* v, 1868, 279.—LAWR., Ann. Lyc. N. Y. viii, 1866, 283.—TURN. B. E. Pa. 1869, 21.—GREGG, Pr. Elmira Acad. 1870 (Che-mung County, N. Y., rare).—ALLEN, Bull. M. C. Z. ii, 1871, 261 (Florida); iii, 1872, 125 (Kansas).—SCOTT, Pr. Bost. Soc. xv, 1872 (West Virginia).—TRIPPE, *ibid.* 236 (Iowa, resident).—MAYN., B. Fla. 1872, 32.—COUES, Key, 1872, 80, fig. 21.—SNOW, B. Kans. 1873, 6 (resident).
Bæolophus bicolor, CAB., Mus. Hein. 1851, 91.
Lophophanes missouriensis, BD., B. N. A. 1858, 384 (in text).

Hab.—Eastern United States. North to the Connecticut Valley, rarely (??) to Nova Scotia, AUD.), and Iowa. West to Kansas and Nebraska. Resident throughout its range.
Not obtained by Captain Raynolds' Expedition, nor by the later ones.
Lieutenant Warren's Expedition.—4731, St. Joseph, Missouri.

In respect of latitudinal distribution the Tufted Titmouse offers much the same case as the Blue-gray Gnat-catcher—both birds appear to be characteristic of a certain faunal area, beyond which they rarely, if ever, pass. Its northern limit appears to be the Connecticut Valley, for Aud-ubon's Nova Scotian record requires confirmation. The species belongs distinctively to the Eastern Province, reaching only to the Lower Mis-souri, Eastern Kansas, and Nebraska. Mr. Allen says that it was "one of the most numerously represented and most noisy species met with at Leavenworth." Though so restricted in its northward range, it is a hardy bird, not migratory, remaining in abundance in the Middle dis-tricts throughout the year. It shares the restless, noisy, and inquisitive characters of the family to which it belongs. The eggs, of the usual shape in this group, are five or six in number, deposited in various holes and crannies; they measure about 0.70 by 0.55 inches, are white, and thickly and pretty evenly sprinkled with minute dots of reddish-brown.

LOPHOPHANES INORNATUS, (Gamb.) Cass.

Plain-crested Titmouse.

Parus inornatus, GAMB., Pr. Phila. Acad. ii, 1845, 265 ; *ibid.* iii, 1847, 154 ; Journ. Phila.
    Acad. i, 1847, 35, pl. 8.
Lophophanes inornatus, CASS., Ill. i, 1853, 19.—BD., B. N. A. 1858, 386 ; Rev. 1864, 78.—
    SCL., Cat. 1862, 14.—HEERM., P. R. R. Rep. x, 1859, pt. vi, 42.—COUES, Pr. Phila.
    Acad. 1866, 79.—COOP., B. Cal. i, 1870, 42.—AIKEN, Pr. Bost. Soc. 1872, 195
    (Eastern Colorado).—COUES, Key, 1872, 80, fig. 22.
    Hab.—Black Hills to the Pacific, and southward in the United States.

This species, which was not observed by either of the expeditions, is
brought into the present connection by the researches of Mr. C. E. Aiken,
who found it a "common winter resident" in Eastern Colorado. I
found it to be an abundant species in Upper Arizona, where it is
apparently resident, though more frequently observed in winter. Its
habits are precisely the same as those of its Eastern congener.

PARUS ATRICAPILLUS, Linn.

Black-capped Chickadee.

Parus atricapillus, LINN., Syst. Nat. i, 1766, 341.—GM., Syst. Nat. i, 1788, 1008.—LATH.,
    Ind. Orn. ii, 1790, 566.—FORST., Philos. Trans. lxii, 1772, 407.—WILS., Am. Orn.
    i, 1808, 134, pl. 8, f. 4.—BP., Journ. Phila. Acad. 1825, 254 ; Syn. 1828, 100 ; List,
    1838, 20.—SW. & RICH., F. B. A. ii, 1831, 226.—AUD., Orn. Biog. iv, 1838, pl.
    353, f. 3 ; Syn. 1839, 79 ; B. Am. ii, 1841, 146, pl. 126.—CASS., Ill. 1853, 17.—BD.,
    B. N. A. 1858, 390.—(?) MAXIM., J. f. O. 1858, 119.—WOODH., Sitgr. Rep. 1853,
    68 (Indian Territory).—ALLEN, Mem. Bost. Soc. 1868, 493 (Iowa).—TRIPPE, Pr.
    Ess. Inst. vi, 1871, 115 (Minnesota) ; Pr. Bost. Soc. xv, 1872, 236 (Iowa).—
    MCILWR., Pr. Ess. Inst. v, 1866, 88 (Canada West).—ALLEN, *ibid.* iv, 1864, 69.—
    VERR., *ibid.* iii, 1862, 150 (Maine, breeds).—BOARDM., Pr. Bost. Soc. ix, 1862,
    126 (Maine, breeds).—ALLEN, Bull. M. C. Z. ii, 1871, 261 (critical).—MAYN., Pr.
    Bost. Soc. xiv, 1871 (New Hampshire, breeding) ; B. Fla. 1872, 30.—TURN., B.
    E. Pa. 1869, 21.—DALL & BANN., Tr. Chic. Acad. i, 1869, 280 (Alaska).—COUES,
    Key, 1872, 81, fig. 25.—SNOW, B. Kans, 1873, 6.
Pœcile atricapillus, BP., Consp. Av. i, 1850, 230.—CAB., Mus. Hein. i, 1851, 91.—COUES,
    Pr. Ess. Inst. vi, 1868, 279.
Parus palustris, NUTT., Man. i, 1832, 79.

    Hab.—Eastern United States, rather northerly, and thence to Alaska. Replaced in
Southern United States (Maryland and Illinois, southward) by var. *carolinensis*, and in
most of the Missouri region by var. *septentrionalis.*
    This form was not noticed by either Expedition.

The typical Chickadee occupies but a limited area of the Missouri
region, being mostly replaced by the larger, more hoary, and longer-
tailed form. It is, however, quoted from Kansas, Western Iowa, and
Minnesota, as above. The var. *carolinensis* represents the opposite extreme, characterized by its small size, little hoariness, tendency to
greater extension of the black on the throat, and particularly by the
shortness of its tail, which is commonly less in length than the wing.
It is the common resident species as far north as Washington, D. C.,
where Dr. Prentiss and myself were probably mistaken in supposing
the true *atricapillus* to occur. The Titmouse builds a nest of mosses
and various other soft vegetable substances, lining it with hair or feathers ; it is snugly hidden in the hole of a tree. The eggs are numerous—
five or six—white, with a delicate rosy blush when fresh, speckled all
over, but most thickly at the larger end, with reddish-brown. They
usually dig a hole for themselves, almost like woodpeckers, choosing a
decayed tree easily excavated after the bark is drilled through ; the
cavity is of large size, though with a small entrance. They also often
occupy knot-holes, which they find to suit their purposes, and similar retreats of various sorts.

PARUS ATRICAPILLUS var. SEPTENTRIONALIS, (Harris) Allen.

Long-tailed Chickadee.

Parus septentrionalis, HARRIS, Pr. Phila. Acad. 1845, 300.—CASS., Ill. i, 1853, 17, 80, pl.
14.—BD., B. N. A. 1858, 389.—SCL., Cat. A. B. 1861, 14.—HAYD., Rep. 1862, 164.—
BD., Rev. 1864, 79.—STEV., U. S. Geol. Surv. Ter. 1870, 464.—AIKEN, Pr. Bost.
Soc. xv, 1872, 195.—SNOW, B. Kans. 1873, 6.
Parus atricapillus var. *septentrionalis*, ALLEN, Bull. M. C. Z. iii, 1872, 174.—COUES, Key,
1872, 81.
Parus septentrionalis var. *albescens*, BD., B. N. A. 1858, p. xxxvii.—COOP., Am. Nat. iii,
1869, 74.

Hab.—Kansas and Missouri to the Rocky Mountains. Northward to the Fur Countries. Southward in alpine regions to New Mexico. Up mountains to the limit of arboreal vegetation.
Not obtained by Captain Raynolds' Expedition.
Lieutenant Warren's Expedition.—8827–8, Black Hills; 4732, Fort Leavenworth; 4733, Big Nemaha River.
Later Expeditions.—60433, Bitter Cottonwood; 60693–4, 60961–8, Fort Bridger, Green River, &c.

A part of these specimens are from the same area and nearly the same locality as Mr. Harris's originals.

Since I have been on the Upper Missouri I have taken pains to secure and measure carefully a number of the Titmice of the region. They are all large, averaging 5.50 in length, with wing from 2.40 to 2.75, and tail from 2.60 to 2.80; the hoariness of the wings and tail is conspicuous. I have found no tail quite 3 inches long, but that dimension is shown by a specimen in my cabinet from the mountains of New Mexico; I doubt that this length is ever exceeded.

The specific identity of the various current "species" of North American Black-capped and -throated Titmice seems to have been first recognized, or rather suspected, by the late Dr. Henry Bryant (Pr. Bost. Soc. 1865, 368), well known as one of the most accomplished ornithologists of this country. But it remained for Mr. Allen to prove the point and explain the natural co-ordination of the several forms. Measuring twenty-seven specimens, all from Massachusetts, he finds the total length to vary an inch—from 4.70 to 5.75; the extent to be equally variable—7.50 to 8.60; the wing to vary from 2.33 to 2.63; the tail from 2.15 to 2.67. These extremes embrace the dimensions of both "*septentrionalis*" and "*carolinensis*," which are thus shown to intergrade with *atricapillus* proper. We can only predicate a variety by taking an average: "*carolinensis*" is the smaller, because more southern, form, with a minimum of hoariness; "*septentrionalis*" is the other extreme; it shows an average length of tail above the average of typical *atricapillus*, and an extreme of length that the latter never presents.

I find that, as Dr. Hayden says, this bird is very abundant in the river-bottom all along the Missouri, where it is one of the few birds that endure the rigors of winter in this bleak region. I observed it in small restless flocks, generally in the shrubbery, in company with tree sparrows, which are also abundant at that season. During the winter they have only the characteristic "chickadee" note, but in spring, at the approach of the breeding season, they utter a peculiarly soft long-drawn note of two syllables, somewhat different in intonation from that of the common species. Mr. Allen found this form in Eastern and Middle Kansas; in the mountains of Colorado, up to about 11,000 feet; in Wyoming; and in Utah. It occupies alpine regions as far south as New Mexico.

Dr. Cooper quotes var. *occidentalis* from the Rocky Mountains of Montana.

PARUS MONTANUS, Gamb.

Mountain Chickadee; White-browed Chickadee.

Parus montanus, GAMB., Pr. Phila. Acad. i, 1843, 259; 1847, 155; Journ. i, 1847, 35, pl. 8,
  f. 1.—CASS., Ill. i, 1853, 18.—WOODH., Sitgr. Rep. 1853, 68 (San Francisco Mts.,
  breeding).—NEWB., P. R. R. Rep. vi, 1857, 79.—HEERM., *ibid.* x, pt. vi, 1859,
  42.—BD., B. N. A. 1858, 394.—COOP. & SUCK., N. H. Wash. Ter. 1860, 194.—
  BD., Rev. 1864, 82.—COOP., Am. Nat. iii, 1869, 75 (Montana); B. Cal. 1870,
  46.—STEV., U. S. Geol. Surv. Ter. 1870, 464.—MERR., *ibid.* 1872, 672.—ALLEN,
  Bull. M. C. Z. iii, 1872, 174 (Colorado).—AIKEN, Pr. Bost. Soc. xv, 1872, 195
  (Colorado).—COUES, Key, 1872, 81.
Pœcile montanus, COUES, Pr. Phila. Acad. 1866, 79 (Arizona).

Not obtained by either of the earlier Expeditions.
Later Expeditions.—60695, Uintah Mountains; 62349-52, Idaho and Wyoming.

Readily distinguished among its allies by the white superciliary
stripe. It is a common and generally distributed inhabitant of the
higher lands of the two western United States Provinces. Its habits
are exactly like those of the common Chickadee. Mr. Aiken saw it in
flocks occasionally through the winter, remarking that it frequents the
shrubbery of the mountain sides, but is not found on the lowlands.
Mr. Allen observed it at intervals throughout the mountains of Colorado,
from about 8,000 feet up to the timber line, but much less numerously
than the common species. Mr. Merriam remarks: "Téton Cañon was
the first place where we observed this species, probably because it was
the first where we found coniferous trees. It is also an abundant species
in the Fire-hole Basin, and from the sources of Snake River to where it
leaves the wooded mountain-sides." I found the bird common in various
coniferous mountainous tracts in New Mexico and Arizona, where it is
resident. Habits not peculiar; egg not seen.

PARUS RUFESCENS, Towns.

Chestnut-backed Chickadee.

Parus rufescens, TOWNS., Journ. Phila. Acad. 1837, 190.—AUD., Orn. Biog. iv, 1838, 371,
  pl. 353.—AUD., Syn. 1839, 80.—AUD., B. Am. ii, 1841, 158, pl. 129.—CASS., B. Cal.
  & Tex. 1853, 18.—BD., B. N. A. 1858, 394.—HEERM., P. R. R. Rep. x, 1859, pt.
  vi, 42.—COOP. & SUCK., Nat. Hist. Wash. Ter. 1860, 194.—BD., Rev. 1864, 83.—
  DALL & BANN., Tr. Chic. Acad. i, 1869, 280 (Sitka).—COOP., Am. Nat. iii,
  1869, 75 (Montana).—COOP., B. Cal. i, 1870, 47.—COUES, Key, 1872, 81.
Pœcile rufescens, BP., Consp. Av. i, 1850, 230.

Hab.—Especially Cascade and Coast ranges to the Pacific, from Sitka to Santa Cruz,
but also extending to the Rocky Mountains (*Cooper*). (In Northern Alaska *P. hudsonicus*
is found instead.)

The centre of abundance of this species appears to be in Washington
Territory, where Drs. Cooper and Suckley found it extremely common,
in coniferous and other evergreen forests, and resident. It is stated to
breed in holes in decayed trunks, and its habits, as described, are the
same as those of its congeners. I have never seen it alive, nor was it
met with by either expedition; but Dr. Cooper has extended its previously recorded range to Montana.

PSALTRIPARUS PLUMBEUS, Bd.

Leaden Titmouse.

Psaltria plumbea, Bd., Pr. Phila. Acad. vii, 1854, 118 (Colorado Chiquito, Ariz.).
Psaltriparus plumbeus, Bd., B. N. A. 1858, 398 ; Rev. 1864, 79.—Kenn., P. R. R. Rep. x,
    1859, pt. iv, 25, pl. 33, f. 2.—Coues, Pr. Phila. Acad. 1866, 79.—Coop., B. Cal. i,
    1870, 49.—Stev., U. S. Geol. Surv. Ter. 1870, 464 (Green River).—Aiken, Pr.
    Bost. Soc. 1872, 195 (Eastern Colorado).—Coues, Key, 1872, 82.

Hab.—Southern Rocky Mountain region.
Not obtained by the earlier Expeditions.
Later Expeditions.—Green River (*Stevenson*).

The distinctive characters of this species are not strong, and it would
not be surprising if it should prove only a geographical race of the Pacific coast species, *P. minimus.*

According to Mr. Aiken, small flocks of the Leaden Titmouse were
occasionally seen during the winter in the foot-hills of Eastern Colorado,
among shrubbery. This, with Mr. Stevencon's record, considerably extends its known range, hitherto confined to Arizona. In that country I
found it abundant. Mr. Aiken is, I think, mistaken in stating that the
iris of the male is brown, and that of the female yellow ; this difference
being entirely fortuitous, independent of sex or age, and perhaps analogous to the diverse coloration of the bill in many species of Jays ; at
least such was my conclusion after examining many specimens. It is
a resident of the mountains of Arizona, where it braves the rigors of
winter without apparent inconvenience, though one is tempted to wonder how such a tiny body, no larger than the end of one's thumb, can
retain its animal heat during exposure to cold that sometimes destroys
large birds like the raven. It is a sociable little creature, generally
going in companies of from half a dozen to fifty, actively engaged in
their search for minute insects, and continually calling to each other
with their curiously squeaky notes. It scarcely knows fear in the presence of man, and will continue its busy search though an observer may
be standing within a few feet of it. I found it oftenest in the shrubbery
of the hillsides and the dense undergrowth which fills the ravines ; it
appeared to have little fancy for the higher growths of oak or pine. It
is surprising what large insects this little creature will sometimes capture ; I saw one struggling with a caterpillar nearly as long as its own
body, and it succeeded, after great exertion, in disposing of the big
mouthful. The nest and eggs I have never seen, nor am I aware that
they have been discovered ; but it is to be presumed that they do not
differ essentially from those of *P. minimus.* This bird builds an astonishingly large nest for such a wee creature—a long purse woven of soft
tree-moss and lichens, some six or eight inches long, suspended by the
contracted brim from a forked twig. The eggs, six or eight in number,
measure about 0.58 by 0.44, and differ from those of the genus *Parus* in
being pure white, without any markings.

Family SITTIDÆ : Nuthatches.

SITTA CAROLINENSIS, Lath.

White-bellied Nuthatch.

Sitta europæa var. *carolinensis*, Gm., Syst. Nat. i, 1788, 440.
Sitta carolinensis, Lath., Ind. Orn. i, 1790, 262.—Wils., Am. Orn. i, 1808, 10, pl. 2, f. 3.—
    Bp., Journ. Phila. Acad. 1825, p. — ; Syn. 1828, 96 ; List, 1838, 10 ; Consp. i, 1850,
    227.—Nutt., Man. i, 1832, 581.—Aud., Orn. Biog. ii, 1834, 299 ; v, 1839, 473 ; pl.

152.—AUD., Syn. 1839, 167.—AUD., B. Am. iv, 1842, 175, pl. 247.—BD., B. N. A.
1858, 374, pl. 33, fig. 4; Rev. 1864, 86.—MAXIM., J. f. O. vi, 1858, 106.—SCL., Ibis,
Apr. 1865.—ALLEN, Bull. M. C. Z. iii, 1872, 174 (Eastern Kansas).—SNOW, B.
Kans. 1873, 6.—SCOTT, Pr. Bost. Soc. Oct. 1872 (breeding in mountains of West
Virginia).—TRIPPE, ibid. 1872, 236 (Iowa).—MAYN., B. Fla. 1872, 35.—COUES,
Key, 1872, 83, fig. 26; and of writers.

Sitta melanocephala, VIEILL., Gal. Ois. i, 1834, 171, pl. —.

Hab.—Eastern United States and British Provinces. West to the Lower Missouri.
Not noticed by either Expedition.

Excepting the lower valley, the species is replaced by the following in
the Missouri region:

SITTA CAROLINENSIS var. ACULEATA, (Cass.) Allen.

Slender-billed Nuthatch.

Sitta aculeata, CASS., Pr. Phila. Acad. viii, 1856, 254.—BD., B. N. A. 1858, 375, pl. 33, f. 3.—
KENN., P. R. R. Rep. x, part iv, 26, pl. 33, f. 4.—HEERM., ibid. part vi, 55.—
COOP. & SUCK., N. H. Wash. Ter. 1860, 193.—BD., Rev. 1864, 86.—COOP.,
Pr. Phila. Acad. 1866, 78.—COOP., Am. Nat. iii, 1869, 74; B. Cal. i, 1870, 54.—
AIKEN, Pr. Bost. Soc. 1872, 195.—MERR., U. S. Geol. Surv. Ter. 1872, 672.

Sitta carolinensis, NUTT., Man. 2d ed. 1840, i, 695 (west coast).—NEWB., P. R. R. Rep. vi,
1857, 79 (western).—(?) SCL., P. Z. S. 1856, 293; 1858, 300; 1859, 363, 373 (Mexico).—(?) SUMICH., Mem. Bost. Soc. i, 1869, 544 (Vera Cruz).

Sitta carolinensis var. *aculeata,* ALLEN, Bull. M. C. Z. 1872, 174.—COUES, Key, 1872, 83.

Hab.—Middle and Western Provinces, United States; south to Cordova, Mexico.

List of specimens.

| 19228 | 166 | Cheyenne River.. | ♂ | Oct. 19, 1859 | F. V. Hayden. | 5.50 | 11.25 | 3.50 |
| 19229 | 167 | .... do .... | .... | .... do ..... | ..... do ...... | 5.00 | 11.00 | 3.50 |

Not obtained by Lieutenant Warren's Expedition.
Later Expeditions.—62297, Lower Geyser Basin, Wyoming (*Merriam*).

The slender-billed form is as abundant in the wooded regions of the
West as its Eastern representative. Its habits are precisely the same.
Neither variety appears to extend much, if any, north of the United
States, in this respect differing from *S. canadensis.*

The distinction between the two varieties consists mainly in the slenderer bill of var. *aculeata.* Since its first introduction into the system,
by Mr. Cassin, in 1856, it has been currently rated as a species, until
reduced to its proper position by Mr. Allen and myself, about simultaneously. Dr. Sclater had, however, previously expressed strong doubts
of its validity, although he did not formally make the reduction, in his
admirable account of the genus *Sitta,* published in the Ibis, April, 1865.

The range of the typical *carolinensis* meets that of *aculeata* in the region embraced in the present report; the former bird being found in
Kansas and Missouri, but apparently not far up the river.

The nidification of the Nuthatches is similar in most respects to that
of the Titmice. They build in holes of trees, constructing a shallow
nest of grasses and similar vegetable substances, lined with hair or
feathers. The eggs of the present species are five or six in number,
white or creamy-white in color, speckled and blotched with reddish-
brown and lavender, sometimes over the whole surface, but oftenest
chiefly about the larger end, where they frequently form, or tend to
form, a wreath. They measure 0.75 to 0.82 in length, by 0.55 to 0.63 in
breadth.

SITTA CANADENSIS, Linn.

Red-bellied Nuthatch.

Sitta canadensis, LINN., Syst. Nat. i, 1766, 177.—GM., Syst. Nat. i, 1788, 441.—LATH.,
Ind. Orn. i, 1790, 262.—BP., Syn. 1828, 96 ; List, 1838, 10 ; Consp. i, 1850, 227.—
NUTT., Man. i, 1832, 583.—AUD., Orn. Biog. ii, 1834, 24, pl. 105 ; Syn. 1839, 167 ;
B. Am. iv, 179, pl. 248.—BD., B. N. A. 1858, 376 ; Rev. 1864, 86.—COUES &
PRENT., Smiths. Rep. 1861, 411.—HAYD., Rep. 1862, 164.—COOP. & SUCK., N.
H. Wash. Ter. 1860, 193.—COOP., Am. Nat. iii, 1869, 74 ; B. Cal. i, 1870, 54.—
COUES, Pr. Phila. Acad. 1866, 79.—SCL., Cat. 1861, 15 ; Ibis, Apr. 1865.—PUTN.,
Pr. Ess. Inst. i, 1856, 214.—VERR., *ibid.* iii, 1862, 150.—ALLEN, *ibid.* iv, 1864, 69.—
MCILWR., *ibid.* v, 1866, 88.—COUES, *ibid.* TRIPPE, *ibid.* vi, 1871,
117.—LAWR., Ann. Lyc. N. Y. viii, 1866, 283.—TURNB., B. E. Pa. 1869, 21.—
STEV., U. S. Geol. Surv. Ter. 1870, 464.—COUES, Key, 1872, 83, fig. 27.—SNOW,
B. Kans. 1873, 6.
Sitta varia, WILS., Am. Orn. i, 1808, 40, pl. 2, f. 4.
"*Sitta stulta*, VIEILL." (BP.)

Hab.—North America at large, in wooded regions, but rather northerly (to 63° or
further). South, however, to the Mexican border.
Not obtained by Captain Raynolds' Expedition.
Lieutenant Warren's Expedition.—5280, Cedar Island, Missouri River; 8889-90, Black
Hills.
Later Expeditions.—60690-2, 60972-3, Fort Bridger, Green River, &c.

As Dr. Hayden remarks, this species is quite rare in the Northwest, the nature of the surface being for the most part unsuited to its wants. It is confined to the wooded streams and the mountains about the various headwaters of the Missouri. In the Eastern United States, the bird is not plentiful south of the Middle States, and is apparently wanting in the Southern States, its place being supplied by the peculiar *S. pusilla*, along with *S. carolinensis*. About Washington, D. C., it was occasionally observed by Dr. Prentiss and myself, but only from October to May. It is resident in New England, breeding abundantly in the northern portions. Audubon gives an interesting note of its nidification : "I found it building its nest," he says, "near Eastport, in Maine, on the 19th of May, before the Bluebird had made its appearance there, and while much ice still remained on the northern exposures. The nest is dug in a low dead stump, seldom more than four feet from the ground, both the male and the female working by turns until they have got to the depth of about fourteen inches. The eggs, four in number, are small and of a white color, tinged with a deep blush and sprinkled with reddish dots. They raise, I believe, only one brood in the season." The eggs are only distinguishable from those of *S. carolinensis* by their smaller size, averaging about 0.60 by 0.48 ; the difference is, however, quite appreciable on comparison. The amount of speckling is undetermined, but the surface is generally pretty evenly covered. They are from four to six in number.

SITTA PYGMÆA, Vig.

Pygmy Nuthatch.

Sitta pygmæa, VIG., Zool. Beechey's Voy. 1839, 29, pl. 4.—AUD., Orn. Biog. v, 1839,·63,
pl. 415.—AUD., Syn. 1839, 168.—AUD., B. Am. iv, 1842, 184, pl. 250.—NEWB., P.
R. R. Rep. vi, 1857, 79.—BD., B. N. A. 1858, 378.—SCL., P. Z. S. 1859, 363
(Xalapa).—COOP. & SUCK., N. H. Wash. Ter. 1860, 193.—BD. Rev. 1864,
88.—SCL., Ibis, 1865.—COUES, Pr. Phila. Acad. 1866, 78.—COOP., Am. Nat. iii,
1869, 74 (Montana).—SUMICH., Mem. Bost. Soc. i, 1869, 544 (Vera Cruz).—COOP.,
B. Cal. i, 1870, 55.—AIKEN, Pr. Bost. Soc. 1872, 195.—COUES, Key, 1872, 83, fig. 27.
Sitta pusilla var. *pygmæa*, ALLEN, Bull. M. C. Z. 1872, 174 (mountains of Colorado, up
to 8,000 feet).

Hab.—Rocky Mountains to the Pacific. North to 49°. South to Xalapa.

This species, which was not noticed by either expedition, extends to the eastern base of the Rocky Mountains, where it was found, in Montana, by Dr. Cooper. Mr. Allen took it in the mountains of Colorado up to 8,000 feet; Mr. Aiken, in the Black Hills. Prof. Sumichrast states that it is resident in the alpine region of Vera Cruz, ascending to the very limit of vegetation on the peaks of Orizaba and Popocatepetl. On the Pacific coast it descends, according to Dr. Cooper, as low as Monterey. It is an abundant species in all suitable places throughout its range, an almost exclusive inhabitant of forests, giving evident preference to those of conifers. In crossing the main chain of the Sierra Madre, at Whipple's Pass, in July, I found it abundant to the summit, in high pine woods; and in the same situations in Upper Arizona it occurs in profusion, and resides permanently. Like the Brown-headed Nuthatch, it is a sociable—almost gregarious—little creature, assembling in noisy restless troops, actively fluttering among the pines and scrambling about their trunks and branches, picking its minute insect prey out of the cracks in the bark. It has a variety of odd, scraping notes, impossible to describe, and makes as much ado about its puny little business as if it were helping the world roll on—as, on second thought, I suppose it does. The mode of nidification is the same as that of other species; the eggs are five or six in number, pinkish-white, dotted with reddish. They would not be distinguishable with certainty from those of *S. canadensis*, but appear to average rather narrower, measuring about 0.62 by 0.48. The young appear first in June; and from the circumstance of finding newly-feathered birds much later in the summer, I presume at least two broods are reared each season.

Communicating with me respecting this species, Mr. Allen observes: "I found it at frequent intervals in our journey from Denver to South Park, usually in quite large parties, associated with Titmice and Kinglets, the whole party keeping up a lively twitter as they passed from tree to tree. It is indistinguishable in notes or habits from its near relation, the Brown-headed Nuthatch of the Southern States. They both hunt the branches of the trees rather than their trunks, often flitting, like Kinglets, about the outer extremities of the branches in their search for insects, thus more resembling both the Kinglets and the Tomtits in their manner of hunting than our common Nuthatches."

In this species the color of the under parts is as variable as that of *S. canadensis*, ranging from fulvous-whitish to rusty-brown. The characters supposed to distinguish it from *pusilla* are very slight, so that it is quite possible Mr. Allen is right in holding it for a variety of the latter.

Family CERTHIIDÆ : Creepers.

CERTHIA FAMILIARIS, Linn.

Brown Creeper.

Certhia familiaris, LINN., and of authors.—VIEILL., Ois. Am. Sept. ii, 1807, 70.—WILS., Am. Orn. i, 1808, 122, pl. 7.—AUD., Orn. Biog. v, 1839, 158, pl. 415.—AUD., B. Am. ii, 1841, 109, pl. 115.—MAYN., Pr. Bost. Soc. xiv, 1871 (New England, breeding south to Massachusetts).—COUES, Key, 1872, 84, f. 28.
Certhia americana, BP., Comp. and Geog. List, 1838.—NUTT., Man. i, 1840, 701.—BD., B. N. A. 1858, 372, pl. 83, f. 2; Rev. 1864, 89.—MAXIM., J. f. O. 1858, 105.—KENN., P. R. R. Rep. x, 1859, pt. iv, 26.—HEERM., *ibid.* pt. vi, 42.—COOP. & SUCK., N. H. Wash. Ter. 1859, 192.—SCL., Cat. A. B. 1861, 15.—SNOW, B. Kans. 1873, 6.—Also of nearly all local writers of Eastern United States.

Certhia mexicana, GLOGER & REICH.—SCL., P. Z. S. 1856, 290; 1858, 297; 1859, 362, 372.—BD., B. N. A. 1858, 923, pl. 83, f. 2; Rev. 1864, 90.—SUMICH., Mem. Bost. Soc. i, 1869, 544 (Vera Cruz).—COOP., Am. Nat. iii, 1869, 74; B. Cal. 1870, 58. (A variety.)
Hab.—Europe. North America at large. Mexico (var.).

No specimens of this species were taken by either of the expeditions, but I bring it into the present connection, since its known range is such as to make it quite certain that it occurs in the Missouri region. It is an inconspicuous bird, liable to be long overlooked in regions where it is not very abundant.

I am unable to perceive any difference between American and European examples, and I am not aware that any tangible characters have been ascribed to our bird by those writers who have technically separated it. The Southwestern American form appears to constitute a slight variety.

The egg of the Creeper is not distinguishable with certainty from that of a Chickadee, but is smaller, measuring only about 0.55 by 0.43. It is white, speckled with reddish-brown.

Family TROGLODYTIDÆ: Wrens.

SALPINCTES OBSOLETUS, (Say) Cab.

Rock Wren.

Troglodytes obsoletus, SAY, Long's Expd. ii, 1823, 4.—NUTT., Man. i, 1832, 435.—AUD., Orn. Biog. iv, 1838, 443, pl. 360.—AUD., B. Am. ii, 1841, 113, pl. 116.—NEWB., P. R. R. Rep. vi, 1857, 80.—HEERM., P. R. R. Rep. x, 1859, pt. vi, 41.
Myiothera obsolcta, BP., Am. Orn. i, 1825, 6, pl. 1, fig. 2.
Thryothorus obsoletus, BP., Comp. and Geog. List, 1838, 11; Rev. Zool. ii, 1839, 98.
Salpinctes obsoletus, CAB., Wieg. Archiv, 1847, 323.—BP., Consp. Av. i, 1850, 224.—BD., B. N. A. 1858, 357; Rev. 1864, 110.—HAYD., Rep. 1862, 163.—SCL., P. Z. S. 1859, 371.—COUES, Pr. Phila. Acad. 1866, 77.—COOP., Am. Nat. iii, 1869, 297 (Upper Missouri), 73 (breeding at Fort Benton).—COOP., Pr. Cal. Acad. 1870, 75 (Colorado River).—COOP., B. Cal. 1870, 64.—ALLEN, Bull. M. C. Z. iii, 1872, 174.—HOLD., Pr. Bost. Soc. xv, 1872, 195 (Black Hills).—STEV., U. S. Geol. Surv. Ter. 1870, 464.—MERR., *ibid.* 1872, 693.—TRIPPE, Pr. Bost. Soc. xv, 1872, 236 (Decatur County, Iowa).—COUES, Key, 1872, 85.
" *Thryothorus latifasciatus*, LICHT." (BP.)

Hab.—United States, from the Central Plains to the Pacific. Iowa (*Trippe.*) Mexico. Not obtained by Captain Raynolds's Expedition.
Lieutenant Warren's Expedition.—8830, Running Water; 5277-9, Powder River; 8831-2, Mauvaises Terres.
Later Expeditions.—60687, Sweetwater (*Stevenson*); 61654, Ogden, Utah (*Merriam*).

This species is especially characteristic of the interior mountainous regions of the West, although, to the southward at least, it reaches the Pacific coast. It is reported from various parts of California, from Cape St. Lucas, and from Mexico. Mr. Allen found it in Colorado, Mr. Merriam in Utah, where it was abundant about White Sulphur Springs, Mr. Holden in Wyoming, and Dr. Hayden states that it is numerous in the "bad lands." I frequently saw it in Upper Arizona, in rocky fastnesses, where its peculiar song always attracted attention. Dr. Cooper states that a nest from a wood-pile on the Upper Missouri was composed of a loose flooring of sticks, lined with a great quantity of feathers, and contained nine eggs of a reddish color, thickly spotted with chocolate. He also found nests at San Diego, under tiled roofs, containing young, in May. According to Mr. Holden, the nest is merely a few sticks and bits of moss put carelessly together: "one was placed under a rock as large as a dog-house, and in it were four young ones, which scampered off while I was removing the rock." The eggs are four to eight in number, measuring 0.72 by 0.60 inches, being thus much rounded. The shell is white, of crystal purity and smoothness, very sparingly sprinkled with minute dots of reddish-brown, chiefly aggregated at, or in a wreath around, the larger end; but a few other specks are commonly scattered over the whole surface. Such are the characters of two sets in the Smithsonian collection, from Fort Defiance, N. M.; the description, it will be observed, differs from that given by Dr. Cooper.

Since writing the preceding I have received an interesting communication from Mr. T. Martin Trippe, who informs me of the common occurrence of this species in Southwestern Iowa, where he states that he saw or shot altogether some fifteen individuals during the month of October, 1872. This occurrence, which Mr. Trippe meanwhile has published, as above, gives a decided extension to the previously known range of the species.

CATHERPES MEXICANUS, (Sw.) Bd.

Mexican Wren; White-throated Wren.

Thryothorus mexicanus, Sw., Zool. Ill. i, 1829, pl. 11.
Salpinctes mexicanus, Cab., Weig. Archiv, 1847, 324; Mus. Hein. i, 1851, 78.—Bp., Consp. i, 1850, 224.—Scl., P. Z. S. 1857, 212; 1858, 297 (Oaxaca).
Troglodytes mexicanus, Gray, Genera, i, 1847, 159.—Heerm., Journ. Phila. Acad. 1853, 263.—Cass., B. Cal. and Tex. 1854, 173, pl. 30.
Catherpes mexicanus, Bd., B. N. A. 1858, 356; Rev. 1864, 111.—Kenn., P. R. R. Rep. x, 1859, pt. iv, 26.—Scl., Cat. 1862, 18.—Coues, Pr. Phila. Acad. 1866, 77.—Sumich., Mem. Bost. Soc. i, 1869, 545 (Vera Cruz).—Coop., B. Cal. i, 1870, 66.—Aiken, Pr. Bost. Soc. 1872, 196 (Middle Colorado).—Coues, Key, 1872, 85.
Catherpes mexicanus var. *conspersus*, Ridgw., Am. Nat. vii, 1872, 2 (Northern form).
Thryothorus guttulatus, Lafres., R. Z. 1839, 99.
Certhia albifrons, Giraud, B. Tex. 1841, pl. 8.
" *Troglodytes albicollis*, Cuv."
" *Troglodytes murarius*, Licht."

The above synonymy includes both the typical Mexican bird and the United States race, which latter is appreciably different, as Mr. Ridgway has shown, and entitled to rank as a geographical race.

Hab.—Var. *conspersus* from the Southwestern United States, from Colorado (*Aiken*) and Utah (*Henshaw*). Typical *mexicanus* from Mexico to Vera Cruz.

It is a matter of much interest that the known range of the White-throated Wren, hitherto reported only from the United States border and southward, should be extended to Colorado, as has lately been done by Mr. Aiken. Even in Arizona I only found it in localities lower than Fort Whipple. I observed it in the southern and western portions of that Territory, always in cañons and other precipitous, rocky places. The note of the species is one of the most striking I ever heard; for a bird of its size it sings with wonderful strength and clearness, uttering a peculiar ringing whistle, the odd intonations of which are exaggerated in the echos awakened among the fastnesses of the rocks. It is a very active, sprightly bird, leaping and fluttering among the rocks almost incessantly. Mr. Aiken found it *in winter* in Colorado, among large masses of rock, on the faces of cliffs. Mr. Allen observes that "the White-throated Wren is one of the most note-worthy birds of those remarkable localities near Colorado City, known as 'Monument Park' and the 'Garden of the Gods,' where alone I observed it in Colorado. Equally with the Rock Wren, it is a lover of cliffs and bare rocky exposures. Whenever it occurs, at least in the breeding season, its presence is sure to be known by its loud ringing notes. At the localities above named it seemed to delight in the reverberation of its notes from the high sandstone walls that give to the Garden of the Gods its peculiar picturesqueness." According to Prof. Sumichrast, it is very common on the plateau of Mexico, "where it probably has its centre of propagation," and is also found in the temperate region of the department of Vera Cruz. "In Orizaba it nests in the houses; its nest, very skillfully wrought with spider's webs, is built in the crevices of old walls, or in the interstices between the tiles under the roofs of houses."

In connection with this northward extension of the White-throated Wren may be noticed the occurrence of *Campylorhynchus brunneicapillus* in Utah, as I am informed by letter from my friend Dr. H. C. Yarrow, U. S. A., who took the species at St. George, in the southwestern portion of the Territory.

THRYOTHORUS LUDOVICIANUS, (Lath.) Bp.

Great Carolina Wren.

a. *ludovicianus.*

Sylvia ludoviciana, LATH., Ind. Orn. ii, 1790, 548.
Troglodytes ludovicianus, LICHT., Verz. 1823, 35.—BP., Obs. Wils. No. 65; Syn. 93.—NUTT., Man. i, 1832, 429.—AUD., Orn. Biog. i, 1831, 399; v, 1839, 466; pl. 78; Syn. 1839, 74; B. Am. ii, 1841, 116, pl. 117.—GIRAUD, B. L. I. 1844, 75.—WOODH., Sitgr. Rep. 1853, 67 (Texas and Indian Territory).—MAYN., B. Fla. 1872, 37.
Thryothorus ludovicianus, BP., List, 1838, 11; Consp. i, 1850, 220.—BD., B. N. A. 1858, 361; Rev. 1864, 123.—SCL., Cat. A. B. 1861, 20.—COUES & PRENT., Smiths. Rep. 1861, 410 (Washington, D. C., not abundant).—LAWR., Ann. Lyc. N. Y. viii, 1866, 283 (Long Island).—COUES, Pr. Bost. Soc. 1868, 108 (South Carolina).—ALLEN, Mem. Bost. Soc. i, 1868, 523 (Indiana).—TURNB., B. E. Pa. 1869, 20 (wintering).—COUES, Pr. Phila. Acad. 1871, 19 (North Carolina).—ALLEN, Bull. M. C. Z. ii, 1871, 266 (Florida); iii, 1872, 125, 175 (Eastern Kansas).—SNOW, B. Kans. 1873, 6.—COUES, Key, 1872, 86, fig. 29.
Troglodytes arundinaceus, VIEILL., Ois. Am. Sept. ii, 1807, 55, pl. 108 (description, not the biography).
Thryothorus arundinaceus, LESS., Rev. Zool. 1840, 263 (exclusive of synonyms).
Thryothorus littoralis, VIEILL., Nouv. Dict. xxxiv, 1819, 56.
Thryothorus louisianæ, LESS., Rev. Zool. 1840, 262.
Certhia caroliniana, WILS., Am. Orn. ii, 1810, 61, pl. 12, f. 5.

Hab.—Eastern United States, south of New England. West into Kansas. New Mexico (*Henry.*) Resident throughout its range. No extralimital record.
Not obtained by any of the Expeditions.

b. *berlandieri.*

Thryothorus berlandieri, COUCH.—BD., B. N. A. 1858, 362, pl. 83, f. 1; Rev. 1864, 124.
Thryothorus ludovicianus var. *berlandieri*, COUES, Key, 1872, 86.

Hab.—Valley of the Rio Grande, and southward. This is the southern race, differing in longer bill and heavier color; the under parts more decidedly rufous, and the sides barred with dusky. Floridan specimens are intermediate.

Although restricted in its northward dispersion, the Carolina Wren is a hardy bird, enduring the winters of the Middle States. There may be an incomplete recession from its more northern abodes, yet it is as common in winter as in summer, at least from Maryland southward. Such is the case about Washington, D. C., where I found it common at all seasons, though never in great abundance. It frequents shrubbery and undergrowth of all sorts, where it hides with great pertinacity, and is oftener heard than seen. Not that it is particularly a timid bird, for it often comes about the gardens and out-houses; but it is retiring and unfamiliar, courting privacy and seclusion. If we attempt to penetrate its hidden resorts, it hurries away into deeper recesses, with a low fluttering near the ground, or scrambling and hopping from one bush to another, very likely mocking us with its rollicking song as soon as it feels perfectly secure. It shares, however, the restlessness and prying curiosity of its tribe; and if we keep still in a favorable spot we may often see it returning slyly to take a look at us, peering from among the leaves with an inquisitive air, all the while "teetering" its body, and performing odd, nervous antics, as if it were possessed with the very spirit of unrest. At such times it chatters in a harsh querulous tone, as if resenting the intrusion; and this is its ordinary note when angry, alarmed, or otherwise disturbed in mind. Its song is quite another thing—loud, clear, strong, and highly musical; indeed I hardly know what bird possesses a richer voice, though many are sweeter songsters. The song is a rapid succession of whistling notes, delivered with great energy and accent; it closely resembles that of the Cardinal Grosbeak, styled in some parts the "Virginia Nightingale," and meriting the compliment. In still weather the Wren can be heard several hundred yards, but is not easy to trace the music up to its source, because the resonant quality of the notes makes the whole copse seem to ring with the sound, and because the restless songster is constantly changing his position.

This Wren is a very early breeder. In the Carolinas it mates in March, nests in April, and the first of its two or three broods are abroad early in May, if not still sooner. Mr. Allen found the young flying at this time even in Kansas. The bird is so capricious in the matter of a nesting place, that we can hardly say what its preference is, if, indeed, it have any choice. It will build in any odd nook or cranny that it fancies—entering an out-house through a knot-hole or a chink between loose boards, like the House Wren; taking the hollow of a tree or stump; settling in the midst of a thick bush; anywhere, in fact, that offers a snug retreat. In Florida, Mr. Maynard says, they like to nest in the palmettoes; and this agreeable writer tells how convenient such resorts are: "The 'boot,'" he explains, "is the base of the dead leaf-stalks which adhere to the tree after the top has decayed and fallen off; they are quite broad, slightly concave, and extend upward in an oblique direction, leaving a space between them and the trunk; the fronds, in falling, often cover the top with a fibrous *debris*, which is impervious to water, and the cavities beneath form a snug nesting place for the Carolina Wrens." Into some such place as we have seen, the Wren puts a great quantity of fibrous, leafy, or grassy material, not being at all particular, but gathering any trash that it finds convenient; and builds a rather bulky nest, more or less like a ball, with a side-entrance. This is freighted with five or six eggs, and very completely filled before the little ones leave it. The eggs are white, dotted very thickly and pretty evenly with reddish-brown and various neutral tints, generally quite over the surface, but sometimes chiefly wreathing around the large end; sometimes the surface is so thickly covered that the ground is almost hidden. But I have never seen any eggs so uniformly dark as those of the Marsh Wren, or even the House Wren, usually are. Several measurements I took ranged from 0.76 by 0.61 to 0.70 by 0.58, averaging about 0.73 by 0.60. The birds are very private about their domestic arrangements, and generally slip off quietly if they have an unwelcome caller. They keep the young ones about them for a few days after they leave the nest, and during this period they are in a state of perpetual panic, showing their intense worry in redoubled restlessness. But the little family is soon dispersed, let us hope, each to a merry life; the parents take a little relaxation from family cares, and then arrange for a new household.

THRYOTHORUS BEWICKII. (Aud.) Bp.

Bewick's Wren.

a. *bewickii.*

Troglodytes bewickii, AUD., Orn. Biog. i. 1831, 96 ; v, 1838, 467 ; pl. 18.—AUD., Syn. 1839,
   74.—AUD., B. Am. ii, 1841, 120, pl. 118.—NUTT., Man. i, 1832, 434.—LESS., Rev.
   Zool. 1840, 264.—WOODH., Sitgr. Rep. 1853, 67 (Indian Territory, very abundant).—TRIPPE, Pr. Ess. Inst. vi. 1871, 115 (Minnesota, common, breeding).
Thryothorus bewickii, BP., List, 1838, 11.—BP , Consp. i, 1850, 221.—BD., B. N. A. 1858, 363 ;
   Rev. 1864, 126.—COUES, Pr. Bost. Soc. xii, 1868, 108 (South Carolina, resident ?).—TURNB., B. E. Pa. 1869, 20 (rare, in summer only).—SNOW, B. Kans.
   6.—COUES, Key, 1872, 86.
Telmatodytes bewickii, CAB., Mus. Hein. 1850, 78.

b. *leucogaster.*

Troglodytes leucogastra, GOULD, P. Z. S. 1836, 89 (Tamaulipas).
Thryothorus leucogaster, BP., Consp. i, 1850, 222 ; Notes Orn. Delattre, 1854, 43.
Thryothorus bewickii, SCL., P. Z. S. 1859, 371 (Oaxaca).—COUES, Pr Phila. Acad. 1866,
   78 (Arizona).
Thryothorus bewickii var. *leucogaster,* BD., Rev. 1864, 127.—COUES, Key, 1872, 86.

c. *spilurus.*

Troglodytes spilurus, VIG., Zool. Beechey's Voy. 1839, 18, pl. 4, f. 1 (California).
Thryothorus spilurus, COOP., B. Cal. i, 1870, 69.
Troglodytes bewickii, NEWB., P. R. R. Rep. vi, 1857, 80.—HEERM., *ibid.* x, 1859, part vi,
   40.—COOP. & SUCK., N. H. Wash. Ter. 1860, 189.
Thryothorus bewickii var. *spilurus,* BD., Rev. 1864, 126.—COUES, Key, 1872, 86.

Hab.—Eastern United States, north to Pennsylvania and Minnesota ; west to Kansas.
Var. *leucogaster* in Southwestern United States and Mexico. Var. *spilurus* along the
whole Pacific coast, United States and southward.
   Obtained by none of the Expeditions.

Like the Carolina Wren, Bewick's is essentially a southern species. Its
northern limit, in the Atlantic States, is Pennsylvania, where it is rare,
and only found in summer. Mr. Turnbull gives it in his list, and Prof.
Baird took it at Carlisle. It appears to be uncommon all along the line.
I do not recollect that I ever saw it in Maryland, Virginia, or either of
the Carolinas, and I never collected a specimen. In the interior, however, it is abundant in some regions; thus, Mr. Ridgway tells me, it is
very common in Southern Illinois, where it replaces the House Wren, to
the nearly complete exclusion of the latter, and has the same semi-domesticated ways, breeding about out-houses and gardens. In the Mississippi Valley, moreover, it proceeds furthest north. Mr. Trippe records
it as common in Minnesota, where it breeds. The egg, of which I have
only seen two or three authentic examples, is white, speckled with lilac
and darker slaty shades of brown, chiefly about the larger end. The egg
resembles that of a Titmouse or Creeper, but the markings are darker
and the size greater—from 0.70 by 0.52 to 0.66 by 0.51.
   In the southwest I found the white-bellied variety of Bewick's Wren
extremely abundant. It was the characteristic Wren about Fort Whipple, in Arizona, though the House Wren was very common there too.
Similarly, var. *spilurus* abounds in the wooded portions of California.
In their habits, these varieties are identical with the common form, except in so far as certain points may be modified to suit circumstances,
especially in the matter of nesting, in which, as is well known, most
birds accommodate themselves very easily to their surroundings. Possessing few, if any, distinctive traits, there is very little to be said of
Bewick's Wren not equally applicable to its numerous relatives, whose
restlessness, curious excitable temper, and odd energetic actions, are
familiar to every one. It is an accomplished and versatile songster ;
though its notes have not the ring and volume of those of the Carolina
Wren, it has a very pretty song of its own, varied at its whim, quite
unlike the simpler trilling of the House or Marsh Wren.

TROGLODYTES AËDON, Vieill.

House Wren.

Troglodytes aëdon, VIEILL., Ois. Am. Sept. ii, 1807, 52, pl. 107.—VIEILL., Nouv. Dict. xxxiv,
1819, 506.—BP., Obs. Wils. 1825, No. 136; Syn. 1828, 92; List, 1838, 11.—Sw. &
RICH., F. B. A. ii, 1831, 316.—AUD., Orn. Biog. i, 1831, 427, pl. 83; Syn. 1839,
75; B. Am. ii, 1841, 125, pl. 120.—GIRAUD, B. L. I. 1844, 73.—BD., B. N. A. 1858,
367; Rev. 1864, 138.—COUES & PRENT., Smiths. Rep. 1861, 410.—SCL., Cat.
1861, 22.—HAYD., Rep. 1862, 163.—MAYN., Nat. Guide, 1870, 195.—ALLEN, Pr.
Ess. Inst. iv, 1864, 68.—McILWR., Pr. Ess. Inst. v, 1866, 88.—COUES, Pr. Ess.
Inst. v, 1868, 278.—LAWR., Ann. Lyc. N. Y. viii, 1866, 283.—TURNB., B. E. Pa.
1869, 20.—ALLEN, Bull. M. C. Z. ii, 1871, 265; iii, 1872, 174.—MAYN., B. Fla. 1872,
39.—HOLD., Pr. Bost. Soc. 1872, 196 (Black Hills).—COUES, Key, 1872, 86.—And
of authors generally.
Troglodytes fulvus, NUTT., Man. i, 1832, 422.
Troglodytes furvus, RICH. List, 1837, 11.
Troglodytes americanus, AUD., Orn. Biog. v, 1839, 310, pl. 179; Syn. 1839, 75; B. Am. ii,
1841, 123, pl. 119.—BD., B. N. A. 1858, 368; Rev. 1864, 141.—VERR., Pr. Ess.
Inst. iii, 1862, 150.—LAWR., Ann. Lyc. N. Y. viii, 1866, 283.—COUES, Pr. Ess.
Inst. v, 278.
Sylvia domestica, WILS., Am. Orn. i, 1808, 129, pl. 8. f. 3.

Hab.—Eastern United States to Nebraska and Dakota. North to Canada and Nova
Scotia. Winters in the Southern States.
Not obtained by Captain Raynolds' Expedition.
Lieutenant Warren's Expedition.—8846, Loup Fork. This single specimen, among Dr.
Hayden's collections, seems referable to typical *aëdon.*
The *T. americanus* of Audubon, a supposed species, which I doubtfully admitted in
1868, has since been shown by Mr. Allen and Mr. Maynard to be inseparable from *T.
aëdon.* It appears to represent simply rather northerly bred birds. The several extra-
limital varieties of the species are not here considered; our western variety is noted
under the next head.

TROGLODYTES AËDON var. PARKMANNI, (Aud.) Coues.

Western House Wren.

Troglodytes parkmanni, AUD., Orn. Biog. v, 1839, 310; Syn. 1839, 75; B. Am. ii, 1841, 133,
pl. 122.—NUTT., Man. 2d ed. 1840, 483.—BD., B. N. A. 1858, 367; Rev. 1864,
140.—HAYD., Rep. 1862, 164.—SCL., Cat. 1861, 23.—COOP. & SUCK., N. H. Wash.
Ter. 1859, 191.—COUES, Pr. Phila. Acad. 1866, 78.—COOP., Pr. Cal. Acad. 1870,
75; B. Cal. 1870, 71.—AIKEN, Pr. Bost. Soc. 1872, 196.—STEV., U. S. Geol. Surv.
Ter. 1870, 464.—MERR., *ibid.* 1872, 673.
Troglodytes sylvestris, GAMB., Pr. Phila. Acad. iii, 1846, 113.
(?) *Troglodytes americanus,* HEERM., P. R. R. Rep. x, 1859, part vi, 41.
Troglodytes aëdon var. parkmanni, COUES, Key, 1872, 87.

Hab.—Western United States, from Nebraska and Dakota to the Pacific.
Not obtained by Captain Raynolds' Expedition.
Lieutenant Warren's Expedition.—4734–35, 4737, 4138, 4741–43, Upper Missouri; 5274–75,
Blackfoot country; 5276, Fort Lookout; 4739, Council Bluffs; 4740, Bald Island; 4736;
North Platte.
Later Expeditions.—60688–9, Green River; 62328–9, Idaho and Montana.

Dr. Hayden's numerous specimens attest the abundance of this variety
in the northwest. I found it to be numerous in the southwest; and, in
fact, it is a common bird throughout the Middle and Western Provinces
of the United States, where it replaces its familiar Eastern representative. It is impossible to separate this form specifically from *aëdon;* it
is merely a little paler (grayer), while certain supposed peculiarities of
habit are shared by *T. aëdon* in those unfrequented districts where its
ways have not been modified by contact with civilization. It is the
most numerous representative and the most uniformly distributed of the
Troglodytidæ of the West. It is especially common in the scanty and
irregular belts of timber that border the streams of the great plains,
and occurs everywhere in the mountains up to about 10,000 feet. Its
notes vary more or less at different localities, but everywhere it seems
to retain its pugnacious disposition, and its bold, inquisitive habits.

ANORTHURA TROGLODYTES var. HYEMALIS, (Vieill.) Coues.

American Winter Wren.

a. *troglodytes proper.*

(The typical form is European—the only Wren of that country.)

b. *hyemalis.*

Sylvia troglodytes, WILS., Am. Orn. i, 1808, 139, pl. 8, f. 6 (not of European writers).
Troglodytes hyemalis, VIEILL., Nouv. Dict. xxxiv, 1819, 514; Ency. Meth. ii, 1823, 470.—
BP., List, 1838, 11; Consp. i, 1850, 222.—SW. & RICH., F. B. A. ii, 1831, 318.—
AUD., Orn. Biog. iv, 1838, 430, pl. 360; Syn. 1839, 76; B. Am. ii, 1841, 128, pl.
121.—NUTT., Man. i, 2d ed. 1840, 481.—GIRAUD, B. L. I. 1844, 72.—SCL., P. Z. S.
1856, 290 (Cordova); Cat. A. B. 1861, 23.—BD., B. N. A. 1858, 369; Rev. 1864,
144.—COOP. & SUCK., N. H. Wash. Ter. 1860, 191.—WHEAT., Ohio Agric. Rep.
1860, No. 126.—VERR., Pr. Ess. Inst. iii, 1862, 152.—ALLEN, *ibid.* iv, 1864, 68.—
MCILWR., *ibid.* v, 1866, 88.—TRIPPE, *ibid.* vi, 1871, 115.—BOARDM., Pr. Bost. Soc.
ix, 1862, 126.—LAWR., Ann. Lyc. N. Y. viii, 1866, 283.—TURNB., B. E. Pa. 1869,
20.—ALLEN, Mem. Bost. Soc. i, 1808, 494.—COOP., Am. Nat. iii, 1869, 74 (Montana); B. Cal. i, 1870, 73.—MAYN., Pr. Bost. Soc. xiv, 1871; B. Fla. 1872, 40.—
SNOW, B. Kans. 1873, 6.
Anorthura hyemalis, COUES & PRENT., Smiths. Rep. 1861, 410.—ALLEN, Bull. M. C. Z. ii,
1871, 267.—COUES, Pr. Bost. Soc. xii, 1868, 107.—MAYN., Guide, 1870, 96.
Anorthura troglodytes, COUES, Key, 1872, 87, fig. 30.
Anorthura troglodytes var. *hyemalis*, COUES, Key, 1872, 351.
Troglodytes hyemalis var. *pacificus*, BD., Rev. 1864, 145.
Troglodytes europæus, BP., Obs. Wils. 1825, No. 127; Syn. 1828, 93.—NUTT., Man. i, 1832, 427.

c. *alascensis.*

Troglodytes alascensis, BD., Tr. Chic Acad. i, 1869, 315, pl. 30, f. 3.—DALL & BANN., *ibid.* 280.
Anorthura alascensis, COUES, Key 1872, 87.
Anorthura troglodytes var. *alascensis*, COUES, Key, 1872, 351.
Troglodytes hyemalis var. *alascensis*, DALL, Pr. Cal. Acad. Feb. 8, 1873.

Hab.—The whole of North America. South to Cordova (*Sclater*). Winters from New
England southward. Var. *alascensis* is a larger, darker, longer-billed race, inhabiting
Alaska, the Aleutians, and Prybilov Islands. The American bird is not specifically dis-
tinct from the European.

Although this species was not noted by any of the Expeditions, it is
properly brought into the present connection, since it is generally distributed over North America. It readily eludes observation in places
where it is not very abundant, being of a shy and retiring disposition
that keeps it near the ground, and for the most part hidden in the dense
undergrowth or broken rocky places it frequents. Its actions are almost
as much like those of a mouse as of a bird; rarely using its wings except for a short flutter from one bush or stone-heap to another, it creeps
slyly and rapidly about, appearing perhaps for an instant, then suddenly
lost to view. It is rather uncommon about Washington, D. C., from
early in October until the latter part of April; I generally found it
along the secluded banks of Rock Creek, and in the little ravines leading down to the stream. Not having met with it elsewhere, I can say
nothing of its habits during the breeding season from personal observation, but will quote from an excellent account:

"The song of the Winter Wren excels that of any other bird of its
size with which I am acquainted. It is truly musical, full of cadence,
energetic and melodious; its very continuance is surprising, and dull
indeed must be the ear that thrills not on hearing it. When emitted, as
it often is, from the dark depths of the unwholesome swamps, it oper-
ates so powerfully on the mind, that it by contrast inspires a feeling of
wonder and delight, and on such occasions has impressed me with a
sense of the goodness of the Almighty Creator, who has rendered every
spot of earth in some way subservient to the welfare of his creatures.

3

"Once when traveling through a portion of the most gloomy part of a thick and tangled wood in the great pine forest, near Mauch Chunk, in Pennsylvania, at a time when I was intent on guarding myself against the venemous reptiles I expected to encounter, the sweet song of this Wren came suddenly on my ear, and with so cheery an effect that I suddenly lost all apprehension of danger, and pressed forward through the rank briars and stiff laurels in pursuit of the bird which I hoped was not far from its nest. But he, as if bent on puzzling me, rambled here and there among the thickest bushes with uncommon cunning, now singing in one spot not far distant, and presently in another in a different direction. After much exertion and considerable fatigue, I at last saw it alight on the side of a large tree, close to the roots, and heard it warble a few notes, which I thought exceeded any it had previously uttered. Suddenly another Wren appeared by its side, but darted off in a moment, and the bird itself, which I had followed, disappeared. I soon reached the spot, without having for an instant removed my eyes from it, and observed a protuberance covered with moss and lichens, resembling the excrescences which are often seen on our forest trees, with this difference, that the aperture was perfectly rounded, clean, and quite smooth. I put a finger into it and felt the pecking of a bird's bill, while a querulous cry was emitted. In a word, I had, the first time in my life, found the nest of a Winter Wren. * * * * Externally it measured seven inches in length and four and a half in breadth; the thickness of its walls, composed of moss and lichens, was nearly two inches; and thus it presented internally the appearance of a narrow bag, the wall, however, being reduced to a few lines where it was in contact with the bark of the tree. The lower half of the cavity was compactly lined with the fur of the American Hare, and in the bottom or bed of the nest there lay over this about half a dozen of the large downy abdominal feathers of our common Grouse, *Tetrao umbellus.*"

Audubon found six eggs in this, and likewise in another nest that he discovered. He describes them as of a delicate blush-color, marked with dots of reddish-brown, more numerous toward the larger end. This agrees with the specimens now before me from a set of six taken from a nest in a crevice of an old log hut, excepting that the surface is thinly and evenly dotted all over, and there is, of course, no blush in the blown specimens. They measure 0.70 by 0.58. In other specimens the markings chiefly encircle the larger end. A nest in the Smithsonian is a compact hollow ball of green moss, mixed with a few pine twigs; it was taken in Maine, where the species is stated to breed in "windfall" country of the evergreen woods, where the fallen trees are piled in confusion.

TELMATODYTES PALUSTRIS, (Wils.) Bd.

Long-billed Marsh Wren.

Certhia palustris, WILS., A. O. ii, 1870, 58, pl. 12, f. 4.—LORD, Pr. Arty. Inst. iv, 1864, 117.
Troglodytes palustris, BP., Obs. Wils. 1825, No. 66; Syn. 1828, 93.—SW. & RICH., F. B. A. ii, 1831, 319 (lat. 55°).—NUTT., Man. i. 1832, 439.—AUD., O. B. i, 1831, 500; v, 1839, 467; pl. 100; Syn. 1839, 77; B. A. ii, 1841, 135, pl. 123.—GIRAUD, B. L. I. 1844, 76.—PUTN., Pr. Ess. Inst. i, 1856, 208.—SCL., P. Z. S. 1856, 290 (Cordova).— SCL., Ibis, i, 1859, 8 (Guatemala).—NEWB., P. R. R. Rep. vi, 1857, 80.—HEERM., *ibid.* x, 1859, pt. vi, 54.—REINH., Ibis, iii, 1861, 5 (Greenland).—TRIPPE, Pr. Ess. Inst. vi, 1871, 115.
Thryothorus palustris, BP., List, 1838, 11.—TURNB., B. E. Pa. 1869, 20.
Cistothorus (Telmatodytes) palustris, BD., B. N. A. 1858, 364; Rev. 1864, 147.—COUES & PRENT., Smiths. Rep. 1861, 410.—ALLEN, Pr. Ess. Inst. iv, 1864, 83.
Cistothorus palustris, COOP. & SUCK., N. H. Wash. Ter. 1860, 190.—HAYD., Rep. 1862, 163.—WHEAT., Ohio Agric. Rep. 1860, No. 123.—LAWR., Ann. Lyc. N. Y. viii,

1866, 283.—Coues, Pr. Phila. Acad. 1866, 79.—Coues, Pr. Ess. Inst. v, 1868, 278.—McIlwr., *ibid.* v, 1866, 87.—Coop., B. Cal. 1870, 75.—Allen, Bull. M. C. Z. ii, 1871, 267; iii, 1872, 175.—Aiken, Pr. Bost. Soc. xv, 1872, 196.—Mayn., Guide, 1870, 98; B. Fla. 1872, 42.—Snow, B. Kans. 1873, 6.
Telmatodytes palustris, Coues, Pr. Bost. Soc. xii, 1868, 108.—Coues, Pr. Phila. Acad. 1871, 20.—Coues, Key, 1872, 87.
Telmatodytes arundinaceus, Cab., Mus. Hein. i, 1850, 78.
Thryothorus arundinaceus, Bp., Consp. i, 1850, 220.
Thryothorus arundineus, Vieill., Nouv. Dict. xxxiv, 1819, 58.
Cistothorus palustris var. *paludicola*, Bd., Rev. 1864, 148 (West coast).

Hab.—In suitable places throughout temperate North America, breeding throughout its range; wintering along our southern border and southward. Greenland. Mexico. Guatemala.
Lieutenant Warren's Expedition.—8838, Sand Hills; 4744, mouth of Big Sioux River. Not obtained by Captain Raynolds' Expedition, nor by the later ones.

This little bird requires a particular condition of surface, which, when met, renders it largely independent of geographical limitations. It inhabits, exclusively, reedy swamps and marshes, nearly throughout the continent, and is extremely abundant in the more favorable situations. In most latitudes it is a migrant, but as it breeds throughout its range, only a part of the individuals passing north for this purpose, the remainder spending the year in their winter homes in the South. It is resident in South Carolina, though the greater number go on northward to breed. On the North Carolina coast I found it abundant during the migrations, and observed it through a part of November, so that possibly some winter as far north as this. In the extensive marshes along the Potomac, overgrown with *Zizania aquatica*, it finds a congenial home; and in some spots scores of the nests may be seen at once. It reaches this latitude about the middle of April, and remains into October. In New England this Wren is only a summer visitor, chiefly along the coast, and it is rare, if really occurring, north of Massachusetts. None of the Maine or New Hampshire lists include it. In the West I found it breeding abundantly in a reedy swamp near Fort Whipple, Arizona, where it arrives in April and remains until November. According to Dr. Cooper, it winters in the Colorado Valley, as high as Fort Mojave. On the Pacific coast the same writer speaks of its wintering north to the Columbia, wherever there is a marsh overgrown with tulé (*Scirpus palustris*). I never seen it in the Missouri region, but Dr. Hayden reports its occasional occurrence in marshy places along the river. Prof. Snow, Mr. Allen, and Mr. Aiken, note its occurrence in Kansas and Colorado.

The nidification of the Marsh Wren is not the least interesting part of its history. It builds a large bulky nest of the tops of coarse grasses and reeds, bent together and woven into a hollow ball, with a little hole in one side, and fastens this globe to the upright stems of the growing reeds, several of which usually pass through its substance. The ball is lined with finer grasses; it is tolerably compact, yet there are often long shreds hanging from it, giving it rather a slovenly appearance. The number of these structures that may sometimes be observed in a small piece of marsh, within a few feet of each other, is astonishing, and apparently out of all proportion to the size of the colony inhabiting the patch of reeds. This has occasioned the surmise that more nests are built than are actually used, the idea being that the nervous, energetic little creatures keep on building while the females are incubating, to amuse themselves, or because they have nothing particular to do and cannot keep still. However this may be, the old nests last a year or so before they decay and fall to pieces, which may partly account for the great numbers to be seen. The eggs, as usual, are numerous—six or eight—sometimes so many as to induce the suspicion that they were not all laid by the same bird. They are very peculiar in appearance, being perhaps the most heavily colored of any found in this country. The usual color is a rich, dark chocolate, but it is extremely variable. Sometimes it is perfectly uniform; again, it is nearly uniform, but with a darker area at the large end or around it; occasionally a whitish ground shows, thickly dotted or smirched with the chocolate, or a nearly uniform brownish-white surface is presented, as if the color had washed out, except in a few dark spots or patches. The egg averages two-thirds by one-half of an inch; in a large number examined, little "runt" eggs are sometimes found. One of these before me measures only 0.54 by 0.47, and I have seen still smaller ones; such are doubtless not fertilized, and correspond to the little eggs that fowls and pigeons often drop at the close of their season, indicating that their power is exhausted. I have seen the same thing in the case of the Barn Swallow, and it is probably not an infrequent occurrence.

On entering a patch of rushes where the Wrens are breeding, we almost instantly hear the harsh screeping notes with which those nearest scold us, in vehement and angry resentment at the intrusion. From further away in the maze of reeds we hear a merry little song from those still undisturbed, and presently we see numbers flitting on feeble wing from one clump of sedge to another, or poised in any imaginable attitude on the swaying stems. Their postures are sometimes very comical; a favorite attitude is with the tail thrown up till it almost covers the back, and the head lowered. In this position they have a peculiar swaying motion, back and forward, as if they were on a pivot, and in this position they sing most frequently. Others may be seen scrambling like little mice up and down the reed-stems or all over their globular nests. They appear among themselves to be excitable to the verge of irascibility, and not seldom quite beyond such moderate limit; but on the whole they form a harmonious little colony which minds its own business, and doubtless makes pleasant company for the blackbirds and other larger species which build among them.

CISTOTHORUS STELLARIS, (Licht.) Cab.

Short-billed Marsh Wren.

a. *stellaris.*

Troglodytes stellaris, LICHT.—NAUM., V. D. iii, 1823, 724.—TRIPPE, Pr. Ess. Inst. vi, 1871, 115 (Minnesota, abundant, breeding).
Cistothorus stellaris, CAB., Mus. Hein. i, 1851, 77.—BD., B. N. A. 1858, 365; Rev. 1864, 146.—SCL., Cat. A. B. 1861, 22.—HAYD., Rep. 1862, 163.—WHEAT., Ohio Agric. Rep. 1860, No. 124 (Cleveland, breeding).—COUES & PRENT., Smiths. Rep. 1861, 410.—ALLEN, Pr. Ess. Inst. iv, 1864, 83.—LAWR., Ann. Lyc. N. Y. viii, 1866, 283.—CÖUES, Pr. Ess. Inst. v, 1868, 279.—COUES, Pr. Bost. Soc. xii, 1868, 108.—SUMICH., Mem. Bost. Soc. i, 1869, 545 (Orizaba).—COUES, Pr. Phila. Acad. 1871, 21.—ALLEN, Bull. M. C. Z. ii, 1871, 167.—TRIPPE, Pr. Bost. Soc. xv, 1872, 236 (Iowa, breeding).—COUES, Key, 1872, 88.—MAYN., Guide, 1870, 96; B. Fla. 1872, 43.—SNOW, B. Kans. 1873, 6.
Thryothorus stellaris, TURNB., B. E. Pa. 1869, 20.
Troglodytes brevirostris, NUTT., Man. i, 1832, 436; Tr. Am. Acad. Sci. i, 1833, 98.—AUD., O. B. ii, 1834, 427; v, 1839, 469; pl. 175; Syn. 1839, 77; B. Am. ii, 1841, 138, pl. 124.—BP., Consp. i, 1850, 222.

b. *elegans.*

Cistothorus elegans, SCL. & SALV., Ibis, 1859, 8.—BD., Rev. 1864, 146.

Hab.—Eastern Province of the United States. Observed west to the Loup Fork of the Platte (*Hayden*). North to Massachusetts and Manitoba (*Coues*). Breeds throughout its range. Winters in the Southern States. Mexico. Var. *elegans* from Mexico to Guatemala.

Lieutenant Warren's Expedition.—9217, Loup Fork of the Platte.
Not obtained by the other Expeditions.

Though inhabiting the same situations as the preceding species, the Short-billed Marsh Wren is not only much rarer, but much more restricted geographically. It occurs along the whole Atlantic coast, from Florida to Massachusetts, beyond which I have observed no record, but according to my experience it is nowhere abundant along this line. In the course of several years collecting in Maryland, Virginia, and the Carolinas, I never happened to find but a single specimen, which I shot in October, in a marsh on the North Carolina coast, where the other species was abundant at the time. According to various authors, the bird is more common in Massachusetts during the summer, arriving about the second week in May, and leaving in October. I think the birds are more plentiful along an interior line of migration, up the Mississippi. Thus Mr. Trippe found them "abundant" and breeding in Minnesota, and I saw them in comparative plenty along the Red River, about Pembina, securing several examples in June. I found them in reedy sloughs on the prairie, where the Yellow-headed Blackbirds and Black Terns were breeding, and also in low sedgy tracts, partly covered with a growth of scrubby willows. Dr. Hayden's specimen is interesting as being the westernmost on record for the United States. Audubon found the species abundant in Texas, where it breeds.

Quite contrary to what might have been expected, the eggs of this species are entirely unlike those of its allies, being pure white, unmarked. They measure 0.63 by 0.48, being thus rather elongate. I never saw a nest; it is said to be similar to that of the Long-billed Wren—a hollow globe with a hole in one side, woven of grasses, reeds or rushes, lined with finer material of the same kind, and placed in a tuft of reeds or tussock of grass. According to Mr. Maynard, the birds are quite noisy in the fresh-water marshes of Massachusetts, frequently singing all night: "Their notes are not fine, but, although monotonous, are more elaborate than those of the Long-billed, and better entitled to the name of song."

Family ALAUDIDÆ: Larks.

The birds of this family differ remarkably from other *Oscines* in the structure of the tarsal envelope, which, instead of consisting on the sides of the tarsus of two undivided plates meeting in a sharp ridge behind, is there formed of a series of scutellæ like those in front, lapping round behind, meeting those of the front in a groove on both inner and outer faces of the tarsus. The back of the tarsus is therefore blunt and rounded in the front. Notwithstanding this peculiarity, they are truly *Oscine*, having the musical apparatus well developed, and being good songsters. The tarsal envelope, while approaching that of the *Clamatorial* birds in character, is not, however, the same as in these, in which a single series of plates, variously arranged, encircles the tarsus, meeting in a groove along the inner face, but being continuous on the outer. In the Larks, the hind claw is elongated and straightened conformably with their terrestrial habits; the bill is conic-elongate, and there are but nine fully-developed primaries. In the genus *Eremophila* there is a peculiar tuft of feathers springing from each side of the head back of the eye, somewhat similar in character to the so-called "horns" of many owls. The species inhabit open grounds, and are gregarious and extensively migratory in most regions. Their food consists of various seeds and insects. We have but a single species, identical with that of the Old World; but it runs into several geographical varieties.

EREMOPHILA ALPESTRIS, (Forst.) Boie.

Horned Lark; Shore Lark.

a. *alpestris.*

Alauda alpestris, FORST., Phil. Trans. lxii, 1772, 398.—LINN., S. N. i, 1766, 289.—GM., S. N. i, 1788, 800.—LATH., Ind. Orn. ii, 1790, 498.—And of earlier authors gener-

ally.—WILS., Am. Orn. i, 1808, 85, pl. 5, fig. 4.—BP., Obs. Wils. 1825, No. 130 ;
Syn. 1828, 102.—NUTT., Man. i, 1832, 455.—AUD., O. B. ii, 1834, 570, pl. 200 ;
Syn. 1839, 96 ; B. A. iii, 1841, 44, pl. 151.—GIRAUD, B. L. I. 1844, 95.—PUTN.,
Pr. Ess. Inst. i, 1856, 209.—TURNB., B. E. Pa. 1869, 4.—(?) TRIPPE, Pr. Ess.
Inst. vi, 1871, 115.
Eremophila alpestris, BOIE, Isis, 1828, 322.—And of authors.—(?) ALLEN, Mem. Bost. Soc.
i, 1868, 496 (Iowa).—MAYN., Guide, 1870, 121 (Massachusetts, in July, perhaps
breeding).—COUES, Key, 1872, 89, fig. 32.
Phileremos alpestris, BREHM, Vog. Dent. 1831, 312.—BP., List, 1838, 37.—KEYS. & BLAS.,
Wirb. Eur. No. 84.—HARTL., Syst. Verz. 1844, 80.
Otocorys alpestris, BP.—GRAY., List of G. of B. 1841, 62.—CAB., Mus. Hein. i, 1851, 121.
Alauda cornuta, WILS., Am. Orn. i, 1808, 87 (in text).—SW. & RICH., F. B. A. ii, 1831,
245.—MAXIM., Reise, i, 1839, 367.
Eremophila cornuta, BOIE, Isis, 1828, 322.—BD., B. N. A. 1858, 403.—COOP. & SUCK., N.
H. Wash. Ter. 1860, 195.—WHEAT., Ohio Agric. Rep. 1860, No. 134.—COUES,
Pr. Phila. Acad. 1861, 221.—COUES & PRENT., Smiths. Rep. 1861, 411.—BOARDM.,
Pr. Bost. Soc. ix, 1862, 126.—VERR., Pr. Ess. Inst. iii, 1862, 150.—ALLEN, *ibid*.
iv, 1864, 69.—MCILWR., *ibid*. v, 1866, 88.—COUES, *ibid*. v, 1868, 280.—LAWR.,
Ann. Lyc. N. Y. viii, 1866, 289.—COUES, Pr. Bost. Soc. xii, 1868, 114.—LORD, Pr.
Arty. Inst. Wool. iv, 118.—DALL & BANN., Tr. Chic. Acad. i, 1869, 281.—COOP.,
B. Cal. i, 1870, 251.—(?) TRIPPE, Pr. Bost. Soc. xv, 1872, 236.
Phileremos cornutus, BP., List, 1838, 37.
Otocorys cornuta, CAB., Mus. Hein. i, 1851, 122.

b. *leucolæma.*

(Pale race, breeding on dry interior plains of the West.)

(?) *Otocoris occidentalis*, MCCALL, Pr. Phila. Acad. v, 1851, 218 (Santa Fé, N. M.).—BD.,
Stansbury's Rep. 1852, 318.
Otocorys alpestris, NEWB., P. R. R. Rep. vi, 1857, 88.
Eremophila alpestris, ALLEN, Bull. M. C. Z. iii, 1872, 176.
Eremophila cornuta, BD., P. R. R. Rep. x, 1859, Beckwith's Route, Birds, 13, pl. 32.—
HAYD., Rep. 1862, 174—STEV., U. S. Geol. Surv. Ter. 1870, 464.—MERR., *ibid*.
1872, 685.—HOLD., Pr. Bost. Soc. xv, 1872, 202.
Eremophila alpestris var. *leucolæma*, COUES.

c. *chrysolæma.*

(Smaller, bright race, from the southwestern plains and southward.)

Alauda cornuta, SW., Phil. Mag. i, 1827, 434 (Mexico).
Eremophila cornuta, COUES, Pr. Phila. Acad. 1866, 79 (Arizona).
Alauda chrysolæma, WAGL., Isis, 1831, 350.—BP., P. Z. S. 1837, 111; Consp. Av. i, 1850, 246.
Otocorys chrysolæma, CAB., M. H. i, 122.—FINSCH, Abhand. Nat. Ver. 1872, 341.
Alauda minor, GIRAUD, B. Texas, 1841.—SCL., P. Z. S. 1855, 66.
Eremophila minor, SCL., Cat. A. B. 1862, 126.
Alauda rufa, AUD., B. Am. vii, 1843, 353, pl. 497.
Otocoris rufa, HEERM., P. R. R. Rep. x, 1859, pt. vi, 45.
Otocorys peregrina, SCL., P. Z. S. 1855, 110, pl. 102 (Santa Fé de Bogota).
Eremophila peregrina, SCL., Cat. A. B. 1861, 127.
Alauda peregrina, GIEBEL, Thes. Orn. i, 1872, 299.
Eremophila cornuta var. *chrysolæma*, BD., B. N. A. 1858, 403.
Eremophila alpestris var. *chrysolæma*, COUES, Key, 1872, 89.

Hab.—North America, breeding northerly; generally dispersed through the United
States by migration. Var. *leucolæma* resident on the dry interior plains from Iowa and
Minnesota westward. Var. *chrysolæma* from the Southwestern Territories and south-
ward to New Grenada.

List of specimens.

19230	239	Deer Creek ...	♀	Jan. 18, 1860	F. V. Hayden.	7.00	12.50	4.75
19231	....	Fort Benton ..	♂	....	...... do	7.50	13.38	4.50
19232	237	Deer Creek ...	♂	Jan. 11, 1860	...... do	6.25	11.25	4.25
19233	279	..... do	♂	Mar. 7, 1859	...... do	7.50	14.00	4.50
19234	278	..... do	....	...... do	...... do	7.00	12.00	4.25
19235	184	Source Chey'e.	....	Nov. 14, 1860	...... do	......	......	......
19236	165	..... do	....	Nov. 4, 1860	...... do	......	......	......

Lieutenant Warren's Expedition.—5314, Medicine Creek ; 5318, Yellowstone ; 5313, Fort
Pierre, Dak. ; 5317, Blackfoot country ; 9241-2, 9244-5, 9256, Black Hills ; 9239-40,
9243, near Bear Butte.
Later Expeditions.—60416, Laramie River ; 60761-4, 60897-934, various localities in
Wyoming ; 61753, Salt Lake, Utah.

The question of the relationships of our various Larks is rather intricate, but we probably have an approximately correct solution of the problem. It is certain, in the first place, that our bird is identical with that of Europe—there is no ground on which to base even varietal distinction of the *ordinary* North American bird. By this is meant those individuals from any part of the country that are extensively migratory, bred far north, and dispersed at other seasons over most of the United States—certainly over all the Eastern States, and apparently, also, to some distance along the Pacific coast. Never continuously exposed to special modifying influences of climate or food, these retain what may be regarded as the normal characters of the species. But in all the open country of the West, from Iowa, Wisconsin, and Minnesota, the birds find congenial breeding ground, and are stationary or nearly so. These birds become impressed with a certain character, due to the special circumstances of environment, which may be summed as *pallor*, corresponding in degree to the atmospheric dryness. It varies in degree from a slight paleness matched by the palest eastern birds, to the maximum in birds of the most arid regions. No specific distinction, of course, can be predicated, nor is it possible to assign a geographical distribution with strictness. In the South the question is complicated by another consideration. Here latitude plays its part in reduction of size, and in brightening the plumage again to an extent scarcely seen in the eastern birds. The result is a bird so different from the ordinary style that it was admitted as a species by Dr. Finsch, although he reduced the dozen or more current species to five. I was particularly struck with the small size and bright color of the Larks of New Mexico, where I found them in the breeding season ; and the same features are found in the Mexican bird. It is, however, impossible to draw any dividing line between them and the ordinary form.

In the Key, I followed Prof. Baird in recognizing only the small, bright southern form, as var. *chrysolœma* of Wagler; but I am now inclined to admit also the pale form to varietal distinction. For this a new name appears to be required. *Alauda rufa* of Audubon apparently included both, but points unmistakably to the southern form, as does also the *Otocorys rufa* of Heermann, and *Alauda minor* of Giraud. The *Otocoris occidentalis* of McCall is based on New Mexican birds of the character above mentioned, though the name, as used by Prof. Baird in 1852 for the bird afterward figured as above (P. R. R. Rep. x, pl. 32), is applicable to the var. *leucolœma*.

Var. *leucolœma*, Coues (No. 2745, coll. E. C., Fort Randall, Mar. 8, 1873). Not smaller than typical *alpestris*. Little or no yellow about the head or throat, and the black markings narrow. Upper parts grayish-brown, with little or no pinkish tinge; the feathers with only obsoletely darker centres.

East of the region above specified the Horned Lark is not known to breed in the United States; and the only record of its occurrence in summer which I have seen, that given by Mr. Maynard, as above, most probably indicates a highly exceptional instance. According to Mr. McIlwraith, a few pairs nest about Hamilton, Canada West. The great majority of the eastern birds repair beyond the latitude of New England, breeding plentifully in Labrador and Newfoundland. I found them very plentiful along the Labrador coast, and on all the rocky moss-clad islands adjoining, where they find the situations in which they delight to nest. Leaving these rugged and inhospitable shores, they enter the United States in October, and by the following month are generally dispersed along the Atlantic as far at least as the Carolinas. They are now in flocks, sometimes of great extent, and scour the open country in search of food. Their return begins in March, and is mostly completed by the end of that month, though stragglers remain in England through the greater part of April. They have no song at this season, beyond the sharp chirping notes with which the flocks call to each other.

The Horned Lark breeds about Pembina, and thence westward in the same latitude. I am also informed that it nests in the vicinity of Racine, Wisconsin, laying sometimes in the middle of April, when the snow is still on the ground. According to Mr. Trippe, it also breeds in Southern Iowa, where it is abundant and nearly resident, being absent only in the depth of winter for a few weeks, and some remaining even then. It nests there early in May, occasionally as late as the 25th. I scarcely think that it endures the winters high on the Missouri. I did not see it through that season at Fort Randall, though it was common after February. Further south, where I have observed it in the west, it is permanently resident, though I presume that a part of the birds to be observed in winter are those that have come from the north.

The nest of the Horned Lark is simply built of dried grasses, and is placed on the ground. Both sexes appear to share the duties of incubation. The eggs are thickly, minutely, and uniformly flecked with light brown on a gray ground, 0.95 by 0.62.

Family MOTACILLIDÆ : Wagtails.

ANTHUS LUDOVICIANUS, (Gm.) Licht.

Titlark; Pipit; Wagtail.

Alauda ludoviciana, GM., Syst. Nat. i, 1788, 793.—LATH., Ind. Orn. ii, 1790, 494.
Anthus ludovicianus, LICHT., Verz. 1823, 37.—BP., List, 1838, 18; Consp. i, 1850, 249.—AUD.,
    Syn. 1839, 94; B. Am. iii, 1841, 40, pl. 50.—GIRAUD, B. L. I. 1844, 94.—SCL., P.
    Z. S. 1856, 296 (Cordova).—SCL. & SALV., Ibis, 1859, 9 (Guatemala).—BD., B. N.
    A. 1858, 232; Rev. 1864, 153.—JONES, Nat. in Bermuda, 1859, 29.—COOP. &
    SUCK., N. H. Wash. Ter. 1860, 176.—COUES, Pr. Phila. Acad. 1861, 220 (Labra-
    dor, breeding); 1866, 67 (Arizona).—REINH., Ibis, iii, 1861, 6 (Greenland).—
    BLACKISTON, Ibis, iv, 1862, 4 (Saskatchewan).—HAYD., Rep. 1862, 159.—ALLEN,
    Mem. Bost. Soc. i, 1868, 494 (Iowa).—DALL & BANN., Tr. Chic. Acad. i, 1869,
    277 (Alaska).—STEV., U. S. Geol. Surv. Ter. 1870, 463.—MERR., *ibid.* 1872, 674.—
    COOP., Pr. Cal. Acad. 1870, 75; B. Cal. i, 1870, 78.—TRIPPE, Pr. Ess. Inst. vi,
    1871, 115 (Minnesota).—ALLEN, Bull. M. C. Z. ii, 1871, 267; iii, 1872, 161, 175
    (breeding in mountains of Colorado).—AIKEN, Pr. Bost. Soc. 1872, 196 (the
    same).—TRIPPE, *ibid.* xv, 1872, 234 (Iowa).—COUES, Key, 1872, 90, fig. 34.—
    SNOW, B. Kans. 1873, 4.—And of recent authors.
Alauda rubra, GM., Syst. Nat. i, 1788, 794.
Anthus rebens, MERR., "Ersch Grub. Encycl."
Alauda pennsylvanica, BRISS., Orn. iii, 1760, 356 (or 413).
Anthus pennsylvanicus, "ZANDER, J. f. O. 1853, extrah. i, 1854, 63;" Naum. iv, 13.
Alauda rufa, WILS., Am. Orn. v, 1872, 89, pl. 42, f. 4.
Anthus spinoletta, BP., Syn. 1828, 90.—NUTT., Man. i, 1832, 450.—AUD., O. B. i, 1832, 408.
Anthus aquaticus, SW. & RICH., F. B. A. ii, 1831, 23, pl. 44.—AUD., O. B. i, 1832, pl. 10.
Anthus pipiens, AUD., O. B. i, 1832, 408, pl. 80.—BP., List, 1838, 18.
Anthus reinhardtii, "HOLBÖLL, Fn. Green. 1846, 25."
Anthus "hypogæus, BP., Compt. Rend. xxxviii, 1856, 65."

Hab.—The whole of North America. Mexico. Guatemala. Bermuda. Greenland.
Accidental in Europe (*Harting*, Br. Birds, 1872, 109).
    Not obtained by Captain Raynolds' Expedition.
    Lieutenant Warren's Expedition.—1844, Black Hills.
    Later Expeditions.—60680, Henry's Fork; 60681, Uintah Mountains; 62298, Snake River.

No birds of this country are more extensively dispersed over the continent, more regular in their times of appearance in the United States or in their departure for the North. Until very recently we had not, to my knowledge, a single authentic instance of its breeding in the United States, although, as I have elsewhere surmised (Pr. Ess. Inst. v, 1868, 268), it may do so in Northern New England. It enters the United States in flocks in September, and becomes thoroughly dispersed as the autumn advances; some pushing to Florida, the Gulf coast, Texas, and Mexico; others wintering as high as the Middle States. I have found it during part of the winter even on the Upper Missouri, with Shore Larks and Snow Buntings. Its vernal migration begins in March at the South, and by the end of the following month the species has mostly passed beyond our limits, though a few loiterers may be sometimes found in May. But precisely as the Shore Lark breeds in the West far south of its Eastern breeding range, so does the Titlark find in the most elevated points of land in the West the necessary conditions of reproduction. Although Mr. Allen did not actually find the nest, there is no question of his having determined that the bird breeds in the mountains of Colorado, for he found young scarcely able to fly, July 20, 1871, on Mount Lincoln, Park County, Colorado, among the snow-fields above timber-line; while he also observed the bird in the Wahsatch Mountains, "probably breeding, above timber-line." These are important observations, not only as first authenticating the breeding of the species in the United States, but as affording a striking illustration of how perfectly complementary to each other are increase of latitude and elevation of land in much that pertains to the distribution of plants and animals. In its summer distribution to the northward, the bird reaches the Arctic coast, and is also found in Greenland.

Of the general habits of the Titlark during the winter, there is no occasion to enlarge. Its thoroughly gregarious disposition; its eminently terrestrial habits; the variety of its food, both animal and vegetable; its timidity, yet its lack of caution; its buoyant, desultory flight; gliding, tremulous gait, accompanied with vibration of the tail, and its querulous voice, are all well known. But with its habits in summer, and particularly its nesting, we are not so familiar. Audubon is one of the few authors who has given us information on this score. He "found it breeding abundantly on the Labrador coast, on moss-covered rocks, as well as in the deep valleys, but never at any great distance from the sea. The nests were usually placed at the foot of a wall of the rocks, buried in the dark mould, and beautifully formed of fine bent grass, arranged in a circular manner, without any hair or other lining. Both birds incubate, sitting so closely, that on several occasions I almost put my foot upon them before they flew. The first nest that I found was on the 29th of June, when the thermometer ranged from 51° to 54°. The eggs were six in number, five-eighths of an inch long and six and one-quarter twelfths in breadth, being rather elongated, though rounded at both ends; their ground color of a deep reddish-chestnut or reddish-brown, considerably darkened by numerous dots of a deeper reddish-brown and lines of various sizes, especially toward the large end."

Although I have myself seen Titlarks everywhere I have been, I never found any breeding except in Labrador, as stated in the above reference. It was there the most numerous of the land birds, excepting perhaps the White-crowned Sparrow, frequenting open, bare and exposed localities, often on the rocky and barren islands, almost untenanted by other species. Here, as elsewhere in maritime localities, the birds are fond of resorting to the sea-shore at low tide, there to ramble in quest of food on the mud and sea-wrack in company with Sandpipers, and not distantly resembling these birds in their manners. Two nests I obtained in July were both placed in a cavity in the ground, about as large as a child's head, on the side of a steep rocky chasm. A flooring of dried grass had been introduced to keep the nest from the wet; the nests were built upon this, of coarse dried grass loosely arranged, and without lining; the exterior diameter was about six inches, the interior three inches, with a depth of two inches. One nest contained five, the other four, eggs, averaging thirteen-sixteenths of an inch long, by nine and one-half sixteenths broad; of a dark chocolate color, indistinctly marked with numerous small spots and streaks of blackish. The parents do not leave the nest until nearly trodden on, then the one that is incubating flutters up with loud cries of distress that soon bring the mate, and the pair hover anxiously over head, at times approaching within a few feet, or even alighting close by, all the while crying out in the most beseeching and plaintive manner. I saw no attempt to deceive by feigning lameness, but the birds often follow one who has disturbed them for some distance.   On such occasions several pairs nesting near each other are often aroused, and join their cries with those of the afflicted parents.

NEOCORYS SPRAGUEI, (Aud.) Scl.

Missouri Skylark.

Alauda spraguei, AUD., B. Am. vii, 1843, 335, pl. 486.
Agrodoma spraguei. BD., Stanbury's Rep. 1852, 329.—BP., C. Rend. xxxviii, 1856, 65.
Neocorys spraguei, SCL., Pr. Zool. Soc. 1857, 5.—BD., B. N. A. 1858, 234.—BLACK., Ibis, 1862, 4.—COUES, Key, 1872, 91.
Anthus spraguei, BD., Rev. 1864, 155.
Otocoris sprangeri, BP., Consp. Av. i, 1850, 246.

Hab.—Region of the Upper Missouri and Sasketchewan.   East to the Red River.

This species is one of the very few characteristic birds of the region particularly treated of in the present work; in fact, it seems chiefly confined to the Upper Missouri.   It is still extremely rare in collections; the type specimen, taken by Audubon at Fort Union, June 19, 1843, long remained unique, and to the present day I have seen but one other, taken by Captain Blackiston on the Sasketchewan (where he found the species not uncommon), and now in the Smithsonian collection, where the type is also preserved.   But since, according to Audubon's account, the bird appears to be abundant, I rest in hopes of seeing it alive before I leave the Missouri.   The original describer says that the nest is sunken in the ground, built entirely of fine grasses, circularly arranged, without lining; and that the eggs are usually four or five in number, seven-eighths long by five-eighths broad, dotted minutely all over, so as to be of a general purplish-gray hue.   He found young in small loose flocks of eight to a dozen, before he left Fort Union, on the 16th of August. He represents manners apparently much in accordance with those ascribed to the European Skylark : "On several occasions my friend, Edward Harris, sought for these birds on the ground, deceived by the sound of their music, appearing as if issuing from the prairies, which they constantly inhabit; and after having traveled to many distant places on the prairie, we at last looked upward, and there saw several of these beautiful creatures singing in a continuous manner, and soaring at such an elevation as to render them more or less difficult to discover with the eye, and at times some of them actually disappearing from our sight in the clear thin air of that country.   On the ground they run prettily, sometimes squatting to observe the movements of the intruder, and at times erecting their body fronting the pursuer.   *   *   *   *   On first rising from the ground they fly in so deep and undulating a manner as to almost preclude their being shot on the wing; and this they continue to do, forming circles increasing in extent until about one hundred yards high, when they begin to sing, and continue to do so for fifteen or twenty minutes at a time, and then suddenly closing their wings, they glide to the prairie.   *   *   *   Sometimes when rising from the ground, as if about to sing, for some forty or fifty yards, they suddenly pitch downward, alight, and run or squat, as already mentioned."

November, 1873.—Since I penned the foregoing, at Fort Randall, last year, my wishes have been gratified in the most satisfactory manner; for during my connection, the past summer, with the Northern Boundary Commission, to results of which I may be permitted to refer in this connection, I became perfectly familiar with the Missouri Skylark.   It is one of the most abundant and characteristic birds of all the region along the forty-ninth parallel of latitude, from just west of the Pembina Mountains to as far as the survey progressed this year—about four hundred miles; I had no difficulty in taking as many specimens as I desired. They were particularly numerous at various points along the Souris or Mouse River, where, during our marches or while we were encamped, they were almost continually hovering about us. The first one that I shot, early in July, was a young of the year, but full grown; and as I found nestlings a month later, probably two broods are reared each season. The ordinary straightforward flight of the bird is performed with a regular rising and falling, like that of the Titlark; but its course, when startled from the ground, is exceedingly rapid and wayward; at such times, after the first alarm, they are wont to hover around in a desultory manner for a considerable time, and then pitch suddenly down to the ground, often near where they rose. Under these circumstances they have a lisping, querulous note. But these common traits have nothing to do with the wonderful soaring action, and the inimitable, matchless song of the birds during the breeding season—it is no wonder Audubon grew enthusiastic in describing it. Rising from the nest, or from its grassy bed, this plain-looking little bird, clad in the simplest colors, and making but a speck in the boundless expanse, mounts straight up, on tremulous wings, till lost to view in the blue ether, and then sends back to earth a song of gladness that seems to come from the sky itself, to cheer the weary, give hope to the disheartened, and turn the most indifferent, for the moment at least, from sordid thoughts. No other bird-music heard in our land compares with the wonderful strains of this songster; there is something not of earth in the melody, coming from above, yet from no visible source. The notes are simply indescribable; but once heard they can never be forgotten. Their volume and penetration are truly wonderful; they are neither loud nor strong, yet the whole air seems filled with the tender strains, and delightful melody continues long unbroken. The song is only heard for a brief period in the summer, ceasing when the inspiration of the love season is over, and it is only uttered when the birds are soaring.

It is not a little singular that the Skylark should have so long continued to be rare in collections, since it is very abundant in the extensive region which it inhabits. In August, after all the broods are on wing, and through September, I have seen it in considerable flocks; and often, when riding along the prairie road, numbers would fly up on my approach, from the ruts ahead, where they were feeding, to settle again at a little distance further on. These wheel-tracks, where the grass was worn away, seemed to be their favorite resorts, where they could run with the greatest ease, and perhaps gather food less easily discovered in the thick grass. They tripped along the tracks with swift and dainty steps, never hopping, and continually vibrated the tail, just like our common Titlark. They were usually associated at such times with numbers of Chestnut-colored Lark-buntings, which seemed to fancy the same places, and with a few of Baird's Buntings. These were the only circumstances under which the Larks could be procured without the great quickness and dexterity required to take them on the wing; for the moment they alight in the grass of the prairie, be it scanty or only a few inches high, they are lost to view, their speckled-gray colors blending completely with the herbage.

On making a camp at Turtle Mountain, a pair of Larks rose from the spot where my tent was to be pitched, and circled about in such evident and painful agitation, that I knew they had a nest somewhere near by. I watched them for a long while, but they would not re-alight to give me any clue to its whereabouts; and though I made careful search for the nest at intervals for several days, during which time I frequently saw the same pair, I was unsuccessful. No nests are harder to find than those of prairie birds, for there is nothing to guide one, and they are not often discovered except by accident, such as stumbling on one and scaring off the parent. But at length, a few days afterward, in finally renewing a particularly thorough search, a little bird, just able to flutter a few feet, was seen and caught, and in a few moments the rest of the family, sitting a few feet apart, were also secured—four in all. They had just left the nest, and yet I could not find it, though a perfectly bare depression of the ground, covered with droppings, just where the birds were, may have been their temporary resting place. My friend, Mr. Allen, was more fortunate on the Yellowstone Expedition which he accompanied the same season, and he obligingly gives me the following account:

"The only nest we found was placed on the ground, and neatly formed of dry fine grass. It was thinly arched over with the same material, and being built in a tuft of rank grass, was most thoroughly concealed. The bird would seem to be a close setter, as in this case the female remained on the nest till I actually stepped over it, she brushing against my feet as she went off. The eggs were five in number, rather long and pointed, measuring about 0.90 by 0.60 inches, of a grayish-white color, thickly and minutely flecked with darker, giving them a decidedly purplish tint."

I saw no Skylarks after about the middle of September, and their numbers sensibly diminished after August. I am entirely ignorant of their winter resorts; we may presume that they scatter over the prairies to the south of their breeding range, but no one appears to have observed them at any other season. Yet the case is not more remarkable than that of Baird's Bunting, which nobody found until last year. These two species are so intimately associated during the breeding season, and have so many characteristics in common, that it would not be surprising if they migrated much together. Before the Larks leave Northern Dakota—if they really do forsake it—they go into moult, and during this period they are very quiet and inconspicuous, keeping hidden for the most part in the grass, whence they are only flushed by accident, rising with apparent reluctance to settle again soon. They are now scattered over the prairie, mixed with Savanna Sparrows, Baird's, and other Buntings of the same region.

As this bird is very little known, the following descriptions, prepared upon examination of over fifty specimens, may be given; that of the young bird, and of the fall plumage, differing materially from the adult, have remained hitherto entirely unknown:

Adult, in breeding season: Eye black. Bill above blackish, below pale flesh color, like the feet. Above dark brown, everywhere variegated with pale gray streaks, constituting the edgings of the feathers, in largest pattern on the middle of the back, smallest on the hind neck. Below dull whitish, with a more or less evident wash of light brown across the breast and along the sides; the breast sharply streaked, the sides less distinctly so, with a few small sparse blackish-brown marks; a more or less evident series of maxillary streaks. Quills dark grayish-brown; the inner ones and the wing-coverts edged with grayish-white, corresponding with the pattern of the back. Middle pair of tail-feathers like the back; next two or three pairs blackish; the outer two pairs mostly or wholly pure white, and the third pair from the outside usually touched with white near the end.

With the reduction of the gray edgings of the feathers of the upper parts, due to wearing away during the summer, the bird becomes darker above, with narrower and sharper variegation, and the pectoral streaks are fainter. After the fall moult the colors again become pure, the streaking of the upper parts is strong and sharp, and the whole under parts acquire much of a ruddy-brown shade.

Young: Edgings of the feathers of the upper parts having a buffy cast, giving a richer complexion to the plumage. Feathers of the back and scapulars having pure white edging, forming conspicuous semicircular markings. Greater coverts and long inner secondaries broadly tipped with white, and outer wing-feathers edged and tipped with white or buffy. Ear-coverts buffy-brown, forming a more conspicuous patch than in the adult. Under parts strongly tinged, except on throat and middle of belly, with buffy-brown, the pectoral and lateral streaks numerous, large, and suffused.

The sexes are indistinguishable, though the male may average a little larger than the female. The bill is slender and weak, compressed and acute, with the culmen concave near the base, and the nostrils quite large, covered with a raised scale. Hind claw remarkably lengthened, little curved, very slender and acute, usually somewhat exceeding its digit in length, but very variable, as is generally the case with such unusual developments.

Length 6.25 to 7.00, but rarely over 6.75. Extent 10.00 to 11.00, rarely more, in one instance 11.50, generally about 10.50. Wing 3.00 to 3.30. Tail about 2.33. Bill about 0.50 along culmen. Tarsus in front 0.80 to 0.90. Hind toe and claw 0.80 to 1.00.

Family SYLVICOLIDÆ : American Warblers.

MNIOTILTA VARIA, (Linn.) Vieill.

Black-and-white Creeping Warbler.

Motacilla varia, LINN., Syst. Nat. i, 1766, 333.
Certhia varia, VIEILL., Ois. Am. Sept. ii, 1807, 69.—AUD., Orn. Biog. i, 1832, 452, pl. 90.
Mniotiltá varia, VIEILL., Anal. 1816, and Gal. Ois. i, 1834, 276, pl. 169.—BP., List, 1838, 11.—AUD., B. Am. ii, 1841, 105, pl. 114.—WOODH., Sitgr. Rep. 1853, 69.—SCL., P. Z. S. 1856, 140.—BD., B. N. A. 1858, 235, and Rev. 1864, 167.—LAWR., Ann. Lyc. viii, 1865, 175 (New Granada).—SALV., P. Z. S. 1867, 135 (Veragua).—SCL. & SALV., P. Z. S. 1870, 780 (Merida).—HAYD., Rep. 1862, 159.—LAWR., Ann. Lyc. ix, 1868, 93 (Costa Rica).—ALLEN, Bull. M. C. Z. iii, 1872, 175.—SCOTT, Pr. Bost. Soc. 1872 (breeding in West Virginia).—COUES, Key, 1872, 92, fig. 35.— TRIPPE, Pr. Bost. Soc. xv, 1872, 234 (Iowa).—SNOW, B. Kans. 1873, 4.—And of all later writers.
Sylvia varia, BP., Synopsis, 1828, 81.
Sylvicola varia, RICH., List, 1837.
Certhia maculata, WILS., Am. Orn. iii, 1811, 22, pl. 19.
Mniotilta borealis, NUTT., Man. i, 2d ed. 1840, 704.
Mniotilta var. longirostris, BD., B. N. A. 1858, page xxxi, No. 167.

Hab.—Eastern North America. North to the fur countries in summer. South to Mexico, Central America, and West Indies (numerous quotations). West to Kansas and the Missouri "as high up as Fort Pierre at least" (*Hayden*).

Lieutenant Warren's Expedition.—4676–81, Lower Missouri.

Not obtained by Captain Raynolds' Expedition, nor by the later ones.

A species confined to the Eastern Province, reaching its western limit on the confines of the Missouri region and in Arkansas. Its northern limit is not exactly defined, unless it be represented by the latitude of Fort Simpson. The extralimital quotations to the southward are very numerous and diversified, showing how generally the bird leaves the United States in the fall; still, a few linger on our extreme border, as shown by Mr. Allen's record of its not uncommon occurrence in Florida throughout the winter (Bull. M. C. Z. ii, 1871, 267). Great numbers enter the United States in March, and some even in February; they reach the middle districts in April, and soon become generally dispersed. Contrary to the rule among our warblers, this bird has a breeding range apparently coextensive with its North American range, which is the more remarkable since it is truly a migratory species. Audubon mentions its breeding in Texas and Louisiana; and others note the same all along its range. There is some discrepancy in the statements of observers respecting its nidification. Audubon states that it breeds in holes in trees, but such appears not to be its habit. Nuttall describes a nest "niched in the shelving of a rock, on the surface of the ground." Dr. Brewer states, that so far as he knows, it always builds on the ground, and mentions a nest found in the drain of a house. The eggs are described as being from three to seven in number, four and one-half eighths to six-eighths long, by one-half an inch to nine-sixteenths broad; oval, nearly equal at both ends, white, speckled with brownish-red and purplish dots, chiefly at the larger end. A nest described by Dr. Brewer was composed externally of coarse hay, and compactly lined with horse-hair; Mr. Nuttall's was of coarse strips of inner hemlock bark, mixed with old leaves and grass, and lined with hair. Dr. Brewer's measured three and one-half inches across outside, by one inch internal depth.

The home of this little bird is one often invaded by the Cow-bird; on several different occasions, of which I am informed, as many as three or four of the alien eggs having been found in it. Its low situation probably favors the Cow-bird in this respect. This Warbler surpasses all others in the agility and ease with which it scrambles in every direction and in every attitude, up, down, and around the trunks or branches of trees, its habits being as strongly pronounced as those of a Creeper itself, and correspondingly different from those of its allies among the true Warblers. It is very abundant throughout the wooded portions of the Eastern United States, and in spring is as noisy as it is active, continually uttering its queer, screeping song in the springtime, during its busy search for insects.

PARULA AMERICANA, (Linn.) Bp.

Blue Yellow-backed Warbler.

Parus americanus, LINN., Syst. Nat. i, 1758, 190.
Motacilla americana, GM., Syst. Nat. i, 1788, 960.
Sylvia americana, LATH., Ind. Orn. ii, 1790, 520.—AUD., Orn. Biog. i, 1832, 78, pl. 15.
Sylvicola amerieana,'AUD., B. Am. ii, 1841, 57, pl. 91.—WOODH., Sitgr. Rep. 1853, 71 (breeding in Indian Territory).
Parula americana, BP., Comp. and Geog. List, 1838, 20.—GOSSE, B. Jam. 1847, 154.—BD., B. N. A. 1858, 238; Rev. 1864, 169.—HAYD., Rep. 1862, 159.—LAWR., Ann. Lyc. ix, 1869, 200 (Yucatan).—ALLEN, Bull. M. C. Z. ii, 1871, 267 (Florida, wintering); iii, 1872, 124, 175.—AIKEN, Pr. Bost. Soc. 1872, 196 (Black Hills).—SCOTT, *ibid.* (West Virginia, in summer).—COUES, Key, 1872, 92.—TRIPPE, Pr. Bost. Soc. xv, 1872, 234 (Iowa).—SNOW, B. Kans. 1873, 4.—And of late writers generally.
Compsothlypis americana, CAB., Mus. Hein. 1850, 20; J. f. O. iii, 1855, 476.
Ficedula ludoviciana, BRISS., Orn. iii, 1760, 500, pl. 26.
Motacilla ludoviciana, GM., Syst. Nat. i, 1788, 983.
Motacilla eques, BODDÆRT, Planches Enlum., 1783, pl. 731, f. 1; pl. 709, f. 1.
Sylvia torquata, VIEILL., Ois. Am. Sept. ii, 1807, 38, pl. 99.
Thryothorus torquatus, STEPH., Shaw's Gen. Zool. xiv, 1826, 94.
Sylvia pusilla, WILS., Am. Orn. iv, 1811, 17, pl. 28.
Sylvicola pusilla, SW., Zool. Journ. iii, 1827, 169.

Hab.—Eastern North America. North to Nova Scotia. West to the Missouri, as far at least as the Platte; to the Black Hills (*Aiken*). Mexico (Xalapa, *Scl.*, P. Z. S. 1857, 202). South to Guatemala (Ibis, 1859, 10). West Indies (Cuba, *Cab.*, J. f. O. iii, 476; Santa Cruz, *Newt.*, Ibis, i, 143; St. Thomas, *Cass.*, Pr. Phila. Acad. 1861, 376; Jamaica, *Gosse*, B. Jam. 154). Greenland (*Reinh.*, Ibis, 1861, 6). Winters from Southern Florida southward.
Lieutenant Warren's Expedition.—4671, mouth of Platte.
Not obtained by Captain Raynolds' Expedition, or by the later ones.

This elegant little species, one of the most prettily marked of the whole group, withdraws almost entirely from the United States in winter, though Mr. Allen has noted its occasional occurrence at that season in Florida, and proceeds as far south as Guatemala. On the vernal migration it reaches the Middle States late in April, and is very abundant during the first half of the following month. The greater number proceed further north, but some appear to breed all along the line, as I have found it about Washington early in August, and Mr. Scott saw it in West Virginia during the summer. We find it in orchards when the fruit trees are blossoming, and in all sorts of woodland, but particularly in high open forests, where it will be observed fluttering and skipping with great activity in the terminal foliage. I never found its nest, and the only one I have examined was taken in Taunton, Massachusetts, early in June. This was an irregular mass of fine, light colored tree-moss, inextricably matted, with a small deep cavity. The single egg in this nest measured 0.70 by 0.57, and was white, finely sprinkled at the large end with reddish dots, having also a few others scattered elsewhere.

The changes of plumage of this dainty little Warbler are great with age, sex and season, and I once procured a curious partial albino, which had the plumage irregularly blotched with pure white.

PROTONOTARIA CITRÆA, (Bodd.) Bd.

Prothonotary Warbler.

Motacilla citræa, BODD., Pl. Enl. 704, f. 2 (1783).
Mniotilta citrea, GRAY, Genera of Birds.
Protonotaria citræa, BD., B. N. A. 1858, 239; Rev. 1864. 173.—WHEAT., Ohio Agric. Rep. 1860, No. 65.—GUNDL., J. f. O. 1861, 324 (Cuba, rare).—COUES & PRENT., Smiths. Rep. 1861, 406 (Washington, D. C., accidental).—SCL., Cat. 1862, 26.—COUES, Pr. Ess. Inst. v, 1868, 21 (quotes "Calais, Me., *Boardman*, Verr. Pr. Bost. Soc. ix, 234").—COUES, Pr. Bost. Soc. xii, 1868, 107 (South Carolina, summer, rare).—TURNB., B. E. Pa. 1869 (straggler).—LAWR., Ann. Lyc. ix, 1868, 94 (Costa Rica); 1869, 200 (Yucatan).—SCL. & SALV., P. Z. S. 1870, 780 (Merida).—COUES, Key, 1872, 93, fig. 36.—SNOW, B. Kans. 1872 (Neosho Falls, breeding).
Helminthophaga citræa, CAB., J. f. O. 1861, 75 (Costa Rica).
Motacilla protonotarius, GM., Syst. Nat. i, 1788, 972.
Sylvia protonotarius, LATH., Ind. Orn. ii, 1790, 542.—VIEILL., Ois. Am. Sept. ii, 1807, 27, pl. 83.—WILS., Am. Orn. iii, 1811, 72, pl. 24, f. 3.—BP., Syn. 1828, 86.—NUTT., Man. i, 1832, 410.—AUD., Orn. Biog. i, 1832, 22; v, 1839, 460; pl. 3.
Sylvia (Dacnis) protonotarius, BP., Journ. Phila. Acad. iv, 1825, 196.
Vermivora protonotarius, BP., List, 1838, 21.—WOODH., Sitgr. Rep. 1853, 72 (Indian Territory, breeding).—HOY, Smiths. Rep. 1864, 438 (Western Missouri).
Helinaia protonotarius, AUD., Syn. 1839, 67.—AUD., B. Am. ii, 1841, 89, pl. 106 (gives Texas to Nova Scotia and Sasketchewan!).
Helmitherus protonotarius, BP., Consp. Av. 1850, 314.
Compsothlypis protonotarius, CAB., Mus. Hein. i, 1850, 20.

HAB.—Eastern United States, southerly. North occasionally to Maryland and Pennsylvania, and even Maine. Ohio. Illinois. Kentucky. Kansas. Missouri. Cuba. Costa Rica. Panama. Merida.

This species was noticed by neither Expedition; it only reaches the lowermost Missouri. According to Dr. Woodhouse, it breeds in the Indian Territory, and it has also been found breeding at Neosho Falls, Kansas, by Mr. B. F. Goss, and at the Kiowa Agency by Dr. Palmer. The nest is built in the hole of a tree, oftenest a deserted Woodpecker's, or even, as in the instance of a nest before me in the Smithsonian, in a mill-frame. It is a slight and inartistic affair, flat and little hollowed, measuring about four inches across outside by scarcely over an inch in depth. It is built of various coarse fibrous strips, woven in with a matting of very fine mossy and downy substances, with some patches of fur, apparently from a rabbit; the lining is chiefly of fine rootlets. It contained five eggs, white, thickly spotted all over, but most heavily at the larger end, with reddish and slaty-brown or neutral tint. An egg of another set from the Kiowa Agency is still more boldly blotched in larger pattern. Two specimens, selected as extremes, measure, respectively, 0.70 by 0.55 and 0.68 by 0.58, the latter being remarkably rounded, while the others are all also quite noticeably obtuse at the smaller end.

HELMITHERUS VERMIVORUS, (Gm.) Bp.

Worm-eating Warbler.

Motacilla vermivora, GM., Syst. Nat. i, 1788, 951.
Sylvia vermivora, LATH., Ind. Orn. ii, 1790, 499.—WILS., Am. Orn. iii, 1811, 74, pl. 24, fig.
    4.—BP., Syn. 1828, 86.—NUTT., Man. i, 1832, 409.—AUD., Orn. Biog. i, 1832, 177;
    v, 1839, 460; pl. 34.
Sylvicola vermivora, RICH., List in Rep. Brit. Assoc. 1837.
Helinaia vermivora, AUD., Syn. 1839, 66.—AUD., B. Am. ii, 1841, 86, pl. 105.—LEMBEYE,
    Aves Cubæ, 1850, 35, pl. 6, f. 4.—PUTN., Pr. Ess. Inst. i, 1856, 277.
Helmitherus vermivorus, BP., Consp. Av. i, 1850, 314.—CAB., Mus. Hein. 1850, 20.—BD., B.
    N. A. 1858, 252.—SCL., P. Z. S. 1859, 363 (Xalapa).—SCL., Cat. 1862, 28.—SCL. &
    SALV., Ibis, 1859, 11 (Guatemala).—CAB., J. f. O. 1860, 329 (Costa Rica).—
    GUNDL., J. f. O. 1861, 326 (Cuba).—WHEAT., Ohio Agric. Rep. 1860, No. 71.—
    COUES & PRENT., Smiths. Rep. 1861, 406 (Washington, D. C., May to Sept.).—
    VERR., Pr. Ess. Inst. iii, 1862, 157 (Maine).—ALLEN, Pr. Ess. Inst. iv, 1864, 82
    (Massachusetts, nesting, *fide* PEAB., Rep. 1839, 312).—COUES, *ibid.* v, 1868, 270
    (New England to Maine in summer, rare).—COUES, Pr. Bost. Soc. xii, 1868, 109
    (South Carolina, April to Oct.).—BD., Rev. 1864, 179.—SCL. & SALV., P. Z. S.
    1867, 135 (Veragua).—LAWR., Ann. Lyc. N. Y. ix, 1868, 94 (Costa Rica); 1869,
    200 (Yucatan).—TURNB., B. E. Pa. 1869, 16 (May to Sept., rather rare).—
    SUMICH., Mem. Bost. Soc. i, 1869, 546 (mountains of Orizaba, migratory).—
    SCOTT, Pr. Bost. Soc. 1872 (breeding in West Virginia).—COUES, Key, 1872, 93,
    fig. 37.—MAYN., B. Fla. 1872, 46 (Florida, wintering).
Helmitherus migratorius, RAF., Journ. Phys. 1819, 417.—HARTL., R. Z. 1845, 342.
Vermivora pennsylvanica, BP., List, 1838, 20.—GOSSE, B. Jam. 1847, 150.—HOY, Smiths.
    Rep. 1864, 438 (Western Missouri).
(?) *Vermivora fulvicapilla,* SW., Birds, ii, 1837, 245.

Hab.—Eastern United States, regularly north to the Middle States, rarely to Southern New England, casually to Maine; no record beyond. West to Missouri, Kansas,
and Indian Territory. In winter, Florida, West Indies, Central America, and Southeastern Mexico.

Like the last, this species only reaches the lowest Missouri, and was not noticed by
either Expedition.

The Worm-eating Warbler is not one of our most abundant species,
and is of southerly distribution, rarely entering New England, and not
being common north of Virginia. I used to find it sparingly about
Washington, where it arrives early in May, and remains through most
of September. I noticed it most frequently in the thickets and undergrowth along Rock Creek, where it may be observed at any time during
the summer. It is a sedate—rather a demure—little bird, without the
vivacity of most warblers. When startled from the dead leaves on the
ground, where it spends most of its time rambling, like the Golden-
crowned Thrush, it flies to a near low limb, and there often sits motionless, or hops listlessly about. The nest and eggs I have never seen.
Mr. Maynard describes the former as being built on the ground (large
for the size of the bird), and composed of grasses, rootlets, and a few
dried leaves. The eggs, he says, are four in number, spotted and dotted,
most thickly at the large end, with reddish-brown, and measuring 0.73
by 0.56. They were discovered by Mr. J. H. Batty "on the eastern slope
of the Orange Mountains, in New Jersey. He was collecting in the
woods, and had wandered into a small open space, when he observed
the bird sitting on the nest. At the first glance he mistook her for a
Golden-crowned Thrush, but upon approaching saw at once what she
was, and knew that he had secured a prize. The bird remained quiet
until he was quite near, and then ran rapidly away for some distance before she took flight. The nest was placed in a little depression on the
ground, and partly covered with dead leaves. Both birds came about
the place uttering a sharp chirp."

HELMINTHOPHAGA PINUS, (Linn.) Bd.

Blue-winged Yellow Warbler.

Certhia pinus, LINN., Syst. Nat. i, 1766, 187.—GM., *ibid.* i, 13th ed. 1788, 478.
Sylvia pinus, LATH., Ind. Orn. ii, 1790, 537.—VIEILL., Ois. Am. Sept. ii, 1807, 44.
Helminthophaga pinus, BD., B. N. A. 1858, 254 ; Rev. 1864, 174.—SCL., P. Z. S. 1856, 291
    (Cordova).—SCL. & SALV., Ibis, 1859, 11 (Guatemala).—SCL., Cat. 1862, 28.—
    COUES & PRENT., Smiths. Rep. 1861 (Washington, migratory, rare).—ALLEN,
    Pr. Ess. Inst. iv, 1864 (Massachuseets, rare ; quotes CAB., Pr. Bost. Soc. vi,
    386).—COUES, *ibid.* v, 1868, 271 (Southern New England, very rare).—MAYN.,
    Guide, 1870, 100 (quotes SAMUELS, "flock at Dedham, Mass.").—ALLEN, Bull.
    M. C. Z. iii, 1872, 124, 175 (Eastern Kansas).—COUES, Key, 1872, 94.—SNOW, B.
    Kans. 1873, 4.
Sylvia solitaria, WILS., Am. Orn. ii, 1810, 109, pl. 15.—BP., Syn. 1828, 87.—NUTT., Man. i,
    1832, 410.—AUD., Orn. Biog. i, 1832, 102, pl. 20.
Sylvicola solitaria, RICH., Rep. Brit. Assoc. 1837.
Vermivora solitaria, JARDINE'S Ed. Wils. 1832.—BP., List, 1838, 21.—WOODH., Sitgr. Rep.
    1853, 73 (abundant and breeding in Indian Territory).—HOY, Smiths. Rep. 1864,
    438 (Western Missouri).
Helinaia solitaria, AUD., Syn. 1839, 69.—AUD., B. Am. ii, 1841, 98, pl. 111.—PUTN., Pr.
    Ess. Inst. i, 1856, 227 (Massachusetts).
Helmitherus solitarius, BP., Consp. Av. i, 1850, 315.
Helminthophaga solitaria, CAB., Mus. Hein. i, 1850, 20.—TURNB., B. E. Pa. 1869, 16.

Hab.—Eastern United States. North rarely to Massachusetts, beyond which no
record. West to Kansas and Indian Territory. Eastern Mexico and Central America
(Cordova, *Scl.*, P. Z. S. 1856, 291 ; Guatemala, *Scl.*, Ibis, i, 11). No West Indian record.
With a range nearly coincident with that of the last species, the present may be
mentioned in the same terms.

The Blue-winged Yellow Warbler was found by Mr. Ridgway breeding at Mount Carmel, Illinois, where a nest containing five eggs was
discovered May 8, 1866, on the ground in a bunch of shrubbery, in the
corner of a field. The nest was built chiefly of fibrous strips, most of
them broad and coarse, and lined with fine grass stems variously interlaced. The eggs, of the usual shape, and measuring about 0.63 by 0.48,
are white, sparsely sprinkled, chiefly at the great end, with blackish
dots, and a few others of lighter dirty brownish.

HELMINTHOPHAGA CHRYSOPTERA, (Linn.) Cab.

Blue Golden-winged Warbler.

Motacilla chrysoptera, LINN., Syst. Nat. i, 1766, 333.
Sylvia chrysoptera, LATH., Ind. Orn. ii, 1790, p. —.—WILS., Am. Orn. ii, 1810, 113, pl. 15,
    f. 5.—BP., Syn. 1828, 87.—BP., Am. Orn. i, 1825, 12, pl. 1, f. 3 (♀).—NUTT., Man.
    i, 1832, 411.—AUD., Orn. Biog. v, 1839, 154, pl. —.
Sylvicola chrysoptera, RICH., List, in Rep. Brit. Assoc. 1837.
Vermivora chrysoptera, BP., List, 1838, 21.
Helinaia chrysoptera, AUD., Syn. 1839, 67.—AUD., B. Am. ii, 1841, 91, pl. 107.—PUTN., Pr.
    Ess. Inst. i, 1856, 227.
Helmiteros chrysoptera, BP., Consp. Av. i, 1850, 315.—SCL., P. Z. S. 1855, 143 (Bogota).—
Helmithophaga chrysoptera, CAB., Mus. Hein. i, 1850, 20 ; J. f. O. 1860, 328 (Costa Rica).—
    BD., B. N. A. 1858, 255 ; Rev. 1864, 175.—WHEAT., Ohio Agric. Rep. 1860.—SCL.
    & SALV., Ibis, 1860, 397 (Guatemala).—LAWR., Ann. Lyc. N. Y. vii, 1861, 293
    (Panama).—GUNDL., J. f. O. 1861, 326 (Cuba, rare).—COUES & PRENT., Smiths.
    Rep. 1861, 406 (Washington, D. C., migratory, rare).—ALLEN, Pr. Ess. Inst. iv,
    1864, 82 (Massachusetts, very rare).—MCILWR., *ibid.* vi, 1866, 85 (Hamilton, two
    specimens).—SALV., P. Z. S. 1867, 135 (Veragua).—COUES, Pr. Ess. Inst. v, 1868,
    271.—COUES, Pr. Bost. Soc. xii, 1868, 106 (South Carolina, migratory).—LAWR.,
    Ann. Lyc. ix, 1868, 94 (Costa Rica).—TURNB., B. E. Pa. 1869, 16.—MAYN., Guide,
    1870, 100 (Massachusetts, breeding).—SCOTT, Pr. Bost. Soc. 1872 (breeding in
    West Virginia).—COUES, Key, 1872, 94, fig. 38.
Motacilla flavifrons, GM., Syst. Nat. i, 1788, 976.
Sylvia flavifrons, LATH., Ind. Orn. ii, 1790, 527.

Hab.—Eastern United States to New England and Canada West (to Nova Scotia,
Audubon). West to the lowermost Missouri. Winters in Central America (*various* quo-
tations). Cuba.
Not noticed by either Expeditien. It appears to be everywhere uncommon.

4

An excellent and very acceptable account of the nesting and eggs of this species has lately been given by Mr. Maynard, who discovered a nest in West Newton, Massachusetts, June 12, 1869. It was placed on the ground, on a small piece of green moss, "partly overshadowed by some ferns and rank weeds; but these must have grown after the nest was built," so that there was no attempt at concealment. "The nest is composed outwardly of large oak-leaves, of the previous year, and grape-vine bark, and is lined, not very smoothly, with fine grass and a few horse-hairs. It is large for the size of the bird, quite deep, and slightly smaller at the top than in the middle. The whole structure is not nearly as neat as would be expected for so small and elegant a bird, and re-minds one strikingly of the nest of the Maryland Yellow-throat. The dimensions are: Depth externally 3.15 inches, internally 2.20; diameter internally in the middle 2.25, at the top 1.90; diameter externally 3.50." The eggs, four in number, measured 0.67 by 0.55, 0.66 by 0.55, 0.66 by 0.55, and 0.67 by 0.50. They were white, spotted and blotched with reddish-brown, thickly at the larger end, where, in one example, the spots formed an irregular wreath, more sparsely elsewhere. There was also a Cow-bird's egg in the nest. The yellow parts of the mother of these eggs were nearly as in the male; there was less white on the tail; the black of the throat and cheeks was replaced by slate; the back was tinged with greenish, instead of being pure pearly gray; and the under parts were yellowish, not white. The writer remarks upon the partial-ity of the species for swampy places, generally on the edges of woods.

Two nests in the Smithsonian from Racine, Wisconsin, taken by Dr. P. R. Hoy, in June, without their outer wall of leaves, are built of fine grasses, neatly bent and woven; one is lined with white horse-hair, the other not. An egg measures 0.68 by 0.49. A large bulky nest from Georgia (Dr. Gerhardt) is chiefly composed of leaves, with fine fibrous lining. An Ohio nest is essentially similar in all respects; it contained two Cow-bird eggs. The egg is sparsely sprinkled all over, but more thickly around the large end.

HELMINTHOPHAGA RUFICAPILLA, (Wils.) Bd.

Nashville Warbler.

Sylvia ruficapilla, WILS., Am. Orn. iii, 1811, 120, pl. 27, f. 3.—AUD., Orn. Biog. i, 1832, 450, pl. 89.

Helminthophaga ruficapilla, BD., B. N. A. 1858, 256; Rev. 1864, 175.—SCL., P. Z. S. 1856, 291 (Cordova); 1858, 298 (Oaxaca); 1859, 373 (Xalapa); Cat. 1862, 29.—WHEAT., Ohio Agric. Rep. 1860, No. 74.—COUES & PRENT., Smiths. Rep. 1861, 406.—BOARDM., Pr. Bost. Soc. ix, 1862, 125 (Calais, Me., very rare)—VERR., Pr. Ess. Inst. iii, 1862, 147 (Norway, Me., rare).—ALLEN, Pr. Ess. Inst. iv, 1864, 59 (Springfield, Mass., breeding).—McILWR., Pr. Ess. Inst. v, 1866, 85 (Hamilton, C. W., summer, common).—COUES, Pr. Ess. Inst. v, 1868, 270.—TURNB., B. E. Pa. 1869, 16—SUMICH., Mem. Bost. Soc. i, 1869, 546 (Orizaba).—COOP., B. Cal. i, 1870, 82 (quotes Fort Tejon, *Xantus*, 1858, and Sierra Nevada, near Lake Tahoe, *Gruber*, 1863, "many specimens").—ALLEN, Bull. M. C. Z. iii, 1872, 124, 175 (Kansas and Utah).—MAYN., Guide, 1870, 99.—MAYN., Pr. Bost. Soc. xiv, 1871; B. Fla. 1872, 63.—COUES, Key, 1872, 94.

Sylvia rubricapilla, WILS., Gen. Index to Am. Orn. vi, 1812, 15.—BP., Journ. Phila. Acad. iv, 1825, 107, No. 159.—BP., Syn. 1828, 87.—NUTT., Man. i, 1832, 412.

Sylvicola (Vermivora) rubricapilla, SW. & RICH., F. B. A. ii, 1831, 220, pl. 42, upper fig. (Cumberland House).

Sylvicola rubricapilla, RICH., Rep. Brit. Assoc. 1837.

Vermivora rubricapilla, BP., List, 1838, 21.—REINH., Viddensk. Meddel. for 1853 (1854), 82 (Greenland).—BREW., Pr. Bost. Soc. 1856, 4 (breeding).

Helinaia rubricapilla, AUD., Syn. 1839, 70.—AUD., B. Am. ii, 1841, 103, pl. 113.—PUTN., Pr. Ess. Inst. i, 1856, 227.

Helmintherus rubricapilla, BP., Consp. 1, 1850, 315.—SCL., P. Z. S. 1856, 291 (Cordova).—SCL., P. Z. S. 1859, 363 (Xalapa).

Helminthophaga rubricapilla, CAB., Mus. Hein. 1850, 20.—SCL., P. Z. S. 1858, 298 (Oaxaca, in Feb. and Aug.).
Mniotilta rubricapilla, REINH., Ibis, iii, 1861, 6 (Greenland).
Sylvia leucogastra, SHAW's Gen. Zool. x, 1817, 622.
"Sylvia nashvillei, VIEILL.—*Sylvia mexicana,* HOLBÖLL."

Hab.—Temperate North America, but especially Eastern United States. North to Canada, and to Cumberland House (*Richardson*); casually to Greenland (*Reinhardt*). Breeds from Massachusetts northward. Numerous Mexican quotations, but none West Indian nor Central American (?). West to Utah (*Allen*) and California (*Cooper*). "Columbia River" (*Audubon*).

Although this species, like most others of the same genus, was not observed by either of the Expeditions, its range includes the Missouri region. It is by no means an exclusively Eastern species, as will be seen by the foregoing citations, its range being more nearly coincident with that of *peregrina* than of either *pinus* or *chrysoptera.*

The nest and eggs I have never found. The following account, given by Mr. Allen, is selected from a number at our disposal. Referring to Springfield, Massachusetts, he says: "Abundant in May and in the early part of autumn. Arrives May 1st to 5th, and for two or three weeks is a common inhabitant of the orchards and gardens, actively gleaning insects among the unfolding leaves and blossoms of the fruit-trees. Nearly all go north, but a few retire to the woods and breed. During June, 1863, I frequently saw them in my excursions in the woods, often three or four males in an hour's walk. Its song so much resembles that of the Chestnut-sided Warbler, that it might readily be mistaken. To this cause, and to the difficulty of seeing such small birds in the dense summer foliage, is doubtless owing to the fact of its being so commonly overlooked by naturalists during the summer months, rather than to its [supposed] extreme rarity in this latitude at that season. I have found the nest of this species for two successive seasons, as follows: May 31, 1862, containing four freshly laid eggs. The nest was placed on the ground, and sunken so that the top of the nest was level with the surface of the ground, and protected and completely concealed above by the dead grass and weeds of the previous year. It was composed of fine rootlets and dry grasses, lined with fine dried grass and a few horse-hairs, and covered exteriorly with a species of fine green moss. The eggs were white, sprinkled with light reddish-brown specks, most thickly near the larger end; longer diameter 0.60, and the shorter 0.50. The following year, June 5, 1863, I found another nest of this species within three or four feet of where the one was discovered the previous year, containing three eggs of this species and one of the Cow-bunting, in all of which the embryos were far advanced. The nest, in every particular, was built and arranged like the one above described, and the egg must have been laid at just about the same time. * * * * The locality of the nests was a mossy bank at the edge of young woods, sloping southward, and covered with bushes and coarse grass. Probably the male of the first nest, mating again, selected the same site for the second nest; and it may have been occupied for a longer time."

HELMINTHOPHAGA VIRGINIÆ, Bd.

Virginia's Warbler.

Helminthophaga virginiæ, BD., B. N. A. 1860 (not 1858), p. xi, pl. 79, f. 1 (Canton Burg-wyn, N. M.); Rev. 1865, 177,—COUES, Pr. Phila. Acad. 1866, 70 (Fort Whipple, Ariz.).—COOP., B. Cal. i, 1870, 85.—AIKEN, Pr. Bost. Soc. 1872, 196 (Eastern Colorado).—COUES, Key, 1872, 94.

Hab.—Southern Rocky Mountain region.

This species, of which until lately only two specimens were known, from the localities above quoted, has more recently been found to be abundant in Nevada and Utah, by Mr. Ridgway, and the present year has been ascertained to breed in Eastern Colorado, by Mr. Aiken, who found a nest with eggs. It was concealed on the ground, in a depression, like that of *H. ruficapilla.* Mr. Ridgway's nest, taken June 9, 1867, at Salt Lake City, is loosely composed of coarse fibrous and fine grassy material; it contains three eggs, which measure 0.68 in length by 0.48 in breadth, and are white, thickly sprinkled all over with purplish-brown and lavender spots, tending to wreathe around the large end.

All the species of *Helminthophaga* occur within our limits, excepting two—*H. bachmani,* an extremely rare species, from the South Atlantic States and Cuba, and *H. luciæ.* recently discovered in Arizona.

HELMINTHOPHAGA CELATA, (Say) Bd.

Orange-crowned Warbler.

a. *celata.*

Sylvia celata, SAY, Long's Exped. i, 1823, 169.—BP., Am. Orn. i, 1825, 45, pl. 5, fig. 2; Syn. 1828, 38.—NUTT., Man. i, 1832, 413.—AUD., Orn. Biog. ii, 1834, 449, pl. 178.
Sylvicola celata, RICH., List, 1837.
Vermivora celata, BP., List, 1838, 21.
Helinaia celata, AUD., B. Am. ii, 1841, 100, pl. 112.
Helmitherus celata, BP., Consp. Av. i, 1850, 315.
Helminthophaga celata, BD., B. N. A. 1858, 257; Rev. 1864, 176.—SCL., P. Z. S. 1858, 298 (Oaxaca); 1859, 373; 1862, 19 (La Parada).—HEERM., P. R. R. Rep. 1859, x, part vi, 40.—COOP. & SUCK., N. H. Wash. Ter. 1859, 178.—HAYD., Rep. 1862, 160.—SCL., P. Z. S. 1862, 19 (Parada, Mex.).—LORD, Pr. Roy. Art. Inst. iv, 1864, 115.—COUES, Pr. Phila. Acad. 1866, 68.—ALLEN, Pr. Ess. Inst. iv, 1864, 60 (Massachusetts).—LAWR., Ann. Lyc. Nat. Hist. N. Y. viii, 1866, 284 (New York).—COUES, Pr. Bost. Soc. 1868, 107 (South Carolina).—COUES, Pr. Ess. Inst. v, 1868, 271 (New England).—DALL & BANN., Tr. Chic. Acad. i, 1869, 278.— COOP., Pr. Cal. Acad. 1870, 75.—COOP., B. Cal. 83.—ALLEN, Bull. M. C. Z. ii, 1871, 268 (Florida).—ALLEN, Bull. M. C. Z. iii, 1872, 175 (Utah; Kansas).— MAYN., B. Fla. 1872, 62.—AIKEN, Pr. Bost. Soc. 1872, 196 (Colorado).—STEV., U. S. Geol. Surv. Ter. 1870, 463.—COUES, Key, 1872, 95.

b. *lutescens.*

Helminthophaga celata var. *lutescens,* RIDGW., Am. Journ. Sci. 1872, 457.

Hab.—North America, at large, but chiefly the Middle and Western Provinces. North to the Yukon and McKenzie River regions. South to Oaxaca, Mex. Var. *lutescens* from the Pacific region. (Some of the above quotations belong here.)
Not obtained by Captain Raynolds' Expedition.
Lieutenant Warren's Expedition.—4672, Bon Homme Island; 4673, mouth of Big Sioux River.
Later Expeditions.—60698–9, Fort Bridger and Little Sandy; 60975, Green River.
A var. *obscurus,* without the concealed orange crown-patch, from the South Atlantic States, lately described by Mr. Ridgway, seems scarcely entitled to recognition by name.

This species, first discovered in the Missouri region, was soon afterward noted by Nuttall from Florida, and Audubon subsequently ascribed to it an extensive Eastern range. He says it is seen "in the Southern States, where it passes the winter, and while crossing the Union in early spring on its way to those northeastern districts, where it breeds. It leaves Louisiana, the Floridas and Carolinas, from the beginning to the end of April; is seen in the Middle States about the 10th of May, and reaches the State of Maine and the British Provinces by the end of that month. On its return, besides settling in the Southern States, it spreads over the provinces of Mexico, from whence individuals in spring migrate by the vast prairies, and along the shores of the western parts of the Union, entering Canada in that direction in the first days of June * * * breeds in the eastern parts of Maine, and in the British Provinces of New Brunswick and Nova Scotia." These data appear to have been for a time overlooked; thus, in 1858, we find Prof. Baird assigning a range only from the "Mississippi River to the Pacific." But the accuracy of Audubon's extensive observations has been of late confirmed. Mr. Allen records the bird as wintering in Florida, on Mr. Boardman's excellent authority, and he found it himself at Springfield, Massachusetts, May 15, 1863. Still the bird appears to be more at home in the West; along the Pacific coast we have advices from the Yukon to Cape St. Lucas. In the interior of the Fur Countries, from Forts Resolution and Simpson; southward to Mexico. It is a common species in most of the Western Territories.

A nest of the Orange-crowned Warbler taken June 12, 1860, by Mr. Kennicott, at Fort Resolution, Great Slave Lake, was built on the ground, inside of a bank, among open bushes, and was much hidden by dry leaves. It contained five eggs. This nest is built outwardly of fibrous strips of bark, interiorly of fine grasses, without other lining. The eggs are very finely dotted all over—thickly about the larger end, more sparsely elsewhere—with pale brown. They measure about 0.67 by 0.50.

HELMINTHOPHAGA PEREGRINA, (Wils.) Cab.

Tennessee Warbler.

Sylvia peregrina, WILS., Am. Orn. iii, 1811, 83, pl. 25, f. 2.—BP., Syn. 1828, 87.—NUTT., Man. i, 1832, 412.—AUD., Orn. Biog. ii, 1834, 307, pl. 154.
Sylvicola peregrina, RICH., List, 1837.
Vermivora peregrina, BP., List, 1838.—HOY, Smiths. Rep. 1864, 438 (Western Missouri).
Helinaia peregrina, AUD., Syn. 1839, 68; B. Am. ii, 1841, 96, pl. 110.
Helmitheros peregrina, BP., Consp. Av. i, 1850, 315.
Helminthophaga peregrina, CAB., Mus. Hein. i, 1850, 20; J. f. O. 1861, 85 (Costa Rica).—BD., B. N. A. 1858, 258; Rev. 1865, 178.—VERR., Pr. Ess. Inst. iii, 1862, 157.—ALLEN, ibid. iv, 1864, 61.—COUES, ibid. v, 1868, 271.—LAWR., Ann. Lyc. 1861, 322 (Panama); viii, 1866, 174 (Veragua); ibid. 284 (New York); ibid. ix, 1868, 94 (Costa Rica).—SALV., P. Z. S. 1867, 135 (Veragua).—SCL., ibid. 1870, 836 (Honduras).—MAYN., Guide, 1870, 100; Pr. Bost. Soc. xiv, 1871, —.—COUES, Key, 1872, 95.—SNOW, B. Kans. 1873, 5.
Sylvia tennesseei, VIEILL., Ency. Meth. ii, 1823, 452.
(?) *Sylvia missouriensis*, MAXIM., J. f. O. vi, 1858, 117.

Hab.—Eastern North America, to high latitudes. Breeds from the northern portions of New England northward, migratory elsewhere. South in winter to Central America. Not obtained by any of the Expeditions.

The Tennessee Warbler appears to be rather rare in the Eastern United States, but more plentiful along its line of migration in the interior. I observed it in great numbers in Minnesota and Eastern Dakota, late in May and early in June, when it was moving along the Red River of the North. Standing in the heavy timber near the bank of the river, I easily procured a dozen specimens in an hour, without moving from my tracks, as the birds came fluttering past in the tree-tops, almost in a continuous band, associating with several other Warblers and with small Fly-catchers. They were extremely active, skipping through the foliage and fluttering through the air, pursuing their insect prey, and uttering a sharp screeping note. I have not myself observed the species further west, but a specimen was taken high up on the Missouri by Mr. Bell, in 1843, as noticed in Prof. Baird's earlier work.

A nest of this species—or rather what appears to be only the inner portion of a nest—was taken by Mr. George Barnston at Michipicoton, Lake Superior, and contained two eggs. The specimen consists entirely of fine dried grass-stems, rather loosely interwoven.

DENDRŒCA ÆSTIVA, (Gm.) Bd.

Blue-eyed Yellow Warbler; Golden Warbler; Summer Warbler.

Motacilla æstiva, GM., Syst. Nat. i, 1788, 996.
Sylvia æstiva, LATH., Ind. Orn. ii, 1790, 551.—VIEILL., Ois. Am. Sept. ii, 1807, 35, pl. 95.—
    AUD., Orn. Biog. i, 1831, 476, pl. 95.—NUTT., Man. i, 1832, 370.
Sylvicola æstiva, SW. & RICH., F. B. A. ii, 1831, 211.—AUD., B. Am. ii, 1841, 50, pl. 88.—
    WOODH., Sitgr. Rep. 1853, 70.—HOY, Smiths. Rep. 1864, 438.
Rhimamphus æstivus, BP., Consp. Av. i, 1850, 311.—SCL., P. Z. S. 1856, 141.
Dendrœca æstiva, BD., B. N. A. 1858, 282; Rev. 1865, 195.—COUES, Key, 1872, 97; and of
    late writers.
Sylvia carolinensis, LATH., Ind. Orn. ii, 1790, 551.
Sylvia flava, VIEILL., Ois. Am. Sept. ii, 1807, 31, pl. 81.
Sylvia citrinella, WILS., Am.·Orn ii, 1810, 111, pl. 15, f. 5.
Sylvia childreni, AUD., Orn. Biog. i, 1831, 180, pl. 35.
Sylvia rathbonia, AUD., Orn. Biog. i, 1831, 333, pl. 65.
"*Rhimanphus citrinus*, RAFINESQUE."

Hab.—Whole of North America, through Mexico and Central America into South
America. In the West Indies, represented by several insular forms, apparently not
specifically distinct.

List of specimens.

| 19204 | 17 | Wind River.. | ♂ | May 25, 1860 | F. V. Hayden.. | 4.50 | 7.75 | 2.50 |

Lieutenant Warren's Expedition.—5292–3, Fort Lookout; 5291, Little Cheyenne River;
5295, Blackfoot country; 4665, near Fort Lookout; 4660, Fort Pierre; 4656, White
River; 4662, Platte River; 5642, Kansas; 5294, Powder River; 8825, Loup Fork; 4658,
4661, 4668–9, "Nebraska."
Later Expeditions.—59855, Colorado; 60427–32, Bitter Cottonwood and La Bonté
Creek; 60702–3, Fort Bridger and Green River, 61660, Utah.

DENDRŒCA VIRENS, (Gm.) Bd.

Black-throated Green Warbler.

Motacilla virens, GM., Syst. Nat. i, 1788, 985.
Sylvia virens, LATH., Ind. Orn. ii, 1790, 537.—VIEILL., Ois. Am. Sept. ii, 1807, 33, pl. 92.—
    WILS., Am. Orn. ii, 1810, 27, pl. 17, f. 3.—BP., Syn. 1828, 80.—NUTT., Man. i,
    1832, 376.—AUD., Orn. Biog. iv, 1838, 70, pl. 399.
Sylvicola virens, BP., List, 1838, 22.—AUD., Syn. 1839, 55.—AUD., B. A. ii, 1844, 42, pl. 84.—
    BP., Consp. Av. i, 1850, 307.—WOODH., Sitgr. Rep. 1853, 70 (Texas and Indian
    Territory).—REINH., Vedensk. Med. 1853, 72, 81 (Greenland).—HOY, Smiths.
    Rep. 1864, 438 (Missouri).—TRIPPE, Pr. Ess. Inst. vi, 1871, 114 (Minnesota,
    breeding).
Rhimanphus virens, CAB., Mus. Hein. i, 1850, 19; J. f. O. iii, 1855, 474 (Cuba).—SCL., P.
    Z. S. 1856, 291 (Cordova).
Mniotilta virens, GRAY.—REINH., Ibis, iii, 1861, 5 (Greenland).
Dendrœca virens, BD., B. N. A. 1858, 267; Rev. 1865, 182.—SCL. & SALV., Ibis, 1859, 11
    (Guatemala).—SCL. P. Z. S. 1859, 373 (Xalapa); Cat. 1862, 29.—GUNDL., J. f. O.
    1861, 326 (Cuba).—LAWR., Ann. Lyc. N. Y. vii, 1861, 293 (Panama); ix, 1868,
    94 (Costa Rica).—SUMICH., Mem. Bost. Soc. i, 1869, 546 (Vera Cruz, "every-
    where").—COUES, Key, 1872, 97, fig. 39; and of late writers generally.
(?) *Sylvia montana*, WILS., v, 113, pl. 44, f. 2 (Blue Mountains, Pa.).—AUD., Orn. Biog.
    v, 294 (California).
(?) *Sylvicola montana*, AUD., B. Am. ii, 69, 98.
(?) *Dendrœca montana*, BD., B. Am. 279; Rev. 190 (most probably; possibly young of *D.
    cærulea;* see COUES, Key, 1872, 105).

Hab.—Eastern North America to the Lower Missouri. Breeds from New England
northward, from New York and higher portions of Pennsylvania (*Audubon, Turnbull*).
Only migratory through most of the United States. Winters in Mexico, Central
America, and Cuba. Accidental in Greenland; also in Europe (Heligoland, *Gœtke,*
Naum. 1858, 423).

In the case of this and several other common birds of the same genus,
which were not noticed by the Expeditions, I shall abridge the current

United States references which demonstrate the now well-known range. I found this species common in pine-woods near Portsmouth, New Hampshire, in June, under circumstances leaving no doubt that it was then breeding; and in the District of Columbia it is very abundant in high, open, mixed woods in May and September, associating with several of its allies.

A nest of the Black-throated Green Warbler, containing three eggs, was obtained by Mr. George Welch at Lynn, Massachusetts. It is composed, first, of fine twigs in small bits, then of various soft, pliant, fibrous substances, composing the bulk of the nest, and lined with fine grasses and rootlets. The substance contains also a few feathers and some downy material. The eggs measure 0.72 by 0.54, and are creamy-white, rather coarsely spotted in a loose wreath around the large end with dark brown and neutral tint shell-markings. This nest measured a little over three inches across by nearly two in depth, and is rather neatly and compactly finished. Another nest, from West Roxbury, Massachusetts, is smaller and deeper, as well as less regular in contour, having apparently been placed in an oblique fork. The materials are much the same, but there is a good deal of horse-hair circularly woven inside. The eggs are four, smaller than the first described (0.67 by 0.50), pure white, with finer speckling more generally distributed, though preserving its distinctively wreathed character. These eggs are sufficiently dissimilar to have been laid by a different species.

DENDRŒCA NIGRESCENS, (Towns.) Bd.

Black-throated Gray Warbler,

Sylvia nigrescens, Towns., Journ. Phil. Ac. vii, 1837, 191.—Aud., O. B. v, 1839, 57, pl. 395.
Vermivora nigrescens, Bp., List, 1838, 21.—Nutt., Man. i, 1840, 471.
Sylvicola nigrescens, Aud., Syn. 1839, 60; B. A. ii, 1841, 62, pl. 94.—Bp., Consp. i, 1850, 308.
Rhimanphus nigrescens, Cab., Mus. Hein. i, 1850, 20.
Mniotilta nigrescens, Gray, Genera of Birds.
Dendrœca nigrescens, Bd., B. N. A. 1858, 270; Rev. 1865, 186.—Scl., P. Z. S. 1858, 298; 1859, 374 (Oaxaca); Cat. 1862, 30.—Heerm., P. R. Rep. x, 1859, pt. vi, 40.—Coop. & Suck., N. H. Wash. Ter. 1860, 180.—Coues, Pr. Phila. Acad. 1866, 69.—Sumich., Mem. Bost. Soc. i, 1869, 547 (Orizaba, rare).—Coop., B. Cal. 1870, 90.—Aiken, Pr. Bost. Soc. 1872, 197 (Colorado).—Coues, Key, 1872, 98.
" *Sylvia halsei*, Gir., B. Tex. 1838, pl. 3 (♀)," (*Sclater*).

Hab.—Rocky Mountains to the Pacific, United States; south through Mexico.

This species has proven not to be so exclusively a Pacific coast one as was formerly supposed. I found it common in the pine-woods about Fort Whipple, the latter part of April until toward October, and have reason to believe that it breeds there; but it is much more plentiful during its migrations. Mr. Aiken's Coloradoan record is the easternmost I have seen; Dr. Hayden did not meet with it, nor did Mr. Allen.

Other western Warblers remaining to be detected on the eastern slopes and foot-hills of the Rocky Mountains, are *D. occidentalis* and *townsendii*, if not also *D. graciæ;* but I have at present no authority for including them in this work.

DENDRŒCA CŒRULESCENS, (Linn.) Bd.

Black-throated Blue Warbler.

Motacilla cærulescens, Gm., Syst. Nat. i, 1788, 960.
Sylvia cærulescens, Lath., Ind. Orn. ii, 1790, 520.—Vieill., Ois. Am. Sept. ii, 1807, 25, pl. 80.—D'Orbig., La Sagra's Cuba, Ois. 1840, 63, pl. 9, figs. 1, 2 (Cuba).

Dendrœca cœrulescens, BD., Rev. 1865, 186.—MAYN., Pr. Bost. Soc. xiv, 1871, No. 25;
    Guide, 1870, 103; B. Fla. 1872, 54.—COUES, Key, 1872, 98.
Motacilla canadensis, LINN., Syst. Nat. i, 1766, 336 *nec* 334.
Sylvia canadensis, LATH., Ind. Orn. ii, 1790, 539.—WILS., Am. Orn. ii, 1810, 115, pl. 15,
    f. 7.—BP., Syn. 1828, 84.—NUTT., Man. i, 1832, 398.—AUD., Orn. Biog. ii, 1834,
    308, pls. 148, 155.—SALLÉ, P. Z. S. 1857, 231 (St. Domingo).
Sylvicola canadensis, SW.—RICH., Rep. Brit. Assoc. 1837.—BP., List, 1838, 23.—AUD., Syn.
    1839, 61.—AUD., B. Am. ii, 1841, 63. pl. 95.—WOODH., Sitgr. Rep. 1853, 71.—
    HOY, Smiths. Rep. 1864, 438 (Missouri).—TRIPPE, Pr. Ess. Inst. vi, 1811, 114
    (Minnesota, breeding).
Mniotilta canadensis, GRAY, Genera of Birds.
Rhimanphus canadensis, CAB., J. f. O. iii, 1855, 473 (Cuba).
Dendrœca canadensis, BD., B. N. A. 1858, 271; and of many late writers.—SCL., P. Z. S.
    1861, 70 (Jamaica); Cat. 1862, 30.—GUNDL., J. f. O. 1861, 326 (Cuba).
Sylvia pusilla, WILS., Am. Orn. v. 1812, 100, pl. 43, fig. 4 (young).
Sylvia leucoptera, WILS., Index, ii, 390.
Sylvia palustris, STEPH., Shaw's Gen. Zool. x, 1817, 722.
Sylvia sphagnosa, BP., Syn. 1828, 85.—NUTT., i, 1832, 406.—AUD., Orn. Biog. ii, 1834,
    279 (♀ and young).
Sylvicola pannosa, GOSSE, Birds Jamaica, 1847, 162 (♀).
Sylvia macropus, VIEILL., *fide* GRAY.

Hab.—Eastern North America to the Lower Missouri (to Upper Missouri, *Audubon*).
Migratory in most of the United States. Breeds from New England, and probably
mountains of Middle States, northward. Winters on Key West, Florida (*Maynard*),
and abundantly in various West Indian Islands. No Mexican nor Central American
quotations.

The United States range of this elegant species seems to be very
nearly coincident with that of the last, but its winter resorts are different, as seen by the above citations. Audubon's quotation of the head-
waters of the Missouri has not been verified by later observations, and
must be held for confirmation; not impossibly, confusion with the somewhat similar *D. nigrescens* led to an erroneous record. Dr. Hayden did
not find it. In the Middle States, where the species is migratory, I
used to find it common every spring and fall, during the migrations;
oftenest in low and tangled woods, but also in open forest in company
with *virens* and others. I am not aware of any specified instances of
its breeding south of the Canadas and Northern New England; but Mr.
Allen notices its recurrence in Massachusetts "in the breeding season,"
and Dr. Turnbull says a few remain to breed in his locality. Audubon
describes a nest from Halifax, Nova Scotia, as being placed on the horizontal bough of a fir, seven or eight feet from the ground, and composed
of bark-slips, mosses, and fibrous roots, lined with fine grass and a warm
bed of feathers. Eggs four to five, rosy-white, sparsely sprinkled with
reddish-brown at the larger end.

DENDRŒCA CŒRULEA, (Wils.) Bd.

Cœrulean Warbler.

Sylvia cœrulea, WILS., Am. Orn. ii, 1810, 141, pl. 17, f. 5.
Sylvicola cœrulea, SW.—RICH., Rep. Bost. Assoc. 1837.—BP., List, 1838, 23.—AUD., Syn.
    1839, 56.—AUD., B. Am. ii, 1841, 45, pl. 86.—BP., Consp. i, 1850, 308.—WOODH.,
    Sitgr. Rep. 1853, 70 (Texas and Indian Territory, abundant, breeding).—PUTN.,
    Pr. Ess. Inst. i, 1856, 207 ("Massachusetts, summer visitant, rare;" a mis-
    take).—HOY, Smiths. Rep. 1864, 438 (Missouri).
Mniotilta cœrulea, GRAY, Genera of Birds.
Dendrœca cœrulea, BD., B. N. A. 1858, 280; Rev. 1865, 191.—SCL., Cat. 1862, 31.—GUNDL.,
    J. f. O. 1861, 326 (Cuba, rare).—LAWR., Ann. Lyc. N. Y. 1861, 322 (Panama);
    ix, 1869, 200 (Yucatan).—COUES & PRENT., Smiths. Rep. 1861, 409 (Washing-
    ton, D. C., probably).—WHEAT., Ohio Agric. Rep. 1860, (quite numerous about
    Columbus that year).—ALLEN, Pr. Ess. Inst. iv, 1864, 83 (quotes PUTNAM).—
    McILWR., *ibid.* v, 1866, 86 (Hamilton, C. W., common May and June; may
    breed).—COUES, *ibid.* v, 1868, 274 (New England; quotes others).—TURNB.,
    B. E. Pa. 1869, 18 ("rare;" from May to end of August).—ALLEN, Bull. M. C. Z.

iii, 1872, 124 (Eastern Kansas, rather common).—COUES, Key, 1872, 99.—SCOTT, Pr. Bost. Soc. 1872 (breeding in West Virginia).—SALV., P. Z. S. 1870, 180 (Veragua).
Sylvia rara, WILS., Am. Orn. iii, 1811, 119, pl. 27, fig. 2. (♀ or young).—BP., Syn. 1828, 82.—NUTT., i, 1832, 225.—AUD., Orn. Biog. i, 1832, 258, pl. 49.
Vermivora rara, JARDINE.
Sylvia azurea, STEPH., Shaw's Gen. Zool. x, 1817, 653.—BP., Am. Orn. ii, 1828, pl. 27; Syn. 1828, 85.—NUTT., Man. i, 1832, 407.—AUD., Orn. Biog. i, 1832, 255, pls. 48, 49.
Sylvia bifasciata, SAY, Long's Exp. Rocky Mountains, 1823, 170.
Sylvia populorum, VIEILL., Enc. Met. ii, 1823, 449.

Hab.—Eastern North America to the Lower Missouri ("Columbia River," *Audubon*). North to Canada (to Nova Scotia, *Audubon*). Cuba (only West Indian record). South in winter to Guatemala, Panama, and New Granada (Bogota, SCL., P. Z. S. 1857, 18). No Mexican quotations (but "entering the United States from Mexico, early in April" (*Audubon*). Not in New England?

It is difficult to trace out the distribution of the species; its geographical record is confused, and many of the earlier citations have not been verified of late. Thus, Audubon says it inhabits "the whole breadth of our country," and that it was found on the Columbia by Mr. Townsend—a statement not now generally credited. The same author's Nova Scotian record has not lately been checked. There is some doubt that the bird ever enters New England; the various accounts seem traceable to one source, which, Dr. Brewer writes me, has proven entirely mistaken. Unequivocal evidence of its presence in Canada is given by Mr. McIlwraith. It is certainly a rare species in the Middle States; Dr. Turnbull so gives it, and at the time Dr. Prentiss and I noticed the birds of the District of Columbia, we had not seen it there, though I have in my cabinet a specimen afterward taken by one of the local collectors. The Mississippi Valley would appear to be the principal United States resort. Mr. Ridgway says it is very abundant in Illinois; Mr. Allen found it not uncommon in the Lower Missouri bottoms, and Dr. Woodhouse mentions its breeding in abundance in the Indian Territory. Recurring again to the perennial Audubon, we find him giving it as numerous in Louisiana, where he says he has seen five or six in a single walk, in August. He describes the nidification as follows: "The nest is placed in the forks of a low tree or bush, more frequently in a dogwood-tree. It is partly pensile, projecting a little above the twigs to which it is attached, and extending below them for nearly two inches. The fibres of vines, and the stalks of rank herbaceous plants, together with slender roots, compose the outer part, being arranged in a circular manner. The lining consists entirely of the dry fibres of the Spanish moss. The female lays four or five eggs, of a pure white color, with a few reddish spots at the larger end."

DENDRŒCA CORONATA, (Linn.) Gray.

Yellow-rump Warbler.

Motacilla coronata, LINN., Syst. Nat. i, 1766, 333.
Sylvia coronata, LATH., Ind. Orn. ii, 1790, 538.—VIEILL., Ois. Am. Sept. ii, 1807, 24, pls. 78, 79.—WILS., Am. Orn. ii, 1810, 138, pl. 17, f. 4; iv, 121, pl. 45, f. 3.—NUTT., Man. i, 1832, 361.—AUD., Orn. Biog. ii, 1834, 303, pl. 153.
Sylvicola coronata, SW. & RICH., F. B. A. ii, 1831, 216.—AUD., B. Am. ii, 1843, 23. pl. 76.— WOODH., Sitgr. Rep. 1853, 71.—HOY, Smiths. Rep. 1864, 437 (Missouri).—MAXIM., J. f. O. vi, 1858, 114.
Dendrœca coronata, GRAY.—BD., B. N. A. 1858, 272.—BD., Rev. 1865, 187.—COUES, Key, 1872, 99, fig. 41; and of late writers generally.—HAYD., Rep. 1862, 160 (to above Fort Pierre).—COOP. & SUCK., N. H. Wash. Ter. 1859, 187 (Washington Territory).—COOP., B. Cal. i, 1870, 89 (California, probably).—DALL & BANN., Tr. Chic. Acad. 1869, 278 (Yukon, breeding).—VERR., Pr. Bost. Soc. ix, 1862, 125 (Calais, Me., breeding).—MARCH, Pr. Phil. Acad. 1863, 292 (Jamaica, breeding).—

GUNDL., Cab. J. f. O. 1861, 326 (Cuba).—JONES, Nat. in Bermuda, 59 (April).—
COUES & PRENT., Smiths. Rep. for 1861 (1862), 407 (Washington, D. C., win-
tering).—TURNB., B. of E. Pa. and N. J. 1869, 17 (wintering).—BRYANT, Pr.
Bost. Soc. vii, 1859 (Bahamas, wintering).—SCL., P. Z. S. 1870, 836 (Honduras).—
LAWR., Ann. Lyc. ix, 1869, 94 (Costa Rica).—AIKEN, Pr. Bost. Soc. 1872, 196
     (Colorado).
Mniotilta coronata, GRAY.—REINH., Ibis, iii, 1861, 5 (Greenland).
Motacilla canadensis et Parus virginianus, LINN.
Motacilla umbria, cincta et pinguis, GM.
Sylvia xanthopygia, VIEILL., Ois. Am. Sept. ii, 1807, 47.
"*Sylvia xanthoroa*, VIEILL."
     Hab.—North America, excepting, so far as known, the Southwestern Territories. In
the northwest, across the continent, thence south along the Pacific coast to Washing-
ton Territory. Colorado (*Aiken*). Arctic coast. Greenland. Mexico, Central America,
and West Indies (*numerous* quotations).
     Lieutenant Warren's Expedition.—4651, mouth of Platte; 4652, 4655, mouth of Ver-
milion; 4654, mouth of Big Sioux; 5300, Medicine Creek.
     Not obtained by Captain Raynolds' Expedition.

   The rather peculiar, as well as very extensive, distribution of this
species may be gathered from the foregoing references, selected from the
great number that have been recorded. The Pacific coast advices are
not so remarkable as they would appear, did we not know that the
Eastern Province trends westward north of the United States, to Alaska,
where many characteristic Eastern birds were noticed by Mr. Dall and
Dr. Bannister. In view of this it is not surprising that individuals
straggle southward along that coast. But it is remarkable, that while
the bird's continental breeding range is not south of Northern New
England, it should also breed in the West Indies. Its wintering range
appears almost anomalous. While some individuals are at that season
in subtropical and tropical America, others are wintering in the Middle
States, if not also in Southern New England.
   The Yellow-rump lays four to six eggs, measuring about 0.72 by 0.54
inches; they are white, spotted chiefly in a wreath about the large end, but
also sparingly over the entire surface, with various shades of brown, none,
however, quite reddish, but some nearly blackish, and with numerous
other shell-markings of neutral tint. A nest from the Yukon (June 7)
is rather rudely built of weed-stalks, grass-stems, and rootlets, and
warmly lined throughout with feathers. Another from the Arctic coast,
east of Anderson River, is entirely composed of soft vegetable fibre, with
a few grass-stems for lining; it was built in a pine-tree, about six feet
from the ground. A third, from Nova Scotia, laid on the horizontal
fork of a tree, is composed chiefly of very slender, stiff rootlets and
similar hard stems, and is much flatter than either of the others.

DENDRŒCA AUDUBONII, (Towns.) Bd.

Audubon's Warbler.

Sylvia audubonii, TOWNS., Journ. Phila. Acad. vii, 1837, 190.—AUD., Orn. Biog. v, 1839,
     52, pl. 395.
Sylvicola audubonii, BP., List, 1838 21.—AUD., Syn. 1839, 52; B. Am. ii, 1826, pl. 77.—
     NUTT., Man. 2d ed. i. 1840, 414.—WOODH., Sitgr. Rep. 1853, 71.
Dendrœca audubonii, BD., B. N. A. 1858, 273.—KENN., P. R. R. Rep. x, 1859, part iii, 24.—
     HEERM., *ibid.* part iv, 39.—COOP. & SUCK., N. H. Wash. Ter. 1859, 181.—SCL.,
     P. Z. S. 1858, 298 (Oaxaca); 1860, 250 (Orizaba); 1864, 172 (Mexico); Cat. A. B.
     1861, 30.—SCL. & SALV., Ibis, 1860, 273 (Guatemala).—HAYD., Rep. 1862, 160.—
     COUES, Pr. Phila. Acad. 1866, 69.—COOP., Am. Nat. iii, 1869, 33; Pr. Cal.
     Acad. 1870, 75; B. Cal. 1870, 88.—STEV., U. S. Geol. Surv. Ter. 1870, 463.—
     MERR., *ibid.* 1872, 67.—ALLEN, Bull. M. C. Z. iii, 1872, 175 (mountains of Colo-
     rado, up to timber-line).—COUES, Key, 1872, 100.

   Hab.—Middle and Western Provinces, United States; East to Fort Laramie; South
to Guatemala. Northern limit yet undefined.

List of specimens.

19202	23	Wind River	♂	May 29, 1860	F. V. Hayden	5.25	9.50	3.00
19203	75	Wind River Mts	....	June 6, 1860	.... do	5.50	9.25	2.75
19234	....	R. Buttes Platte	....	May 12, 1860	G. H. Trook	5.75	9.25	3.25

Lieutenant Warren's Expedition.—8826, Laramie Peak; probably about the eastern limit of the species.
Later Expeditions.—60701, Fort Bridger; 62345-6, Wyoming.

In most localities through its range, this species is as common as its Eastern representative, *D. coronata*, with which it corresponds precisely in habits.

The only nest of this species that I have seen is in the Smithsonian, from Vancouver's Island, where it was secured by Mr. Hepburn. It is built in the crotch formed by three forks of an oblique stem, and is obliquely conical in shape to correspond. The exterior is rather coarse fibrous strips of bark and weeds, variously intertwined; the main substance is of fine grasses and mosses, mixed with large feathers and twine, and the interior is lined with an abundant deposit of horse-hair.

DENDRŒCA BLACKBURNIÆ, (Gm.) Bd.

Blackburnian Warbler.

Motacilla blackburniæ, GM., Syst. Nat. i, 1788, 977.
Sylvia blackburniæ, LATH., Ind. Orn. ii, 1790, 527.—VIEILL., Ois. Am. Sept. ii, 1807, 36, pl. 96.—WILS., Am. Orn. iii, 1811, 64, pl. 23, f. 3.—BP., Syn. 1828, 80.—NUTT., Man. i, 1832, 379.—AUD., Orn. Biog. ii, 1834, 208; v, 1839, 73; pls. 135, 399.
Sylvicola blackburniæ, JARD., ed. Wils. 1832.—RICH., List, 1837.—BP., List, 1838, 22; Consp. 1850, 307.—AUD., Syn. 1839, 57.—AUD., B. Am. ii, 1841, 48, pl. 87.—HOY, Smiths. Rep. 1864, 438 (Missouri).
Mniotilta blackburniæ, GRAY, G. of B.
Rhimanphus blackburniæ, CAB., Mus. Hein. i, 1850, 19; J. f. O. 1860, 328 (Costa Rica).—SCL., P. Z. S. 1855, 143 (Bogota); 1856, 130 (Veragua).
Dendrœca blackburniæ, BD., B. N. A. 1858, 274; Rev. 1865, 189.—SCL., P. Z. S. 1859, 363 (Xalapa); 1860, 64 (Ecuador); Cat. 1862, 30.—SCL. & SALV., Ibis, i, 1859, 11 (Guatemala); P. Z. S. 1870, 780 (Merida).—BRYANT, Pr. Bost. Soc. vii, 1859 (Bahamas).—LAWR., Ann. Lyc. vii, 62 (Panama); ix, 1868, 94 (Costa Rica).—SUMICH., Mem. Bost. Soc. i, 1869, 547 (Orizaba, rare).—MCILWR., Pr. Ess. Inst. vi, 1866, 85 (migratory at Hamilton, C. W.).—ALLEN, Pr. Ess. Inst. iv, 1864, 62 (chiefly migratory, but some breed in Massachusetts).—ALLEN, Bull. M. C. Z. iii, 1872, 175 (Kansas and Utah).—COUES, Key, 1872, 100; and of most late writers.
Sylvia parus, WILS., Am. Orn. v, 1812, 114, pl. 44, f. 3.—BP., Syn. 1828, 82.—NUTT., i, 392.—AUD., Orn. Biog. ii, 1834, 205, pl. 134.
Sylvicola parus, AUD., Syn. 1839, 55.—AUD., B. Am. ii, 1841, 40, pl. 83.—EMM., Cat. B. Mass. 1835, 3.—PEAB., Rep. B. Mass. 1839, 310.—LINSL., Cat. B. Conn., Am. Journ. Sci. xliv, 1843, 257.—PUTN., Pr. Ess. Inst. i, 1856, 226.
Mniotilta parus, GRAY, Genera of Birds.
Rhimamphus parus, BP., Consp. i, 1850, 311.
Sylvia lateralis, STEPH., Shaw's Gen. Zool. xii, 1817, 659.
"(?) *Motacilla chrysocephala et incana*," GM., i, 1788, 971 and 976.—Also of LATHAM and VIEILLOT.
"(?) *Sylvia melanorhoa*," VIEILL., Nouv. Dict. xi, 1817, 180; Enc. Met. ii, 1823, 444.

Hab.—Eastern United States and British provinces. West to Kansas and Utah (*Allen*). Breeds from Massachusetts northward, and apparently in the mountains of the Middle States. Winters in Mexico and Central America. Scarcely West Indian (*Bryant*).

As is now well known, Wilson described the young of this species as the "Hemlock Warbler," *S. parus*, in which he was followed by many writers. Audubon magnified the error by uniting with it the autumnal Warbler of Wilson, which is the young of the Bay-breasted. Bonaparte did still worse, in putting the "Hemlock Warbler" in a different genus.

This species, famed for its delicacy of coloring, is common along the
Atlantic States during the migrations, in high, open woods, associated
with *virens, castanea, striata,* and others.   Not before quoted from beyond the mouth of the Missouri, its known range has lately been
extended to Utah.   Audubon speaks of its occurrence in Nova Scotia,
Newfoundland, and Labrador, and on the Magdeleine Islands, describing a nest and eggs from the former locality.

DENDRŒCA STRIATA, (Forst.) Bd.

Black-poll Warbler.

Muscicapa striata, FORST., Phil. Trans. lxii, 1772, 383, 428.
Motacilla striata, GM., Syst. Nat. i, 1788, 976.
Sylvia striata, LATH., Ind. Orn. ii, 1790, 527.—VIEILL., Ois. Am. Sept. ii, 1807, 22, pls. 75,
    76.—WILS., Am. Orn. iv, 1811, 40, pl. 30, f. 3 ; vi, 1812, 101, pl. 54, f. 3.—NUTT.,
    Man. i, 1832, 383.—AUD., Orn. Biog. ii, 1834, 201, pl. 133.
Sylvicola striata, SW. & RICH., F. B. A. ii, 1831, 218.—AUD., B. Am. ii, 1841, 28, pl. 78.—
    WOODH., Sitgr. Rep. 1853, 70.—HOY, Smith. Rep. 1864, 438 (Missouri).
Mniotilta striata, GRAY.—REINH., Ibis, iii, 1861, 6 (Greenland).
Rhimanphus striatus, CAB., Mus. Hein. i, 1850, 20.
Dendrœca striata, BD., B. N. A. 1858, 280 ; Rev. 1864, 192.—COUES, Pr. Phila. Acad. 1861,
    220.—HAYD., Rep. 1862, 161.—DALL & BANN., Tr. Chic. Acad. i, 1869, 278
    (Alaska).—SCL. & SALV., P. Z. S. 1870, 780 (Merida).—COUES, Key, 1872, 100,
    fig. 42, and pl. 2, figs. 15, 16.—Also of all local lists of Eastern United States.
Dendrœca pinus! COUES, Pr. Phila. Acad. 1861, 220 (error).   (Labrador.)

Hab.—Eastern North America ; North to Arctic Ocean ; Northwest to Alaska ; West
to Nebraska.   Greenland (REINH., Veddensk. Meddel. 1854, 73 ; Ibis, iii, 1861, 6).   Cuba
(CAB., J. f. O. iii, 1855, 475 ; GUNDL., ibid. 1861, 326).   Bahamas (BRYANT, Pr. Bost. Soc.
vii, 1859).   Bogota (SCL., P. Z. S. 1855, 143).   (?) Chili (*Confer D. atricapilla,* LANDB.,
Weigm. Arch. 1864, 56 ; SCL., P. Z. S. 1867, 321).
    Lieutenant Warren's Expedition.—4644-50, Nebraska.
    Not obtained by Captain Raynolds' Expedition.
    Strongly marked as this species is in its complete dress, of either sex, as described in
the Key, p. 100, there is difficulty in identifying the young bird in the fall, when it
bears an extraordinary resemblance to the young of the Bay-breasted Warbler.   The
upper parts of the two are almost precisely alike, but there is, probably, always an appreciable difference below.   Young *striata* has a clear pale yellowish wash, if any, on
the white of the under parts, fading into pure white on the under tail-coverts at least,
and usually has at least a few dusky streaks on the sides ; while the tinge of the under parts of *castanea* is buffy or ochrey, especially observable on the belly, flanks and
under tail-coverts, just where *striata* is the whitest, and it has no dusky streaks on the
sides.
    In the extent of its migrations this species is surpassed by none of its allies, and
equalled by few, if any ; its dispersion will prove more extensive than that of any other
Warbler, should the *D. atricapilla* be found identical, as it probably will.   It is known
to breed beyond the United States, from Labrador to Fort Yukon, where its eggs were
procured by Mr. Kennicott.   The southernmost breeding localities I have found quoted
are the Umbagog Lakes, and Calais, Maine (*Verrill* and *Boardman*).   It is very abundant throughout the Eastern United States during the migrations, but appears to leave
the country altogether in the fall, wintering further south.   Audubon's quotation,
"Columbia River," requires confirmation, but will most probably be proved correct ;
in that event the case will apparently correspond to that of *D. coronata.*

Two nests of this species, from Great Slave Lake and Fort Yukon,
respectively, are entirely similar in material and structure.   Both were
taken in June, one with four, the other with five eggs.   They are built
of soft weedy material, bleached and gray, and withered almost to dis-
integration, mixed with grasses, and lined with finer stems of the same.
The eggs are finely sprinkled with brown and neutral tint, chiefly in a
wreath about the larger half of the egg, and have also a few larger
blackish spots and scrawls, very sharply marked.   The size is 0.70 by
0.52.   Two nests without eggs, taken by Dr. Brewer at Grand Menan,
are quite different in appearance and material, as well as heavier and

more compact. They are built chiefly of moss, mixed with small twigs, weedy and fibrous material, and rootlets; but are lined, like the others, entirely with fine grasses.

DENDRŒCA CASTANEA, (Wils.) Bd.

Bay-breasted Warbler.

Sylvia castanea, WILS., Am. Orn. ii, 1810, 97, pl. 14, f. 4.—BP., Syn. 1828, 80.—NUTT., Man. i, 1832, 382.—AUD., Orn. Biog. i, 1832, 358, pl. 69.
Sylvicola castanea, RICH., List, 1837.—BP., List, 1838, 22; Consp. i, 1850, 308.—AUD., Syn. 1839, 53.—AUD., B. Am. ii, 1841, 34, pl. 80.—HOY, Smiths. Rep. 1864, 438 (Missouri).
Mniotilta castanea, GRAY, Genera of Birds.
Rhimanphus castaneus, CAB., Mus. Hein. i, 1850, 19.
Dendrœca castanea, BD., B. N. A. 1858, 276; Rev. 1865, 189.—SCL. & SALV., Ibis, i, 1859, 11 (Guatemala); CASS., Pr. Phila. Acad. 1860, 193 (Darien).—LAWR., Ann. Lyc. N. Y. 1861, 322 (Panama).—MAYN., Guide, 1870, 103.—COUES, Key, 1872, 101; and of most late writers.
Sylvia autumnalis, WILS., Am. Orn. iii, 1811, 65, pl. 23, f. 3.—NUTT., Man. i, 1832, 390.—AUD., Orn. Biog. i, 1832, 449, pl. 88.

Hab.—Eastern North America ; North to Hudson's Bay ; West to the Lower Missouri. Breeds from Northern New England northward. Winters in Central America. Migrant only in most parts of the United States. No Mexican nor West Indian quotations.

The earlier authors left the history of this species very incomplete, having had, from some cause, little opportunity of becoming acquainted with it; nevertheless, it is a common bird of the Eastern United States. I observed it every season when collecting about Washington, D. C., and took a large number of specimens. It passes through the Middle States in May and returns in September, being found during the whole of these months, sometimes, particularly in the fall, in abundance. It may be looked for in any woods, where the other species of the genus stop to rest and feed during their journeys, and in orchards—the last a favorite resort of Warblers of various kinds in the spring when the apple, pear, peach, and cherry-trees are in blossom, the birds doubtless being attracted by the different minute insects that infest our fruit trees. The breeding places of the Bay-breasted Warbler, not to mention its nest and eggs, were for a long while unknown; latterly the desired information has been supplied. Mr. C. J. Maynard, a very good observer and collecter, has published a satisfactory account. He took two nests with eggs, June 8th, at Umbagog, where, he says, the species is the most abundant of the *Sylvicolidæ*. Both were placed on the horizontal branch of a hemlock-tree, fifteen or twenty feet from the ground, and seemed large for the size of the bird, resembling those of the Purple Finch. They were built of fine, dead larch twigs, mixed in one instance with long tree-moss, in the other with a few grass-stems, and smoothly lined with black fibrous rootlets, some moss and rabbit's hair. External diameter five and one-half to six inches, internal two and one-half to three; depth outside two and one-half to three, the cavity one and one-fourth to one and one-half; they differed in shape, the broader nest being the shallower one. One contained three eggs, the other two; the five ranged from 0.65 to 0.71 long, by 0.50 to 0.53 broad. The ground color was bluish-green, more or less thickly speckled with brown all over, the markings becoming confluent, or nearly so, at or around the larger end, where the brown was mixed with some lilac or umber markings.

DENDRŒCA PENNSYLVANICA, (Linn.) Bd.

Chestnut-sided Warbler.

Motacilla pennsylvanica, LINN., Syst. Nat. i, 1766, 333.
Sylvia pennsylvanica, LATH., Ind. Orn. ii, 1790, 540.
Dendrœca pennsylvanica, BD., B. N. A. 1858, 279; Rev. 1865. 191.—SCL. & SALV., Ibis,
    1859, 21; 1860, 273 (Guatemala).—SCL., P. Z. S. 1870, 836 (Honduras).—SALV.,
    P. Z. S. 1867, 136 (Veragua).—LAWR., Ann. Lyc. ix, 1868, 94 (Costa Rica); 1869,
    200 (Yucatan).—HAYD., Rep. 1862, 161 (to mouth of Platte River).—ALLEN,
    Bull. M. C. Z. iii, 1872 (Leavenworth, Kans.).—COUES, Key, 1872, 101, fig. 43;
    and of all late local writers of Eastern United States.
Sylvia icterocephala, LATH., Ind. Orn. ii, 1790, 538.—VIEILL., Ois. Am. Sept. ii, 1807, 31,
    pl. 90.—WILS., Am. Orn. i, 1808, 99, pl. 14, f. 5.—AUD., Orn. Biog. i, 1832, 306,
    pl. 59.—NUTT., Man. i, 1832, 380.
Sylvicola icterocephala, AUD., B. Am. ii, 1841, 35, pl. 81; and of other earlier writers.—
    HOY, Smiths. Rep. 1864, 435 (Missouri).
Dendrœca icterocephala, SCL., P. Z. S. 1859, 363, 373 (Xalapa; Oaxaca).

Hab.—Eastern United States; little if any beyond New England, where it breeds
abundantly. Apparently retires altogether from the United States in winter. Bahamas (*Bryant*). Honduras (*Sclater*). Panama (*Lawrence*).
Lieutenant Warren's Expedition.—4670, mouth of Platte River.
Not obtained by Captain Raynolds' Expedition.

According to my experience, the Chestnut-sided Warbler is a very
common species of the Eastern United States, passing through in great
numbers during the migrations, where it is found in orchards and open
woods in company with several other species. It is rather southerly in
distribution, apparently not passing much, if any, beyond the United
States, in the northern parts of which it breeds. It retires far south in
winter. The numerous nests in the Smithsonian collection agree in
being placed in an upright crotch, generally of several stems, and are
all more or less lengthened perpendicularly to fit such situations, with a
rather narrow but deep cavity. The twigs preserved with the nests are
all small, and in one case the nest was only a yard from the ground.
The exterior is a rather loosely woven mass of weedy, downy, and fibrous
substances; the interior is more closely woven of fine grasses, with a
tolerably firm and even brim. Sometimes there is horse-hair lining,
sometimes not. None of the nests contain more than four eggs; several only three; one is occupied alone by a Cow-bird's. The shell is
white; the markings are chiefly confined to the larger end, only rarely
a few dots being sprinkled over the whole surface, and they form, or
tend to form, in many cases, a wreath about the large end. The wreath
is sometimes close and heavy, consisting of confluent blotches, in other
instances is a circle of separate fine dots. The markings are of all
shades, from light reddish to various darker browns, mixed with neutral
tints. The size is about 0.68 by 0.50.

DENDRŒCA MACULOSA, (Gm.) Bd.

Black-and-yellow Warbler.

Motacilla maculosa, GM., Syst. Nat. i, 1788, 984.
Sylvia maculosa, LATH., Ind. Orn. ii, 1790, 536.—VIEILL., Ois. Am. Sept. ii, 1807, pl. 93.--
    AUD., Orn. Biog. i, 1831, 260; ii, 1834, 145; v, 1839, 458; pl. 50, 123.—NUTT.,
    Man. i, 1832, 370.
Sylvicola maculosa, SW. & RICH., F. B. A. ii, 1831, 213, pl. 40.—AUD., B. Am. ii, 1841, 65,
    pl. 93.—HOY, Smiths. Rep. 1864, 435 (Missouri).
Rhimanphus maculosus, CAB., Mus. Hein. 1851, 20.
Dendrœca maculosa, BD., B. N. A. 1858, 284; Rev. 1865, 206.—SCL., P. Z. S. 1859, 363,
    373 (Xalapa).—SCL. & SALV., Ibis, 1859, 11 (Guatemala).—BRYANT, Pr. Bost.
    Soc. vii, 1859, p. — (Bahamas).—GUNDL., J. f. O. 1861, 326 (Cuba).—LAWR.,
    Ann. Lyc. N. H. N. Y. 1861, 322 (Panama).—SCL., P. Z. S. 1862, 19 (Mexico).—

MAYN.—Pr. Bost. Soc. xiv, 1871 (Umbagog, breeding).—COUES, Key, 1872, 102, fig. 44; and of all late local writers of Eastern United States.
Sylvia magnolia, WILS., Am. Orn. iii, 1811, 63, pl. 23, f. 3.

Hab.—Eastern North America; in summer, New England to Hudson's Bay; migratory through the States; in winter, beyond the United States, as above quoted.
Lieutenant Warren's Expedition.—4643, mouth of Vermilion River.
Not obtained by Captain Raynolds' Expedition.

Mr. C. J. Maynard has given us an excellent account of the nest and eggs of this species. A nest, taken the second week in June, 1870, at Umbagog, "was placed on the forked branch of a low spruce, about three feet from the ground, on a rising piece of land, leading from a wood-path. The nest, which contained four eggs, was constructed of dry grass, spruce twigs, roots, etc., and was lined with fine black roots, the whole being a coarse structure for so dainty looking a Warbler. The eggs were more spherical than any Warbler's I have ever seen. The ground color is a creamy-white, blotched sparingly over with large spots of lilac and umber." The dimensions of these eggs were: 0.62 by 0.52, 0.61 by 0.52, 0.62 by 0.50, 0.63 by 0.52 (hundredths of the inch). Another nest, taken June 8, 1871, was on a low hemlock, about four feet from the ground. "It is composed outwardly of a few scattered dead twigs of larch, interwoven with stalks of weeds and dry grass. It is lined with black horse-hair; this dark lining formed a strange contrast with the faded appearance of the outer part. The whole structure is very light and airy in appearance, strongly reminding one of the nest of *D. pennsylvanica*. Dimensions of the nest are: External diameter three inches, internal diameter two, external depth one and three-fourths, internal depth one and one-fourth." The four eggs in the nest measured 0.65 by 0.50, 0.62 by 0.47, 0.64 by 0.46, 0.65 by 0.48. They were ashy-white, blotched and clouded with brown and lilac, chiefly around and about the larger end, and sparsely dotted with brown elsewhere; they differed in the size and amount of the brown spottings. Two other nests are also described, which, with their eggs, were similar to the others in every essential respect.

DENDRŒCA DISCOLOR, (Vieill.) Bd.

Prairie Warbler.

Sylvia discolor, VIEILL., Ois. Am. Sept. ii, 1807, 37, pl. 98.—BP., Syn. 1828, 83.—NUTT., Man. i, 1832, "294" (by error for 394).—AUD., Orn. Biog. i, 1831, 76, pl. 14.—LEMB., Aves Cubæ, 1850, 32, pl. 6, f. 2.
Sylvicola discolor, JARD., ed. Wils., 1832.—RICH., List, 1837.—BP., List, 1838.—AUD., Syn. 1839.—AUD., B. Am. ii, 1841, 68, pl. 97.—GOSSE, B. Jam. 1847, 159.
Mniotilta discolor, GRAY, Genera of Birds.
Rhimanphus discolor, CAB., J. f. O. iii, 1855, 474 (Cuba, winter).
Dendrœca discolor, BD., B. N. A. 1858, 290; Rev. 1865, 213.—BRYANT, Pr. Bost. Soc. vii, 1859 (Bahamas).—NEWTON, Ibis, i, 1859, 144 (St. Croix).—GUNDL., J. f. O. 1861, 326 (Cuba).—ALLEN, Pr. Ess. Inst. iv, 1864, 64 (Massachusetts, usually rare).—COUES, *ibid.* v, 1868, 274 (north to Massachusetts, common).—COUES, Pr. Bost. Soc. xii, 1868, 110 (South Carolina).—COUES, Pr. Phila. Acad. 1871, 20 (coast of North Carolina, very numerous).—COUES, Key, 1872, 103.—ALLEN, Bull. M. C. Z. ii, 1871, 268 (undoubtedly resident in Florida in the whole year); iii, 1872, 125 (Kansas, May, rather frequent).
Sylvia minuta, WILS., Am. Orn. iii, 1811, 87, pl. 25, f. 4.

Hab.—Eastern United States, as far north as Massachusetts; west to Kansas. Breeds throughout its range. Winters in Florida, and abundantly in most of the West Indian islands. No Mexican nor Central American record.

The pretty little Prairie Warbler was one of my earliest bird-acquaintances, and one I have always been fond of, on this and other accounts. When we were shooting birds pretty much all the time we could find, or "make," in spite of the college dons, in our early home at Washington, Dr. Prentiss and I knew just where to look for it, and it did not take long to get a few of the delicate birds, in their season. We were generally back in time for recitation, and even if that performance went lame in consequence, it did not seem much matter, comparatively. The inflection of the Prairie Warbler's notes was a much more agreeable theme than that of a Greek verb, and I am still uncertain whether it was not quite as profitable. There was a little glade just by the college, bordering Rock Creek, closed in by high woods—a sloping, sandy field, run waste with scattered cedars—where we could be sure of finding the Warblers any day, from the 20th of April, for two or three weeks. Ten to one we would not *see* the little creatures at first; but presently, from the very nearest juniper, would come the well-known sounds. A curious song, if song it can be called—as much like a mouse complaining of the tooth ache as anything else I can liken it to—it is simply indescribable. Then perhaps the quaint performer would dart out into the air, turn a somersault after a passing midge, get right side up, and into the shrubbery again in an instant; or if we kept still, with wide-open eyes, we would see him perched on a spray, settling firmly on his legs, with his beak straight up in the air, the throat swelling, and hear the curious music again. After that would come the inevitable tragedy—for tragedy it *is*, and I cannot, after picking up warm bloody little birds for years, make anything else out of it, or learn to look on it with indifference.

I did not see this bird in Kansas, where my friend Allen found it, nor, of course, further westward; but a few years afterward, when the eccentric course of military migration stranded me on a sandbar on the North Carolina coast, there were the Prairie Warblers as plenty, as unmusical and interesting, as ever. Excepting the ubiquitous Yellowrumps, they were the only Warblers that showed bad taste enough to come voluntarily about Fort Macon in any considerable numbers. But they appear to fancy rather barren, sandy places, very likely because they have grown fond of certain kinds of bugs, and if so, they must have been contented there. Arriving the latter part of April, they became very numerous in May, all through the juniper patches, clumps of live-oak, and scrubby "yupon" tracts, singing at their best and catching insects in the air. I consider them very expert fly-catchers, quite equal in this respect to most of their tribe; and my experience has been to show that they are not so terrestrial as Audubon intimates. He says that "while on the ground, where it remains a good deal, it searches among the leaves slowly and carefully;" but I never saw anything of the kind. But as he says, the bird's ordinary flight is weak and vacillating, not often protracted further than from one bush to another; it appears to find coming down easier than going up was. I also agree with him that it goes singly—never in troops; but I have certainly seen many more at once than the three or four he allows to a thirty acre lot.

As above intimated, the Prairie Warbler breeds along the Atlantic coast, but only a few about Washington, where I never discovered the nest; nor was I more fortunate in either of the Carolinas. Wilson, Nuttall, and Audubon, who described the nidification and the eggs as they believed them to be, give such entirely different accounts, that, in the uncertainty, the following notice, which I owe to my kind friend, Dr. Brewer, may be the more acceptable. Dr. Brewer corroborates Nuttall's account, in the interesting article intended for his forthcoming work:

"Both Wilson and Audubon were evidently at fault in their descriptions of the nest and eggs. These do not correspond with more recent and positive observations. Its nest is never pensile. Mr. Nuttall's descriptions, on the other hand, are made from his own observations, and are evidently correct. He describes a nest that came under his observation, as scarcely distinguishable from that of the *D. œstiva*. It was not pensile, but fixed in a forked branch, and formed of strips of the inner bark of the red-cedar, fibres of asclepias, and caterpillar's silk, and thickly lined with the down of the *Gnaphalium plantagineum*. He describes the eggs as having a white ground, sharp at one end, and marked with spots of lilac-purple and of two shades of brown, more numerous at the larger end, where they formed a ring. He speaks of their note as slender, and noticed their arrival about the second week of May, leaving the middle of September.

"At another time Mr. Nuttall was attracted by the slender, filing notes of this bird, resembling the suppressed syllables *'tsh-'tsh-'tsh-'tshea*, beginning low and gradually growing louder. With its mate it was busily engaged collecting flies and larvæ among a clump of locust-trees in Mount Auburn. Their nest was near, and the female, without any precautions, went directly to it. Mr. Nuttall removed two eggs, which he afterward replaced. Each time, on his withdrawal, she returned to the nest, and resorted to no expedients to entice him away.

"Several nests of this Warbler have been obtained by Mr. Welch in Lynn. One was built on a wild rose, only a few feet from the ground. It is a snug, compact, and elaborately woven structure, having a height and a diameter of about two and one-half inches. The cavity is two inches wide and one and one-half deep. The materials of which the outer parts are woven are chiefly the soft inner bark of small shrubs, mingled with dry rose-leaves, bits of vegetable wood, woody fibres, decayed stems of plants, spiders' webs, etc. The whole is bound together like a web by cotton-like fibres of a vegetable origin. The upper rim of this nest is a marked feature, being a strongly interlaced weaving of vegetable roots and strips of bark. The lining of the nest is composed of fine vegetable fibres and a few horse-hairs. This nest, in its general mode of construction, resembles all that I have seen; only in others the materials vary—in some dead and decayed leaves, in others remains of old cocoons, and in others the pappus of composite plants being more prominent than the fine strips of bark. The nests are usually within four feet of the ground. The eggs vary from three to five, and even six.

"The late Dr. Gerhardt found this bird the most common Warbler in Northern Georgia. There its nests were similar in size, structure, and position, but differed more or less in the materials of which they were made. The nests were a trifle larger and the walls thinner, the cavities being correspondingly larger. The materials were more invariably fine strips of inner bark and flax-like vegetable fibres, and were lined with the finest stems of plants, in one case with the feathers of the Great Horned Owl. In that neighborhood the eggs were deposited by the 15th of May.

" In Massachusetts the Prairie Warbler invariably selects wild pasture-land, often not far from villages, and always open or very thinly wooded. In Georgia their nests were built in almost every kind of bush or low tree, or on the lower limbs of post-oaks, at the height of from four to seven feet. Eggs were found once as early as the 2d of May, and once as late as the 10th of June. They arrived there by the 10th of April, and seemed to prefer hillsides, but were found in almost any open locality.

" In Southern Illinois, Mr. Ridgway cites this species as a rather rare bird among the oak barrens where it breeds. He also met with it in orchards in the wooded portions, in April, during the northward migration of the *Sylvicolidæ.*

"The eggs are of an oval shape, pointed at one end, and measure 0.68 by 0.48 of an inch. They have a white ground, marked with spots of lilac and purple, and two shades of umber-brown."

DENDRŒCA DOMINICA, (Linn.) Bd.

Yellow-throated Warbler.

Motacilla dominica, LINN., Syst. Nat. i, 1766, 334.
Dendrœca dominica, BD., Rev. 1865, 209 (Colima, &c.).—LAWR., Ann. Lyc. ix, 1869, 200 (Yucatan).—SUMICH., Mem. Bost. Soc. i, 1869, 547 (Orizaba, Aug.).—ALLEN, Bull. M. C. Z. ii, 1871, 268 (Florida, in winter).—COUES, Key, 1872, 103.—SCOTT, Pr. Bost. Soc. 1872 (West Virginia).—MAYN., B. Fla. 1872, 60.
Motacilla superciliosa, BODD., Pl. Enl. 686, f. 1.
Mniotilta superciliosa, GRAY, Genera of Birds.
Dendrœca superciliosa, BD., B. N. A. 1858, 289.—SCL., P. Z. S. 1859, 363 (Xalapa); 1859, 373 (Oaxaca); 1861, p. — (Jamaica); 1863, 368 (Mexico); Cat. 1862, 33.—SCL. & SALV., Ibis, iii, 1860, 274 (Guatemala).—WHEAT., Ohio Agric. Rep. 1860, No. 94 (quite common).—COUES & PRENT., Smiths. Rep. 1861, 408 (Washington, D. C., accidental; spec. in 1842).—GUNDL., J. f. O. 1861, 326 (Cuba, common).—MARCH, Pr. Phila. Acad. 1863, 293 (Jamaica, June).—COUES, Pr. Bost. Soc. xii, 1868, 109 (South Carolina, common).—TURNB. B. E. Pa. 1869, 42 (straggler).—SNOW, B. Kans. 1873, 5 (Neosho Falls, in June).
Motacilla flavicollis, GM., Syst. Nat. i, 1788, 959.
Sylvia flavicollis, LATH., Ind. Orn. ii, 1790, 518.—WILS., Am. Orn. ii, 1810, 64, pl. 12, f. 6.
Motacilla pensilis, GM., Syst. Nat. i, 1788, 960.
Sylvia pensilis, LATH., Ind. Orn. ii, 1790, 520.—VIEILL., Ois. Am. Sept. ii, 1807, 11, pl. 72.—BP , Syn. 1828, 79.—NUTT., i, 1832, 374.—AUD., Orn. Biog., i, 1831, 434, pl. 85.
Sylvicola pensilis, RICH., Rep. Br. Assoc., 1837.—BP., List, 1838; Consp. i, 1850, 307.—AUD., Syn. 1839, 53.—AUD., B. Am. ii, 1841, 32, pl. 79.—GOSSE, B. Jam. 1847, 156.
Rhimanphus pensilis, CAB., J. f. O. iii, 1855, 474 (Cuba).—SCL., P. Z. S. 1856, 291 (Cordova).

Hab.—Eastern United States, north to Maryland; to New Jersey (*Audubon*); to Pennsylvania (*Turnbull*); to New York (*Dekay*); to Connecticut (*Linsley*). Ohio, Illinois, and Kansas. Cuba. Jamaica. St. Domingo (*Sallé,* P. Z. S. 1857, 231). Mexico, on west coast to Colima. Guatemala. Winters from Florida southward. (A var. *albilora* is described from the Mississippi Valley by Mr. Ridgway, Am. Nat. vii, 1873, 606.)

This is essentially a Southern species, which I have not been able to trace further north than Washington, D. C. Audubon, however, gives it to New Jersey; and Turnbull, in his admirable List, notes it as a straggler to the lower counties of New Jersey and Pennsylvania. The Rev. Mr. Linsley included it among the birds of Connecticut, but apparently upon information at second hand; and its occurrence in New England is very questionable. (See COUES, Pr. Ess. Inst. v, 1868, 270.) Mr. Lawrence omits it from his New York list. In Ohio, Mr. J. M. Wheaton states that it was common one season: "It seems," he adds, "quite partial to the vicinity of running water, and is usually seen on trees and fences near rivers. In its habits it approaches the Titmice and Creepers, frequently hanging and walking, head downward, on fence rails." I have noted similar habits of the species in South Carolina. Prof. Snow's reference is particularly interesting, indicating that the bird breeds in Kansas. It would also appear, from various accounts, to breed in the West Indies. It has not, to my knowledge, been observed to winter anywhere in the United States, excepting in Florida.

Since the foregoing paragraph was prepared, Mr. W. D. Scott has printed an interesting note respecting the occurrence and probable breeding of the species in Kanawha County, West Virginia. Two individuals, male and female, were taken in July.

One of the most remarkable nests I ever saw, was built by a Yellow-throated Warbler at Wilmington, North Carolina, where it was secured and forwarded to the Smithsonian by Mr. Norwood Giles. It is built in a large mass of Spanish moss (*Tillandsia usneoides*), and composed chiefly of that material. A part of the mass which hung from an oak bough, two feet downward and a foot across, was caught up and closely woven together with a little fibrous substance and much plant-down, to form a swinging bed for the nest, with a lateral entrance which will admit the hand. Inside is the nest proper, of the usual dimensions, very neatly wrought of the moss, with a smooth, even border, and lined with plant-down and a few fine grasses. The eggs of this nest were of the usual form, measuring 0.70 by 0.52, white, with a wreath of sepia-brown, blackish and lilac spots around the larger end.

My acquaintance with the species is limited to observing it on a few occasions in and around the city of Columbia, South Carolina. According to Mr. Maynard, the Yellow-throats "are found throughout the entire extent of Florida, where they are resident, though the majority leave in May with other Warblers, and return early in November; they frequent piney woods and hummocks, associating with Titmice, Nuthatches, etc. I have shot this species on the banks of the St. John's, where it was searching for insects in the low trees in the numerous swamps there; and again I have seen them on the topmost boughs of the high trees in the trackless piney woods. They are very slow of movement for Warblers, and have many of the habits of the Black-and-white Creeper, clinging to the limbs and running up and down the tree-trunks, after the manner of that species. I have even seen one climbing about the roof of a house. They are very unsuspicious, and may be found almost any day in autumn and early winter on the live and water oaks which grow in the streets of Jacksonville. The songs of this bird are simple, and resemble the trills of the Pine Warbler—or, perhaps, the continuous lisping chirp of the Black-and-white Creeper sounds more nearly like it. I think the species must breed in Florida, as I have seen specimens taken in the State in June."

I am favored with the following communication from Mr. J. M. Wheaton, of Columbus, Ohio, under date of May 1, 1873, respecting the appearance of this species in Ohio: "It is one of the earliest and most constant of our Warblers. I saw the first one this year on the 21st of April. That night we had frost, with snow for three successive days afterward. On the 25th I saw three, on the 26th one (in the city), on the 27th three, and on the 28th five or six, two of which I shot. No other Warbler made its appearance until the 30th, when the Summer Yellowbird arrived. The Yellow-throat prefers the trees along the banks of streams. The two specimens which I secured agree with your description ('Key,' p. 103), except that the back is not streaked, and each feather is obsoletely margined with ashy." These specimens were evidently not quite in perfect plumage.

DENDRŒCA PALMARUM, (Gm.) Bd.

Yellow Red-poll Warbler.

Motacilla palmarum, GM., Syst. Nat. i, 1788, 951.
Sylvia palmarum, LATH., Ind. Orn. ii, 1790, 544.—VIEILL., Ois. Am. Sept. ii, 1807, 21, pl. 73.—BP., Am. Orn. ii, pl. 10, f. 2.—BP., Syn. 1828, 83.—D'ORBIG., La Sagra's Cuba, Ois. 1840, 61, pl. 8.
Sylvicola palmarum, SALLÉ, P. Z. S. 1857, 231 (St. Domingo).
Dendrœca palmarum, BD., B. N. A. 1858, 288; Rev. 1865, 207.—BRYANT, Pr. Bost. Soc. viii, 1859 (Bahamas).—GUNDL., J. f. O. 1861, 326 (Cuba).—SCL., P. Z. S. 1861, 71 (Jamaica).—COUES & PRENT., Smiths. Rep. 1861, 408 (Washington, D. C., migratory).—COUES, Pr. Ess. Inst. v, 1868, 274 (migratory in New England,

68   DENDRŒCA PALMARUM, YELLOW RED-POLL WARBLER.

some perhaps breeding).—COUES, Pr. Bost. Soc. xii, 1868, 109 (South Carolina,
wintering).—ALLEN, Bull. M. C. Z. ii, 1871, 268 (Florida, wintering).—MAYN.,
B. Fla. 1872, 52; Guide, 1870, 104.—COUES, Key, 1872, 104.

Sylvia petechia, WILS., Am. Orn. vi, 1812, 19, pl. 28, f. 4 (not of early authors, which refers to species like *æstiva*).—NUTT., i, 1832, 364.—AUD., Orn. Biog. ii, 1834, 259,
360, pls. 163, 164.

Sylvicola petechia, SW. & RICH., F. B. A. ii, 1831, 215, pl. 41.—AUD., Syn. 1839, 58.—AUD.,
B. Am. ii, 1841, 55, pl. 90.—HOY, Smiths. Rep. 1864, 437 (Missouri).—TRIPPE,
Pr. Ess. Inst. vi, 1872, 114 (Wisconsin).

"Seiurus petechia, McCUL., Bost. Journ. N. H. iv, 406."

Sylvicola ruficapilla, BP., List, 1838; Consp. i, 1850, 307.   (Not *Motacilla r.*, GM.)

Rhimanphus ruficapillus, CAB., J. f. O. iii, 1855, 473 (Cuba).

Hab.—Eastern North America to the Lower Missouri.   North to Labrador, Hudson's
Bay, and Fort Simpson.   No record of breeding in the United States south of Maine.
Winters in the Southern States, from the Carolinas to Texas; Bahamas, Cuba, Jamaica,
and St. Domingo.   No Mexican or Central American quotations.

The Palm Warbler is an extremely abundant bird in the Southern
States in winter, and equally common in the rest of the United States
during the migrations, but has not been observed to breed south of the
British possessions, excepting in Maine, where, according to Mr. Boardman, it occasionally nests near Calais.   It passes rapidly through the
Middle and Western States very early in the spring, sometimes reaching
the Connecticut Valley before the snow is gone, and returns more leisurely in autumn, lingering late by the way.   It is found in New England
through October, and has even been seen in Massachusetts in November.   Its habits are somewhat peculiar, some of them, such as the continual jetting of the tail and fondness for the ground, recalling the
Seiuri rather than a bird of its own genus.   Unlike most Warblers, it
is rarely, if ever, found in high thick woods, being partial to coppices,
hedge-rows, straggling shrubbery, and especially old waste fields, where
it delights to ramble and flutter in company with Yellow-rumps and various kinds of Sparrows.   It keeps much on the ground, running among
the weeds and stubble, and even on the open dust of the wayside, with
a peculiar tremulousness, something like that of the Titlark.   Its song,
if it have one, I have never heard; its only note, with us, is a slight
"tsip," indistinguishable from that of several of its allies.   This is corroborated by Dr. Brewer, as I learn from an early proof-sheet of his
work.   He says: "They have no other song than a few simple and feeble notes, so thin and weak that they might almost be mistaken for the
sounds made by the common grasshopper."   I am entirely ignorant of
the nidification, which is described by Dr. Brewer as follows:

"The Red-Poll usually selects for the site of its nest the edge of a
swampy thicket, more or less open, placing it invariably upon the ground.
They are usually not large, about three and a half inches in diameter and
two and a half in depth, the diameter and depth of the cavity averaging
each only half an inch less.   The walls are compactly and elaborately
constructed of an interweaving of various fine materials, chiefly fine dry
grasses, slender strips of bark, stems of the smaller plants, hypnum and
other mosses.   Within, the nest is warmly and softly lined with down
and feathers.

"Mr. Kennicott met with a nest of this bird at Fort Resolution, June
18.   It was on the ground, on a hummock, at the foot of a small spruce,
in a swamp.   When found it contained five young birds.

"Their eggs are of a rounded-oval shape, and measure 0.70 of an inch
in length by 0.55 in breadth.   Their ground-color is a yellowish or creamy-
white, and their blotches, chiefly about the larger end, are of a blending
of purple, lilac, and reddish-brown."

DENDRŒCA PINUS, (Wils.) Bd.

Pine-creeping Warbler.

Sylvia pinus, WILS., Am. Orn. iii, 1811, 25, pl. 19, fig. 4.—BP., Syn. 1828, 81.—NUTT.,
  Man. i, 1832, 387.—AUD., Orn. Biog. ii, 1834, 232, pl. 111.
Thryotharus pinus, STEPH., Shaw's G. Z. xiv, 194.
Sylvicola pinus, JARD.; RICH. & BP., Lists.—AUD., Syn. 1839, 54.—AUD., B. Am. ii, 1841,
  37, pl. 82.—WOODH., Sitgr. Rep. 1853, 70 (Texas).—TRIPPE, Pr. Ess. Inst. vi,
  1871, 114 (queries it from Minnesota).
Rhimamphus pinus, BP., Consp. i, 1850, 311.
Dendrœca pinus, BD., B. N. A. 1858, 277; Rev. 1865, 190 (not of COUES, Phila. Acad. 1861,
  220, which = *striata!*).—COUES & PRENT., Smiths. Rep. 1861, 407 (Washington,
  D. C., breeding, but not wintering).—MCILWR., Pr. Ess. Inst. vi, 1866, 86 (Ham-
  ilton, C. W.).—COUES, Pr. Ess. Inst. v, 1868, 272 (New England, breeding, not
  wintering).—COUES, Pr. Bost. Soc. xii, 1868, 109 (South Carolina, resident).—
  TURNB., B. E. Pa. 1869, 18 (migratory).—ALLEN, Bull. M. C. Z. ii, 1871, 263
  (Florida, resident).—MAYN., Guide, 1870, 103 (Massachusetts, migratory, a few
  breeding); B. Fla. 1872, 49.—COUES, Key, 1872, 104.
Sylvia vigorsii, AUD., Orn. Biog. i, 1832, 153, 30.
Vireo vigorsii, NUTT., Man. i, 1832, 318.

Hab.—Eastern United States to the Lower Missouri. North to Canada and New
Brunswick, but *not* to Labrador. Bermuda (*Jones,* Nat. in Berm. 1859, 59; only extralimital record). Breeds throughout its United States range; resident from the Carolinas southward.

Like the Palm Warbler, with which it is often found associated, the
Pine-creeping is a migrant betimes in the spring, and a loiterer in the
fall. The range, as well as the movement of the two species, is somewhat coincident, but that of the present bird is more restricted, not extending into the West Indies, nor reaching so far north. The quotation
"Labrador" originated in an error of mine some years since. On a re-
examination lately of the specimen I thought was *pinus,* I find that it is
a newly-fledged Black-poll Warbler, in the spotted plumage common to
very young birds of many species of Warblers and Thrushes, corresponding to the equally early and transient streaked stage of many
Sparrows. The earliness of the vernal movement is attested by the
bird's presence in New England by the end of March, sometimes when
the ground is still covered with snow. Audubon affirms that it winters
in the Middle States, but I think the alleged fact has not been since confirmed. Dr. Turnbull does not so state; and for my own part I could
never detect the species in Maryland or Virginia between October and
March. I found it, however, at all seasons in South Carolina, where it
is extremely abundant, and one of the very few species breeding there.
It nests there remarkably early for a Warbler, the first broods being
abroad by the second week in April. The northward migration of that
portion of the great body of birds that winter in the Southern States
begins in March, about the time that those not intending to move off set
about mating and nesting. The return movement is delayed in its completion until November by the stragglers.

The nest is built of a variety of soft vegetable substances, plant-down,
&c., usually mixed with fine rootlets, and often with hair or feathers,
and set on a foundation of coarse fibrous and weedy material. It measures about three inches across by two deep, and generally presents a
pretty firm brim of circularly disposed fibres. It is placed on trees.
The eggs are commonly four in number, about 0.70 by 0.50, of the usual
shape, white, speckled and spotted with different shades of brown,
usually tending to wreathe around the larger end, sometimes generally
distributed.

As its name implies, the Pine-creeping Warbler is partial to coniferous
woods, but by no means confined to such forests; in fact I have observed

it in almost every situation in which any Warbler could be expected. Mr. Allen has accurately indicated the variability of its resorts: "During the last weeks of April and the early part of May, they frequent open fields, obtaining much of their food from the ground, associating with *D. palmarum*, and at this time closely resembling it in habits. A little later they retire to the pine forests, where they almost exclusively remain during summer, keeping mostly in the tops of the taller trees. During a few weeks, about October 1st, they again come about the orchards and fields." This note refers to Massachusetts. In Florida, where the same writer found it abundant in winter, he states that it is much on the ground at that season, and that it comes into full song in February, from which latter circumstance we may conclude it is then pairing. The song is rather weak and monotonous—a chirring trill, insusceptible of adequate translation into words; and during most of the year only a slight chirp is heard. The bird is of a sociable if not gregarious nature, usually going in straggling companies of its own kind, and often mixing with Titmice, Kinglets, and Nuthatches, the whole throng gaily and amicably flitting through the shady woods, scrambling incessantly on and all around the branches of the trees in eager, restless quest of their minute insect food.

SEIURUS AUROCAPILLUS, (Linn.) Sw.

Golden-crowned Thrush; Orange-crowned Accentor.

Motacilla aurocapilla, LINN., Syst. Nat. i, 1766, 334.—GM., *op. cit.* 1788, 982.
Turdus aurocapillus, LATH., Ind. Orn. ii, 1790, 328.—WILS., Am. Orn. iii, 1810, 88, pl. 14, f. 2.—NUTT., Man. i, 1832, 355.—AUD., Orn. Biog. ii, 1834, 253, pl. 143.
Sylvia aurocapilla, BP., Journ. Phila. Acad. iv, 1826, 35; Syn. 1828, 77.
Seiurus aurocapillus, SW., Zool. Journ. iii, 1827, 171.—SW. & RICH., F. B. A. ii, 1831, 227.—D'ORBIG., La Sagra's Cuba, 1840, 55.—AUD., B. Am. iii, 35, pl. 148.—BD., B. N. A. 1858, 260; Rev. 1865, 214.—MOORE, P. Z. S. 1859, 55 (Honduras).—MAXIM., J. f. O. 1858, 177.—JONES, Berm. 27.—HAYD., Rep. 1862, 160.—HOY, Smiths. Rep. 1864, 437 (Missouri).—SUMICH., Mem. Bost. Soc. i, 1869, 547 (Orizaba, &c.).—LAWR., Ann. Lyc. ix, 1868, 94 (Costa Rica); 1869, 200 (Yucatan).—DALL & BANN., Tr. Chic. Acad. i, 1869, 268 (Alaska, breeding).—SCL., P. Z. S. 1856, 293 (Cordova).—SALLÉ, *ibid.* 1857, 231 (St. Domingo).—NEWTON, Ibis, i, 1842 (Santa Cruz).—CAB., J. f. O. iii, 471 (Cuba).—GOSSE, B. Jam. 752.—SCL., P. Z. S. 1861, 70.—CAB., J. f. O. 1861, 80 (Costa Rica).—SALV., P. Z. S. 1870, 184 (Chiriqui).—ALLEN, Bull. M. C. Z. ii, 1871, 269 (Florida, wintering).—ALLEN, *op. cit.* iii, 1872, 125 (Eastern Kansas, May).—COUES, Key, 1872, 105, fig. 45; and of all late United States writers.
Accentor aurocapillus, RICH., List, 1837.
Enicocichla aurocapilla, GRAY.
Henicocichla aurocapilla, CAB.—GUNDL., J. f O. 1861, 326 (Cuba).—SCL., Cat. 1862, 25; P. Z. S. 1870, 836 (Honduras).
Turdus coronatus, VIEILL., Ois. Am. Sept. ii, 1807, 8, pl. 64.

Hab.—Eastern Province North America; west to Platte and Yellowstone, and thence to Alaska. Winters sparingly in Florida and along Gulf coast, but the greater number enter the West Indies, Mexico, and Central America (*numerous quotations*). Mazatlan. Breeds almost throughout its North American range.
Lieutenant Warren's Expedition.—4714, 4717, mouth of Platte River; 4715, Bald Island; 4716, James River; 4718-29, Vermilion River; 5257, Medicine River.
Not obtained by Captain Raynolds' Expedition.

Chiefly characteristic of the Eastern Province. Audubon's Columbia River reference has never been confirmed, but is by no means improbably correct, since we have the bird from Denver, Colorado, from near the Yellowstone, and in Alaska. The extralimital quotations are both numerous and diversified, showing how generally dispersed the species is at that season, and how far south it proceeds. It is one of our most abundant woodland birds in summer, noted for its loud, monotonous notes, for its habit of rambling and scratching on the ground, among fallen leaves, like a Towhee, and for its curious arched-over nest. Upon its arrival in the Middle States, about the second week in April, it is shy and silent for a week or two, as if getting accustomed to its new resorts; when, grown bolder, it no longer courts concealment, but mounts the lower boughs of the trees in the open woodland, and its loud harsh notes fill the air. There is nothing of the half-aquatic nature of its relatives in this bird; it prefers dry woods, especially where there is a thick undergrowth. Its nest is placed on the ground, usually among dead leaves, on an inclined surface, and though usually arched over, with a lateral opening, is often of simpler construction. It is built of leaves, moss, and dried grasses; the eggs are four or five in number, white, speckled with reddish-brown. Probably more than one brood is reared each season; the young, almost from the first, are quite like the parents, excepting that the orange-brown is not so bright. The species is very constant in size and coloring.

SEIURUS NOVEBORACENSIS, (Gm.) Nutt.

Water Thrush.

Motacilla noveboracensis, GM., Syst. Nat. i, 1788, 958.
Sylvia noveboracensis, LATH., 1nd. Orn. ii, 1790, 518.—VIEILL., Ois. Am. Sept. ii, 1807, 26, pl. 82.—BP., Syn. 1828, 77.
Turdus (Seiurus) noveboracensis, NUTT., Man i, 1832, 353.
Seiurus noveboracensis, BP., Comp. and Geog. List, 1838.—BP., Consp. Av. i, 1850, 306.— AUD., Syn. 1839, 93.—AUD., B. Am. iii, 37 (in part; confounds it with *S. ludovicianus*).—BD., B. N. A. 1858, 261; Rev. 1865, 215.—DALL & BANN., Tr. Chic. Acad. i, 1869.—HAYD., Rep. 1862, 160.—COOP., Am. Nat. iii, 1862, 32 (Hell Gate).—SUMICH., Mem. Bost. Soc. i, 1869, 547 (Orizaba).—LAWR., Ann. Lyc. 1868, 94 (Costa Rica); 1869, 200 (Yucatan).—COUES, Key, 1872, 106, pl. 2, figs. 9, 10, 11; and of late United States writers.
Henicocichla noveboracensis, CAB., Schomb. Guiana, iii, 1848, 666; Mus. Hein. 1851, 16; J. f. O. 1860, 324.—SCL., Cat. 1861, 25.—GUNDL., J. f. O. 1861, 326.—SCL. & SALV., P. Z. S. 1869, 251 (Venezuela).—SCL., P. Z. S. 1870, 836 (Honduras).
Enicocichla noveboracensis, GRAY, Genera of Birds.
Turdus aquaticus, WILS., Am. Orn. iii, 1811, 66, pl. 23, f. 5.—AUD., Orn. Biog. v, 1839, 284, pl. 433.
Seiurus aquaticus, SW. & RICH., F. B. A. ii, 1831, 229, pl. 43.
Sylvia anthoides, VIEILL., Nouv. Dict. d'H. N. 1817, 208.
Seiurus tenuirostris, SW., Phil. Mag. i, 1827, 369.—GAMB., Pr. Phila. Acad. i, 1843, 261.
Seiurus sulfurascens, D'ORBIG., La Sagra's Cuba, Ois. 1840, 57, pl. 6.
Seiurus gossii, BP., Consp. Av. i, 1850, 306.
"(?) *Anthus l'herminieri*, LESS., Rev. Zool. 1839, 101."

Hab.—Eastern North America, straggling westward along the United States Boundary to Montana (*Cooper*) and Washington Territory. Alaska. Arizona. Mexico. West Indies. Central America. Northern South America.
Lieutenant Warren's Expedition.—4721, 4818, mouth of Vermilion River.
Not obtained by Captain Raynolds' Expedition.

Formerly supposed to belong to the Eastern Province, this bird has later been shown to inhabit so many other portions of North America, that it may fairly be inferred that it occurs also in the remaining localities whence, simply through lack of observations, it has not been recorded. I inspected, when working up the birds of the Northwest Boundary Survey, some of the first western specimens, taken in Washington Territory. Mr. Dall has shown its occurrence in Alaska, and others throughout British America, quite to the Arctic Ocean. Dr. Cooper found it in Idaho. The extralimital quotations are numerous and almost universal. It is a very abundant species in the Eastern United States, and has a very extensive breeding range. It winters in Florida and along the Gulf coast, as well as much further south.

Several nests with eggs are in the Smithsonian, from various arctic localities, as Fort Yukon and La Pierre House. They appear to have been built on the ground, and are composed chiefly of moss, compactly matted and mixed with little sticks and straws—in one instance with a large amount of disintegrating fibrous material, circularly woven. The eggs, four or five in number, measure from 0.75 by 0.58 to 0.82 by 0.60; they are pure white, probably with a rosy blush when fresh, speckled all over, but most thickly at and around the larger end, with various shades of reddish and darker brown, with lilac or lavender. In some the markings are all in fine dots; in others they constitute larger spots, often confluent in a wreath. The nests are about four inches across by two-thirds as much in depth.

SEIURUS LUDOVICIANUS, (Aud.) Bd.

Large-billed Water Thrush.

(?) *Turdus motacilla*, VIEILL., Ois. Am. Sept. ii, 1807, 9, pl. 65 (almost certainly).
Seiurus motacilla, BP., Consp. Av., i, 1850, 306 (quotes VIEILL. and queries AUD.).
Henicocichla motacilla, CAB., J. f. O. 1857, 240 (Cuba).—GUNDL., *ibid.* 1861, 326.
Turdus ludovicianus, AUD., O. B. i, 1832, 99, pl. 19. (In Syn., unites it with *noveboracensis*.)
Seiurus ludovicianus, BP., List, 1838.—BD., B. N. A. 1858, 262, pl. 80, fig. 2.—SCL., P. Z. S.
    1859, 363 (Xalapa); 1859, 373 (Oaxaca); 1861, 70 (Jamaica).—SCL. & SALV.,
    Ibis, ii, 1860, 273 (Guatemala).—BD., Rev. 1864, 217 (Colima, &c.).—COUES &
    PRENT., Smiths. Rep. 1861, 407 (Washington, common April and May).—LAWR.,
    Ann. Lyc. viii, 1866, 284 (New York); ix, 1868, 94 (Costa Rica).—SALV., P. Z.
    S. 1870, 181.—COUES, Pr. Ess. Inst. v, 1868, 271 (probably in Southern New
    England).—COUES, Pr. Bost. Soc. xii, 1868, 110 (South Carolina).—ALLEN, Am.
    Nat. iii, 1869, 577 (Massachusetts, two instances).—TURNB., B. E. Pa. 1869, 17
    ("not rare").—SNOW, B. Kans.—SCOTT, Pr. Bost. Soc. 1872 (West Virginia).—
    COUES, Key, 1872, 106, pl. 2, fig. 8).
Henicocichla ludoviciana, SCL., Cat. 1862, 25 (Orizaba).
Henicocichla major, CAB., Mus. Hein. i, 1850, 16 (Xalapa).

Hab.—Eastern United States. North to Massachusetts (*Allen*) and Michigan (*Baird*). West to Kansas (*Snow*) and the Wachita River (*Clark*). Cuba and Jamaica. Various Mexican localities. Guatemala.

I still endorse the specific validity of this bird, having seen no specimens I could not at once distinguish from *noveboracensis*. Mr. Allen seems to incline to the contrary view. Audubon, plate 19 of the folio edition, represents it unmistakably, and his letter-press seems to be based chiefly upon it, but in the Synopsis, and in the octavo reprint, he unites the synonymy, description and biography of the two species. Vieillot's figure and description point here so unmistakably, that it may be found necessary to call the species *Seiurus motacilla*.

For the appearance of this species in the present connection, we have the authority of Prof. Snow, who found it in Kansas, and marks it in his list as breeding there. Dr. Cooper obtained a specimen in Missouri. I have myself only met with it in the District of Columbia, where, with Dr. Prentiss, I found it to be not at all uncommon. We gave the following note: "From the 20th of April to the 10th of May, it may always be obtained, by an acute collector, in the dense laurel brakes which border the banks of, and fill the ravines leading into, Rock Creek and Piney Branch. We think we have seen it in June, which would prove it to breed here, as is, indeed, very probable. We have not detected it in the fall. It is usually very shy, darting at once into the most impenetrable brakes, but we have sometimes seen it quite the reverse, and have shot a pair, one after the other, as they sat in full view before us, unconcernedly wagging their tails. We have nearly always found it in *pairs*, even as early as April 20th. Its note is a sparrow-like chirp, like that made by striking two pebbles together, but it has also a loud, most beautiful and melodious song, the singularity of which first drew our attention to it."

I am informed by a letter from Mr. Maynard, that the species has been found in great abundance in West Virginia. This was before publication of the fact by Mr. W. D. Scott, who found it abundant in Kanawha County, "in damp places generally, mainly along the edges of the river."

My anticipation of its occurrence in Massachusetts has since been unquestionably confirmed by Mr. Allen, who mentions two instances of its capture in that State.

The Large-billed Water Thrush has been found breeding on the Wachita River, where the nest and eggs were secured by Mr. J. H. Clark, and at the Kiowa Agency, where Dr. Palmer also procured them. The one of these two nests in the best condition was built upon a layer of leaves, apparently upon the ground, composed otherwise entirely of rootlets and fine grasses. The other contained five eggs; they are more globular than any of those of *S. noveboracensis* I have seen, but not otherwise different; and other sets would probably not be distinguishable. The roundest one of them measures only 0.69 by 0.59.

OPORORNIS FORMOSUS, (Wils.) Bd.

Kentucky Warbler.

Sylvia formosa, WILS., Am. Orn. iii, 1811, 85, pl. 25, f. 3.—BP., Obs. Wils. 125.—BP., Syn. 1828, 34.—NUTT., Man. i, 1832, 399.—AUD., Orn. Biog. i, 1831, 196, pl. 38.
Sylvicola formosa, JARD., ed. Wils. 1832.—RICH., List, 1837.—BP., List, 1838.—MAXIM., J. f. O. vi, 1858, 113.
Myiodioctes formosus, AUD., Syn. 1839, 50.—AUD., B. Am. ii, 1841, 19, pl. 74.—BP., Consp. i, 1850, 315.—LEMB., Aves Cubæ, 1850, 37.—GUNDL., J. f. O. 1861, 326 (Cuba).
Sylvania formosa, WOODH., Sitgr. Rep. 1853, 70 (Texas and Indian Territory).
Oporornis formosus, BD., B. N. A. 1858, 247; Rev. 1864, 218.—SCL. & SALV., Ibis, i, 1859, 10 (Guatemala).—LAWR., Ann. Lyc. N. Y. vii, 62 (Panama).—SCL., P. Z. S. 1862, 19 (Playa Vicente, Mex.).—SCL., Cat. 1862, 28.—WHEAT., Ohio Agric. Rep. 1860, No. 69.—COUES & PRENT., Smiths. Rep. 1861, 406 (Washington, D. C., breeding).—LAWR., Ann. Lyc. N. Y. viii, 1866, 284 (New York); ix, 1868, 94 (Costa Rica).—COUES, Pr. Ess. Inst. v, 1868, 269.—COUES, Pr. Bost. Soc. xii, 1868, 110 (South Carolina, migratory).—TURNB., B. E. Pa. 1869, 16 (in summer).—COUES, A. N. v, 1871, 197 (Kansas).—RIDGW., ibid. 1872, 431 (Illinois).—ALLEN, Bull. M. C. Z. iii, 1872, 125, 175 (Kansas).—SNOW, B. Kans. 5.—SCOTT, Pr. Bost. Soc. 1872 (breeding in West Virginia).—COUES, Key, 1872, 106, fig. 46.
Trichas (Sylvicola) formosa, HOY, Smiths. Rep. 1864, 438 (Missouri).
"(?) *Sylvia æquinoctialis*, VIEILL., O. Am. Sept. ii, 1807, 26, pl. 81 (Pennsylvania; *nec* GM.)."

Hab.—Eastern United States. North to the Connecticut Valley. West to Kansas and the Indian Territory. Missouri (*Hoy*). South to Guatemala and Panama. Cuba. Breeds in most of its United States range. Winters extralimital.

This beautiful species is perhaps more abundant in the Mississippi Valley than elsewhere, and ascends the Missouri to Leavenworth at least, if not further. I observed it near Fort Riley, in Kansas, in May, and Allen found it breeding at the same season, the nest being nearly completed by the middle of the month. According to Dr. Woodhouse, it is "common in Texas and the Indian Territory, frequenting the borders of streams whose banks are covered with low bushes, procuring its insect prey," which Audubon remarks consists largely of spiders, as that of *O. agilis* also does. Its unusual abundance in Southern Illinois is attested by Mr. Ridgway. Earlier accounts—even those down to the date of Baird's Review—placed the Atlantic coast limit at Maryland, but since then the species has been traced to the borders of New England. I have several specimens, shot about Washington, D. C., where I occasionally observed the bird, always in the low shrubbery to which it is so evidently partial, and generally in places near water. Its song I have never heard, the only note with which it ever saluted me being the ordinary chirp. I am not aware that the species has been traced up the

Mississippi Valley beyond the Missouri, where Dr. Hoy found it in great abundance in the western part of the State.   He says: "They live and nest in the underbrush, the male occasionally hopping upon a low branch of a tree to pour forth his *whittishée, whittishée*, repeated two or three times, then disappearing in the tangled brush.   This song is so precisely like that of the Yellow-throat, that it requires a practiced ear to distinguish the one from the other."

The nest, says Audubon, "is small, beautifully constructed, and usually attached to several stems of rank weeds.   The outer parts are formed of the bark of stalks of the same weeds, in a withered state, mixed with a finer kind, and some cottony substances.   It is beautifully lined with the cottony or silky substance that falls from the cotton-wood tree.   The eggs are from four to six, of a pure white color, finely sprinkled with bright red dots."   Two nests before me, taken early in June, in Georgia and Kansas, respectively, differ somewhat from such a one as Audubon describes.   One of them appears to have lost an outer part it probably had; the other, complete, is a large bulky structure, five or six inches across, composed externally of a mass of dried leaves and small sticks; the lining is of fine rootlets.   The eggs are as Audubon says—the fine dotting occurs sparsely all over the surface, but most thickly at and around the larger end, and besides the reddish sprinkling there are other dots of neutral tint.   Dimensions 0.68 by 0.55.

GEOTHLYPIS TRICHAS, (Linn.) Cab.

Maryland Yellow-throat.

Turdus trichas, LINN., Syst. Nat. i. 1766, 293.—GM., *op. cit.* 13th ed. 1788, 811.
Sylvia trichas, LATH., Ind. Orn. ii, 1790, 519.—VIEILL., Ois. Am. Sept. ii, 1807, 28, pls.
        28, 29.—NUTT., Man. i, 1832, 401.—AUD., Orn. Biog. i, 1832, 120; v, 1839, 463,
        pls. 23, 240.—D'ORBIG., Sagra's Cuba, 1840, 67.
Geothlypis trichas, CAB., Mus. Hein. 1850, 16.—BD, B. N. A. 1858, 241; Rev. 1865, 220.—
        COOP. & SUCK., N. H. Wash. Ter. 1860, 177.—GUNDL., J. f. O. 1861, 326.—SCL.,
        Cat. A. B. 1862, 27.—HAYD., Rep. 1862, 160.—MARCH, Pr. Phila. Acad. 1863,
        293.—LORD, Pr. Roy. Arty. Inst. Wool. iv, 1864, 115.—JONES, Nat. Berm. 29.—
        COUES, Pr. Phila. Acad. 1866, 69 (Arizona).—LAWR., Ann. Lyc. ix, 1868, 94
        (Costa Rica); 1869, 200 (Yucatan).—SCL., P. Z. S. 1870, 836 (Honduras).—COOP.,
        B. Cal. 1870, 95.—STEV., U. S. Geol. Surv. Ter. 1870, 463.—MERR., *ibid.* 1872,
        674.—ALLEN, Bull. M. C. Z. iii, 1872, 175.—ALLEN, *op. cit.* ii, 1871, 269.—AIKEN,
        Pr. Bost. Soc. 1872, 197 (Black Hills).—COUES, Key, 1872, 107, fig. 47; also of
        all Eastern United States writers.
Ficedula trichas and *marilandica* of BRISSON.
Sylvia marilandica, WILS., Am. Orn. i, 1808, 88, pl. 6, f. 1, and ii, 163, pl. 18, f. 4.—BP.,
        Syn. 1828, 85.
Trichas marilandica, BP., List, 1838; Consp. i, 1850, 310.—AUD., Syn. 1839, 65; B. Am.
        ii, 1841, 78, pl. 102.—WOODH., Sitgr. Rep. 1853, 71.—HOY, Smiths. Rep. 1864, 438.
Regulus mystaceus, STEPH., Shaw's Gen. Zool. xiii, 1826, 232.
Trichas personatus, Sw., Zool. Journ. iii, 1827, 16.
Trichas brachydactylus, Sw., An. in Men. 1838, 295.
Sylvia roscoe, AUD., Orn. Biog. i, 1832, 124, pl. 24.
Trichas roscoe, NUTT., Man. i, 2d ed. 1840, 457.
Trichas delafieldii, HEERM., P. R. R. Rep. x, 1859, 40 (whether of *Aububon?*)

Hab.—The whole of the United States, and South through Mexico and most of the West Indies, to Guatemala.   Breeds throughout its United States range, and winters sparingly on our southern border.   Resident individuals of Mexico constitute var. *melanops* (*G. melanops*, BD., Rev. 1865, 222).   Those resident in the Bahamas form an insular race *rostratus* (*G. rostratus*, BRYANT, Pr. Bost. Soc. 1866, 67).   (See RIDGW., Am. Journ. Sci. 1872, 458.)

List of specimens.

19340	....	(No locality)...	....	(Not dated)..	G. H. Trook..	......	......	......

Lieutenant Warren's Expedition.—4674-5, "Nebraska;" 8834-37, Loup Fork.
Later Expeditions.—60426, La Bonté Creek ; 62343-4, Utah and Montana.
Excellent analytical accounts of the species of this genus have been given by Baird, Rev. 219-228, and by Salvin, Ibis, 1872, 147-152; while later, Mr. Ridgway, as above cited, has furnished an admirable synthesis, showing the relations of the forms which other writers had differentiated, and thus managing to reduce the eleven or twelve current species to five. The connection between climate and color is proven to be a relation of cause and effect.

GEOTHLYPIS PHILADELPHIA, (Wils.) Bd.

Mourning Warbler.

a. *philadelphia.*

Sylvia philadelphia, WILS., Am. Orn. ii, 1810, 101, pl. xiv, f. 6.—BP., Syn. 1828, 85.— NUTT., Man. i, 1832, 404.—AUD., Orn. Biog. v, 1839, 78.
Trichas philadelphia, JARD., ed. Wils. 1832.—RICH., List, 1837.—BP., List, 1838.—BP., Consp. i, 1850, 310.—REINH., Vid. Med. 1853, 73; Ibis, 1861, 6 (Greenland).— TRIPPE, Pr. Ess. Inst. vi, 1871 (Minnesota, breeding abundantly).—HOY, Smiths. Rep. 1864, 438 (Western Missouri, breeding).
Geothlypis philadelphia, BD., B. N. A. 1858, 243, pl. 79, f. 3 ; Rev. 1865, 226.—LAWR., Ann. Lyc. N. Y. 1861, 322 (Panama).—SCL., Cat. 1862, 27 (Orizaba).—ALLEN, Pr. Ess. Inst. iv, 1864, 59 (Massachusetts, rare).—HAML., Rep. Sec'y Maine Board Agric. 1865, p. — (Waterville, Me., breeding).—McILWR., Pr. Ess. Inst. v, 1866, 85 (Hamilton, C. W., very rare).—LAWR., Ann. Lyc. N. Y. viii, 1866, 283 (New York) ; ix, 1868, 94 (Costa Rica).—COUES, Pr. Ess. Inst. v, 1868, 269 (rare summer resident in New England).—COUES, Pr. Bost. Soc. xii, 1868, 110 (South Carolina, rare, migratory).—TURNB., B. E. Pa. 1869, 16 (rare, particularly in autumn).—MAYN., Guide, 1870, 99 (Massachusetts, rare).—MAYN., Pr. Bost. Soc. xiv, 1871 (breeding commonly at Umbagog).—ALLEN, Bull. M. C. Z. iii, 1872, 126 (Topeka, Kans., in May).—SNOW, B. Kans. 5.—SALV., Ibis, Apr. 1872.— RIDGW., Am. Journ. Sci. 1872, 459.—COUES, Key, 1872, 107.

b. *macgillivrayi.*

Sylvia macgillivrayi, AUD., Orn. Biog. v, 1839, 75, pl. 399, figs. 4, 5.
Trichas macgillivrayi, AUD., Syn. 1839, 64; B. Am. ii, 1841, 74, pl. 100.—BP., Consp. i, 1850, 310.
Sylvicola macgillivrayi, MAXIM., J. f. O. vi, 1858, 118.
Geothlypis macgillivrayi, BD., B. N. A. 1858, 244, pl. 99, f. 4 ; Rev. 1865, 227.—SCL., P. Z. S. 1859, 363, 373 (Xalapa, Oaxaca) ; Cat. 1862, 27 (Guatemala).—CAB., J. f. O. 1861, 84 (Costa Rica).—LAWR., Ann. Lyc. ix, 1868, 94 (Costa Rica).—COOP. & SUCK., N. H. Wash. Ter. 1860, 177.—COUES, Pr. Phila. Acad. 1866, 70 (Arizona).— COOP., Am. Nat. iii, 1869, 32 (Rocky Mountains) ; Pr. Cal. Acad. 1870, 75 (Colorado River) ; B. Cal. i, 1870, 96.—SALV., Ibis, 1872, 148.—AIKEN, Pr. Bost. Soc. 1872, 197 (Black Hills).—COUES, Key, 1872, 107.
Geothlypis philadelphia var. macgillivrayi, ALLEN, Bull. M. C. Z. iii, July, 1872, 175 (mountains of Colorado, below 9,000 feet).—RIDGW., Am. Journ. Dec. 1872, 459.
Sylvia tolmiœi, TOWNS., Journ. Phila. Acad. viii, 1839 (1840), 139, 159 ; Narr. 1839, 343.
Trichas tolmiœi, NUTT., Man. i, 2d ed. 1840, 460.
Trichas vegeta, BP., Consp. i, 1850, 310 (based on *Sylvia vegeta*, LICHT., Mus. Berol ; *cf.* CAB., J. f. O. 1861, 84).

Hab.—The typical form in the Eastern Province of North America, north regularly to the British provinces, casually to Greenland. South to Costa Rica, Panama and Bogota. West to Kansas. No record of wintering in the United States, the West Indies or Mexico. Breeds in New England. The var. *macgillivrayi* from the Middle and Western Provinces, north to British Columbia; east to Colorado and Laramie. Winters in Mexico and Central America. Breeds in all its United States range.
Later Expeditions.—60700, Box Elder Creek (var. *macgillivrayi*).
Although in the Key I kept Macgillivray's Warbler specifically separate from the Mourning Warbler, I am now prepared to agree with Mr. Allen in ranking it as a geographical race of the latter. Mr. Ridgway has also adopted the same view, upon his independent investigations. He shows some additional characters of general applicability, besides the presence of white eyelids in the western bird ; this form being longer-tailed (2.25 to 2.50 instead of 2.00 to 2.15), with darker lores, the black contrasting with the ash and white of contiguous parts, and the black centres of the pectoral feathers never forming a continuous blotch, as is the case with higher-plumaged specimens of *philadelphia.*

In the East, it is the nearly unanimous testimony of observers that the Mourning Warbler is rare. It is, moreover, a particularly shy and retiring bird, courting the privacy of dense shrubbery, and quiet in its ways; so that even were it common it might ordinarily elude observation. It seems also to migrate rapidly, as well as stealthily. Mr. Maynard is one of the few naturalists fortunately enabled to use the word "common" in speaking of this bird from his personal observations; he found it so at Umbagog, where it was breeding, in June; and states that Mr. C. W. Brewster took newly-fledged young at Franconia, "in spring." "It frequents," he continues, "the bushes along fences, stone-walls, and the edges of woods. The male may be seen in the early morning perched on the top rail of a fence, or dead branch of a tree, singing. The song is loud and clear, somewhat resembling that of the Water Thrush."

It is perhaps more abundant than anywhere else, in the breeding season, along the Red River, between Dakota and Minnesota, but I never saw it further west. It frequents the dense shrubbery along the banks of the river, and is rather difficult to observe, the female especially. But the male often mounts quite high in the trees overhead, singing, during the mating season and while the female is incubating. The nest must be very carefully concealed, for after repeated close search in places where I knew there was a nest, I never succeeded in finding one.

Mr. T. Martin Trippe has been equally successful in making the acquaintance of this species, finding it breeding abundantly in Minnesota. "The Mourning Warbler haunts the edges of the tamarack swamps and the damp thickets that adjoin them. I made frequent search for the nest, but was not fortunate enough to find it, though I repeatedly saw the old birds feeding the young in the latter part of June and early in July. They are similar in their habits to the Maryland Yellow-throat, but are not so exclusively devoted to thickets and underbrush, frequently ascending to the tops of the tamaracks, for which they show a great predilection." The author speaks of the "agreeable" song, and, like the one just quoted, compares it to that of the Water Thrush.

Both forms of this species occur in the Missouri region—one entering Kansas from the East, the other reaching Laramie in the opposite direction. Macgillivray's Warbler appears to be more abundant than its eastern representative, and more generally diffused during the breeding season. I found it to be a common though not abundant summer resident in the mountainous parts of Arizona, where it arrived late in April and departed in September. My specimens were procured with some difficulty, owing to the closeness of its coverts and its secretive habits, which are just the same as those of *philadelphia*. Dr. Cooper notes its arrival in the Colorado Valley, at Mojave, at the same time, but very pertinently observes they probably came there earlier, since he had found them on the Columbia River by the third of May. He describes a nest that he found at Puget's Sound, in June, as being built without attempt at concealment, about a foot above the ground, in a small bush, and formed wholly of dry grasses, rather loosely put together. The eggs, he states, are white, speckled with reddish.

Mr. Allen sends me a pleasant manuscript note: "The western race of the Mourning Warbler (*Geothlypis philadelphia* var. *macgillivrayi*), or Macgillivray's Warbler, is a common summer inhabitant of the mountains of Colorado, from the base of the foot-hills up to about 9,000 feet. On Bear and Turkey Creeks it was the most numerous representative of the *Sylvicolidæ*, keeping chiefly in the thick shrubbery bordering the streams. Although its sweet notes were heard at frequent intervals, its very retiring habits rendered it a rather difficult species to secure. Occasionally, however, a male would mount to the highest point of the thicket to pour forth his warbling melody, almost unrivalled in sweetness by that of any other of the forest songsters."

The nest is a rather slight but neat structure, placed on the ground, composed of various soft fibrous materials and fine grasses, mostly circular arranged, lined with fine rootlets. The eggs, judging from several sets before me, collected by Mr. Ridgway, lack the sharp speckling of reddish-brown found mostly throughout this family, being variously blotched, in an entirely irregular manner, with very dark brown, and smirched with several shades of lighter dirty brown, together with some obscure neutral shell-markings; the ground is white, as usual. Extremes of size and shape which have offered, are 0.70 by 0.50 and 0.65 by 0.52.

ICTERIA VIRENS, (Linn.) Bd.

Yellow-breasted Chat.

a. *virens*.

Turdus virens, LINN., Syst. Nat. i, 1758, 171.
Icteria virens, BD., Rev. 1865, 228.—SUMICH., Mem. Bost. Soc. i, 1869, 54.—LAWR., Ann. Lyc. ix, 1868, 95 (Costa Rica); ix, 1869, 200 (Yucatan).—ALLEN, Bull. M. C. Z. iii, 1872, 175.—COUES, Key, 1872, 108, fig. 48.
Muscicapa viridis, GM., Syst. Nat. i, 1788, 936.
Icteria viridis, BP., Obs. Wils. 1826; Syn. 1828, 69; List, 1838; Consp. Av. i, 1850, 331.—NUTT., Man. Orn. i, 1832, 299.—AUD., Orn. Biog. ii, 1834, 223; v, 1839, 433, pl. 137; SYD. 1839, 163; B. Am. iv, 160, pl. 244.—WOODH., Sitgr. Rep. 1853, 73.—BD., B. N. A. 1858, 248; and of late local writers.—HOY, Smiths. Rep. 1864, 437 (Missouri, breeding).—COOP., Am. Nat., Aug. 1869 (Fort Union, breeding).—SCL., P. Z. S. 1870, 836 (Honduras).—CAB., J. f. O. viii, 403 (Costa Rica).
Icteria dumicola, VIEILL., Ois. Am. Sept. ii, 1807, 85, pl. 55.
Pipra polyglotta, WILS., Am. Orn. i, 1808, 90, pl. 6, f. 2.
(?) *Icteria auricollis*, LICHT.—BP., Consp. Av. 1850, 331.
(?) *Icteria velasquezii*, BP., P. Z. S. 1837, 117; Consp. 1850, 331.—SCL. & SALV., 1859, 12.

b. *longicauda*.

Icteria longicauda, LAWR., Ann. Lyc. Nat. Hist. N. Y. vi, 1863, 4.—NEWB., P. R. R. Rep. vi, 1857, 81.—BD., B. N. A. 1858, 249, pl. 34, f. 2.—HEERM., P. R. R. Rep. x, 1859, 55.—SCL., Cat. 1861, 42.—HAYD., Rep. 1862, 160.—COUES, Pr. Phila. Acad. 1866, 71.—COOP., Pr. Phila. Acad. 1870, 75.—COOP., B. Cal. 1870, 98.—AIKEN, Pr. Bost. Soc. 1872, 197 (Colorado).—MERR., U. S. Geol. Surv. Ter. 1872, 674.
Icteria virens var. *longicauda*, COUES, Key, 1872, 108.

Hab.—The typical form to the high central plains; thence replaced by the other. True *virens* north only to Connecticut Valley.
Lieutenant Warren's Expedition.—4725, "Nebraska;" 4724, mouth of White River; 5304, 5308, 5307, 5310-11, Fort Lookout; 5306, Little Cheyenne; 4647-48, Fort Pierre.
Later Expeditions.—61655-59, Ogden, Utah; 61794, Devil's Creek, Idaho. Var. *longicauda*.
Not obtained by Captain Raynolds' Expedition.
It has proven impossible to distinguish the several supposed species enumerated in the above synonymy. Nevertheless, I am at present indisposed to follow Dr. Cabanis to the length of uniting them all without varietal qualification. In the dryer portions of the Western United States the species becomes, like other birds of that region, less highly colored, the olive taking a grayish cast noticeably different from the rich clear shade of Eastern specimens. This change is accompanied by an increase in *average* length of tail, although this feature does not always obtain. I predicate a var. *longicauda* upon this basis. Dr. Hayden's specimens appear to belong here. There is some uncertainty attaching the determination of the two described Mexican species; but as well as I can judge, they are referable to true *virens* rather than to var. *longicauda*.

This is a southern species not exceeding the limits of the "Carolinian Fauna," as defined by Mr. Allen (Bull. M. C. Z. ii, 1871, 394). A form extends through Mexico to Guatemala. I have seen no West Indian references. The bird does not appear to winter anywhere in the United

States; it breeds throughout its United States range. It is very abundant in suitable places in most portions of the Missouri region. Thus Mr. Allen writes: "I never saw it in greater abundance than in and about the woodlands of Eastern Kansas. At Topeka, during the last half of May, it was especially numerous and noisy, several males being almost constantly in view from a single point, hovering in the air in their well-known manner over the low thickets that border the forests along the Kaw River, engaged in musical rivalry. Further westward they occur with more or less frequency along the streams wherever they are skirted with thickets, and also along the partially wooded streams that descend into the plains from the foot-hills of the Rocky Mountains, as well as among the foot-hills up to about 7,800 feet. I also met with them in the vicinity of Cheyenne, and at Ogden, Utah."

MYIODIOCTES MITRATUS, (Gm.) Aud.

Hooded Fly-catching Warbler.

Motacilla mitrata, GM., Syst. Nat. i, 1788, 977.
Sylvia mitrata, LATH., Ind. Orn. ii, 1790, 528.—VIEILL., Ois. Am. Sept. ii, 1807, 23, pl. 77.—BP., Syn. 1828, 79.—NUTT., Man. i, 1832, 373.—AUD., Orn. Biog. ii, 1834, 68.
Sylvania mitrata, NUTT., Man. i, 1840, 2d ed. 333.—WOODH., Sitgr. Rep. 1853, 69 (Texas and Indian Territory).
Setophaga mitrata, JARD., ed. Wils. 1832.—GRAY, Genera of Birds.—D'ORBIG., La Sagra's Cuba, Ois. 1840, 89.
Wilsonia mitrata, BP., List, 1838, 23.—ALL., Bull. M. C. Z. iii, 1872, 175 (Eastern Kansas).— ALLEN, Pr. Ess. Inst. iv, 1864, 83 (Massachusetts).—ALLEN, Mem. Bost. Soc. i, 1868, 516 (Illinois).
Myiodioctes mitratus, AUD., Syn. 1839, 48.—AUD., B. Am. ii, 1841, 12, pl. 71.—BP., Consp. i, 1850, 315.—SCL., P. Z. S. 1856, 281 (Cordova); 1858, 358 (Honduras); Cat. 1862, 33.—BD., B. N. A. 1858, 292; Rev. 1865, 239.—SCL. & SALV., Ibis, 1859, 11 (Guatemala).—JONES, Nat. Berm. 1859, 26.—GUNDL., J. f. O. 1861, 326 (Cuba).— LAWR., Ann. Lyc. viii, 63 (Panama).—WHEAT., Ohio Agric. Rep. 1860.--COUES & PRENT., Smiths. Rep. 1861, 409.—LAWR., Ann. Lyc. N. Y. viii, 1866, 284 (near New York, rare, breeding).—COUES, Pr. Ess. Inst. v, 1868, 275 (Massachusetts and Connecticut).—COUES, Pr. Bost. Soc. xii, 1868, 110 (South Carolina, migratory).—TURNB., B. E. Pa., 1869, 19 (rather rare).—SUMICH., Mem. Bost. Soc. i, 1869, 547 (Orizaba).—LAWR., Ann. Lyc. ix, 1869, 200 (Yucatan).—SNOW, B. Kans. 1873, 5.—COUES, Key, 1872, 109, fig. 49.
Sylvicola mitrata, MAXIM., J. f. O. vi, 1858, 113.
Myioctonus mitratus, CAB., Mus. Hein. 1850, 18; J. f. O. iii, 1855, 472 (Cuba).
Muscicapa cucullata, WILS., Am. Orn. iii, 1811, 101, pl. 26, f. 3.
Muscicapa selbyi, AUD., Orn. Biog. i, 1831, 46, pl. 9.—NUTT., Man. i, 1832, 296.

Hab.—Eastern United States; north to the Middle States regularly; to Connecticut (*Linsley*, Am. Journ. Sci. xliv, 1843, 257) and Massachusetts (*Samuels*, App. Secy's Rep. Agric. 1863, p. xxii) rarely. Ohio. West to Kansas (*Cooper, Allen*). Bermudas. Cuba. Jamaica. Eastern Mexico, and south to Panama.

As will be seen by the foregoing, this is essentially a southern bird, the northern limit of which falls short of the United States border. It does not appear to winter anywhere within the United States, which it enters in March, and where it breeds throughout its range. I have rarely met with it in the Atlantic States, where I consider it not common; but it appears to be more plentiful in the Mississippi Valley. Westward it has been noted in the Indian Territory by Dr. Woodhouse, and in Kansas as far as Fort Leavenworth, which constitutes the limit of its extension as now known, unless the Prince Maximilian's quotation, which I have not verified, represents a locality beyond. It is not noted by Mr. Trippe among the birds of Minnesota. Mr. W. D. Scott found it common and breeding in Kanawha County, West Virginia (Pr. Bost. Soc., Oct. 1872).

MYIODIOCTES PUSILLUS, (Wils.) Bp.

Wilson's Green Black-capped Fly-catching Warbler.

Muscicapa pusilla, WILS.. Am. Orn. iii, 1811, 103, pl. 26. f. 4.
Wilsonia pusilla, BP., List, 1838, 23.—ALLEN, Pr. Ess. Inst. iv, 1864, 64 (Massachusetts, May and Aug., rare; "probably breeds").—ALLEN, Bull. M. C. Z. iii, 1872, 175 (Colorado, to above timber-line; Utah; Wyoming).
Sylvania pusilla. NUTT., Man. i, 2d ed. 1840, 335.
Myiodioctes pusillus, BP., Consp. Av. i, 1850, 315.—BD., B. N. A. 1858, 293 (United States, from Atlantic to Pacific; south to Guatemala).—SCL., P. Z. S. 1856, 291 (Cordova); 1858, 299 (mountains of Oaxaca, in winter); 1859, 363 (Xalapa).—SCL. & SALV., Ibis, 1859, 11 (Guatemala).—COOP. & SUCK., N. H. Wash. Ter. 1860, 182 (Fort Steilacoom, abundant).—WHEAT., Ohio Agric. Rep. 1860.—COUES & PRENT., Smiths. Rep. for 1861 (1862), 409 (migratory).—VERR., Pr. Bost. Soc. 1862, 125 ; Pr. Ess. Inst. iii (Maine, summer visitant, not common).—BD., Rev. 1864, 240 (various parts of British America, &c.).—LORD, Pr. Roy. Art'y Inst. Wool. iv, 1864, 115 (British Columbia).—COUES. Pr. Phila. Acad. 1866 (Arizona, summer resident in mountains).—COUES, Pr. Ess. Inst. v, 1868, 274 (New England, migratory, summer, and probably breeding).—COUES, Pr. Bost. Soc. N. H. 1868, 111 (South Carolina, migratory).—LAWR., Ann. Lyc. N. Y. viii, 1866, 285 (New York); ix, 1868, 95 (Costa Rica).—TURNB., B. E. Pa. 1869, 19 (migratory).—SUMICH., Mem. Bost. Soc. i, 1869, 547 (Vera Cruz, migratory, "everywhere").—STEV., U. S. Geol. Surv. Ter. 1870, 464.—MERR., *ibid.* 1872, 675.—DALL & BANN., Tr. Chic. Acad. i, 1869, 278 (Alaska, breeding at Sitka).—COOP., Pr. Cal. Acad. 1870, 75 ; B. Cal. 101.—AIKEN, Pr. Bost. Soc. 1872, 197 (Colorado).—COUES, Key, 1872, 109, fig. 50 (North America, at large).
Myioctonus pusillus, CAB., Mus. Hein. 1851, 18.—CAB., J. f. O. 1860, 325 (Costa Rica.)
Motacilla pileolata, PALL., Zoog. R.-A. i, 1811, 497. (Pacific variety.)
Myiodioctes pusillus var. *pileolata*, RIDGW., Am. Journ. Sci. 1872, 457. (A variety.)
Sylvia wilsonii, BP., Obs. Wils. 1826, No. 127.—NUTT., Man. i, 1832, 408.
Muscicapa wilsonii, AUD., Orn. Biog. ii, 1834, 148, pl. 124.
Setophaga wilsonii, JARD., ed. Wils. Am. Orn. 1832.
Myiodioctes wilsonii, AUD., Syn. i, 1839, 50.—AUD., B. Am. ii, 1841, 21, pl. 75 (Labrador, Newfoundland).—PUTN., Pr. Ess. Inst. i, 1856, 206 (Massachusetts, summer, rare).
Sylvania wilsonii, WOODH., Sitgr. Rep. 1853, 69 (Texas and Indian Territory).

Hab.—North America. Mexico. Central America. No West Indian record.
Later Expeditions.—60704-10, Fort Bridger and Henry's Fork ; 62347-8, Lower Geyser Basin and Téton Lakes.

Brighter colored examples, from the humid Pacific regions, constitute Mr. Ridgway's "var. *pileolata*" (Am. Journ. Sci. 1872, 457), to which the various Pacific coast references, given above, pertain.

Not obtained by either of the earlier Expeditions, but beyond a doubt overlooked. The foregoing quotations illustrate very fully the distribution of the species. It doubtless breeds in New England, but I have no authentic advices that such is the case. I have found no record of its wintering in the United States.

Mr. Allen communicates the following interesting note :

"The Black-capped Warbler (*Wilsonia pusilla*) is a common inhabitant of the subalpine and alpine districts in the Colorado Mountains, breeding from about 8,000 feet up to about timber-line. In the dwarfed willows and other low shrubs that grow for some distance above the limit of trees, we found it by far the most numerous of all the insectiverous birds. It was here more plentiful even than at lower points, and may hence be regarded as an eminently alpine species. Although evidently breeding, we failed to discover its nests. It manifests great anxiety when its chosen haunts are invaded, and during our excursions at the above-described locality, we were almost constantly scolded by one or more pairs of these birds. Later in the season we met with this species at Cheyenne, and near Colorado City and Denver, and also found it common in the vicinity of Ogden, Utah, in September."

I have met with the species in various parts of the East, where, however, it appears to be less abundant than it is in many western regions. In the mountainous districts of Arizona it is a common summer resident from May to September, and doubtless breeds, though I have no information of its nest and eggs.

MYIODIOCTES CANADENSIS, (Linn.) Aud.

Canadian Fly-catching Warbler.

Muscicapa canadensis, LINN., Syst. Nat. i, 1766, 327.—GM., *ibid.* 13th ed. 1788, 937.—WILS.,
    Am. Orn. iii, 1811, 100, pl. 26, f. 2.—AUD., Orn. Biog. ii, 1834, 17, pl. 103.
Setophaga canadensis, JARD., ed. Wils. 1832.—RICH., List, 1837.—GRAY, Gen. of Birds.
Myiodioctes canadensis, AUD., Syn. 1839, 49.—AUD., B. Am. ii, 1841, 14, pl. 72.—(??)BREW.,
    Pr. Bost. Soc. vi, 5 (Lynn, Mass., breeding).—SCL., P. Z. S. 1854, 111; 1858, 451
    (Ecuador); 1855, 143 (Bogota).—PUTN., Pr. Ess. Inst. i, 1856, 206 (Massachu-
    setts, in summer).—BD., B. N. A. 1858, 294.—SCL. & SALV., Ibis, i, 1859, 11
    (Guatemala).—LAWR., Ann. Lyc. N. Y. vi, 1862; viii, 1866, 286; ix, 1868, 95
    (Costa Rica).—BD., Rev. 1865, 240.—WHEAT., Ohio Agric. Rep. 1840.—COUES
    & PRENT., Smiths. Rep. 1861, 409 (migratory, abundant).—BOARDM., Pr. Bost.
    Soc. ix, 1862, 125 (Maine, breeding, common).—VERR., Pr. Ess. Inst. iii, 1862,
    146 (ditto).—McILWR., Pr. Ess. Inst. v, 1866, 86 (Hamilton, C. W., in summer).—
    COUES, Pr. Ess. Inst. v, 1868, 274.—COUES, Pr. Bost. Soc. xii, 1868, 111 (S. Car.,
    migratory, common).—TURNB., B. E. Pa. 1869, 19 (frequent, Apr., Oct.).—MAYN.,
    Guide, 1870, 105; Pr. Bost. Soc. xiv, 1871.—COUES, Key, 1872, 109, fig. 51.
Euthlypis canadensis, CAB., Mus. Hein. 1850, 18.—ALLEN, Pr. Ess. Inst. iv, 1864, 65.
Sylvia pardalina, BP., Obs. Wils. 1826; Syn. 1828, 79.—NUTT., Man. i, 1832, 372.—LINS.,
    Am. Journ. Sci. xliv, 1843, 256.
Sylvicola pardalina, BP., List, 1838, 22.—BREW., Pr. Bost. Soc. vi, 1857, 4, (Mass., breeding).
Myiodioctes pardalina, BP., Consp. i, 1850, 315.
Muscicapa bonapartii, AUD., Orn. Biog. i, 1831, 27, pl. 5 (young).
Setophaga bonapartii, SW. & RICH., F. B. A. ii, 1831, 225, pl. 47.—RICH., List, 1837.
Wilsonia bonapartii, BP., List, 1838.
Sylvania bonapartii, NUTT., Man. i, 2d ed. 1840, 332.
Myiodioctes bonapartii, AUD., Syn. 1839, 49; B. Am. ii, 1841, 17, pl. 73.—BD., B. N. A. 295.
Setophaga nigricincta, LAFRES., R. Z. 1843, 292; 1844, 79.

Hab.—Eastern North America. North to Labrador (*Audubon*) and Cumberland
House (lat. 54°, *Richardson*). West to the Lower Missouri. South to Ecuador. No
West Indian record. Breeds from the Middle States and Massachusetts, occasionally;
from Maine, regularly, northward. Winters entirely beyond the United States.

No species of *Myiodioctes* was noticed by either Expedition. The
present one has not, to my knowledge, been actually taken anywhere on
the Missouri; but I admit it, with this remark, because there is no reasonable doubt whatever of its occurrence in Missouri and Eastern
Kansas.

It is too late now to argue in favor of the identity of "*M. bonapartii*"
with this species; this has become a settled issue. It is curious to note
how, in striving to separate the supposed species, Audubon was led un-
wittingly to deny to *canadensis* any occurrence in the Southern States;
he says "from Kentucky northward," but the fact is, as indicated in the
foregoing paragraph, that the species has a southward extension equal
to that of almost any United States species of the family, excepting *D.
striata*, which probably goes to Chili. It is abundant in the woodland
of the Carolinas, Virginia, and Maryland, during the migrations; some
individuals stop to breed in the Middle States and Southern New England, but the majority reach a latitude in British America correspondent to that of most other species of the family. Its habits are not
peculiar in comparison with those of its congeners.

The nest of this species is a rude and bulky structure, which would
scarcely be attributed to so delicate a bird. The description is taken
from the only one I have seen, collected at Lynn, Massachusetts, by Mr.
G. Welch. It is irregular in contour, about four inches in one diameter
and nearly six in the other, though less than two inches deep. It is
composed chiefly of dried pine-needles, closely laid together, but with
these are mixed a number of leaves, chiefly outside and below, some
fibrous strips and weed-stalks. The cavity itself is very small, neatly finished, and lined with a quantity of black horse-hair. This nest contained

three eggs, white, spotted with reddish-brown and lavender, chiefly at the larger end, where many of the spots are confluent, but also sparingly sprinkled over the whole surface. Size 0.68 by 0.52. The nest is placed on the ground.

SETOPHAGA RUTICILLA, (Linn.) Sw.

Redstart.

Muscicapa ruticilla, LINN., Syst. Nat. i, 1766, 326.—GM., Syst. Nat. i, 1788, 935.—VIEILL., Ois. Am. Sept. ii, 1807, 66, pl. 35, 36.—WILS., Am. Orn. i, 1808, 103, pl. 6, fig. 6.—AUD., Orn. Biog. i, 1831, 202; v, 1839, 428; pl. 40.—AUD., B. Am. i, 240, pl. 68.
Setophaga ruticilla, Sw., Zool. Journ. iii, 1827, 358.—Sw. & RICH., F. B. A. ii, 1831, 223.—BD., B. N. A. 1858, 297; Rev. 1865, 256.—HAYD., Rep. 1862, 161.—COOP., Am. Nat. Aug. 1869, 33 (Fort Union, breeding; obtained eight nests).—LAWR., Ann. Lyc. viii, 1866, 174; ix, 1868, 96 (Costa Rica).—SALV., P. Z. S. 1867, 136 (Veragua); 1868, 166 (Venezuela).—SCL. & SALV., P. Z. S. 1870, 780 (Merida).—ALLEN, Bull. M. C. Z. iii, 1872, 175 (Kansas; mountains of Colorado, up to about 8,000 feet; Ogden, Utah).—STEV., U. S. Geol. Surv. Ter. 1870, 463.—COUES, Key, 1872, 110; and of all late writers.
Sylvania ruticilla, NUTT., Man. i, 1832, 291.
Motacilla flavicauda, GM., Syst. Nat. i, 1788, 997 (♀).

Hab.—Chiefly Eastern North America. North to Fort Simpson. West to Utah. South through Mexico and Central America to Ecuador. West Indies.

List of specimens.

| 19205 | 24 | Wind River...... | ♂ | May 28, 1860 | F. V. Hayden. | 5.75 | 8.00 | 2.50 |
| 19206 | 34 | ...... do .... | ♀ | .... do ..... | ..... do ...... | 5.25 | 7.25 | 2.25 |

Lieutenant Warren's Expedition.—4691, "Nebraska;" 4687-90, 8843, Upper Missouri River; 4688, Big Sioux River; 4689, mouth of Platte River; 5271, Medicine Creek.
Later Expeditions.—60424-5, La Bonté Creek.

According to several observers, the Redstart is one of the commonest birds along the Missouri River bottoms, breeding abundantly. Dr. Cooper obtained numerous nests at various points between Fort Union and Milk River, and traced the species westward to the Cœur d'Aleñe Mountains. Mr. Allen says it occurs with considerable frequency as a summer resident in the foot-hills west of Denver, where it evidently breeds, and is doubtlessly sparingly represented wherever there are woodlands or thickets, thence eastward to the Atlantic coast, as well as westward throughout the lower mountain valleys, as he found it common about Ogden, Utah, in autumn. In the mountains he did not observe it above 8,000 feet.

The Redstart builds an elegant little nest in the fork of a tree, of various soft downy substances matted together, and usually also with fibrous strips. Those built chiefly of down are exquisitely soft and neatly finished with a firm, smooth, circular brim, quite narrow. The interior is lined with a considerable quantity of very fine rootlets, or horse-hair, or both, for the most part circularly arranged. The whole nest is only about two and one-half inches across outside, and the same in external depth; the cavity is usually rather deeper than broad. A nest taken at Racine, Wisconsin, by Dr. Hoy, is curiously fixed entirely to one side of an upright fork, setting away from the support altogether, excepting on a small part of its circumference, which is continued downward into the crotch, and to which the rest of the nest is attached more intimately than it is to the fork itself. The eggs, in the examples before me, are mostly four in number; they are white, quite thickly sprinkled all over, but especially spotted at or around the large end, with usual shades of brown and lilac. Different specimens measure from 0.60 by 0.49 to 0.70 by 0.51. The bird breeds in Kansas, and also very abundantly along the Red River, in June.

6

Family TANAGRIDÆ: Tanagers.

PYRANGA RUBRA, (Linn.) Vieill.

Scarlet Tanager.

Tanagra rubra, LINN., Syst. Nat. i, 1706, 314.—GM., i, 1788, 889.—WILS.. Am. Orn. ii, 1810, 42, pl. 11, f. 3, 4.—BP., Syn. 1828, 105.—NUTT., Man. i, 1832, 465.—AUD., Orn. Biog. iv, 1838, 388, pl. 354, f. 3, 4.
Pyranga rubra, VIEILL., Ois. Am. Sept. i, 1807.—SW. & RICH., F. B. A. ii, 1831, 273.—JARD., ed. Wils. 1832, i, 192.—BP., List, 1838, 35; Consp. 1850, 241 (quotes pl. Enlum. 127 ♂, 156 ♀; *Desm.*, Tang. pl. 34).—AUD., Syn. 1839, 136.—AUD., B. Am., iii, 1841, 226, pl. 209.—GIR., B. L. I. 1844, 135.—WOODH., Sitgr. Rep. 1853, 82 (Texas and Indian Territory).—GOSSE, B. Jam. 1847, 235.—SCL., P. Z. S. 1855, 156 (Bogota); 1856, 123 (Cuba, Jamaica); 1858, 73 (Ecuador); Cat. 1862, 80 (Bogota).—MAXIM., J. f. O. vi, 1858, 270.—BD., B. N. A. 1858, 30.—SUMICH., Mem. Bost. Soc. i, 1869, 550 (Vera Cruz).—LAWR., Ann. Lyc. 1861, 331 (Panama); ix, 1868, 99 (Costa Rica).—GUNDL., Rep. 238 (Cuba).—ALLEN, Bull. M. C. Z. iii, 1872, 175 (Eastern Kansas).—SNOW, B. Kans. 1873, 5.—COUES, Key, 1872, 111; and of late writers.
Phœnisoma rubra, SW., Birds, ii, 1837, 284.
Phœnicosoma rubra, CAB., Mus. Hein. i, 1850, 24.
Pyranga erythromelas, VIEILL., Enc. Met. 800; Nouv. Dict. xxviii, 293.

Hab.—Eastern United States and British provinces (north to 59°, *Richardson*). West to Kansas and Indian Territory only. Breeds at large through its United States range; none winter. South in winter through Mexico and Central America, to Ecuador. Cuba. Jamaica.

The Missouri extension of this species is very limited, probably not reaching above Leavenworth.

The egg of the Scarlet Tanager is pale dull greenish, minutely freckled all over with light reddish-brown, the markings often aggregated into a wreath around the larger end. Size about 0.90 by 0.65.

PYRANGA ÆSTIVA, (Gm.) Vieill.

Summer Redbird.

a. *æstiva.*

Muscicapa rubra, LINN., Syst. Nat. i, 1766, 326.
Tanagra æstiva, GM., Syst. Nat. i, 1788, 889.—WILS., Am. Orn. i, 95, pl. 6, f. 3.—BP., Syn. 1828, 105.—NUTT., Man. i, 1832, 469.—AUD., Orn. Biog. i, 1831, 232; v, 1839, 518, pl. 44.
Pyranga æstiva, VIEILL., Enc. Met. 799; Nouv. Dict. xxviii, 291.—BP., P. Z. S. 1837, 117; List, 1838, 35; Consp. i, 1850, 241.—LINS., Am. Journ. xliv, 1848, 261 (Connecticut).—WOODH., Sitgr. Rep. 1853, 82.—SCL., P. Z. S. 1855, 156 (Bogota); 1856, 123 (Cuba, Jamaica); 142, 303 (Cordova); 1858, 73 (Ecuador); 358 (Honduras); 1859, 364 (Xalapa); 377 (Oaxaca); 1860, 293; Cat. 1862, 80.—SCL. & SALV., Ibis, 1859, 15 (Guatemala); P. Z. S. 1867, 278 (Mosquito coast); 1870, 836.—TAYLOR, Ibis, 1860, 111.—PUTN., Pr. Ess. Inst. i, 1866, 224.—BD., B. N. A. 1858, 301.—CAB., J. f. O. 1860, 329 (Costa Rica).—ALLEN, Pr. Ess. Inst. iv, 1864, 83.—COUES, Pr. Ess. Inst. v, 1868, 275.—LAWR., Ann. Lyc. vii, 1861, 297 (Panama); viii, 1865, 176 (New Granada); ix, 1868, 99 (Costa Rica).—RIDGW., Pr. Phila. Acad. 1869, 130 ("to Nova Scotia").—SUMICH., Mem. Bost. Soc. i, 1869, 548 (Vera Cruz).—SNOW, B. Kans. 1873, 5.—MAYN., Guide, 1870, 109 (Massachusetts).—COUES, Key, 1872, 111, fig. 52ª; plate ii, figs. 19, 20; and of late writers.

b. *cooperi.*

Pyranga æstiva, COOP., Pr. Cal. Acad. 1861, 122.—COUES, Pr. Phila. Acad. 1866, 71 (refers to one of Dr. Cooper's specimens, afterward called *cooperi* by Mr. Ridgway).
Pyranga hepatica, COUES, Pr. Phila. Acad. 1866, 71 (excl. syn. In part. Intended to indicate the true *hepatica*, but erroneously included my Rio Grande specimens, afterward made types of *P. cooperi*).
Pyranga cooperi, RIDGW., Pr. Phila. Acad. 1869, 130 (Rocky Mountains).—COOP., B. Cal. i, 1870, 142.
Pyranga æstiva var. *cooperi*, COUES, Key, 1872, 111, fig. 52ᵇ.

Hab.—The typical form from the Eastern United States, north to Connecticut (*Linsley*) and Massachusetts (*Jillson*, quoted by Putnam, Allen, Coues, and Maynard; straggling even to Nova Scotia, *Ridgway, loc. cit.* spec. in Mus. Smiths.). West to Kansas and the Indian Territory. South through a part of the West Indies (Cuba; Jamaica) and Eastern Mexico to Central America, New Granada, Ecuador, and Peru. Var. *cooperi* from Southern Middle Province, latitude 35°. South through Western Mexico.

This species, like the last, merely reaches the eastern extremity of the Missouri region. With a range generally coincident with that of *P. rubra*, the Summer Redbird is somewhat more southerly, being rare or casual even in Southern New England, beyond which I have found no record, excepting Mr. Ridgway's citation, based on a specimen in the Smithsonian, of "Nova Scotia." The bird breeds throughout its United States range, but wholly withdraws from this country in winter, penetrating very far south.

As stated in the Key, *Pyranga cooperi* is not a tenable species, but may be recognized as a geographical race. In Cooper's late work, "*Pyranga hepatica*, Coues," is cited as synonymous, but is so only in part. I included, under the head of *hepatica*, page 71 of the Academy's Proceedings for 1866, my Rio Grande specimens, afterward made types of var. *cooperi*; but this is simply a mistake, not to be held to overbalance the rest of my notice, which was based on *hepatica* proper, as shown by the synonyms adduced.

The egg of the Summer Redbird is not distinguishable with certainty from that of the Scarlet Tanager, though it averages rather larger. It also closely resembles that of the Rose-breasted Grosbeak.

PYRANGA LUDOVICIANA, (Wils.) Bp.

Louisiana Tanager.

Tanagra ludoviciana, WILS., Am. Orn. iii, 1811, 27, pl. 22, fig. 1.—AUD., Orn. Biog. iv, 1838, 385; v, 1839, 90, pl. 354, 400. (Name geographically inappropriate.)
Tanagra (*Pyranga*) *ladoviciana*, BP., Syn. 1828, 105.—NUTT., Man. i, 1832, 471.
Pyranga ludoviciana, BP.—AUD., Syn. 1839, 137.—AUD., B. Am. iii, 1841, 211, pl. 210.—
      SCL., P. Z. S. 1856, 125.—BD., B. N. A. 1858, 303.—HEERM., P. R. R. Rep. x, 1859,
      52.—COOP. & SUCK., N. H. Wash. Ter. 1860, 182.—SCL., P. Z. S. 1856, 125 (Guatemala); 1859, 377 (Oaxaca); 1857, 213 (Orizaba); 1862, 19 (Parada, Mex.);
      Ibis, 1859, 15 (Guatemala).—COUES, Pr. Phila. Acad. 1866, 71.—COOP., Am. Nat.
      iii, 1869, 33.—COOP., B. Cal. 1870, 145.—SUMICH., Mem. Bost. Soc. i, 1869, 550
      (Vera Cruz).—ALLEN, Bull. M. C. Z. 1872, 175.—AIKEN, Pr. Bost. Soc. 1872, 198
      (Colorado).—COUES, Key, 1872, 112.—MERR., U. S. Geol. Surv. Ter. 1872, 678.
Pyranga erythropis, VIEILL., Nouv. Dict. d'Hist. Nat. xxviii, 1819, 291.

Hab.—Upper Missouri and eastern foot-hills of the Rocky Mountains to the Pacific. Mexico. South to Guatemala. Not north of the United States?

List of specimens.

19207	22	Wind River ...	♂	May 24, 1860	F. V. Hayden.	6.25	11.00	3.75
19208	80	Snake River...	....	June 18, 1860	...... do	6.50	10.50	3.75
19334	....	Pryor's Fork...	♂	June 22, 1860	G. H. Trook...	6.75	11.25	3.75
19335	....	.... do	....	..... do	...... do	6.75	11.25	3.75

Lieutenant Warren's Expedition.—8822, Black Hills; 8823, Laramie Peak.
Later Expeditions.—61662, Wyoming; 61663, Utah; 62278–86, Idaho.

The elegant Louisiana Tanager has been ascertained to breed in the vicinity of Laramie Peak, where several examples have been procured in a higher state of plumage than that usually described as adult—the whole head and throat intense scarlet, the middle of the back pure black, and the rump rich chrome-yellow. Dr. Hayden's specimens are also interesting in establishing an extreme limit of the species, as far as now known. It has been more recently taken by Mr. Allen, in the mountains of Colorado, from the plains up to about 8,000 feet. I found the bird in the mountains of Arizona, where it was a rather rare summer resident from the middle of April until the end of September; and I have no doubt that it breeds about Fort Whipple, although I did not succeed in establishing the fact. The birds were exclusively confined to the pine forests; in their manners they appeared to me to closely resemble the eastern species. Dr. Cooper noticed the arrival of this species near San Diego, in small parties, on the 24th of April, and states that they reach Puget Sound about May 15th. "The males," he remarks, "come some time in advance, clothed in their full summer livery, and are more bold and conspicuous than the females, which are rarely seen without close watching. They frequent trees, feeding on insects and berries, and singing much in the same manner as the other species." He continues: "I saw none of them in the coast range toward Santa Cruz, or at Santa Barbara, in summer, and suppose that they must seek the higher and more northern regions at that season. I found this species in September, 1860, in the higher Rocky Mountains, near the sources of the Columbia, in latitude 47°, and they probably remain until October within this State. * * * I saw none along the Colorado Valley, probably because they migrate more on the line of the mountain ranges."

Dr. George Suckley has given an interesting account: "The beautiful Louisiana Tanager is quite abundant in certain seasons in the vicinity of Fort Steilacoom. In 1854 but a limited number made their appearance, while, on the contrary, in the summer of 1856, I could readily have obtained a hundred specimens. I have had frequent opportunities of studying their habits, and have never yet seen them descend to the low bushes or the ground, as stated by Nuttall, the reverse being the rule (at least at Puget Sound); the difficulty being generally to find the bird sufficiently low down on fir-tree branches to allow fine shot to reach it with any degree of certainty. * * * The favorite habitat of the species, in those localities where I have observed it, is among the tall, red fir-trees belonging to that magnificent species, the *Abies douglasii*. They seemingly prefer the edges of the forest, rarely retiring to its depths unless for concealment when alarmed. In early summer, at Fort Steilacoom, they are generally seen during the middle of the day sunning themselves in the firs, occasionally darting from one of these trees to another, or to some of the neighboring white-oaks (*Q. garryana*) on the prairies. Later in the season they may be seen very actively flying about in quest of insect food for their young. On July 10, 1856, I saw one of these birds carrying a worm or insect in its mouth, from which I inferred that the young were then hatched out. Both sexes, during the breeding season, are much less shy; the males, during the day-time, frequently sitting on some low limb, rendering the scene joyous with their delightful melody."

The stomach of a specimen examined by Dr. Suckley contained insects, principally *Coleoptera*, among them many fragments of a large *Buprestis*, found generally on the Douglas fir-trees.

Mr. Allen writes to me, that "the Louisiana Tanager is the only representative of the *Tanagridæ* I observed at any point west of Eastern Kansas. In Colorado it occurs from the plains up to about 8,000 feet in the mountains, about the base of which it may be regarded as a rather common species. In song and general habits it strikingly resembles the Scarlet Tanager of the East, its song, in fact, being scarcely distinguishable from that of the eastern bird."

A set of eggs taken in the Uintah Mountains, July 7, 1869, by Mr.

Ridgway, are noticeably different from those of the other species of this genus, being a much clearer green, and more sparingly dotted with mere points of very dark purplish-brown. A few specks are sprinkled over the whole surface, but the tendency is to aggregate just at the larger end, where the spots, though so numerous, preserve their distinctness. In size and shape the eggs are not very different from those of *P. rubra*, though perhaps averaging a little larger and especially thicker. The nidification is essentially the same.

Family HIRUNDINIDÆ: Swallows.

HIRUNDO HORREORUM, Barton.

American Barn Swallow.

a. *erythrogaster.*

Hirundo erythrogaster, Bodd., P. E. 1783, pl. 724.—Scl., Cat. Am. Birds, 1862, 39; P. Z. S. 1867, 340.
Hirundo rufa, Gm., Syst. Nat. i, 1788, 1018.—Bp., Consp. i, 1850, 339 (in part).—Burm., Syst. Ueb. iii, 148.
Hirundo cyanopyrrha, Vieill., Nouv. Dict. 1817, 510; Ency. Meth. ii, 1823, 528.

b. *horreorum.*

Hirundo rufa, Vieill., Ois. Am. Sept. i, 1807, 60, pl. 30.—Bp., Syn. 1828, 64; List, 1838, 9.—Nutt., Man. i, 1832, 601.—Woodh., Sitgr. Rep. 1853, 64.—Cass., Ill. 1855, 243.—Cab., J. f. O. iv, 1856, 3 (Cuba).—Brew., N. A. O. i, 1857, 91, pl. 5, figs. 63–67.—Reinh., Ibis, iii, 1861, 5 (Greenland).—Gundl., J. f. O. 1861, 328 (Cuba).
Hirundo horreorum, Bart., Frag. N. H. Pa. 1799, 17.—Bd., B. N. A. 1858, 308; Rev. 1865, 294.—Scl. & Salv., Ibis, i, 1859, 13 (Guatemala).—Newt., Ibis, i, 1859, 63 (Santa Cruz, migratory).—Lawr., Ann. Lyc. N. Y. 1861, 310 (Panama); 1864, 98 (Sombrero).—Sumich., Mem. Bost. Soc. i, 1869, 547 (Vera Cruz).—Gundl., Ofv. 1869, 584 (St. Bartholomew).—Salv., P. Z. S. 1870, 184 (Veragua).—Hayd., Rep. 1862, 161.—Coop. & Suck., N. H. Wash. Ter. 1860, 184.—Coues, Pr. Phila. Acad. 1866, 72 (Arizona).—Coop., Am. Nat. iii, 1869, 33 (Montana).—Dall & Bann., Tr. Chic. Acad. i, 1869, 279 (Alaska).—Coop., B. Cal. i, 1870, 103.—Finsch, Abh. Nat. iii, 1872, 28 (Alaska).—Merr., U. S. Geol. Surv. Ter. 1872, 676.—Allen, Bull. M. C. Z. iii, 1872, 176 (Colorado, up to timber-line).—Coues, Key, 1872, 113, fig. 54.—Snow, B. Kans. 1873, 5; and of late United States writers.
Hirundo americana, Wils., Am. Orn. v, 1812, 34, pl. 8, f. 1, 2.—Sw. & Rich., F. B. A. ii, 1831, 329.—Lemb., Aves Cubæ, 1850, 44, pl. 7, f. 2.
Hirundo rustica, Aud., Orn. Biog. ii, 1834, 413, pl. 173; Syn. 1839, 35; B. Am. i, 1840, 181, pl. 48.—Giraud, B. L. I. 1844, 35.—Jones, Nat. Berm. 34.

Hab.—Var. *horreorum;* North and Middle America. North to Alaska. Greenland. West Indies. *H. erythrogaster* is the South American form.
Lieutenant Warren's Expedition.—5206–8, Yellowstone River.
Later Expeditions.—62295–6, Lower Geyser Basin, Wyoming.
Not obtained by Captain Raynolds' Expedition.
In the above heading this species is retained under the name given in the Key, and used by nearly all later American writers, although there is no probability that it is specifically distinct from the South American form, *H. erythrogaster*. The synonymy is distinguished above, for convenience, and our species may stand as *H. erythrogaster* var. *horreorum*, though even the varietal distinctions are very slight.

The Barn Swallow occurs throughout the Missouri region, especially during the migrations, and breeds in suitable localities, although it is much less numerous than it is in most wooded and settled parts of the country. It appears to withdraw altogether from the United States in winter, though a few Swallows are usually among the earliest arrivals, in southern portions, even in February. Their great powers of flight enable them to pass rapidly from one country to another, according to the exigencies of the weather.
There is no occasion here to enter into details of the well-known nidi-

fication and eggs of our Swallows. I will indicate the general character. In *Hirundo* and *Petrochelidon* the eggs are alike spotted, heavily and sharply, upon a white ground, with various reddish-brown and darker brown shades. In *Tachycineta bicolor* and *thalassina*, in *Cotyle* and *Stelgidopteryx*, and in *Progne purpurea*, the eggs are pure white, unmarked.

TACHYCINETA BICOLOR, (Vieill.) Cab.

White-bellied Swallow.

Hirundo bicolor, VIEILL., Ois. Am. Sept. i, 1807, 61, pl. 31.—BP., Syn. 1828, 65.—AUD., Orn. Biog. i, 1831, 491; v, 417; pl. 98; Syn. 1839, 35; B. Am. i, 1840, 175, pl. 46.—NUTT., Man. i, 1832, p. —.—GIRAUD, B. L. I. 1844, 36.—LEMB., Aves Cubæ, 1850, 46.—WOODH., Sitgr. Rep. 1853, 65.—CASS., Ill. 1855, 244.—NEWB., P. R. R. Rep. vi, 1857, 78.—BREW., N. A. O. i, 1857, 100, pl. 4 (egg).—BD., B. N. A. 1858, 310; Rev. 1865, 297.—COOP. & SUCK., N. H. Wash. Ter. 1860, 185.—JONES, Nat. Berm. 34.—LORD, Pr. Roy. Arty. Inst. iv, 1864, 15 (British Columbia).—DALL & BANN., Tr. Chic. Acad. i, 1869, 279 (Alaska).—COOP., B. Cal. i, 1870, 106.— FINSCH, Abh. Nat. iii, 1872, 29 (Alaska).—COUES, Pr. Phila. Acad. 1871, 21 (North Carolina, in January).—ALLEN, Bull. M. C. Z. iii, 1872, 176 (up to timber-line).—TRIPPE, Pr. Bost. Soc. xv, 1872, 235 (Iowa).—HART., Br. Birds, 1872, 125 (accidental in England).—SNOW, B. Kans. 1873, 5; and of most writers.
Chelidon bicolor, LESS.—BP., List, 1838, 8.
Tachycineta bicolor, CAB., Mus. Hein., 1850, 48; J. f. O. iv, 1856, 5 (Cuba).—GUNDL., J. f. O. 1861, 330 (Cuba).—SUMICH., Mem. Bost. Soc. i, 1869, 547 (plateau of Mexico).— ALLEN, Bull. M. C. Z. ii, 1871, 269 (Florida, in winter).—COUES, Key, 1872, 113.
Herse bicolor, BP. Consp. Av. i, 1850, 341.
Petrochelidon bicolor, SCL., P. Z. S. 1857, 201; 1859, 364 (Xalapa); Cat. 1862, 40.—SCL. & SALV:, Ibis, i, 1859, 13 (Guatemala).
Hirundo viridis, WILS., Am. Orn. v, 1812, 49, pl. 38.
"*Chelidon viridis*, BOIE, 1826." (*Bp.*)
Hirundo leucogaster, STEPH., Shaw's Gen. Zool. x, 1817, 105.
Chelidon leucogastra, BOIE, Isis, 1844, 171.

Hab.—Temperate North America. North to Great Slave Lake and Alaska. Mexico, in summer. South to Guatemala. Cuba. Bermudas. Accidental in England (*Wolley*, Zoologist, 1858, 3806; *Newton, ibid.* 1860, 7145; P. Z. S. 1860, 131). Breeds in most of its United States range. Winters in Florida, Cuba, and Central America.
Not noticed by the Expeditions.

The White-bellied Swallow appears to be rarer in the Missouri region than the other species are, or than it is in most other parts of the United States, much of the country being not well suited to its wants. It is occasionally seen in the Southern States in midwinter, as in the instances above given.

TACHYCINETA THALASSINA, (Sw.) Cab.

Violet-green Swallow.

Hirundo thalassina, Sw., Phil. Mag. i, 1827, 365.—BP., List, 1838, 9.—AUD., Orn. Biog. iv, 1838, 597, pl. 385; Syn. 1839, 36; B. Am. i, 1840, 186, pl. 49.—WOODH., Sitgr. Rep. 1853, 64.—CASS., B. Cal. and Tex. i, 1855, 245.—BREW., N. A. Oöl. i, 1857, 102 (not the fig.!).—NEWB., P. R. R. Rep. vi, 1857, 78.—BD., B. N. A. 1858, 311; Rev. 1865, 299.—MAXIM., J. f. O, 1858, 101.—HEERM., P. R. R. Rep. x, 1859, 36.— COOP. & SUCK., N. H. Wash. Ter. 1859, 185.—LORD, Pr. Roy. Arty. Inst. Wool. iv, 1864, 115 (British Columbia).—COUES, Pr. Phila. Acad. 1866, 72 (Arizona).— COOP., Pr. Cal. Acad. 1870, 75; B. Cal. ii, 1871, 107.—ALLEN, Bull. M. C. Z. iii, 1872, 149 (Colorado, up to 8,000 feet).
"*Cecropis thalassina*, LESS."
Chelidon thalassina, BOIE, Isis, 1844, 171.
Herse thalassina, BP., Consp. Av. i, 1850, 341.
Tachycineta thalassina, CAB., Mus. Hein. 1850. 48.—SUMICH., Mem. Bost. Soc. i, 1869, 547 (Vera Cruz, abundant, breeds).—MERR., U. S. Geol. Surv. Ter. 1872, 676.— COUES, Key, 1872, 113.
Petrochelidon thalassina, SCL. & SALV., Ibis, 1859, 13 (Guatemala).—SCL., Cat. 1861, 39.— SCL., P. Z. S. 1864, 173 (city of Mexico).

Hab.—Middle and Western Provinces. North to British America. South through Mexico to Guatemala.

List of specimens.

19208	31	Wind River...	♂	May 26, 1860	F. V. Hayden.	4.75	12.75	4.75
19210	15	...... do	♂	..... do	...... do	5.25	12.50	4.75
19211	14	...... do	♂	..... do	...... do	5.25	12.25	4.50
19350	....	G. Bull Creek.	♂	June 7, 1860	G. H. Trook ..	5.00	12.00	4.50
19351	....	...... do	♂	June 5, 1860	...... do	5.25	12.00	4.75

Not obtained by Lieutenant Warren's Expedition.
Later Expeditions.—61665, Utah.

A fine series of this lovely Swallow was procured by Captain Reynolds, and its eggs are also in the collection. The locality is apparently at about the northeast limit of distribution of the species. It does not appear to be recorded north of Washington Territory and Vancouver. In winter it retires beyond the United States, reaching to Guatemala. Its breeding range appears to comprise all suitable localities in that portion of the United States it occupies, as well as parts of Mexico; to the southward, it chiefly occupies elevated and wooded situations. I found it abundant in the Raton Mountains of New Mexico, in June; it was then doubtless breeding. In Arizona, as I have already recorded (*l. c.*), it is very abundant, being the characteristic Swallow of the pine regions, where it breeds; it arrives at Fort Whipple about the 20th of March, and remains until late in September. Dr. Cooper noticed its arrival in the Santa Clara Valley, California, as early as March 15th, and further observes that it "frequents chiefly the groves of oaks along the sides of the valleys and across the whole coast range, excepting the windy and cold neighborhood of the sea. They range at least as far north as the Straits of Fuca, and across the interior to the eastern base of the Rocky Mountains." Dr. Suckley reports its arrival at Puget Sound about the 10th of May. Mr. Allen found it in July and August, in Colorado, in the Garden of the Gods, about Castle Rock, and at Lake Pass.

A well known and often recorded point in the economy of the Swallows, is the readiness with which they modify their ways of nesting according to circumstances. Those species, like the Barn Swallow, the White-bellied and Cliff Swallows, and the Purple Martin, which inhabit populous countries, have almost completely changed their modes of nidification, now breeding in the convenient places afforded by buildings, or in shelters expressly provided for their use. In the case of the Cliff Swallows, the change is of very recent date, and many records are preserved of the precise time when, in particular localities, the birds deserted cliffs to build under eaves, or when, adopting this habit, they appeared and bred in places where they were before unknown. With the Purple Martins the modification occurred earlier, and I am not aware that the time is recorded. But in the west both these birds still adhere to their primitive ways. Along the Missouri I saw great numbers of nests of Cliff Swallows stuck in batches on the high vertical water-worn exposures; and in Arizona the Martins occupied the blasted tops of tall pine-trees, in colonies, having driven off the Woodpeckers, rightful proprietors of the holes that riddled the trunks. It becomes an interesting speculation whether the Bank Swallow will ever abandon its burrows, and so far modify its fossorial nature as to build in chinks and crannies, or affix a nest anywhere about a building. As far as is now known, the Violet-green Swallow retains its primitive habits, but the same easy adaptability to varying circumstances may be observed in this case, warranting the inference that before long it will accept the conditions that civilization imposes, and breed about buildings like its allies.

At Fort Whipple the Violet-green Swallows resided during the summer in small, loose colonies, in high, open pine woods, preferably about the edges of the timber. They could not contest with the Woodpeckers, as the Martins did, for recent holes, but they occupied deserted ones, as well as knot-holes or other crannies in the trees. According to Dr. Cooper, on the Pacific coast they frequent the high prairies bordered with *oaks* and other deciduous trees, breeding in knot-holes or in deserted Woodpeckers' holes. Mr. Allen found them breeding in holes in the *rocks*. Mr. Nuttall states, on the authority of Mr. Townsend, that along the Columbia River they used to breed in the deserted nests of the Cliff Swallow.

The speckled egg figured and described by Dr. Brewer, as of this species, has since been ascertained to belong to another. The eggs are four or five in number, and pure white, like those of the Bank Swallow.

According to Mr. Allen's manuscript, "the Violet-green Swallow, the most delicately and brilliantly colored of our *Hirundines*, was met with in considerable abundance in Colorado, from the base of the mountains up to about 8,000 or 10,000 feet. Like the White-bellied Swallow, it lives generally in colonies, a considerable number of pairs commonly breeding in the same vicinity. We met with several such colonies on our route from Denver to South Park, but as we also passed long distances during the same journey without meeting with the species at all, it is probably to be regarded as rather locally distributed. They appear to generally nest in abandoned Woodpeckers' holes, but at the "Garden of the Gods," and on the "divide" between Denver and Colorado City, we found them breeding in holes in the rocks, at the former locality, in company with the Rocky Mountain Swift (*Panyptila saxatilis*)."

Since writing the foregoing I have received the desired evidence of the change of nidification of this species, above noted as to be expected. Referring to Idaho Springs, Clear County, Colorado, Mr. Trippe informs me that the Violet-green Swallow is abundant, *nesting under the eaves of houses*, like the Cliff Swallow, and also in hollow trees. "It arrives," he adds, "toward the close of May, and soon becomes numerous, up to an altitude of 10,500 feet, occasionally even venturing higher. It disappears from the higher regions in August, and in September leaves the country."

PETROCHELIDON LUNIFRONS, (Say.) Scl.

Cliff Swallow; Eave Swallow.

Hirundo lunifrons, SAY, Long's Exp. ii, 1823, 47.—WOODH., Sitgr. Rep. 1853, 64.—CASS., Ill. 1855, 243.—BREW., N. A. O. i, 1857, 94, pl. 5, figs. 68–73.—NEWB., P. R. R. Rep. vi, 1851, 78.—BD., B. N. A. 1858, 309.—COOP. & SUCK., N. H. Wash. Ter. 1860, 124.—LAWR., Ann. Lyc. N. Y. 1861, 317 (Panama, winter).—HAYD., Rep. 1862, 161.—LORD, Pr. Arty. Inst. Wool. iv, 1864, 16 (British Columbia).—VERR., Pr. Bost. Soc. 1864, 276 (biogr.).—DALL & BANN., Tr. Chic. Acad. i, 1869, 279 (Alaska).—COOP., Am. Nat. iii, 1869, 33 (Missouri, "in swarms"); B. Cal. 1870, 104.—STEV., U. S. Geol. Surv. Ter. 1870, 463 (Wyoming).—ALLEN, Bull. M. C. Z. iii, 1872, 176 (Colorado, up to timber-line).—TRIPPE, Pr. Bost. Soc. xv, 1872, 235 (Iowa).—SNOW, B. Kans. 1873, 5; and of most writers.
Petrochelidon lunifrons, SCL., Cat. A. B. 1862, 40.—BD., Rev. 1865, 288.—COUES, Key, 1872, 114.—HOLD., Pr. Bost. Soc. xv, 1872, 197 (Black Hills).—MERR., U. S. Geol. Surv. Ter. 182, 676 (Idaho).
Hirundo opifex, CLINT., Ann. Lyc. N. Y. i, 1824, 161.
Hirundo respublicana, AUD., Ann. Lyc. N. Y. i, 1824, 164.
Hirundo fulva, BP., Am. Orn. i, 1825, 63, pl. 7, f. 1; Syn. 1828, 64; List, 1838, 9.—NUTT., Man. i, 1832, 603.—AUD., Orn. Biog. i, 1831, 353, pl. 58; Syn. 1839, 35; B. Am.

i, 1840, 177, pl. 47.—GIRAUD, B. L. I. 1844, 38.—MAXIM., J. f. O. vi, 1858, 100.—
HEERM., P. R. R. Rep. x, 1859, pt. vi, 36.
Herse fulva, BP., Consp. Av. i, 1850, 341 (in part).
Hirundo melanogaster, SW., Phil. Mag. i, 1827, 336 (Mexico).
Petrochelidon melanogastra, CAB., Mus. Hein. i, 1850, 47.
Petrochelidon swainsoni, SCL., P. Z. S. 1858, 296; 1859, 376; Cat. A. B. 1862, 40.—BD.,
Rev. 1865, 290.—SUMICH., Mem. Bost. Soc. i, 1869, 547 (Vera Cruz).

Hab.—North America at large, breeding almost throughout, in suitable places.
Mexico. South to Panama. Not West Indian.

List of specimens.

| 19212 | 93 | Smith's Fork . | ..... | June 7, 1860 | F. V. Hayden. | 5.50 | 11.50 | 4.25 |

Lieutenant Warren's Expedition.—4776-80, Bijoux Hills.
Later Expeditions.—60420-3, Wyoming; 61774, Idaho.
Without present opportunity of direct comparison of several closely related species
or varieties of the West Indies and South America, the above synonymy is made only
with reference to the North American bird, and the Mexican, which is certainly not
distinct. The differences assigned to *swainsoni,* in both size and shade of color, are
found in every sufficient series of the North American bird; thus, of two specimens,
both shot at Washington, D. C., one has a whitish and the other a brown frontlet. I
scarcely think that even varietal distinction can be predicated in this case. The West
Indian form (true *fulva* of Vieillot) appears to constitute all insular race worthy of recognition, in lacking the steel-blue pectoral spot, and in other features. But there
seems to be little probability of its proving not to intergrade with *lunifrons.*

Prof. Verrill has recently elucidated some interesting facts relative to
the distribution of this species, substantiating its occurrence in Eastern
North America, long before the time when it was erroneously supposed
to have immigrated from the west. My present belief in the matter is,
that the Cliff Swallow is, and always has been, amenable to the ordinary
laws of migration, and spread over nearly all of North America, the
South Atlantic States perhaps excepted. The numerous recorded dates
of its appearance and breeding in particular localities, merely mark the
times when the birds forsook their natural breeding places and built
under eaves, which enabled them to pass the summer where formerly
they were unable to breed for want of suitable accommodations.

Dr. Hayden notices the abundance of this species along the Missouri,
and of its nests on the vertical sides of the river bluffs: "Near the
mouth of the Niobrara River, the chalk bluffs and cretaceous formation
No. 3 form lofty vertical walls, which are sometimes completely covered
with their nests." In passing up the river last year, I noticed the same
thing. Mr. Allen's observations are correspondent: He says it is "a
common inhabitant of the central plateau of the continent, throughout
which extensive region small colonies may be observed breeding on the
rocky escarpments of the plains and in the mountains. It, however,
even here manifests its preference for the eaves of buildings for nesting
sites, and wherever settlements occur it soon abandons its ancient cliffs
for these apparently more congenial locations. This species and the
White-bellied Swallow were the most common *Hirundines* in South Park,
and both these species and the Barn Swallow were observed in fine
weather coursing above the tree-line summits of the Snowy Range."

COTYLE RIPARIA, (Linn.) Boie.

Bank Swallow.

Hirundo riparia, LINN., Syst. Nat. i, 1766, 344.—GM., Syst. Nat. i, 1788, 1019.—LATH.,
Ind. Orn. ii, 1790, 575.—WILS., Am. Orn. v, 46, pl. 38.—BP., Syn. 1828, 65; List,
1838, 9.—SW. & RICH., F. B. A. ii, 1831, 333.—NUTT., Man. i, 1832, 607.—AUD.,
Orn. Biog. iv, 1838, 584, pl. 385; Syn. 1839, 36; B. Am. i, 1840, 187, pl. 50.—

GIR., B. L. I. 1844, 37.—LEMB., Aves Cubæ, 1850, 47, pl. 7, f. 3.—JONES, Nat. Berm.
    34.—FOWLER, Am. Nat. iii, 1869, 116; and of earlier authors generally.
Hirundo riparia americana, MAXIM., J. f. O. vi, 1858, 101.
Cotyle riparia, BOIE, Isis, 1822, 550.—BP., Consp. Av. 1850, 342.—WOODH., Sitgr. Rep.
    1853, 65.—CASS., Ill. 1855, 247.—CAB., J. f. O. 1856, 4 (Cuba).—NEWB., P. R. R.
    Rep. vi, 1857, 78.—BREW., N. Am. Oöl. 1857, 105, pl. 4, f. 49.—BD., B. N. A. 1858,
    313; Rev. 1865, 319.—HEERM., P. R. R. Rep. x, 1859, pt. vi, 36.—GUNDL., J. f.
    O. 1861 (330).—HAYD., Rep. 1862, 162.—MARCH, Pr. Phila. Acad. 1863, 297 (Ja-
    maica).—DALL & BANN., Tr. Chic. Acad. i, 1869, 280 (Alaska).—COUES, Pr.
    Phila. Acad. 1866, 72 (Arizona).—COOP., B. Cal. i, 1870, 110 (California).—ALLEN,
    Bull. M. C. Z. ii, 1871, 269 (Florida, in winter); iii, 1872, 176.—TRIPPE, Pr. Bost.
    Soc. 1872, 235.—AIKEN, *ibid.* 198.—MERR., U. S. Geol. Surv. Ter. 1872, 677.—
    SNOW, B. Kans. 1873, 5.—COUES, KEY, 1872, 114; and of nearly all late writers.
Hirundo cinerea, VIEILL., Nouv. Dict. d'Hist. Nat. xiv, 1817, 526.
Cotyle fluviatilis et microrhynchos, BREHM, Vög. Deutschl. i, 142, 143.

Hab.—Europe. The whole of North America. Bermudas. Cuba. Jamaica. Breeds
throughout the greater part of its North American range. Winters from the southern
coast southward. Not common on the Pacific side. Brazil (*Pelz.*, Orn. Braz. i, 18.

List of specimens.

| 19213 | 64 | Wind River... | ♀ | May 26, 1860 | F. V. Hayden. | 5.00 | 10.75 | 4.00 |

Lieutenant Warren's Expedition.—5209–10, Yellowstone.
Later Expeditions.—61664, Utah.
Notable as one of the few species of *Oscines*, American and European specimens of
which are absolutely identical.

Ascending the Missouri in the spring of 1864, I saw thousands of these
birds along the banks, which were, in suitable places, riddled with their
holes. Again, in the fall of 1872, higher up the river, I observed multitudes of their deserted nests, often in the soft ground capping the bluffs
where, a little below, the bottle-shaped nests of the Cliff Swallows were
fastened in great masses.

STELGIDOPTERYX SERRIPENNIS, (Aud.) Bd.

Rough-winged Swallow.

Hirundo serripennis, AUD., Orn. Biog. iv, 1838, 593; Syn. 1839, 37; B. A. i, 1840, 193, pl. 51.
Cotyle serripennis, BP., Consp. Av. i, 1850, 342.—CASS., Ill. i, 1855, 247.—BREW., N. A.
    Oöl. i, 1857, 106, pl. 4, f. 50.—BD., B. N. A. 1858, 313.—HEERM., P. R. R. Rep. x,
    1859, pt. vi, 36.—KENN., *ibid.* pt. iv, 24.—NEWB., *ibid.* vi, 1857, 79.—COOP. &
    SUCK., N. H. Wash. Ter. 1860, 186.—SCL., Cat. A. B. 1862, 41; (?) P. Z. S. 1856,
    285 (Cordova); (?) 1859, 364 (Jalapa)—(?) SCL. & SALV., Ibis, i, 1859, 13 (Gua-
    temala), 126.—(?) OWEN, Ibis, iii, 1861, 61 (Guatemala)—LORD, Pr. Roy. Arty.
    Inst. iv, 1864, 116 (British Columbia).—COOP., Pr. Cal. Acad. 1870, 75; B. Cal.
    1870, 110.—ALLEN, Bull. M. C. Z. iii, 1872, 176 (Kansas and Utah).—SNOW,
    B. Kans. 1873, 5 (common).
Stelgidopteryx serripennis, BD., Rev. 1865, 316.—COUES, Pr. Phila. Acad. 1866, 72 (Arizona);
    Key, 1872, 114.

Hab.—United States, from Atlantic to Pacific, excepting perhaps New England.
British Columbia. South into Mexico (? to Guatemala; compare *C. fulvipennis*, SCL.,
P. Z. S. 1859, 364; Ibis, 1860, 31).
Not obtained by any of the Expeditions.
It appears to me improbable that the *Cotyle fulvipennis*, based on a young bird, is distinct from the present species. My Arizona birds-of-the-year, as described (*l. c.*), seem
to answer the description of *fulvipennis*, though they have subsequently been found
inseparable from *serripennis*. It would not be surprising, indeed, if it proved necessary
to unite the several supposed species described from Central and South America, and
Mexico. The ascribed characters seem very slight, and of a kind readily accounted
for by differences in sex, age, and season of the specimens examined, with, of course,
discrepancies due to climatic influences. A series will probably be established of several geographical races.

This species was not noticed by any of the Expeditions, but its known
range includes the Missouri region. It is stated to be common in Kan-

sas, where it breeds. I found it breeding in the mountains of Arizona, where it arrives late in April, and remains through the greater part of September. Dr. Heermann records its breeding in Texas; Mr. Allen notes its occurrence, in summer, in different parts of the west; Drs. Cooper and Suckley found it from May to August near the Columbia River. These records, joined with those we have from the Eastern States, show that the species, like other Swallows, has a breeding range about co-extensive with its dispersion in the United States. In some places it is stated to burrow, like the Bank Swallow, in soft earth; elsewhere it has been found breeding about the piers and abutments of bridges, &c.

PROGNE PURPUREA, (Linn.) Boie.

Purple Martin.

Hirundo subis, LINN., Syst. Nat. i, 10th ed. 1758, 192; 12th ed. 1766, 344.
Progne subis, BD., Rev. 1865, 274.—COUES, Pr. Phila. Acad. 1866, 72; Pr. Ess. Inst. v, 1868, 276.—SUMICH., Mem. Bost. Soc. i, 1869, 547 (Orizaba).—STEV., U. S. Geol. Surv. Ter. 1870, 463.—ALLEN, Bull. M. C. Z. iii, 1872, 56.
Hirundo purpurea, LINN., Syst. Nat. i, 1766, 344.—GM., Syst. Nat. i, 1788, 1020.—LATH., Ind. Orn. ii, 1790, 578.—WILS., Am. Orn. v, 58, pl. 39, f. 2, 3.—BP., Syn. 1828, 64.—AUD., Orn. Biog. i, 1831, 115; v, 1839, 408; pl. 23; Syn. 1839, 37; B. Am. i, 1840, 170, pl. 45.—NUTT., Man. i, 1832, 598.—GIR., B. L. I. 1844, 34.—JONES, Nat. Berm. 34.—MAXIM., J. f. O. vi, 1858, 101.—TRIPPE, Pr. Ess. Inst. vi, 1871, 114 (Minnesota).
Progne purpurea, BOIE, Isis, 1826, 971.—BP., List, 1838, 8; Consp. i, 1850, 337.—WOODH., Sitgr. Rep. 1853, 65.—CASS., Ill. 1855, 47.—NEWB., P. R. R. Rep. vi, 1857, 79.—BREW., N. A. O. 1857, 103, pl. 4, f. 47.—BD., B. N. A. 1858, 314.—HEERM., P. R. R. Rep. x, 1859, pt. vi, 35.—COOP. & SUCK., N. H. Wash. Ter. 1860, 186.—SCL., Cat. 1862, 38.—HAYD., Rep. 1862, 162.—BLAK., Ibis, 1863, 65 (Saskatchewan).—McILWR., Pr. Ess. Inst. v, 1866, 87 (Canada).—COOP., B. Cal. 1870, 113.—COUES, Key, 1872, 114; and of most late writers.
Hirundo violacea, GM., Syst. Nat. i, 1788, 1026.
Hirundo (Cecropis) violacea, LESS., Compl. Buff. viii, 498.
Hirundo cærulea, VIEILL., O. A. S. i, 1807, 57, pls. 26, 27.
Hirundo versicolor, VIEILL., Nouv. Dict. d'Hist. Nat. xiv, 1817, 509.
Hirundo ludoviciana, CUV., Regne Anim. i, 1817, 374.
(?) *Hirundo chalybea*, MAXIM., Beitr. iii, 354.
(?) *Progne cryptoleuca*, BD., Rev. 1865, 277 (= *Hirundo purpurea*, D'ORBIG., La Sagra's Cuba, Ois. 1840, 94; *Progne purpurea*, CAB., J. f. O. iv, 1856, 3). Cuba.
(?) *Progne elegans*, BD., Rev. 1865, 275 (Vermejo River, Paraguay; supposed identical with *P. elegans*, DARW., Voy. Beagle, 38, Buenos Ayres).
(?) *Progne furcata*, BD., Rev. 1865, 248 (Chili).
(Other references to the supposed *P. purpurea* of South America are : BURM., Syst. Ueb. iii, 140; SCHOMB., Guiana, 671; TSCHUDI, Fn. Peru, ii, 132; PELZ., Orn. Bras. i, 16.—See SCLATER, P. Z. S. 1872, 605. The Galapagoes species or variety is : *P. concolor*, GOULD, P. Z. S. 1837, 22; *P. modesta*, GOULD, Voy. Beagle, 39, pl. 5.)

Hab.—United States and British provinces (north to Canada and the Saskatchewan). Mexico. (?) Cuba. (?) Greater part of South America. Breeds in most of its United States range; winters beyond. Accidental in Great Britain (*Yarrell*, Br. Birds, 2d ed., ii, 257; 3d ed., ii, 267; *Gray*, List, Br. B. 34; *Harting*, Br. Birds, 125).
Lieutenant Warren's Expedition.—4505-8, Cedar Island; 4770-4, "Nebraska;" 5204, Fort Union; 5205, Blackfoot country.
Later Expeditions.—60418-19, Bitter Cottonwood, Wyoming.
Not obtained by Captain Raynolds' Expedition.

Family AMPELIDÆ : Waxwings.

AMPELIS GARRULUS, Linn.

Bohemian Waxwing.

Lanius garrulus, LINN., Fn. Suec. 82.
Ampelis garrulus, LINN., Syst. Nat. i, 1766, 297.—BP., Consp. Av. i, 1850, 336.—BD., B. N. A. 1858, 307 (southwest to Fort Riley, Kansas; also, p. 923, "millions" on Powder

River).—BD., Rev. i, 1866, 405.—WHEAT., Ohio Agric. Rep. 1860 (Northern Ohio, "often taken in winter").—COOP., Pr. Cal. Acad. ii, 1861, 122 (Fort Mojave, Colorado River, Arizona; southernmost locality on record).—VERR., Pr. Ess. Inst. iii, 158 (Maine; accidental in winter, and rare).—BOARDM., Pr. Bost. Soc. ix, 1862, 126 (Calais, Maine).—ALLEN, Pr. Ess. Inst. iv, 1864, 66 (accidental winter visitant, Springfield, Massachusetts).—COUES, Pr. Ess. Inst. v, 1868, 276 (New England; rare and irregular in the north, accidental in the south to Connecticut; *Dr. Wood*).—LAWR., Ann. Lyc. viii, 1866, 285 (New York).— TURNB., B. E. Pa. 1869, 42 ("occasional near Philadelphia; not uncommon on Lake Superior")—DALL & BANN., Tr. Chic. Acad. i, 1869, 280 (breeding at Fort Yukon).—ALLEN, Am. Nat. 1869, 579 (Southern New England).—AIKEN, Pr. Bost. Soc. 1872, 198 (mountains of Colorado).--COOP., Pr. Cal. Acad. 1870, 75; B. Cal. i, 1870, 127.—MAYN., Guide, 1870, 107 (Massachusetts).—COUES, Key, 1872, 115, fig. 55.

Bombycivora garrula, TEMM., Man. i, 1815, 77.—NAUM., Vög. Deutschl. ii, 1822, 143.
Bombycilla garrula, BP., Zool. Journ. iii, 1828, pl. 16, f. 2.—SW. & RICH., F. B. A. ii, 1831, 237.—NUTT., Man. i, 1832, 579.—AUD., Orn. Biog. iv, 1838, 462, pl. 363; Syn. 1839, 165; B. Am. iv, 1842, 169, pl. 246.—PEAB., Rep. B. Mass. 1839, 290.—GIR., B. L. I. 1844, 165.—PUTN., Pr. Ess. Inst. i, 1856, 228.—MAXIM., J. f. O. vi, 1858, 188.
Bombyciphora poliocœlia, MEYER, Vög. Liv- u. Esthl. 1815, 104.
Bombycilla bohemica, BRISS.—LEACH, Cat. 1816, 18.—EYT., Cat. 8.—BREHM., V. D. 219.
Parus bombycilla, PALL., Zoog. R.-A. i, 548.

Hab.—A species of circumpolar distribution, wandering irregularly southward in flocks, in winter, to about 35° north in America.

List of specimens.

19214	273	Deer Creek ...	♂	Feb. 13, 1860	F. V. Hayden.	7.50	11.75	4.50
19215	274	..... do	♀	..... do	...... do	7.75	12.25	4.00
19216	226	..... do	♂	Jan. 7, 1860	...... do	8.50	13.60	4.60
19217	272	..... do	♀	Feb. 13, 1860	...... do	7.50	11.25	4.25
19218	275	..... do	♂	..... do	...... do	7.50	13.50	4.25
19220	277	..... do	♂	..... do	...... do	8.00	14.00	4.75
19221	271	..... do	♂	..... do	...... do	8.00	14.00	4.75
19219	276	..... do	♂	..... do	G. H. Trook ..	8.00	14.06	4.75

A fine series of this species, not very common in American collections, was taken on Deer Creek in winter. Prof. Baird mentions that Mr. Drexler saw "millions" on Powder River, in flocks "rivalling in extent those of the Wild Pigeon."

The singularly erratic movements of this species are well known, but not so easily accounted for, since the exigencies of the weather and scarcity of food do not seem sufficient, in every instance, to explain the case. It seems, however, most nearly parallel with that of the Wild Pigeon. The occasional occurrence of the bird in small numbers in winter, through New England and the other Atlantic States, as far as Philadelphia, is noticed in the records above quoted. The only Eastern United States region where it seems to be of regular occurrence in winter, is the vicinity of the Great Lakes. Mr. T. McIlwraith reports (Proc. Ess. Inst. v, 1866, 87), that at Hamilton, Canada West, it is a winter visitant, "sometimes appearing in vast flocks, and not seen again for several years." We also have advices from Kansas, and from the Colorado Valley, latitude 35°. We have no United States record from the Pacific coast, but Dr. Cooper gives an interesting note in his later work, above quoted: "It is probable," he says, "that they reside, during summer, about the summits of the loftiest mountains of the interior ranges, if not of the Sierra Nevada, as I have seen them in September at Fort Laramie, and the specimen obtained on the Colorado was a straggler from some neighboring mountains. It appeared January 10th, after a stormy period which had whitened the tops of the mountains with snow, and was alone, feeding on the berries of the mistletoe, when I shot it."

I am informed by Mr. Trippe that the species is "abundant during winter" at Idaho Springs, Colorado, "arriving during the latter part of

November, or in December. It affects particular regions in the mountains, being very numerous in some localities, and rare in others; but it is seldom seen in the foot-hills. It begins to leave the country toward the close of February, and by the middle of March has nearly disappeared, only straggling flocks remaining until the close of the month."

Mr. Dall reports that this bird "is quite common near Nulato, but does not arrive until the 10th of June, or later."

"For many years authentic eggs of the Bohemian Chatterer were greatly sought after, but it was not until 1856 that any were brought to the notice of the scientific world, when the late Mr. Wolley discovered them in Lapland. Early duplicates from his collection were sold at five guineas each; and although a good many have been since obtained, they are yet considered as great prizes. A nest, with its eggs, of those collected by Mr. Wolley, has been presented to the [Smithsonian] Institution by Mr. Alfred Newton. The only instances of their discovery in America, are of a nest and one egg by Mr. Kennicott, on the Yukon, in 1861, and a nest and single egg on the Anderson River, by Mr. MacFarlane, both of which, with the female parents, are in the possession of the Institution." (*Baird.*)

European references to the nidification of this bird are given by Baird, as follows: *Newton*, Ibis, 1861, 92, pl. 4; *Nordmann*, Cab. Journ. vi, 1858, 307, and vii, 1859, pl. 1. The egg is precisely like a Cedar-bird's, but larger; two specimens in the Smithsonian, both from the Yukon, measure, respectively, 1.05 by 0.69, and 0.87 by 0.67.

AMPELIS CEDRORUM, (Vieill.) Gray.

Cedar Bird; Cherry Bird; Carolina Waxwing.

Ampelis garrulus var. β, LINN., Syst. Nat. i, 1766, 297.
Bombycilla cedrorum, VIEILL., Ois. Am. Sept. i, 1807, 88, pl. 57.—VIEILL., Gal. Ois. i, 1834, 186, pl. 118.—CAB., Mus. Hein. i, 1850, 55; J. f. O. iv, 1856, 3 (Cuba).—GUNDL., J. f. O. 1861, 328 (Cuba).
Ampelis cedrorum, SCL., P. Z. S. 1856, 299 (Cordova); 1858, 302 (Oaxaca); 1859, 364 (Xalapa); 1864, 172 (city of Mexico).—BD., B. N. A. 1858, 318; Rev. 1866, 407.— SCL. & SALV., Ibis, 1859, 13 (Guatemala).—HEERM., P. R. R. Rep. x, 1859, 56.— COOP. & SUCK., N. H. Wash. Ter. 1860, 187.—TAYLOR, Ibis, 1860, 111 (Honduras).—HAYD., Rep. 1862, 162.—MARCH, Pr. Phila. Acad. 1863, 294 (Jamaica).— LORD, Pr. Roy. Arty. Inst. iv, 1864, 116 (British Columbia).—SUMICH., Mem. Bost. Soc. i, 1869, 547 (Vera Cruz, abundant in winter).—COOP., Am. Nat. iii, 1869, 34; B. Cal. i, 1870, 129 (California).—ALLEN, Bull. M. C. Z. iii, 1872, 176 (Eastern Kansas).—AIKEN, Pr. Bost. Soc. 1872, 198 (Black Hills).—COUES, Key, 1872, 115, pl. 56; and of all late United States writers.
Bombycilla carolinensis, BRISS., Orn. ii, 1760, 337.—BP., List, 1838, 9.—AUD., Orn. Biog. i, 1831, 227, pl. 43; Syn. 1839, 165; B. Am. iv, 1842, 165, pl. 245.—NUTT., i, 1832, 248.—GIR., B. L. I. 1844, 163.
Ampelis carolinensis, GOSSE, B. Jamaica, 1847, 197 (winter).—BP., Consp. Av. i, 1850, 336.
Ampelis americana, WILS., Am. Orn. i, 1808, 107, pl. 7, f. 1.
Bombycilla americana, SW. & RICH., F. B. A. ii, 1831, 239.—JONES, Nat. in Bermuda, 1859, 29 (winter).

Hab.—North America generally, up to 54° north (*Richardson*). Mexico and Central America. Bermuda. Jamaica. Cuba. Accidental in England (*Newt.*, Zool. 1851, 3277; 1852, 3507; *Gray*, List Br. B. 1863, 81).
Lieutenant Warren's Expedition.—5318-19, Yellowstone River.
Not obtained by Captain Raynolds' Expedition.

MYIADESTES TOWNSENDII, (Aud.) Cab.

Townsend's Flycatching Thrush.

Ptiliogonys townsendii, AUD., Orn. Biog. v, 1839, 206, pl. 419, f. 2.—AUD., Syn. 1839, 46.— AUD., B. Am. i, 1840, 243, pl. 69.—NUTT., Man. i, 2d ed. 1840, 361.—GAMB., Pr. Phila. Acad. i, 1843, 263.—NEWB., P. R. R. Rep. vi, 1857, 82.

Myiadestes townsendii, CAB., Wiegm. Archiv, i, 1847, 208.—SCL., P. Z. S. 1857, 5; 1858, 97.—BD., B. N. A. 1858, 321; Rev. 1866, 429.—KENN., P. R. R. Rep. x, 1859, Whipple's Route, 25.—HEERM., *ibid.* Williamson's Route, 38.—HAYD., Rep. 1862, 162.—LORD, Pr. Roy. Arty. Inst. iv, 1864, 116 (British Columbia).—COUES, Pr. Phila. Acad. 1866, 72.—COOP., Am. Nat. iii, 1869, 34.—ALLEN, Bull. M. C. Z. iii, 1872, 176.—AIKEN, Pr. Bost. Soc. 1872, 249 (Colorado, resident).—STEV., U. S. Geol. Surv. Ter. 1870, 464 (Wyoming).—COUES, Key, 1872, 117, fig. 57. (*Not of* BREW., Pr. Bost. Soc. 1873, 109; the nest and eggs there described being those of *Phænopepla nitens!*)

Hab.—Middle and Western Provinces of the United States, in mountainous regions. North to British Columbia. East to the Black Hills. Not south of the United States, if the *M. unicolor* and *M. obscurus* be different.

List of specimens.

| 19225 | 162 | Pump. Butte . | .... | Oct. 22, 1859 | F. V. Hayden. | 8.25 | 12.50 | 4.50 |

A clue to the true position of this genus is found in the fusion of the tarsal plates, and in the spotted plumage of the young, warranting the inference that it belongs among the *Turdidæ.* This fact was noticed by Dr. Suckley and myself while preparing a report upon the Birds of the Northwest Boundary Survey, in 1862, and is adverted to by Baird in his Review, in my paper in the Philadelphia Academy's Proceedings, and in the "Key." The eminent vocal powers of all the species of the genus bear out the inference.

Dr. J. S. Newberry has given a very interesting account of the bird. Noticing its occurrence in the Des Chutes Basin, he continues: "It does not inhabit dense forests, nor prairies entirely destitute of trees, but chooses surfaces covered with a scattered growth of pine and cedar. We first met with it in the cañon of Mptolyas River, at the base of Mt. Jefferson. As we picked our way with infinite difficulty down the side of this gorge, my attention was attracted by the delightful song of, to me, a new bird, of which a few were sitting in the pines and cedars which, by a precarious tenure, held a footing on the craggy face of the cliff. The song, so clear, full, and melodious, seemed that of a *Mimus;* of the bird I could not see enough to judge of its affinities. The next day we followed down the river in the bottom of the cañon; all day the deep gorge was filled with a chorus of sweet sounds from hundreds and thousands of these birds, which, from their monotonous color, and their habit of sitting on the branch of a tree projecting into the void above the stream, or hanging from some beetling crag, and flying out in narrow circles after insects, precisely in the manner of Flycatchers, I was disposed to associate with them. Two days afterward, in the cañon of Psucseeque Creek, of which the terraced banks were sparsely set with low trees of the western cedar, I found these birds numerous, and had every opportunity of hearing and seeing them, watching them for hours while feeding and singing, and procuring specimens of both male and female. With the first dawn of day they began their songs, and at sunrise the valley was vocal with their notes. Never, anywhere, have I heard a more delightful chorus of bird-music. Their song is not greatly varied, but all the notes are particularly clear and sweet, and the stream of pure gushing melody is as spontaneous and inspiring as that of the Song Sparrow."

This bird appears to feed mostly upon cedar-berries, and its abundance is to be in a measure determined by the presence of the juniper. Thus Dr. Cooper says: "I saw only a few of this species among some junipers on the western slope of the mountains, not far from the summit, in September, 1863. The scarcity of the juniper on the western slope, toward the north, seems to be the reason why this bird is not more frequent there; as, according to all accounts, they are found wherever that tree grows in abundance, especially on the mountain ranges of the great interior basin, and their extensions to the north and south." The same excellent observer adds his testimony to that of Dr. Newberry respecting the bird's vocal powers : "Although plain in plumage and retiring in habits, this bird is one of the most interesting in the western country ; for, like its not distant relative, the European Nightingale, it compensates by its delightful melody for its deficiencies in beauty. Having seen them in the Rocky Mountains, where they seemed merely plain and silent flycatchers, my astonishment, when I first heard one sing in the Sierra Nevada, was indeed great ; and if I had not shot the bird immediately, I could not have believed that one belonging to the same family as the nearly silent Waxwings and *Phœnopepla*,* could sing with such power, variety, and sweetness. Their song can be compared to nothing uttered by any other bird I have heard in the United States, for it excels that of the Mockingbird in sweetness, besides being entirely original. It has the melancholy slowness, but without the interruptions, of that of the Wood-Thrush, and agrees better with the descriptions of that of the Nightingale of Europe.

Mr. Allen observed this bird in the mountains of Colorado, up to timber-line. I found it rather rare, in summer, in Upper Arizona.

I am favored by Mr. Trippe with the following interesting communication, designed for the present work : "This exquisite songster is a permanent resident of the mountains of Colorado, and may be seen at all times of the year, from the lower valley of the country up to timber-line, and in midsummer even beyond it, to the highest limit of the shrubby willows and junipers. It is never a familiar bird, shunning the vicinity of houses and cultivated fields, and seeking the rockiest mountain sides and darkest cañons as its favorite haunts, yet avoiding the sombre depths of dense forests, though occasionally found therein. During the winter it feeds on berries and such insects as it can find, but in the warmer months subsists almost entirely upon the latter, which it captures with the address of the most skilful Flycatcher. It is never gregarious, and usually solitary, associating together only from the time of pairing, which is in the early part of May, until the young are able to shift for themselves. It frequently alights on the top of a dead limb or tree, from which it keeps a bright lookout for passing insects, and returns several times to the same perch after capturing its prey ; it also frequents the lower boughs, and at times alights upon the ground and searches among the leaves for food. In its flight it bears some resemblance to the Cedar-bird, with which, indeed, it has many common traits. In summer and fall its voice is rarely heard ; but as winter comes on, and the woods are well-nigh deserted by all save a few Titmice and Nuthatches, it begins to utter occasionally a single bell-like note that can be heard distinctly at a great distance. The bird is now very shy ; and the author of the clear, loud call, that I heard nearly every morning from the valley of Clear Creek, was long a mystery to me. Toward the middle and latter part of winter, as the snow begins to fall, the Fly-catching Thrush delights to sing, choosing for its rostrum a pine tree in some elevated position, high up above the valleys ; and not all the fields and groves, and hills and valleys of the Eastern States, can boast a more exquisite song ; a song in which the notes of the Purple Finch, the Wood-Thrush, and the Winter Wren, are blended into a silvery cascade of melody, that ripples and dances down the mountain sides as clear and sparkling as the mountain brook, filling the woods and val-

* The supposition that *Phœnopepla nitens* is songless, is entirely erroneous. "It has a superb song, powerful and finely modulated." COUES, Proc. Phila. Acad. 1866, 71 ; Key, 1872, 116.

leys with ringing music. At first it sings only on bright, clear mornings; but once fairly in the mood, it sings at all hours and during the most inclement weather. Often while traveling over the narrow, winding mountain roads, toward the close of winter, I have been overtaken and half-blinded by sudden, furious storms of wind and snow, and compelled to seek the nearest tree or projecting rock for shelter. In such situations I have frequently listened to the song of this bird, and forgot the cold and wet in its enjoyment. Toward spring, as soon as the other birds begin to sing, it becomes silent as though disdainful of joining the common chorus, and commences building its nest in May, earlier than almost any other bird. During this season it deserts the valleys, and confines itself to partially wooded hill-tops."

I never found the nest of this bird myself, nor have I ever seen it. The only one thus far known was discovered by Mr. Ridgway, *in the rift of a rock*. He describes it to me as being large and bulky, built of sticks and grasses. Unfortunately it was empty, and the eggs continue entirely unknown. For those described, with the nest, by Dr. Brewer, as above quoted, are not of this species, but of *Phœnopepla nitens*, as I ascertained by examining them myself. They are correctly labelled in Lieutenant Bendire's collection. Dr. Brewer's mistake is apparently the result of a slip of the pen.

Family VIREONIDÆ: Greenlets.

VIREO OLIVACEUS, (Linn.) Vieill.

Red-eyed Vireo.

Muscicapa olivacea, LINN., S. N. i, 1766, 327.—WILS., Am. Orn. ii, 1810, 55, pl. 12, f. 3.
Lanius olivaceus, LICHT., Verz. 1823, 49.
Vireo olivaceus, VIEILL.—BP., Obs. Wils. 1826, 124; Syn. 1828, 71.—SW. & RICH., F. B. A. ii, 1831, 233.—AUD., Orn. Biog. ii, 1834, 287, pl. 150; Syn. 1839, 162.—NUTT., Man. i, 1832, 312.—AUD., B. Am. iv, 155, pl. 243.—GIR., B. L. I. 1844, 157.— WOODH., Sitgr. Rep. 1853, 76.—BD., B. N. A. 1858, 331.—ALLEN, Bull. M. C. Z. 1872, 176 (mountains of Colorado, up to 11,000 feet; Ogden, Utah).—COUES, Key, 1872, 120, fig. 59; and of most late United States writers.
Vireosylvia olivacea, BP., List, 1838, 26; Consp. i, 1850, 329.—REINH., Viddensk. Med. for 1853 (1854), 82 (Greenland).—REINH., Ibis, iii, 1861, 7 (Greenland).—SCL., P. Z. S. 1855, 151 (Bogota); 1859, 137, 363 (Xalapa); 1870, 836 (Honduras); Cat. A. B. 1862, 43.—A. & E. NEWTON, Ibis, 1859, 145 (Santa Cruz).—SCL. & SALV., Ibis, 1859, 12 (Guatemala).—LAWR., Ann. Lyc. vii, 1860, 246 (Cuba); ix, 1868, 96 (Costa Rica).—MOSLEY, Nat. Hist. Tutbury, 1863, 385, pl. 6; Ibis, 1864, 394; Zoologist, 1864, 8965; *fide* HARTING, Man. Br. B. 1872, 99 (accidental in England).—BD., Rev. 1866, 333.—ALLEN, Bull. M. C. Z. ii, 1871, 270 (a few wintering in Florida).—B. B. & R., N. A. B. i, 1874, 363;* and of many late United States writers.
Phyllomanes olivaceus, CAB., Mus. Hein. i, 1850, 63.—CAB., J. f. O. 1860, 404 (Costa Rica).—GUNDL., J. f. O. 1861, 324 (Cuba).
(?) *Vireo virescens*, VIEILL., Ois. Am. Sept. i, 1807, 84, pl. 53.—GRAY, G. of B. i, 1844, pl. 75.
Vireo bogotensis, BRY., Pr. B. S. vii, 1860, 227 (Bogota).—LAWR., A. L., 1863 (Panama).

Hab.—Eastern North America to Hudson's Bay. Greenland. West beyond the limits of the Eastern Province to Ogden, Utah. Fort Bridger. Bitterroot Valley. Kootenay, Washington Territory (*Kennerly*). Missouri River, 800 miles above its mouth (*Pearsall*). Some winter in Florida. Greenland. Cuba. Trinidad, FINSCH, P. Z. S. 1870, 565 (with *agilis*). Panama. In Mexico nearly replaced by the closely allied species *V. flavoviridis*. Extremely abundant throughout the Eastern United States. Accidental

---

* *A History of North American Birds.* By S. F. BAIRD, T. M. BREWER, and R. RIDGWAY. Illustrated by 64 colored plates and 593 woodcuts. Vols. I, II: Land Birds— Boston: Little, Brown & Co., 1874. The reception of the earlier volumes of this great work (Feb., 1874), as the present publication reaches this point in printing, will enable me to cite it in succeeding pages.

in England (near Derby, May, 1859; Mosley, N. H. Tutbury, 1863, 385, pl. 6; Zoologist, 1864, p. 8965; Harting, Br. Birds, 1872, 99).
Lieutenant Warren's Expedition.—8695, Fremont, Platte River.
Not obtained by Captain Raynolds' Expedition.

There is a very great uniformity among the eggs of our *Vireonidæ;* with specimens before me of *olivaceus, gilvus, bellii, noveboracensis, solitarius,* and *flavifrons,* I can see no difference, except in size. They are all pure white, very sparingly sprinkled, chiefly about the larger end, with fine sharp dots of dark brown. *Solitarius* and *flavifrons,* on the whole, may average a little the heaviest spotting: in one case of *noveboracensis* there are no spots, but its fellow from the same nest is spotted. Likewise, a whole set of *V. bellii* are immaculate, and in another set there is but a mere speck here and there over the surface. Eggs of *bellii,* the smallest, measure 0.70 or less by about 0.50; those of *noveboracensis* are a trifle larger; a specimen of *gilvus* is 0.74 by 0.54; *flavifrons, solitarius,* and *olivaceus,* are 0.80 to 0.85 by 0.55 to 0.60. Nidification is essentially the same throughout; a thin-walled, cup-shaped nest, of various fibrous material, is suspended by the brim betwixt the forks of a twig.

VIREO PHILADELPHICUS, Cass.

Brotherly-love Vireo.

Vireosylvia philadelphica, Cass., Pr. Phila. Acad. v, 1851, 153; vi, pl. 1, fig. 1.—Scl. & Salv., Ibis, 1859, 12 (Guatemala).—Bd., Rev. 1866, 340.—Lawr., Ann. Lyc. N. Y. ix, 1868, 96 (Costa Rica).—Salv., P. Z. S. 1870, 187 (Veragua).—B. B. & R., N. A. B. i, 1874, 367.
Vireo philadelphicus, Bd., B. N. A. 1858, 335, pl. 78, fig. 3 (Wisconsin and Ohio).—Wheat., Ohio Agric. Rep. 1860, No. 114.—Coues & Prent., Smiths. Rep. 1861, 410.— Hamlin, Rep. Maine Board Agric. 1865 (Waterville, Me.; only New England record).—Coues, Pr. Ess. Inst. v, 1868, 277.—Allen, Mem. Bost. Soc. i, 1868, 517 (Illinois).—Turnb., B. E. Pa. 1869, 19 (very rare).—Coues, Key, 1872, 120, fig. 62.
Vireosylvia cobanensis, Scl., P. Z. S. 1860, 463; Ann. Mag. N. H. 1861, 328. (Vera Paz.)

Hab.—Eastern North America. North to Hudson's Bay; south to Central America. No Mexican or West Indian quotations.

From the rarity of this species along the Atlantic coast, and its comparative frequency of occurrence in the interior, it would seem probable that it migrates chiefly through the Mississippi, and I confidently anticipate that it will be found breeding in the Missouri region. It is more than likely that Mr. Trippe's queried citation (Minnesota, Pr. Ess. Inst. vi, 1871, 117) really does belong here, and not to *gilvus.* Dr. Brewer informs me by letter that one was shot near Calais, Maine, by Mr. Boardman, in the spring of 1872, and others found the latter part of May in northwestern Maine, by Mr. Brewster—an occurrence not mentioned by Mr. Maynard in his late excellent paper. Dr. Brewer adds that it is "abundant" every spring, about May 24th, in Wisconsin. I found it quite common along the Red River of the North, about Pembina, in June, and it doubtless breeds there. It frequented the heavy timber of the river-bottom, in company with *V. olivaceous* and *V. gilvus.*

VIREO GILVUS, (Vieill.) Bp.

Warbling Vireo.

a. *gilvus.*

Muscicapa gilva, Vieill., Ois. Am. Sept. i, 1807, 65, pl. 34.
Vireo gilvus, Bp., Obs. Wils. 1825, No. 123; Syn. 1828, 70; List, 1838, 26.—Nutt., Man. i, 1832, 309.—Aud., Orn. Biog. ii, 1834, 114; v, 1839, 433; Syn. 1839, 161; B. Am.

7

1842, 149, pl. 241.—Gir., B. L. I. 1844, 161.—Woodh., Sitgr. Rep. 1853, 76.—Bd., B. N. A. 1858, 335.—Coues, Key, N. A. Birds, 1872, 120, fig. 63.—Trippe, Pr. Bost. Soc. xv, 1872, 236 (Iowa, breeding).—Snow, B. Kans. 1873, 5 (Kansas, breeding); and of most United States writers.

Vireosylvia gilva, Cass., Pr. Phila. Acad. 1851, 153.—Scl., P. Z. S. 1856, 298 (Cordova); 1858, 302 (Oaxaca).—Bd., Rev. 1866, 342.—Sumich., Mem. Bost. Soc. i, 1869, 548 (Vera Cruz; migratory).—B. B. & R., N. A. B. i, 1874, 368.

Muscicapa melodia, Wils., Am. Orn. v, 1812, 85, pl. 42, f. 2.

b. *swainsoni.*

Vireo swainsoni, Bd., B. N. A. 1858, 336 (in text).—Coues, Ibis, 1865, 164 (Arizona).— Coues, Pr. Phila. Acad. 1866, 73 (Arizona).

Vireosylvia swainsoni, Bd., Rev. 1866, 343.—Aiken, Pr. Bost. Soc. 1872, 198 (Colorado).— Stev., U. S. Geol. Surv. Ter. 1870, 464 (Wyoming).

Vireosylvia gilva var. *swainsoni*, Coop., B. Cal. i, 1870, 116.—B. B. & R., N. A. B. i, 1874, 371.

Vireo gilvus var. *swainsoni*, Coues, Key, 1872, 121, fig. 64.

Vireo gilvus, Coop. & Suck., N. H. Wash. Ter. 1859, 188.—Coop., Am. Nat. iii, 1869, 35 (Rocky Mountains).—Allen, Bull. M. C. Z. iii, 1872, 156, 176 (Kansas, Colorado, Utah; includes both varieties).

Hab.—Of true *gilvus*, Eastern North America to high central plains; north to Fort Simpson. Var. *swainsoni*, wooded regions from Plains to Pacific, United States.

Lieutenant Warren's Expedition.—4729, Missouri River; 5305, Fort Lookout.

Later Expeditions.—60769, Green River, Wyoming (var. *swainsoni*).

Not obtained by Captain Raynolds' Expedition.

These specimens are referable to the *gilvus* proper, excepting No. 60769. "*swainsoni*" seems to be scarcely distinguishable even as a variety. A supposed difference in the wing-formula proves not to hold always. The bird is, however, paler and grayer, like others from the same region.

The Warbling Vireo is stated by Dr. Hayden to be abundant along the wooded bottoms of the Missouri, where, however, I never observed it, though I found it quite common on the Red River of the North. It is numerously represented throughout the greater part of the United States east of the Mississippi; reaching the middle districts about the middle of April, and remaining through the greater part of September, breeding in gardens and the streets of cities, among the high shade trees, rather than in the forests.

VIREO FLAVIFRONS, Vieill.

Yellow-throated Vireo.

Vireo flavifrons, Vieill., Ois. Am. Sept. i, 1807, 85, pl. 54.—Bp., Syn. 1828, 70.—Nutt., Man. i, 1832, 302.—Aud., Orn. Biog. ii, 1834, 119; v, 1839, 428; pl. 119; Syn. 1839, 160; B. Am. iv, 1842, 141, pl. 238.—Gir., B. L. I. 1844, 159.—Woodh., Sitgr. Rep. 1853, 82 (Texas and Indian Territory).—Scl., P. Z. S. 1857, 227 (Vera Cruz); 1860, 257 (Orizaba).—Scl. & Salv., Ibis, 1859, 12 (Guatemala).—Cab., J. f. O. iii, 468 (Cuba); 1860, 405 (Costa Rica).—Gundl., J. f. O. 1861, 324 (Cuba).—Bd., B. N. A. 1858, 341.—Hamlin, Rep. Maine Board Agric. 1865 (Waterville; only Maine record).—McIlwr., Pr. Ess. Inst. v, 1866, 87 (Hamilton, C. W., in summer).—Trippe, Pr. Ess. Inst. vi, 1871 117 (? Minnesota).—Snow, B. Kans. 1873, 5 (breeding).—Coues, Key, 1872, 121, fig. 65.

Lanivireo flavifrons, Bd.—Lawr., Ann. Lyc. ix, 1868, 96 (Costa Rica).—Allen, Bull. M. C. Z. ii, 1871, 279 (wintering in Florida).—B. B. & R., N. A. B. i, 1874, 379.

Vireosylvia flavifrons, Bd., Rev. 1866, 346.

Muscicapa sylvicola, Wils., Am. Orn. i, 1808, 117, pl. 7, f. 3.

Hab.—Eastern United States and British provinces, west to Kansas only. Cuba (rare). Mexico and Central America, to Costa Rica and Guatemala. Breeds from Maryland and Virginia northward. Stated to winter in Florida, as it does further south.

VIREO SOLITARIUS, (Wils.) Vieill.

Blue-headed or Solitary Vireo.

Muscicapa solitaria, WILS., Am. Orn. ii, 1810, 143, pl. 17, f. 6.
Vireo solitarius, VIEILL., Nouv. Dict. xi, 1817.—BP., Syn. 1828, 70; List, 1838, 26.—AUD.,
    Orn. Biog. i, 1831, 147; 1839, 432; pl. 28; Syn. 1839, 160.—GIR., B. L. I. 1844,
    160.—NUTT., Man. iv, 1832, 305.—AUD., B. Am. iv, 1842, 144, pl. 229.—CASS., Pr.
    Phila. Acad. 1851, 150.—SCL., P. Z. S. 1856, 298 (Cordova); 1859, 363 (Xalapa).—
    BD., B. N. A. 1858, 340.—COOP. & SUCK., N. H. Wash. Ter. 1859, 189.—SCL. &
    SALV., Ibis, 1860, 31 (Guatemala).—CAB., J. f. O. iii, 486 (Cuba).—GUNDL., J. f.
    O. 1861, 324 (Cuba).—TRIPPE, Pr. Ess. Inst. vi, 1871, 117 (Minnesota, breeds).—
    COUES, Key N. A. Birds, 1872, 121, 66.—GENTRY, Pr. Phila. Acad. 1873, 354
    (nest); and of most late United States writers.
Vireosylvia solitaria, BD., Rev. 1866, 347.—COOP., B. Cal. 117.—SUMICH., Mem. Bost. Soc.
    1869, 548 (Vera Cruz).
Lanivireo solitarius, BD.—B. B. & R., N. A. B. i, 1874, 373.
Vireo cassini, XANTUS, Pr. Phila. Ac. 1858, 117.—BD., B. N. A. 1858, 340, pl. 78, f. 1. (Var?)
Lanivireo solitarius var. *cassini*, B. B. & R., N. A. B. i, 1874, 377 (considered tenable
    variety).

Hab.—Whole United States, except Southern Rocky Mountain region, where replaced
by *V.* var. *plumbeus.* Canada (*McIlwraith*, Pr. Ess. Inst. v, 1866, 87). South to Guatemala in winter. Cuba.
Lieutenant Warren's Expedition.—4727-28, mouth of Vermilion River.
Not obtained by Captain Raynolds' Expedition.

In the paper above quoted, Mr. Thomas G. Gentry makes the following observations on the nidification of this species:

"Audubon, in describing the nest of *Vireo solitarius*, Vieill., affirms
it 'is prettily constructed and fixed in a partially pensile manner between two twigs of a low bush, on a branch running horizontally from
the main stem, and formed externally of gray lichens, slightly put together, and lined with hair chiefly from the deer and raccoon.' My
experience has been quite different. Out of the many nests which I
have seen and examined, I cannot recall a single specimen that will
answer to the above description. I have five nests of this species, four
of which are perfectly similar in structure; the remaining one formed of
the culms of a species of *Aira*, constituting an exceptional case, and the
only one that has ever fallen under my notice. They are all shallow,
loose in texture, scarcely surviving the season for which they were designed, and placed between two twigs of a cedar or a maple tree at a
considerable elevation from the ground, on a branch nearly horizontal
to the main axis. They are built entirely of clusters of male flowers of
Quercus palustris, which, having performed their allotted function, don
their brownish hue at the very period when they can be utilized.

"Here is evidently a change within a moderately short period, rendered necessary by external causes. This necessity may have grown
out of inability to procure the favorite materials, or a desire for self-
preservation. In the case of the species under consideration, it cannot
be denied that the utter inability, without unnecessary physical effort,
to procure the hair of the afore-mentioned animals, particularly in sections where *they* have been compelled to retreat before the advance of
man, may have been one of the causes which have induced the change.
I am satisfied, however, that it has not been the leading one, but that
self-preservation has operated in this case for individual and family good.
The adaptation of the colors of the female bird to the tints of surrounding objects, during the trying period of incubation, and the establishment of certain resemblances to familiar external objects, are two of the
ways in which it manifests itself."

VIREO SOLITARIUS var. PLUMBEUS, (Coues) Allen.

Plumbeous Vireo.

" *Vireo* most like *solitarius*," COUES, Ibis, 1865, 164.
Vireo solitarius, COOP., Pr. Cal. Acad. 1870, 175 (Colorado Valley).
Vireo plumbeus, COUES, Pr. Phila. Acad. 1866, 73 (Arizona).—COUES, Key, 1872, 122, fig. 6.
Vireosylvia plumbea, BD., Rev. 1866, 349 (same spec.).—AIK., P. B. S. 1872, 198 (Colorado).
Vireo solitarius var. *plumbeus*, ALLEN, Bull. M. C. Z. iii, 1872, 176.—COUES, Key, 1872, 351.
Lanivireo solitarius var. *plumbeus*, B. B. & R., N. A. B. i, 1874, 377.

Hab.—Southern Rocky Mountain region. North to Laramie Peak (*Hitz*). South to Colima (*Xantus*). "Western edge of the plains of Colorado, and in the mountains up to about 10,000 feet; Ogden, Utah" (*Allen*).

Although this bird was not procured by the Expeditions, its occurrence in the region of the Upper Missouri is shown by specimens obtained at Laramie Peak by Dr. R. B. Hitz.

Typical examples look so different from ordinary *solitarius* that I confidently described it as a distinct species. Some of Mr. Allen's specimens, however, which he kindly submitted to my inspection, show an approach to typical *solitarius*, and I am now inclined to rate it as one of the numerous duller-colored races of birds found in the same region.

I found it very abundant in the pine woods around Fort Whipple, Arizona, in summer, from April 25th until October. It unquestionably breeds there, although I did not find its nest. I shot it in July and August. Mr. Aiken took it in Colorado in May, and, according to Mr. Trippe's manuscript, it arrives at Idaho Springs, in that Territory, in the latter part of May, a week or so before the Warbling Vireo makes its appearance. "It ranges up the mountains to 9,000 feet, and is quite numerous somewhat lower, while the Warbling Vireo is comparatively rare at such heights, and does not reach above 8,000 feet." In all points of habit it is the counterpart of its eastern representative.

VIREO NOVEBORACENSIS, (Gm.) Bp.

White-eyed Vireo.

Muscicapa noveboracensis, GM., Syst. Nat. i, 1788, 947.
Vireo noveboracensis, BP., Obs. Wils. 1825 ; Syn. 1828, 70 ; List, 1838, 26.—NUTT., Man. i, 1832, 306.—AUD., Orn. Biog. i, 1831, 328 ; v, 1839, 431 ; pl. 63 ; Syn. 1839, 161 ; B. A. iv, 1842, 146, pl. 240.—GIR., B. L. I. 1844, 158.—CASS., Pr. Phila. Acad. 1851, 150.—WOODH., Sitgr. Rep. 1853, 75 (Texas, New Mexico, and Indian Territory).—CAB., J. f. O. iii, 469 (Cuba).—BD., B. N. A. 1858, 358 ; Rev. 1866, 354.— SCL., P. Z. S. 1857, 204, 228 (Xalapa and Vera Cruz).—MAXIM., J. f. O. vi, 1858, 187.—JONES, Nat. Berm. 1859, 71.—SCL. & SALV., Ibis, ii, 1860, 274 (Guatemala).—GUNDL., J. f. O. 1861, 324 (Cuba).—SCL., Cat. 1862, 42.—COUES, Pr. Ess. Inst. v, 1868 (New England).—COUES, Am. Nat. 1871, 197 (Kansas).—TRIPPE, Pr. Ess. Inst. vi, 1871, 117 (Minnesota).—ALLEN, Bull. M. C. Z. ii, 1871, 270 (Florida, wintering); iii, 1872, 176 (Kansas).—SNOW, B. Kans. 1873, 5.—COUES, Key, 1872, fig. 68.—B. B. & R., N. A. B. i, 1874, 385 ; and of most late writers.
Vireo musicus, VIEILL., Ois. Am. Sept. i, 1807, 83, pl. 50.
Muscicapa cantatrix, WILS., Am. Orn. ii, 1810, 266, pl. 18, fig. 6.

Hab.—Eastern United States. Minnesota. Not recorded from Maine. "Nova Scotia" (*Audubon*). Westward regularly to Kansas, Indian Territory, and Western Texas; occasionally to eastern foot-hills of the Rocky Mountains. "Columbia River" (*Audubon*; not since verified). South to Guatemala. Cuba (rare). Bermudas (resident, common). Eastern Mexico. Breeds through most of its United States range. Winters from South Carolina, Georgia, the Gulf States, and southward.

List of specimens.

| 13124 | 38 | U. Missouri .. | ♀ | (No date).... | F. V. Hayden.. | ...... | ...... | ...... |

This neat and pleasant little bird has a more extensive range than has usually been attributed to it, but how far it is casual only in some of the localities quoted, remains to be seen. A bird of the Eastern Province, it would certainly not be expected to occur on the Missouri, but this is the case, and gives some color to Audubon's unsupported citation of the Columbia. Eastward I have not traced it beyond Southern New England. I found it in Kansas, with the Red-eyed and Bell's Vireos. In the Middle States it is very abundant from April to October, breeding in shrubbery and moist, tangled places; although by an unaccountable oversight, it is omitted from Coues and Prentiss' Washington list, we found it plentiful there every season. It is a bird that seems to affect particular districts and avoid others equally within its general range; for instance, Mr. Allen did not find it at Springfield, though it is common enough in some parts of Massachusetts. Nuttall says he saw it in South Carolina in January, and it certainly winters in other of the Southern States. Its sprightly manners, and loud, clear song, make it a conspicuous and agreeable bird.

VIREO BELLII, Aud.

Bell's Vireo.

Vireo bellii, AUD., B. Am. vii, 1844, 333, pl. 485.—BP., Consp. Av. i, 1850, 330.—CASS., Pr. Phila. Acad. 1851, 150.—WOODH., Sitgr. Rep. 1853, 76.—BD., B. N. A. 1858, 337.—SCL., Cat. 1861, 42.—HOY, Smiths. Rep. 1864, 438 (Missouri).—BD., Rev. 1866, 358.—COUES, Ibis, Apr. 1865 (Kansas).—RIDGW., Am. Nat. 1873, 199 (Illinois).—ALLEN, Bull. M. C. Z. iii, 1872, 176.—COUES, Key N. A. Birds, 1872, 123, fig. 40.—SNOW, B. Kans. 1873, 5 (common).—TRIPPE, Pr. Bost. Soc. xv, 1872, 236 (Decatur County, Iowa).—B. B. & R., N. A. B. i, 1874, 389. (*Not of* COOPER.)

Hab.—Missouri region to Texas. Not observed in Southern Rocky Mountain region, where replaced by *V. pusillus*, COUES, a closely related species or variety. East to prairies of Illinois (*Ridgway*). South to Tehuantepec, Mexico (*Sumichrast*).

This species, originally described from the Upper Missouri (Fort Union, &c.), appears to have been overlooked by Dr. Hayden. Both Mr. Allen and myself found it abundant in Kansas; others have noted its occurrence in Missouri, Arkansas, and in Texas. Mr. Ridgway has lately announced its presence in Illinois, the easternmost locality as yet recorded. According to Mr. Trippe, as above cited, it breeds abundantly in Decatur County, Iowa, where it is the commonest species of the genus. "It arrives the second week in May, and is seldom seen after the middle of August. In its habits it bears a strong resemblance to the White-eyed Vireo, preferring the thickets and underbrush to the trees. Its notes are quite different from those of any other Vireo, being somewhat like those of the Blue-bird in early spring, but quicker and more hurried."

In its manners and general habits it is nearly a counterpart of *V. noveboracensis*, to which it is also similar in physical character, although bearing a still closer resemblance to *V. gilvus*.

Family LANIIDÆ : Shrikes.

COLLURIO BOREALIS, (Vieill.) Bd.

Butcher Bird; Northern Shrike.

Lanius excubitor, FORST., Phil. Trans. lxii, 1772, 382.—WILS., Am. Orn. i, 1808, 74, pl. 5, fig. 1.—AUD., Orn. Biog. ii, 1834, 534, pl. 192. (Not of European writers.)
Lanius borealis, VIEILL., Ois. Am. Sept. i, 1807, 90, pl. 50.—SW. & RICH., F. B. A. ii, 1831, 111, pl. 33.—AUD., Syn. 1839, 157.—AUD., B. Am. iv, 1842, 130, pl. 236.—GIR.,

B. L. I. 1844, 155.—GRAY, Gen. of Birds, 1847, 294.—CASS., Pr. Phila. Acad, 1857,
212.—MAXIM., J. f. O. vi, 1858, 190 (Upper Missouri).—JONES, Nat. in Bermuda,
1857, 51.—DRESSER & SHARPE, P. Z. S. 1870, 591.—TURNB., B. E. Pa. 1869, 19.—
FINSCH, Abh. Nat. 1872, 39 (Alaska).—TRIPPE, Pr. Ess. Inst. vi, 1871, 117.
Collyrio borealis, BD., B. N. A. 1858, 324.—COOP. & SUCK., N. H. Wash. Ter. 1859, 188.—
COUES & PRENT., Smiths. Rep. for 1861 (1862), 409.—HAYD., Rep. 1862, 162.—
COUES, Pr. Phila. Acad. 1866, 73.—LORD, Nat. Vanc. ii, 1866, 295.—COOP., Am.
Nat. iii, 1869, 35.—DALL & BANN., Tr. Chic. Acad. i, 1869, 280.—STEV., U. S.
Geol. Surv. Ter. 1870, 464.—MERR., *ibid.* 1872, 677.
Collurio borealis, BD., Rev. 1866, 440.—COUES, Pr. Ess. Inst. v, 1868, 277.—COOP., B. Cal.
i, 137.—AIKEN, Pr. Bost. Soc. 1872, 198 (Colorado).—COUES, Key, 1872, 125, fig.
73.—MERR., U. S. Geol. Surv. Ter. 1872, 677.—B. B. & R., N. A. B. i, 1874, 415.
Lanius septentrionalis, BP., Syn. 1828, 72 ; P. Z. S. 1837, 112 ; Consp. i, 1850, 363 ; R. &
M. Z. 1853, 294.—CASS., Pr. Phila. Acad. 1857, 213.—MURRAY, Edinb. N. Phil.
Journ. xi, 1859, 223.
Collyrio chemungensis, GREGG, Pr. Elmira Acad. i, 1870 (p. 9 of reprinted list). (Young).

Hab.—North America. In winter, south to about 35°. Alleghanies, breeding (*Turn-
bull*). Bermuda (*Jones*).
Lieutenant Warren's Expedition.—4552, Fort Pierre.
Later Expeditions.—60996-98, Rock Creek and Green River, Wyoming ; 62270, Idaho.
Not obtained by Captain Raynolds' Expedition.

The Shrike appears to be common on the Upper Missouri in winter ;
I have several times seen it at that season about Fort Randall. I have
also happened to meet with it twice in widely separated localities, but
in each instance at about the extreme southern limit, viz., at Washington, D. C., and at Fort Whipple, Arizona. The only record of its breeding in the United States that I have found, is Mr. Turnbull's statement,
that "many nestle on the mountain ridges of the Alleghanies."

Mr. Trippe informs me that the Butcher-bird is "quite common in Colorado, in October, about the Middle Park, and during the winter along
the edge of the plains. Late in November one was observed at Idaho
Springs to catch and kill a Snow-bird, and carry it off in its bill up the
side of a mountain."

The eggs of our two species of Shrike are indistinguishable, though
those of *borealis* average a trifle the largest—about 1.10 by 0.80. The
ground is dull white, blotched or freckled all over with a peculiar shade
of dull grayish-brown, in some instances deepening into grayish-choco-
late. The variations in precise amount of spotting, as well as in size
and shade of the markings, is interminable.

COLLURIO LUDOVICIANUS var. EXCUBITOROIDES, (Sw.) Coues.

White-rumped Shrike.

b. *excubitoroides.*

Lanius excubitoroides, SW., F. B. A. ii, 1831, 115, pl. 35.—GAMB., Pr. Phila. Acad. 1847,
200.—CASS., *ibid.* 1857, 213.—WOODH., Sitgr. Rep. 1853, 77 (Texas).—HEERM.,
P. R. R. Rep. x, 1859, 55.—SCL., P. Z. S. 1864, 173 (city of Mexico).—DRESS. &
SHARPE, P. Z. S. 1870, 595.
Collyrio excubitoroides, BD., B. N. A. 1858, 527, pl. 75, f. 2.—KENN., P. R. R. Rep. x, 1859,
25.—HAYD., Rep. 1862, 162.—COUES, Pr. Phila. Acad. 1866, 73 (Arizona).—
McILWR., Pr. Ess. Inst. v, 1866, 87 (Hamilton, C. W.).—COOP., Am. Nat. Aug.
1869, 34 (Fort Union, breeding ; eggs six).—COOP., Pr. Cal. Acad. 1870, 75.
Collurio excubitoroides, BD., Rev. 1866, 445.—COUES, Pr. Ess. Inst. v, 1868, 277.—ALLEN,
Mem. Bost. Soc. i, 1869, 504, 517 (Illinois).—SUMICH., Mem. Bost. Soc. N. H. i,
1869, 548 (Vera Cruz).—COOP., B. Cal. i, 1871, 138.—AIKEN, Pr. Bost. Soc.
1872, 198 (Colorado).
Collurio ludovicianus var. *excubitoroides*, COUES, Key, 1872, 125.—B. B. & R., N. A. B.
1874, 421.
Lanius ludovicianus, MAXIM., J. f. O. 1858, 191 (Upper Missouri).
Collurio ludovicianus, ALLEN, Mem. Bost. Soc. i, 1868, 499 (Iowa).—ALLEN, Am. Nat. 1869,
579 (refers to Canadian and New York examples).—ALLEN, Bull. M. C. Z. iii,
1872, 176 (Kansas ; Colorado, Utah).—(?) PURDIE, Am. Nat. vii, 1873, 115 (Mass.)

(??) *Lanius elegans*, Sw., F. B. A. ii, 1831, 122 (*said to be* from the fur countries; original specimen identified by *Dresser* and *Sharpe* (P. Z. S. 1870, 595) as belonging to *C. lahtora* of Asia and Africa).
Lanius elegans, NUTT., Man. i, 2d ed. 1840, 287.—CASS., Pr. Phila. Acad. 1857, 213.—BD., B. N. A. 1858, 328, foot-note; pl. 75, f. 1.
Collyrio elegans, BD., B. N. A. 1858, page xxxv.
Collurio elegans, BD., Rev. 1866, 444.—COOP., B. Cal. i, 1870, 140.
Lanius mexicanus, BREHM, J. f. O. ii, 1854, 145.—SCL., Cat. 1862, 46.
Collurio ludovicianus var. *robustus*, BD., Am. Nat. vii, 1873, 609 (same specimen as formerly called *C. elegans*).—B. B. R., B. N. A. i, 1874, 420 (the same).

Hab.—Middle Province of North America, to the Saskatchewan. East through Kansas, Iowa, Ohio, Illinois, and Wisconsin, to New York and Canada West, probably into New England. In the Southern States replaced by typical *ludovicianus*. On the Pacific coast not observed north of California. South through Mexico.

List of specimens.

19222	164	Pump. Butte..	....	Nov. 18, 1859	F. V. Hayden.	......	......	......
19224	191	...... do	♂	Oct. 23, 1859	...... do	10.00	12.50	4.75
19223	....	....	....	....	Dr. Hines.....	......	......	......

Lieutenant Warren's Expedition.—8902-04, Upper Missouri River; 5312, Yellowstone River; 4649, White River; 8801-03, L'eau qui court.
Later Expeditions.—60435, La Bonté Creek, Wyoming; 60768, Pacific Creek, Wyoming; 61752, Utah; 62271, Idaho.

As I stated in the "Key," "extreme examples of *ludovicianus* and *excubitoroides* look very different, but they are observed to melt into each other when many specimens are compared, so that no specific character can be assigned." The change takes place in the States just east of the Mississippi; typical *ludovicianus* I have only seen from the South Atlantic States. Whatever the original *L. elegans* of Swainson may have been, there seems to be little doubt that the *elegans* of Baird and Cooper is the same as the *excubitoroides* of the same authors. The doubt is, whether the specimen of Dr. Gambel's, marked "California," really came from that State; for some of Gambel's birds so labelled were certainly procured elsewhere (for example, his *Tyrannus bairdii*, which is a South American species, the *Tyrannus atrifrons* of Sclater—a species of *Myiodynastes*). The features of this specimen, if it be really American, may have been individual peculiarities. I consider there is as yet nothing upon which to base the belief that we have more than a single species of Shrike in this country (aside from *C. borealis*), and that is *C. ludovicianus*, of which a variety, with the above synonymy, occurs in the regions above specified.

I have not yet met with this bird on the Missouri. Dr. Hayden reports it as being quite abundant, "especially along the Platte to the Laramie Mountains, Black Hills, and Bad Lands. I found it breeding abundantly in Northern Dakota, beyond the Missouri Coteau, securing newly-fledged young late in July. The nest, just deserted, was placed in a dense thicket, in the crotch of a bush, about five feet from the ground. It was a large, bulky, and inartistic structure, upon a foundation, of loosely interlaced twigs, as large as a man's hat. The nest proper was about six inches wide outside, and three deep, composed entirely of the stems and tops of a species of white weed growing in the vicinity, inextricably matted with plaits of fibrous inner bark; there was no special lining or any circular disposition of the material. The nest was very foul with excrement and, apparently, a scurfy exfoliation from the plumage of the young.

Mr. Allen, in the American Naturalist as quoted, gives the interesting record of the breeding of *excubitoroides* in New York State. A nest of six eggs were taken in 1869, near Buffalo, New York. Mr. McIlwraith states that it is a summer resident, not very rare, at Hamilton, Canada West, where, however, it had not been observed until five or six years before 1865. Its occurrence in New England, although highly probable, remains to be confirmed. Several of the earlier authors, however, mention a New England Shrike, not *C. borealis*. See also PURDIE, *op. cit.*

Family FRINGILLIDÆ : Finches, etc.

HESPERIPHONA VESPERTINA, (Coop.) Bp.

Evening Grosbeak.

Fringilla vespertina, Coop., Ann. Lyc. N. Y. i, 1825, 220 (Michigan).—BP., Syn. 1828, 113, No. 188.—BP., Zool. Journ. iv, 1828, 2.—BP., Am. Orn. ii, 75, pl. 15, fig. 1.— NUTT., Man. i, 1832. 594.—AUD., Orn. Biog. iv, 1838, 515 ; v, 235 ; pls. 373, 425.
Coccothraustes vespertina, SW. & RICH., F. B. A. ii, 1831, 269, pl. 68.—BP., List, 1838, 30.— AUD., Syn. 1839, 134.—AUD., B. Am. iii, 1841, 217, pl. 207.
Hesperiphona vespertina, BP., C. R. xxxi, 1850, 424.—BP., Consp. Av. i, 1850, 505.—BD., B. N. A. 1858, 409.—COOP. & SUCK., N. H. Wash. Ter. 1860, 196.—SCL., P. Z. S. 1860, 251.—KIRTL., " Ohio Farmer" for March 24, 1860 (Ohio ; Racine, Wis., *Dr. Hoy*).—WHEAT., Ohio Agric. Rep. for 1860.—COUES, Pr. Phila. Acad. 1866, 80.— LAWR., Ann. Lyc. N. Y. viii, 1866, 289 (near New York City).—COUES, Pr. Ess. Inst. v, 1868, 280, 312.—MCILWR., Pr. Ess. Inst, v, 1866, 88 (Woodstock, Canada).—SUMICH., Mem. Bost. Soc. i, 1869, 550 (Monte Alto, 36 miles from city of Mexico).—COOP., B. Cal. i, 174.—AIKEN, Pr. Bost. Soc. 1872, 199 (Sherman, Wyo.).—COUES, Key, 1872, 127.—B. B. & R:, N. A. B. i, 1874, 449, pl. 22, f. 1.
Hesperiphona vespertina var. *montana*, B. B. & R., N. A. B. i, 1874, 449, pl. 22, f. 4 (individual, not geographical, variation).
Coccothraustes bonapartii, LESS., Ill. Zool. 1834, pl. 34 (♀).
Loxia bonapartii, LESS.

Hab.—Rocky Mountains to the Pacific, United States. North to the Saskatchewan (*Richardson*). Eastward along the northern tier of States to Lake Superior regularly, to Ohio, Canada, and New York City, casually. South to the table-lands of Mexico. Not procured by either of the Expeditions.
"Black Hills, ♀, June 3, 1824" (*Townsend*), AUDUBON, *op. cit.* Mr. Aiken also saw several, January 20, 1872, in the foot-hills near Sherman, Wyoming Territory.

PINICOLA ENUCLEATOR, (Linn.) Cab.

Pine Grosbeak.

Loxia enucleator, FORST., Phil. Trans. lxii, 1772, 383.—LINN., Syst. Nat. i, 1766, 299.— GM., Syst. Nat. i, 1788. 845.—WILS., Am. Orn. i, 1808, 80. pl. 5, f. 2.
Fringilla enucleator, MEYER, "Vög. 74."—TEMM., Man., Orn i, 1815, 198.
Corythus enucleator, CUVIER.—BP., Am. Orn. pl. 16, f. 3 ; List, 1838, 36.—BP. & SCHL., Monog. Lox. 9, pls. 11, 12.—GOULD, B. Eur. pl. 204.—AUD., Syn. 1839, 127.— AUD., B. Am. iii, 1841, 179, pl. 199.—GIR., B. L. I. 1844, 128.—PUTN., Pr. Ess. Inst. i, 1856, 211 (Massachusetts, rare).—TRIPPE, Pr. Ess. Inst. vi. 1871, 116 (Minnesota, winter visitant) ; and of many authors.
Pyrrhula enucleator, BP., Syn. 1828, 119.—NUTT., Man. i, 1832. 535.—AUD., Orn. Biog. iv, 1838, 414, pl. 358.—TEMM., M. i, 1820, 333.—NAUM., V. D. iv, 1824, 403, pl. 112.
Pyrrhula (Corythus) enucleator, SW. & RICH., F. B. A. ii, 1831, 262, pl. 53.—KEYS. & BLAS., 40.
Strobilophaga enucleator, VIEILL., N. D. H. N. ix, 609.—GRAY, G. of B. i, 337.
Pinicola enucleator, CAB., Mus. Hein. i, 1851, 167.—FINSCH, Abh. Nat. iii, 1872, 54 (Alaska).—COUES, Key, 1872, 127.—B. B. & R., N. A. B. i, 1874, 453, pl. 21, f. 1, 2.
Coccothaustes canadensis, BRISS., Orn. iii, 250, pl. 12, f. 3.
Corythus canadensis et C, splendens et Cangustirostris, "BREHM."
Pinicola canadensis, CAB., Mus. Hein. i, 1851, 167 (Illinois).—BD., B. N. A. 1858, 410.— COUES, Pr. Phila. Acad. 1861, 221 (Labrador, breeding).—COUES & PRENT., Smiths. Rep. 1861, 411 (accidental at Washington, D. C., in winter).—WHEAT., Ohio Agric. Rep. 1860, No. 136.—BOARDM., Pr. Bost. Soc. ix, 1862, 126 (Calais, Me., winter, common).—VERR., Pr. Ess. Inst. iii, 160 (ditto at Norway, Me.).— ALLEN, Pr. Ess. Inst. iv, 1864, 69 (Massachusetts, winter, rare).—MCILWR., Pr. Ess. Inst. v, 1866, 88 (Hamilton, C. W., irregular).—COUES, Pr. Ess. Inst. v, 1868, 280.—LAWR., Ann. Lyc. viii, 1866, 288 (New York).—COOP., Pr. Cal. Acad

Jan. 1868 (Sierra Nevada).—DALL & BANN., Tr. Chic. Acad. i, 1869, 281 (Alaska).—TURNB., B. E. Pa. 1869, 21 (rather rare).—STEV., U. S. Geol. Surv. Ter. 1870, 464 (Wyoming).—MAYN., Guide, 1870, 109 (Massachusetts, winter).— COOP., B. Cal. i, 1870, 151 (resident in Sierra Nevada of California).— SNOW, B. Kans. 1873, 6.

Pinicola americana, CAB., Mss.—BP., Consp. Av. i, 1850, 528.
"*Loxia flamingo*, SPARRM., Mus. Carls. pl. 17 (var.")*, (Gray).*
"*Loxia psittacea*, PALL.*" (Gray).*

Hab.—In this country, occupies the whole of British America, migrating regularly into the northern tier of States in winter, and occasionally to Maryland, Ohio, Illinois, and Kansas. Apparently resident in the Sierra Nevada of California, and certainly so in the Rocky Mountains within the United States. South to Colorado, where it breeds. "Breeds from Maine northward" (*Audubon*).
Later Expeditions.—60637, Uintah Mountains, September 20, 1870.

This species was not met with by either of the earlier Expeditions, and must be a rare winter visitant, if it occur at all, in most portions of the Missouri region, the greater part of which is topographically unsuited to its wants. We have, however, authentic information of its presence even so far south as Kansas. Prof. Snow places it in his list, with the remark: "occurs in winter; taken by Sidney Smith, of Leavenworth." Mr. Trippe says it appears in Wisconson "about the middle of November, and remains throughout the winter, feeding on the buds and seeds of the alder, birch, &c., as well as of the weeds that abound on the prairies." He observed a much larger proportion of old birds than there is in the flocks that visit New York, though these are still far outnumbered by the females and young. I found it rather common, and breeding, on the coast of Labrador, in patches of juniper and other thick woods. Audubon has a note of Nuttall's finding it on the Lower Missouri.

In the Rocky Mountains it finds its southernmost extension, as well as breeding range. This fact, but lately ascertained, is attested by young birds in the Smithsonian collection, and very fully by the following interesting communication which Mr. Trippe has sent me from Idaho Springs, Colorado:

"The Pine Grosbeak is irregularly distributed in this part of the mountains, being rarely seen in certain localities, while it is very common in others. It is probably resident, as I have observed it throughout the summer and fall months in the woods near timber-line, below which it does not wander very far, none being seen below 9,500 feet, even in the depth of winter, although it is probable that stragglers occasionally descend even to the foot-hills at times. It is very tame, frequently alighting and feeding within a few feet of one with the greatest composure. Its food seems to consist principally of pine seeds, but it is also fond of those of the birch and alder, and occasionally descends to the ground, where it picks up the seeds of various plants, and probably a few insects. During late summer and winter it has a very pleasing song—clear, sweet, and flowing, like that of the Purple Finch. I cannot say at what season it breeds, but am inclined to think that it must be very early, as young birds are fully feathered and have left their parents in June, before the snow has disappeared from the woods.

"Individuals vary in size—though the coloration of the adults is quite constant—and average larger than winter specimens from the Atlantic States, a length of nine or nine and one-half inches being not uncommon, while occasionally old males will measure ten and even a little over. In one specimen (an adult male, shot July 10th near James Peak) the length is 10.15 inches; the tip of the upper mandible is decurved beyond and below that of the lower 0.13 of an inch."

Two specimens of the rare and little-known egg of the Pine Grosbeak are in the Smithsonian. One taken in New Brunswick, May 7, 1865, by Mr. G. A. Boardman; the other from James' Bay. The color is a peculiar pale bluish-gray, or pale bluish with a glaucous shade, thickly speckled at the larger end with reddish-brown, and elsewhere sparingly sprinkled with the same and a few darker dots. A specimen measures 0.97 by 0.65.

CARPODACUS PURPUREUS, (Gm.) Gray.

Purple Finch.

Fringilla purpurea, GM., Syst. Nat. i, 1788, 923.—LATH., Ind. Orn. ii, 1790, 446.—WILS., Am. Orn. i, 1808, 119, pl. 7, f. 4 ; v, 1812, 87, pl. 43, f. 3.—BP., Syn. 1828, 114.—AUD., Orn. Biog. i, 1831, 24 ; v, 500, pl. 4.—SW. & RICH., F. B. A. ii, 1831, 264.—NUTT., Man. i, 1832.
Erythrospiza purpurea, BP., List, 1838, 34.—AUD., B. Am. iii, 1841, 170, pl. 196.—GIR., B. L. I. 1844, 126.—TRIPPE, Pr. Ess. Inst. vi, 1871, 116 (Minnesota).
Carpodacus purpureus, GRAY.—BP., C. A. i, 1850, 533.—NEWB., P. R. R. Rep. vi, 1857, 88.—BD., B. N. A. 1858, 412.—HEERM., P. R. R. Rep. x, 1859, 50.—HAYD., Rep. 1862, 164.—COUES, Key, 1872, 128, pl. 75.—B. B. & R., N. A. B. i, 1874, 463, pl. 21, f. 7, 8 ; and of nearly all late United States writers.
Carpodacus californicus, BD., B. N. A. 1858, 413, pl. 72, f. 23.—COOP. & SUCK., N. H. Wash. Ter. 1860, 196.—COOP., B. Cal. i, 1870, 154.
Carpodacus purpureus var. *californicus,* B. B. & R., N. A. B. i, 1874, 465, pl. 21, f. 10, 11.

Hab.—United States from Atlantic to Pacific, excepting, probably, the Southern Rocky Mountain region, where replaced by the following species. North to the Saskatchewan and Labrador. Winters in the Southern States.
Lieutenant Warren's Expedition.—4853, Vermilion River.
Not obtained by Captain Raynolds' Expedition.

Dr. Hayden's suspicion that this species does not occur on the uppermost Missouri may prove correct. I have found it, however, as high up as Fort Randall. This was in October; I observed small flocks in shrubbery, feeding on and near the ground. Very cold weather setting in soon after, no more were observed, and I think that they all moved off southward. I found it breeding on Turtle Mountain, Dakota, in July. The egg is clear pale bluish, irregularly dotted, but chiefly in a wreath around the large end, with very dark blackish-brown—almost black in some instances; in others lighter. An average egg is 0.80 by 0.60; but I have seen specimens from 0.85 by 0.57 (abnormally elongate) to 0.75 by 0.56.

I have failed to substantiate any tangible distinctions between the bird of the Pacific coast and the ordinary form.

CARPODACUS CASSINI, Bd.

Cassin's Purple Finch.

Carpodacus cassini, BD., Pr. Phila. Acad. 1854, 119.—BD., B. N. A. 1858, 414.—KENN., P. R. R. Rep. x, 1859, 27, pl. 27, f. 1.—LORD, Pr. Roy. Arty. Inst. iv, 1864, 119 (British Columbia).—COUES, Pr. Phila. Acad. 1866, 80.—SCL., P. Z. S. 1869, 362 (city of Mexico).—COOP., B. Cal. i, 155.—MERR., U. S. Geol. Surv. Ter. 1872, 678.—COUES, Key, 1872, 128.—B. B. & R., N. A. B. i, 1874, 460, pl. 21, f. 4, 5.
(?) *Carpodacus purpureus,* ALLEN, Bull. M. C. Z. iii, 1872, 176 (Colorado and Utah).

Hab.—Southern Rocky Mountain region. North to British Columbia, between Cascades and Rocky Mountains. Table-lands of Mexico. (SCL. & SALV., P. Z. S. 1869, 362.)

List of specimens.

19250	77	W. River Mts.	♂	June 5, 1860	F. V. Hayden.	6.50	11.25	3.50
19251	66	......do......	♂	.....do......	......do......	6.50	11.00	3.75

Later Expeditions.—62326–26, Yellowstone and Snake Rivers.

Not obtained by Lieutenant Warren's Expedition.

Although it might be argued with some reason that this is merely a variety of *purpureus*, I am at present inclined to treat it as a distinct species, for I have seen no specimens, of many examined, that were not instantly recognizable by the peculiarities given in the above-quoted works. Dr. Hayden's specimens are interesting as representing the northeasternmost recorded locality.

I have only myself observed this species in Arizona, about Fort Whipple, where it was common, and resident. It is found westward to the Sierra Nevada, but probably not beyond. Dr. Cooper found it in large numbers about Lake Tahoe, and noticed a peculiar call-note. So little has been placed on record of its habits, that the following paragraph from Mr. Trippe, referring to his observations at Idaho Springs, Colorado, is the more acceptable :

"Abundant; breeds. A few remain all winter in sheltered localities in Bergen's Park, but the greater number seek some warmer climate, returning as soon as the severest portion of the season has passed by. In March and April they frequent the dense thickets of willows that line the banks of nearly all the streams in places, and have at that time a low, sweet warbling song, which becomes louder in May, and then fully equals that of the Purple Finch. They breed as high as 10,000 feet, but are not uniformly distributed, as I never saw them abundant outside of Bergen's Park. During summer and fall they frequent the pine trees in which they nest; and during this season the female sings nearly as sweetly as the male. I strongly suspect that the *C. purpureus* mentioned by Allen as abundant in the South Park, was this species, which he does not give at all. The latter is common, while the former is at least so rare that I never saw it in a year's careful observation."

The only sets of eggs I have seen are not distinguishable from some specimens of *C. purpureus*, though on an average they are probably rather larger. As in the case of that species, very pale sets occur, corresponding to the whitish eggs of Blue-birds. The nidification is wholly similar to that of *C. purpureus*. The eggs, supposed to be of this species, lately described by Dr. Brewer, are those of *C. frontalis*. They were from the South Arizona collection of Lieutenant C. Bendire, who writes me that they were wrongly identified. *C. cassini* probably does not breed in that locality. (*Cf.* BREW., Pr. Bost. Soc. xvi, 1873, 109.)

CARPODACUS FRONTALIS, (Say) Gray.

Crimson-fronted Finch; House Finch; Burion.

a. *frontalis.*

Fringilla frontalis, SAY, Long's Exped. R. Mts. ii, 1824, 40.
Fringilla (Pyrrhula) frontalis, GAMB., Pr. Phila. Acad. i, 1843, 262.
Pyrrhula frontalis, BP., Am. Orn. i, 1825, 49, pl. 6, figs. 1, 2.
Erythrospiza frontalis, BP., P. Z. S. 1837, 112; List, 1838, 35.—GAMB., J. P. Ac. 1847, 53.
Carpodacus frontalis, GRAY, Genera of Birds.—BP., Consp. i, 1850, 533.—McCALL, Pr. Phila. Acad. 1851, 219.—NEWB., P. R. R. Rep. vi, 1857, 88.—BD., B. N. A. 1858, 415.—KENN., P. R. R. Rep. x, 1859, pt. iv, 28.—COUES, Pr. Phila. Acad. 1866, 80.—COUES, Ibis, 1866, 267.—COOP., B. Cal. i, 1870, 156.—AIKEN, Pr. Bost. Soc. 1872, 199 (Arkansas River, Col.).—COUES, Key, 1872, 129.
Carpodacus frontalis var. *frontalis,* RIDGW., Am. Journ. v, 1873, 40.—B. B. & R., N. A. B. i, 1874, 466, pl. 21, f. 3, 6.
Carpodacus familiaris, McCALL, Pr. Phila. Acad. vii, 1852, 61.—WOODH., Sitgr. Rep. 1853, 88.—CASS., Ill. 1854, 73, pl. 13.—HEERM., P. R. R. Rep. x, 1859, pt. vi, 50.
Carpodacus obscurus, McCALL, Pr. Phila. Acad. 1851, 220.
Carpodacus "*californicus,*" COUES, Ibis, 1865, 164 (*lapsu*).
Carpodacus "*cassini,*" BREW., Pr. Bost. Soc. xvi, 1873, 109 (error in identification of eggs).

b. *rhodocolpus.*

Carpodacus rhodocolpus, CAB., Mus. Hein. 1851, 166.—SCL., P. Z. S. 1856, 304; 1857, 127.
Carpodacus frontalis var. *rhodocolpus*, RIDGW., Am. Journ. Sci. v, 1873, 39.—B. B. & R.,
    N. A. B. i, 1874, 463, pl. 21, f. 9.

c. *hœmorrhous.*

Pyrrhula frontalis, SW., Syn. Mex. B. in Phil. Mag. i, 1827, 435, No. 52.
Erythrospiza frontalis, BP., "Osserv. Reg. anim. Cuv., p. 80."—(?) AUD., Syn. 1839, 125;
    B. Am. iii, 1841, 175, pl. 197 ((*Fringilla frontalis* of the folio ed., pl. 424).
Carpodacus frontalis, BP. & SCHL., Mon. *Lox.* 15, pl. 16.
Fringilla hœmorrhoa, WAG., Isis, 1831, 525.
Carpodacus hœmorrhous, SCL., P. Z. S. 1856, 304 (Cordova); 1858, 303; 1859, 380 (Oaxaca);
    Cat. 1862, 122.—BD., B. N. A. 1858, 417.—SUMICH., Mem. Bost. Soc. i, 1869, 550.
Carpodacus frontalis var. *hœmorrhous*, RIDGW., *l. c.*

Hab.—Southern Rocky Mountains and Sierra Nevada, United States. North to the
headwaters of the Platte or further, and on the Pacific side to Oregon. Var. *rhodocolpus*
from the Pacific coast, Southern California, to Colima. Var. *hœmorrhous* from the Table
Lands of Mexico.

While I am willing to follow Mr. Ridway in adopting a Mexican var. *hœmorrhous*, I
do not feel satisfied of the necessity for recognizing var. *rhodocolpus*—at least my collections do not bear out the asserted differences. Comparing one from New Mexico
with another from Southern California, both males in good plumage, the red of the
former is seen to "spread" *more* than that of the latter, instead of the reverse, as
ought to be the case, according to Mr. Ridgway. Still he has examined much more
material than I have, and I presume his definition is borne out, as a rule; and this is
all, I believe, that is claimed in such cases. Some of the above quotations under var.
frontalis include, or refer to, var. *rhodocolpus*. Females and young of the several varieties are indistinguishable.

I met with great numbers of "Burions" on first entering New Mexico,
and traced them thence across the continent to the Pacific, at San Pedro.
In the Mexican towns they were as plentiful, fearless and familiar, as
the English Sparrows have become in many of our eastern cities, breeding in all sorts of nooks about the buildings, as well as in the forks of
trees in the court-yards and streets. It is a pleasing feature in the dirty
Mexican settlements which, with questionable taste, it selects as its
abode, and where the air is vocal all the day long with its delightful
melody. They are seldom molested by the worthless population, who
have only just energy enough to bask by day in the sun rolling cigar-
ettes, and cheat each other at cards by night; consequently the little
birds thrive, and no doubt live as happily as if they were appreciated.
The materials of the nests are as various as the location; but the structure is usually of grasses, lined with finer dried roots or hair. The eggs,
five or six in number, are about three-fourths of an inch long by three-
fifths wide, and pale bluish, marked, chiefly near the larger end, with
specks and lines of blackish-brown. Two or three broods are reared
each year. Among the situations chosen for the nest, Dr. Cooper mentions trees, logs and rocks, "the top rail of a picket-fence, inside a win-
dow-shutter, in the holes of walls, under tile or thatch roofs, in hay-
stacks and barns, in the interstices between the sticks of a Hawk's nest,
and in the old nest of an Oriole;" to which Dr. Heermann adds, cactuses
and Woodpeckers' holes. In the Rio Grande towns, where Barn Swallows were breeding plentifully, the House Finches used to occupy last
year's Swallows' nests, and not unfrequenly would take possession by
force, after an animated contest, of a nest just finished, making its disconsolate owners, who had little chance against the spirited interlopers,
build another nest. But as a rule, the Finches and Swallows lived amicably, the former rather prefering the trees in the areas, while the gentle Swallows nestled under the eaves on projecting rafters.

In the interior of Arizona, where towns were not, and have not yet
become, the established order of things, I found the Burions no more

familiar than most small birds are, frequenting open hillsides and ravines, often in company with Cassin's Purple Finches. They were abundant, and apparently residents, though more numerous in the spring and fall than at other seasons. I also found them in good feather and full song in November, at San Pedro, when I enjoyed the hospitalities of my friend Dr. Cooper, then post surgeon at Drumm Barracks. He told me that further south, at San Diego, they begin to build early in March. Under the name of Linnets, they are often kept in cages in California, as the Arkansas Goldfinch is in New Mexico.

Mr. Trippe informs me that the Crimson-fronted Finch is only an occasional visitor to Clear Creek County, Colorado, small flocks sometimes visiting the lower valleys in late spring. It does not breed in the county, so far as his observations go, though it is not improbable that a few nest in Bergen's Park.

LOXIA CURVIROSTRA var. AMERICANA, (Wils.) Coues.

American Red Crossbill.

b. *americana*.

Loxia curvirostra, FORST., Phil. Trans. lxii, 1772, No. 23.—BP., Syn. 1828, 117.—NUTT. Man. i, 1832, 583.—AUD., Orn. Biog. ii, 1834, 559 ; v, 511 ; pl. 197 ; Syn. 1839 128 ; B. Am. iii, 186 ; pl. 200.—GIR., B. L. I. 1844, 130.—TRIPPE, Pr. Ess. Inst vi, 1871, 117 (Minnesota, very common, breeds).
Loxia curvirostra var. *americana*, COUES, Key, 1872, 351.—B. B. & R., N. A. B. i, 1874 484, pl. 23, f. 1, 4.
Curvirostra americana, WILS., Am. Orn. iv, 1811, 44, pl. 31, f. 1, 2.—BD., B. N. A. 1858, 426.—COOP. & SUCK., N. H. Wash. Ter. 1860, 198.—WHEAT., Ohio Agric. Rep. 1860, —.—HAYD., Rep. 1862, 165.—ALLEN, Pr. Ess. Inst. iv, 1864, 70.—BOARDM., Pr. Bost. Soc. ix, 1862, 126 (Calais, Me. ; said to breed in winter).—COUES, Pr. Ess. Inst. v, 1868, 281.—TURNB., B. E. Pa. 1869, 21 (winter, and resident in the Alleghanies).—DALL & BANN., Tr. Chic. Acad. i, 1869, 281 (Sitka).—COOP., B. Cal. i, 1870, 148 (resident in the Sierra Nevada).—MAYN., Pr. Bost. Soc. xiv, 1871, —.—MAYN., N. Guide, 1870, 111.—COUES, Key, 1872, 129, pl. 3, figs, 13, 14, 15.
Loxia americana, BP., List, 1838, 38 ; Consp. 1850, 527.—NEWB., P. R. R. Rep. vi, 1857, 87.—LAWR., Ann. Lyc. N. Y. viii, 1868, 288 (New York).—FINSCH, Abh. Nat. iii, 1872, 56 (Alaska).

c. *mexicana*.

Loxia mexicana, STRICKL., Jard. C. O. 1851, 43 (city of Mexico).—BD., B. N. A. 1858, 94.— SCL., P. Z. S. 1859, 365 ; 1864, 174.—SALV., Ibis, 1866, 193 (Guatemala).
Curvirostra mexicana, SUMICH., Mem. Bost. Soc. Nat. Hist. i, 1869, 551 (Orizaba).—STEV., U. S. Geol. Surv. Ter. 1870, 464.
Curvirostra americana var. *mexicana*, COUES, Key, 1872, 129.
Loxia curvirostra var. *mexicana*, COUES.—B. B. & R., N. A. B. i, 1874, 488.

Hab.—Northern North America. South into most of the States in winter (on the Atlantic usually to Philadelphia). Resident in Maine, and southward, in alpine regions, to Pennsylvania. Breeds in Minnesota. Resident in the Sierra Nevada of California. South along the alpine regions of Mexico to Guatemala (var. *mexicana*).
Lieutenant Warren's Expedition.—8962-63, Laramie Peak.
Later Expeditions.—59881, 60091, Colorado ; 60386-87, Wyoming.
Not obtained by Captain Raynolds' Expedition.

Mr. Trippe has furnished me the following observations made in Clear Creek County, Colorado : "Like the Pine Grosbeak, the Crossbill is irregularly distributed throughout the county, flocks of hundreds being occasionally seen, while, as a rule, it is not commonly to be met with in this part of the mountains. It ranges much lower than the former bird, breeding from 7,000 feet, if not lower, all the way up to timber-line; nesting, as near as can be judged from the appearance of the young birds, in April and May, according to the elevation, or about the breaking up of winter. In June flocks composed of young and old may be seen roving through the woods occasionally, and alighting on dead limbs and tree tops, where their bright colors and noisy chatter are sure to attract the attention of passers-by. They are not at all shy, and 'sometimes alight in trees in the midst of large towns. Their food is the same as the Pine Grosbeak's—the seeds of pines, birches, &c.; and as they sometimes alight in the thickets of rose-bushes, raspberries and other shrubbery, they probably add haws and berries to their bill of fare. In June I have heard it sing very agreeably; its notes are much like those of the Pine Grosbeak, and show the family resemblance which runs through the songs of all the members of this group of the *Fringillidæ*. Among a series of specimens, some will be found having much larger bills than others, showing an approach to var. *mexicana*. A male, taken in Bergen Park, had the bill 0.78 in length.

The eggs of this species are four or five in number, about 0.85 by 0.52 in size, very pale greenish, variously marked in dots and blotches, with different shades of lilac and purplish brown. Dr. Brewer notes a nest taken in Vermont, early in March, when the ground was covered with snow, from the upper branch of a leafless elm. "The birds were very tame and fearless, refusing to leave their eggs, and had to be several times taken off by hand." Even after the nest had been taken in hand the bird resumed its place upon it.

LOXIA LEUCOPTERA, Gm.

White-winged Crossbill.

Loxia leucoptera, GM., Syst. Nat. i, 1788, 844.—BP., Syn. 1828, 117.—BP., Am. Orn. ii, —.—SW. & RICH., F. B A. ii, 1831, 263.—NUTT., Man. i, 1832, 540.—AUD., Orn. Biog. iv, 1838, 467, pl. 364; Syn. 1839, 129; B. Am. iii, 1841, 190, pl. 201.—GIR., B. L. I. 1844, 131.—BP., Consp. Av. i, 1850, 527.—REINH., Ibis, iii, 1861, 8 (Greenland).—GOULD, B. Gr. Brit. v, 1864, pl. — (England).—LAWR., Ann. Lyc. N. Y. viii, 1866, 288.—FINSCH, Abh. Nat. iii, 1872, 55 (Alaska).—B. B. & R., N. A. B. i, 1874, 488, pl. 23, f. 2, 3.
Curvirostra leucoptera, WILS., Am. Orn. iv, 1811, 48; pl. 31, f. 3.—BD., B. N. A. 1858, 427.— WHEAT., Ohio Agric. Rep. 1860, —.—HAYD., Rep. 1862, 165.—ALLEN, Pr. Ess. Inst. iv, 1864, 70.—BOARDM., Pr. Bost. Soc. ix, 1862, 126 (Calais, Me., breeding in winter).—MCILWR., Pr. Ess. Inst. v, 1866, 88.—COUES, Pr. Ess. Inst. v, 1868, 281.—TURNB., B. E. Pa. 1869, 22.—DALL & BANN., Tr. Chic. Acad. i, 1869, 281.— STEV., U. S. Geol. Surv. Ter. 1870, 464.—MAYN., Nat. Guide, 1870, 111.—MAYN., Pr. Bost. Soc. xiv, 1871, —.—COOP., B. Cal. i, 1870, 149 (not in California).— COUES, Key. 1872, 129, fig. 76.
Loxia falcirostra, LATH., Ind. Orn. i, 1790, 371.
Crucirostra leucoptera, BREHM, Naum. i, 1853, 254, f. 20.

Hab.—Northern North America, from ocean to ocean. South in winter into the United States, as far west as the Rocky Mountains (no United States Pacific coast record). Resident in Northern New England; breeding in winter, and, according to Audubon, breeding in Pennsylvania and New Jersey. Wyoming in summer. South ordinarily to Philadelphia. Greenland, one instance. Accidental in Europe. (See HARTING, Man. Brit. Birds, 1872, 116.)

List of specimens.

19152	81	W. side W. Riv. Mts.	♂	June 5, 1860	F. V. Hayden.	6.25	10.50	3.25
19153	78	.... do	♂	..... do	..... do	6.25	10.25	3.25

Lieutenant Warren's Expedition.—8964-65, Laramie Peak, August 25, 1857.
Later Expeditions.—60639, Box Elder Creek, Wyoming, August 21, 1870.

Dr. Hayden's specimens are of unusual interest. They afford the only record I have been able to find of the occurrence of the species in the United States west of the Mississippi; while the dates of collection— June, August—render it unquestionable that the birds breed where they were procured. Dr. Brewer describes a saucer-shaped nest of lichens, encased in spruce-twigs, lined with hair and bark shreds, four inches in diameter, with a cavity an inch and a half deep; the egg pale blue, spattered at large end with fine dots of black and ashy-lilac; the size 0.80 by 0.56. It was taken in New Brunswick.

It is remarkable that so many of these birds should have been taken in Great Britain where, however, *L. americana* has not been found. Mr. Harting, as above quoted, enumerates four instances in which they were observed, on one of which occasions "a large flock" made its appearance near Banff, in 1859. He also says: "Some years since Dr. Dewar, of Glasgow, when six hundred miles off Newfoundland, observed a number of these birds crossing the Atlantic before a stiff westerly breeze. Many alighted on the rigging, and ten or twelve were secured."

LEUCOSTICTE TEPHROCOTIS, Sw.

Gray-crowned Finch.

a. *tephrocotis.*

Linaria (Leucosticte) tephrocotis, Sw., F. B. A. ii, 1831, 265, pl. 50 (Saskatchewan, May, 1827).
Leucosticte tephrocotis, Sw., Classif. B. ii, 1837.—BP., C. A. i, 1850, 536.—BD., Stansbury's Rep. 1852, 317 (Salt Lake City, Utah).—BD., B. N. A. 1858, 430.—STEV., U. S. Geol. Surv. Ter. 1872, 464 (Wyoming).—COOP., B. Cal. i, 1870, 174 (California).— ALLEN, Bull. M. C. Z. iii, 1872, 162 (Mt. Lincoln, Park county, Col., July, breeding above timber-line).—COUES, Key, 1872, 130.—B. B. & R., N. A. B. i, 1874, 504, pl. 23, f. 8, 9.
Erythrospiza tephrocotis, BP., C. & G. List, 1838, 34.—AUD., Syn. 1839.—AUD., B. Am. iii, 1841, 176, pl. 198 (Swainson's type).
Fringilla tephrocotis, NUTT., Man. Orn. ii, 1834, App. 593.—AUD., O. B. v, 1839, 232, pl. 424.
Leucosticte campestris, BD., in Cooper's B. Cal. i, 1870, 163 (Colorado, *Wernigk;* slightly approaching the next var.).
Leucosticte tephrocotis var. *campestris,* COUES, Key, 1872, 130.—B. B. & R., N. A. B. i, 1874, 507, pl. 23, f. 7.
Leucosticte tephrocotis var. *australis,* ALLEN, Mss. (midsummer plumage). *

b. *griseinucha.*

Passer arctous var. γ, PALLAS, Zoog. R.-A. ii, 1811, 23.
Fringilla (Linaria) griseinucha, BRANDT, Bull. Imp. Acad. St. Peters. 1844, 36.
Montifringilla (Leucosticte) griseinucha, BP. & SCHL., Mon. Lox. 1850, 35, pl. 41.
Montifringilla griseinucha, FINSCH, Abh. Nat. iii, 1872, 57 (Alaska).
Leucosticte griseinucha, BP., Consp. Av. i, 1850, 537.—BD., B. N. A. 1858, 430.—ELLIOT, B. N. A. pl. 11.—DALL & BANN., Tr. Chic. Acad. i, 1869, 282, pl. 28, f. 2.—COOP., B. Cal. i, 1871, 161 (not California, but Oonalashka and St. George's, Alaska).— DALL, Pr. Cal. Acad. Feb. 1873 (Oonalashka Island).
Leucosticte tephrocotis var. *griseinucha,* and var. *littoralis,* COUES, Key, 1872, 130, 352, fig. 77.—B. B. & R., N. A. B. i, 1874, 508, 507, pl. 23, f. 5, 6.
Leucosticte griseigenys, GOULD, P. Z. S. 1843, 104.—GOULD, Voy. Sulphur, i, 1844, 42, pl. 22.
Leucosticte littoralis, BD., Tr. Chic. Acad. i, 1869, 318, pl. 28, f. 1.—DALL & BANN., *ibid.* 282.—COOP., B. Cal. i, 1870, 162 (Sitka, British Columbia; Fort Simpson).
Montifringilla littoralis, FINSCH, Abh. Nat. iii, 1872, 58 (Alaska).

Hab.—Northwestern North America and Saskatchewan to the Pacific. South to Colorado, Utah, and Northern California. Var. *griseinucha* from the Pacific coast from British Columbia northward, and Aleutian Islands. In the interior to Fort Simpson.

---

* This cannot well be a variety—if it is anything more than midsummer plumage, it is a good species. Mr. Allen's originals, labelled as cited, were submitted to Prof. Baird and myself. Prof. Baird's opinion is recorded in his work, *l. c.;* my own is here given. In the Appendix to the third volume of his work, now in press, however, a var. *australis,* in which I do not concur, will be recognized.

List of specimens.

19255	265	Deer Creek	♂	Feb. 22, 1860	F. V. Hayden.	6.50	12.50	4.00
19256	241	...... do	♀	Jan. 17, 1860	..... do	6.50	12.50	4.50
19257	262	...... do	♂	Feb. 23, 1860	..... do	6.50	12.50	4.50
19259	266	...... do	♀	Feb. 22, 1860	..... do	6.00	11.00	4.00
19262	264	...... do	♀	...... do	..... do	6.25	11.50	4.50
19263	267	...... do	....	Mar. 7, 1860	..... do	6.25	12.50	4.50
19264	270	...... do	♀	Feb. 28, 1860	..... do	......	......	......
19265	244	...... do	....	Jan. 17, 1860	..... do	6.00	11.50	4.25
19266	243	...... do	....	...... do	..... do	6.50	11.75	4.00
19267	246	...... do	....	...... do	..... do	6.00	12.00	4.00
19268	142	...... do	♀	Jan. 2, 1860	..... do	6.50	12.50	3.75
19269	247	...... do	0	Jan. 17, 1860	..... do	5.75	11.50	3.75
19270	263	...... do ....,	♂	Feb. 22, 1860	..... do	6.25	11.75	4.25
19271	269	...... do	♂	...... do	..... do	6.25	11.25	4.50
19273	245	...... do	♂	Jan. 17, 1860	..... do	6.50	12.00	4.00
19274	246	...... do	♀	...... do	..... do	5.75	11.00	3.50
19258	141	...... do	....	Nov. 22, 1859	G. H. Trook..	6.50	12.50	4.50
19254	268	...... do	♂	Feb. 28, 1860	..... do	6.50	12.50	4.50
19260	145	...... do	....	Nov. 22, 1859	..... do	6.50	12.50	4.50
19261	143	...... do	....	...... do	..... do	6.50	12.50	4.50
19272	147	...... do	♀	Nov. 21, 1859	..... do	6.50	12.50	4.50

Later Expeditions.—60633, Uintah Mountains.

One of the most interesting results of Dr. Hayden's ornithological researches is the discovery that this highly-prized bird, hitherto considered so rare, is abundant in the Wind River Mountains, where, as shown by the above list, numerous specimens were procured by himself and Mr. Trook in the winter of 1859–'60. Originally described from the Saskatchewan, the same specimen afforded the subject of Audubon's plate, and the subsequent United States quotation from Great Salt Lake remained single until the present discovery. Since this, however, the records have multiplied, until the distribution above given has been determined. In January, 1862, Dr. C. Wernigk sent the bird from Denver, Colorado, to the Smithsonian ; this specimen became the basis of the untenable *L. "campestris."* In the birds of California, Dr. Cooper states that he saw a specimen brought from somewhere east of Lake Tahoe, in Washoe. "They were said to be plentiful there in the very cold winter of 1861–'62, and doubtless visited the similar country east cf the Northern Sierra Nevada within this State." It remained, however, for Mr. Allen to show that the bird breeds in the United States. He found it, in summer, "common above the timber-line on Mount Lincoln [Colorado] breeding among the snow-fields." He also mentions other specimens killed at Central City, Colorado, in March, 1869, by Mr. F. E. Everett.

Mr. Allen's specimens, which he kindly transmitted to me for examination, differ materially from any previously-known plumage of *L. tephrocotis*, as he himself says in giving a careful description of them (*op. cit.* 162). Not to duplicate his description, it will be sufficient to state here that the peculiarities lie in the darkness of the general chocolate or liver-brown ; the heightening of the customary rosy to crimson ; the entire absence of silvery-ash on the head, the whole crown being sooty blackish ; and in the black instead of whitish bill. He remarks that, "whether they represent more than the breeding plumage or *L. tephrocotis*, or a well-marked southern form of that species, I am at present uncertain, being without summer specimens of that species." I have myself no doubt whatever that they represent the worn midsummer state of the breeding plumage, and nothing more. Everything seems to indicate this ; and if analogy be pertinent in the case, we may instance the closely-allied *Ægiothus linaria*, which in midsummer often shows a precisely parallel condition.

Inspection of Swainson's remarkably faithful plate will give a good idea of the normal condition of typical *tephrocotis*, with which all the United States specimens I have seen, excepting these of Mr. Allen's, agree perfectly. We have just seen how southern individuals at least, under certain circumstances, lose the hoary ash of the head altogether. In this variability of the ash we find the clue to the correct interpretation of some northern styles that have been currently accepted as distinct species. In the extreme case of *griseinucha* (Brandt), the ash envelopes nearly the whole head, including the chin, leaving only a black frontlet of varying width. Such a specimen looks quite unlike typical *tephrocotis*, and would certainly be held a distinct species, were the intermediate links unknown. Such, however, is not the case; in the Smithsonian series alone, which I have examined, we find almost every imaginable gradation in the extent of the ash, so that it becomes impossible to draw a dividing line anywhere. It is necessary, therefore, to treat *griseinucha* as a variety of *tephrocotis*. As stated in the Key (p. 352), it does not seem to be necessary to recognize more than one variety, "*campestris*" of Baird being referable to *tephrocotis* proper, and "*littoralis*" of Baird agreeing sufficiently with var. *griseinucha*.

It is interesting to observe, that in the closely allied but apparently distinct species, *L. arctoa* of Siberia, and of the Kurile and Aleutian Islands, a great part of the plumage takes on a rosy-tinted, silvery-ash hue.

We have little information respecting the habits of the Gray-crowned Finch; they probably agree in the main with those of Red-polls and Linnets. Mr. Holden gives a note upon this subject, and one also bearing upon the dark plumage above discussed. Speaking of the mountainous southeastern extremity of Wyoming, he says: "These birds are never found here in summer; they come in small flocks in the coldest part of winter. Their food is small seeds and insects. I have found some with the crops so full of seeds as to distort the birds. They become very fat, and are good eating. In one specimen, a young male I think, the plumage is almost *black*—in fact it *is* black, except the wings and after-half of the body."

I find the following notes in Mr. Trippe's Mss.:

"During the winter I saw several flocks of this bird near Central City, where they were feeding in the dry gulches and about gardens, acting like Lapland Longspurs; but did not observe them elsewhere, though I looked carefully for them throughout a large extent of country. During summer and autumn the Gray-crowned Finch is common above timber-line, where it breeds, ranging higher than the Titlark, and being usually found in the vicinity of snow-fields and the frozen lakes near the summit of the range. It is rather shy in such localities, though exceedingly tame in winter; its flight is in undulating lines, like the Crossbill's, and the only note I have heard it utter is a kind of 'churr,' like the call of the Scarlet Tanager. In the latter part of September small flocks, composed of one or two families, may be seen together; and still later in the season they gather into large flocks. They stay above timber-line till the close of October or the middle of November, being much hardier than the Titlark; and only descend when driven away by the furious winter storms. * * * * Since the above was penned, great flocks of the Gray-crowned Finch have appeared near Idaho Springs. In their habits and actions they are very similar to the *Plectrophanes*. They are perpetually roving from place to place; feed upon the seeds of weeds and grasses; and are never at rest for more than a moment at a time, constantly whirling about in close, dense masses, like so many

Longspurs. · During summer there is no ash whatever on the head; but in some thirty or forty specimens killed during the past week (December) the ash is present in every one. In three or four this color extends below the eyes and over the cheeks; and in two it embraces the throat. Bill, black in summer, yellow in winter with a black tip." Mr. Dall has given us an interesting note upon var. *griseinucha*: "This species abounds on the Prybilov and Aleutian Islands. A number of specimens were obtained on St. George's in August, although they were moulting at the time. * * * * This beautiful bird had no song at that season except a clear chirp, sounding like '*wéet-a-wéet-a-wee-weet.*' It was on the wing a great part of the time, avoiding alighting on the ground, but darting rapidly in a series of ascending and descending curves, now swinging on the broad top of an umbelliferous plant, and now alighting on some ledge of the perpendicular bluff, jumping from point to point, and seemingly delighting in testing its own agility. Their nest is a simple hollow on one of these ledges, provided with a few straws or bits of moss. They lay four white eggs in May (0.97 by 0.67). In August the young were fully fledged. They are granivorous, apparently, but I found two or three small beetles in the crop of one which I skinned."

The same author's later article, above quoted, is as follows: "This is one of the most abundant small birds of the [Aleutian] islands, and is especially common at Oonalashka, where it is resident. On the 24th of May we found a nest situated in a crevice of a rocky bank on the shore of Captain's Harbor, Oonalashka. It was of grass, very neatly sewed together, and lined with fine grass and a few feathers. It contained five white eggs in a fresh condition, and was about twelve feet above the beach. The bird was most common on the grassy banks and rocky bluffs near the shore; I do not remember ever having seen one on the higher hills or mountains. It is usually found singly or in pairs."

ÆGIOTHUS LINARIA, (Linn.) Cab.

Red-poll Linnet.

Fringilla linaria, LINN., Syst. Nat. i, 1766, 322.—GM., Syst. Nat. i, 1788, 917.—WILS., Am.
 Orn. iv, 41, pl. 30, f. 4; ix, 126.—TEMM., Man. Orn. 1820, 373 (*nec* 1835).—BP.,
 Syn. 1828, 112.—NUTT., Man. i, 1832, 512.—AUD., Orn. Biog. iv, 1838, 533, pl. 375.
Fringilla (Acanthis) linaria, KEYS. & BLAS., Wirbel. Europ. 1840, 161.
Passer linaria, PALL., Zoog. R.-A. ii, 1811, 25.
Spinus linarius, KOCH, Syst. Zool. 233.
Linota linaria, BP., List, 1838, 34.—HOLBOËLL, Fn. Groen. 1846, 29?
Acanthis linaria, BP., Consp. i, 1850, 541.—BP. & SCH., Mon. Lox. 48, pl. 52.
Ægiothus linarius, CAB., Mus. Hein. 1851, 161.—BD., B. N. A. 1858, 428.—COUES, Pr. Phila.
 Acad. 1861, 382.—DALL & BANN., Tr. Chic. Acad. i, 1869, 281 (Alaska).—COOP.,
 B. Cal. 1870, 159.—COUES, Key, 1872, 130, pl. 3, figs. 1, 2, 4, 5.—MAYN., Guide,
 1870, 110.—STÉV., U. S. Geol. Surv. Ter. 1870, 464.—B. B. & R., N. A. B. i, 1874,
 493, pl. 22, f. 3, 5; and of most late writers.
Linaria minor, SW. & RICH., F. B. A. ii, 1831, 267.—AUD., Syn. 1839, 114; B. Am. iii,
 1841, 122, pl. 179.—GIR., B. L. I. 1844, 116.—TRIPPE, Pr. Ess. Inst. vi, 1871, 116
 (Minnesota).
Fringilla borealis, VIEILL., Nouv. Dict. xxi, 341; *nec* Temm.
Linaria americana, MAXIM., J. f. O. vi, 1858, 338.
Ægiothus fuscescens, COUES, Pr. Phila. Acad. 1861, 222 (Labrador); 1861, 380; 1869,
 186.—ELLIOT, B. N. A. pl. 10. (Midsummer plumage.)
Ægiothus linaria var. *fuscescens*, COUES, Key, 1872, 131, pl. 3, f. 3.

Hab.—The typical form in North America, from Atlantic to Pacific, ranging irregularly southward, in flocks, in winter, to the Middle States (sometimes a little beyond) and corresponding latitudes in the West. No late record of breeding in the United States. ("Breeds in Maine, Nova Scotia," &c., *Audubon*.)
 Not obtained by the earlier Expeditions.
 Later Expeditions.—60977–88, various Wyoming localities.

I am now inclined to the opinion, that my *Æg. fuscescens*, originally described from Labrador as a distinct species, and subsequently, in the Key, reduced to a variety, will finally prove to have been based merely upon the midsummer plumage of ordinary *linaria*. At this season the whole plumage becomes much darker—partially as a mechanical effect of the wearing away of the lighter edgings of the feathers—the bill blackens, and the nasal *plumulæ* are somewhat deficient. This would correspond precisely with the now determined summer condition of *Leucosticte tephrocotis.* Var. *exilipes* is better marked; it appears to consist of the more nearly stationary individuals, this particular form having been rarely, if ever, observed in the United States. The small size of the bill and feet, heavy nasal *plumulæ*, and hoariness of plumage, all indicate a boreal race. By those who separate the Greenland *"canescens"* as a species, *exilipes* is rated as a variety of the latter rather than of *linaria*; but the Greenland bird may be merely one link in a chain, rather better marked than usual, in consequence of its isolation and continual subjection, for an indefinite period, to special modifying influences. The synonymy of *exilipes* is as follows:

Linota borealis, BP., List. 1838, 34.
Fringilla borealis, AUD., Orn. Biog. v, 1839, 87, pl. 400 ; *nec* Vieill.
Linaria borealis, AUD., B. Am. iii, 1841, 120, pl. 178 ; *nec* Temm.
Ægiothus canescens, ROSS, Edinb. Phil. Journ. 1861, 163 ; *nec* Auct.
Ægiothus exilipes, COUES, Pr. Phila. Acad. 1861, 385 ; 1869, 187.—ELLIOT, B. N. A. pl. 9.
Ægiothus linaria var. *exilipes*, COUES, Key, 1872, 131, pl. 3, f. 6.
Ægiothus canescens var *exilipes*, RIDGW., Mss.—B. B. & R., N. A. B. i, 1874, 493, pl. 22, f. 2.

In Minnesota, according to Mr. Trippe, "the Lesser Red-poll appears in vast numbers about the middle of October, and remains during the entire winter, proceeding northward, however, some weeks before the Snow Buntings and Longspurs." The Red-poll lays four or five eggs of a pale bluish-green color, speckled chiefly in a wreath round the large end with confluent blotches of pale-reddish brown, purplish-brown, and a few darker-brown tints. Sometimes an egg is obsoletely freckled all over with pale reddish-brown. The size is about 0.70 by 0.50. Great numbers were observed, and many specimens secured, by Lieutenant Mullan's Expedition, while surveying for a military road from Walla-Walla to Fort Bridger. Like other species of this roving tribe, the Red-poll may be expected to occur in winter, at irregular periods, throughout the greater part, if not the whole, of the Missouri region. A considerable flock made their appearance at Fort Randall, Dakota, in the early part of March, and remained for several days.

The same gentleman writes me that he saw large flocks, in the latter part of November, in Western Kansas and Eastern Colorado, feeding on the seeds of various prairie weeds. In Clear Creek County, Colorado, it is "abundant in winter and spring, ranging from the foot-hills up to 10,000 feet, and probably somewhat higher. The Lesser Red-poll haunts the willow and alder thickets along the brooks, and also the poplar groves on the hill-sides. About the middle of April it disappears, returning late in November or December."

CHRYSOMITRIS PINUS, (Wils.) Bp.

Pine Linnet.

Fringilla pinus, WILS., Am. Orn. ii, 1810, 133, pl. 17, f. 1.—BP., Syn. 1828, 111.—NUTT., Man. i, 1832, 511.—AUD., Orn. Biog. ii, 1834, 455 ; v, 509 ; pl. 180.
Linaria pinus, AUD., Syn. 1839, 117 ; B. Am. iii, 1841, 125, pl. 180.—GIR., B. L. I. 1844, 115.
Chrysomitris pinus, BP., List. 1838, 33 ; Consp. Av. i, 1850, 515.—BD., B. N. A. 1858, 425.—
    COOP. & SUCK., N. H. Wash. Ter. 1860, 197 (summer).—HAYD., Rep. 1862, 165.—
    SCL. & SALV., P. Z. S. 1869, 362 (city of Mexico).—SUMICH , Mem. Bost. Soc.
    i, 1869, 550 (plateau and alpine region of Vera Cruz).—COOP., B. Cal. i, 1870,
    173.—ALLEN, Bull. M. C. Z. iii, 1872, 176 (mountains of Colorado, up to timber-
    line, in summer, doubtless breeding).—AIKEN, Pr. Bost. Soc. 1872, 199 (Wyo-
    ming).—MERR., U. S. Geol. Surv. Ter. 1872, 679.—FINSCH, Abh. Nat. iii, 1872,
    60 (Alaska).—COUES, Key, 1872, 131, pl. 3, f. 11, 12—B. B. & R., N. A. B. i, 1874,
    480, pl. 22, f. 16 ; also of late local writers.
Chrysomitris macroptera, DUBUS, Esquisses Orn. pl. 23.—BP., Consp. Av. i, 1850, 515
    (Mexico ; no tangible characters).

Hab.—North America generally. United States chiefly in winter, in roving flocks, but breeds down to sea-level, as far south at least as Massachusetts (COUES, Pr. Ess. Inst. v, 1868, 280; MAYN., Nat. Guide, 1870, 110), and in alpine regions much further. South along the Rocky Mountains into Mexico.

Lieutenant Warren's Expedition.—5393-94, Little Missouri River (September).
Later Expeditions.—62339-40, Idaho, in July and August.
Not obtained by Captain Raynolds' Expedition.

The erratic movements of this species, according to exigencies of the weather and consequent scarcity of food, render it difficult to define its limits with precision. It sometimes appears in localities where it was before unknown, and at unwonted times.

Prof. Sumichrast states (*l. c.*) that it is found in the alpine region of Vera Cruz to the height of 2,000 metres, and that he thinks it does not descend below 1,000 metres.

In Colorado, according to Mr. Trippe, "the Pine Finch is not very common. It breeds from 7,000 feet up to timber-line. I did not observe this species during winter, but think it probably remains nearly stationary, like the Pine Grosbeak and Red Crossbill. It frequents the pine trees principally, but often descends to the weeds and thistles, acting precisely like the Yellow-bird. In spring it sings very agreeably, very much like the latter bird, but in a lower voice; and like it, has the habit of singing in a lively, rambling sort of way, for an hour or more at a time." The eggs of this species are pale greenish, speckled with rusty-brown, 0.70 by 0.50. Dr. Brewer describes a neat nest of pine twigs lined with hair.

CHRYSOMITRIS TRISTIS, (Linn.) Bp.

American Goldfinch; Thistle-bird; Yellow-bird.

Fringilla tristis, LINN., Syst. Nat. i, 1766, 320.—GM., Syst. Nat. i, 1788, 907.—WILS., Am. Orn. i, 1808, 20, pl. 1, f. 2.—BP., Am. Orn. i, p. 57, pl. 8, f. 4.—BP., Syn. 1828, 111.—AUD., Orn. Biog. i, 1831, 172; v, 510; pl. 33.—NUTT., Man. i, 1832, 507.
Carduelis tristis, BP., Obs. Wils. 1825, No. 96.—AUD., Syn. 1839, 116; B. Am. iii, 1841, 129, pl. 181.—GIR., B. L. I. 1844, 117.—MAXIM., J. f. O. vi, 1858, 281.
Chrysomitris tristis, BP., List, 1838, 33; Consp. Av. i, 1850, 517.—BD., B. N. A. 1858, 421.—COOP. & SUCK., N. H. Wash. Ter. 1859, 197.—ALLEN, Bull. M. C. Z. iii, 1872, 176.—COOP., B. Cal. i, 1871, 167.—STEV., U. S. Geol. Surv. Ter. 1870, 464.—MERR., *ibid.* 1872, 679.—AIKEN, Pr. Bost. Soc. 1872, 199 (Wyoming).—COUES, Key, 1872, 131, pl. 3, f. 7, 8, 9, 10.—B. B. & R., N. A. B. i, 1874, 471, pl. 22, f. 7, 8; and of late writers generally.
Astragalinus tristis, CAB., Mus. Hein. i, 1851, 159.—ALLEN, Pr. Ess. Inst. iv, 1864, 69.—COUES, Pr. Ess. Inst. v, 1868, 280.—RÜSS, J. f. O. 1871, 19.
Carduelis americana, SW. & RICH., F. B. A. ii, 1831, 268.

Hab.—North America generally.
Lieutenant Warren's Expedition.—4824-25, Running Water; 4659, Fort Pierre; 5391, Fort Lookout; 5392, Blackfoot country.
Later Expeditions.—60388-91, 60976, Wyoming; 61666-67, 62335-38, Utah and Idaho.
Not obtained by Captain Raynolds' Expedition.

The egg is white, with a rosy blush when fresh, and usually the faintest possible bluish hue when blown. The size is about 0.65 by 0.52. The egg of *C. lawrencei* is not distinguishable, but may average rather smaller. The habits of both species are essentially the same.

CHRYSOMITRIS PSALTRIA, (Say) Bp.

Arkansas Goldfinch; Mexican Siskin.

a. *psaltria.*

Fringilla psaltria, SAY, Long's Exped. ii, 1823, 40.—BP., Am. Orn. i, 1825, 54, pl. 6, f. 3; Syn. 1828, 111.—NUTT., Man. i, 1832, 510.—AUD., Orn. Biog. v, 1839, 85, pl. 394.
Carduelis psaltria, AUD., Syn. 1839, 117; B. Am. iii, 1841, 134, pl. 183.

Chrysomitris psaltria, BP., List, 1838, 33; Consp. **i**, 1850, 516.—GAMB., Journ. Phila.
Acad. i, 1847, 52.—BD., B. N. A. 1858, 422.—CASS., Pr. Phila. Acad. 1865, 93.—
COUES, *ibid.* 1866, 80.—COOP., B. Cal. 1870, 168.—ALLEN, Bull. M. C. Z. iii, 1872,
178 (Kansas(?) and Utah).— COUES, Key, Oct. 1872, 132.—RIDGW., Am. Journ.
iv, Dec. 1872, 454.—B. B. & R., N. A. B. i, 1874, 474, pl. 22, f. 9, 10.

b. *arizonæ.*

Chrysomitris mexicana var. *arizonæ*, COUES, Pr. Ph. Ac. 1866, 82.—COOP., B. Cal. i, 1870, 170.
Chrysomitris psaltria var. *arizonæ*, COUES, Key, Oct. 1872, 132, fig. 72.—RIDGW., Am.
Journ. iv, Dec. 1872, 454.—B. B. & R., N. A. B. i, 1874, 476, pl. 22, f. 11.

c. *mexicana.*

Carduelis mexicana, SW., Phil. Mag. i, 1827, 435.—WAGLER, Isis, 1831, 525.
Chrysomitris mexicana, BP., List, 1838, 33; Consp. i, 1850, 516.—SCL., P. Z. S. 1855, 65;
1856, 303 (Cordova); 1858, 303 (Oaxaca); 1859, 365, 380; Cat. 1862, 124.—SCL.
& SALV., Ibis, 1859, 19 (Guatemala); 1860, 34.—BD., B. N. A. 1858, 423.—LAWR.,
Ann. Lyc. N. Y. 1861, 331 (Panama).—CASS., Pr. Phila. Acad. 1865, 93.—COUES,
ibid. 1866, 82.—SUMICH., Mem. Bost. Soc. i, 1869, 550 (Vera Cruz).—SALV., P. Z.
S. 1870, 190 (Veragua).
Astragalinus mexicanus, CAB., Mus. Hein. i, 1851, 159; J. f. O. 1861, 7 (Costa Rica).
Chrysomitris psaltria var. *mexicana*, COUES, Key, Oct. 1872, 133, fig. 80.—RIDGW., Am.
Journ. iv, Dec. 1872, 455.—B. B. & R., N. A. B. i, 1874, 478, pl. 22, f. 12, 13.
(?) *Fringilla catotol*, GM., Syst. Nat. i, 1788, 914 (probably, but indeterminable).
Fringilla melanoxantha, LICHT.—WAGLER, Isis, 1835, 525 (=*Cocozton*, HERDAN).
Fringilla texensis, GIR., B. Tex. 1841, pl. 5, f. 1 (type examined).

d. *columbiana.*

Chrysomitris columbiana, LAFRES., Rev. Zool. 1843, 292.—SCL., P. Z. S. 1855, 759.—BD.,
B. N. A. 1858, 423.—CASS., Pr. Phila. Acad. 1865, 93.—SUMICH., Mem. Bost. Soc.
i, 1869, 550.
Astragalinus columbianus, CAB., Mus. Hein. i, 1851, 159.
(?) *Chrysomitris nana*, BP., Consp. i, 1850, 516 (♀, indeterminable, but probably this
variety, to judge from locality—"Columbia").
Chrysomitris xanthogastra, DUBUS, Bull. Acad. Belg. xxii, 1855, 150.
Chrysomitris mexicana var. *columbiana*, COUES, Pr. Phila. Acad. 1866, 82.
Chrysomitris psaltria var. *columbiana*, COUES, Key, Oct. 1872, 133 (in text).—RIDGW.,
Am. Journ. iv, Dec. 1872, 455.—B. B. & R., N. A. B. i, 1874, 471.

Hab.—The typical form from the Southern Rocky Mountain region, and somewhat
eastward. West to the Pacific. North at least to the sources of the Platte. In New
Mexico and Arizona, shades insensibly into var. *arizonæ;* this merges into var. *mexicana*, of all Mexico; and this into the Central American var. *columbiana.*
Not noticed by the Expeditions.

The Arkansas Goldfinch is only known to occur along the southern border of the Missouri region, about the sources of the Platte (near 40°). Mr. Allen, indeed, queries it from Middle Kansas, where it will probably be found, but his observations lacked certainty. He found it at Ogden, Utah. It is not mentioned by Prof. Snow, nor by Messrs. Holden and Aiken. I found it common in Northern Arizona from the latter part of April until toward October, in shrubby ravines and weedy places, feeding on buds and seeds, in flocks, much in the manner of the common Thistle-bird. The male, as in this last, takes on a plumage like that of the female, in August. These birds were mostly very like true *psaltria*, showing the approach to var. *mexicana* much less than those I noticed along the Rio Grande and near Fort Wingate, New Mexico, where specimens were secured, in high breeding dress, with only a trace of olive on the black of the upper parts.

The nidification of this species is similar to that of *C. tristis*, and the eggs are not distinguishable from those of the latter. An account of the habits of the Arizona variety, from my observations in the West, will be found in Prof. Baird's work, above cited.

PLECTROPHANES NIVALIS, (Linn.) Meyer.

Snow Bunting; Snow-flake.

Emberiza nivalis, LINN., Syst. Nat. i, 1766, 308 (according to Gray, type of the genus).—
FORST., Philos. Trans. lxii, 1772, 403.—GM., Syst. Nat. i, 1788, 866.—LATH., Ind.
Orn. i, 1790, 397.—WILS., Am. Orn. iii, 1811, 86, pl. 21, fig. 2.—BP., Syn. 1828,
103.—NUTT., Man. i, 1832, 458.—AUD., Orn. Biog. ii, 1834, 515; v, 496; pl. 189.
Emberiza (Plectrophanus) nivalis, BP., Obs. Wils. 1825, No. 89.—SW. & RICH., F. B. A.
ii, 1831, 247.
Plectrophanus nivalis, MEYER, and authors generally.—BP., List, 1838, 37.—AUD., Syn.
1839 ; B. Am. iii, 55, pl. 155.—GIR., B. L. I. 1844, 97.—MAXIM., J. f. O. vi, 1858,
345.—BD., B. N. A. 1858, 432.—COUES & PRENT., Smiths. Rep. for 1861 (1862),
411 (Washington, D. C.).—ALLEN, Pr. Ess. Inst. iv, 1864, 70 (breeding in 1862
near Springfield, Mass.).—NEWB., Ibis, 1865, 502 (Spitzbergen.)—DALL & BANN.,
Tr. Chic. Acad. i, 1869, 282 (Alaska, breeding).—TURNB., B. E. Pa. 1869, 22 ("of
frequent occurrence," Dec. to Mar.).—MAYN., Guide, 1870, 112 (Massachu-
setts).—COOP., B. Cal. i, 1870, 177 (does not state it has occurred in California).—
TRIPPE, Pr. Ess. Inst. vi, 1871, 116 (Minnesota, Nov. to May).—ALLEN, Bull.
M. C. Z. iii, 1872, 177 (Kansas).—FINSCH, Abh. Nat. iii, 1872, 54 (Alaska).—
COUES, Key, 1872, 133.—B. B. & R., N. A. B. i, 1874, 512, pl. 24, f. 2.
Emberiza montana, GM., Syst. Nat. i, 1788, 867.—LATH., Ind. Orn. i, 1790, 398.
Emberiza mustelina, GM., Syst. Nat. i, 1788, 867.
Emberiza glacialis, LATH., Ind. Orn. i, 1790, 398.
Hortulanus glacialis et montanus, LEACH, Cat. 1816, 15, 16.
Plectrophanes borealis, montanus, mustelinus, BREHM, V. D. 305, 306.

Hab.—Arctic America and Greenland, and corresponding latitudes in the Old World.
Irregularly southward in winter in the United States, to about 35°, in roving flocks.
Washington, D. C. Georgia. Ohio. Illinois. Kentucky. Kansas. Deer Creek.

List of specimens.

19237	282	Deer Creek	♂	Mar. 4, 1860	F. V. Hayden.	6.75	13.25	4.25
19239	211	..... do	♀	Dec. 24, 1859	..... do	6.75	11.50	4.00
19240	281	..... do	♀	Mar. 4, 1860	..... do	6.25	11.50	4.00
19241	228	..... do	♂	Dec. 23, 1859	..... do	6.75	12.75	4.50
19242	....	..... do	♂	..... do	..... do	6.50	11.75	4.00
19243	235	..... do	....	Jan. 4, 1860	..... do	6.50	12.75	4.25
19238	236	..... do	♂	Jan. 18, 1860	G. H. Trook..	7.00	12.25	4.50
19244	207	..... do	♂	Dec. 14, 1859	..... do	6.50	12.50	4.25
19245	148	..... do	♂	Dec. 21, 1859	..... do	7.00	11.75	4.25

The Snow-flake is extremely abundant in the Missouri region in winter. They reached Fort Randall November 15, 1872, after a severe
cold snap with a light snow-fall, and as I write (January, 1873), great
numbers are swirling over the ground around, and in the fort. They
keep pretty closely in flocks numbering from a dozen or so to several
hundred, and, though they spread over the ground a good deal in running about after seeds, they fly compactly, and wheel all together. In
their evolutions they present a pretty sight, and have a not displeasing
stridulent sound, from mingling of the weak chirrups from so many
throats. They are quite unsuspicious, trooping about our very door-
steps in search of food, unconscious of real danger ; but their natural
timidity, as well as restlessness, is so great, that they seem to constantly
take causeless alarm, scurrying off in an instant, but, perhaps, only to
return to the same spot immediately. They are readily approached
within a few feet, and as readily taken with horse-hair snares, in box-
traps, or by other simple devices. They do not appear to suffer with
the cold, although the thermometer has been down to 30° below zero ;
those that I secured were in good condition, and proved excellent eating. Their crops were usually found crammed with the small seeds of
a plant that grows here in profusion. It may not be generally known
that these little Sparrows have a definitely circumscribed dilation of the

œsophagus, to all intents and purposes a true crop. I am familiar with the appearance presented by the capacious and distensible gullets of birds of the genus *Chrysomitris*, when full of seeds; but this appears altogether different. Happening to be skinning some Sharp-tailed Grouse at the same time, it struck me that the Snow-bird had the proportionally larger crop of the two. In six or eight individuals examined, this organ always lay completely to the right side, partly in the depression between the one of the legs of the furcula, but mostly protuberant; it pushed out so far, when completely distended, as to make the contour of the bird outside the feathers noticeably unsymmetrical. It is capable of holding a fair tea-spoonful of seeds. At this season the bill is yellowish, usually black-tipped, instead of entirely black; it dries to a brownish shade. Warm brown clouds all, or nearly all, the upper parts; mixes with black of the back; it is darkest on the crown, where often quite blackish; usually forms a marked auricular patch and pectoral collar, with more or less wash along the sides, leaving the rest of the under parts white. Specimens of course vary interminably in amount of brown clouding, but the pattern just mentioned, or a tendency to form such a pattern, may almost invariably be seen.

The general southward dispersion of the species in winter may be gathered from the above. Of its breeding in the United States I have found but two records. One is that given by Audubon (p. 56). He says a nest was found on a declivity in the White Mountains of New Hampshire, in July, 1831; it was described to him as being fixed on the ground among low bushes, and formed like that of the Song Sparrow's; and that it contained young. Mr. Allen, on the authority of Mr. C. W. Bennett, says that a pair spent the summer of 1862, and reared their young, at Springfield, Massachusetts.

At Fort Randall, the birds disappeared during some open weather early in March, but came back with a severe snow storm some weeks afterward, and were seen until April. They occasionally alight in troops on the roofs of sheds and houses, or string along fences. I have but rarely seen them on trees. When in this position they do not seem to be easy or even comfortable. They sit still, apparently busy balancing; on attempting to change their position they move awkwardly, seemingly as if afraid they would fall, putting one foot down after the other, and recovering a lapse with a flutter of the wings. Their feet evidently do not grasp small twigs with security.

The few nests of the Snow-flake I have seen were built with a great quantity of a kind of short curly grass which grows in the Arctic regions, mixed with moss, the whole forming a very substantial structure, with walls an inch or more thick, and a small, deep cavity. This is warmly lined with a quantity of large feathers, from some waterfowl. They are built on the ground, often covered and hidden by tussocks of grass or even slabs of rock. The eggs are exceedingly variable in coloration as well as size. Thus, one measures 0.65 by 0.70, and another 0.97 by 0.62; an average is about 0.90 by 0.65. The ground is white or whitish, in some instances flecked all over with neutral tint shell-markings, overlaid by deep brown spots and scratches, especially at the butt. In other cases the former are wanting and we have a heavy wreath of confluent blotches of dull brown around the larger end; and again the whole surface may be obscurely mottled with pale chocolate.

PLECTROPHANES LAPPONICUS, (Linn.) Selby.

Lapland Longspur.

Fringilla lapponica, LINN., Syst. Nat. i, 1766, 317.—FORST., Philos. Trans. lxii, 1772, 404.
Emberiza lapponica, NILSS., Orn. Luec. i, 157.—BP., Am. Orn. i, 53, pl. 13, f. 1.—BP., Syn. 1828, 440.—NUTT., Man. i, 1832, 463.—AUD., Orn. Biog. iv, 1838, 473, pl. 365.
Emberiza (Plectrophanes) lapponioa, Sw. & RICH., F. B. A. ii, 1831, 248, pl. 48.
Plectrophanes lapponica, SELBY, Linn. Trans. xv, 156, pl. 1.—BP., List, 1838, 36.—AUD , Syn. 1839, 98 ; B. Am. iii, 1841, 50, pl. 152.—GIR., B. L. I. 1844, 99.—BD., B. N. A. 1858, 433.—WHEAT., Ohio Agric. Rep. 1860 (Ohio.)—BOARDM., Pr. Bost. Soc. ix, 1862, 126 (Calais, Me., in winter only, not common).—VERR., Pr. Ess. Inst. iii, 158.—MCILWR., Pr. Ess. Inst. v, 1866, 89 (Hamilton, C. W., until May).— COUES, Pr. Ess. Inst. iv, 1868, 281.—TURNB., B. E. Pa. 1869, 42 (very rare, in severe winters only).—DALL & BANN., Tr. Chic. Acad. i, 1869, 283 (Alaska, breeding).—MAYN., Nat. Guide, 1870, 112 (Ipswich, Mass., with *P. nivalis* and *E. alpestris*).—COOP., B. Cal. i, 1870, 178 (but it does not appear to have ever been found in California).—MAYN., Pr. Bost. Soc. xiv, 1871, 115 (Minnesota, until May, and probably breeds).—FINSCH, Abh. Nat. iii, 1872, 54 (Alaska).— COUES, Key, 1872, 133, fig. 81.—B. B. & R., N. A. B. i, 1874, 515, pl. 24, f. 7.
Centrophanes lapponica, KAUP, Sk. Ent. Eur. Thierw. 1829.—CAB., Mus. Hein. 1851, 127.—ALLEN, Pr. Ess. Inst. iv, 1864, 84.
Fringilla calcarata, PALLAS., Itin. ii, App. 710.
Emberiza calcarata, TEMM., Man. 1815, 190.
Plectrophanes calcarata, MEYER, TASCH., Deuts. 57.—BOIE, Isis, 1822, 554.
Centrophanes calcarata, GRAY, List, Gen. of B., App. 1842, 11.

Hab.—A species, like *P. nivalis*, of circumpolar distribution ; in this country inhabits all the arctic regions, coming south in winter to Philadelphia, Kentucky (*Audubon*), Illinois (*Ridgway*), Kansas (*Cooper*), and Colorado (*Trippe*). Not yet observed in the United States west of the Rocky Mountains. Not known to breed in the United States, and very rarely found in full plumage in the United States.

List of specimens.

19246	284	Deer Creek	....	Mar. 7, 1860	F. V. Hayden.	5.50	9.75	3.00
19247	234	..... do	♀	Jan. 18, 1860	..... do	6.25	10.35	3.75
19248	....	..... do	♀	..... do	..... do	6.25	10.75	3.45
19249	187	Source Chey'ne.	....	....	G. H. Trook..	......	......	......

The general southward extension of this species is seen from the above remarks. Although included by Dr. Cooper in the Birds of California, I do not know that it has ever been taken on the Pacific coast of the United States, nor indeed anywhere west of the Rocky Mountains. Dr. Hayden's specimens, above enumerated, probably represent the south-westernmost record to date. I find no quotations for the Atlantic States beyond Pennsylvania. It appears to extend furthest south in the interior; it was observed in large flocks in Kentucky by Audubon. Mr. Trippe's notice is interesting as indicating the probable breeding of the bird in Minnesota. He says it comes there about the middle of September and remains until December, when it moves southward, and its place is supplied by the Snow Bunting ; and that it is very abundant in Southern Iowa in the depth of winter and in early spring. He has since informed me that a large flock was seen by him in the Middle Park, Colorado, in the latter part of October. Messrs. Dall and Bannister report it as very abundant in Alaska, where it arrives the second week in May, and breeds. Both these writers attest its eminent musical ability. Collections of Messrs. Ross, Kennicott, and others, now in the Smithsonian, show that it is very abundant in summer in the vicinity of Great Slave Lake and McKenzie's River. The species enters the Missouri region from the north early in October, according to my observations, but I have as yet found it nowhere abundant.

Of two sets of eggs of the Lapland Longspur before me, both collected by Mr. H. W. Elliott on the Prybilov Islands, Bering's Sea, one contains six, the other four specimens. The eggs are rather pointed at the smaller end, and measure about 0.80 by 0.62. They are very dark colored, reminding one of the Titlark's; the color is a heavy clouding or thick mottling of chocolate-brown, through which the greenish-gray ground is little apparent. The nests are built of mosses and fine, soft, dried grasses, and lined with a few large feathers from some water-fowl; they were placed on the ground, under tussocks, in grassy hummocks. The female did not leave the nest until nearly trodden upon.

PLECTROPHANES PICTUS, Sw.

Painted Lark Bunting.

Emberiza (*Plectrophanes*) *picta*, Sw. & RICH., F. B. A. ii, 1831, 250, pl. 49 (perfect spring plumage; Saskatchewan).—NUTT., Man. i, 1832, 589.
Emberiza picta, AUD., Orn. Biog. v, 1839, 91, pl. 400.
Plectrophanes pictus, BP., List, 1838, 37; Consp. i, 1850, 463.—AUD., Syn. 1839, 99; B. Am. iii, 1841, 52, pl. 153 (from the original specimen).—BD., B. N. A. 1858, 434 (Minnesota and Illinois).—DALL & BANN., Tr. Chic. Acad. i, 1869, 283 (Fort Yukon and McKenzie River region).—COUES, Key, 1872, 134.—B. B. & R., N. A. B. i, 1874, 518, pl. 24, f. 4. 5.
Centrophanes pictus, CAB., Mus. Hein. i, 1851, 127.
Emberiza smithii, AUD., B. Amer. vii, 1844, 337, pl. 487 (Illinois, in winter). (Young.)
Centrophanes smithii, CAB., Mus. Hein. i, 1851, 127.

Hab.—Yukon, McKenzie, Saskatchewan, and Missouri River regions, to the prairies of Illinois in winter.

This species was not noticed by either of the Expeditions; yet there is no doubt whatever of its occurrence in the regions explored. The only United States quotations I have found are those above given. Audubon states that he found the bird "very abundant" on low prairie about a lake near Edwardsville, Illinois. Richardson had but his single Saskatchewan specimen. The Smithsonian collections, of great extent, and embracing many perfectly plumaged specimens, attest the abundance of the bird in the McKenzie River region. It does not appear to breed anywhere in the United States. In Northern Dakota it makes its appearance the latter part of September, but, according to my observations, only in limited numbers. It associates intimately with *P. ornatus*, and has much the same habits and general appearance. No eggs are more variable than those of *Plectrophanes*, and *P. pictus* is no exception to the rule in this regard. The very extensive series in the Smithsonian exhibits some specimens exactly like those of *P. lapponicus*, with a corresponding range of variation, and others like *P. ornatus*, but always larger than the latter, being of the size of *P. lapponicus*. None of the specimens, however, are as darkly and uniformly chocolate as some examples of *P. lapponicus* are. These eggs are nearly all from the Anderson River region, with a few from Great Slave Lake.

The following is a more sufficient description of the young bird than that given in the Key: *Male*—Length, 6.50; extent, 11.25; wing, 3.75; tail, 2.50; tarsus, 0.75; middle toe and claw, about the same; hind toe and claw, rather less (*P. ornatus* is much less in all its dimensions). Bill, dusky brown above and at tip, paler below; feet, light brown (drying darker); toes, rather darker. Entire under parts, rich yellowish-brown, or buffy (in *P. ornatus* never thus); paler on the chin and throat, which, with the fore-breast, are obsoletely streaked with dusky; the tibiæ white. Tail, white only on the two or three outer feathers (in *P. ornatus* all the feathers, exceping sometimes the central pair, are white at the base). Upper parts much as in the adult, but the sharp, distinctive head-markings wanting, or only obscurely indicated.

PLECTROPHANES ORNATUS, Towns.

Chestnut-collared Bunting; Black-bellied Longspur.

Plectrophanes ornatus, Towns., Journ. Phila. Acad. vii, 1837, 189.—Aud., Syn. 1839, 99.—
Aud., B. Amer. iii, 1841, 53, pl. 154.—Nutt., Man. i, 2d ed. 1840, 537.—Bp., List,
1838, 37; Consp. i, 1850, 463.—Woodh., Sitgr. Rep. 1853, 88 (Indian Territory).—
Bd., B. N. A. 1858, 435.—Hayd., Rep. 1862, 165.—Dress., Ibis, 1865, 486 (Texas).—
Allen, Bull. M. C. Z. iii, 1872, 135.—Coues, Key, 1872, 134.—B. B. & R., N. A.
B. i, 1874, 520, pl. 24, f. 3.
Emberiza ornata, Aud., Orn. Biog. v, 1839, 44, pl. 394, f. 1.
Centrophanes ornatus, Cab., Mus. Hein. i, 1851, 127.
Plectrophanes melanomus, Bd., B. N. A. 1858, 436 (Black Hills to Mexico).—Heerm., P.
R. R. Rep. x, 1859, Parke's Route, Birds, p. 13 (New Mexico).—Hayd., Rep.
1862, 165 (Black Hills and Niobrara River).—Scl., P. Z. S. 1860, 251 (Orizaba).—
Dress., Ibis, 1865, 486 (Texas).—Coues, Pr. Phila. Acad. 1866, 84 (Arizona).—
Sumich., Mem. Bost. Soc. i, 1869, 551 (Plateau of Vera Cruz to Orizaba).
Plectrophanes ornatus var. *melanomus,* B. B. & R., N. A. B. i, 1874, 521, pl. 24, f. 6.

Hab.—Interior of British America; whole Missouri region; prairies of Kansas, breed-
ing (*Allen*). Breeds very abundantly in Dakota. South through the Rocky Mountain
region to the table-lands of Mexico. West of the Rocky Mountains, only observed in
Arizona (*Coues.*)
Lieutenant Warren's Expedition.—4827, Bijoux Hills; 5377-79, Medicine Creek; 5917,
Fort Pierre; 8924, 8926, Black Hills; 8925, Running Water.
Not obtained by Captain Raynolds' Expedition.

This is an abundant and characteristic species of the Missouri region.
Originally described from this country, it has since been traced far north
in the interior of the British Possessions, and southward, in elevated
regions, to Vera Cruz and Orizaba.

The time for discussing the claims of *P. melanomus* as a distinct species, passed when the variations in plumage of *P. ornatus* became
known. The results of a critical examination I made when this Report
was originally drafted, some years since, are now suppressed; for in the
interim Mr. Allen has satisfactorily stated the case. In the paper above
cited, he has the following remarks:

" The plumage varies greatly in color in different individuals of even
the same sex, the variation being generally in respect to the purity and
intensity of the colors. The most highly-colored males have the breast
and middle of the abdomen more or less strongly tinged with very bright
ferrugineous; others have these parts pure black; while in others still,
the black is obscured by the feathers having brownish-white tips. The
lesser wing-coverts vary from gray to black. The red tinge on the
abdomen seems merely indicative of a high state of plumage, those thus
marked also having the lesser coverts black; but they are also black in
some specimens that are not tinged with red. *Plectrophanes melanomus*
is merely the ferrugineous phase of this species. The highest colored
female (the sex determined by dissection) was nearly as bright colored
as the paler-colored males, having the chestnut collar and the black
on the breast, nearly as distinct as some of the males. It was nearly
as large, and, until dissected, was supposed to be an immature male."

In Dakota, where I observed the bird during the breeding season in
the greatest abundance, few were found with the sienna color on the
under parts, and then only as a trace. The summer birds rarely show
the black bend of the wing, but this is assumed in perfection, as a rule,
after the fall moult, which occurs in September.

Mr. Allen sends me the following notice, prepared for this work:
" The Chestnut-collared Bunting was found on the plains about Fort
Hays, in considerable abundance. They live in summer in large scattered colonies, generally many pairs being found at the same locality,
while they may not be again met with in a whole day's travel. We

found them very shy for so small birds, and were obliged to obtain all our specimens (some thirty in number) by shooting them on the wing at long range. They breed, of course, on the ground, constructing a rather slight but neat nest of dry grass and the stems of small plants. The eggs appear to be commonly five in number, blotched and streaked with rusty on a white ground, full sets of which were obtained the first week in June. This species has the curious habit of circling round the observer, with a buoyant, undulatory flight, generally high in the air, and usually keeping all the while well out of range, uttering, meanwhile, its rather sharp but musical call notes. I met with it in winter from Fort Hays westward, nearly to the Colorado line, indicating that it is resident here the whole year. We failed to meet with it, however, about Cheyenne in August, or anywhere to the westward of Western Kansas; neither does it appear in Mr. Aiken's list of the birds observed by him near Cañon City, Colorado, nor in Mr. Holden's list of the birds seen by him in the vicinity of Sherman."

Under head of *P. melanomus*, Dr. Heermann has the following:

"I first remarked this bird, associated with the *P. maccownii*, at a large prairie-dog village, some miles west of Puerto del Dado. Fresh meat having become scarce in camp, and desiring a few birds for supper, I fired into a flock covering densely quite a large space. T.ree dozen fell at the first discharge, and among them I was pleased to find this species and *P. maccownii*. From this point to the Rio Grande we found both of these species abundant wherever we struck isolated water-holes, these being the only spots for miles around where drink can be obtained. When fired at, they rise as if to fly away; but forced by thirst to return, after describing a few curves, to the only spot where their parched tongues can find relief, they may, if the hunter feels so inclined, be freely slaughtered. I have often seen from one hundred to one hundred and fifty brought down in four or five discharges of a gun. While on a trip to the Rocky Mountains, in 1843, I met * * * * *P. ornatus* in small flocks and pairs, scattered over the prairies of the Platte River, and was fortunate enough to discover one of their nests. Built on the ground, it was composed of fine grasses, lined with hair. The eggs, four in number, were white, with black lines at the larger end, and a few faint neutral-tint blotches scattered over the surface.

I took a single specimen in October, 1864, on a grassy plain near Fort Whipple, Arizona, the only one observed in the Territory.

The Chestnut-collared Bunting breeds in profusion on the plains of Northern Dakota. On the bare plains, away from a single land-mark, it is perhaps the most abundant bird of all, though Baird's Bunting and the Missouri Sky-lark are not far behind in this respect. All three associate intimately together, and there is a great general similarity in their habits. The nest of the present species is placed on the ground, effectually concealed beneath some little tuft of grass; it is a slight affair, merely a few fine grasses and slender weed-stems, for the most part circularly disposed, and considerably hollowed. Like the nests of most other sparrows that breed on the ground, it is sunken in a depression so as to be flush with the general surface. It measures about three and one-half inches across outside, and more than half as much in depth; the bottom is very thin in comparison with the brim, which is well defined. The eggs are usually four in number, measuring about four-fifths of an inch long by three-fifths broad, and are not peculiar in shape. They are grayish-white, more or less clouded, and mottled obscurely with pale purplish-gray, which confers the prevailing tone; this is overlaid with numerous surface-markings of points, scratches, and small spots of dark brown, wholly indeterminate in distribution and number, but always conspicuous, being sharply displayed upon the subdued ground color. I think that two or three broods are reared each season, for I have found fresh eggs and newly hatched birds the same day, July 18th, when a week before I had shot young birds already on the wing; and again, I have found fresh eggs so late as the first week in August. When the nest is approached, the female generally walks quietly off, after a little flutter, threading her way through the grass till she is at a safe distance, and then taking wing. Should the young be hatched, however, both parents will hover together close over-head, in evident distress, with beseeching cries.

The young birds keep much together until they are well on wing, when they form larger flocks by uniting several families together. As soon as the care of the last brood is over, they are joined by the parents, now, in August, moulting, and in poor plumage, forming troops of great extent, which scurry over the prairies in search of food. Later still, in September, they are joined by numbers of the *P. pictus* from the north, and a few *P. lapponicus*, all associating together, and having much the same habits; they remain in this part of the country until the middle of October, at least, and then probably wend their way South.

This bird has a peculiar note, difficult of description, but easily learned; in the breeding season it is a fine songster, having a soft and pleasing, though rather weak twitter. Its ordinary flight, when undis-turbed, is perfectly undulatory, as much so as that of the *Chrysomitris*, and with each impulse of the wings it utters its chirp. When startled from the ground it flies hastily, in a wayward course, which makes it difficult to shoot; the various members of a flock fly separately, but generally straggle after each other, to settle again at no great distance and resume their rambling search for food. Like the other small birds of the prairie, it haunts the roads where, as the grass is worn away from the wheel-tracks, it feeds and runs with the greatest ease. I never saw one alight except on the ground. In flight, it may always be recognized by the amount of white on the tail. In size, it varies from $5\frac{3}{4}$ to $6\frac{1}{4}$ in length, by $10\frac{1}{4}$ to $10\frac{3}{4}$ in extent. With the renewal of the feathers, the birds come into a much purer and richer plumage than that worn dur-ing the summer. Young male birds very early show some black on the under parts, but the distinctive head-markings do not appear to be assumed until the following spring. A large number of the old fall birds have perfectly black bend of the wing; but few show, in any plumage in this region, the rich, rusty-red edgings of the feathers of the under parts, which is so conspicuous in more southerly examples.

PLECTROPHANES MACCOWNII, Lawr.

Maccown's Bunting.

Plectrophanes maccownii, LAWR., Ann. Lyc. N. Y. vi, 1851, 122 (Western Texas).—MAC., Ann. Lyc. vi, p. 14.—CASS., Ill. 1855, 228, pl. 39.—BD., B. N. A. 1858, 437.— HEERM., P. R. R. Rep. x, 1859, Parke's Route of 32° parallel, Birds, 13.—HAYD., Rep. 1862, 165.—DRESS., Ibis, 1865, 487 (Texas).—STEV., U. S. Geol. Surv. Ter. 1870, 464.—ALLEN, Bull. M. C. Z. iii, 1872, 145, 177 (Cheyenne, Wyoming Ter., abundant, breeding; Western Kansas, in winter).—COUES, Key, 1872, 134.— B. B. & R., N. A. B. i, 1874, 523, pl. 24, f. 1.

Hab.—Middle Province United States; north to the Black Hills; east to Western Kansas, Western Texas, and New Mexico.
Lieutenant Warren's Expedition.—8954-6, Black Hills.
Later Expeditions.—60396, Wyoming.
Not obtained by Captain Raynolds' Expedition.

Since its discovery by Captain Maccown, then of the United States

Army, in Western Texas, this species has been noticed in various parts of New Mexico, by Drs. A. L. Heermann and T. C. Henry, and by other naturalists further north, as above quoted. It has been usually observed in company with *P. ornatus*, and its United States range appears to be much the same, although, as yet, we have no accounts of its occurrence in the British Possessions or in Mexico. I am informed, by letter from Mr. T. Martin Trippe, that vast numbers were seen in winter in the Arkansas Valley, and throughout Eastern Colorado.

" Maccown's Bunting," writes Mr. Allen to me, " was abundant in the vicinity of Cheyenne in August, and the occurrence of partially-fledged young seemed to indicate that it had bred in the immediate vicinity. I also observed it near Laramie City during the same months, and found it common, in winter, in the northwestern counties of Kansas. In habits, notes, and general appearance, it is scarcely distinguishable, at a little distance, from the Chestnut-collared Bunting."

A nest of Maccown's Bunting taken on Heart River, Dakota, July 7, 1873, by Mr. Allen, was built on the ground, and is constructed of decomposing woody fibre and grasses, with a lining of finer grasses. In its present state of preservation it is too much distorted to permit description of its shape. It contained four eggs, closely resembling the lighter-colored varieties of the *P. ornatus*, but without the purplish-gray clouding of the latter. The ground is dull white; the markings are obscure and rather sparse mottling, with some heavier, sharp, scratchy ones, both brown, of different intensity. A specimen measures 0.80 by 0.60.

CENTRONYX BAIRDII, (Aud.) Bd.

Baird's Sparrow.

Emberiza bairdii, AUD., B. Am. vii, 1843, 359, pl. 500.
Coturniculus bairdii, BP., Consp. Av. i, 1850, 481.
Centronyx bairdii, BD., B. N. A. 1858, 441.—COUES, Key, 1872, 135 (not of MAYN., Nat. Guide, 113, the supposed "Centronyx" from Massachusetts proving to be a *Passerculus*. See MAYN., Am. Nat. vi, 1872, 637; ALLEN, *ibid.* 631; BREW., *ibid.* vi, 1872, 307; COUES, Key, 352).—B. B. & R., N. A. B. i, 1874, 531, pl. 25, fig. 3.— HENSH., Am. Nat. viii, 1874, p. — (Arizona).
Passerculus bairdii, COUES, Am. Nat. vi, 1873, 697.
Ammodromus bairdii, GIEBEL, Nomenc. Av. i, 328.
Centronyx ochrocephalus, AIKEN, Am. Nat. vii, 1873, 237 (El Paso, Colorado. Autumnal plumage. See SCOTT, *ibid.* 564; COUES, *ibid.* 694).

Hab.—Central Plains. North to the British Provinces. South to New Mexico and Arizona. East nearly to the Red River of the North. West to the Rocky Mountains. Not procured by any of the Expeditions.

Upon insufficient examination of the type, a faded specimen in worn plumage, preserved in the Smithsonian, I ventured the hasty and, as it proved, unfounded surmise that this was not a valid species, having an idea that some obscure plumage of a young *Plectrophanes* was in question. The following descriptions are drawn up from about *seventy-five* specimens I collected in Dakota last year.

Adult, in breeding plumage.—With a general resemblance to *Passerculus savanna*. Inner secondaries less elongated, only rarely equaling the primaries in the closed wings. First four quills about equal, and longest. Hind toe and claw about equaling the middle toe and claw, its claw about equaling the digit. (No evident or constant difference from *Passerculus* in proportions of the toes.) Tail shorter than the wing, lightly double-rounded (central and outer pair of feathers both a little shorter than the intermediate ones). Top of head streaked with black and rich brownish-yellow, or buff, the former predominating laterally, the latter chiefly as a median stripe, but also suffusing the nape and sides of head in greater or less degree. Back varied with brownish-black and gray, together with a little bay, the two latter colors forming the edgings of the interscapulars and scapulars. Rump variegated with gray and chestnut-brown, different in shade from that of the back. Under parts dull white, usually with a faint ochrey tinge on the breast, but often without; a circlet of small, sharp, sparse, dusky streaks across the breast, continuous with others, longer and mostly lighter, along the whole sides, and with others, again, extending up the sides of the neck into small, vague maxillary and auricular markings. When the feathers are perfectly arranged these lateral head-markings are seen to be a post-ocular stripe just over the auriculars, a post-auricular spot, a streak starting from the angle of the mouth, and another heavier one parallel with and below this, running directly into the pectoral ones. Quills without special markings, excepting the elongated inner secondaries, which correspond with the scapulars. Tail the same, slightly whitish-edged. Upper mandible mostly dark, lower pale. Feet flesh-colored. Length, 5.10 to 5.85; extent, 8.60 to 9.85; wing 2.75 to 3.00 (in one case 3.05; average, about 5⅞ by 9¼ by 2⅘); tail, 2.00 to 2.25; culmen, about 0.40; tarsus, in front, about 0.75; middle toe and claw, and hind toe and claw, each, rather less. The female averages rather smaller than the male, but is otherwise similar.

Autumnal plumage.—Soft, with brighter, more suffused colors, in bolder pattern. Whole top and sides of head, as well as nape and part of neck, suffused with rich buff, in many instances as bright a golden-brown as that on the head of *Seiurus aurocapillus.* A paler, rather ochraceous, shade of the same also suffusing the whole fore under-parts. Pectoral and lateral dusky streaks, as well as the two rows on each side of the throat, large, heavy, diffuse. Bay and whitish edgings of the secondaries broad and conspicuous, constrasting with the black central fields. Whitish edgings of tail-feathers the same; and, in general, the same character is stamped over all the upper plumage.

Newly-fledged young have each feather of the dorsal plumage conspicuously bordered with white, producing a set of semicircles, much as in *Neocorys spraguei.* There is the same general buffy suffusion of the head and fore-parts noted in the last paragraph, but the tint is dull and ochrey. The markings below have a short, broad, guttiform character. When just from the nest, the edging of the secondaries and tail-feathers is of a peculiar pinkish-rusty shade.

Although we here retain the nomenclature of the Key, the structural peculiarities of *Centronyx* are so slightly different from *Passerculus* that the bird might, very properly, be included in the latter genus, as we have already suggested. The characters given by Prof. Baird, from the original specimen, do not all hold throughout a large series.

Not the least singular thing in the history of this species is the length of time which elapsed after its discovery before anything further was learned about it. Considering how often and how thoroughly the region it inhabits has been explored by naturalists, and how abundant the bird is now known to be, it is the more surprising that it should have so long eluded observation. No second specimen was known for thirty years, until Mr. Aiken and myself took it, in Colorado and in Dakota, respectively; and the same year, as I am informed, Mr. Henshaw has obtained it further south. The question may arise, has the bird really been, all this time, so common and widely dispersed, or has it only recently become so? Sprague's Lark offers a nearly parallel case; and instances like these suggest the probability of a kind of *rotation* in the abundance of birds, analogous to that occurring among plants, no less than a change in geographical distribution not dependent upon the ordinary laws of migration.

However this may be, the fact is that Baird's Bunting is extremely abundant in Dakota, in some places outnumbering all other birds together. I did not see it immediately along the Red River, but at once encountered it beyond the low Pembina range of mountains, thirty or forty miles west of the river, as soon as I came upon the high prairie. This was the second week in July, when I shot some young birds just fledged, though the great majority were then breeding. In two days, July 14 and 15, I took thirty specimens, and more might have been procured; during the summer about seventy-five were preserved, showing all stages. Almost without exception my earlier specimens were males, which attracted attention as they sat singing on the low bushes of the prairie, the females lying concealed in the grass, incubating or attending to the young. The song is peculiar, consisting of two or three distinct syllables, in a mellow, tinkling tone, running into an indefinite trill; it may be suggested by *zip-zip-zip-zr-r-r-r.* In their general appearance and habits, the birds are so nearly the same as the Savanna Sparrows that it was two or three days before I learned to distinguish them at gunshot range. They do not go in flocks, yet there is a sort of colonization among them, for we may ride a mile or two over the prairie without seeing any, and then come upon numerous pairs breeding together. I think it probable that a second brood is usually reared each season, as I have shot equally young birds six weeks apart. After the duties of incubation, the plumage is renewed, it having become greatly worn and faded. When the young are all on wing, they associate together with their parents, in loose straggling troops, mixing freely with the Chestnut-collared Buntings and the Sky-larks. Their numbers sensibly diminish in September, and they apparently move south during the month, as I saw none after the 1st of October. In September, in this latitude, there is a good deal of cold weather, and not unfrequently a heavy snow-fall, sending the more delicate birds away early. The birds feed upon various seeds, as usual, as well as upon insects, even sizable grasshoppers, which in this region seem to be eaten by almost every bird and animal.

Although I made many a search whilst the birds were evidently breeding, I never succeeded in stumbling upon a nest. Fortunately, however, I am enabled to complete the history of the species with a description of the nest and eggs, taken July 1, 1873, on Big Muddy Creek, Dakota, by Mr. J. A. Allen, Naturalist of the Yellowstone Expedition. These are the first specimens which have been brought to the notice of naturalists. The nest was built, as was to be expected, on the ground, and is very similar to that of *Plectrophanes ornatus*—a slight structure of grasses and weed-bark, circularly disposed, about four inches across outside. It contained five fresh eggs, most nearly resembling those of the Bay-winged Bunting, but smaller, and decidedly more rounded. They measure 0.80 by 0.65. The ground is dull white, speckled all over, but very irregularly, with light reddish-brown (pale sienna), and having a few larger blotches of the same and a darker shade, owing to heavier laying on of the pigment. In a number of instances the coloration would probably not be distinguishable with certainty from those of *Pooecetes*. The general pattern of the coloration is much as in *Plectrophanes ornatus*, but the general effect is quite different, and, in the single set before me, peculiar.

Mr. Henshaw's Arizona specimens (*Wheeler's* Exped. of 1873) show a condition of plumage leading him to believe that the species breeds in the locality where he procured them, as is undoubtedly the case. He found the birds very numerous, and secured a large series.

PASSERCULUS SAVANNA, (Wils.) Bp.

Savanna Sparrow.

a. *savanna*.

Fringilla savanna, WILS., Am. Orn. iii, 1811, 55, pl. 22, f. 2; iv, 1811, 72, pl. 34, f. 4.—BP., Syn. 1828, 109.—NUTT., Man. i, 1832, 489.—AUD., Orn. Biog. ii, 1834, 63; v, 1839, 516; pl. 109.
Linaria savanna, RICH., List. 1837.
Emberiza savanna, AUD., Syn. 1839, 103.—AUD., B. Am. iii, 1841, 68, pl. 160.—GIR., B. L. I. 1844, 102.
Passerculus savanna, BP., List, 1838, 33; Consp. Av. i, 1850, 480.—CAB., Mus. Hein. 1851, 131.—BD., B. N. A. 1858, 442.—HAYD., Rep. 1862, 165.—DALL & BANN., Tr. Chic. Acad. i, 1869, 283.—ALLEN, Bull. M. C. Z. ii, 1871, 272, (critical discussion).—ALLEN, M. C. Z. iii, 1872, 177 (edge of plains to above timber-line).—COUES, Key, 1872, 135, fig. 82.—B. B. & R., N. A. B, i, 1874, 534, pl. 24, f. 8; and of late writers generally.

Passerculus savanna var. *alaudinus*, B. B. & R., N. A. B. 1874, pl. 24, f. 11.
Ammodromus savanna, GRAY, Genera of Birds.
Passerculus alaudinus, BP., Comp. Rend. xxxvii, 1853, 918 (California).—BD., B. N. A.
    1858, 446.—HEERM., P. R. R. Rep. ix, 1859, 49.—COUES, Pr. Phila. Acad. 1861,
    223 (Labrador); 1866, 84 (Arizona).—COUES, Ibis, 1866, 268.—COUES, Pr. Ess.
    Inst. v, 1868, 281.—DRESS., Ibis, 1865, 487.—ELLIOT, B. N. A. pl. 13.—DALL &
    BANN., Tr. Chic. Acad. 1869, i, 284 (Alaska).—STEV., U. S. Geol. Surv. Ter. 870,
    464.—MERR., U. S. Geol. Surv. Ter. 1872, 679.—SUMICH., Mem. Bost. Soc. i,
    1869, 552 (Vera Cruz).—COOP., B. Cal. i, 1870, 181.—SCL., P. Z. S. 1858, 302
    (Oaxaca).
Zonotrichia alaudina, FINSCH, Abh. Nat. iii, 1872, 51 (Alaska).

b. *anthinus.*

(Slender-billed, with numerous small sharp dark spots below.   Marshes, Pacific coast.)

Passerculus anthinus, BP., Comp. Rend. xxxvii, 1853, 919.—BD., B. N. A. 1858, 445.—SCL.,
    Cal. A. B. 1862, 112.—COUES, Ibis, 1866, 268.—(?) DALL & BANN., Tr. Chic. Acad.
    i, 1869, 284 (rather "*alaudinus*").—COOP., B. Cal. i, 187, 183.—ELLIOT, B. N.
    A. pl. 13.
Passerculus savanna var. *anthinus*, COUES, Key, 1872, 136.—B. B. & R., N. A. B. i, 1874,
    539, pl. 24, f. 10.

c. *sandvicensis.*

(Large northern coast form.)

Emberiza sandwichensis, GM., Syst. Nat. i, 1788, 875.
Passerculus sandwichensis, BD., B. N. A. 1858, 444.—COOP. & SUCK., N. H. Wash. Ter.
    1860, 199, pl. 28, f. 2.—DALL & BANN., Tr. Chic. Acad. i, 1869, 284.—COOP., B.
    Cal. i, 1870, 180.
Passerculus savanna var. *sandvicensis*, COUES, Key, 1872, 136.—B. B. & R., N. A. B. i,
    1874, 538, pl. 24, f. 9.
Emberiza arctica, LATH., Ind. Orn. i, 1790, 414.
Fringilla arctica, VIG., Voy. Blossom, 1839, 20.—BRANDT, Ic. Ross. ii, 6.
Euspiza arctica, BP., Consp. i, 1850, 469.
Zonotrichia arctica, FINSCH, Abh. Nat. iii, 1872, 46 (Alaska).
Emberiza chrysops, PALL., Zoog. R. A. ii, 1811, 45, pl. 48, fig. 1 (Oonalashka).

Hab.—North America, at large.   Migratory.   Breeds from the Middle States north-
ward (to Labrador at least and to the Yukon), and in mountainous parts of the United
States elsewhere.   Winters from the Middle States southward.   Mexico.   Cuba (CAB.,
J. f. O. iv, 1856, 6).
    Lieutenant Warren's Expedition.—4807, Vermilion River; 4808, Big Sioux River; 8786,
North Fork of the Platte; 8756-57, 8768, Black Hills.
    Later Expeditions.—59888-89, Colorado; 60407, 60663-67, Wyoming; 62310, Idaho.
Not obtained by Captain Raynolds' Expedition.
    The characteristics of our *Passerculi*, too hastily, it appears, assumed to indicate sev-
eral distinct species, will be found more or less fully discussed by some of the authors
above cited.   My present view, as stated in the Key, is that "*alaudinus*" is entirely
indistinguishable, but that *anthinus* and *sandvicensis* represent local varieties that it is
usually possible to recognize.   We might, perhaps, indicate by the name of "*alaudinus*" the pale race of the dry middle region, but for the fact that its original describer
indicates it as being from "California."

Savanna Sparrows are extremely abundant in the Missouri region,
especially during the migrations.   They remain during the winter in
the milder portions, and breed in the northern portions as well as beyond, in the region just north of the Coteau.   This may be toward the
southern limit of their breeding range.   They are found during the
breeding season. both in the valleys of the rivers and out on the high
prairie, where they associate intimately with Baird's and the Chestnut-
collared Buntings, forming a part of the small prairie *avifauna*.   Their
habits and general appearance are so similar to those of Baird's Bunting that the two species are only distinguished with some difficulty at
gun-shot range.   The nuptial song is sweet and simple; at other seasons
they have only a weak chirp.   The nest is placed on the ground, in all
the instances that have come under my observation, and closely resembles that of the Bay-winged Bunting, excepting that in the specimens

I have seen, at any rate, it has a considerable lining of horse-hair. The eggs, generally four, sometimes five, in number, are rather peculiar in the heaviness of their coloring, being so thickly and uniformly mottled with several shades of reddish-brown that the ground-color—a light gray, with faint greenish shade—scarcely appears. Different specimens, however, vary much in the amount of the mottling. In Northern Dakota the eggs are generally laid the first and second weeks in June. They are a trifle over three-fourths of an inch long by about three-fifths in breadth. One nest I found contained two Cow-bird eggs.

POOECETES GRAMINEUS, (Gm.) Baird.

Bay-winged Bunting; Grass Finch.

a. *gramineus.*

Fringilla graminea, GM., Syst. Nat. i, 1788, 922.—BP., Syn. 1828, 108.—AUD., Orn. Biog. i, 1831, 473; v, 502; pl. 90.—NUTT., i, 182, 482.
Emberiza graminea, WILS., Am. Orn. iv, 1811, 51, pl. 31, f. 5.—AUD., Syn. 1839, 102.— AUD., B. Am. iii, 1841, 65, pl. 153.—MAXIM., J. f. O. vi, 1858, 342.—TRIPPE, Pr. Ess. Inst. vi, 1871, 116 (Minnesota, breeding abundantly in pine-barrens).
Fringilla (Zonotrichia) graminea, SW. & RICH., F. B. A. ii, 1831, 254 (Saskatchewan, May to September).
Zonotrichia graminea, BP., List, 1838, 31; Consp. Av. i, 850, 478.—NEWB., P. R. R. Rep. vi, 1857, 85.—HEERM., P. R. R. Rep. x, 1859, 47.
Pooecetes gramineus, BD., B. N. A. 1858, 447.—HAYD., Rep. 1862, 165.—B. B. R., N. A. B. i, 1874, 545.
Pooecetes gramineus, COUES, Key, 1872, 136; and of late authors generally.

b. *confinis.*

Pooecetes gramineus var. *confinis,* BD., B. N. A. 1858, 448 (in text. Pale western race).— MERR., U. S. Geol. Surv. Ter. 1872, 680.—COUES, Key, 1872, 136.

Hab.—United States from Atlantic to Pacific; north to the Saskatchewan at least. Breeds from Maryland to corresponding latitudes northward. Winters in countless multitudes in the Southern States. The pale var. *confinis* from the Middle Province.

List of specimens.

| 19281 | 65 | Snake River ... | ♀ | June 17, 1860 | F. V. Hayden. | 6.00 | 10.60 | 3.25 |

Lieutenant Warren's Expedition.—4507-08, 4505, Yellowstone River; 4506, 4504, Fort Union; 8943-44, Black Hills; 8942, 8945, 8947, South Fork.
Later Expeditions.—54311, 59887, 60398-406; 60744-59, various Wyoming localities; 61674-7, Utah; 61777-8, Idaho; 62308-9, Wyoming. (All var. *confinis.*)

Dr. Hayden's collections show that this species is abundant in the Missouri region, as it is in all suitable localities elsewhere in the United States. Allen found it common at Denver, as well as along the western edge of the plains, and occasionally thence upward to above timber line on the Snowy Range. I have met with it abundantly in all parts of the West where I have been.

Mr. Trippe kindly furnishes the following notes from Idaho Springs, Colorado: "The Bay-winged Bunting is very abundant, breeding from the plains up to timber-line, though not numerous above 9,000 feet. It arrives at Idaho Springs early in May, and has become very common by the 20th, extending up to timber-line wherever it can find congenial haunts. It frequents the open valleys of the larger streams and the grassy hill-sides, where its manners are much as in the East. It has quite a variety of songs; one almost precisely like that of the Eastern bird; another so different that the two would scarcely be supposed to come from the same author—of these the latter is by far the most common—and variations between them, different individuals varying greatly in their songs.

9

"This Western race is certainly as well entitled to rank as a geo-graphical species or variety as any of the Western *Empidonaces* for instance. The bay on the wings is often reduced to a faint trace, and sometimes extinguished altogether; the white of the tail is lessened in extent, and the whole aspect of the bird certainly presents a strong contrast to the typical *gramineus.*"

The Bay-winged Bunting builds a nest on the ground in an open field, anywhere, clear of any special surroundings. It is sunk to the level of the surface, and is rather large outside, though the cavity is small and deep, owing to the great thickness of the walls—an inch or even more. It is built entirely of grass and weed-stalks, having usually a layer of quite fine grasses at the bottom, where it is thinnest, and with a mass of the coarser material around the sides, forming the broad brim. It is finished inside with little art—with a few horse-hairs, or some finer grass, in many instances, but often without any special lining what-ever. An average nest, gathered somewhat compactly together, will measure about four inches across by two deep, with a cavity but two inches across and nearly as deep. I have only found four eggs, laid the latter part of May or early in June. They are rather narrow, measur-ing on an average 0.80 by 0.55. The ground-color is grayish-white; this is marked all over in a wholly indeterminate manner with spots, splashes, and even larger areas of dull reddish-brown, with a good deal of fine sprinkling of the same color, as well as, occasionally, dots of heavier, darker brown. The female does not spring from her nest until almost trodden upon, when she flutters in silence languidly away, re-peatedly falling as if hurt, and arising again, in hopes of drawing atten-tion from the nest to herself; at a little distance she finally disappears in the herbage.

The charming song of the "Vesper-bird" has been fittingly de-scribed by one of the most enthusiastic and agreeable of writers upon birds—I mean John Burroughs, in his welcome little volume entitled "Wake Robin." "Have you heard the song of the Field-Sparrow?" he asks. "If you have lived in a pastoral country, with broad upland pastures, you could hardly have missed him. Wilson, I believe, calls him the Grass-Finch, and was evidently unacquainted with his powers of song. The two white lateral quills of his tail, and his habit of running and skulking a few yards in advance of you as you walk through the fields, are sufficient to identify him. Not in meadows or orchards, but in high, breezy pasture-grounds, will you look for him. His song is most noticeable after sundown, when other birds are silent, for which reason he has been aptly called the Vesper-Sparrow. The farmer follow-ing his team from the field at dusk catches his sweetest strain. His song is not so brisk and varied as that of the Song-Sparrow, being softer and wilder, sweeter and more plaintive. Add the best parts of the lay of the latter to the sweet vibrating chant of the Wood-Sparrow (*Spizella pusilla*), and you have the evening hymn of the Vesper-bird—the poet of the plain, unadorned pastures. Go to those broad, smooth, up-lying fields, where the cattle and sheep are grazing, and sit down on one of the warm, clean stones, and listen to this song. On every side, near and remote, from out the short grass which the herds are cropping, the strain rises. Two or three long, silver notes of rest and peace, ending in some subdued trills or quavers, constitute each separate song. Often you will catch only one or two of the bars, the breeze having blown the minor part away. Such unambitious, unconscious melody! It is one of the most characteristic sounds in Nature. The grass, the stones, the stubble, the furrow, the quiet herds, and the warm twilight among the hills, are all subtilely expressed in this song; this is what they are at least capable of."

Speaking of music, and while I have a favorite author in hand, let me reproduce another passage—not alone for its truth and beauty, but because it tells something few know—something about the voice of the Golden-crowned Thrush that I never knew myself till I found it here, familiar as I thought I was with that pretty and dainty bird: "Coming to a dryer and less mossy place in the woods, I am amused with the Golden-crowned Thrush, which, however, is no Thrush at all, but a Warbler, the *Seiurus aurocapillus*. He walks on the ground ahead of me with such an easy, gliding motion, and with such an unconscious, pre-occupied air, jerking his head like a Hen or Partridge, now hurrying, now slackening his pace, that I pause to observe him. If I sit down, he pauses to observe me, and extends his pretty rambling on all sides, apparently very much engrossed with his own affairs, but never losing sight of me. Satisfied that I have no hostile intentions, the pretty pedestrian mounts a limb a few feet from the ground, and gives me the benefit of one of his musical performances, a sort of accelerating chant. Commencing in a very low key, which makes him seem at a very uncertain distance, he grows louder and louder, till his body quakes and his chant runs into a shriek, ringing in my ears with peculiar sharpness. This lay may be represented thus: ' Teacher, *teacher*, TEACHER, TEACHER, **TEACHER**!'—the accent on the first syllable, and each word uttered with increased force and shrillness. No writer with whom I am acquainted gives him credit for more musical ability than is displayed in this strain; yet in this the half is not told. He has a far rarer song, which he reserves for some nymph whom he meets in the air. Mounting by easy flights to the top of the tallest tree, he launches into the air with a sort of suspended, hovering flight, like certain of the Finches, and bursts into a perfect ecstacy of song—clear, ringing, copious, rivaling the Goldfinch's in vivacity, and the Linnet's in melody. This strain is one of the rarest bits of bird-melody to be heard. Over the woods, hid from view, the ecstatic singer warbles his finest strain. In the song you instantly detect his relationship to the Water-Wagtail (*Seiurus noveboracensis*)—erroneously called Water-Thrush—whose song is likewise a sudden burst, full and ringing, and with a tone of youthful joyousness in it, as if the bird had just had some unexpected good fortune. For nearly two years this strain of the pretty walker was little more than a disembodied voice to me, and I was puzzled by it as Thoreau was by his mysterious Night-Warbler, which, by the way, I suspect was no new bird at all, but one he was otherwise familiar with. The little bird himself seems disposed to keep the matter a secret, and improves every opportunity to repeat before you his shrill, accelerating lay, as if this were quite enough, and all he laid claim to. Still, I trust I am betraying no confidence in making the matter public here. I think this is pre-eminently his love-song, as I hear it oftenest about the mating season. I have caught half-suppressed bursts of it from two males chasing each other with fearful speed through the forest."

COTURNICULUS PASSERINUS, (Wils.) Bp.

Yellow-winged Sparrow.

Fringilla passerina, WILS., Am. Orn. iii, 1811, 76, pl. 26, f. 5.—BP., Syn. 1828, 109.—AUD., Orn. Biog. ii, 1834, 180, v, 497, pl. 130.
Fringilla (Spiza) passerina, BP., Obs. Wils. 1825, No. 111.
Emberiza passerina, AUD., Syn. 1839, 103.—AUD., B. Am. iii, 1842, 73, pl. 162.—GIR., B. L. I. 1844, 103.—PUTN., Pr. Ess. Inst. 1856, 210 (summer; common).

Coturniculus passerinus, BP., List, 1838, 32; Consp. 1850, i, 481.—CAB., J. f. O. 1856, 7 (Cuba).—BD., B. N. A. 1858, 450.—SCL., P. Z. S. 1859, 379 (Oaxaca).—SCL. & SALV., Ibis, 1859, 18 (Guatemala).—KENN., P. R. R. Rep. x, 1859, iv, 28 (Bill Williams' R., Arizona).—HEERM., P. R. R. Rep. x, 1859, vi, 49 ("abundant").—HAYD., Rep. 1862, 166.—DRESS., Ibis, 1865, 487 (Texas).—COUES, Pr. Phila. Acad. 1866, 84 (Arizona; refers to Kennerly).—ALLEN, Pr. Ess. Inst. iv, 1864, 71 (Massachusetts, May to September, breeding).—COUES, Pr. Ess. Inst. v, 1868, 282 (New England, abundant, summer resident).—MCILWR., Pr. Ess. Inst. v, 1876, 89 (Hamilton, C. W., rare, in summer).—BOARDM., Pr. Bost. Soc. ix, 1862, 126 (rare, in summer, from April).—VERR., Pr. Ess. Inst. iii, 158 (Maine, rare; quotes Boardman).—LAWR., Ann. Lyc. N. Y. viii, 1866, 287 (New York).—COUES & PRENT., Smiths. Rep. for 1861 (1862), 412 (Washington, D. C., abundant, in summer, April to October, breeding).—COUES, Pr. Bost. Soc. xii, 1868, 116 (South Carolina, resident, common).—SUMICH., Mem. Bost. Soc. i, 1869, 552 (Vera Cruz, in winter).—CAB., J. f. O. viii, 411 (Costa Rica).—LAWR., Ann. Lyc. ix, 1868, 103 (Costa Rica).—ALLEN, Bull. M. C. Z. iii, 1872, 136, 177 (Kansas and Utah).—COOP., B. Cal. i, 1870, 189.—COUES, Key, 1872, 137.—B. B. & R., N. A. B. i, 1874, 553, pl. 25, f. 4. (Of the above, western references belong to next var.)
Ammodromus passerinus, GRAY, G. of B. ii, 373.—WOODH., Sitgr. Rep. 1853, 86 (very common in the Indian Territory, in Texas, and in some parts of New Mexico.)
Fringilla savannarum, "GM."—NUTT., Man. i, 1832, 494; *ibid.* 2d ed. i, 1840, 570.—PEAB., Rep. Birds Mass. 1839, 324.
(?) *Fringilla caudacuta*, LATH., Ind. Orn. i, 1790, 459.—NUTT., Man. i, 1832, 505.
Coturniculus tixicrus, GOSSE, B. Jam. 1847, 242.—BP., Consp. Av. 1850, 481.—SCL., P. Z. S. 1861, 74 (Jamaica); Cat. A. B. 1862, 116. (Resident in Jamaica.)

b. *perpallidus*.

Coturniculus passerinus var. *perpallidus*, RIDGW., Mss.—COUES, Key, 1872, 137 (pale form, from dry, western regions).—B. B. & R., N. A. B. i, 1874, 556.

Hab.—United States. Not on the Pacific coast? Mexico. Cuba. Jamaica. Porto Rico. South to Costa Rica and Guatemala. Var. *perpallidus* from the West.
Lieutenant Warren's Expedition.—8184, Shawnee Mission; 8936-69-78, Loup Fork of the Platte River.
Not obtained by Captain Raynolds' Expedition.

The earlier accounts of Nuttall, Townsend, and Audubon, mention the Yellow-winged Sparrow as occurring on the Columbia. Although this record has not been checked by later observations, what we now know of the distribution of the species makes it appear most probably correct. It is true that in the higher latitudes of the United States we have no quotations from regions west of the Rocky Mountains; but further south the species is known to range across New Mexico and Arizona; and Dr. Cooper states that Mr. Hepburn procured several specimens in California. Mr. Allen quotes Ogden, Utah. The pertinence of Audubon's remark hence appears. "Some of this species," he says, "on their way from their unknown winter abode northward, pass toward the middle and eastern districts of our Atlantic coast, while others diverge to reach the Oregon section (in which this bird has been found by Mr. Townsend), passing over our Southern States unobserved, although when proceeding toward the Texas, in April, 1837, I found them abundant on their way eastward."

This is a rather southerly bird, even more so than the Bay-winged Bunting. I can find no record beyond the United States, excepting Mr. McIlwraith's, and his locality is south of some of the Maine quotations. In the latter State, according to all observers, it is rare; I do not think it is common north of the Connecticut Valley. It increases in numbers southward, and in the Middle States, Maryland, and Virginia, it is very abundant, breeding in old, weedy fields. I found it in South Carolina, at such various seasons, as to lead me to believe that it is resident there. Its great abundance in the Platte country is attested by Dr. Hayden's numerous specimens. Mr. Allen found it "abundant everywhere on the plains" of Kansas, and secured several nests with the full complement (usually five) of fresh eggs, early in June. According to Prof. Sumichrast, the species winters in Vera Cruz.

Mr. Allen institutes an interesting comparison between the colors of this species in different sections of the country. "On comparing Florida specimens with northern ones, the former are found to be far more brightly colored than the latter. Between northern and southern specimens of the same species greater differences in color are rarely observable than in this, the differences being far greater than occur between many conspecific geographical races to which has been awarded specific rank. The difference consists in the much brighter and blacker tints of the southern form. Massachusetts specimens, although lighter than Florida ones, are still much darker than those from the plains." To the last-mentioned pale form Mr. Ridgway has applied the name *perpallidus*. Mr. Allen observes that it is one of the characteristic summer birds of the plains, ranging to the eastern foot-hills of the Rocky Mountains, and very common in Salt Lake Valley. It breeds abundantly in Kansas.

The song of the Yellow-winged Sparrow is a humble effort, rather weak and wheezy, but quite curious, more resembling the noise made by some grasshoppers than the voice of a bird. It is only heard in the breeding season, when the little performer mounts a tall mullein in his chosen pasture, or the fence-rail around it, settles himself firmly on his legs, and throwing up his head, utters the chirring notes *ad libitum*. At other seasons he has only a weak chirp. The bird is very timid, keeping almost always on the ground, amid the weeds and grass, where he runs like a mouse. On being forced up, he starts quickly, with a wayward, jerky flight, but seldom goes far before pitching into the grass again. The nest is placed on the ground, in a field, and resembles that of other Sparrows that build on the ground. As many as nine eggs are said to have been found in one nest, but the number is usually four or five. They are pure white, speckled with rich, clear, reddish-brown, chiefly at the larger end, but sparingly also all over the surface. The egg is usually rather globose—0.75 by 0.60 for an average instance.

COTURNICULUS HENSLOVII, (Aud.) Bp.

Henslow's Bunting.

Emberiza henslowi, AUD., Orn. Biog. i, 1831, 360; v, 498, pl. 77.—AUD., Syn. 1839, 104.—
    AUD., B. Am. iii, 75, pl. 163.—GIR., B. L. I. 1844, 104.
Fringilla henslowi, NUTT., Man. i, 1840, 2d ed. 571.
Coturniculus henslowi, BP., List, 1838, 32; Consp. i, 1850, 481.—BD., B. N. A. 1858, 451.—
    WHEAT., Ohio Agric. Rep. 1860.—HAYD., Rep. 1862, 166.—COUES & PRENT.,
    Smiths. Rep. 1861 (1862), 412.—WHEEL., Pr. Bost. Soc. vii, 137 (Berlin, Mass.).—
    ALLEN, Pr. Ess. Inst. iv, 1864, 71 (Springfield, Mass.).—LAWR., Ann. Lyc. N. Y.
    viii, 1868, 287 (New York).—COUES, Pr. Ess. Inst. v, 1868, 282 (Massachusetts,
    rare).—COUES, Pr. Bost. Soc. xii, 1868, 115 (South Carolina).—TURNB., B. E. Pa.
    1869, 22 (rather rare).—ALLEN, Bull. M. C. Z. ii, 1871, 279 (Florida, in winter).
    MAYN., Guide, 1870, 117.—COUES, Key, 1872, 137.—TRIPPE, Pr. Bost. Soc. xv,
    1872, 237 (Iowa, common, breeds).—SNOW, B. Kans. 1873, 7.—B. B. & R., N. A.
    B. i, 1874, 550, pl. 25, f. 5.
Ammodromus henslowi, GRAY, G. of B. ii, 373.

    Hab.—Eastern United States to Massachusetts. West to the Loup Fork. "Winters in Carolina, Alabama, Louisiana, and Florida; breeds from Maryland to New York" (*Audubon*).
    Lieutenant Warren's Expedition.—8938, Loup Fork of the Platte.
    Not obtained by Captain Raynolds' Expedition.

The obtaining of this specimen greatly extends the known range of the species, and fixes the westernmost limit thus far recorded. Audubon speaks of its great abundance in several of the Atlantic States, but no later observers have found it to be so. With me, it has been one of the rarest of our sparrows. I have seen it on but one or two occasions, about Washington, D. C. It has been found breeding in Massachusetts. The eggs are not distinguishable from those of *C. passerinus.*

COTURNICULUS LECONTEI, (Aud.) Bp.

Leconte's Sparrow.

Emberiza lecontii, Aud., B. Am. vii, 1843, 338, pl. 488.—Maxim., J. f. O. vi, 1858, 340.—
Ammodromus lecontii, Gray, G. of B. ii, 374.
Coturniculus lecontii, Bp. Consp. Av. i, 1850, 481.—Bd., B. N. A. 1858, 452.—Coues, Key, 1872, 137.—Coues, Am. Nat. vii, 1873, 748 (biography, &c.).—B. B. & R., N. A. B. i, 1874, 552, pl. 25, f. 6.

Hab.—Central Plains, from Northern Dakota to Texas.

This long-lost species, of which I, for one, never expected to see an example, believing it to have been based upon some particular condition of *C. passerinus* or *C. henslovii,* has at length been re-discovered. While at the Smithsonian, in 1872, I was shown a specimen, No. 50222, from Texas, which had been identified by Mr. Ridgway with *Emberiza lecontii* of Audubon. On careful examination, I could not refer it to any species known to me, while at the same time I found that it agreed in all essential particulars with Audubon's description and plate; so that I did not hesitate to endorse Mr. Ridgway's view. As stated in the Key, it resembles *C. henslovii;* the bill is much smaller; the fore and under parts and sides of the head are buff, with black touches on the sides; there is no yellow loral stripe; the median stripe on the crown is buff, passing into white posteriorly. The length of the specimen is $4\frac{1}{4}$ inches; the wing, $2\frac{1}{8}$; tail, $1\frac{7}{8}$. This is a young bird.

Audubon says that the species is common on the Upper Missouri, where, let us hope, other specimens will be found.

December, 1873.—Since the foregoing was penned, I have been so fortunate as to find the bird myself, and secure several examples. These represent the old and young of both sexes, and are particularly interesting, since they show that we have hitherto misapprehended the characters of the species. For Audubon's account (his type is lost), with which the Texas specimen agrees, indicates only the extensively buffy, diffusely marked, soft plumage of the *young,* for which the adult differs materially, necessitating a revision of the diagnosis of the species. In form the species differs notably from its congeners in the shape and relatively greater length of the tail, which is rather over two inches long, decidedly exceeding the wings, reaching beyond the outstretched feet, and remarkably graduated, the lateral feathers being from *one-third* to *one-half* an inch shorter than the central. The tail-feathers are all extremely narrow and acuminate, even more so than in the Sharp-tailed Fnch, *Ammodromus candacutus.* In fact the bird is quite as much an *Ammodromus* as a *Coturniculus,* furnishing an excellent connecting link for those who are disposed to unite these so called genera. The wings are very short and much rounded; when closed, the primaries hardly exceed the longest secondary by one-fourth of an inch, although the secondaries are not at all elongated. The bill is not so turgid as in *C. passerinus;* the younger birds have it smaller than it is in that species, as stated in the Key, but in the adults the difference is less notable. Specimens measure from 4.90 to 5.10 in length, by 6.90 to 7.10 in extent; the wing is 1.90 to 2.00; the tail, 2.00 to 2.25. The general buffiness varies in intensity and extent with age and wear of the feathers; it is greatest in birds of the year; an old male, moulting (August 9th), shows scarcely any. There is no yellow on the edge of the wing, nor a loral yellow spot, as in *C. passerinus ;* there are no blackish maxillary or pectoral streaks, as in *C. henslovii*, the markings of the under part of the adult being confined to sparse, sharp, blackish touches along the sides. In the younger birds, however, these may usually be traced across the breast, as is also the case with young *passerinus*, the adult of which is not, or not noticeably, marked below. But even the youngest specimen shows no maxillary streaks. There are some peculiarities in the shade and pattern of the variegation of the upper parts; the markings of the adults being bold, sharply contrasted and heavily colored. The bill of the old bird is dark horn-blue, lighter bluish below; that of the young is reddish-brown, paler below; the feet are flesh-colored at all ages.

My article in the American Naturalist, here reproduced in substance, continues:

"I only noticed the birds on one occasion,[*] August 9th, when a number were found together in the deep green sea of waving grass that rolled over an extensive moist depression of the prairie. Five specimens were secured in the course of an hour, not without difficulty; for the grass being waist-high, the only chance was a snap-shot, as the birds, started at random, flitted in sight for a few seconds; while it was quite as hard to find them when killed. Several seen to fall were not recovered after diligent search. In their mode of flight, the birds resembled Wrens; a simile which suggested itself to me at the time, was that of a bee returning home laden with pollen; they flew straight and steadily enough, but rather feebly, as if heavily freighted for their very short wings. The only note I heard was a chirring, like the noise of a grasshopper. Although I found no nest, the circumstances of observation leave no doubt that the birds bred here. They were in company with a number of short-billed Marsh Wrens; their neighbors of the drier prairie around were Chestnut-collared Buntings, Baird's Buntings, and Sprague's Larks, all very numerous."

These observations were made near Turtle Mountain, on the border of Dakota, latitude 39°, while I was Surgeon and Naturalist of the Northern Boundary Survey, season of 1873. The nest and eggs remain unknown; another year they may be brought to light.

MELOSPIZA LINCOLNI, (Aud.) Bd.

Lincoln's Sparrow.

Fringilla lincolnii, AUD., Orn. Biog. ii, 1834, 539, pl. 193.—NUTT., Man. i, 2d ed. 1840, 569.
Linaria lincolnii, RICH., List, 1837.
Passerculus lincolnii, BP., List, 1838, 33.
Peucæa lincolnii, AUD., Syn., 1839, 113.—AUD., B. A. iii, 1841, 116, pl. 177.—BP., Consp. Av. 1850, 481; C. R. 185920.—HEERM., P. R. R. Rep. x, 1859, pt. vi, 494, (California).
Zonotrichia lincolnii, WOODH., Sitgr. Rep. 1853, 85.—FINSCH, Ab. Nat. iii, 1872, 76 (Alaska).
Melospiza lincolnii, BD., B. N. A. 1858, 483.—SCL., P. Z. S. 1858, 303 (Oaxaca); 1859, 365 (Xalapa).—SCL. & SALV., Ibis, 1850, 18 (Guatemala).—KENN., P. R. R. Rep. x, 1849, part iv, 29 (Arizona).—HAYD., Rep. 1862, 167 (abundant).—COUES, Pr. Phila. Acad. 1866, 88 (Arizona, *Kennerly*).—ALLEN, Pr. Ess. Inst. iv, 1864, 73.—COUES, Pr. Ess. Inst. v, 1868, 283.—LAWR., Ann. Lyc. N. Y. viii, 1866, 286 (New York).—TURNB., B. E. Pa. 1869, 23 (rather rare, spring and fall).—ALLEN, Mem.

---

[*] But after I had written the article for the Naturalist, being then in the field, I found the species again, early in September, on the head-waters of Mouse River, about the margins of reedy pools, in situations exactly corresponding to those the *Ammodromi* inhabit along the coast.

Bost. Soc. i, 1869, 505 (Illinois).—SUMICH., Mem. Bost. Soc. i, 1869, 552 (Vera Cruz).—DALL & BANN., Tr. Chic. Acad. i, 1869, 285.—MAYN., Nat. Guide, 1870, 120 (Massachusetts, very rare).—ALLEN, Bull. M. C. Z. iii, 1872, 177 (Eastern Kansas; Colorado Mountains, from 8,000 feet to above timber-line; Ogden, Utah).—STEV., U. S. Geol. Surv. Ter. 1870, 465 (Wyoming).—COOP., B. Cal. i, 1870, 216.—HOLD., Pr. Bost. Soc. 1872, 200 (Black Hills).—TRIPPE, *ibid.* 238 (Iowa, common).—COUES, Key, 1872, 138.—SNOW, B. Kans. 1873, 7.—B. B. & R., N. A. B. ii, 1874, 31, pl. 27, f. 13.

Helospiza lincolni, BD.—ALLEN, Pr. Ess. Inst. iv, 1864, 72 (Massachusetts).
Passerculus zonarius, BP.—SCL., Pr. Zool. Soc. 1856, 305.

Hab.—Whole of North America. Mexico. Guatemala.
Lieutenant Warren's Expedition.—4811, Iowa Point; 4898, Bald Island; 4809, Platte River; 4814, Big Sioux River; 4816, Blackfoot country; 4810, 4812-13, 4815, Vermilion River.
Later Expeditions.—59890-93, Middle Park, Colorado; 61052-57, Henry's Fork and Green River, Wyoming.
Not obtained by Captain Raynolds' Expedition.

Since described by Audubon from "Labrador to New York" this bird has occurred at various points, until its range has been determined to include the whole continent. It does not, however, appear to be equally distributed. In the Atlantic States it is apparently rare; in the course of all my collecting I never saw it, and the above quotations, including nearly all that exist, are unanimous in attesting its scarcity. In the West, however, the case is different. In Iowa, according to Mr. Trippe, as above quoted, it is common in spring and fall; and from Colorado, the same observer writes as follows: "Lincoln's Finch is abundant, and migratory; it breeds from about 9,500 or 10,000 feet up to timber-line. It arrives at Idaho Springs early in May, and soon becomes very common, haunting the thickets and brush-heaps by the brooks, and behaving very much like the Song Sparrow. During the breeding season it is most abundant among the bushes near and above timber-line, nesting as high as it can find the shelter of the willows and junipers. Reappearing in the valleys in October, it lingers by the streams for a few weeks, and then disappears." Mr. Allen also informs me that it is "an abundant summer resident of the mountains of Colorado, from about 8,000 feet to above the limit of trees. It is found chiefly in the vicinity of wooded streams and in moist or swampy thickets, being essentially a woodland bird. Its song is rather feeble, but pleasant and varied, and generally uttered for a considerable period from some elevated point of the thicket. It is one of the few species that are as abundant at the timber-line as at lower points. I also met with it sparingly in Eastern Kansas in May, and found it abundant in the vicinity of Ogden, Utah, in September." Dr. Hayden found it "abundant" throughout the western territory. Mr. Ridgway informs us of its great numbers in winter in Southern Illinois. Finally, my own observations attest how numerous it is in Dakota during the migrations. Arriving from the North in September, it frequents the shrubbery along the streams for a month or more before it passes on South. Under these circumstances I have found it in company with Ridgway's and Harris's Finches. It is one of the more timid and retiring of our Sparrows, at least at this season. When I startled it from its ramblings in the low herbage outside the shrubbery, it would instantly seek shelter in the thickest cover, flying low, direct, and with a jerky flight like that of the Song and Swamp Sparrows; nor would it venture out again for a long while. It does not habitually, at this season, perch on the tops or outer twigs of bushes, except momentarily, seeming to feel insecure unless hidden from view; it rarely lifts itself more than a few feet from the ground. Altogether, its habits seem to be nearest those of the Swamp Sparrow. I have never heard its song. In the fall it has only a weak chirp, but in the breeding season it is said to be a "sweet songster."

The only United States record of breeding I have, is the above mention of its nesting in the Rocky Mountains. As attested by our numerous and extensive collections from British America and Alaska, it pushes very far north in the spring, breeding in abundance in these high latitudes. Audubon found the young flying in Labrador July 4th, but did not discover the nest or eggs. The eggs, of which an immense series from Great Slave Lake and the Yukon, are in the Smithsonian, are of the same general pattern as those of the Song Sparrow, and present the endless variation in coloration shown in the latter. The various shades of reddish and other brown blotching is generally heavy and uniformly distributed, but in some specimens wreathes around the larger end. The egg averages smaller than a Song Sparrow's—about 0.80 by 0.60.

MELOSPIZA PALUSTRIS, (Wils.) Bd.

Swamp Sparrow.

(??) *Fringilla georgiana*, LATH., Ind. Orn. i, 1790, 460.
Fringilla georgiana, NUTT., Man. i, 1832, 502.
Fringilla (Ammodromus) georgiana, NUTT., Man. i, 2d ed. 1840, 588.
Fringilla palustris, Wils., Am. Orn. iii, 1811, 49, pl. 22, fig. 1.—BP., Syn. 1828, 110.—
    AUD., Orn. Biog. i, 1831, 331, v. 508, pl. 64.
Fringilla (Spiza) palustris, BP, Obs. Wils. 1825, No. 105.
Passerculus palustris, BP., List, 1838, 33 —BP., Consp. Av. i, 1850, 481.
Ammodromus palustris, AUD, Syn. 1839, 111.—AUD., B. Am. iii, 1841, 110, pl. 175.—
    GIR., B. L. I. 1844, 114.—PUTN., Pr. Ess. Inst. 1856, 218 (Massachusetts, sum-
    mer).—TRIPPE, Pr. Ess. Inst. vi, 1871, 116 (Minnesota, "common").
Melospiza palustris, BD., B. N. A. 1858, 483.—WHEAT., Ohio Agric. Rep. 1860.—SCL., Cat.
    1862, 114.—COUES & PRENT., Smiths. Rep. 1861 (1862), 413 (Washington, D. C.,
    migratory.—VERR., Pr. Ess. Inst. iii, 151 (Maine, breeding).—BOARDM., Pr.
    Bost. Soc. ix, 1862 (Maine, breeding).—HAYD., Rep. 1862, 167 (Lower Missouri,
    rare)—McILWR., Pr. Ess. Inst. v, 1866, 89 (Hamilton, C. W., common in sum-
    mer).—COUES, Pr. Ess. Inst. v, 1868, 283 (New England).—COUES, Pr. Bost.
    Soc. 1868, 116 (South Carolina, winter).—LAWR., Ann. Lyc. N. Y. 1868, 286.—
    ALLEN, Mem. Bost. Soc. i, 1868, 505 (Illinois, October, abundant).—TURNB., B.
    E. Pa. 1869, 23.—ALLEN, Bull. M. C. Z. ii, 1871, 279 (Florida, winter, common).—
    COUES, Phila. Acad. 1871, 22 (North Carolina, common).—MAYN., Pr. Bost. Soc.
    xiv, 1871 (north to Quebec, *Couper*).—TRIPPE, *ibid.* xv, 1872, 238 (Iowa).—
    ALLEN, Bull. M. C. Z. iii, 1872, 177 (Eastern Kansas, May).—COUES, Key, 1872,
    138.—SNOW, B. Kans. 1873, 7.—B. B. & R., N. A. B. ii, 1874, 34, pl. 28, f. 1, 2.
Helospiza palustris, BD.—ALLEN, Pr. Ess. Inst. iv, 1864, 73 (Massachusetts).

Hab.—Eastern and part of Middle Province of North America. West to Utah (*Dr. H. C. Yarrow*). North to Newfoundland and Labrador (*Audubon*); ordinarily to New England and Canada. Winters in the Southern States, Carolinas to Texas. (No extralimital record.)

Lieutenant Warren's Expedition.—4806, Vermilion River.
Not obtained by Captain Raynolds' Expedition.

The Swamp Sparrow is chiefly a bird of the Eastern Province, the specimen just recorded being the westernmost I have seen, and perhaps representing the normal limit of distribution in that direction. But I am recently advised by Dr. Yarrow of its occurrence in Southern Utah. I have found it myself in Northern Dakota, as far north as the headwaters of Mouse River, where it is rather common in the shrubbery along the streams during the migrations. How far it may penetrate in the interior of British America I do not know; but, although unnoticed by Swainson and Richardson, it probably reaches a high latitude in summer, since it was found by Audubon to be plentiful in Labrador. It is generally distributed throughout New England in summer, breeding in suitable places. According to my observations, it is only a bird of passage in the Middle States, but Wilson states that, of the numbers that pass through Pennsylvania, a few remain during the summer. On the coast of North Carolina I saw some after May, but I judge these were merely late migrants, not about to breed there. In the same locality I saw others through November, and it is quite possible that some may winter there, as they certainly do in South Carolina, and thence throughout the Southern States to Texas. I have not met with any extralimital quotations, a circumstance confirming the winter residence of the species as just stated.

The nest of the Swamp Sparrow is usually placed on the ground, in low, moist places, at the foot of a bunch of rank grass or reeds; sometimes in a tussock, more rarely off the ground, in a low bush. It is built of various dried grasses, weeds, roots, and other fibrous material, and lined with fine rootlets. The eggs, four or five in number, are usually dull grayish or faintly bluish-white, speckled all over with reddish-brown and various other shades, the markings sometines tending to aggregate in a wreath about the larger end, sometimes not; often so close as to hide the ground-color altogether. They measure about 0.78 by 0.55 in size. Two, and sometimes three, broods are reared in a season, and fledglings are to be observed through part of August.

The food and general economy of this species are not peculir, but it has nevertheless its distinctive traits. It is a very abundant bird, but its retiring habits withdraw it from general observation. It is not so decidedly gregarious as some of its allies, and is oftener found skulking alone through rank herbage and tangled undergrowth than in flocks; still, in the fall, I have found considerable numbers together, about the edges of reedy swamps, sharing the shrubbery with the Song Sparrows and the reeds with the species of *Ammodromus*, between which it forms, in one sense, a connecting link. I have also seen it, though more rarely, in open, wet, grassy places. During the vernal migration, at Washington, D. C., I used to look for it in the undergrowth fringing tiny streams flowing through open woods, and rarely failed to find it, if I looked close enough, in the very heart of such recesses, the skirts of which were full of White-throated Sparrows and other more conspicuous species. I never saw it take a long flight in the open woods ; generally it was seen flitting from bush to bush, just over the ground or water, flirting the tail, and uttering its peculiar note. Its chirp is remarkably different from that of any other species, and, with its general *reddishness*, seems to distinguish it from its associates. The song I have never heard. Nuttall says that occasionally, mounted on the top of a low bush or willow-tree, it chants "a few trilling, rather monotonous, minor notes, resembling, in some measure, the song of the Field Sparrow, and appearing like *twé, tw' tw' tw' tw' tw twe*, and *twl' tw'l 'tw tw' twé*, uttered in a pleasing and somewhat varied warble."

MELOSPIZA MELODIA, (Wils.) Bd.

Song Sparrow.

a. *melodia*.

(?) *Fringilla fasciata*, GM., Syst. Nat. i, 1786, 922. (Very probable.)
Fringilla melodia, WILS., Am. Orn. ii, 1810, 125, pl. 16, fig. 4.—BP., Syn. 1828, 108.—
    AUD., Orn. Biog. i, 1831, 126 ; v, 507 ; pl. 25 ; Syn. 1839, 120 ; B. Am. iii, 1841,
    147, pl. 189.—NUTT., Man. i, 1832, 486.—GIR., B. L. I. 1844, 121.—PUTN., Pr. Ess.
    Inst. 1856, 211.—TRIPPE, *ibid.* vi, 1871, 116.
Zonotrichia melodia, BP., List, 1838, 31 ; Consp. Av. 1850, 478.
Melospiza melodia, BD., B. N. A. 1858, 477.—HAYD., Rep. 167.—COUES, Key, 1872, 139.—
    B. B. & R., N. A. B. ii, 1874, 19, pl. 27, fig. 6 ; also of nearly all late writers.

b. *fallax.*

(?) *Zonotrichia fasciata*, GAMB., J. A. N. S. 2d ser. i, 1847, 49.
Zonotrichia fallax, BD., Pr. A. N. S. vii, 1854, 119 ("New Mexico" = Arizona).
Melospiza fallax, BD., B. N. A. 1858, 481; 1860, 481, pl. 27, fig. 2.—KENN., P. R. R. Rep.
    x, 1859, p.. iv, 29, pl. 27, fig. 2.—COUES, Pr. Phila. Acad. 1866, 52 (Arizona).—
    COOP., B. Cal. i, 1870, 215.
Melospiza melodia var. *fallax*, RIDGW.—COUES, Key, 1872, 139.—B. B. & R., N. A. B. ii,
    1874, 22, pl. 27, fig. 10.
Melospiza melodia, COUES, Ibis, 1865, 165.

c. *heermanni.*

Melospiza heermanni, BD., B. N. A. 1858, 478; 1860, 478, pl. 70, fig. 1 (California).—COOP.,
    Orn. Cal. i, 1870, 212.
Melospiza melodia var. *heermanni*, RIDGW.—COUES, Key, 1872, 139.—B. B. & R., N. A. B.
    ii, 1874, 24, pl. 27, fig. 9.

d. *gouldii.*

Melospiza gouldii, BD., B. N. A. 1858, 479; 1860, 455, pl. 71, fig. 1 (California).
Melospiza melodia var. *gouldii*, COUES, Key, 1872, 139.
Ammodromus samuelis, BD., Pr. Bost. Soc. vi, 1858, 381 (California).
Melospiza melodia var. *samuelis*, B. B. & R., N. A. B. ii, 1874, 26, pl. 27, fig. 7.

e. *mexicana.*

"(??) *Melospiza pectoralis*, v. MÜLLER."
Melospiza melodia var. *mexicana*, RIDGW., B. B. & R., N. A. B. ii, 1874, 18 (Puebla, Mex.)

f. *guttata.*

Fringilla cinerea ("GM."), AUD., Orn. Biog. v, 1839, 22, pl. 390, fig. 1; Syn. 1839, 119; B.
    Am. iii, 1841, 145, pl. 187. (Not of *Gmelin*.)
Passerella cinerea, BP., List, 1838, 31; Consp. i, 1850, 477.
Fringilla (*Passerella*) *guttata*, NUTT., Man. i, 2d ed. 1840, 581.
Zonotrichia guttata, GAMB., J. A. N. S. 2d ser. i, 1847, 50.
Melospiza melodia var. *guttata*, RIDGW.—COUES, Key, 1872, 139.—B. B. & R., N. A. B. ii.
    1874, 27, pl. 27, fig. 12 (excl. ref. *Dall* and *Bannister*).
Melospiza rufina, BD., B. N. A. 1858, 480.—COOP. & SUCK., N. H. Wash. Ter. 1860, 204.—
    COOP., B. Cal. i, 1870, 214 (excl. Syn. *rufina*, *Brandt*).

g. *rufina.*

Emberiza rufina, BRANDT, Desc. Av. Rossic. 1836, pl. 2, 5 (*Bonaparte*).
(?) *Passerella rufina*, BP., Consp. Av. i, 1850, 477.
Melospiza rufina, DALL & BANN., Tr. Chic. Acad. i, 1869, 285.
Melospiza melodia var. *rufina*, RIDGW.—COUES, Key, 1872, 139.—B. B. & R., N. A. B. ii,
    1874, 29, pl. 27, fig. 11 (not *rufina* of *Baird*, 1858, which = var. *guttata*).
Melospiza guttata et *cinerea*, FINSCH, Abh. Nat. iii, 1872, 41.

h. *insignis.*

(?) *Fringilla cinerea*, GM., Syst. Nat. i, 1788, 922 (*cinereous Finch*); PENN., Arct. Zool.
    ii, 68 (Oonalashka).
(?) *Zonotrichia cinerea*, "GR."—BP., Consp. 1850, 478.
Melospiza insignis, BD., Tr. Chic. Acad. i, 1869, 319, pl. 29, fig. 2.—DALL & BANN., ibid.
    285.—FINSCH, Abh. Nat. iii, 1872, 44 (Kodiak).
Melospiza melodia var. *insignis*, RIDGW.—COUES, Key, 1872, 140.—B. B. & R., N. A. B. ii,
    1874, 30, pl. 27, fig. 8.

Hab.—The ordinary Eastern type extends westward to the dry, central plains. North to the Canadas and Nova Scotia. Winters as far north as the Middle States, if not in Southern New England (Coos County, New Hampshire, November, with snow, *Maynard*). Breeds throughout its range, and is, in most localities, one of the most abundant and familiar of all Sparrows. (No extralimital record.) Var. *fallax* from the Southern Middle Province. Var. *heermanni* from California east to the Humboldt Mountains. Var. *gouldii* from the California coast, San Francisco, and southward. Var. *guttata* from the Pacific coast north to British Columbia. Var. *rufina* from Pacific coast north of British Columbia. Var. *insignis* from Kodiak and Oonalashka.

    I adopt the several varieties of this species from Mr. Ridgway's account, published in the work above cited. He very kindly gave me his identifications, for use in the Key, in advance of his own publication. The reader is referred to the work in question for an exhaustive analysis of this perplexing group.

Lieutenant Warren's Expedition.—4817, Bald Island ; 8750, Loup Fork of the Platte.
Later Expeditions.—Var. *fallax*: 60640–5, 61032–51, 61119, various Wyoming locali-
ties; 61673, Utah; 62303–6, Idaho.
Not obtained by Captain Raynolds' Expedition.

Dr. Hayden's Missouri region specimens represent the typical form,
but one at least approximates to the pale western race (var. *fallax*).
This author remarks that it is not abundant in the Northwest, and the
same is the case in most of the unsettled localities of the West, affording a parallel with the scarcity of the Robin under the same circumstances. Allen found it abundant only at Ogden, Utah. I did not find
it in Northern Dakota.

PEUCÆA CASSINI, (Woodh.) Bd.

Cassin's Pine Finch.

Zonotrichia cassini, WOODH., Pr. Phila. Acad. vi, 1852, 60 (Texaᵃ).
Passerculus cassini, WOODH., Sitgr. Rep. 1853, 85, pl. 4.
Peucæa cassini, BD., B. N. A. 1858, 485 (Texas. In part. The Sonora specimen there
      included is *P. æstivalis* var. *arizonæ*. See RIDGW., Am. Nat. vii, 1873, 616).—
      HEERM., P. R. R. Rep. x, 1859, Parke's Route, Birds, 12, pl. 4, fig. 2 (Texas).—
      SCL., Cat. A. B. 1862, 115 (Mexico; compared with type).—DRESS., Ibis, 1865,
      (Texas, eggs).—SUMICH., Mem. Bost. Soc. i, 1869, 551 (Orizaba, resident).—
      COOP., B. Cal. i, 1870, 219 (California).—RIDGW., Am. Nat. vii, 1873, 617 (in
      text).—SNOW, B. Kans. 1873, 7.—COUES, Check-list, App. No. 170 *bis*.—B. B. &
      R., N. A. B. ii, 1874, 42, pl. 28, fig. 5.
Ammodromus cassini, GR.—GIEBEL, Nomenc. Av. i, 328.
Peucæa æstivalis var. *cassini*, ALLEN, Bull. M. C. Z. iii, 1872, 137 (Middle Kansas). (Not
      of COUES, Key, 1872, 140, which was intended for what has since been called
      var. *arizonæ*. See COUES, Check-list, App. No. 170ᵃ).

Hab.—Texas to California, and southward into Mexico. North to Kansas.

The type of "*Zonotrichia cassini*" may be a young bird, but other specimens in the
Smithsonian appear adult, and most probably warrant Mr. Ridgway's separation of
the species from *æstivalis*, although at one time I was of the contrary opinion. It must
not be confounded with the pale race of *æstivalis* (var. *arizonæ*) which occurs in the
same region. It was this pale race which I wrongly called var. *cassini* in the Key; the
mistake is corrected in the Check-list, upon examination of ample material with Mr.
Ridgway.

This species is brought into the present connection upon its occurrence in Kansas, where it was found by Mr. Allen to be "rather common along the streams, where its low but peculiarly sweet song is heard
at morning and evening, beginning with the first approach of dawn and
continuing at evening considerably after nightfall. It is very retiring,
and it was only after several attemps that I discovered the author of
the sweet notes that at these still hours added greatly to the pleasure
of camping on the plains." Dr. Heermann notices it as follows : " My
attention having been attracted by the sound of a new note while at
Comanche Springs, Texas, I found, after some observation, that it proceeded from this bird. Rising with a tremulous motion of its wings
some twenty feet or more, it descends again in the same manner to
within a few yards of the spot whence it started, accompanying its
entire flight with a lengthened and pleasing song. The country there-
about is very barren, being covered with low stunted bushes, into
which the bird takes refuge on being alarmed, gliding rapidly through
the grass and shrubbery, adroitly and effectually evading its pursuer.
I observed them during four or five days of our travel, when they disappeared. They were probably migrating at the time, though their
continued and oft-repeated song gave notice they were about preparing
for the duties of incubation."

The species of *Peucæa* differ from all their allies in laying a pure crystal-white egg without markings. That of the present species measures 0.75 by 0.60, being thus quite globose. Four or five are the complement. The nest is placed on the ground.

JUNCO HYEMALIS, (Linn.) Scl.

Eastern Snow-bird.

a. *hyemalis*.

Fringilla hyemalis, LINN., Syst. Nat. i, 1758, 183.—BP., Syn. 1828, 109.—SW. & RICH., F. B. A. ii, 1831, 259.—AUD., Orn. Biog. i, 1831, 72; v, 505; pl. 13.—MAXIM., J. f. O. vi, 1858, 277.

Emberiza hyemalis, LINN., S. N. i, 1766, 308 (*Passer nivalis*, CATES., i, 36).—LATH., I. O, i, 399.
Struthus hyemalis, BP., List, 1838, 31; C. Av. i, 1850, 475.—WOODH., Sitgr. Rep. 1853, 83.
Niphæa hyemalis, AUD., Syn. 1839, 106.—AUD., B. Am. iii, 88, pl. 167.—GIR., B. L. I. 1844, 108.—PUTN., Pr. Ess. Inst. 1856, 210 (Oct. to May).—TRIPPE, Pr. Ess. Inst. vi, 1811, 116 (Minnesota, breeding).
Junco hyemalis, SCL., P. Z. S. 1857, 7.—BD., B. N. A. 1858, 468.—WHEAT., Ohio, Agric. Rep. 1860, No. 152.—COUES, Pr. Ph. Ac. 1861, 224 (Labrador, breeding).—HAYD., Rep. 1862, 167.—SCL., Cat. 1862, 115.—COUES & PRENT., Smiths. Rep. 1861 (1862), 412 (middle of Oct. till May).—ALLEN, Pr. Ess. Inst. iv, 1864 (Springfield, Mass., Oct. 1 to Dec., and early Mar. till May; breeds in mountains of Berkshire).—VERR., Pr. Ess. Inst. iii, 1862, 151 (Norway, Me., winter, spring, and fall, breeding in White Mountains and at Umbagog lakes).—VERR., Pr. Bost. Soc. 1862, 132 (Anticosti, "common all summer").—BOARDM., Pr. Bost. Soc. 1862, 127 (Calais, Me., summer, very common, breeds).—DRESS., Ibis, 1865, 488 (Texas).—COUES, Pr. Ess. Inst. v, 1868, 282.—COUES, Pr. Bost. Soc. xii, 1868, 115 (South Carolina, Oct. to Apr.).—COUES, Pr. Phila. Acad. 1866, 85 (Arizona, winter, accidental, three specimens).—TURNB., B. E. Pa. 23 (Oct. to Apr.; also, breeding on the Alleghanies).—DALL & BANN., Tr. Chic. Acad. i, 1869, 284 (Nulato, Alaska, common, arriving June 1, breeding).—ALLEN, Bull. M. C. Z. ii, 1871, 278 (Florida, January, common).—MAYN., Nat. Guide, 1870, 119 (Massachusetts, abundant everywhere, middle Oct. to late May).—MAYN., Pr. Bost. Soc. xiv, 1871 (New Hampshire, common, breeding in June in districts north of Franconia).—AIKEN, Pr. Bost. Soc. 1872, 201 (Wyoming).—TRIPPE, Pr. Bost. Soc. xv, 1872, 237 (Iowa).—COUES, Key, 1872, 141.—SNOW, B. Kans. 1873, 7.—RIDGW., Am. Nat. vii, 1873, 613 (critical).—B. B. & R., N. A. B. i, 1874, 580, pl. 26, fig. 5.
Fringilla hudsonia, FORST., Phil. Tr. lxii, 1772, 428.—GM., Syst. Nat. i, 1788, 926.—WILS., Index, vi, 1812, p. xiii.
Fringilla nivalis, WILS., Am. Orn. ii, 1810, 129, pl. 16, f. 6.—NUTT., Man. i, 1832, 491.

b. *aikeni*.

Junco hyemalis var. *aikeni* (RIDGW., Mss.).—AIKEN, Pr. Bost. Soc. xv, 1872, 201 (Colorado).—RIDGW., Am. Nat. vii, 1873, 613, 615 (characterized by two white wing-bands across tip of median and greater coverts, and an additional feather of the tail white).—COUES, Check-list, App. No. 174ª; see Key, 1872, 141 (in text).— B. B. & R., N. A. B. i, 1874, 584, pl. 26, fig. 6.

Hab.—Eastern Province of North America; in the United States, seen as far west as the Black Hills, thence trending northwest to Alaska. Some straggle southward, west of the Rocky Mountains (Washington Territory, *Suckley;* Utah, *Henshaw;* Colorado, *Aiken;* Arizona, *Coues*). Breeds from Maine and New Hampshire northward, and in mountains south to the Middle States, and even to the Graylock Range. Winters from Iowa and Massachusetts, southward. No recorded extralimital localities. Var. *aikeni* only as yet from mountains of Colorado.

Lieutenant Warren's Expedition.—4816, Vermilion River; 5393, Cannon-ball River; 8959, Black Hills.

Not obtained by Captain Raynolds' Expedition.

Besides its general distribution, the course and periods of its migrations, as well as its nesting and wintering, may be accurately traced by the above indications. Dr. Hayden's specimen, No. 8959, probably represents the extreme *normal* western range of the species in the United States. It breeds in mountains far south of the latitudes where it nests

at ordinary altitudes.   The eggs are white or whitish, often with a faint
grayish tint, occasionally slightly flesh-colored, sprinkled more or less
thickly and uniformly with reddish-brown, or pale chocolate, and often,
also, a few dark-brown dots.   The tendency is to aggregation, at or
around the but.   They measure 0.80 by 0.60.   All the species of *Junco*
lay similar eggs, and the nidification is essentially the same.

JUNCO OREGONUS, (Towns.) Scl.

Oregon Snow-bird.

Fringilla oregona, Towns., J. A. N. S. Phila. vii, 1837, 188; Narr. 1839, 345.—Aud., Orn.
   Biog. v, 1839, 68, pl. 398.
Struthus oregonus, Bp., List, 1838, 31; Consp. Av. i, 1850, 475.—Woodh., Sitgr. Rep.
   1853, 83.—Newb., P. R. R. Rep. vi, 1857, 88.
Niphœa oregona, Aud., Syn. 1839, 107; B. Am. iii, 1841, 91, pl. 168.
Junco oregonus, Scl., P. Z. S. 1857, 7; Cat. 1862, 115.—Lord, Pr. Arty. Inst. 1864, iv,
   120.—Bd., B. N. A. 1858, 466.—Kenn., P. R. R. Rep. 1859, part iv, 28.—Heerm.,
   ibid. part vi, 47.—Coop. & Suck., N. H. Wash. Ter. 1860, 202.—Hayd., Rep.
   1862, 166.—Coues, Pr. Phila. Acad. 1866, 85.—Dall & Bann., Tr. Chic. Acad.
   i, 1869, 284.—Coop., B. Cal. i, 1870, 199.—Stev., U. S. Geol. Surv. Ter. 1870,
   464.—Merr., *ibid.* 1872, 681.—Finsch, Abh. Nat. iii, 1872, 53 (Alaska).—Allen,
   Bull. M. C. Z. iii, 1872, 118, 167.—Hold.—Aiken, Pr. Bost. Soc. 1872, 200 (Wyoming).—Coues, Key, 1872, 141.— B. B. & R., N. A. B. i, 1874, 584, pl. 26, f. 2.
Junco hyemalis var. *oregonus*, Ridgw., Am. Nat. vii, 1873, 613 (critical).
Fringilla hudsonia, Licht., Abh. Ak. Berlin, 1839, 424, *nec* Forst.
Fringilla atrata, Brandt, Ic. Rosso-As. pl. 2, fig. 8.

Hab.—Western and Middle Provinces of North America; straggling to edge of the
Eastern Province.

List of specimens.

| 19279 | 73 | W. side R. Mts. | .... | June 5, 1860 | F. V. Hayden. | 5.75 | 9.00 | 2.75 |
| 19280 | 41 | S. of Cheyenne. | .... | June 2, 1860 | ......do...... | ...... | ...... | ...... |

Lieutenant Warren's Expedition.—No. 5372, Medicine Creek; 5374, Great Bend of Missouri River.
   Later Expeditions.—61022-7, Green River, &c., Wyoming; 62316-23, Idaho and Wyoming.

The Warren specimens indicate a nearly extreme eastern range of the
species; still, we have advices of its occurrence in Kansas, both at Fort
Leavenworth and at Fort Riley, which brings it fairly within the limits
of the Eastern Province.   It has only occurred in winter, however, in
these localities.
   The date of capture of the Raynolds' examples renders it probable
that the bird breeds in those places.   Just as we have seen the Eastern
Snow-bird breeding in mountains, in latitudes below those where it
breeds down to sea-level, so the Oregon species resides in summer, at
least, down to the 35° parallel, if not further.   Dr. Cooper, indeed,
observes that it summers in the mountainous parts of California, probably down to the 32° parallel; he observed it at San Diego until April,
when he judged that it retired to the high mountains a few miles from
the coast, to breed.   He found it nesting on the coast mountains south
of Santa Clara, in May, the young flying by the 13th of that month, and
has given a description of the nest.   "It was built in a cavity among
the roots of a large tree on a steep bank; formed of leaves, grasses, and
fine root-fibres, and covered outside with an abundant coating of green
moss."   Another nest that he found May 20th, on the very summit of
the mountains, was "slightly sunk in the ground under a fern (*Pteris*)
and formed like the other, but with less moss around the edge; some

cow's and horse's hair was also used in the lining." It contained three eggs, measuring 0.74 by 0.60, bluish-white, with blackish and brown spots of various sizes thickly sprinkled on the larger end.

My own experience with this bird has been only in the winter time. I found it extremely abundant in the mountains of Arizona, from the middle of October until the middle of April; and loiterers remained until May. I judge that it breeds in the neighboring higher mountains, as the San Francisco and Bill Williams. In habits, it seemed the counterpart of the familiar eastern bird. During pleasant, open weather, it used to keep in the recesses of the woods and shrubbery, but in snow-storms, and during severe weather, when seeds were scarce and hard to find, it would come trooping about our tents, and especially around the stock corrals, gleaning a subsistence from the waste grain that dropped from the feed-troughs of our horses. Under such circumstances it was sometimes emboldened even to enter a vacant tent; and I caught several alive by scattering some bread crumbs in a small "A"-tent standing near mine, the flap of which was fixed so it could be pulled down with a string. Its ordinary note is a soft chirp, which I could not dis-tinguish from that of the common Snow-bird; in the spring, just before leaving for its breeding-grounds, it has a rather pleasing song, also like that of its eastern relative.

JUNCO CINEREUS var. CANICEPS, (Woodh.) Coues.

Gray-headed Snow-bird.

b. caniceps.*

Struthus caniceps, WOODH., Pr. Phila. Acad. vi, 1852, 202 (New Mexico and Texas).— WOODH., Sitgr. Rep. 1853, 83, pl. 3.
Junco caniceps, BD., B. N. A. 1858, 468, pl. 72, fig. 1.—HAYD., Rep. 1862, 167.—COUES, Pr. Phila. Acad. 1866, 85.—COOP., B. Cal. i, 1870, 201.—ALLEN, Bull. M. C. Z. iii, 1872, 177.—AIKEN, Pr. Bost. Soc. 1872, 200 (Wyoming).—GRAY, Hand-list, No. 7370.—B. B. & R., N. A. B. i, 1874, 587, pl. 26, f. 3.
Junco cinereus var. *caniceps*, COUES, Key, 1872, 141.
Junco hyemalis var. *caniceps*, RIDGW., Am. Nat. vii, 1873, 613 (critical).
Junco dorsalis, HENRY, Pr. Phila. Acad. x, 1858, 117 (New Mexico).—BD., B. N. A. 1858, 468, pl. 28, fig. 1 (tending to characteristics of *cinereus* proper).
Junco annectens, BD., in COOP. B. Cal. i, 1870, 564 (intermediate between *caniceps* and *oregonus*; probably a hybrid).

Hab.—Middle Province (Southern Rocky Mountain region), United States. North to the Black Hills and Laramie Peak.
Lieutenant Warren's Expedition.—8960-61, Laramie Peak.
Not obtained by Captain Raynolds' Expedition.

As observed in my late work, the descent with modification of all the described forms of *Junco* from a common stock, is undoubted if not unquestionable, although the diversion has become so great that it would be scarcely expedient to consider them all as a single species. The various forms may be reduced to three, *hyemalis*, *oregonus*, and *caniceps*, with their varieties. The first of these has no pinkish-rufous on the sides below, and in full plumage the dark parts are nearly uniform blackish-plumbeous; the adult female is grayer, even brownish, especially on the inner quills, and the young of the first autumn and winter are extensively brownish. *Oregonus* has an opaque, blackish head, and fore-parts sharply contrasted with reddish of the back, and the white of the

---

* The synonymy of *a. cinereus*, is: *Fringilla cinerea*, Sw., Phil. Mag. i, 1827, 435.— *Junco cinereus*, CAB., Mus. Hein. 1850, 134.—BD., B. N. A. 1858, 465.—SCL., P. Z. S. 1856, 306; 1857, 7; 1858, 304; 1859, 365.—SUMICH., Mem. Bost. Soc. i, 1869, 551 (alpine region of Vera Cruz, 2,000 to 3,500 metres, abundant and characteristic).—*Junco phœonotus*, WAGL., Isis, 1831, 526.—"*Fringilla rafidorsis*," LICHT. *Hab*: Mexico. In this form the rusty-red extends over the upper surface of the wings, and the bill is black and yellow. An allied form is *J. alticola*, SALV., P. Z. S. 1863, 189; Ibis, 1866, 193, from the mountains of Guatemala. It is the *J. hyemalis* var. *alticola* of RIDGW., *l. c.*

under-parts shaded with pinkish-brown on the sides. Young birds of this form come very near immature *hyemalis*; Mr. Ridgway has noted intermediate specimens (Pr. Phil. Acad. 1869, 126), and complete inosculation of the two is claimed by Mr. Allen. In both of these the white of the under-parts is abruptly defined against the dark colors. In "*caniceps*," the main color is pale grayish-plumbeous, fading insensibly into the white below; the lores are definitely blackish, and the interscapular region alone is ferruginous—this color forming a small triangular area; the bill is pinkish-white, as in the foregoing. This form passes through "*dorsalis*" into the extreme of typical *cinereus*, in which the characters are as given in a preceding foot-note; while on the other hand specimens have been found showing pinkish-brown sides, and otherwise tending to the characters of *oregonus*—these constitute *J. "annectens"* of Baird. The probability that some of these intermediate specimens are really hybrids is very strong, but has not been proven by detection of opposite sexes of the two actually breeding together; so it remains an open question. Mr. Allen inclines to dispose of the matter of hybridism upon the hypothesis that the doubtful specimens are simply examples of intergradation of character, according to climatic or other influences resulting from geographical distribution. However this may be, it is certain that all three forms, in their typical development, occur together. This is the case in Arizona, for instance, where I found them all. To show how intimately they are associated, I may state that once, on firing into a flock of Snow-birds, I picked up, after the single discharge, several *oregonus*, one pure *caniceps*, and a single typical *hyemalis*.

The Gray-headed Snow-bird is not nearly so common in Arizona, in winter, as the Oregon species; still, I frequently observed it in company with the latter, and obtained several specimens. It arrived at the same time as *oregonus*, and departed with it, probably to breed in the neighboring higher mountains. It undoubtedly breeds at Laramie, since Dr. Hayden's specimens were taken in August. It appears to be common in Colorado, from the eastern bases of the foot-hills up the mountains to above timber-line.

In the American Naturalist, as above cited, Mr. Ridgway takes the view that *all* the forms of *Junco* are geographical races of one species. He discusses the matter very ably and upon good grounds. Referring the reader especially to this article, I submit, in further elucidation of the difficult problem, the following notes received from Mr. T. Martin Trippe, premising, however, that in so doing I am not necessarily committed to his conclusions. (The biographical notes refer to Idaho Springs, Colorado.)

Junco hyemalis var. *hyemalis*.—Eastern Snow-bird. This Snow-bird is never abundant, nor does it breed in Clear Creek County; the only period during which it is at all common being March and the early part of April. During fall and winter, it is a rare visitor; but among the foot-hills, and edge of the plains, it is abundant, as Mr. Aiken, of Fountain, informs me, during November and March, but is rarely met with in midwinter. I have never seen it higher than 8,000 feet, and it is far more common below 7,000. It is similar in its habits and notes to the eastern bird, and is almost always found in flocks with the succeeding variety.

J. hyemalis var. *oregonus*.—Oregon Snow-bird. Where this species begins and *hyemalis* ends, it would puzzle even Brehm to decide; for while it is easy to select two specimens representing the species as described in the books, a large series collected at the same time and from the same place, will show all possible gradations between the two, many individuals combining the characteristics of both. Thus, the rusty-rufous back of *oregonus* is sometimes found without the purplish sides, which are supposed to belong to the latter bird; or, *vice versâ*, specimens of *hyemalis* with scarcely a wash of rusty on the back, are occasionally marked by decidedly purplish sides. Of all the varieties these two are the most unstable and seem to blend most perfectly with each other. They associate together, and have the same habits and notes; they appear and disappear about the same time; but of the two, *oregonus* is most abundant, being twice or thrice as numerous as *hyemalis*. Mr. Aiken informs me that the present variety arrives in his vicinity—which is a short distance south of this region, on the edge of the plains—about the middle of October, and remains till April, thus showing a slightly more southern habitat than that of the preceding race.

J. caniceps.—Chestnut-backed Snow-bird. Abundant, and the only species that breeds here. The Chestnut-backed Snow-bird arrives about the middle or latter part of March, two or three weeks previous to the departure of the two preceding races, with whom it associates as long as they remain. As the snow disappears, it gradually works its way upward, and by the middle of June has disappeared from the regions below 8,000 feet. It breeds most abundantly in the upper woods, from the extreme limit of the willows down to 1,000 or 1,200 feet below timber-line; and more sparingly below that point as far down as 8,500 feet, and occasionally as low as 7,500 and even 7,000 feet. In October it descends to the lower valleys, and soon disappears altogether. On the plains it is common in December and March, but rare during midwinter. In habits it resembles *hyemalis;* its twitter is the same, but its song is different. Of all the varieties that are found in this region, this is the most constant in its markings. Among scores of specimens, I never met with any that exhibited in any marked degree the characteristics of any of the other races combined with those of the Chestnut-backed species.

J. annectens.—Chestnut-sided Snow-bird. This race or species is supposed by some ornithologists to be a hybrid between *oregonus* and *caniceps,* a supposition showing the danger of generalization on too narrow grounds, for there is nothing to support the idea except the combination of certain characteristics belonging to those two races; and on the same principle *Colaptes chrysoides* might be supposed to be a hybrid between *C. auratus* and *C. mexicanus.* The Chestnut-sided Snow-bird is as well marked, and almost as constant in its coloration, as *J. caniceps,* and far more so than *oregonus, hyemalis,* or *aikeni.* It is common only in spring, associating with other varieties, and remaining till April, being the last to leave of the migratory species. It ranges rather higher than either the Oregon or the Black Snow-bird, occasionally extending as high as 9,500 feet, or higher. In winter I have not noticed it, but am informed by Mr. Aiken that it is very abundant on the plains from early in October till May, and that it out-numbers *caniceps* and *oregonus* together—a singular fact, if it is a "hybrid." Undoubt-edly it does occasionally mix with both these varieties, as specimens sometimes show a tendency to one or other of them, usually toward the latter; but I have never seen any that I could not refer, without hesitation, to one or the other of three species—*caniceps, annectens,* or that which embraces *hyemalis, oregonus,* and *aikeni* as sub-varieties.

J. aikeni.—White-winged Snow-bird. Abundant; does not breed. This race is evi-dently the most northern of the five, as it arrives latest (in November) and departs earliest (in March), ranging higher also than any of the others, up to 10,000 feet, and probably further still. In its notes and habits the White-winged Snow-bird differs somewhat from its congeners. Its song is louder and sweeter; it is less gregarious in its nature; and it frequents brushy hill-tops and mountain-sides, high up above the valleys, and rarely visited by the other species during the winter. It is the only Snow-bird at all common during winter, choosing as its favorite haunts the bushy ravines and hollows, as well as the valleys of the larger streams, and wandering thence far up on the mountains, associating in small parties only, more than six or eight being rarely seen together. During the coldest weather, only the well-marked typical birds are seen, among which are both males and females, the former being most numerous; but toward the close of winter the females become more abundant, and among a large series of specimens, obvious approaches to both *hyemalis* and *oregonus* may be distin-guished, especially toward the former. The intergradation, however, is by no means as perfect as that between the two latter races, and a specimen that cannot be de-cidedly referred to either *aikeni* or *oregonus-hyemalis* is unusual. The white wing-bands vary very much; in the largest males they are almost always broad and well-defined; in the small males and females they are narrower, sometimes almost obsolete, occa-sionally wanting on one wing and present on the other, and sometimes wholly want-ing or indicated by the faintest trace. In the latter case, the other characteristics of the bird are those of *hyemalis,* while the peculiar features of the latter bird or of *ore-gonus* are never to be seen where the white wing-bands are well defined. Well-devel-oped males frequently have white lores or white spots on the head and neck.

Without a very large number of specimens from different localities, it is difficult to discuss, intelligently, the relations of these races or species; but from a careful study of their habits, notes, distribution, and migration in this region, as well as the com-parison of a large number of specimens, I cannot help drawing the conclusion that at least three, or perhaps four, of the various forms have, in the words of Dr. Coues, "passed the merely varietal stage and become nascent species, though still unstable in character." These may be arranged as follows:

I. *Junco caniceps.* Sp. ch. Interscapular region bright rufous. Breeds abundantly in the mountains of Colorado, from 9,000 feet up to timber-line. Retreats south of the Territory in winter.

II. *J. annectens.* Sp. ch. Sides clear cinnamon-fulvous. Abundant in Colorado during winter and spring, but breeds north of the Territory.

III. *J. hyemalis.* With three varieties:

    a. *aikeni.* Var. ch. Two broad, well-defined white bands on the wing-coverts. Abundant in winter, retiring north earlier than the other races, and evidently the most northern in its distribution. Intergrades with the fol-lowing form, though not as intimately as that does with the succeeding.

    b. *hyemalis.* Var. ch. No wing-bands; upper parts with no rufous, except a rusty tinge in autumn. Less abundant than the others, reaching here its western limit; breeding north of the Territory. Intergrades impercept-ibly with the next.

    c. *oregonus.* Var. ch. Back and wings with a decided rusty-brown wash. Abundant, reaching here its eastern limit. Breeds northward, retiring from Colorado with the preceding, or a little later.

10

SPIZELLA MONTICOLA, (Gm.) Bd.

Canadian, or Tree Sparrow.

Fringilla montana, FORST., Philos. Tr. lxii, 1772, 405; not of *Linnæus*.
Fringilla monticola, GM., Syst. Nat. i, 1788, 912.
Spinites monticolus, CAB., Mus. Hein. i, 1851, 134.
Spizella monticola, BD., B. N. A. 1858, 472.—KENNERLY, P. R. R. Rep. x, 1859, iv, 29
    (Colorado Chiquito, Arizona, December).—COOP. & SUCK., N. H. Wash. Ter.
    1860, 203 (Fort Dalles, January).—COUES, Pr. Phila. Acad. 1861, 224 (Labrador,
    summer, abundant).—SCL., Cat. 1862, 114.—HAYD., Rep. 1862, 167.—COUES &
    PRENT., Smiths. Rep. for 1861 (1862), 412 (Washington, D. C., November to
    April, very abundant).—BOARDM., Pr. Bost. Soc. ix, 1862, 127 (Calais, Me., in
    summer, common, breeding early).—VERR., *ibid.* 138 (Anticosti, breeding).—
    VERR., Pr. Ess. Inst. iii, 151 (Norway, Me., spring and fall).—ALLEN, Pr. Ess.
    Inst. iv, 1864, 72 (Springfield, Mass., October to May; also, breeding in East-
    ern Massachusetts in 1855; see Pr. Bost. Soc. v, 213*).—MCILWR., Pr. Ess. Inst.
    v, 1866, 89 (Hamilton, C. W., winter, common, not known to breed).—COUES,
    Pr. Phila. Acad. 1866, 87 (Arizona, *fide Kennerly*).—COUES, Pr. Ess. Inst. v, 1868,
    283.—COUES, Pr. Bost. Soc. xii, 1868, 115 (South Carolina, November to
    March).—DALL. & BANN., Tr. Chic. Acad. i, 1869, 285 (Alaska, breeding).—
    TURNB., B. E. Pa. 1869, 23 (October to April).—COOP., B. Cal. i, 1870, 205 (queried
    as occurring in mountains of California).—ALLEN, Bull. M. C. Z. iii, 1872, 177
    (Western Kansas, in winter).—MAYN., Guide, 1870, 119 (Massachusetts, early
    November to late April).—MAYN., Pr. Bost. Soc. xiv, 1871.—AIKEN, *ibid.* 1872,
    200 (Wyoming).—STEV., U. S. Geol. Surv. Ter. 1870, 465.—COUES, Key, 1872,
    142.—SNOW, B. Kans. 1873, 7.—B. B. & R., N. A. B. ii, 1874, 3, pl. 27, f. 5.
Zonotrichia (Spizella) monticola, GRAY, Hand-list, No. 7398.
Passer canadensis, BRISS., Orn. iii, 1760, 102.
Fringilla canadensis, LATH., Ind. Orn. i, 1790, 434.—BP., Syn. 1828, 109.—NUTT., Man. i,
    1832, 495.—AUD., Orn. Biog. ii, 1834, 511; v, 1839, 504; pl. 188.—MAXIM., J. f. O.
    vi, 1858, 280.
Emberiza canadensis, SW. & RICH., F. B. A. ii, 1831, 252.—AUD., Syn. 1839, 105.—AUD., B.
    Am. iii, 1841, 83, pl. 166.—GIR., B. L. I. 1844, 107.—PUTN., Pr. Ess. Inst. i, 1856
    210 (Essex County, Mass., October to May).—TRIPPE, Pr. Ess. Inst. vi, 1871
    (Minnesota, not very common; not observed in summer).
Spizella canadensis, BP., List, 1838, 33; Consp. Av. i, 1850, 480.
Fringilla arborea, WILS., Am. Orn. ii, 1810, 12, pl. 16, fig. 3.

Hab.—North America at large, excepting, probably, the Gulf States. Infrequent or
casual in the United States west of the Rocky Mountains. Winters high up on the
Missouri, and in corresponding latitudes eastward. Breeds north of the United States,
to high latitudes, but also, like the Snow-bird, in mountains within our ilmits.

List of specimens.

19283	282	Deer Creek....	....	Mar. 7, 1860	F. V. Hayden.	6.00	9.00	3.00
19284	283	...... do	....	..... do	..... do			
19285	284	...... do	....	..... do	..... do	6.00	9.00	3.00
19286	237	...... do	....	Jan. 27, 1860	..... do	6.00	9.25	3.25
19287	....	...... do	....	....	..... do			

Lieutenant Warren's Expedition.—4509, Cedar Island; 4510, Medicine River.
Later Expeditions.—61028-31, 61153-62, various Wyoming localities.

The movements of this interesting species, as well as its general distribution, may be traced in the above quotations. Its western records
are still meagre, but sufficient to represent its range in that quarter; it
appears to be, like the Eastern Snow-bird, little if anything more than a
straggler west of the Rocky Mountains, some individuals apparently
straying southward in that direction from their breeding places in
Alaska. Eastward, the Tree Sparrow is one of the most abundant
species, wintering in great profusion in the Middle States, Maryland,
and Virginia, and some reaching the Carolinas, beyond which it has not,
to my knowledge, been traced. It also winters as high as New England,

---

*.But this instance proves to be not authentic, the Chipping Sparrow having been
mistaken for the Tree Sparrow. See *Samuels*, Orn. and Oöl. of New England, 318.

and even the Canadas; for, as we shall presently see, it is a hardy little
bird, capable of enduring extreme cold, and only forced southward by
scarcity of food. Its breeding range is extensive; on the Atlantic coast
it nests from Labrador to Maine. The general similarity of its distribution to that of the Snow-bird leads me to believe it will yet be found
passing the summer in the mountains of the Middle States. It occurs
through the greater portion of British America in summer, from Atlantic to Pacific. It has been found in Kansas in August, and may
breed in that State.

At Fort Randall I found these birds as abundant as I have ever seen
them anywhere, during pleasant weather in the month of October. All
the undergrowth of the river-bottom was full of them, in troops sometimes numbering hundreds, singing as gaily, it seemed to me, as in
spring-time. With the colder weather of the following month, so many
moved off that I thought none would remain to endure the rigor of
winter, but such proved to be not the case. The remainder simply
retreated to the deepest recesses of the shrubbery, where, protected
from the biting winds, if not from the cold, they passed the winter, and
to all appearances very comfortably. I account for their remaining at
this inclement season, by the profusion of seeds of various kinds that
are to be obtained during the whole winter; certainly, those that I shot
were in good condition, and generally had the crop well filled. Their
seclusion and quietness at this season is remarkable, and causes them
to be in a great measure overlooked. On several occasions, when the
thermometer was far below zero, the river frozen solid for two feet deep,
and snow on the ground, I have unexpectedly come upon little groups of
these birds, hiding away close to the ground among and under a net-
work of vines and rank herbage, close enough to collect and retain a
mantle of snow. When startled at such times they have a low, pleasant
chirp as they flutter into sight among the bushes, scattering a little, but
only to collect again and seek their snug retreat as soon as left to themselves. Whether rendered careless by the cold, or through a natural
heedlessness, they are very tame at such times; they sit unconcernedly
on the twigs, it may be but a few feet distant, chirping cheerfully, with
the plumage all loosened and puffy, making very pretty "roly-poly"
looking objects. There is a particular kind of plant here, the seeds of
which endure all winter, furnishing a favorite repast. In a clump of
these tall weeds dozens of the birds may be seen together, busily feeding. Some, more energetic, spring up and cling to the swaying pan-
icles, picking away, while others gather about the stem, getting a good
dinner, without trouble, off the seeds that their neighbors above rattle
down. At such times the whole company keep up an animated conversation, expressing their satisfaction, no doubt, in their own language;
it is more than chirping, and not quite singing—a low, soft, continuous
chanting, as pleasing as it is indescribable. The Tree Sparrow is, indeed, one of the sweet-voiced of our Sparrows, and one very fond of
singing, not only in the spring, but at other seasons; times are hard
with it indeed when it cannot, on occasion, tune its gentle pipe.

According to Mr. Trippe, in Colorado the Tree Sparrow is "abundant
during winter in all the willow and alder thickets along the streams,
from the plains up to 7,000 feet, and occasionally up to 8,500. It arrives
in November and disappears in April."

Accounts of the egg of this species are conflicting, and mostly erroneous. Mr. Hutchins said it was pale brown, marked with darker spots, a
statement copied by Nuttall and repeated even by Dr. Cooper. Audubon
wrote it was uniform deep blue, just like a Chipping Sparrow's, but

larger. The egg is, in fact, much like that of the Song Sparrow, being pale bluish, speckled and blotched with different shades of reddish-brown. It measures about three-fourths of an inch long by three-fifths in breadth. The immense series in the Smithsonian, from the Anderson River and Yukon region, show the same wide range of variation that the Song Sparrow's egg displays, being thus different from the eggs of other *Spizellæ.* The nidification varies, the nest being placed indifferently on trees, bushes, or the ground.

SPIZELLA SOCIALIS, (Wils.) Bp.

Chipping Sparrow.

a. *socialis.*

Fringilla socialis, WILS., Am. Orn. ii, 1810, 127, pl. 16, f. 5.—BP., Syn. 1828, 109.—NUTT., Man. i, 1832, 497.—AUD., Orn. Biog. ii, 1834, 21,; v, 1839, 517 ; pl 104.
Emberiza socialis, AUD., Syn. 1839, 105 ; B. A. iii, 1841, 80, pl. 165.—GIR., B. L. I. 1844, 106.
Spinites socialis, CAB., Mus. Hein. i, 1851, 133.
Spizella socialis, BP., List, 1838, 33 ; Consp. i, 1850, 480.—BD., B. N. A. 1858, 473.—COUES, Key, 1872, 142, fig. 86—B. B. & R., N. A. B, ii, 1874, 7, pl. 27, f. 1 ; and of late authors generally.
Zonotrichia (Spizella) socialis, GRAY, Hand-list, No. 7397.

b. *arizonæ.*

Spizella socialis var. *arizonæ,* COUES, Key, 1872, 143 (Arizona).—B. B. & R., N. A. B. ii, 1874, 11.

Hab.—Temperate North America, from Atlantic to Pacific, especially United States. Breeds chiefly in Middle and Northern States. Winters in the Southern States and south into Mexico. Cuba. Extremely abundant. (Among extralimital quotations are :.Oaxaca, *Scl.,* P. Z. S. 1858, 304 ; Xalapa, *ibid.* 1859, 365 ; Cordova, *ibid.* 1856, 305 ; Cuba, *Lawr.,* Ann. Lyc. vii, 1860, 269 ; Vera Cruz, *Sumich.,* Mem. Bost. 1869, 552.)
Lieutenant Warren's Expedition.—4805, Bald Island; 5411, Fort Lookout.
Later Expeditions.—60671-72, Green River and Little Sandy ; 61779, 62311-14, Idaho and Wyoming.
Not obtained by Captain Raynolds' Expedition.

SPIZELLA PUSILLA, (Wils.) Bp.

Field Sparrow.

(?) *Little Brown Sparrow,* CATESBY, Car. i, 35 (*Motacilla juncorum,* GM., i, 952 ; *Sylvia juncorum.* LATH., ii, 511.
Fringilla juncorum, NUTT., Man. i, 1832, 499 ; 2d ed. i, 1840, 577.
Fringilla pusilla, WILS., i, 1810, 121, pl. 16, f. 2.—BP., Syn. 1828, 110.—AUD., Orn. Biog. ii, 1834, 229, pl. 139.
Emberiza pusilla, AUD., Syn. 1839, 104 ; B. Am. iii, 1841, 77, pl. 164.—GIR., B. L. I. 1844, 105.
Spinites pusillus, CAB., Mus. Hein. i, 1851, 133.
Spizella pusilla, BP., List, 1838, 33 ; Consp. i, 1850, 480.—BD., B. N. A. 1858, 473.— COUES, Key, 1872, 143.—B. B. & R., N. A. B. ii, 1874, 5, pl. 27, f. 2 ; and of late authors generally.
Zonotrichia (Spizella) pusilla, GRAY, Hand-list, No. 7396.

Hab.—Eastern United States ; breeding from Virginia northward ; wintering from the same point southward.
Lieutenant Warren's Expedition.—4800-01, Big Sioux River ; 4802, Fort Leavenworth, Kans. ; 5412-13, Knife River.
Not obtained by Captain Raynolds' Expedition.

SPIZELLA PALLIDA, (Sw.) Bp.

Clay-colored Sparrow.

Emberiza pallida, Sw. & RICH., F. B. A. ii, 1831, 251.
Spizella pallida, BP., List, 1838, 33 (not of the Conspectus).—BD., B. N. A. 1858, 474.— SCL., P. Z. S. 1859, 365, 379.—SCL., Cat. 1862, 114.—HAYD., Rep. 1862, 167.—

ALLEN, Bull. M. C. Z. iii, 1872, 177.—TRIPPE, Pr. Bost. Soc. 1872, 237 (Iowa).—
COUES, Key, 1872, 143.—SNOW, B. Kans. 1873, 7.—B. B. & R., N. A. B. ii, 1874,
    11, pl. 27, f. 3.
Spinites pallidus, CAB., Mus. Hein. i, 1851, 133.
Zonotrichia (Spizella) pallida, ,GRAY, Hand-list, No. 7400.
Emberiza shattuckii, AUD., B. Am. vii, 1843, 347, pl. 493.
Spizella shattuckii, BP., Consp. i, 1850, 480.

Hab.—From the Saskatchewan and Upper Missouri to Eastern Kansas. To Texas
(*Baird*). East into Iowa (*Trippe*), Wisconsin (*Hoy*), and Illinois (*Holden*).
    Lieutenant Warren's Expedition.—No. ——, Cheyenne River; 4803, "Nebraska;"
4804, Bijoux Hills; 5414, Blackfoot country.
    Not obtained by Captain Raynolds' Expedition.

The typical form of this species appears to be one of the more characteristic birds of the high central plains. It was originally described by Swainson from the region of the Saskatchewan. Dr. Richardson says that it was very abundant at Carlton House, and as familiar as the Chipping is in the Eastern States. Audubon's account of "*Emberiza pallida*" presents nothing incompatible with the typical form; but the specimens, on which his description was based, procured by Townsend in the "Rocky Mountains," and now in the Smithsonian, have been identified by Prof. Baird with *breweri*, which renders it necessary to turn "*pallida*, AUD.," over to the latter variety, although indeed his quotations, and the habitat he assigns, are those of true *pallida*. He afterward described the typical Missouri bird as *E. shattuckii*, giving the following account:

"This handsome little species is found quite abundant throughout the country bordering on the Upper Missouri. It inhabits with particular partiality the small valleys found here and there along the numerous ravines running from the interior, and between such hills as I have already mentioned. Its usual demeanor resembles much that of the Chipping Bunting, *Emberiza socialis* of Wilson, and like it, it spends much of its time in singing its monotonous ditties, while its mate is engaged in the pleasing task of incubation. When approached, it will dive and conceal itself either amid the low bushes around, or will seek a large cluster of wild roses, so abundant in that section of country, and the fragrance of which will reach the olfactory nerve of the traveler or gunner for many paces.

"The nest of the Shattuck Bunting is usually placed on a small horizontal branch, seven or eight feet from the ground; and I believe it is occasionally placed in the broken and hollow branches of trees. The eggs, four or five in number, are blue, spotted with reddish-brown toward the large end, and placed in a nest so slightly formed of slender grasses, circularly lined with horse or cattle hair, as to resemble as much as possible the nest of the species to which it is allied." These observations differ somewhat from my own, given beyond.

I found this bird in small numbers on the Republican Fork of the Kansas River, near Fort Riley, in May, frequenting shrubbery along the stream, and also open, weedy places away from the water; but I noticed nothing peculiar in its manners, which were the same as those of the Chip-bird. Mr. Allen found it common at Topeka, in the same State, associating there with *S. socialis*. He also quotes "*pallida*" from Utah; but as he does not recognize the distinction of var. *breweri*, his observations undoubtedly refer to the latter.

The eastward extension of *S. pallida* has only been of late generally recognized; it seems to correspond somewhat with that of *Vireo belli*. In Iowa, according to Mr. Trippe, it is common in spring; "frequents the thickets and copses along the margins of the woods, and has somewhat the habits of the Red-poll, feeding on the buds of the elm and other trees in early spring."

It is singular that the eggs of our *Spizellæ* should differ so much among themselves, for the rule is that congeneric birds lay similar eggs. Thus, *S. monticola* lays an egg like that of *Melospiza ;* the egg of *S. pusilla* is not distinguishable from that of *Junco*, except in size, and is altogether different from the clear green, blackish-dotted eggs of *S. socialis* and *pallida*.

The Clay-colored Sparrow's nest abundantly in Dakota, and especially along the Red River, in the open, low underbrush by the river-side, and among the innumerable scrub-willow copses of the valley. They pair here the latter part of May, when the males come into full song; the nests are built and the complement of eggs laid, usually by the middle of June. During this month, while the females are incubating, the males mount the tops of the bushes and sing continually—indeed I know of no more assiduous and persistent songster than this little bird is, although his vocal efforts are of an humble sort. His ditty is a simple stave of three notes and a slight trill—nothing like the continuous song of the Chip-bird. In places where the birds are plentiful, several males may be in sight at once, each on his own bush-clump, while his mate is nesting below. As soon as incubation is over, the habit is entirely changed, and the males become as inconspicuous as their consorts. The pairing season, during which the males may be seen continually chasing the females about in the bushes, is of short duration ; and, preliminaries adjusted, both birds set to work in earnest at their nest, with such success that it is completed and the eggs laid in a week or two. Most of my nests were taken during the first two weeks in June. In one case, in which I visited a nest daily, I found that an egg was laid each day, till the complement of four was filled. I have not found more than four eggs in a nest, and sometimes only three. They are of a light-green color, rather scantily and sharply speckled with sienna and other rich shades of brown—sometimes very dark brown. Generally the dotting is chiefly confined to the larger end, with only a speck here and there over the general surface; the dots are sometimes in an area at the butt, sometimes partially confluent and wreathed around it. The eggs measure about 0.62 by 0.50. The nest is always placed low ; I never found one so high as a yard from the ground, and generally took nests within a few inches, in the crotch of a willow or other shrub, or in a tuft of weeds. The nest is inartistically built of fine dried grass-stems and the slenderer weed-stalks, with perhaps a few rootlets ; it is sometimes lined quite thickly with horse-hair, sometimes not, then having instead some very fine grass-tops. It varies a good deal in size and shape, according to its situation, but may average about three inches across by two deep, with a cavity two inches wide by one and a half deep. In those cases where I approached the setting bird, she left the nest when I was a few steps away, and fluttered directly into concealment, without attempting any artifice or venturing to protest against the spoilation of her home.

It is most probable that two broods may be reared, even in this high latitude, but I cannot so assert, as I found no nests nor heard the nuptial songs after June. In July the birds appear in greater numbers than ever, from the accession of the year's broods, and now go in little troops in the shrubbery along with several other kinds of Sparrows. I found them in all wooded and shrubby situations in Dakota, but never out on the high prairie. Early in the fall, in Dakota, they are joined by numbers of Lincoln's, Gambel's, and Harris's Finches, all of which flutter through the shrubbery together. They depart for the South early in

October, according to my observations, though some may linger later. In the spring their return may be noted on the Missouri River, in the region about Fort Randall for instance, toward the end of April, at the same time that the Bay-winged Buntings and Lark Finches arrive.

SPIZELLA PALLIDA var. BREWERI, (Cass.) Coues.

Brewer's Sparrow.

Emberiza pallida, AUD., Orn. Biog. v, 1839, 66, pl. 398, f. 2; Syn. 1839, 103; B. Am. iii, 1841, 71, pl. 161 (*nec* Sw.). (See last article.)
Spizella pallida, BP. Cousp. Av. i, 1850, 480.—WOODH., Sitg. Rep. 1853, 83 (New Mexico).—HEERM., P. R. R. Rep. x, 1859, part vi, 48 (Texas to California).—COUES, Ibis, 1865, 164 (Arizona).
Spizella breweri, CASS., Pr. Phila. Acad. viii, 1856, 40.—BD., B. N. A. 1858, 475.—KENN., P. R. R. Rep. x, 1859, part iv, 29.—COUES, Pr. Phila. Acad. 1866, 87.—STEV., U. S. Geol. Surv. Ter. 1870, 465.—COOP., B. Cal. i, 1870, 209.
Zonotrichia (Spizella) breweri, GRAY, Hand-list, No. 7399.
Spizella pallida var. *breweri*, COUES, Key, 1872, 143.—B. B. & R., N. A. B. ii, 1874, 13, pl. 27, f. 4.

Hab.—Southern Rocky Mountain region, especially New Mexico and Arizona. Texas. California.

List of specimens.

| 19282 | 76 | Pierre's Hole... | .... | June 26, 1860 | F. V. Hayden. | 5.00 | 7.50 | 2.25 |

Later Expeditions.—60408-15, Bitter Cottonwood and Fort Fetterman; 60673-4, Big Sandy and Green River.
Not obtained by Lieutenant Warren's Expedition.

Brewer's Sparrow is of common occurrence in the region above given. Its habits, as I observed them in the southwest, are the same as those of the typical form.

NOTE.—A North American species of this genus, not occurring in the Missouri region, as far as now known, is the following:

SPIZELLA ATRIGULARIS, (*Cab.*) *Baird.*

Spinites atrigularis, CAB., Mus. Hein. i, 1851. 133.
Spizella atrigularis, BD., B. N. A. 1858, 476; 1860, pl. 55, f. 1; Mex. B. Surv. ii, pt. ii, 1859, Birds, 16, pl. 17, f. 1.—COUES, Pr. Phila. Acad. 1866, 87 (Arizona).—COOP., B. Cal. i, 1870, 210.—COUES, Key, 1872, 144.—B. B. & R., N. A. B. ii, 1874, 15, pl. 26, f. 11, 12.
Struthus atrimentalis, COUCH, Pr. Phila. Acad. vii, 1854, 67.
Spizella evura, COUES, Ibis, 1865, 118, 164 (*Young*).
Spizella cana, BD., Mus. Smiths. (*Young*).

Hab.—Mexico, and southwest border of the United States. Arizona (*Coues*). California (*Xantus*).

ZONOTRICHIA ALBICOLLIS, (Gm.) Bp.

White-throated Sparrow.

Fringilla albicollis, GM., Syst. Nat. i, 1788, 926.—WILS., Am. Orn. iii, 1811, p. 51, pl. 22, f. 2.
Zonotrichia albicollis, BP., Consp. Av. 1850, 478.—CAB., Mus. Hein. 1851, 132.—BD., B. N. A. 1858, 463.—HAYD., Rep. 1862, 166.—COUES, Key, 1872, 144, fig. 88.—B. B. & R., N. A. B. i, 1874, 574, pl. 26, p. 10; and of most late authors.
Fringilla pennsylvanica, LATH., Ind. Orn. 1790, 446.—BP., Syn. 1828, 108.—SW. & RICH., F. B. A. ii, 1831, 256 (*Zonotrichia*).—AUD., Orn. Biog. i, 1831, 42; pl. 8; Syn. 1839, 121; B. Am. iii, 1841, 153, pl. 191.—MAXIM., J. f. O. vi, 1858, 276.
Zonotrichia pennsylvanica, BP., List, 1838, 32.

Hab.—Eastern Province of North America, to the 65th parallel. Not observed in Alaska. Breeds from Northern New England and Minnesota northward, especially in the interior. Winters in the United States from Maryland (from New York, *Nuttall*) southward. West to the Indian Territory, Kansas, and Dakota. Accidental in Europe (Aberdeenshire, Scotland, August 17, 1867; Zoologist, 1869, 1547; *Turnbull*, B. E. Pa. 1869, 23; *Newton*, P. Z. S. 1870, 52; England, *Rowley*, P. Z. S. 1872, 681).

Lieutenant Warren's Expedition.—4990-91, Big Nemaha River; 4788, Wood's Bluff; 4785, 4787, Blackbird Hills; 4782, 4784, 4796, Big Sioux River; 4783, 4786, 4789, Vermilion River; 4501, White Earth River; 4502, Cedar Island.
Not obtained by Captain Raynolds' Expedition.

I have not deemed it necessary to cite the voluminous records substantiating the above-mentioned range and movements of this familiar species. Dr. Hayden's specimens represent, as far as we now know, the westernmost limit in the United States. For the Eastern States, I have found no record of the bird's breeding south of the northerly parts of New England—not even in the highest parts of the Middle States, where, however, some may yet be found to nestle, like the Tree Sparrow and Snow-bird. Mr. McIlwraith does not give it as breeding at Hamilton, Canada West; but Mr. Trippe found it nesting in the tamarack swamps and windfalls of Minnesota, as it probably does at other points on our northern frontier. It does not appear to reach Alaska, although the westward trend of the Eastern Zoological Province reaches to the Pacific in that latitude. Judging from the dates of collection of Dr. Hayden's numerous specimens, they were migrating at the time of observation. The bird occupies the whole Southern States in winter; and, selecting a middle point in its migrations, we may clearly trace its movements. Thus, in Maryland and Virginia, where I became familiar with it during several years of observation, many spend the winter in sheltered situations; but the great increase in their numbers during spring and fall show that the great body of them moves further south. They are extremely abundant in the month of October, while most are passing through, and again in May. Many linger until the middle of May, when they are off for the north, leaving not a single straggler. They frequent, on the whole, different places in the spring and fall. At the former season, they enter the woods in large numbers, less closely associating than during the fall, and ramble over the ground, doubtless in search of insects, the last year's supply of seeds being in a great measure exhausted. In autumn, they are found principally trooping together in shrubbery, along hedge-rows, the brier-patches of old fields, and similar resorts, where the seeds they like are plenty. Audubon's account of their manners at this season is too faithful and vivid to ever grow out of date:

"How it comes and how it departs are quite unknown to me. I can only say that, all of a sudden, the edges of the fields bordering on creeks or swampy places, and overgrown with different species of vines, sumac-bushes, briers, and the taller kinds of grasses, appear covered with these birds. They form groups, sometimes containing from thirty to fifty individuals, and live together in harmony. They are constantly moving up and down among these recesses, with frequent jerkings of the tail, and uttering a note common to the tribe. From the hedges and thickets they issue one by one, in quick succession, and ramble to the distance of eight or ten yards, hopping and scratching, in quest of small seeds, and preserving the utmost silence. When the least noise is heard, or alarm given, and frequently, as I thought, without any alarm at all, they all fly back to their covert, pushing directly into the thickest part of it. A moment elapses, when they become reassured, and, ascending to the highest branches and twigs, open a little concert, which, although of short duration, is extremely sweet. There is much plaintive softness in their note, which I wish, kind reader, I could describe to you; but this is impossible, although it is yet ringing in my ear, as if I were in those very fields where I have so often listened to it with delight. No sooner is their music over than they return to the field, and thus continue alternately sallying forth and retreating during the greater part of the day. At the approach of night they utter a sharper and shriller note, consisting of a single *twit*, repeated in smart succession by the whole group, and continuing until the first hooting of some owl frightens them into silence. Yet, often during fine nights, I have heard the little creatures emit, here and there, a twit, as if to assure each other that ' all's well.' "

The musical abilities of this pretty Sparrow, to which Audubon so feelingly alludes, are of a high order, though the song is rather notable for its limpid sweetness than for power and brilliancy. An attempt is made to express the sound in the name commonly given to the species, in some sections, "Peabody-bird." It seems to say, *pee-a'body, a'body, a'body, a'body*, beginning clear, high, and loud, with prolonging of the first syllable; then rising still higher and shortly accenting the second note; then trilling the remainder with a falling inflexion and decreasing volume; this latter part being repeated three or four times, the *a'* still accented, but with diminishing emphasis. I think it might be readily written in musical notes, but I am unable to do so.

Audubon does not appear to have known the nest and eggs of this bird, since he copies Richardson's account. It builds on the ground, usually among bushes, in various situations; the nest is made of dried grass, weed-stems, and moss, lined with thready rootlets or very fine grasses. The eggs are four or five in number, measuring, on an average, nine-tenths of an inch long by three-fifths, or a little more, in breadth, and are dull-whitish, with spots and splashes of surface-brown and similar shell-markings of neutral-tint. It breeds in the latter part of May and in June; I do not know whether more than one brood is reared each season.

The change of plumage of the head of this species offers an interesting point, apparently not yet determined. Only the male, it appears, gets the pure black of the crown, and only during the breeding season. Though I have shot great numbers in the fall, I do not recollect that I ever got one at that season in perfect head-feathering, so that it becomes probable that the breeding livery is put off with a late summer moult. And even in spring, in the Middle States, the number of brown-headed, or, at any rate, of imperfectly black-crowned individuals, is out of all proportion to those in breeding dress. I used to take a few such in May, just before they moved off, but they were rarities. This circumstance may be accounted for by Mr. Allen's observation, that the male does not attain its mature colors until the *second* spring. "The young males," he observes, "sing equally well with the adults, and probably breed in this plumage. Observing many birds singing in the garb of the female drew my attention to the subject, and dissection showed them invariably to be males. This accounts for the great proportion of birds in the livery of the female, both in spring and fall, often observed." These remarks may bear as well upon other species of the same genus. I am not aware that other writers have indicated that the female of this species is songless; I was certainly myself unaware of the fact, if, indeed, it be so.

The eggs of *Zonotrichia albicollis*, and of *leucophrys*, with its varieties, are not distinguishable from each other. They are of the same general character as those of *Melospiza*—heavy marking, in interminable variety, with different reddish and darker brown shades, upon a dull, pale greenish or grayish ground. These markings may be large blotches, or mere marbling in fine points; at the butt of the egg the reddish coloration is frequently nearly uniform.

ZONOTRICHIA LEUCOPHRYS, (Forst.) Sw.

White-crowned Sparrow.

Emberiza leucophrys, FORST., Philos. Tr. lxii, 1772, 382, 403, 426.—GM., Syst. Nat. i, 1788,
    874.—WILS., Am. Orn. iv, 1811, 49, pl. 31, f. 4.
Fringilla leucophrys, BP., Syn. 1828, 107.—NUTT., Man. i, 1832, 479.—AUD., Orn. Biog. ii,
    1834, 88; v, 1839, 515; pl. 114.—AUD., Syn. 1839, 121.—AUD., B. Am. iii, 1841,
    157, pl. 192.—PUTN., Pr. Ess. Inst. 1856, 211 (Essex County, Mass., very rare,
    May and Sept.).—TRIPPE, *ibid*. vi, 1871, 116 (Minnesota, common, breeding).
Fringilla (Zonotrichia) leucophrys, Sw. & RICH., F. B. A. ii, 1831, 255.
Zonotrichia leucophrys, BP., List, 1838, 32; Consp. Av. i, 1850, 478.—WOODH., Sitgr. Rep.
    1853, 84 (Indian Territory, Texas, New Mexico; but mixes it with var. *inter-
    media*).—KENN., P. R. R. Rep. (error for *intermedia?*).—BD., Pr. Phila. Acad. 1859,
    p. — (Cape St. Lucas!).—REINH., Ibis, iii, 1861, 7 (Greenland, breeding).—
    WHEAT., Ohio Agric. Rep. 1860.—COUES, Pr. Phila. Acad. 1861, 223 (Labrador,
    abundant, breeding).—HAYD., Rep. 1862, 166.—COUES & PRENT., Smiths. Rep.
    1861, (1862), 412 (Washington, D. C., winter, until May 10, rare and irregular).—
    BOARDM., Pr. Bost. Soc. ix, 1862, 126 (Calais, Me., not common).—VERR., Pr.
    Ess. Inst. iii, 151 (Norway, Me., spring and fall, rare).—ALLEN, Pr. Ess. Inst.
    iv, 1864, 71 (Springfield, Mass., rare in spring and autumn, "possibly breeds").—
    —COUES, *ibid*. v, 1868, 282.—COUES, Pr. Bost. Soc. xii, 1868, 115 (South Caro-
    lina, Oct. to Apr., not common).—LAWR., Ann. Lyc. N. Y. viii, 1868, 286.—
    ALLEN, Mem. Bost. Soc. i, 1868, 517 (Northern Illinois, May, quite common).—
    TURNB., B. E. Pa. 1869, 22 (Sept. to May, rather rare).—MAYN., Guide, 1870,
    118 (Massachusetts, very rare migrant).—MAYN., Pr. Bost. Soc. xiv, 1871
    (common, and breeding at Quebec; various New England localities).—STEV.,
    U. S. Geol. Surv. Ter. 1870, 464 (Wyoming).—MERR., *ibid*. 1872, 681 (Montana).—
    COOP., B. Cal. i, 1870 (Cape St. Lucas, in winter).—ALLEN, Bull. M. C. Z. iii,
    1872, 156, 163, 177 (mountains of Colorado, to above timber-line, *in July*).—
    AIKEN, Pr. Bost. Soc. 1872, 200 (Sherman, Wyo.; "common wherever there is
    brush").—COUES, Key, 1872, 144.—B. B. & R., N. A B., i, 1874, 566, pl. 25, f. 9, 10.
(?) *Spizella maxima*, BP., Comp. Rend. 1853, —.

Hab.—Eastern North America to the Rocky Mountains. Greenland (*Reinhardt*).
Cape St. Lucas in winter (*Xantus*). Not given by *Allen* among winter birds of Florida,
nor by *Dall* and *Bannister* as occurring in Alaska.
    Lieutenant Warren's Expedition.—4794, Vermilion River; 5403, Knife River; 9238,
Black Hills.
    Later Expeditions.—59882-6, Colorado; 60656-9, 62301-2, Wyoming; 62300, Montana.
Not obtained by Captain Raynolds' Expedition.

Like other naturalists who have visited the forbidding shores of Labrador, I found the White-crowned Sparrow one of the most abundant of
the summer birds of that country. Labrador and Newfoundland,
indeed, appear to be the principal breeding resorts of the species along
the Eastern coast. The nest appears to be always placed on the ground;
the situations generally selected are thick patches of low heath, and the
still more dense growths of scrubby conifers. It is composed chiefly of
mosses, but lined with a quantity of very fine dried grasses or rootlets,
set evenly round and round. The eggs are four or five in number,
about seven-eighths of an inch long, and pale greenish, speckled and
blotched, particularly toward the larger end, with brown and neutral
tint. The descriptions of some of the earlier authors are certainly erroneous, probably relating to the egg of the Tit-lark, which breeds abundantly with the White-crowned Sparrow, and, like it, builds a mossy
nest on the ground. I found nestlings but a few days old the last week
in July; these were perhaps of a second brood, as many birds of the
year were flying about the same time. The southward migration begins,
according to Audubon, as early as the middle of August; this statement is confirmed by the presence of the birds in New England, and
even in the Middle States, in September. The migration is very extensive, the birds scattering all over the United States, and wintering as
far north, at least, as Maryland. Audubon says that they pass beyond
Texas; but he does not appear to have made any personal observation

to that effect, and I cannot lay my hand on a Mexican quotation. I can hardly understand the scarcity—much less the irregularity—of the occurrence of the birds along the Atlantic States, considering the numbers that breed to the northward, unless the migration is performed obliquely and in the interior. At Washington, for example, I found that they were not to be depended upon at all. Dr. Prentiss and I used to look for them in October, and especially in April, and some years we found a good many, while at others there appeared to be none at all. They seemed, on the whole, more frequent in spring than in the fall, and all those we secured were in breeding dress. They remained sometimes until the second week in May; frequented the same situations as the White-throats, often associating with them, and showing very similar traits.

I have not met with any authentic record of this bird breeding along the Atlantic, in the United States, not even in Northern New England, where some might be expected to pass the summer, and where, indeed, they may yet be found. Mr. Cooper gives a Quebec reference. In the West, however, the case is different. According to Mr. Trippe, they breed in Minnesota; and Mr. Allen gives the particularly interesting instance of occurrence high in the mountains of Colorado in July—a date that leaves no reasonable doubt of their breeding in that elevated locality. The parallelism between the present case and that of the Tit-lark, already mentioned, is here extended and perfected. Beyond this point the species is less easily traced, for it directly becomes mixed up with var. *intermedia*. Dr. Kennerly has, however, noted the occurrence of *leucophrys* in Western Arizona; while Prof. Baird records it from Cape St. Lucas. I am somewhat surprised not to find the species in Dall's List, and think it will yet be detected in Alaska.

The song of this species bears a close, general resemblance, to that of the White-throat, but is, nevertheless, instantly distinguishable. It is a less enterprising vocal effort, of only five or six syllables, like *pĕé, dĕé, dĕ dĕ dĕ*, the two first long drawn, rising, the rest hurried and lowering. Unlike the White-throat, this species has no evident sexual color-markings, the female sharing with the male the pure black and white of the crown; the young, however, have the black replaced by rich, warm brown.

A single specimen of this species was obtained at Leavenworth, Kansas, by Mr. Allen, who says that in the mountains of Colorado it was frequent in all favorable localities from about 8,000 feet up to above timber-line. "It was one of the most abundant birds met with along the northern and western borders of South Park, but was nowhere more numerous than at the upper verge of the timber on the Snowy Range. It is essentially a woodland species."

The following interesting notice is communicated by Mr. Trippe. "This Sparrow appears in the lower valleys of Clear Creek County, Colorado, in the first or second week of May, and soon becomes very abundant, frequenting the shrubby banks of the streams, and occasionally venturing some distance upon the hill-sides, but, as a rule, keeping close to the brooks and creeks. As the snow disappears it ascends higher and higher, reaching timber-line by the middle of June, and going up to the extreme limit of the willows and junipers, being nowhere more abundant than in those dense thickets that shut the upper edge of the timber. By far the greater number pass the breeding season there, but a few nest lower down, as far as 8,500 feet, below which it does not occur during summer. In habits, during the breeding season, it resembles the Song Sparrow, seeking its food in the grass and among the dry leaves in the thickets. It sings constantly during June and July, and occasionally in August, mounting to the top of some high bush, the dead limb of a pine, or any convenient perch well elevated above the surrounding shrubbery, and chanting its ditty at short intervals for half an hour or more at a time—a lively, agreeable song, fine and clear, and frequently heard from a score or more of birds at once, with a most pleasing effect. While his mate is setting, the male sings almost constantly throughout the day, and sometimes even late into the evening, long after dark—I have heard it at midnight, and even as late as one or two o'clock. It is very tame; a pair had their nest within a few feet of our camp at Chicago Lake, and all the bustle and noise did not drive the female from her nest, while her mate would pick up crumbs which we threw to him, almost at our feet. It commences building in July, and the young are hatched about the 20th ; the nest is placed on the ground in a clump of bushes, composed of coarse grass and weeds, and lined with fine grass. The eggs are usually four, of a pale bluish-green, very thickly speckled and dotted with reddish-brown, the latter color almost wholly obscuring the former at the larger end. In September it begins to descend; by October is abundant at Idaho, and by November has disappeared. It is by no means as numerous in the lower valleys during fall as in spring, passing through much more quickly, a peculiarity shared by many species whose migrations are similar, as *Myiodioctes pusillus*, *Dendrœca auduboni*, and others."

ZONOTRICHIA LEUCOPHRYS, var. INTERMEDIA, Ridgw.

Ridgway's Sparrow.

Zonotrichia gambeli, BD., B. N. A. 1858, 460 (in part. Includes the original *Fringilla gambeli* of NUTT., Man. i, 2d ed. 1840, 556 ; GAMB., Pr. Phila. Acad. 1843, 262, or *Zonotrichia gambeli*, GAMB., Journ. Phila. Acad. i, 1847, 50, which is the Pacific coast form, appreciably different).—HAYD., Rep. 1862, 166.—COUES, Pr: Phila. Acad. 1866, 84 (Arizona).—DALL & BANN., Tr. Chic. Acad. i, 1869, 284 (Alaska).—STEV., U. S. Geol. Surv: Ter. 1870, 464 (Wyoming).—MERR., *ibid*. 1872, 681.—HOLD., Pr. Bost. Soc. xv, 1872, 199 (Black Hills).—TRIPPE, *ibid*. 237 (Iowa).
Zonotrichia leucophrys var. *gambeli*, ALLEN, Bull. M. C. Z. iii, 1872, 157, 177.—COUES, Key, 1872, 145 (in part ; includes the true *gambeli*).
Zonotrichia leucophrys var. *intermedia*, RIDGW., Mss.—COUES, Check-list, App. No. —.

Hab.—Rocky Mountain region, Alaska to Mexico. Middle Dakota (*Coues*). Eastward, rarely, to Iowa (*Trippe*).
Lieutenant Warren's Expedition.—4793, Durion's Hill ; 4795, Vermilion River.
Later Expeditions.—60646-55, 60989-95, 60993, 61019, various Wyoming localities ; 62299, Idaho.

Mr. Ridgway has lately shown that the western style of *leucophrys*, so similar to the typical form as to be only distinguished by the different loral pattern, and which is usually called "*gambeli*," is not the *gambeli* of Nuttall. The latter is confined to the Pacific coast, and is a very curious form, having almost exactly the plumage and general appearance (excepting the head-markings) of *Z. coronata*. Examining these forms, we agree with him in making a varietal distinction. There is nothing in the Pacific coast race (true *gambeli*) of the peculiar purplish-ashy tinge of plumage that marks *leucophrys* and var. *intermedia*, and the bend of the wing is decidedly yellowish.

Among the numerous Warren examples of *leucophrys*, are two referable to var. *intermedia*, as are all of the large series taken by Stevenson and Merriam, as above quoted. They are found associated in many Rocky Mountain localities, and also further east, with true *leucophrys*. Mr. Allen only found *leucophrys* in Kansas and Colorado, meeting with var. "*gambeli*" (*intermedia*) in Utah. The latter I found abundant in Arizona, at various seasons, though most plentifully during the migrations ; and I believe it is resident in the Territory, the varied conditions of surface of which offer suitable retreats at the different seasons. In Dakota I encountered it in numbers as far east as 102° of longitude, during the fall migration ; no *leucophrys* proper was observed. Mr. Trippe has noted it from Iowa, the easternmost locality on record.

ZONOTRICHIA QUERULA, (Nutt.) Gamb.

Harris's Sparrow.

Fringilla querula, NUTT., Man. i, 2d ed., 1840, 555 (Westport, Mo.).
Zonotrichia querula, GAMB., Journ. Phila. Acad. i, 1847, 51.—BP., Consp. Av. i, 1850, 478.—
    BD., B. N. A. 1858, 462.—ALLEN, Bull. M. C. Z. iii, 1872, 127, 177.—COUES, Key,
    1872, 145.—TRIPPE, Pr. Bost. Soc. xv, 1872, 237 (Iowa).—SNOW, B. Kans. 1873,
    7.—B. B. & R., N. A. B. i, 1874, 577, pl. 26, fig. 4, 7.
Fringilla harrisii, AUD., B. Am. vii, 1843, 331, 484.
Fringilla comata, MAXIM., Reise Nord-Am. ii, 1841, — ; J. f. O. vi, 1858, 279.
Zonotrichia comata, BP., Consp. Av. i, 1850, 479.

Hab.—Region of the Missouri.   East to Eastern Iowa.
Lieutenant Warren's Expedition.—4797, Fort Leavenworth; 4798, Upper Missouri River;
4799, Bald Island ; 5400, Medicine Creek.
Not obtained by Captain Raynolds' Expedition.

Harris's Finch and Sprague's Lark may be regarded as the most characteristic birds of the Missouri region. The former has not yet been found away from the river at any distance. Nuttall's original is said to be from Westport, in the State of Missouri ; Audubon's came from the Black-Snake Hills, in the Kickapoo country, and Fort Croghan. Dr. Hayden took several at the various points above mentioned. Latterly Mr. Allen found the species "exceedingly abundant" at Fort Leavenworth, in May ; "it was found almost exclusively in the forests, and generally in company with *Z. albicollis*, which it resembles in habits, and somewhat in song." He informs me that he has specimens in the Museum of Comparative Zoology from various points in Iowa. Prof. Snow states that in Kansas the bird is often taken in winter, probably resident, and abundant in May along the Missouri. In Iowa, according to Mr. Trippe, it is abundant in spring and fall in Decatur County : "This beautiful Sparrow is one of the commonest of the *Fringillidœ* that pass through Decatur County in spring and fall, associating at such times with the other Sparrows and Finches, and frequenting similar haunts. Its notes in the fall are a simple, loud chirp, not distinguishable from that of the White-throated Sparrow, and, occasionally, a low, sweet warble ; in the spring it has a curious song, beginning very much like that of the latter bird, but ending in a few harsh, drawling notes, sounding like a faint mimicry of the scream of the Night-Hawk, and totally unlike the first part of the song."

In October of the past year I found Harris's Finches in numbers at Fort Randall. They were loitering in small troops in the undergrowth of the river-bottom, along with Towhee Buntings and hundreds of Tree Sparrows, all enjoying at their ease the genial sunshine of the lingering season. This was the first time I had ever seen the birds alive, and I was struck with their size and beauty—even among the bushes they looked noticeably larger than their eastern allies, reminding me rather of the *Z. coronata* I observed some years since on the coast of California. I saw none with black head—this part and the neck appearing at a distance grayish-brown, with irregular dark markings on the throat and breast. They uttered at intervals the usual sparrow-like chirp, but I heard no song. I was not collecting at the time, my outfit having been delayed *en route* in following me, but their image haunted me for several days, until, borrowing a gun, and securing some shot (big enough to kill ducks with, but the smallest I could get), I started after them again, expecting of course to find them, and gather a good suite illustrating the immature plumage. But I had missed my chance. I ransacked the same tract for hours without success, and at complete loss to account for their sudden disappearance, till I recollected we had just had a cold snap and a storm. No doubt this sent them trooping off; but however this may be, I am satisfied that not a single individual passed the winter in the vicinity.

The cold in winter becomes intense at Fort Randall, the thermometer sometimes marking thirty or forty degrees below zero. The surrounding country is "flat, windy, and comfortable," furnishing as bleak and dreary a prospect as can well be imagined. Even the shelter afforded by the thick undergrowth and low position of the river-bottom, defended as it is in a measure by bluffs and hills, is insufficient to allure any but a few of the hardiest birds to pass the inclement season. The river freezes solid, and the water-birds betake themselves elsewhere; some Hawks and Owls remain, indeed, but the other winter land-birds of the immediate vicinity, as far as I have made them out, may almost be counted on the fingers. There are Sharp-tailed Grouse in plenty, and Quails too, though these smaller birds sometimes freeze to death. There is a stray pinnated Grouse now and then. Sorry-looking Crows wing about and croak dismally, and gangs of Magpies screech noisily through the trees. Snow-birds fleck the open, with Shore-larks, during a part of the season, and probably Longspurs; troops of Tree Sparrows cower under the bushes. Cheery companies of Titmice stand the cold, and Hairy Woodpeckers hammer at the old cottonwoods as industriously as ever. A Shrike is seen now and then on his patient perch; but hereabout the short list ends.

The following spring, at the time I suppose the Finches came back to Fort Randall, I was too busy, writing portions of this work and attending to other matters incident to my transfer to a different field of operations, to look after them; and it was not until late in September of the same year that I found the birds again and secured my first specimens. This time I was encamped on the Mouse River, in Northern Dakota, and with the onset of the migration among the *Fringillidæ* came Harris's Finches in plenty. Where they came from I have no idea, further than that it was north of 49°; for, singular as it may appear, the breeding range of the species continues undiscovered, and nobody has yet seen the nest or eggs. I presume the bird has some special, restricted breeding localities, of which, in due time, we shall learn. The birds came from the north, just as the White-throat does, silently and unperceived; all at once the shrubbery along the river-bottom was thronged with them, as well as with Lincoln's and Ridgway's Finches. In their general appearance they recall Fox Sparrows, being so large and somewhat reddish-colored, with heavy dark markings underneath, when seen from a distance. They go in little troops, loitering in the patches of briers that lead out from the continuous undergrowth into the ravines making down to the streams; and their habit, when disturbed, of mounting the topmost twigs of the bushes to gain a better view, together with their size, renders them very conspicuous. They had no song at this season, nor indeed any note excepting a weak chirp. I saw none with completely black head and throat, as in spring, although at the same season a certain portion of the Ridgway Sparrows were in complete dress. The following description of the ordinary fall plumage is given, as no sufficient account of it has yet appeared:

Male.—Bill, light reddish-brown, paler at base below; feet, flesh-colored, obscured on the toes; eyes, brown. Crown, grayish-black, every feather with a distinct, narrow, pale gray edge all around, producing a peculiar effect; this area bounded with a light ochrey-brown superciliary and frontal line. Sides of head like the superciliary, but the auricular patch rather darker grayish-brown, and the loral region obscurely whitish. Chin, pure white, bounded on each side by a sharp maxillary line of blackish, with a rusty-red tinge. On the lower throat, a large, diffuse and partially discontinuous blotch of this same blackish-red, cutting off the white chin from the white of the rest of the under parts, connecting with the maxillary streaks, and stretching along the sides of the neck and breast in a series of rich dusky-chestnut streaks. On the middle of the breast the blotch generally runs out into the white in a sharp point, but its size and shape vary interminably. The markings here described are all included in the jet-black hood and breast-plate of the perfect spring dress; and between the two extremes every intermediate condition may be observed at various seasons. The rest of the plumage does not differ very materially from that of the adults. This is, excepting *Z. coronata*, the largest of our Sparrows. Length, 7.00 to nearly 8.00 inches; extent, 11.00 or more; wing, 3.50; tail, rather more; bill, along culmen, 0.45; tarsus, 1.00; middle toe and claw rather less. In the fall the sexes are not distinguishable by any outward mark.

NOTE.—The only remaining North American species of the genus is the following:

ZONOTRICHIA CORONATA, (*Pall.*) Bd.

Emberiza coronata, PALL., Zoog. R.-A. ii, 1811, pl. —.
Zonotrichia coronata, BD., B. N. A. 1858, 461.—COOP. & SUCK., N. H. Wash. Ter. 1860, 201.—HEERM., P. R. R. Rep. x, 1859, pt. vi, 48 (breeding).—DALL & BANN., Tr. Chic. Acad. i, 1869, 284 (Alaska).—COOP., B. Cal. i, 1870, 197.—COUES, Key, 1872, 145.—B. B. & R., N. A. B. i, 1874, 573, pl. 26, f. 1.
Emberiza atricapilla, AUD., Orn. Biog. v, 1839, 47, pl. 394.
Fringilla atricapilla, AUD., Syn. 1839, 122; B. Am. iii, 1841, 162, pl. 193.
Fringilla aurocapilla, NUTT., Man. i, 2d ed. 1840, 555.
Zonotrichia aurocapilla, BP., Consp. i, 1850, 478.—NEWB., P. R. R. Rep. vi, 1857, 88.

Hab.—Pacific coast, from Alaska to Southern California, and probably eastward to the Rocky Mountains.

CHONDESTES GRAMMACA, (Say) Bp.

Lark Finch.

Fringilla grammaca, SAY, Long's Exp. i, 1823, 139.—BP., Am. Orn. i, 1825, 47, pl. 5, f. 3.— BP., Syn. 1828.—NUTT., Man. i, 1832, 480.—AUD., Orn. Biog. v, 1839, 17, pl. 390.
Chondestes grammaca, BP., List, 1838, 32; Consp. Av. i, 1850, 479.—WOODH., Sitg. Rep. 1853, 86.—BD., B. N. A. 1858, 456.—BD., Pr. Phila. Acad. Nov. 1859 (Cape St. Lucas).—HEERM., P. R. R. Rep. x, 1859, part vi, 48.—COOP. & SUCK., N. H. Wash. Ter. 1860, 200.—WHEAT., Ohio Agric. Rep. 1860 (Ohio, three specimens).— HAYD., Rep. 1862, 166.—SCL., P. Z. S. 1859, 379 (Oaxaca).—DRESS., Ibis, 1865, 488 (Texas).—ALLEN, Pr. Ess. Inst. iv, 1864, 84 (Massachusetts).—MAYN., Guide, 1870, 142 (Massachusetts).—COUES, Pr. Phil. Acad. 1866, 84 (Arizona).—ALLEN, Mem. Bost. Soc. i, 1868, 495, 517 (Iowa and Illinois).—SUMICH., *ibid.* 1869, 552 (Vera Cruz, in winter).—COUES, Pr. Ess. Inst. v, 1868, 281 (Massachusetts).— STEV., U. S. Geol. Surv. Ter. 1870, 464.—MERR., *ibid.* 1872, 680.—COOP., B. Cal. i, 1870, 103.—ALLEN, Bull. M. C. Z. iii, 1872, 177.—HOLD., Pr. Bost. Soc. 1872, 201 (Wyoming).—TRIPPE, *ibid.* 237 (Iowa, breeding).—SNOW, B. Kans. 1873, 7.—COUES, Key, 1872, 146, fig. 90.—B. B. & R., N. A. B. i, 1874, 562, pl. 31, f. 1· *Emberiza grammaca*, AUD., Syn. 1839, 101.—AUD., B. Am. iii, 1841, 63, pl. 158.—" BP., Am. Orn. 8ᵛᵒ ed. iii, 65, pl. 158."—PUTN., Pr. Ess. Inst. i, 1856, 244 (Gloucester, Mass., one specimen, in 1845, *S. Jillson*).—MAXIM., J. f. O. vi, 1858, 343.
Chondestes strigatus, SW., Phil. Mag. i, 1827, 435 (Mexico).

Hab.—Prairies and plains of the West, from Illinois and Iowa, &c., to the Pacific; occasional in Ohio; accidental in Massachusetts. Cape St. Lucas. South into Mexico.

List of specimens.

| 19348 | .... | Yellowstone R.. | ♂ | July 12, 1870 | G. H. Trook.. | 6.75 | 11.00 | 3.75 |
| 19349 | .... | ....do...... | .... | ....do...... | ....do...... | 6.50 | 11.00 | 3.50 |

Lieutenant Warren's Expedition.—4820–21, Upper Missouri River; 4822–23, Big Sioux River; 5382–83, Powder River; 5384–85, Fort Lookout; 9228–31, 9233–36, 1938, Loup Fork of Platte River; 9232, Frémont, on Platte River; 9237, Sand Hills.
Later Expeditions.—60397, Bitter Cottonwood Creek; 61668–71, 61776, Utah; 62307, Wyoming.

This is one of the most abundant and characteristic birds of the prairie regions of the West. In the spring of 1864, in company with my respected friend, Dr. George Engelmann, the eminent botanist, I observed it in great numbers in the suburbs of Saint Louis, and various accounts exhibit its occurrence in the flat, open country of several States still further eastward. A solitary instance of its occurrence, entirely accidental, in Massachusetts, is recorded. In the West it appears universally dispersed, and it is conspicuous, among its congeners, by its striking colors, agreeable song, and pleasing manners, as well as by its abundance in all suitable localities. Although essentially a prairie bird, it is not confined to the plains, nor is it exclusively terrestrial; it is observed also in wooded, broken, even mountainous regions, alighting on trees and bushes as often as its allies, the birds of the genera *Zonotrichia, Pooecetes*, &c. I found it frequently in the openings about pine-woods, in the higher portions of Arizona, where it is very numerous in spring and fall during the migrations, though less so at other seasons. Although I did not find its nest, I am convinced it breeds there, having taken very young birds late in the summer. (It breeds in Colorado, according to Mr. Trippe.) In the fall it collects in small troops, rambling in the grass near bushes or small trees, to which it betakes itself on alarm, like the Fox Sparrow and other species.

In the spring of 1873 I observed its arrival at Fort Randall in large numbers, late in April, along with *Spizella pallida*. It appeared in straggling troops about the fort, entering the parade-ground, where, perching upon the young and struggling shade-trees of that very unconfined establishment, it would make its first essays in the way of nuptial song—music that, later in the season, becomes stronger, more attractive, and almost incessant. Further north than this, along the forty-ninth parallel, I never observed the bird.

The Lark Finch nests on the ground, like the other prairie *Fringillidæ*, building a rather rude structure of grasses and weeds, lined with very fine tortuous rootlets. It is constructed about the first of June. The eggs are laid during the same month. A nest before me, taken by Mr. Allen on the Big Muddy, contains seven eggs. The eggs of this species are very peculiar in coloration, being white, curiously streaked in zigzag, much like the Blackbird's (*Agelæus*). The markings are sharp and distinct, and heavy in color—a rich, dark reddish-brown or chocolate; sometimes, where the pigment is thickest, being almost blackish. The markings straggle all over the surface, and are usually accompanied with a few spots of the same color. The egg is noticeably globose, very much rounded at the smaller end, measuring about 0.75 by 0.65. Other specimens, however, are more elongate, measuring as much as 0.85. According to Mr. Ridgway, the nest is sometimes placed on bushes or trees.

PASSERELLA ILIACA, (Merr.) Sw.

Fox Sparrow.

Fringilla iliaca, MERR., Beit. Gesch. Vög. ii, 1786–7, 49, pl. 10.—GM., Syst. Nat. i, 1788, 923.—BP., Syn. 1828, 112.—NUTT., Man. i, 1832, 514.—AUD., Orn. Biog. ii, 1834, 58; v, 1839, 512; pl. 108.—AUD., Syn. 1839, 119.—AUD., B. Am. iii, 1841, 139, pl. 185.—PUTN., Pr. Ess. Inst. i, 1856, 211.—TRIPPE, Pr. Ess. Inst. vi, 1871, 116 (Minnesota, migratory, uncommon).
Fringilla (Zonotrichia) iliaca, SW. & RICH., F. B. A. ii, 1831, 257.
Passerella iliaca, SW., Class. B. ii, 1837, 228.—BP., List, 1838, 31; Consp. Av. i, 1850, 477.—WOODH., Sitgr. Rep. 1853, 82 (Indian Territory, abundant, migratory).—BD., B. N. A. 1858, 488.—WHEAT., Ohio Agric. Rep. 1860.—COUES & PRENT., Smiths. Rep. for 1861 (1862), 413 (Washington, D. C., October to April, but chiefly

November and March).—BOARDM., Pr. Bost. Soc. ix, 1862, 127 (Calais, Me., migratory, common).—VERR., *ibid.* 138 (Anticosti, common, breeds).—VERR., Pr. Ess. Inst., iv, 1864, 73 (Springfield, Mass., October, November, March, April, sometimes February).—COUES, Pr. Ess. Inst. v, 1868, 283 (New England, migratory).—COUES, Pr. Bost. Soc. xii, 1868, 116 (South Carolina, November to April).—LAWR., Ann. Lyc. N. Y. viii, 1868, 287.—TURNB., B. E. Pa. 1869, 13 (October to March).—DALL & BANN., Tr. Chic. Acad. i, 1868, 285 (Alaska, summer, breeding abundantly).—MAYN., Guide, 1870, 120 (Massachusetts, migratory); and Pr. Bost. Soc. 1871 (Quebec, breeding).—ALLEN, Bull. M. C. Z. ii, 1871, 279 (Florida, rare).—TRIPPE, Pr. Bost. Soc. 1872, 238 (Iowa).—COUES, Key, 1872, 147, fig. 91.—SNOW, B. Kans. 1873, 7.—B. B. & R., N. A. B. ii, 1874, 50, pl. 78, f. 2.

Fringilla rufa, WILS., Am. Orn. ii, 1811, 53, pl. 22, f. 4.—LICHT., Vᴏᴢ. 1823, No. 428.
Fringilla ferruginea, WILS., Cat. vi, 1812.
" *Emberiza pratensis*, VIEILL."
Passerella obscura, VERR., Pr. Bost. Soc. ix, 1862, 153 (Anticosti).

Hab.—Eastern Province of North America. North to 68°, and to the Yukon. Breeds from the British Provinces northward. Not observed to nest anywhere in the United States. Winters in the Middle States sparingly, in the Southern States very abundantly. West in the United States only to the edge of the Central Plains. Accidental in California (spec. in Mus. S. I.).
Not obtained by any of the Expeditions.

The Fox Sparrow enters the Middle States from the North in October, and by the first of the following month has become abundant. Some linger here through the winter in sheltered situations, but the greater number repair further south early in December, to reappear the latter part of February, thus escaping the coldest weather. During the winter they are dispersed over the Southern States, beyond which, however, they do not appear to pass, as I have found no record. In March they again become plentiful in the Middle States; and, having already taken up their line of migration toward their homes in the North, their coming is with song of gladness and all the busy stir of the opening season. They are not all off until April, and during the sunny days that precede their departure, the males are fond of mounting the little bushes, or even the trees, to warble a few exquisitely sweet notes, the overture of the joyous music which, later in the year, enlivens the northern solitudes, whither the birds resort to nest. So musical is the Fox Sparrow, indeed, that even in autumn, when the transient glow and fervor of the nuptial period has subsided and commonplace occupations alone engage him, he forgets the dull season at times, and lisps fugitive strains of sweet memories awakened by the warmth and glamour of the Indian summer. But this is a mere fragment—the shadow of a song stealing across the mind, not the song itself, which we only hear in perfection when the bird's life is quickened in the sunny, showery April, and he leaves us with cheery "good-bye," promising to come again. What one of our fringilline birds is so entirely pleasing as this, my favorite? Strong, shapely, vivacious, yet gentle, silver-tongued; clad most tastefully in the richest of warm browns; and, that nothing may be wanting to single him out from among his humbler relatives, a high-bred bird, exclusive, retiring. We do not find him mixing indiscriminately with the throng of Sparrows that accompany him in his journeyings and spend the winter with him. With a few select associates of his own kind, perhaps only two or three families that were reared together, he chooses his own retreat, and holds it against intrusion. In some little glade, hedged about with almost impenetrable briers, you will come upon him and his friends, nestling among the withered leaves on the ground, gently calling to each other in the assurance of safety. On your unwelcome appearance, they will hurriedly take flight together, throwing themselves into the thickest shrubbery. You will find such company, again, in the ravines over-grown with *smilax* and brambles that lead down to the brook; and as you pass along neglected fences, fringed with tall, rank weeds, you may surprise the birds out for a morning's ramble, and make them hurry back in alarm to the shelter of heavier undergrowth.

I have never known a single Fox Sparrow to nest in the United States, nor even loiter within our limits through the summer; though Audubon states, upon perhaps insufficient grounds, that it remains in abundance during the season around Boston. Nor did I find a nest in Labrador, where it is said to breed, as well as in various British provinces north of us. "The nest," says Audubon, "which is large for the size of the bird, is usually placed on the ground, among moss or tall grass, near the stem of a creeping fir, the branches of which completely conceal it from view. Its exterior is loosely formed of dry grass and moss, with a care-fully-disposed under-layer of finer grasses, circularly arranged; and the lining consists of very delicate fibrous roots, together with some feathers from different species of water-fowl." The eggs, he adds, are laid from the middle of June to the 5th of July. The nest is not always, how-ever, placed on the ground, but sometimes in a bush or low tree, eight or ten feet high.

The eggs show the same style as those of *Zonotrichia* and *Melospiza* in heavy coloring, wholly indeterminate in size and shape of the mark-ings, upon a pale greenish-gray ground; and in some instances the whole egg assumes a nearly uniform dark chocolate hue, much like that of *Plectrophanes lapponicus*. The reddish-brown blotching is usually, however, much as in a Song Sparrow's or White-throated Sparrow's. The size of the egg is about 0.95 by 0.68.

PASSERELLA TOWNSENDII var. SCHISTACEA, (Bd.) Coues.

Slate-colored Sparrow.

a. *townsendii.*

(?) *Fringilla unalaskensis*, GM., Syst. Nat. i, 1788, 875 (*Oonalashka Bunting*, LATH., Syn. ii, 202; PENN., 52).
Passerella unalaskensis, FINSCH., Abh. Nat. iii, 1872, 53 (Alaska).
Fringilla townsendii, AUD., Orn. Biog. v, 1839, 236, pl. 424, f. 7; Syn. 1839, 119; B. Am. iii, 1841, 43, pl. 187.
Fringilla (Passerella) townsendii, NUTT., Man. i, 1840, 533.
Passerella townsendii, BP., Consp. i, 1850, 477.—BD., B. N. A. 1858, 489.—COOP. & SUCK., N. H. Wash. Ter. 1860, 204.—DALL & BANN., Tr. Chic. Acad. i, 1869, 285.— COUES, Key, 1872, 352.—B. B. & R., N. A. B. ii, 1874, 53, pl. 28, f. 8.
Passerella iliaca var. *townsendii*, COUES, Key, 1872, 147.
Fringilla meruloides, VIG., Zool. Beech. Voy. 1839, 19 (Monterey).
(?) *Emberiza (Zonotrichia) rufina*, KITTL., Denk. 1858, 200 (Sitka).

Hab.—Pacific Coast, North America. Alaska to Southern California.

b. *schistacea.*

Passerella schistacea, BD., B. N. A. 1858, 490, pl. 69, fig. 3 (Platte River and Fort Tejon).— SNOW, B. Kans. 1873, 7.
Passerella iliaca var. *schistacea*, ALLEN, Bull. M. C. Z. iii, 1872, 168 (Ogden, Utah).— COUES, Key, 1872, 147.
Passerella townsendii var. *schistacea*, COUES, Key, 1872, 352.—B. B. & R., N. A. B. ii, 1874, 56, pl. 28, f. 9.
Passerella megarhyncha, BD., B. N. A. 1858, 925, pl. 69, fig. 4 (larger billed form from California).—COOP., B. Cal. i, 1870, 222.
Passerella townsendii var. *megarhyncha*, B. B. & R., N. A. B. ii, 1874, 57, pl. 28, f. 10.
Passerella schistacea var. *megarhyncha*, RIDGW., "Rep. Geol. Exp. 40th parallel" (in press).

Hab.—Central region, Kansas to California.

No example of a *Passerelline* form was taken by either expedition ; but the *P.* " *schistacea* " was originally based upon a specimen from the Platte, within the region embraced in the present report.

I am much inclined to doubt the distinctness of any of the currently reputed species of *Passerella*, but, as I observed in the Key, it may be as well to allow *P. townsendii* to rest upon its characters until its intergradation with *iliaca* is proven. In any event, *P* "*schistacea*" goes with *townsendii*, as a paler variety.

CALAMOSPIZA BICOLOR, (Towns.) Bp.

Lark Bunting.

Fringilla bicolor, TOWNS., Journ. Phila. Acad. vii, 1837, 189 ; Narr. 1839, 346.—AUD., Orn. Biog. v, 1839, 19, pl. 390.
Calamospiza bicolor, BP., List, 1838, 30 ; Consp. Av. i, 1850, 475.—BD.,B. N. A. 1858, 492.—
BD., Pr. Phila. Acad. Nov. 1859 (Cape St. Lucas).—HEERM., P. R. R. Rep. x, 1859, Route 32d par., Birds, 13 (Texas, New Mexico, Arizona).—HAYD., Rep. 1862, 166.—DRESS., Ibis, 1865, 490 (Texas) —COUES, Pr. Phila. Acad. 1866, 86 (Arizona).—STEV., U. S. Geol. Surv. Ter. 1870, 465 (Wyoming).—COOP., B. Cal. i, 1870, 225.—ALLEN, Bull. M. C. Z. iii, 1872, 137, 177.—HOLD., Pr. Bost. Soc. 1872, 201 (Wyoming).—COUES, Key, 1872, 147.·—SNOW, B. Kans. 1873, 7.—B. B. & R., N. A. B. ii, 1874, 61, pl. 29, f. 2, 3.
Corydalina bicolor, AUD., Syn. 1839, 130.—AUD., B. Am. iii, 1841, 195, pl. 202.—MAXIM., J. f. O. vi, 1858, 347.
Dolichonyx bicolor, NUTT., Man. i, 2d ed. 1840, 203.

Hab.—United States, Plains to the Rocky Mountains. Southward to Mexico, and across to Lower California.

List of Specimens.

19276	34	Fort Benton...	♂	July 6, 1860	F. V. Hayden.	6.12	11.25	3.60
19352	....	Bighorn Mts...	♂	May 30, 1860,	G. H. Trook..	7.00	11.25	3.25
19353	....	...... do	♂	..... do	...... do	7.00	11.25	3.25

Lieutenant Warren's Expedition.—5375, seventy miles above Yellowstone ; 5076, Medicine Butte ; 8928-29-31, Loup Fork of Platte.

Later Expeditions.—60392-5, Camp Curling and Bitter Cottonwood ; 60760, North Butte.

The Lark Bunting is one of the most singularly specialized of all our fringilline forms. As implied in its name, it has somewhat the habits of a Lark, and shares the long inner secondary quills. An eminently terrestrial bird, yet the hind claw is neither lengthened nor straightened as is usual with passerine birds frequenting the ground almost exclusively. The bill is that of a Grosbeak, being shaped almost exactly like that of *Goniaphea cœrulea* for instance, and the sexual differences in plumage are as great as in that bird. But a more remarkable circumstance still is the seasonal change of plumage, which is exactly correspondent with that of the Bobolink, to which the species bears a general similarity in coloration. This fact was first noticed, I believe, by Mr. Allen, in the paper above quoted : "After the moulting season, the males assume the plumage of the female, the change in color being similar to that of the males of *Dolichonyx oryzivora*." There is still another curious analogy, that the same writer has brought out : " It has habits that strongly recall the Yellow-breasted Chat, singing generally on the wing, hovering in the same manner as that bird, while its notes are so similar to those of the Chat, as to be scarcely distinguishable from them."

This author remarks that he found the bird very wary and difficult to shoot—a fact at variance with my own experience. I found it common from the plains in Kansas to the Raton Mountains, westward of which I never saw it. In some places it was extremely abundant, and fairly to be considered the characteristic species. This was in June when the birds were breeding, apparently in straggling groups, keeping up somewhat of association, but by no means intimate companionship, still less flocking; each pair finding its own business sufficiently interesting and absorbing. As I was traveling by coach at the time, I had no opportunity of looking for the nests. Judging from the fact that I saw scarcely any females, the birds were then either incubating or brooding over their young. The more conspicuous and voluble males were almost constantly in view, fluttering over the grass, every now and then starting up on tremulous wing, almost perpendicularly in the air, hovering and singing the while, till they dropped as if exhausted. Sometimes several were in view at once, and I used to watch their vocal rivalry with unflagging interest, as each strove, it seemed, to rise the higher, and carol the louder its joyous song.

The *Calamospiza* nests on the ground in open prairie, building, as usual in such cases, a rather rude structure of grasses and slender weed-stalks, with merely a little finer material of the same sort for lining. The nest is sunk flush with the surface of the ground. The eggs are commonly five in number, sometimes only four. They are of a clear pale bluish-green, and look almost exactly like those of a Bluebird, in fact, could not be distinguished with certainty, though rather larger and thicker. Rarely a set of eggs is found very sparsely dotted, as frequently happens with these pale greenish eggs; but I have never seen a white one, like the curious white eggs Bluebirds sometimes lay. The egg varies in size and shape from 0.80 to 0.95 in length, by about 0.65 in breadth. Cow-birds' eggs are frequently found in the nest.

The following was prepared by Mr. Allen for this work: "The Lark Bunting, though of rather local distribution and limited range, must be regarded as one of the most characteristic and interesting birds of the plains. Generally in the breeding season a number of pairs are found in the same vicinity, while again not an individual may be met with for many miles. At other seasons it is eminently gregarious, roving about in considerable flocks. In its song and the manner of its delivery it much resembles the Yellow-breasted Chat (*Icteria virens*), like that bird rising to a considerable distance in the air, and poising itself by a peculiar flapping of the wings during its utterances, then abruptly descending to the ground to soon repeat the manoeuvre. It is a very strong flier, and seems to delight in the strongest gales, singing more at such times than in comparatively quiet weather. I met with several colonies not far from Fort Hays in June and July, and later at Cheyenne, Laramie, and in South Park, and in the elevated open table-lands, between South Park and Colorado City. They were also frequent along the route from Colorado City to Denver, sometimes considerable flocks being met with. They were then moulting, and the parti-colored flocks of young and old were quite unsuspicious and easily approached. During the breeding season we found them exceedingly shy and difficult to procure, and were unsuccessful in our efforts to discover their nests."

EUSPIZA AMERICANA, (Gm.) Bp.

Black-throated Bunting.

Emberiza americana, Gm., Syst. Nat. i, 1788, 872.—Wils., Am. Orn. i, 1808, 411; iii, 1811, 86; pl. 3, f. 2.—Nutt., Man. i, 1832, 461.—Aud., iv, 1838, 579, pl. 384; Syn. 1839, 101; B. Am. iii, 1841, 58, pl. 156.—Emm., Cat. B. Mass. 1835, 4.—Peab., Rep. B. Mass. 1839, 319.—Gir., B. L. I. 1844, 100.—Putn., Pr. Ess. Inst. i, 1856, 227.— Maxim., J. f. O. vi, 1858, 341.
Fringilla (Spiza) americana, Bp., Obs. Wils. 1825, No. 85.

Fringilla americana, BP., Syn. 1828, 107.
Cœlebs americana, LESS., Tr. Orn. 1831, 440.
Euspiza americana, BP., List, 1838, 32: Cousp. i, 1850, 469.—WOODH.. Sitgr. Rep. 1853,
    87 (Indian Territory, Texas, New Mexico).—BD., B. N. A. 1858, 494.—WHEAT.,
    Ohio Agric. Rep. 1860 (plentiful).—LAWR., Ann. Lyc. vii, 1861, 298 (New
    Granada).—COUES & PRENT., Smiths. Rep. 1861, (1862) 413 (Washington,
    D. C., May to Sept., abundant).—HAYD., Rep. 1862, 168.—ALLEN, Pr. Ess.
    Inst. iv, 1864, 84 (Massachusetts, rare, or occasional).—COUES, Pr. Ess. Inst.
    v, 1868, 284 (northeast to Massachusetts).—LAWR., Ann. Lyc. vii, 1861, 298
    (Panama); 1865, 181 (Nicaragua); viii, 1868, 286 (New York); ix, 1868, 103
    (Costa Rica).—COUES, Pr. Bost. Soc. xii, 1868 (South Carolina in summer, *fide
    Gibbes*).—ALLEN, Mem. Bost. Soc. i, 1868, 505 (Western Iowa, very abundant,
    breeding), and 517 (Northern Illinois, common).—TURNB., B. E. Pa. 1869, 24
    (May to Sept., plentiful.)—DRESS., Ibis, 1865, 490 (Texas).—SALV., P. Z. S.
    1867, 142 (Veragua).—CASS., Pr. Phila. Acad. 1860, 140 (Turbo).—SUMICH.,
    Mem. Bost. Soc. i, 1869, 552 (Vera Cruz, wintering).—SCL. & SALV., Ibis, i,
    1859, 18 (Gautemala).—MAYN., Guide, 1870, 120 (Massachusetts, three instan-
    ces noted).—ALIEN, Bull. M. C. Z. iii, 1872, 177 (Kansas and Colorado).—
    TRIPPE, Pr. Bost. Soc. 1872, 238 (Iowa, breeding).—COUES, Key, 1872, 148.—
    SNOW, B. Kans. 1873, 7.—B. B. & R., N. A. B. ii, 1874, 65, pl. 28, f. 11, 12.
Euspina americana, CAB., Mus. Hein. i, 1851, 133.
Fringilla flavicollis, GM., Syst. Nat. i, 1788, 926.
Fringilla mexicana, MÜLLER, Syst. Nat. Suppl. 165.
Emberiza mexicana, GM., S. Nat. i, 1788, 873.—LATH., Ind. Orn. i, 1790, 412. (P. E. 386, 1.)
Passerina nigricollis, VIEILL., Enc. Meth. 931.

Hab.—United States, west to Kansas and Nebraska, and even Colorado. North to
Connecticut regularly (LINSL., Am. Journ. Sci. 1843, 261), to Massachusetts occasionally ;
no record beyond. No record of wintering in the United States. Winters in Mexico
and Central America, and New Granada (numerous quotations).
    Lieutenant Warren's Expedition.—5381, 9286, Fort Lookout ; 9261. 9265, 9258, 9263,
9260, 9254, 9248, 9270, 9269, Loup Fork of the Platte ; 9256, 9262, 9264, 9249, Elkhorn
River ; 9257, Frémont, on Platte.
    Not obtained by Captain Raynolds' Expedition, or by the later ones.

From its winter abode in tropical America, the Black-throated Bunting enters the United States in April, in small troops. Vast numbers
pass up the Mississippi Valley, some finding their final resting place in
Iowa, but others lingering to breed all along the route. Many spread
westward over the prairies of Kansas and Nebraska, and a part of the
host reaches the Middle Atlantic States by the latter part of the month,
some even penetrating eastward to Southern New England, which
forms their terminus. Rearing their young in nearly all parts of this
great extent of land, from Texas to Nebraska, and New England, they
depart before the approach of cold weather to their homes far south.
    Making no claim to the brilliancy of coloration that many of its
spizine allies possess, this Bunting is nevertheless a handsome bird,
with tasteful color contrasts, a trim form, and a peculiarly smooth, neat
plumage. As a vocalist, however, we must rate it a very humble performer ; its song is short and simple, even weak, and grows monotonous
with repetition through the season of incubation, when the male, from
the highest perch he can find near his nest, cheers his faithful mate
with the assurance of his presence and protection. He seems to say,
" Look! look! see me here! see!" And if we do not like his performance, we may remember we are not asked to listen.
    The nest of this species is almost invariably placed on the ground,
but occasionally in a thick grass-clump, over a foot high. The eggs are
four or five in number, of precisely the same pale blue shade as in the
last species, being thus exactly like Bluebird eggs. They are said to
be sometimes dotted, and I have no doubt such is the case, though I
have seen none not perfectly plain. The size is 0.80 by 0.65.
    As was remarked by Audubon, the Black-throated Bunting appears
to avoid certain districts, both in its migrations and for breeding, giving preference to fertile portions of the country, and in settling down to

breed will make capricious choice of particular spots and confine itself to them. . About Washington, it was most plentiful in the skirts of the city itself, in gardens and orchards, and in fields about the edges of woods. It abounds on the western prairies, to the edge of the sterile plains. The fact of its becoming abundant in regions where it was scarce before, is also attested, but remains unexplained. Thus, according to Audubon, it was rare in Ohio, and Dr. Kirtland, writing in 1838, admits the insufficiency of his authority, but believes it " to be an occasional visitor ; " whereas Mr. J. M. Wheaton, commenting upon this circumstance, in 1860, gives it as one of the most numerous birds of that State. It is there known as the " Little Field Lark ; " while in Illinois, Mr. Ridgway tells me, it is called " Judas-bird " and " Dick-sissel," both names being in allusion to its song.

GONIAPHEA LUDOVICIANA, (Linn.) Bowd.

Rose-breasted Grosbeak.

Loxia ludoviciana, LINN., Syst. Nat. i, 1766, 306.—WILS., Am. Orn. ii, 1810, 135, pl. 17, f. 2.
Fringilla ludoviciana, BP., Am. Orn. ii, 79, pl. 15, f. 2.—BP., Syn. 1828, 113.—NUTT., Man. i, 1832, 527.—AUD., Orn. Biog. ii, 1834, 166 ; v, 1839, 513 ; pl. 127.
Pyrrhula ludoviciana, SABINE, Franklin's Journ. Zool. App. 675.
Guiraca ludoviciana, SW., Phil. Mag. i, 1827, 438.—BP., List, 1838, 30 ; Consp. Av. i, 1850, 501.—BD., B. N. A. 1858, 497.—WHEAT., Ohio Agric. Rep. 1860.—COUES & PRENT., Smiths. Rep. 1861 (1862), 413 (Washington, D. C., summer, rare).—HAYD., Rep. 1862, 168 (abundant along Missouri).—ALLEN, Pr. Ess. Inst. iv, 1864 (Springfield, Mass., summer, not abundant).—BOARDM., Pr. Bost. Soc. ix, 1862, 127 (Calais, Me., summer, rare).—VERR., Pr. Ess. Inst. iii, 151 (Norway, Me., not common).—MCILWR., Pr. Ess. Inst. v, 1866, 90 (Hamilton, C. W., summer).—COUES, Pr. Ess. Inst. v, 1868, 284 (throughout New England).—COUES, Pr. Bost. Soc. xii, 1868, 116 (South Carolina, rare, migratory).—TURNB., B. E. Pa. 1869, 24 (May to Sept., rather rare).—SUMICH., Mem. Bost. Soc. i, 1869, 552 (Vera Cruz, winter).—MAYN., Guide, 1870, 120 (Massachusetts, May to Sept., common, breeds).—MAYN., Pr. Bost. Soc. xiv, 1871, — (north to Quebec, *Couper*).—TRIPPE, *ibid.* xv, 1872, 238 (Iowa, breeds).—SNOW, B. Kans. 1873, 8.
Coccothraustes (Guiraca) ludoviciana, SW. & RICH., F. B. A. ii, 1831, 271.
Goniaphea ludoviciana, "BOWDITCH."—ALLEN, Bull. M. C. Z. iii, 1872, 177 (Eastern Kansas).—COUES, Key, 1872, 148, fig. 92.
Coccoborus ludovicianus, AUD., Syn. 1839, 133.—AUD., B. Am. iii, 1841, 209, pl. 205.—PUTN., Pr. Ess. Inst. i, 1856, 212 (Massachusetts).—GIR., B. L. I. 1844, 133.—MAXIM., J. f. O. vi, 1858, 267.—TRIPPE, Pr. Ess. Inst. vi, 1871, 117 (Minnesota).
Hedymeles ludovicianus, CAB., Mus. Hein. i, 1851, 1853 ; J. f. O. iv, 1856, 9 (Cuba) ; 1861, 7 (Costa Rica).—SCL., P. Z. S. 1855, 133, 154 (Bogota) ; 1856, 301 (Cordova) ; 1859, 365 (Xalapa) ; 1860, 293 (Ecuador).—SCL. & SALV., Ibis, i, 1859, 17 (Guatemala).—SCL., Cat. 1862, 100 (Guatemala and Bogota).—LAWR., Ann. Lyc. N. Y. vii, 1861, 297 (Panama) ; viii, 1868, 287 (New York) ; ix, 1868, 102 (Costa Rica) ; 1869, 200 (Yucatan).—ALLEN, Mem. Bost. Soc. 1868, 496, 505, 517 (Iowa and Illinois).—B. B. & R., N. A. B. ii, 1874, 70, pl. 30, f. 4, 5.
Coccothraustes rubricollis, VIEILL., Gal. Ois. i, 1824, 67, pl. 58.
Loxia rosea, WILS., *loc. cit.*
Loxia obscura, GM., Syst. Nat. i, 1788, 862.—LATH., Ind. Orn. i, 179, 379.
Fringilla punicea, GM., Syst. Nat. i, 1788, 921.—LATH., Ind. Orn. i, 1790, 444.

Hab.—Eastern Province of North America, north to Labrador and the Saskatchewan. Breeds from the Middle States northward. Winters in Mexico and Central America. South to Ecuador. Cuba.
Lieutenant Warren's Expedition.—4848, Ponca Island ; 4849, Vermilion River ; 4850, Running Water ; 4852, Bijoux Hills.
Not obtained by Captain Raynolds' Expedition.

I have nowhere found this beautiful bird more abundant than along the Red River of the North, and there may be no locality where its nidification and breeding habits can be studied to greater advantage. On entering the belt of noble timber that borders the River, in June, we are almost sure to be saluted with the rich, rolling song of the rose-

breasted male, and as we penetrate into the deeper recesses, pressing
through the stubborn luxuriance of vegetation into the little shady
glades that the bird loves so well, we may catch a glimpse of the shy
and retiring female, darting into concealment, disturbed by our approach. She is almost sure to be followed the next moment by her
ardent spouse, solicitous for her safety, bent on reassuring her by his
presence and caresses. Sometime during this month, as we enter a
grove of saplings, and glance carefully overhead, we may see the nest,
placed but a few feet from the ground, in the fork of a limb. The
female, alarmed, will flutter away stealthily, and we may not catch
another glimpse of her, nor of her mate even, though we hear them
both anxiously consulting together at a little distance. The nest is not
such an elegant affair as might be desired; it is, in fact, bulky and rude,
if not actually slovenly. It is formed entirely of the long, slender,
tortuous stems of woody climbers, and similar stout rootlets; the base
and outer walls being very loosely interlaced, the inner more compactly
woven, with a tolerably firm brim of circularly-disposed fibres. Sometimes there is a little horse-hair lining, oftener not. A very complete
nest before me is difficult to measure from its loose outward construction, but may be called six inches across outside, by four deep; the
cavity three inches wide, by one and a half deep. The nest contained
three eggs, which I think is the usual number in this latitude; four I
have only found once. The eggs are usually rather elongate, but obtuse
at the smaller end. Different specimens measure, 1.00 by 0.75, 1.08 by
0.70, 1.03 by 0.75, 1.02 by 0.72, 0.96 by 0.76; by which dimensions the
variation in shape is denoted. The average is about that of the first
measurement given. They are of a light and rather pale green color,
profusely speckled with dull reddish-brown, usually in small and also
rather diffuse pattern, but sometimes quite sharply marked; the sharper
markings are usually the smallest. There is sometimes much confluence,
or at least aggregation, about the greater end, but the whole surface is
always marked. Most of these eggs were taken in the latter part of
June, some by the end of the month; in all, incubation was in progress.

GONIAPHEA MELANOCEPHALA, (Sw.) Gray.

Black-headed Grosbeak.

Guiraca melanocephala, Sw., Philos. Mag. i, 1827, 438.—Bp., List, 1838.—Bp., Consp. Av. i,
1850, 502.—Bd., B. N. A. 1858, 498.—Coop. & Suck., N. H. Wash. Ter. 1860, 206.—
Hayd., Rep. 1862, 168.—Coues, Pr. Phila. Acad. 1866, 88 (Arizona, May to
October).—Sumich., Mem. Bost. Soc. i, 1869, 551 (Vera Cruz, alpine region and
plateau, 1,200 to 2,500 metres, resident).—Coop., B. Cal. i, 1870, 228.—Merr.,
U. S. Geol. Surv. Ter. 1872, 683 (Utah and Idaho).—Snow, B. Kans. 1873, 8.
Coccothraustes melanocephalus, Rich., Pr. Brit. Assoc. for 1836 (1837).
Pitylus melanocephalus, Gray, Gen. of B. ii, 362.
Fringilla melanocephala, Aud., Orn. Biog. iv, 1838, 519, pl. 373.
Coccoborus melanocephalus, Aud., Syn., 1839, 133.—Aud., B. Am. iii, 1841, 214, pl. 206.—
Heerm., P. R. R. Rep. x, 1859, part vi, 51.
Hedymeles malanocephalus, Cab., Mus. Hein. i, 1851, 153.—Scl., P. Z. S. 1857, 213
(Orizaba); 1858, 303; 1859, 58, 365 (Xalapa); Cat. 1862, 100.—B. B. & R., N.
A. B. ii, 1874, 73, pl. 30, fig. 1, 2.
Goniaphea (Hedymeles) melanocephala, Gray, Hand-list, No. 7547.
Goniaphea melanocephala, Coues, Key, 1872, 149.—Allen, Bull. M. C. Z. iii, 1872, 178
(Kansas, Colorado, and Utah).
Fringilla xanthomaschalis, Wagl., Isis, 1831, 525.
Pitylus guttatus et (?) *Guiraca tricolor*, Less., R. Z. ii, 1839, 102.—" *F. epopœa*, Licht."

Hab.—United States, Middle and Western Provinces, retiring into Mexico in winter.
Resident on the table-lands of Mexico. No Central American or valid West Indian
record.

List of specimens.

19355	....	Stinking Creek.	♂	June 13, 1860	G. H. Trook..	8.25	12.75	4.25
19356	....	Bighorn River.	♂	June 5, 1860	..... do	7.50	13.00	4.25
19357	....	M. of Passoagie.	♂	June 24. 1860	..... do	......	......	......
19358	....	Bighorn River.	♀	June 4, 1860	..... do	8.25	13.00	4.25

Lieutenant Warren's Expedition —4850–2, Bijoux Hills; 5586, Powder River.
Later Expeditions.—61635–90, Ogden, Utah; 62274, Idaho.

This interesting western ally and representative of our Rose-breasted
Song Grosbeak, is of common and very general occurrence in the Middle
and Western Provinces of the United States. The easternmost instance
is, I believe, that recorded by Mr. Allen, who found the bird in Middle
Kansas, breeding, in June. He saw young birds on the 11th, and the
eggs of a second brood toward the end of the month. I have not
observed any references beyond the United States to the northward;
in the other direction the bird appears to extend through Mexico, on
the Table-lands. Many reside in that country; others, obeying the
mysterious impulse of migration, enter the United States in April, and
become extensively dispersed, as we have just seen, retreating to their
warm winter quarters in the fall. In the mountains of Arizona I found
it to be an abundant summer resident from the beginning of May until
the end of September. It appeared to shun the pine woods, preferring
ravines wooded with deciduous trees and upgrown to shrubbery, as
well as the thick willow-copses that fringe the mountain streams. Like
others of the same beautiful genus, it is a brilliant and enthusiastic
vocalist, its song resembling that of the Rose-breasted Grosbeak, and
having much similarity to that of the Baltimore Oriole. As I have
elsewhere remarked, its ordinary chirp, or call note, strikingly resembles
that of Gambel's Plumed Quail—so closely, indeed, that I never could
tell which of the two I was about to see, both species often being found
together in the creek bottoms. It feeds at times extensively upon willow buds, and similar soft, succulent vegetable matter; also upon seeds
and berries, in their season, and upon various insects. Mr. Allen has
noted its fondness for peas, causing it to be ungraciously regarded by
the agriculturists of Utah.

According to Dr. Cooper, a nest "found May 12, at the eastern base of
the Coast Range, was built on a low, horizontal branch of an alder,
consisting of a few sticks and weeds, very loosely put together, and
with a lining of roots and grasses. The eggs were only three, pale
bluish-white, thickly spotted with brown, densely so near the large end;
size, 0.95 by 0.70." Dr. Heermann's account of the nidification is substantially correspondent, except as to the situation of the nest, which,
he says, is "formed with little care of twigs very loosely thrown together, and lined with roots; it is placed on the branches of a bush. The
eggs, four in number, are greenish-blue, marked with irregular spots
of umber-brown, varying in intensity of shade." In nearly a dozen
specimens, I can find no reliable differences from the egg of the Rose-
breasted Grosbeak.

During Mr. Allen's western reconnoisance, the species was first met
with at Fort Hays, and afterward at various localities near the foot-
hills of the Rocky Mountains, and in the valleys, up to about 8,000 feet.
Its song and breeding habits, according to his observations, agree with
those of the Rose-breasted Grosbeak, and the nidification is very similar. Mr. Merriam, who found the species to be quite numerous among
the scrub-oaks at the foot of the Wahsatch Mountains, obtained a nest
on the 22d of July, in Téton Basin, Idaho. "It was on a cottonwood

sapling, about five feet above the ground, and was composed of pieces of grass and vines laid carefully together, with their ends sticking out four or five inches; it contained two fresh eggs." Mr. Trippe writes to me as follows:

"The Black-headed Grosbeak arrives in the lower valleys of Bergen's Park, Colorado, about the 20th of May, and by the 1st of June has become quite numerous throughout the park. It rarely ventures higher than 7,500 feet, however, as it is rare in the valley of Clear Creek, and, indeed, quite uncommon outside of Bergen's Park, but is abundant from there down to the plains. It is the exact counterpart of the Rose-breasted Grosbeak in its flight, manner of feeding, and general habits and actions, and its song closely resembles that of the latter bird, but is nevertheless distinguishable. In September it disappears from the upper range in the mountains."

GONIAPHEA CŒRULEA, (Linn.) Gray.

Blue Grosbeak.

Loxia cœrulea, LINN., Syst. Nat. i, 1766, 306.—WILS., Am. Orn. iii, 1811, 78, pl. 24, f. 6.
Guiraca cœrulea, Sw., Philos. Mag. i, 1827, 438 (Mexico).—BP., List, 1838, 30.—WOODH.,
　Sitgr. Rep. 1853, 81 (Indian Territory and Texas, very common).—NEWB., P. R.
　R. Rep. vi, 1857, 88.—BD., B. N. A. 1858, 499.—SCL., P. Z. S. 1859, 365 (Xalapa);
　378 (Oaxaca); Cat. 1862, 101.—HAYD., Rep. 1862, 168.—COUES & PRENT.,
　Smiths. Rep. 1861 (1862), 413 (Washington, D. C., May to Sept., breeding,
　rather rare).—BOARDM., Pr. Bost. Soc. ix, 1862, 127 (Calais, Me., "very uncer-
　tain, but common in the spring of 1861").—VERR., Pr. Ess. Inst. iii, 158
　(Maine, "accidental").—COUES, Pr. Phila. Acad. 1866, 88 (Arizona, summer).—
　LAWR., Ann. Lyc. N. Y. viii, 1866, 286 (New York, rare); ix, 1868, 102 (Costa
　Rica); ix, 1869, 200 (Yucatan).—COUES, Pr. Ess. Inst. v, 1868, 284 (New
　England, rare or occasional).—COUES, Pr. Bost. Soc. xii, 1868, 116 (South
　Carolina, summer, not uncommon).—TURNB., B. E. Pa. 43 (rare straggler).—
　SUMICH., Mem. Bost. Soc. i, 1869, 552 (Vera Cruz, wintering).—COOP., B. Cal.
　i, 1870, 230 (whole of California).—B. B. & R., N. A. B. ii, 1874, 77, pl. 29, f. 4, 5.
Fringilla cœrulea, LICHT., Verz. 1823, 22.—BP., Syn. 1828, 114.—NUTT., Man. i, 1832, 529.—
　AUD., Orn. Biog. ii, 1834, 140; v, 1839, 508; pl. 122.
Coccoborus cœruleus, Sw., Class. B. ii, 1837, 277.—AUD., Syn. 1839, 132.—AUD., B. Am. iii,
　1841, 204, pl. 204.—CAB., Mus. Hein. i, 1852, 152; J. f. O. iv, 1856, 9 (Cuba).—
　PUTN., Pr. Ess. Inst. i, 1856, 228 (Massachusetts, casual).—HEERM., P. R. R.
　Rep. x, part vi, 1859, 51.—FINSCH, Abh. Nat. 1870, 339 (Mazatlan).
Cyanoloxia cœrulea, BP., Consp. Av. i, 1850, 502.
Goniaphea cœrulea, SCL., P. Z. S. 1856, 301 (Cordova).—GRAY, Hand-list, No. 75, 35.—
　COUES, Key, 1872, 149, fig. 93.

Hab.—United States, southerly, from Atlantic to Pacific. In the east, north to Middle States regularly; to Connecticut Valley occasionally; to Maine casually. In the interior, north to the Platte. In the west, north through California. Breeds throughout its United States range. Winters in Mexico and Central America. Cuba (*Cabanis*).
　Lieutenant Warren's Expedition.—9285-87, Loup Fork of the Platte.
　Not obtained by Captain Raynolds' Expedition.

This is essentially a southern bird, whose desultory northward extension is perceived from the foregoing quotations. It appears to visit the Middle States regularly, yet rarely, and is not common north of Maryland—in fact, I know of no locality in the United States where it can be said to be abundant. I used to get it every season about Washington, where it breeds; it was quite common in the old fields and pastures just north of the city. I have also shot young birds in Arizona, in August. The nest is placed in the crotch of a bush or dwarfish shrub —rarely on the lower limbs of trees—generally in an old, neglected field, half overrun with shrubbery, or on the adjoining edge of an open piece of woods. It is built of fine, dried grasses, rather inartistically, and lined with rootlets or hair. The eggs are of the palest blue shade

—much like those of an Indigo-bird. I have never seen one with any markings whatever. The variations in size, even 'in the few specimens before me, are very great. Thus, one measures a full inch long by only 0.60 broad, and is as pointedly pyriform as a Sandpiper's; another is only 0.78 by 0.65, and is almost globular, and equally rounded at each end.

CYANOSPIZA AMŒNA, (Say) Bd.

Lazuli Finch.

Emberiza amœna, SAY, Long's Exp. Rocky Mts. ii, 1823, 47.
Fringilla (Spiza) amœna, BP., Am. Orn. i, 1825, 61, pl. 6, f. 5.
Fringilla amœna, BP., Syn. 1828, 106.—NUTT., Man. i, 1832, 473; 2d ed. i, 1840, 546.—AUD., Orn. Biog. v. 1839, 64, 230, pls. 398 424.
Spiza amœna, BP., List, 1838, 35.—AUD., Syn. 1839, 109.—AUD., B. Am. iii, 1841, 100, pl. 171.—WOODH., Sitgr. Rep. 1853, 87.—HEERM., P. R. R. Rep. x, 1859, part vi, 46.—MAXIM., J. f. O. 1858, 283.
Cyanospiza amœna, BD., B. N. A. 1858, 504.—COOP. & SUCK., N. H. Wash. Ter. 1860, 205.—HAYD., Rep. 1862, 168.—COUES, Pr. Phila. Acad. 1866, 89.—COOP., B. Cal. i, 1871, 233.—ALLEN, Bull. M. C. Z. iii, 1872, 178.—MERR., U. S. Geol. Surv. Ter. 1872, 683 (Utah).—HOLD., Pr. Bost. Soc. 1872, 201 (Wyoming).—COUES, Key, 1872, 149.—SNOW, B. Kans. 1873, 8.—B. B. & R., N. A. B. ii, 1874, pl. 30, f. 11, 12.
Passerina amœna, GRAY, Hand-list, 1870, ii, 97, No. 7436.

Hab.—United States, from the Plains to the Pacific; southward into Mexico. No Central American record.

List of Specimens.

| 19275 | 30 | Wind River.... | ♂ | May 25, 1860 | F. V. Hayden. | 5.00 | 8.50 | 2.75 |
| 19354 | .... | Yellowstone R.. | ♂ | June 22, 1860 | G. H. Trook.. | 5.50 | 8.76 | 3.00 |

Lieutenant Warren's Expeditions.—5395-98, Fort Lookout; 5399, Fort Pierre; 8948, Laramie Peak.
Later Expeditions.—61691 to 61712, Ogden, Utah; 62324, Idaho.

The prettily-colored and delicate little Lazuli Finch is found to be common in most suitable places within its range, where it entirely replaces its Eastern ally, the Indigo-bird. It breeds at large, apparently, in the portions of the United States just indicated, but its winter resorts are not so clear; at least I do not find among the works at hand any such satisfactory indications as I could desire.

I do not agree with some who say that the song of the Lazuli Finch is entirely different from that of the Indigo-bird; on the contrary, to my ear at least, it has sounded very similar. It is a simple and even feeble strain, rather monotonous, and given in a tripping, desultory way, as if the little performer were tired or indifferent. At such a time he is usually observed on some prominent outpost, near a grove, or in an open place overgrown with shrubbery; and if we see him frequently resorting to the same perch, meanwhile flying into the low cover at intervals, we may be sure his home and mate are there concealed. The first batch of eggs are laid early in May, in a grassy, hair-lined nest of considerable bulk, let down in the crotch of a low bush, much like that of the Black-throated Finch (*Poozpiza bilineata*); the eggs are three to five in number. An excellent description has been given by Dr. Cooper: "A nest found May 7, in a low bush close to a public road, about three feet from the ground, was built very strongly supported by a triple fork of the branch, composed of grass-blades firmly interwoven, the inside lined with much horse-hair and cobweb. The outside measured three inches in height, three and three fourths in

CYANOSPIZA CYANEA, INDIGO-BIRD.

width; inside it was two wide, one and three-fourths deep. The eggs,
partly hatched, were pale bluish-white, and measured 0.75 by 0.56 inch."
He also describes nests similar in position, but of fibrous roots and bark
strips as well as grasses, with a lining of plant-down or horse-hair, and
containing four or five eggs. These last correspond with three found
in Utah by Mr. Merriam; "one was on a scrub-oak about three feet
high, and the other two were about two feet above the ground. The
eggs, generally four in number, are laid about the first or middle of
June, in a beautiful downy nest, composed of fine grasses and wool,
lined with hair."

According to Mr. Trippe, " the Lazuli Finch is abundant in Colorado
from the plains up to about 6,000 feet, stragglers wandering into Bergen's Park, where a few pairs breed, but never venturing beyond 7,000
or 8,000 feet, and rarely reaching that limit. A pretty little bird, with
much the manners and voice of the Indigo-bird, and a weak, rambling
song, in which the relationship of the two birds is quite apparent."

CYANOSPIZA CYANEA, (Linn.) Bd.

Indigo-bird.

Tanagra cyanea, LINN., Syst. Nat. i, 1766, 315.
Emberiza cyanea, et (?) *cœrulea*, et (?) *cyanella*, GM., Syst. Nat. 1788, 876, 887.
Fringilla cyanea, WILS., Am. Orn. i, 1810, 100, pl. 6, f. 5.—BP., Am. Orn. ii, pl. 11, fig. 3
    (♀).—BP., Syn. 1828, 107.—NUTT., Man. i, 1832, 473.—AUD., Orn. Biog. i, 1832,
    377; v, 1839, 503; pl. 74.
Passerina cyanea, "VIEILL., 1816."—GRAY, Hand-list, ii, 1870, 97, No. 7435 (according
    to *Gray*, type of the genus, antedating *Cyanospiza, Baird*, 1858).
Spiza cyanea, BP., List, 1838, 35.—AUD., Syn. 1839, 109; B. Am. iii, 1841, 96, pl. 170.—
    GIR., B. L. I. 1844, 110.—WOODH., Sitgr. Rep. 1853, 87.—PUTN., Pr. Ess. Inst. i,
    1856, 210.—SCL., P. Z. S. 1856, 304 (Cordova).—RUSS, J. f. O. 1871, 18.
Cyanospiza cyanea, BD., B. N. A. 1858, 505.—SCL. & SALV., Ibis, 1859, 18 (Guatemala).—
    SCL., Cat. 1862, 107 (Mexico and Guatemala).—BOARDM., Pr. Bost. Soc, ix,
    1862, 128 (Maine, "rare").—MCILWR., Pr. Ess. Inst. vi, 1866, 90 (Canada West,
    common).—SUMICH., Mem. Bost. Soc. i, 1869, 552 (Vera Cruz, winter).—LAWR.,
    Ann. Lyc. viii, 180 (Nicaragua); ix, 1868, 103 (Costa Rica); 1869, 201 (Yuca-
    tan).—SALV., P. Z. S. 1870, 190 (Veragua).—ALLEN, Bull. M. C. Z. ii, 1872,
    178 (Eastern Kansas).—COUES, Key, 1872, 150.—SNOW, B. Kans. 1873, 8 (very
    common).—B. B. & R., N. A. B., ii, 1840, 82, pl. 30, f. 13, 17.
Cyanoloxia cyanea, BP., Consp. Av. i, 1850, 502.

Hab.—Eastern Province of the United States. North to Canada and Maine. West
to Kansas and Indian Territory. South through Texas to Mexico and Central America,
where it winters. Breeds through most of its United States habitat, from Texas to
Canada. Cuba (CAB., J. f. O. iv, 1856, 8).

Although obtained by neither Expedition, this bird is known to range
along the Lower Missouri, having been found in Kansas by several
observers.

The habits of the dainty Indigo-bird need not be here given; they
are familiar to all interested in ornithology. The egg is variously
described as pure white, plain blue, or bluish, speckled with reddish.
The fact appears to be, not that these statements are conflicting or any
of them erroneous, but that different eggs vary accordingly. It seems
to be the general rule with normally bluish eggs, that they range in
shade from quite blue to white, and are occasionally speckled. Such,
for instance, is the case with the eggs of *Poospiza bilineata*, as noted by
me in the "American Naturalist" for 1873, p. 323; and I presume it will
so prove to be with those of *Cyanospiza amœna*, as it is with *Calamospiza
bicolor*, *Euspiza americana*, and even *Turdus fuscescens*. Nevertheless,
all the numerous eggs before me are plain white, with a faint blue shade.
A fair specimen measures 0.72 by 0.52. Eggs of *C. amœna* are indistin-

guishable. Those of *Guiraca cærulea* are the same in color, but of course larger. But another species, commonly placed in the genus *Cyanospiza*, namely, *C. ciris*, lays an entirely different egg—pure white, heavily speckled with reddish-brown, dark brown, or purplish-gray. This style of egg is much as in *Junco*, or in *Spizella pusilla*.

CARDINALIS VIRGINIANUS, (Briss.) Bp.

Cardinal Grosbeak; Virginian Redbird.

a. *virginianus*.

Coccothraustes virginiana cardinalis dicta, BRISS., Orn. iii, 1760, 252.
Cardinalis virginianus, BP., List, 1838, 35 ; Consp. Av. i, 1850, 501.—WOODH., Sitgr. Rep. 1853, 81 (Texas and Indian Territory).—BD., B. N. A. 1858, 509.—MAXIM., J. f. O. vi, 1858, 268.—WHEAT., Ohio Agric. Rep. 1860, No. 162.—COUES & PRENT., S. I. Rep. 1861, 413 (Washington, D. C., resident, abundant).—HAYD., Rep. 1862, 163.—ALLEN, Pr. Ess. Inst. iv, 1864, 85 (Massachusetts, accidental in summer, on *Nuttall's* authority).—COUES, *ibid.* v, 1868, 284 (the same).—DRESS., Ibis, 1865, 491 (Texas).—LAWR., Ann. Lyc. N. Y. viii, 1866, 286 (New York Island).— TURNB., B. E. Pa. 1869, 24 (frequent, and wintering).—ALLEN. Bull. M. C. Z. iii, 1872, 178 (Kansas).—COUES, Key, 1872, 151, fig. 96.—SNOW, B. Kans. 1873, 8.— B. B. & R., N. A. B. ii, 1874, 100, pl. 30, f. 6, 7.
Loxia cardinalis, LINN., Syst. Nat. i, 1766, 300.—GM., Syst. Nat. i, 1788, 847.—LATH., Ind. Orn. i, 1790, 375.—WILS., Am. Orn. ii, 1810, 38, pl. 6, f. 1, 2.
Fringilla (Coccothraustes) cardinalis, BP., Obs. Wils. 1825, No. 79.
Coccothraustes cardinalis, VIEILL., Nouv. Dict. d'Hist. Nat.
Fringilla cardinalis, BP., Syn. 1828, 113.—NUTT., Man. i, 1832, 519.—AUD., Orn. Biog. ii, 1834, 336, pl. 159.
Pitylus cardinalis, AUD., Syn. 1839, 131; B. Am. iii, 1841, 198, pl. 203.—GIR., B. L. I. 1844, 132.—HOY, Smiths. Rep. 1864, 438 (Missouri).

b. *coccineus*.

Cardinalis virginianus, SCL., P. Z. S. 1856, 302 (Cordova); 1859, 365 (Xalapa); Ibis, 1859, 104; Cat. Am. B. 100 (in part).—LAWR., Ann. Lyc. ix, 1860, 201 (Yucatan).— SUMICH., Mem. Bost. Soc. 1869, 552 (Vera Cruz).
Cardinalis virginianus var. *coccineus*, RIDGW., Am. Journ. Sci.—B. B. & R., N. A. B. ii, 1874, 99.

c. *igneus*.

Cardinalis igneus, BD., Pr. Phila. Acad. 1859, 305 (St. Lucas).—COUES, Pr. Phila. Acad. Jan. 1868 (South Arizona).—ELLIOT, B. N. A. pl. 16.—COOP., B. Cal. i, 1870, 238.
Cardinalis virginianus var. *igneus*, COUES, Key, 1872, 1851.—B. B. & R., N. A. B. ii, 1874, 103, pl. 30, f. 10.
Cardinalis virginianus, LAWR., Ann. Lyc. N. Y. 1872 (Tres Marias).—FINSCH, Abh. Nat. 1870, 339.

d. *carneus*.

Cardinalis carneus, LESS., R. Z. 1843, 209 (Acapulco and Realejo).—BP., Consp. Av. i, 1850, 501.
Cardinalis virginianus var. *carneus*, RIDGW., Am. Journ.—B. B. & R., ii, 1874, 99.

Hab.—The typical form from the Eastern United States, west to Kansas, Nebraska, Indian Territory, Texas (and New Mexico?). North to the Middle States commonly, to New York rarely, to Connecticut casually, to Massachusetts accidentally, and in the West to Missouri. Not south of the Rio Grande. Stationary or scarcely migratory. Var. *coccineus* is the resident form beyond the United States, through Eastern Mexico to Central America. More richly-colored, and without the grayish edgings of the dorsal plumage. Var. *igneus*, in which the black frontlet is narrowed or wanting at the base of the culmen, is from Arizona and Lower California, and southward. Var. *carneus*, with stiffened coronal feathers, as in the very different *C. phœniceus*, is from Western Mexico. The last-mentioned variety I have not seen ; the others run extremely close to typical *virginianus*.

Mr. Allen has prepared some interesting tables showing the range of variation in this species and others. He finds the southern resident birds, as might be expected, smaller than those of the Middle States. The former measure as follows : Males— length, 7.75 to 9.10 ; extent, 11.00 to 11.78 ; wing, 3.50 to 3.85 ; tail, 3.40 to 4.20 ; tarsus,

0.62 to 0.80. Females—7.50 to 8.75; 10.70 to 11.75; 3.25 to 2.85; 3.40 to 4.10; 0.62 to 0.75.
Average, male—8.46; 11.43; 2.63; 3.87. Average, female—8.27; 11.27; 3.53; 3.75.
Lieutenant Warren's Expedition.—4854, Iowa Point.
Not obtained Captain Raynolds' or the later Expeditions.

The Cardinal lays rather a peculiar egg, some specimens reminding one of a Night-Hawk's, in coloration at least, and others being more like those of the Rose-breasted Grosbeak in the pattern of markings. The ground is white, in all of about fifty cases noticed. The spotting is of every shade of brown, from pale-reddish to heavy chocolate, but it is usually rather dark, and there is a great show of the various purplish-brown or stone-gray shell markings. The markings vary from fine uniform dotting or marbling to heavy spotting, but I see none with very large masses of color. Size a little over an inch by rather less than three-fourths of an inch, but very variable. The egg of *Pyrrhuloxia sinuata* is altogether similar.

PIPILO ERYTHROPHTHALMUS, (Linn.) Vieill.

Ground Robin; Marsh Robin; Towhee Bunting; Chewink.

a. *erythrophthalmus.*

Fringilla erythrophthalmus, LINN., Syst. Nat. i, 1766, 318.—BP., Syn. 1828, 112.—NUTT., Man. i, 1832, 515.—AUD., Orn. Biog. i, 1832, 150; v, 1839, 511; pl. 29.
Emberiza erythrophthalma, GM., Syst. Nat. i, 1788, 874.—WILS., vi, 1812, 90, pl. 53.
Pipilo erythrophthalmus, VIEILL., Gal. Ois. i, 1824, 109, pl. 80.—BP., List, 1838, 35.—AUD., Syn. 1839, 124.—AUD., B. Am. iii, 1841, 167, pl. 195.—GIR., B. L. I. 1844, 124.—BP., Consp. Av. i, 1850, 487.—WOODH., Sitgr. Rep. 1853, 81 (New Mexico (?), Texas, and Indian Territory).—BD., B. N. A. 1858, 512.—HAYD., Rep. 1862, 168.—ALLEN, Bull. M. C. Z. iii, 1872, 178.—COUES, Key, 1872, 151.—SNOW, B. Kans. 1873, 8.—B. B. & R., N. A. B. ii, 1874, 106, 109, pl. 31, f. 2, 3; and of authors generally.
Pipilo ater, VIEILL., Nouv. Dict. d'Hist. Nat. xxxiv, 1819, 292.

b. *alleni.*

(Smaller, white-eyed, with less white on wings and tail. Florida.)

Pipilo erythrophthalmus var. *alleni*, COUES, Am. Nat. v, 1871, 366; Key, 1872, 152.—B. B. & R., N. A. B. ii, 1874, 112, with figs.
Pipilo leucopis, MAYN., B. of Fla. (in press).

Hab.—Eastern Province of North America to Minnesota (*Trippe*), Canada (*McIlwraith*), and Labrador (*Audubon*). In northern portions of its range perfectly migratory, and only seen in summer. Resident in the Southern States, and even as high as Pennsylvania, in sheltered situations (*Turnbull*). Breeds in most places throughout its range. Reaches westward through part of Kansas, and on the Missouri River to about 43°. Fort Randall (*Hayden*). Meets var. *arcticus* in Northern Dakota.
Lieutenant Warren's Expedition.—4832, Iowa Point; 4835, St. Joseph's; 4834, Wood's Bluff; 4828-29, 4833, 4836, Bald Island, Missouri River.
Not obtained by Captain Raynolds' Expedition.
According to the authority last quoted on this subject, extensive series of Eastern *Pipilo* present the following measurements of the males, the females being a little smaller in each case:
Northern specimens.—Length, 7.50 to 8.80; extent, 10.00 to 10.25; wing, 3.17 to 3.90; tail, 3.30 to 3.93; tarsus, 0.98 to 1.13. Average: Length, 8.19; extent, 11.32; wing, 3.43; tail, 3.66; tarsus, 1.06.
Floridan specimens (var. *alleni*).—Length, 7.20 to 8.50; extent, 9.50 to 11.30; wing, 2.80 to 3.50; tail, 3.25 to 3.90; tarsus, 0.80 to 1.00. Average: Length, 7.88; extent, 9.88; wing, 3.13; tail, 3.56; tarsus, 0.94.
The little difference in total length of Northern and Southern, compared with that in the wing and in alar extent, is owing to the greater relative length of the tail of the Floridan form.
Audubon states that in the young the eye is sometimes yellowish-white, and that occasionally the two eyes of the same individual are not of the same color. A late anonymous writer says that the eyes turn white in winter. The Floridan form appears to be resident in that State, and to always have white or whitish eyes. Its song "is quite

different from that of the northern bird, being ordinarily only about half as long, and uttered with much less spirit. There is probably a large proportion of northern birds among the *Pipilones* of Florida in winter; while probably in summer the majority are of the southern type above described, as are doubtless those of Middle and Southern Florida at all seasons" (Bull. M. C. Z. ii, 1871, 282). The amount of white on the tail is less—that on the outer feather of var. *alleni* about equaling that on the next quill of ordinary *erythrophthalmus*.

Specimens from the Red River region show an interesting approach to var. *arcticus* in the presence of small, concealed white spots. It may be necessary, after all, to bring the species into the same series with *maculatus*, and consider all the forms as varieties of one species.

In the Middle Atlantic districts, as Maryland for instance, the Towhee is chiefly a migrant, appearing in great numbers the third or fourth week in April, and so continuing until the middle of May; while in the fall it is still more numerous during the month of October. Still, I used to find one or more families settled to breed each summer, and generally saw the streaked birds of the year in July. I never ascertained that any wintered about Washington, but should guess this to be the case, since the Rev. Dr. Turnbull states that some pass that season in the most sheltered situations in Pennsylvania and New Jersey. With the coming of other seed-eaters from the north, early in October, the Towhee suddenly appears. As we walk along the weedy old "snake" fences and thick hedges, or by the briery tracts marking the course of a tiny water-thread through a field, scores of the humble gray Sparrows flit before us; while ever and again the jaunty Towhee, smartly dressed in black, white, and chestnut, comes into view, flying low, with a saucy flirt of the tail, and dashes again into the covert as quickly as it emerged, crying "*tow-hée*" with startling distinctness. In the spring it is less conspicuous, and more likely to be found in low, tangled woods, amid laurel brakes and the like; on the ground, rustling and busily scratching the matting of last year's leaves that covers the earth, doubtless in search of insects. Its notes are then louder, and oftener heard. Some say that the males precede the females in migrating; this may average true, but I have constantly found the sexes together at both seasons. This is only a partially gregarious bird, large gatherings being seldom witnessed. In fact it seems to prefer the society of the smaller and plainer Sparrows, among which it shines without difficulty, doubtless patronizing them in the genteel way, customary with big folks, that is so exasperatingly oppressive to the recipients.

The Towhee Bunting nests always on the ground, usually at the foot of a bush by an old log, or in weedy rubbish, which, with the deep set of the nest in the ground, very effectually conceals it. The only one I have happened to find so far, was sunk to the level of the surface, resting upon a straggling bed of leaves, like those strewn all around, built of weed-stalks and small sticks, loosely interlaced, and finished carelessly with a slight lining of fine, dried grass. It contained five eggs— *three* Cow-bird's and two of its own, which must have been sufficiently discouraging. After this infliction, when I came to take the nest away altogether, the poor birds seemed perfectly stupefied with despair. The female flew to a bush near by, with a plaintive chirp that soon brought her mate, and there the two sat motionless, side by side, too sick at heart, it seemed, to even remonstrate.

This was a case contrary to the general rules, that the Cow-bird lays but one egg in a nest, and selects the nest of a bird whose eggs are smaller than her own. The Towhee's egg measures about 0.95 by 0.70; the Cow-bird's about 0.75 by 0.60. There is a remarkable similarity in coloration between the two—so much do they resemble each other, that in the instance noted above I wondered at first how the Towhee had come to lay three "runt" eggs. The ground is white, but uniformly and so completely and thickly freckled in fine pattern with dull, pale reddish-brown, as show as much of this color as of the white. The Cow-bird's egg is minutely freckled in the same way, but the colors are darker and more sharply marked.

Two broods of Towhees are usually reared each season, and sometimes three. The young are very different from the adult, being streaky all over; yet at a very early age the black of the male, and the rich brown of the opposite sex, respectively appear.

PIPILO MACULATUS var. ARTICUS, (Sw.) Coues.

Arctic Spotted Towhee.

a. maculatus.

Pipilo maculatus, Sw., Philos. Journ. 1827 (Mexico).—"JARD. & SELB., Ill. pl. 31, 34."— BP., Consp. i, 1850, 487.—SCL., P. Z. S. 1858, 304 (Oaxaca); 1859, 380.—COUES, Key, 1872, 152.—B. B. & R., N. A. B. ii, 1874, 105.

b. oregonus.

Pipilo oregonus, BELL., Ann. Lyc. N. Y. v, 1852, 6 (Oregon).—BP., C. R. xxxvii, 1853, 932; Consp. i, 1850, 487.—BD., B. N. A. 1858, 513.—COOP. & SUCK., N. H. Wash. Ter. 1860, 200.—LORD, Pr. Roy. Arty. Inst. iv, 1864, 120 (British Columbia).— COOP., B. Cal. i, 1870, 241.
Pipilo maculatus var. *oregonus*, COUES, Key, 1872, 152.—B. B. & R., N. A. B. ii, 1874, 116, figs.
Fringilla arctica, AUD., Orn. Biog. v, 1839, 49, pl. 394, *nec* Sw.
Pipilo arctica, AUD., Syn. 1839, 123; B. Am. iii, 1841, 164, pl. 194.

c. arcticus.

Pyrgita (Pipilo) arctica, Sw. & RICH., F. B. A. ii, 1831, 260, pls. 51, ♂, 52, ♀.
Pipilo arcticus, NUTT., Man. i, 1832, 589; 2d ed. i, 1840, 610.—BP., List, 1838, 35; Consp. i, 1850, 487.—BELL, Ann. Lyc. N. Y. v, 1852, 7.—WOODH., Sitgr. Rep. 1853, 81.— BD., B. N. A. 1858, 514 (also, var. *subarcticus*, ID., *ibid.* 515, in text).—HAYDN., Rep. 1862, 168.—DRESS., Ibis, 1865, 492 (Texas).—HOLD., Pr. Bost. Soc. 1872, 202 (Wyoming).—STEV., U. S. Geol. Surv. Ter. 1870, 465.
Pipilo erythrophthalmus var. *arcticus*, ALLEN, Bull. M. C. Z. iii, 1872, 178.
Pipilo maculatus var. *arcticus*, COUES, Key, 1872, 152.—B. B. & R., N. A. B. ii, 1874, 119, pl. 31, f. 5, 6.

d. megalonyx.

Pipilo megalonyx, BD., B. N. A. 1858, 515, pl. 73.—HEERM., P. R. R. Rep. x, 1859, pt. vi, 51.—COUES, Pr. Phila. Acad. 1866, 89.—COOP., B. Cal. i, 1870, 242.
Pipilo maculatus var. *megalonyx*, COUES, Key, 1872, 152.—B. B. & R., N. A. B. ii, 1874, 113.

Hab.—Middle Province. North to the Saskatchewan. South along the Rocky Mountains, where it runs into *megalonyx*, of New Mexico, Arizona, and California; west to Oregon and Washington, there inosculating with *oregonus*. East to about 43° north latitude on the Missouri, where it meets *erythrophthalmus*. The typical form Mexican.

List of specimens.

| 19277 | 178 | Powder River.. | ♂ | Sept. 24, 1860 | G. H. Trook.. | 8.00 | 11.25 | 3.50 |

Lieutenant Warren's Expedition.—4839-40-45, Bon Homme Island; 4841, The Tower; 4842-43-44-47, Bijoux Hills; 5387, Fort Pierre; 5389, Yellowstone River; 5388-90, Fort Lookout.
Later Expeditions.—60382-5, Wyoming.

The connection of the several spotted *Pipilos* of the west and of Mexico, I believe first noted by *Dr. Sclater*, has been amply confirmed by subsequent investigation. They unquestionably intergrade completely, forming geographical races of one species. The question is, whether to this series *P. erythrophthalmus* should not also be added. In the Key, I kept it apart and presented the considerations favoring this view, viz., the entire absence of spotting on the scapulars and back, the stronger sexual distinctions, and the different note—the cry of the western species resembling that of the Cat-bird.

It would not, however, be at all surprising if complete intergradation between *erythroph-thalmus* and *arcticus* were proven by specimens from the Lower Missouri, gaining first a spot or two, and then gradually assuming the fully speckled state. In that event, I should not hesitate to combine the whole in one series, beginning with the black unspotted *erythrophthalmus*, with clear brown female, and ending with the olive-shaded, spotted *maculatus* and its nearly similar female.

Dr. Hayden has shown exactly where the two forms meet along the Missouri, at about 43°. In Northern Dakota var. *arcticus* occurs east to about 102° longitude, and my Red River specimens of *erythrophthalmus* show an approach toward it.

Excepting the curiously different call-note, the western forms are all precisely like the eastern in habits and manners. The large-clawed form is very abundant in New Mexico, Arizona, and California. The sexes of this race are not obviously distinguishable by any outward mark—in fact, on cutting open a supposed male on one occasion, I found an egg inside. Mr. Trippe sends me the following items :

" The Arctic Towhee appears in the vicinity of Idaho Springs about the middle of May, and in the course of a week or two becomes rather common, though never very abundant. It becomes rare above 8,500 feet, and above 9,000 disappears altogether, being most numerous from 7,500 feet down to the plains. In habits and appearance, it is quite similar to the Eastern Towhee, but is much shyer and is easily frightened, when it hides in the bushes until all appearance of danger has passed by. Sometimes, though rarely, I have heard it utter the "chewink" of *P. erythrophthalmus*, or a note almost exactly like it, though a little lower and more wiry ; but its usual call is quite different. It does not sing near as frequently as the latter bird, but when it does, acts in the same manner, mounting to the lower limb of a tree and chanting its simple ditty at short intervals for half an hour or more. This song is almost the same as the Eastern Towhees ; and it has, also, the same fine drawn, wiry note. It disappears in September."

NOTE.—The *Pipilo fuscus*, SW. (*mesoleucus*, BD. ; cf. COUES, Key, 152), has been taken near Cañon City, Colorado, by Mr. C. E. Aiken, and may extend to the head-waters of the Platte. A pair were killed in winter.

PIPILO CHLORURUS, (Towns.) Bd.

Green-tailed Finch ; Blanding's Finch.

Fringilla chlorura, TOWNS.—AUD., Orn. Biog. v, 1839, 336.
Zonotrichia chlorura, GAMB., Journ. Phila. Acad. i, 1847, 51, pl. 9.
Embernagra chlorura, BP., Consp., i, 1850, 483.—HEERM., P. R. R. Rep. x, 1859, part vi,
    46.—SCL., Cat. 1862, 117.
Pipilo chlorurus, BD., B. N. A. 1858, 519.—HEERM., *l. c.* part v, 15.—HAYD., Rep. 1862,
    169.—COUES, Pr. Phila. Acad. 1866, 90.—COOP., B. Cal. i, 1870, 248.—STEV.,
    U. S. Geol. Surv. Ter. 1870, 465.—MERR., *ibid.* 1872, 684.—ALLEN, Bull. M. C. Z.
    iii, 1872, 178.—COUES, Key, 1872, 153.—B. B. & R., N. A. B. ii, 1874, 131, pl. 31, f. 4.
Fringilla blandingiana, GAMB., Pr. Phila. Acad. i, 1843, 260.
Zonotrichia blandingiana, WOODH., Sitgr. Rep. 1853, 85.
Embernagra blandingiana, CASS., Ill. 1853, 70, pl. 12.
Pipilo rufipileus, LAFRES., R. Z. xi, 1848, 176.—BP., Consp. i, 1850, 487.
Kieneria rufipileus, BP., Comp. Rend. xl, 1855, 356.

Hab.—Southern Rocky Mountain region. North to Laramie. Across from Texas to Southern California. Winters on the southern United States border (Colorado Valley and San Diego, *Cooper*).

List of specimens.

19278	16	Wind River ...	♂	May 28, 1860	F. V. Hayden.	7.25	9.75	3.00

Lieutenant Warren's Expedition.—9270-77-78, Laramie Peak.
Later Expeditions.—60660-62, Little Sandy Creek, Uintah Mountains, and Green River, Wyoming ; 62292-94, Conant Creek, and Téton Basin, Idaho.
In continuing to refer this species to the genus *Pipilo*, I follow custom ; but I am unable to appreciate any obvious differences from *Zonotrichia*.

Within the general range just mentioned the movements of this species remain to be precisely ascertained. The bird probably breeds in mountains throughout its range, and lower down in higher latitudes. It has been ascertained to breed in Colorado. Dr. Hayden's specimens may represent its limit in one direction. In the higher portions of Arizona, I ascertained its presence in numbers, but only during the migrations, in April and May, and in September. It appeared to be a shy, retiring bird, courting the seclusion of tangled undergrowth, where it might easily be overlooked, unless diligently sought for. I generally observed it in small, straggling companies, associated with other fringilline birds. Dr. Cooper states that it winters in the Colorado Valley, as well as in Lower California.

In a late communication to me, Mr. Allen observes: "This is one of the most interesting birds met with in the wooded portions of the great central plateau of the continent. In the mountains of Colorado it ranges from the foot-hills up to the limit of trees, and throughout the mountain valleys is one of the more common species. It affects the moister thickets near the streams, and possesses a peculiar and very pleasing song. In habits or notes it has but little resemblance to the group of Towhees with which it is commonly associated by systematic writers, presenting in these respects far more resemblance to the group of Sparrows so familiarly represented in the Atlantic States by the common White-throat, from which it only differs structurally in its relatively longer tail." Mr. Trippe's notes upon the same subject will be read with interest: "The Green-tailed Finch is abundant throughout Clear Creek County, from its lower valleys up to within 700 or 800 feet of timber-line, breeding throughout; but is most numerous, during the nesting season, from 7,500 to 9,000 feet. It arrives at Idaho early in May, and soon becomes abundant, remaining till the close of September or early part of October. It is a sprightly, active little bird, with something wren-like in its movements and appearance. It is equally at home among the loose stones and rocks of a hill-side (where it hops about with all the agility of the Rock Wren), and the densest thickets of brambles and willows in the valleys, amidst which it loves to hide. It is rather shy, and prefers to keep at a good distance from any suspicious object; and if a cat or dog approaches its nest, makes a great scolding, like the Cat-bird, and calls all the neighbors to its assistance; but if a person walks by, it steals away very quietly and remains silent till the danger is passed. It has a variety of notes which it is fond of uttering; one sounds like the mew of a kitten, but thinner and more wiry; its song is very fine, quite different from the Towhee's, and vastly superior to it. It builds its nest in dense clumps of brambles, and raises two broods each season, the first being hatched about the middle of June."

The eggs of this species have recently been brought in by Mr. H. W. Henshaw, one of the naturalists of Lieutenant Wheeler's Survey. They are rather peculiar, being of a pale greenish or grayish-white, freckled all over with rich reddish-brown, the speckling being aggregated in a wreath or area about the larger end of the egg. Some specimens are much more minutely and obsoletely dotted than others, but in all the cases I have seen the markings are quite regular. Mr. G. H. Trook also took the eggs on Snake and Henry River. The nest is placed indifferently on the ground or in a low bush. The egg measures 0.90 by 0.68. The egg is of the same general character as that of *P. erythrophthalmus* and its allies; but entirely different from the whole *P. fuscus* group, in which the style is curiously as in *Agelæus*—a pale greenish ground, sharply spotted, scratched and streaked with blackish.

Family ICTERIDÆ: American Starlings.

DOLICHONYX ORYZIVORUS, (Linn.) Sw.

Bobolink; Reed-bird; Rice-bird

Emberiza oryzivora, LINN., Syst. Nat. i, 1766, 311.—(*Hortulanus carolinensis*, BRISS., Orn.
iii, 282, pl. 15, f. 3; *Emberiza caroliniensis*, KLEIN, 92).—GM., i, 1788, 880.—
LATH., Ind. Orn. i, 1790, 408.—WILS., Am. Orn. ii, 1810, 48, pl. 12, f. 1, 2.
Passerina oryzivorus, VIEILL., Nouv. Dict. d'Hist. Nat. 1817, 3.
Dolichonyx oryzivorus, SW., Zool. Journ. iii, 1827, 351.—SW. & RICH., F. B. A. ii, 1831,
278.—BP., List, 1838, 29; Consp. i, 1850, 437.—AUD., Syn. 1839, 138.—AUD., B.
Am. iv, 1842, 10, pl. 211.—GOULD, Voy. Beagle, 1841, 106 (Galapagoes).—GIR.,
B. L. I. 1844, 137.—GOSSE, B. Jam. 1847, 229.—WOODH., Sitgr. Rep. 1853, 81
(Texas and Indian Territory, migratory).—CAB., J. f. O. iv, 1856, 11 (Cuba).—
BD., B. N. A. 1858, 522.—MAXIM., J. f. O. 1858, 266.—BRYANT, Pr. Bost. Soc. vii,
1859 (Bahamas).—SCL., P. Z. S. 1858, 72; Cat. 1862, 134 (Bolivia; St. Martha).
MARCH, Pr. Phila. Acad. 1863, 299 (Jamaica).—SCL. & SALV., P. Z. S. 1870, 781
(Venezuela).—HAYD., Rep. 1862, 169 (very common to Fort Pierre).—COOP.,
Am. Nat. iii, 1869, 78.—TRIPPE, Pr. Ess. Inst. vi, 1871, 117 (Minnesota, not
common).—SNOW, B. Kans. 1873 (breeding; rare).—ALLEN, Bull. M. C. Z. iii,
1872, 178 (Ogden, Utah).—MERR., U. S. Geol. Surv. Ter. 1872, 686 (Utah).—
COUES, Key, 1872, 154, fig. 97.—CASS., Pr. Phila. Acad. 1866, 16 (Rio Negro,
Rio Napo, La Plata).—LAWR., Ann. Lyc. N. Y. 1864, 99 (Sombrero).—PELZ.,
Orn. Braz. iii, 199 (Brazil).—B. B. & R., N. A. B. ii, 1874, 149, pl. 32, f. 4, 5.
Icterus agripennis, BP., Obs. Wils. 1824, No. 87; Syn. 1828, 53.—NUTT., Man. i, 1832, 185.—
AUD., Orn. Biog. i, 1831, 283; v, 1839, 486; pl. 54.
Dolichonyx agripennis, RICH., Rep. Brit. Assoc. 1837.
Psarocolius caudacutus, WAGL., Syst. Av. 1827, 32 (*Bd.* and *Cass.*).
Dolichonyx oryzivorus var. *albinucha*, RIDGW., Mss.—COUES, Check-list, App.

Hab.—Eastern North America. North to the Saskatchewan (latitude 40°, *Rich.*).
West to the Rocky Mountains and somewhat beyond. Utah (*Allen*); Nevada (*Ridgway*); Wyoming (*Hayden*); Montana (*Cooper*). South to Bolivia, La Plata, &c. Galapagoes. Breeds from the Middle States and Kansas northward. Does not winter
anywhere in the United States. West Indies, Central and South America (numerous
quotations).
Lieutenant Warren's Expedition.—5360, Fort Pierre; 8951-52, Loup Fork of Platte.
Later Expeditions.—61728-30, Ogden, Utah ("abundant").

The entire change of plumage which the male of this species under-
goes twice a year is none the less interesting because it is so well known
a fact in its economy. When the bird reaches the Middle districts,
which is usually not until May, the males, as a rule, are already in
nearly perfect breeding attire, but in the vast majority of instances still
show touches of yellowish on the belly and legs. At this period they
are very conspicuous, associated in flocks, sometimes great in extent,
moving restlessly about the meadows and orchards, overflowing with
glad music. Their number seems out of all proportion to that of the
females, but this is probably due to the silent and more retiring ways
of the latter sex. They really pass through, in the vernal migration,
quite rapidly, though they do not appear to be at all in a hurry, as we
see them by day. They throw themselves in a field, scatter on the
ground, feeding, and at the slightest alarm, or in mere wantonness,
suddenly fly *en masse* to the nearest tree, fence, or bush, and begin to
sing, producing an indescribable medley, hushed in an instant only to
be resumed. Sometimes they sing as merrily, though with less con-
certed action, while they are rambling in the grass. Their day-time
leisure for song and food is easily explained; for they migrate, at this
season, almost entirely by night. Every night in early May, as we walk
the streets, we can hear the mellow metallic clinking coming down
through the darkness, from birds passing high over head, and sounding
clearer in the stillness. By the middle of May they have all passed;

a few, it is stated, linger to breed south of New England, but the main body passes on, spreading over that portion of the Union and the neighboring British Provinces, occupying in pairs almost every meadow. The change of plumage with the finishing of the duties of reproduction is rapid and complete before the return movement is made, although this takes place in August. As far north at least as Maryland, I never saw or heard of a decidedly black individual, among the millions that repass that State late in the summer and during September. The males are, indeed, distinguishable by their superior size and a sort of diffuseness of tawny coloration, not quite like the cleaner and lighter pattern of the females, aside from the black traces that frequently persist; but the difference is not great. They are now songless—who ever heard Bobolink music in the fall?—they have a comfortable, self-satisfied *chink*, befitting such fat and abandoned gourmands as they are, thronging in countless hordes the wild-rice tracts and the grain fields, loafing and inviting their souls. So they go, until the first cold snap, that sends them into winter quarters at once—chiefly in the West Indies, but also much further south. They have successively filled the *rôle* of Bobolink, Reed-bird, Rice-bird, and Butter-bird; and as soon as the season relaxes once more, in March, they will re-enter the United States, and do it all over again.

The Atlantic Coast is the favorite highway of this species, but it travels also by other routes in the interior. It goes up the Mississippi Valley; there some stop to breed, as low at least as the mouth of the Missouri, but numbers keep on, pushing past the United States, and resting at last in the region of the Saskatchewan. The very considerable westward extension of the species has been only lately determined. Thus Mr. Allen and Mr. Merriam both found it "common" in September at Ogden, in Utah, where it is said to breed. Dr. Hayden remarks that it is "very common at Fort Pierre," and "one of the most abundant birds on the western prairies." Dr. Cooper has an interesting note from an extreme locality: "At several points in the valley of the Bitterroot River, I heard and saw at a distance what I took for the Bobolink, the flight and flying-call exactly resembling that bird's. At Cœur d'Alene Mission I again met with it, but could not get near enough to shoot it or determine the species, though they frequented a wheat-field for several mornings. I know no bird likely to be mistaken for it, and, having been found at Fort Bridger, a few probably go north to 47° 30′, as they go to latitude 54° east of the mountains." The westward extension of several eastern birds in this latitude is apparently an indication of the oblique westward trend of the Eastern Province, which reaches the Pacific in Alaska. It breeds very abundantly, in June, on the prairies bordering the Red River of the North, to 49° at least.

The Bobolink makes a rude and flimsy nest of dried grass on the ground, and lays four or five eggs, 0.85 long by about 0.63 broad, dull bluish-white, sometimes brownish-white, spotted and blotched with dark chocolate or blackish-brown surface-marks, and others of paler hue in the shell. The general effect is much as in *Passerculus*, or *Pooëcetes*, but the variability is very great. The nest is cunningly hidden, and often further screened from threatened observation by ingenious devices of the parents.

It appears to me most probable that this species and the Cow-bird will require removal from the family *Icteridœ*, where they have long rested, to a position nearer that assigned by the original and several early describers.

MOLOTHRUS PECORIS, (Gm.) Sw.

Cow-bird; Cowpen-bird; Cow-Blackbird.

a. *pecoris*.

Fringilla pecoris, GM., Syst. Nat. i, 1788, 910 (♀).—LATH., Ind. Orn. ii, 1790, 443.—
   LICHT.,̈ Verz. 1823, Nos. 230, 231.—SABINE, Frankl. Journ. 676. (*F. virginiana* of
   Brisson; Cowpen Finch of *Pennant*, Arct, Zool. ii, 371, No. 241.)
Emberiza pecoris, WILS., Am. Orn. ii, 1810, 145, pl. 18, figs. 1, 2, 3.
Passerina pecoris, VIEILL., Nouv. Dict. d'Hist. Nat. xxv, 1819, 22.
Icterus pecoris, BP., Obs. Wils. 1824, No. 88; Syn. 1828, 53.—NUTT., Man. i, 1832, 178.—
   AUD., Orn. Biog. i, 1831, 493 ; v, 1839, 233, 400; pls. 99, 424.
"*Psarocolius pecoris*, WAGL., Syst. Av. 1827, No. 30" (*fide Cabanis*).
Molothrus pecoris, SW. & RICH., F. B. A. ii, 1831, 277.—BP., List. 1838, 29; Consp. i, 1850,
   436.—AUD., Syn. 1839, 139; B. Am. iv, 1842, 16, pl. 212.—GIR., B. L. I. 1844,
   139.—BD., B. N. A. 1858, 524.—TRIPPE, Am. Nat. iii, 1869, 291 (biography).—
   STEV., U. S. Geol. Surv. Ter. 1870, 465.—COUES, Key, 1872, 155.—B. B. & R., N.
   A. B. ii, 1874, 154, pl. 32, f. 6, 7 ; and of writers generally.
Molobrus pecoris, SUNDEVALL, Meth. Nat. Av. Disp. Tentamen, 1872, 22 (after CAB.,
   Mus. Hein. 192).
Molothrus ater, GRAY, Hand-list, ii, 1870, 36, No. 6507 (after BODD., Pl. Enl. 606, fig. 1).
"*Oriolus fuscus*, GM., Syst. Nat. i, 1788, 303" (thus identified by *Cabanis* and *Gray*;
   queried by *Baird*; probably belongs here).
"*Oriolus minor*, GM., Syst. Nat. i, 1788, 394 " (*apud Cabanis* and *Cassin*); also of *Latham*.
"*Icterus emberizoides*, DAUDIN " (*fide Gray* and *Cabanis*).
Fringilla ambigua, NUTT., Man. i, 1832, 484 (unquestionably !).

b. *obscurus*.

Sturnus obscurus, GM., Syst. Nat. i, 1788, 804 (*S. nova-hispaniæ*, BRISS., ii, 448).
Sturnus junceti, LATH., Ind. Orn. ii, 1790, 326 (= *S. obscurus*, GM.)
Molothrus obscurus, CASS., Pr. Phila. Acad. 1866, 18 (Lower California and Mexico).—
   COOP., B. Cal. i, 1870, 260.—GRAY, Hand-list, ii, 1870, 36, No. 6508.
Molothrus pecoris, var. *obscurus*, COUES, Key, 1872, 155 (Arizona and southward).—B. B.
   & R., N. A. B. ii, 1874, 154 (in text), pl. 32, f. 8.
Molothrus pecoris, (?) SCL., P. Z. S. 1857, 213 ; 1859, 365; 1860, 252.—COUES, Pr. Phila.
   Acad. 1866, 90.

Hab.—The typical form throughout temperate North America (excepting Pacific coast?). North to 68°. Breeds abundantly from about 35° northward, and winters in great numbers in the Southern States. Var. *obscurus* in Arizona, Lower California, and southward.

  Lieutenant Warren's Expedition.—4355, Fort Pierre ; 4365, 5368, mouth of the Yellowstone ; 5327, Medicine Hill ; 9334, 9336-7, Loup Fork.
  Later Expeditions.—60450, La Bonté Creek, Wyoming.

  The bird I have designated as var. *obscurus*, or the Dwarf Cow-bird, as above, and also in the Key, is strikingly smaller than the typical form. Indeed, Mr. Cassin was led to make it a distinct species, which, however, it is not. It is precisely like the ordinary bird in color, but is much smaller, the male only about equaling the female of true *pecoris*. The female of var. *obscurus* is under 7 inches long, with the wing about 3⅛, and the tail 2½ ; the female of *pecoris* is 7 to 7½ inches long, the wing nearly 4, the tail nearly 3 ; while an average male *pecoris* measures full 8 inches, the wing over 4, and the tail over 3.

  Earlier authors described the Cow-bird under a variety of names, and not always accurately, causing uncertainty if not confusion. But we may be reasonably sure that *pecoris*, the name usually adopted, is not the one having priority. Turning back a few pages of Gmelin, from p. 910 (*pecoris*), we find on p. 804 a certain *Sturnus obscurus*, evidently a Cow-bird, and usually held identical with *pecoris*, but which, from the reference to *S. novæ-hispaniæ* of Brisson, is the dwarf Mexican form. So far as this goes, the above quotations ought in strictness to be reversed, giving us *Molothrus obscurus* and *M. obscurus* var. *pecoris*. But back still further in Gmelin, we find *Oriolus minor* (p. 394) and *O. fuscus* (p. 393), both probably Cow-birds. It appears, however, that we need not employ any of Gmelin's names ; for, according to Mr. G. R. Gray, the *ater* of Boddært is this species, and antedates them all. It would appear, therefore, that the proper name of the species is *Molothrus ater* (BODD.), GRAY, and of its variety, *M. ater* var. *obscurus* (GM.), COUES. Even the generic name has given trouble, for both Cabanis and Sundevall understand, upon philological grounds, that Swainson should have written *Molobrus* instead of *Molothrus*.

There is no doubt whatever that the *Fringilla ambigua* of Nuttall. which Audubon once* hastily surmised to be a young White-crowned Sparrow, is nothing but a very young Cow-bird, as questioningly suggested by Baird. A newly-feathered bird in my cabinet, shot in the middle of July, at Washington, answers perfectly to Nuttall's description.

Parasitism, in the zoological sense of the term a frequent condition of lower forms of life, is sufficiently rare among higher animals to excite special interest; and the exceptional absence of the strong parental instincts of birds is particularly noteworthy. Considering that conscious volition—that choice, in a word—determines the whole process of perpetuation of the species in the Cow-bird, denying all but the purely sexual of conjugal relations, abrogating parental relations, and rendering family relations impossible, we must concede a case of parasitism having almost an ethical significance, to such an extreme is it pushed. Certain low organisms, like the *Entozoa*, for example, only exist under conditions fulfilled within the bodies of higher animals, presenting a case not so widely different from that exhibited in the relation between a plant-germ and the soil in which it grows; but they work detriment to their host, and even its death, by the irritation of their presence in myriads, or their actual consumption of substance, and in this respect are more exactly comparable to the true epiphytes, like the mistletoe, drawing sap directly from the other plants upon which they fix. Another kind of parasitism is illustrated by numerous insects, sometimes designated as *Epizoa*, which are independent organisms, self-supporting, yet habitually seeking to live upon other animals. Such answer more nearly to the peculiar signification of a parasite, in its etymological sense of an " uninvited guest," than the *Entozoa* do, and lead up to cases of parasitism in its literal signification. Among mammals we have pure parasitism in the asserted relations of the jackal and lion, the former being literally "beside the table" of the latter. The Jaegers are similarly and more forcibly parasitic, feeding at the expense and to the annoyance of Gulls; so are some Gulls, in their turn, parasites of the Pelicans, picking small fry out of the very beak of these industrious fishers. The Bald Eagle is a bold parasite of the Osprey, accomplishing by violence what is usually done by intrigue. But all such cases relate simply to procuring of food; only a few extremely "advanced thinkers" among birds and the human species dispense with family ties, duties, and delights, throwing the burthensome results of their sexual propensities upon society. It is not difficult to trace, in either case, the demoralizing effect upon the individuals themselves, or the mischief wrought at large. But it may be straining an analogy to compare cases, however similar, in one of which resides a moral quality which we must presume to be absent in the other.

However this may be, it is singular that this particular kind of parasitism should occur in the isolated cases of birds so unlike, as Cuckoos and Cow-birds, and only there, so far as we know. The egg of the Cow-bird is less than an inch long, by about two-thirds of an inch wide; it varies a great deal in size, as is seen on comparing any large series. Given the existence of the habit of laying in other birds' nests, we should have anticipated its occurrence throughout some particular group, rather than its seemingly "sporadic" character. But there are no accidents in the order of nature; if we could but see far enough, not

---

* 8vo ed. iii, 159. But later (iv, 20) he says that the young Cow-bird from which he made his drawing was sent to him by Nuttall, and that it was the *same specimen* as that described by Nuttall as the "Ambiguous Sparrow"—" nothing else than a young Cow-pen-bird, scarcely fledged."

only would the connection between the habits of the Cow-bird and
Cuckoo be plain, but we should discern how such peculiar modifications of its instinct were effected. The production of the traits in
question is a theme fruitful of speculation, if not of solid information.
Ages ago, it might be surmised, a female Cow-bird, in imminent danger
of delivery without a nest prepared, was loth to lose her offspring, and
deposited her burthen in an alien nest, perhaps of her own species,
rather than on the ground. The convenience of this process may have
struck her, and induced her to repeat the easy experiment. The found-
lings duly hatched, throve, and came to maturity, stamped with their
mother's individual traits—an impress deep and lasting enough to similarly affect them in turn. The adventitious birds increased by natural
multiplication, till they outnumbered the true-born ones; what was en-
gendered of necessity was perpetuated by unconscious volition, and
finally became a fixed habit—the law of reproduction for the species.
Much current reasoning on similar subjects is no better nor worse than
this, and it all goes for what it is worth.

There are several species of the genus *Molothrus* in the warmer parts
of America; their habits, so far as we know, are like those of our representative. The position of the genus is a little uncertain; it has strong
affinity with the Blackbirds (*Icteridæ*), yet it is difficult to see in what
respects it differs from certain fringilline birds. But in any event, there
is nothing whatever in the structure of the birds to give a hint of their
peculiar habits. Attending the central fact of reproductive parasitism
are numerous circumstances worthy of attention, since they all tend to
insure the perpetuation of these species under anomalous conditions,
and react against the multiplication of the various birds which are
selected as foster-parents. It is mysterious, indeed; the infliction is
certainly an unmitigated evil to the birds who are drawn into the connection, and yet we cannot rationally conceive of the existence of such
thing, except as a means of some greater good. Can it not be possible
that this special check upon the increase of certain kinds of birds preserves the delicate balance of some of Nature's forces?

I do not feel at all sure that the small relative size of the Cow-bird's
egg should be accounted a circumstance favorable to the bird, as some
have believed, reasoning that a larger egg could not be adequately incubated by the small species usually selected as nurses. No *à priori*
reason appears why the egg should not have been of ordinary dimensions, and a different series of birds been called upon to incubate it;
while, as the facts stand, it is clear that the *bigness* of the egg, in comparison with those among which it is usually deposited, and not its
smallness relative to the Cow-bird's bulk, is the favoring element. For
the larger egg must mechanically obstruct the incubation of the smaller
ones, and so receive the greater share of warmth from the bird's body.
But perhaps both the circumstances may be brought into reasonable
connection. Were the Cow-bird's egg of ordinary dimensions relative
to the bulk of the species, it might be susceptible of successful incubation only by other birds large enough to remove or destroy it, as would
certainly be done when practicable; it is therefore unusually small, in
order that it may be committed to the charge of birds able to hatch it,
yet too weak to eject it; and now its superiority in size to the eggs of
such birds becomes a favorable circumstance.

It is stated that the Cow-bird's egg hatches sooner than that of most
birds, the period of incubation being not over ten days. But I am not
aware that the evidence in this case is either sufficient, explicit, or precise; it would be well to have it checked by many additional observa-

tions. A difficulty, not usually recognized, meets us here, in the variable circumstances of incubation. An egg habitually intrusted to numerous different birds, from the size of a Thrush down to that of the tiny Blue-gray Gnatcatcher, is necessarily subjected to a varying temperature (within, however, narrow limits), hastening or retarding development of the embryo ; even the material of so many different nests, considered as conductors of heat, may exercise a slight disturbing influence. Under these fluctuating circumstances the duration of incubation may yet be proven inconstant ; and it cannot be supposed to bear a single definite relation to that of each of the birds concerned. Of its prior maturity, as a rule, however, there seems to be no doubt, and the resulting advantage is obvious. The young Cow-bird immediately demands and receives attention, so that incubation of the other eggs may remain unfinished ; and if the latter are hatched, the chances of the younger and weaker birds against the alien are very problematical. They may be trampled to death, or smothered, even if they are not forcibly ejected ; and they generally fail to receive sufficient nourishment, of which the lion's share falls to the intruder.

There is another and a very singular element of success for the Cow-bird. However indignant and despairing the nurses may be supposed to feel about it at first, they generally make a virtue of necessity ; and when they have once made up their minds to accept the unpleasant situation, they do their whole duty by it, even to the neglect of their rightful offspring. As not unfrequently occurs in other cases, they become, so far as we can judge by their actions, really fond of the foundling, and, at any rate, they give assiduous attention to its wants, and care for it as tenderly as if it were their own.

It does not appear that the Cow-bird ever attempts to take forcible possession of a nest. She watches her chance while the owners are away, slips in by stealth, and leaves the evidence of her unfriendly visit to be discovered on their return, in the shape of the ominous egg. The parents hold anxious consultation in this emergency, as their sorrowful cries and disturbed actions plainly indicate. If their nest was empty before, they generally desert it, and their courage in giving up a cosy home results in one Cow-bird the less. Sometimes even after there is an egg of their own in the nest, they have nerve enough to let it go, rather than assume the hateful task of incubating the strange one. But if the female has already laid an egg or two, the pair generally settle into the reluctant conviction that there is no help for it ; they quiet down after awhile, and things go on as if nothing had happened. Not always, however, will they desert even an empty nest ; some birds have discovered a way out of the difficulty—it is the most ingenious device imaginable, and the more we think about it the more astonishing it seems. They build a two-story nest, leaving the obnoxious egg in the basement. I want no better proof that birds possess a faculty indistinguishable, so far as it goes, from human reason ; and such a case as this bears impressively upon the general question of the difference between reason and that faculty we designate by the vague and misleading term "instinct." The evidence has accumulated till it has become conclusive, that the difference is one of degree, not of kind—that instinct is a lower order of reason—the arrest, in brutes, at a certain stage, of a faculty reaching higher development in man. Instinct, in the ill-considered current sense of term, could never lead a Summer Yellowbird up to building a two-story nest to let a Cow-bird's eggs addle below. Such "instinct" is merely force of habit, inherited or acquired—a sum of tendencies operating unknowingly and uniformly upon the same recurring circumstances, devoid of conscious design, lacking recognized prevision; totally inadequate to the requirements of the first special emergency. What bird, possessed of only such a faculty as this, could build a two-story nest to get rid of an objectionable deposit in the original single-story fabric? It argues as intelligent a design as was ever indicated in the erection of a building by a human being. No question of inherited tendency enters here; and if it did, the issue would be only set back a step no nearer determination, for there must have been an original double nest, the result of an original idea. Nor is this wonderful fore-thought very rarely exhibited; considering what proportion the double nests discovered bear to the ordinary ones brought to our notice, among the millions annually constructed, we can easily believe that the inge-nious device is in fact a frequent resort of the birds plagued by the Cow-bunting. And how can we sufficiently admire the perseverance and energy of a bird which, having once safely shut up the terrible egg in her cellar, and then having found another one violating her premises, *forthwith built a third story?* She deserved better of fate than that her house should at last be despoiled by a naturalist. This was a Summer Yellowbird, to whom the price of passing thus into history must have seemed hard.

The Cow-bird's foster-parents are numerous; the list of those so deter-mined is already large, and when completed will probably comprise pretty much all of the species nesting within the Cow-bird's breeding range, from the size of a Thrush down to that of the Gnatcatcher. It is unnecessary to recite the long list; I will mention, however, the Wood Thrush, Yellow-breasted Chat, and Towhee Bunting, as showing that the foster-birds are not always *smaller* than the Cow-bird itself. The Summer Yellowbird, the Maryland Yellow-throat, and the Red-eyed Vireo, are among those most persistently victimized. On the prairies of the west, where the Cow-birds are very numerous, and breeding birds restricted in number of species if not of individuals, I had almost said that in a majority of the nests taken in June will be found a Cow-bird's egg.

In the nature of the case it is impossible to say what is the normal number of eggs usually deposited each season by a single bird—that is if more than one be laid, as is probable. We can only presume, quite reasonably, that the laying is of four or five eggs, as usual among the allied species. Neither do we know whether the same individual ever deposits more than one egg in the same nest—at least I am not aware of observations on this score, and they would be necessarily very diffi-cult, if not impossible, to make. Finding several Cow-bird's eggs in a nest, as frequently happens, proves nothing to this effect, for the same nest might easily enough be used by different Cow-birds in succession. It is rare to find more than two of the alien eggs together; I have found three in a Towhee-Bunting's nest, and even *five* have been discovered in the same nest. Singularly enough, these unusual numbers were in the nest of the same species. Thus Mr. T. Martin Trippe, in his inter-esting article on the Cow-bird (Am. Nat. iii, 291), cites a remarkable case: "I never heard of more than two instances where there were more than two eggs of the Cow-bird in a single nest. Prof. Baird and Dr. Brewer once found three eggs in the nest of a Black-and-white Creeper, and I once had the good fortune to discover a nest of the same bird containing *five* eggs of the parasite, together with three of her own. In the latter case incubation had begun, and all of the eggs contained em-bryos." We may consider this pair of Creepers relieved, on the whole, by Mr. Trippe's visit—the mother-bird rescued from drowning in the inundation of so many "well-springs," and the father saved the necessity of hanging himself from the nearest convenient crotch.

It is interesting to observe the female Cow-bird ready to lay. She becomes disquieted; she betrays unwonted excitement, and ceases her busy search for food with her companions. At length she separates from the flock, and sallies forth to reconnoitre, anxiously indeed, for her case is urgent, and she has no home. How obstrusive is the sad analogy! She flies to some thicket, or hedge-row, or other common resort of birds, where, something teaches her—perhaps experience—nests will be found. Stealthily and in perfect silence she flits along, peering furtively, alternately elated or dejected, into the depths of the foliage. She espies a nest, but the owner's head peeps over the brim, and she must pass on. Now, however, comes her chance; there is the very nest she wishes, and no one at home. She disappears for a few minutes, and it is almost another bird that comes out of the bush. Her business done, and trouble over, she chuckles her self-gratulations, rustles her plumage to adjust it trimly, and flies back to her associates. They know what has happened, but are discreet enough to say nothing—charity is often no less wise than kind.

Polygamy is rare among higher birds; in no creatures are the parental and conjugal instincts more strongly developed or beautifully displayed. But the Cow-bird illustrates this mode of life, and not in the lordly manner of the barn-yard cock, so devoted to his harem, so gallant and just to all. As in this species there is no love of offspring, neither can there be conjugal affection; all family ties are dispensed with. The association is a mere herding together in quest of food in similar resorts. The Cow-birds never mate; their most intimate relations are no sooner effected than forgotten; not even the decent restrictions of a seraglio are observed; it is a perfect community of free-lovers, who do as the original Cynics did. The necessary courtship becomes in consequence a curiously mixed affair. During the period corresponding to the mating season of orderly birds, the patriarchs of the sorry crew mount up the trees and fences, to do what they call their singing. They posture and turn about, and ruffle their feathers to look bigger than Nature made them; if their skins were not tough they would certainly burst with vanity. They puff out their throats and pipe the most singular notes, perhaps honestly wishing to please their companions of the other sex—at any rate, to their own satisfaction. Meanwhile the females are perched near by, but without seeming very enthusiastic—rather taking it all as a matter of course, listening at times, it may be, but just as likely preening their plumage, with other thoughts and an ulterior purpose. The performance over, it is a very little while afterward when the whole band goes trooping after food in the nearest cattle-yard or pasture.

Cow-birds appear to be particularly abundant in the West; more so, perhaps, than they really are, for the numbers that in the East spread equally over large areas are here drawn within small compass, owing to lack of attractions abroad. Every wagon-train passing over the prairies in summer is attended by flocks of the birds; every camp and stock-corral, permanent or temporary, is besieged by the busy birds, eager to glean subsistence from the wasted forage. Their familiarity under these circumstances is surprising. Perpetually wandering about the feet of the draught-animals, or perching upon their backs, they become so accustomed to man's presence that they will hardly get out of the way. I have even known a young bird to suffer itself to be taken in hand, and it is no uncommon thing to have the birds fluttering within a few feet of one's head. The animals appear to rather like the birds, and suffer them to perch in a row upon their back-bones, doubtless finding the scratching of their feet a comfortable sensation, to say nothing of the riddance from insect parasites.

A singular point in the history of this species is its unexplained disappearance, generally in July, from many or most localities in which it breeds. Where it goes, and for what purpose, are unknown; but the fact is attested by numerous observers. Sometimes it reappears in September in the same places, sometimes not. Thus, in Northern Dakota, I saw none after early in August.

AGELÆUS PHŒNICEUS, (Linn.) Vieill.

Red-winged Blackbird.

a. *phœniceus.*

Oriolus phœniceus, LINN., Syst. Nat. i, 1766, 161.—GM., Syst. Nat. i, 1788, 386.—LATH., Ind. Orn. i, 1790, 428.
Agelœus phœniceus, VIEILL., "Analyse, 1816."—Nouv. Dict. d'Hist. Nat. xxxiv, 539.— GRAY, Gen. of B. ii, 347 ; List of Brit. B. 1863, 92 (said to be accidental in England).—SW. & RICH., F. B. A. ii, 1831, 280.—BP., List, 1838, 30 ; Consp. i, 1850, 430.—AUD., Syn. 1839, 141 ; B. Am. iv, 1842, 31, 216.—GIR., B. L. I. 1844, 141.—WOODH., Sitgr. Rep. 1853, 80.—SCL., P. Z. S. 1857, 205 ; 1859, 58, 381 ; Cat. 1862, 133 (Orizaba ; Guatemala).—SCL. & SALV., Ibis, i, 1859, 19 (Guatemala).—DRESS., Ibis, 1865, 492 (Texas).—MAXIM., J. f. O. vi, 1858, 263.—BD., B. N. A. 1858, 526 ; Mex. B. Surv. ii; 1859, pt. ii, 18.—KENN., P. R. R. Rep. x, 1859, iv, 30.—BRYANT, Pr. Bost. Soc. vii, 1859 (Bahamas).—COOP. & SUCK., N. H. Wash. Ter. 1860, 207.—HAYD., Rep. 1862, 169.—CASS., Pr. Phila. Acad. 1866, 90.—LAWR., Ann. Lyc. N. Y. ix, 1868, 104 (Costa Rica).—SUMICH., Mem. Bost. Soc. i, 1869, 553 (Orizaba).—COOP., B. Cal. i, 1870, 261.—TRIPPE, Pr. Ess. Inst. vi, 1871, 117 (Minnesota).—ALLEN, Bull. M. C. Z. ii, 1871, 284 (Florida); iii, 1872, 178 (Kansas to Utah).—STEV., U. S. Geol. Surv. Ter. 1870, 465.— MERR., *ibid.* 1872, 686.—SNOW, B. Kans. 1873, 8.—COUES, Pr. Phila. Acad. 1866, 90 (Arizona) ; Key, 1872, 156, pl. 4.—B. B. & R., N. A. B. ii, 1874, 159, pl. 33, f. 1, 2, 3 ; and of late authors generally.
Icterus phœniceus, DAUD.—LICHT., Verz. 1823, No. 128.—BP., Obs. Wils. 1825, No. 68 ; Syn. 1828, 52.—NUTT., Man. i, 1832, 169.—AUD., Orn. Biog. i, 1831, 348 ; v, 1839, 487 ; pl. 67.
Psarocolius phœniceus, WAGL., Syst. Av. 1827, No. 10.
Sturnus predatorius, WILS., Am. Orn. iv, 1811, 30, pl. 30, fig. 1.

b. *assimilis.*

Agelaius assimilis, GUNDL., J. f. O. iv, 12 ; Pr. Bost. Soc. vi, 316 (Cuba, breeding).
Agelœus phœniceus var. *assimilis*, B. B. & R., N. A. B. ii, 1874, 159.

c. *gubernator.*

Psarocolius gubernator, WAGL., Isis, 1832, 281.
Agelaius gubernator, BP., Comp. and Geog. List. 1838, 30 ; Consp. i, 1850, 430.—AUD., Syn. 1839, 141 ; B. Am. iv, 1842, 29, pl. 215.—WOODH., Sitgr. Rep. 1853, 89 (California).—SCL., P. Z. S. 1857, 127, 213 ; 1859, 365 ; Cat. 1862, 136 (Xalapa).— NEWB., P. R. R. Rep. vi, 1857, 86 (California).—BD., *ibid.* ix, 529.—KENN., *ibid.* x, 1859, pt. iv, 31.—HEERM., *ibid.* pt. vi, 53.—COOP., B. Cal. i, 1870, 263.
Icterus gubernator, NUTT., Man. i, 2d ed. 1840, 187.
Agelœus phœniceus var. *gubernator*, COUES, Key, 1872, 156.—B. B. & R., N. A. B. ii, 1874, 163, pl. 33, f. 4, 8.

d. *tricolor.*

Icterus tricolor, NUTT., Man. i, 2d ed. 1840, 186.—AUD., Orn. Biog. v, 1839, 6, pl. 388.
Agelœus tricolor, BP., Comp. and Geog. List, 1838, 30 ; Consp. i, 1850, 430.—AUD., Syn. 1839, 141 ; B. Am. iv, 1842, 27, pl. 214.—WOODH., Sitgr. Rep. 1853, 80.—NEWB., P. R. R. Rep. vi, 1857, 86.—BD., *ibid.* ix, 1858, 530 ; Mex. B. Surv. ii, 1859, pt. ii, 18 (Colorado River).—CASS., Pr. Phila. Acad. 1866.—COOP., B. Cal. i, 1870, 265.— B. B. & R., N. A. B., ii, 1874, 165, pl. 33, f. 5, 6, 7.
Agelœus phœniceus var. *tricolor*, COUES, Key, 1872, 156.

Hab.—The typical form throughout temperate North America, and south to Central America. Breeds in suitable places from Texas to the Saskatchewan, and along the whole Atlantic coast. Winters from about 35° southward. Said to have occurred in England. Var. *assimilis* in Cuba. Var. *gubernator* along the Pacific coast, from British Columbia into Mexico. Var. *tricolor* resident in California.

Lieutenant Warren's Expedition.—4757, Big Nemaha; 5325–26, Medicine Creek; 9332, 9331, 9339, 9333, 9330, along the Platte.

Later Expeditions.—61058–89, Green River; 61725–56, Ogden, Utah.

We have been furnished by Mr. Allen with elaborate tables of measurements, showing the sexual and individual differences in size and proportions of specimens from the same locality, as well as the variation in the same respects, according to geographical distribution. The difference in size consists in the inferiority of southern birds, according to a well understood law; it is coupled, as usual, also, with attenuation of the bill. In color, southern birds differ in the more intense lustre of the black and brighter red. Following are the dimensions; the numbers in parentheses are the several averages. Massachusetts males: Length, 8.40 to 9.85 (9.16); extent, 13.95 to 15.35 (14.71); wing, 4.43 to 5.00 (4.69); tail, 3.12 to 3.90 (3.63); bill, 0.75 to 0.91 (0.88). Massachusetts females: Length, 7.35 to 8.55 (7.53); extent, 11.25 to 13.55 (12.24); wing, 3.63 to 4.26 (3.86); tail, 2.65 to 3.15 (2.93); bill, 0.70 to 0.82 (0.75). Southern males: Length, 8.25 to 9.55 (9.02); extent, 13.60 to 14.90 (14.41); wing, 4.34 to 4.80 (4.62); tail, 3.35 to 3.90 (3.61); bill, 0.85 to 1.00 (0.91). Southern females: Length, 7.50 to 8.00 (7.73); extent, 11.85 to 12.85 (12.44); wing, 3.63 to 3.90 (3.83); tail, 2.75 to 3.20 (2.99). Californian specimens are correspondent. Independent of all extrinsic influences, the normal inherent variation in dimensions amounts to fifteen per cent.

The so-called species, *A. gubernator*, has not the slightest claim to specific rank—in fact it can hardly be rated as a fair variety. Of the same size and shape as ordinary *phœniceus*, with the same scarlet carpus, it only differs, in extreme cases, in not having this red bordered with tawny. This is produced by the restriction of the brownish-yellow of the middle wing-coverts (in *phœniceus* occupying the whole length of these feathers) to the basal portion of the feathers, their projecting ends being black, and so failing to produce a tawny bordering of the red. But every imaginable stage is a matter of observation in different specimens, from one extreme to the other; and in some cases of *phœniceus* most of the greater coverts are likewise tawny, producing a brownish-yellow patch, nearly as large as the scarlet one itself.

Var. *tricolor* is better marked, in its smaller size and attenuated bill (thus agreeing, however, with Floridan *phœniceus*), dark blood-red wing-patch, and pure white border. The better distinction in this case corresponds to the geographical restriction and comparative isolation of this local race. That it is no more, however, than a variety, seems fairly inferable; the difference in the shade of red is no greater than that observable in specimens of *phœniceus* proper, while the bordering of the red in the latter is sometimes nearly pure white.

The Red-shouldered Marsh Blackbird is of common occurrence in all suitable places throughout the Missouri region; but from its nature it is somewhat localized, being found only in wooded and watered portions, except while journeying; and I am not aware that it ever gathers in such vast numbers as throng the more congenial marshy tracts of the Eastern States. Some modification in habits is the necessary result of topographical as well as climatic changes, which birds experience in their ordinarily extensive dispersion. In Arizona, for instance, I found Redwings common in the pine-woods, miles away from any water, excepting a tiny mountain stream that afforded no special conveniences for them.

The Tricolor variety is extremely abundant and resident in the fertile portions of Southern California. It very rarely crosses the intermediate desert to the Colorado River; this arid tract forming a barrier to the eastward progress of many species, of great efficacy in distinguishing the littoral fauna from that of the Colorado Valley. One who has traveled this region will not be surprised that birds with any fancy for green, watery places, decline the same journey. At Wilmington and Drumm Barracks I found the Tricolors flocking in vast numbers, in November. They thronged the streets of the town, and covered the military parade-ground; alone, so far as their congeners were concerned, but on intimate association with hundreds of Brewer's Blackbirds. Both species were almost as tame as poultry, and the boys used to stone them, to their mutual amusement, I should say, for the birds were never hit, and rather seemed to like the sport. Often, as I sat in my quarters on a bright sunny day, the light would be suddenly obscured, just as by a quickly passing cloud, and a rushing noise ensued as the compact flock swirled past the window. They often alighted by hundreds on the roofs of the barracks, almost hiding the shingles, and every picket of a long paling fence near by would sometimes be capped by its bird. They were very noisy, chattering from daylight till dark—all the time they could see to fly about. Nobody troubled them much; but Hawks of various kinds—the Harrier, the Western Red-breast, and the Lanier—were continually dashing in among them, with terrible swooping, bringing death to not a few, and dismay everywhere. At this season the sexes kept mostly apart; the flocks of males seemed to largely outnumber the females. Very few of those I shot and examined were in perfect plumage, much of the black being varied with different shades of brown and yellowish, and the white wing-bar being imperfect. In spring the birds resort together to marshy spots, breeding in loose communities. The nests and eggs do not differ appreciably from those of the common Redwing.

XANTHOCEPHALUS ICTEROCEPHALUS, (Bp.) Bd.

Yellow-headed Blackbird.

Icterus icterocephalus, BP., Am. Orn. i, 1835, 27, pl. 3.—NUTT., Man. i, 1832, 176; 2d ed. 1840, 187.
Agelæus icterocephalus, CAB., Mus. Hein. i, 1851, 188.
Xanthocephalus icterocephalus, BD., B. N. A. 1858, 531; Mex. B. Surv. ii, 1859, pt. ii, 18.— CASS., Pr. Phila. Acad. 1866, 11 (several near Philadelphia).—COUES, Pr. Phila. Acad. 1866, 91 (New Mexico and Arizona).—DRESS., Ibis, 1865, 492.—COUES, Am. Nat. v, 1871, 195 (biography).—COOP., B. Cal. i, 1870, 267.—SNOW, B. Kans. (breeding).—ALLEN, Am. Nat. iii, 1869, 636 (Watertown, Mass.).—MAYN., Guide, 1870, 122 (same case).—ALLEN, Bull. M. C. Z. iii, 1872, 178 (Kansas to Utah).—ALLEN, Mem. Bost. Soc. i, 1868, 498 (Iowa); 518 (Illinois).—TURNB., B. E. Pa. 43 (casual).—STEV., U. S. Geol. Surv. Ter. 1870, 465.—MERR., *ibid.* 1872, 686.—SNOW, B. Kans. 1873, 8.—AIKEN, Pr. Bost. Soc. 1872, 202 (Wyoming).—COUES, Key, 1872, 156, fig. 98.—B. B. & R., N. A. B. ii, 1874, 167, pl. 32, f. 9, pl. 33, f. 9.
Icterus xanthocephalus, BP., Journ. Phila. Acad. v, 1826, 222; Syn. 1828, 52.—AUD., Orn. Biog. v, 1839, 6, pl. 388.
Agelaius xanthocephalus, SW. & RICH., F. B. A. ii, 1831, 281 (north to 58°).—BP., List, 1838, 29.—AUD., Syn. 1839, 140.—AUD., B. Am. iv, 1842, 24, pl. 213.—WOODH., Sitgr. Rep. 1853, 80.—NEWB., P. R. R. Rep. vi, 1857, 86.—HEERM., *ibid.* x, 1859, pt. vi, 52.—MAXIM., J. f. O. vi, 1858, 261.—TRIPPE, Pr. Ess. Inst. vi, 1871, 117 (Minnesota).
Agelaius longipes, SW., Syn. Mex. B. in Philos. Mag. i, 1827, 436, No. 57.
Icterus perspicillatus, LICHT., "Mus. Berol."
Psarocolius perspicillatus, WAGL., Isis, 1829, 758.
Xanthocephalus perspicillatus, BP., Consp. i, 1850, 431.
Agelæus perspicillatus, REINH., Ibis, iii, 1861, 7 (Nenortalik, Greenland, Sept. 2, 1820).
"*Icterus frenatus*, LICHT., Isis, 1843, 59.—REINH., Kroyer's Tidskrift, iv; Vidensk. Meddel. for 1853 (1854), 82 (Greenland)."

Hab.—Western North America. North to the Saskatchewan and Red River (*Richardson*). East regularly to Iowa and Illinois (*Allen*), and Wisconsin (*Coues*). Casually to Greenland (*Reinhardt*), Pennsylvania (*Cassin, Turnbull*), and Massachusetts (*Allen*). West to the Pacific. South into Mexico. Cape Saint Lucas, Florida (Mus. S. I.). Cuba (CAB., J. f. O. vii, 1857, 350).

List of specimens.

19367	....	Devil's Gate...	♂	May 15, 1860	G. H. Trook.	10.75	17.25	......
19368	....	Sweetwater ...	....	May 17, 1860	......do	......	......	......

Lieutenant Warren's Expedition.—5323, near Fort Pierre.
Later Expeditions.—60737, Green River; 61783-4, 61786-7, Idaho.

I am inclined to agree with Dr. Cabanis and others, that it is unnecessary to separate this species generally from *Agelæus*. In form it differs from the latter only very slightly, and its general economy is the same.

The eastward extension of the species is greater than was not long since supposed. Essentially a prairie bird, it reaches regularly the flat open portions of the States immediately east of the Mississippi, occurring in Minnesota, Iowa, Missouri, Wisconsin, and Illinois, if not also more rarely in Michigan and Ohio. Its presence in Greenland is doubtless casual; all the above quotations appear to relate to a single instance. Other exceptional records are above quoted for Massachusetts and Pennsylvania. Mr. Allen says a specimen was taken near Watertown, in October, 1869, by Mr. Maynard; and Mr. Turnbull says "Dr. Jackson mentions that this species is occasionally seen along the Alleghany Mountains, where a flock appeared in 1857. Mr. John Krider. shot a young male near Philadelphia." Allen states that it is "said to breed in great numbers in the Calumet marshes of Illinois," and also in the Skunk River marshes of Iowa. He saw birds in Iowa, in July, about grassy ponds near Boonesboro'. I met with a few on the prairies of Wisconsin, in April, 1864, and the following month found it abundant in Kansas, and again in New Mexico, where thousands were breeding in a marshy place near Laguna, just west of the Rio Grande; they were also seen in Eastern Arizona, but not in such plenty. I do not recollect meeting any in California, but Dr. Cooper states that they are numerous in all the valleys of the State, especially where there are grassy meadows or marshes. "They winter in large numbers in the middle districts, and some wander at that season to the Colorado Valley and San Diego, though I doubt if any pass the summer so far south." He alludes in this connection to Dr. Newberry's finding them swarming about Klamath Lake, and adds, that he never saw them near the Columbia, though they are abundant east of the Rocky Mountains up to 58°. Dr. Heermann mentions the appearance of immense flocks at Fort Inge, Texas. Dr. Woodhouse speaks of its abundance in Texas and the Indian Territory, and states that it winters about San Francisco, in California. I have not seen it higher on the Missouri than Leavenworth, but Dr. Hayden says it is quite common throughout the northwest, in marshy spots on the prairies. Finally, Sir John Richardson gives it as very numerous in the interior of the fur countries, to about 58° in summer, reaching the Saskatchewan by the 20th of May.

The Yellow-headed Blackbird breeds in suitable places throughout the region indicated in the above paragraph. However generally distributed over dry places and even deserts it may be at other seasons, in the breeding time it shows its affinity to the true *Agelæi* by resorting to marshy spots, sometimes by thousands. The nest is placed in a tuft of upright reeds or rank grasses, some of which pass through its walls, fastening it securely, like that of a Marsh Wren, though it may sway with the motion of the rushes. Probably, to render it light enough to be supported on such weak foundation, no mud is used in its composition; the structure is entirely woven and plaited with bits of dried reeds, and long, coarse, aquatic grasses, not lined with any different material, although the inside strands are the finer. The brim of the nest is elevated and somewhat folded over, making a thick, firm edge; but I am not aware that the fabric is ever actually "canopied over like that of the Meadow-lark," as stated by Townsend and repeated by Cooper. The whole thing measures five or six inches across, and is nearly as deep. The eggs may be from three to six in number; two selected specimens measured 1.04 by 0.75, and 1.15 by 0.76. They are pale grayish-green, spotted all over with several shades of reddish-brown, sometimes so thickly, especially at the larger end, as to hide the ground-color. This speckling instead of streaking, is more like that of the eggs of the *Scolecophagi* than of the *Agelæi*. During incubation the males appear to desert their mates, as is certainly the case with the Boat-tailed Grackle. I have found the birds nesting in June, in New Mexico, and during the same month in Northern Dakota.

At other seasons these Blackbirds are very generally dispersed. They gather about stock-yards and corrals, come into the emigrants' camp at evening, and ramble fearlessly among the animals in search of food, often in company with flocks of Cow-birds. They are eminently terrestrial birds, as indicated by their long, strong legs, and large rasorial claws, and always walk or run, instead of hopping on the ground. They retire in cold weather from the northerly portions of their habitat.

STURNELLA MAGNA, (Linn.) Bd.

Meadow-lark; Field-lark.

a. *magna.*

Alauda magna, LINN., Syst. Nat. i, 1758, 167 (*ex Catesby,* pl. 33); 1766, 289.—GM., *ibid.* ed. 13th, 1788, 801.—WILS., Am. Orn. iii, 1811, 20, pl. 19.
Sturnella magna, BD., B. N. A. 1858, 535; and of many late authors.—HAYD., Rep. 1862, 169 (to 43°).—ALLEN, Mem. Bost. Soc. i, 1868, 496.—TRIPPE, Pr. Bost. Soc. xi, 1872, 239 (Iowa).—HART., Brit. B. 1872, 118 (England).—COUES, Key, 1872, 157, fig. 99, and pl. 6, figs. 1, 2, 3, 4.—B. B. & R., N. A. B. ii, 1874, 174, pl. 34, f. 2.
Sturnus ludovicianus, LINN., Syst. Nat. i, 1766, 290.—GM., i, 1788, 802.—LATH., Ind. Orn. i, 1790, 323.—BP., Journ. Phila. Acad. iv, 1824, 180; Syn. 1828.—NUTT., Man. i, 1832, 147.—AUD., Orn. Biog. ii, 1834, 216; v, 1839, 492; pl. 136.
Sturnella ludoviciana, SW., F. B. A. ii, 1831, 282.—BP., List, 1838, 29; Consp. i, 1850, 429.—AUD., Syn. 1839, 148; B. Am. iv, 1842. 70, pl. 223.—CAB., Mus. Hein. i, 1851, 192.—ALLEN, Bull. M. C. Z. ii, 1871, 288.
Sturnella collaris, VIEILL. Anal. 1816; Gal. Ois. i, 1824, 134, pl. 90.
Sturnus collaris, WAGL., Syst. Av. i, 1827, No. 1; Isis, 1831, 527.
Cacicus alaudarius, DAUD., (*fide Cabanis*).

b. *neglecta.*

Sturnella neglecta, AUD., B. Am. vii, 1843, 339, pl. 487.—WOODH., Sitgr. Rep. 1853, 78.—NEWB., P. R. R. Rep. vi, 1857, 86.—BD., B. N. A. 1858, 537.—KENN., P. R. R. Rep. x, 1859, pt. iv, 31.—HEERM., *ibid.* pt. vi, 54.—COOP. & SUCK., N. H. Wash. Ter. 1860, 208.—HAYD., Rep. 1862, 109.—DRESS., Ibis, 1865, 492 (Texas).—CASS., Pr. Phila. Acad. 1866, 23.—COUES, Pr. Phila. Acad. 1866, 91.—COOP., B. Cal. i, 1870, 270.—HOLD., Pr. Bost. Soc. 1872, 203 —TRIPPE, Pr. Bost. Soc. 1872, 239 (Iowa, with the preceding).—STEV., U. S. Geol. Surv. Ter. 1870, 465.—MERR., *ibid.* 1872, 687.—SNOW, B. Kans. 1873, 8.
Sturnella ludoviciana var. *neglecta,* ALLEN, Bull. M. C. Z. iii, 1872, 178.
Sturnella magna var. *neglecta,* COUES, Key, 1872, 157.—B. B. & R., N. A. B. ii, 1874, pl. 34, f. 1.
"(?) *Sturnella hippocrepis,* HEERM., Journ. Phila. Acad. ii, 1853, 269 (Suisun)."

c. *hippocrepis.*

(Cuba.)

Sturnella hippocrepis, WAGL., Isis, 1832, 281.—LAWR., Ann. Lyc. vii, 1860, 266.—SCL., Ibis, 1861, 179; Cat. 1862, 139 (Cuba).—CASS., Pr. Phila. Acad. 1866, 24.
Sturnella magna var. *hippocrepis,* B. B. & R., N. A. B. ii, 1874, 172.

d. *mexicana.*

(Mexico and Central America.)

(?) *Sturnella magna,* SW., Syn. Mex. B. Philos. Mag. i, 1827, 436 (Mexico).
Sturnella hippocrepis, SCL., P. Z. S. 1856, 30, 301; 1859, 58, 365, 381; Cat. 1862, 139.—SCL. & SALV., Ibis, i, 1859, 19; 1860, 34.
Sturnella mexicana, SCL., Ibis, iii, 1861, 179.—LAWR., Ann. Lyc. iii, 1865, 177 (New Granada).—CASS., Pr. Phila. Acad. 1866, 24.
Sturnella magna var. *mexicana,* B. B. & R., N. A. B. ii, 1874, 172.

e. *meridionalis.*

(South America.)

Sturnella ludoviciana, (?) SCL. P. Z. S. 1856, 29, 142.—(?) LAWR., Ann. Lyc. ix, 1868, 104.
Sturnella meridionalis, SCL., Ibis, 1861, 179.—CASS., Pr. Phila. Acad. 1866, 24.
Sturnella magna var. *meridionalis,* B. B. & R., N. A. B. ii, 1874, 172.

Hab.—The typical form in Eastern North America to Nova Scotia, and north to 53°. Breeds throughout its range. Winters from Maryland (sometimes Pennsylvania) southward. (Accidental in England; SCL., Ibis, 1861, 176; LLOYD., The Field, Mar. 11, 1871; HART., Man. Brit. B. 1872, 118.) At the edge of the western prairies begins to shade into var. *neglecta,* which reaches its maximum departure on the dry central plains. Individuals indistinguishable from typical *magna* in Kansas, Iowa, and Eastern Dakota, and reappearing on the moist Pacific coast. Individuals like *neglecta* occur in Pennsylvania. Extralimital races, all inseparably connected, are distributed as above noted.

Lieutenant Warren's Expedition.—a. *magna,* 9325-7, Loup Fork.—b. *neglecta,* 9307, 9312-19, 9321, Loup Fork; 9332, Platte; 4748, 4751, 4752, "Nebraska;" 5334, 5338, Fort Union; 5336, 5341, Yellowstone; 5335, 5339, Fort Pierre; 5330, Fort Lookout; 5329, Little Cheyenne; 4749, The Tower.

Later Expeditions.—var. *neglecta,* 54312-15, 60,444-6, 60738-43, 60808-12, 61060-9, various Wyoming localities; 61732-3, Utah.

Cases like the present have, until very recently, proven stumbling-blocks. All the facts were long in our possession before they received adequate and reasonable explanation; they were simply noted and left as found. It would be a curious and not unprofitable enquiry, how much the progress of philosophic ornithology has been retarded by the trammels of the binomial nomenclature, which practically forced us to either recognize as a species what we now call a race, or sink it into an unmeaning synonym. To cite a striking example in this very case of *Sturnella*: Dr. Cabanis, in 1856; Dr. Finsch, in 1870; and Mr. Allen, in 1871, all came to the same conclusion, that there is but a single species of the genus. But in a synonymical notation of this fact, such as that given by Mr. Allen, Bull. M. C. Z. ii, 288, the differences of race are ignored as completely as the resemblance is brought out. So far as his synonymy goes, all the *Sturnellas* are repeated exactly alike, which is by no means the case. The bringing into general use of the term " var." is a great practical help, albeit an instrument too clumsy for the nice work of the future, we may confidently anticipate. I can to-day foresee naturalists' reversion to a polynomial nomenclature, in which three or more words shall express to a nicety the shades of their zoölogical meaning. Linnæus conferred an inestimable boon upon a century of naturalists; but an effective mode of expressing the ideas then current has proven inadequate for present purposes. I raise my voice emphatically in favor of freedom from the binomial shackles.

I have not personally investigated the relationships of the extralimital forms, but the current views of those who have, accord with my belief. The case of *Sturnella magna neglecta* is settled and explained; *Magna* shades directly into *neglecta,* and develops its peculiarities precisely according to the mean annual rain-fall, and consequently the average humidity of the atmosphere of the regions in which it resides. The change is imperceptibly effected; distinguishable examples sometimes occur together; the characters culminate in the most sterile regions. The peculiarities of *neglecta* are casually exhibited in the East. I was once shown some unlabelled specimens, which I did not hesitate to call "*neglecta,*" and was considerably taken aback on learning they were shot near Philadelphia, by Mr. Krider.

A difference in the song, "attested by all observers from Lewis and Clarke down to the present day," is very curious. My own experience in this matter agrees exactly with that of Mr. Allen, who I will quote: "At the little village of Denison, in Iowa, where I first noticed it in song, it was particularly common, and half-domestic in its habits, preferring, apparently, the streets and grassy lanes, and the immediate vicinity of the village, to the remoter prairie. Here, wholly unmolested and unsuspicious, it collected its food; and the males, from their accustomed perches on the house-tops, daily warbled their wild song for hours together. * * * * The song, however, was so new to me that I did not at first have the slightest suspicion its author was the Western Meadow-lark, as I found it to be, the time being between daylight and sunrise, and the individual in question singing from the top of the court-house. It differs from that of the Meadow-lark in the Eastern States in the notes being louder and wilder, and at the same time more liquid, mellower, and far sweeter. They have a pensiveness and a general character remarkably in harmony with the half-dreary wildness of the primitive prairie, as though the bird had received from its surroundings their peculiar impress; while if less loud their songs would hardly reach their mates above the strong winds that almost constantly sweep over the prairies in the hot months. It differs, too, in the less frequency of the harsh, complaining chatter so conspicuous in the Eastern birds, so much so that at first I suspected this to be wholly wanting."

It has often occurred to me, and I make the suggestion for what it may be worth, that a different acoustic property of the dry, rarified air of the West may in some measure determine the peculiarity of the song. In further illustration of this interesting subject, I will quote the remarks of Mr. Trippe, who evidently inclines to keep the two forms apart:

"If this bird is merely a variety of *S. magna*, it is certainly a very remarkable one. * * * * Careful observations for the last two years have convinced me of the following facts, viz., that there are two varieties or species of the Meadow-lark in Southern Iowa, that possess totally different songs and notes, and that these differences are constant. The Common Lark is here by far the most abundant; its notes are *precisely similar* to those of the same bird in the East, and its habits, also, nearly or quite the same. The Western Lark, on the contrary, *never* utters the peculiar, long-drawn whistle of the common species—at least I never heard it—and it has a number of notes which the latter never utters, one in particular, which resembles a note of the Red-winged Blackbird. The Western Lark, like the common species, has a rapid chatter, but so different, in every bird that I have heard, that the difference was at once appreciable; indeed, it is more striking than the resemblance. The Western Lark is here quite a timid species, compared with the other at least, which is quite as tame as the Bluebird or Chipping Sparrow. The former is never heard after the 1st of September, although it arrives as soon as, or a little before, the other—early in March—while the latter remains until November. I have never heard a bird whose notes were intermediate between the two. Here, then, we have the remarkable fact of two varieties—if they are such—of the same species, existing side by side, seldom or never mingling, and each preserving its peculiar notes and habits; yet resembling each other so closely in form and plumage that the most experienced ornithologists are unable to draw the dividing line between them."

In Dakota, along the Red River, I found *S. neglecta* alone, although the *Fauna* there is almost exclusively Eastern. The same was the case at Fort Randall, and, in fact, all along that portion of Dakota towards Sioux City, Iowa, where the birds are exceedingly numerous—perhaps the most abundant of all the prairie species. They reach this locality early in April, and soon begin to sing. In May we cannot ride a mile anywhere without seeing them, while their peculiar notes, one of the most delightful voices of the prairie, are continually heard. In April, before pairing, hundreds used to frequent daily the parade-ground of Fort Randall, where, as the grass was yet scarcely sprouted, good opportunity was offered of observing their characteristic habit—one not so generally known as it should be, since it is related to the peculiar shape of the bill. The birds may be seen scattered all over the ground, busily tugging at something; and on walking over the scene of their operations, the ground, newly-softened by the spring thaw, is seen to be riddled with thousands of little holes, which the birds make in search of food. These holes are quite smooth—not a turning over of the surface of the ground, but a clean boring, like that made by sinking in the end of a light walking-stick; just as if the birds inserted the bill and then worked it about till the hole was of sufficient size. Whether they bored at random, or were guided by some sense in finding their prey, and what particular objects they were searching for, I did not ascertain; but the habit was so fixed and so continually persevered in as to attract general attention. Silent, or nearly so, upon their first arrival, the birds became highly musical during April, singing in rival groups from the trees and fences in the intervals of their search for food; and at length they paired and scattered over the prairie to breed. None pass the winter in this latitude; they depart late in October. Further west, on the boundless prairie, they occur everywhere, but not, according to my observations at least, in such large numbers as they do about settlements, since they appear to prefer more fertile regions, where, doubtless, their food is most plenty.

ICTERUS SPURIUS, (Linn.) Bp.

Orchard Oriole; Chestnut Hangnest.

a. *spurius.*

Oriolus spurius, LINN., Syst. Nat. i, 1766, 162.—GM., i, 1788, 389.
Icterus spurius, BP., Syn. 1828, 51; List, 1838, 29.—NUTT., Man. i, 1832, 165.—AUD., Orn. Biog. i, 1831, 221; v, 1839, 485; pl. 42.—AUD., Syn. 1839, 144.—AUD., B. Am. iv, 1842, 46, pl. 219.—GIR., B. L. I. 1844, 144.—BD., B. N. A. 1858, 547.—CASS., Pr. Phila. Acad. 1860, 140 (Atrato).—SCL., P. Z. S. 1856, 301 (Cordova); 1859, 365 (Xalapa); 1859. 380.—LAWR., Ann. Lyc. viii, 1865, 177 (New Granada).—McILWR., Pr. Ess. Inst. v, 1866, 90 (Canada, casual).—COUES, Pr. Ess. Inst. v, 1868, 285 (Southern New England).—SUMICH., Mem. Bost. Soc. 1869, 553 (Orizaba).— TRIPPE, Pr. Bost. Soc. 1872, 239 (Iowa, breeding).—ALLEN, Bull. M. C. Z. iii, 1872, 178 (Kansas and Colorado).—SNOW, B. Kans. 1873, 8.—COUES, Key, 1872, 158.—B. B. & R., N. A. B. ii, 1874, 190, pl. 34, f. 4, 5, 6; and of most authors.

Icterus (Bananivorus) spurius, SCL., Cat. 1862, 130.
Yphantes spurius, BP., Consp. i, 1850, 432.
Xanthornus spurius, CAB., Mus. Hein. 1851, 184.—LAWR., Ann. Lyc. ix, 104 (Costa Rica).
Pendulinus spurius, CASS., Pr. Phila. Acad. 1867, 61.
Oriolus varius et (?) *capensis,* GM., Syst. Nat. i, 1788, 390, 392.
Xanthornus varius, GRAY, Gen. of B.—WOODH., Sitgr. Rep. 1853, 79.
Turdus ater, GM., Syst. Nat. i, 1788, 831.
Oriolus castaneus, LATH., Ind. Orn. i, 1790, 181 (= *O. varius,* GM.).
Icterus castaneus et *flavus,* DAUD.
Psarcolius castaneus, WAGL., Syst. Av. 1829.
Turdus jugularis, LATH., Ind. Orn, i, 1790. 361 (= *T. ater,* GM.).
Oriolus mutatus, WILS., Am. Orn. i, 1808, pl. 4, figs. 1, 2, 3, 4.
Hyphantes solitarius ; et *Pendulinus nigricollis* et *viridis,* VIEILL.

b. *affinis.*

Xanthornus affinis, LAWR., Ann. Lyc. v, 1851, 113.—WOODH., Sitgr. Rep. 1853, 79.—SCL.
 & SALV., Ibis, 1859, 20 (Guatemala) ; 1860, 34.
Bananivorus affinis, SCL., P. Z. S. 1859, 365.
Pendulinus affinis, CASS., Pr. Phila. Acad. 1867, 61.
Icterus spurius var. *affinis,* COUES, Key, 1872, 158.

Hab.—Throughout the United States east of the Rocky Mountains; rare in Northern New England, and only casually to the Canadas. Breeds throughout its United States range. South in winter into Central America. Cuba. Var. *affinis* from Texas south-ward.
 Lieutenant Warren's Expedition.—9339, Loup Fork; 5343-53, Nebraska and Dakota. Not obtained by Captain Raynolds' nor by the later Expeditions.

The Orchard Oriole is abundant in the eastern portions of the Mis-souri, and of common occurrence along the wooded streams of the mountains. It is a slightly southerly species, more so than the next. It is not included by Mr. Trippe among Minnesota birds, and is very rare or casual in Northern New England and the British Provinces, its regular limit appearing to be the Connecticut Valley. It breeds throughout its United States range. Var. *affinis* consists of the smaller Southern birds.

ICTERUS BALTIMORE, (Linn.) Daud.

Baltimore Oriole; Golden Robin; Firebird; Hangnest.

Oriolus baltimore, LINN., Syst. Nat. i, 1766, 162.—GM., Syst. Nat. i, 1788, 381.—WILS.,
 Am. Orn. i, 1808, 23, pl. 1, f. 3 ; vi, 88, pl. 53, f. 4.
Icterus baltimore, DAUD., Tr. Orn. ii, 348.—BP., Syn. 1828, 51 ; List, 1838, 29.—NUTT.,
 Man. i, 1832, 152.—AUD., Orn. Biog. i, 1831, 66 ; v, 1839, 278 ; pls. 12, 423 ; Syn.
 1839, 143 ; B. Am. iv, 1842, 37, pl. 217.—BD., B. N. A. 1858, 548.—HAYD., Rep.
 1862, 170.—LAWR., Ann. Lyc. viii, 1865, 177 (New Granada).—SUMICH., Mem.
 Bost. Soc. i, 1869, 553 (Orizaba).—SNOW, B. Kans. 1873, 8.—TRIPPE, Pr. Bost.
 Soc. xv, 1872, 239 (Iowa).—ALLEN, Bull. M. C. Z. iii, 1872, 178 (Kansas, Wy-oming, and Colorado).—COUES, Key, 1872, 158.—RODNEY, Am. Nat. 1871.—B.
 B. & R., N. A. B. ii, 1874, pl. 35, f. 5.
Yphantes baltimore, VIEILL., Ency. Meth. 708 ; Gal. Ois. i, 1824, 124, pl. 87.—BP., Consp.
 Av. i, 1850, 432.—WOODH., Sitgr. Rep. 1853, 79.
Psarocolius baltimore, WAGL., Syst, Av. 1827, No. 26.
Hyphantes baltimore, CAB., Mus. Hein. 1851, 183.—LAWR., Ann. Lyc. ix, 104 (Costa Rica).
Icterus baltimorensis, BP., P. Z. S. 1837, 116.—SCL. & SALV., Ibis, 1859, 20 (Guatemala).—
 COUES, Pr. Ess. Inst. v, 1868, 285.—TRIPPE, *ibid.* vi, 1871, 117 (Minnesota).
Hyphantes baltimorensis, SCL., P. Z. S. 1859, 57, 365 ; Cat. 130 (Xalapa).
Icterus baltimorus, McILWR., Pr. Ess. Inst. v, 1866, 90 (Canada West).

Hab.—United States, east of the Rocky Mountains. North regularly to the British Provinces. Breeds chiefly toward the northern portions of its range, but generally dispersed in summer over the United States. Passes to Mexico and Central America (numerous quotations). Cuba (CAB., J. f. O. iv, 10).
 Lieutenant Warren's Expedition.—9341, Loup Fork ; 9342, Elkhorn River ; 5359, Yel-lowstone River ; 5357-58, Powder River ; 6715, Fort Lookout ; 4745, Farm Island.
 Respecting the specific name of this species, it may be observed : That if Linnæus' name, *baltimore,* is to be changed at all, it should be altered into *baltimorei,* not *balti-morensis ;* for the allusion is to the colors of Lord Baltimore's dress, not to the city of that name.

The range of this Oriole is nearly coincident with that of the last, and, like it, it is generally dispersed along wooded streams of the Northwest. It regularly goes, however, somewhat further north, apparently reaching the British border all along. It breeds in all suitable places in its Missouri range, which reaches and somewhat overlaps that of the succeeding species. It is extremely abundant about Pembina, Dakota, where it breeds in June, but was not observed by me west of the Red River Valley. The specimens from this region, as well as those from Kansas, are remarkable for the brilliancy and intensity of the golden-orange, which in some cases become almost scarlet.

The following interesting communication was prepared for the work by Mr. Thomas G. Gentry, of Germantown, Pennsylvania:

"The nidification of this species is so familiar to nearly all that it may seem presumptuous upon my part to say anything in connection therewith. Nuttall has so beautifully and faithfully delineated the characteristic nest of this species that it would be worse than folly for me to attempt an improvement thereon. But there is a novelty, hitherto unnoticed, so far as I am aware, in a couple of nests in my collection, of which a description cannot be considered amiss.

"In the scores of nests which I have had the pleasure to examine, exclusive of the above exceptions, all were begun as Nuttall affirms, 'by firmly fastening natural strings of the flax of the silk-weed or swamp-hollyhock, or stout artificial threads, around two or more forked twigs, corresponding to the width and depth of the nest. With the same materials, willow-down, or any accidental ravellings, strings, thread, sewing-silk, tow, or wool, that may be lying near the neighboring houses, or around the grafts of trees, they interweave and fabricate a sort of coarse cloth into the form intended, toward the bottom of which they place the real nest, made chiefly of lint, wiry grass, horse and cow hair,' &c.

"To one of the nests referred to, the above partial description answers satisfactorily; but it does appear that the birds had, through some cause or other, manifested but little judgment, so to speak, in the selection of a suitable site; for we find, in order to make the best of a bad bargain, they were constrained to erect a permanent roof to their dwelling by interwoven strings, through their deprivation of the verdant and agreeable canopy which the leaves would naturally afford. In the other, economy seems to have been of paramount importance, for this nest is a faithful counterpart of the real one of Nuttall's description, minus, to be sure, the inclosing pouch.

"No. 1 is somewhat cylindrical in shape, with the long axis or distance from top to bottom slightly in excess of the short, or the distance from side to side, the former being about five and the latter nearly four and a half inches. It is composed of strings compactly woven together, with a slight interspersing of hairs of the horse and cow; the whole forming a structure comfortable and cozy, and well calculated to protect its inmates from the inclemency of the weather. So nicely is the roof adjusted to the nest, that even the most critical investigation cannot discern the union. The entrance is a circular opening situated in the superior third of the nest, facing southwardly.

"No. 2 is an inverted cone, with a blunt apex. The greatest diameter at top is four inches, and the less three and a half; depth, four and a half inches. It was built between two forks of a pear-tree. It is composed almost entirely of the hairs of the horse and cow, firmly but densely woven together. So slight is the texture that it can be readily seen through. This specimen presents the appearance of an ordinary nest without its customary covering. In Northumberland County, of the State of Pennsylvania, where this nest was found in the summer of 1866, I am told that it is the characteristic style of nest. It is more than likely that in districts far removed from the busy haunts of men, owing to a lack of the usual materials, the birds are constrained to use the hairs of the domestic as well as those of wild animals in the structure of their domiciles. In times very remote, before the introduction of civilized man into the country, there is no doubt that the above was the only style of architecture known to the species.

" It is evident that in those days of primitive gloom, and even at the present time in thickly-wooded sections, a very dense nest is not at all desirable, since the birds obtain the protection which they require from the weather in the beautiful covering which Nature throws around them. Now, in sections where the forests have disappeared by the strokes of the pioneer's axe, such a shelter would not afford the comfort and security which the inmates demand. Now, as birds are not slow to discern what best comports with their security, surely the Oriole, which displays so much taste and ingenuity, would readily perceive that a more compact and thicker structure would be necessary. History shows that the highest and most elaborate style of architecture which man is now capable of achieving is but the outgrowth of the simpler and less complicated forms that preceded it. Reasoning, therefore, from analogy, the highest style which the Baltimore Oriole has been able to accomplish the typical nest, is but an outgrowth of the one which I have described.

" From the plausible remarks advanced, the inclosing pouch is but an improvement superadded to the main structure, it being a subsequent operation. This is apparent from the manner in which the initial stages of the nests of *Vireo olivaceus* and *V. noveboracensis* are accomplished.

" In the first of these anomalous forms of nests still further improvement is manifest in the closely-woven roof. In the open nests this protection is but partially secured in the clusters of leaves that depend from above, the site being doubtless selected with a view to this natural arrangement. As reason tends to improvement, and as birds are possessed of a share of this great gift, so it is natural to suppose that they must vary their style of nest-building in favorable directions when it will subserve the individual and family good."

ICTERUS BULLOCKII, (Sw.) Bp.

Bullock's Oriole.

Xanthornus bullockii, Sw., Syn. Mex. B. Phil. Mag. i, 1827, 436.
Agelaius bullockii, RICH., List, Rep. Br. Assoc. 1837.
Icterus bullockii, BP., List, 1838, 29.—AUD., Orn. Biog. v, 1839, 9, pls. 388, 433.—AUD., Syn. 1839, 143.—AUD., B. Am. iv, 1842, 43, pl. 218.—NEWB., P. R. R. Rep. vi, 1857, 87.—BD., B. N. A. 1858, 549; Mex. B. Surv. ii, 1858, pt. ii, 20.—MAXIM., J. f. O. vi, 1858, 259.—COOP. & SUCK., N. H. Wash. Ter. 1860, 209.—HAYD., Rep. 1862, 170.—LORD, Pr. Roy. Art. Inst. iv, 121 (British Columbia).—COUES, Pr. Phila. Acad. 1866, 91.—COOP., B. Cal. i, 1870, 273.—COUES, Am. Nat. v, 1871, 678 (biography).—HOLD., Pr. Bost. Soc. 1872, 203.—ALLEN, Bull. M. C. Z. iii, 1872, 178.—MERR., U. S. Geol. Surv. 1872, 685, 708 (eggs).—SNOW, B. Kans. 1873, 8.—COUES, Key, 1872, 158, fig. 100.—B. B. & R., N. A. B. ii, 1874, 199, pl. 34, f. 3, 7.
Yphantes bullockii, BP., Consp. i, 1850, 432.—HEERM., P. R. R. Rep. x, 1859, pt. vi, 52.
Hyphantes bullockii, CASS., Pr. Phila. Acad. 1867, 62.
Psarocolius auricollis, MAXIM., Reise, i, 1839, 367 (Dakota).

Hab.—Entire Missouri region (rare above Fort Pierre, *Hayden*) to the Pacific, and southward along the Table-Lands of Mexico. North to British Columbia. Breeds in suitable places throughout its United States range. Passes beyond the United States in winter. (City of Mexico, SCL., P. Z. S. 1869, 362).

List of specimens.

19359	....	Popoagie.......	♂	May 23, 1860	G. H. Trook..	......	12.25	4.00
19360	....	Bighorn Mts...	♂	May 29, 1860	.....do......	8.50	12.00	3.15
19361	....	Bighorn River.	♂	May 25, 1860	.....do......	7.75	12.25	4.25
19362	....	Popoagie.......	♀	May 24, 1860	.....do......	8.00	12.00	4.00
19288	18	Wind River....	♂	May 29, 1860	F. V. Hayden.	8.25	12.00	4.00
19289	19	Wind River....	♀	May 29, 1860	.....do......	7.55	11.25	3.50
19290	29	Wind River....	♀	May 26, 1860	.....do......	7.50	12.00	3.75

Lieutenant Warren's Expedition.—5354, Farm Island.
Later Expeditions.—61713–24, Ogden, Utah; 61782–85, Devil's Creek, Idaho.

The occurrence of this species eastward into Kansas, where, Prof. Snow remarks, it is "quite frequent," has been lately determined. Its range thus largely overlaps that of the Baltimore Oriole, both being found over a considerable portion of the Missouri region, along the wooded streams. From the Rocky Mountains to the Pacific it is the characteristic species, entirely replacing the Baltimore. I have seen but one record (above given) of its occurrence in British America. It appears, however, to rarely penetrate to the uppermost Missouri. It is strictly migratory, like our other representatives of the family, wintering in Mexico. It appears over our border in March, but the migration is not completed until the following month, when the forests it loves to dwell in are clothed in verdure. My experience with the species enabled me to give, on a former occasion, the following account:

"In the pine-clad mountains of Arizona and New Mexico, I never saw it until about the middle of April; then, and until the cool weather of September, I was almost daily gratified with the sight of the gaily-hued birds gleaming through the sombre foliage like tiny meteors, and with the sound of their musical voices awakening echoes along the deepening aisles of the woodland.

"In the countries just mentioned, the belts of thick cotton-wood and willows that generally fringe the streams are favorite resorts, perhaps because the pliant twigs are best suited to their wants in constructing their nests. All the Orioles are wonderful architects, weaving pensile nests of soft, pliable, fibrous substances, with a nicety and beauty of finish that human art would vainly attempt to rival. These elegant fabrics are hung at the end of slender twigs, out of reach of ordinary enemies; and though they may swing with every breath of wind, this is but cradle-rocking for the callow young, and it is a rude blast indeed that endangers the safety of their leafy home.

"Little time passes after their arrival before the modestly-attired females, rambling silently through the verdure, are singled out and attended each by her impetuous consort, who sings his choicest songs, and displays the prowess she admires most. His song is an elegant paraphrase of the Baltimore's, with all its richness and variety, though an ear well skilled in distinguishing birds' notes can readily detect a difference. Their courtship happily settled, the pair may be seen fluttering through the thicket they have chosen, in eager search for a building-place; and when a suitable one is found, no time is lost in beginning to weave their future home. It is a great mistake to suppose that birds of the same species always build in the same way. Though their nests have a general resemblance in style of architecture, they differ greatly according to their situation, to the time the birds have before the nest must be used for the reception of the eggs, and often, we are tempted to think, according to the taste and skill of the builders. In their work of this sort, birds show a remarkable power of selection, as well as of adapting themselves to circumstances; in proof of which we have only to examine the three beautiful specimens now lying before us. Each is differently constructed; and while all three evince wonderful powers of weaving, one of them in particular is astonishingly ingenious, displaying the united accomplishments of weaving and basket-making. Before proceeding, we may premise that the idea of the nest is a sort of bag or purse, closely woven of slender pliant substances, like strips of fibrous bark, grass, hair, twine, &c., open at the top, and hung by its rim in the fork of a twig or at the very end of a floating spray.

"The first nest was built in a pine-tree; and if the reader will call to mind the stiff nature of the terminal branchlets, each bearing a thick bunch of long, straight needle-like leaves, he will see that the birds must have been put to their wits' end, though very likely he will not be able to guess how they made shift with such unpromising materials. They made up their minds to use the leaves themselves in the nest, and with this idea they commenced by bending down a dozen or twenty of the stiff, slender filaments, and tying their ends together at the bottom. If you have ever seen a basket-maker at work, with his upright pieces already in place, but not yet fixed together with the circular ones, you will understand exactly what the birds had thus accomplished. They had a secure frame-work of nearly parallel and upright leaves naturally attached to the bough above, and tied together below by the bird's art. This skeleton of the nest was about nine inches long, and four across the top, running to a point below; and the subsequent weaving of the nest upon this basis was an easy matter to the birds, though, if one were to examine a piece of the fabric cut away from the nest, he could hardly believe that the thin yet tough and strong felting had not been made by some shoddy contractor for the supply of army clothing. Yet it was all designed in a bird's little brain, and executed with skilful bill and feet.

"Perhaps the young birds that were raised in the second nest did not appreciate their romantic surroundings, but their parents were evidently a sentimental pair. If they did not do their courting 'under the mistletoe,' at any rate they built a cosy home there, tinting the sober reality of married life with the rosy hue of their earlier dreams. The nest was hung in a bunch of the *Arceuthobium oxycedri*, an abundant epiphytic plant, that on the western wilds represents the mistletoe, and recalls the cherished memories of holiday gatherings. The nest was a cylindrical purse, some six inches deep and four broad, hanging to several sprays of the mistletoe, which were partly interwoven with the nest to form a graceful drapery. The felting material was long, soft, vegetable fibre of a glistening silvery lustre, in artistic contrast with the dark-hued foliage. A few hairs were sewn through and through, for greater security, and the pretty fabric was lined with a matting of the softest possible plant-down, like that of a button-wood or an *Asclepias*.

"The general shape and the material of the third nest were much the same as those of the last; it was, however, suspended from the forked twig of an oak, and draped, almost to concealment, with leaves. But it had a remarkable peculiarity, being arched over and roofed in at the top with a dome of the same material as the rest, and had a little round hole in one side just large enough to let the birds pass in. Such a globular nest as this is probably exceptional; but now it will not do to say that Orioles always build pensile pouches open at the top.

"The eggs of this species are four or five in number, and rather elongated in form, being much pointed at the smaller end. They measure, on an average, just an inch in length by about two-thirds as much in greatest diameter, which is much nearer the larger than the smaller end. In color they are very pale bluish, or rather whitish, with a faint, dull blue shade, and are everywhere irregularly overrun with fine, sharp hair lines of blackish-brown, or blackish with a slight tinge of purplish. These curious zigzag markings are characteristic of the eggs of a majority of the birds of the family (*Icteridæ*). They have no definite style, but wander at random over the surface, and in no two specimens are they alike. Thus, in one specimen, the lines, fine as hairs, are wound round and round the butt, with such regularity that they hardly ever interfere; in others they are snarled up in different places, and sometimes, particularly at a sharp turning-point, the lines spread into little spots; and there are often a few such isolated markings in various places over the. egg."

Further accounts of the nidification of this beautiful species are given. Mr. Merriam, who found it very abundant in Utah, and collected in June no less than sixteen nests, containing over sixty eggs, says:

"They build a beautiful hanging nest, often ten and a half inches deep, and composed of fibres of grass, flax, and the inner bark of vines, which is generally lined with wool. The first lot were deep and solid; were composed chiefly of the fibres of flax and dry grass, and had a grayish appearance, while the second lot—which were built by the same birds after their first had been taken—were not very deep, had evidently been made in haste, and were principally composed of the inner bark of small bushes and vines, giving them a brownish look. They generally conceal their nests among the leaves on the top of a willow, from eight to ten feet above the ground, in such a position that it rocks to and fro whenever there is a little wind."

SCOLECOPHAGUS FERRUGINEUS, (Gm.) Sw.

Rusty Grackle.

Oriolus ferrugineus, GM., Syst. Nat. i, 1788, 393.—LATH., Ind. Orn. i, 1790, 176.
Gracula ferrvginea, WILS., Am. Orn. iii, 1811, 41, pl. 21, f. 3.
Quiscalus ferrugineus, BP., Obs. Wils. 1824, No. 46; Syn. 1828, 55.—NUTT., Man. i, 1832, 199.—AUD., Orn. Biog. ii, 1834, 325; v, 1839, 483; pl. 147; Syn. 1839, 146; B. Am. iv, 65, pl. 222.—GIR., B. L. I. 1844, 146.—MAXIM., J. f. O. vi, 1858, 204.— TRIPPE, Pr. Ess. Inst. vi, 1871, 117 (west to Red River).
Scolecophagus ferrugineus, SW. & RICH., F. B. A. ii, 1831, 286.—BP., List, 1838, 28.—GRAY, Gen. of B.—WOODH., Sitgr. Rep. 1853, 78.—BD., B. N. A. 1858, 551.—COUES, Pr. Phila. Acad. 1861, 225 (Labrador, breeding).—CASS., *ibid.* 1866, 412.—HAYD., Rep. 1862, 170.—DALL & BANN., Tr. Chic. Acad. i, 1869, 285 (Alaska).—MAYN., Pr. Bost. Soc. xiv, 1871 (Maine and New Hampshire, breeding).—SNOW, B. Kans. 1872 (Kansas, migratory).—COUES, Key, 1872, 159.—B. B. & R., N. A. B. ii, 1874, 203, pl. 35, f. 4.
(?) *Oriolus niger*, GM., i, 1788, 393.
Scolecophagus niger, BP., Consp. i, 1850, 423.—CAB., Mus. Hein. i, 1851, 195.
Turdus hudsonicus, noveboracensis et *labradorius*, GM., i. 1788, 818, 832.
" *Oriolus leucocephalus,* et *Gracula quiscala* var., LATH."
Pendulinus ater, VIEILL., Nouv. Dict. d'Hist. Nat.
" *Chalcophanes virescens*, WAGL., Syst. Av. App. *Oriolus*, No. 9."

Hab.—Eastern Province of North America. West to Kansas, Nebraska, and Dakota; thence obliquely in British America to the Pacific in Alaska. Breeds from Northern New England northward. In winter, generally dispersed over the Middle, Southern, and Western States.

Lieutenant Warren's Expedition.—No. 5322, near Sioux City, Iowa.

There are some interesting points in the geographical distribution of this species as compared with that of *S. cyanocephalus*. During the breeding season their *habitats* are entirely separate, but they overlap during the fall migration, if not also in winter. In the East, the Rusty Grackle breeds from Northern New England (and perhaps further south in mountains) northward, throughout a great part of the British Pos-sessions, from Labrador entirely across to Alaska. Now, to take an intermediate point—say Fort Pembina, on the Red River, the extreme northeast corner of Dakota. Here, in the spring and summer, the Rusty Grackle is not known, while Brewer's Blackbird occurs in great abundance, breeding. In the fall, however, the Rusty Grackle enters Dakota from the north on its migration, and mixes with the other species. I have even found them so associated over three hundred miles further west, on the head-waters of the Mouse River, where they came in September; and for a month the flocks of Blackbirds about our camps contained both species of *Scolecophagus*, associating so inti-mately that the same shot would generally drop individuals of both kinds. Their habits at this season are identical, but the specific char-acters are always, so far as I know, preserved intact. I have never seen any doubtful specimens of either species.

Mr. Holden's record of *S. ferrugineus* breeding in Wyoming in com-pany with the other species is undoubtedly erroneous; no such associ-ation occurs at this season; when the two are found together, the indi-viduals of *S. ferrugineus* are altogether a different lot, come from the North. The case is by no means unparalleled; in fact, a great many birds in migrating take up different lines of migration in the spring and fall. This brings species often into association at certain seasons, while never found together at other times; and it accounts satisfactorily for their abundance, during migration, at one season and scarcity at another. Of this latter fact we have a striking example in the Con-necticut Warbler (*Oporornis agilis*), a bird so abundant in New England and elsewhere in the East, in the fall, that hundreds have been taken in one season, while it is rarely ever seen in the spring, as at that season it appears to migrate inland, up the Mississippi Valley, being, according to accounts, not uncommon at some points during the vernal migration.

SCOLECOPHAGUS CYANOCEPHALUS, (Wagl.) Cab.

Blue-headed Grackle; Brewer's Blackbird.

Psarocolius cyanocephalus, WAGL., Isis, 1829, 758.
Scolecophagus cyanocephalus, CAB., Mus. Hein. i, 1851, 195.—BD., B. N. A. 1858, 552.—
    HEERM., P. R. R. Rep. x, 1859, pt. vi, 53.—COOP. & SUCKL., N. H. Wash.
    Ter. 1860, 209.—HAYD., Rep. 1862, 170.—DRESS., Ibis, 1865, 403 (Matamoras
    and San Antonio, breeding).—CASS., Pr. Phila. Acad. 1866, 413.—COUES, Pr.
    Phila. Acad. 1866, 90 (Arizona, resident).—SUMICH., Mem. Bost. Soc. i, 1859,
    553 (plateau of Mexico, abundant).—SNOW, B. Kans. 1873, 8 (Eastern Kansas).—
    STEV., U. S. Geol. Surv. Ter. 1870, 465.—MERR., *ibid.* 1872, 687.—AIKEN, Pr.
    Bost. Soc. 1872, 203 (Wyoming).—ALLEN, Bull. M. C. Z. iii, 1872, 178.—COUES,
    Key, 1872, 160.—B. B. & R., N. A. B. ii, 1874, 206, pl. 35, f. 3.
Scolecophagus mexicanus, Sw., Two Cent. and a Quarter, 1838, 302, No. 66.—GRAY, Gen.
    of B.—BP., Consp. i, 1850, 432.—NEWB., P. R. R. Rep. vi, 1857, 86.
"*Icterus æneus*, LICHT." (*Bp.*)
Quiscalus breweri, AUD., B. Am. vii, 1843, 345, pl. 492.
Scolecophagus "*ferrugineus*," HOLD., Pr. Bost. Soc. 1872, 203 (error) (Wyoming, breeding).

Hab.—United States, from Eastern Kansas and Minnesota to the Pacific. South into Mexico. Breeds throughout its United States range. Migratory from extremes of its range.

List of specimens.

| 19369 | .... | S. Fork Stink. C. | ♀ | June 14, 1860 | G. H. Trook.. | 9.00 | 14.75 | 5.00 |

Lieutenant Warren's Expedition.—5320, Fort Randall, Dakota; 4753–56, Upper Mis-souri River.
    Later Expeditions.—60451–57, 60721–36, 61070–73, various Wyoming localities; 61710, 61731, Utah; 62272–73, Idaho and Wyoming.

The *habitat* of this species is observed to overlap that of the preceding, along the line through Eastern Kansas, Nebraska, and Dakota, as well as in the country immediately along the Red River. Prof. Snow states that it is " quite common even in Eastern Kansas;" and at Pembina, on the Red River, I found it breeding abundantly. Further south, in Dakota, I have not observed it east of Fort Randall, where it is common; and beyond this, in the Missouri region, it almost replaces the eastern species, which, however, reaches, in Dakota, during the fall migration, to about 103° west longitude at least.

I took a single male bird at Fort Randall, in November, after all the migrants had passed southward; but its occurrence was due, I ascertained, to an injury of one wing, which kept it from flying off with the rest; and I am satisfied that none winter so far north as this, though, on the Pacific coast, according to Dr. Cooper, the species is resident as far north as the Columbia. In Arizona, at various seasons, and late in the fall in Southern California, I found the birds in great abundance, and enjoyed excellent opportunities of studying their habits.

This species appears to leave both latitudinal extremes of its range periodically, and probably all the individuals change their abode twice a year; yet the oscillation of the whole body is insufficient to remove them entirely from most localities, the birds being simply more or less abundant according to season. Thus casual observation in Arizona would lead to the belief that the species was there a winter visitant only, while I am satisfied that they reside in the Territory. In September and October their ranks are recruited by constant arrivals from the north, and they are very abundant until the following May. Then the flocks break up; the incomplete migration ensues, and the remainder scatter about to breed. Unlike some Blackbirds, the *Scolecophagi* do not breed in extensive communities, nor do they necessarily resort to swampy localities. Several pairs, however, are often attracted to the same spot, and more than one nest may be found on the same tree or high bush. The nest is placed in a crotch several feet from the ground; it is a bulky structure, like a miniature Crow's nest, but deeper and more compact. The basement and outer wall is an interlacement of short, crooked twigs, matted with a variety of softer materials, and may rarely be plastered with mud. This substance, however, is not used in great quantity, often apparently no more than what sticks to the weeds and roots. The nest is finished inside with a quantity of hair, rootlets, &c. The eggs differ entirely from those of the *Agelœi*, being speckled, not streaked, like those of the *Xanthocephalus*. They are hardly distinguishable from those of the Rusty Grackle. They vary in number from four to six, measuring an inch or more by a little over three-fourths of an inch (a selected specimen was 1.05 by 0.78). They are a dull, olivaceous-gray, sometimes a clearer pale-bluish or greenish-gray, thickly scattered all over with various shades of brown, from quite blackish or dark chocolate to light umber. None of the spots are large; they are very irregular in outline, occasionally quite linear; they vary in number, sometimes being numerous enough to hide the ground-color. A nest of Brewer's Blackbird before me, taken by Mr. Allen, June 24, 1873, on Heart River, Dakota, was placed only a few inches from the ground. It is large and bulky, with many projections of the small sticks which form the exterior, and are mixed with grasses and weed-stalks throughout the nest. The lining is distinct, of fine, tortuous rootlets, very neatly disposed in a circular manner. It contained five eggs, with large embryos. The ground is grayish, but it is everywhere so thickly mottled, or rather clouded, with dull chocolate-brown as to give the prevailing effect. A specimen measures 1.19 by 0.80; the shape is tumid, with an obtuse smaller end.

Several kinds of Blackbirds are abundant in Arizona, but the present surpasses them all in numbers, and in its general diffusion plays the part that the Cow-bird takes in the farms of the East, and that the Yellow-headed Blackbird fulfils in the settlements on the plains. They are eminently gregarious when not breeding. Yet I never saw such countless numbers as those of the Red-winged Blackbird during its migrations. Troops of twenty, fifty, or a hundred are commonly seen; they have no special fondness for watery places, but scour the open, dry ground, and scatter among straggling pines and oaks; they come fearlessly into the clearings about houses, the traveler's camp, and the stock-yards, gleaning plentiful subsistence from man's bounty or wastefulness. Much of their time is spent on the ground, rambling in hurried, eager search for grain and insects; they generally run with nimble steps, hopping being the exception, when they have satisfied their hunger, and are moving leisurely with no particular object in view. The movements are all easy and graceful, the bird's trim form and glossy color setting it off to great advantage. At full speed the head is lowered and fixed; in slower progress it is held upright, bobbing in time with each step. When a flock is feeding, they pass over a good deal of ground, without seeming to examine it very closely; every one tries to keep ahead of the next, and thus they scurry on, taking short flights over each other's head. At the least alarm, the timid birds betake themselves to the nearest tree, perching in various attitudes. A favorite posture, so easy as to appear negligent, is with the body held nearly upright, the tail hanging loosely straight down, while the head turns in various ways, with the whim of the moment. When excited, the bird often sits low down, firmly on its legs, with elevated and widespread tail, constantly flirted, while its watchful eye peers down through the foliage. However compactly a flock may fly up into a tree, they generally scatter as they alight all over the branches, so that it is rarely that more than two or three can be brought down at a shot. On the ground the case is quite different; there they often huddle so close together that the whole flock may be decimated. Their behavior in the presence of man is a curious mixture of timidity and heedlessness; they come to the very door-step, and yet a sudden movement, or a shout, sends them affrighted into the nearest trees. The next moment they begin to straggle back again, at first singly or in little squads, till the more timid ones are reassured and come streaming down together, when the busy search for food is resumed.

Their hunger satisfied for the time, the birds betake themselves to the trees, often passing the whole period of digestion snugly ensconced in the thick foliage. Then their concert opens; and if the music is neither sweet nor soft, it is sprightly, and not disagreeable, for it suggests the careless joviality and lazy good humor of Blackbirds with their stomachs full, and satisfactory prospect of future supply. The notes are energetic, rapid, and varied, with a peculiar delivery, which, like the yelping of the prairie wolves, gives the hearer a very exaggerated idea of the number of the performers. The usual note is like the sound of pebbles smartly struck together, rapidly repeated an indefinite number of times; it is varied at irregular intervals by a long-drawn liquid whistle, which has a peculiarly pleasing effect in breaking the monotony of the other notes, and mellowing the whole performance. The ordinary call-note is exactly between the rough guttural "*chuck*" or the Redwing and the clear metallic "*chink*" of the Reed-bird.

In the fall, when seeds of all sorts and various insects are most readily procured, the birds grow fat, and furnish very good eating. They are tender, like nearly all small birds, and their flesh lacks the peculiar taste and odor, not entirely agreeable, that that of the Redwing acquires at the same season, when the bird feeds mostly on wild oats (*Zizania*). At this season the lustre of the plumage is obscured, and its uniformity interrupted by dull gray edging of the feathers. But even in autumn some males are found nearly as richly clad as in the spring-time, and I do not think that even the dullest colored females and young are ever so decidedly rusty-brown as the Eastern Grackle. The sexes may be known by their disparity in size, aside from the difference in plumage; moreover, the eye of the male is clear lemon-yellow, that of the female brown. The perfect male is lustrous greenish-black, changing abruptly to purplish and violet on the head; length, $9\frac{1}{2}$ to $10\frac{1}{2}$; extent, 16 or 17; wing, about $5\frac{1}{2}$; tail, $4\frac{1}{2}$; bill, 0.85; tarsus, about $1\frac{1}{8}$. The female only averages 9 in length, with an extent of about 15, and other dimensions are correspondingly smaller than those of the male. She is dull brownish, blackening on the back, wings, and tail, where there is often a greenish lustre, and with a plumbeous cast on the under parts; the head, neck, and breast, ochrey-brown. The female and young are distinguished from those of *S. ferrugineus* with some difficulty, but they average larger, with the bill heavier at the base, and are probably never so decidedly rusty-brown.

Since the preceding was written, Mr. Allen has sent me an interesting addendum: "Brewer's Blackbird is one of the most common representatives of the *Icteridæ* at the western edge of the plains, and throughout the mountains of Colorado. I found it abundant both at Denver and Cheyenne, and along all the wooded streams southward to Colorado City. It was also numerous at all favorable localities along the mountain streams; it occurred in large flocks in South Park, and was met with on the Snowy Range, even above timber-line. I met with it also at various points in Southern Wyoming, west of Cheyenne, and saw it in the Great Salt Lake Valley, in autumn, in flocks of several hundred. It is at all times more or less gregarious, and from its size, color, and habits, might readily be mistaken at a little distance for the Purple Grackle of the East. The latter species, however, was not seen west of Middle Kansas."

Mr. Trippe also furnishes his observations upon the species at Idaho Springs, Colorado: "Abundant; migratory; breeds. The Blue-headed Blackbird arrives in Bergen's Park early in spring, as soon as the marshes and wet meadows begin to thaw. In this park, as well as in all others that I have visited, it is very abundant, but only ventures outside of these limits in straggling parties, foraging up and down the valleys for food, especially early in the spring and late in the fall, when the supply has become precarious. In its habits and actions it shows more resemblance to the Crow Blackbird than to the Rusty. It is very social, and constantly in flocks, even in the breeding season associating in small parties on its way to and from its feeding grounds. It nests in wet meadows and brushy swamps, whence it makes excursions to the neighboring plowed fields and hills. The nest is built late in May, and the female begins to set early in June. It is placed on any dry spot in the swamp, the centre of a clump of bushes being preferred, and is always on the ground. It is large for the size of the bird, neatly constructed of weeds, grass, and bark, and smoothly lined with rootlets, fine bark, and hair. The eggs are five, of a pale bluish-green, very thickly splashed and speckled with pale chocolate-brown. Late in fall this bird leaves the mountains, and gathers in large flocks on the plains."

QUISCALUS PURPUREUS, (Bart.) Licht.

Purple Grackle; Crow Blackbird.

a. *purpureus.*

Gracula quiscala, LINN., Syst. Nat. i, 1758, 109 ; 1766, 165.—GM., i, 1788, 397.—LATH.,.
  Ind. Orn. i, 1790, 191.—WILS., iii, 1811, 44, pl. 21, f. 4.
Chalcophanes quiscalus, WAGL., Syst. Av. 1827.—CAB., Mus. Hein. i, 1851, 196.
Gracula purpurea, BART., Trav. in Florida, 1791, 290.
Quiscalus purpureus, LICHT.—GRAY.—WOODH., Sitgr. Rep. 1853, 79.—CASS., Pr. Phila.
  Acad. 1866, 403.—RIDGW., *ibid.* 1869, 133.—ALLEN, Bull. M. C. Z. ii, 1871, 291
  (includes several species); iii, 1872, 178.—COUES, Key, 1872, 160, fig. 102 ; pl.
  5, figs. 1, 3, 4, 5.—B. B. & R., N. A. B. ii, 1874, 214, 215, pl. 37, f. 1.
Quiscalus versicolor, VIEILL., Nouv. Dict. xxviii, 1819, 488; Gal. Ois. i, 171, pl. 108.—
  BP., Obs. Wils. 1824, No. 45; Am. Orn. i, 1825, 45, pl. 5, f. 1; Syn. 1828, 54;
  List, 1838, 28 ; Consp. i, 1850, 424.—SW. & RICH., F. B. A. ii, 1831, 485.—NUTT.,
  Man. i, 1832, 194.—AUD., Orn. Biog. i, 1831, 35 ; v, 1839, 481; pl. 7; Syn. 1839,
  146 ; B. Am. iv, 1842, 58, pl. 221.—BD., B. N. A. 1858, 555.—HAYD., Rep. 1862,.
  170.—TRIPPE, Pr. Ess. Inst. vi, 1871, 187.—SNOW, B. Kans. 1873, 8.
(?) *Oriolus ludovicianus* et *hudsonius,* GM., i, 1788, 387.
"Sturnus quiscalus, DAUDIN."
Gracula barita, ORD, Journ. Phila. Acad. i, 1818, 253.
Quiscalus nitens, LICHT., Verz. Doubl. 1823, 18, No. 164 (et *"fulgida,* LICHT.")
Quiscalus purpuratus, SW., Lardner's Cycl. 1838, 299.
Chalcophanes purpuratus, CAB., Mus. Hein. 1851, 196.

b. *æneus.*

Quiscalus æneus, RIDGW., Pr. Phila. Acad. 1869, 134 (*cf.* AUD., pl. 7; COUES, Key, 161).
Quiscalus purpureus var. æneus, B. B. & R., N. A. B. ii, 1874, 218.

c. *aglæus.*

Quiscalus baritus, BD., B. N. A. 1858, 556, pl. 32 (*an auct?*).
Quiscalus aglæus, BD., Am. Journ. Sci. 1866, 84.—CASS., Pr. Phila. Acad. 1866, 404.—
  RIDGW., *ibid.* 1869, 135.
Quiscalus purpureus var. aglæus, COUES, Key, 1872, 161, pl. 5, figs. 2, 6.—B. B. & R.,
  N. A. B. ii, 1874, 221, pl. 37, f. 2.
(For other probable synonyms of this species, and names of local races, see SW.,
Lardner's Cycl. 299, 300, 355 ; CASS., Pr. Phila. Acad. 1866, 404 *et seq.* ; ALLEN, Bull. M.
C. Z. ii, 1871, 291.)

Hab.—North America, east of the Rocky Mountains. North to Labrador, Hudson's
Bay, and the Saskatchewan. Breeds throughout its range. Winters in the Southern
States. Var. *aglæus* from Southern Florida.
  Lieutenant Warren's Expedition.—4761, Big Nemaha; 4766, 4762, 4758, 4760, 4767, Bald
Island, Missouri River.

The Crow Blackbird has lately been traced west to the Rocky Mountains; it is abundant in the eastern part of the Missouri region. It has
been several times accredited to California, but the evidence remains
insufficient. The variety *æneus* is very abundant along the Red River
of the North, breeding in hollows of trees, and later in the season I
have found it far west on the Mouse River, in the same latitude.
  Mr. Thomas T. Gentry sends me the following paragraph : " This
familiar bird reaches the latitude of Philadelphia, usually about the
middle of March. As I write (March 21), many small flocks may be
seen in various directions, fluttering and chattering among the trees.
Nest-building has been observed even as early as March 15; but then
only in sheltered situations, such as the south slopes of a hill. Here
the nests are built chiefly in the branches of coniferous trees. Usually,
but one brood is reared each season, but I have observed instances of a
second brood, when the season has been unusually propitious. In such
cases the first batch of young appeared in April, the other in July.
Though sometimes annoying to the agriculturist by its mischief in the
corn-fields, this bird has nevertheless some good qualities recommend-

ing it to favor. It is obviously of great service in the destruction of insects. But it has one very bad trait, perhaps not generally known. Like the Crow, a not distant relative, it is fond of birds' eggs and tender nestlings, and it destroys a great many, particularly Robins. Coward-like it lurks about the Robin's vicinity until the parents are away, when it pounces on the nest, seizes an egg or a young one, and hastily retreats. But wary and vigilant as it is, sometimes it is caught in the act, and forced to seek safety by rapid flight from the impetuous attacks of the owners. I had been aware of its fondness for eggs for several years, but only lately learned of this carnivorous propensity, which is doubtless the natural outgrowth of its habit of sucking eggs." About Washington, the present year (1874), the Grackles appeared in considerable number early in March, frequenting the various parks of the city with Robins, Bluebirds, Red-wings, and other early arrivals.

The following (the only additional North American species of *Quiscalus*), has not been found in the Missouri region:

QUISCALUS MAJOR, *Vieill.*

a. *major.*

Gracula barita, WILS., Ind. Am. Orn. vi, 1812.
Quiscalus baritus, PEAB., Rep. Orn. Mass. 1839, 285 (Massachusetts; probably a mistake).—LINSL., Am. Journ. xliv, 1843, 260 (Connecticut; probably a mistake).
Gracula quiscala, ORD, Journ. Phila. Acad. i, 1818, 253.
Quiscalus major, VIEILL., Nouv. Dict. xxviii, 1819, 487.—BP., Am. Orn. iv, 1825, 35, pl. 4; List, 1838, 28; Consp. i, 1850, 424.—NUTT., Man. i, 1832, 192.—AUD., Orn. Biog. ii, 1834, 504; v, 1838, 480; pl. 187; Syn. 1839, 146; B. Am. iv, 1842, 52, pl. 220.—BD., B. N. A. 1858, 555.—DRESS., Ibis, 1865, 494 (Texas).—CASS., Pr. Phila. Acad. 1866, 409.—ALLEN, Pr. Ess. Inst. iv, 1864, 85 (Massachusetts; probably a mistake).—COUES, Pr. Ess. Inst. v, 1868, 286 (New England; probably a mistake).—ALLEN, Bull. M. C. Z. ii, 1871, 295 (Florida).—COUES, Pr. Bost. Soc. xii, 1868, 117 (South Carolina).—COUES, Ibis, 1870, 367 (biography).—COUES, Pr. Phila. Acad. 1871, 25 (North Carolina).—COUES, Key, 1872, 160.—COUES, Check-list, 1874, No. 224.—B. B. & R., N. A. B. ii, 1874, 222, pl. 36, f. 3, 4.
Chalcophanes major, TEMM., Cab. Mus. Hein. 1851, 96.

b. *macrourus.*

Quiscalus macrourus, SW., An. in Men. 1838, 299, f. 51ª.—SCL., P. Z. S. 1856, 300 (Cordova); Ibis, i, 1859, 20 (Guatemala); *ibid.* ii, 1860, 112 (Honduras).—BD., B. N. A. 1858, 554; 1860, 554, pl. 58; Mex. B. Surv. ii, 1859, Birds, 20, pl. 20.—CASS., Pr. Phila. Acad. 1860, 138 (Carthagena).—CAB., J. f. O. ix, 1861, 82 (Costa Rica).—LAWR., Ann. Lyc. viii, 181 (Nicaragua); *ibid.* ix, 104 (Costa Rica).—DRESS., Ibis, 1865, 493 (Texas).—CASS., Pr. Phila. Acad. 1867, 410 (critical).—SUMICH., Mem. Bost. Soc. i, 1869, 553 (Vera Cruz).—COUES, Key, 1872, 160, fig. 159.
Chalcophanes macrourus, CAB., Mus. Hein. i, 1851, 196.
Quiscalus major var. *macrourus*, B. B. & R., N. A. B. ii, 1874, 225, pl. 36, f. 1, 2.

Hab.—The typical form along the South Atlantic and Gulf coast, from the Carolinas to Texas; not authentic in New England. Var. *macrourus* from Texas south into Central America.

Family CORVIDÆ : Crows, etc.

Subfamily CORVINÆ : *Ravens and Crows.*

CORVUS CORAX, Linn.

Raven.

Corvus corax, LINN., *auctorum;* Planches Enlum. 495.—NAUM., Vog. pl. 53.—GOULD, B. E. pl. 220.—SCHL., Not. sur *Corv.* pl. 1.—WILS., Am. Orn. ix, 1825, 136, pl. 75, f. 3.—BP., Syn. 1828, 56.—DOUGH., Cab. Nat. Hist. i, 1830, 270, pl. 24.—SW. & RICH., F. B. A. ii, 1831, 290.—NUTT., Man. i, 1832, 202.—AUD., Orn. Biog. ii,

1834, 476, pl. 101; Syn. 1839, 150; B. Am. iv, 1843, 78, pl. 224.—GIR., B. L. I. 1844, 149.—BP., Consp. i, 1850, 387.—WOODH., Sitgr. Rep. 1853, 78.—HEERM., P. R. R. Rep. x, 1859, pt. vi, 54.—ALLEN, Mem. Bost. Soc. i, 1868, 525 (Indiana); Bull. M. C. Z. iii, 1872, 178.—FINSCH, Abh. Nat. iii, 1872, 40 (Alaska).

Corvus var. *ferrœnsis*, BRUNN.; *C. leucomelas*, WAGL.; *C. leucophœus*, VIEILL., Gal. Ois. pl. 100 (individuals streaked with white).

Corvus corax var. *littoralis*, HOLBÖLL, Kroyer's Tidskrift, iv, 1843, 390 (Greenland and Labrador).

Corvus corax (var ?), COUES, Key, 1872, 162.

Corvus corax var. *carnivorus*, B. B. & R., N. A. B. ii, 1874, 234, pl. 37, f. 6.

Corvus maximus, SCOP., Ann. i, 34, No. 45.

Corvus clericus, SPARRM., Mus. Carls. pl. 2.

Corvus major, VIEILL., et *C. montanus*, TEMM.; LE VAILL., Ois. Afr. pl. 61.—BP., Consp. i, 1850, 387 (*sp. apocrypha*).

Corvus carnivorus, BART., Trav. Fla. 1793, 290.—BD., B. N. A. 1858, 560.—COOP. & SUCK., N. H. Wash. Ter. 1860, 210, pl. 21.—WHEAT., Ohio Agric. Rep. 1860.— COUES, Pr. Phila. Acad. 1861, 225 (Labrador); *ibid*. 1866, 91 (Arizona).— HAYD., Rep. 1862, 70.—LORD, Pr. Roy. Arty. Inst. iv, 1864, 121 (British Columbia.—DRESS., Ibis, 1865, 494 (Texas).—DALL & BANN., Tr. Chic. Acad. 1869, 285 (Alaska).—COOP., Pr. Cal. i, 1870, 282.—STEV., U. S. Geol. Surv. Ter. 1870, 465; and of most late American writers.

Corvus cacalotl, WAGL., Isis, 1831, 527 (Mexico).—BP., P. Z. S. 1837, 115; Consp. i, 1850, 387.—MAXIM., Reise, ii, 1841, 289.—MAXIM., J. f. O. 1858, 195.—NEWB., P. R. R. Rep. vi, 1857, 82.—KENN., P. R. R. Rep. x, 1859, pt. iv, 31, pl. 20.— BD., B. N. A. 1858, 563.—SCL., Ibis, i, 1859, 21 (Guatemala).—SUMICH., Mem. Bost. Soc. i, 1869, 553 (Vera Cruz).

Corvus sinuatus, WAGL., Isis, 1829, 748 (Mexico).

Corvus catototl, BP., Comp. List, 1838, 28.

Corvus nobilis, GOULD, P. Z. S. 1837, 79.—BP., Consp. i, 1850, 386 (Mexico).

Corvus " *splendens*, GOULD," BP., P. Z. S. 1837, 115 (error). Not of VIEILL.

Corvus lugubris, AGAS., Pr. Bost. Soc. ii, 1846, 188.

" *Corvus thibetanus*, HODGS."

" *Corvus vociferus*, CAB."

Gray's Hand-list, Nos. 6181–84, and 6189–90.

Hab.—In North America, generally distributed. Throughout British America. Everywhere in United States west of the Mississippi (according to *Aiken*, Am. Nat. vii, 16, the Ravens of Colorado are chiefly *C. cryptoleucus*). Rare, or wanting in different parts of Eastern United States. On the Atlantic coast, regularly south to Maine, where it nests (*Boardman*); rarely to Southern New England, New York, Pennsylvania, and New Jersey. Formerly breeding in Middle States and mountainous parts of South Carolina (*Audubon*). Kentucky (*Audubon*). Ohio (*Wheaton*). Indiana (*Haymond*; formerly numerous, became exceedingly rare in 1856). . Not found in the Gulf States, excepting Texas. South into Mexico (*C. "cacalotl," "sinuatus," "splendens," and "nobilis"*). Guatemala.

List of specimens.

| 19300 | 202 | Loc. not given . | .... | .... | F. V. Hayden. | 25.00 | 47.00 | 16.00 |

Lieutenant Warren's Expedition.—5186, Fort Randall, Dakota; 4546, source Little Missouri River; L'Eau qui court; 5787, Fort Pierre.

Later Expeditions.—54316, 60813, Wyoming.

It is impossible to distinguish our Raven specifically from the European, and the grounds for separating even a *C. corax* var. *carnivorus* are very slight. The American bird may *average* a trifle larger, with a correspondingly more robust bill; but the difference in these respects is entirely within the normal individual variability of the bird, being equaled if not exceeded among specimens from each country. As to the Raven of Mexico, described as distinct under a variety of names, it appears to be somewhat more richly iridescent, as a consequence of its subtropical habitat; from the same circumstances, the bill and feet may average relatively larger.

It is unnecessary to mention particular localities in the West, where the Raven is more or less numerous; it is so generally distributed, that its great abundance, scarcity, or absence at various points merely represent incidents in the career of individuals, drawn together by abundance of food or other favoring circumstances, and dispersed under opposite conditions. In fact, the restriction of its range in the United States is probably reducible to a fortuitous matter, since this bird, like some others, sooner or later finds the advance of civilization unsupportable, and retires to regions more congenial to its wild and wary nature.

CORVUS CRYPTOLEUCUS, Couch.

White-necked Raven.

Corvus cryptoleucus, COUCH, Pr. Phila. Acad. vii, 1854, 66 (Tamaulipas).—BD., B. N. A.
1858, 565; Mex. B. Surv. ii, pt. ii, 1859, Birds, p. 20.—COOP., B. Cal. i, 1870,
284.—DRESS., Ibis, 1865, 494 (Eagle Pass, Texas).—COUES, Key, 1872, 162.—
AIKEN, Am. Nat. vii, 1873, 16 (Cheyenne, Wyo. Ter.).—AIKEN, Pr. Bost. Soc.
1872, 203 ("very common along the base of the mountains").—B. B. & R., N.
A. B. ii, 1874, 242.

Hab.—Texas, New Mexico, and Arizona. North to Colorado and Wyoming. South
into Mexico. Said to be abundant on the Llano Estacado. Found near Tucson, Arizona, by Lieutenant Bendire (*epist.*)

The known range of this species has been lately extended by Mr. C.
E. Aiken, who found it near Cheyenne; this brings it within the region
of the Missouri. Its peculiar character, of snowy-white bases of the
cervical feathers, has not been observed in any other of the North
American *Corvi,* but it occurs in a number of extralimital species. It
is described as being considerably smaller than the Common Raven, and
otherwise different; but its relationship to some of its allies might perhaps be profitably investigated. In our Raven and Crows the bases of
the neck-feathers are plumbeous-gray. The eggs of the White-necked
Raven are said to resemble those of the Common Raven, but to be paler,
and, it is to be presumed, smaller.

Mr. Trippe writes me, that in Colorado the White-necked Raven "is
abundant along the edge of the plains in winter; not common in the
mountains; not observed during spring and summer. I did not succeed
in taking any specimens of this bird, but have no doubt that it is the
White-necked Raven. It is called "Crow" by the inhabitants, to distinguish it from the Raven proper. Its croak is different from that of the
Eastern Crow, being much harsher; in flight and actions it is very similar to that bird. I have seen this species, one hundred miles or more
east of the mountains, feeding on dead buffalo."

CORVUS AMERICANUS, Aud.

Common Crow.

a. *americanus.*

Corvus corone, WILS., Am. Orn. iv, 1811, 79, pl. 25, f. 3.—BP., Syn. 1828, 56.—SW. & RICH.
F. B. A. ii, 1831, 291.—NUTT., Man. i, 1832, 209.
Corvus americanus, AUD., Orn. Biog. ii, 1834, 317; v, 1839; 477; pl. 156; Syn. 1839,
156; B. Am. iv, 1842, 87, pl. 225.—BP., List, 1838, 29; Consp. i, 1850, 385.—
NUTT., Man. i, 2d ed. 1840, 221.—MAXIM., Reise, i, 1839, 140; J. f. O. vi, 1858,
198.—GIR., B. L. I. 1844, 151.—NEWB., P. R. R. Rep. vi, 1857, 82.—BD., B. N. A.
1858, 566.—HEERM., P. R. R. Rep. x, 1859, vi, 54.—DRESS., Ibis, 1865, 494
(Texas).—COOP. & SUCK., N. H. Wash. Ter. 1860, 211, pl. 23.—COUES, Pr.
Phila. Acad. 1861, 226 (Labrador).—STEV., U. S. Geol. Surv. Ter. 1870, 465.—
ALLEN, Bull. M. C. Z. iii, 1872, 178.—SNOW, B. Kans. 1873, 8.—HOLD., Pr. Bost.
Soc. 1872, 203 (Wyoming).—COUES, Key, 1872, 162.—B. B. & R., N. A. B. ii,
1874, 243, pl. 37, f. 5; and of authors generally.

b ? *caurinus.*

Corvus caurinus, BD., B. N. A. 1858, 569.—COOP. & SUCK., N. H. Wash. Ter. 1860, 24, pl.
24.—DALL & BANN., Tr. Chic. Acad. i, 1869, 286.—COOP., B. Cal. i, 1870, 285.—
FINSCH, Abh. Nat. iii, 1872, 41.—B. B. & R., N. A. B. ii, 1874, 248.
Corvus americanus var. *caurinus,* COUES, Key, 1872, 163.

c. *floridanus.*

Corvus americanus var. *floridanus,* BD., B. N. A. 1858, 568.—COUES, Key, 1872, 163.—B. B.
& R., N. A. B. ii, 1874, 247.

Hab.—Temperate North America (to 55°, *Richardson*), excepting, probably, most of the high central plains and the Southern Rocky Mountains, where the Raven abounds. Var. *caurinus* along the Pacific coast, from Sitka to Lower California. Var. *floridanus* is a larger-billed strain from Southern Florida.

Lieutenant Warren's Expedition.—5188, mouth of Powder River; 5189-91, Fort Union, Dakota; 5192, Vermilion River.

Later Expeditions.—60461, La Bonté Creek, Wyoming.

The *Corvus caurinus* is probably not specifically distinct, but may represent a littoral variety, distinguished by its smaller size, and some particular mode of life, circumstances probably mutually explanatory. It is hardly necessary to recognize "*floridanus*" by name, since it merely illustrates the usual relative increase in size of the bill and feet shown by birds of corresponding latitudes.

Although apparently rare or quite wanting in a great part of the West, in the interior, as above indicated, the Crow occurs along the whole Missouri River. It is associated in most places with the Raven, but in general their numbers are reciprocal. The Raven spreads more over the plains, while the Crow is more partial to the wooded river-bottoms and the immediate vicinity of the water-courses. At Fort Randall, where the Raven is comparatively rare, the Crow is common and resident. I found many Crows along Mouse River, in Northern Dakota, but no Ravens. I never saw a single Crow in Colorado, New Mexico, or Arizona, where the Raven was my constant companion during all my journeying and residence.

The Fish Crow, which is not found in the Missouri region, has the following synonymy:

CORVUS OSSIFRAGUS, *Wilson.*

Corvus ossifragus, WILS., Am. Orn. v, 1812, 27, pl. 37, f. 2.—BP., Obs. Wils. 1825, No. 39; Syn. 1828, 57; List, 1838, 27; Consp. i, 1850, 385.—WAGL., Syst. Av. 1827, *Corvus* No. 12.—NUTT., Man. i, 1832, 216.—AUD., Orn. Biog. ii, 1834, 268; v, 1839, 479; pl. 146; Syn. 1839, 151; B. Am. iv, 1842, 94, pl. 226.—BD., B. N. A. 1858, 571; 1860, 571, pl. 67, f. 2.—COUES & PRENT., Smiths. Rep. 1861, 414 (Washington, D. C., common).—ALLEN, Pr. Ess. Inst. i, 1864, 85 (Southern New England, occasional).—COUES, *ibid.* v, 1868, 286 (the same).—LAWR., Ann. Lyc. N. Y. viii, 1866, 289 (New York).—COUES, Pr. Bost. Soc. xii, 1868, 117 (South Carolina).—TURNB., B. E. Pa. 1869, 26.—COUES, Pr. Phila. Acad. 1871, 26 (North Carolina).—ALLEN, Bull. M. C. Z. ii, 1871, 297 (Florida).—COUES, Key, 1872, 162.—B. B. & R., N. A. B. ii, 1874, 251, pl. 37, f. 7.

Hab.—Coast of the United States, from New England to Florida.

PICICORVUS COLUMBIANUS, (Wils.) Bp.

Clarke's Crow; American Nutcracker.

Corvus columbianus, WILS., Am. Orn. iii, 1811, 29, pl. 20, f. 2.—BP., Obs. Wils. 1825, No. 38; Syn. 1828, 57.—NUTT., Man. Orn. i, 1832, 218.

Nucifraga columbiana, AUD., Orn. Biog. iv, 1838, 459, pl. 362; Syn. 1839, 156; B. Am. iv, 1842, 127, pl. 235.—BP., List, 1838, 28.—NUTT., Man. i, 1840, 251.

Nucifraga (Picicorvus) columbiana, GRAY, Hand-list, ii, 1870, 9, No. 6165.

Picicorvus columbianus, BP., Consp. i, 1850, 384.—NEWB., P. R. R. Rep. vi, 1857, pt. iv, 83.—BD., B. N. A. 1858, 573, 925.—KENN., P. R. R. Rep. x, 1859, pt. iv, 32.—COOP & SUCK., N. H. Wash. Ter. 1860, 212.—HAYD., Rep. 1862, 171 (to Fort Laramie).—COUES, Pr. Phila. Acad. 1866, 91.—LORD, Pr. Roy. Arty. Inst. iv, 121 (British Columbia); Nat. in Vancouver (breeding near Fort Colville).—DALL & BANN., Tr. Chic. Acad. i, 1869, 286 (Sitka).—COOP., B. Cal. i, 1870, 289.—STEV., U. S. Geol. Surv. Ter. 1870, 465.—COUES, Ibis, 1872, 52 (biography).—ALLEN, Bull. M. C. Z. iii, 1872, 178.—HOLD.-AIKEN., Pr. Bost. Soc. 1872, 203 (Wyoming).—COUES, Key, 1872, 162, fig. 104.—B. B. & R., N. A. B. ii, 1874, 255, pl. 38, f. 4.

"*Corvus megonyx,* WAGL."—(*Gray.*)

Hab.—Chiefly the coniferous belt of the West, in mountainous regions, from about 3.000 feet up to the highest peaks. North to Sitka (*Bischoff*). Northeast to Milk River, Montana (200 miles east of Rocky Mountains., lat. about 49°, *Suckley*). East to Fort

208   PICICORVUS COLUMBIANUS, CLARKE'S CROW.

Kearney (Nebraska, long. 99° 6′ W. Greenwich, *Cooper*).   South on high lands to Mexico?
(to Albuquerque, New Mexico, *Kennerly*; Fort Whipple, Arizona, *Coues*; Fort Tejon,
California, *Xantus*).   Found breeding at Fort Colville, Washington Territory (*Lord*).

List of specimens.

19291	37	Grosventres R. .	♂	June 2, 1860	F. V. Hayden.	12.25	16.50	7.50
19292	38	...... do	....	..... do	..... do	11.50	20.50	6.75
19293	32	Mud River.... .	...	May 30, 1860	..... do	......	17.50	6.75
19294	....	Popoagie Creek.	♂	May 20, 1860	G. H. Trook..	......	......	.....

Lieutenant Warren's Expedition.—8870–74, Black Hills, Dakota; 8875, Rawhide Peak,
Wyoming.
Later Expeditions.—54317–19, Wyoming; 59856–9, Colorado; 60817–18, Pacific Creek,
Wyoming; 61087, Green River; 11159 (*young*), Wyoming.

The range of this species is nearly coincident with the zone of coniferous vegetation in the West.   It rarely descends below an altitude of
3,000 feet, and has been observed on peaks 10,000 feet high.   A hardy
bird, finding its food at all seasons, Clarke's Crow is not a true
migrant; that is to say, it does not move north and south at regular
periods.   But the individuals are never thoroughly localized; they are
restless birds, scurrying continually among the mountains.   The nearest
approach to a regular movement appears to be their flying down mountains in severe weather, and returning to the more elevated situations
to breed.   This seems to be the case, at any rate, in latitudes from 45°
southward, although they nest quite low down in more northern situations.   Thus, at Fort Whipple, near 35° 30′, and 4,000 or 5,000 feet high,
I never saw them in summer; but they were irregularly common from
October to March, and I have no doubt they breed in the neighboring
San Francisco Mountains.   I have never seen the nest or eggs.   Mr. J.
K. Lord, who found the bird in immense flocks, in May, near Fort Colville, and subsequently breeding there, states that a nest was placed in
the top of a pine, 200 feet high; "it was composed of fir-twigs, bark,
leaves of pine, and fine root-fibres, with some moss and gray lichen—
very large and shallow."

Like others of this omnivorous family, Clarke's Crow is an indiscriminate feeder upon vegetable substances, giving preference, however, to
the seeds of the pine, berries of the cedar, and acorns.   Prying into a
pine-cone with its long and peculiarly-shaped beak, it gouges out the
seeds, often hanging, while thus engaged, head downward, like a
Thistle-bird swing under the globular ament of a button-wood.   It also
eats insects of various kinds, and has been observed pecking at dead
bark to obtain them, and making short sallies in the air for the same
purpose, like a Woodpecker.   It sometimes descends to the ground in
search of food, walking easily and firmly, like a true Crow; but we may
infer, from the length and sharpness of its claws, that it does not spend
much of its time on the ground.

According to my observations, made at all seasons, excepting during
the breeding time, Clarke's Crow is decidedly a gregarious bird.   Flocks
of fifty or a hundred are oftener witnessed than single birds, and Mr.
Lord speaks of their appearance "by thousands."   They are very noisy
birds, uttering a harsh, discordant scream of great volume and penetration, and extremely wary, under ordinary circumstances, like most
of the larger *Corvi*.   The ordinary flight is rapid, straight, and steady,
accomplished by regular and vigorous wing-beats; but when flying
only from tree to tree, the birds swing themselves in an undulatory
course, with the wings alternately spread and nearly closed, much in
the manner of the Woodpeckers.

The following interesting passages occur in Mr. Trippe's Manuscripts: "At Idaho Springs, in Colorado, Clarke's Crow is by no means rare; nearly, or quite, resident; breeds. Eight or ten years ago, as I have been informed by old residents, this bird was exceedingly numerous, and during winter, very tame and bold, approaching close to the cabins and homes of the settlers, and devouring everything left exposed to its voracity. At present it is seldom seen in numbers; but singly, or in small parties, is not uncommon from about 9,000 feet up to timber-line during the warmer months, descending to the lower valleys, and probably to the foot-hills, during the depth of winter, a few remaining in the county throughout the year. As soon as the weather has commenced to moderate a little, they begin ascending again, working upward in advance of all other birds.

"The habits of Clarke's Crow are well indicated by its name, for they are a compound of those of the Woodpecker and Crow. At times it will alight on a dead limb, and hammer it precisely as a Woodpecker does, the loud rattling being audible at a great distance; at others, its actions are so similar to that of a Crow, that one might readily mistake it for a smaller species of that bird were it not for its colors. It frequently alights on the top of a tree, and utters its hoarse notes to call or alarm its companions, constantly looking around in every direction to detect any approaching danger, just as the Crow is in the habit of doing. It is rather a shy bird than otherwise, yet not so wild but that it may be shot by using a little caution in approaching it. Its flight is bold and strong, with rather quick and rapid strokes, like the Blue Jay's; at times, after flying a little way from its perch, it will sail on its wings in a wide circle, returning to the same tree. Near timber-line I have seen dozens of them all performing this manœuvre together, sometimes flying hundreds of feet above the trees and returning to them when tired. It occasionally visits the slaughter-houses, and, like a true Crow, seems to be quite omnivorous, cramming its hungry maw with everything that will satisfy its voracious appetite. In spring, when other food is scarce, it even attacks the cones and buds of *Pinus ponderosa* and *P. contorta;* and nothing seems to come amiss. A tame one which I saw preferred raw meat, but ate anything given to it with apparent relish.

"Clarke's Crow probably breeds very early, as young birds are able to fly in the middle of May; its nest, however, I was never able to find, nor even gain any idea of where it is placed. The young are cared for by the parents a short time after leaving the nest, and are then left to shift for themselves—hence, as the first brood is hatched so early, they may raise a second; but I never saw any young birds after the latter part of June, and am inclined to think, therefore, that they raise but a single brood. Of notes, this bird possesses several, all of which are harsh, grating, and crow-like, many being quite loud. It is tamed as easily as the Crow or Raven, and soon becomes quite as familiar and impudent, showing all the propensities to theft and mischief that mark those birds."

GYMNOKITTA CYANOCEPHALA, (Maxim.) Bp.

Blue Crow; Cassin's Jay; Maximilian's Jay.

Gymnorhinus cyanocephalus, MAXIM., Reise, ii, 1841, 21.
Gymnokitta cyanocephala, BP., Consp. i, 1850, 382.—CASS., B. Cal. and Tex. i, 1854, 165, pl. 28.—NEWB., P. R. R. Rep. vi, 1857, 83.—MAXIM., J. f. O. vi, 1858, 193.—BD., B. N. A. 1858, 574.—KENN., P. R. R. Rep. x, 1859, pt. iv, 32.—COUES, Pr. Phila.

14

Acad. 1866, 91; Ibis, 1872, 152 (biography); Key, 1872, 163.—COOP., B. Cal. i, 1870, 292.—AIKEN, Pr. Bost. Soc. xv, 1872, 204 (Wyoming).—B. B. & R., N. A. B. ii, 1874, 260, pl. 38, f. 2.

Psilorhinus cyanocephalus, GRAY, Genera of Birds.
Nucifraga (*Gymnokitta*) *cyanocephala*, GRAY, Hand-list, ii, 1870, 10, No. 6166.
Cyanocephalus wiedi, BP., Oss. Stat. Zool. Eur. Vert. 1840-'41, 1842; see Ibis, 1873, 103.
Cyanocorax cassini, McCALL, Pr. Phila. Acad. v, 1851, 216.

Hab.—Western United States, from the eastern foot-hills and spurs of the Rocky Mountains to the opposite slopes of the Cascade and Coast Ranges.

List of specimens.

19370	....	Bighorn Mts...	♂	June 1, 1860	G. H. Trook..	10.50	18.00	6.00
19371	....	...... do	♀	..... do	..... do	10.50	18.00	6.00
19372	....	...... do	♀	..... do	..... do	......	......	......
19373	153	Tullock Creek.	♂	Sept. 3, 1890	F. V. Hayden.	11.00	10.00	6.50

Not obtained by Lieutenant Warren's Expedition.
Later Expeditions.—59860-3, Wyoming.

The following account, like that of Clarke's Crow, is reproduced, in substance, from my article in the "Ibis," as above quoted:

For many years this species was considered a rarity, to be highly prized, and may still remain among the *desiderata* of many or most European collectors; but of late a great many specimens have been gathered, notably in California, by the late Captain John Feilner, and in Arizona, by myself. Prince Maximilian's original examples are stated to have come from one of the tributaries of the Upper Missouri, which locality, if not beyond the bird's ordinary range, is certainly far from its centre of abundance. Dr. Hayden does not appear to have met with it in that region, and probably Maximilian's quotation indicates nearly the northeastern limit of the species, which would thus prove very nearly coincident with that of Clarke's Crow. Colonel McCall found his *Cyanocorax cassini* abundant near Santa Fé, New Mexico; Dr. Kennerly met with great numbers near San Miguel and at Fort Webster, in the same Territory; and Captain Feilner procured his fine suite of specimens at Fort Crook, Califonia. Dr. J. S. Newberry is our principal Oregon reference. I have seen no Washington Territory record; but data are to be anticipated from this quarter, corresponding to those respecting Clarke's Crow. In the matter of altitude, the present species has not been proven to occur so high up as Clarke's Crow has; but the evidence is only negative. It breeds at or near its limit of altitude, descending in winter to the lower border of the pine-belt, if not a little beyond.

At Fort Whipple, in Arizona, where my observations were made, the bird may be considered a permanent resident. Though we did not observe it breeding in the immediate vicinity, we found newly-fledged young in the neighboring higher mountains, showing that it nests there. Like most of its tribe—in fact, like most birds largely subsisting on varied animal and vegetable substances—it is not strictly migratory, except, perhaps, at its highest point of dispersion. A descent of a few thousand feet from mountain tops appears to answer the purpose of the southward journeying most migratory species perform, as far as food is concerned, while its hardy nature enables it to endure the rigors of winter in regions frequently snow-bound. It feeds principally upon juniper-berries and pine-seeds; also upon acorns, and probably other small, hard fruit.

Notwithstanding its essentially corvine form, the habits of this bird, like its colors, are rather those of Jays. It is a garrulous and vociferous creature, of various and curiously modulated chattering notes when at ease, and of extremely loud, harsh cries when in fear or anger. The former are somewhat guttural, but the latter possess a resonance different both from the hoarse screams of *Cyanura macrolopha*, and the sharp, wiry voice of the *Cyanocitta*. Like Jays, it is a restless, impetuous bird, as it were of an unbalanced, even frivolous, mind; its turbulent presence contrasting strongly with the poised and somewhat sedate demeanor of the larger black *Corvi*. With these last, however, it shares a strong character—its attitudes when on the ground, to which it habitually descends, being crow-like; and its gait, an easy walk or run, differing entirely from the leaping progression of the true Jays. It shares a shy and watchful disposition with its relatives on both sides of the family; its flight is most nearly like that of the *Picicorvus*. It is highly gregarious, in the strict sense of the term. Immense as the gatherings of Crows frequently are, these birds seem to associate rather in community of interest than in obedience to a true social instinct; each individual looks out for himself, and the company disperses for cause as readily as it assembles. It is different with these small, Blue-Jay Crows; they flock, sometimes in surprising numbers, keep as close together as Blackbirds, and move as if by a common impulse. As usual, their dispersion is marked, if not complete, at the breeding season; but the flocks reassemble as soon as the yearlings are well on wing, from which time until the following spring hundreds are usually seen together. On one occasion at least, I witnessed a gathering of probably a thousand individuals.

The nest and eggs of this bird apparently remain unknown.

Subfamily GARRULINÆ: *Jays.*

PICA MELANOLEUCA var. HUDSONICA, (Sab.) Coues.

American Magpie.

a. *melanoleuca.*

Corvus pica, LINN., Fn. Suec. 92; Syst. Nat. i, 1766, 157; and of early authors.
Pica melanoleuca, VIEILL., Nouv. Dict. d'Hist. Nat. xxvi, 121.
Pica albiventris, VIEILL., Fn. Franç. 119, pl. 55, f. 1.
Pica europœa, BOIE, Isis, 1822, 551.
Pica rusticorum, LEACH, Cat. 1816, 18.
Pica caudata, FLEMING, Br. An. 1828, 87; and of many authors.
Pica varia, SCHL., Rev. Crit. Ois. Eur. 1844, 54.
Pica germanica, septentrionalis, et hiemalis, BREHM, V. D. 1831, 177, 178.

b. *hudsonica.*

Corvus pica, FORST., Phil. Trans. lxxii, 1772, 382.—WILS., Am. Orn. iv, 1811, 75, pl. 35, f. 2.—BP., Obs. Wils. 1825, No. 40; Syn. 1828, 57, No. 62.—SW. & RICH., F. B. A. ii, 1831, 292.—NUTT., Man. i, 1832, 219.—AUD., Orn. Biog. iv, 1838, 408, pl. 357.
Corvus hudsonicus, SAB., App. Franklin's Journey, 1823, 25, 671.
Pica hudsonica, BP., List, 1838; Consp. i, 1850, 383.—MAXIM., Reise, i, 1839, 508; J. f. O. 1858, 197.—NEWB., P. R. R. Rep. vi, 1857, 84.—BD., B. N. A. 1858, 576.—WOODH., Sitgr. Rep. 1853, 77.—COOP. & SUCK., N. H. Wash. Ter. 1860, 213.—HAYD., Rep. 1862, 171.—LORD, Pr. Arty. Inst. iv, 121 (British Columbia).—DALL & BANN., Tr. Chic. Acad. i, 1869, 286 (Alaska).—FINSCH, Abh. Nat. iii, 1872, 39 (Alaska).—COOP., B. Cal. i, 1870, 296.—SNOW, B. Kans. 1873, 8 (Shawnee County, Kans.).—HOLDEN-AIKEN, Pr. Bost. Soc. 1872, 204 (Wyoming, abundant, breeding).—STEV., U. S. Geol. Surv. Ter. 1870, 465.—MERR., *ibid.* 1872, 687.
Cleptes hudsonicus, GAMB., Journ. Phila. Acad. i, 1847, 47.
Pica melanoleuca, AUD., Syn. 1839, 157; B. Am. iv, 1842, 99, pl. 227.
Pica melanoleuca var. *hudsonica*, COUES, Key, 1872, 164, fig. 106.
Pica caudata var. *hudsonica*, ALLEN, Bull. M. C. Z. iii, 1872, 178 (Kansas, &c.).—B. B. & R., N. A. B. ii, 1874, 266, pl. 38, f. 1.

c. *nuttalli.*

Pica nuttallii, AUD., Orn. Biog. iv, 1838, 450, pl. 362; Syn. 1839, 152; B. Am. iv, 1842,
    104, pl. 228.—NUTT., Man. i, 1840, 236.—WOODH., Sitgr. Rep. 1853, 77.—NEWB.,
    P. R. R. Rep. vi, 1857, 84, pl. 26.—BD., B. N. A. 1858, 578.—HEERM., P. R. R.
    Rep. x, 1859, pt. vi, 54.—COOP., B. Cal. i, 1870, 295.
Cleptes nuttallii, GAMB., Journ. Phila. Acad. i, 1847, 46.
Pica melanoleuca var. *nuttallii*, COUES, Key, 1872, 164.
Piva caudata var. *nuttallii*, B. B. & R., N. A. B. ii, 1874, 270, pl. 38, f. 2.

Hab.—Western and Northern America. Eastward occasionally to Lake Superior and Hudson's Bay (*Richardson*). Western Kansas (*Pond*) and Iowa (*Coues*) to
the Pacific. Alaska (*Dall*). Breeds in mountains of New Mexico (*Coues*). Var. *nuttallii*
in California, apparently to the exclusion of the normal form. The typical form in
Europe.

List of specimens.

19295	201	Deer Creek	....	....	Nov. 20, 1860	F. V. Hayden.	19.00	26.00	8.25
19296	158	...... do	....	....	Oct. 31, 1860	G. H. Trook..	20.00	26.00	8.75
19297	193	...... do	....	....	....	...... do	19.50	25.50	8.00

Lieutenant Warren's Expedition.—4547, 5196, Fort Pierre; 5193, Running Water; 5197,
Great Bend, Missouri River; 5198, Fort Berthold; 5194–95, 5199, Fort Randall; 9060,
Fork of Cheyenne River; 9057–58–59, 9062–63, 9067, Black Hills.
    Later Expeditions.—54320, 60459–60, 60814–16, 61074–81, 61155, various Wyoming
localities; 61780, Idaho.

In ascending the Missouri I saw the first Magpie near Sioux City,
Iowa, a point immediately on the border of its eastward dispersion.
Mr. Trippe does not include the species in his Minnesota list, nor does
Dr. Head, United States Army, mention it among the birds of Fort
Ripley, in that State. Prof. Snow includes it among Kansas birds,
stating that it has been seen in Shawnee County. Mr. Allen found it
in the mountains of Colorado, up to at least 11,000 feet, and elsewhere
in the West. Further south, Dr. Kennerly informs us that he met with
it soon after crossing the Rio Grande, and saw it from time to time on
his journey thence into California. But in following almost in Dr. Kennerly's tracks through part of New Mexico and most of Arizona, I did
not meet with a single one, and must conclude that it is rare in that
region. I, however, found it breeding east of the Rio Grande, in the
Raton Mountains, in June. A nest that I there found in a dense thicket
was a large globular mass, about eighteen inches in diameter, suspended
in a thick bush about ten feet high. Its walls were composed of closely-
interlaced twigs, and very thick, leaving but a small cavity, the entrance to which was a hole in one side, large enough to admit the hand.
The lining was a little dried grass. The nest contained six young ones,
nearly ready to fly—a fact that disposes of one of the alleged distinctive characters of the American as compared with the European Magpie, namely, that it has but two young. The eggs measure from 1.40 to
1.20 in length by about 0.90 in breadth ; the ground-color dull pale
bluish or greenish, sometimes merely grayish-white, thickly marked all
over with spots and dots of several shades of olive-brown and clearer
brown, with neutral-tint and pale-purplish or lavender shell-markings.
    Mr. Aiken describes a somewhat differently built nest: "The nest,
which is quite a curious structure, is usually placed in a small scrubby
tree, about ten feet from the ground. They commence to build about
the last of March, and the eggs are laid two or three weeks later. The
foundation of the nest is of twigs, firmly cemented with mud. On this
is placed the nest proper, which is composed of finer twigs, plastered
with mud, and lined with rootlets. Outside of this a wall of dead twigs
is built up from the foundation, and arched over at the top, the whole
structure forming a rounded mass from one to three (!) feet in diameter.

The entrance is an unconspicuous hole in the side.   Full number of eggs, eight.   Young begin to fly about June 1."

Magpies are very common at Fort Randall through the winter, as at other points higher up the river.   They keep mostly in troops in the wooded river-bottom, and, notwithstanding the severity of the weather, they are not familiar and impudent, as they are represented to be in times of scarcity.   In fact I have always found them wary and watchful, on the alert for suspicious approach, and rather difficult to shoot. When a flock is feeding, as they habitually do, down among the bushes, one or more are perched, apparently as sentinels, on the high trees overhead, and the hidden birds below are instantly warned of danger by their discordant screams.   I have more than once succeeded in getting within range of one of these picket-guards, and at the report of my gun, scores of birds, of whose presence I was entirely unaware, have sprung up from the bushes all around, where they had been feeding in perfect silence.   I once procured several specimens unexpectedly and unintentionally, the birds having come to feed upon the carcase of a horse I had poisoned to secure wolves.   Six or eight magpies were found dead next morning, besides several coyotés and a skunk.   It is stated that this method has also been successfully employed to destroy the birds, when, from their numbers and under stress of hunger, they proved a nuisance by alighting on the sore backs of horses and mules to pick at the raw flesh.   An Indian boy at Fort Randall succeeded in capturing a number alive with a common "figure-of-four" trap, showing that their native cunning is sometimes at fault.   During the whole season of 1873 I did not see a single Magpie along the northern border of Dakota.

This variety is scarcely at all found in California, where the yellow-billed form is common west of the Sierra Nevada.   That *P. nuttallii* is not a valid species is sufficiently proven by the facts, that the same peculiarity occurs in the European bird, and that in several species of this family the bill is indifferently black or yellow.   I continue to regard the yellow-billed race as simply illustrating the perpetuation of a fortuitous condition.   Messrs. Baird and Ridgway agree to the reduction.

The following observations, made by Mr. Trippe in Colorado, will be read with interest :

"Common; resident; breeds.   The Magpie abounds from the plains up to 10,000 feet, rarely venturing higher than that limit, while it is most numerous below 8,500.   It is a social bird, although not gregarious, being usually found in pairs or small parties of from three to six or eight, but quite often goes alone.   It is very voracious, living upon seeds, carrion, insects, &c., and being especially fond of the eggs and young of other birds, of which it destroys very great quantities.   It is easily caught and tamed, even when old, and soon becomes very cunning and mischievous, exhibiting the same traits as the Crow, and, like that bird, is said to imitate the human voice with some aptitude.   It has almost an infinite variety of notes, some low, gurgling, and musical, some harsh and discordant, others squeaky and grating.   It is very noisy at times, and quite silent at others, when engaged in robbing birds' nests or foraging near dwellings or barns.   It has a loud, rapid chatter, uttered as an alarm cry, and, with its extensive vocabulary, seems at no loss to convey its ideas to its fellows.   It prefers, as a rule, the vicinity of streams, and the brushy valleys, but often wanders among the pine groves on the hill-sides, and pays frequent visits to the vicinity of slaughter-houses.   It is common along road-sides, where its bright plumage and harsh cries attract the attention of the traveler.

The Magpie is not a shy bird, but if frequently shot at soon learns to keep out of range. Among the foot-hills, the Magpie begins building in April; the nest is quite an elaborate affair, and occupies several days in its construction. It is placed in the fork of a small, bushy tree— which is never a pine—from six to fifteen feet from the ground, and composed externally of stout sticks, ingeniously placed and wedged together. Upon this is a layer of smaller twigs, and then a layer of fine clay one-half or three-quarters of an inch in thickness, which, being applied soft and well worked in, becomes very hard, and binds the whole structure firmly together. On this again is a soft lining of fine twigs, hair, feathers, and any proper material which they can find. Over the whole, rising from the walls of the nest, is a dome of twigs and sticks, very ingeniously and securely woven together, and framing a shelter for the bird while setting. There are two openings, opposite each other, evidently to make room for the long tail of the bird, which could never be brought within the nest. The eggs are five, of a pale greenish, very thickly obscured with spots and dashes of pale purplish-brown, varying somewhat in intensity and being somewhat thicker at the larger end. In the foot-hills, the young are hatched about the first of June, at Idaho Springs nearly three weeks later, or not for two months after the appearance of the broods of *Picicorvus columbianus*—a singular fact, considering the intimate relations of the two birds, and their similar habits, range and food."

CYANURUS CRISTATUS, (Linn.) Sw.

Blue Jay.

Corvus cristatus, LINN., i, 1766, 157.—GM., i, 1788, 369.—WILS., Am. Orn. i, 1808, 11, pl. 1, fig. 1.—DOUGHTY, Cab. 1832, 62, pl. 6.—BP., Syn. 1828, 58.—NUTT., Man. i, 1832, 224.—AUD., Orn. Biog. ii, 1834, 11; v, 1839, 475; pl. 102.
Garrulus cristatus, VIEILL., Ency. Meth. 890; Gal. Ois. 160, pl. 102; Dict. 1817, 477.—SW. & RICH., F. B. A. ii, 1831, 293.—AUD., B. Am. iv, 110, pl. 231.--GIR., B. L. I, 1844, 153.—MAXIM., J. f. O, 1858, 192.—TRIPPE, Pr. Ess. Inst. vi, 1871, 177 (Minnesota, resident).
Pica cristata, WAGL., Syst. Av., 1827, *Pica* No. 8.
Cyanurus cristatus, SW., F. B. A. ii, 1831, 495.—BD., B. N. A. 1858, 580; and of most late writers.—DRESS., Ibis, 1865, 494 (Texas).—MCILWR., Pr. Ess. Inst. v, 1868, 90 (Canada West, resident).—ALLEN, Bull. M. C. Z. iii, 1872, 178 (Kansas).—SNOW, B. Kans. 1873, 8.—COUES, Key, 1872, 165.—B. B. & R., N. A. B. ii, 273, pl. 42, fig. 3.
Cyanocorax cristatus, BOIE.—BP., List, 1838, 27.—WOODH., Sitgr. Rep. 1853, 77 (Indian Territory).
Cyanocitta cristata, STRICKL., Ann. Mag. 1845, 261.—CAB., Mus. Hein. i, 1851, 221.
Cyanogarrulus cristatus, BP., Consp. Av. i, 1850, 376.

Hab.—Eastern North America. North to the Fur Countries (to 56°, *Richardson*). West to Kansas, Eastern Nebraska, and Dakota. Common on the Red River. Breeds throughout its range. Resident throughout its United States range.

This abundant and familiar species of the Eastern States was unnoticed by either Expedition, and although Audubon states that it "proceeds up the Missouri River to the eastern declivities of the Rocky Mountains," it does not appear to have been of late observed further west than as above indicated.

CYANURUS STELLERI var. MACROLOPHUS, (Bd.) Allen.

Long-crested Jay.

a. *stelleri*.

Corvus stelleri, GM., i, 1788, 370.—LATH., Ind. i, 1790, 158.—PALL., Zoog. i, 393,—BP., Zool. Journ. iii, 1827, 49; Syn. 1828, 433; Am. Orn. ii, 1828, 44, pl. 13, fig. 1.— NUTT., Man. i, 1832, 229.—AUD., Orn. Biog., iv, 1838, 453, pl. 362, fig. 2.

Garrulus stelleri, VIEILL., Enc. Meth. 893; Dict. 1817, 481.—Sw. & RICH., F. B. A. ii, 1831, 294 (not pl. 54 ?).—AUD., Syn. 1839, 154; B. Am. iv, 1842, 107, pl. 230.
Cyanurus stelleri, Sw., F. B. A. ii, 1831, 495.—BD., B. N. A. 1858, 581.—HEERM., P. R. R. Rep. x, 1859, pt. vi, 55.—COOP. & SUCK., N. H. Wash. Ter. 1860, 214.—LORD, Pr. Roy. Arty. Inst. iv, 1864, 122 (British Columbia, nesting).—DALL & BANN., Tr. Chic. Acad. i, 1869, 286.—COOP., B. Cal. i, 1870, 298 (includes *frontalis*).—COUES, Key, 1872, 165.—RIDGW., Am. Journ. v, 1873, 43.—B. B. & R., N. A. B. ii, 1874, 277, pl. 39, fig. 1.
Pica stelleri, WAGL., Syst. Av. 1827.
Cyanocorax stelleri, BOIE.—BP., List, 1838, 27.—FINSCH, Abh. Nat. iii, 1872, 40 (Alaska).
Cyanocitta stelleri, STRICKL.—CAB., Mus. Hein. 1851, 221.—NEWB., P. R. R. Rep. vi, 1857, 85.
Cyanogarrulus stelleri, BP., Consp. Av. i, 1850, 377.

b. *frontalis*.

Cyanura stelleri var. *frontalis*, RIDGW., Am. Journ. v, 1873, 43.—B. B. & R., N. A. B. ii, 1874, 279, pl. 39, fig. 2.

c. *macrolophus*.

Garrulus stelleri, Sw. & RICH., F. B. A. ii, pl. 54 (the text refers to true *stelleri;* the plate seems to represent var. *macrolophus*).
Cyanocorax stelleri, WOODH., Sitgr. Rep. 1853, 77.
Cyanocitta macrolopha, BD., Pr. Phila. Acad. 1854, 118.
Cyanura macrolopha, BD., B. N. A. 1858, 582.—KENN., P. R. R. Rep. x, 1859, 32.—COUES, Pr. Phila. Acad. 1866, 92 (Arizona).—COOP., B. Cal. i, 1870, 300.—STEV., U. S. Geol. Surv. Ter. 1870, 465.—MERR., *ibid*. 1872, 688.—COUES, Am. Nat. v, 1871, 770 (biography).—ELLIOT, B. N. A. pl. 17.—AIKEN, Pr. Bost. Soc. 1872, 205.
Cyanuri stelleri var. *macrolopha*, ALLEN, Bull. M. C. Z. 1872, 178.—COUES, Key, 1872, 165, fig. 107.—B. B. & R., N. A. B. ii, 1874, 281, pl. 29, fig. 3.
Cyanura coronata var. *macrolopha*, RIDGW., Am. Jour. v, 1873, 43.

d. *diadematus*.

Cyanogarrulus diadematus, BP., Consp. Av. i, 1850, 377.
Cyanocitta diademata, SCL., Cat. Am. Birds, 1862, 143.
Cyanura coronata var. *diademata*, RIDGW., Am. Journ. v, 1873, 42.
Cyanura stelleri var. *diademata*, B. B. & R., N. A. B. ii, 1874, 272.

e. *coronatus*.

Garrulus coronatus, Sw., Phil. Mag. i, 1827, 437, No. 67.—JARD. & SELBY, Illust. pl. 64.
Pica coronata, WAGL., Isis, 1829, 750.
Cyanurus coronatus, Sw., F. B. A. ii, 1831, 495.—BD., B. N. A. 1858, 583.—SCL., P. Z. S. 1859, 381.—SCL. & SALV., Ibis, 1859, 22.
Cyanacorax coronatus, BP., P. Z. S. 1837, 115.—GRAY, Gen. of B.
Cyanogarrulus coronatus, BP. Consp. i, 1850, 377.
Cyanocitta coronata, STRICKL.—CAB., Mus. Hein. 1851, 222.—SCL., P. Z. S. 1858, 302, 359; Cat. 1862, 142.—TAYLOR, Ibis, 1860, 112.
Cyanura coronata var. *coronata*, RIDGW., Am. Journ. v, 1873, 42.
Cyanura stelleri var. *coronata*, B. B. & R., N. A. B. ii, 1874, 272, pl. 39, fig. 4.

Hab.—The typical form from the Northern Pacific slopes, from Sitka southward. Shading, in the Cascade, Coast Range, and Sierra Nevada of California, into var. *frontalis*. Var. *macrolophus* in the central Rocky Mountain region of the United States (and eastward to Fort Lyons, in the Arkansas Valley). Inosculating with *stelleri* proper about the head-waters of the Columbia; separated from it thence southward by the Great Basin. Passing, on the Table-lands of Mexico, into var. *diadematus*, and this last passing southward into var. *coronatus*.

List of specimens.

19298	72	Spring Creek ..	....	June 27, 1860	F. V. Hayden.	12.50	18.00	5.75

Lieutenant Warren's Expedition.—8856-7, Laramie.
Later Expeditions.—54325, 62243, Wyoming; 60436, Laramie Peak; 62241-2, Idaho.

All the specimens collected are of the var. *macrolopha*.
The intergradation of the various supposed species of *Cyanurus* quoted above, was noted by Prof. Baird in 1858, and subsequently by myself; but it remained for Mr. Ridgway to point out exactly the links in the connected chain and define them with precision. I cannot do better than to quote from his lucid exposition : " *C. stelleri* ex-

ists under two very well-marked, though of course intergrading, forms; the typical *stelleri* is confined to the northern coast region, from Sitka to the Columbia River, and is characterized by a short crest, entirely black head without any blue on the forehead; by sooty-black body and uniform blue of wings, belly, rump and tail. From the Columbia, southward along the Sierra Nevada to Southern California, it is modified into a well-marked form (var. *frontalis*), which has a longer crest, the head and crest grayish-brown with conspicuous blue streaks on the forehead, brownish-ashy body, and two different shades of blue—the indigo of the tail and secondaries being abruptly contrasted with the light azure of the rump, primaries, abdomen, and tail-coverts. This form * * * * approximates closely to *C. macrolopha* of a parallel latitude, *but does not grade into it*, there never being a white supraocular spot, barred greater coverts, or other peculiar features of the Rocky Mountain and Mexican form. That the northern race of *C. stelleri* should grade into *C. macrolopha*, while the southern one does not, seems to be easily explained by the following facts: The habitat, longitudinally, of *C. coronata* var. *macrolopha*, is exceedingly limited, it being confined to the central ranges of the Rocky Mountain system; thus it is everywhere separated from the habitat of *stelleri* var. *frontalis*, which is equally restricted longitudinally by that broad desert expanse, the Great Basin, which affords no sheltering woods, such as are furnished on the two boundary barriers, the Sierra Nevada and the Rocky Mountains, which each represents. The northern limit of the range of *C. macrolopha* passes just a little beyond the southern limit of the habitat of the northern race of the coast stock, and at a latitude where the Great Basin becomes greatly reduced in width, or even terminates, and where its two great mountain systems become less distinctly separated. Consequently the coast stock cannot grade into the Rocky Mountain one, by approaching its habitat, until [except] before it becomes modified into var. *frontalis*. * * * * The coast stock reaches its southern limit with the Sierra Nevada, and this of course prevents it from passing into *C. coronata* var. *diademata*."

It will be observed that in this article Mr. Ridgway keeps the mountain and coast stocks specifically separated, assigning the former to *C. coronata* as a variety. He, however, admits their intergradation, saying: "As a summary of these facts, it appears evident that the series of forms under consideration is divided into two well-marked stocks, but that they intergrade at one point. The conclusion then must be, that they are all modifications of one primitive species, or we must accept as the only alternative the hypothesis of hybridization." And again, speaking of the mountain varieties, he says: "It is possible, however, that even the *C. stelleri* may yet also have to be combined with these," apparently overlooking the fact that both Mr. Allen and myself (*ll. cc.*) had already made the combination he indicates. Messrs. Baird and Ridgway now combine the whole series as one species with five varieties, a procedure which I endorsed without hesitation.

Having enjoyed excellent facilities for studying the habits and manners of the Long-crested Jay in the pine-clad mountains of Arizona, I offered, on a previous occasion, an account substantially as follows:

When I was traveling westward, in the spring of 1864, I saw some of these Jays in the Raton Mountains, in New Mexico, which I believe to be about their eastern limit, at least in this latitude, for they were strongly attached to pine-clad mountains, and are found as high up as timber grows. In crossing the Rocky Mountains, through Whipple's Pass, I did not happen to meet with any; to the westward still, in the lofty forests of the San Francisco Mountains, they were abundant, and at that time (July) had just reared their families, and were rambling through the tops of the trees together. The old birds were in sorry plight, literally with a "crest-fallen" air, and full of pin-feathers. But when I came across them the third time, in the pineries about Fort Whipple, they were in good trim once more, and saucy as ever. They live in the mountainous parts of Arizona all the year, for they are able to endure severe cold, being of hardy nature, and well clothed with soft, thick plumage, while their food is such as can be procured at any season. Thus being non-migratory, their permanent habitat may be given with some accuracy; it includes the wooded Rocky Mountain region at large. To the north, and especially about the Columbia River, they become mixed up with Steller's Jay, which is the boreal extreme, reaching into Alaska; while in the opposite direction they run into the *Cyanura coronata* on the Table-lands of Mexico.

All Jays make their share of noise in the world; they fret and scold about trifles, quarrel over anything, and keep everything in a ferment when they are about. The particular kind we are now talking about is nowise behind his fellows in these respects—a stranger to modesty and forbearance, and the many gentle qualities that charm us in some little birds and endear them to us; he is a regular fillibuster, ready for any sort of adventure that promises sport or spoil, even if spiced with danger. Sometimes he prowls about alone, but oftener has a band of choice spirits with him, who keep each other in countenance (for our Jay is a coward at heart, like other bullies) and share the plunder on the usual terms in such cases, of each one taking all he can get. Once I had a chance of seeing a band of these guerrillas on a raid; they went at it in good style, but came off very badly indeed. A vagabond troop made a descent upon a bush-clump, where, probably, they expected to find eggs to suck, or at any rate a chance for mischief and amusement. To their intense joy, they surprised a little Owl quietly digesting his grasshoppers, with both eyes shut. Here was a lark! and a chance to wipe out a part of the score that the Jays keep against Owls for injuries received time out of mind. In the tumult that ensued, the little birds scurried off, the Woodpeckers overhead stopped tapping to look on, and a snake that was basking in a sunny spot concluded to crawl into his hole. The Jays lunged furiously at their enemy, who sat helpless, bewildered by the sudden onslaught, trying to look as big as possible, with his wings set for bucklers and his bill snapping; meanwhile twisting his head till I thought he would wring it off, trying to look all ways at once. The Jays, emboldened by partial success, grew more impudent, till their victim made a break through their ranks and flapped into the heart of a neighboring juniper, hoping to be protected by the tough, thick foliage. The Jays went trooping after, and I hardly know how the fight would have ended had I not thought it time to take a hand in the game myself. I secured the Owl first, it being the interesting Pygmy Owl (*Glaucidium*), and then shot four of the Jays before they made up their minds to be off. The collector has no better chance to enrich his cabinet than when the birds are quarreling, and so it has been with the third party in a difficulty, ever since the monkey divided cheese for the two cats.

It is difficult to describe the notes of this Jay, he is such a garrulous creature, and has such a variety of outcries. He ordinarily screams at the top of his voice, until he is tired or something attracts his attention. This cry is something like that of a Blue Jay, but hoarser and heavier; its base quality distinguishes it in a moment from the harsh outcry of either Woodhouse's or Maximilian's Jay, both of which birds run higher up the scale. He has also a call sounding like the rataplan of a Flicker; and again, when greedily regaling on acorns, or hopping aimlessly about, or peering curiously down through the pine fronds to watch a suspicious character, he talks to himself in a queer way, as if thinking aloud, and chuckling over some comical notions of his own. Such loquacity has given a good name (*Garrulinæ*) to the whole tribe of Jays.

The Long-crested Jay will eat anything eatable. It is said Jays kill and devour small birds, and doubtless they do so on occasion, though I do not think it is habitual with them. They suck eggs, despoiling many a pretty nest; and if they cannot catch winged insects, fat larvæ and beetles do not come amiss; but after all, they are principally vegetarians, feeding mainly upon seeds, hard fruits, and berries. In the mountains where the Long-crested Jay lives, pine-seeds afford most of its fare. I have often watched the bird hammering away at a pine-cone, which he would sometimes wedge in a crotch, and sometimes hold under his feet. Though most at home in the pineries, where this particular source of supply is unfailing, he often strays into the adjoining oak openings, and into juniper patches, after acorns or berries, or to pick a quarrel with Woodhouse's Jay and frighten the Sparrows. Wherever he goes he has it pretty much his own way, hated and feared by the other birds, whom he silences with a scream and subdues by a show of authority. But who of his kind has not enemies? Cassin's Flycatcher, almost as noisy and audacious, has many a set-to with him, and even the nimble little Wood Pewees pester him sometimes. The Woodpeckers tease him persistently; they can scramble about faster than he can follow, and laugh at him from the other side of a bough, till he quite loses his temper. But after all our Jay has his good points, and I confess to a sneaking sort of regard for him. An elegant, dashing fellow, of good presence if not good manners; a tough, wiry, independent creature, with sense enough to take precious good care of himself, as any one who wants his skin will discover. As one approaches the tall pine where he is rollicking, his restless, bright brown eye marks the suspicious object. Now on the alert, he leaps like a squirrel from bough to bough, till he reaches the top, when he is off with a scream that makes the woods echo his triumph and disdain. It is of no use to follow when he is thoroughly alarmed. But on some other occasion he may be inclined to take another peep, for his curiosity is great, and thus expose himself through a rift in the foliage. This moment is the chance; and with the report of the gun comes his shriek of agony as he tumbles all bloody from the bough he just mounted in pride and strength.

The foregoing account may be supplemented by Mr. Trippe's observations in Colorado, where he found the species "abundant and resident, ranging up to timber-line and down to the plains, breeding, probably, throughout—certainly from 7,000 feet up to timber-line. The Long-crested Jay scarcely changes its habitat the year round, those living highest up descending a little in the severest weather, but even in mid-winter it is common at elevations of 10,000 feet and over. This species is known as the Blue Jay throughout the mountains, and is one of the most abundant and conspicuous of all the birds. From its noisy famil-iarity, its splendid plumage, and its universal presence in every locality, it is quite sure to attract the attention of the tourist and stranger. It has all the pertness, garrulity and vivacity, of the Eastern Blue Jay; and never being molested it becomes very tame, alighting close to the door of the miner's cabin to pick up whatever crumbs and bits of food it may happen to find, and evincing the same familiarity that *C. cristata* displays in Iowa and Kansas. Its notes are harsh and jay-like—at times guttural and rasping. Its favorite haunts are the valleys, and hill-sides thinly scattered with pines; yet it also frequents the densest pine forests, and adapts itself to all localities. Its nest I could not find, nor even dis-cover at what time of the year it breeds. It occasionally robs the nests of other birds, like the Eastern Blue Jay. In December I found this bird quite common in the valley of the Arkansas River, near old Fort Lyon and the mouth of Sand Creek."

The egg of Steller's Jay is pale, dull bluish-green, more or less thickly, but usually quite uniformly, sprinkled all over with small olive-brown and clearer brown spots. Size, 1.25 by 0.85, to 1.35 by 0.90.

APHELOCOMA FLORIDANA var. WOODHOUSEI, (Bd.) Allen.

Woodhouse's Jay.

a. *floridana.*

Corvus floridanus, BARTR., Trav. 1791, 291.—BP., Syn. 1828, 58.—NUTT., Man. i, 1832, 230.—
    AUD., Orn. Biog. i, 1831, 444, pl. 87.
Garrulus floridanus, BP., Am. Orn. ii, 1828, 59, pl. 14, f. 1.—AUD., Syn, 1839, 154; B. Am.
    iv, 1842, 118, pl. 233.
Cyanurus floridanus, SW., F. B. A. ii, 1831, 495.
Cyanocorax floridanus, BP., List, 1838, 27.
Cyanocitta floridana, BP., Consp. 1850, 377.—BD., B. N. A. 1858, 586.—ALLEN, Bull. M. C.
    Z. ii, 1871, 298.—B. B. & R., N. A. B. ii, 1874, 285, pl. 40, f. 4.
Aphelocoma floridana, CAB., Mus. Hein. 1851, 221.—COUES, Key, 1872, 165, f. 108.
Garrulus cyaneus, VIEILL., Nouv. Dict. d'Hist. Nat. xii, 1817, 476 (no description).
Garrulus cœrulescens, VIEILL., *ibid.* 480.—ORD, Journ. Phila. Acad. i, 1818, 347.
Pica cœrulescens, WAGL., Syst. Av. 1827, *Pica* No. 11.

b. *woodhousei.*

Cyanocorax californica, WOODH., Sitgr. Rep. 1853, 77 (Arizona).
Cyanocitta woodhousei, BD., B. N. A. 1858, 585, pl. 59; Mex. B. Surv. ii, 1859, Birds, 20,
    pl. 21.—COUES, Pr. Phila. Acad. 1866, 92 (Arizona).—COOP., B. Cal. i, 1870, 304.—
    AIKEN, Pr. Bost. Soc. 1872, 205 (Colorado).—STEV., U. S. Geol. Surv. Ter. 1870,
    465.—MERR., *ibid.* 1872, 688.
Aphelocoma floridana, var. *woodhousei*, ALLEN, Bull. M. C. Z. iii, 1872, 179 (Ogden,
    Utah).—COUES, Key, 1872, 166.
Cyanocitta californica var. *woodhousei*, B. B. & R., N. A. B. ii, 1874, 291, pl. 40, f. 3.

c. *californica.*

Garrulus californicus, VIG., Zool. Beechey's Voy. 1839, 21, pl. 5.
Cyanocitta californica, STRICKL., Ann. Mag. xv, 1845, 342.—GAMB., Journ. Phila. Acad.
    i, 1847, 45.—BP., Consp. i, 1850, 377.—NEWB., P. R. R. Rep. vi, 1857, 85.—BD.,
    B. N. A. 1858, 584.—KENN., P. R. R. Rep. x, 1859, pt. iv, 32.—HEERM., *ibid.* pt. vi,
    55.—COOP., B. Cal. i, 1870, 302.—SCL., P. Z. S. 1857, 127; 1858, 302; 1859, 381;
    Cat. 1862, 143.—B. B. & R., N. A. B. ii, 1874, 288, pl. 40, f. 1.
Cyanocorax californica, GAMB., Pr. Phila. Acad. iii, 1847, 201.
Aphelocoma californica, CAB., Mus. Hein. 1851, 221.—BP., Compt. Rend. xxxii, 1853, 828.
Aphelocoma floridana var. *californica*, COUES, Key, 1872, 166.
Corvus ultramarinus, AUD., Orn. Biog. iv, 1838, 456, pl. 362.
Garrulus ultramarinus, AUD., Syn. 1839, 154; B. Am. iv, 1842, 115, pl. 232 (*nec* Bp.).
Cyanocitta superciliosa, STRICKL., Ann. Mag. xv, 1845, 260 (*fide* Bd., type of genus).
"*Corvus palliatus*, DRAPIEZ."

d. *sumichrasti.*

Cyanocitta sumichrasti, RIDGW., Rep. Geol. Surv. 40th parallel, p. — (still in press).
Cyanocitta californica var. *sumichrasti*, B. B. & R., N. A. B. ii, 1874, 283 (Mexico).
Aphelocoma floridana var. *sumichrasti*, COUES.

Hab.—The typical form in Florida only. Var. *woodhousei* from the Southern Rocky
Mountain region, Utah into Mexico. Var. *californica* from the Cascade Mountains and
Sierra Nevada of California to the Pacific.

Not obtained by either of the earlier Expeditions.

Later Expeditions.—59864, 61082, Wyoming; 61754-55, Utah.

The three forms above given, after being currently reported as distinct species for
several years, were united by Dr. Schlegel, whose example was followed by Mr. Allen.
But it appears that there are some tangible differences, warranting a geographico-
varietal separation. Mr. Allen subsequently modified his first impressions to agree
with the determination as given in the Key, above quoted. Messrs. Baird and Ridgway keep *floridana* separate, uniting only *woodhousei* with *californica;* but all three
forms appear to constitute links in a single chain. As for the generic name, both Gray
and Cabanis state that *Cyanocitta* (STRICKLAND) was based upon the crested species, and,
therefore, is a synonym of *Cyanurus*, Sw. Prof. Baird states, however, that *Cyanocitta*
has as type *C. californica.* I have no opportunity, just at present, of satisfying myself
which is right.

The northernmost record of var. *woodhousei* I have seen, is that given
by Mr. Allen, who found it at Ogden, in Northern Utah, thus bringing
its range to the confines of the region embraced in the present work.

220   APHELOCOMA FLORIDANA VAR. WOODHOUSEI.

I judge it remains to be detected somewhere further north still, along the mountains. It is very abundant in the upper parts of Arizona, where I saw it almost daily for two years. It may be called the characteristic species of the subfamily in this region; for, although Maximilian's and Steller's Jays are equally abundant, Woodhouse's is the more widely and equally distributed in all sorts of places, with the exception, perhaps, of the recesses of pine woods, which are generally relinquished in favor of the crested species. Its preference, however, is for oak openings, rough, broken hill-sides, covered with patches of juniper, manzanita, and yuccas, brushy ravines and wooded creek-bottoms. The ordinary note is a harsh scream, indefinitely repeated with varying tone and measure; it is quite noticeably different from that of either Maximilian's or Steller's, having a sharp, wiry quality lacking in these. It is always uttered when the bird is angry or alarmed, and consequently is oftener heard by the naturalist; but there are several other notes. If the bird is disporting with his fellows, or leisurely picking acorns, he has a variety of odd chuckling or chattering syllables, corresponding to the absurd talk of our Blue Jay under the same circumstances. Sometimes again, in the spring-time, when snugly hidden in the heart of a cedar bush with his mate, whom he has coaxed to keep him company, he modulates his harsh voice with surprising softness to express his gallant intention; and if one is standing quite near, unobserved, he will hear the blandishments whispered and cooed almost as softly as a Dove's. The change, when the busy pair find they are discovered, to the ordinary scream, uttered by wooer and wooed together, is startling.

The food is varied, as with all birds of this family; but acorns seem a favorite article of diet. To procure them with the least trouble, the bird sometimes robs the store that the Californian Woodpecker has stuck in the bark of trees. The flight of the bird is firm and direct. When going far, and high over head, in flocks, the wing-beats are regular and continuous; among trees and bushes, the short flights are more dashing and unsteady, performed with a vigorous flap or two and a sailing with widely-spread wings and tail. The tail is often jerked in the shorter flights, especially those of ascent or the reverse, and its frequent motion, when the bird is not flying, is like that seen in *Pipilo* or *Mimus*. Among the branches the bird moves with agile hops, like all true Jays, and its movements when on the ground have the same buoyant ease; it never walks, like Maximilian's and other Crows. I never succeeded in finding a nest; it is to be presumed that its nidification and eggs are much the same as those of the California variety. According to Dr. Cooper, the latter builds "a large and strong nest of twigs, roots, grass, &c., in a low tree or bush, and lays about five eggs, dark-green, with numerous pale-brown blotches and spots." He found eggs laid at San Diego about the 5th of April.

Since the preceding paragraph was written, the surmise has been verified. Mr. Aiken, who found the bird a common resident in Southeastern Wyoming, says: "Nest composed outwardly of dead twigs, then of fine roots, and lined with fine rootlets or horse-hair. The eggs, four or five in number, are laid about May 1. They are of a light bluish-green color, and with the reddish-brown specks thickest at the large end. Their average length is 1.06 inches; breadth, 0.80 inch." The egg of *Aphelocoma*, of which numerous examples are before us, is distinguishable from that of *Cyanurus*, in most cases, by its richer, deeper green ground, and much bolder marking of heavy spots, especially large, numerous, and heavily colored about the great end.

PERISOREUS CANADENSIS var. CAPITALIS, Bd.

Canada Jay.

a. *canadensis.*

Corvus canadensis, LINN., Syst. Nat. i, 1766, 158.—FORST., Phil. Trans. 1772, 382.—GM.,
   Syst. Nat. i, 1788, 376.—WILS., Am. Orn. iii, 1811, 33, pl. 21, f. 1.—SAB., App.
   Franklin's Journ. 572.—BP., Obs. 1824, No. 42; Syn. 1828, 58.—NUTT., Man. i,
   1832, 232.—AUD., Orn. Biog. ii, 1834, 53; v, 1839, 208; pl. 107.
Garrulus canadensis, SW. & RICH., F. B. A. ii, 1831, 295.—AUD., Syn. 1839, 155; B. A. iv,
   1842, 121, pl. 234.—PUTN., Pr. Ess. Inst. i, 1856, 228 (Massachusetts, casual).—
   TRIPPE, *ibid.* vi, 1871, 117 (Minnesota, resident; breeds).
Perisoreus canadensis, BP., List, 1838, 27; Consp. i, 1850, 375.—CAB., Mus. Hein. 1851, 219.—
   BD., B. N. A. 1858, 590.—COUES, Pr. Phila. Acad. 1861, 226 (Labrador).—VERR.,
   Pr. Ess. Inst. iii, 152 (Norway, Me., winter).—BOARDM., Pr. Bost. Soc. ix, 1862,
   127 (Calais, Me., resident).—LAWR., Ann. Lyc. viii, 1866, 289 (New York Island,
   in summer, accidental).—McILWR., Pr. Ess. Inst. v, 1866, 91 (Canada West).—
   COUES, Pr. Ess. Inst. v, 1868, 286.—TURNB., B. E. Pa. 1869, 43 (winter strag-
   gler).—MAYN., Pr. Bost. Soc. xiv, 1871, p. — (Umbagog, in June).—COUES.,
   Key, 1872, 166.—B. B. & R., N. A. B. ii, 1874, 299, pl. 41, f. 3.
Dysornithia canadensis, SW., F. B. A. ii, 131, 495.
Garrulus brachyrhynchus, SW. & RICH., F. B. A. ii, 296, pl. 55.—NUTT., Man. ii, 1834, 599.
Garrulus fuscus, VIEILL., Nouv. Dict. d'Hist. xii, 1817, 479; Ency. Meth. 892.
" *Pica nuchalis*, WAGL."—" *Coracias mexicanus*, TEMM."

b. *obscurus.*

Perisoreus canadensis, NEWB., P. R. R. Rep. vi, 1857, 85 (California).—COOP. & SUCK.,
   N. H. Wash. Ter. 1860, 216 (Washington Territory).—DALL & BANN., Tr.
   Chic. Acad. i, 1869, 286 (Alaska).—COOP., B. Cal. i, 1870, 397.—FINSCH, Abh.
   Nat. iii, 1872, 40 (Alaska).
Perisoreus canadensis var. *obscurus*, RIDGW., Bull. Ess. Inst. v, 1874, 199.—COUES, Check-
   list, 1874, App. No. 239ᵃ.—B. B. & R., N. A. B. ii, 1874, 302.

b. *capitalis.*

Perisoreus canadensis, HAYD., Rep. 1862, 171.—ALLEN, Bull. M. C. Z. iii, 1872, 179 (mount-
   ains of Colorado, &c.).—STEV., U. S. Geol. Surv. Ter. 1870, 465 (Wyoming).—
   MERR., *ibid.* 1872, 689 (Idaho and Wyoming).
Perisoreus canadensis var. *capitalis*, BD.—RIDGW., Bull. Ess. Inst. v, 1874, 199.—B. B. &
   R., N. A. B. ii, 1874, 302, pl. 41, f. 4.—COUES, Check-list, 1874, App. No. 239ᵃ.

Hab.—North America, to about 39° (further south along high ranges). Breeds from
New York, New England, and Minnesota, northward, and in the Rocky Mountains to its
southernmost observed limit. Rare straggler to the Middle Atlantic States in winter.
Var. *capitalis* is the Rocky Mountain form. Var. *obscurus* from Alaska to California.

List of specimens.

19299	210	H. waters Grosv..	....	June 7, 1860	F. V. Hayden.	10.75	17.75	5.75

Lieutenant Warren's Expedition.—8847, Laramie Peak; 8848-52, 8855-58, Black Hills.
Later Expeditions.—59865, Colorado; 60819-22, Uintah Mountains; 61083-6, Henry's
Fork and Green River; 62244-48, 62250-53, Idaho and Wyoming.

Dr. Hayden speaks of this bird as occurring in " myriads " in the
Black Hills, and the dates of his observation leave no doubt of its
breeding in that region. In California, Drs. Newberry and Cooper
found it common north of 39°; and in Colorado, at about this parallel,
Mr. Allen observed it in July, and noted its abundance. The birds
mentioned in his list of the vicinity of Mount Lincoln, Park County,
Colorado, doubtless breed at or near that point, as he says " the region
is strictly alpine in its features. Our camp was in the valley of the
Platte, at an altitude of about 12,000 feet, from whence excursions were
made every day by some of the party to the region above the timber,
which is here about 13,000 feet above the sea level. Three species
(*Anthus ludovicianus, Leucosticte tephrocotis,* and *Lagopus leucurus*) were

obtained above timber-line, that are truly arctic in their summer distribution   *   *   *   *   *   *   Wilsonia pusilla, Zonotrichia leucophrys, and Melospiza lincolni, were nowhere more abundant than among the dwarfed willows and birches just above the general limit of the trees." All the
notes of this paragraph refer to var. capitalis.

In Minnesota, Mr. Trippe ascertained that this bird breeds in the
dense tamarack swamps. It is also known to breed in Maine. With
these exceptions, the United States record east of the Rocky Mountains,
and south of Northern New England, is entirely of straggling birds,
rare and only in winter, saving only Mr. Lawrence's note of an accidental summer occurrence. But Mr. Merriam informs me that it breeds in
the Adirondacks. ·In Colorado, says Mr. Trippe, the Canada Jay [var.
capitalis] is abundant and resident, breeding. " I have never," he continues, " seen the Canada Jay 'below 9,000 feet, even in mid-winter; and
but rarely below 9,500 or 10,000. During the warmer months it keeps
within a few hundred feet of timber-line, frequenting the darkest forests
of spruce, and occasionally flying a little way above the trees. It is
quite tame, coming about mining camps to pick up whatever is htrown
out in the way of food, and evincing much of the curiosity that is characteristic of the family. In winter, its supply of food is very precarious,
and it is often reduced to mere skin and bones; at such times it will
frequently weigh no more than a plump Snow-bird or Sparrow, and
undoubtedly starves to death sometimes. During the latter part of
autumn, its hoarse croaking is almost the only sound to be heard in the
cold sombre forests that lie near timber-line."

The egg of Perisoreus is altogether different from that of Cyanurus
and Cyanocitta, much nearer Pica, but still peculiar. The ground is
grayish-white, marked all over, but nearly always most heavily at the
but, or in a wreath around it, with several shades of a dark neutral
tint, mixed usually with some olive-brown spots. The markings in several specimens before me are all quite fine, even those that are confluent at the larger end. Size, 1.20 by 0.70. The nest is built on the
limbs of trees, of hay, feathers, &c.

APPENDIX TO OSCINES.

A.

[NOTE.—A portion of Mr. T. M. Trippe's series of interesting observations upon the birds of Colorado, having failed to reach me in time for insertion in the earlier pages of this work, they are here introduced, together with various additional data respecting the species thus far treated. The remainder of Mr. Trippe's notes is in substance incorporated, *passim*, in the work.]

The period during which my notes were made, extends from January, 1873, to the early part of December of the same year; the field of observation, Clear Creek County, Colorado, with two or three adjacent townships of Gilpin and Jefferson counties. During different parts of the year, excursions were made throughout the whole of this region; and although these were not as frequent as could have been desired for a complete account of the avi-fauna, yet they were so often repeated that I believe very few birds escaped me, except such as are rare visitors or mere stragglers.

Clear Creek County lies on the eastern slope of the Rocky Mountains, extending from the summit of the main range some twenty to twenty-five miles eastward, and about the same distance north and south, the centre line being in latitude 39° 40' nearly. It is traversed by a number of streams, whose valleys lie from 300 to 1,500 or 2,000 feet below the surrounding ridges and peaks. The general course of the main stream, South Clear Creek, is nearly due east; but the smaller tributaries, running at various angles to this course, so cut up and divide the surface as to present a confused assemblage of isolated peaks and ridges, disposed in no regular order or system, and divided by deep valleys and ravines, which, toward the range, become in many instances, precipitous, rocky cañons. Bordering the country on the east, lies Bergen's Park; an open park-like tract of rolling, grassy prairie, interspersed with groves of pines, low hills, and wet, marshy swales, a miniature of the great parks lying to the westward of the range. The elevation of the western edge of the county,—the dividing ridge of Atlantic and Pacific waters,—is between 11,000 and 12,000 feet, isolated peaks rising 1,500 or 2,000 feet higher; from this the general surface slopes eastward at the average of about 300 feet per mile, the slope being much greater nearer the range however, and diminishing as the distance from it increases, to the eastern border of the county, which has an elevation, in its lowest part, of between 6,500 and 7,000 feet above the sea. Bergen's Park, lying for the most part in Jefferson County, has an elevation varying between 7,000 and 7,500 feet.

The streams are for the most part mountainous torrents, rarely with a fall less than one hundred feet per mile, and, near the range, three or four times that, being frequently a simple succession of cascades and waterfalls for miles. These waters, save when muddied by the placer workings, are always clear and cold, and abound with the black-speckled trout and two or three species of chub and sucker, the latter, however, being only found in the lower valleys, where the current is less rapid than higher up toward the range. Near timber-line, nestled under the very shadows of the main divide, most frequently faced by perpendicular cliffs of rock, or abrupt, precipitous and craggy slopes, are numbers of small, deep lakes, varying from mere pools to one hundred acres or more in size, and usually bordered on one or more sides by deep, cold bogs, wherein grow various species of arctic willows and other alpine plants. Their surface is covered with ice from the end of October till early in July, some with northern exposure not being free from ice till late in August; and their waters are always of an icy coldness, owing to their depth and the melted snow which is constantly pouring into them. Some few of the deepest are tenanted by trout; but the majority are void of life, save various forms of insects which pass the larva state in them. One or two lakes at a lower elevation, near 10,000 feet, swarm with the curious *Siredons* or *Amblystomœ*. Under these conditions, the absence of aquatic birds will not be surprising; and with a single exception no wader or swimmer can be said to be characteristic of the region.

Great as is the diversity of the surface, the climate is perhaps still more variable. The season of 1873 was in no way a remarkable one; there was less snow than usual, but otherwise it was a fair average of the weather since the settlement of the country. During January, February, and the first half of March, the weather was delightful beyond comparison. No snow nor rain fell, with the exception of three or four days in February; the mercury never sank below zero; the days were bright, cloudless, and mild, even warm, 20° or 25° Fahrenheit being a common temperature at 7 a. m., while at midday it rose to 50° or 60°. On the 7th of February the mercury stood at 71° in the shade at noon, at an elevation of 8,000 feet. After the middle of March wintry weather set in; there was a constant succession of snow-storms, violent winds and biting frosts, continuing till May. On the first of June, at an elevation of 7,800 feet, the poplars and willows had but just begun to put forth their leaves; but once started, the season advanced with great rapidity, and by the 15th, the deciduous trees had attained a complete foliage up to the highest limit of the poplars, 10,500 or 11,000 feet. In autumn, the difference between this climate and that of eastern localities in the same latitude, is less marked. The leaves of the poplars and willows begin to change color toward the close of September, and a month later have all fallen; but it is usually not till the middle or close of November that winter weather sets in. Heavy snows sometimes fall in October, however, but unusual severity is generally followed by a very mild, open winter. The nights are always cool, even in midsummer, while at mid-day the heat is at times oppressive, even at great elevations; but in exposed localities this is moderated by the strong winds that are almost constantly blowing.

Above and near timber-line, which varies from 10,000 to 11,000 feet, the climate partakes of an alpine nature. The immense accumulations of snow do not begin to melt rapidly till about the middle of June; but once started, they disappear very fast; the streams are swollen to thrice their usual size, and by the first of July only isolated snow-fields remain, many of which are of great extent, and have sufficient depth and solidity to exist throughout the summer. Frosts are almost of nightly occurrence, and during summer scarcely a day passes without frequent thunder-storms, with hail, sleet and rain. Light snows begin to fall in September, but it is not until November that heavy snow-storms set in, and the range is usually passable till the middle of winter, or even later, the heaviest snows falling in April and May.

Many of the wider valleys have limited tracts of great fertility, and the immense quantities of potatoes, rye and barley, raised on the scattered mountain ranches, attest the adaptation of the soil to such crops. Yet the sum total of all the tillable land scarcely amounts to as much as one or two per cent. of the whole; while the remainder consists of rocky ridges and peaks, gravelly hills, gently sloping plateaus of sand and glacial detritus, far above the valleys, and insusceptible of irrigation, and a general surface so rough, craggy and inaccessible, as to be quite beyond the capabilities or desires of the agriculturist. Nevertheless, on all the mountain-sides which are not absolutely precipices of bare rock, in every nook and corner and crevice where the soil can lodge, various grasses grow in great luxuriance, and furnish abundant food for numerous herds of cattle, the wild deer and sheep. Vast forests of pines and firs formerly covered the whole face of the country, except the valleys and a few hill-sides, too rocky or too barren even to support conifers; but since the settlement of the country, large tracts of timber have been cut down and their places supplied, to a great extent, by young groves of poplars. Two species of *Pinus* (*P. ponderosa* et *P. contorta*) range up to within [1,000 feet of timber-line; two others (*P. aristata* et *P. flexilis*) are small alpine species; while *Abies mencziesii* et *A. engelmanni* form large forests, the former almost monopolizing the region near timber-line. Of *Populus* there are three species, one growing extensively on the hill-sides, and extending up to 10,500 or 11,000 feet (*P. tremuloides*); the two others, mainly confined to the valleys of the larger streams, where they grow amid dense thickets of willows, and not reaching much over 9,000 feet (*P. angustifolia* et *P. balsamifera*). These few species, with *Juniperus virginianus*, which often grows to a large size, and extends, in a dwarfed form, far above timber-line, comprise the limited sylva of the country. A species of *Alnus*, or small *Betula*, various *Salices*, and a *Negundo*, grow in the rich bottom-lands, and flourish in rank profusion on the banks of the streams, forming the densest thickets, and frequently reaching a height of twenty feet or more. Different species of *Rubus*, *Rosa*, *Cerasus*, *Ribes*, and other small bush-plants abound in the valleys and form thick copses on the hill-sides, along with *Clematis*, *Humulus*, *Vitis*, and other climbers. Among the annual and biennial plants, however, the deficiency in number of species of the larger forms is compensated. Although the species are quite different, the genera are for the most part the same as in the eastern mountainous States, the order of flowering the same, and, to a certain extent, there is the same relative proportions among families and genera. Among distinctive features may be mentioned the abundance of various forms of *Borraginaceæ*—*Echinospermum*, *Lithospermum*, *Cynoglossum*, *Mertensia*, &c.; the many species of *Euphorbia*, *Senecio*, and *Erigeron*, and the various alpine plants, *Primula*, *Actinella*, &c. Yet, considering the vast intervening distance, the general aspect is strikingly like that of the Alleghany region. The genera *Viola*, *Castelleia*, *Saxifraga*, *Caltha*, *Mimulus*, *Pedicularis*, *Polemonium*, *Phlox*, *Helianthus*, *Solidago*, *Aster*, *Erigeron*, *Senecio*, *Cirsium*, *Trifolium*, *Silene*, *Aquilegia*, *Ranunculus*, *Claytonia*, *Rosa*, *Rubus*, *Nabalus*, *Ambrosia*, *Bidens*, *Rudbeckia*, and scores of others, are abundantly represented, and, as in New York, are the predominating features of the flora.

In the fauna we find, perhaps, more points of difference from the eastern mountainous regions. The various genera of mammalia are the same, but nearly all the species are different. Among animals common to the two faunæ, may be mentioned *Felis concolor*, *Lynx rufus*, *Cani occidentalis*, *Gulo luscus*, *Lutra canadensis*, *Ursus americanus*, and *Cervus canadensis*, all large and, with a single exception, carnivorous species. The smaller and granivorous mammals are quite distinct, and many new genera are introduced, while others are wanting. *Cervus leucurus*, *C. macrotis*, *Aploceros montanus*,

Lepus artemisia, L. campestris, Erethizon epixanthus, Arctomys flaviventer, and various species of *Sciurus, Spermophilus, Tamias, Mephitis, Neotoma, Blarina,* and the small rodentia are common, all differing from the eastern representatives of the genera, or even generically distinct. Above and near timber-line, and occasionally wandering a long way below it, is found the Little Chief Hare, *Lagomys princeps,* an essentially alpine form.

Reptiles are rare in the mountains. A species of rattlesnake is common in the foothills, but is seldom found higher than 6,500 feet. A *Bufo* and a *Rana* are occasionally seen in the valleys of the larger streams as high as Georgetown; while a *Tropidonotus* and a large blackish snake (*Coluber?*) occur sparingly as high as 9,000 feet. In some few lakes *Siredon* or *Amblystoma* are found. With the lower animals the difference between eastern and western forms is much greater than it is among the higher.

Of the one hundred and twenty species of birds I have found here, eighty-three were observed throughout the breeding season; of these sixty-four were quite common, while nineteen were more or less rare, and but seldom observed. Of the thirty-seven remaining species, twenty-one were common and sixteen rare. Fifty-three species, or nearly one-half, are different from eastern forms and peculiar to the West; but of these, twenty-one are considered by many ornithologists to be merely geographical races, leaving thirty-two species characterizing this region as distinct from the eastern avi-faunal provinces. Twenty-two of the breeding species do not rear their young below 7,500 feet, and three, only, above timber-line.

Taking into account the varied climate, surface, and general features, the number of birds that are common during the breeding season seems surprisingly small when compared with those found in less diversified regions. Southern Iowa, a rolling prairie country, has at least a number greater by twenty or twenty-five; and certain portions of the State, embracing the marshy haunts of aquatic birds, have nearly twice as many. Nor is the paucity of species compensated for by the number of individuals. The vast, gloomy forests, the rocky precipitous mountain sides, the deep ravines and sandy hill-tops scattered with straggling pines, even the broad open valleys are, save on rare occasions, remarkably poor in bird-life. The greatest number of birds is to be found in the parks; but even these have more or less of the dreary, desolate aspect of the great plains. It is only in a region where prairies and mountains, woods and open meadow, and marsh and lake, are in close proximity, that we can look for a great variety of species; and where the mountains, the plains, the forests or the prairies, extend alone over great areas, the forms of bird-life, as well as all others, must be more limited.

The small areas to which the local mountain avi-faunæ are confined, and the sharp lines which divide them, may be seen by a comparison with the lists of J. A. Allen, who, in 1871, made an exploration of the fauna of the South Park and adjacent mountains. Five species are given as common in that region, which were not observed at all in Clear Creek County, or else so rarely as to leave no doubt that they were mere stragglers; three or four others were more or less frequent, which in the latter region were scarce or entirely wanting; while, on the other hand, four species were common in Clear Creek County, and four or five more or less frequent, that are entirely wanting in Allen's lists, or else given as quite rare. Yet the two regions are contiguous, have nearly the same physical characteristics, and are divided simply by a spur from the main range. The same abrupt transitions may be noticed in the flora, a small ridge limiting the range of species and marking a local flora. The main range—Sierra Madre—of course, is the most important of these dividing lines, but the subsidiary and independent ridges often mark out areas almost as distinctly. Nor does elevation appear to have that decided influence which it is generally supposed to exert. The different temperatures, of course, depend ultimately upon it; and plant and animal life are so intimately related to climate that the one can scarcely vary without producing a change in the other. Yet other causes combine to modify the influence of mere altitude, to a degree wholly unexpected by one who has not studied the subject in all its actual aspects. Thus, the limit of the growth, supposed by most persons to be represented by a nearly constant figure, varies so greatly that on Mount Lincoln it is about 13,000 feet (Allen), while at the South Boulder Pass it is several hundred feet below the summit of the range, which is given by Prof. Hayden at 10,200 feet, the latter point being not more than thirty or thirty-five miles north of the former. Berthoud's Pass, indeed, is in no place above timber-line, though, according to the same authority, it is 600 feet higher (10,800), and is less than ten miles south of it. Thus, with a difference of 3,000 feet or more in the altitude of timber-line within so short a distance, and corresponding modifications in the altitudes of all the local floræ and faunæ, it will be seen that an attempt to mark out zones of certain elevations, corresponding to similar zones as determined by latitude, would be quite futile. Yet, in a general way, it may be said that near the summit of the peaks and higher portions of the range is an arctic region, characterized by the Ptarmigan and Gray-crowned Finch, and the presence of perpetual snow-fields; that below this is a sub-arctic belt, in which various forms of alpine willows and northern plants flourish, and inhabited by

15

the Titlark, Green Black-capped Warbler, Lincoln's Finch, and White-crowned Sparrow; next, a Hudsonian belt, extending from 500 to 1,000 feet below the timber-line, in which may be found sub-alpine plants and such birds as the Canada Jay, Audubon's Warbler, Brown Creeper, &c.; then, of varying extent, a Canadian zone; below this, an Alleghenian; and, finally, on the plains, a Carolinian. It is quite impossible to fix any precise limits to these various faunæ, however; they pass into each other quite gradually, and extend to such different elevations, according to the different influences to which they are exposed, that sometimes two of them will be side by side for some distance through the same altitudes, with merely a ridge intervening.

Nevertheless, the temperature of a region, although it modifies the plant and insect life to a great extent, determines entirely the range of birds. *Junco hyemalis* abounds on the plains and up to 8,000 feet during winter, yet, in company with three of the other four varieties that spend the winter in the same localities, it migrates to the north on the approach of the breeding season, while *J. caniceps* alone ascends the mountains, and finds the requisite climate in the higher forests, which the others seek at higher latitudes. Yet it is well known that the Snow-bird breeds in the Alleghanies further south than this region; and there appears no obvious reason for a northern migration, when it could easily find any desired temperature by ascending the mountains in company with its congener, *J. caniceps*. On arriving from the north, most birds appear among the foot-hills and along the edge of the plains, some days in advance of their arrival higher up in the mountains; and the same thing occurs during the vernal migrations, showing that most of the species prefer migrating along the edge of the plains rather than through the mountains. Even so northern a species as *Ampelis garrulus*, which, during midwinter, is rare among the foot-hills, frequently gathers there in large flocks, in spring, preparatory to its leaving the country. The boundary between plains and mountains appears to be a highway for all the migratory species in spring and autumn.

The most prominent characteristic of the avi-fauna of this region—which may be taken as a fair type of the Rocky Mountain chain between the thirty-eighth and forty-first parallels—is, perhaps, the remarkable number of birds which are represented further east by very closely-allied races or species. Of these there are over twenty; and while some are plainly varieties shading into the eastern forms by such imperceptible gradations as to leave no doubt of their specific identity, others cannot be so summarily disposed of. No one has shown, for instance, that *Geothlypis macgillivrayi* is connected by gradual, intermediate stages, with *G. philadelphia;* or that *Junco caniceps* is similarly related to the other forms of its genus. But are we to accept this definition of a species? Are only such forms entitled to specific rank which cannot be shown to intergrade with others? The tendency of the day is decidedly in that direction; yet, if logically carried out, this system will eventually lead to startling results. If *Pipilo erythrophthalmus* can be shown to gradually pass into *P. arcticus* toward the Rocky Mountains, and into *P. alleni* in Florida; and if the former changes into *oregonus* and *megalonyx* on the Pacific coast, and thus all these forms are to constitute a single species, what reason is there for still keeping apart the various races of *Colaptes*, which intergrade quite as closely? *Carpodacus cassini* is considered a good species; yet its points of difference from *C. purpureus* are fewer and less marked than those separating *Contopus virens* and *C. richardsonii*, which are now thrown together under the same specific name. New links and new intermediate forms are constantly coming to light; and if, on discovering the gradation between any two forms previously held as good species, we are at liberty to combine them as races of the same species, will it not be equally proper to combine other forms together, even though some of the intervening links are wanting, where analogy and experience point to that conclusion? It is the exact reverse of Brehm's system, which led that ornithologist to find no end of species, where others could see but one.

The results of this system of reasoning are already beginning to manifest themselves. Different forms are thrown together with the utmost freedom, and we are learnedly referred to "well-known laws" of geographic and climatic variation. Yet there are cases where these "laws" will not work at all, and then they are quietly ignored. In the Rocky Mountains, for example, a species of Wren is found, so well marked in its notes, plumage, and habits, that the older ornithologists considered it quite distinct; but being somewhat like the eastern House Wren, only grayer and paler, it is at once referred to that species, and its changed color accounted for by the "law" that, in this region, the dry air and bright sunlight exercise a bleaching influence. In the same locality, and existing under precisely similar physical conditions, is a species of Flycatcher, also supposed by Audubon and the older school to be a distinct species, but which these modern ornithologists pronounce to be "var." *richardsoni* of the eastern Wood Pewee. Unfortunately, in this case, the bird happens to be *darker* than its eastern relative, and so we have not a word concerning the "laws of climatic variation" and the "mean amount of rain-fall." Nor do the chief exponents of this new method of reasoning find any limits to their course when once fairly started. In a review of a certain genus of the *Tyrannidæ* (*Myiarchus*), one of our present writers has declared that the examination of a large number of specimens has resulted in his accepting a much smaller number of species than had previously been received as valid, and significantly adds that, had a still more complete series been before him, he would probably have reduced the number still further. So then, in his mind, recognition of specific rank is something almost dependent upon the number of specimens one has for comparison—the larger the series, the fewer the species.* Another equally well-known author, in a recent review of the fifteen species of the genus *Certhiola*, remarks that "it is a nice question what are really species in this genus, and what merely races or varieties, but it would probably be not far from correct to assume that the various forms described are simply modifications of one primitive species, produced by geographical distribution and external physical conditions." Is there any reason to suppose that, since the primitive species has become thus modified by geographical distribution and external physical conditions, that it was not, itself, one of the modifications of a still more primitive form? Yet the progenitors of this "primitive species," which has split into no less than fifteen different races, must have undergone variations brought about by changed geographical habitats and different physical conditions; unless, indeed, they were special creations, and confined to a single narrow locality, a supposition which we have quite as much reason for applying to all the recent forms of *Certhiola* as to the one original form.

In considering the question of specific distinction, too little importance has been attached to the habits and notes of the different races, while there seems to be no intrinsic reason why a difference in these points should not be considered of as much weight as a variation in the plumage. A series of Meadow-larks may be laid out, representing a gradual transition between the Eastern and Western forms, yet the notes of the two are so different that, in a region where they both abound, either may be distinguished at once by its voice; and a bird whose song is intermediate between the two, is so rare that, in a residence of two years in a region where both were abundant, I never heard one. Here, then, is an instance where the different forms may *always* be distinguished by their *notes*, though sometimes ambiguous in their plumage. Again, *Contopus richardsonii* resembles *Sayornis fuscus* in its habits more than it does the Wood Pewee, *C. virens*, while its notes are as different from those of the latter bird as the western Lark's are from the eastern's. If Macgillivray's Warbler is a geographical variety of the Mourning Warbler, it is difficult to comprehend how it could have suffered such a complete loss of musical power, seeing that its habits are unchanged, and that the external physical influences are very nearly similar. Perhaps, however, the "dry, thin air" can account for it; but if this is the case, it would be interesting to know why the same air has failed to change the voices of the Robin and Hermit Thrush in the slightest degree.† All the western species which are closely allied to, or intergrade with eastern forms, vary from the latter, more or less, in their notes and habits, sometimes so much that a resemblance can scarcely be recognized. That this may be partly due to changed conditions of life, is undeniable, yet, under the supposition that it has been wholly brought about by such cause, it is very difficult to see why the same changes have effected opposite results in birds of the same family and of the same mode of life. And if these supposed races are found to meet and occupy the same regions, each preserving its peculiarities of notes, plumage, and habits, with a great degree of constancy, how can they properly be called "geographical" varieties, or their differences be accounted for on the supposition of different physical conditions? Yet of one species, at least (*Sturnella magna*), this is absolutely true. And admitting the influence of these external causes to be sufficient to produce such results, the question at once arises: How wide must be the gap that separates congeneric "species;" where shall the limit of variation produced by such causes be placed?

But however ornithologists may differ as to the proper rank of these forms, their existence is undeniable, whether classed as species, varieties, or races, and it becomes necessary to distinguish them apart in ornithological nomenclature. The usual method is to give the name of the first-discovered race, together with the specific title of the form referred to as a variety. Thus, Macgillivray's Warbler is spoken of as *Geothlypis philadelphia* var. *macgillivrayi*. To follow out this method, every bird of which there is more than a single form should be designated by three‡ names, generic, specific, and

---

* Quite true. We can only predicate and define species at all from the mere circumstance of *missing links*. "Species" are the twigs of a tree separated from the parent stem. We name and arrange them arbitrarily, in default of a means of reconstructing the whole tree according to nature's ramifications.—E. C.

† Is it not quite reasonable to suppose that different animals may possess a different degree of susceptibility to modifying influences, and that some may be able to resist such influences altogether? We must not presume upon uniform plasticity of organization.—E. C.

‡ I strongly advocate a return to polynomial nomenclature, as the only fit instrument of expression of nice shades of zoological meaning. Many of us, in effect, are already using trinomials, the true nature of which is but partially concealed by intervention of the term "var."—E. C.

varietal; but in view of the now frequent consolidation of old species, and the constant discovery of new geographical races, such a method threatens to become quite cumbrous and inconvenient.

Throughout my notes the nomenclature of Coues, as given in his "Key to North American Birds," is followed. All the statements are the result of my personal observations, except some few which are based upon the accounts of trustworthy persons, and of which separate mention is made.

TURDUS MIGRATORIUS, *Robin.* Very abundant; migratory; breeds. The Robin is perhaps the commonest bird to be found in the county. It arrives in Bergen's Park in the middle of March, and slowly makes its way into the mountains, reaching the elevation of 10,000 feet nearly a month later, and advancing as the season progresses to the extreme limit of timber. From the plains up to timber-line it abounds in great numbers all through the breeding season, and is nowhere more abundant than in the extreme upper edge of the forests, nesting in the very topmost trees. They raise two broods, commonly; occasionally only one, and rarely three. At an elevation of 8,000 feet the first brood is hatched in the fore part of June, and the second toward the middle of July; near timber-line the second brood is not hatched till late in July, or even the early part of August. The nest is placed in the fork of a pine, and is precisely similar to those of eastern birds in construction and material. During the latter part of July and early part of August the young birds from lower down ascend to the upper forests, and abound in the woods near timber-line. They frequently wander to the very top of the range, feeding on the grasshoppers that swarm in countless multitudes above the tree limit, toward the close of summer. They also frequent the edges of the little lakes and pools which are very numerous at high elevations, where they pick up the larvæ of various insects. In September they flock in great numbers to the blueberry patches, of which fruit they seem extravagantly fond. Early in the autumn they begin to descend, gradually working their way downward, until in November they all have disappeared, except a few stragglers who linger about the juniper bushes until banished by the deep snows of December.

T. SWAINSONI, *Olive-backed Thrush.* Seen in May and September only. Late in October I saw great numbers of this bird near the Hot Sulphur Springs, in the Middle Park. A sudden violent storm had occurred a day or two previous, and the snow lay on the ground a foot deep. Great numbers of Titlarks, Song Sparrows, Blackbirds, Bluebirds, and many other species, including the Olive-backed Thrush, had gathered about the tepid pools, attracted by the warmth, and were busily searching for food along the muddy banks and in the shallow water, though apparently without much success, as the water is surcharged with sulphur. [This species is stated to breed about New Haven, Connecticut, and also in the mountains of Pennsylvania.—E. C.]

T. FUSCESCENS, *Veery.* Seen but once in July, at an elevation of 8,400 feet. I looked carefully for the Veery in the lower parts of the county, as Allen states that it is not uncommon from the foot-hills up to 8,500 feet, but with the single exception mentioned I did not see it. [The eggs of this species are occasionally spotted.—E. C.]

T. PALLASI, *Hermit Thrush.* Abundant; migratory; breeds. The Hermit Thrush arrives toward the end of May, and by the middle of June is abundant about timber-line, below which it does not range more than 1,000 or 1,200 feet during the nesting season. It is shy and retiring in its habits, seeking the seclusion of the darkest forests, and the subdued light of deep, rocky cañons, where the dense foliage and precipitous walls shut out the sun and a perpetual twilight prevails. It is an exquisite songster, and sings at all hours of the day; its notes are something like those of the Wood Thrush, but louder, wilder, and with very much of the melancholy sweetness that marks the Western Meadow-lark's song. No one who visits its haunts in June or July can fail to be delighted by the singing of the Hermit Thrush; and when several are heard together, as is frequently the case, the blending and echoing of so many sweet tones lends an indescribable charm to the sublime and romantic scenery, amid which only are they ever heard; a charm heightened by the mysterious concealment of the singers. Never very tame, it is so shy while singing as to be almost unapproachable, and only the utmost address will enable one, at such times, to obtain sight of the bird. Its voice is very loud and clear, and may be heard at a great distance. In September they descend from the higher regions, and by October have disappeared from the county. Among several specimens there was no appreciable difference from eastern birds.

OREOSCOPTES MONTANUS, *Mountain Mockingbird.* A single specimen was taken at Idaho Springs, May 10. It is a curious fact that many birds, on their first arrival in spring, venture much higher and further into the mountainous regions than the localities in which they pass the breeding season. The migratory instinct, probably, impels them to penetrate into the mountains, until, finding the temperature too cool for their comfort, they recede until they have found their proper habitat.

MIMUS CAROLINENSIS, *Cat-bird.* Common, from the plains up to 7,800 feet, and ranging a few hundred feet higher. The Cat-bird arrives among the foot-hills early in May, and gradually advances into the mountains, reaching its highest point by the 20th. As is the case with many other birds, it presents some strong points of dissimilarity from the eastern representatives of the species. One would scarcely recognize the shy, almost silent bird, that sedulously hides itself from view in the thickest shrubbery, as the tame loquacious Cat-bird of the east, and, indeed, might never suspect its existence in localities where it was not uncommon, from superficial observations. Although quite numerous at Idaho, where I saw it nearly every day for weeks, I never but once heard the cat-like mew so common elsewhere as to have given the bird its name, and only once or twice heard it attempt a song. Yet though so different in some respects, in others it is precisely the same as its eastern relatives. In form, colors, size, carriage, and expression, I could detect not the slighest difference, while its favorite haunts and food are the same. It disappears in August.

The Brown Thrush, given by Allen as extending up to 7,500 feet, does not occur in the county at all, or at least but very rarely. [Dr. Rothrock found it in Colorado.—E. C.]

[To the synonyms of this species add : *Antimimus rufus*, SUND., Meth. Av. Disp. Tent. 1872, 13 (type *rufus*).—E. C.]

SIALIA ARCTICA, *Bluebird.* Abundant from the plains up to timber-line, breeding everywhere. Similar in its general habits to the Eastern Bluebird, the Arctic Bluebird arrives in Bergen's Park early in March, and gradually working its way into the mountains, reaches an elevation of 10,000 feet about the close of the month, preceding the Robin by a few days. In Bergen's Park the first brood is not hatched till June; it probably raises two broods, although of this I cannot be certain. It nests in hollow trees and similar places, and being quite familiar, though not as tame as its eastern cousin, takes possession of the little bird-houses put up for its convenience by the miners and ranchmen. Its flight and habits seem to be the same; but it lacks the carol of the latter bird, its only note being a disconsolate, mournful sort of plaint, somewhat like the fall note of the eastern bird. The young families of Bluebirds may be seen with their parents throughout the latter part of summer, frequently wandering far above timber-line, and even up to the highest peaks. It remains until late in fall, migrating both in spring and autumn in flocks. In the early part of November I saw a bird at Hay's City, Kansas, which I am almost certain was this species; but not being able to shoot it, I could not identify it beyond all doubt.

S. MEXICANA, *Western Bluebird.* Of this species I shot two or three, and saw as many more, in the first week in June, in Bergen's Park, where they probably breed. Of their habits I learned nothing, except that they frequented the tops of the pine-trees, and rarely descended to the lower limbs or ground.

CINCLUS MEXICANUS, *Dipper.* Rather common, though nowhere very numerous. The Dipper frequents all the mountain-streams up to timber-line, and is a constant resident. It is an odd little bird, both in its notes and manners, and attracts the attention of the tourist and miner, as well as the naturalist, from the singularity of its movements. C. being startled from the side of a brook, it flies off, flitting down the stream, close to the surface, uttering a rapid, chattering note; and having flown a certain distance, alights on a stone or drift-log, in or close to the water's edge. Upon alighting it begins bobbing up and down, bending the knees as though curtseying, and eyes the intruder suspiciously. Having satisfied itself of safety, it walks into the water, picking here and there, and getting beyond its depth, spreads its wings and disappears beneath the surface. Apparently as much at home under the water as above, it flies some distance beneath the surface, and stays under for a minute or more. At times it alights on the surface of the water and floats down the rapid stream like cork, till it has found footing. In winter it frequently goes beneath the ice, walking under with the utmost composure, and reappearing at some air-hole a few yards off. Its nest is a large globular structure, with an entrance on one side; it is composed of moss, lined with grass, and is very neatly built. It is frequently placed in a hollow or crevice in the rocks, by the side of a stream. I did not succeed in finding either the eggs or young. Although its ordinary note is the rapid chatter referred to before, it has a very beautiful song, which it utters, however, very rarely, and then only in August, after the young birds are able to shift for themselves. Like the Hermit Thrush, it seeks the wildest, darkest ravines, and is very timid while singing. It song is clear, sweet, and varied, more wren-like than anything else, yet peculiarly its own, and, only to be heard amid the most romantic scenery, mingled with the music of mountain torrents, has a charm that is wanting to other and finer songs.

The Dipper is called "Water Turkey" by the miners and mountaineers. One of them told me that it passed the colder part of the winter in the mud, and that he had taken one out from under the ice in a torpid state. During the coldest weather it descends from the higher regions to the lower and more open valleys, where the streams are larger and less obstructed with ice, and it finds a better and more accessible supply of food.

REGULUS CALENDULUS, *Ruby-crowned Kinglet.* Abundant; migratory; breeds from 9,500 or 10,000 feet up to timber-line. The Ruby-crowned Wren arrives at Idaho Springs in the first week of May, and disappears toward the close of the month. During the breeding season it is very abundant in the upper woods, but is never seen below 9,500 feet. In September it begins to descend, reaching Idaho about the 20th, and finally disappearing in October. It is a fine songster; and its lively, animated strains, of canary-like sweetness and clearness, may be heard at all hours of the day, in the cool, damp woods, near the upper limit of tree-growth. The female sings at times, and nearly as loudly and sweetly as the male. *R. satrapa* I have not seen in these mountains.

[To the synonyms of this species add: *Corthylio calendula*, CAB., J. f. O. i, 1853, 83 (type of the genus), and *Sylvia (Reguloides) calendula*, GRAY, Hand-list, i, 1869, 216, No. 3068.—E. C.]

[The first nest of *Regulus calendula* which has reached naturalists was taken by Mr. J. H. Batty, in Colorado, July 21, 1873. It was placed on a spruce-bough, about 15 feet from the ground, and contained five young and one egg. The nest is astonishingly large for the bird; I am not sure that its shape is preserved accurately, but the whole could scarcely be got in the largest coffee-cup. It is composed of an inextricably but loosely-woven mass of feathers and hair, mixed with short bits of straws and a little moss.—E. C.]

PARUS ATRICAPILLUS var. SEPTENTRIONALIS, *Long-tailed Titmouse.* Common; resident; breeds. Precisely similar in habits, notes, and actions, to the typical *P. atricapillus.* This species does not range as high as the Mountain Titmouse, rarely venturing beyond 9,000 feet, while its usual range is from the plains up to about 8,000 feet.

P. MONTANUS, *Mountain Titmouse.* Abundant; breeding from about 8,000 feet up to timber-line. In winter it descends nearly to the plains, but may be found, in the most inclement weather, nearly or quite up to timber-line. Not distinguishable from the former in its notes and habits.

SITTA CAROLINENSIS var. ACULEATA, *Slender-billed Nuthatch.* This species arrives at Idaho about the 1st of April, and gradually extends upward, breeding from about 8,000 or 8,500 feet, up to timber-line. It is not very common, but by no means rare. In its motions and habits it is the exact counterpart of the White-breasted Nuthatch, but its notes are quite different. The common, piping note is nearly the same, though in a different key; but the loud spring-call is very different. It is far coarser, louder, and more rapid in *aculeata*—so loud and rattling in fact, that I have mistaken it for the call of the Red-shafted Flicker—while there is none of the soft, musical tone that marks the spring-note of *S. carolinensis.* The notes, in fact, are almost as widely apart as those of *Sturnella magna* and *S. neglecta*, and one unacquainted with the bird would never suspect its relationship on first hearing its call. In October it retires toward the foot-hills, where it may be found all winter.

S. PYGMÆA, *Pygmy Nuthatch.* Abundant and resident; breeding from about 6,000 feet up to 8,500 or 9,000. Scarcely migratory, remaining in nearly the same localities throughout the year. The Pygmy Nuthatch is a delicate little fellow, with more of the habits and voice of *S. canadensis* than of the white-breasted species; a similarity carried out by the coloration of the tail, and their half-warbler-like movements at times. They are very active, and incessantly on the move, creeping over the trunks and limbs of the pines, and tapping vigorously here and there, like a Woodpecker, and far louder than the other Nuthatches do. Very social, it is fond of gathering in flocks with the Mountain Titmouse, whose habits lead it into similar places, and in whose society it roams through the woods in busy, twittering groups, exploring every decayed limb and fallen trunk, peering with sharp eyes into each crack and cranny that might form the lurking place of its insect food, and examining the pine and fir cones for the same purpose, hanging from them in all possible positions, precisely like a Pine Finch. Like the Canada Nuthatch, they will chase and capture an insect on the wing; and frequently descend to the ground, alighting, warbler-like, on low bushes, and then flitting back to the pine boughs. Their notes are various; a sort of shrill piping, like that of the red-breasted species; a deep-toned variation of the same note, uttered only in spring; and a twittering note, uttered at times while feeding together, and used as a rallying or warning cry, and when about to take wing.

CERTHIA FAMILIARIS, *Brown Creeper.* Abundant during the winter, from 7,000 feet up to 9,000 feet, and probably ranging considerably higher and lower. Breeds sparingly in the upper woods, within a few hundred feet of timber-line. Appears at Idaho late in the fall, and becomes very common as soon as the weather becomes cold, great numbers coming in from other regions. Similar in all respects to the eastern bird.

[Add to the synonyms of this species: *Certhia fusca*, BART., Frag. Nat. Hist. Pa. 1799. If the American bird is to be distinguished, it is to be called *C. familiaris* var. *fusca.*—E. C.]

SALPINCTES OBSOLETUS, *Rock Wren.* Abundant; migratory; breeds. The Rock Wren arrives at Idaho about the 20th of May, and extends its range up to, and a little above, timber-line. It breeds most abundantly between 6,500 and 9,500 feet, rarely nesting higher that the latter elevation, though found during summer from 12,000 feet down to the plains. It is a constant resident of the piles of loose rock which lie scattered on the mountainsides, in which it finds its food and rears its young, and to which it retreats for safety on being alarmed. On its first arrival it is rather shy, but soon becomes tame and even familiar, haunting piles of boulders and small stones in the placer diggings, close to the miners' cabins. It rarely ventures far from its favorite rocky retreats ; but occasionally visits the road-sides to pick up flies and other insects, and sometimes hops over the roofs of cabins and mills, and not infrequently chooses the ridge as a convenient place from which to serenade its mate. It has a curious, rapidly repeated note, that sounds like the whirring of wings ; its song is very beautiful, louder and sweeter than that of the House Wren, though not as varied. While singing, the bird usually perches on the top of a heap of stones, and stands erect, with head thrown up, like the Carolina Wren. At such times it is quite timid, and if alarmed, instantly ceases the song and looks anxiously around, bobbing itself up and down every little while, like the Dipper, and presently creeps down into the stone-heap. Late in autumn its feathers become much worn from constant creeping among the rocks. In September it disappears.

[To synonyms of *T. aëdon* add: *Hylemathrous aëdon*, CAB., J. f. O. 1860, 407.—E. C.]

TROGLODYTES AËDON var. PARKMANI, *Parkman's Wren.* This bird, now regarded as a variety of *Troglodytes aëdon*, nevertheless presents many distinguishing characteristics from the latter bird, not only in size and color, but in notes and habits ; and hence, though merely a geographical race, may well be designated as Parkman's Wren, in distinction from the typical House Wren. It arrives at Idaho in the middle of May, and soon becomes abundant, extending its range up to 10,500 feet, and occasionally venturing nearly up to timber-line. In many of its habits it is very similar to the House Wren ; but it frequently haunts rocky hill-sides and cliffs and ledges of rock, which I have never observed the latter to do. As is the case with many other birds, its notes differ strikingly from those of its eastern relatives. It has far more variety in its song, which at times is precisely the same as that of the House Wren, and at others is very different, yet always wren-like—clear, ringing, and changeable. It has one note which I never heard the latter bird utter—a rapid chirruping note, more like the rattling noise produced by a grasshopper or cricket than that of a bird, quite similar, in fact, to the peculiar sound produced by the Rock Wren, referred to previously. This note it rarely utters, however ; nor is it as fond of the scolding chatter that the House Wren uses so frequently to express its anger or alarm. It nests wherever it can find a chink or cranny to build in—between the logs of a miner's cabin, in deserted mills, among the timbering about the mouths of old shafts and tunnels, and in any snug little nook it can find. It raises two and sometimes three broods ; and, between 8,000 and 10,500 feet, the last brood is hatched in the latter part of July. The eggs and nest are similar to those of eastern birds; the number of the former is usually five, though sometimes only four. It disappears in September.

[*Telmatodytes palustris* was taken by MERRIAM (No. 62327, Idaho): U. S. Geol. Surv. Ter. 1872, 673.—E. C.]

[*Cistothorus stellaris.* Satisfactory evidence of the presence of this species at Utah Lake was obtained by Mr. Henshaw during the last season.—E. C.]

[To synonyms of *Anorthura troglodytes* var. *hyemalis* add : *Troglodytes parvulus* var. *hyemalis*, B. B. & R., N. A. B. i, 1874, 155.—E. C.]

EREMOPHILA ALPESTRIS var. CHRYSOLÆMA, *Western Horned Lark.* This bird is not abundant in the mountains, there being few localities suitable to its habits. It is rather common in Bergen's Park, and may be seen occasionally in the mountain valleys and meadows and on hill-sides, as well as above timber-line, breeding from the foot-hills up to the summit of the range, wherever it can find a spot adapted to its tastes. Although abundant on the plains throughout winter, it does not enter the mountains till spring. On the 11th of July I found several pairs in an extensive grassy plain near James' Peak, at least a thousand feet above timber-line, that were evidently breeding there, although I looked in vain for their nests. They were a little larger, apparently, than specimens from the plains, and very brightly colored.

ANTHUS LUDOVICANUS, *Brown Lark.* Abundant ; migratory; breeds in great numbers above timber-line. The Titlark arrives at Idaho Springs in the early part of May, frequenting open hill-sides, and showing a partiality to the plowed fields of mountain ranches. By June it has ascended to the summit of the range, and commences nesting almost as soon as the snow has sufficiently melted to allow the ground to dry and the grass to come up, incubation beginning in the first and second weeks in July. The nest is placed under the shelter of a projecting stone, and is very neatly constructed of coarse grass externally, lined with fine grass, and is about three inches and a half in diameter. The eggs are five in number ; the ground-color dark brownish-purple, almost hidden by spots and splashes of purplish-black. Eggs from different nests vary somewhat in the intensity of the colors, some being much lighter and grayer than others, but the general aspect is always quite dark. There is also considerable variation in the colors and size of individual birds; in some the legs being black, in others lighter, occasionally light brown ; some having two bands of white on the wings, and others having no trace of them whatever; some being much darker beneath than others ; with other variations. Notwithstanding which, I could not define any well-marked or constant varieties, as, among a large number of specimens, the various forms of coloration and size seemed to shade imperceptibly into each other.

In its habits and notes, the Titlark is precisely the same as the abundant, well-known bird that abounds in the Northern States throughout spring and fall—restless, vacillating creatures, ever on the move, querulous and fidgety. They are more shy during summer, however, not willingly permitting one to approach nearer than fifty or sixty yards. During the breeding season the males have a song unheard at other times, with which they serenade their mates. Rising in the air at an angle of forty-five degrees, with a fluttering, uncertain flight, they commence singing when they are up a little way, and continue till they have reached the height of a hundred yards or so; then descending, fluttering their wings as before, till they light on a stone or sod, not far from where they started. They have several different variations, all consisting of two or three notes, quickly repeated over and over again, with quite a musical and pleasing effect. One of these variations sounds very much like the plaint of a little chicken lost from its brood. As one approaches their nests, they hover silently about, uttering, at intervals, a chirp expressive of their anxiety. During their stay above timber-line—they do not ever go below it during the breeding season—they prefer wet, springy places, which abound near the summit of the range. They may often be seen running over the vast snow-banks that remain on northern slopes throughout the year. In August and September they gather into flocks, and begin descending into the valleys, reaching Idaho toward the close of the latter month. Many remain above timber-line until October, and some few throughout the month, or as long as they can find open ground to feed in. In November they finally disappear.

[To the synonyms of *Helminthophaga ruficapilla* add: *Helminthophaga ruficapilla* var. *ocularis* et var. *gutturalis*, B. B. & R., N. A. B. i, 1874, 191, which may not necessarily be recognized by varietal name.—E. C.]

DENDRŒCA ÆSTIVA, *Yellow Warbler.* The Yellow Warbler is abundant along the foot-hills, and ranges as high as 6,500 feet. Stragglers undoubtedly wander as far as Bergen's Park, although I did not observe any there.

D. CORONATA, *Yellow-crowned Warbler.* Abundant; migratory; does not breed. Appears at Idaho in the latter part of April, and goes up as high as 8,500 or 9,000 feet; disappearing about the 10th of May, a few days before the following species. In fall I did not observe it; probably it does not venture in the mountains, to any extent, in that season. [It has also been taken in Colorado by Mr. Henshaw.—E. C.]

D. AUDUBONI, *Audubon's Warbler.* Abundant; migratory; breeds from about 9,500 feet up to timber-line. Audubon's Warbler arrives at Idaho about the middle of May, but goes higher up into the mountains to breed, rarely being seen below 9,000 feet during the latter part of June and July, in which months it rears its young, preferring, during this season, the dense, dark forests of black spruce. In spring it haunts the same localities as the Yellow-crowned Warbler, but is more partial to the under-shrubbery, and frequently ventures into open fields and clearings, alighting on bushes and weeds, and even on the ground, exhibiting much of the manners of the Red-polled Warbler. Its usual note is one very similar to that of the Barn Swallow; its song is a simple little carol, like that of the preceding species. In August it begins to descend, by September it is common in the lower parts of the country, and by October has disappeared.

D. NIGRESCENS, *Black-throated Gray Warbler.* A single specimen seen at Idaho Springs, May 23.

GEOTHLYPIS MACGILLIVRAYI, *Macgillivray's Warbler.* Common; migratory; breeds up to a little above 9,000 feet. Very similar in habits to the Mourning Warbler. Arrives in the latter part of May and disappears in August and September.

MYIODIOCTES PUSILLUS, *Green Black-capped Flycatcher.* Abundant; breeding in great numbers in the bushes near timber-line. First seen at Idaho, May 5, but not common till the 22d. By the middle of June all had left the valleys, and at the close of the month I found them very numerous in the dense coppices of brush that extend for some hundred feet above timber-line. They breed in July, reappearing at Idaho toward the close of September, finally disappearing in the following month. It has quite a sprightly little song, and is very active, flitting rapidly from bush to bush, and rarely ascending among the trees.

SETOPHAGA RUTICILLA, *Redstart.* Apparently not very common; breeds. First appeared at Idaho Springs May 20, from which date until the 1st of June a few were daily seen; subsequently I saw but a single individual, a female, near timber-line, in July.

Geothlypis trichas and *Helminthophaga celata* are abundant along the edge of the plains, but probably never wander as high up as Clear Creek County.

PYRANGA LUDOVICIANA, *Louisiana Tanager.* This bird arrives at Idaho toward the close of June, and soon becomes quite common, remaining till late in August or early in September. It does not extend its range beyond 9,000 feet, but breeds from that limit, or a little lower, all the way down to the plains. It bears a close resemblance to the Scarlet Tanager, both in notes and habits; rambling leisurely through the pine woods, and singing at intervals from the tree tops; descending at times to the lower branches and bushes, where its bright yellow is almost as conspicuous as the flaming scarlet of his eastern cousin ; feeding on much the same food, and capturing insects on the wing with equal skill. His chirp is the same as the Scarlet Tanager's, and his song very similar; yet a difference may be detected—a difference to the prejudice of the western bird. As a general rule, the western races are a little inferior in song to their eastern relatives of the same species and genus, although there are many exceptions to this—the Robin, for instance. Birds of colder and more densely wooded regions have sweeter, fuller, and more melodious voices than their kindred of warmer and more arid districts.

B.

The following interesting notes were communicated to me by Dr. J. M. Wheaton, of Columbus, Ohio, favorably known by his excellent List of the Birds of that State, so often quoted in the present work.—E. C.

OLIVE-BACKED THRUSH (*T. swainsoni*). This is the most abundant of the *Hylocichla* during the migrations. It presents greater variations of color and size than any other. By far the greater number of individuals belong to the typical variety *swainsoni*, but we have as extremes var. *aliciæ*, the Gray-cheeked Thrush, and a small variety, length 6½ inches, bill only ⅔, with the olive of the back suffused with tawny, in this respect resembling var. *ustulatus* of the Pacific coast, but having the spots on the breast darker. The buff of this variety is much more decided, especially on the eyelids and line from above the eye to the bill. On very high colored fall specimens the buff of the breast is sometimes prolonged in a pale median line to the middle of the belly. The obscure bar at the base of the secondaries and inner primaries is creamy buff in *swainsoni* proper, white in var. *aliciæ*, and brownish-white in the small variety.

The Gray-cheeked variety arrives a few days later in the spring than the Wood or Wilson's Thrush, the typical Olive-back nearly a week later, followed shortly after by the small variety, which, in 1873, remained till June 1, and was the most terrestrial in its habits, frequenting brush heaps in sparse, wet woodland. In the fall the Gray-cheeked variety makes its appearance sooner than the others.

BLUE WARBLER (*D. cærulea*). Not common in most places ; is tolerably common in Central Ohio. I have found them in considerable numbers in May and June. Towards the close of June I have found the young fully fledged in oak woods, where they probably breed. The song ot this bird bears considerable resemblance to that of the Bay-wing Bunting, though less loud.

YELLOW-THROATED WARBLER (*D. dominica*). Has perhaps a northern limit in this State. In this vicinity they are among the most regular and earliest to arrive of the family. I have noted them before the arrival of the Yellow Warbler, and even before the last frosts and snow. They commonly follow the streams in their migrations, and may be readily recognized by their comparatively loud and frequent note, which almost exactly resembles that of the Indigo-bird on its first arrival. They soon disperse through the woodland and appear in the shade-trees and gardens of the city. I have never found them breeding. They return south in September by the same route as in the spring migration.

CEDAR BIRD (*A. cedrorum*). I have taken one spring specimen in very high plumage, in which the *six* central tail feathers possessed the waxen tips. The length of the specimen was 7.05 inches, the color much darker than usual.

BROTHERLY-LOVE VIREO (*Vireo philadelphicus*). I saw them on September 16, to the number of twenty to thirty, in beech woodland, accompanying the Red-eyed Vireos on their southern migration.

LOGGERHEAD SHRIKE (*C. ludovicianus*). Usually considered to be confined to the South Atlantic and Gulf States, and the white-rumped variety (*excubitoroides*), heretofore supposed to have its eastern limit in Illinois; but both occur not uncommonly with us, and appear to be on the increase. They arrive early in April. My observations coincide with those made by Mr. Trippe in Iowa (Naturalist, 1873, 497), except that we have specimens which might be considered typical *ludovicianus*. On the 31st of May, 1873, I captured a family of these birds, the male of which was clearly of the white-rumped variety, but lighter than Illinois specimens of the same. The female presented the typical features of *ludovicianus*. The length of the male was 9 inches ; the female, 8¼. The young were just from their nest in a hedge. They were light ashy, dusky waved above, decidedly waved below, and with the head-stripe *not meeting* in front of the eye, and considerably restricted. My observations are not sufficiently extended to venture an opinion, but from such as I have made, I would not be surprised if it should be determined, that to the north and west the White-rumped Shrike passed insensibly into the northern bird (*borealis*), as with us it does into the southern form.

SONG SPARROW (*M. melodia*). Dr. Abbott, in the Naturalist, 1870, page 378, calls attention to a variation in the song of this bird, and asks if others have noticed it. With us it is resident in comparatively small numbers in winter. During the fall months its song is seldom or never heard. In December I have observed them perched in the top of a forest tree, singing with vivacity a continuous song, which was altogether different from their usual spring notes. The position and song were such that I failed to recognize the bird, and on two occasions have shot them before suspecting the true nature of the case. When alarmed in this position, they drop almost perpendicularly to the ground, as in the habit of the Brown Thrush, a miniature of which, in attitude and song, they seem to be. I have heard the same song near the ground, but not often. Late in January their winter song is freely varied with passages from their well-known summer notes, and by the first of March the peculiar notes of winter have all disappeared.

LARK FINCH (*C. grammaca*). Usually considered to find its eastern limit in Illinois, is a summer resident in this locality. I am of the opinion that both it and the Shrike, above mentioned, are comparatively recent additions to our fauna. I first saw it in 1860, since which time it has increased in numbers, and at present is not uncommon. It nests in meadows, and the young take to trees as soon as they are able to fly. I suspect, from not meeting either these birds or the Shrikes after the breeding season is fairly over, that they join their comrades in the west before going south. [This species has occurred in Florida (spec. in Mus. S. I.)—E. C.]

NIGHT-HAWK (*C. popetue*). I have noticed, when skinning this bird, that the male, in spring, exhales a strong hircine odor. If this is common to all birds of the family, it may have added apparent reason to the superstition from which the family name is derived.

CHIMNEY SWALLOW (*C. pelasgia*). No writer seems to have mentioned what many have noticed in this bird, that the broad line of black extending from the nostrils along the bill to the gape, across the lores, in front of and above the eyes, is composed of feathers of different structure from those of the general plumage. These are short and thick set, remarkably velvety both to the eye and touch.

There is another curious anomaly in this remarkable bird, which I have not seen mentioned : On the under-surface of the wing a linear bare space will be noticed, extending from the carpal-joint to the base of the first primary. This seems to have been caused by friction, and suggests that the bird uses the wings to assist the feet and spiny tail in clinging to the chimney-side. That certain birds do make use of their wings as supports has been affirmed in the pages of the Naturalist ; but if this is really the case do they not violate the law laid down for them by Owen (?), who says (Anat. of Vert. vol. ii, p. 6) : "In no case do the anterior limbs (wings) take any share in stationary support or prehension."

NOTE.—Neither of the North American species of so-called *Poospiza* has occurred, to my knowledge, in the Missouri region, but either may yet be found in the southwestern portion.

These birds seem scarcely congeneric with the type of *Poospiza*, *Emberiza nigro-rufa*, D'ORBIG., and, in the extreme subdivision which at present obtains, may be distinguished under the following names :

AMPHISPIZA, Coues, n. g. (type Emberiza bilineata, Cass.)

AMPHISPIZA BILINEATA, *Coues.*

Emberiza bilineata, CASS., Pr. A. N. S. P. v, 1850, 104, pl. 3 (Texas); Ill. 1854, 150, pl. 23.
Poospiza bilineata, SCL., P. Z. S. 1857, 7.—BD., B. N. A. 1858, 470 ; Mex. B. Surv. ii, part
        ii, 1859, Birds, 15.—HEERM., P. R. R. Rep. x, 1859, Parke's Route, Birds, 14.—
        COOP., B. Cal. i, 1870, 203.—DRESS., Ibis, 1865, 483 (Texas).—COUES, Pr. Phila.
        Acad. 1866, 86 (Arizona).—COUES, Key, 1872, 140.—B. B. & R., N. A. B. i, 1874,
        590, pl. 26, fig. 8.
    Hab.—Middle Province of the United States. North 40°. South into Mexico.

AMPHISPIZA BELLII, *Coues.*

Emberiza bellii, CASS., Pr. Phila. Acad. v, 1850, 104, pl. 4 (California).
Poospiza bellii, SCL., P. Z. S. 1857, 7.—BD., B. N. A. 1858, 470.—HEERM., P. R. R. Rep. x,
        1859, pt. vi, 46.—COUES, Pr. Phila. Acad. 1866, 86 (Arizona).—COOP., B. Cal. i,
        1870, 204.—ALLEN, Bull. M. C. Z. iii, 1872, 177 (Ogden, Utah, var. *nevadensis*,
        RIDGW.).—COUES, Key, 1872, 141.—B. B. & R., N. A. B. i, 1874, 593, pl. 26, f. 9.
Zonotrichia bellii, ELLIOT, B. N. A. i, pl. 14.

    Hab.—Of *A. bellii* proper, Southern California. Of *A. bellii* var. *nevadensis* (*Ridgway*,
Rep. Birds 40th parallel, in press ; *B. B. & R.*, N. A. B. i, 1874, 594), Middle Province of
the United States, to 40°, and somewhat beyond.

SUBORDER CLAMATORES: NON-MELODIOUS PASSERES.

Family TYRANNIDÆ: American Flycatchers.

MILVULUS FORFICATUS, (Gm.) Sw.

Swallow-tailed Flycatcher; Scissor-tail.

Muscicapa forficata, GM., Syst. Nat. i, 1788, 931 (Moucherolle à queue fourchue de Mexi-
    que, BUFF., P. E. 677).—VIEILL., Ois. Am. Sept. i, 1807, 71.—STEPH., Shaw's
    Gen. Zool. x, 413, pl. 3.—BP., Am. Orn. i, 1825, 15, pl. 2, f. 1 ; Syn. 1828, 275.—
    NUTT., Man. i, 1832, 275.—AUD., Orn. Biog. iv, 1838, 426, pl. 359, f. 3.
Tyrannus forficatus, TEMM., Tabl. Meth. 24.—SAY, Long's Exp. ii, 1823, 224.—NUTT.,
    Man. i, 2d ed. 1840, 309.
Milvulus forficatus, Sw., Classif. B. ii, 225.—RICH., List, 1837.—BP., List, 1838, 25.—AUD.,
    Syn. 1839, 38.—AUD., B. Am. i, 1840, 197, pl. 53.—BP., Consp. i, 1850, 192 ; Not.
    Delat. 87.—WOODH., Sitgr. Rep. 1853, 73 (Texas and Indian Territory).—SCL.,
    P. Z. S. 1857, 204 (Xalapa).—BD., B. N. A. 1858, 169.—CAB., Mus. Hein. ii, 1859,
    79.—SCL., Ibis, 1859, 439 ; Cat. 1862, 237.—SCL. & SALV., Ibis, 1859, 121 (Gua-
    temala).—TAYLOR, Ibis, 1860, 114 (Honduras).—CAB., J. f. O. ix, 1861, 252
    (Costa Rica).—LAWR., Ann. Lyc. ix, 1868, 116.—SUMICH., Mem. Bost. Soc. i,
    1869, 556 (Vera Cruz).—GRAY, Hand-list, i, 1869, 365, No. 5563.—SNOW, B.
    Kans. 1873 3 (Fort Riley, Kans.).—ABBOTT, Am. Nat. vii, 1872, 367 (accidental
    at Trenton, N. J.).—COUES, Key, 1872, 169, fig. 110ª.—B. B. & R., N. A. B.
    ii, 1874, 311, pl. 43, f. 1.
Tyrannus mexicanus, STEPH., Shaw's Gen. Zool. xiii, pt. ii, 1826, 135.
Muscicapa spectabilis, LICHT., "Mus. Berol."

Hab.—Lower Mississippi Valley, Texas, and southward into South America.

This peculiarly elegant species, not inaptly called "bird of paradise"
by the Texans, is merely a straggler to the Missouri water-shed. The
single instance I know of its occurrence in this region, is that cited by
Prof. Snow, on Prof. Baird's authority. It is abundant in this country
only in some parts of Texas ; Dr. Woodhouse, however, gives it as not
uncommon in the Indian Territory. Like its equally graceful relative,
the Fork-tailed Flycatcher, *M. tyrannus*, it has been known to wander
even to New Jersey, where a specimen was lately captured near Trenton. Some years ago, Dr. Prentiss and I stated that a *Milvulus*, probably *forficatus*, had been seen at Washington, D. C., by Mr. C. Drexler.
I only mention this to throw discredit upon it ; having since found reason to believe that we were imposed upon by the collector.

The eggs of this Flycatcher are not with certainty distinguishable
from those of a Kingbird ; they are, however, rather smaller, and perhaps on an average a little more nearly globular. Size, scarcely 0.90
by 0.70.

TYRANNUS CAROLINENSIS, (Gm.) Temm.

Kingbird; Bee-martin.

Lanius tyrannus, LINN., Syst. Nat. i, 1766, 136 (CATESBY, i, 55, pl. 55 ; BRISS., ii, 391 ;
    P. E. 537).—GM., Syst. Nat. i, 1788, 302.—LATH., Ind. Orn. i, 1790, 81.
Lanius tyrannus var. *carolinensis* et *ludovicianus*, GM., i, 1788, 302.—LATH., Ind. Orn. i,
    1790, 82 (P. E. 676).
Tyrannus carolinensis, TEMM., Tabl. Meth. 24.—CAB., Mus. Hein. ii, 1859, 79.—BD., B.
    N. A. 1858, 171.—COOP. & SUCK., N. H. Wash. Ter. 1860, 167.—HAYD., Rep.
    1862, 157.—LORD, Pr. Roy. Arty. Inst. 1864, 113 (British Columbia).—LAWR.,

Ann. Lyc. viii, 1865, 183 (Nicaragua).—Coop., B. Cal. i, 1870, 311.—Snow, B.
Kans. 1873, 3.—Allen, Bull. M. C. Z. iii, 1872, 179 (Utah and Wyoming).—
Stev., U. S. Geol. Surv. Ter. 1870, 463.--Merr., ibid. 1872, 689.—Hold.-Aiken,
Pr. Bost. Soc. 1872, 205.—Coues, Key, 1872, 169, pl. 2, figs. 1, 2; fig. 110ᵇ; fig.
111.—B. B. & R., N. A. B. iii, 1874, 316, pl. 43, f. 4; and of most late writers.
Muscicapa rex, Bart., Frag. Nat. Hist. Pa. 1799, 18.
Muscicapa tyrannus, Wils., Am. Orn. i, 1808, 66, pl. 13, f. 1.—Bp., Syn. 1828, 66.—Nutt.,
Man. i, 1832, 265.—Aud., Orn. Biog. i, 403, v, 420; pl. 79; Syn. 1839, 40; B.
Am. i, 204, pl. 56.—Gir., B. L. I. 1844, 39.
Tyrannus pipiri, Vieill., Ois. Am. Sept. i, 73, pl. 44.—Cab., J. f. O. 1855, 478.—Scl.,
Cat. 1862, 236.--Gundl., Rep. 1865, 239 (Cuba).—Coues, Pr. Phila. Acad. 1871,
26.—Scl. & Salv., P. Z. S. 1866, 189 (Peru); 1870, 837 (Honduras).
Tyrannus intrepidus, Vieill., Gal. Ois. i, 1824, 214, pl. 133; Ency. Meth. 849.—Sw., Philos.
Mag. i, 1827, 368; Quart. Journ. xx, 1826, 274.—Sw. & Rich., F. B. A. ii, 1831,
137.—Bp., List, 1838, 24.—Woodh., Sitgr. Rep. 1853, 73.—Scl., P. Z. S. 1857,
232; 1858, 302 (Oaxaca).—Moore, ibid. 1859, 55 (Honduras).—Scl., Ibis, 1859,
439.—Sumich., Mem. Bost. Soc. i, 1869, 557 (Vera Cruz).
" *Myiarchus intrepidus*, Burm.," Verz. Mus. Hal. 46 (*Cabanis*).
Muscicapa animosa, Licht., Verz. 1823, 54, No. 558.
Tyrannus leucogaster, Steph., Gen. Zool. xiii, pt. ii, 1826, 132.
Tyrannus vieillotii, Sw., F. B. A. ii, 1831, 138 (= Gal. Ois. pl. 133).

Hab.—North America at large. North to " 57° or further " (*Richardson*). West to
the Rocky Mountains, beyond which only observed in Washington and Oregon Territories, and British Columbia. Breeds throughout. Winters on our extreme southern
border (*Audubon*), and thence into Mexico, Central and South America, to Peru. Cuba.
Lieutenant Warren's Expedition.—4692, 4695, Upper Missouri; 5235-36, near Fort
Pierre, Dakota; 5237-38, Farm Island, Missouri River; 8095, Frémont, on Platte.
Later Expeditions.—60440, 60765, Wyoming; 61770-1, 62287, 62289, Idaho.

The Missouri furnishes to this and other species a highway across the
central plains, of which it readily avails itself, and, crossing the mountains of Montana, it occurs in Oregon and Washington Territories. As
Mr. Allen observes in a letter to me, it is "abundant throughout Eastern and Middle Kansas, and more or less common at Colorado City,
Denver, Cheyenne and Ogden, indicating for it a more general western
range than it was formerly supposed to have, and showing that it may
readily reach the coast region of Oregon by way of the passes north of
the mountains of Colorado, and perhaps, also, by way of the Great
Utah Basin and the valley of the Columbia. In Colorado it disappears
near the base of the foot-hills, no species of the genus being met with
above about 7,000 feet." Mr. Trippe also attests its abundance in Colorado, on the plains, and it even straggles as high up as Idaho Springs.
Through Northern Dakota, during the whole summer, I found it to be
one of the most abundant of all the birds wherever there was any
timber.

TYRANNUS VERTICALIS, Say.

Arkansas Flycatcher.

Tyrannus verticalis, Say, Long's Exp. ii, 1823, 60.--Nutt., Man. ii, 1840, 360.—Bp., List,
1838, 35; Consp. i, 1850, 192.—Bd., B. N. A. 1858, 173.—Heerm., P. R. R. Rep.
x, 1859, pt. vi, 37.—Coop. & Suck., N. H. Wash. Ter. 1860, 168.—Hayd., Rep.
1862, 157.—Lord, Pr. Arty. Inst. iv, 1864, 113 (British Columbia).—Bryant, Pr.
Bost. Soc. x, 1865, 96 (Plympton, Me.).—Coues, Pr. Phila. Acad. 1866, 59.—
Coop., B. Cal. i, 1870, 312.—Snow, B. Kans. 1873, 3.—Stev., U. S. Geol. Surv.
Ter. 1870, 463.—Merr., ibid. 1872, 690.—Allen, Bull. M. C. Z. 1872, 179 (Kan-
sas and westward).—Aiken., Pr. Bost. Soc. 1872, 205.—Coues, Key, 1872, 170,
figs. 110ᵃ, 112.—B. B. & R., N. A. B. ii, 1874, 324, pl. 43, f. 2.
Muscicapa verticalis, Bp., Am. Orn. i, 1825, 18, pl. 2, fig. 2.—Bp., Syn. 1828, 67.—Nutt.,
Man. i, 1832, 273.—Aud., Orn. Biog. iv, 1838, 422, pl. 359; Syn. 1839, 39; B.
Am. i, 1840, 199, pl. 54.
Laphyctes verticalis, Cab., Mus. Hein. ii, 1859, 77.

Hab.—Western United States, from Middle Kansas and Western Iowa (Allen, Mem
Bost. Soc. i, 1868, 498), to the Pacific, especially abundant on the high central plains.

British Columbia. Accidental at Moorestown, New Jersey (Mus. Acad. Phila.; TURNB., B. E. Pa. 41), and at Plympton, Maine (as above).
Lieutenant Warren's Expedition.—5263, 5265, Yellowstone ; 5264, Knife River ; 5258, 5259, 5260, 5262, Fort Lookout ; 5240, 5242, 5243, 5246, 5252, 5253, 5256, Farm Island, Missouri River ; 5261, 5266, mouth Powder River ; 8893, 8898, 8899, Loup Fork.
Later Expeditions.— 60437-9, 61135, Wyoming ; 61748-51, Utah ; 61772, 61781, Idaho.

The very extensive series taken by Lieutenant Warren's Expedition, demonstrates the abundance of the species in the Upper Missouri and Platte regions. Speaking of its occurrence with the Kingbird, Dr. Hayden says that the two are often found together, but notices that this species " does not make its appearance, however, till we reach a point about one hundred miles below Fort Pierre, and thence to the mountains. The *T. carolinensis* diminishes in numbers, while the *T. verticalis* becomes exceedingly abundant, occurring in vast numbers along the wooded portions of streams." We may accept this as indicating, in general, the respective bearing of the species upon the regions in question, but *T. verticalis* is certainly found much further east than Dr. Hayden supposed, as will be observed by the above citations. I never saw it, to my knowledge, in Arizona, but Dr. Cooper observed it at Fort Mojave, on the Colorado. He describes a nest, taken at Santa Barbara, in the following terms : " This nest was built on a branch of low oak, near the town, was five inches wide, and constructed of lichens, twigs, coarse grass, and wool, lined with hair ; the four eggs it contained were creamy-white, spotted with purple of two shades near the large end, measuring 0.94 by 0.70." The habits and manners of the species are, in all essentials, the same as those of Kingbird, familiar to all.

Mr. Allen has favored me with an interesting communication prepared for the present report: "The Arkansas Flycatcher occurs abundantly as far east as Fort Hays, Kansas, where it is one of the most numerous and characteristic of the woodland birds. It seems even more pugnacious than its relative, the Kingbird, the males fighting with each other almost constantly; and it is equally alert in driving other birds from the vicinity of its nest. Its notes are harsher and louder than those of the Kingbird, though at times rather more musical; they are marked by the same general character. It is more graceful on the wing than the latter bird, possessing rather superior powers of flight, yet resembling it closely in general habits. It constructs a rather bulky and conspicuous nest, composed outwardly of the coarse stems of plants, softly lined with finer material, generally hair ; it is placed on the outer and higher branches of quite large trees. The eggs, commonly five in number, in size, shape, and color so closely resemble those of the Kingbird as not to be always distinguishable. Dozens of pairs were breeding in the narrow belt of timber bordering Big Creek, on the Military Reservation at Fort Hays. We also found them nesting in isolated trees at the heads of ravines, sometimes several miles from any other tree or shrub.

"The species is probably a common inhabitant of the plains, along all the timbered portions of the streams, from Middle Kansas westward to the Rocky Mountains. Along the South Platte and its tributaries, near Denver, it is one of the most conspicuous species, but it ranges only a little way into the foot-hills. None were met with in South Park, nor at any point in Colorado, above 7,000 feet. During the latter part of August they were abundant on Crow Creek, in the vicinity of Cheyenne, although the arboreal vegetation was limited to a few dwarfed clumps of willows. It was here partially gregarious, loose flocks of several dozens being sometimes met with, composed almost wholly of young birds. These roving parties had doubtless wandered here from the open woodlands, the nearest of which were about a hundred miles distant. We also met with a few individuals at Ogden, Utah, and it doubtless occupies the intervening country at all favorable points."

In Utah, according to Mr. Merriam, "Arkansas Flycatchers are numerous in the Great Salt Lake Basin, as they are among the cottonwoods and bushes that border most of the streams between Salt Lake and Fort Hall. From the 5th to the 28th of June I collected four of their nests; they were placed on willows or cottonwoods, from eight to fifteen feet above the ground; were composed of fibrous roots, pieces of dead sage-brush (*Artemisia*), dry grass, &c., lined with wool and other soft substances. The first nest that I found was really very beautiful, as well as curious; it was composed of fibrous roots, stalks of dry grass, wool, pieces of sage-brush, with here and there a few leaves, and is lined with wool, fibrous bark, and thread, with a feather occasionally showing itself; there is much wool on the outside and all through the nest, giving it a soft, downy appearance. This beautiful structure contained four cream-colored eggs, spotted with reddish and dark brown, the spots being most numerous near the large end."

TYRANNUS VOCIFERANS, Sw.

Cassin's Flycatcher.

Tyrannus vociferans, Sw., Quart. Jour. Sci. xx, 1826, 273; Phil. Mag. i, 1827, 368.—BD., B. N. A. 1858, 174; Mex. B. Surv. ii, 1859, pt. ii, 8, pl. 10.—SCL., P. Z. S. 1859, 383 (Oaxaca).—SCL. & SALV., Ibis, 1859, 121 (Vera Paz).—SCL., Ibis, 1859, 439: Cat. 1862, 235 (Mexico).—COUES, Pr. Phila. Acad. 1866, 59 (Arizona).—SUMICH., Mem. Bost. Soc. i, 1869, 557 (Vera Cruz).—COOP., B. Cal. i, 1870, 314.—AIKEN, Pr. Bost. Soc. 1872, 205 (Southeast Wyoming.—MERR., U. S. Geol. Surv. Ter. 1872, 690.—COUES, Key, 1872, 170, fig. 110ᵈ.—B. B. & R., N. A. B. ii, 1874, 327, pl. 43, f. 5.
Laphyctes vociferans, CAB., Mus. Hein. ii, 1859, 77.
Tyrannus cassini, LAWR., Ann. Lyc. N. Y. v, 1852, 39, pl. 3, fig. 2 (Texas).
Muscicapa satelles, LICHT., "Mus. Berol." (*Cabanis*).

Hab.—Southwestern United States; Western Texas to Southern California. North to the vicinity of the Black Hills. South through Mexico to Guatemala. "A few of this species winter at Santa Cruz, latitude 37°; * * * * resident as far north as Los Angeles" (*Cooper*).
Later Expeditions.—61747, Cheyenne, Wyoming.

Mr. Aiken's memorandum of the occurrence of the species near the Black Hills is the northernmost record I have found, and it extends the known range of the bird into the Missouri region. This observer first noticed it the second week in May, in the same places where he found *T. verticalis*. Further south it is an abundant and characteristic species, mostly replacing *T. verticalis* in New Mexico and Arizona. I found it plentiful in both these Territories, from the main chain of the Rocky Mountains, at Whipple's Pass, westward. It is only a summer resident in upper Arizona, where it arrives about the middle of April, and remains until toward October, frequenting all wooded localities. Its habits, according to my observations, are precisely the same as those of *T. verticalis;* the nidification and the eggs are similar.

MYIARCHUS CRINITUS, (Linn.) Cab.

Great Crested Flycatcher.

a. *crinitus.*

Muscicapa crinita, LINN., Syst. Nat. i, 1766, 325.—WILS., Am. Orn. ii, 1810, 75, pl. 13, fig. 2.—BP., Syn. 1828, 67.—NUTT., Man. i, 1832, 271.—AUD., Orn. Biog. ii, 176; v, 423; pl. 129; Syn. 1839, 40; B. Am. i, 1840, 209, pl. 57.—PUTN., Pr. Ess. Inst. i, 1856, 206 (Massachusetts).

Tyrannus crinitus, Sw., Quart. Journ. xx, 1826, 271.—BP., Comp. List, 1838, 25.—NUTT., i, 1840, 302.—MAXIM., J. f. O. 1858, 182.
Myiobius crinitus, GRAY, Genera of Birds, i, 248.
Tyrannula crinita, BP., Consp. Av. i, 1850, 189.—HARTL., Verz. Mus. Brem. 49.—KAUP, P. Z. S. 1851, 51.—WOODH., Sitgr. Rep. 1853, 73.
Myiarchus crinitus, CAB., J. f. O. 1855, 479.—BD., B. N. A. 1858, 178.—SCL. & SALV., Ibis, i, 1859, 121, 440.—DRESS., Ibis, 1865, 473 (Texas).—MCILWR., Pr. Ess. Inst. vi, 1866, 83 (Canada West).—SNOW, B. Kans. 1873, 3.—ALLEN, Bull. M. C. Z. iii, 1872, 179 (Kansas).—COUES, Pr. Phila.·Acad. 1872, 63 (critical).—COUES, Key, 1872, 171.—B. B. & R., N. A. B. ii, 1874, 334, pl. 43, fig. 3.
Myionax crinitus, CAB., Mus. Hein. ii, 1859, 73 (type).
Myiarchus (Myionax) crinitus, SCL., Cat. Am. B. 232.
Pyrocephalus (Myionax) crinitus, GRAY, Hand-list, No. 5518.
Muscicapa ludoviciana, GM., Syst. Nat. i, 1788, 934.
Tyrannus ludovicianus, VIEILL., Ois. Am. Sept. i, 1807, pl. 45.
Tyrannus irritabilis, VIEILL., Enc. Meth. ii, 1823, 847.
"*Muscicapa virginea*, MÜLLER."
"*Muscicapa virginea cristata*, BRISS., Orn. ii, 412; Planch. Enl. 569, fig. 1 " (*Gray*).

For extralimital vars. *b.* and *c.*, see COUES, Pr. Phila. Acad. 1872, 65, 67. In there assigning *T. irritabilis*, Vieillot, to the South American bird (*Suiriri pardoyrojo*, Azara, ii, 143, No. 195, Paraguay), I fell into error following Bonaparte, who makes this identification. I am apprized by Dr. Sclater that Vieillot's name is really based upon Buffon (P. E., as above); and is therefore the true North American *crinitus*.

Hab.—Eastern United States and British Provinces, but rarely beyond the Connecticut Valley. Not given by Trippe as Minnesotan. West to Eastern Kansas and Indian Territory. Breeds throughout its United States range. Migratory. Entirely withdraws from the United States to winter in Central America, especially in Guatemala. Costa Rica (*Lawrence*, Ann. Lyc. ix, 1868, 115). Cuba? (*Gundlach*, 239); no other West Indian quotations found. (Minnesota? *Hatch*, Pr. Minn. Acad. i, 54.)

This species was not observed by any of the Expeditions, and its Missouri range is restricted, apparently, to the lowermost portions of the river. According to the observations of Mr. Allen and others, as well as of my own, it occurs abundantly in Eastern Kansas, gradually becoming less numerous with the restriction of timber to the westward, being already rare in Middle Kansas. Mr. Allen only saw one during his six weeks stay at Fort Hays.

No eggs of this country are more peculiar than those of the *Myiarchi*, and they are alike in all our species of the genus. It is difficult to convey an adequate idea of the curious pattern of coloration. Upon a buff or rich clay-color ground are drawn *lengthwise* unnumbered markings of rich, dark purplish-chestnut, or purplish-chocolate, with others of a paler shade of the same. The markings are of a peculiar sharp, scratchy character, as if made with a fine pen. At the butt the scratches are usually expansive and confluent, but elsewhere are distinct, and maintain for the most part their longitudinal direction, although in many samples the scratches run in every way. The size of the egg of *crinitus* is about 0.85 by 0.62.

MYIARCHUS CINERASCENS, (Lawr.) Scl.

Ash-throated Flycatcher.

Tyrannula cinerascens, LAWR., Ann. Lyc. N. Y. v, 1851, 109.—NEWB., P. R. R. Rep. vi, 1857, 81.
Myiarchus cinerascens, SCL., Ibis, 1859. 121 (? Guatemala), 440; P. Z. S. 1859, 384 (Oaxaca); 1871, 84; Cat. 1862, 233 (excl. syn. *T. mexicanus*, KAUP).—COUES, Pr. A. N. S. 1872, 69 (critical).—COUES, Key, 1872, 171.
Myiarchus crinitus var. *cinerascens*, B. B. & R., N. A. B. ii, 1874, 337, pl. 43, fig. 6.
Myiarchus mexicanus, BD., B. N. A. 1858, 179 (*nec* KAUP; *nec M. mexicanus*, LAWR., Ann. Lyc. ix, 1869, 202).—HEERM., P. R. R. Rep. x, 1859, pt. vi, 37, pl. 4.—COUES, Pr. Phila. Acad. 1866, 59.—SUMICH., Mem. Bost. Soc. i, 1869, 557 (Vera Cruz).—COOP., B. Cal. i, 1870, 316.—AIKEN, Pr. Bost. Soc. 1872, 205 (near Black Hills).
Myiarchus mexicanus var. *pertinax*, BD., Pr. Phila. Acad. 1859, 303 (Cape St. Lucas).
Myionax mexicanus, CAB., Mus. Hein., ii, 1859, 74.

Hab.—Southwestern United States. North to the Black Hills (*Aiken*); Utah (*McCarthy*); Nevada (*Ridgway*). South through Mexico. Texas to the Pacific; Cape St. Lucas; Mazatlan (*Grayson*); Guatemala(?). Said by Dr. Cooper to winter in the Colorado Valley as high as Fort Mojave.

The characters of this species, and its synonymy, will be found fully discussed in my paper of 1872, above cited.

As in the case of the preceding species, Mr. Aiken again furnishes a northernmost quotation, carrying the known range into Wyoming. It had before been brought from Utah and Nevada, but its centre of abundance in the United States appears to be somewhat further south. I found it numerous in the mountains of Arizona, there occupying the place of *crinitus*, as Cassin's does of the Arkansas Flycatcher. It is there only a summer resident, arriving late in April, and remaining through most of September. Avoiding the depths of the pineries, it resorts to the oak openings, brushy ravines, and the fringes of wood along the streams. Its habits and manners recall those of *crinitus* in every particular. I never found the nest, which is thus described by Dr. Heermann: "The nest, found in the hollow of a tree, or in a deserted squirrel's or Woodpecker's hole, is composed of grasses lined with feathers. The eggs, five in number, are cream-colored, marked and speckled with purplish-red dashes and faint neutral-tint blotches."

The species is of very general distribution in Mexico, in many places associated with the resident variety of *crinitus* (var. *cooperi* of that country). In the United States it is migratory, retiring to or beyond our boundary in the fall.

SAYORNIS SAYUS, (Bp.) Bd.

Say's Flycatcher.

Muscicapa saya, Bp., Am. Orn. i, 1825, 20, pl. 2, fig. 3; Syn. 1828, 67.—Nutt., Man. i, 1832, 277.—Aud., Orn. Biog. iv, 1838, 428, pl. 359; Syn. 1839, 41; B. Am. i, 1840, 217, pl. 59.
Tyrannula saya, Sw. & Rich., F. B. A. ii, 1831, 142, pl. 45.—Bp., List, 1838, 24; Consp. i, 1850, 189.—Newb., P. R. R. Rep. vi, 1857, 81.—Woodh., Sitgr. Rep. 1853, 74.
Tyrannus saya, Nutt., Man. i, 1840, 311.
Tyrannus sayii, Maxim., J. f. O. 1858, 183.
Myiobius sayus, Gray, Genera of Birds, i, 249.
Ochthoëca saya, Cab., Wieg. Archiv, 1847, 255.
Aulanax sayus, Cab., J. f. O. 1856, 2.
Sayornis sayus, Bd., B. N. A. 1858, 185; Mex. Bound. ii, 1859, Birds, 9.—Kenn., P. R. R. Rep. x, 1859, pt. iv, 24.—Heerm., *ibid.* pt. vi, 37.—Hayd., Rep. 1862, 158.—Coues, Pr. Phila. Acad. 1866, 60 (Arizona).—Allen, Bull. M. C. Z. iii, 1872, 179 (Colorado and Wyoming).—Aiken, Pr. Bost. Soc. 1872, 205.—Stev., U. S. Geol. Surv. Ter. 1870, 463.—Merr., *ibid.* 1872, 690.—Coues, Key, 1872, 172.—B. B. & R., N. A. B. ii, 1874, 347, pl. 45, fig. 3.
Theromyias sayi, Cab., Mus. Hein. ii, 1859, 67 (type).
Tyrannula pallida, Sw., Phil. Mag. i, 1827, 367.
Sayornis pallidus. Scl., P. Z. S. 1857, 127, 204; 1859, 366 (Xalapa); Cat. 1862, 199 (Orizaba).—Scl. & Salv., Ibis, 1859, 438

Hab.—Western North America, from the high central plains to the Pacific. North to latitude 60° (*Richardson*). South to Mexico. Breeds apparently throughout most of its range (Texas, Dress., Ibis, 1865, 473), and winters along our southern border.
Lieutenant Warren's Expedition.—5237, Knife River; 5268, Fort Union; 5269, Cannonball River, 8293-4, Black Hills.
Later Expeditions.—54305, 60448, 60763, Wyoming; 61769, Utah.

This is an abundant species throughout its range, in suitable places, and one of the hardier birds of the family, proceeding as far north, apparently, as any, and further than most. It is also one of the earliest migrants, in this respect agreeing with *S. fuscus* of the East. From its winter quarters along our southern border, in the valleys of the Colo-

rado and Gila, and in Southern California, it begins to move in February, and by the following month has accomplished the first stages of
its journey. According to Dr. Richardson, it reaches the Saskatchewan
early in May. It returns very leisurely, tarrying by the way, not fairly
resuming its winter station until November.

In its habits it is nearest *S. nigricans*, but also in a noticeable degree
resembles the arboreal species of the East. It is a bird of open country,
the Flycatcher of the plains. As we ride through the rank herbage of
the innumerable ravines that trend toward the water-courses of the
west, among the sage-brush of the still more inhospitable regions, or in
less forbidding valleys, environed by forests, that lie among the mountains, Say's Flycatcher may often be seen, singly or in pairs, perched
on the stunted vegetation. We may approach quite near without
alarming it, hear its sharp note, observe its characteristic attitude as
it sits in wait for passing insects, ready for instant action, and then see
it sally into the air to capture its prey with a click of the bill. It has
the same vibrating motion of the tail so characteristic of *S. fuscus*. The
nidification is essentially similar to that of this species, in the construction of the nest, if not in its position. Sometimes mud is used in its
composition, sometimes not. The eggs, of the usual number for this
family, are pure white, unmarked, as in *S. fuscus*, and also *S. nigricans*.

SAYORNIS FUSCUS, (Gm.) Bd.

Pewit Flycatcher; Phœbe-bird.

Muscicapa fusca, GM., Syst. Nat. i, 1788, 93 (*M. carolinensis fusca*, BRISS., iv, 367.)—
    VIEILL., Ois. Am. Sept. i, 1807, 68, pl. 40; Ency. Meth. 829.—BP., Obs. Wils.
    1825, No. 115; Syn. 1828, 68.—AUD., Orn. Biog. ii, 1834, 122; v, 1839, 424; pl.
    120; Syn. 1839, 43; B. Am. i, 1840, 223, pl. 63.—GIR., B. L. I. 1844, 42.
Tyrannula fusca, RICH., List in Rep. Brit. Assoc. 1837.—BP., List, 1838, 24.
Tyrannus fuscus, NUTT., Man. i, 1840, 312.
Myiarchus fuscus, CAB., Wieg. Arch. 1847, 248.—SCL., P. Z. S. 1859, 366; Ibis, 1859, 440.
Aulanax fuscus, CAB., J. f. O. iv, 1856, 1.
Sayornis fuscus, BD., B. N. A. 1858, 184.—SUMICH., Mem. Bost. Soc. i, 1869, 557 (Vera
    Cruz).—HAYD., Rep. 1862, 158.—DRESS., Ibis, 1865, 473 (Texas).—SNOW, B.
    Kans. 1873, 3.—ALLEN, Bull. M. C. Z. iii, 1872, 179.—COUES, Key. 1872, 172, fig.
    113b.—GENTRY, Pr. Phila. Acad. 1873, 292 (nesting).—B. B. & R., N. A. B. ii,
    1874, 343, pl. 45, fig. 2.
Empidias fuscus, CAB., Mus. Hein. ii, 1859, 69 (type).—SCL., Cat. 1862, 234 (Mexico).—
    LAWR., Ann. Lyc. N. Y. viii, 1866, 290.
Pyrocephalus (Empidias) fuscus, GRAY, Hand-list, i, 1869, 363, No. 5539.
Muscicapa atra, GM., Syst. Nat. i, 1788, 946.—NUTT., Man. i, 1832, 278.
Muscicapa phœbe, LATH., Ind. Orn. ii, 1790, 489.
Muscicapa nunciola, WILS., Am. Orn. ii, 1810, 78, pl. 13, f. 4.
Myiobius nunciola, GRAY, Genera of Birds, i, 248.
Tyrannula nunciola, BP., Consp. i, 1850, 189.—WOODH., Sitgr. Rep. 1853, 74.

Hab.—Eastern United States and British Provinces. West to the Vermilion River,
or further. South into Mexico (Xalapa, *De Oca*, Mus. Lawr.). Winters abundantly in
all the Southern States. Breeds throughout its United States range. One of the very
earliest migrants in the spring, reaching the Canadas by the middle of April.
    Not noticed by the Expeditions.

The following fresh observations on the nidification of this species,
by Mr. Gentry, in the paper above quoted, are reproduced entire, as
being of sufficient interest:
"It is the commonly received opinion that birds of the same species
uniformly build their nests of the same materials and in the same form
and situation, though they inhabit different climates. This, however,
is not invariably the case, as a few observations will show. On the
north branch of the Susquehanna, some months since, I procured several

nests of our common Phœbe-bird, *Sayornis fuscus*, which in size, structure, and materials, might be taken for nests of species distinct from the one under consideration. As these nests were found upon the horizontal beams of a wagon-shed, they would not seem to require such compactness of structure as when built in more exposed situations.

"After a careful examination of several nests from different localities, I find that they are usually circular at the top, with a depth externally differing but little from the average diameter. By measurement I obtain the following dimensions: Diameter from side to side, $3\frac{1}{2}$ inches, depth 3 inches; diameter of cavity within, $2\frac{1}{2}$ inches, making the thickness of the lateral walls $\frac{1}{2}$ inch; depth of cavity, $1\frac{1}{2}$ inch, indicating a thickness at the bottom of $1\frac{1}{2}$ inch. These nests are composed of fine roots, grasses, fine mosses, and hairs, which are plastered together, and to the objects upon which they are built, by pellets of mud; within they are lined with soft grasses, lint, hairs, and sometimes with wool and feathers.

"No. 1 of deviation is nearly circular, with an average diameter of 4 inches and a depth of 2 inches, being considerably depressed. Diameter of cavity $2\frac{1}{2}$ inches, depth 1 inch; thickness of lateral walls $\frac{3}{4}$ inch, at the bottom 1 inch. The nest is constructed wholly of the silk of corn, with a few strings and hairs on the inside for a lining; the absence of moss and clay pellets being a noticeable feature of the nest; such ordinarily indispensable materials evidently not being requisite, if the site of the nest affords any criterion for judging.

"No. 2 of these anomalous forms is circular, with a diameter of 5 inches, and a depth of $2\frac{1}{2}$ inches on the outside; within, $2\frac{1}{4}$ inches in diameter and 2 inches in depth; lateral walls, $1\frac{1}{4}$ inch in thickness; inferior, $\frac{1}{2}$ inch. The entire nest is composed of the inner bark of the chestnut, plucked, doubtless, from fence rails, and reduced to very fine strips for the inner part of the nest, and gradually attaining a width of nearly one-fourth of an inch on the exterior.

"In an intermediate form between the ordinary form and the first deviation therefrom, I find the diameter $4\frac{1}{2}$ inches externally, depth 2 inches; cavity $2\frac{1}{2}$ inches, and depth $1\frac{1}{2}$ inch; lateral walls, each, 1 inch; inferior, $\frac{1}{2}$ inch. This nest is formed of fine grasses, hair, wool, and an abundance of moss externally; within it is lined by fine grasses and hairs; the absence of clay would seem to imply an unexposed place for its site, to which theory looseness of its structure most assuredly adds weight.

"That a species which has always been known to build a nest so characteristic as the Pewee should deviate so considerably and suddenly, as it seems to be, from its ordinary habit of nest-building, is remarkable. But such is the fact, as the mother-bird was discovered in the act of incubation. It has been suggested that possibly these nests were stolen property, and not the work of the bird in question. But this, I am satisfied, is not the case. The individuals of some species do take forcible possession of the abodes of others, or the cavities in which such are secreted, but I have never known the intruders to occupy the same, except in the case of *Molothrus pecoris* of America, and *Cuculus canorus* of England. As these birds never build, but deposit their eggs in the nests of other birds, I am hardly disposed to grant the propriety of considering them in this light. It is well known that *Troglodytes aëdon* does, when prompted by a mischievous spirit, drive away *Icterus baltimore* and *Sayornis fuscus* from their rightful property, and take up her abode therein, but not without having previously constructed her rude nest of coarse sticks, well lined with feathers and down.

"So strong is the attachment of birds to the nests of their own construction, that the parental instinct is often lost sight of. Proofs could be cited to sustain this assertion. One, however, will suffice. Two years ago, in Atlantic County, New Jersey, I came across a nest of the Robin, which, on account of its curious arrangement, I desired to possess. Unable to wait until the unfledged brood had taken their departure, I conceived the plan of removing them to another nest of the same species, not so neatly constructed or so tastefully arranged. But, as I had anticipated, the mother deserted her offspring; the love for home predominating over every other feeling.

"These deviations from the usual style of nest-building by the Pewee would seem to argue against the belief generally entertained, that instinct, being a positive determination given to the minds of animals for certain purposes, must necessarily be perfect, when viewed in connection with those purposes; but to say that they doubtless imply a *change of instinct* is to perplex the understanding by a perversion of language. But to ascribe these changes to the operations of reason influenced by motives, does seem to be the most rational view to take of the subject. That reason does enter into the inferior creatures, and dictate many of the changes of habit which mark their career, has been shown in many instances; but I cannot forbear to record one which came under my observation in the spring of 1871. While watching a pair of *Ampelis cedrorum*, engaged in the building of a nest on a branch of an apple-tree, it occurred to me that, by supplying them with materials, I might secure a nest neater and more compact than those usually made. The birds entered into the project with readiness, and carried away every piece of colored string and cotton fabric with which I supplied them. After I had ceased to furnish the materials they would fly repeatedly to the branch where the articles were deposited, as if imploring my services. The result was a nest firmer, more symmetrical, and more elegant in proportions than any I had ever observed. If instinct had been the controlling principle in this case, the birds would not have given my labors so much attention; but admitting that they had been actuated by reasoning faculties in their selection, the whole thing is perfectly plausible. Instinct is always the same thing; it never advances, never retrogrades; but reason tends to improvement, when it can serve a good purpose.

"As the nests which form the subject-matter of this paper were found within a short distance of each other, it would seem that circumstances peculiar to the neighborhood had rendered a deviation from the common form necessary. Observation teaches us that when danger or any other circumstance renders a change in the character of the nest necessary, that deviation is made in an equal degree and in the same manner by all the birds of one species, and that it does not extend beyond the limits of the region where alone it can serve a good purpose."

CONTOPUS BOREALIS, (Sw.) Bd.

Olive-sided Flycatcher.

Tyrannus borealis, Sw., F. B. A. ii, 1831, 141, pl. 35.
Myiobius borealis, GRAY, Gen. of B. i, 248.
Contopus borealis, BD., B. N. A. 1858, 188.—COOP. & SUCK., N. H. Wash. Ter. 1860, 169.—SCL., Cat. 1862, 230 (not of P. Z. S. 1858, 301; 1859, 43; which are *C. pertinax*).—VERR., Pr. Ess. Inst. iii, 145 (Norway, Me., probably breeding, not very common; quite common about Umbagog).—ALLEN, Pr. Ess. Inst. iv, 1864, 54 (Massachusetts, not very rare; May 15 to Sept. 15).—COUES, *ibid.* v, 1868, 264.—MCILWR., *ibid.* v, 1866, 84 (Toronto, two specimens).—LAWR., Ann.

Lyc. N. Y. viii, 1866, 290; ix, 1868, 115 (Costa Rica).—Coues, Pr. Bost. Soc. xii, 1868, 118 (South Carolina).—Turnb., B. E. Pa. 1869, 13 (very rare).— Coop., B. Cal. i, 1870, 323.—Mayn., Guide, 1870, 125 (Massachusetts, breeds, not very rare).—Mayn., Pr. Bost. Soc. 1871 (Northern New England).—Aiken, ibid. 1872, 206 (Wyoming).—Snow, B. Kans. 1873, 3 (migratory).—Allen, Bull. M. C. Z. iii, 1872, 179 (Colorado Mountains up to 12,000 feet; Wahsatch Mountains; Utah).—Merr., U. S. Geol. Surv. Ter. 1872, 691 (Idaho).—Coues, Key, 1872, 173.—Salv., P. Z. S. 1870, 199 (Veragua).—B. B. & R., N. A. B. ii, 1874, 353, pl. 44, f. 1.

Sayornis borealis, Wheat., Ohio Agric. Rep. 1860, Birds, No. 48.

Pyrocephalus (Contopus) borealis, Gray, Hand-list, i, 1869, 362, No. 5507.

Muscicapa inornata, Coop. & Nutt., Nutt., Man. i, 1832, 282, 285.

Muscicapa cooperi, Nutt., Man. i, 1832, 282 (not Tyrannula cooperi, of Hartl., Chili, nor of Kaup, Mexico, nor Myiarchus cooperi of authors).—Aud., Orn. Biog. ii, 1834, 422, pl. 174; Syn. 1839, 41; B. Am. i, 1840, 212, pl. 58.—Putn., Pr. Ess. Inst. i, 1856, 206 (Massachusetts).

Tyrannus cooperi, Bp., List, 1838, 24.—Nutt., Man. i, 1840, 298.—Reinh., Ibis, Jan. 1861, 7 (Greenland).

Tyrannula cooperi, Bp., Consp. Av. i, 1850, 189.

Contopus cooperi, Cab., J. f. O. iii, 1855, 479; ix, 1861, 248 (Costa Rica); Mus. Hein. ii, 1859, 72 (excl. syn. C. borealis, Sclater).

Contopus mesoleucus, Scl., P. Z. S. 1859, 43; Ibis, 1859, 122, 440.—Sumich., Mem. Bost. Soc. i, 1869, 557 (Vera Cruz).

Muscicapa villica, Licht., "Mus. Berol." (Cabanis).

Hab.—Entire temperate North America. Mexico. Greenland (Reinhardt). Common, and breeds in parts of New England. Rare in Middle and Southern Atlantic States. More abundant in the West. South to Central America.

List of specimens.

| 19189 | 131 | Wind River ... | .... | May 24, 1860 | F. V. Hayden. | 7.25 | 12.50 | 4.25 |

Later Expeditions.—61739, Utah; 62289-90, Idaho.

The very general dispersion of this species in North America only gradually become apparent. It was discovered by Sir John Richardson on the Saskatchewan, at Cumberland House, in latitude 54°, and described in 1831 by Mr. Swainson, as above cited. It was rediscovered by Mr. Nuttall, a specimen being obtained near Cambridge, Massachusetts, in June, 1830. This gentleman obtained several others in the same vicinity, and described its notes and manners accurately. The nest, he states, was on "the horizontal branch of a tall cedar-tree, forty or fifty feet from the ground. It was formed much in the manner of the Kingbird's, externally made of interlaced dead twigs of the cedar, internally of the wiry stolons of the common cinquefoil, dry grass, and some fragments of branching Lichen or Usnea. It contained three young, and had probably four eggs. The eggs had been hatched about the 20th of June, so that the pair had arrived in this vicinity about the close of May. The young remained in the nest no less than twenty-three days." The same author speaks of the eggs as "yellowish-creamy white, with spots of reddish-brown, of a light and dark shade." This is exactly the character of the specimens before me. The size is about 0.84 by 0.66. About the same time Dr. Brewer communicated a note to Mr. Audubon, describing the nest as follows: "Measures five inches in external diameter and three and a half inches in internal, and is about half an inch deep. It is composed entirely of roots and fibres of moss. It is, moreover, very rudely constructed, and is almost wholly flat, resembling the nest of no other Flycatcher I have seen, but having some similitude to that of the Cuckoo." New England quotations have continually multiplied, many referring to the breeding of the bird from Massachusetts northward; quite lately, Mr. Brewster says, in Mr. Maynard's book above quoted, that it nests generally in the fork of a pine-tree, the only nest found by him in any other situation being placed on the outer limb of an apple-tree. Mr. Audubon mentions the Magdaleine Islands and Labrador as other localities. In the reverse direction, the bird has been traced in New York, New Jersey, and Pennsylvania, but I never saw it in Maryland or Virginia ; and in including it in my South Carolina list I relied entirely upon Prof. R. W. Gibbes, of Charleston. He very likely included it on the strength of Audubon's statement of its occurrence in Georgia. The rarity of the bird, along the whole Atlantic coast south of New England, may be inferred from the foregoing.

Turning now to the west, we find Audubon again quoting Nuttall for its occurrence "in the dark fir-woods of the Columbia." This is corroborated by Dr. Cooper, who says that the Olive-sided Flycatcher "is very common, arriving early in May, and frequenting the borders of woods, where, from the summit of some tall, dead tree, its loud, melancholy cry resounds through the day, during the whole of summer. It frequents the small pine-groves along the coast, as well as in the interior, and remains until late in September." More recently, the same observer gives the species as "resident" in most parts of California, stating that he found them rather common in the coast-range toward Santa Cruz, where they had nests in May; and saw them at Lake Tahoe in September. Dr. Hayden's, Mr. Allen's, and Mr. Aiken's Rocky Mountain references are above given. There is little doubt that the bird breeds in places in these regions. In Colorado, according to Mr. Trippe, it breeds, though it is not very common. "This Flycatcher," he says, " arrives at Idaho Springs late in May, and remains till late in August or early in September. It is quite uncommon, only three or four pairs having been observed throughout the summer, and these at widely different points, each pair apparently monopolizing a wide range. It keeps in the tops of the trees, and is an active flycatcher; its voice is loud and distinct; and its nest is placed in the top of a pine, and zealously guarded from all intrusion with as much fierceness and energy as the Kingbird's." I did not observe it any season in Arizona, but the presumption is that it visits that Territory, since it is known to go south, through Mexico, and to Central America. But in that region its place seems to be mostly taken by the *C. pertinax*, a closely allied, but perfectly distinct Mexican species, there finding, probably, its northern limit. I took a young bird of *C. pertinax* at Fort Whipple, August 20, doubtless hatched in the vicinity. The differences between *C. pertinax* and *C. borealis* are correctly expressed in my paper (Pr. Phila. Acad. 1866, 60) and in my later work, as above quoted. Both are true " Pewees," and in their general economy closely resemble *C. virens*.

CONTOPUS VIRENS, (Linn.) Cab.

Wood Pewee.

Muscicapa virens, LINN., Syst. Nat. i, 1766, 327.—GM., 936.—LATH., Ind. Orn. ii, 482.—
    LICHT., Verz. 1823, 563.—BP., Syn. 1828, 68.—NUTT., Man. i, 1832, 285.—AUD.,
    Orn. Biog. ii, 1834, 93 ; v, 1839, 425 ; pl. 115 ; Syn. 1839, 42 ; B. Am. i, 1840, 231,
    pl. 64.—GIR., B. L. I. 1844, 43.—TRIPPE, Pr. Ess. Inst. vi, 1871, 114 (Minnesota).
Tyrannula virens, BP., List, 1838, 24 ; Consp. i, 1850, 189.—WOODH., Sitgr. Rep. 1853, 74.
Myiobius virens, GRAY, Gen. of B. i, 1840, 249.
Tyrannus virens, NUTT., Man. i, 1840, 316.
Myiarchus virens, CAB., Wieg. Arch. 1847, 248.—SCL., P. Z. S. 1855, 150.
Contopus virens, CAB., J. f. O. iii, 1855, 479 ; ix, 1861, 248 (Costa Rica); Mus. Hein. ii,
    1859, 71.—SCL., P. Z. S. 1859, 44.—SCL. & SALV., Ibis, 1859, 122, 441.—SCL., Cat.
    1862, 231 (Vera Paz; Guatemala).—BD., B. N. A. 1858, 190.—DRESS., Ibis, 1865,
    474 (Texas, breeding).—GUNDL., Rep. 1865, 239 (Cuba).—MCILWR., Pr. Ess. Inst.
    vi, 1866, 84 (Canada).—LAWR., Ann. Lyc. ix, 1868, 115 (Costa Rica).—SUMICH.,
    Mem. Bost. Soc. i, 1869, 557 (Orizaba).—SCL. & SALV., P. Z. S. 1870, 837 (Hon-

duras).—ALLEN, Bull. M. C. Z. iii, 1872, 179 (Kansas).—COUES, Key, 1872, 173, fig. 113ᶜ.—B. B. & R., N. A. B. ii, 1874, 357, pl. 44, fig. 3.
Pyrocephalus (Contopus) virens, GRAY, Hand-list, i, 1869, 361, No. 5506.
Muscicapa querula, VIEILL., Ois. Am. Sept. 1, 1807, 68, pl. 39 (*nec Wils.*).
Muscicapa rapax, WILS., Am. Orn. ii, 181, 81, pl. 13, f. 5.

Hab.—Eastern United States and British Provinces. Not much west of the Mississippi; only to borders of central plains. South to New Granada. Mexico. Breeds throughout its United States range. Said by Audubon to winter in Louisiana and Florida; observation unchecked by later accounts. Winters in Mexico and Central America to New Granada. A late migrant in the spring; entering the United States in March, and reaching the middle districts usually about the end of the next month. Extremely abundant, in wood-land, in most localities.

I am indebted to Mr. Gentry for the following notes : "This species usually makes its appearance in the eastern part of Pennsylvania in the latter part of April, and commences building about the middle of May. It prefers the loneliness of the forest generally, to the busy haunts of man. It is described by writers as being more retired in its habits than its cousins, as well as more suspicious. In my early ornithological peregrinations, I had always encountered it far from the scenes of active life, its nest being found in the recesses of dense forests, saddled upon the horizontal limb of some gigantic, high-towering oak. Last spring I was surprised to meet with several within a few yards of occupied dwellings, in the midst of a rather thickly settled portion of our town. These nests were fixed upon the horizontal branches of apple-trees, at elevations less than ten feet from the ground. The trees had been often visited by several of my pupils, who had even whiled their leisure moments away underneath their sheltering boughs, while the mother-birds sat within their cozy nests overhead, apparently in the enjoyment of calm satisfaction and perfect security.

"It is true that birds originally conceive very unfavorable opinions of man, and seek safety and immunity from his presence in interminable forests and impenetrable undergrowth, under the fancied belief that he is their inveterate foe; but through the habit of association, or accidental intrusion into his presence, they have learned more of his nature, particularly in these latter times when the law is their protection, and from holding him aloof as a being to be hated, they begin to see his good qualities, and draw near to his dwellings and render to him manifold services.

"Nuttall's description of the nest of this species, which has the credit of being the best that is recorded, may have been a faithful portraiture thereof in his day, and no doubt will be found to hold good in various sections, as it does in New England, according to the authority of Samuels; but in this section of the country it is somewhat different, and needs remodeling. Instead of being 'universally saddled upon an old moss-grown and decayed limb,' I have frequently seen it resting between the forked twigs of an oak, and one that was in a perfectly living condition. 'The body of the fabric' occasionally consists of 'wiry grass or root-fibres,' but I have never detected the "small branching lichens held together with cobwebs and caterpillars' silk, moistened with saliva.' In a nest which I have before me, which can be taken as a type, the bulk of it is made up entirely of small strips of liber plucked from trees and fence-rails, tow, and wool, arranged in a circular manner, and pressed compactly together by the body of the bird. One of the most prominent features of the nest is its external coating of bluish-gray crustaceous lichens, of the kind that are found upon the trunks of trees, which give it a very close resemblance to that of the Hummingbird, which it nearly rivals in symmetry and beauty.

"When the nests are saddled upon the limb there is much saving of material, economy doubtless being practised at the expense of the com-fort of the young.   The bottom of the nest is so slight, that upon being detached from the branch it presents a sieve-like appearance.   In those that have been placed in the angle constituted by two uniting twigs, there has always been an abundance of material, thus making a soft and comfortable nest for the tender brood.

"The habit of constructing the nest upon the superior face of a branch was doubtless acquired in order to secure protection, the nest in this po-sition presenting to an enemy at a distance the semblance of an anoma-lous growth, overgrown with moss, such as are sometimes found upon the diseased branches of the oak.

"I have taken the nests of this species during the latter part of July and the early part of August, with eggs, but whether a second laying or not I am not prepared to say ; possibly the work of birds that had been debarred the essential duties of incubation earlier in the season, since this desire is so innate as to be foregone with difficulty."

CONTOPUS (VIRENS var ?) RICHARDSONII, (Sw.) Bd.

Western Wood Pewee.

Tyrannula richardsonii, Sw., F. B. A. ii, 1831, 146, pl. 46, lower fig. (very wrongly colored).
Muscicapa richardsonii, AUD., Orn. Biog. v, 1839, 299, pl. 434.
Contopus richardsonii, BP., B. N. A. 1858, 189.—SCL., Cat. 1862, 231 (Vera Paz).—HAYD.,
    Rep. 1862, 158.—DRESS., Ibis, 1865, 474 (Matamoras, breeding).—COUES, Pr.
    Phila. Acad. 1866, 61 (Arizona).—LAWR., Ann. Lyc. N. Y. ix, 1868, 115 (Costa
    Rica).—COOP., Am. Nat. iii, 1869, 31 (Montana).—COOP., B. Cal. i, 1870, 325.
    AIKEN, Pr. Bost. Soc. 1872, 206 (Colorado).—STEV., U. S. Geol. Surv. Ter. 1870,
    463.—MERR., *ibid.* 1872, 691.
Pyrocephalus (Contopus) richardsonii, GRAY, Hand-list, 1869, 362, No. 5510.
Tyrannula phœbe, BP., Comp. List, 1838, 24 (not *Muscicapa phœbe*, LATH.).
Muscicapa phœbe, AUD., Syn. 1839, 42 ; B. Am. i, 1840, 219, pl. 61 (Labrador quotation
    probably erroneous).
Tyrannus phœbe, NUTT., Man. i, 1840, 319.
Tyrannus atriceps, D'ORBIG., (*fide* Gray).
Contopus bogotensis, SCL., P. Z. S. 1858, 459.
Tyrannula bogotensis, BP., Comptes Rend.
Contopus plebeius, CAB., Mus. Hein. ii, 1859, 71 (Mexico); J. f. O. ix, 1861, 248 (Costa Rica).
Contopus sordidulus, SCL., P. Z. S. 1859, 43 ; Ibis, 1859, 491 (Orizaba).—SCL. & SALV.,
    Ibis, 1859, 122 (Guatemala).—SUMICH., Mem. Bost. Soc. i, 1869, 557 (alpine
    region of Vera Cruz).
Contopus veliei, BAIRD & COUES ; COUES, Pr. Phila. Acad. 1866, 61 (in text ; seasonal
    state of plumage).
Contopus virens var. *richardsonii*, ALLEN, Bull. M. C. Z. iii, 1872, 179 (Colorado and
    Utah).—COUES, Key, 1872, 174.—B. B. & R., N. A. B. ii, 1874, 360, pl. 44, f. 4.

Hab.—Western North America, from high central plains to the Pacific.   North to the Saskatchewan.   South through Mexico and Central America to New Granada.   (?) "Lab-rador" (*Audubon*).   Breeds in suitable places throughout its range.   Migrates entirely beyond the United States in the fall.

Lieutenant Warren's Expedition.—8892, Loup Fork of Platte River.
Later Expeditions.—59854, Berthoud's Pass ; 60441, 60449, Bitter Cottonwood, Wyom-ing ; 61740, Utah ; 62291, Idaho.

As already observed by Professor Baird, there are material discrepancies between Swainson's account of *Tyrannula richardsonii* and the subject of the present article ; but the most striking of these, the different wing formula, may be reconciled upon the supposition that the type of Swainson's species was a young bird.   This seems the more reasonable, because of the coloration of the plate—certainly wrong for an adult, yet after all not so far out of the way for the *very* young bird, which is rusty-tinged, as in allied species.   Upon the whole, in view of the facts that Swainson's bird was a *Contopus*, and that the present is the only one ever known to inhabit the ascribed locality, the identification may be safely made.

I should not be surprised if, after all, it proved that Mr. Allen and others were hasty in reducing this bird to a variety of *C. virens*.   It is true, indeed, as stated in the "Key," that I failed to appreciate any perfectly constant differences, or, in fact, any decided peculiarities, in examining the very large series submitted to me by several kind friends. But even in dried skins certain slight differences may be observed to hold with considerable constancy. The colors are *darker* (they should be lighter, paler, in a geographical variety from the dry, western region); the olive-brown of the upper parts is more fuscous, the olive-gray shading of the sides is heavier, and reaches almost or entirely uninterrupted quite across the breast, leaving only the upper part of the throat, and the belly, whitish. The wings average longer, owing to elongation of the primaries, by which the tip is carried further from the ends of the secondary quills. It is also a significant fact, that Audubon—one of the acutest of observers, and certainly not one who can be accused of wanton species-making— has left no hint that he even suspected its identity with *virens*. If he be not mistaken in his investigations in Labrador respecting this species, the mode of nidification is totally different from that of the eastern Wood Pewee. The note is harsher and more abrupt—has little of the plaintive, drawling intonation so characteristic of *C. virens*. When I reached the Rio Grande, fresh from eastern woods, where I saw the Wood Pewee almost every day in summer, and had been familiar with it for years, the western Pewee's note was one of the first that saluted my ears from the heavy timber bordering the river; and I well remember how peculiar it sounded, making me sure my old friend was not before me; and likewise through Arizona, it never occurred to me that the birds might be the same as *C. virens*. So we return to the question, and it is an open one, whether such field observations as those of Audubon's, Allen's, Trippe's, and mine, should not be allowed to turn the scale in favor of specific distinctness, although in this case they are not very satisfactorily borne out by inspection of specimens in the closet. We may have to acknowledge, in some cases, that species are better determined in the field than in the closet. If this be true in any case, it holds with the little Flycatchers.

The Western Wood Pewee is exceedingly abundant in Arizona, from the beginning of May until the latter part of September. I found it in all sorts of woodland, but more particularly in high, open forests. On entering a piece of woods the ear was sure to be saluted by the curious notes of the bird, and one, or more likely several, would be seen, sentinel-like, on the ends of dead branches, in wait for passing insects. At least two broods are reared in this latitude. The bird appears to breed indifferently throughout its range; in the northward migration, individuals drop off all along, only a small fraction reaching the extreme limit of the species; but in the fall they sweep southward with one accord, being delicate birds, unable to endure the cold of even our southern districts. It would appear that a portion of them are resident in Mexico and Central America; and to these, no doubt presenting some slight peculiarities not shared by the migratory and northern-bred birds, the names *bogotensis*, *sordidulus*, and *plebeius* have been applied. In most of its extent it appears to be separated a little from *C. virens;* but the two forms meet in their tropical winter quarters, and also, if Audubon made no mistake, again at their northern terminus, on the cold and foggy shores of Labrador.

Information received from Mr. Allen since the above was written increases the suspicion that Audubon may not have been entirely correct in his description of the nidification, even if the Labrador record be not itself invalidated. My esteemed correspondent, remarking that the bird is more or less common at the western edge of the plains wherever there are trees, and also throughout the mountains of Colorado, up to about 12,000 feet, continues: "Though generally distinguishable from the Eastern Wood Pewee on comparison of dried skins, it is more easily recognized by the difference in its notes and breeding habits. The nest is built in the forks of a small branch, instead of being "saddled" on a horizontal limb, like that of the eastern bird. It is neat and compact, resembling, both in position and general form, that of the Least Flycatcher (*Empidonax minimus*) of the Atlantic States, and hence differs widely from that described by Audubon as observed by him in Labrador. Its notes are harsh and less varied than those of its eastern relatives, lacking almost entirely the plaintive character so distinctive of the latter. The usual eastern type was not met with west of Eastern Kansas, the western form being the only one seen in Colorado. The latter was especially frequent near Fairplay, in South Park, where it was breeding, but all the nests obtained contained half-grown young." The eggs are very similar to those of *C. virens.*

The following has been obligingly communicated by Mr. Trippe: "This bird arrives in Bergen's Park, Colorado, in the latter part of May, and soon becomes abundant, extending its range up to over 10,000 feet, and perhaps as high as timber-line. It breeds from about 7,000 feet upward. The nest is planted in the fork of a tree and resembles that of *Empidonax minimus,* being quite different from that of the Eastern Wood Pewee; the eggs, however, are entirely similar. The young are hatched late in June, and only one brood is raised. It is one of the first birds to leave in autumn, departing about the middle of August. In notes and habits it is very different from *C. virens.* Instead of haunting the thickest woods, it roams over the open country, shunning the deep shade of the forests, and acting in all respects like *Sayornis fuscus;* while its notes are far harsher and quicker than the slow, melancholy plaint of the Eastern Wood Pewee, and only faintly resemble it. The two varieties, in fact, are as well marked as any that are supposed to belong to the same species of this family."

EMPIDONAX ACADICUS, (Gm.) Bd.

Acadian, or small Green-crested Flycatcher.

(?) *Muscicapa acadica,* GM., Syst. Nat. i, 1788, 947.—LATH., Ind. Orn. ii, 1790, 480.— VIEILL., Ois. Am. Sept. i, 1807, 71 (not of *Nuttall*).
Muscicapa acadica, BP., Syn. 1828, 68.—AUD., Orn. Biog. ii, 1834, 256; v, 1839, 429; pl. 144; Syn. 1839, 42; B. Am. i, 1840, 221, pl. 62.—GIR., B. L. I. 1844, 40.—(?) PUTN., Pr. Ess. Inst. i, 1856, 206 (more likely *minimus*).
Tyrannula acadica, SW.—BP., Comp. and Geog. List, 1838, 24; Consp. i, 1850, 189.— WOODH., Sitgr. Rep. 1853, 74 (Indian Territory).
Myobius acadicus, GRAY, Genera of Birds, i, 219.
Myiarchus acadicus, CAB., Wieg. Arch. 1847, 248.
Empidonax acadicus, CAB., Mus. Hein. ii, 1859, 70.—BD., B. N. A. 1858, 197.—SCL., Cat. 1862, 229.—COUES & PRENT., Smiths. Rep. 1861, 404.—WHEAT., Ohio Agric. Rep. No. 52.—ALLEN, Pr. Ess. Inst. iv, 1864, 54.—DRESS., Ibis, 1865, 475 (Texas).—LAWR., Ann. Lyc. N. Y. viii, 1866, 290.—McILWR., Pr. Ess. Inst. v, 1866, 84 (Canada West, rare).—COUES, Pr. Ess. Inst. v, 1868, 264.—TURNB., B. E. Pa. 1869, 14.—BREW., Am. Nat. i, 1867, 119 (important).—COUES, Key, 1872, 174.—B. B. & R., N. A. B. ii, 1874, 374, pl. 44, f. 11.
Pyrocephalus (Empidonax) acadicus, GRAY, Hand-list, i, 1869, 361, No. 5492.
(?) "*Platyrhynchus virescens,* VIEILL., Nouv. Dict. d'Hist. Nat. xxvii, 22" (*fide Cabanis*).
Muscicapa querula, WILS., Am. Orn. ii, 1810, 77, pl. 13, f. 3 (*nec Vieillot*).
"*Muscicapa subviridis,* BARTR., p. 289" (quoted in *Jard.* ed. Wils.).
"*Muscicapa pusilla,* LEMB., Av. Isl. Cuba, 1850, 129" (*fide Lawr.*).
"*Tyrannula pusilla,* GUNDL., J. f. O. 1855, 480" (*fide Lawr.*).
"*Empidonax pusillus,* CAB., J. f. O. 1855, 480" (*fide Lawr.*).

Hab.—Eastern United States; rarely north into New England, and no authentic record beyond Massachusetts. Canada West (*McIlwraith*). West to the Mississippi and slightly beyond. Breeds abundantly in the Middle Districts. Cuba (LAWR., Ann. Lyc. N. Y. vii, 1860, 265; GUNDL., Rep. 240). ("*Acadicus*" geographically wrong.)

The present is the most distinct and easily recognized of the four species of the genus inhabiting the Eastern States. Nevertheless, it has been frequently confounded with others, notably by New England writers, many or most of whose citations really refer to *minimus* or *traillii*—especially the former. Thus, Nuttall says it is one of "our most common summer birds" in Southern New England; but his whole account evidently refers to *minimus.* Mr. Allen more correctly says it is rather rare in Massachusetts, while Mr. Maynard, a trustworthy observer, never recognized it from that State. The only record beyond Massachusetts I have found, is Audubon's citation of " Nova Scotia." This may be correct, but is more likely a mistake. The fact is, that if there is any biographical circumstance distinguishing this species prominently from its allies, it is its restricted northern range. It does *not* ordinarily proceed beyond the Middle States, where it breeds in abundance, in this differing from *traillii*, *minimus* and *flaviventris*, which are chiefly seen in the Middle States during the migration. At Washington, D. C., the Acadian Flycatcher is, through the summer, very abundant, almost as much so as the Pewee itself. It arrives from the South the last week in April, and remains through September. Dr. Prentiss and I observed *E. flaviventris* there in July, leading to the belief that it may breed in that vicinity; but with this exception *acadicus* was the only species of the genus we ever found between the periods of migration. It was the only species of the genus observed in summer in West Virginia by Mr. Scott.

The *Muscicapa acadica* of Gmelin is not certainly determinable, but has become current with later authors for this species, as accurately indicated by Wilson under the name of *querula*. I notice a quotation of a *Muscicapa subviridis* of Bartram, which, if belonging here, antedates *querula ;* if *acadica* be set aside as indefinite or inapplicable, is the proper name to be applied. Most of the earlier descriptions of our Flycatchers, except Wilson's, apply with about equal propriety to several different ones, so that the identification is usually made, if at all, by some collateral evidence. For instance, even Audubon's *description* of *"acadica"* rather indicates *minimus*, with which he was not at the time acquainted ; and the rest of his account, though apparently relating to the true *acadicus*, requires some modification. Prof. Baird made a perfect discrimination of the species in 1858; and in the " Key" I endeavored to set forth its peculiarities in such a pointed manner that there need be no subsequent misapprehension respecting it. By an inadvertence the *M. acadica* of Nuttall is quoted as synonymous. It is, as I have said, the most strongly marked of all our species; and how little acquainted with it New England writers were may be inferred from the fact, that so late as 1871 we find Mr. Maynard saying (Pr. Bost. Soc.) that he cannot see the difference between it and *traillii*. (*Cf.* Am. Nat. vii, 1873, 42). I should not be surprised, indeed, if it proved that even Mr. Allen, whose reliability is justly rated so high, confounded it with *traillii*, and that, consequently, the bird remains to be detected in New England.

The western limit of this species is much restricted, barely reaching the eastern border of the Missouri region. The only trans-Mississippian quotation I have seen is Dr. Woodhouse's, giving the bird as common in the Indian Territory.

Setting Nuttall's account aside altogether, as unquestionably relating entirely to *minimus*, we will notice Wilson's and Audubon's. The former's description is unmistakable, and he says, nearly correctly: " It inhabits the deepest, thick-shaded solitary parts of the woods; sits generally on the lower branches; utters, every half minute or so, a sudden, sharp squeak, which is heard a considerable way through the woods; and, as it flies from one tree to another, has a low, querulous note, something like the twitterings of chickens nestling under the wings of a hen. It arrives from the South about the middle of May; *builds on the upper side of a limb*, in a low, swampy part of the woods, and lays five *white* eggs." The italics here, which are mine, indicate that portion of the account which is erroneous. Audubon described the nesting as follows:

"Early in May, in our Middle Districts, the small Green-crested Flycatcher constructs its nest. * * * * It is placed in the darkest shade of the woods, in the upright forks of some middle-sized tree, from eight to twenty feet above the ground, sometimes so low as to allow a man to look into it. *In some instances I have found it on the large horizontal branches of an oak, when it looked like a knot. It is always neat and well finished*, the inside measuring about two inches in diameter, with a depth of an inch and a half. The exterior is composed of strips of the inner bark of various trees, vine-fibres, and grasses, matted together with the down of plants, wool, and soft moss. The lining consists of fine grass, a few feathers, and horse-hair. The whole is light, elastic, and firmly coherent, and is glued to the twigs or *saddled on the branch with great care. The eggs are from four to six, small, and pure white.*"

I have italicized the passages of this account that appear to be more or less completely at variance with the facts. The next notice I will call attention to is Mr. Giraud's. He says, in his "Birds of Long Island," of this species, that "in habits it is solitary; generally seen on the lower branches of the larger trees; utters a quick, sharp note; arrives among us in the latter part of May, and retires southward early in September." Mr. E. A. Samuels gives the bird as a rare summer inhabitant of any of the New England States, seldom coming so far north." He states his lack of personal experience, and even this sentence is probably grounded on Allen, whom I believe to have been mistaken in this case. Mr. Samuels, however, describes the eggs accurately, and for the first time, upon five specimens furnished him by J. P. Norris, Esq., of Philadelphia, and presumably from that locality. They "are of a pale, creamy-white color, with a few thin spots of reddish-brown scattered over their larger end. They vary in size from 0.78 inch in length by about 0.56 in breadth, to 0.72 inch in length by 0.55 in breadth. The form is like that of *traillii*, but the spots are larger and more numerous."

In the American Naturalist, as above quoted, Dr. Brewer gives to several writers one of the overhaulings he can adm nister effectively on occasion, and, among other things, takes an opportunity of showing up the misunderstanding and confusion that have prevailed respecting the Acadian Flycatcher. On my applying to him for information he did not give at this time, he writes me as follows: "I do not think the bird occurs in New England, even in the Connecticut Valley, and believe that Mr. Allen has mixed it up with *traillii*. I have myself no evidence of its breeding northeast of Philadelphia; but it is shy and retiring in its habits, and would readily escape notice, so that its presence in New Jersey, New York, and New England, may not be uncommon and yet we not know of it." He also kindly inclosed a passage from his then forthcoming work; it runs as follows:

"The nest is generally placed on a drooping limb of a beech or a dogwood-tree, at the height of from six to ten feet from the ground. It is never saddled on a limb, like that of a Wood Pewee, neither is it pensile, like those of the Vireos, but is built in the fork of a small limb, and securely fastened thereto by a strip of bark. The nest itself is mostly made of fine strips of bark or weed-stalks, woven together without much care as to neatness or strength, and so very slight is the structure that you may often count the eggs in the nest from below.

"The eggs are generally three in number, and are of a rich creamcolor, thinly spotted near the greater end.

"A beautiful nest of this species was found by Mr. George O. Welch near Indianapolis. It was fully identified and the parent shot. This nest has a diameter of *four* inches and a height of *two*. Its base is composed, to a large extent, of dry grasses, intermingled with masses of withered blossoms of different herbaceous plants. Above this is constructed a somewhat rudely-interwoven nest, composed of long, fine, wiry stems of grasses. The cavity is two inches wide, and is less than one in depth. The eggs, three in number, are exceedingly beautiful, *and differ from all the eggs of this genus,* having more resemblance to those of *Contopi.* They have an elongated oval shape, and are quite pointed at one end. They measure 0.78 by 0.56 of an inch. Their ground is a rich cream-color, tinged with a reddish-brown shading, and at the larger end the eggs are irregularly marked with scattered and vivid blotches of red and reddish-brown."

EMPIDONAX TRAILLII, (Aud.) Bd.

Traill's Flycatcher.

a. *traillii.*

Muscicapa traillii, AUD., Orn. Biog. i, 1832, 236; v, 1839, 426; pl. 45; Syn. 1839, 43; B. Am. i, 1840, 234, pl. 65.
Tyrannula traillii, RICH., Rep. Br. Assoc. 1837.—BP., List, 1838, 24; Consp. i, 1850, 189.— WOODH., Sitgr. Rep. 1853, 74.
Tyrannus traillii, NUTT., Man. i, 1840, 323.
Myiobius traillii, GRAY, Genera of Birds, i, 249.
Empidonax traillii, BD., B. N. A. 1858, 193.—CAB., Mus. Hein. ii, 1859, 70 (reference to Audubon is wrong).—SCL., Cat. 1862, 229.— WHEAT., Ohio Agric. Rep. 1860, No. 50.—COUES & PRENT., Smiths. Rep. 1861, 404.—VERR., Pr. Ess. Inst. iii, 146 (Norway, Me.).—LAWR., Ann. Lyc. N. Y. viii, May, 1863 (New Granada); viii, 1866, 290 (New York); ix, 1868, 114 (Costa Rica); ix, 1868, 202 (Yucatan).— ALLEN, Pr. Ess. Inst. iv, 1864, 54.—McILWR., *ibid.* v, 1866, 84.—COUES, *ibid.* v, 1868, 265.—TURNB., B. E. Pa. 1869, 13.—MAYN., Guide, 1870, 125; Pr. Bost. Soc. 1871, p. —.—SNOW, B. Kans. 1873, 3.—ALLEN, Bull. M. C. Z. iii, 1872, 179 (Kansas).—COUES, Key, 1872, 175.
Empidonax pusillus var. *traillii,* B. B. & R., N. A. B. ii, 1874, 369, pl. 44, f. 8.

b. *pusillus.*

(?) *Platyrhynchus pusillus,* SW., Syn. Mex. B. in Phil. Mag. i, 1827, 366.
(?) *Tyrannula pusilla,* SW. & RICH., F. B. A. ii, 1831, 144, pl. 46, upper fig. (uncertain— just as likely to have been *minimus*).—GAMB., Pr. Phila. Acad. iii, 1847, 156.— BP., Consp. i, 1850, 189.
Muscicapa pusilla, AUD., Orn. Biog. v, 1839, 288, pl. 434; Syn. 1839, 44; B. Am. i, 1840, 236, pl. 66 (quotes " Labrador" and " Newfoundland ").
Tyrannus pusillus, NUTT., Man. i, 1840.
Myiobius pusillus, GRAY, Genera of Birds, i, 249.
Empidonax pusillus, (?) CAB., J. f. O. 1855, 480.—CAB.. Mus. Hein. ii, 1859, 70 (Mexico).— BD., B. N. A. 1858, 194.—SCL., Ibis, 1859, 441; Cat. 1862, 229.—COOP. & SUCK., N. H. Wash. Ter. 1860, 170.—COUES, Pr. Phila. Acad. 1866, 61.—SUMICH., Mem. Bost. Soc. i, 1869, 557 (Vera Cruz).—SNOW, B. Kans. 1873, 4.—AIKEN, Pr. Bost. Soc. 1872, 206 (Wyoming).—MERR., U. S. Geol. Surv. Ter. 1872, 691.— B. B. & R., N. A. B. ii, 1874, 366, pl. 44, f. 9.
Empidonax traillii, COOP., B. Cal. i, 1870, 327.
Empidonax traillii var. *pusillus,* COUES, Key, 1872, 175.

Hab.—Eastern United States and British Provinces, west to the central plains, whence to the Pacific replaced by var. *pusillus.* South to New Granada. The western form through Mexico.
Late Expedtions.—81741-6, Ogden, Utah; 61773, Idaho.

I have found it impracticable to distinguish the western bird as a species, and in treating it varietally it proves difficult to assign any very tangible characters. It may be noted, in this connection, that Dr. Cooper has, on several occasions, insisted that the Californian bird is indistinguishable from *traillii.* Audubon's type was taken in Arkansas, and he accredits the species with a range thence to the

Columbia, where he also locates *pusillus*. But it is best to accept *traillii* as the eastern bird, taking *pusillus*, as defined by Baird more particularly, for the western form, if this be considered worthy of a name.

In the East I never found Traill's Flycatcher abundant, having observed it only in its passage through the Middle districts, chiefly in May and September. According to New England writers, it breeds in that section; and Mr. Maynard has given a valuable note respecting it: "This species has a most peculiar note, like the syllables ' *ke-win'k* ' ; this is not so quickly given as the ' *se-wic'k* ' of *E. minimus*, and is somewhat harsher. There is, perhaps, thirty seconds' interval between each *kewin'k*. The birds while singing were perched on the top of a low alder. It appears to frequent these thickets, generally by the side of streams, for Mr. Brewster has repeatedly observed it in similar localities at Gorham, where it had the same song and habits. When the bird is freshly killed, the bill bears a striking resemblance to that of *E. flaviventris*, and having the under mandible yellow, delicately veined with purple. But in the dried state this yellow fades into brown, and loses its veining. The whole bird then appears much like the larger and darker types of *E. minimus*. Indeed, were it not for the slightly larger and broader bill, and generally olivaceous or greenish-yellow stripe at the base of the upper mandible and sides of the head of *E. traillii*, it would be difficult to determine the skins of the two species." I entirely agree with the author so far, though the rest of his article is not so pertinent. *E. minimus* does grade up to *traillii* in size, the colors are very nearly the same, and the proportions of the parts scarcely different; yet no one who has had any experience in the field would say that they were not different birds.

This species appears to entirely withdraw from the United States in the fall, to winter in Central America.

I found var. *pusillus* an abundant Flycatcher of the West. At Fort Whipple, in Arizona, it is the commonest and characteristic species of its group, arriving in the middle of April, and remaining through September. According to my note-book, the under mandible in my specimens was dusky flesh-color. They averaged about 6 inches long by 9 in extent, thus being quite as large as ordinary *acadicus*. A young bird was strongly suffused with olivaceous-yellow below, nearly as in *flaviventris*, and had the under mandible bright yellow, like the inside of the mouth. The species was not noticed by Dr. Hayden in the Missouri region, but we have various quotations demonstrating a general range from the central plains to the Pacific, north to the fur countries, and south far into, if not quite through, Mexico. Mr. Merriam gives the following account of its nidification:

" This western race of *E. traillii* was very common in the Salt Lake Valley, where I collected seven specimens and three nests. They build a neat, compact little nest, which they place in the fork of a rose or other small bush, about five feet above the ground. It is composed of fibrous grasses, flax, wool, and other soft substances, interwoven with a few leaves of swamp-grass. It is a curious fact that this bird places all the wool and other soft, downy substances on the *outside* of its nest, lining it with the rough stalks of dry grass."

The eggs of this species (*traillii*), to judge from numerous specimens before me, may be distinguished from those of *acadicus* in lacking much or all of the creamy tinge of the latter, and in the markings being, for the most part, large, bold, and blotched, rather than sharply dotted. The fact that the eggs are colored instead of colorless at once distinguishes them from those of *E. minimus*, and is a point to be regarded in discussing the specific relationships of the two.

EMPIDONAX MINIMUS, Bd.

Least Flycatcher.

Muscicapa "acadica, GM." of NUTT., Man. i, 1832, 288; not of authors.
Tyrannula minima, W. M. & S. F. BAIRD., Pr. Phila. Acad. i, 1843, 284; Am. Journ. Sci.
    July, 1844.—BP., Consp. Av. i, 1850, 190.
Muscicapa minima, AUD., B. Am. vii, 1844, 343, pl. 491.
Empidonax minimus, BD., B. N. A. 1858, 195.—SCL., P. Z. S. 1859, 384 (Oaxaca); Ibis,
    1859, 122 (Guatemala); 1859, 441 (Orizaba); Cat. 1862, 229 (Coban, Dueñas,
    &c.).—SCL. & SALV., Ibis, 1859, 122.—HAYD., Rep. 1862, 158.—WHEAT., Ohio
    Agric. Rep. 1860, No. 51.—COUES & PRENT., Smiths. Rep. 1861, 404.—VERR.,
    Pr. Ess. Inst. iii, 146 (breeding commonly about Norway, Me.).—ALLEN, Pr.
    Ess. Inst. vi, 1864, 54.—MCILWR., *ibid.* v, 1866, 84.—COUES, *ibid.* v, 1868, 265.—
    DRESS., Ibis, 1865, 474 (Texas).—LAWR., Ann. Lyc. N. Y. viii, 1866, 290.—
    TURNB., B. E. Pa. 1869, 14 (chiefly migratory, but some breeding).—ALLEN,
    Mem. Bost. Soc. i, 1868, 498, 505, 517 (Iowa and Illinois).—MAYN., Guide, 1870,
    126; Pr. Bost. Soc. 1871.—SCL. & SALV., P. Z. S. 1870, 837 (Honduras).—SNOW,
    B. Kans. 1873, 4.—ALLEN, Bull. M. C. Z. iii, 179 (Kansas).—COUES, Key, 1872,
    175.—B. B. & R., N. A. B. ii, 1874, 372, pl. 44, f. 10.

Hab.—Eastern North America to the high central plains; up the Missouri to Fort
Union. Breeds abundantly from Southern New England northward. Winters in
Central America.

Lieutenant Warren's Expedition.—4698, "Nebraska" (probably Dakota); 4699, 4700-1,
L'Eau qui court; 4702, Vermilion River; 5270, near Powder River.

It is singular that a bird so abundant as this is in the Eastern United
States should have been overlooked by Wilson and Audubon, or, what
is more probable, confounded with *E. acadicus.* Nuttall was perfectly
familiar with it, though he thought it was the Acadian Flycatcher. It,
however, escaped Audubon's attention, having only been brought to his
notice, by Prof. Baird, just as he was finishing his work. It is very
common in the Middle States during the migrations. At Washington,
D. C., it usually arrives the last week in April, and is seen for about
two weeks only; it returns the last of August, and loiters through most
of September. Its arrival is about a week earlier, on an average, than
that of *E. flaviventris.* I never found it in summer, and Prof. Baird, in
Audubon, states that it is not seen about Carlisle, Pennsylvania, after
May; but Dr. Turnbull says that a few remain to breed. It breeds
abundantly in most parts of New England; in Massachusetts Mr. Allen
found it as numerous as all the other *Empidonaces* put together. Some
individuals press on into the Hudson's Bay country, and in the West
its extension is much greater than that of typical *traillii* or *flaviventris*,
particularly along the Missouri itself, and the Red River, where the
wooded river-bottoms afford it congenial shelter. Dr. Hayden saw it
occasionally "throughout the West," and Audubon mentions it from
the Yellowstone. Like others of the genus, it penetrates to Central
and Northern South America in winter, and it is also quoted from portions of Mexico.

It is not ordinarily found in gloomy woods, like *E. acadicus,* nor even
in heavy timber of any kind; it prefers the skirts of woods, coppices, and
even hedge-rows. It is readily distinguishable from *acadicus* by this
circumstance alone, to say nothing of the several personal peculiarities—
so to speak—slight traits, almost impossible to describe intelligently,
but which the field naturalist learns to recognize in a moment. Its
usual voice is lower and more plaintive, though one of its call-notes is
sharp and jerky; and its flight is slightly different, owing to the marked
difference in the shape of the wing. In all these particulars it comes
much nearer *traillii* and *flaviventris,* as has been already hinted.

The Least Flycatcher is more numerous during the breeding season
along the Red River of the North than I have found it to be anywhere

else. It probably reaches the latitude of Pembina about the third week in May, as I found it common on my arrival the first of June. It is confined entirely to the wooded river-bottom, where, in the shadow of the lofty trees, it may be observed at any time, perched on an outermost twig, uttering its peculiar note, and dashing into the air to secure the passing insect, clicking its mandibles; returning to its post to sit upright and motionless, after a rustle of its wings and tail as it alights. Early in June it was in company with Traill's Flycatcher, but as the breeding season advanced the latter appeared to pass on; at least, I found none nesting. Most of the numerous nests I took were procured the third and fourth weeks in June, at which latter date incubation was generally advanced.

The bird generally nests on a sapling or shrub, within ten or twelve feet from the ground. One nest I reached without climbing, and another was placed on a slender swaying elm, about forty feet high; these were the extremes of situation I observed. It is always placed, so far as I discovered, in an upright crotch of several forks, preferably between twigs no thicker than a finger. The high nest just mentioned was situated on the bending trunk itself, but it rested, as usual, between a little set of twigs that grew upright. It is very deeply let down into the crotch, and usually bears deep impressions of the boughs. The female sets very closely; one I almost covered with my hand before she fluttered off, although I stood for several moments within a yard of her. On being frightened away, she retreats but a little distance, and flies from one twig to another, uttering a mournful note. The nest is a neat little structure; if it were only stuccoed with lichens it would be as elegant as that of a Blue-gray Gnatcatcher, which it scarcely exceeds in size. The basis of the nest is a substantial intertwining of fine fibrous inner bark, and the decomposing outer substance of various weeds. With this is matted a great quantity of soft plant-down, making a soft yet firm and warm fabric. The interior is finished variously with a special lining of plant-down, confined with a slight layer of horse-hair or the finest possible grass-tops. The brim of the nest is firm and even, with a circular arrangement of the fibres; inside, the lining is simply interlaced. In size, these elegant structures vary a good deal; the smallest one before me is under two inches and a half across outside, and less than two deep; another, which was let down very deeply in a narrow crotch, is nearly three inches, both in depth and width, and is quite unsymmetrical. The cavity is quite large for the outside dimensions, in some instances the walls being barely coherent along the track of the supporting twigs; it is not, or but little, contracted at the brim, and is about as deep as wide.

The eggs are generally four in number, sometimes only three; I did not find five in any one of the six nests collected. One contained a Cowbird's egg. The eggs are pure white, unmarked. They vary much in size and shape. Out of twenty examples, a large elongate one measures 0.68 by 0.52; a small globular one, 0.59 by 0.50; a normal one, 0.65 by 0.50.

EMPIDONAX FLAVIVENTRIS, Bd.

Yellow-bellied Flycatcher.

a. *flaviventris.*

Tyrannula flaviventris, W. M. & S. F. BAIRD, Pr. Phila. Acad. i, 1843, 283; Am. Journ. Sci. April, 1844.
Muscicapa flaviventris, AUD., B. Am. vii, 1844, 341, pl. 490.
Empidonax flaviventris, BD., B. N. A. 1858, 198.—SCL., P. Z. S. 1859, 366; Ibis, 1859, 441; Cat. 1862, 229 (Xalapa, Vera Paz, Dueñas).—SCL. & SALV., Ibis, 1859, 122

(Guatemala).—WHEAT., Ohio Agric. Rep. 1860, No. 53.—COUES & PRENT., Smiths. Rep. 1861, 404 (migratory, perhaps breeding).—VERR., Pr. Ess. Inst. iii, 146 (Maine, summer).—ALLEN, *ibid.* iv, 1864, 55 (Massachusetts, May and June).—McILWR., *ibid.* v, 1866, 84.—COUES, *ibid.* v, 1868, 265.—LAWR., Ann. Lyc. N. Y. viii, 1863, 8 (New Granada); viii, 1866, 290; ix, 1868, 114 (Costa Rica).—SCL. & SALV., P. Z. S. 1870, 837 (Honduras).—ALLEN, Mem. Bost. Soc. i, 1868, 518 (Illinois).—TURNB., B. E. Pa. 1869, 14 (breeding in New Jersey).—SUMICH., Mem. Bost. Soc. i, 1869, 557 (Vera Cruz).—MAYN., Guide, 1870, 126; Pr. Bost. Soc. 1871 (breeding commonly at Franconia, N. H.).—COOP., B. Cal. i, 1870, 328.—SNOW, B. Kans, 1873, 4.—COUES, Key, 1872, 175.—B. B. & R., N. A. B. ii, 1874, 378, pl. 44, f. 12.
Tyrannula minuta, BP., Consp. i, 1850, 189 (so identifies *Muscicapa minuta*, WILS!).
(?) " *Tyrannula pusilla*, REINH., Vidensk. Meddel. for 1853 (1854), 82.—GLOGER, J. f. O. 1854, 426."—REINH., Ibis, Jan. 1861, 7. (These citations refer to a specimen taken in Godthaab, Greenland, in 1853).
Empidonax hypoxanthus, BD., B. N. A. 1858, 198 (in text).

b. *difficilis.*

Empidonax difficilis, BD., B. N. A. 1858, 198 (in text); pl. 76, f. 2.—COOP. & SUCK., N. H. Wash. Ter. 1860, 170, and " p. xv, errata."—COUES, Pr. Phila. Acad. 1866, 62 (Arizona).—SCL., Cat. 1862, 230.
Empidonax flaviventris var. *difficilis*, ALLEN, Bull. M. C. Z. iii, 1872, 179 (Utah).—COUES, Key, 1872, 176 (in text).—B. B. & R., N. A. B. ii, 1874, 380.

Hab.—North America, at large. (?) Greenland. South through Mexico and Central America to New Granada. Breeds from the Middle States northward. The typical form eastern. Var. *difficilis* western.

In size between average *traillii* and *minimus*, this species differs from these and all our other Flycatchers by the decided yellowness of the under parts—a coloration so distinctive that the bird is always recognizable on sight. The Prince Bonaparte identifies it with the long lost " *Muscicapa minuta* "—the Small-headed Flycatcher of Wilson, Audubon, and Nuttall—a very questionable reference.

This species reaches the Middle States a little later than the three other eastern species of the genus—not ordinarily until the very last of April or first week in May. It is found in high open woods as well as in thickets, thus differing somewhat in the situation it affects from *minimus*. Dr. Prentiss and I have taken it at Washington, at different times in July, probably indicating that it breeds in the vicinity, as it certainly does a little further north: Dr. Turnbull mentions Trenton, New Jersey, as a locality where Dr. Slack found it nesting. According to Mr. Maynard, whose opportunities for observation appear to have been ample, it breeds abundantly in Northern New England. In his excellent Manual of Taxidermy, he remarks: " May 31, 1869, I shot the first specimen I had ever seen living; the next day I took eight of both sexes in a few hours. Between this time and the 10th of June I took two or three more;" this was in Massachusetts. The writer continues: " I do not doubt that it has occurred in previous seasons, but, being unaccustomed to its low note—which is like the syllable *pea* very plaintively prolonged—and its retiring habits, I had not detected it before. The specimens were all taken in low, swampy thickets, with the exception of the first, which was shot on a tall oak. It keeps near the ground, is rather shy, and upon the appearance of an intruder instantly ceases its song. 'Shot a specimen on May 25, 1869, in Watertown, Massachusetts, singing, with its peculiar note, in an apple-tree. I have shot the female singing in the same manner, in August, 1867, in Franconia, New Hampshire. The only note I ever heard was the low *pea* (*Brewster*).'" In his later publication, after speaking of the abundance and breeding of the bird in Northern New England, Mr. Maynard remarks that in the dark swamps at Upton he first heard the breeding note; "it was like the syllables *kil-lic*, very gravely given, with a long interval between each utterance. The song was even less energetic than that of *traillii*. While singing, the birds were perched on low limbs. Both male and female used this note."

Var. *difficilis* is generally dispersed in the West in all suitable wooded places. It reaches the mountainous parts of Arizona by the middle of April, and remains through most of September, inhabiting the more open pine woods, the brush of ravines, and the mixed timber along streams. Dr. Cooper observed its arrival at San Diego, April 15th. Mr. Allen took it at Ogden, Utah, along with *obscurus* and *hammondii*. Dr. Hayden did not observe it in the Missouri region, where, however, it unquestionably occurs and doubtless breeds.

The egg of *flaviventris* is pure white, unmarked, and not distinguishable from that of *E. minimus*.

EMPIDONAX HAMMONDII, (Xantus) Bd.

Hammond's Flycatcher.

Tyrannula hammondii, XANTUS, Pr. Phila. Acad. 1858, 117.
Empidonax hammondii, BD., B. N. A. 1858, 199, pl. 76, f. 1.—SCL., Cat. 1862, 230.—COUES, Pr. Phila. Acad. 1866, 62 (Arizona).—SUMICH., Mem. Bost. Soc. i, 1869, 557 (Vera Cruz).—COOP., B. Cal. i, 1870, 330.—ALLEN, Bull. M. C. Z. 1872, 179 (Utah and Wyoming).—COUES, Key, 1872, 176.—B. B. & R., N. A. B. ii, 1874, 383, pl. 44, f. 7.

Hab.—Rocky Mountains to the Pacific, United States, from British to Central America.
Later Expeditions.—60767, Pacific Springs, Wyoming.

This appears to be, in effect, the western representative of *minimus ;* and in spite of the tolerably well-marked characters, my present impression is, that it will prove to be a geographical race of the species just mentioned. Originally described from Southern California, its range has latterly been extended, as above. Specimens were taken by the late regretted Kennerly, upon the northwest boundary of the United States and British America.

My personal acquaintance with its life-history is limited to finding it a rather rare summer visitant in Northern Arizona, where it arrives late in April, and remains until the third week in October. Dr. Cooper noted its arrival at Santa Cruz, March 13, 1866, and found it numerous during the summer. "April 27th," he writes, "I found the first nest, built on a horizontal branch of box-elder (*Negundo*), about eighteen feet from the ground; but in pulling down the branch the eggs were broken. I found four others afterward, from four to ten feet high, either on horizontal branches or in forks of small trees, and containing three or four eggs or young. The last found with eggs was as late as June 29th— probably a second attempt of a pair before robbed. All were thick walled, composed externally of dry moss and downy buds, with a few leaves and strips of bark, then slender fibres of bark, a few hairs and feathers often lining the inside. The size outside was about four inches wide, two and a half high; the cavity two inches wide, one and a half deep; the walls nearly one and a half thick. The eggs were white, with brown blotches and specks near the large end, mostly in a circle. They measured 0.68 by 0.52 inch." Dr. Cooper's next paragraph, however, should be reproduced with the above: "These birds frequented only the darkest groves along the river, had very few simple calls of two or three monotonous notes, and were so shy that I did not get near enough to determine the species positively." Under these circumstances, it is almost unnecessary to add, the above description of the nest and eggs must be taken subject to confirmation. As the eggs of *hammondii* are pure white, unmarked, like those of *minimus*, the whole account probably refers to var. *pusillus* of *trailli*.

17

EMPIDONAX OBSCURUS, (Sw.) Bd.

Wright's Flycatcher; Gray Flycatcher.

(?) *Tyrannula obscura*, Sw., Syn. Mex. B. in Philos. Mag. i, 1827, 367.
Empidonax obscurus, Bd., B. N. A. 1858, 200; Mex. B. Surv. ii, 1859, pt. ii, 8, pl. 11, f. 3.—
    Scl., P. Z. S. 1862, 19; Cat. 1862, 230 (La Parada, Mexico).—Coues, Pr. Phila.
    Acad. 1866, 62 (Arizona).—Sumich., Mem. Bost. Soc. i, 1869, 557 (Vera Cruz).—
    Coop., B. Cal. i, 1870, 329.—Allen, Bull. M. C. Z. iii, 1872, 179 (Colorado and
    Utah).—Aiken, Pr. Bost. Soc. 1872, 206 (Colorado).—Coues, Key, 1872, 176.—
    B. B. & R., N. A. B. ii, 1874, 381, pl. 44, f. 6.
Empidonax wrightii, Bd., *l. c.* (in text).

Hab.—Rocky Mountains to the Pacific, United States. Observed north to Colorado. South through Mexico.

This species enters the United States from Mexico the latter part of March, or early in April, and remains until October, some proceeding as far north as the above-cited localities, and probably further. I have only observed it in Arizona. Mr. Allen has obligingly placed the following notes at my disposal:

"The Gray Flycatcher was the commonest and almost the only species of *Empidonax* met with in the mountains of Colorado. It was generally observed in rather wet, swampy localities, dense willow thickets seeming to form its favorite resorts. It is very retiring in its habits, keeping almost constantly concealed in thick copses, where it silently hunts its insect prey, and is hence a difficult species to collect. Though it may be approached within a few yards, it eludes capture by keeping in the middle of the close willow clumps, exposing itself to view only when obliged to fly across an open space, taking its departure from the side furthest from the observer, and flying low and hurriedly to the nearest point of concealment. The several nests found contained young, and were always placed some distance within the thick copse the birds had chosen for their home. The nests were usually built in the forks of small branches, and in thickness and general appearance greatly resembled the ordinary nests of the summer Yellow-bird (*Dendrœca œstiva*).

Mr. Trippe's manuscript contains the following interesting notes of the four Flycatchers occurring in Colorado:

"*Empidonax obscurus.* Abundant; migratory; breeds. This Flycatcher arrives at Idaho Springs about the middle of May, and soon becomes abundant, extending up all the valleys to over 10,000 feet, and probably ranging up to timber-line, wherever it can find localities suitable for its habitat. It is rather a shy little bird, with more of the habits and appearance of *acadicus* than any other of the genus. It loves the densest thickets of poplars and willows, and rarely ventures far from the streams, never ascending the mountain-sides. It breeds from about 7,500 feet up to its highest limit.

"*E. difficilis.* Abundant on the plains and up to 6,800 or 7,000 feet; and found, also, though unfrequently, up to timber-line, near which one was shot in July. This species frequents the valleys and similar localities to the preceding, but often wanders among the mountains a considerable distance from the streams, and instead of constantly hiding itself amidst the densest shrubbery, frequently mounts to the dead tops of trees from which it may have an extended view, and watch for insects, which it captures with great address and returns to the same perch again. It has one or two low notes like those of *E. minimus*, and a loud, musical call, like "*pé-té, pé-té,*" quickly repeated.

E. hammondii. Two or three specimens which were taken in June and July, near Idaho Springs, answered pretty well to the description of this species, and being nearer to it than to any other form found in this region, may properly be referred to it.   On the plains *E. pusillus* was met with in small numbers in June, but not observed elsewhere. It will be seen that four different species or varieties of *Empidonax*, are found in the same region within a short distance ; one, *obscurus*, breeding from 7,000 or 7,500 feet up to timber-line, or nearly to it ; another, *difficilis*, from the plains up to the lower limit of the former, and sometimes straggling higher ; a third, *pusillus*, restricted entirely to the plains ; and a fourth, *hammondii*, occurring, probably, only as a straggler.   All these varieties are much alike in their habits and notes, yet all present distinguishing characteristics in both ; and although among a large series of specimens some will be found that are intermediate, apparently, the greater number of adults can be referred with certainty to one or the other of the type forms."

To complete an account of the North American small olivaceous Flycatchers, all of which, with these exceptions, have been given, I introduce the following species, particularly as I think they may yet be found in the southwestern part of the Missouri region :

EMPIDONAX FULVIFRONS var. PALLESCENS, *Coues.*

a. *fulvifrons.*

Muscicapa fulvifrons, GIR., 16 Sp. Texas B. 1841, pl. 2 (probably Mexico).
Empidonax fulvifrons, SCL., P. Z. S. 1858, 301.
Mitrephorus fulvifrons, SCL., P. Z. S., 1859, 45 ; Ibis, 1859, 442.—B. B. & R., N. A. B. ii, 385.
Empidonax rubicundus, CAB., Mus. Hein. ii, 1859, 70.

b. *pallescens.*

(??) *Tyrannula affinis*, Sw., Phil. Mag. i, 1827, 336 (very uncertain).
Empidonax pygmæus, COUES, Ibis, 1865 (in text).
Mitrephorus pallescens, COUES, Pr. Phila. Acad. 1866, 63 (Arizona).—COOP., B. Cal. i, 386.
Mitrephorus fulvifrons, ELLIOT, B. N. A. i, pl. 19.
Mitrephorus fulvifrons var. *pallescens*, COUES, Key, 1872, 176.—B. B. & R., N. A. B. ii, 1874, 386, pl. 44, fig. 13.

Hab.—Mexico.   North into Arizona and New Mexico.

CONTOPUS PERTINAX, *Cab.*

Contopus borealis, SCL., P. Z. S. 1858, 301 ; 1859, 43 ; Ibis, i, 1859, 122, 440 (*nec* BD.).
Contopus pertinax, CAB., Mus Hein. ii, 1859, 72.—SCL., Cat. 1862, 231.—COUES, Pr. Phila.
    Acad. 1866, 60 (first introduced to United States; Fort Whipple, Arizona).—
    ELLIOT, B. N. A. i, pl. 8.—COOP., B. Cal. i, 1870, 324.—COUES, Key, 1872, 173.—
    B. B. & R., N. A. B. ii, 1874, 356, pl. 44, f. 2.

Hab.—Mexico and Guatemala.   North into Arizona and New Mexico.   (Mr. H. W. Henshaw recently took quite a number of both these species in Arizona.)

ORDER PICARIÆ: PICARIAN BIRDS.

SUBORDER CYPSELI: CYPSELIFORM BIRDS.

Family CAPRIMULGIDÆ: Goatsuckers.

ANTROSTOMUS VOCIFERUS, (Wils.) Bp.

Whippoorwill; Night-jar.

" *Caprimulgus minor*, FORST., Cat. An. N. A. 1771, 13." (*Cass.*)
" *Caprimulgus europæus*, BARTON, Frag. Nat. Hist. Pa. 1799, 14." (*Cass.*)
" *Caprimulgus virginianus*, LINN.—GM."—VIEILL., Ois. Am. Sept. i, 1807, 55, pl. 23 (mixed
   with *Chordeiles popetue*).
" *Caprimulgus clamator*, VIEILL., Nouv. Dict. d'Hist. Nat. 1817, 324."
Caprimulgus vociferus, WILS., Am. Orn. v, 1812, 71, pl. 41, fig. 1, 2, 3.—BP., Syn.
   1828, 62.—Sw. & RICH., F. B. A. ii, 1831, 336.—NUTT., Man. i, 1832, 614.—AUD.,
   Orn. Biog. i, 1832, 443 ; v, 405 ; pl. 82; Syn. 1839, 32 ; B. Am. i, 1840, 155, pl. 42.—
   GIR., B. L. I. 1844, 31.—PUTN., Pr. Ess. Inst. i, 1856, 205.—MAXIM., J. f. O. vi,
   1858, 98.—TRIPPE, Pr. Ess. Inst. vi, 1871, 114 (Minnesota, very abundant, May
   to September).
Antrostomus vociferus, BP., List, 1838, 8; Consp. i, 1850, 60.—CASS., Journ. Phila. Acad.
   ii, 1852, 122; Ill. 1855, 236.—BREWER, N. Am. Oöl. i, 1857, 84.—BD., B. N. A.
   1858, 148.—SCL., P. Z. S. 1859, 367 ; Cat. 1862, 280 (Xalapa and La Parada).—
   SALV., Ibis, ii, 1860, 275 (Guatemala).—SCL., P. Z. S. 1866, 137.—McILWR., Pr.
   Ess. Inst. v, 1866, 83 (Canada).—ALLEN, Mem. Bost. Soc. i, 1868, 498, 506 (Iowa,
   and Illinois, very abundant).—ALLEN, Bull. M. C. Z. ii, 1871, 300 (Florida, wintering) ; iii, 1872,129, 179 (Leavenworth, Kans.).—TRIPPE, Pr. Bost. Soc. xv,
   1872, 232 (Iowa, abundant, breeding).—SNOW, B. Kans. 1873, 3.—COUES, Key,
   1872, 180, fig. 116.—B. B. & R., N. A. B. ii, 1874, 413, pl. 46, f. 2.
Caprimulgus vociferans, WARTH., J. f. O. xvi, 1868, 369.

Hab.—Eastern United States and British Provinces. North to about 50°. West to
the Plains. South through portions of Mexico to Guatemala. Breeds in most of its
United States range. Winters from the Gulf coast southward. Apparently replaced
in the West Indies by the closely related species, if not var., *A. cubanensis* (LAWR., Ann.
Lyc. vii, 1860, 260—*vociferus* of *D'Orbigny, Lembeye*, and *Gundlach*).
Not obtained by the Expeditions.

The Whippoorwill extends only to the eastern border of the Missouri
region, being replaced further west by the following species. It is said
to be rare in Kansas (where I did not find it), but abundant in Iowa,
there breeding. But even in the Carolinas, where it is a common and
characteristic bird during the summer, I did not think it present in such
numbers as I found it along the Red River of the North, between Dakota and Minnesota. At Pembina, every night in June we were sere-
naded by a chorus of these strange voices, penetrating the darkness, it
seemed, from all points at once along the line of heavy timber that
skirted the river.

The reproduction of this species is similar to that of the Night-hawk,
which was also breeding at the same time. It lays on the ground, in
the woods, constructing no proper nest, and depositing only two eggs.
These are elliptical, nearly or quite equal at both ends, about 1.25 long
by 0.85 wide, and are curiously scratched and mottled all over with
brown surface markings and paler purplish-gray shell colors upon a
whitish ground. The egg is quite variable in amount of intensity of
coloration, some specimens being heavily marbled, while others appear
as if faded or bleached, from indistinctness of the tracery.

ANTROSTOMUS NUTTALLI, (Aud.) Cass.

Nuttall's Whippoorwill.

Caprimulgus nuttalli, AUD., Orn. Biog. v, 1839, 335 ; B. Am. vii, 1844, 350, pl. 495 (Upper
    Missouri).—WOODH., Sitgr. Rep. 1853, 63 (Arizona).
Antrostomus nuttalli, CASS., Journ Phila. Acad. ii, 1852, 123 ; Ill. i, 1855, 237.—BREW.,
    N. Am. Oöl. i, 1857, 86.—NEWB., P. R. R. Rep. vi, 1857, 77.—BD., B. N. A. 1858,
    149.—KENN., P. R. R. Rep. x, 1859, pt. iv, 23.—HEERM., *ibid,* pt. vi, 35.—COOP.
    & SUCK., N. H. Wash. Ter. 1860, 166.—HAYD., Rep. 1862, 157.—COUES, Ibis,
    1865, 158.(Kansas).—DRESS., Ibis, 1865, 470 (Texas).—COUES, Pr. Phila. Acad.
    1866, 58 (Arizona).—SCL., P. Z. S. 1866, 137.—COOP., B. Cal. i, 1870, 340.—
    ALLEN, Bull. M. C. Z. iii, 1872, 179 (Kansas, Colorado, and Utah).—SNOW, B.
    Kans. 1873, 3.—MERR., U. S. Geol. Surv. 1872. 692 (Utah).—AIKEN, Pr. Bost.
    Soc. xv, 1872, 206 (Wyoming).—COUES, Key, 1872, 181.—COUES, Am. Nat. vii,
    1873, 325 (eggs).—B. B. & R., N. A. B. ii, 1874, 417, pl. 46, f. 3.

Hab.—United States, west of the Mississippi. Mexico (*Salvin*).

List of specimens.

19187	184	Powder River..	....	Sept. 9, 1859	G. H. Trook..	8.00	17.50	6.00
19188	157	Bighorn River .	....	....	F. V. Hayden.	.....	......	.....

Lieutenant Warren's Expedition.—8876, Black Hills ; 5200, Yellowstone River.
Later Expeditions.—61734-5, Ogden, Utah.

In the Conspectus, at page 61, Bonaparte makes an *Antrostomus californianus,* with
which, he says, *A. nuttalli* should be compared. The latter being the only Californian
species, we might suppose the two to be the same. Such, however, is not the case ; the
description indicates a bird belonging to the second of Dr. Sclater's two sections of the
genus, namely, that one in which there is a white wing-spot ; and the bird seems related to *A. nigrescens* of South America, the assigned locality being most probably erroneous. Dr. Sclater appears to have overlooked the name in his synonymy of the
American *Caprimulgidæ.*

Nuttall's Whippoorwill was discovered by Audubon, on the Upper
Missouri, thirty years ago ; but it is only recently that much material
has come into the possession of naturalists. The bird is, nevertheless,
very abundant in most parts of the West, where it is the characteristic,
in fact the only, species of the genus. Audubon gave a pleasant account of its discovery, but nothing specially to the point respecting its
biography, excepting the fact that its note differs from that of the
eastern species in omitting one syllable. He rendered it by the word
"*oh'-will,*" which is perfectly expressive, though we now generally write
"*poor'-will.*" This cry is very lugubrious, and in places where the birds
are numerous the wailing chorus is enough to excite vague apprehen-
sions on the part of the lonely traveler, as he lies down to rest by his
camp-fire, or to break his sleep with fitful dreams, in which lost spirits
appear to bemoan their fate and implore his intercession. It is not
strange that a heated fancy should riot in the circumstances of desolation and imminent peril under which the emigrant or the explorer must
often be placed in the western wilderness. Experience comes vividly
to mind as I write, of night after night, when I have gradually lost consciousness with a mind peopled with all manner of wierd images. Closing my eys to the stars in the broad expanse above, my only coverlet,
and to the ruddy gleam from the embers of the camp fire, with a thought
of home and perhaps a silent aspiration, it might be long before the
sense of hearing, unnaturally strained, would desert its post. The monotonous tread of the sentinel would fall heavily on the ear ; the horses
would seem to champ as never before ; the bands of vagrant coyotés
would howl with redoubled energy, and all the while the Poor-wills
shouted their alarm. Sleep, in apprehension, if not really expectation

of danger before morning, is a strange state of mind—like a gun at full cock, perfectly quiescent, yet on the very edge of action. A shot, even a shout, at such a time, would bring a whole camp to its feet in a second of time. So the hours wear on, till darkness and tension of mind relax together, and imagination is dissipated in the very homely, prosy fact of breakfast.

Like others of its family, Nuttall's Whippoorwill is oftener heard than seen. When flushed from its retreat in the day time, among the shrubbery or tall weeds, it rises hurriedly with wayward flight, dashes a few yards, and realights. There is something about it at such times that strongly recalls the Woodcock, and the bird is quite as difficult to shoot on the wing. I saw it under such circumstances in Kansas, near Fort Riley, one of its easternmost recorded localities. It was not, apparently, very common in that region, but great numbers are found in the warmer parts of Arizona and New Mexico. Their breeding range appears to be coextensive with their United States distribution. I have observed one Mexican quotation; the species appears to winter on or near our southern border, as the eastern Whippoorwill does in corresponding localities.

An interesting and important item in the history of this species has only recently come to light. Unlike most species of its genus—of its subfamily, in fact—of which the eggs are known, it lays colorless instead of variegated eggs. Of this fact I was first informed by my Arizona correspondent, Lieutenant C. Bendire, United States Army. He gave me a minute account of the nesting, which is terrestrial, and essentially similar to that of other species of the group. Lieutenant Bendire found the eggs near Tuscon, in Arizona; there were two, laid on the ground, in a depression, at the foot of a bush, among dense vegetation. Eggs were also taken by Mr. Ridgway in Nevada, and by Mr. Merriam in Utah. They are white, unmarked, about an inch, or rather over, in length, by four-fifths broad. Both sexes incubate.

The following interesting passage occurs in the Allen Mss., before unpublished:

"Nuttall's Whippoorwill was first met with on my western expedition at Topeka, Kansas, where it was by no means infrequent. We often heard it at night near the outskirts of the city, and repeatedly met with it in the day time in the darker and denser portions of the woodlands bordering on the Kaw River, reposing on the ground, like the common Whippoorwill of the Eastern States. When flushed it passed rapidly, with a noiseless, skimming flight, through the more open parts of the undergrowth, soon realighting again on the ground. In the mountains of Colorado we again met with it at a few points in great numbers, as high even as 8,000 feet above the sea. At our camp of July 12, on Turkey Creek, just above the cañon, scores were heard singing on the neighboring slopes throughout the beautiful moon-lit night, but our pursuit of them was fruitless, as they could be seen only as they flitted from point to point when disturbed. We afterward heard them in considerable numbers at the Garden of the Gods, near Colorado City, and found them very numerous in September at the mouth of Ogden Cañon, near Ogden City, in Utah. Here, as soon as the dusk of the evening rendered it difficult to distinguish such small objects with distinctness, the whole hill-sides seemed to be alive with the tantalizing abundance of these birds. Like the common Whippoorwill of the East, they seem to sing at intervals throughout the season, and at this date (September) appeared fully as musical as during the breeding season. It lingers at its summer home till the autumn is far advanced, as we found it at Ogden as late as October 6, quite far up the slope of the mountains, in the midst of a driving snow-storm—the first of the season—the snow having then already accumulated to the depth of several inches."

Mr. Merriam gives the following note in his report: "This rare bird was only found on the rocky slopes at the foot of the Wahsatch Mountains; here, on the 12th of June, I obtained their eggs; they were pure white, without spots, and were laid in a slight cavity in the bare ground, without any nest. They contained full-grown embryos, and would doubtless have hatched in a few hours. The male bird was shot as he left the nest, and as the feathers were worn off his belly by setting, it is evident that both male and female take part in the incubation."

Introduction of the following species completes an account of the North American species of the *Caprimulgidæ*:

ANTROSTOMUS CAROLINENSIS (*Gm.*) *Gould.*

Caprimulgus carolinensis, GM., Syst. Nat. i, 1788, 1028.—LATH., Ind. Orn. ii, 1790, 584.—
    WILS., Am. Orn. vi, 95, pl. —, fig. -.—BP., Syn. 1828, 61.—NUTT. i, 1832, 612.—
    AUD., Orn. Biog. i, 273; v, 401; pl. 52; Syn. 31; B. Am. i, 151, pl. 41.—WARTH.,
    J. f. O. 1868, 368.
Antrotomus carolinensis, GOULD.—CASS., Ill. i. 1855, 236.—CAB., J. f. O., iv, 6 (Cuba).—
    BD., B. N. A. 1858, 147.—CAB., Mus. Hein. ii, 1859, 90.—SCL., P. Z. S. 1866, 136;
    Cat. 1862, 280.—DRESS., Ibis, 1865, 70 (Texas).—COUES, Pr. Bost. Soc. xii, 1868,
    118 (South Carolina).—LAWR., Ann. Lyc. ix, 1868, 120 (Costa Rica).—SALV., P.
    Z. S. 1870, 303 (Veragua).—ALLEN, Bull. M. C. Z. ii, 1871, 300.—COUES, Key,
    1872, 180.—B. B. & R., N. A. B. ii, 1874, 410, pl. 46, fig. 1.
Caprimulgus rufus, VIEILL., O. A. S. i, 1807, 57, pl. 25.
Caprimulgus brachypterus, STEPH., G. Z. x, 159.

Hab.—South Atlantic and Gulf States. Cuba. South to Guatemala

CHORDEILES TEXENSIS, *Lawr.*

Chordeiles brasiliensis, LAWR., Ann. Lyc. N. Y. v, 1851, 114 (*nec* GM.).—CASS., Ill. 1855, 238.
Chordeiles sapiti, BP., Consp. Av. i, 1850, 63.
Chordeiles texensis, LAWR., Ann. Lyc. N. Y. vi, 1856, 167.—BD., B. N. A. 1858, 154, pl. 44;
    Mex. B. Surv. ii, 1859, Birds, 7, pl. 6.—SCL., Cat. 1862, 279; P. Z. S. 1866, 134
    (Guatemala).—COOP., B. Cal. i, 1870, 345.—DRESS., Ibis, 1865, 471 (Texas).—
    COUES, Pr. Phila. Acad. 1866, 58 (Arizona).—LAWR., Ann. Lyc. ix, 1868, 120
    (Costa Rica), 204 (Yucatan).—COUES, Key, 1872, 181.
Caprimulgus texensis, WARTH., J. f. O. 1868, 376.
Chordeiles sapiti var. *texensis*, B. B. & R., N. A. B. ii, 1874, 406, pl. 46, fig. 5.

Hab.—Southwestern United States, and south to Guatemala.

CHORDEILES VIRGINIANUS, (Gm.) Bp.

Night-hawk; Bull-bat; Pisk; Piramidig.

a. *virginianus.*

Caprimulgus virginianus, BRISS., Orn. ii, 1760, 477 (*partim*).—GM., Syst. Nat. i, 1788,
    1028.—LATH., Ind. Orn. ii, 1790, 585.—BP., Syn. 1828, 62.—AUD., Orn. Biog. ii,
    1834, 273; v, 1839, 406; pl. 147.—NUTT., Man. i, 1832, 619; ii, 1834, 609.
Caprimulgus (Chordeiles) virginianus, SW. & RICH., F. B. A. ii, 1831, 337.
Chordeiles virginianus, BP., List, 1838, 8; Consp. i, 1850, 63.—AUD., B. Am. i, 1840, 159,
    pl. 43; Syn. 1839, 32.—GIR., B. L. I. 1844, 72.—WOODH., Sitgr. Rep. 1853, 63.—
    CASS., Pr. Phila. Acad. 1851, 186; Ill. 1855, 238.—BREW., N. Am. Oöl. i, 1857,
    87.—NEWB., P. R. R. Rep. vi, 1857, 79.—SCL., Cat. 1862, 279; P. Z. S. 1866, 132
    (Brazil).—SALV., P. Z. S. 1870, 303 (Veragua).—COUES, Key, 1872, 181, fig. 117.
Chordeiles virginianus, CAB., Mus. Hein. ii, 1859, 86.
Caprimulgus popetue, VIEILL., O. A. S. i, 1807, 56, pl. 24 (♀).—BP., Obs. Wils. 1825, 177.
Chordeiles popetue, BD., B. N. A. 1858, 151.—HEERM., P. R. R. Rep. x, 1859, pt. vi, 36.—
    COOP. & SUCK., N. H. Wash. Ter. 1860, 166.—LAWR., Ann. Lyc. May, 1860
    (Cuba).—HAYD., Rep. 1862, 157.—SNOW, B. Kans. 1873, 3.—ALLEN, Bull. M. C. Z.
    ii, 1871, 300 (excl. syn. *sapiti, brasiliensis* et *texensis*); iii, 1872, 179.—COOP.,
    B. Cal. i, 1870, 342.—AIKEN, Pr. Bost. Soc. 1872, 206.—B. B. & R., N. A. B. ii,
    1874, 401.
Caprimulgus americanus, WILS., Am. Orn. v, 1812, 65, pl. 40, figs. 1, 2.
Chordeiles americanus, DEKAY, N. Y. Zool. ii, 1844, pl. 27, fig. 60.

b. *henryi.*

Chordeiles henryi, CASS., Ill. 1855, 239.—BD., B. N. A. 1858, 153, 922 ; P. R. R. Rep. x, 1859, pt. iii, 13, pl. 17.—SCL., Cat. 1862, 279 ; P. Z. S. 1866, 133.—DRESS., Ibis, 1865, 476 (Matamoras).—COUES, Pr. Phila. Acad. 1866, 58.—COOP., B. Cal. i, 1870, 344.—STEV., U. S. Geol. Surv. Ter. 1870, 463.—MERR., *ibid.* 1872, 692.— SNOW, B. Kans. 1873, 3.
Chordeiles popetue var. *henryi,* ALLEN, Bull. M. C. Z. iii, 1872, 179.—B. B. & R., N. A. B. ii, 1874, 404, pl. 46, f. 4.
Chordeiles virginianus var. *henryi,* COUES, Key, 1872, 181.

c. *minor.*

Chordeiles virginianus, LEMB., Aves Isl. Cuba, 1850, 51.—GOSSE, B. Jam. 1847, 33.
Chordeiles minor, CAB., J. f. O. 1856, 5 ; Mus. Hein. ii, 1859, 86.—LAWR., Ann. Lyc. May, 1860.—SCL., P. Z. S. 1861, 77 ; Cat. 1862, 279 ; P. Z. S. 1866, 433 (Cuba and Jamaica).—MARCH, Pr. Phila. Acad. 1863, 286 (Jamaica).
Chordeiles gundlachii, LAWR., Ann. Lyc. vi, 1856, 165 (Cuba).

Hab.—Entire temperate North and Middle America. North to Hudson's Bay (MUR-RAY, Edinb. Phil. Journ. 1860). Cuba and Jamaica, migratory. Bahamas (BRYANT, Pr. Bost. Soc. vii, 1859). South to Brazil (PELZ. Orn. Braz. i, 14). Var. *henryi* from the Southern Rocky Mountain region. Var. *minor* in Cuba and Jamaica (resident).

List of specimens.

49336	....	Stinking Creek.	....	....	G. H. Trook..	......	......	......

Lieutenant Warren's Expedition.—8877, Black Hills ; 8878, Loup Fork ; 5201-03, forty miles above St. Pierre.
Later Expeditions.—59851, Colorado ; 60417, Laramie ; 60772, Pacific Springs ; 61775, 62254-5, Idaho ; 6225, Wyoming. (All var. *henryi.*)
The bird described as *C. henryi* is merely the paler form prevailing in the dryer and unwooded parts of the West ; the gray and tawny shades in excess of the darker colors, and the white patches more extensive. It is not larger than ordinary *virginianus,* though so stated to be ; and the plate above cited, in the Pacific Railroad Report, is highly exaggerated in coloring. The West Indian form, apparently resident, I can-not distinguish as a species ; the only ascribed character, its smaller size, is readily attributable to its southern habitat. The fact that the true *virginianus* also occurs in Cuba is no rebutting evidence, for I suppose the individuals of the latter to have been migrants ; and, as is well known, the bird performs very extensive journeys—quite from the Arctic regions to Brazil.
Mr. Allen is clearly wrong in allocating the *C. texensis* (*Lawrence*), *sapiti* (*Bonaparte*), and *brasilianus, auct.,* among the synonyms of *virginianus.* I cannot here discuss the question whether or not these names are synonymous *inter se ;* but they are, beyond all question, permanently distinct from *virginianus,* as Mr. Allen himself afterward became aware. I should judge that " *texensis,*" which is abundant along our Mexican border, constitutes a large northern race of *C. acutipennis* (*Boddaert*), with which *sapiti* (*Natt-erer, Bonaparte*) is synonymous. It may require to stand as *C. acutipennis* var. *texensis.*

The Night-hawk is as abundant in most parts of the West as else-where in North America, particularly in the spring and fall, during the migration. I have seen it at these seasons wherever I happened to be ; and it also breeds throughout most of the country. It retires south-ward in the fall, entirely withdrawing from the United States.

Mr. Allen's notice is corroborative of these statements. "It ap-pears," he says in a letter to me, "to be everywhere a common inhab-itant of the great central plateau of the continent. About Fort Hays, Kansas, it was as abundant in June as I ever found it in any portion of the Atlantic States, and presenting essentially the same habits. It breeds on the bare ground, where, during our ornithological tramps, we often flushed them from their quiet repose on the heated earth. We also frequently found them assembled in the timber along Big Creek, several being sometimes observed in a single tree. They were also abundant in the mountains of Colorado, being more or less common up to the altitude of about 11,000 feet."

The Night-hawk nests on the ground, lays two eggs, and the young are hatched downy. This is a singular circumstance, in which the *Caprimulgidæ* resemble the lower orders of birds, and not the higher groups with which they are associated. The chicks are not, however, hatched entirely clothed; for the first two or three days they are only densely flocculent on the under parts, the upper being but sparsely downy; soon, however, they are uniformly covered with down, variegated above, plain below. The design of this provision is evidently protection from the damp ground on which the young rest. In the several instances of nesting I have found, there was nothing whatever between the birds and the earth; but occasionally, it is said, a few leaves or straws lie underneath them. A favorite nesting place, in the West, is the little mounds of loose soil thrown up by the gophers, either in open fields or by the edge of woods. The birds are also said to lay on the mould of stumps and logs, but I have never found eggs in such situations. One of the two eggs may be hatched sooner than the other; in one instance I found an interval of three days to elapse, during which I frequently visited a nesting place. The female, on each occasion, remained near her charge until nearly trodden upon, and then fluttered off, making believe she was crippled, as perfectly as I ever saw the pious fraud performed in my life. Not having much, if any, legs to be lame in, she simulated a broken wing, fluttering and pitching about in the grass, at no time more than a few feet off. The statement that the bird will remove her young, if disturbed, is true. The bird I am alluding to carried them to another hillock, after my second visit, but only a couple of yards away. The male, on each occasion, came dashing overhead, sometimes darting close down, but did not join the mother in her attempts to decoy me away.

I have found the Night-hawk nesting in the Carolinas and Dakota, as it apparently does in most of its United States range. The eggs are nearly elliptical, blunt at the smaller end, where nearly as large and rounded as at the other. They measure about 1.30 by 0.90, but vary a good deal. The coloration is blended, intricate, and difficult of description. The ground-color is a pale stone-gray, sometimes grayish-white, obscurely mottled all over with pale purplish-gray or neutral shell-markings, over which is laid a marbling or scratchy fret-work of dark olive-gray. The tone of the markings—rather, the number and intensity of the markings, resulting in the general tone of coloration—is extremely variable, some very pale, scarcely clouded, eggs being met with.

Family CYPSELIDÆ: Swifts.

PANYPTILA SAXATILIS, (Woodh.) Coues.

White-throated or Rock Swift.

Acauthylis saxatilis, WOODH.. Sitgr. Rep. 1853, 64.—CASS., Ill. i, 1855, 252.
Panyptila saxatilis, COUES, Key, 1872, 182.
Cypselus melanoleucus, BD., Pr. Phila. Acad. 1854, 118.—CASS., Ill. i, 1855, 248.
Panyptila melanoleuca, BD., B. N. A. 1858, 141.—KENN., P. R. R. Rep. x, 1859, pt. iv, 23.—
    HEERM., *ibid.* pt. v, 10; pt. vi, 35, pl. 18, lower fig.—SCL. & SALV., Ibis, 1859,
    125 (biography).—COOP., Pr. Cal. Acad. 1861, 122 (Cajon Pass, Southern California).—COUES, Phila. Acad. 1866, 57.—SCL., P. Z. S. 1865, 607.—COOP., B.
    Cal. i, 1870, 347.—ALLEN, Bull. M. C. Z. iii, 1872, 151, 180 (Colorado).—AIKEN,
    Pr. Bost. Soc. xv, 1872, 206.—B. B. & R., N. A. B. ii, 1874, 424, pl. 45, f. 5.

Hab.—Southern Rocky Mountain region to the Pacific. North to headwaters of the Platte at least. South to Guatemala.
Not noticed by the Expeditions.

Respecting the *Acauthylis saxatilis* of Dr. Woodhouse, I remarked on a former occasion that there was no doubt of its being the same as the bird subsequently described by Prof. Baird; and although I did not then consider it necessary to make the change of nomenclature, this has since appeared to me to be required. While encamped at "Inscription Rock" (the original locality of *saxatilis*), I saw great numbers of these Swifts; but as I had been obliged to leave my gun behind, to accomplish the difficult and rather dangerous ascent of the cliffs, I failed to secure specimens, though the birds occasionally flew almost in my face, so that I could positively identify them. The only material discrepancy in Woodhouse's description is the mention of a white rump; but I am perfectly satisfied the observer mistook the character of the white lateral flank-patches, which often in life overlie the rump till they nearly or quite meet across it. The Violet-green Swallow shows exactly the same thing.

From Inscription Rock, which lies a day's march west of Whipple's Pass, between this and Zuñi, to the San Francisco Mountains, I saw the Swifts almost daily—always when we passed the peculiar cliffs they frequent. In favorable places they were congregated in immense numbers, and were evidently nesting in the rocks. But their strongholds were impregnable, at least from the front, and as it would have delayed the party a day to make a détour and scale the crags from behind, I cannot say whether they built a nest against the open rocks or in the crevices, though they certainly did so upon the face of the cliffs. With them were associated large numbers of Swallows, particularly the *H. lunifrons*. They generally fly very high—far out of gunshot-range, and with extraordinary rapidity. I shall never forget my disappointment when, on this account, I failed to secure specimens under the most advantageous circumstances I could reasonably expect. It was at sundown when we encamped by some small pools, where the dank, hot, lower atmosphere was loaded with gnats and mosquitoes, upon which the birds came skimming down quite to the ground to feed, as well as to sip the water in passing. The associate Swallows outnumbered them ten or twenty to one, and it added so much to the difficulty of shooting them, that I had to occupy precious seconds in picking out the right birds, among the hundreds dashing down to the pool, and I invariably fired either prematurely or just too late; and when the darkness closed in I had not got a single Swift.

The species was observed in the same zoological area by Drs. Kennerly and Heermann, both of whom have recorded remarks agreeing in purport with my own. Dr. Cooper extended the known range of the species to the Pacific. "About twelve miles north of San Diego," he writes, "I found them rather numerous about some high rocky bluffs, close to the sea-shore. They were there March 22, and may have been about a month previously, but generally fly so high during the day that they are at first betrayed by their harsh twitter when scarcely perceptible in the zenith. Occasionally they start off like lightning for several miles and back, as if it were only a slight curve in their course; sometimes they sweep for a moment near the ground, and the next disappear in the sky." This naturalist seems to think they winter about the cañons of the Colorado, noting that Dr. Kennerly found them February 16, but this appears to me improbable. Swallows often appear in our Middle districts in February, allured by a few warm days to perform a flight from the far South; and the appearance of these Swifts in February is nothing remarkable for the hot region of Colorado. Messrs. Sclater and Salvin record the species from Guatemala, and a flight through Mexico, toward the close of winter, would be a mere bagatelle to birds of such powers of wing.

The White-throated Swift, for all that is at present known, barely reaches the southern border of the Missouri region, being noted from points in Colorado not far from the headwaters of the Platte. Mr. Aiken records its arrival at Cañon City, April 18; Mr. Allen found it somewhat further north, and it probably goes as far at least as the Black Hills. The last-mentioned gentleman's note is as follows: "Observed only at the 'Garden of the Gods,' near Colorado City, where a considerable colony were nesting in holes and crevices in the cliffs, usually far above gunshot. They seemed very shy, and flew mostly near the tops of the highest rocks. Upon ascending the rocks most frequented by them, they moved to other points, and thus managed to keep generally out of range. By spending a considerable part of two days, we procured only four specimens, though several others which were killed fell in inaccessible places. They fly with great velocity, and are very tenacious of life. As they swoop down to enter their nests ('almost with the velocity of a bullet,' he says in a letter), the rushing sound produced by their wings can be heard to a considerable distance. *Hirundo thalassina* was also breeding here in similar situations."

CHÆTURA PELAGICA, (Linn.) Bd.

Chimney Swift.

Hirundo pelagica, LINN., Syst. Nat. i, 1758, 192.
Chætura pelagica, B. B. & R., N. A. B. ii, 1874, 432, pl. 45, f. 7.
" *Hirundo carolinensis*, BRISS., Orn. ii, 1760, 501."
" *Herundo cerdo*, BARTR., Trav. Fla. 1791, 292.—BART., Frag. N. H. Pa. 1799, 18."
Hirundo pelasgia, LINN., Syst. Nat. i, 1766, 345.—VIEILL., Ois. Am. Sept. i, 1807, 73, pl. 33.—WILS., Am. Orn. v, 1812, 48, pl. 39, f. 1.
Cypselus pelasgius, BP., Syn. 1828, 63.—NUTT., Man. i, 1832, 609.—AUD., Orn. Biog. ii, 1835, 329; v, 1839, 419; pl. 158.—DEKAY, N. Y. Zool. 1844, pl. 27, f. 58.—MAXIM., J. f. O. vi, 1858, p. —.
Chætura pelasgia, STEPH., Shaw's Gen. Zool. xiii, 1825, 76.—BP., Comp. List, 1838, 8.—AUD., Syn. 1839, 33; B. Am. i, 1840, 104, pl. 44.—BD., B. N. A. 1858, 144.—HAYD., Rep. 1862, 156.—SCL., Cat. 1862, 262; P. Z. S. 1863, 100; 1865, 610.—TRIPPE, Pr. Ess. Inst. vi, 1871, 114 (Minnesota; not common).—SNOW, B. Kans. 1873, 3.—ALLEN, Bull. M. C. Z. ii, 1871, 301; iii, 1872, 180.—COUES, Key, 1872, 183, fig. 119; and of authors generally.
Acanthylis pelasgia, TEMM.—BP., Consp. i, 1850, 64.—WOODH., Sitgr. Rep. 1853, 63.—CASS., Ill. i, 1855, 249.—BREW., N. A. Ool. i, 1857, 108.
Hemiprocne pelasgia, STREUBEL, Isis, 1848, 362.

Hab.—Eastern United States and British Provinces.
Lieutenant Warren's Expedition.—4781, Bijoux Hills.

It is difficult at present to fix the western limit of this species, owing to several circumstances. The accounts of the earlier writers, who ascribe to it a range to the Pacific, must remain in abeyance until it is decided whether *C. vauxii* be a distinct species or only a variety; for it is certain that this is the bird they had in view. Others mention its abundance along the eastern base of the Rocky Mountains, and in New Mexico; I never recognized it in the latter Territory, and I do not find that later observers, such as Allen, Aiken, and Holden, have there met with it. The westernmost locality of which I am personally cognizant, is that above quoted. Finally, Prof. Snow's remark, that it was formerly rare, but is now becoming common in Kansas, would appear to indicate a shifting of its western extension, very probably with the advance of civilization. Dr. Hayden says that it is rare in the northwest, where I have yet to meet with it. I am entirely in the dark respecting its winter-quarters. I find no mention of its wintering in the United States, and Allen notices its entering Florida late in March; yet after faithful search among the papers of Lawrence, Sclater, Salvin, and others, I have failed to lay my hand on a West Indian, Mexican, or Central American reference. Dr. Sclater, usually explicit, is silent in the matter, in his critical notice of the *Cypselidæ*.

The Chimney Swift reaches the Middle States early in April, and leaves toward October. It is abundant in our towns and cities, and familiar to all. The following account of its nidification, the most interesting point in its economy, leaves nothing to be desired. Dr. Brewer writes:

"The nest of the Chimney Swallow is one of the most remarkable structures of the kind to be found among the handiwork of even this interesting family, nearly all of whom are far from being undistinguished for their architectural accomplishments. It is composed of small twigs of nearly uniform size, which are interwoven into a neat semi-circular basket. In selecting the twigs with which to construct the nest, the Swift seems to prefer to break from the tree such as are best adapted to its wants, rather than to gather those already scattered upon the ground. This is done with great skill and adroitness, while on the wing. Sweeping on the coveted twig, somewhat as a Hawk rushes on its prey, it parts it at the desired place, and bears it off to its nest. This fact is familiar to all who have attentively observed its habits. Each of these twigs is firmly fastened to its fellows by an adhesive saliva, secreted by the bird, and the whole structure is strongly cemented to the side of the chimney in which it is built, by means of the same secretion. When dry, this saliva hardens into a glue-like substance, apparently firmer even than the twigs themselves. In separating a nest from the side of a chimney, I have known portions of the brick to which it was fastened to give way sooner than the cement with which it had been secured. When moistened, however, by long or heavy rains, the weight of their contents will sometimes cause them to part, and precipitate the whole to the bottom. The young birds cling very tenaciously to the sides of the chimney, with their strong claws and muscular feet, and often save themselves from falling in such accidents, by this means, even at a very early age, and before they have attained their sight. As the nest, even when undisturbed, soon becomes too small for them, the young leave it long before they are able to fly, and climb to the top of the chimney, where they are fed by their parents."

The eggs, four to six in number, are pure white, unmarked, sub-elliptical in shape, and measure 0.75 by 0.50, or slightly more.

Remaining North American species of this family are only as follows:

CHÆTURA VAUXII (*Towns.*), De Kay.

Cypselus vauxii, TOWNS., Journ. Phila. Acad. viii, 1839, 148 (Colorado River).
Chætura vauxii, DEKAY, N. Y. Zool. ii, 1844, 36.--BD., B. N. A. 1858, 145, pl. 18.—KENN.,
    P. R. R. Rep. x, pt. iv, 1859, pl. 18, f. 2.—COOP. & SUCK., N. H. Wash. Ter.
    1860, 165.—SCL. & SALV., P. Z. S. 1860, 37 (no specific name).—SCL., Cat. 1862,
    282; P. Z. S. 1863, 100 (Guatemala); 1865, 611 (critical).—LAWR., Ann. Lyc.
    ix, 1868, 204 (Yucatan).—COOP. B. Cal. i, 1870, 351.—COUES, Key, 1872, 183.
Acanthylis vauxii, BP., Consp. i, 1850, 64; Comptes Rend. 1854, 660.—CASS., Ill. 1855,
    250.—NEWB., P. R. R. Rep. vi, 1857, 78.
Chætura (palagica var. ?) *vauxi*, B. B. & R., N. A. B. ii, 1874, 435.

Hab.—Pacific Coast, United States, south to Guatemala.

NEPHŒCETES NIGER var. BOREALIS (*Kenn.*), Coues.

a. *niger*.

Hirundo nigra, GM., Syst. Nat. i, 1788, 1025.—LATH., Ind. Orn. ii, 1790, 577 (Antilles;
    based on *H. apos dominicensis*, BRISS., ii, 514, pl. 46, f. 3).
Cypselus niger, GOSSE, B. Jam. 1847, 63; Ill. pl. 10.—LAWR., Ann. Lyc. N. Y. vi, 1858,
    268 (Cuba).
Cypseloides niger, SCL., P. Z. S. 1865, 615.

b. *borealis.*

Cypselus borealis, KENN., Pr. Phila. Acad. ix, 1857, 202.
Cypseloides borealis, SCL., P. Z. S. 1865, 615.
Nephocætes niger, BD., B. N. A. 1858, 142.—ELLIOT, B. N. A. i, pl. 20.—COOP., Orn. Cal. i,
    1870, 349.—SUMICH., Mem. Bost. Soc. i, 1869, 562 (Vera Cruz).
Nephæcetes niger var. *borealis,* COUES, Key, 1872, 183.
Nephæcetes niger, B. B. & R., N. A. B. ii, 1874, 429, pl. 45, f. 4.

Hab.—The typical form in Cuba and Jamaica. Var. *borealis* from the Pacific coast,
United States; south into Mexico.

Family TROCHILIDÆ: Hummingbirds.

The Hummers constitute a very large family of very small birds, and form one of
the most remarkable groups in ornithology. Sharply distinguished from all other
birds, no less by their general appearance than by their technical characters, they are
recognizable at a glance by the casual observer, and some representatives are familiar
objects to all, from the vast numbers that are set up all over the civilized world merely
for ornamental purposes, and the gratification of the curious. They compete with
Ostrich and Bird of Paradise plumes, Rooster's hackles, Gull's breasts, and other miscellaneous objects of natural history in the decoration of woman's head-apparel; and
are prominent features of bird-stuffer's show-cases. Beautiful even under such conditions, in the more favorable circumstances of their native haunts they are the most
lovely of the feathered denizens of the air, gorgeous in color, exquisite in form, wonderful in action.

Notwithstanding the ease with which these birds as a group may be known, some
technical comments will not be out of place here. With ordinal characters of *Picariæ,*
they associate a medium to extremely long and very slender, subulate or even acicular
bill, usually straight and acute, with inflected tomia, serrate or not, and short unbristled
gape. In some remarkable species, as the *Docimastes ensiferus,* the bill is actually longer
than all the rest of the bird, a thing not elsewhere known among birds; and in general,
it is longer than the head. The tongue is peculiar; it resembles that of the Woodpeckers, in its length and lumbriciform slenderness, as well as its susceptibility of
being protruded to great distance by means of its posterior prolonged "horns," that
curve around the skull; but in structure it is double-barrelled, consisting of two
thready tubes, an arrangement which, in connection with the tube-like sloping of the
mouth, facilitates the extraction of honey from the nectaries of flowers, by a peculiar
process that may be true voluntary suction, or a sort of capillary attraction, or partly
both.

The wings are remarkable in several respects. In general, they are thin, sharp, and
pointed, with long, stiff, curved primaries, rapidly graduated, and short secondaries,
resulting in the shape especially to be called falcate. They have but six remiges, in
addition to the ten primaries. The upper arm-bone is extraordinarily short; perhaps
representing the extreme of this condition among birds. The breast-bone is very large,
and has an enormous keel; this is in relation to the immensely developed pectoral muscles that move the wing. The whole conformation illustrates perfectly a well-known
law, yet one not often mentioned, respecting the movements of the wing of a bird, viz.,
that the nearer to the body the longest quill-feather is, the more rapidly is the wing
moved. We will assume, for example, what is very near the truth, that a Humming-
bird and an Albatross have about the same relative length of wing in the "hand" or
pinion portion that bears the ten primaries, and the same relative length of these
quills. In the Albatross, this portion of the wing is widely separated from the body
by the length of the humerus and fore-arm; in the former, the reverse extreme exists;
and we see the result in the long, measured sweep of the ocean-bird's wing and the
rapid strokes of the other's. This is in strict accordance with a mechanical law
respecting the ratio between time of motion and distance traversed. Given, say, a
Hummer's wing two inches from flexure to tip of first primary, and one inch from
flexure to shoulder-joint; this would make the point of the wing describe an arc of a
circle with a radius of three inches; and a certain amount of muscular contraction
effects this in a certain time. Now, lengthen fore-arm and upper-arm till they are
each about two inches long, which would be something like the relative lengths in an
Albatross' wing; this would make the point of the wing move in the arc of a circle
with a radius of six inches. Now, the muscular force remaining the same, it is evident that the point of the wing could not move through this much larger arc in the
same time; *i. e.,* the wing-strokes would be necessarily slower. It is interesting to
observe how, in some other birds, a similar result is brought about by different means.
In a Partridge, for instance, without special shortening of upper-arm or fore-arm, the
longest quill-feather is brought nearer the body by the roundness of the wing; that is,

the successive shortening of several outer primaries; and this bird, as is well known, makes correspondingly more rapid wing-beats and vigorous, whirring flight. In the Humming-bird the quickness of the wing-vibration reaches the maximum; so rapid is it that the eye cannot follow the strokes, but merely perceives a film on each side of the body. The flight of the bird is also the most rapid; frequently the eye cannot follow the bird itself. It is almost needless to add, that the peculiar sound, from which the family takes its English name, is not vocal, but produced by the wings, just as it is in the cases of so many insects.

The tail is moderate, in most Hummers, but is too various in size and shape to be concisely characterized here. It sometimes greatly exceeds the length of the body. None of our representatives have any special developments of this member. It always has ten rectrices. The feet are small and short, and usually naked, though clothed in some; the toes normal; the claws rather large, relatively, and sharp. The feet are scarcely used for progression; the birds take to their wings for the briefest locomotion.

The birds are noted for their gorgeous coloring, due in most part, and in the vast majority of instances, to the iridescent glitter of their plumage; the metallic sheen is specially noticeable upon the throat, forming the characteristic gorget of the male sex. This is commonly wanting in the female, and she is also duller, usually, and otherwise so different in color as to be frequently mistaken for a different species. The sexual difference is sometimes so great, and affects such changes in size and shape of parts, that even genera have been framed upon it, or the sexes of the same species referred to different genera. Various greens, particularly of the golden series, are among the commonest body-colors; purples and violet-blacks oftenest tint the wings and tail; the brilliant gorget changes hue in different lights, and here only, among birds, the rainbow finds adequate material expression.* The crown is sometimes as brilliant as the throat. Velvety-black and snowy-white occur. A part of the species are crested; others have the gorget prolonged into a ruff; many have white, cottony tufts upon the flanks.

The general interest that attaches to the Hummers causes them to be eagerly sought after, and one good result of their search, to offset the lamentable wanton destruction of the beautiful little creatures for mercenary ends, has been the unparalleled advance of our knowledge of the species within comparatively few years. Now, we know at least three hundred species, apparently valid, aside from the unnumbered nominal ones that have been introduced into the system. The family is confined to America, and has its centre of abundance in the tropical parts of South America, especially New Granada, although some representatives are found from Alaska to Patagonia, and others live on snowy Andean peaks. The species have been almost endlessly subdivided into subfamilies and genera; but, while the latter are undeniably many, perhaps but two of the former may be recognized with certainty and entire propriety. One of these, *Phaëthornithinæ*, embraces only about a tenth of the family, and is composed of the duller-colored species, especially inhabitants of the dense forests of the Amazon. The other, *Trochilinæ*, comprehends the great variety, and is the only one represented in North America, at least with the limitation of *Phaëthornithinæ* just alluded to. The localization of many species is a singular fact in the history of the family; not a few are strictly confined, so far as is now known, to particular valleys or particular mountain peaks, only a few miles in area. Others however, are widely dispersed, as our Ruby-throat and the western Rufous-backed Hummer, which reaches from Alaska into Mexico. Few of the genera now usually adopted have many species; quite often but a single one.

There has been much conflict of opinion concerning the food of these birds. From their hovering so constantly about flowers, it was for a long time believed that they were nourished solely upon the sweets extracted from the nectaries. Then insects were found in their stomachs, and opinion veered to the opposite extreme. But doubtless both views are correct; we know that the birds are extensively insect-eaters, and the few that have been preserved alive in confinement have been easily fed upon syrup or sugar and water. Besides being the most active of birds, they are spirited, even irascible, and at times extremely pugnacious; the males have fierce encounters in airy tournament. They are not properly gregarious, though so many often collect at favorite feeding-grounds. They build exquisite nests, sometimes pensile, but ordinarily saddled upon a small bough or in a crotch, tastefully adorned outside, and at the same time effectively concealed, by being stuccoed over with bits of moss or lichen; within, they are warmly lined with the most delicate silky, cottony, or downy vegetable substances. They never lay more than two eggs, which are white; and the period of incubation is stated to be twelve or fourteen days.

Wilson knew but one North American Humming-bird, and Audubon only two or

---

* It may not be generally known that under certain conditions the plumage of our dullest birds will show rainbow-colors. A Sparrow's wing, for instance, held up to a strong light, and half-spread, will give the spectrum, by decomposition of the solar ray in passing through the fine barbules and barbicels, like that seen upon a soap-bubble.

three more. In 1858, Prof. Baird nearly doubled the number, including seven in his work. In 1872, I was enabled to recognize eleven species in the "Key"; one of these, however, was purely adventitious. Since this time, a large and beautiful species (*Eugenes fulgens*) has been discovered by Mr. Henshaw to occur over our Mexican border, where, doubtless, additional species will eventually be found.

TROCHILUS COLUBRIS, Linn.

Ruby-throated Hummingbird.

Trochilus colubris, LINN., Syst. Nat. i, 1766, 191.—LATH., Ind. Orn. i, 1790, 312.—VIEILL., Enc. 569; Ois. Am. Sept. i, pls. 31, 32; Ois. Dor. i, 66, 69, 70, pls. 31, 32, 33 (" *Rubis* ").—WILS., Am. Orn. ii, 1810, 26, pl. 10, figs. 3, 4.—JARD., Humm. i, 85, pl. 5.—BP., Syn. 1828, 98; Comp. List, 1838, 10; Consp. i, 1850, 81.—SW. & RICH., F. B. A. ii, 1831, 323.—NUTT., Man. i, 1832, 588.—AUD., Orn. Biog. i, 1832, 248; v, 1839, 544; pl. 47; Syn. 1839, 170; B. Am. iv, 1842, 190, pl. 253.— GIR., B. L. I. 1844, 169.—GOULD, Monog. iii, pl. 131; Introd. 86.—MAXIM., J. f. O. vi, 1858, 104.—BD., B. N. A. 1858, 131.—CAB., J. f. O. iv, 1856, 98 (Cuba); Mus. Hein. iii, 1860, 57.—SCL., P. Z. S. 1856, 287 (Cordova); 1859, 367.—SCL. & SALV., Ibis, i, 1859, 129 (Guatemala).—SALV., Ibis, 1860, 266.—SALV., P. Z. S. 1870, 203 (Veragua).—DRESS., Ibis, 1865, 470 (Texas).—SNOW, B. Kans. 1873, 3.—ALLEN, Bull. M. C. Z. ii, 1871, 301; iii, 1872, 180.—COUES, Key, 1872, 184.— B. B. & R, N. A. B. ii, 448, pl. 47, f. 2.
Mellisuga colubris, STEPH., Shaw's Gen. Zool. xiv, 247.—GRAY, Gen. of B. i, 113.—WOODH., Sitgr. Rep. 1853, 65.
Ornismyia colubris, LESS., Troch. 1, pl. 1; Ois. Mou. 151, pl. 48.—DEV., R. M. Z. 1852, p.—.
Cynanthus colubris, JARD., Humm. ii, 143.
Trochilus aureigaster, LAWR., (*fide Bd.*).

Hab.—North America, east of the Rocky Mountains. North to 57°, at least. South to Brazil. Cuba. Winters in Florida (?)

No Hummers appear to have been observed by Dr. Hayden; but two certainly inhabit the Missouri region, while a third (*S. rufus*), if not also a fourth (*Stellula calliope*), may occur. The present species is of common occurrence in Kansas, has been taken in the Saskatchewan region, and ranges also over the intermediate ground. I found it quite common and breeding, at Pembina, in June.

SELASPHORUS PLATYCERCUS, (Sw.) Bp.

Broad-tailed Hummingbird.

Trochilus platycercus, Sw., Syn. Mex. B. in Philos. Mag. i, 1827, 441.
Selasphorus platycercus, BP., Consp. i, 1850, 82.—GOULD, Monog. iii, 1852, pl. 140; Introd. 89.—SCL., P. Z. S. 1856, 288 (Cordova); 1858, 297.—SCL. & SALV., Ibis, i, 1859, 129 (Guatemala).—BD., B. N. A. 1858, 135, 922.—BD., U. S. & Mex. B. Surv. ii, 1859, pt. ii, 6, pl. 5, f. 1, 2.—CAB., Mus. Hein. iii, 1860, 56.—COOP., Pr. Cal. Acad. 1861, 68; B. Cal. i, 1870, 357.—ALLEN, Bull. M. C. Z. iii, 1872, 180 (Colorado, Wyoming, and Utah).—HOLD., Pr. Bost. Soc. 1872, 206 (Wyoming).— COUES, Pr. Phila. Acad. 1866, 57 (Arizona), and Key, 1872, 185.—B. B. & R., N. A. B. ii, 1874, 462, pl. 47, f. 5.
Mellisuga platycerca, GRAY, Gen. of B. i, 113.
Ornismyia tricolor, LESS, Colibris, 125, pl. 14 (Brazil); Troch. 1831, 156, pl. 60 (Mexico).—JARD., Nat. Libr. ii, 77, pl. 13.
Cynanthus tricolor, JARD., Humm. ii, 144.
Ornismyia montana, LESS., Troch. 1831, 161, plt. 63, 64 (young).
Trochilus montanus, JARD., Humm. ii, 67.

Hab.—Rocky Mountains and Sierra Nevada to the Black Hills. Texas. South into Mexico.
Not obtained by the Expeditions.

This species, one of the several ascertained of late years to inhabit the United States, long after its original description as a bird of Mexico, was first entered in our fauna by Prof. Baird, upon specimens taken at El Paso, Texas, by Mr. J. H. Clark. Its range was almost simultaneously ascertained to extend through New Mexico, where Dr. W. W. Anderson obtained it, at Canton Burgwyn, to Fort Bridger, then Utah, now in the new Territory of Wyoming, where Mr. C. Drexler secured examples. In June, 1864, I found it on the very summit of the Rocky Mountains of New Mexico, at Whipple's Pass. It appeared to be quite common; many were seen feeding among the wild roses then in full bloom, and excellent examples were procured. I did not recognize it at Fort Whipple, where the other species of the genus, *S. rufus*, was numerous through the summer. Dr. Cooper found it at Lake Tahoe, at an altitude of 6,000 feet, where it was breeding, his specimens being young. He records his anticipation of its extension northward to the Blue Mountains, near Snake River, in Oregon. Mr. Allen found it common at Ogden, Utah, in September, at Cheyenne, Wyoming, and also in Park County, Colorado, where he saw it repeatedly among the flowers growing far above the timber-line of Mount Lincoln, as more fully stated in the following memorandum he obligingly gave me:

"The Broad-tailed Hummer was common from Cheyenne southward along the base of the mountains to Colorado City, and throughout the mountains was everywhere abundant, even to above the timber-line. Its flight is exceedingly swift, and characterized by a sharp whistling sound; but in all other respects it might be readily mistaken for the common Ruby-throat of the East. Its nest was not discovered, but hardly a day passed without a considerable number of the birds being observed, often several individuals being in sight at once. The great abundance of flowers throughout the mountain valleys, and which here and there also nearly cover the ground, even far above the limit of trees on the Snowy Range, renders this mountain region highly favorable to the existence of this interesting species, and offers a ready explanation of its abundant occurrence here." Our last record is a note, by Mr. C. H. Holden, relating to his observations among the Black Hills:

"These little birds were quite common. On one occasion, while skinning a Hawk, I threw a piece of flesh into a small dead tree near me. In an instant three of the birds were poised before the meat, mistaking it, no doubt, for some gaudy flower. But one nest was found. It contained two young ones about a week old. I was struck by the wisdom displayed by the birds in placing their nest. A small tree had fallen over the brook, which was here eight feet wide. The nest was placed on one of the under branches in such a way that the trunk of the tree would effectually keep out the rain. The nest was lined with a species of cotton obtained in the vicinity." Mr. Trippe writes as follows from Colorado:

S. platycercus, Broad-tailed Hummingbird. Abundant; migratory; breeds. The Broad-tailed Hummingbird arrives in the vicinity of Idaho Springs about the middle of May, and extends upward as the season advances, reaching timber-line by the 15th of June, and during summer roaming far above it. It is very common, and universally distributed, wandering over all the mountain-sides and throughout all the valleys; and even penetrating at times the depths of the forest—in short, wherever it can find flowers, it is at home. The sound produced by its wings is very peculiar, and quite unlike the humming of the Ruby-throat; it is a loud, rattling noise, more like the shrill chirrup of a locust than the buzzing of wings. It is an expert insect-catcher, and frequently perches on the dead limb of a tree, or some tall, dry bush, whence it keeps a sharp lookout for passing insects, which it pursues with lightning-like rapidity, and after capturing them returns to the same perch. At times it utters a sharp, quick note, especially when angry or alarmed. It has the habit, during early summer, of mounting forty or fifty yards straight up in the air, poising itself a moment or two, and then darting down again, repeating the same manœuvre several times in succession. Sometimes a score or more may be seen darting up and down together in this way for half an hour or more.

This Hummingbird, breeds from the plains up to timber-line, and probably raises two broods each season, as I have found young birds just hatched, as late as the middle of August. Its nest is an exquisite little affair, so cunningly covered with lichens as to look precisely like the limb on which it rests. One which I found was placed on a swaying bough directly over a mountain-torrent, and within two or three feet of the water. The young are cared for and fed by the old birds for some time after they leave the nest. They disappear in September. Mrs. Maxwell, of Boulder, who has paid much attention to the birds of this region for the last few years, informs me that she has seen on two or three occasions, a Hummingbird with a flaming-red throat and breast, much larger than the present species, a straggler from Mexico, perhaps, as yet undetected within the limits of the United States [very possibly *Eugenes fulgens.*—E. C.].

Family ALCEDINIDÆ : Kingfishers.

CERYLE ALCYON, (Linn.) Boie.

Belted Kingfisher.

Alcedo alcyon, LINN., Syst. Nat. i, 1766, 180.—GM., Syst. Nat. i, 1788, 451.—LATH., Ind. Orn. i, 1790, 257 (*Ispida carolinensis cristata*, BRISS., iv, 512; *Belted Kingfisher*, CATES., Car. i, pl. 69; Arct. Zool. ii, No. 169; Gen. Syn. ii, 637; also, *Martin-pêcheur de la Louisiane*, P. E. 715; Gen. Syn. ii, 637, and *M.-p. huppé* de St. Domingue, P. E. 593).—VIEILL., Enc. Meth. 283.—WILS., Am. Orn. iii, 1811, 59.—BP., Syn. 1828, 48.—SW. & RICH., F. B. A. ii, 1831, 339.—AUD., Orn. Biog. i, 1831, 394, pl. 77; Syn. 1839, 173; B. Am. iv, 205, pl. 255.—NUTT., Man. i, 1832, 594.—GIR., B. L. I. 1844, 172.—MAXIM., J. f. O. vi, 1858, 102.—TRIPPE, Pr. Ess. Inst. vi, 1871, 117.
Ceryle alcyon, BOIE, Isis, 1828, 316.—BP., P. Z. S. 1837, 108; List, 1838, 10; Consp. Vol. Anis. 10; Consp. Av. 160.—GRAY, Gen. of B. i, 82; GOSSE, B. Jam. 1847, 81 (Jamaica).—WOODH., Sitgr. Rep. 1853, 65.—CASS., Ill. 1855, 254; Cat. Halc. Mus. Phila. 4.—CAB., J. f. O. iv, 1856, 101 (Cuba); GUNDL., Rep. 1866, 292 (Cuba).—BREW., N. A. Orn. 1857, 110, pl. 4, f. 52 (egg).—NEWB., P. R. R. Rep. vi, 1857, 79.—BD., B. N. A. 1858, 158.—HEERM., P. R. R. Rep. x, 1859, pt. vi, 57.—MOORE, P. Z. S. 1859, 53 (Honduras).—NEWT., Ibis, i, 1859, 67 (Santa Cruz).—SCL., Ibis, i, 1859, 131 (Belize).—TAYLOR, *ibid.* ii, 1860, 116 (Honduras).— BRY., Pr. Bost. Soc. vii, 1859 (Bahamas).—SCL., P. Z. S. 1857, 233; 1859, 236, 367; 1860, 253 (Orizaba).—MURRAY, Edinb. Philos. Journ. 1860 (Hudson's Bay).—COOP. & SUCK., N. H. Wash. Ter. 1860, 167.—COUES, Pr. Phila. Acad. 1861, 217 (Labrador).—LAWR., Ann. Lyc. 1861, 318 (New Granada).—HAYD., Rep. 1862, 157.—CAB., Journ. 1862, 162 (Costa Rica).—DRESS., Ibis, 1865, 471 (Texas).—BRY., Pr. Bost. Soc. 1866 (Porto Rico and St. Domingo).—COUES, Pr. Phila. Acad. 1866, 59 (Arizona).—LAWR., Ann. Lyc. ix, 1868, 118 (Costa Rica).— SUND., Ofv. V. A. 1869, 585 (St. Bartholomew).—DALL & BANN., Tr. Chic. Acad. i, 1869, 275 (Alaska).—COOP., B. Cal. i, 1870, 336.—STEV., U. S. Geol. Surv. Ter. 1870, 463 (Wyoming).—ALLEN, Bull. M. C. Z. ii, 1871, 300 (Florida); iii, 1872, 179 (mountains up to 9,000 feet).—AIKEN, Pr. Bost. Soc. xv, 1872, 206 (Colorado).—TRIPPE, *ibid.* 233 (Iowa).—FINSCH, Abh. Nat. iii, 1872, 29 (Alaska).— HART., Man. Br. Birds, 1872, 124 (Ireland!).—COUES, Key, 1872, 188.—SNOW, B. Kans., 1873, 3.—B. B. & R., N. A. B. ii, 1874, 392, pl. 45, f. 6.—SHARPE, Monog. *Alcedinidæ.*
Ispida alcyon, SW., Classif. of Birds, ii, 1837, 336.
Megaceryle alcyon, REICH., Handbuch, i, 1851, 25, pl. 412, figs. 3108, 3109.
Streptoceryle alcyon, CAB., Mus. Hein. i, 1859, 151.
Chloroceryle alcyon, SCL., Cat. Am. Birds, 1862, 264.
Alcedo ludoviciana, GM., Syst. Nat. i, 1788, 452 (P. E. 715, *v. suprà*).
Alcedo jaguacati, "DUMONT, Dict. Sci. Nat. i, 1816, 455."
Alcedo guacu, "VIEILL., Nouv. Dict. d'Hist. Nat. xix, 1818, 406."

Hab.—Over the waters of all North and Middle America, and many of the West Indian Islands. Resident, or imperfectly migratory, being in the north forced away by the freezing of the waters. Breeds nearly throughout its range. Accidental in Ireland (in 1845, *Thompson*, B. Irel. i, 373).

Lieutenant Warren's Expedition.—4657, Little Missouri ; 5234, Yellowstone.

Later Expeditions.—59849-50, Colorado ; 60458, 60806-7, Wyoming.

Family CUCULIDÆ: Cuckoos.

NOTE.—The Ground Cuckoo, *Geococcyx californianus*, is entered upon the Holden-Aiken List (Pr. Bost. Soc. xv, 1872), as a resident species ; but since, in the preparation of two different Mss. for the press, the editor neglected to preserve indications of localities with desirable precision, it is uncertain whether the species should be included in the present work or not. The List covers ground partly in the water-shed of the Missouri, and partly beyond it, for Mr. Aiken's observations extend as far south as Cañon City, Colorado. The case is parallel with that of *Pipilo fuscus* (" *mesoleucus* "). Until recently, I was unaware of the extension of the Ground Cuckoo beyond the latitude of New Mexico and Arizona, excepting in the Sacramento Valley, California, to Fort Reading (latitude 40¼°) ; Mr. Aiken's record is interesting in this regard. To this may be added the occurrence of the species on the Arkansas, near Fort Lyons, as recorded by me, Am. Nat. vii, 1873, 751.

COCCYZUS ERYTHROPHTHALMUS, (Wils.) Bp.

Black-billed Cuckoo.

Cuculus erythrophthalmus, WILS., Am. Orn. iv, 1811, 16, pl. 27, fig. 2.—STEPH., Shaw's Gen. Zool. xiv, 208.—HART., Br. Birds, 1872, 124 (Ireland).

Coccyzus erythrophthalmus, BP., Obs. Wils. 1825, No. 48 ; Syn. 1828, 42 ; Consp. i, 1850, 111.—AUD., Orn. Biog. i, 1832, 170, pl. 32 ; Syn. 1839, 187 ; B. Am. iv, 1842, 300, pl. 276.—GIR., B. L. I. 1844, 183.—GRAY, Gen. of B. ii, 457.—WOODH., Sitgr. Rep. 1853, 92.—GLOGER, J. f. O. 1854, 224.—LEOTAUD, Ois. de Trin. 352.—SCL. & SALV., Ibis, 1860, 276 (Guatemala).—SCL., P. Z. S. 1859, 252 ; 1864, 122 ; 1870, 168 ; Cat. 1862, 323.—COUES, Key, 1872, 199.—SNOW, B. Kans. 1873, 2.—LAWR., Ann. Lyc. ix, 1868, 128 (Costa Rica).—GUNDL., Rep. F. N. i, 1866, 295 (Cuba).

Piaya erythrophthalma, LESS., Traité Orn. 1831, 141.

Erythrophrys erythrophthalmus, BP., Comp. List, 1838, 40.

Coccygus erythrophthalmus, CAB., J. f. O. 1856, 104 (Cuba, breeds).—BD., B. N. A. 1858, 77.—HAYD., Rep. 1862, 154.—CAB. & HEINE, Mus. Hein. iv, 1862, 76.—LAWR., Ann. Lyc. vii, 1862, 23 (New Granada).—McILWR., Pr. Ess. Inst. v, 1866, 83 (Canada).—TRIPPE, Pr. Ess. Inst. vi, 118 (Minnesota) ; Pr. Bost. Soc. xv, 1872, 233 (Iowa).—B. B. & R., N. A. B. ii, 1874, 484, pl. 48, f. 5.

Coccyzus dominicus, NUTT., Man. i, 1832, 556 (not of authors).

Hab.—North America to the Rocky Mountains (Wyoming, *Trook*). North to Labrador. South through Mexico and Central America to the valley of the Amazon. Cuba, rarely ; no other Antillean record. Said to winter in Florida. Accidental in Europe (Killead, Antrim County, September 25, 1871 ; BLAKE-KNOX, Zool. 1872, 2943 (" *americanus*," error ; CLERMONT, *ibid*, p. 3022) ; HARTING, Br. Birds, 1872, 124.—Italy, BOLLE, J. f. O. 1858, 457 ; SELYS-LONG., Ibis, 1870, 452 ; SALVAD., Fn. Ital. Ucc. 1871, 42.

List of specimens.

19337	....	P. F. Bighorn R	....	June 15, 1860	G. H. Trook..	12.00	15.00	5.50
19338	....	.... do	....	....	....	12.00	15.00	5.50

Lieutenant Warren's Expedition.—5332, Fort Lookout ; 5233, Moreau River ; 8979-81, Platte River ; 8982, Loup Fork.

These specimens indicate the westernmost locality as yet on record for this species, which was not previously known to cross the central plains. It is true that Dr. Newberry quotes the species for California, but he does so with a double query ; he secured no specimens, and the cries he heard, if those of any Cuckoo, were doubtless of *C. americanus*.

This species is found throughout most of Eastern North America with *C americanus*, and yet there is a notable difference in their distribution, the Black-billed Cuckoo being the more northerly bird. Audubon has recorded both species from Labrador, but in rather vague terms, and does not appear to have actually taken any specimens; I think it safe to infer that all the Cuckoos he may have seen there were of this species. In New England the Black-billed is the more common of the two, and I think that there the Yellow-billed finds its ordinary northern limit; in fact, it is extremely rare in many localities. This relative distribution is susceptible of numerous illustrations. Thus, Mr. McIlwrath gives the Black-billed as a common summer resident at Hamilton, Canada West, while of the Yellow-billed he says he never saw but one specimen in Canada. Allen and Maynard's testimony for Massachusetts, though necessarily less pointed, is to the same general effect. In the Middle States, on the contrary, we find Dr. Turnbull giving the Yellow-billed as rather the more common of the two. At Washington, D. C., the Yellow-billed is very abundant, especially in the spring and fall, but also breeds plentifully; it arrives late in April, and remains through September. There the Black-billed is much less numerous, even when both are migrating, and breeds but sparingly. In his Kansas list, Prof. Snow gives both species without remark, but marks the Yellow-billed only, as breeding. The latter appears to breed everywhere in its United States range, the former rarely south of the Middle districts.

The habits of the two species are very similar, and the birds are commonly confounded by unscientific observers. The notes of the Black-billed are less harsh and not so often repeated. The nesting is much the same; the eggs deeper green, smaller (1.10 by 0.80), and less elliptical.

I found the Black-billed Cuckoo breeding in the Pembina Mountains, forty miles west of the Red River. At date of July 12 the nest contained a single young bird, just ready to fly; the others, if any, having already left. The nest, in this instance, was remarkable in position, being placed in the crotch of an oak bush less than two feet from the ground, in a dense thicket on a hill-side. There was a large basement of loosely-interlaced twigs, on which was placed a matted platform with scarcely any depression, of dried leaves and poplar catkins. The young one could not quite fly, but scrambled off as I approached, and I had some little difficulty in catching it; during the capture, the old bird came about within a few feet of me, and answered the cries of the young with a curious guttural note. The young has the feathers of the upper parts all edged with whitish, and a faint tawny-gray shade on the breast; the bill and feet are pale-bluish; the iris is brown.

COCCYZUS AMERICANUS, (Linn.) Bp.

Yellow-billed Cuckoo.

Cuculus dominicensis, BRISS., Orn. iv, 110, pl. 9.
Cuculus dominicus, LINN., Syst. Nat. i, 1766, 170.—GM., i, 416.—LATH., Ind. Orn. i, 221.—
    (Not *Coccygus dominicus* of NUTT., or of BP., Consp., or of SCL., Cat.)
Coccygus dominicus, BD., Pr. Phila. Acad. 1863, 154.
Piaya dominica, GRAY, Genera of Birds, ii, 457.
Cuculus carolinensis, BRISS., Orn. iv, 112 (Coucou de la Caroline, P. E. 816).—WILS., Am.
    Orn. iv, 1811, 13, pl. 28, f. 1.
Erythrophrys carolinensis, SW., Classif. Birds, ii, 1837, 322.
Cuculus americanus, LINN., Syst. Nat. i, 1766, 170.—GM., i, 416.—LATH., Ind. Orn. i, 1790,
    219.—STEPH., Shaw's Gen. Zool. ix, 93.—SCHL., Rev. Crit. Ois. Eur. 1844. 51.—
    HART., Man. Br. Birds, 1872, 124 (Great Britain).
Coccyzus americanus, BP., Obs. Wils. 1825, No. 47; Consp. i, 1850, 111.—NUTT., Man. i,
    1832, 551.—AUD., Orn. Biog. i, 1832, 18; v, 1839, 520; pl. 2; Syn. 1839, 187; B.

Am. iv, 1842, 293, pl. 275.—GOULD, B. Eur. pl. 242.—GRAY, Gen. Birds, ii, 457.—
GOSSE, B. Jam. 279.—WOODH., Sitgr. Rep. 1853, 92.—LEOTAUD, Ois. Trin. 350.—
NEWT., Ibis, 1859, 149.—SCL., P. Z. S. 1860, 252; 1864, 120; 1870, 165; Ibis,
1860, 43; Cat. 1862, 322.—LAWR., Ann. Lyc. ix, 1868, 128 (Costa Rica).—GRAY,
Hand-list, ii, 1870, 210, No. 8914.—GUNDL., Rep. F. N. i, 295 (Cuba).—COUES,
Key, 1872, 190, fig. 126.
Piaya americana, LESS., Traité Orn. 1831, 142.
Erythrophrys americanus, BP., Comp. and Geog. List, 1838, 40.
Cureus americanus, BP., Cat. Metod. Ucc. Europ. 1842, 50.
Coccystes americanus, KEYS. & BLAS., Wirbelth. Europ. 1840, 149.
Coccygus americanus, CAB., J. f. O. 1856, 104; 1862, 167; Mus. Hein. iv, 1862, 75.—BD.,
B. N. A. 1858, 76.—HAYD., Rep. 1862, 155.—COOP., B. Cal. i, 1870, 371.—SNOW,
B. Kans. 1873, 2.—ALLEN, Bull. M. C. Z. iii, 1872, 180.—TRIPPE, Pr. Bost. Soc.
xv, 1872, 233 (Iowa).—B. B. & R., N. A. B. ii, 1874, 477, pl. 48, f. 4 ("3" err.).
Coccyzus pyrrhopterus, VIEILL., Nouv. Dict. d'Hist. Nat. viii, 270; Ency. Met. iii, 1343.
Cuculus cinerosus, TEMM., Man. Orn. iv, 1835, 277.
Coccystes flavirostris, GLOGER, J. f. O. 1854, 223.
Coccyzus bairdii, SCL., P. Z. S. 1864, 120.—GRAY, Hand-list, ii, 1870, 211, No. 8923.—
"PELZELN, Orn. Bras. 273."
(?) *Coccygus julieni*, LAWR., Pr. Phil. Acad. 1863, 106, Ann. Lyc. viii, 1864. 42, 99 (Som-
brero).

Hab.—Eastern United States and part of the British Provinces. West to the Rocky
Mountains. Also observed in California. South through Mexico and various West
India Islands and Central America into South America as far as Buenos Ayres. Acci-
dental in Europe. See Gould's & Schlegel's works; also, HART., Man. 1872, 124 (five
British instances, with the references).
Lieutenant Warren's Expedition.—8980, 8987, Platte River; 8983, 8985, Loup Fork of
Platte; 8986, Elkhorn River.
Confusion has arisen in the employ of the name *dominicus* for different species. Nutt-
all applied it to our Black-billed Cuckoo; Bonaparte used it for a species, of which he
says (correctly or not) "*rostro nigerrimo;*" Sclater, for the West Indian Mangrove
Cuckoo; Baird apparently relegated it to the insular variety of *americanus*, afterwards
named *bairdii* by Sclater. But, as Cabanis and Heine determined, there is no doubt
whatever that it is merely a synonym of *americanus.*
I am satisfied of the necessity of reducing the *C. bairdii*, SCL., to *americanus*, and the
same may be found necessary with *C. julieni.*
Cabanis and Heine have made two species of the rusty-bellied, yellow-billed "Mangrove" Cuckoos; it does not appear, however, that there is more than one species, the
synonymy of which may be arranged as in the accompanying foot-note.*

Having already compared the North American distribution of this
species with that of the Black-billed, it only remains to note its Pacific

---

* COCCYZUS SENICULUS, (*Lath.*) *Vieill.*

Cuculus minor, GM., i, 411 (ex P. l. 813.) (*Nomen ineptum.*)
Coccyzus minor, GRAY, Gen. of B. ii, 457; Hand-list, ii, 1870, 210, No. 8917.
Cuculus seniculus, LATH., Ind. Orn. i, 219.—STEPH., Gen. Zool. ix, 125.
Coccyzus seniculus, VIEILL., Ency. Meth. 1346.—BR., Consp. i, 1850, 111.—SCL., Cat. 1862,
323; P. Z. S. 1864, 121.—TAYLOR, Ibis, 1864, 170.
Coccygus seniculus, CAB. & HEINE, Mus. Hein. iv, 78.
Coccygus helviventris, CAB., Schomb. Guiana, iii, 714.

Hab.—Continental Tropical America. Trinidad; Dominica; Guadeloupe; Martinique.

C. SENICULUS var. NESIOTES.

Coccyzus seniculus, NUTT. Man. i, 1832, 558.—AUD., Orn. Biog. ii, 1834, 390, pl. 169; Syn.
1839, 188; B. Am. iv, 1842, 303, pl. 277.— GOSSE, B. Jam. 1847, 281.—SALLÉ, P. Z.
S. 1857, 234.—NEWT., Ibis, 1859, 150.—CASS., Pr. Phila. Acad. 1860, 377.—SCL.,
P. Z. S. 1861, 79.—COUES, Key, 1872, 190.
Erythrophrys seniculus, BP., Comp. and Geog. List, 1838, 40.
Piaya minor, LESS., Traité Orn. 1831, 141.
Coccygus minor, CAB., J. f. O. 1856, 104.—BD., B. N. A. 1858, 78.—B. B. & R., N. A. B. ii,
1874, 482, pl. 48, f. 3 ("4" err.).
Coccyzus dominicus, (?) BP., Consp. i, 1850, 112 (gives black bill).—SCL., Cat. 1862, 323
(not of Linnæus).
Coccygus nesiotes, CAB., Mus. Hein. iv, 1862, 78.—TAYLOR, Ibis, 1864, 170.—SCL., P. Z. S.
1864, 121.—GRAY, Hand-list, ii, 1870, 210, No. 8918.

Hab.—Greater Antilles and Florida.

coast record. Early observers gave "Oregon" as a locality which has remained unchecked to date, and, in fact, it is only recently that the California quotations have been confirmed. Before, it rested upon "hearsay," literally, for several persons who thought they heard its cry may have been mistaken, easily enough. In the first place, the hooting of the Burrowing Owl is so similar to the notes of the Rain Crow, that I should have been deceived myself on one occasion had I not been forewarned by my friend Cooper; and secondly, as this gentleman observes, the noise made by the Spade-footed Toad (*Scaphiopus*) is also very similar. Specimens have, however, been actually procured by Mr. F. Gruber in Napa Valley.

The peculiar notes of this bird, sounding like the syllables *koo-koo-koo*, indefinitely repeated, are probably uttered more frequently during the atmospheric changes preceding falling weather, and have given rise to the name "Rain Crow," by which both our species are universally known to the vulgar. The Yellow-billed is rather the noisier bird of the two, and its voice is more forcible. It is a rather shy and unfamiliar species, inhabiting high, open woods, as well as the large shade-trees of parks and cities, and generally remains high among the branches. When dashing about, in active pursuit of the various large-winged insects that form its chief food, they are conspicuous objects, the metallic olive-gray flashing in the sun, and the snowy under parts contrasting with verdure. But ordinarily they are hidden birds, oftener heard than seen; they pass from one tree to another stealthily, with a rapid, gliding, noiseless flight, and often rest motionless as statues for a long time, especially when crying out, or when they have detected a suspicious object. They court the seclusion of the thickest foliage. Their curiosity is not small, and they may be observed to frequently peer down with inquisitive looks through the dense foliage, trying to make out some unusual object. Although not parasites, like the European species, devoid of parental instinct, they have their bad traits, being even worse enemies of various small, gentle birds; for they are abandoned thieves, as wicked as Jays in this respect, continually robbing birds of their eggs, and even, it is said, devouring the helpless nestlings.

The nidification is not remarkably peculiar, the nest being like that of a Crow in miniature, composed artlessly of many small sticks and some grass, rather loosely interlaced, and forming a flattish, unsubstantial structure, usually saddled on a large horizontal branch. The eggs are pale greenish, rather broadly oval, measuring about $1\frac{1}{8}$ inches long by $\frac{7}{8}$ in breadth. But the oviposition is very unusual. The fact is, that the bird begins to set as soon as the first egg is laid, and successively deposits the rest at such intervals that a nest may be found with a fresh egg in it, another partially incubated, a newly-hatched bird, and one or more young more advanced. I have verified this fact; but in place of my observations I will give an extract from Audubon, which leaves nothing to be desired:

"A nest, which was placed near the centre of a tree of moderate size, was reached by a son of the gentleman on whose grounds we were. One of the old birds, which was sitting upon it, left its situation only when within a few inches of the climber's hand, and silently glided off to another tree close by. Two young Cuckoos, nearly able to fly, scrambled off from their tenement among the branches of the tree, and were caught by us after awhile. The nest was taken, and carefully handed to me. It still contained three young Cuckoos, all of different sizes, the smallest apparently just hatched, the next in size probably several days old, while the largest, covered with pin-feathers, would have been able to leave the nest in about a week. There were also in the nest two eggs, one containing a chick, the other fresh or lately laid. The two young birds which escaped from the nest clung so firmly to the branches with their feet that our attempts to dislodge them were of no avail, and we were obliged to reach them with the hand. On now looking at all these young birds our surprise was indeed great, as no two of them were of the same size, which clearly showed that they had been hatched at different periods; and I should suppose the largest to have been fully three weeks older than any of the rest. Mr. Rhett assured us that he had observed the same in another nest placed in a tree within a few paces of his house, and which he also showed to us. He stated that *eleven* young Cuckoos had been successively hatched and reared in it, by the same pair of old birds, in one season, and that young birds and eggs were to be seen in it at the same time for many weeks in succession.

"On thinking since of this strange fact, I have felt most anxious to discover how many eggs the Cuckoo of Europe drops in one season. If it, as I suspect, produces as our bird does, not less than eight or ten, or what may be called the amount of two broods, in a season, this circumstance would connect the two species in a still more intimate manner than theoretical writers have supposed them to be allied. And if our Cow-pen bird also drops eight or ten eggs in a season, which she probably does, that number might be considered the amount of two broods, which the Red-winged Starling usually produces."

The Yellow-billed Cuckoo is stated to winter in Southern Florida. It is a partially nocturnal species, in so far at least as the fact of its often crying out in the night, and being apparently in motion, may warrant the statement. Besides the insects above mentioned as its food, it eats various grubs, even wood-inhabiting molluscs, and also plucks different kinds of berries and other soft fruits.

Family PICIDÆ: Woodpeckers.

In all our representatives of this family, the nesting and eggs are so similar that it becomes unnecessary to refer to the subject under heads of each species. The birds all lay in holes of trees, dug by themselves, depositing the eggs—generally to the number of five or six, but sometimes more or fewer—upon the chips and dust at the bottom. The eggs are of a more nearly globular shape than is usual among birds, with a shell of crystal smoothness and purity, white, unmarked. Almost the only difference in the eggs of the species is in size, which corresponds in general with that of the parent, though, in the cases of our two largest species, the size appears disproportionately small. Thus, an egg of *H. pileatus* measures only 1.25 by 0.98, thus being not much bigger than a good-sized Flicker's egg (1.18 by 0.88).

HYLOTOMUS PILEATUS, (Linn.) Bd.

Pileated Woodpecker.

Picus pileatus, LINN., Syst. Nat. i, 1766, 173 (*Picus niger maximus capite rubro.* CATES., i, 17; *P. virginianus cristatus*, BRISS., iv, 29; *Pic noir huppé de Louisiane*, BUFF., P. E. 718).—GM., i, 1788, 425.—LATH., Ind. i, 1790, 225.—VIEILL., Ois. Am. Sept. ii, 1807, 58, pl. 110.—WILS., Am. Orn. iv, 1811, 27, pl. 29, f. 2.—STEPH., Gen. Zool. ix, 158, pl. 32.—WAGL., Syst. Av. 1827.—VIEILL., Nouv. Dict. xxvi, 84; Ency. iii, 1313.—BP., Syn. 1828, 44.—SW. & RICH., F. B. A. ii, 1831, 304.—LESS., Tr. Orn. 1831, 229.—NUTT., Man. i, 1832, 567.—AUD., Orn. Biog. ii, 1834, 74; v, 1839, 533; pl. 111; B. Am. iv, 226, pl. 257.—MAXIM., J. f. O. vi, 1858, 352.—SUND., Consp. Av. Pic. 1866, 8.
Dryotomus pileatus, SW., Classif. Birds, ii, 1837, 308.—BP., Comp. List, 1838, 39.
Dryocopus pileatus, BOIE.—BP., Consp. Av. i, 1850, 132.—SCL., Cat. 1862, 332.—GRAY, Hand-list, ii, 1870, 188, No. 8635.
Dryopicus pileatus, BP., Not. Orn. Delattre, 1854, 85.—MALH., Mon. i, 34, pl. 11, figs. 5, 6, 7.
Driocpicus pileatus, BP., Consp. Vol. Zygod., Aten. Ital. 1854, 8.

Campephilus pileatus, REICH., Hand-buch Sp Orn. 391, pl. 647, figs. 4317, 4318.
Hylatomus pileatus, BD., B. N. A. 1858, 107; and of most United States writers.
Hylotomus pileatus, COOP., B. Cal. i, 1870, 396.—COUES, Key, 1872, 192, fig. 128.—SNOW,
    B. Kans. 1873, 3. (rare).—B. B. & R., N. A. B. ii, 1874, 550, pl. 56, f. 5, 6.
Ceophlœus pileatus, CAB., J. f. O. 1862, 176.
Phlœotomus pileatus, CAB. & HEINE, Mus. Hein. iv, 1863, 102.
    Hab.—Timbered regions of North America at large.

This large species was not noticed by either of the Expeditions, and is doubtless of rare, if more than casual, occurrence in most parts of the Missouri region, which is not heavily wooded enough to suit its habits. It varies greatly in size according to latitude.

PICUS VILLOSUS, Linn.

Hairy Woodpecker.

a. *villosus*. (Wing-coverts profusely white-spotted.)

a'. *majores*. (Northern examples, 10 to 11 inches long.)

Picus villosus, FORST., Phil. Trans. lxii, 1772, 383.—SW. & RICH., F. B. A. ii, 1831, 305.—
    DALL & BANN., Tr. Chic. Acad. i, 1869, 274.
Picus villosus var. *major*, BD., B. N. A. 1858, 84.—SUND., Consp. Av. Pic. 1866, 16.
Picus villosus var. *canadensis*, B. B. & R., N. A. B. ii, 1874, 503.
Picus leucomelas, BODD., Tabl. P. E. 1783, pl. 345, f. 1 (*Pic du Canada*, BUFF.).—GRAY,
    Hand-list, ii, 1870, 185, No. 8599.—CASS., Pr. Phila. Acad. 1863, 199.
Dryobates leucomelas, CAB. & HEINE, Mus. Hein. iv, 1863, 67.
Picus canadensis, GM., i, 437 (*Picus varius canadensis*, BRISS., Orn. iv, 45, No. 16, pl. 2, f.
    2, ♀).—LATH., Ind. Orn. i, 1790, 230.—STEPH., Gen. Zool. ix, 173.—VIEILL.
    Nouv. Dict. xxvi, 92; Ency. iii, 1318.—AUD., Orn. Biog. v, 1839, 188, pl. 417,
    Syn. 1839, 177; B. Am. iv, 1842, 235; pl. 258.—BP., Consp. i, 1850, 137.—REICH.;
    Hand-buch Sp. Orn. 373, pl. 638, figs. 4250, 4251.—MALH., Mon. Pic. i, 78, pl,
    21, f. 4.
Picus phillipsii, AUD., Orn. Biog. v, 1839, 186, pl. 417; Syn. 1839, 177; B. Am. iv, 1842,
    238, pl. 259 (young, with yellow crown).—NUTT., Man. i, 1840, 686.—MALH.,
    Mon. Pic. i, 84, pl. 21, f. 5.—GRAY, Hand-list, ii, 1870, 185, No. 8601.
Picus philipsii, GRAY, Gen. of B. ii, 435.
Picus philipsi, BP., Consp. Av. i, 1850, 138.
Picus philippsii, REICH., Hand-buch Sp. Orn. 364, pl. 632, figs. 4204, 4205.
Trichopicus philipsi, BP., Consp. Vol. Zygod., Aten. Ital. 1854, 8.
Picus septentrionalis, NUTT., Man. i, 1840, 684 (= *phillipsii*).

b'. *medii*. (Intermediate examples, 9 to 10 inches long.)

Picus villosus, LINN., Syst. Nat. i, 1766, 175 (KALM, It. iii, 43; *P. varius medius quasi
    villosus*, CATES., i, 19; *P. varius virginianus*, BRISS., iv, 48; *Pic varie de Virginie*,
    BUFF., P. E. 754).—GM., Syst. Nat. i, 1788, 435.—LATH., Ind. Orn. i, 1790, 232
    (England).—VIEILL., Ois. Am. Sept. ii, 1807, 64, pl. 120.—WILS., Am. Orn. i,
    1808, 150, pl. 9.—STEPH., Gen. Zool. ix, 171.—VIEILL., Nouv. Dict. xxvi, 71;
    Ency. 1305.—NUTT., Man. i, 1832, 575.—BP., Syn. 1828, 46; List, 1838, 39; Consp.
    i, 1850, 137.—AUD., Orn. Biog. v, 1839, 164, pl. 416; Syn. 1839, 179; B. Am. iv,
    1842, 244, pl. 262.—GRAY, Gen. of B. ii, 435.—REICH., Hand-buch Sp. Orn. 374, pl.
    638, figs. 4252, 4253, 4254.—MALH., Mon. Pic. i, 75, pl. 21, f. 1, 2.—GRAY, Hand-
    list, ii, 1870, 184, No. 8592.—COUES, Key, 1872, 193.—CASS., Pr. Phila. Acad.
    1863, 199.—SNOW, B. Kans. 1873, 3.—ALLEN, Bull. M. C. Z. iii, 1872, 180.—
    FINSCH, Abh. Nat. iii, 1872, 60 (Alaska).—HAYD., Rep. 155.—HART., Man. Brit.
    Birds, 1872, 122 (accidental in England; three instances).
Picus villosus var *medius*, BD., B. N. A. 1858, 84.—SUND., Consp. Av. Pic. 1866, 16.
Picus villosus var. *villosus*, B. B. & R., N. A. B. ii, 1874, 503, pl. 49, f. 3, 4, 5.
Trichopicus villosus, BP., Consp. Vol. Zygod., Aten. Ital. 1854, 8.
Trichopipo villosus, "CAB. & HEINE, Mus. Berol."
Dryobates villosus, CAB. & HEINE, Mus. Hein. iv, 1863, 66.
Picus leucomelanus, WAGL., Syst. Av. 1827 (young).—MALH., Mon. Pic. i, 85.
Picus martinœ, AUD., Orn. Biog. v, 1839, 81, pl. 417; Syn. 1839, 178; B. Am. iv, 1842,
    240, pl. 260 ("Canada;" but ascribed dimensions not those of the large northern
    race; young).—GRAY, Gen. of B. ii, 435.—BP., Consp. i, 1850, 138.—REICH.,
    Hand-buch, 364, pl. 632, figs. 4206, 4207.

Picus martini, BP., Comp. List, 1838, 39.—MALH., Mon. Pic. 82, pl. 22, f. 1, 2.
Trichopicus martinæ, BP., Consp. Vol. Zygod., Aten. Ital. 1854, 8.
Picus rubricapillus, NUTT., Man. i, 1840, 685 (= *martinæ*).

c.' *minores*. (Southern examples, 8 to 9 inches long.)

Picus auduboni, SW., F. B. A. ii, 1831, 306, figs. 5, 6, 7, on next page (Georgia).—TRUD.,
    Journ. Phila. Acad. vii, 1837, 404 (young, with yellow on crown).—AUD., Orn.
    Biog. v, 1839, 194, pl. 417; Syn. 1839, 181; B. Am. iv, 1842, 259, pl. 265.—BP.,
    Comp. List, 1838, 39.—GRAY, Gen. of B. ii, 435.—BP., Consp. i, 1850, 138.—REICH.,
    Hand-buch, 363, pl. 632, fig. 4203.—MALH., Mon. Pic. i, 87, pl. 22, f. 4.
Trichopicus auduboni, BP., Consp. Vol. Zygod., Aten. Ital. 1854, 8.
Picus villosus var. *minor*, BD., B. N. A. 1858, 85.—SUND., Consp. Av. Pic. 1866, 16.
Picus villosus var. *auduboni*, B. B. & R., N. A. B. ii, 1874, 503.
Picus villosus, BRY., Pr. Bost. Soc. 1859 (Bahamas).—ALLEN, Bull. M. C. Z. ii, 1871, 302
    (Florida).
Picus cuvieri, MALH., Mon. Pic. i, 85, pl. 22, f. 3 (young female).

b. *harrisii*. (Wing-coverts scarcely or not spotted.)

a'. *majores*.

Picus harrisii, AUD., Orn. Biog. v, 1839, 191, pl. 417; Syn. 1839, 178; B. Am. iv, 1842,
    242, pl. 261 (smoky-bellied).—GRAY, Gen. of B. ii, 435.—NUTT., Man. i, 1840,
    627.—GAMB., Journ. Phila. Acad. i, 1847, 54.— BP., Consp. i, 1850, 138.—REICH.,
    Hand-buch Sp. Orn. 364, pl. 632, figs. 4308, 4209.—BD., B. N. A. 1858, 87.—LORD,
    Pr. Arty. Inst. iv, 111.—COOP. & SUCK., N. H. Wash. Ter. 1860, 159.—STEV.,
    U. S. Geol. Surv. Ter. 1870, 463.—MERR., *ibid*, 1872, 693.—MALH., Mon. Pic. i,
    73, pl. 20, f. 1, 2, 3.—SUND., Consp. Av. Pic. 1866, 17.
Trichopicus harrisii, BP., Consp. Vol. Zygod., Aten. Ital. 1854, 8.
Trichopipo harrisii, CAB., "Mus. Berol."
Dryobates harrisii, CAB. & HEINE, Mus. Hein. iv, 68.

b'. *medii*.

Picus harrisii, KENN., P. R. R. Rep. x, 1859, pt. iv, 21.—HEERM., *ibid*. pt. vi, 57.—COUES,
    Pr. Phila. Acad. 1866, 52.—COOP., B. Cal. i, 1870, 375.—AIKEN, Pr. Bost. Soc.
    1872, 206.
Picus villosus var. *harrisii*, ALLEN, Bull. M. C. Z. iii, 1872, 180.—COUES, Key, 1872, 194.—
    B. B. & R., N. A. B. ii, 1874, 507.
Picus hyloscopus, GRAY, Hand-list, ii, 1870, 185, No. 8604.
Dryobates hyloscopus, CAB. & HEINE, Mus. Hein. iv, 1863, 69.

c'. *minores*.

Picus jardinei, MALH., R. Z. 1845, 374; Mon. Pic. i, 103, pl. 25, f. 4, 5.—GRAY, Gen. of B.
    iii, App. p. 21; Hand-list, ii, 1870, 186, No. 8614.—BP., Consp. i, 1850, 137.— SCL.,
    P. Z. S. 1856, 308; 1857, 214; 1859, 367, 388; Cat. 1862, 334 (Xalapa).—SCL. &
    SALV., Ibis, 1859, 136.—CASS., Pr. Phila. Acad. 1863, 200.—SUND., Consp. Av.
    Pic. 1866, 17.
Phrenopicus jardinii, BP., Consp. Vol. Zygod., Aten. Ital. 1854, 8.
Trichopipo jardini, CAB. & HEINE, "Mus. Berol."
Dryobates jardinei, CAB. & HEINE, Mus. Hein. iv, 1863, 69.
Picus harrisii, CAB., J. f. O. 1862, 175.
'*Picus incarnatus*, LICHT.," "Mus. Berol." (*fide* CAB. = "*inornatus*," error, BP.).

Hab.—The entire wooded portions of North America—the typical form east of the
Rocky Mountains, reaching the Pacific, however, in Alaska. Var. *harrisii* from the
Rocky Mountains to the Pacific. Each variety grading in size according to latitude.
(England).

List of specimens (var. *harrisii*).

19179	250	Deer Creek	♀	Jan. 4, 1860	F. V. Hayden.	......	......	......	

Lieutenant Warren's Expedition.—4638, Sioux River; 5226, Powder River; 5227-28,
Fort Lookout. (Typical *villosus*).
Later Expeditions.—60360, 60802-3, Wyoming; 62260, Idaho (var. *harrisii*).
The very interesting parallel relations subsisting between different forms of this
species, as sketched in the foregoing synonymy, may be properly amplified.
We have first to note that typical *villosus*, of the Eastern United States, exhibits a
profusion of white spots on the wings, usually in six or seven pairs on the primaries,
with several pairs on all the secondaries, and one or more such spots on each of the
wing-coverts. In the other extreme, typical *harrisii*, there are fewer pairs (five or

six) on the primaries, and none on the inner secondaries and wing-coverts. The change begins in birds from the eastern slopes of the Rocky Mountains, and is effected by imperceptible degrees. Laying a few scores of specimens side by side, in linear series representing the change in longitude, one may see the spots disappear one by one, or by pairs, proving the complete intergradation of the two forms. This has been known to several ornithologists for some years, and hints to this effect have repeatedly been given; but, so far as I am aware, it was not formally recognized, by reduction of *harrisii* to a variety, until this was done simultaneously by Mr. Allen and myself.

We will next observe that the original of *Picus harrisii*, from the Columbia River, has the under parts of a peculiar smoky-gray tinge, with also more or less evident thin black stripes along the sides. This appears chiefly in specimens from Oregon and Washington Territories, and I think is something more than mechanical soiling of the feathers with carbonaceous matter from the trees, although this agent undoubtedly sometimes effects a like result. All my New Mexican and Arizonian specimens are as pure white below as in the eastern variety, and usually lack all traces of stripes along the sides.

Resting upon these facts respecting the distinctions between the eastern and western form, we will take up the remarkable variation in size that both exhibit in a perfectly parallel manner. Specimens of typical *villosus* occur ranging from 8 to 11 inches long; and this difference is found to depend upon latitude, size increasing *pari passu* with heightening of latitude, by insensible degrees. But there is nothing exceptional about this; on the contrary, it is merely a strong illustration of the prevailing rule with widely-distributed birds, the individuals of which are stationary or nearly so. With the maximum size of the northern birds there is associated an increase of whiteness, also in conformity with a general rule. These two particulars, size and hoariness, give the bird a peculiar aspect, so readily distinguishable that the *Picus "leucomelas"* or *"canadensis"* has passed for a species with many writers. But I see no necessity of recognizing it by even varietal name; if we did, we should also, to be consistent, separate the *Hylotomus pileatus* into races founded on size, the variation being fully as great in this case. The smaller size of the South Atlantic and Gulf States' *villosus* is recognizable, on an average, but is not so strongly marked; in coloration they are precisely the same as the ordinary bird of the Middle States.

In the West, the boreal extension of var. *harrisii* is cut off by the topography of that region, the westward trend of the mountains bringing the eastern zoological province to the very Pacific, and giving us var. *villosus* instead of *harrisii*. Consequently, typical var. *harrisii* is itself the largest form. It about equals ordinary *villosus* of the Middle States. The New Mexican and Southern Californian specimens are slightly smaller than those of Washington Territory, but not notably so, the chief distinction being the color of the under parts, as already noted (*hyloscopus, Cabanis*). But the Mexican extension of the species, as well as I can judge by descriptions, is strongly marked by its small size, being quite as much *under* the average as *P. "leucomelus"* is *over* the average. This is the *P. jardinei* of authors. The parallelism is thus seen to be complete; in the east, a series with a marked northern maximum of size and less conspicuous minimum; in the west, a marked southern minimum and less conspicuous northern maximum; in both cases, the variation directly and precisely according to latitude; while the intergradation of the two according to longitude is perfect.

It is too late to say much about the various nominal species established upon conditions of immaturity; they have already been satisfactorily disposed of. But, although so admirable and long-experienced a field-naturalist as Audubon might well be excused for proposing *harrisii* and *gairdneri*, at a time when climatic variation had no place in the conceptions of naturalists, it is incomprehensible that, after years of study in the field, and shooting perhaps hundreds of Hairy Woodpeckers, he should never have found out that the young males have more or less of the vertex red or yellow, instead of an occipital crescent of scarlet. This crown-patch is sometimes perfectly square, and bright yellow, almost exactly as in *Picoides;* but it is oftener diffuse, of a bronzy or coppery hue, mixed with white, &c. ~ *P. "phillipsii"* is the young of the northern race; *P. "martinæ"* may be so too, being from Canada, but the ascribed dimensions ("length, 9¼") are those of ordinary *villosus*, to which it may be as well to relegate it. *"Septentrionalis"* and *"rubricapillus"* of Nuttall are the same as *"phillipsii"* and *"martinæ,"* respectively. *"Picus auduboni"* is one of the curiosities of ornithological literature, inasmuch as Swainson and Trudeau, without the slightest reference to each other, each proposed the same name for the same bird in the same plumage, and not a valid species either.

This species moults the quills and tail-feathers very tardily; they persist with decreasing vitality, until just before they drop they are often found faded, toward their ends at least, into brownish-*white*.

This condition has crept into some of the published plates. Another individual peculiarity is, that the occipital scarlet band of the male is often discontinuous behind, being thus resolved into two supra-auricular spots, almost exactly as in *Picus querulus*. This may have induced Gray to put *jardinei* alongside *P. borealis* in the subgenus *Phren-*

opicus. Great as the variation of size is in this species, the minimum does not appear to inosculate with the maximum of *pubescens.* There is a constant gap between full-grown birds of about an inch (*P. gairdneri* being usually between seven and eight inches); and, besides, the white tail-feathers of *villosus,* as against the barred ones of *pubescens,* are perfectly distinctive.

In the Missouri region, *P. villosus* proper is the prevailing type; only mixing with or shading into the var. *harrisii* among the mountains. The birds are very abundant in the timbered bottoms along the Missouri, as at Fort Randall and elsewhere. My Randall examples are pure *villosus,* of rather large size, averaging 9¼ or 9½ long, 16 or 17 in extent, the wing 4¾ or 5. One was shot that had apparently broken its leg, and the union at a considerable angle threw the foot outward; notwithstanding this, the bird was scrambling as actively as any one could. This species is very noticeable among the few birds that endure the rigor of winter on the Upper Missouri, apparently without the slightest inconvenience. On entering the crackling, dry weed-patches of the bottom, at such times the ear is often saluted with the shrill, startling "*quank*" of the active bird, unseen in the low covert until, disturbed at its meal in the snug retreat, it takes a long, swift swing up into the nearest tree, or disappears in festoons further into the under-wood.

PICUS PUBESCENS, Linn.

Downy Woodpecker.

a. *pubescens.*

Picus pubescens, LINN., Syst. Nat. i, 1766, 175 (*P. varius minimus,* CATES., 21; *P. varius virginianus minor,* BRISS., Orn. iv, 50).—GM., i, 1788, 435.—LATH., Ind. Orn. i, 1790, 232.—VIEILL., Ois. Am. Sept. ii, 1807, 65, pl. 121.—WILS., Am. Orn. i, 1808, 153, pl. 9, f. 4.—STEPH., Gen. Zool. ix, 170.—VIEILL., Ency. iii, 1311; Nouv. Dict. xxvi, 82.—BP., Syn. 1828, 46.—LESS., Tr. Orn. 1831, 228.—NUTT., Man. i, 1832, 576.—AUD., Orn. Biog. ii, 1834, 81; v, 1839, 539; pl. 112; Syn. 1839, 180; B. Am. iv, 249, pl. 263.—BP., List, 1838, 39.—GRAY, Gen. of B. ii, 435.—BP., Consp. i, 1850, 138.—REICH., Hand-buch Sp. Orn. 374, pl. 638, fig. 4255-57.—BD., B. N. A. 1858, 89.—CASS., Pr. Phila. Acad. 1863, 201.—MALH., Mon. Pic. i, 119, pl. 29, f. 8, 9, 10.—SUND., Consp. Av. Pic. 1866, 17.—GRAY, Hand-list, ii, 1870, 184, No. 8590 (excl. syn. *auduboni,* SW.).—DALL & BANN., Tr. Chic. Acad. i, 1869, 274.—SNOW, B. Kans. 1873, 3.—HAYD., Rep. 1862, 155.—ALLEN, Bull. M. C. Z. ii, 1871, 304; iii, 1872, 180.—FINSCH, Abh. Nat. iii, 1872, 60 (Alaska).—COUES, Key, 1872, 194, fig. 131.—HART., Man. Br. Birds, 1872, 122 (England).—B. B. & R., N. A. B. ii, 1874, 509, pl. 49, f. 6, 7; and of authors generally.
Picus (Dendrocopus) pubescens, SW., F. B. A. ii, 1831, 307.
Trichopicus pubescens, BP., Consp. Vol. Zygod. Ateneo Ital. 1854, 8.
Trichopipo pubescens, CAB. & HEINE, "Mus. Berol."
Dryobates pubescens, CAB. & HEINE., Mus. Hein. iv, 1863, 62.
Picus (Dendrocopus) medianus, SW., F. B. A. ii, 1831, 308 (New Jersey).
Picus medianus, NUTT., Man. ii, 1834, 601.—GRAY, Gen. of B. ii, 435.—BP., Consp. i, 1850, 138.—REICH., Hand-buch Sp. Orn. 375.—MALH., Mon. Pic. i, 122.—GRAY, Hand-list, ii, 1870, 184, No. 8594.
Trichopicus medianus, BP., Consp. Vol. Zygod. 1854, 8.
Picus (Deudrocopus) meridionalis, SW., F. B. A. ii, 1831, 308 (Georgia).
Picus meridionalis, GRAY, Gen. of B. ii, 435.—BP., Consp. i, 1850, 138.—REICH., Hand-buch Sp. Orn. 375.—MALH., Mon. Pic. i, 124.—GRAY, Hand-list, ii, 184, No. 8505.
Trichopicus meridionalis, BP., Consp. Vol. Zygod. Ateneo Ital. 1854, 8.
Picus lecontei, JONES, Ann. Lyc. N. Y. iv, 1848, 489, pl. 17 (malformed specimen, lacking hallux).
Tridactylia (!) *lecontei,* BP., Consp. Zygod. 1854, 8 (made type of a genus!)
Picoides (!) *lecontei,* MALH., Mon. Pic. i, 132, pl. 40, f. 7.

b. *gairdneri.*

Picus gairdneri, AUD., Orn. Biog. v, 1839, 317; Syn. 1839, 180; B. Am. iv, 1842, 252.— REICH., Hand-buch Sp. Orn. 375.—MALH., Mon. Pic. i, 123.—BD., B. N. A. 1858, 91, pl. 85, fig. 2, 3.—HEERM., P. R. R. Rep. x, pt. vi, 57.—COOP. & SUCK., N. H. Wash. Ter. 1860, 159.—CASS., Pr. Phila. Acad. 1863, 201.—LORD, Pr. Roy. Arty.

Inst. iv, 1860, 111.—SUND., Consp. Av. Pic. 1866, 17.—COOP., B. Cal. i, 1870, 377.—AIKEN, Pr. Bost. Soc. 1872, 206.—STEV., U. S. Geol. Surv. Ter. 1870, 462.
Picus gardneri, GRAY, Gen. of B. ii, 435.
Picus gardineri, SCL., P. Z. S. 1857, 127.
Trichopicus gairdneri, BP., Consp. Vol. Zygod. Ateneo Ital. 1854, 8.
Dryobates gairdneri, CAB. & HEINE, Mus. Hein. iv, 1863, 64.
Picus (Dryobates) gardneri, GRAY, Hand-list, ii, 1870, 184, No. 8591.
Picus meridionalis, NUTT., Man. i, 1840, 690.—GAMB., Journ. Phila. Acad. i, 1847, 55.
Picus turati, MALH., Mon. Pic. i, 125, pl. 29, f. 5, 6.—CASS., Pr. Phila. Acad. 1863, 202.
Dryobates turatii, CAB. & HEINE, Mus. Hein. iv, 1863, 65.
Picus (Dryobates) turati, GRAY, Hand-list, ii, 1870, 185, No. 8597.
Picus homorus, " CAB. & HEINE, Mss."
Dryobates homorus, CAB. & HEINE, Mus. Hein. iv, 1863, 65.
Picus (Dryobates) homorus, GRAY, Hand-list, ii, 1870, 185, No. 8596.
Picus pubescens var. *gairdneri*, COUES, Key, 1872, 194.—B. B. & R., N. A. B. ii, 1874, 512.

Hab.—Entirely correspondent with that of *P. villosus*. (Accidental in England.)

List of specimens of var. *gairdneri*.

19180	168	Source Cheyenne	♂	Oct. 27, 1859	F. V. Hayden.	......	......	......

Lieutenant Warren's Expedition.—4639-40, Platte River; 4641, Bonhomme, Dakota (typical *pubescens*).
Later Expeditions.——60361, 61088-89, Wyoming (*gairdneri*).

This case of the Lesser Spotted Woodpecker is exactly parallel with that of the last species; it passes from *pubescens* to var. *gairdneri* in the same region, and both forms show a gradation of size and some minor changes, according to latitude. It is unnecessary, therefore, to enlarge upon the matter. There is no question of the pertinence of the various synonyms above enumerated.

Although the range of the two species is substantially the same, they being found together in most localities, yet, upon the whole, the Downy is rather more southern than the Hairy, at least in the matter of abundance of individuals. On the Atlantic coast, up to the Middle districts, the Downy is the more numerous. It is abundant about Washington, D. C., where the Hairy is comparatively rare. Mr. Allen says the same for Florida. In the Missouri region, throughout which both species are found in timbered places, the Hairy is the prevailing form. I was rather surprised to find, in Arizona, that the latter occurred to the almost entire exclusion of the other, which, in fact, I never identified there to my satisfaction. The habits of the species differ in no appreciable respect. Neither is there the slightest difference in the character of their plumage, as implied in the names " Downy" and " Hairy"— words that have only a quasi-application to these or any other Woodpeckers.

Such synonymical lists as may be prepared in this case and the preceding one, and countless other instances, do not reflect creditably upon a late state of our science—a state that we may hope soon to be able to call " late" in the same sense in which the word is used respecting defunct persons. The vagaries of nomenclature are exhibited in strong light by such an affair as the genus *Tridactylia*, based on a malformation, either congenital or merely accidental. I may remark, in this connection, that I once shot, at Washington, D. C., a specimen of *Colaptes auratus* showing the same thing, the right inner hind toe being wanting. It did not occur to me, however, to propose a genus *Tridactylocolaptes*, nor even to describe the bird as a new species of *Picoides*. Yet my knowledge of birds at that time was much more limited than either Bonaparte's or the monographer Malherbe's should be presumed to have been.

PICOIDES ARCTICUS, (Sw.) Gray.

Black-backed Three-toed Woodpecker.

"*Picus varius cayanensis*, ♀, BRISS., Orn. iv, 57 " (fide CAB.; nomen geogr. ineptum, lapsu ("canadensis"), sec. SUND.).
Picus tridactylus, BP., Am. Orn. iii, 1828, 243, pl. 14, f. 2; Syn. 1828, 46.—AUD., Orn. Biog. ii, 1834, 198; v, 1839, 538; pl. 132.—NUTT., Man. i, 1832, 578. (*Not of European writers.*)
Picus (Apternus) arcticus, Sw., F. B. A. ii, 1831, 313, pl. 57.
Picus arcticus, AUD., Syn. 1839, 182; B. Am. iv, 266, pl. 268.—NUTT., Man. i, 1840, 691.— PUTN., Pr. Ess. Inst. i, 1856, 214 (Massachusetts; very rare).—SUND., Consp. Av. Pic. 1866, 15.
Apternus arcticus, Sw., Classif. B. ii, 1837, 306.—BP., Consp. List, 1838, 39; Consp. Av. i, 1850, 139.—REICH., Hand-buch Sp. Orn. 36; pl. 630, f. 4189, 4191.—NEWB., P. R. R. Rep. vi, 1857, 91.
Picoides arcticus, GRAY, Gen. of B. ii, 434; pl. 108, fig. 7; Hand-list, ii, 1870, 181, No. 8539.—BD., B. N. A. 1858, 98.—MALH., Mon. Pic. i, 174, pl. 39, f. 5, 6.—BOARDM., Pr. Bost. Soc. ix, 1862, 123 (Maine; probably resident).—LORD, Pr. Roy. Arty. Inst. iv, 1864, 112 (Cascade Mountains).—VERR., Pr. Ess. Inst. iii, 144 (Norway, Me.; very common, except in summer).—ALLEN, Pr. Ess. Inst. iv, 1864, 52 (Massachusetts; very rare or accidental, in winter).—McILWR., *ibid.* v, 1866, 83 (Hamilton, C. W.; rare, in winter).—COUES, *ibid.* v, 1868, 262.— TURNB., B. E. Pa. 1869, 41 (occasional in mountains of Northern Pennsylvania, Pocono).—MAYN., Guide, 1870, 129 (Massachusetts, very rare); Pr. Bost. Soc. 1871, p. —.—COOP., Pr. Cal. Acad. 1868 (Lake Tahoe); B. Cal. i, 1870, 385 (Sierra Nevada of California).—TRIPPE, Pr. Ess. Inst. vi, 1871, 118 (?).—MERR., U. S. Geol. Surv. Ter. 1872, 694.—COUES, Key, 1872, 194.—B. B. & R., N. A. B. ii, 1874, 530, pl. 50, f. 1.
Tridactylia arctica, CAB. & HEINE, Mus. Hein. iv, 1863, 27.
"*Picus kochii*, NAUM.—GLOGER, Hand-buch Nat. Gesch. Vog. Eur. 462" (CAB.)

Hab.—Northern North America, into the Northern United States in winter, and in all probability resident along our northern frontier, as well as further south in mountainous regions. Rarely south in winter to Massachusetts; casually to Pennsylvania (*Audubon, Turnbull*). South to Sierra Nevada (*Cooper*).
Late Expeditions.—62261, Lower Geyser Basin, Wyoming.

Although this species has not, to my knowledge, been yet taken in the Missouri region, there is no doubt whatever of the propriety of including it in the present work, as a species to be found at least in the mountainous and northern portions. Mr. Trippe gives it as probably breeding in Minnesota, and Dr. Cooper has a more explicit notice. "I found this bird," he writes, "quite numerous about Lake Tahoe, and the summits of the Sierra Nevada above 6,000 feet altitude, in September, and it extends thence northward, chiefly on the east side of these and the Cascade Mountains, as I never saw it near the Lower Columbia. At the lake, they were quite fearless, coming close to the hotel, and industriously tapping the trees in the early morning and evening. * * I noticed their burrows in low pine-trees near the lake, where they had doubtless raised their young. I found them silent birds, though probably in the spring they have a great variety of calls. The only note I heard was a shrill, rattling cry, sufficiently distinct from that of any other Woodpecker."

PICOIDES AMERICANUS, Brehm.

Banded Three-toed Woodpecker.

a. *americanus.*

(? ?) "*Picus varius cayanensis*, ♂, BRISS., Orn. iv, 54" = *Pic tacheté de Cayenne*, P. E. 553 = *Apternus cayanensis*, REICH., Hand-buch, 363; nomen ineptum; avis fictita? Inde *P. undulatus*, VIEILL., Ois. Am. Sept. ii, 1807, 69; Enc. Meth. iii, 1319 ("digitibus quatuor") = *P. undatus*, TEMM., Tabl. Meth. 63, et *P. undosus*, CUV., R. A. i, 1829, 451.—(MALH., Mon. i, 184, 185).

Picus tridact *lus* var. *β.*, GM., Syst. Nat. i, 1788. 439.—LATH., Ind. Orn. i, 1790, 243.
Picus (*Apternus*) *tridactylus*, SW., F. B. A. ii, 1831, 311, pl. 56 (*nec Linn.*).
Picoides tridactylus var. *americanus*, B. B. & R., N. A. B. ii, 1874, pl. 50, f. 2.
Tridactylia undulata, STEPH., Gen. Zool. ix, 220.—CAB. & HEINE, Mus. Hein. iv, 1863, 28.
Picus hirsutus, WAGL., Syst. Av. 1827, Gen. Pic. No. 102 (*nec* STEPH., G. Z. ix, 219, pl. 38; *nec* VIEILL., Ois. Am. Sept. ii, 1807, 68, pl. 124; Enc. iii, 1324; Nouv. Dict. xxvi, 103, qui sp. Amer. refert, sed spec. Europ. descripsit).—AUD., Orn. Biog. v, 1839, 184, pl. 217, f. 3, 4; Syn. 1839, 183; B. Am. iv, 1842, 268, pl. 269.—NUTT., Man. i, 1840, 622.—PUTN., Pr. Ess. Inst. i, 1856, 229.
Apternus hirsutus, BP., List, 1838, 39; Consp. Av. i, 1850, 139.—REICH., Hand-buch, 361, pl. 630, f. 4192, 4194.—FINSCH, Abh. Nat. iii, 1872, 61 (Alaska).
Picoides hirsutus, GRAY, Gen. of B. ii, 434.—BD., B. N. A. 1858, 98.—VERR., Pr. Ess. Inst. iii. 157 (Maine, in winter).—COUES, *ibid.* v, 1868, 262 (straggling to Massachusetts).—ALLEN, Am. Nat. iii, 1870, 572 (Lynn, Mass.).—MAYN., Guide, 1870, 129 (same instance).
Picoides americanus, BREHM, Vog. Deutschl. 1831, 195; "Vollst. Vogelf. 71."—MALH., Mon. Pic. i, 176, pl. 39, f. 1, 2.—SCL., Cat. 1862, 335.—GRAY, Cat. Brit. Mus. iii, 1868, 30.—DALL & BANN., Tr. Chic. Acad. i, 1869, 274.—GRAY, Hand-list, ii, 1870, 181, No. 8537.—COUES, Key, 1872, 194.
Picoides americanus var. *fasciatus*, BD., in Coop. B. Cal. i, 1870, 385.
Apternus americanus, SW., Classif. B. ii, 1837, 306.
Picus americanus, SUND., Consp. Av. Pic. 1866, 15.
Picus arcticus, DEKAY, N. Y. Zool. 1844, 190, pl. 17, f. 36 (*nec* SW.).

b. dorsalis.

Picoides dorsalis, BD., B. N. A. 1858, 100, pl. 85, f. 1.—MALH., Mon. Pic. i, 179.—HAYD., Rep. 1862, 155 (type specimen).—MERR., U. S. Geol. Surv. Ter. 1872, 694.
Tridactylia dorsalis, CAB. & HEINE, Mus. Hein. iv, 1863, 26.
Picus dorsalis, SUND., Consp. Av. Pic. 1866, 14.
Picoides americanus var. *dorsalis*, BD., in Coop. B. Cal. i, 1870, 386.—ALLEN, Bull. M. C. Z. iii, 1872, 180 (mountains of Colorado, from 8,000 feet up to timber-line).—COUES, Key, 1872, 194.

Hab.—The typical form in Arctic and Northern North America, straggling into the United States in winter, to Massachusetts. Var. *dorsalis* from the Rocky Mountain region as far south as Colorado.
Lieutenant Warren's Expedition.—8809, Laramie Peak, ♂, Aug. 25, 1857; type of *dorsalis.*
Later Expeditions.—62262, Lower Geyser Basin, Wyoming.

As observed by Sundevall, and afterward by Baird, our three species of *Picoides* chiefly differ in the amount of white on the back, from none in *arcticus*, to a long continuous white stripe in var. *dorsalis*, much as in *P. villosus.* But although it may be only a step from the darkest-backed *hirsutus* to *arcticus*, I am not aware that the step is ever actually taken by intermediate specimens, and I therefore retain the species as distinct. Between *americanus* and var. *dorsalis*, on the contrary, the intergradation is complete. The character of *dorsalis* lies in the disappearance of the one or more transverse black bars on each white feather of the back, leaving an uninterrupted white stripe—the successive steps toward this end being as clearly traceable as are those of the changes in the white spots of *P. villosus* and *pubescens.* Sundevall showed that the name *hirsutus*, of Vieillot, usually applied to this species, was based upon the European bird, although ascribed to North America; and that the *P. undulatus* of the same author, probably a fictitious species, is based upon P. E. 533, said to be from "Cayenne," to have *four* toes, and to be otherwise entirely incompatible with the present species.

The Banded Three-toed Woodpecker is very rare in the United States—apparently more so than *P. arcticus.* I have not learned of its occurrence further south than Massachusetts, where Mr. Welch lately took specimens at Lynn. The dorsal variety, on the other hand, is a common bird of the Rocky Mountain region, especially about Laramie, and to judge from the dates of observation of the specimens secured, it is undoubtedly there resident. Dr. Hayden's specimen, above quoted, furnished the type of the description of *P. dorsalis.*

SPHYRAPICUS VARIUS, (Linn.) Bd.

Yellow-bellied Woodpecker.

a. varius.

Picus varius, LINN., Syst. Nat. i, 1766, 176 (*P. varius minor, ventre luteo*, CATES., i, 21; *varius carolinus*, BRISS., iv, 62; P. E. 785).—GM., i, 438.—LATH., Ind. Orn. i, *P.* 232.—VIEILL., Ois. Am. Sept. ii, 1807, 63, pls. 118, 119.—WILS., Am. Orn. i, 1808,

147, pl. 9, f. 2.—BP., Am. Orn. i, pl. 8, f. 2 ; Syn. 1828, 45 ; List, 1838, 39 ; Consp. i, 1850, 138.—WAGL., Syst. Av. 1827, No. 16 ; Isis, 1829, 509.—NUTT., Man. i, 1832, 574.—LESS., Tr. Orn. i, 1831, 228.—AUD., Orn. Biog. ii, 1834, 519 ; v, 1839, 537 ; pl. 190 ; Syn. 1839, 182 ; B. Am. iv, 1842, 263, pl. 267.—GRAY, Gen. of B. ii, 435.— REICH., Handbuch Sp. Orn. 376, pl. 639, f. 4258, 4259 ; J. f. O. 1856, 102.— MAXIM., J. f. O. vi, 1858, 416.—SCL., P. Z. S. 1856, 308 ; 1858, 305 ; 1859, 367, 388.—REINH., Ibis, iii, 1861, 8 (Greenland ; two instances).—SUND., Consp. Av. Pic. 1866, 33.

Picus (Dendrocopus) varius, SW. & RICH., F. B. A. ii, 1831, 309.
Pilumnus varius, BP., Consp. Vol. Zygod. Ateneo. Ital. 1854, 8.
Sphyrapicus varius, BD , B. N. A. 1858, 103.—MALH., Mon. Pic. i, 157, pl. 37, figs. 2, 4.— COUES, Key, 1872, 195, f. 131.—SNOW, B. Kans. 1873, 3.—BRY., Pr. Bost. Soc. x, 1865, 91 (anatomy) ; and of most late authors.
Sphyropicus varius, SCL. & SALV., Ibis, 1859, 136 (Guatemala).—SCL., Cat. 1862, 335 (Orizaba).—B. B. & R., N. A. B. ii, 1874, 539, pl. 51, f. 1, 2.
Cladoscopus varius, CAB. & HEINE, Mus. Hein. iv, 1863, 80.
Picus (Sphyrapicus) varius, GRAY, Hand-list, ii, 1870, 186, No. 8617.
Picus atrothorax, LESS., Traité Orn. i, 1831, 229.—PUCH., R. M. Z. vii, 1855, 21.
" *Picus galbula*, TEMM., Mus. Lugd."—MALH., Mon. Pic. i, 157.

b. *nuchalis.*

Sphyrapicus varius var. *nuchalis*, BD., B. N. A. 1858, 103 (in text.).—MALH., Mon. Pic. i, 161.—ALLEN, Bull. M. C. Z. iii, 1872, 180.—COUES, Key, 1872, 195.
Sphyropicus varius var. *nuchalis*, RIDGW., Am. Journ. Sci. 1873, 40.—B. B. & R., N. A. B. ii, 1874, 542, pl. 51, f. 3. 4.
Sphyrapicus nuchalis, BD., B. N. A. 1858, 921, pl. 35.—COUES, Pr. Phila. Acad. 1866, 53 (anatomy, &c.).—STEV., U. S. Geol. Surv. Ter. 1870, 463.
Sphyropicus nuchalis, COOP., B. Cal. i, 1870, 390.
Cladoscopus nuchalis, CAB. & HEINE, Mus. Hein. iv, 1863, 82.
Picus varius, HEERM., P. R. R. Rep. x, 1859, pt. vi, 58.
Sphyrapicus varius, HAYD., Rep. 1862, 155.—HOLD., Pr. Bost. Soc. 1872, 207.
Picus varius occidentalis, SUND., Consp. Av. Pic. 1866, 34.

c. *ruber.*

Picus ruber, GM., Syst. Nat. i, 1788, 429.—LATH., Ind. Orn. i, 1790, 228.—STEPH., Gen. Zool. ix, 160.—WAGL., Syst. Av. 1827, P. No. 15.—AUD., Orn. Biog. v, 1839, 179, pl. 416 ; Syn. 1839, 181 ; B. Am. iv, 1844, 261, pl. 266.—HEERM., P. R. R. Rep. x, 1859, pt. vi, 57.—MALH., Mon. Pic. i, 132, pl. 31, figs. 1, 2.—SUND., Consp. Av. Pic. 1866, 32.
Picus (Sphyrapicus) ruber, GRAY, Hand-list, ii, 1870, 186, No. 8616.
Melanerpes ruber, RICH., List, 1837.—BP., List, 1838, 39 ; Consp. i, 1850, 115.—GRAY, Gen. of B. ii, 444.—GAMB., Journ. Phila. Acad. 1844, 56.—REICH., Hand-buch Sp. Orn. 382, pl. 642, f. 4287, 4288.—SCL., P. Z. S. 1857, 127.
Pilumnus ruber, BP., Consp. Vol. Zygod. Ateneo Ital. 1854, 8.
Sphyrapicus ruber, BD., B. N. A. 1858, 104.—COOP. & SUCK., N. H. Wash. Ter. 1860, 160.— COUES, Key, 1872, 195.
Sphyropicus ruber, COOP., B. Cal. i, 1870, 392.
Cladoscopus ruber, CAB. & HEINE, Mus. Hein. iv, 1863, 82.
Sphyropicus varius var. *ruber*, RIDGW., Am. Journ. Sci. iv, 1873, 40.—B. B. & R., N. A. B. ii, 1874, 544, pl. 51 fig. 6.
Picus flaviventris, VIEILL., Ois. Am. Sept. ii, 1807, 67 ; Nouv. Dict. xxv, 95 ; Enc. iii, 1320.
" *Picus niger*, VIEILL., Nouv. Dict. xxvi, 90."

Hab.—The typical form in Eastern North America, north to 61° at least. South to Guatemala (numerous extralimital quotations). Mexico. Cuba. Bahamas. Green- land. Var. *nuchalis* from the Rocky Mountain region and Great Basin. Var. *ruber* from Cascade Mountains and Sierra Nevada to the Pacific.

List of specimens (nuchalis).

19181	33	Wind River Mts.	♂	May 28, 1860	F. V. Hayden.	8.00	14 50	5.00
19182	74	......do......	♂	June 6, 1860	......do.....	7.50	15.00	5.00
19183	25	......do......	♂	May 26, 1860	......do.....	7.75	15.00	4.75
19184	28	......do......	♂	May 27, 1860	......do.....	7.75	15.50	5.00
19185	....	Popoagie Creek.	♂	May 25, 1860	G. H. Trook..	8.25	17.00	5.25

Lieutenant Warren's Expedition.—(*varius* and *nuchalis*); 4631–33, Big Sioux River; 4635, mouth of Platte River ; 4636–37, near Council Bluffs ; 8807, Laramie.
Later Expeditions.—60804–05, 61090–92, 61095, Wyoming.

Probably no genus of the *Picidæ* is more strongly marked than this one. Without very striking external peculiarities, the structure of the tongue and associate parts is remarkably different from that obtaining in any of the North American species at least, and may justly claim higher taxonomic value than that subsisting among any of the details of contour of our remaining species. The peculiarities are fully set forth in my paper above cited. Assertions of misinformed authors to the contrary notwithstanding, the *S. "williamsoni"* or *thyroideus* is a typical *Sphyrapicus*, as I determined by examination of the hyoid apparatus in freshly-killed specimens. The regimen of both species, correspondently with their anatomical features, is peculiar; they denude trees of their bark in areas, instead of drilling holes, and feed extensively upon soft sap-wood, as well as upon various fruits and insects.

I intimated a suspicion of the specific identity of *S. ruber* and *varius* in the Key, as above cited. I had not, at the moment of writing, specimens enough to satisfy myself of the complete intergradation of the two forms, through var. *nuchalis*, which is simply the first step toward var. *ruber*. But this has been satisfactorily determined by Mr. Ridgway. His remarks are so pertinent that I will transcribe them, in giving them my unreserved endorsement:

"This tendency to an extension of red, as we approach the Pacific coast, is strictly paralleled in the case of *Sphyrapicus varius*. Taking specimens of this species from the Atlantic States (typical *S. varius*), it is noticed that in the male the red patch on the throat is entirely cut off from the white rictal stripe by a continuous maxillary stripe of black, while the nuchal band is brownish-white; and that the ♀ has the throat entirely white. Not more than one per cent. have a tinge of red on the nape in the male, or a trace of it on the throat in the female. In specimens from the Rocky Mountains (var. *nuchalis*) we find that *all* have the nuchal band more or less red, while the female invariably has the throat at least one-third of this color; the male, too, has the black maxillary stripe interrupted, allowing the red of the gular patch to touch, for quite a distance, the white stripe beneath the eye, while it invades, for a greater or less extent, the black pectoral crescent. Another step is seen in specimens from the region between the Rocky Mountains and the Cascade Range, in which the red is extended still more; first, the black auricular stripe has a few touches of red, the black pectoral crescent is mixed with red feathers, and the light area surrounding it (sulphur-yellow in the more eastern styles) is more or less tinged with red. Then, as we continue westward, the red increases, until, in specimens from the coast region of California, Oregon, Washington Territory, and British Columbia (var. *ruber*), it overspreads the whole head, neck and breast, in extreme examples entirely obliterating the normal pattern, though usually this can be distinctly traced. With this increase in the extent of red there is also a gradually increased amount of black, strictly parallel to that in *Picus villosus* (var *harrisii*) and *P. pubescens* (var. *gairdneri*) from the same regions."

The Yellow-bellied Woodpecker is common in the wooded bottoms of the Missouri region. Kansas and other eastward examples are pure *varius*, but most incline toward var *nuchalis*, which becomes completely established on the first slopes of the mountains. I found *varius* breeding commonly along the Red River of the North.

SPHYRAPICUS THYROIDEUS, (Cass.) Bd.

Black-breasted or Williamson's Woodpecker.

Picus thyroideus, CASS., Pr. Phila. Acad. v, 1851, 349 (♀).—HEERM., Journ. Phila. Acad. ii, 1853, 270.—SUND., Consp. Av. Pic. 1866, 32.
Picus (Sphyrapicus) thyroideus, GRAY, Hand-list, ii, 1870, 186, No. 8618.
Melanerpes thyroideus, CASS., Ill. B. Cal. and Tex. 1854, 201, pl. 32.
Pilumnus thyroideus, BP., Consp. Vol. Zygod. 1854, 8.
Colaptes thyreoideus, REICH., Hand-buch Sp. Orn. 411.
Sphyrapicus thyroideus, BD., B. N. A. 1858, 106.—HAYD., Rep. 1862, 155.—COUES, Pr. Phila. Acad. 1866, 54.—MALH., Mon. Pic. i, 162, pl. 37, f. 2.—COOP., B. Cal. i, 1870, 394.—MERR., U. S. Geol. Surv. Ter. 1872, 694.—COUES, Key, 1872, 195.— HENSH., Am. Nat. viii, 1874, 242.
Sphyropicus thyroideus, B. B. & R., N. A. B. ii. 1874, 547, pl. 56, fig. 6.
Cladoscopus thyroideus, CAB. & HEINE, Mus. Hein. iv, 1863, 84.
" *Picus nataliæ*, MALH., J. f. O. 1854, 171."
" *Centurus nataliæ*, REICH., Hand-buch Sp. Orn. 411."
Picus williamsoni, NEWB., P. R. R. Rep. vi, 1857, 89, pl. 34, f. 1 (♂).—SUND., Consp. Av. Pic. 1866, 32.
Sphyrapicus williamsoni, BD., B. N. A. 1858, 105.—HAYD., Rep. 1862, 155.—MALH., Mon. Pic. i, 163, pl. 36, f. 4.—COUES, Pr. Phila. Acad. 1866, 54.—COOP., B. Cal. i, 1870, 393.—ALLEN, Bull. M. C. Z. iii, 1872, 180.—MERR., U. S. Geol. Surv. Ter. 1872, 694.—COUES, Key, 1872, 195.
Sphyropicus williamsoni, B. B. & R., N. A. B. ii, 1874, 545, pl. 51, fig. 5.
Cladoscopus williamsoni, CAB. & HEINE, Mus. Hein. iv, 1863, 82.
Melanerpes (Cladoscopus) williamsoni, GRAY, Hand-list, ii, 1870, 201, No. 8820.
Melanerpes rubrigularis, SCL., P. Z. S. 1858, i, pl. 131 ; Ann. Mag. Nat. Hist. 1858, 127 (♂).

Hab.—Rocky Mountains to the Pacific, United States.
Lieutenant Warren's Expedition.—8803-04, Laramie Peak, August 24, 1857.
Later Expeditions.—62363 (♂), Wyoming ; 62259 (*iuvenis*), Montana.

The foregoing synonymy will doubtless be viewed with surprise by those not previously aware of Mr. Henshaw's discovery that "*williamsoni*" is the male and "*thyroideus*" the female, of one and the same species. No point in our ornithology could have been more novel and unexpected than was Mr. Henshaw's announcement of the fact, which he determined beyond reasonable question, that he found the two supposed species paired and rearing a family in the same hole. It is not uninstructive now to look back upon the history of the supposed species. In the first place we notice that the two have always been accredited with the same geographical range, and have generally been found together; at least, most papers containing a notice of one, also give the other. Next we observe, in most cases, hesitation and evident uncertainty in descriptions of the sexual differences of each supposed species, the female of "*williamsoni*" and the male of "*thyroideus*" having been groped for indeed, but not found. Nor is there, in the fairly large amount of material received at the Smithsonian, an unquestionable specimen of the opposite sex of either of the supposed species. As indicating how far we may sometimes go astray, these birds have been placed in several different genera, so widely have the sexes of one species been dissociated ; while the biographical notices which have appeared are not entirely concordant, showing how much our written history of living birds may be tempered by evidently fortuitous circumstances of observation, or transient impressions of an observer.

On the systematic position of the species there is no room for question. Prof. Baird correctly assigned it to the genus *Sphyrapicus*, of which it is a typical representative, having all the strong lingual peculiarities of *S. varius*, as I showed in my paper above cited.

I frequently observed this Woodpecker in the pineries about Fort Whipple, where it is resident and not uncommon, though less abundant than either the *Melanerpes formicivorus* or *Colaptes mexicanus*. It appeared to be nearly confined to the pine woods, and proved rather a wary bird, frequenting for the most part the upper portions of the tall trees. It has an abrupt, explosive outcry, much like that of other species of Woodpeckers, and also an entirely different call-note. This sounds to me like a number of rolling *r*'s, beginning with a guttural *k*—*k'-r-r-r*—each set of *r*'s making a long syllable. This note is leisurely given, and indefinitely repeated, in a very low key. The general habits of this species are most nearly like those of *S. varius*, but its geographical distribution is much more restricted, and the bird is not, apparently, migratory. It is an inhabitant more especially of mountainous regions of the west, within the pine belt—the same faunal area of which *Picicorvus* and *Gymnokitta* are characteristic.

Mr. Trippe writes me as follows of Williamson's Woodpecker in Colorado: "Common; migratory; breeds. This Woodpecker arrives in the neighborhood of Idaho Springs in the early or middle part of April, and soon becomes rather common, extending its range up to 10,000 feet, and perhaps higher, but is most numerous between 6,000 and 9,000 feet. It is rather unequal in its distribution, being abundant in certain localities and quite scarce in others, but a short distance away."

CENTURUS CAROLINUS, (Linn.) Sw.

Red-bellied Woodpecker.

Picus carolinus, LINN., Syst. Nat., 1766, 174 (*P. ventre rubro*, CATES., i, 19).—WILS., Am. Orn. i, 1808, 113, pl. 7, fig. 2.—BP., Syn. 1828, 45.—NUTT., Man. i, 572.—AUD., Orn. Biog. v, 1839, 169, pl. 415; Syn. 1839, 183; B. Am. iv, 1842, 270, pl. 270.— GIR., B. L. I. 1844, 179.—MAXIM., J. f. O. 1858, 418.—SUND., Consp. Av. Pic. 53.
Centurus carolinus, SW., Class. B. ii, 1837, 310 ("*carolinensis*").—BP., List, 1838, 40 ; Consp. i, 1850, 119.—WOODH., Sitgr. Rep. 1853, 91.—BD., B. N. A. 1858, 109.—HAYD., Rep. 1862, 156.—CAB., J. f. O. 1862, 324.—DRESS., Ibis, 1865, 469 (Texas).— ALLEN, Pr. Ess. Inst. iv, 1864, 53 (Massachusetts, "accidental").—COUES, *ibid.* v, 1868, 262 (rare or accidental in Southern New England).—MCILWR., *ibid.* v, 1866, 83 (Chatham, C. W., three specimens).—ALLEN, Mem. Bost. Soc. i, 1868, 499, 519, 525 (Iowa, Illinois, and Indiana).—ALLEN, Bull. M. C. Z. ii, 1871, 306 (Florida); iii, 1872, 180 (Kansas).—SNOW, B. Kans. 1873, 3 (abundant).—COUES, Key, 1872, 196.—B. B. & R., N. A. B. ii, 1874, 554, pl. 52, fig. 1, 4.
Zebrapicus carolinus, MALH., Mon. Pic. ii, 234, pl. 103, figs. 7, 8.
Picus zebra, BODD., Planch. Enlum. 602.
Picus griseus, VIEILL., Ois. Am. Sept. ii, 1807, 52, pl. 116.
"*Picus erythrauchen*, WAGL., Syst. Av. 1827."

Hab.—United States to the Rocky Mountains. North rarely to Southern New England ("Nova Scotia," *Audubon*). Canada West. Not found in Minnesota (*Trippe*). Fort Thorn, New Mexico (*Henry*).

Lieutenant Warren's Expedition.—4653, St. Joseph's, Mo.; 4624, Nemaha Reserve.

This is a rather southern species, very abundant south of 35°, but not common north of the Middle districts. It very rarely extends into New England, whence we have but few quotations, and none north of Massachusetts. Audubon, indeed, gives it from Nova Scotia, but such a range has not, to my knowledge, been confirmed of late. Mr. McIlwraith notes three specimens captured in Canada West. I used to find it frequently about Washington. Mr. Trippe remarks upon its apparent absence in Minnesota with surprise, since "during the winter it is exceedingly abundant in Southern Iowa, from which section great numbers migrate on the approach of spring. I supposed that it crossed over the prairies of Iowa and the southern part of Minnesota, and passed the breeding season in the woods of the northern part of the latter State. I found this to be a mistake, however, as I did not see a single individual during the whole year." In Kansas it is plentiful; I found it in May in the timber along Republican River. It must, however, be considered a rare bird in most portions of the Missouri region.

MELANERPES ERYTHROCEPHALUS, (Linn.) Sw.

Red-headed Woodpecker.

Picus erythrocephalus, LINN., Syst. Nat. i, 1766, 174 (CATES., i, 20 ; BRISS., iv, 53, pl. 3, fig. 1; Planch. Enlum. 117).—VIEILL., Ois. Am. Sept. ii, 1807, 60, pls. 112, 113.—WILS., Am. Orn. i, 1808, 142, pl. 9, fig. 1.—BP., Syn. 1828, 45.—WAGL., Isis, 1829, 518.—NUTT., Man. i, 1832, p.—AUD., Orn. Biog. i, 1832, 141, pl. 27 ; Syn. 1839, 184; B. Am. iv, 1842, 274, pl. 271.—GIR., B. L. I. 1844, 180.—MAXIM., J. f. O. 1858, 419.—PUTN., Pr. Ess. Inst. i, 1856, 214 (Massachusetts, rare).—TRIPPE, *ibid.* vi, 1871, 118 (Minnesota, abundant).—SUND., Consp. Av. Pic. 1866, 50.
Melanerpes erythrocephalus, Sw., F. B. A. ii, 1831, 316 (Lake Huron).—BP., List, 1838, 40 ; Consp. i, 1850, 115.—GAMB., Journ. Phila. Acad. 1847, 55.—WOODH., Sitgr. Rep. 1853, 91.—BD., B. N. A. 1858, 113.—HAYD., Rep. 1862, 156.—VERR., Pr. Ess. Inst. iii, 1862, 145 (Maine, rare).—ALLEN, *ibid.* iv, 1864, 53 (Massachusetts, rare).—McILWR., *ibid.* v, 1866, 83 (Canada West, common).—COUES, *ibid.* v, 1868, 263 (New England, rare).—DRESS., Ibis, 1865, 469 (Texas).—COOP., B. Cal. i, 1870, 402.—STEV., U. S. Geol. Surv. Ter. 1870, 463 (Wyoming).—SNOW, B. Kans. 1873, 3.—ALLEN, Bull. M. C. Z. iii, 1872, 180 (Kansas and Colorado).—HOLD., Pr. Bost. Soc. 1872, 207 (Wyoming).—COUES, Key, 1872, 196.—B. B. & R., N. A. B. ii, 1874, 564, pl. 54, fig. 4.
Picus obscurus, GM., Syst. Nat. i, 1788, 429 (juvenile).

Hab.—Temperate Eastern North America to the Rocky Mountains. Not authenticated on the Pacific Coast? Now rare in New England. Breeds from Texas to Nova Scotia. Utah (*Ridgway*). California (*Gambel*).
Lieutenant Warren's Expedition.—4625-30, Nemaha River; 5230-31, Yellowstone River; 5529, Fort Lookout; 8808, Frémont, on Platte River.
Later Expeditions.—60348-54 Bitter Cottonwood and La Bonté Creeks.

From time to time we have had accounts of the supposed occurrence of this species on the Pacific coast, and elsewhere west of the Rocky Mountains. Thus, Richardson mentions a specimen said to have come from the Columbia River; Gambel gives it from the coast of California; Cooper includes it in his work, as in many other cases, upon supposition of its occurrence in California, "as it extends to the Rocky Mountains and perhaps over them." None of these records are satisfactory, however; the most western ones upon which full reliance can be placed being those from the headwaters of the Missouri and its tributaries, and from Salt Lake City. Of these there is no question. Dr. Hayden speaks of the species as one of the most abundant birds along the wooded bottoms of the Missouri. Mr. Holden and Mr. Stevenson found it in Wyoming, and Mr. Allen in Colorado, from the plains up to about 11,000 feet. Mr. Trippe, also, found it common in Bergen's Pass.

The Woodpeckers, as a rule, are non-migratory birds, owing to their hardy nature, and the character of their food, which can be obtained at all times. Most of our species are pretty thoroughly localized; such are all those of Southern portions, as the Ivory-bill and Red-cockaded in the East, the *Melanerpes formicivorus* in the West, &c., as well as the robust species of *Picus* proper, *Picoides*, and *Sphyrapicus*. But even some of these journey with the season, and others, notably the Red-bellied, the Golden-winged, and the present species, are migrants in most regions—perhaps irregularly so, indeed, but still not entirely stationary. Taking an intermediate locality, as the District of Columbia, for instance, we find the Red-bellied and the Flicker there the whole year; but both of these are partially migratory, the former being most abundant in summer, while the latter is so during the spring and fall, most individuals going further north to breed and further south to winter. The Red-head is more decidedly migratory, and most abundant in summer. I never found it between October and April. This corresponds with Dr. Turnbull's observations, made in Pennsylvania and New Jersey, where, he says, it arrives the latter part of April and departs in September or the beginning of October. That even this species, however, sometimes lingers through the winter in Pennsylvania is shown by Prof. Baird's record of Carlisle specimens, among which are observed captures in December and February. I do not think that any Red-heads endure the severe winters of the Upper Missouri, *P. villosus* and *pubescens* being the only species I have observed in Dakota at this season.

ASYNDESMUS TORQUATUS, (Wils.) Coues.

Lewis's Woodpecker.

Picus torquatus, WILS., Am. Orn. iii, 1811, 31, pl. 20, fig. 3.—BP., Syn. 1828, 46.—NUTT., Man. i, 1832, 577.—AUD., Orn. Biog. v, 176, pl. 416; Syn. 1839, 184; B. Am. iv, 1842, 280, pl. 272.—SUND., Consp. Av. Pic. 1866, 51.
Melanerpes torquatus, BP., Consp. Av. i, 1850, 115.—HEERM., Journ. Phila. Acad. ii, 1853, 270.—NEWB., P. R. R. Rep. vi, 1857, 90.—BD., B. N. A. 1858, 115.—HEERM., P. R. R. Rep. x, 1859, pt. vi, 58.—COOP. & SUCK., N. H. Wash. Ter. 1860, 161.—HAYD., Rep. 1862, 156.—COOP., B. Cal. i, 1870, 406.—ALLEN, Bull. M. C. Z. iii, 1872, 180.— AIKEN, Pr. Bost. Soc. 1872, 207.—STEV., U. S. Geol. Surv. Ter. 1870, 463.—MERR., *ibid.* 1872, 695.—B. B. & R., N. A. B. ii, 1874, 561, pl. 54, fig. 5.
Celeus torquatus, WOODH., Sitgr. Rep. 1853, 90 (excl. syn. *Gm., Less., Wagl.*)
Asyndesmus torquatus, COUES, Pr. Phila. Acad. 1866, 56.—COUES, Key, 1872, 197.
Melanerpes (Asyndesmus) torquatus, GRAY, Hand-list, ii, 1870, 201, No. 8818.
Picus montanus, ORD, Guthrie's Geog. 2d Am. ed. 1815, 316.
" *Picus lewisii*, DRAPIEZ." (*fide G. R. Gray*).

Hab.—Eastern slopes and foot-hills of the Rocky Mountains to the Pacific, United States.

List of specimens.

19185	82	Snake River ...	♀	June 17, 1860	F. V. Hayden	11.50	22.00	6.75
19186	10	Wind R. Mts...	♂	May 26, 1860	......do......	11.75	22.00	6.75
19331	....	Yellowstone R ..	....	June 23, 1860	G. H. Trook..	11.00	22.00	6.50
19332	....	Bighorn Mts...	♂	June 15, 1860	......do......	11.50	22.00	6.50
19333	....	.... do	....	June 20, 1860	......do......	11.00	21.50	6.00
19334	....	.... do	....	June 20, 1860	......do......	11.00	21.50	6.00

Lieutenant Warren's Expedition.—No. 4668, Cheyenne River; 8810-15, Laramie Peak. *Later Expeditions.*—59844-46, Colorado; 54303, 60355, Wyoming, 62274-76, Idaho.

The plumage of this remarkable Woodpecker is peculiar, both in texture and color; no other species of our country shows such a rich metallic iridescence, or such intense crimson, and in none is the plumage so curiously modified into a bristly character. Unlike most species, again, the sexes are not certainly distinguishable. The young, however, differ very materially, the under parts being dull gray, only here and there slashed with red, the face lacking the crimson velvety pilous area, and the upper parts being much less lustrous.

This fine species, like *Sphyrapicus thyroideus*, is chiefly a bird of the vast forests that clothe most of our mountain ranges with permanent verdure. With this limitation its distribution is extensive, as noted above. My own experience with the bird in life is confined to the vicinity of Fort Whipple, in Arizona, where it is a very common species. A bird of singular aspect, many of its habits are no less peculiar. One seeing it for the first time would hardly take it for a Woodpecker, unless he happened to observe it clambering over the trunk of a tree, or tapping for insects, in the manner peculiar to its tribe. When flying, the large, dark bird might rather be mistaken for a Crow Blackbird; for, although it sometimes swings itself from one tree to another, in a long festoon, like other Woodpeckers, its ordinary flight is more firm and direct, and accomplished with regular wing-beats. It alights on boughs, in the attitude of ordinary birds, more frequently than any of our other species, excepting the *Colaptes*, and, with the same exception, taps trees less frequently than any. It may often be seen circling high in the air, around the tree-tops, apparently engaged in capturing passing winged insects; and, as it is particularly gregarious—let me say, of a sociable disposition—many are sometimes thus occupied together in airy evolutions about the withered head of some ancient woodland monarch falling to decay. At the sight, as the birds passed and repassed each other in vigorous flight, while the sheen of their dark-green plumage flashed in the sunbeams, I could not help fancying them busy weaving a laurel-wreath fitting to crown the last days of the majestic pine that had done valorous battle with the elements for a century, and was soon to mingle its mould with the dust whence it sprang.

Unlike its gay, rollicking associates, the Californian Woodpeckers, Lewis' is a shy and wary bird, not easily destroyed. In passing from one part of the forest to another, it prefers, apparently through cautiousness, to pass high over the tops of the trees rather than to thread its way through their mazes. It generally alights high up, and procures its food at the same elevation. I do not remember to have ever seen one descend among bushes, still less to the ground, as Flickers are wont to do, in search of ants and other insects. At most times they are rather silent birds for this family, but during the mating season, which always calls out whatever vocal powers birds possess, their harsh notes resound through the forest with startling distinctness. I have never identified one of their nests, but there is no question of their breeding in the summits of the pines, generally a projecting top blasted by lightning or decayed in natural process. In July the young may be seen scrambling in troops about the tree tops, before they are grown strong enough to fly; and a curious sight they are. Having seen more of them together than were at all likely to have been hatched in the same nest, I have no doubt that different families join each other as soon as the young are on wing, haunting favorable resorts. The association of Californian Woodpeckers and "Sapsuckers" with these more aristocratic birds seems partly a matter of sufferance, partly of necessity, for the smaller and more agile birds can scramble out of the way when, as often happens, Lewis' makes hostile demonstrations.

In Colorado, according to Mr. Trippe, "Lewis' Woodpecker is common among the foot-hills, extending up to 7,000 feet, and occasionally to 8,000. It is rarely seen within the limits of Clear Creek County, but is common lower down. It is a common visitor, arriving a little later than the Red-headed Woodpecker."

COLAPTES AURATUS, (Linn.) Sw.

Golden-winged Woodpecker; Flicker.

Cuculus auratus, LINN., Syst. Nat. 10th ed. i, 1758, 112.
Picus auratus, LINN., Syst. Nat. i, 1766, 174.—FORST., Phil. Trans. lxii, 1772, 383.—
    VIEILL., Ois. Am. Sept. ii, 1807, 66, pl. 123.—WILS., Am. Orn. i, 1808, 45, pl. 3,
    f. 1.—BP., Syn. 1828, 44.—NUTT., Man. i, 1832, 561.—AUD., Orn. Biog. i, 1832,
    191; v, 1839, 540; pl. 37; Syn. 1839, 184; B. Am. iv, 1842, 282, pl. 273.—SUND.,
    Consp. Av. Pic. 1866, 71.—TRIPPE, Pr. Ess. Inst. vi, 1871, 118 (Minnesota).
Colaptes auratus, SW., Zool. Journ. iii, 1827, 353.—SW. & RICH., F. B. A. ii, 1831, 314.—
    BP., List, 1838, 40; Consp. i, 1850, 113.—WOODH., Sitgr. Rep. 1853, 91 (Indian
    Territory).—BD., B. N. A. 1858, 118.—MAXIM., J. f. O. 1858, 420.—REINH., Ibis,
    iii, 1861, 8 (Greenland; quotes MÖSCHLER, J. f. O. 1856, 335).—DRESS., Ib's, 1865,
    470 (Texas).—HAYD., Rep. 1862, 156.—ALLEN, Mem. Bost. Soc. i, 1868, 499

(Iowa).—DALL & BANN., Tr. Chic. Acad. 1869, 275 (Yukon River, Alaska).—
FOWLER, Am. Nat. iii, 1869, 422 (biography).—SNOW, B. Kans. 1873, 3.—ALLEN,
Bull. M. C. Z. iii, 1872, 180 (East Kansas).—HART., Man. Brit. Birds, 1872, 123
(England).—COUES., Key, 1872, 197, fig. 132.—B. B. & R., N. A. B. ii, 1874, 575,
pl. 55, f. 1. 2; and of most authors.
Geopicus auratus, MALH., Mon. Pic. ii, 255, pl. 109, figs. 5, 6, 7.

The following synonyms refer to specimens intermediate in varying degree between
auratus and *mexicanus*:

Colaptes ayresii, AUD., B. Am. vii, 1843, 348, pl. 494 (Fort Union, Upper Missouri River;
mostly *auratus*, but with red moustaches). (Not of HEERM., P. R. R. Rep. x,
1859, pt. vi, 59, California, which is *C. chrysoides*.)
Colaptes hybridus, BD., B. N. A. 1858, 122 (excl. syn. *Geopicus chrysoides*, MALH; gives
all the stages).—HAYD., Rep. 1862, 156.—STEV., U. S. Geol. Surv. Terr. 1870,
463.—SNOW, B. Kans. 1873, 3.
Picus aurato-mexicanus, SUND., Consp. Av. Pic. 1866, 72.

Hab.—Eastern North America, to the slopes and foot-hills of the Rocky Mountains,
where in many localities it becomes mixed with *C. mexicanus*. Alaska (*Dall*). Greenland
(*Reinhardt*). Accidental in Europe (Amesbury Park, Wilts, England, one instance;
"MARSH, Zool. 1859, p. 6327"; HART., Brit. Birds, 1872, 123). Breeds throughout its
range; resident from the Middle States southward.

List of specimens from the Warren Expedition.—A, true *auratus*: 4620, Fort Leavenworth; 4619, Upper Missouri; 5221, Fort Lookout; 8868, fifty miles above mouth of
Platte River; 8866-67, Frémont, Platte River; 8861-62, 8864-65, Loup Fork.—B, *aurato-
mexicanus*: 5214, Fort Pierre; 5225, near Fort Pierre; 5220, 5222-23, Squaw Butte Creek;
5215, Powder River; 5211, 5216, Fort Union; 5224, White Earth River; 5212-13, 5217-19,
Yellowstone River; 8863, Loup Fork; 8869, fifty miles above mouth of Platte. Of the
foregoing specimens, not typical *auratus*, Nos. 5211-13 have red or orange predominating on the shafts, and are nearer *mexicanus* than *auratus*; the remainder are yellow-
shafted, and nearer *auratus*.
Later expeditions.—60357-9 (Wyoming); 60800, North Platte; 61093, Green River (all
"*hybridus*").

Dr. Hayden's numerous examples are principally those that enabled Prof. Baird to
elucidate one of the most remarkable cases in American ornithology—the perfect intergradation of two such distinct species as *auratus* and *mexicanus*. This author adopted,
without qualification, the hypothesis of hybridization, remarking, in proposing the
name the *hybridus*: "By the above name I intend to cover a remarkable series of
Woodpeckers, from the Upper Missouri and Yellowstone, combining the characteristics
of *Colaptes auratus* and *mexicanus*, in proportions varying with almost each individual,
and leading irresistably to the conclusion that they are the descendants of originals of
the species mentioned above, mixed up by interbreeding of successive generations, to
a degree unparalleled in the annals of ornithology." He traces the successive steps of
departure from the typical *auratus* into *mexicanus*, and forcibly illustrates the gradations with a comparative tabulation of the varying characters. The first deviation
is the appearance of red feathers in the black maxillary patches;* these increase till
they prevail, finally to the exclusion of the black, resulting in the wholly red patch of
the *mexicanus*. With this occurs the diminution and final extinction of the scarlet
nuchal crescent, where coincidently we find the characteristic golden-yellow on the
wing and tail passing through an intermediate orange into the red of *mexicanus*, a
change accompanied with another affecting the peculiar lilac-brown of the throat and
olive-brown of the back, which become respectively merged into ashen and purplish-
gray.
If there ever were a case of hybridization to an unlimited extent, resulting in fertile
offspring, that again and again interbred, this would appear to be one; and it has been
so accepted by the majority of ornithologists without hesitation. But we may well
pause before committing ourselves to an hypothesis of hybridization on such an immense scale. In the light of late researches upon the question of climatic variation
according to inflexible and infallible laws, most of the lesser instances of supposed
hybridity have seemed less weighty. The present may be considered a test case—the
strongest argument of those who maintain hybridity.
A slight circumstance may give a clue to the case, and lead up to impartial considerations. As stated in the "Key" (p. 198), I am informed by Mr. Allen that *Floridan*
examples of *C. auratus* sometimes show red touches in the black maxillary patches.

*These black patches are supposed to be entirely wanting in the female. But Mr.
W. D. Scott says (Pr. Bost. Soc. Oct. 1872): "An immature female (sex noted by careful dissection) had a dark cheek-patch, differing only from that of the mature male in
having gray feathers mixed with the black. In an adult female the outlines of the
cheek-patch can be plainly seen."

Mr. J. H. Batty tells me of a *New Jersey* specimen, got a few years since, with mixed red and black cheek patches. As *C. mexicanus* never occurs in these regions, hybridity is there impossible; and the fact is demonstrated that *C. auratus* may thus tend toward the characters *mexicanus* by its own inherent susceptibility to change under climatic influences. The important bearing of this fact cannot easily be over-estimated; the circumstance is, in my judgment, strongly against the theory of hybridization.

So far as I am aware, the assumed case of *C. "hybridus"* was first called seriously into question by Mr. Allen. This writer says (p. 118): "Few congeneric species, it would seem, need be more distinct than *Colaptes auratus* and *C. mexicanus*, the one occupying the eastern and the other the western side of the continent. Yet a mixed race has been long known to exist in the region where their habitats adjoin, in which every possible combination of the characters of the two birds is presented, and which shade off gradually on the one side into *C. auratus*, and on the other into *C. mexicanus;* these, as it were, engrafted characters not entirely fading out in either direction for a distance of several hundred miles; while to the southwestward is a smaller synthetic race (*C. chrysoides*) partaking mainly of the characters of *C. auratus*. When but comparatively few instances were known, in which specimens combined in various degrees the characters of two quite distinct species, their synthetic character was generally explained by the theory of hybridity; but the irrefragibility of the evidence now at hand in proof of the gradual intergradation of such forms over large areas—the transition being so gradual as to occupy hundreds of miles in the passage—and also coincident with a similarly gradual change in the conditions of environment, together with the demonstrable evidence of the power of climatic influence, seems to furnish a far more satisfactory explanation of these perplexing phenomena. But an advocate of the theory of hybridity might still assume that this gradual transition over a wide area is no objection to the theory, since the gradual fading out of the impression of contact in either direction from the line of junction of the respective habitats of two forms is just the result that would be anticipated from such a sexual intermingling of the forms in question. But the real objection to the theory—granting the possibility of hybridization on such a gigantic scale, which seems really improbable—is, that widely different forms occur also at different points in latitude, between which each successive stage of gradual differentiation can be readily traced, where hybridity can scarcely be supposed to account for the gradual change. Furthermore, a differentiation is now known in so many cases that it amounts to the demonstration of climatic variation as a general law, by means of which a species may be safely predicted to take on a given character under certain specific climatic conditions. If the theory of hybridity be urged to account for the intergradation of forms occurring at localities differently situated in respect to latitude, as has been sometimes done, it evidently falls under the weight it has to support; and yet there seems to be little better evidence in its behalf in cases where the intergrading forms happen to be differently situated in respect to longitude."

For my own part, I am strongly inclined to endorse this view, though I do not deny that there is much to be said against it. No weak argument, indeed, is comprehended in the statement, that if *C. auratus* and *mexicanus* are not "good species," then there are none such in ornithology. But I would reply, as I did on a former occasion, that it is only in virtue of missing links that we are enabled to predicate species in any case. If all the steps in a line of descent with modification were before our eyes, we could no more draw specific, or generic, or ordinal lines of distinction, than we could say where a circle begins. This particular case of *Colaptes* seems to be exactly parallel with that of *Sphyrapicus varius* and *ruber*—it is merely pushed to a further extreme, and appears in stronger light, because of the greater amount of differentiation suffered. Such being my view, I may be justly accused of inconsistency in not formally reducing *C. mexicanus* to *C. auratus* var. *mexicanus;* and I would say, that such an action may yet be deemed advisable, or even prove necessary. But our nomenclature is merely a matter of convenience, of little more significance than the index of a book; the present case is unique in some respects; and, especially, the hypothesis of hybridity is not yet actually disproven.

In Northern Dakota, beyond the Missouri water-shed, the true *C. auratus* occurs, without the slightest admixture of *mexicanus*, at least four hundred miles west of the Red River—much further west than the point on the Missouri region where the gradation commences, "*hybridus*" having been noted even from Kansas, and being the prevailing Missouri form.

COLAPTES MEXICANUS, Sw.

Red-shafted Woodpecker; Mexican Flicker.

Picus cafer, GM., Syst. Nat. i, 1788, 431.—LATH., Ind. Orn. ii, 1790, 242 (supposed to be from Cape of Good Hope).

Picus lathami, WAGL., Syst. Av. 1827, *Picus* No 85 (same as *P. cafer*).
Colaptes mexicanus, Sw., Syn. Mex. B. in Phil. Mag. i, 1827, 440; F. B. A. ii, 1831, 315.—
    SCL., P. Z. S. 1858, 305 (Oaxaca).—NEWB., P. R. R. Rep. vi, 1857, 91.—MAXIM.,
    J. f. O. vi, 1858, 421.—BD., B. N. A. 1858, 120.—KENN., P. R. R. Rep. x, 1859, pt.
    iv, 22.—HEERM., *ibid.* pt. vi, 59.—COOP. & SUCK., N. H. Wash. Ter. 1860, 163.—
    LORD, Pr. Roy. Arty. Inst. iv, 112 (British Columbia).—DRESS., Ibis, 1865, 470
    (Texas).—COUES, Proc. Phila. Acad. 1866, 56.—DALL & BANN., Tr. Chic. Acad.
    i, 1869, 275 (Sitka).—SUMICH., Mem. Bost. Soc. i, 1869, 562 (Vera Cruz).—COOP.,
    B. Cal. i, 1870, 408.—STEV., U. S. Geol. Surv. Ter. 1870, 463.—MERR., *ibid.* 1872,
    695.—ALLEN, Bull. M. C. Z. iii, 1872, 180.—HOLD., Pr. Bost. Soc. 1872, 207.—
    COUES, Key, 1872, 198.—SNOW, B. Kans. 1873, 3.—B. B. & R., N. A. B. ii, 1874,
    578, pl. 55, f. 3, 4; and of most late authors.
Picus mexicanus, AUD., Orn. Biog. v, 1839, 174, pl. 416; Syn. 1839, 185; B. Am. iv, 1842,
    295, pl. 274.—SUND., Mon. Pic. 1866, 72.
Picus (Colaptes) mexicanus, NUTT., Man. Orn. ii, 1834, 603.
Geopicus mexicanus, MALH., Mon. Pic. ii, 262, pl. 110, f. 4, 5.
Picus rubricatus, "LICHT., Mus. Berol."—WAGL., Isis, 1829, 516.
Colaptes rubricatus, BP., P. Z. S. 1837, 109; List, 1838, 40, Consp. i, 1850, 114 (not of
    GRAY & MITCH., Gen. of B. pl. 111, which is *C. mexicanoides*, LAFR.; nor *Geo-
    picus rubricatus* of MALH., Mon. Pic. ii, 265, pl. 110, f. 1, 2, which is also *mexi-
    canoides*, LAFR.).
Colaptes collaris, VIG., Zool. Journ. iv, 1820, 384; Zool. Beechey's Voy. 1839, 23, pl. 9
    (not of BP., Consp. i, 1850, 114, which is *mexicanoides*).
Colaptes mexicanoides, WOODH., Sitgr. Rep. 1853, 91 (not of LAFR.).

Hab.—Eastern slopes and foot-hills of the Rocky Mountains, to the Pacific. North
to Sitka. South into Mexico. East to Kansas.
    Late Expeditions.—59847–48, Soda Springs, Colorado; 54304, 50356, 60797–99, 62258,
Wyoming; 62259, Idaho.

As will have been gathered from the preceding article, the greater
part of the Missouri region is occupied either by the true *C. auratus* or
by the mixed form, the typical *mexicanus* being chiefly confined to the
western border, among the head-waters of the Missouri and its greater
tributaries. I did not observe it north of the Missouri water-shed. Dr.
Hayden says that he found it most abundant about the Bad Lands and
the sources of the Missouri. Prof. Baird, however, in 1858, quoted
individuals from the Republican Fork of the Kansas River, and Prof.
Snow speaks of a flock which remained about the timber, near Lawrence,
for two or three weeks in December. The northernmost record I have
seen is Mr. Dall's; he speaks of its being taken at Sitka by Bischoff.
The true *auratus* is found in Alaska, north of the main range of mountains. In the Rocky Mountains the bird becomes fairly established,
mostly freed from admixture with *auratus*, and occurs thence, in all
suitable regions, to the Pacific coast. I found it as common in some
parts of New Mexico and Arizona as the Flicker is in the East, the
habits of the two being identical in all essential respects. In Colorado,
says Mr. Trippe, the species is common and migratory. " It breeds
from the plains up to timber-line. The Red-shafted Flicker appears
near Idaho Springs about the middle of April, and soon becomes rather
common. It is never a very abundant bird, but is to be seen, more or
less frequently, throughout the mountains, having very much the same
habits as the Golden-winged Woodpecker. It is shy and difficult of
approach. In October and November it disappears.

" Mrs. Maxwell, of Boulder, informs me that a Yellow-winged Flicker
has appeared in the groves that fringe the streams near that town,
within the last few years, and is gradually becoming more abundant.
From her descriptions I should suppose it to be *C. auratus*, but probably
it is some form of *C. hybridus*."

Family ARIDÆ : Parroquets.

CONURUS CAROLINENSIS, (Linn.) Kuhl.

Carolina Parroquet.

Psittacus carolinensis, LINN., Syst. Nat. i, 1766, 141 (CATES., i, 11 ; BRISS., iv, 350).—
    WILS., Am. Orn. iii, 1811, 89, pl. 26, f. 1.—BP., Syn. 1828, 41.—NUTT., Man. i,
    1832, 545.—AUD., Orn. Biog. i, 1832, 135, pl. 26.
Conurus carolinensis, "KUHL, Nov. Act. Acad. Cæs. Leop.-Car. 1830."—BP., List, 1838, 38 ;
    Consp. i, 1850, p. 1.—WOODH., Sitgr. Rep. 1853, 89 (Texas and Indian Terri-
    tory.—MAXIM., J. f. O. v, 1857, 97.—BD., B. N. A. 1858, 67.—HAYD., Rep. 1862,
    154 (Missouri River below Platte).—COUES, Pr. Bost. Soc. 1868, 119 (South
    Carolina, formerly).—ALLEN, Mem. Bost. Soc, i, 1868, 525 (Indiana, formerly).—
    TURNB., B. E. Pa. 1869, 41 (at rare intervals).—ALLEN, Bull. M. C. Z. ii, 1871,
    308 (Florida, still abundant) ; iii, 1872, 130 (Kansas, formerly).—TRIPPE, Pr.
    Bost. Soc. xv, 1872, 233 (Iowa).—SNOW, B. Kans. 1873, 2 (Kansas, now occa-
    sional).—COUES, Key, 1872, 199, fig. 133.—B. B. & R., N. A. B. ii, 1874, 587, pl.
    56, f. 1, 2.—FINSCH, Die Papageien, i, 1867, 475.
"*Centurus*" (err.) *carolinensis*, AUD., Syn. 1839, 189 ; B. Am. iv, 1842, 306, pl. 278.
Psittacus ludovicianus, GM., Syst. Nat. i, 1788, 347.
Conurus ludovicianus, GRAY, Cat. B. M. *Psit.* 1859, 36 (North America).
Psittacus luteicapillus, VIEILL., Ency. Meth. p. 1402.
Psittacus thalassinus, VIEILL., Ency. Meth. 1377.

Hab.—Southernmost Atlantic and Gulf States ; up the Mississippi Valley to Missouri ; up the Missouri River to the Platte.

Lieutenant Warren's Expedition.—Nos. 4606–18, Bald Island, Missouri River, Nebraska.

According to Gray (Hand-list, ii, 147, No. 8113), the *Conurus carolinensis* of Kuhl is
not this but a Brazilian species, *C. chrysogenys* of authors, perhaps referable to the *P.
æruginosus* of Linnæus ; and he quotes "*pertinax* p. FINSCH" as synonymous.

Among the more interesting ornithological results of Dr. Hayden's investigations
may be mentioned his discovery that this species is abundant at a higher point than
usually recognized—" along the thickly-wooded bottoms as far up the Missouri as Fort
Leavenworth, possibly as high as the mouth of the Platte, but never seen above that
point." Dr. Woodhouse, in 1853, recorded it as quite numerous in the timber-lands of
the large streams of the Indian Territory and Eastern Texas. I never found it along
the Missouri, or anywhere in Kansas, and neither did Mr. Allen, who merely mentions,
on the authority of Dr. C. A. Logan, that it was formerly common in Eastern Kansas,
but had not recently been observed. Prof. Snow, however, remarking upon its former
abundance in the woods of Eastern Kansas, states that it is still seen in thinly-settled
districts. In Iowa, according to Mr. Trippe, the Parrot still occurs. "A resident of
Decatur County told me that he had several times seen a flock of Parrots in the southern part of the county, on a tall, dead cottonwood-tree, known to the neighboring
people as the 'parrot-tree,' from its having been frequented at intervals by the same
flock for several years."

A comparison of the earlier with the more recent accounts of the general distribution of the Carolina Parroquet, shows that it has been steadily contracting year by
year. About a century ago, we are informed by Prof. Barton, writing in 1790, a flock
appeared in January in the neighborhood of Albany, New York, and excited great con-
sternation, being regarded as of evil portent. We have various records of occurrences
in Pennsylvania, so that, even in 1869, Prof. Turnbull allowed it to hold a place in his
list of casuals. I retained it in my South Carolina list, with the remark that it seemed
hardly entitled to remain there, although it was abundant in that State not many
years since. Audubon (1832) has an interesting paragraph upon this subject :

"Our Parrakeets are very rapidly diminishing in number, and in some districts,
where twenty-five years ago they were plentiful, scarcely any are now to be seen. At
that period they could be procured as far up the tributary waters of the Ohio as the
Great Kanawha, the Scioto, the heads of Miami, the mouth of the Manimee at its junction with Lake Erie, on the Illinois River, and sometimes as far northeast as Lake
Ontario, and along the Eastern districts as far as the boundary-line between Virginia
and Maryland. At the present day very few are to be found higher than Cincinnati,
nor is it until you reach the mouth of the Ohio that Parrakeets are met with in considerable numbers. I should think that along the Mississippi there is not now half the
number that existed fifteen years ago."

In 1838, Dr. J. P. Kirtland stated, that "the Parrakeets do not usually extend their
visits north of the Scioto, though I am informed, perhaps on doubtful authority, that
thirty years since flocks of them were seen on the Ohio at the mouth of Big Beaver,
thirty miles below Pittsburgh." Mr. J. M. Wheaton admits it in his Ohio list, but with

the remark, on a subsequent page, that it is not probable they extend their migrations into the State at the present time. Although not given in Allen's Illinois list, they still exist in the southern part of that State, or did within ten or fifteen years. For their occurrence in Indiana he quotes the authority of Dr. Haymond, who states, in 1856, that they were formerly very numerous along White Water River, but had not been seen for several years.

Among the causes of this retrocession—perhaps the principal cause—is their persecution and destruction, partly for the damage they do in grain-fields, partly in pure wantonness. They may be readily killed by any pot hunter or idler, merciless advantage being taken, to slaughter them by scores, of the heedless distraction and concern they show when any of their number are brought down. Mr. Allen's paragraph may well be here reproduced. In speaking of their abundance in Florida, he says: "Hundreds are captured every winter on the Lower St. Johns, by professional bird-catchers, and sent to northern cities. Thousands of others are destroyed wantonly by sportsmen. Concerning this needless slaughter, Mr. Boardman thus writes: 'The little Parrakeet must soon be exterminated. Some of our Enterprise party would sometimes shoot forty or fifty at a few discharges, for sport, as they hover about when any are shot until the whole flock is destroyed.' From its habit of feeding upon the tender maize in autumn, it is somewhat injurious to the farmer, and for this cause, also, many are killed. It is also more or less hunted as a game-bird. It is well known that the Parrokeet formerly inhabited large portions of the United States where it is now never seen, and the cause of its disappearance has been deemed a mystery. Such facts as these, however, seem to render clear what its ultimate fate must be in the United States—extermination."

The egg of the Parroquet is nearly equal at both ends, of rather rough texture, and measures about 1.40 by 1.05. The color is white; but the only specimen before me shows much yellowish discoloration, like that on the eggs of many geese and ducks.

ORDER RAPTORES: BIRDS OF PREY:

Family STRIGIDÆ: Owls.

STRIX FLAMMEA var. AMERICANA, (Aud.) Schl.

American Barn Owl.

a. *flammea.*

≈trix aluco, BRISS., Orn. i, 503.
Strix flammea, LINN., Syst. Nat. i, 1766, 133 (Fn. Suec. No. 73; *Noctua guttata*, FRISCH,
    97; *Aluco minor*, ALD., i, 536).—GM., Syst. Nat. i, 1788, 293.—LATH., Ind. Orn. i,
    1790, 60.—DOND., Orn. Beyt. i, 164.—DAUD., Tr. Orn. ii, 197.—SHAW, G. Z. vii,
    1809, pl. 33.—BECHST., Naturg. Deutschl. ii, 947.—MEY., Tasch. D. V. i, 79.—
    TEMM., Man. i, 1815, 52.—LEACH, Cat. 1816, 11.—BREHM, V. D. i, 106.—VIEILL.,
    Fn. Franç. 46, pl. 22, fig. 1.—ROUX, Orn. Prov. i, 81, pls 54, 55.—BRESCH., Ann.
    Sc. Nat. 2d ser. v, pl. i, pl. 2 (anat.)—LESS., Man. i, 114; Tr. 112.—CUV., R. A.
    2d ed. i, 342.—NAUM., V. D. 1822, i, 483, pl. 47, fig. 2.—MACG., Hist. Br. B. iii,
    473; Rap. Br. B. 343.—JARD., Br. B. i, 253, pl. 27.—THOMPS., B. Irel. i, 92.—
    MORRIS, Br. B. 205, pl. 29.—EYT., Cat. Br. B. 6.—BP., List, 1838, 7.—KEYS. &
    BLAS., Wirb. Eur. 1840, 31.—SCHL., Rev. Crit. Ois. Eur. 15.—GRAY, Gen. of B. i,
    1844, 41.—BAILL., Orn. Sav. i, 188.—WEBB & BERTH., H. N. Canar. Orn. 8.—
    MÜLL., J. f. O. ii, 398.—BOLLE, *ibid.* 447.—DEGL., Orn. Eur, i, 137.—STRICKL.,
    Orn. Syn. 1855, 178.—GRAY, Cat. Br. B. 1863, 28; and of authors generally.
Strix flammea var. *flammea*, RIDGW.—B. B. & R., N. A. B. iii, 1874, 11.
Aluco flammeus, FLEMING, Brit. Anim. 57.
Strix alba, SCOP., Ann. i, 21, No. 14.—GM., Syst. Nat. i, 1788, 293.—LATH., Ind. Orn. i,
    1790, 61.—DAUD., Tr. Orn. ii, 200.—SHAW, G. Z. vii, 247.
Strix guttata, BREHM, Vög. Deutschl. i, 106, pl. 7, fig. 3.
L'Effraye, BUFF., P. E. 440.—LEVAILL., Ois. Afr. i, 164.
White or Barn Owl of AUTHORS.

b. *javanica.*

Strix flammea, PEARS., Journ. A. S. B. x, 630.—BLYTH, *ibid.* xiv, 186; Ann. N. H. xii, 93
Strix flammea var. *javanica*, RIDGW.—B. B. & R., N. A. B. iii, 1874, 13.
Strix javanica, GM., Syst. Nat. i, 1788, 295.—LATH., Ind. Orn. i, 1790, 64.—DAUD., Tr.
    Orn. ii, 202.—HORSF., Linn. Trans. xiii, 139; Isis, 1825, 1055.—SYKES, P. Z. S.
    ii, 81; Journ. A. S. B. iii, 420.—LESS., Man. i, 109.—JERD., Madras Journ. x, 85.—
    BP., Consp. Av. i, 1850, 55.—GRAY, Gen. of B. pl. 15; List B. Brit. Mus. 109.—
    STRICKL., Orn. Syn. 1855, 180.

c. *delicatula.*

Strix flammea, VIG., Linn. Trans. xv, 190.—LESS., Isis, 1832, 112.
Strix flammea var. *delicatula*, RIDGW.—B. B. & R., N. A. B. iii, 1874, 13.
Strix delicatula, GOULD, P. Z. S. iv, 140; Syn. B. Aust. iii, pl. 60, fig. 1; Intr. B. Aust.
    23; B. Aust. i, pl. 31.—BLYTH, J. A. S. B. xvii, 346.—GRAY, List B. Brit. Mus.
    109.—KAUP, Mon. *Strig.* Cont. Orn. 1852, 119.—BP., Consp. Av. i, 1850, 54.

d. *americana.*

Strix flammea, WILS., Am. Orn. vi, 1812, 57, pl. 50, fig. 2.—BP., Syn. 1828, 38; Isis, 1832,
    1140.—NUTT., i, 1832, 139.—AUD., Orn. Biog. ii, 1834, 403; v, 388; pl. 171.—
    VIG., Zool. Beechey's Voy. 16; Zool. Journ. iii, 438.—GRAY, List B. Brit. Mus.
    1844, 54.
Ulula flammea, JARD., ed. Wils. ii, 264.
Strix americana, AUD., Syn. 1839, 25.—AUD., B. Am. i, 1840, 127, pl. 34.—BREW., ed.
    Wils. 687.—DEKAY, Nat. Hist. N. Y. 1844, 31; pl. 13, fig. 28. (Not of *Gmelin*.)
Strix flammea americana, SCHL., Mus. Pays-Bas, 1862, *Striges*, p. 4.
Strix flammea var. *americana*, COUES, Key, 1872, 201, fig. 134.
Strix pratincola, BP., List, 1838, 7; Consp. i, 1850, 55.—CASS., Ill. 1854, 116.—BREW., N.
    A. O. i, 62, pl. 4, fig. 38.—NEWB., P. R. R. Rep. vi, 1857, 76.—BD., B. N. A. 1858,
    47.—SCL., P. Z. S. 1859, 390 (Oaxaca)—HEERM., P. R. R. Rep. x, 1859, pt. vi, 34.—

WHEAT., Ohio Agric. Rep. 1860, No. 20.—DRESS., Ibis, 1865, 330 (Texas).—
COUES, Pr. Phila. Acad. 1866, 49 (Arizona).—LAWR., Ann. Lyc. N. Y. viii, 1866,
281 (New York, rare).—DRESS., Ibis, 1862, 49 (Texas).—COUES., Pr. Ess. Inst. v,
1868, 312 (Massachusetts).—COUES, Pr. Bost. Soc. 1868, 119 (South Carolina).—
BRYANT, Pr. Bost. Soc. 1867, 65.—ALLEN, Am. Nat. iii, 570 (Springfield, Mass.;
Sachem's Head, Conn.; Stratford, Conn.); *ibid.* 646 (Lynn, Mass.).—TURB., B. E.
Pa. 1869, 8.—COOP., B. Cal. i, 1870, 415.—COUES, Pr. Phila. Acad. 1871, 27 (North
Carolina).—SNOW, B. Kans. 1873, 2.
Strix flammea var. *pratincola*, RIDGW.—B. B. & R., N. A. B. iii, 1874, 13.
Strix perlata, ("LICHT."), KAUP, Tr. Z. S. iv, 1859, 247.

e. *furcata.*

Strix flammea ex Insulis Antill.
Strix pratincola, GOSSE, B. Jam. 1847, 23.
Strix furcata, TEMM., Pl. Color. 432 (Cuba).—D'ORB., La Sagra's Cuba, Ois. 34.
Strix flammea var. *furcata*, RIDGW.—B. B. & R., N. A. B. iii, 1874, 12.

f. *guatemalæ.*

Strix flammea var. *guatemalæ*, RIDGW.—B. B. & R., N. A. B. iii, 1874, 11.

g. *perlata.*

Strix flammea, DARW., Zool. Voy. Beag. 34.—SCHOMB., Guiana, 732.—SPIX, Av. Bras. i, 21.
Strix flammea var. *perlata*, RIDGW.—B. B. & R., N. A. B. iii, 1874, 12.
Strix perlata, LICHT., Verz. 1823, 59.—MAXIM., Beit. iii, 363 (excl. syn.)—HARTL., Ind.
Azara, 3.—TSCHUDI, Wiegm. Arch. 1844, 267.—BRIDGES, P. Z. S. xi, 110; Ann.
Nat. Hist. xiii, 500.—KAUP, Mon. *Strig.* Cont. Orn. 1852, 119.—STRICKL., Orn.
Syn. 1855, 180 (excl. syn. *furcata*, TEMM.).

Hab.—The *Strix flammea* type of Owl is found in nearly all warm and temperate
parts of the globe. Var. *flammea*: Europe, Africa. Var. *javanica*: parts of Asia,
Java, &c. Var. *delicatula*: Australia, &c. Var. *americana*: North America and
Mexico; not beyond the United States; rather southerly; rarely north to New England and the Columbia. Var. *furcata*: West Indies (Cuba, Jamaica). Var. *guatemalæ*: Central America. Var. *perlata*: South America generally.

The foregoing appear to be unquestionably geographical races of a single species,
slightly modified, by climate and other circumstances, in size, form, or coloring, but
not sufficiently impressed to be permanently separable. In a number of other offshoots
of this same *Strix* stock the modification has progressed further, and become sufficiently
profound for the characterization of "species." Instances in point are the following:
S. PUNCTATISSIMA, Gray (Zool. Voy. Beagle, iii, 34, pl. 4), from the Galapagoes; S. CAN-
DIDA, of Tickell (J. A. S. B. ii, 572 = *S. longimembris*, Jerd., Madras Journ. x, 86), from
Southern Asia; S. CAPENSIS, Smith (Ill. S. Afr. Zool. 9; Müll., J. f. O. ii, 398), of South
Africa, where *S. flammea* is also found; another form, S. POENSIS, Fraser, P. Z. S. 1842,
189, is described from Fernando Po; S. NOVÆ-HOLLANDIÆ, Steph. (Shaw's Gen. Zool.
xiii, pt. ii, 61 = *S. personata*, Vig., P. Z. S. i, 50; Gould, B. Aust. i, pl. 29 = *S. cyclops*,
Gould, P. Z. S. iv, 140 = *Dactylostrix personata*, Kaup, Mon. Strig. Cont. 1852, 119),
of Australia; S. CASTANOPS, Gould (P. Z. S. iv, 140; B. Aust. pl. 28 = *Dactylostrix castanops*, Kaup, *l. c.*), of Tasmania; S. TENEBRICOSA, Gould (P. Z. S. 1845, 80; B. Aust. i,
pl. 30 = *Megastrix tenebricosa*, Kaup, Op. Cit. 120), of Australia. The last three are
especially well marked, and have been placed, as above noted, in different subgenera.
A still more distinct form, though most nearly related to *Strix* proper, is the PHODILUS
BADIUS of Southern Asia, Java, Sumatra, &c. Its synonymy is given below.*

The American Barn Owl is an abundant bird on both sides of the
continent, south of a certain latitude. Unlike many of its relatives,
warmly clothed and of a hardy nature, withstanding great cold, it appears of rather delicate and sensitive organization. In the Missouri
region it has only occurred, to my knowledge, in Kansas, where it
breeds, though it is rarely found, according to Prof. Snow. I ascer-

---

* *Strix badia*, HORSF., Zool. Res. 1821, pl. 37; Linn. Trans. xiii, 139; Isis, 1825, 698,
1055.—TEMM., Pl. Col. 318.—LESS., Man. i, 114; Tr. Orn. 112.—CUV., R. A. 2d
ed. i, 342.—SW. Class. B. ii, 216.
Athene badia, HODGS.—GRAY, Zool. Misc. 82.
Phodilus badius, GEOFF., Ann. Sc. Nat. xxxi, 1830, 201.—BLYTH, J. A. S. B. n. s. xix, 513.—
GRAY, Gen. of B. i, 1844, pl. 15, fig. 1; List B. Brit. Mus. 110.—BP., Consp. Av.
i, 1850, 55.—STRICKL., Orn. Syn. 1855, 183.—KAUP, Mon. *Strig.* Cont. Orn.
1852, 118.

tained its occurrence in Arizona; once, wading through a reedy lagoon at mid-day, I disturbed a Barn Owl, which rose silently and flapped along till I brought it down. It is a common bird in California—appar ently the most abundant species of its family in the southern part of the State; and, according to Dr. Cooper, it extends its range to the Columbia, in lat. 46°. Dr. Newberry observed an interesting modifica- tion of its habits by circumstances, which cause it to inhabit holes in the perpendicular cliffs bordering the shore of San Pablo Bay. The same fact has been noted by Mr. Dall, in the case of *Brachyotus palustris*, in the Aleutian Islands; so that our Burrowing Owl is not the only species that lives in holes in the ground. In the Atlantic States, the Barn Owl is not abundant north of the Carolinas; I found it on the coast of North Carolina, in the salt marshes. It occurs, however, regu- larly, if rarely, in New York, Pennsylvania, and New Jersey. Dr. Turnbull observes: " Not rare, and more frequent in spring and autumn. Its nest is generally found in a hollow tree, near marshy meadows." Its occurrence in New England must be regarded as exceptional, and it has not been observed in that section further north than Massachusetts. In 1843 (Am. Journ. xliv, 253), Rev. J. H. Linsley reported the capture of a specimen at Stratford Conn. According to Mr. Allen, as above quoted, Dr. Wood took one at Sachem's Head, Connecticut, October 28, 1865. The first specimen known from Massachusetts was procured near Springfield, in May, 1866, as stated in my paper above quoted; another was shot near Lynn, in the same State, in 1863, as recorded by Mr. Allen. This completes the New England quotations to date.

The egg of this species is colorless, and measures about $1\frac{4}{5}$ in length by $1\frac{1}{4}$ in greatest breadth. Little or no preparation is made for the re- ception of the eggs, which are simply dropped on the débris—often the bones and the remains of the birds' food—in the cavities or recesses to which the birds resort to breed. The eggs are said to vary from three to six in number.

BUBO VIRGINIANUS, (Gm.) Bp.

Great Horned Owl.

a. *virginianus.*

Strix virginianus, GM., Syst. Nat. i, 1788, 287.—LATH., Ind. Orn. i, 1790, 52 (BRISS., i, 484; Eagle Owl, Arct. Zool. ii, 228; Virginian Eared Owl, EDW., 60; Gen. Syn. i, 119).—DAUD., Tr. Orn. ii, 210, pl. 13.—SHAW, G. Z. vii, pl. 30.—TEMM., Tabl. Meth. p. 7.—WILS., Am. Orn. vi, 1812, 52, pl. 50, f. 1.—BP., Syn. 1828, 37; Isis, 1832, 1139.—RICH. & SW., F. B. A. ii, 1831, 82 (Subg. *Bubo*).—NUTT., Man. i, 1832, 124.—AUD., Orn. Biog. i, 1832, 313; v, 393; pl. 61.—DEKAY, N. Y. Zool. 1844, pl. 10, fig. 22.—PEAB., Rep. Orn. Mass. 1839, 87.—THOMPS., N. H. Vt. 65.
Bubo virginianus, BP., List, 1838, 6; Consp. i, 1850, 48.—AUD., Syn. 1839, 29; B. Am. i, 1840, 143, pl. 39.—GIR., B. L. I. 1844, 27.—KAUP, Monog. Cont. Orn. 1852, 116; Tr. Z. S. iv, 1859, 241.—CASS., Ill. 1854, 177.—BREW., N. A. O. 1857, 64.—MAXIM., J. f. O. vi, 1858, 23.—BD., B. N. A. 1858, 49.—SCL., P. Z. S. 1859, 390 (Oaxaca).— SCL. & SALV., Ibis, ii, 1860, 276 (Guatemala).—SCL., P. Z. S. 1860, 253 (Ori- zaba).—COOP. & SUCK., N. H. Wash. Ter. 1860, 154.—BLAK., Ibis, iii, 1861, 320.—LORD, Pr. Roy. Arty. Inst. iv, 1864, 111.—DRESS., Ibis, 1865, 330 (Texas).—COUES, Pr. Phila. Acad. 1866, 49 (Arizona).—LAWR., Ann. Lyc. N. Y. ix, 132 (Costa Rica).—DALL & BANN., Tr. Chic. Acad. i, 1869, 272 (Alaska).— SCL. & SALV., P. Z. S. 1869, 155 (Peru).—SALV., P. Z. S. 1870, 116 (Veragua).— COOP., B. Cal. i, 1870, 418.—FINSCH., Abh. Nat. iii, 1872, 26 (Alaska).—COUES, Key, 1872, 202, f. 135.—B. B. & R., N. A. B. iii, 1874, 62; and of authors.
Bubo virginianus atlanticus, CASS., Ill. 1854, 178.
Otus virginianus, STEPH., Shaw's G. Z. xiii, pt. ii, 57.
Ulula virginiana, JAM., ed. Wils. i, 100.
(?) *Strix maximus,* BARTR., Trav. Fla. 1790, 285 (" capite aurito, corpore niveo ").

Strix pythaules, BARTR., Trav. Fla. 1790, 289.
Bubo ludovicianus, DAUD., Tr. Orn. ii, 1800, 210.
Bubo pinicola, VIEILL., Ois. Am. Sept. i, 1809, 51.

b. *pacificus.*

Bubo virginianus var. *pacificus*, CASS., Ill. 1854, 178.—COUES, Key, 1872, 202.—B. B. & R., N. A. B. iii, 1874, 61, 65.

c. *arcticus.*

Strix (Bubo) arcticus, SW. & RICH., F. B. A. ii, 1831, 86, pl. 30.
Heliaptex arcticus, SW., Classif. B. i, 328 ; ii, 217.
Bubo virginianus var. *arcticus*, CASS., Ill. 1854, 178.—BLAK., Ibis, iii, 1861, 320.—COUES, Key, 1872, 202.—B. B. & R., N. A. B. iii, 1874, 60, 64.
Bubo sub-arcticus, HOY, Pr. Phila. Acad. vi, 1852, 211 (Wisconsin).—CASS., Ill. 1854, 117.

d. *magellanicus.*

Strix magellanicus, GM., Syst. Nat. i, 788, 286 (*Hibou des terres Magellaniques*, P. E. 385).—DAUD., Tr. Orn. ii, 1800, 210.—LESS., Voy. Coquille, i, 617 ; Isis, 1833, 76.
Bubo magellanicus, GRAY, List B. Br. Mus., 1844, 46.
Bubo virginianus var. *magellanicus*, CASS., Ill. 1854, 178.—B. B. & R., N. A. B. iii, 1874, 61.
Strix bubo var. δ., LATH., Ind. Orn. 1790, 52 (*Magellanic Eared Owl*, Gen. Syn. i, 118).
Strix nacurutu, VIEILL., N. D. d'Hist. Nat. vii, 44 ; Enc. iii, 1281 (*Nacurutu*, Azara, i, 192.
Bubo crassirostris, VIEILL., Ois. Am. Sept. 1807, pl. 19.
Bubo macrorhynchus, TEMM., Pl. Color. 62.

Hab.—The Western Hemisphere. Common and generally distributed in wooded regions in the United States. Var. *magellanicus* in South America.

List of specimens.

19126	179	Powder River..	♀	Oct. 5, 1859	G. H. Trook..	23.00	56.70	17.00
19127	202	Deer Creek	♀	Nov. 21, 1859	....do	19.50	49.00	14.00
19128	183	Powder River..	♂	Oct. 1. 1859	....do	21.00	52.00	15.00

Lieutenant Warren's Expedition.—5180–81, Fort Union, Dakota.

I divide the synonymy of this species in the conventional method, without feeling in any considerable degree impressed with the necessity of so doing, but rather believing that, with the exception of the alpine and boreal var. *arcticus*, the races are variously inter-related, and not satisfactorily co-ordinated with geographical distribution. This appears to be Mr. Cassin's later view ; for after establishing the races in 1854, he subsequently remarked : " These varieties are evidently not to be recognized as at all strictly geographical, nor so much so as intimated in our notice of them alluded to above." I have not myself critically examined the South American bird, which appears to average darker ; but Dr. Schlegel states that some specimens are like North American ones in every respect. Var. *pacificus* would also appear to be a dark form, but it is not confined to the coast whence the name is derived, nor are all the birds of that region alike, some being entirely indistinguishable from the ordinary Atlantic styles. In the " Key," I adopted the variety entirely at the instance of Mr. Ridgway, who has made our raptorial birds a special study, and followed him in presenting it as a dark, littoral form, " extending from Oregon northward, coastwise, to Labrador," although I confess that I do not quite comprehend this peculiar alleged distribution. Var. *arcticus* is the most easily recognized, being very pale-colored, frequently quite whitish, and not distantly resembling the Snowy Owl. This peculiarity of coloring seems to mark, in varying degree, alpine specimens, even so far south as New Mexico.

The Great Horned Owl occurs in suitable localities throughout the Missouri region, as elsewhere in North America. It is by no means rare, and, conspicuous in its size, falls under frequent observation. It occurs chiefly in wooded regions, where the various animals it preys upon find shelter, and where it is itself in a measure concealed from view. It is not migratory. In temperate latitudes, the eggs are laid in winter; and even in the fur countries, according to Sir John Richardson, the young are hatched in March. It breeds indifferently, according to circumstances, in hollow trees, or even in the crevices of rocks ; in such cases the eggs are simply deposited on some grass or feathers. But, perhaps oftener, a large, bulky, rude nest, of sticks and twigs, lined with grass and feathers, is placed among the branches of a tree, generally at a great height. The eggs are colorless, subspherical, measuring about 2¼ inches in length by 2, or a little less in breadth. They are said to range from three to six in a clutch. The only instance of breeding of which I have become personally aware was at Pembina, Dakota, where, early in June, I found two young birds in the timber-belt along the river. Both parents were observed, perched on the tree-tops, near the nest, and flying boldly, apparently not in the least incommoded by the light of day. That they could see perfectly well, was evidenced by the care they took to keep at a distance. The young, two in number, were found on a prostrate log; where the nest was I had no idea—perhaps it was in the hollow of a large blasted tree that overshadowed the log. The young were entirely unfledged; the downy covering was entirely white. On approach, they resented the liberty in the usual manner, clicking the bill, hissing, and throwing themselves into an upright posture. They could scarcely stand, however, and were easily secured. I took them with me, and they were amusing pets for a whole summer, during which time they traveled with me several hundred miles. They got their feathers in due season, and became very finely plumaged by the fall. The first plumage, after the down disappeared, was of a much more uniformly fulvous cast than that ensuing when the dark gray mottling, and distinctive white of the under parts, was assumed. The birds ate freely from the first—in fact were voracious, grew rapidly, and became more tame than any other birds of prey I have ever kept. They would suffer themselves to be handled without impatience, and would occasionally fly up on my shoulder. Early in their lives they had two different notes, one of hunger or loneliness, a querulous explosive syllable, and the other a harsh cry of anger, or remonstrance, when rudely handled, or too nearly approached by an unfamiliar object. They did not begin to hoot until they were about four months old, and then only while at liberty during the night. For they became so thoroughly tame, that, as their wings grew, enabling them to take short flights, I used to release them in the evening from the tether by which they were usually confined. They enjoyed the liberty, and eventually used to stay away all night, doubtless foraging for themselves for their natural prey, and returning to their shelter behind my tent in the morning.

These Owls were most active during the night; yet it would be a great mistake to suppose their vision is much restricted in the day-time, notwithstanding that they belong to a group of Owls commonly regarded as nocturnal. They passed most of the day, indeed, crouching in the shadow of the tent, and it was only toward sundown that they became active, flying the length of their tether in the attempt to reach the ridge of the tent; yet their vision was acute at all hours. I often saw them look up and follow with their eyes the motions of a grasshopper or butterfly, flickering several yards up in the air. On one occasion, in particular, I saw them both gazing steadfastly, and on looking up to see what had attracted their attention, I was myself blinded by the glare, for the direction was exactly in the sun's eye. But a few moments afterward I discovered a pair of white Cranes, floating in circles half a mile high. The Owl's eyes endured a glare that my own could not, and the birds certainly saw the objects, for they slowly moved the head as the Cranes passed over. The best of the supposed performances of an Eagle soaring in the sun's eye, could not excel this. Nor was the inner eyelid drawn over the ball to shade it. I had abundant evidence, on this and numerous other occasions, that the movements of the bird's iris are entirely under the control of the will, instead, as commonly supposed, of being automatic, depending upon the stimulus of light. I frequently saw them instantaneously contract or relax the quivering iris in accommodating their vision to different objects, or different distances; and moreover, they could move the two irides independently of each other. For they often looked at objects with one eye only, the other being sleepily half-closed; and on such occasions the pupils were generally of different sizes. They varied in diameter from that of a small split-pea, to that of a finger-ring; in the latter condition the iris was a mere margin, about a tenth of an inch in diameter. In the night-time, I always found the pupil largely if not fully dilated; at every stage of contraction it remained perfectly circular.

SCOPS ASIO, (Linn.) Bp.

Red Owl; Mottled Owl; Screech Owl.

a. *asio.*

Strix asio, LINN., Syst. Nat. i, 1766, 132 (*Noctua aurita minor*, CATES., i, 7; *Asio scops carolinensis*, BRISS., i, 497).—GM., Syst. Nat. i, 1788, 287.—LATH., Ind. Orn. i, 1790, 54.—DAUD., Tr. Orn. ii, 1800, 216.—SHAW, G. Z. vii, 1809, 229.—WILS., Am. Orn. v, 1812, 83, pl. 42, f. 1.--BP., Syn. 1828, 36; Isis, 1832, 1139.—AUD., Orn. Biog. i, 1832, 486; v, 1839, 392; pl. 97.—NUTT., Man. i, 1832, 120.—BREW., ed. Wils. 687.
Scops asio, BP., Comp. List, 1838, 6; Consp. i, 1850, 45.—LESS., Tr. Orn. 107.—KAUP, Mon. *Strig.* Cont. Orn. 1852, 112.—CASS., Ill. 1854, 179.—STRICKL., Orn. Syn. 1855, 199.—BREW., N. A. Oöl. 1857, 65.—BD., B. N. A. 1858, 51.—COOP. & SUCK., N. H. Wash. Ter. 1860, 155?—COOP., B. Cal. i, 1870, 420.—MAYN., Nat. Guide, 1870, 131.—COUES, Key, 1872, 202, fig. 136—B. B. & R., N. A. B. iii, 1874, 49; and of most authors.
Bubo asio, VIEILL., Ois. Am. Sept. i, 1807, 53, pl. 21.—AUD., Syn. 1839, 29; B. Am. i, 1840, 147, pl. 40.—DEKAY, N. Y. Zool. 1844, pl. 12, figs. 25, 26.—GIR., B. L. I. 1844, 28.—MAXIM., J. f. O. 1858, 23.
Hibou asio, TEMM., Planch. Color. No. 80.
Otus asio, STEPH., Gen. Zool. xiii, pt. ii, 57.
Ephialtes asio, GRAY, Gen. of B.—WOODH., Sitgr. Rep. 1853, 62.
Strix nævia, GM., Syst. Nat. i, 1788, 289.—LATH., Ind. Orn. i, 1790, 55.—DAUD., Tr. Orn. ii, 1800, 217.—SHAW, Gen. Zool. vii, 230.—WILS., Am. Orn. iii, 1812, 16, pl. 19, f. 1.
Asio nævia, LESS., Man. Orn. i, 117.
Otus nævius, CUV., R. A. i, 2d ed. 341.
Surnia nævia, JAM., ed. Wils. i, 96, 99.
Bubo striatus, VIEILL., Ois. Am. Sept. i, 1807, 54, pl. 21.
"*Ephialtes ocreata*, LICHT., Mus. Berol."

b. *kennicottii.*

Scops kennicottii, ELLIOT, Pr. Phila. Acad, 1867, 69; B. Am. p. xxvii, pl. 11.—DALL & BANN., Tr. Chic. Acad. i, 1869, 273.—BD., *ibid*. 311, pl. 27 (Sitka).—FINSCH, Abh. Nat. iii, 1872, 28 (Alaska).
Scops asio var. *kennicottii*, COUES, Key, 1872, 203.—B. B. & R., N. A. B. iii, 1874, 53.

c. *maccallii.*

Ephialtes choliba, LAWR., Ann. Lyc. N. Y. vi, 1853, 4 (not of *Vieill.*).
Scops maccallii, CASS., Ill. 1854, 180.—STRICKL., Orn. Syn. 1855, 200.—BREW., N. A. Oöl. 1857, 66.—BD., B. N. A. 1858, 52, pl. 39; Mex. B. Surv. ii, 1859, pt. ii, Birds, 4, pl. 1.—DRESS., Ibis, 1865, 330 (Texas). (*Not Scops trichopsis*, WAGL., Isis, 1832, 276: See SCL. & SALV., P. Z. 1868, 57.*)
Scops asio var. *maccallii*, COUES, Key, 1872, 203.—B. B. & R., N. A. B. iii, 1874, 52.

d. *floridanus.*

(?) *Scops asio*, CAB., J. f. O. iii, 465 (Cuba).
Scops asio var. *floridanus*, RIDGW.—B. B. & R., N. A. B. iii, 1874, 51.

---

* Mr. Ridgway has called my attention to the fact, that *S. trichopsis* of Wagler, to which *maccallii* is referred by Sclater and Salvin, as above quoted, is a perfectly distinct species, as, on examination of typical specimens, I find it to be.

e. *enano.*

(?) *Scops maccallii*, SCL., P. Z. S. 1858, 296 (Oaxaca).—SCL., Ibis, 1859, 220 (Guatemala).
Scops asio var. *enano,* LAWR., MSS.—B. B. & R., N. A. B. iii, 1874, 48.

Hab.—North America at large. Var. *kennicottii* is the large, dark, northern form, from Alaska, &c. Var. *maccallii* is a small, pale, southern form, from the southwestern border and southward. Var. *floridanus,* from Georgia, Florida (and Cuba ?). Var. *enano,* from Mexico and Guatemala.*

This little Owl does not appear to have been noticed by either of the Expeditions, as we find no specimens in the collection. It inhabits, however, the wooded tracts of the Missouri region, and is abundant in some parts, as in Kansas.

Without going into the history of the long controversy respecting the "Red" and "Mottled" Owls—which would involve scores of quotations†—it will be sufficient to state, that not only are these two birds identical, as indeed has been admitted by most observers since Wilson, but that, moreover, the plumages are purely fortuitous, and characteristic of neither sex, age, nor season. The same rufescent phase occurs in other species of Owls—notably, among ours, in the little *Glaucidium ferrugineum*, which I recently introduced to our fauna (Key, 206)—and is apparently analogous to the melanotic condition of many Hawks.

OTUS VULGARIS var. WILSONIANUS,(Less.) Allen.

American Long-earedOwl.

a. *vulgaris.*

Strix otus, LINN., Syst. Nat. i, 1766, 132 ; and of early authors generally.
Bubo otus, SAVIG., Descr. Egypte, i, 109.
Asio otus, LESS.,.Man. Orn. i, 116.
Ulula otus, MACGIL., Rap. B. Br. 403.
Ægolius otus, KEYS & BLAS., Wirb. Eur. 1840, 32.
" *Otus soloniensis,* GM., Syst. Nat. i, 1788, 203 " (*Gray*).
" *Otus albicollis* et *italicus,* DAUD., Tr. Orn. ii, 213" (*Strickland*).
Otus sylvestris, arboreus et *gracilis,* BREHM, V. D. i, 121, 122, 123.
Otus vulgaris, FLEM., Brit. An. 56 ; and of many authors.
Otus europœus, STEPH., Gen. Zool. xiii, pt. ii, 1826, 57.
Otus communis, LESS., Tr. Orn. 1831, 110.
Otus aurita, MONT., Orn. Dict. ed. Rennie, 262.
Otus asio, LEACH, Syst. Cat. 1816, 11.

b. *wilsonianus.*

(?) *Strix americana,* GM., Syst. Nat. i, 1788, 288.
Otus americanus, BP., Comp. List, 1838, 7 ; Consp. i, 1850, 50.—KAUP, Mon. Strig. Cont. Orn. 1852, 113 ; Tr. Z. S. iv, 1859, 233.—MAXIM., J. f. O. vi, 1858, 25.—ALLEN, Pr. Ess. Inst. iv, 1864, 51.
Strix peregrinator BARTR., Trav. in Fla. 1791, 289.
Asio peregrinator, STRICKL., Orn. Syn. 1855, 207.
Strix otus, WILS., vi, 1812, 73, pl. 51, f. 3.—BP., Syn. 1828, 37.—NUTT., Man. i, 1832, 130.—AUD., Orn. Biog. iv, 1835, 573, pl. 83.—PEAB., Rep. Orn. Mass. 1839, 88.
Strix (Asio) otus, SW. & RICH., F. B. A. ii, 1831, 72.
Ulula otus, JAM., ed. Wils. i, 104.

---

* Another small species of *Scops,* occurring over our southern border, is the following : SCOPS FLAMMEOLA, *Licht.*

Scops flammeola, LICHT., Nomen. Mus. Berol. 7.—KAUP, Monog. Tr. Z. S. iv, 1859, 226.—SCHL., M. P.-B. *Oti,* p. 27.—SCL., P. Z. S. 1858, 96.—SCL. & SALV., P. Z. S. 1868, 57 ; Exot. Orn. vi, 1868, 99, pl. 50.—ELLIOT, B. N. A. i, pl. 28.—COOP., B. Cal. i, 1870, 422.—COUES, Key, 1872, 203.—B. B. & R., N. A. B, iii, 1874, 58.

It was found breeding at Fort Crook, California, by the late Captain John Feilner, United States Army.

†Those who wish to examine the subject may refer to the following among other articles : BP., Journ. Phila. Acad. iii, 1824, 357.—MICHNER, *ibid.* vii, 1834, 53.—HOY, Pr. Phila. Acad. vi, 1853, 306 ; and Trans. Wisc. Agric. Soc. ii (1852), 1853, 344.—CABOT, Journ. Bost. Soc. ii, 1838, 126.—ALLEN, Am. Nat. ii, 1868, 327 ; Bull. M. C. Z. ii, 1871, 338.

Otus wilsonianus, LESS., Tr. Orn. i, 1831, 110.—CASS., Ill. 1854, 181.—BREW., N. A. Oöl.
    1857, 67.—BD., B. N. A. 1858, 53.—HAYD., Rep. 1862, 153.—COOP. & SUCK., N.
    H. Wash. Ter. 1860, 155.—COUES, Pr. Phila. Acad. 1866, 50 (Arizona).—COOP., B.
    Cal. i, 1870, 426.—SNOW, B. Kans. 1873.—MERR., U. S. Geol. Surv. Ter. 1872, 695.
Otus vulgaris, JARD., ed. Wils. ii, 278.—AUD., Syn. 1839, 28; B. Am. i, 1840, 136, pl. 37.—
    GIR., B. L. I. 1844, 25.
Otus vulgaris americanus, SCHL., Mus. Pays-Bas, 1862, *Oti,* p. 2.
Otus vulgaris var. *wilsonianus,* ALLEN, Bull. M. C. Z. iii, 1872, 180.—COUES, Key, 1872,
    204.—B. B. & R., N. A. B. iii, 1874, 18.

Hab.—Europe, &c. Var. *wilsonianus.* Temperate North America, at large.

List of specimens.

19130	290	Willow Springs.	♂	April 7, 1860	F. V. Hayden.	14.50	36.00	11.50
19131	174	Powder River..	....	Oct. 1, 1859	G. H. Trook..	14.00	37.00	12.50
19330	....	Popoagie Creek.	♂	....	...... do	13.00	35.00	11.00

Lieutenant Warren's Expedition.—4536, 4538, White River; 4537, Fort Pierre.
Later Expeditions.—61760, Devil's Creek, Idaho.

I quote the principal synonyms of the Old World form, without, however, additional references. In the uncertainty at present attending the determination of several names of American forms, I only quote those of special pertinence here.

This species is of not uncommon occurrence in the northwest, as in suitable places elsewhere throughout temperate North America.

"This species is quite common in Eastern Pennsylvania throughout the year. It is more retiring in its nature than *Nyctale acadica*. The latter prefers an orchard, in close proximity to man; while the former, according to the writer's experience, evinces by its actions a partiality for deep forests of evergreens, where the hum and stir of busy farm-life is nearly unknown. The nests are usually constructed of rude sticks, sometimes of boughs with the leaves adherent thereto, externally, and generally, but not always, lined with the feathers of birds. The same nest is made use of for several successive years. The female begins to lay early in April, and sometimes produces two broods in a season. The eggs are never more than four in number; sometimes as low as two have been observed. It is stated, by both Audubon and Wilson, that the nests of other birds, when of sufficient size, are generally used in which to rear its young. Although it has not been my fortune to know of such a case by personal experience, yet I cannot doubt the observations of these learned authorities. One of the best authenticated cases is that related by Wilson, where one of these Owls had taken possession, forcibly, as I am led to infer, of the nest of the Qua-bird (Night Heron), and was actually setting. The common Crow occasionally builds in similar situations in this latitude, and there is a possibility that its abandoned nests are sometimes appropriated, but this is mere presumption. Within three quarters of a mile of Chestnut Hill (upper part of Germantown), existed an immense forest of pines, within a comparatively recent period, which was the great place of rendezvous of the Long-eared Owl, during the dreary winter months, and where, in the spring-time, the females deposited their eggs in rude and unsightly nests of their own construction. The numbers that thronged this thicket of pines was prodigious, so there were very few of the trees, if any, that had not supported one or more nests. The many fragments of the bones of mammals and birds, and the other remains of the same that laid in piles upon the ground, bore testimony to the wholesale destruction of life that was carried on. Within the last two years, during which time many of the trees have yielded to the woodman's axe, the number that visit the wood is small in comparison. The birds have mostly gone to more congenial localities, and but a few remain of all that mighty host."—(*Gentry.*)

BRACHYOTUS PALUSTRIS, (Bechst.) Gould.

Short-eared Owl.

(a. *general references.*)

"*Strix noctua major*, BRISS., Orn. i, 511." (This is one of the bases of *Strix ulula*, L., 1766.)
"*Noctua minor*, GM., Nov. Comm. Petrop. xv, 447, pl. 12."
"*Strix stridula*, ——, Nov. Act. Reg. Ac. Suec. 1783, 47." (*Strickland.*)
"*Strix arctica*, SPARRM., Mus. Carls. pl. 51.—DAUD., Tr. Orn. ii, 197."
Strix brachyotus, GM., Syst. Nat. i, 1788, 289.—LATH., Ind. Orn. i, 1790, 55.—DAUD., Tr.
    Orn. ii, 1800, 216.—BECHST., Naturg. ii, 909.—SHAW, G. Z. vii, 1809, 223.—
    TEMM., Man. i, 89; iii, 51; Tabl. Meth. 7.—MEY., Tasch. i, 73.—FRISCH., V. D.
    pl. 98.—VIEILL., Fn. Franç. 43, pl. 20, f. 3,—ROUX, Orn. Prov. i, 75, pl. 49.—
    BAILL., Orn. Sav. i, 177.—BREW., Br. B. 2d ed. i, 58, 60.—YARR., Br. B. i, 121.—
    PENN., Br. Z. i, 1812, 260, pl. 32.—SELYS-LONGCH., Fn. Belg. 59.—MORR., Br. B.
    173, pl. 23.
Otus brachyotus, BOIE, Isis, 1822, 549.—STEPH., G. Z. xiii, pt. ii, 1826, 57.—HODG., J. A.
    S. B. 1837, 369.—JENYNS, Man. 92.—NAUM., V. D. i, 1822, 459, pl. 45.—EYT.,
    Cat. Br. B. 6.—SCHL., Rev. Crit. 14.—GRAY, Gen. of B. i, 1844, 40.—RÜPP., Syst.
    Uebers. 12.—CUV., R. A. ed. 2, i, 341.—LESS., Tr. Orn. 1831, 111.—JARD., Br. B.
    i, 285.—SW., Classif. B. ii, 1837, 217.—BP., Cat. Ucc. Eur. 1842, 23.—SELBY, Ill.
    Br. B. i, 88.—FLEM., Br. An. 56.—MONT., Orn. Dict. ed. Rennie, 241.—THOMPS.,
    B. Irel. i, 88.—WATT., B. Irel. 24.—PEALE, U. S. Exp. Ex. 75.—KAUP, Mon. *Strig.*
    Contr. Orn. 1852, 114; Tr. Z. S. iv, 1859, 236.—HUDS., P. Z. S. 1870, 799.—CASS.,
    Cat. *Strig.* Acad. Phila. 1849, 11.
Asio brachyotus, MACGIL., Brit. B. iii, 461.—STRICKL., Orn. Syn. 1855, 209.
Ulula brachyotus, MACGIL., Rapac. B. Br. 412.
Ægolius brachyotus, KEYS & BLAS., Wirb. Eur. 1840, 32.
Strix accipitrina, PALL., Itin. i, 455.—GM., Sib. Reise, ii, 163—GM., Syst. Nat. i, 1788, 295.—
    DAUD., Tr. Orn. ii, 1800, 185.
"*Strix ulula*, GM., Syst. Nat. i, 1788, 294 (*nec* LINN.)".—LATH., Ind. Orn. i, 1790, 60.—
    DAUD., Tr. Orn. ii, 1800, 196.—SHAW, G. Z. vii, 1809, 270.
Asio ulula, LESS., Man. i, 116.
Otus ulula, CUV., R. A. i, 1817, 328.
"*Strix passerina* var. B., LATH., Ind. Orn. i, 1790, 66."
Strix palustris, BECHST., V. D. ii, 344.—SIEMSS., Hand-buch, 35.—LATH., Ind. Orn. Suppl.
    13.—SHAW, G. Z. vii, 1809, 227.—MEY., Zool. Ann. i, 332.
Otus palustris, GOULD, Zool. Voy. Beagle, pt. iii, p. 33.—BREHM, V. D. i, 123.—BRIDGES,
    P. Z. S. ix, 110; Ann. Nat. Hist. xiii, 500.
Brachyotus palustris, GOULD, B. Eur. pl. 40.—BP., List, 1838, 7.
Brachyotus palustris europæus, BP., Consp. i, 1850, 51.
Strix tripennis, SCHRANK, Fn. Boica, 112.
Strix brachyura, NILSS., Fn. Suec. i, 62.
Strix caspia, SHAW, G. Z. vii, 1809, 272.
Strix ægolius, PALL., Zoog. R. A. i, 309.
Otus microcephalus, LEACH, Syst. Cat. 1816, 11.
Otus agrarius, BREHM, V. D. i, 124.

(b. *American references.*)

Strix brachyotus, FORST., Phil. Trans. lxii, 1772, 384.—WILS., Am. Orn. iv, 1812, 64, pl.
    32, f. 3.—BP., Syn. 1828, 37.—NUTT., Man. i, 1832, 132.—AUD., Orn. Biog. v,
    1839, 273, pl. 432.—THOMPS., N. H. Vermont, 66.—PEAB., Rep. Orn. Mass. 89.
Strix brachyota, Sw. & RICH., F. B. A. ii, 1831, 75.
Otus brachyotus, AUD., Syn. 1839, 28; B. Am. i, 1840, pl. 38.—JARD., ed. Wils. ii, 63.—
    GIR., B. L. I. 1844, 26.—CASS., Ill. 1854, 182.—REINH., Ibis, iii, 1861, 5 (Green-
    land).—ALLEN, Bull. M. C. Z. ii, 1871, 340.—SCL. & SALV., P. Z. S. 1868, 143.—
    PELZ., Orn. Bras. i, 10.—HUDS., P. Z. S. 1870, 799.
Otus (Brachyotus) brachyotus, B. B. & R., N. A. B. iii, 1874, 22.
Ulula brachyotus, JAM., ed. Wils. i, 106.—PHILIPPI, Cat. (Chili).
Otus brachyotus americanus, MAXIM., J. f. O. vi, 1858, 27.
Otus palustris, DEKAY, N. Y. Zool. ii, 28, pl. 12, f. 27.
Brachyotus palustris, BP., List, 1838, 7.•—COUES, Pr. Phila. Acad. 1871, 27; Key, 1872, 204.
Brachyotus palustris americanus, BP., Consp. i, 1850, 51.
Brachyotus cassini, BREW., Pr. Bost. Soc. 1856, —.—BREW., N. Am. Oöl. 1857, 68.—CAB.,
    J. f. O. iii, 465 (Cuba).—GUNDL., Rep. 1865, 225 (Cuba).—BD., B. N. A. 1858,
    54.—NEWB., P. R. R. Rep. vi, 1857, 76.—HEERM., *ibid.* x, 1859, pt. vi, 34.—SCL.,
    P. Z. S. 1859, 390 (Oaxaca).—COOP. & SUCK., N. H. Wash. Ter. 1860, 155.—
    HAYD., Rep. 1862, 154.—DRESS., Ibis, 1865, 330.—COUES, Pr. Phila. Acad. 1866,

50.—SCL. & SALV., P. Z. S. 1868, 143 (Buenos Ayres).—DALL & BANN., Tr. Chic. Acad. i, 1869, 273.—COOP., B. Cal. i, 1870, 428.—STEV., U. S. Geol. Surv. Ter. 1870, 462.—SNOW, B. Kans. 1873, 2.—DALL, Pr. Cal. Acad. Feb. 1873 (Aleutian Islands).

c. galapagoensis.

Brachyotus galapagoensis, GOULD, P. Z. S. 1837, 10.
Otus galapagoensis, DARW., Voy. Beagle, iii, 32, pl. 3.—BP., Consp. Av. i, 1850, 51.— GRAY, Gen. of B.; List B. Brit. Mus. 108.
Asio galapagoensis, STRICKL., Orn. Syn. 1855, 211.

Hab.—Europe. Asia. Greenland. America. West Indies. Var. *galapagoensis* from the Galapagos.
Lieutenant Warren's Expedition.—4634, Grindstone Creek; 4539, White River.
Later Expeditions.—60633, Sweetwater, Wyoming.

The specific name of this species is highly appropriate, such is its preference for low, moist, and even swampy or marshy resorts. The greater part of the Missouri region being not particularly adapted to its wants, it is not so common or so generally diffused in this part of the country as in some other portions. I procured one specimen at Fort Randall, in the winter of 1872-'73. It is, however, one of the few species not confined to woods, but occurring in open prairie, sometimes many miles from timbered land. It nests on the ground, laying its eggs either in a bare depression, or upon a few sticks, or feathers, or a little grass. The eggs, usually four or five in number, are dull white, less nearly spherical than usual in this family, and measure about an inch and a half in length by one and a fourth in breadth. But its nesting varies with circumstances. Mr. Dall recently found it breeding in burrows, on the island of Oonalashka; "the hole is horizontal, and the inner end usually a little higher than the aperture; lined with dry grass and feathers." The burrows were not over two feet deep, usually excavated in the side of a steep bank.

Being so generally diffused in this country, it is not a little surprising that Dr. Brewer should have been led to say, in 1857, there was no authentic case of its occurrence, south of Pennsylvania, in the United States. It is decidedly the commonest Owl about Washington, D. C., especially in winter. I frequently observed it in the salt-marshes of the North Carolina coast at various seasons, and Mr. Allen records it as quite common in the marshes of Florida. On one occasion I observed a gathering of twenty or thirty individuals on the Colorado River, below Fort Mojave; others have noted similar instances of its sociable disposition. The birds were sitting quite closely together in the rank herbage bordering the river; some flapped hurriedly off as the steamboat came abreast of them, while others stood to their perches as we passed. In California, Dr. Cooper observes that he has not seen it south of the Santa Clara Valley. It occurs in the West Indies, and the South American form is conspecific. I am unable to appreciate any constant or tangible differences between the European and American bird, although the latter may average slightly larger, and a shade darker.

SYRNIUM CINEREUM, (Gm.) Aud.

Great Gray Owl.

a. cinereum.

Strix cinerea, GM., Syst. Nat. i, 1788, 291.—LATH., Ind. Orn. i, 1790, 58 (based on Sooty Owl, Arct. Zool. ii, 232, No. 120; Cinereous Owl, Syn. Suppl. 45).—VIEILL., Nouv. Dict. d'Hist. Nat. vii, 23; Enc. Meth. iii, 1289; Ois. Am. Sept. i, 48.— BP., Am. Orn. pl. 23; Ann. Lyc. N. Y. ii, 436; Isis, 1832, 1140.—NUTT., Man. i,

1832, 128.—Sw. & RICH., F. B. A. ii, 1831, 77, pl. 31.—AUD., Orn. Biog. iv, 1838, 364, pl. 351.—TYZEN., R. Z. 1851, 571.
Scotiaptex cinerea, Sw., Classif. B. ii, 1837, 217.
Ulula cinerea, BP., Consp. i, 1850, 53 (in part).
Syrnium cinereum, BP., List, 1838, 6.—AUD., Syn. 1839, 26; B. Am. i, 130, pl. 35.—BREW., ed. Wils. 1840, 687.—DEKAY, N. Y. Zool. ii, 26, pl. 13, f. 29.—ABBOTT, Pr. Bost. Soc. i, pp. 57, 99 (Massachusetts).—PUTN., Pr. Ess. Inst. i, 1856, 204 (Massachusetts).—CASS., Ill. 184.—STRICKL., Orn. Syn. 1855, 188.—NEWB., P. R. R. Rep. vi, 1857, 77 (Sacramento Valley, Cal., and Oregon).—BD., B. N. A. 1858, 56.—KAUP, Tr. Z. S. iv, 1859, 256.—COOP. & SUCK., N. H. Wash. Ter. 1860, 156.—WHEAT., Ohio Agric. Rep. 1860, No. 25.—BOARDM., Pr. Bost. Soc. ix, 1862, 123 (Maine, rare).—ALLEN, Pr. Ess. Inst. iv, 1864, 81 (Massachusetts).—VERR., *ibid.* iii, 1862, 144 (Maine, rare).—COUES, *ibid.* v, 1868, 260 (New England).—MCILWR., *ibid.* v, 1866, 82 (Canada West, in winter, rare).—TURNB., B. E. Pa. 1869, 40 ("several times found in New Jersey.").—DALL & BANN., Tr. Chic. Acad. i, 1869, 273 (Alaska).—MAYN., Guide, 1870, 130 (Massachusetts).—HATCH, Bull. Minn. Acad. i, 1874, 52 (Minnesota, common).—RIDGW., Ann. Lyc. N. Y. x, 1874, 379 (Illinois).
Syrnium (Scotiaptex) cinereum, B. B. & R., N. A. B. iii, 1874, 30.
Syrnium lapponicum var. *cinereum*, RIDGW., *apud* COUES, Key, 1872, 204; but *cinereum* (1788) has priority over *lapponicum* (1800).
"*Strix acclamator*, BART., Trav. 1790, 285" (more likely *S. nebulosum*).
"*Strix fuliginosa*, SHAW, Gen. Zool. vii, 1809, 244."

b. *lapponicum.*

Strix lapponica, RETZ., Fn. Suec. 1800, 79, No. 30.—SPARRM., Mus. Carls.—NILSS., Orn. Suec. i, 58.—MEYER, Taschenb. iii, 20.—TEMM., Man. Orn. pt. i, 81; pt. iii, 44.—WERN., Atl. Ois. Eur. pl.—TYZEN., R. Z. 1851, 576.
Ulula lapponica, LESS., Man. Orn. i, 113; Tr. Orn. 108.—CUV., R. A. 2d ed. i, 342.
Surnia lapponica, GOULD, B. Eur. pl. 42.
Syrnium lapponicum, STRICKL., Orn. Syn. 1855, 188.
Strix barbata, PALL., Zool. R. A. i, 318, pl. 2.
Strix microphthalma, TYZEN.
Syrnium microphthalmum, GRAY.
Syrnium cinereum, BP. List, 1838, 6; Cat. Ucc. Eur. 23.
Ulula cinerea, BP., Consp. Av. i, 1850, 53.

Hab.—Northern North America, south in winter to Massachusetts (to New Jersey, *Turnbull*), Illinois (*Ridgway*), and California. Var. *lapponicum* from corresponding latitudes in the Old World.

Although this species was not noticed by the Expeditions, it is introduced as one undoubtedly occurring in the Missouri region in winter. Dr. Cooper states that it is "common" in the dense spruce forests of the Columbia, and probably resident in that latitude. According to Dr. Newberry, proofs of its occurrence even to the Sacramento Valley have been obtained. It is given in Mr. Wheaton's Ohio list, and has frequently occurred in New England as far south as Massachusetts. Dr. Turnbull's notice extends the record to New Jersey, Mr. Ridgway's to Illinois. It is said by Dr. Hatch to be very common in Minnesota.

SYRNIUM NEBULOSUM, (Forst.) Boie.

Barred Owl.

a. *nebulosum.*

Strix nebulosa, FORST., Tr. Philos. Soc. lxii, 1772, 386, 424.—GM., Syst. Nat. i, 1788, 291.—LATH., Ind. Orn. i, 1790, 58.—DAUD., Tr. Orn. ii, 1800, 191.—SHAW, G. Z. vii, 1809, 245; Misc. pl. 25.—VIEILL., Ois. Am. Sept. 1807, pl. 17; Nouv. Dict. d'Hist. Nat. vii, 32; Enc. Meth. iii, 1292.—WILS., Am. Orn. iv, 1812, 61, pl. 33, f. 2.—JARD., ed. Wils. ii, 57.—BP., Syn. 1828, 38; Isis, 1832, 1140.—Sw. & RICH., F. B. A. ii, 1831, 81.—NUTT., Man. i, 1832, 133.—AUD., Orn. Biog. i, 1832, 242; v, 1839, 386; pl. 46.—DEKAY, N. Y. Zool. 1844, pl. 10, f. 21.
Syrnium nebulosum, BOIE.—GRAY, Gen. of B.—GOULD, B. Eur. pl. 46.—AUD., Syn. 1839, 27; B. Am. i, 1840, 132, pl. 36.—WOODH., Sitgr. Rep. 1853, 63.—CASS., Ill. 1854, 184.—BREW., N. A. Oöl. 1857, 72.—BD., B. N. A. 1858, 56.—KAUP, Cont. Orn.

1852, 12; Tr. Z. S. iv, 1859, 256.—MAXIM., J. f. O. vi, 1858, 28.—DRESS., Ibis, 1865, 330 (Texas).—HAYD., Rep. 1862, 154.—ALLEN. Mem. Bost. Soc. i, 1868, 499 (Western Iowa); 506 (Illinois).—COOP., B. Cal. i, 1870, 431 (but never found in California).—ALLEN, Bull. M. C. Z. ii, 1871, 340 (Florida).—TRIPPE, Pr. Ess. Inst. vi, 1871, 114 (Minnesota).—SNOW, B. Kans. 1873, 2 (Kansas, common).—COUES, Key, 1872, 204, fig. 137.
Ulula nebulosa, STEPH., G. Z. xiii, pt. ii, 60.—CUV., R. A. 2d. ed. i, 342.—JAMES., ed. Wils. i, 107; iv, 280.—LESS., Man. i, 113; Tr. 108.—BP., List, 1838, 7; Consp. Av. i, 1850, 53.—SCHL., Mus. Pays-Bas, *Striges*, 1862, p. 11.
Strix chichictli, GM., Syst. Nat. i, 1788, 296.
(?) *Strix acclamator*, BARTR., Trav. in Fla. 1791, 289.
Strix varius, BART., Frag. N. H. Pa. 1799, 11.
Strix fernandica, SHAW, Gen. Zool. vii, 1809, 263.

b. *sartorii*.

Syrnium nebulosum var. *sartorii*, RIDGW.—B. B. & R., N. A. B. iii, 1874, 29 (Mirador).

c. *fulvescens*.

Syrnium fulvescens, SALV., P. Z. S. 1868, 58 (Guatemala).
Syrnium nebulosum var. *fulvescens*, RIDGW.—B. B. & R., N. A. B. iii, 1874, 29.

Hab.—North America, east of the Rocky Mountains. Chiefly United States. Var. *sartorii* in Mexico. Var. *fulvescens* in Central America.
Lieutenant Warren's Expedition.—No. 4607, Missouri River.

This specimen of Dr. Hayden's remains, as it was when taken, the westernmost on record for the species. The Barred Owl is one of the few which does not appear to be equally distributed, having never yet been observed west of the Rocky Mountains, where it is to some extent replaced by the allied but perfectly distinct *S. occidentale*, discovered by Mr. Xantus, at Fort Tejon, California, and subsequently observed in Arizona, by Lieutenant Bendire, United States Army. It appears to be somewhat a southerly bird, very abundant in the woods of the South Atlantic and Gulf States; but, although common in New England, is rather sparingly represented in British America, the home of the Great Gray Owl, *S. cinereum*. It breeds in March, laying five or six white subspherical eggs in the hollow or among the branches of a tree, sometimes taking possession of a deserted Hawk's or Crow's nest, sometimes building for itself. The eggs measure about 2 inches in length by 1⅔ in breadth. Although Wilson states to the contrary, the sexes of this bird are not appreciably different in size, nor otherwise distinguishable by external characters. The average size appears to be 20 inches in length, 47 in extent, the wing 13½, the tail 9.

The third and only other species of *Syrnium* of North America, *S. occidentale*, will probably, in time, be found in the Missouri region. Its synonymy is given below.*

NYCTEA SCANDIACA, (Linn.) Newt.

Great White or Snowy Owl.

Strix capite aurito, corpore albido, LINN., Fn. Suec. 1746, 16; ex *Bubo scandianus*, RUDEB., Ic. ined. (*fide* WALDEN).
Strix scandiaca, LINN., Syst. Nat. i, 1766, 132 (ex *præced.*).—MALMG., J. f. O. 1865, 396.
Nyctea scandiaca, NEWT., 4th ed. Yarr. Br. B. pt. iii, 1872, 187.—DRESS., B. Eur. pt. —.
Nyctea scandiaca var. *arctica*, RIDGW.—B. B. & R., N. A. B. iii, 1874, 70.
Strix alba freti-hudsonis, BRISS., Orn. i, 1760, 522.
Strix nyctea, LINN., Syst. Nat. i, 1766, 132 (ex *Aluco albus diurnus*, EDW., 61.—BRISS., i, 522).—BRÜNN., Orn. Bor. 1764, 7.—FORST., Phil. Trans. lxii, 1772, 385.—GM., Syst. Nat. i, 1788, 201.—FABR., Fn. Groen. No. 16.—LATH., Ind. Orn. i, 1790,

---

* *Syrnium occidentale*, XANTUS, Pr. Phila. Acad. 1859, 193.—BD., B. N. A. 1860, pl. 66 (not in ed. of 1858).—COUES, Key, 1872, 204.—B. B. & R., N. A. B. iii, 1874, 38.

Hab.—California (Fort Tejon, *Xantus*). Arizona (*Bendire*).

57.—DAUD., Tr. Orn. ii, 1800, 188.—BECHST., Naturg. ii, 925 ; V. D. ii, 350.—
MEYER, Tasch. i, 75.—VIEILL., Ois. Am. Sept. pl. 18 ; Fn. Fr. 48, pl. 23, f. 2.—
SHAW, Gen. Zool. vii, 1809, 240.—SAB., Parry's 1st Voy. Suppl. 193.—RICH.,
Parry's 2d Voy. App. 342.—PALL., Zoog. R. A. i, 1831, 312.—WILS., Am. Orn.
iv, 1812, 53, pl. 32, f. 1.—BP., Syn. 1828, 34 ; Isis, 1832, 1139.—TEMM., Man. pt.
i, p. 82 ; pt. iii, p. 45 ; Tabl. Meth. 6.—NAUM., V. D. 241, pl. 33, f. 66; ed. nov.
j, 417, pl. 41.—YARR., Br. B. i, 134.—FLEM., Br. An. 58.—SCHINZ, Fn. Helv. 56.—
MONT., Dict. (ed. Rennie) 471.—MORR., Br. B. i, 194, pl. 27.—WERN., Atl. Ois.
pl. 45.—SW. & RICH., F. B. A. ii, 1831, 88.—NUTT., Man. i, 1832, 116.—AUD.,
Orn. Biog. iv, 1834, 135 ; v, 1839, 382 ; pl. 121.—THOMPS., Hist. Vt. 64.—PEAB.,
Rep. Orn. Mass. 1839, 84.—SCHL., Rev. Crit. Ois. Eur. 17.
Noctua nyctea, CUV., R. A. i, 1817, 332.—BOIE, Isis, 1822, 770.—LESS., Man. i, 110 : Tr.
101.—BREHM, Isis, 1834, 240.—BREHM, V. D. 103.—JENYNS, Man. Br. Vert.
23.—SCHL., M. P.-B. 1862, *Striges*, 45.
Syrnium nyctea, KAUP, Sk. Ent. Eur. Thierw. 1829, pp. 59, 190.
Surnia nyctea, SELBY, Ill. Br. Orn. i, 1833, 95, pl. 23.—EDMONST., Mem. Wern. Soc. iv,
157.—JAMES., ed. Wils. i, 92.—GOULD, B. Eur. pl. 43.—JARD., Br. B. i, 303.—
THOMPS., B. Irel. i, 95.—EYT., Cat. Br. B. 6.—KEYS & BLAS., Wirb. Eur.
33.—AUD., Syn. 1839, 21 ; B. Am. i, 1840, 113, pl. 28.—DEKAY, N. Y. Zool. 1844,
pl. 9, f. 20.—GIR., B. L. I. 1844, 22.—PUTN., Pr. Ess. Inst. i, 1856, 204.—KAUP,
Tr. Z. S. iv, 1859, 214.
Syrnia nyctea, MACGIL., Hist. Br. B. iii, 1840, 407 : Rep. B. Gr. Brit. 348.—THOMPS., Ann.
Nat. Hist. i, 241 ; iii, 107.—JARD., ed. Wils. ii, 46.—WATT., B. Irel. 27.
Strix wapacuthu, GM., Syst. Nat. i, 1788, 291 (*ex Wapacuthu Owl*, PENN., Arct. Zool. ii,
1785, 231, No. 119).—LATH., Ind. Orn. i, 1790, 58 (Gen. Syn. Suppl. 49).—DAUD.,
Tr. Orn. ii, 1800, 189.—SHAW, Gen. Zool. vii, 1809, 243.—VIEILL., Ois. Am. Sept. 47.
Nyctea wapacuthu, STEPH., Shaw's Gen. Zool. xiii, 1826, 63, No. 2.
Strix arctica, BART., Trav. in Fla. 1791, 289.
Strix nivea, THUNB., Sv. Ak. Handlung, 1798, 84.—DAUD., Tr. Orn. ii, 1800, 190 (*la Chou-
ette blanche*, LEVAIL., Ois. Afr. i, 1799, 174, pl. 45).—ZAWAD., Fn. Wirb. 1840, 45.
Noctua nivea, BREHM, Isis, 1834, 246.
Nyctea nivea, GRAY, Gen. of B. i, 1844, 34, pl. 12, f. 2 ; List, B. Br. Mus. 86 ; Cat. Gen.
8.—BP., Consp. Av. i, 1850, 36.—CASS., Ill. 1854, 190.—BREHM, Vogelf. 1855, 35.—
BREW., N. Am. Oöl. 1857, 79.—BD., B. N. A. 1858, 63.—KIRKP., Ohio Agric. Rep.
1858.—WHEAT., *ibid.* 1860, No. 28 (Ohio).—COUES & PRENT., Smiths. Rep. 1861,
402, (Washington, D .C.).—BOARDM., Pr. Bost. Soc. ix, 1862, 123 (Calais, Me.,
probably breeding).—VERR., Pr. Ess. Inst. iii, 1862, 144 (Norway, Me., in winter).—ALLEN, *ibid.* iv, 1864, 52 and 97 (Massachusetts, Nov. to May 20).—
McILWR., *ibid.* v, 1866, 82 (Hamilton, C. W., in winter).—COUES, *ibid.* v, 1868,
261 (New England, in winter).—DRESS., Ibis, 1865, 330 (Texas).—LAWR.,
Ann. Lyc. N. Y. viii, 1866, 259.—COUES, Pr. Bost. Soc. xii, 1868, 120 (South
Carolina).—TURNB., B. E. Pa. 1869, 9 (winter, rather rare).—DALL & BANN.,
Tr. Chic. Acad. i, 1869, 273 (Alaska).—DALL, Pr. Phila. Acad. Feb. 1873 (Aleu-
tian Islands).—COOP., B. Cal. i, 1870, 447 (never found in California).—SNOW,
B. Kans. 1873, 2 (Kansas, rare in winter).—COUES, Key, 1872, 205, fig. 138.
Nyctea nivea europœa et *americana*, A. BREHM, Verz. Samml. C. L. Brehm, 1866, 2.
Strix bubo var. *albus*, DAUD., Tr. Orn. ii, 1800, 210 (ex LINN.).
Strix candida, LATH., Ind. Orn. Suppl. 1801, p. xiv, No. 3 (*ex* LEVAIILL.—*Ermine Owl*,
LATH., Syn. Suppl. ii, 1802, 60, No. 7).
Nyctia candida, SW., Classif. B. ii, 1837, 217.
Nyctea candida, BREHM, Vogelf. 1855, 35.—BP., List, 1838, 6.—KAUP, Mon. *Strig.* Cont.
Orn. 1852, 107.
Strix erminea, SHAW, Gen. Zool. vii, 1809, 251.
Nyctea erminea, STEPH., Gen. Zool. xiii, pt. ii, 1826, 63, No. 1.
Harfang, BUFF., P. E. 458.

Hab.—Northern portions of the Northern Hemisphere, ranging irregularly southward in winter. In North America, resident from the Canadas and probably from
Maine, northward. Regularly enters the Northern States in winter, frequently wandering to the Middle States, casually to the Southern States, even to Texas (*Dresser*).
Kansas (*Snow*). Kentucky and South Carolina (*Audubon*). Bermuda (*Jardine*).

Although apparently unnoticed by either Expedition, the Snowy
Owl visits the Missouri region in winter, as it does the corresponding
latitudes of the Eastern States. Its wanderings are more extensive
than those of either the Hawk Owl or the Great Gray Owl, as will be
seen by the above quotations, and are remarkable for a bird whose
whole aspect betokens a nature fitted to endure the utmost rigor of
climate. We have advices of its presence in winter in *nearly* all the

States east of the Mississippi, and in Kansas and Texas; while the silence of the records in the West may be in greatest part due to the fact, that few explorations are conducted—even individual observations being restricted—during the inclement season, when its visits are made, if at all. But I have learned, from several residents in the vicinity of Fort Randall, of its occasional appearance on the Missouri at that point. I find no United States quotations west of the Rocky Mountains; for although the species is admitted in Dr. Cooper's work, this author admits "there is as yet no intimation of the occurrence in California of this large Owl." In New England and a part of the Middle States, the Snowy Owl is sometimes common in winter. Mr. Cassin remarks that it is occasionally so numerous as to sell for a mere trifle in the Philadelphia markets. It does not, however, entirely withdraw from the arctic regions even in winter, at which season Mr. Dall saw it flying over the frozen Yukon. The probability is, that it is resident in the forests of Maine. Mr. Boardman instances a pair seen in spring that probably had a nest in the vicinity of Calais; and its capture in Massachusetts, as late as the 20th of May, is recorded by Mr. Allen.

According to those who have studied the bird in its native regions, it is not exclusively nocturnal, but hunts by day without inconvenience; feeds on hare and grouse as well as smaller game, and is expert in fishing; nests on the ground, and lays three or four white eggs measuring about 2⅝ inches in length by 2 in breadth.

SURNIA ULULA var. HUDSONIA, (Gm.) Coues.

American Hawk Owl.

a. *ulula.*

Chouette à longue quene de Sibérie, BUFF., P. E. 463; Ois. Sonn. iv, pl. 30, fig. 1.
Chouette épervière, BUFF., Ois. Sonn., iv, 128.
Strix ulula, LINN., Syst. Nat. i, 1766, 133 (based on Fn. Suec. 78; BRISS., i, 511, &c.).—
    DONND., Beit. i, 169.—NILSS., Skand. Fn. i, 64.
(???) *Strix ulula* var. *b.*, LATH., Ind. Orn. i, 1790, 60 (quotes *S. arctica*, SPARR., Mus. Carls.
    iii, p. 5).
Surnia ulula, BP., Cat. Ucc. Eur. p. 22.—GRAY, Gen. of B. i, 1844, pl. 12, fig. 1.—KAUP,
    Mon. *Strig.* Cont. Orn. 1852, 107.—GRAY, Hand-list, i, 1869, 39.—DRESS., B. Eur.
    pt. xii, 1872.
"*Strix funerea*, LINN., Fn. Suec, 1761, 25, No. 75" (this is also the primary basis of Syst.
    Nat. i, 1766, 133, No. 11, with which, however, is cited *S. canadensis*, BRISS.).—
    LATH., Ind. Orn. ii, 1790, 60.—TEMM., Man. i, 1820, 86.—SCHL., Rev. Crit. 1844, 17.
Noctua (*Surnia*) *funerea*, CUV., R. A. 1817, i, 332.
Surnia funerea, BP., List, 1838, 6.—GOULD, B. Eur. pl. 45.—LESS., Man. i, 110.—SW.,
    Classif. B. ii, 218.—BREHM, V. D. i, 101.—KEYS & BLAS. Wirb. Eur. 1840, 32.
Strix uralensis, SHAW, Gen. Zool. vii, 1809, 277, pl. 35 (*nec* PALL.).
Strix nisoria, MEYER, Tasch. i, 1810, 84.—BECHST., Naturg. ii, 984.—NAUM., V. D. 1822,
    i, 427, pl. 42, fig. 2.
Syrnium nisoria, KAUP, Sk. Ent. Eur. Thierw. 1829, 59.
Noctua nisoria, CUV., R. A. 2d ed. i, 1829, 344.
Surnia nisoria, BREHM, V. D. i, 102, pl. 7, fig. 1.
Strix doliata, PALL., Zoog. R.-A. i, 1811, 316, pl. 1.
(??) "*Strix arctica*, SPARRM., Mus. Carls. 51."—(GRAY; rather *Brachyotus palustris*).
"*Strix accipitrina*, BECHST., Vog. Deutsch. ii, 372, pl. 12."

b. *hudsonia.*

Strix canadensis, BRISS., Orn. i, 1760, 518, pl. 37, fig. 2.—SHAW, Gen. Zool. vii, 1809, 273.
Surnia canadensis, STEPH., Shaw's Gen. Zool. xiii, pt. ii, 1826, 62.
Strix freti-hudsonis, BRISS., Orn. i, 1760, 520 ("Little Hawk Owl," EDW., ii, 1747, pl. 62;
    whence *Caparacoch*, BUFF., i, 1770, 306).
Strix funerea, LINN., Syst. Nat. i, 1766, 133 (partly; includes the European).—FORST.,
    Philos. Trans. lxii, 1772, 3-5.—BP., Syn. 1828, 25.—SW. & RICH., F. B. A. ii,

1831, 92.—Nutt., Man. i, 1832, 115.—Peab., Rep. Orn. Mass. 83.—Brew , ed.
Wils. 686.—Thomps., Vermont, 64.—Aud., Orn. Biog. iv, 350, pl. 378.—DeKay,
N. Y. Zool. 1844, pl. 9, fig. 19.
Surnia funerea, Duméril, Zool. Anal. 1806, 34.—Bp., List, 1836, 6.—Jard., ed. Wils. ii,
270; Br. B. i, 514.—Aud., Syn. 1839, 21; B. Am. i, 1840, 112, pl. 27.—Dress. &
Sharpe, B. Eur. pt. xii, Aug. 1872 (North America and Great Britain).
Noctua (Surnia) funerea, Jenyns, Man. Br. Vert. 526.
Syrnia funerea, Macgil., Hist. Brit. Birds, iii, 1840, 404 (*fide* Dr. & Sh.).
Noctua funerea, Yarrell, Hist. Brit. Birds, i, 1843, 139 (*fide* Dr. & Sh.).
Strix caparoch, Müller, Syst. Nat. Suppl. 1779, i, 69.
Strix hudsonia, Gm., Syst. Nat. i, 1788, 295.—Wils., Am. Orn. vi, 1812, 64, pl. 50, fig. 6
(Philadelphia).
Surnia hudsonia, Jameson, ed. Wils. i, 90.
Surnia borealis, Lesson, Traité d' Orn. i, 1831, 100.
Strix ulula of Authors, partly; excluding Continental European references.
Surnia ulula, Cass., Ill. 1854, 191 (excl. part of the synonymy).—Brew., N. A. Oöl. 1857,
80 (excl. part of syns.).—Bd., B. N. A. 1858, 64 (excl. pt. syn.).—Wheat., Ohio
Agric. Rep. 1860, No. 29.—Hoy, Tr. Wisc. Agric. Soc. 1852; Pr. Phila. Acad. 1853
(Wisconsin).—Board., Pr. B. Soc. ix, 1862, 123 (Calais, Me., breeding).—Verr.,
Pr. Ess. Inst. iii, 1862, 144 (Maine, autumn and winter).—Allen, *ibid.* iv, 1864,
81 (Massachusetts).—McIllwr., *ibid.* v, 1866, 82 (Hamilton, C. W., rare in winter).—Coues, *ibid.* v, 1868, 261 (New England).—Lawr., Ann. Lyc. N. Y. viii,
1866, 281 (New York, rare).—Samuels, B. New Engl. 1867, 80; Rep. Agric. Mass.
1863, App.—Cooper *apud* Samuels, 81 (Quebec, winter).—Allen, Am. Nat. iii,
1870, 569 (Massachusetts).—Turnb., B. E. Pa. 1869, 41 (occasional in severe
winters).—Coop., B. Cal. i, 1870, 448 (not found in California).—Dall & Bann.,
Tr. Chic. Acad. i, 1869, 274 (Alaska, very common, breeding).—Merr., U. S.
Geol. Surv. Ter. 1872, 696.
Surnia ulula var. *hudsonia*, Coues, Key, 1872, 205.—B. B. & R., N. A. B. iii, 1874, 75.

Hab.—Northern North America. Breeds from Maine northward. In winter occa-
sionally south to Pennsylvania and Illinois (*Ridgway*, Ann. Lyc. N. Y. x, 1874, 379).
Bermudas (*Drummond, Jardine*, Contr. Orn. 1850, 37). Not yet observed west of the
Rocky Mountains. "Great Britain." Typical *ulula* European.
Later Expeditions.—62240, Madison River, Montana.

Contrary to the opinion entertained by ornithologists, of the absolute identity of the
American and European Hawk Owls, they prove to form two distinguishable geographical races, the American bird being recognized without difficulty by its darker
color, and the broader reddish-brown bars of the whole breast and belly, only a small
gorget being left white. According to the authors of the splendid work on the Birds
of Europe, from which a part of the foregoing synonymy is borrowed, it is the American
form, and not that of Continental Europe, which inhabits Great Britain, apparently to
the entire exclusion of the other.

The distribution of the American Hawk Owl is quite fully worked out
in a communication I had the pleasure of contributing to the work just
mentioned, and may be gathered with approximate accuracy from the
foregoing quotations. The bird does not appear to ever wander so far
south as the Snowy Owl frequently does; excepting the Bermuda instance, I have never heard of it south of Pennsylvania and Illinois, nor
has it been observed west of the Rocky Mountains. It is common in
the northern half of New England, in winter, and known to breed in
some parts of Maine; from Massachusetts southward its occurrence is
rare and fortuitous.

As is well known, this species is the most diurnal in its habits of any
of the family, retiring to rest at night like an ordinary bird; and it is
the most hawk-like Owl, not only in its habits, but in physical aspect.
It feeds chiefly upon the field-mice (*Arvicolæ*) which swarm in the sphag-
nous vegetation of arctic lands; also upon small birds, grasshoppers and
other insects. It is stated to breed oftenest in the hollows of trees, but
sometimes to construct a nest of sticks, grass, and feathers, among the
branches. The eggs range from five to eight in number, are white, and
measure from $1\frac{3}{8}$ to $1\frac{5}{8}$ in length by $1\frac{1}{8}$ to $1\frac{1}{4}$ in breadth. Both sexes incubate. The parents are represented as very spirited in the defence of
their home: the male bird will even attack and wound an intruder with

its talons, sometimes meeting death in the rashness of its onslaught. When wounded it displays similar courage, boldly facing the enemy and preparing to defend itself with all its might—"calmly and silently it maintains its ground, or springs from a short distance on its foe. So, bravely it dies, without a thought of glory and without a chance of fame; for of its kind there are no cowards."

"This species is seldom met with except in the arctic regions. Occasionally, during severe winters, it is driven as far south as the latitude of Philadelphia, owing to a scarcity of food in its natural haunts. Samuels affirms that he 'has known several specimens to be taken in Vermont and New Hampshire,' and expresses the belief that it builds occasionally in the New England States. The writer and a very intimate friend of his, who is a taxidermist, have taken specimens as early as the middle of October. In the former's collection is a beautiful specimen of a female that was shot on the 15th day of last October, the thermometer indicating a rather high temperature at the time. It was shot in the middle of the day, while careering hawk-like through the air, doubtless in quest of the field-mouse, which is found in meadow grounds in profusion, and which it prizes most assuredly as one of its daintiest morsels.

"The southern appearance of individuals on many occasions, so early in the fall, in rather mild weather, leads to the supposition that it is either a summer resident in small numbers, and performs the essential duties of nidification and incubation here[?], or else, having attended to these important concerns in more northern climes, journeys southward, where it meets with a temperature which it has recently learned to regard as more congenial than the rigors of an arctic autumn. The writer is sanguine of the discovery of nests in this latitude. Like many birds on their entrance into a new territory, this species may be shy and reserved, and consequently nidificates in out-of-the-way situations. Familiarity with the country and its denizens, acquired by a few years' occupancy, may operate in the production of changes of habits and disposition. Distrustfulness will undoubtedly give place to confidence, and more of its history will be known.

"It is said by some writers that the species is crepuscular rather than nocturnal. The writer's experience has been the former. There is no doubt that it frequently hunts in the twilight; but the movements of the bird during the day-time, both in watching for its prey and in its capture, are certain evidence to his mind of the truth of the assertion. While on the alert for its prey, it stations itself upon the topmost bough of a tree, and, as soon as the object of its desire comes in view, pounces down upon it like a hawk, and bears it away to devour it at its leisure. Frequently it goes abroad in search of prey, skimming above meadows and low fields, at a slight elevation, until its object is secured."—(*Gentry*.)

NYCTALE TENGMALMI var. RICHARDSONI, (Bp.) Ridgw.

Richardson's Owl.

a. *tengmalmi*.

Strix noctua, TENG., Act. Stockh. i, 1783.
Strix tengmalmi, GM., i, 291.—LATH., i, 64.—DAUD., ii, 205.—SHAW, G. Z. vii, 1809, 267.—
    TEMM., Man. 1815, 54; i, 94; iv, 49.—VIEILL., Gal. i, pl. 23; Fn. Franç. 48, pl.
    23, f. 1.—NAUM., V. D. i, 1822, 501, pl. 48, f. 2, 3.—DEGL., Orn. Eur. i, 134.—
    SOHL., Rev. Crit. 1844, 15.
Athene tengmalmi, BOIE, Isis, 1822, 771.

Noctua tengmalmi, CUV., R. A. i, 1829, 549.—LESS., Tr. Orn. 1831, 102.—SELBY, Brit. Orn.
2d ed. i, 105, pl. 26.—JARD., Brit. Birds, i, 270.—JEN., Man. 1835, 94.
Ægolius tengmalmi, KAUP, Sk. Ent. Eur. Th. 1829, 34.
Ulula tengmalmi, BP., Oss. Cuv. R. A. 53; Isis, 1833, 1052.—MACGIL., Brit. Birds, iii, 445.
Scotophilus tengmalmi, SW., Classif. B. ii, 217.
Nyctale tengmalmi, BP., List, 1838, 7.—GRAY, Gen. of B. i, 40.—KEYS & BLAS., Wirb.
Eur. 1840, 32.—STRICKL., Orn. Syn. 1855, 175.
"*Strix funerea*, LINN., Fn. Suec. 25" (*Gray*).
Nyctale funerea, BP., Cat. Ucc. Eur. 1842, 24; Consp. Av. 1850, 54.—GRAY, Cat. B. Brit.
Mus. 94; List Brit. Birds, 1863, 22.—KAUP, Mon. *Strig.* Cont. Orn. 1852, 104.
"*Strix passerina*, MEYER, Zool. Ann. i, 333.—PALL., Zoog. R. A. i, 323."
Strix dasypus, BECHST., Naturg. Deut. ii, 972.—MEYER, Tasch. i, 82; Naturg. vi, pl. 2;
Vög. Liv. Esthl. 37.
Nyctale dasypus, GRAY, Gen. of B.
Nyctale planiceps, pinetorum et abietum, BREHM, V. D. 1831, 112, 113.

b. *richardsoni*.

(?) *Strix passerina*, FORST., Phil. Trans. lxii, 1772, 385 (Penn. Arct. Zool. ii, Suppl. 60.)
Strix tengmalmi, SW. & RICH., F. B. A. ii, 1831, 94, pl. 82 (not of authors).—NUTT., Man.
i, 1834, 562.—AUD., Orn. Biog. iv, 559, pl. 380.—PEAB., Rep. Orn. Mass. 91.
Nyctale tengmalmi, DALL & BANN., Tr. Chic. Acad. i, 1869, 273 (Alaska).—ALLEN, Am.
Nat. iii, 1870, 646 (Massachusetts, three instances).
Nyctale tengmalmi var. richardsoni, RIDGW., Am. Nat. vi, 1872, 285.—COUES, Key, 1872,
205.—B. B. & R., N. A. B. iii, 1874, 40.
Ulula tengmalmi, AUD., Syn. 1839, 24; B. Am. i, 1840, 122, pl. 32.—PUTN., Pr. Ess. Inst.
i, 1856, 226 (Massachusetts).—? TRIPPE, ibid. vi, 1871, 113 (Minnesota).
Nyctale richardsoni, BP., Comp. List, 1838, 7; Consp. i, 1850, 64.—KAUP, Mon. *Strig,*
Cont. Orn. 1852, 105.—CASS., Ill. i, 1854, 185.—STRICKL., Orn. Syn. 1855, 176.—
BREW., N. Am. Oöl. 1857, 73.—BD., B. N. A. 1858, 57.—BOARDM., Pr. Bost. Soc.
ix, 1862, 123 (Maine, probably resident, not common).—VERR., Pr. Ess. Ihst.
iii, 1862, 157 (Maine).—ALLEN, ibid. iv, 1864, 52 (Massachusetts, rare, in winter).—MCILWR., ibid. v, 1866, 82 (Canada West, rare, in winter).—COUES, ibid.
v, 1868, 260 (New England).—MAYN., Nat. Guide, 1870, 133 (Massachusetts).—
HATCH, Bull. Minn. Acad. i, 1874, 52 (Minnesota, occasionally, in winter).
Nyctala richardsoni, GRAY, Hand-list, i, 1869, 51, No. 555.

Hab.—The typical form from Europe, Asia, and Northern Africa. Var. *richardsoni*
from Northern North America; south regularly to the United States frontier; in winter
rarely through New England, beyond which no record on the Atlantic. Northern
Ohio (*Winslow*).

Having been at first considered the same as its European representative, and afterward held to be a distinct species, this interesting Owl
has at length settled into its true position as a geographical race of *N.
tengmalmi* of Europe, as ascertained by Mr. Ridgway's studies. It differs
from its congener, just as the American Hawk Owl does, in an excess
of darker colors; the legs being ochrey-brown, much variegated with
darker, instead of white, with little marking; and there is more dark
color on the crissum. It is, perhaps, the most decidedly boreal of our
species of the family; for although it does not range further north than
some, such as the Hawk Owl, the Snowy, and the Great Gray Owl, its
southern limit is more restricted. It has never been observed as far
south as all of the three just mentioned are known to range in winter.
On the Atlantic coast I find no record for Pennsylvania or New Jersey,
though it is stated to have been procured in Connecticut by Dr. W.
W. Wood, while Mr. Allen gives several instances of its capture in Massachusetts. In Maine, according to Mr. Boardman, it is resident; it has
been noticed in Wisconsin by Dr. Hoy, and the queried Minnesotan
record, by Mr. Trippe, is doubtless correct, as it has been lately checked
by Dr. Hatch. Sir John Richardson speaks of its very great abundance
in the region of the Saskatchewan, whence it undoubtedly visits the
Upper Missouri in winter.

Owls of this genus are among the most perfectly nocturnal birds of
the family, and appear confined to wooded regions. The food is princi-

pally insects, although mice and the smallest birds are also captured. The egg of the present bird is colorless, like that of other Owls, and measures 1¼ inches in length by 1 inch in breadth.

NYCTALE ACADICA, (Gm.) Bp.

Acadian or Saw-whet Owl.

Strix acadica, GM., Syst. Nat. i, 1788, 296.—DAUD., Tr. Orn. ii, 1800, 206.—VIEILL., Ois. Am. Sept. i, 1807, 49.—BP., Syn. 1828, 38; Isis, 1832, 1140.—SW. & RICH., F. B. A. ii, 1831, 97.—JARD., ed. Wils. ii, 66.—NUTT., Man. i, 1832, 137.—AUD., Orn. Biog. ii, 1834, 567; v, 1839, 397; pl. 199.—PEAB., Rep. Orn. Mass. 1839, 70.—DEKAY, N. Y. Zool. 1844, pl. 11, fig. 23.

Nyctale acadica, BP., Comp. List, 1838, 7; Consp. Av. i, 1850, 44,—GRAY, Gen. of B. 1844, App. p. 3.—KAUP, Tr. Zool. Soc. iv, 206.—STRICKL., Orn. Syn. i, 1855, 176.—NEWB., P. R. R. Rep. vi, 1857, 77.—CASS., Ill. 1854, 186.—BREW., N. A. Oöl. 1857, 74.—SCL., P. Z. S. 1858, 295 (Oaxaca).—CASS., B. N. A. 1858, 58.—COOP. & SUCKL., N. H. Wash. Ter. 1860, 156.—WHEAT., Ohio Agric. Rep. 1860, No. 27.—COUES & PRENT., Smiths. Rep. 1861, 402.—BOARDM., Pr. Bost. Soc. ix, 1862, 123 (Maine, resident).—VERR., Pr. Ess. Inst. iii, 1862, 144 (Maine, resident).—ALLEN, *ibid.* iv, 1864, 52 (Massachusetts, resident).—MCILWR., *ibid.* v, 1866, 82 (Canada West).—COUES, *ibid.* v, 1868, 260.—COUES, Pr. Phila. Acad. 1866, 50 (Arizona).—COUES, Pr. Bost. Soc. xii, 1868, 119 (South Carolina).—LAWR., Ann. Lyc. N. Y. viii, 1866, 281 (New York).—TURNB., B. East Pa. 1869, 9 (rare, chiefly in winter).—LORD, Pr. Roy. Arty. Inst. 1864 (British Columbia).—COOP., B. Cal. i, 1870, 436.—SNOW, B. Kans. 1873, 2.—RIDGW., Am. Nat. vi, 1872, 284 (critical).—HART., Brit. Birds, 1872, 95 (England, very doubtfully; quotes MILN., Zool. 1860, 8104).—COUES, Key, 1872, 205.—ALLEN, Am. Nat. vii, 1873, 427.—B. B. & R., N. A. B. iii, 1874, 43.—RIDGW., Ann. Lyc. x, 1874, 378 (Illinois).

Nyctala acadica, GRAY, Hand-list, i, 1869, 51, No. 556.

Scotophilus acadicus, SW., Classif. B. ii, 1837, 217.

Noctua acadica, RICH., 1837.

Ulula acadica, AUD., Syn. 1839, 24; B. Am. i, 1840, 123, pl. 33.—PUTN., Pr. Ess. Inst. i, 1856, 204 (Massachusetts).—SCHLEGEL, M. P.-B., 1862, *Striges*, p. 8.

(?) *Strix passerina*, FORST., Phil. Trans. lxii, 1772, 385 (PENN., Arct. Zool. 1785, 236).—WILS., Am. Orn. iv, 1812, 66, pl. 34, f. 1.

Strix acadiensis, LATH., Ind. Orn. i, 1790, 65 (Syn. pl. 5, f. 2).—SHAW, G. Z. vii, 266.

Strix albifrons, SHAW, Nat. Misc. v, 1794, pl. 171; Gen. Zool. vii, 1809, 238.—LATH., Ind. Orn. Suppl. 14.

Bubo albifrons, VIEILL., Ois. Am. Sept. i, 1807, 54.

Scops albifrons, STEPH., Shaw's Gen. Zool. xiii, pt. ii, 1820, 51.

Nyctale albifrons, CASS., Ill. 1854, 187.—CASS., B. N. A. 1858, 57.—COUES, Pr. Phila. Acad. 1866, 50.—MCILWR., Pr. Ess. Inst. vi, 1866, 82 (Canada).—COOP., B. Cal. i, 1870, 435.—VERR., Am. Nat. 1871, 119 (Maine).

Nyctala albifrons, GRAY, Hand-list, i, 1869, 52, No. 557.

Strix frontalis, LICHT., Abhandl. Akad. Berol. 1838, 430.

Nyctale kirtlandii, HOY, Pr. Phila. Acad. vi, 1852, 210.—CASS., Ill. 1853, 63, pl. 11.

Strix phalænoides, DAUD., Tr. Orn. ii, 1800, 206.—LATH., Ind. Orn. Suppl. 16.—VIEILL., Ois. Am. Sept. i, 1807, pl. 15.—SHAW, G. Z. vii, 1809, 268.

Athene phalænoides, GRAY, Gen. of B. fol. 1844, sp. 43.

Athene wilsoni, BOIE, Isis, 1828, 315.

"*Strix dalhousei*, HALL, Ms., Macg. ed. Cuv. R. A. 1829, pl. 8."

Hab.—Temperate North America, from Atlantic to Pacific; chiefly, however, Northern United States and adjoining British territory; ranging southward, in wooded mountainous regions, into Mexico. Oaxaca (SCL., P. Z. S. 1856, 295).

Having been long aware that the so-called "White-fronted Owl," *Strix albifrons*, *S. frontalis*, and *N. kirtlandii*, of various authors, was simply the young of the present species, I was pleased to see the case so clearly set forth as it was in Mr. Ridgway's article above quoted—a paper instigated by Mr. Elliot's late erroneous identification of these names as pertaining to the young of *N. tengmalmi*. In both species of *Nyctale*, the plumage is much the same, and its changes are entirely correspondent. The young have the disc dark brown, contrasted with white supercilia, the forehead plain, and the under parts unvariegated, fading from a dark brown on the breast to ochrey-brown on the belly. In the adults the disc is mostly white, the forehead is sharply streaked, and the under parts are white, with lengthwise chocolate-brown markings. Specific characters of the two birds are perceived in the greatly inferior size of *acadica*, a different relative length of wings and tail, a difference in the cere and nostrils, and the black instead of yellow bill.

In the paper above cited, Mr. Allen has the following on the supposed rarity of "*albifrons*:" "Although the White-fronted Owl (*Nyctale albifrons*, CASS.) is now conceded by most, if not all, American ornithologists to be the young of the Saw-whet (*N. acadica*), its supposed rarity, in comparison with the adult, renders the following record of recent instances of its capture in Canada of considerable interest. Mr. Ridgway, in a paper published in this journal in May, 1872, in noticing Mr. D. G. Elliot's mistake of considering the *N. albifrons* to be the young of *N. tengmalmi*, has carefully elaborated the evidence of its being the young of *N. acadica*. This relationship had been previously suspected, and now seems to be fully confirmed. Mr. McIlwraith, under date of Hamilton, Ontario, Canada, January 20, 1873, writes as follows: 'In looking over the Naturalist of April, 1871, I observe a notice of the capture of a specimen of the White-fronted Owl in Maine, and the writer of the note, Prof. A. E. Verril, says that the only other instance of its occurrence in the United States of which he is aware, is the specimen taken by Dr. Hoy, at Racine. I am a little surprised at this, for, though not coming much in contact with collectors, I have seen or heard of this [supposed] species now and then for a number of years back. My first knowledge of it was from Cassin's account, and the figure given of it in his Birds of America. Shortly afterward I recognized it in a small case in the possession of the Rev. Professor Ingles, now of the Dutch Reformed Church, Brooklyn, New York, where it was called 'Saw-whet—young.' The case was brought from Montreal. I next met it in Toronto, where Mr. Passmore, taxidermist, had two specimens, one of which I obtained, and have now in my collection. Again, I heard from Mr. P. H. Gibbs, of Guelph, that there were several about his evergreens near the house, one of which he shot. About the same time Mr. Booth, naturalist, of Drummondville, told me of a specimen he had obtained. Dr. Anderson of Point Levi, opposite Quebec, had his alive for a time; and I heard of still another in the hands of R. K. Winslow, esq., of Cleveland, Ohio. From the foregoing it would seem to be more common in Canada than it is further south. The opinion seems to be generally held by those with whom I have conversed upon the subject, that it is the young of the Saw-whet; and yet it is somewhat singular that it is not as often met with as its supposed parents. In the month of October, a few years since, I had six in the Saw-whet form brought me by a lad, who got them all near the same place on his father's farm. The theory recently advanced by Mr. Elliot, in the 'Ibis,' of its being the young of the Sparrow Owl (*Nyctale tengmalmi*), I do not think at all probable; I have the two side by side, and cannot observe any resemblance to warrant such a conclusion, the difference in size alone being sufficient to show the distinction. My own opinion is that it will be found to be the young of Saw-whet; but is it not possible that they do not all assume the same garb—that there may be here a freak of nature, so to speak, such as there is in the case of the Screech Owl, where we find both red and gray.'"

The Acadian Owl is not so boreal a bird as its congener, being found throughout the United States in suitable places, and in the more southerly portions of British America. I have found no decidedly arctic quotations. It is, however, more numerous in the northern half of the United States; and although it has been traced far into Mexico, its southward extension appears to be mainly along wooded mountain ranges, the altitude of which compensates, in a faunal sense, for the decrease of latitude. Fitted to endure great cold, it is resident in our northern districts. I procured a specimen, in the depth of winter, at Boar's Head, on the New Hampshire coast, and another at Fort Randall, in January, when the temperature had been ranging far below zero. The last-named, a fine adult example, was brought to me alive by Lieut. W. J. Campbell, who found it in the possession of an Indian, and I kept it for some time in my study before it died, probably of inanition. It refused food, and after death its body was found greatly emaciated. Although so puny and weak, the little bird showed good spirit, setting back with an air of defiance when approached, snapping its little bill, and pecking as hard as it could when I took it in hand; but after soothing it for a few moments, it would seem appeased, roost quietly on my finger, and apparently like to have its poll quietly scratched. In its noiseless fluttering about the room by night it more resembled a big bat than a bird; in perching, as it did by preference, on the edge of the table or of a pile of books, it stood with its claws bent inward, so that their convexities, and not the points, rested against the support.

The food of this interesting little Owl, which is not so large as a Robin, though it appears bulkier, consists chiefly of insects. Its nesting, according to Wilson and Audubon, is various: sometimes it builds in the branches of trees, while at other times it will occupy the deserted nests of other birds, or lay in a hollow tree. The eggs are pure white, subspherical, of crystalline clearness, measuring 1¼ inches by 1⅞ inches.

Mr. Gentry informs me of a curious circumstance in regard to this Owl. Referring to the association of the Burrowing Owl of the West with the prairie-dog, he continues: "In the hollow of an oak-tree, not far from Germantown, lives an individual of the common chickaree squirrel (*Sciurus hudsonius*), with a specimen of this little Owl as his sole companion. They occupy the same hole together in perfect harmony and mutual good-will. It is not an accidental temporary association, for the bird and the squirrel have repeatedly been observed to enter the same hole together, as if they had always shared the apartment. But what benefit can either derive from the other?"

While speaking of this small species, it may not be amiss to mention some other little Owls of this country. Small as it is (the specimen above mentioned measured only 7½ inches long, with an extent of 19 inches, the wing 5⅓ inches, the tail 2⅞ inches), it surpasses several pygmies found on the west coast and southward. The Pygmy Owl, *Glaucidium passerinum* var. *californicum*, of the whole Pacific region, is the most abundant and best known of these. A closely allied Mexican species of the same genus, and of about the same size (*G. ferrugineum*), has lately been detected in Arizona by Lieut. C. Bendire, U. S. Army. His specimen gave the first intimation of its presence in the United States, as I stated in the American Naturalist, vol. vi, p. 370. It will be found fully described in the "Key," p. 206. Another, still smaller, and very curious lilliputian Owl, was discovered at Fort Mojave, Arizona, by Dr. J. G. Cooper, and has more recently been observed at Mazatlan and on the island of Socorro, by Col. A. J. Grayson. It is the type of a new genus I instituted in 1866, calling it *Micrathene whitneyi*. This species is only about six inches long, has the tarsi nearly bare, and is otherwise peculiar. I have the following accounts to present of these two species from my Arizona MSS.:

PYGMY OWL.*—G. PASSERINUM var. CALIFORNICUM, (*Scl.*) *Ridgw.*

* The following is the synonymy of this species:

a. *passerinum.*

Strix passerina, LINN., Syst. Nat. i, 1766, 133.—RETZ., Fn. Suec. 86.—GM., Syst. Nat. i, 1788, 296.—LATH., Ind. Orn. i, 1790, 65.—NILSS., Orn. Suec. i, 69, pl. 3.—VIEILL., Enc. Meth. iii, 1285.—GOULD, B. Eur. pl. 50.—DEGL., Orn. Eur. i, 136; and of authors generally.
Glaucidium passerinum, BOIE, Isis, 1826, 976.—BP., List, 1838, 6; Cat. Ucc. Eur. 22; Consp. Av. i, 1850, 36.—BREHM, Vög. Deutschl. 108.—SH. & DR., B. Eur. pt. iii.
Surnia passerina, KEYS & BLAS., Wirb. Eur. 1840, 32.
Microptynx passerinum, KAUP, Mon. *Strig.* Cont. Orn. 1852, 107.
Athene passerina, GRAY, Gen. of B. i, 1845, 35.
Noctua passerina, SCHL., M. P.-B., *Striges*, 1862, 41.
Strix pusilla, DAUD., Tr. Orn. 1800, 205 (*ex Levaillant*).
Strix pygmæa, BECHST., Nat. Deutschl. iv, 1805, 978, pl. 24.—MEYER, Taschenb. i, 83.
Noctua pygmæa, SHAW, Gen. Zool. vii, 63.
Strix acadica, TEMM., Man. i, 1820, 96 (not of *Gmelin*).
"*Athene africana*, GRAY," BP., Consp. Av. i, 1850, 36 (under *G. passerinum*).

b. *californicum.*

(?) "*Strix elata*, NATT., Mus. Vindob." *apud* BP., Consp. Av. i, 1850, 36.
(?) *Glaucidium elata*, BP., Consp. Av. i, 1850, 36 ("*Similis S. passerinæ, sed cauda longiori;*" most probably this form; Mexico).
Strix passerinoïdes, AUD., Orn. Biog. v, 1839, 271, pl. 432 (not of *Temminck*).

The specimens I took at Fort Whipple enabled me to credit the Territory with this fine little species, before only known in the United States as a bird of California, Oregon, and Washington. It inhabits the whole Pacific Slope, as now appears, and extends southward into Mexico. Audubon referred it to *Strix passerinoides*, Temminck, and Mr. Cassin, at first, to *S. infuscata* of the same author. Both these names appear to have been bestowed upon the same species, which is South American, and entirely different from the Mexican and United States bird, which is more closely allied to the European *passerina*. Dr. Sclater proposed, in 1857, to separate the North American from the Mexican, under the name of *G. californicum*.

I saw the Pygmy Owl several times at Fort Whipple, and secured two specimens, which were fortunately male and female. The peculiarly retiring and unobtrusive habits of the Owls renders them difficult of observation, and less frequently met with than their numbers would lead us to expect. Judging with due regard for this fact, I take it that this bird is common in the wooded regions and mountainous portions of Arizona. One of my specimens was moulting; the other, taken in winter, was in perfect plumage. This warrants the belief that the species is resident about Fort Whipple, and that it breeds there, though I was not fortunate enough to discover the nest, which, with the eggs, remains almost unknown, so far as I am aware. It will probably be found to mate and lay very early in the year—in March, if not in February. As a well-known general rule, the Owls breed earlier than most birds, for some unexplained reason, but probably on account of their nocturnal habits, and the quiet seclusion in hollow trees and other sheltered places, in which most of their time is spent. Removed in a great meas-

---

Surnia passerinoides, AUD., Syn. 1839, 23; B. Am. i, 117, pl. 30.
Glaucidium infuscatum, CASS., Ill. 1854, 189.—NEWB., P. R. R. Rep. vi, 1857, 77 (not of Temminck).
Glaucidium gnoma, CASS., Baird's B. N. A. 1858, 62 (not of *Wagler*).—HEERM., P. R. R. Rep. x, 1859, pt. vi, 31.—COOP. & SUCK., N. H. Wash. Ter. 1860, 158.—CAB., J. f. O. 1862, 336; Ueb. Berlin. Mus. 1869, 207.—LORD, Intellect. Observer, 1865, 409 (biography).—COUES, Pr. Phila. Acad. 1866, 50 (Arizona).
Glaucidium californicum, SCL., P. Z. S. 1857, 4.
Glaucidium passerinum var. *californicum*, RIDGW., *apud* COUES, Key, 1872, 206.—RIDGW., Pr. Bost. Soc. xvi, 1873, 92, 94 (critical examination of all the forms of the genus).—B. B. & R., N. A. B. iii, 1874, 81.

Hab.—The true *passerinum* is European. Var. *californicum* is from the Western Province of North America. North to Oregon. East to Colorado. South on the table-lands of Mexico. I regard it as very probable that the *Strix elata* of *Natterer's* Mss., which is said by Bonaparte to differ from *passerinum* in the greater length of the tail, is really this variety; for the length of tail is precisely one of the main characters adduced by Mr. Ridgway in his excellent monograph of the genus. Should this prove to be the case, the bird will be known as *G. passerinum* var. *elatum*.

The only other North American species of this genus is the following:

GLAUCIDIUM FERRUGINEUM, (*Maxim.*) *Kaup.*

Strix ferruginea, MAXIM., Reise, i, 1820, 105; Beit. iii, 234.—TAMM., P. C. 199. (Identified by Strickland with the *Sparrow Owl* of LATH., Gen. Hist. i, 373, pl. 17.)
Noctua ferruginea, STEPH., Gen. Zool. xiii, pt. ii, 69.—LESS., Man. i, 111; Tr. Orn. 104.—CUV., R. A. 2d ed. i, 346.—TSCH., Wiegm. Arch. 1844, 267; Fn. Peru. 19, 117.
Surnia ferruginea, BP., Osserv. Cuv. R. A. 56; Isis, 1833, 1053.
Athene ferruginea, GRAY, Gen. of B; List B. Brit. Mus. 92.—BP., Consp. Av. i, 1850, 38.—STRICKL., Orn. Syn. 1855, 162.
Glaucidium ferrugineum, KAUP, Mon. Strig. Cont. Orn. 1852, 104.—BURM., Th. Bras. ii, 141, 146.—CAB., Ueb. Berl. Mus. 1869, 206.—COUES, Am. Nat. vi, 1872, 370 (Arizona, *Bendire;* first introduction to fauna of United States).—COUES, Key, 1872, 206.—RIDGW., Pr. Bost. Soc. xvi, 1873, 100 (critical).—B. B. & R., N. A. B. iii, 1874, 85.

Hab.—Eastern South America, and whole of Middle America, to the southern border of the United States.

ure from the effects of sunlight, its vivifying and invigorating influence seems replaced by the analogous effect of the warmth of their accustomed haunts, and the same purpose of fostering vitality to be subserved. Sedentary habits, and luxurious day-dreams in snug seclusion, may have on these birds the same effect of exciting into early and uncontrollable action certain vital functions, that is known to be produced in our own species by a similar mode of life.

The brief notice of this species that Dr. Heermann has left is incorrect in one portion, for he says that it may sometimes " be caught perched on the branch of a tree, *napping*, during the day-time." The fact is, that it shows a decided tendency toward diurnal habits, and though thus often found abroad in the day-time, it will not likely be " caught napping." It has appeared to me, in fact, as little inconvenienced by the glare of day as the Burrowing Owl is, and it pursues its insect prey by day as well as by night with activity and success. Dr. Newberry speaks more to the point: " It flies about," he writes, "with great freedom and activity by day, pursuing small birds. upon which it subsists, apparently as little incommoded by the light as they are;" thought I doubt that birds form a great portion of its food. It is so small, and its rapacious powers, if not nature, so limited, that it must confine its pursuit to the most insignificant game. The stomachs of my specimens were found to be filled with fragments of grasshoppers and beetles, some of which were yet scarcely altered by digestion, showing that they must have been very recently captured. Each of the birds was killed about noon. The following account of the bird is so good, and agrees so well with my own observations, that I reproduce it from the Natural History of Washington Territory. The first paragraph is by Dr. Cooper, the other by Dr. Suckley:

" This (the smallest Owl found in the Territory) I have seen only once, though it seems to be not very uncommon. On the 1st of November, 1854, I observed it among a flock of Sparrows, which did not seem at all frightened by its presence. For some time I thought it was one of them, though its large head and owl-like flight seemed to me strange. It was plainly diurnal in habits, not seeming to seek any shelter from the sunshine. Its stomach contained only insects, and it is probable that it does not often attack birds."

" I have obtained two specimens of this Owl at Puget Sound, where it seems to be moderately abundant. It appears to be diurnal in its habits, gliding about in shady situations in pursuit of its prey. I saw a bird of this kind, about midday, in a shady alder swamp near Nisqually. It flitted noiselessly past me several times, alighting near by, on a small branch, as if to examine the intruder. It seemed quite tame, and entirely unsophisticated. I noticed that in flying the tail was kept rather widely spread. Near a small lake in the neighborhood of Fort Steilacoom I frequently heard the voice of a small Owl, the notes of which were subdued and clear, like the low, soft notes of a flute. As the only small Owl I ever saw in the neighborhood belonged to this species, it is probable that the sounds heard came from an individual of the kind."

The last sentence gives the only intimation of the notes of this bird that we have; and, unless the writer was mistaken in his surmise, which is quite possible, it is something new in the history of the family, for no Owl is known to emit sounds at all comparable to the notes of a flute. The voices of most of these night birds are among the most uncouth, inharmonious, and lugubrious sounds that ever break the stillness of the dark scene. With an average of musical ability that birds are favored with, they compare as the creaking and puffing of disordered organ-bellows to sounds from the keys of the instrument. No wonder that in classic times it was written of Owls:

> "Est illis *strigibus* nomen ; sed nominis hujus
> Causa quod horrendâ stridere nocte solent;"

nor that later and more professedly ornithological observers of nature should have heavily taxed their vocabularies in selection of epithets to express the vocal eccentricities of Owls, not to allude to the liberties that lay writers, whether of prose or verse, have taken, in a superstitious, legendary mood, with the weird associations of these "monks who chant midnight mass in the great temple of Nature."

I am inclined to repeat in this connection a liberal proposition, made by one of the most delightful of writers on birds. In his history of the rapacious birds of Great Britain, Mr. Macgillivray quotes a poetic passage respecting Owls, and adds, in his original way, "the reader may here supply a chapter on superstitions, which the author forgot!" For the Pygmy Owl, unknown to poetic and legendary fame, living to our remembrance only in times when nature is questioned fearlessly, not tremblingly as of old when ignorance served all purposes, has never been regarded as of weird, uncanny import. Not a single irrational attribute has attached to it; nor need it be sought in greater obscurity than the shade of its favorite pines. With little experience of man, it has had no opportunity of gaining that sort of wisdom credibly supposed to flow from such contact; still less has it the supernatural lore attributed to the bird of Minerva. It is a very straightforward, ingenious, unsuspicious little bird, meddling with no affairs but its own, and innocent enough to expect like treatment from others, expectations, however, not always realized.

NOTE.—That there may be in future no misunderstanding regarding this Owl, and for the purpose of comparing it with Whitney's, which bears some superficial resemblance, I give the following concise description, believed to be in every way pertinent. Facial disk imperfect; no ear-tufts; tarsi densely feathered to the toes, which are covered with hairs; claws strong, sharp, much curved; tail rather long, even; wings medium, or rather short; the fourth primary longest; iris, bright yellow; bill, cere, and feet, dull greenish-yellow; soles, chrome-yellow; mouth, livid flesh-color; upper parts one shade of dark-brown, everywhere dotted with small circular spots of white; a collar of mixed blackish-brown and white, around the back of the neck; breast with a band of mottled-brown, separating the white throat from the white of the rest of the under parts, which all have irregular lengthwise streaks of reddish-brown. Wings and tail dusky-brown; the feathers marked on both webs with a row of round white spots, largest on the inner; under wing-coverts white, crossed obliquely by a blackish bar. Length of the male 7.00 inches, or a little less; extent of wings, 14.50; wing, 3.75; tail, 3.00; of the female, length 7.50; extent, 15.50, &c. In the female the upper parts are rather lighter, with fewer larger spots, and a nearly obsolete nuchal collar; but both sexes vary in the tint of the upper parts, which ranges from pure deep brown to pale grayish, almost olivaceous brown, probably according to age and season, the newer feathers being darker than they are when old and worn.

WHITNEY'S OWL *—MICRATHENE WHITNEYI, (*Cooper*), Coues.

This singular little Owl is one of the most noteworthy and interesting of the many late additions to our knowledge of western birds. Until recently, the last-noticed species was properly regarded as the smallest of its family in North America; but it somewhat surpasses Whitney's in size. The latter is not so long as many of our Sparrows, being the

---

* *Athene whitneyi*, COOP., Pr. Cal. Acad. 1861, 118 (Fort Mojave, Arizona). *Micrathene whitneyi*, COUES, Pr. Phila. Acad. 1866, 51.—ELLIOT, B. N. A. i, p. xxix, pl. —.—COOP., B. Cal. i, 1870, 442.—GRAYS., *apud.* LAWR., Ann. Lyc. N. Y. (Socorro).—COUES, Key, 1872, 207.—B. B. & R., N. A. B. iii, 1874, 87.

Hab.—Arizona, Southern California, and southward to Socorro.

least among our raptorial birds, if not the smallest known Owl. It was discovered at Fort Mojave, in 1860, by Dr. J. G. Cooper, to whose exertions in developing the zoology of the West we are so much indebted. We learn from Dr. Cooper's account that it is an arboreal, not a terrestrial species, is partly diurnal, and feeds upon insects. It is probably a rare bird, to judge from its having remained so long undetected. But Mr. A. J. Grayson lately found it on Socorro Island, off the coast of Mexico, while several specimens have been taken in Arizona, by Lieut. C. Bendire, and Mr. H. W. Henshaw. The former found it breeding in the hollow of a mezquite stump.

NOTE.—As this species is still not generally known, I deviate from my usual course to present the following description : Bill small and weak, narrow at the base, which is hidden among recurved and closely appressed bristly feathers. Facial disk imperfect. No ear-tufts. Wings very long, but rounded, the first primary only ⅞ the third and fourth, which are equal and longest; second equal to sixth. Tail of moderate length, not graduated; the rectrices broad at the tip. Tarsi nearly naked, the feathers extending but a little way below the heel-joint; rest of the tarsus, and the upper surfaces of the toes, sparsely covered with short bristly hairs. Middle toe and claw about as long as the tarsus; hind toe lengthened. Claws remarkably small, weak, and little curved ; hardly more than insessorial, instead of raptorial, in character. The foregoing are rather the generic than the specific characters, and are those upon which the genus *Micrathene* was established. It agrees with *Athene*, to which the bird was referred by its discoverer, in the imperfect disk and mostly naked tarsi; but is otherwise quite different and more nearly related to *Nyctale, Glaucidium*, &c., from which again, it is notably distinct ; nor do I know of any established genus of Owls to which the species could probably be referred. It presents an entirely peculiar combination of characters. The slight claws are an especial feature. The following account of the colors, &c., is compiled from the original description, as the specimen itself is not at hand at time of writing. Above light brownish-gray, thickly spotted with angular pale brown dots, especially on the crown ; those on the back larger ; back also obsoletely barred with wavy lines of the same color. A concealed white collar on back of neck, forming a bar across the middle of the feathers, which are plumbeous at base and brown at tip. Quills with three to six spots on each web, those of the inner webs white, those of outer web of the fourth, third and second, white, the others brown. A row of white spots on lesser coverts ; four on upper, seven on lower series, with a row of light brown spots between ; outer secondaries with a few white spots ; outer scapulars with a white stripe, edged by pale brown stripes nearer the back ; outer wing-feathers dark brown, with pale, ashy dots near the ends of the secondaries. Rectrices like the primaries, the light spots forming five broken bars and a narrow terminal bar. Feathers above the eye white, with black spotted shafts ; below it, light brown, obsoletely barred with dark ; bristles at base of bill black on terminal half. Chin and throat white, the lower feathers light brown, the white forming a broad crescent from side to side. Sides of neck narrowly barred with ashy and light and dark brown ; breast imperfectly barred and blotched with the same colors ; toward the abdomen, the brown forming large patches, margined with grey and white. Sides more grayish, tinged with yellowish, the flanks plumbeous; tibiæ narrowly barred with light and dark brown. Tarsal bristles white; those of the toes yellowish. Bill, pale green ; iris, bright yellow. Length. 6.25 ; extent, 15.25 ; wing, 4.50 ; tail, 2.25 ; tarsus, 0 90 ; middle toe and claw, 1.30 ; hind toe and claw, 0.50 ; gape, 0.45 ; height of bill, 0.30 ; width at base, 0.40.

SPEOTYTO CUNICULARIA var. HYPOGÆA, (Bp.) Coues.

Burrowing Owl.

a. *cunicularia.*

Strix cunicularia, MOL., Sagg. Stor. Nat. Chili, 1872, 343.—GM., Syst. Nat. i, 1788, 292.— LATH., Ind. Orn. i, 1790, 63 (*Noctua coquimbana*, BRISS., i, 525 ; *Coquimbo Owl*, LATH., Gen. Syn. i, 145).—DAUD., Tr. Orn. ii, 201.—MEYEN, N. Act. Leop. Car. xvi, Suppl. 70.—LICHT., Verz. 59.—MAXIM., Beit. iii, 248 ; Reise, ii, 191, 344.
Ulula cunicularia, FEUILLÉE, Journ. Obs. Phys. 562.
Noctua cunicularia, DARW., Journ. Res. 145.—D'ORB., Voy. 128.
Otus cunicularia, CUV., Règne Anim. i, 2d ed. 341.
Surnia cunicularia, BP., Observ. Cuv. R. A. 50.
Nyctipetes cunicularia, SW., Classif. Birds, ii, 1837, 218.

Athene cunicularia, BP., Consp. i, 1850, 38.—DARW., Voy. Beagle, iii, 31.—SCHOMB., Gniana, ii, 731.—BRIDGES, P. Z. S. xi, 109 ; Ann. Nat. Hist. xiii, 500.—GRAY, Gen. of B. sp. 19; List Br. Mus. 92.—PEALE, U. S. Expl. Ex. 1848, 77.—HARTL., Ind. Syst. Azara, 4.
Pholeoptynx cunicularia, KAUP, Mon. *Strig.* Cont. Orn. 1852, 106.—SCL. & SALV., P. Z. S. 1868, 143 (Buenos Ayres).
Strix grallaria, SPIX, Av. Braz. i, 21.—TEMM., P. C. 146.
Noctua grallaria, STEPH., Gen. Zool. xiii, pt. ii, 67.—LESS., Man. i, 111 ; Tr. Orn. 102.
Noctua urucurea, LESS., Tr. Orn. 103.—TSCH., Wieg. Arch. 1844, 267 ; Fn. Peru, 116.
Athene patagonica, PEALE, U. S. Expl. Exped. 1848, 78.

b. *guadeloupensis.*

Speotyto cunicularia var. *guadeloupensis*, RIDGW.—B. B. & R., N. A. B. iii, 1874, 90.

c. *hypogæa.*

Strix cunicularia, VIEILL., Ois. Am. Sept. i, 1807, 48.—SAY, Long's Exp. ii, 36, 200.—BP., Am. Orn. i, 1825, 68, pl. 7, f. 2 ; Syn. 1828, 36.—NUTT., Man. i, 1832, 118.—AUD., Orn. Biog. v, 1839, 264, pl. 432.
Surnia cunicularia, AUD., Syn. 1839, 23 ; B. Am. i, 1840, 119, pl. 31.—DEKAY, N.Y. Zool. ii, 23.
Athene cunicularia, BP., List, 1838, 6 (not of Consp.).—CASS., B. N. A. 1858, 60 (*nec* MoLINA).—KENN., P. R. R. Rep. x, 1859, pt. iv, 20.—HEERM., *ibid.* pt. vi, 33.—COOP. & SUCK., N. H. Wash. Ter. 1860, 157.—KAUP, Tr. Z. S. iv, 201.—CANF., Am. Nat. ii, 1869, 583 (biography).—COOP., B. Cal. i, 1870, 437.
Ulula cunicularia, JARD., ed. Wils. 1832, iii, 325.
Speotyto cunicularia var. *hypogæa*, COUES, Key, 207.—B. B. & R., N. A. B. iii, 1874, 90.
Strix hypugæa, BP., Am. Orn. i, 1825, 72.
Athene hypogæa, BP., Consp. i, 1850, 39 (*hypogæa*).—WOODH., Sitgr. Rep. 1853, 62 (*hypugæa*).—CASS., Ill. 1854, 188 (*hypugæa*).—BREW., N. Am. Oöl. 1857, 75 (*hypugæa*).—CASS., B. N. A. 1858, 59 (*hypugæa*).—NEWB., P. R. R. Rep. vi, 1857, 17.—COOP. & SUCK., N. H. Wash. Ter. 1860, 157.—HAYD., Rep. 1862, 154 (*hypugæa*).—COOP., B. Cal. i, 1870, 448 (*hypugæa*).—STEV., U. S. Geol. Surv. Ter. 1870, 462 (*hypugæa*).—MERR., *ibid.* 1872, 696 (*hypugæa*).—ALLEN, Bull. M. C. Z. iii, 1872, 180 (Kansas and Utah).—SNOW, B. Kans. 1873, 2 (*hypugæa*).—HOLD., Pr. Bost. Soc. 1872, 208 (*hypugæa*).
Athene (*Speotyto*) *hypogæa*, GRAY, Hand-list, i, 1869, 43, No. 437.
Strix californica, AUD., Orn. Biog. pl. 432 (name on plate).
Athene socialis, GAMB., Pr. Phila. Acad. iii, 1846, 47.—SCL., P. Z. S. 1857, 201 (Xalapa).—DRESS., Ibis, 1865, 330 (Texas).

NOTE.—As the older authors generally made no distinction of the races, the term *cunicularia* includes all, in most cases.

Hab.—The true *cunicularia* is South American ; var. *guadeloupensis* is considered by Mr. Ridgway as a local form, of Guadeloupe. Var. *hypogæa* is the North American form, occurring in open places in the United States west of the Mississippi, and in Middle America. In addition, Gray gives Antillean forms of *Speotyto* under the names of *domingensis, Müll.* (*dominicensis, Gm.*), and *fusca, Vieill.;* the latter is, however, an entirely different bird, while the former is scarcely identifiable.

List of specimens.

| 19132 | 163 | Powder River.. | ♀ | Sept. 13, 1859 | G. H. Trook.. | 9.00 | 23.50 | 7.00 |
| 19133 | 192 | Tongue River.. | ♂ | .... | ...... do ..... | 9.50 | 25.00 | 7.00 |

Lieutenant Warren's Expedition.—5182–84, Fort Pierre ; 9965, Running Water ; 9066–67, Loup Fork of Platte.
Later Expeditions.—54300–01, 60090, 60342–47, Wyoming ; 59843, Soda Springs, Colorado ; 60634–36, Big Sandy Creek ; 61637, Utah ; 61761–64, Idaho.

After examination of many Burrowing Owls from all parts of the West, in the field as well as in the closet, I am of the decided opinion that the differences alleged to exist between the birds of opposite sides of the Rocky Mountains have no foundation in fact. The ascribed distinctions fall largely within the limit of individual variation, and may be observed in any sufficient series of specimens from a single locality. Nor am I, indeed, fully satisfied of the necessity of separating the North from the South American bird, although in view of some slight average distinctions they may be held, conventionally at any rate, as climatic races.

The Burrowing Owl is the only bird of its family inhabiting, in any numbers, the entirely treeless regions of the West, and may be considered characteristic of the plains. Wherever it can find shelter in the holes of such animals as wolves, foxes, and badgers, and especially of the various species of marmot squirrels, there it is found in abundance; and in not a few instances small colonies are observed living apart from their ordinary associates, in holes apparently dug by themselves. They constitute a notable exception to the general rule of arboricole habits in this family, being specially fitted by their conformation for the sub-terranean mode of life for which they are designed, and are further-more exceptional in their gregarious disposition, here carried to the ex-treme. The diffusion of the species in the West is so general that there is little occasion to mention particular localities. They are met with in suitable situations throughout nearly all the Missouri region, except the easternmost, and are especially abundant to the south and west. The most eastern point I have found them was a little beyond Fort Riley, in Kansas; they were observed in great numbers thence to and along the Arkansas River. I saw them near Fort Wingate, in New Mexico. They occur in various parts of Arizona, living with the western spermo-phile, *Cynomys* var. *gunnisoni*, and on the coast of Southern California I found them plentiful in the burrows of *Spermophilus beecheyi*, which are numerous on the plain that stretches from Los Angeles to the seashore. In the northwest, Dr. Hayden remarks, he does not remember to have ever seen a prairie-dog village that was not inhabited by one or more pairs of the birds. Southward they extend into Mexico; to the north I am not aware that they have been observed beyond the United States border, and I saw none along the northern boundary of Dakota. But Dr. Suckley found them at Fort Benton, at the head of navigation on the Missouri, and, with Dr. Cooper, in Oregon and Washington Terri-tories. In further illustration of their distribution, I insert the following communication from Mr. Allen, which also contains some interesting biographical items:

" We found the Burrowing Owl a more or less frequent inhabitant of the prairie-dog "towns," from Middle Kansas westward to the base of the mountains in Colorado, and in Southern Wyoming; also in the Great Salt Lake Valley, in Utah, where they occupied the deserted holes of badgers and coyotés in the absence of those of prairie-dogs. Contrary to the experience of Townsend and Say, we found them usually wary and difficult to approach, and, when once fully aroused, they were almost sure to keep out of reach. Occasionally, however, they showed but little timidity. They appear to live in small colonies of several pairs, these colonies being generally quite widely separated. We often trav-eled a whole day on the plains, passing most of the time through a suc-cession of prairie-dog villages, without perceiving any indication of the presence of the Owls. In twice crossing South Park we saw none what-ever, and in a journey thence eastward over the mountains to Colorado City, we met with the Owls but once or twice, although the western prairie-dog (*Cynomys* var. *gunnisoni*) occurred in abundance. Though a wide-ranging species, they appear to be quite locally distributed, by no means inhabiting all the prairie-dog villages, as some writers have rather con-fidently affirmed. Mr. Townsend says that 'the Indians assert, with great confidence, that it retires into its burrow and spends the winter in a torpid state.' I found, however, both the prairie-dogs and the Bur-rowing Owls abroad and very active on pleasant days in December and January, on the plains of Western Kansas, although the temperature often fell nearly to zero (Fahrenheit) during the nights following. I was also assured by old residents of the plains that both these animals are frequently seen abroad during pleasant weather throughout the winter."

Having been noticed by the earlier writers in special connection with the singular settlements of the prairie-dog (*Cynomys ludovicianus*), and the life relations of the two creatures being really intimate in very many localities, an almost inseparable association of ideas has been brought about, which is only partly true; and it was a long time before the whole truth in the case became apparent. When competent observers, familiar with the animals, disagree, as they have, respecting the kind and degree of relation between the bird and the mammals, we need not be surprised at conflict of opinion in the books of naturalists who never saw either of them alive. The case is further complicated by the introduction of the rattlesnakes; and no little pure bosh is in type respecting the harmonious and confidential relations imagined to subsist between the trio, which, like the "happy family" of Barnum, lead Utopian existences. According to the dense bathos of such nursery tales, in this underground Elysium the snakes give their rattles to the puppies to play with, the old dogs cuddle the Owlets, and farm out their own litters to the grave and careful birds; when an Owl and a dog come home, paw-in-wing, they are often mistaken by their respective progeny, the little dogs nosing the Owls in search of the maternal font, and the old dogs left to wonder why the baby Owls will not nurse. It is a pity to spoil a good story for the sake of a few facts, but as the case stands, it would be well for the Society for the Prevention of Cruelty to Animals to take it up. First, as to the reptiles, it may be observed that they are like other rattlesnakes, dangerous, venomous creatures; they have no business in the burrows, and are after no good when they do enter. They wriggle into the holes, partly because there is no other place for them to crawl into on the bare, flat plain, and partly in search of Owls' eggs, Owlets, and puppies, to eat. Next, the Owls themselves are simply attracted to the villages of prairie-dogs as the most convenient places for shelter and nidification, where they find eligible ready-made burrows, and are spared the trouble of digging for themselves. Community of interest makes them gregarious to an extent unusual among rapacious birds; while the exigencies of life on the plains cast their lot with the rodents. That the Owls live at ease in the settlements, and on familiar terms with their four-footed neighbors, is an undoubted fact; but that they inhabit the same burrows, or have any intimate domestic relations, is quite another thing. It is no proof that the quadruped and the birds live together, that they are often seen to scuttle at each other's heels into the same hole when alarmed; for in such a case the two simply seek the nearest shelter, independently of each other. The probability is, that young dogs often furnish a meal to the Owls, and that, in return, the latter are often robbed of their eggs; while certainly the young of both, and the Owls' eggs, are eaten by the snakes. In the larger settlements there are thousands upon thousands of burrows, many occupied by the dogs, but more, perhaps, vacant. These latter are the homes of the Owls. Moreover, the ground below is honey-combed with communicating passages, leading in every direction. If the underground plan could be mapped, it would resemble the city of Boston, with its tortuous and devious streets. The dogs are continually busy in fair weather in repairing and extending their establishments; the main entrances may be compared to the stump of a hollow tree, the interior of which communicates with many hollow branches that moreover intersect, these passages finally ending in little pockets, the real home of the animals. It is quite possible that the respective retreats of a dog and an Owl may have but one vestibule, but even this does not imply that they nest together. It is strong evidence in point, that usually there are the fewest Owls in the towns most densely populated by the dogs, and conversely. Scarcity of food, of water, or some obscure cause, often makes the dogs emigrate from one locality to another; it is in such "deserted villages" that the Owls are usually seen in the greatest numbers. I have never seen them so numerous as in places where there were plenty of holes, but where scarcely a stray dog remained.

As already intimated, the Owls are by no means confined to the dog-towns, nor even to the similar communities of other gregarious spermophiles. They sometimes occupy the underground dens of wolves, foxes, and badgers. In South America, the representative race lives among the bizcachas (*Lagostomus trichodactylus*) that inhabit the Pampas. On some occasions the birds have been found alone, residing apparently in burrows excavated by themselves, as already stated. They are by no means nocturnal; able to endure the sunlight without inconvenience, they may be observed abroad at all hours. It has been stated that, in the autumn, at the approach of cold weather, they retire into their burrows to hybernate—a fable matching the one that ascribes to Swallows the habit of diving into the mud to pass the winter in repose along with torpid frogs. In most localities the birds are abroad the year round; their disappearance, in inclement regions, is accomplished, if at all, by ordinary migration. In California I saw them, bright and lively as crickets, in November.

I never undertook to unearth the nest of a Burrowing Owl, but others have been more zealous in the pursuit of knowledge under difficulties. Dr. Cooper says that he once dug two fresh eggs out of a burrow, which he followed down for three feet, and then traced five feet horizontally, at the end of which he found an enlarged chamber, where the eggs were deposited on a few feathers. In his interesting note in the *American Naturalist*, Dr. C. S. Canfield gives a more explicit account of the nesting: "I once took pains to dig out a nest of the *Athene cunicularia*. I found that the burrow was about four feet long, and the nest was only about two feet from the surface of the ground. The nest was made in a cavity of the ground, of about a foot in diameter, well filled with dry, soft horse-dung, bits of an old blanket, and fur of a coyoté (*Canis latrans*) that I had killed a few days before. One of the parent birds was on the nest, and I captured it. It had no intention of leaving the nest, even when entirely uncovered with the shovel and exposed to the open air. It fought bravely with beak and claws. I found *seven* young ones, perhaps eight or ten days old, well covered with down, but without any feathers. The whole nest, as well as the birds (old and young), swarmed with fleas. It was the filthiest nest I ever saw. In the passage leading to it there were small scraps of dead animals, such as pieces of the skin of the antelope, half dried and half putrified; the skin of the coyoté, &c.; and near the nest were the remains of a snake that I had killed two days before, a large *Coluber?* two feet long. The birds had begun at the snake's head, and had picked off the flesh clean from the vertebræ and ribs for about one-half its length; the other half of the snake was entire. The material on which the young birds rested was at least three inches deep. * * * * There are very few birds that carry more rubbish into the nest than the *Athene;* and even the Vultures are not much more filthy. I am satisfied that the *A. cunicularia* lays a larger number of eggs than is attributed to it in Dr. Brewer's book (four). I have frequently seen, late in the season, six, seven, or eight young birds standing around the mouth of a burrow, isolated from others in such a manner that I could not suppose that they belonged to two or more families."

The same writer has some further remarks, so strongly corroborative of what has preceded, that I will quote his words again. Speaking of the hundreds, perhaps thousands, of the birds he had seen in California, he continues : " Where I have seen them, they always live in the de-serted or unoccupied burrows of the ground squirrel (*Spermophilus beecheyi*). I came to the conclusion that they were able to drive out the *Spermophiles* from their habitations, but I am not certain of this. It is true that there were, in that region, a large number of unoccupied burrows wherever there was a colony of *Spermophiles ;* so that there was no lack of unoccupied habitations for the Owls to take possession of. But I have noticed that wherever there was a large number of the Owls, very few or no *Spermophiles* lived. *One* or *two* Owls would occa-sionally be seen among a colony of *Spermophiles ;* but they never ap-peared to enter the same hole or burrow with a squirrel, and I have never seen a squirrel enter a burrow that was occupied by Owls, how-ever much tempted by fear he might be to enter the first hole he should come to. True, the *Spermophile* never likes to enter any burrow but his own, and will run past any number of inviting entrances, in order that he may at last hide himself in his own domicile. But aside from this, I believe that the squirrels are afraid of the Owls, and do not dare to intrude upon them."

The notes of the Burrowing Owl are peculiar. The birds do not " hoot," nor is there anything lugubrious or foreboding in their cry. Sometime they chuckle, chatter, and squeal in an odd way, as if they had caught a habit of barking from the "dogs" they live with, and were trying to imitate the sound. But their natural cry is curiously similar to that of the Rain Crow, or Cuckoo of America—so much so, that more than one observer has been deceived. They scream hoarsely when wounded and caught, though this is but seldom, since, if any life remains, they scramble quickly into a hole and are not easy to recover. The flight is perfectly noiseless, like that of other Owls, owing to the peculiar downy texture of the plumage. By day they seldom fly far from the entrance of their burrow, and rarely, if ever, mount in the air. I never saw one on wing more than a few moments at a time, just long enough for it to pass from one hillock to another, as it does by skimming low over the surface of the ground in a rapid, easy, and rather graceful manner. They live chiefly upon insects, especially grasshoppers; they also feed upon lizards, as I once determined by dissection, and there is no doubt that young prairie-dogs furnish them many a meal. Under ordinary circumstances they are not very shy or difficult to procure; I once secured several specimens, in a few minutes, and, I fear, left some others to languish and die in their holes. As commonly observed, perched on one of the innumerable little eminences that mark a dog-town, amid their curious surroundings, they present a spectacle not easily forgotten. Their figure is peculiar, with their long legs and short tail; the element of the grotesque is never wanting; it is hard to say whether they look most ludicrous as they stand stiffly erect and motion-less, or when they suddenly turn tail to duck into the hole, or when engaged in their various antics. Bolt upright, on what may be imagined their rostrum, they gaze about with a bland and self-satisfied, but earn-est air, as if about to address an audience upon a subject of great pith and moment. They suddenly bow low, with profound gravity, and rising as abruptly, they begin to twitch their face and roll their eyes about in the most mysterious manner, gesticulating wildly, every now and then bending forward till the breast almost touches the ground, to propound the argument with more telling effect. Then they face about to address the rear, that all may alike feel the force of their logic; they draw themselves up to their fullest height, outwardly calm and self-contained, pausing in the discourse to note its effect upon the audience, and collect their wits for the next rhetorical flourish. And no distant likeness between these frothy orators and others is found in the celerity with which they subside and seek their holes on the slightest intimation of danger.

[NOTE.—The foregoing pages include all the species of *Strigidæ* at present known to inhabit North America, north of Mexico.]

Family FALCONIDÆ : Diurnal Birds of Prey.

CIRCUS CYANEUS var. HUDSONIUS, (Linn.) Schl

Marsh Hawk; Harrier.

a. *cyaneus.*

Falco cyaneus, LINN., Syst. Nat. i, 1766, 126 (*Accipiter cœruleus,* EDW., v, 33, pl. 225).— RETZ, Fn. Suec. 64.—GM., Syst. Nat. i, 1788, 276.—LATH., Ind. Orn. i, 1790, 39.— DAUD., Tr. Orn. ii, 1800, 174.—SHAW, Gen. Zool. vii, 163.—TEMM., Man. Orn. 1815, 26 ; and of earlier authors generally.
Circus cyaneus, BOIE, Isis, 1822, 549 ; 1828, 306.—LESS., Man. i, 105.—FLEM., Br. An. 53.—MACGIL., Rap. Br. B. 298 ; Hist. Br. B. iii, 366.—KEYS & BLAS., Wirb. Eur. 1840, 31.—SCHL., Rev. Crit. 1844, 6.—GRAY, Gen. of B. i, 32, pl. 11, f. 1.—GOULD, B. Eur. pl. 33.—BREHM, V. D. 93 ; Isis, 1832, 839 ; and of late authors generally.
Circus (Strigiceps) cyaneus, KAUP, Mus. Senck. 1845, 258.—GRAY, List Br. B. 1863, 17.
Buteo cyaneus, JENYNS, Man. Brit. Vert. An. 89.
Strigiceps cyaneus, BP., Consp. Av. i, 1850, 35.
Falco pygargus, LINN., Syst. Nat. i, 1766, 126 (*Pygargus* ANTIQ. ; *Acc. falco torquatus,* BRISS., i, 345).— RETZ, Fn. Suec. 65.—GM., Syst. Nat. i, 1788, 227.—LATH., Ind. Orn. i, 1790, 39.—NAUM., V. D. i, 1822, 391, pl. 38, 39 ; and of many authors.
Circus pygargus, CUV., R. A. i, 1817, 324.—STEPH., Shaw's G. Z. xiii, pt. ii, 41.—EYT., Cat. Br. B. 5.—SW., Classif. B. ii, 1837, 212.
Strigiceps pygargus, BP., List, 1838, 5.
Falco macrourus, GM., Syst. Nat. i, 1788, 269.—LATH., Ind. Orn. i, 1790, 29 (based on *Accipiter macrourus,* S. G. GM., It. i, 48 ; N. C. Petrop. xv, 439, pl. 8 ; LEPECH., It. i, 59).—DAUD.. Tr. Orn. ii, 1800, 90.—SHAW, G. Z. vii, 160 (*Strickland*).
Falco griseus, GM., Syst. Nat. i, 1788, 275.—LATH., Ind. Orn. i, 1790, 37.—DAUD., Tr. Orn. ii, 1800, 114.
Falco albicans, GM., Syst. Nat. i, 1788, 276.—LATH., Ind. Orn. i, 1790, 38 (based on *Acc. laniarius albicans,* BRISS., i, 367).
Falco montanus β, GM., Syst. Nat. i, 1788, 278.—LATH., Ind. Orn. i, 1790, 48 (based on *Acc. falco montanus cinereus,* BRISS., i, 355).
Falco bohemicus, GM., Syst. Nat. i, 1788, 279.—LATH., Ind. Orn. i, 1790, 43.
Falco cinereus, POSEG., It. 29.
Falco rubiginosus, POSEG., It. 29.—LATH., Ind. Orn. i, 1790, 27.—DAUD, Tr. Orn. ii, 1800, 167.—SHAW, G. Z. vii, 170.
Falco ranivorus, LATH., Ind. Orn. Suppl. ii, 7 (*Strickland*).
Falco strigiceps, NILSS., Orn. Suec. i, 21.
Circus gallinarius, SAVI., Descr. Egyp. i, 91.—LESS., Tr. Orn. 84.—VIEILL., Nouv. Dict. d'Hist. Nat. iv, 459 ; Fn. Franç. 26, pl. ii, f. 1, 2.
Circus variegatus, VIEILL.,, Nouv. Dict. d'Hist. Nat. iv, 466 ; Enc. Meth. iii, 1216.
Circus ægithus, LEACH, Cat. 1816, 9.
Circus cinereus, BREHM, V. D. 94 ; Isis. 1832, 843.
Accipiter variabilis, PALL., Zoog. R. A. i, 364.
Pygargus dispar, KOCH., Syst. Baier. Zool. 128.

b. *hudsonius.*

Falco hudsonius, LINN., Syst. Nat. i, 1766, 128 (*Pygargus canadensis,* EDW., 107 ; *Accipiter freti-hudsonis,* BRISS., vi, App. 18).—GM., i, 1788, 277.—DAUD., Tr. Orn. ii, 173.— SHAW, Gen. Zool. vii, 165

Circus hudsonius, VIEILL., Ois. Am. Sept. i, 1807, 36, pl. 9.—CASS., Ill. i, 1854. 108.—
    BREW., N. A. Oöl. 1857, 42.—CASS., B. N. A. 1858, 38.—NEWB., P. R. R. Rep. vi,
    1857, 74.—KENN., *ibid.* x, 1859, pt. iv, 19.—HEERM., *ibid.* pt. vi, 33.—COOP. &
    SUCK., *ibid.* xii, 1859, 150.—HAYD., Rep. 1862, 153.—COUES, Pr. Phila. Acad.
    1866, 49.—RIDGW., Pr. Phila. Acad. 1870, 141.—STEV., U. S. Geol. Surv. Ter,
    1870, 462.—MERR., *ibid.* 1872, 698.—SNOW, B. Kans. 1873, 2; and of most authors.
Circus (Strigiceps) hudsonius, GRAY, Hand-list, i, 1869, 37, No. 365.
Strigiceps hudsonius, Bp., Consp. Av. i, 1850, 35.
Falco uliginosus, GM., Syst. Nat. i, 1788, 278.—LATH., Ind. Orn. i, 1790, 40.—DAUD., Tr.
    Orn. ii, 1800, 173.—SAB., App. Frank. Journ. 671.—WILS., Am. Orn. vi, 1812,
    67, pl. 51, f. 2 (*Marsh Hawk*, EDW., pl. 291; Arct. Zool. ii, No. 105; Gen. Syn. i, 90).
Circus uliginosus, VIEILL., Ois. Am. Sept. i, 1807, 37.—DEKAY, N. Y. Zool. ii, 20, pl. 3, f. 6, 7.
Circus (Strigiceps) uliginosus, KAUP, Mus. Senck. 1845, 258.
Strigiceps uliginosus, BP., List, 1838, 5.—KAUP, Mon. *Falc.* Cont. Orn. 1850, 58.
Falco variegatus, GM., Syst. Nat. i, 1788, 276.
Circus variegatus, VIEILL., Ois. Am. Sept. i, 1807, 37.
Falco albidus, GM., Syst. Nat. i, 1788, 276.
Falco buffonii, GM., Syst. Nat. i, 1788, 277.—DAUD., Tr. Orn. ii, 172.
Falco cyaneus, vars. β et γ, LATH., Ind. Orn. i, 1790, 40.
Falco glaucus, sub-cœruleus, et ranivorus, BARTR., Trav. 1791, 290.
Falco europogistus, BOSC.—DAUD., Tr. Orn. ii, 1800, 110.
Circus europogistus, VIEILL., Ois. Am. Sept. i, 1807, 36, pl. 8.
Falco hyemalis var., LATH., Ind. Orn. Suppl. 8 (*Strickland*).
Falco æruginosus var., SHAW, Gen. Zool. vii, 117 (*Strickland*).
Falco picatus, SHAW, Gen. Zool. vii, 167 (*Strickland*).
Falco cœsius, ORD, Guthrie's Geog. 2d Am. ed. 315.
Falco cyaneus, BP., Am. Orn. ii, 30, pl. 12; Syn. 1828, 33, sp. No. 22; Isis, 1832, 1038.—
    NUTT., Man. i, 1832, 109.—AUD., Orn. Biog. iv, 1838, 396, pl. 356.—PEAB., Rep.
    Orn. Mass. 1839, 82.
Circus cyaneus, AUD., Syn. 1839, 19.—AUD., B. Am. i, 1840, 105, pl. 26.—GIR., B. L. I.
    1844, 21.—WOODH., Sitgr. Rep. 1853, 61.
Buteo (Circus) cyaneus? var.? *americanus*, SW. & RICH., F. B. A. ii, 1831, 55, pl. 29.
Circus cyaneus hudsonius, SCHL., M. P.-B. 1862, *Circi*, p. 2.
Circus cyaneus var. *hudsonius*, ALLEN, Bull. M. C. Z. iii, 1872, 181.—COUES, Key, 1872, 210,
    fig. 159.—B. B. & R., N. A. B. iii, 1874, 214.

c. cinereus.

Circus cinereus, VIEILL., Nouv. Dict. d'Hist. Nat. iv, 1816, 454; Enc. Meth. iii, 1213.—
    DARW., Voy. Beag. iii, 30.—D'ORBIG., Syn. Av. Mag. Zool. 1837; Voy. Am.
    Merid. 110.—BRIDGES, P. Z. S. ix, 109; Ann. Nat. Hist. xiii, 500.—GRAY, Gen.
    of B.; List B. Br. Mus. 80.—STRICKL., Orn. Syn. 1855, 254.
Circus cyaneus var. *cinereus*, RIDGW.—B. B. & R., N. A. B. iii, 1874, 214.
Circus compestris, VIEILL., Enc. Meth. iii, 1213.
Circus histrionicus, QUOY, Zool. Journ. ii, 271.—KING, *Ibid.* 425; Isis, 1830, 1182; Voy.
    Beag. i, 532.—LESS., Tr. Orn. 85.
Falco histrionicus, QUOY, Voy. Uranie, 93, pl. 15, 16.
Strigiceps histrionicus, BP., Consp. Av. i, 1850, 35.
Spiziacircus histrionicus, KAUP, Mon. *Falc.* Cont. Orn. 1850, 59.

Hab.—Europe, Asia. Var. *hudsonicus* throughout North America. Var. *cinereus* in
South America.

List of specimens.

| 19121 | 160 | .... | ♂ | .... | G. H. Trook.. | 18.00 | 41.00 | 14.00 |
| 19122 | 181 | E. F'k. Tongue R. | ♀ | Sept. 15, 1859 | ......do ...... | 22.00 | 43.50 | 15.50 |

Lieutenant Warren's Expedition.—5160, Cedar Island; 5161, Fort Randall, Dakota;
5162, Running Water.
    Later Expeditions.—59841, Colorado; 60339-41, Wyoming; 60625, Uintah Mountains;
60626-7, North Platte River; 62237, Idaho.

With this species I begin an account of our diurnal *Reptores* that
might be indefinitely prolonged were I disposed to enlarge upon " natural affinities" at the reader's expense. Mr. William Swainson, an ingenious and not entirely unimaginative writer, who entertained peculiar
ideas and was not fastidious in choosing the means to uphold them,
found the Marsh Hawk a more attractive, if not a more profitable, sub-

ject of speculation than we are now likely to discover it to be. Since mere opinions in such cases usually seem more valuable to their authors than others find them, it is the more to be regretted that science requires us to disagree with the wit who met the objection that facts did not support his theory, by remarking, so much the worse for the facts. So far from agreeing respecting the natural affinities of the Marsh Hawk, ornithologists have not succeeded in agreeing upon a name for it. If one will collate the synonyms of the species, he must be prepared to contemplate a great license ornithology has taken in the manufacture of nominal species. Ornithology wears a histrionic mask, never wholly laid aside ; and has its comic aspect, which becomes prominent when we see what is often said about birds—how many parts they are made to play in books, for which nature never designed them, when we note their appearance in different characters at the hands of successive literary costumers. After the play of birds, to which authors invite us, is over, it is well, sometimes, to go into the woods and fields with the birds, and see how they look with their dominos off.

It is sufficient for my present purpose to state, that the Marsh Hawk combines, to a notable degree, the characters of several raptorial types, being, in particular, a link between Hawks and Owls ; and that our bird is a geographical variety of the European. These facts established, the theories that might be based upon them may be disregarded. Audubon's plate is a good portrait of the bird. It has a queer owlish physiognomy, produced by the shape of the head, and especially by the ruff of modified feathers, which, in its higher development, is characteristic of the *Strigidæ*. This analogy is strengthened by a peculiar soft texture of the plumage. Yet the bird is not in the least degree nocturnal, as some of the Buzzards are to a certain extent. In its general habits and structure, the Harrier is allied to ordinary Buzzards ; yet its long wings and tail are nearer those of Hawks of the genus *Accipiter*, birds whose spirit, however, it lacks. Its changes of plumage and sexual differences are peculiar. It differs from most Hawks in its mode of nesting. Briefly, then, birds of the genus *Circus* look like Owls, behave like Buzzards, nest like Vultures, and change color like no other birds of the group to which they belong.

The terrestrial nidification of this bird, in which it stands apart from its kind and approaches the *Cathartes*, is well known ; but accounts of the nesting are at variance in detail. Some say that the nest is built of "sticks, reeds, straw, leaves, and similar materials heaped together, and is lined with feathers, hair, or other soft substances"—a statement too comprehensive to be successfully attacked. Such a nest would be so comfortable that it is a wonder the birds have not the good taste to use it. It has been said, again, that the only materials used " were dried grasses, which were woven together rather neatly." To this statement exception is taken by a writer whose science is better than his grammar, in this wise : " I should doubt the power they possess in so combining the materials of their nest as to cause them to appear to be woven. In many instances they merely trample down the grass in the meadow, and lay their eggs on the bare turf; and when they pretend to build a nest, it will not compare in architecture with that of the common hen." This is rather severe on the Marsh Hawk, though probably true. But Audubon speaks of a nest that he saw : " It was made of dry grass, * * * * pretty regularly and compactly disposed, especially in the interior, on which much care appeared to be bestowed. No feathers or other materials had been used in its construction, not even a twig." This account of Audubon's applies very nearly to the only nest of the Marsh Hawk I ever discovered myself—one that I found at Pembina, Dakota, June 3, 1873. It was on the ground, in the midst of a large patch of wild roses, near the border of the woods along the river. There was no depression of the ground; the cavity of the nest was slight; its diameter, about twelve inches; its height, about three inches The base was a few rose-bush twigs, upon which rested a mass of dried grasses, rather neatly and for the most part circularly disposed; there was no special lining whatever. The eggs are variously rated by writers from three to six in number. In this instance there were five, slightly incubated at the date mentioned. Four or five appears to be the ordinary number. The eggs are broadly oval, and nearly equal in contour at both ends. My specimens measured as follows: 1.87 by 1.45; 1.86 by 1.45; 1.82 by 1.44; 1.80 by 1.45; 1.80 by 1.42. They were dull white, with the faintest possible greenish shade; there were no evident spots, but much mechanical soiling. In numerous other specimens I have examined, the bluish or greenish shade is much stronger; and, authors to the contrary notwithstanding, some sets display markings, often pale and obscure it is true, but too evident to be easily overlooked. These consist of irregular surface-markings, in small spots and larger blotches, of pale brown, with other shell-spots of lilac, lavender, or pale neutral tint. In this wide range of variation, eggs from the same nest not seldom differ, though any one clutch is usually much the same throughout. I have seen much smaller eggs than those the measurements of which are above given.

In the case just given, I had seen the pair of birds for several days, but could not trace them to their nest; at length, however, I stumbled upon it by accident; the female was setting, and did not fly up until I was within a few feet of her, my approach being hidden by the bushes. She flew hurriedly away, with loud cries, which soon brought the male; and the pair circled for some minutes overhead. The male was quite shy and perfectly mute; the female, on the contrary, circled close overhead, and continually uttered a harsh note. I contented myself with securing the nest and eggs, not caring to take the life of the devoted mother. The same season I almost constantly saw Marsh Hawks throughout Northern Dakota; they were the most abundant and universally distributed of all the rapacious birds. In July, at Turtle Mountain, several pairs had bred in the vicinity of one of our camps; and on one occasion I secured a family of five, newly on wing—the male alone escaping. Here, as elsewhere, the brown birds are much more numerous than those in blue plumage; in fact, I saw scarcely a dozen of the latter during the whole season. These birds showed little of the wariness most Hawks display, and almost any number could have been secured. The craws of those examined contained insects, especially grasshoppers, with remains of small quadrupeds and reptiles.

The geographical distribution of the North American Marsh Hawk is coextensive with the continent. In most localities it is one of the most abundant representatives of the family, and may be seen the whole year. But it is, at least partially, migratory; that is to say, the same individuals do not reside permanently in all localities, nor even in those where the bird, as a species, is seen at all seasons. In general, the majority of individuals are bred further north than those places where they reside most of the year; and the further south we proceed, the fewer birds are found during the summer. In most parts of British America, over the vast extent of which the bird ranges, it is stated that it is seen during only a portion of the year, when the food supply is assured.

The presence of water seems a necessary condition of its existence. Along the Missouri River it is the most abundant of the Hawks, not even excepting the Sparrow Hawk. I took numerous individuals at Fort Randall. On the coast of the Carolinas, over the salt-marshes, I found it more plentiful than all other Hawks together. In traveling by rail through the flat, fertile, and well-watered districts of Minnesota and Iowa, in October, I was surprised at the number of these birds I saw; they were almost continually in view, and sometimes several would be seen at a time circling over the prairie, almost as if hunting in packs. The bird may be recognized at any reasonable distance by its peculiar configuration, produced by the length of the wings and tail, its easy sailing flight, the singular bluish and white coloration of the adult male, and the conspicuous white patch on the root of the tail of the female and young. Probably none of our Hawks can be called properly gregarious, but the Marsh Hawk comes the nearest to being so; the young are said to hunt for some time in company, a statement that my observations probably confirm. When mated, the pairs of old birds display the affection and fidelity for which most rapacious birds are noted, keeping close company as long as their cares and delights are shared.

The Marsh Harrier belongs among the "ignoble" birds of the falconers, but is neither a weakling nor a coward, as one may easily satisfy himself by handling a winged bird. Still, under ordinary circumstances, its spirit is hardly commensurate with its physique, and its quarry is humble. It lacks the splendid action that insures success, in the pursuit of feathered game, to the dashing Falcons and true Hawks; with all its stroke of wing, it acquires no such resistless impetus. Audubon, indeed, says that at times, when impelled by hunger, it will attack Partridges, Plovers, and even Teal; but he adds, that he once saw a Marsh Hen come off victorious in a battle with the Harrier. It ordinarily stoops to field-mice, small reptiles, and insects. It is particularly fond of frogs; these goggle-eyed and perspiring creatures suffer more from the Harriers than from all the schoolboys that ever stoned them of a Saturday afternoon. The birds thus particularly resemble the Rough-legged Buzzards in the nature of their prey, and we can see a reason why they are so tenacious of their watery preserves. They hover at no great height, keenly surveying the ground below, and drop directly on their quarry when it is descried. They rarely pursue their prey or transport it to any distance when secured, preferring to make a meal on the spot. Hence, it frequently happens that, when walking in reedy covert, the gunner puts up a Marsh Hawk, disturbed at its repast in the thick vegetation that served alike to screen the bird and cover his own advance. At such a time, as the bird flaps up and makes off at its best pace, it may be brought down with the greatest ease. With wings of ample dimensions—even to be called long in proportion to its weight—the bird nevertheless does not fly very fast; it proceeds ordinarily with regular, easy strokes, three or four times in succession, and then sails until the impulse is exhausted. It often courses very low over the ground, and rather swiftly, turning, passing and repassing, "quartering" the ground like a well-broken dog. This is the habit that has given it the name of "Harrier," and, in some sections, the less elegant designation of "Bog trotter." The old male is also sometimes called "Blue Hawk."

NAUCLERUS FORFICATUS, (Linn.) Ridgw.

Swallow-tailed Kite.

Falco forficatus, LINN., Syst. Nat. i, ed. x, 1758. (Prior name.)
Nauclerus forficatus, RIDGW.—B. B. & R., N. A. B. iii, 1874, 192.—MERR., Am. Nat. viii, 1874, 88 (Florida).
Falco furcatus, LINN., Syst. Nat. i, 1766, 129 (CATES., Car. pl. 4; BRISS., Orn. i, 418; P. E. 72).—GM., Syst. Nat. i, 1788, 262.—LATH., Ind. Orn. i, 1790, 22.—DAUD., Tr. Orn. ii, 1806, 152.—SHAW, G. Z. vii, 1809, 107.—FLEM., Br. An. 52.—WILS., Am. Orn. vi, 1812, 70, pl. 51, fig. 3.—NUTT., Man. i, 1832, 95.—AUD., Orn. Biog. i, 1830, 368; v, 1839, 371; pl. 72.—DEKAY, N. Y. Zool. 1844, pl. 7, fig. 55.
Milvus furcatus, VIEILL., O. A. S. i, 1807, pl. 10.—JEN., Man. 86 —EYT., Cat. Br. B. 66.
Elanus furcatus, VIG., Zool. Journ. i, 340.—STEPH., G. Z. xiii, pt. ii, 49.—CUV., R. A. 2d ed. i, 334.—BP., Syn. 1828, 31.—JAMES., ed. Wils. i, 75.—JARD., ed. Wils. ii, 275.
Elanoides furcatus, VIEILL., Enc. Meth. 1204.—GRAY, G. of B. i, 24, pl. 9, fig. 9.—STRICKL., Orn. Syn. 1855, 141.—OWEN, Ibis, ii, 1860, 240 (biography).—SALV., P. Z. S. 1867, 158 (Veragua).—LAWR., Ann. Lyc. N. Y. ix, 1868, 134 (Costa Rica).
Nauclerus furcatus, VIG., Zool. Journ. ii, 1825, 387; Isis, 1830, 1043.—LESS., Man. i, 1828, 101; Tr. Orn. 73.—SW., Classif. B. ii, 1837, 210.—BP., List, 1838, 4; Consp. Av. i, 1850, 21.—AUD., Syn. 1839, 14; B. Am. i, 1840, 78, pl. 18.—GOULD, B. E. pl. 30.—WOODH., Sitgr. Rep. 1853, 60.—CASS., Ill. 1854, 105.—BREW., N. A. O. 1857, 38.—BD., B. N. A. 1858, 36.—SCL., Ibis, i, 1859, 220 (Guatemala).—WHEAT., Ohio Agric. Rep. 1860, No. 14.—COUES & PRENT., Smiths. Rep. 1861, 402.—LAWR., Ann. Lyc. N. Y. vii, 1861, 289 (Panama); viii, 1866, 280.—COUES, Pr. Bost. Soc. xii, 1868, 120 (South Carolina).—TURNB., B. E. Pa. 1869, 40.—ALLEN, Am. Nat. iii, 1870, 645 (Massachusetts).—RIDGW., Pr. Phila. Acad. 1870, 144.—TRIPPE, Pr. Ess. Inst. vi, 1871, 113 (Minnesota).—ALLEN, Bull. M. C. Z. iii, 1872, 130.—COUES, Key, 1872, 211.—SNOW, B. Kans. 1873.—DRESS., Ibis, 1865, 325 (Texas).—HATCH, Bull. Minn. Acad. i, 1874, 51 (Minnesota).—RIDGW., Ann. Lyc. x, 1874, 380 (Illinois).—HART., Br. B. 1872, 88 (Great Britain, five instances, with references).
Elanoides yetapa, VIEILL., Enc. Meth. iii, 1823, 1205.

Hab.—South Atlantic and Gulf States. On the Atlantic coast not regularly beyond Virginia, but casually to Massachusetts. Up the whole Mississippi Valley, however (Kansas, *Snow, Allen;* Iowa, *Cooper;* Minnesota, lat. 47°, *Trippe*). Up the Missouri to Fort Leavenworth, at least (*Coues*). Cuba (*Cabanis, J. f. O. ii, p. lxxxiii*). South to Brazil (*Cabanis, J. f. O. v, 41; Reinh.*, Vid. Med. 1870, 65). Accidental in Europe.

Marked among its kind by no ordinary beauty of form and brilliancy of color, the Kite courses through the air with a grace and buoyancy it would be vain to rival. By a stroke of the thin-bladed wings and a lashing of the cleft tail, its flight is swayed to this or that side in a moment, or instantly arrested. Now it swoops with incredible swiftness, seizes without a pause, and bears its struggling captive aloft, feeding from its talons as it flies; now it mounts in airy circles till it is a speck in the blue ether and disappears. All its actions, in wantonness or in severity of the chase, display the dash of the athletic bird, which, if lacking the brute strength and brutal ferocity of some, becomes their peer in prowess—like the trained gymnast, whose tight-strung thews, supple joints, and swelling muscles, under marvellous control, enable him to execute feats that to the more massive or not so well conditioned frame would be impossible. One cannot watch the flight of the Kite without comparing it with the thorough-bred racer.

The Swallow-tailed Kite is a marked feature of the scene in the Southern States, alike where the sunbeams are redolent of the orange and magnolia, and where the air reeks with the pestilent miasm of moss-shrouded swamps that sleep in perpetual gloom. But, imbued with a spirit of adventure, possessed of unequaled powers of flight, it often wanders far from its southern home; it has more than once crossed the ocean, and become a trophy of no ordinary interest to the ardent collector in Europe. On the Atlantic coast its natural limit appears to be the lower portions of Virginia, similar in physical and zoölogical characters to the Carolinas; but it has more than once occurred in the Middle States. The Rev. Dr. Turnbull mentions an instance of its capture near Philadelphia, in 1857, probably the same that Mr. Cassin speaks of. The name occurs in Mr. Lawrence's New York List, and Dr. DeKay figures it among the birds of that State. But its greatest extension is through the Mississippi Valley, where it regularly occurs above the mouth of the Missouri. Dr. Woodhouse found it common in Texas and the Indian Territory, and especially so along the Arkansas River. Dr. Hoy records it from Wisconsin. Prof. Snow says it is rare in Kansas, where, however, Mr. Allen states that several pairs arrived about May 15, 1871, near Topeka. The northernmost quotation I have found is that of Mr. Trippe, who observed the bird in Minnesota, north of Mille Lac, at latitude 47°, and states that it is rather common, especially in the immediate vicinity of the Mississippi. Finally, I may add, I had the pleasure of observing it myself in Missouri, opposite Fort Leavenworth, in May, 1864, when a magnificent specimen shaped its course across my path, so near that I could see the flash of its eye as it swept by in full career. It was a beautiful sight, upon which no one could look unmoved, nor without feeling that his excited senses borrowed a plume from the bird itself to follow in imagination when the Kite was lost to view.

I have before me an egg of this species, from the Smithsonian collection, taken in Iowa. It measures 1.90 by 1.50; one end is smaller than the other, though the greatest diameter is nearly equidistant from either. The ground-color is white, but tinged, as if soiled or otherwise mechanically discolored, with a faint brownish shade; it is marked with large irregular blotches of rusty and chestnut-brown, most numerous around the *smaller* end. Besides these there are some specks and small spots of blackish-brown. Audubon describes other eggs, no doubt correctly, as being "of a greenish-white color, with a few irregular blotches of dark brown at the larger end," and states they were from four to six in number. "The nest," he observes, "is usually placed on the top branches of the tallest oak or pine-tree, situated on the margin of a stream or pond. It resembles that of the common Crow externally, being formed of dry sticks, intermixed with Spanish moss, and is lined with coarse grasses and a few feathers."

As if in compensation for its powers of flight, this bird's legs are so short as to be scarcely serviceable for locomotion, and it rarely, if ever, alights on the ground. Its food is principally reptiles and insects. It is found in winter in Central and South America, and is said, whether or not with entire truth I do not know, to withdraw altogether from the United States in September, to return in April. It appears to breed indifferently throughout its normal United States range.

ACCIPITER FUSCUS, (Gm.) Gray.

Sharp-shinned Hawk; Pigeon Hawk.

Falco fuscus, GM., Syst. Nat. i, 1788, 280.—LATH., Ind. Orn. i, 1790, 43.—DAUD., Tr. Orn. ii, 1800, 86.—SHAW, Gen. Zool. vii, 161.—BP., Syn. 1828, 433.—NUTT., Man. i, 1832, 87.—AUD., Orn. Biog. iv, 1838, 522, pl. 474.—PEAB., Rep. Orn. Mass. 1839, 78.—BREW., ed. Wils. 1840, 685.
Accipiter fuscus, BP., Comp. List, 1838, 5; Consp. i, 1850, 32.—WOODH., Sitgr. Rep. 1853, 61.—CASS., Ill. i, 1854, 95; Pr. Phila. Acad. 1855, 279.—BREW., N. A. Oöl. 1857, 18.—BD., B. N. A. 1858, 18.—SCL., P. Z. S. 1858, 295 (Oaxaca).—SCL., Ibis, i, 1859, 218 (Central America).—BRY., Pr. Bost. Soc. vii, 1859 (Bahamas).—COOP.

& SUCK. N. H. Wash. Ter. 1860, 146.—BLAK., Ibis, iii, 1861, 317.—SCL., P. Z. S.
1864, 178.—DRESS.. Ibis, 1869, 324.—COUES, Pr. Phila. Acad. 1866, 43 (Arizona).—
SCL. & SALV., P. Z. S. 1869, 280 (Mosquito Coast).—DALL & BANN., Tr. Chic.
Acad. i, 1869, 271.—GRAY, Hand-list, i, 1869, 32, No. 304. — LAWR., Ann.
Lyc. N. Y. ix, 134 (Costa Rica).—SALV., P. Z. S. 1870, 216 (Veragua).—COOP.,
B. Cal. i, 1870, 466.—ALLEN, Bull. M. C. Z. ii, 1871, 319.—STEV., U. S. Geol.
Surv. Ter. 1870, 462.—MERR., ibid. 1872, 69, 9.—SNOW, B. Kans. 1873.—COUES,
Key, 1872, 212 ; and of most late authors.
Astur fuscus, AUD., Syn. 1839, 18 ; B. Am. i, 1840, 100, pl. 25.—DEKAY, N. Y. Zool. 1844,
ii, 17, pl. 2, f. 2.—GIR., B. L. I. 1844, 19.
Nisus fuscus, KAUP, Mon. Falc. Cont. Orn. 1850, 64.—FINSCH, Abh. Nat. iii, 1872, 26
(Alaska).—B. B. & R., N. A. B. iii, 1874, 224.
Falco dubius, GM., Syst. Nat. i, 1788, 281.—LATH., I. O. i, 1790, 44.—DAUD., Tr. Orn. 122.
Accipiter striatus, VIEILL., Ois. Am. Sept. i, 1807, 42, pl. 14 ; Enc. Meth. iii, 1265.
Falco velox, WILS., Am. Orn. v, 1812, 116, pl. 45, f. 1.—BP., Syn. 1828, 29 ; Isis, 1832, 1137.
Accipiter velox, VIG., Zool. Journ. i, 338.—STEPH., Gen. Zool. xiii, pt. ii, 31.
Astur velox, JAMES., ed. Wils. i, 68.
Falco pennsylvanicus, WILS., Am. Orn. vi, 1812, 13, pl. 46, f. 1.
Nisus pennsylvanicus, CUV., R. A. 2d ed. i, 334.
Nisus pennsylvaticus, LESS., Tr. Orn. i, 1831, 59.
Accipiter pennsylvanicus, VIG., Zool. Journ. i, 338.—STEPH., Gen. Zool. xiii, pt. ii, 32.—
SW. & RICH., F. B. A. ii, 1831, 44.—JARD., ed. Wils. ii, 210.—SW., Classif.
B. ii, 1837, 215.
Astur pennsylvanicus, LESS., Man. Orn. i, 92.—JAMES., ed. Wils. i, 70.
Sparvius lineatus, VIEILL., Enc. Meth. iii, 1823, 1266.
Nisus malfini (juv.), LESS., Traité d'Orn. i, 1831, 58.
Accipiter ardosiacus, VIEILL., Enc. Meth. iii, 1274.
'——— *cooperi,* ♀ , and *fringillarius,* partly, KAUP" (*fide* GRAY).

Hab.—The whole of North America. South to Panama.

List of specimens.

| 19116 | 154 | Powder River.. | ♀ | Oct. 1, 1859 | G. H. Trook.. | 14.00 | 25.00 | 8.50 |
| ? 19117 | 182 | Rosebud ...... | .... | Sept. 9, 1859 | Dr. Hines.... | ...... | ...... | ...... |

Late Expeditions.—60624, Uintah Mountains ; 62234-5, Wyoming.

Although not noticed by Dr. Hayden during the Warren explorations, this handsome and spirited little Hawk was observed by naturalists of the Raynolds' Expedition, and ranges over the whole of the Missouri region, as elsewhere on our continent. It is one of the best known,
and, in most sections, one of the more abundant of our birds of this
family. It preys chiefly upon small birds and quadrupeds, captured in
the dashing manner of all the species of this group, and, like its small
allies, feeds to some extent upon insects. It nests in trees, or on rocks,
preferably the former, laying four or five eggs. They are difficult of concise description, because so variable. The white ground-color has often
a livid or even purplish tint, and is marked, often so thickly as to be
obscured, with large, irregular splashes of various shades of brown,
interminably changeable in number, size, and pattern, sometimes inclining to form masses or a wreath, sometimes more evenly distributed.
The egg is of nearly equal size at both ends, and measures about 1.45
by 1.15.

ACCIPITER COOPERI, (Bp.) Gray.

Cooper's Hawk ; Chicken Hawk.

a. *cooperi.*

Falco cooperi, BP., Am. Orn. ii, 1828, p. 1, pl. 1, f. 1 ; Syn. 1828, 433 ; Isis, 1830, 1137.—
NUTT., Man. i, 1832, 90.—JAMES., ed. Wils. iv, 3.—PEAB., Rep. Orn. Mass. 78.
Astur cooperi, BP., Comp. List, 1838, 5 ; Consp. i, 1850, 31.—AUD., Syn. 1839, 18 ; B. Am.
i, 1840, 98, pl. 24.—NEWB., P. R. R. Rep. vi, 1857, 74.—MAXIM., J. f. O. vi, 1858, 13.

Accipiter cooperi, GRAY, List B. Br. Mus. 38.—CASS., Ill. 1854, 96.—BREW., N. A. Oöl.
    1857, 20, pl. 5, f. 55 (egg).—BD., B. N. A. 1858, 16 ; Mex. B. Surv. ii, 1859, pt.
    ii, p. 3.—SCL., P. Z. S. 1859, 389 (critical).—HEERM., P. R. R. Rep. x, 1859, pt.
    vi, 33.—COOP. & SUCK., N. H. Wash. Ter. 1860, 145.—BLAK., Ibis, iii, 1861, 317.—
    DRESS., Ibis, 1865, 323 (Texas).—COUES, Pr. Phila. Acad. 1866, 43.—ALLEN,
    Bull. M. C. Z. ii, 1871, 321.—SCL. & SALV., Exot. Orn. i, 1869, 170.—LAWR., Ann.
    Lyc. N. Y. ix, 1868, 134 (Costa Rica).—COOP., B. Cal. i, 1870, 464.—SNOW, B.
    Kans. 1873.—COUES, Key, 1872, 212, fig. 140.
Accipiter (Cooperastur) cooperi, GRAY, H. L. i, 1869, 32, No. 312 (" *Cooperastur*," BP., 1854).
Falco stanleyi, AUD., Orn. Biog. i, 186, pl. 36 (*Astur*) ; ii, 245, pl. 141, 3.—NUTT., Man. i,
    1832, 91.
!*Nisus cooperi*, RIDGW., Pr. Bost. Soc. xvi, 1873, 59.—B. B. & R., N. A. B. iii, 1874, 230.
.*Accipiter mexicanus*, SW., F. B. A. ii, 1831, 45.—CASS., Ill. 1854, 96.—STRICK., Orn. Syn.
    1855, 109.—BD., B. N. A. 1858, 17.—COOP. & SUCK., N. H. Wash. Ter. 1860, 146.—
    COUES, Pr. Phila. Acad. 1866, 43 (Arizona).—COOP., B. Cal. i, 1870, 465.—STEV.,
    U. S. Geol. Surv. Ter. 1870, 462.
Accipiter (Cooperastur) mexicanus, GRAY, Hand-list, i, 1869, 33, No. 313.
Nisus cooperi var. *mexicanus*, RIDGW., Pr. Bost. Soc. xvi, 1873, 59.—B. B. & R., N. A. B.
    iii, 1874, 231.
"———— *beskii*, LICHT. ; *pileatus*, juv. KAUP" (*fide* GRAY).

b. *gundlachi*.

Astur cooperi, LEMB., Aves Isl. Cuba, 1850, 17.
Nisus pileatus, LEMB., Aves Isl. Cuba, 1850 ; Suppl.
Astur pileatus, GUNDL., J. f. O. 1854, p. —.
Accipiter gundlachi, LAWR., Ann. Lyc. N. Y. vii, 1860, 252.—GUNDL., Rep. 224.—SCL. &
    SALV., Exot. Orn. i, 170.
Accipiter (Cooperastur) gundlachi, GRAY, Hand-list, i, 1869, 33, No. 319.

Hab.—Temperate North America, and southward. Var. *gundlachi*, Cuba.
    Lieutenant Warren's Expedition.—5163, Fort Berthold ; 5164, White Earth River,
Dakota ; 5165, mouth of the Yellowstone.
    Later Expeditions.—60623, Uintah Mountains.
    As may be gathered from the above, the habitat assigned to Cooper's Hawk includes
that of the so-called *Accipiter mexicanus*. This last is a pure figment, described by Mr.
Swainson, who was apparently ignorant of *A. cooperi*, and perpetuated mainly by Mr.
Cassin, whose authority has had weight in this instance with all American writers,
until quite recently. The most that can be claimed for the supposed *mexicanus* is, that
it consists of rather smaller and more heavily colored, because more southern, specimens, of *A. cooperi;* but even in extreme cases, the difference is insufficient to warrant
retention of the name. Dr. Hayden's specimens, originally referred to " *mexicanus*"
by Mr. Cassin, are no smaller than ordinary *cooperi*, and not otherwise perceptibly
different ; as in too many other cases, the identification, in all probability, was made
upon some supposed points of geographical distribution that were groundless. So far
as I know, the identity of *mexicanus* with *cooperi* was first published by Mr. Allen,
although others, myself among the number, had previously become convinced of the
fact. There is little to add to Mr. Allen's satisfactory exposition of the case. This
pretended species disposed of, we have in this country two species of *Accipiter*, identical in coloration, and nearly so in form, but instantly distinguished by the great disparity in size—the difference being relatively as great as that subsisting between *Picus
villosus* and *P. pubescens*, and the two cases being precisely parallel. The largest females
of *A. fuscus* grade up closely toward the small males of *cooperi*, but there appears to be
a constant small gape between them, which, taking sex for sex, is much greater. The
female *fuscus* is 12 to 14 long, the extent about 26, the wing 7 to 8, the tail 6 to 7 ;
the male *cooperi* is 16 to 18 long, about 30 in extent, the wing 9 to 10, the tail about
8. There is also a difference in the feet, those of *fuscus* being much slenderer, comparatively as well as absolutely, and relatively longer; the whole foot is not over 3¼
long, while that of *cooperi* is at least 4, generally more. In adult male *fuscus* the tarsal scutella frequently fuse, leaving a perfectly smooth shank—a state not observed
in *cooperi*.

    Notwithstanding the abundance of this Hawk in the United States,
its perfectly adult plumage is rarely noted, and in fact I have never seen
a description I considered entirely satisfactory—that given in the
" Key" is accurate, but, like most of my accounts, necessarily much
abbreviated. The adult bird is not only bluish-gray on the upper parts,
but has a decided shade of the same on the breast and sides. A fine
male I procured at Washington showed this very plainly; yet it has
been supposed specifically distinctive of the Cuban variety. As usually

observed, in youth, the upper parts are dark brown, deepest on the head, where often quite blackish, and the under parts are white or whitish, lengthwise streaked with brown. This latter marking gradually changes, both in pattern and color, to a fine rusty red, in transverse bars alternating with white. The upper parts simultaneously grow bluish-gray; the under finally acquire a similar glaucous shade. There is nothing peculiar in this, however, for it is the rule among Hawks, that those which on the under parts were barred crosswise when adult, are striped lengthwise when young. The coloration and changes of plumage of *A. fuscus* are precisely the same.

The birds of this genus are closely allied to the true *Asturs*, or Goshawks, differing mainly in smaller size, slenderer build, and consequently inferior prowess; but they are " noble" birds of prey, scarcely yielding in spirit and action to the typical Falcons themselves. Cooper's is one of the largest of the genus, and an audacious highwayman it is. An idea of its daring may be gathered from Audubon's account of an exploit he witnessed: " This marauder sometimes attacks birds far superior to itself in weight, and sometimes possessed of a courage and strength equal to its own. As I was one morning observing the motions of some Parakeets near Bayou Sara, in Louisiana, in the month of November, I heard a cock crowing not far from me, and in sight of a farm-house. The Hawk next moment flew past me, and so close that I might have touched it with the barrel of my gun, had I been prepared. Not more than a few seconds elapsed before I heard the cackling of the hens, and the war-cry of the cock, and at the same time observed the Hawk rising, as if without effort, a few yards in the air, and again falling toward the ground with the rapidity of lightning. I proceeded to the spot, and found the Hawk grappled to the body of the cock, both tumbling over and over, and paying no attention to me as I approached. Desirous of seeing the result, I remained still until, perceiving that the Hawk had given a fatal squeeze to the brave cock, I ran to secure the former; but the marauder had kept a hawk's eye upon me, and, disengaging himself, rose in the air in full confidence. The next moment I pulled trigger, and he fell dead to the ground."

On the other hand, Cooper's Hawk has occasionally been tamed, exhibiting an intelligent docility, and no small degree of regard for its master. I witnessed an interesting instance of this while in the southwest, riding twenty miles one day to see some tamed Hawks that had grown quite famous locally. I find the following account of the visit in one of my old note-books: " Our errand told, we were made at home directly, for ' Tennessee Bill,' as our host was known in these parts, was proud of his pets, and doubtless gratified we had come so far to see them; besides, he was not sorry to hear the news from ' the fort,' living all alone as he did. He tendered such hospitality as his log-cabin afforded—of the kind that, however varied in substance, is always much the same ' in spirit.' Whoso drinks in the West is entitled to all the rights, privileges, and immunities said to be accorded him who tastes salt in Arabia; but, although I have no objection to salt in its place, I consider its place as limited, and, on the whole, prefer our own customs. Bill promised that the birds should be duly forthcoming—' providin' they're anyways about here,' he added. He stepped to the door, and blew a long, shrill whistle with his fingers in his mouth. No answer, and he whistled again, when, like a far echo, we heard a cry from the woods. ' Jes' so; I suspicioned they were off down the crik, huntin' on their own hook; thar they come; think I've got some grub for em; sold, ain't they?' In a moment three Hawks came dashing toward the

house, with eager cries. Catching sight of strangers, they veered off
at the last moment, and, with a graceful upward curve, settled in a tall
cottonwood overhead. There they stood, peering with outstretched
necks down through the foliage, eager, curious, yet distrustful, and
occasionally uttering a whining note. Bill explained that they were
afraid of us, but said he 'reckoned he'd fetch 'em down,' and entered
the house for his rifle. I was surprised, for I thought he was going to
kill one; but my companion called to my mind that Bill was still in the
habit of shooting small birds for them to eat, as he had done when they
were quite young. The birds redoubled their clamor as their owner
reappeared, gun in hand, and leaped lower down among the branches.
He stepped forward a few paces, and then, appetite overcoming their
mistrust, they sailed down, and flapped about over his head as he
walked toward the bushes. Crack! ping! He knocked the head off an
unlucky Sparrow, picked it up, held it out in his hand, and made a
queer, chuckling noise, like a hen clucking to her chickens. The boldest
settled lightly on his shoulder, then slid down his arm, seized the bird,
and flew off, with the other two in full pursuit. This was the first time
I ever saw a Hawk at liberty come at a call, and take food from its
master's hands. It was worth the ride."

These three birds had been taken when very young from their nest
in the crotch of a cottonwood over the cabin, reared in captivity until
well grown, and then allowed their liberty, with the above gratifying
result. Both the parents had been shot. The nest, which was pointed
out to me, looked, from where I stood, like a Crow's. I did not venture
on a perilous climb to examine it more closely. Such is the situation
generally chosen. Audubon describes the nest as composed externally
of numerous crooked sticks, and lined with grasses and a few feathers.
Dr. Brewer mentions two, both lined with pieces of bark; one of them
was between one and a half and two feet broad, the external layer of
sticks hardly an inch thick, " with only a slight depression in the centre,
hardly enough to keep the eggs from rolling out." The eggs I have examined measured from 1.80 by 1.55 to 2.10 by 1.60—figures showing the
variation both in size and shape—they average about 1.90 by 1.50.
They resemble those of the Marsh Hawk so closely as to be not certainly distinguishable, but they are usually more globular, and with a
more granulated shell. The greatest diameter is at or very near the
middle; difference in shape of the two ends is rarely appreciable. All
were more uniform in color than those of most Hawks, resembling the
pale, scarcely marked examples occasionally laid by most kinds of
Hawks; none were conspicuously dark-marked. The ground is white,
faintly tinted with livid or greenish-gray; if marked, it is with faint,
sometimes almost obsolete, blotches of drab, liable to be overlooked
without close inspection; only an occasional specimen is found with
decided, though still dull and sparse, markings of pale brown. Three
or four eggs are the usual nest-complement; in the Northern and Middle
States they are laid in May. Mr. Samuels speaks of a pair that nested
near Newton, Massachusetts, and were robbed of their eggs four times
in succession. "They built different nests in the same grove, and laid
in the four litters four, four, five, and three eggs, respectively. The
eggs of the last litter were very small, but little larger than those of
the Sharp-shinned Hawk."

The range of Cooper's Hawk is, in a measure, complementary to that
of the Goshawk; not that the two are never found together, for such is
the case in all our Northern States; but one is as decidedly southern as
the other is northerly. The present species does not appear to pene-

trate any great distance into the British possessions, like its smaller
relative, the Sharp-shinned; and I have found no indication whatever
of its presence far north. It is abundant in most parts of the United
States; particularly so in New England, where it is perhaps the most
numerous of all the birds of prey. It appears to breed indifferently in
all suitable places throughout its United States range; and, to judge
by the well-known rule of difference in size according to latitude, it is a
resident bird. Gulf-coast examples average about two and a half inches
smaller than others from New England. Possessed of spirit commensurate with its physical powers, it preys upon game little if any humbler
than that of our more powerful Falcons. It attacks and destroys hares,
Grouse, Teal, and even the young of larger Ducks, in the state in which
they are known as ' flappers,' besides capturing the usual variety of
smaller birds and quadrupeds. It occasionally seizes upon reptiles or
picks up insects. In securing its prey it gives chase openly, and dives
down on its quarry with almost incredible velocity. Its ordinary flight
is rapid, easy, and soaring, performed with alternate flapping and sailing. When brought down winged, it shows undaunted front, and fights
desperately to the last gasp.

ASTUR ATRICAPILLUS, (Wils.) Jard.

The American Goshawk.

Falco atricapillus, WILS., Am. Orn. vi, 1812, 80, pl. 52, f. 3.—WAGL., Isis, 1831, 517.—NUTT.,
    Man. i, 1832, 85.—PEAB., Rep. Orn. Mass. 77.—THOMPS., Nat. Hist. Vermont, 62.
Hierofalco atricapillus, CUV., R. A. 2d ed. i, 323.
Sparvius atricapillus, VIEILL., Ency. Meth. iii, 1823, p. 1266.
Astur atricapillus, JARD. & SELBY, Illust. 1825, pl. 121.—BP., Comp. List, 1838, 5; Consp.
    i, 1850, 31.—KAUP, Monog. *Falc.,* 1850, 66.—CASS., Ill. 1854, 93; Pr. Phila. Acad.
    1855, 279.—BREW., N. Am. Oöl, 1857, 17.—NEWB., P. R. R. Rep. 1857, vi, 74.—
    BD., B. N. A. 1858, 15.—COOP. & SUCK., N. H. Wash. Ter. 1860, 144.—LORD,
    Pr. Roy. Arty. Inst. iv, 110 (British Columbia).—WHEAT., Ohio Agric. Rep. 1860,
    No. 6.—COUES & PRENT., Smiths. Rep. 1861, 401 (Washington, D. C., very
    rare, in winter).—BLAK., Ibis, iii, 1861, 316.—BOARDM., Pr. Bost. Soc. ix, 1862,
    122 (Calais, Me. ; resident, common, breeds).—VERR., Pr. Ess. Inst. iii, 1862,
    141 (Norway, Me.; resident, common, breeds).—ALLEN, Pr. Ess. Inst. iv, 1864,
    50 (Massachusetts, winter).—MCILWR., Pr. Ess. Inst. v, 1866, 80 (Hamilton,
    Canada West, rather rare).—COUES, Pr. Ess. Inst. v, 1868, 255.—LAWR., Ann.
    Lyc. N. Y. viii, 1866, 280 (New York).—TURNB., B. E. Pa. 1869, 6 (rare).—DALL
    & BANN., Tr. Chic. Acad. i, 1869, 271 (Alaska, common, resident).—COOP., B.
    Cal. i, 1870, 467 (Sierra Nevada).—SNOW, B. Kans. 1873 (rare).—MAYN., Pr.
    Bost. Soc. xiv, 1871 (Northern New England, common, resident).—FINSCH, Abh.
    Nat. iii, 1872, 26 (Alaska).—COUES, Key, 1872, 212.
Falco palumbarius, BP., Syn. 1828, 28; Isis, 1832, 1137.—AUD., Orn. Biog. ii, 241, pl. 141.
Accipiter palumbarius, SW. & RICH., F. B. A. ii, 1831, 39, pl. 26.
Astur palumbarius, AUD., Syn. 1839, 18; B. Am. i, 1840, 95, pl. 23.—GIR., B. L. I, 1844, 18.
Astur palumbarius var. *atricapillus,* RIDGW., Pr. Bost. Soc. xvi, 1874, 57.—B. B. & R.,
    N. A. B., iii, 1874, 237.
Astur palumbarius var. *striatulus,* RIDGW.—B. B. & R., N. A. B. iii, 1874, 240.
Falco regalis, TEMM., Planches Coloriées, No. 495.
Dœdalion pictum, LESS., Traité d'Ornith. i, 1831, 67 (see PUCHER., R. Z. 1850, 211).

Hab.—British America, and the Northern half of the United States—the latter chiefly
in winter; farthest south along the Rocky Mountains and Sierra Nevada ("*striatulus*").

List of specimens.

| 19115 | .... | Deer Creek..... | .... | Mar. 28, 1860 | G. H. Trook.. | 24.50 | 44.50 | 14.00 |

Late Expeditions.—58982, Colorado.

It is still a question whether the American Goshawk is specifically distinct from that
of Europe. Authorities are about equally divided in opinion, and both sides speak
with little, if any, reserve. My own comparisons have not been sufficiently extensive;

but careful examination of the material at my command shows me decided differences, constant enough to fairly warrant specific discrimination, although I should not be surprised if larger series led to a different result. But "var. *striatulus*" is untenable.

This noble Hawk, one of the handsomest birds of the family when in perfect plumage, is a decidedly boreal bird, entirely wanting in the southern portions of the United States, appearing only in winter, and in small numbers, in the Middle districts, but common along our northern frontier. I have myself never seen it alive. According to the records examined, its southward extension is from Maryland to Ohio, Kentucky, Kansas, and California. It is, as a rule, rare even in Southern New England, where, however, it appears some winters in considerable numbers. Mr. Allen remarks that it was common in Massachusetts in the winter of 1859-'60; and Mr. Samuels states that the same season he received a dozen or fifteen specimens from the vicinity of Boston. Audubon says his figure was drawn from a specimen taken in Kentucky, and speaks of its breeding in New York and Pennsylvania. Such instances of breeding as this must be, I think, exceptional. The only region in the United States where it is reported as regularly resident is Northern New England, where, both Mr. Boardman and Prof. Verrill state it is of common occurrence, and breeds. On the west coast, Mr. Dall gives it as abundant and resident in the Yukon region. According to Drs. Cooper and Suckley, it is of frequent occurrence in Oregon and Washington Territories. The specimen above quoted is the only one I have ever seen from the Missouri region, where the species appears to be rare, though doubtless of regular occurrence. Prof. Snow remarks upon an individual killed near Lawrence, in Kansas.

According to Dr. Brewer, the egg of the Goshawk is $2\frac{5}{16}$ long by $1\frac{1}{16}$ broad, nearly spherical, roughly granulated, soiled white, with a faint bluish shade, "marked irregularly with large but quite faint blotches of drab and yellowish-brown." It thus closely resembles that of Cooper's Hawk, differing chiefly in its larger size; and the nidification is represented as being the same in essential particulars. In the nature of its prey, its mode of securing it, its general habits and nature, we find it also much the same, the only difference resulting from its superior prowess, if not more ferocious nature.

FALCO MEXICANUS var. POLYAGRUS, (Cass.) Coues.

American Lanier, or Prairie Falcon.

a. *mexicanus*.

Falco mexicanus, LICHT., Mus. Berol. (Monterey, *Deppe*).—SCHL., Abh. Geb. Zool. u. Vergl. iv, 1841, 15; M. P.-B. 1862, *Falcones*, p. 18.—BP., Consp. i, 1850, 24.— GRAY, Hand-list, i, 1869, 20, No. 179.—RIDGW., Pr. Phila. Acad. 1870, 140 (includes both varieties).
Falco (Hierofalco) laniarius var. *mexicanus*, RIDGW., Pr. Bost. Soc. xvi, 1873, 44.—B. B. & R., N. A. B. iii, 1874, 109.

b. *polyagrus*.

Falco polyagrus, CASS., Ill. 1853, 88, 121, pl. 16.—BD., B. N. A. 1858, 12.—KENN., P. R. R. Rep. x, 1859, pt. iv, 19 (Arizona.)—HEERM., *ibid.* pt. vi, 31.—COOP. & SUCK., N. H. Wash. Ter. 1860, 143 (Oregon).—HAYD., Rep. 1862, 152.—DRESS., Ibis, 1865, 323 (Texas).—COUES, Pr. Phila. Acad. 1866, 42 (Arizona).—GRAY, Hand-list, i, 1869, 20, No. 178.—COOP., B. Cal. i, 1870, 458 (California).—SNOW, B. Kans. 1873 (Kansas).—STEV., U. S. Geol. Surv. Ter. 1870, 462 (Wyoming).
Falco mexicanus, RIDGW., Am. Nat. vi, 1872, 430 (Illinois).—COUES, Key, 1872, 213.
Falco (Hierofalco) laniarius var. *polyagrus*, RIDGW., Pr. Bost. Soc. xvi, 1873, 44.—B. B. & R., N. A. B. iii, 1874, 123.

Hab.—The typical form from Mexico. Var. *polyagrus* from Western United States. East to Illinois (*Sargent*).

List of specimens.

19113	68	Grosv. Fork	....	....	June 18, 1860	F. V. Hayden.	......	......	......

Lieutenant Warren's Expedition.—5167, Fort Randall, Dakota; 5168-69, Knife River, Missouri.

Later Expeditions.—60333, Laramie Peak; 60334, Camp Carling, Wyoming; 60616, Uintah Mountains; 61094, Sulphur Springs.

The specific identity of Mr. Cassin's *Falco polyagrus* with the little known *F. mexicanus* of Prof. Lichtenstein may be considered established. The discrepancies noted in my article, above cited, are in part at least due to age, sex, or other fortuitous circumstances. There may be, however, as Mr. Ridgway has probably shown, certain differences due to climatic influences which may warrant recognition of two varieties. But I am not at present prepared to follow Mr. Ridgway in referring these forms to the old world *F. laniarius*, although they are unquestionably very closely related. As Mr. Cassin pointed out, the resemblance is also very great to the Indian Jugger—*F. jugger*, GRAY, Ill. Ind. Zool. ii, pl. 26; JERD., Ill. Ind. Orn. pl. 44; in fact, the specimens I have examined, excepting some very old ones, come nearer the representations I have seen of *F. jugger* than of *laniarius* proper. This form, *jugger*, is also referred by Mr. Ridgway to *laniarius* as a variety, but, until its varietal relationship is established, it may be best to keep the two apart, and also to recognize the American form as specifically distinct.

The comparatively late discovery of this bird as an inhabitant of the United States is particularly interesting, not only as giving us a hitherto unknown representative of the familiar Lanier group of Falcons of the Old World, but also as adding another to the numerous instances of close alliance of *Western* American birds to certain Old World forms.

This interesting bird is of general distribution in open country throughout the West, and rather common. It appears to be essentially a prairie species, a circumstance probably explaining its occurrence in Illinois, where it was noted by Mr. J. D. Sargent and Mr. R. Ridgway. Prof. Snow catalogues it as rare in winter in Kansas. Dr. Hayden remarks that it is found at various points along the Missouri and on the Platte, though not abundantly. Several observers found it in New Mexico and Arizona. On the Pacific coast it is known to occur at various points, from Fort Dalles, Oregon, where it was procured by Dr. Suckley, to Monterey, whence came one of the types of the species. It appears to be particularly abundant in the open portions of Southern California, where Dr. Cooper told me he often saw it, in company with the Ferruginous Buzzard, resting on the ground or flying low over the surface in the neighborhood of the villages of the California ground squirrel (*Spermophilus beecheyi*), for which animals it was doubtless on the watch. The only time I ever saw it alive was in this region. While at Drumm Barracks, one of these birds dashed past, returned in an instant, and alighted on the roof of the house, while Dr. Cooper and I were standing on the porch. It had evident designs upon the Blackbirds, thousands of which were scurrying about. Watching the bird for a few moments, and perceiving it had no intention of leaving at that particular time, I went into the house for my gun, and loaded for its especial benefit. The bird watched the whole proceedings, eyeing me audaciously, and never stirred from its perch until I made an irresistible appeal. I found it to be a young bird, the iris brown, the feet dull bluish, the claws black, the bill bluish-black, with the base of the under mandible yellow.

This Falcon is inferior to none of our country in strength and spirit, unless it be that the Gyrfalcon surpasses it in this respect. It even attacks and overpowers the great hares of the West (*L. callotis* and allies)—animals actually larger and heavier than itself. With its nidification I am unacquainted; I have, however, examined its eggs, of which no description has hitherto appeared. A set now in the Smithsonian was collected by Dr. Hayden in the Wind River Mountains, in June, 1860. They are rather unusually pointed at the smaller end, though probably other examples might tend more nearly to the ordinary sub-spherical shape prevailing among the eggs of rapacious birds. They measure 2 inches in length by a trifle over 1½ in breadth. The ground color is dull white, but scarcely apparent, so thickly is it clouded over with dull brown, forming here and there patches of deeper shade. In one specimen there is a decided purplish tint. To this identification of its breeding range we may append the notice of its unfledged young, found by Dr. Heermann near San Francisco.

FALCO COMMUNIS, Gm.

Peregrine Falcon; Duck Hawk.

a. *communis.*

Falco communis, GM., Syst. Nat. i, 1788, 270.—LATH., Ind. Orn. i, 1790, 30 (*Acc. falco communis*, BRISS., Orn. i, 321).—DAUD., Tr. Orn. ii, 1800, 92.—SHAW, Gen. Zool. vii, 124.—SAVI., Descr. Egyp. i, 101.—MEYER, Tasch. i, 57.—WILS., Mem. Wern. Soc. ii, 595.—CUV., R. A. 2d ed. 320.—RAFFL., Linn. Trans. xiii, 278.—LESS., Tr. Orn. i, 88, pl. 16, fig. 1.—SCHL., Krit. Ueb. 14; Rev. Crit. 2; Fn. Jap. 1; Traité Fancon. —; M. P.-B. i, 1862, *Falc.* 1.—BP., Consp. Av. i, 1850, 23.
Falco peregrinus, GM., Syst. Nat. i, 1788, 272.—LATH., Ind. Orn. i, 1790, 33 (BRISS., Orn. i, 341).—DAUD., Tr. Orn. ii, 1800, 97.—SHAW, Gen. Zool. vii, 128.—STEPH., *ibid.* xiii, pt. ii, 39.—TEMM., Man. 1815, 34.—LEACH, Cat. 1816, 11.—KAUP, Classif. Säug. u. Vög. 110.—BREHM, V. D. i, 63.—FLEM., Br. An. 49.—JERD., Mad. Journ. x, 1839, 79.—PALL., Zoog. R. A. i, 1811, 327, pl. 3, 4.—JENYNS, Man. 82.—NAUM., V. D. i, 1822, 285, pl. 24, 25.—MACGIL., Hist. Br. B. iii, 294; Rap. B. Gr. Br. 159.—EYT., Cat. 1.—BP., List, 1838, 4.—KEYS. & BLAS., 1840, 28.—GRAY, Gen. of B. i, 19.—HODG., Gray's Zool. Misc. 1844, 81.—GOULD, B. Eur. pl. 21.—KUHL, Beit. Zool. i, 78 (anat.).—RUPP., Neue Wirb. 44; Syst. Uebers. 11.—HARDY, Rev. Zool. 1844, 289.—VIEILL., Fn. Franç. 29, pl. 13, figs. 1, 2.—KAUP, Mus. Senck. 257.—BAILLY, Orn. Sav. i, 45.—S.-LONGCH., Fn. Belg. 50—LUBB., Fn. Norf. 17.—ROUX, Orn. Prov. i, 49, pl. 29, 30.—BECHST., Tasch. 33.—MEYER, Tasch. i, 55.—FRISCH, V. D. pl. 83.—SELBY, Ill. Brit. Orn. i, 39, pl. 15, 15*.—JARD., Br. B. i, 115, pl. 4.—THOMPS., B. Ireland, i, 33.—WATT., B. Ireland, 4.—MORRIS, Br. B. 88, pl. 13.—STRICKL., Orn. Syn. 1855, 81.—GRAY, List Br. B. 1863, 11; and of authors generally.
Falco orientalis, GM., Syst. Nat. i, 1788, 264.—LATH., I. O. i, 1790, 22.—DAUD., Tr. ii, 76.
Falco tartaricus, GM., Syst. Nat. i, 1788, 272 (BRISS., Orn. i, 345).
Falco calidus, LATH., Ind. Orn. i, 1790, 41 (*Behree Falcon*, Syn. Suppl. 35).
Falco lunulatus, DAUD., Tr. Orn. ii, 1800, 122 (*Strickland*).
Falco abietinus, BECHST., Naturg. Deutschl. ii, 759.
Falco pinetarius, SHAW, Gen. Zool. vii, 195 (*Strickland*).
Falco gentilis, WILS., Mem. Wern. Soc. ii, 587 (*Strickland*).
Falco micrurus, HODG., Gray's Zool. Misc. 1844, 81.
Falco griseiventris, BREHM, Isis, 1833, 778.
Falco cornicum, BREHM, V. D. i, 62.

b. *melanogenys.*

Falco peregrinus, VIG., Linn. Trans. xv, 183; Isis, 1830, 260 (*Strickland*).
Falco melanogenys, GOULD, P. Z. S. v, 139; Syn. B. Aust. 3; Introd. B. Aust. 19; B. Aust. i, pl. 8.—GRAY, Gen. of B.; List B. Brit. Mus. 51; Hand-list, i, 1869, 19, No. 167.—BP., Rev. Zool. 1850. 484; Consp. i, 1850, 23.—KAUP, Mon. *Falc.* Cont. Orn. 1850, 56.—STRICKL., Orn. Syn. 1855, 84.
Falco macropus, SW., An. in Menag. 341.
Falco communis var. *melanogenys*, RIDGW.—B. B. & R., N. A. B. iii, 1874, 129.

c. *anatum.*

Falco niger, GM., Syst. Nat. i, 1788, 270 (BRISS., i, 327). (*Strickland.*)
Falco nævius, GM., Syst. Nat. i, 1788, 271 (BRISS., i, 329.) (*Strickland.*)
Falco communis, COUES, Key, 1872, 213, f. 141.
Falco communis var. *anatum*, RIDGW., Pr. Bost. Soc. 1873, 45.—B. B. & R., N. A. B. iii, 132.

Falco peregrinus var. b. *anatum*, BLAS., List B. Eur. 3.—RIDGW., Pr. Phila. Ac. 1870, 139.
Falco peregrinus, WILS., Am. Orn. ix, 1814, 120, pl. 76.—JAMES., ed. Wils. i, 51.—JARD.,
    ed. Wils. iii, 251.—BREW., ed. Wils. 677, 683.—SAB., Linn. Trans. xii, 529.—BP.,
    Journ. Phila. Acad. i, 1824, 342; Syn. 1828, 27; Isis, 1832, 1136.—SW. & RICH.,
    F. B. A. ii, 1831, 23.—RICH., App. Parry's 2nd Voy. 342.—NUTT., Man. i, 1832,
    53.—AUD., Orn. Biog. i, 1832, 85; v, 1839, 365; pl. 16; Syn. 1839, 16; B. Am. i,
    1840, 84, pl. 20.—GIR., B. L. I. 1844, 14.—HALD., Pr. Phila. Acad. i, 1841, 54
    (breeding in United States).— DEKAY, Nat. Hist. N. Y. 1844, 13, pl. 3, f. 8.—
    LEMB., Av. Cubæ, 1850, pl. 1, fig. 2.—WOODH., Sitgr. Rep. 1853, 60.—ALLEN,
    Am. Nat. iii, 1869, 514.—TAYLOR, Ibis, 1864, 80 (Trinidad).—TRIPPE, Pr. Ess.
    Inst. vi, 1871, 113 (Minnesota).—ALLEN, Bull. M. C. Z. ii, 1871, 316; iii, 1872,
    180.—RUSS, J. f. O. 1871, 49.—PHILLIPPI, Cat. 1869 (Chili).
Falco anatum, BP., List, 1838, 4 ; R. Z. 1850, 484; Consp. i, 1850, 23.—GOSSE, B. Jam.
    1847, 16.—CASS., Ill. 1854, 86.—BREW., N. A. Oöl. 1857, 8.—BD., B. N. A., 1858, 7.—
    BRY., Pr. Bost. Soc. vii, 1859; 1867, 66 (Bahamas).—CAB., J. f. O. ii, p. lxxxiii.—
    GUNDL., Repert. 1865, 225.—NEWT., Ibis, i, 1859, 63 (Santa Cruz).—WOOD,
    "Hartford Times," June 24, 1861.—BLAKISTON, Ibis, 1861, 315.—BOARDM., Pr.
    Bost. Soc. ix, 1862, 122 (Grand Menan, breeding).—MARCH, Pr. Phila. Acad.
    1863, 304 (Jamaica).—ALLEN, Pr. Ess. Inst. iv, 1864, 50; 1865, 153 (breeding).—
    SALV., P. Z. S. 1867, 158 (Veragua).—COUES, Pr. Ess. Inst. v, 1868, 254 (New
    England).—MCILWR., Pr. Ess. Inst. v, 1866, 80 (Canada West).—TURNB., B.
    E. Pa. 1869, 6 (breeding on Alleghanies and cliffs along Susquehanna).—DALL
    & BANN., Tr. Chic. Acad. i, 1869, 270 (Alaska).—COOP., B. Cal. i, 1870, 457.—
    SNOW, B. Kans. 1873; and of most late American writers.
Falco nigriceps, CASS., Ill. 1853, 87 (California); Pr. Phila. Acad. 1855, 277 ; Gillis' U. S.
    Astron. Exp. ii, 1855, pl. 14 (Chili); B. N. A. 1858, 8, pl. 11.—STRICKL., Orn.
    Syn. 1855, 85.—COOP. & SUCK., N. H. Wash. Ter. 1860, 142, pl. 11.—GRAY,
    Hand-list, i, 1869, 19, No. 166.—COOP., B. Cal. i, 1870, 456.
(?) *Falco communis* var. *pealei*, RIDGW., B. B. & R., N. A. B. iii, 1874, 137 (northwest coast;
    melanotic ; may require varietal recognition).
(?) *Falco cassini*, SHARPE, Ann. Mag. N. H. Mar. 1873 (Straits of Magellan).

e. *minor.*

Falco communis minor, SCHL., Traité Faucon. ; M. P.-B. i, 1862, 4.
Falco minor, BP., Consp. Av. i, 1850, 23; R. Z. 1850, 484.—STRICKL., Orn. Syn. 1855, 83.—
    GRAY, Hand-list, i, 1869, 19, No. 168.
Falco peregrinus, SMITH, S. Afr. Quart. Journ. 236 (*Strickland*).
Falco peregrinus var. *capensis*, SUND. (*Gray*).
Falco peregrinoides, ALIQ., (*Bp.*)—SMITH, *l. c.* 235 (*Strickland*).

Hab.—Nearly cosmopolitan. Var. *communis*, from most parts of the Old World. Var.
melanogenys, from Australia and Java. Var. *anatum*, generally distributed in America.
Var. *minor* from South Africa.

Lieutenant Warren's Expedition.—5166, mouth of Vermilion River.

Without feeling at all assured of even varietal distinctions in this case (excepting
var. *minor*), I arrange the synonymy as above. The several sets of names may be
readily combined if desired, while it would be less easy to separate them if the
synonymy were compiled indiscriminately. I quote several names, for the identification of which I am not responsible, on the authorities cited in the respective cases.
    The American Duck Hawk appears to have been first separated from the Old World
Peregrine by Prince Bonaparte, in 1838; but no characters were, to my knowledge,
then ascribed to it, and it is very doubtful that any exist. It may be presumed
that this author was misled by a then supposed, but since proved groundless, difference in the nidification ; more likely, however, he proceeded upon some theory respecting geographical distribution. The name has, however, been very generally adopted,
even by those who have demurred against it. One of the highest authorities on birds
of prey, Dr. Schlegel, states, after examination of various examples from North and
South America and Mexico, that " le *Faucon commun* de l'Amérique ne diffère en au-
cune façon du nôtre." Such is nearly my own view; and even Bonaparte, in 1850,
confesses that his *anatum* is " forsan a *F. communi* spec. haud diversus." Mr. Ridgway,
however, claims good varietal characters for our bird A later candidate for recognition is found in the *F. nigriceps* of CASSIN, which, like *F. anatum*, rests upon some
ascribed characters, being said to be smaller, darker, &c. But these features appear
to be fortuitous, belonging to the category of individual peculiarities; and since pure
anatum has been determined to occur within areas supposed to be occupied by *nigriceps*,
even its character as a geographical race disappears. Of the Australian *F. melanogenys*,
Dr. Schlegel has remarked : " La variété accidentelle foncée de l'Australie * * * *
ne mérite pas même le nom de conspecies."

A more distinct form than either of the foregoing is, according to nearly all authorities, that found in South Africa (var. *minor*), it being constantly smaller.

Following Dr. Schlegel, I omit from the above synonymy the names of the Indian Red Falcon (*F. ruber indicus*, ANTIQ.; *F. communis indicus*, GM.; *F. shaheen*, JERD., Madras Journ. x. 81; Ill. Ind. Orn. pl. 12; *F. sultaneus*, HODG., Zool. Misc. 81; *F. ruber*, SCHL., M. P.-B. i, 1862, 5; *F. peregrinator*, GRAY & BP., *au* SUND.?), which seems to be entitled to specific separation. By some authors, both early and late, it is rated as a variety of *communis*, while others hold it to be distinct.

The Peregrine occurs at intervals in all suitable places in North America, and it is not a little remarkable that its extensive breeding range should have only lately been ascertained. Even so late as 1857, Dr. Brewer stated that he had only recently become aware of its breeding in the United States, and that only one authentic instance of its occurrence during the breeding season south of Newfoundland had come to his knowledge. He appends a foot-note, containing information from Prof. Haldeman of its breeding on a cliff along the Susquehanna, near Columbia, Pennsylvania, and also, probably, at Harper's Ferry in Virginia. More recently Mr. Allen, with the assistance of Mr. C. W. Bennett and Dr. W. Wood, of East Windsor Hill, Connecticut, have been conspicuous in elaborating the history of the species, and especially in establishing the fact that it regularly breeds on several of the mountains on and near the Connecticut River Valley. Mr. Boardman reports the same item from Grand Menan, where, he says, the bird is resident, and regularly breeds on the cliffs. Dr. Wood, in the newspaper above quoted, states that four nearly fledged young were taken from a nest on Talcott Mountain, near Hartford, June 1, 1861, the female parent being shot. Writing in 1864, Mr. Allen states that Mr. Bennett took young birds, "a few years since," on Mount Tom, near Springfield, Massachusetts. Shortly afterward Mr. Allen announced the discovery of the eggs by Mr. Bennett, on Mount Tom, April 19, 1864; these were the first known to have been procured in New England, or, indeed, in the United States. The unusual interest attaching to his article induces me to quote at some length:

"Although the Duck Hawk has been long known to breed at the localities in Massachusetts mentioned above [Mounts Tom and Holyoke], those conversant with the fact were not aware that any special interest was attached to it, or that its eggs and breeding-habits were very little known to ornithologists; and so, until very recently, no particular efforts have been made to procure the eggs. Mr. Bennett, becoming aware of this, resolved to procure the eggs. He accordingly visited Mount Tom for this purpose, April 6th of the present year [1864], when he searched the whole ridge of the mountain, discovered the old birds and the particular part they most frequented, and also the site of a nest, where the young had been raised. The old birds were continually near this spot, and manifested much solicitude when it was approached, often flying within six or eight rods, and once the female came within three, screaming and thrusting out her talons, with an expression of great rage and fierceness. The birds did not appear at all shy, being easily approached quite nearly, though in walking, the cracking of sticks and the clinking of splinters of trap-rock made no little noise. One of the birds appeared to keep close to the eyrie, and both would approach whenever it was visited, screaming at and menacing the intruder, notwithstanding that at that time there were no eggs. Mr. Bennett, suspecting that incubation had commenced, visited the locality again on the 9th, but only saw the old nest, the birds behaving as before. Ten days later he made another visit, and, creeping carefully to the summit of the cliff, at a point near the eyrie already spoken of, he saw the female, on looking over the cliff, sitting on the nest, and but five or six yards distant. She eyed him fiercely for an instant, and then, scrambling from the nest to the edge of the narrow shelf supporting it, launched into the air. In a twinkling Mr. Bennett's unerring aim sent her tumbling dead at the foot of the precipice, several hundred feet below. The nest contained four eggs, which were soon safely secured, and the body of the female was obtained from the foot of the cliff. The male soon coming about was shot at, but he was too shy to come within range, excepting once, when the gun was being reloaded. The eggs were all laid after April 9th, and their contents showed, April 19th, that they had been incubated but a day or two. Incubation seems, in this case, to have commenced several weeks later than usual, which may have been owing to the late snows and unusual coldness of the weather this year during the first half of April.

"The situation of the eyrie was near the highest part of the mountain, about one-third of the length of the mountain from its south end, on a narrow shelf in the rock, eight or ten feet from the top of a nearly perpendicular cliff, 150 or 200 feet in height, and was inaccessible except to a bold climber, and at one particular point. The nest was merely a slight excavation, sufficient to contain the eggs; no accessory material had been added. The site had been previously occupied, and probably for several years; and for weeks before the eggs were laid was carefully guarded by the bold and watchful birds."

These four eggs averaged 2.22 long by 1.68 broad, with 2.32 by 1.71, and 2.16 by 1.65 as maxima and minima, respectively. The smallest was larger than the one measured by Dr. Brewer (2.00 by 1.56), which he obtained in Labrador. They also varied considerably in contour, and in heaviness and extent of coloration they showed a series from the darkest and most nearly uniform to the lightest and most sparsely marked, in which latter the contrast between the white ground and the blotches was striking. Of the darkest egg the writer says: "The general color is chocolate-brown, darker and more dense and uniform about the ends, the part about the middle being lighter, varied with small irregular blotches and specks of a darker tint than the ground-color. The color of the smaller end is a nearly uniform dull red-ochre. There is also an irregular belt of scattered and apparently very superficial blotches of very dark brown or nearly black." Two other eggs, as already mentioned, graded toward the lightest, which is thus described: "The greater end of the egg, which in the eggs of most birds is the end most subject to markings and to the greatest depth of color, is white, sprinkled sparingly with reddish specks; while the smaller end is deep bright brick-red, here and there relieved by small specks and patches of white ground-color. About the middle of the egg the colors are in more equal proportions, the white patches becoming larger on the smaller end toward the middle, and the red patches on the larger end increase toward the same point, where the colors meet and become mixed in irregular patches of various sizes, from mere dots to blotches."

Viewing such variation as this, in size, form, and color, among eggs of the same clutch, we see how utterly worthless are such discrepancies as a means of deciding a mooted question of specific identity, or the reverse, in nearly-allied birds. Yet some ornithologists will compare a single egg with another, gravely note the differences, and thereupon proceed to an argument with still denser gravity. Corresponding discrepancies in the mode of nidification serve as a basis for equally flimsy arguments. Take the present case of the Duck Hawk, breeding on Mount Tom on the bare ground, while in other instances it is known to build a large, bulky nest of sticks and other coarse material, as noticed by Dr. Wood on Talcott Mountain, and by Audubon on the cliffs of the Labrador coast. The eggs of this species are also stated to be from two to five in number, four being the usual nest-complement. Oölogy is attractive and in many respects satisfactory, but it is certainly the most unsafe department of ornithology.

Mr. Allen continues the subject in his later communication to the American Naturalist, as above quoted: " One or more pairs of these birds have been seen about Mounts Tom and Holyoke every season since the first discovery of their eggs at the former locality, in 1864. Mr. Bennett has since carefully watched them, and his frequent laborious searches for their nests have been well rewarded. In 1866 he took a second set of eggs, three in number, from the eyrie previously occupied. In 1867 the male bird was killed late in April, and this apparently prevented their breeding there that year, as they probably otherwise would have done; at least no nest was that year discovered. In 1868 Hawks of this species were seen about the mountains, and, although they reared their young there, all effort to discover their nest was ineffectual. The present year (1869) they commenced to lay in the old nesting-place, but as they were robbed when but one egg had been deposited, they deserted it, and chose a site still more inaccessible. Here they were equally unfortunate; for, during a visit to the mountain in company with Mr. Bennett, April 28, we had the pleasure of discovering their second eyrie, and from which, with considerable difficulty, three freshly-laid eggs were obtained. Not discouraged by this second misfortune, they nested again, this time depositing their eggs in the old eyrie, from which all, excepting the last set of eggs, have been obtained. Again they were unfortunate, Mr. Bennett removing their second set of eggs, three in number, May 23d, at which time incubation had just commenced. The birds remained about the mountain all the summer, and, from the anxiety they manifested in August, it appears not improbable that they laid a third time, and at this late period had unfledged young."

Accounts from the West are meagre. The only indications from the Missouri region I have seen are Dr. Hayden's and Prof. Snow's. Mr. Dall found the bird in Alaska; a pair nested on a dead spruce, and had young nearly ready to fly June 1st. Dr. Cooper observes that it is resident along the whole coast of Southern California, but migratory north of the Columbia. It breeds in cavities of the lofty, inaccessible cliffs overhanging the water, both along the main-land and on the islands. " On Santa Barbara Island, in May, a pair which probably were still feeding their young, swept boldly around my head, when I must have been fully half a mile from the nest, and I shot the female, a very fine specimen. I have seen one pursue a Swallow, and, turning feet upward, seize it flying with perfect ease."

FALCO COLUMBARIUS, Linn.

Pigeon Hawk.

Falco columbarius, LINN., Syst. Nat. i, 1766, 128 (*Ac. palumbarius*, CATES., i, 3; *Ac. carolinensis*, BRISS., i, 378).—FORST., Philos. Tr. lxii, 1772, 382.—GM., Syst. Nat. i, 1788, 281.—LATH., Ind. Orn. i, 1790, 44.—DAUD., Tr. Orn. ii, 1800, 83.—SHAW, Gen. Zool. vii, 188.—CUV., R. A. 2d ed. i, 322.—WILS., Am. Orn. ii, 1810, 107, pl. 15, f. 3.—JARD., ed. Wils. i, 254.—JAMES., ed. Wils. i, 61.—BREW., ed. Wils. 683.—BP., Syn. 1828, 38; Isis, 1832, 1136.—NUTT., Man. i, 1832, 60.—LESS., Tr. Orn. 92 —RICH. & SW., F. B. A. ii, 1831, 35.—SW., Classif. B. ii, 1837, 212.—AUD., Orn. Biog. i, 1832, 466; v, 368; pl. 92; Syn. 1839, 16; B. Am. i, 1840, 88, pl. 21.—BP., List, 1838, 4.—GIR., B. L. I. 1844, 17.—DEKAY, N. Y. Zool. i, 1844,

4, pl. 4, f. 9.—JARD., Ann. N. H. xviii, 118 (Tobago).—BLAK., Ibis, iii, 315.—
COOP. & SUCK., N. H. Wash. Ter. 1860, 142.—COOP., B. Cal. i, 1870, 460.—
RIDGW., Pr. Phila. Acad. 1870, 140.—? ALLEN, Bull. M. C. Z. iii, 1872, 180.—
COUES, Key, 1872, 214.
Falco (Hypotriorchis) columbarius of many authors.—CASS., B. N. A. 1858, 9.
Tinnunculus columbarius, VIEILL., Ois. Am. Sept. i, 1807, pl. 11 ; Nouv. Dict. d'Hist. Nat.
xii, 104 ; Enc. Meth. iii, 1236.
Nisus columbarius, CUV.
Astur columbarius, BOIE.
Hypotriorchis columbarius, GRAY, Gen. of B.; List B. Br. Mus. 55.—BP., Consp. i, 1850,
26.—WOODH., Sitgr. Rep. 1853, 60.—CASS., Ill. 1854, 90 (includes next species).—
BREW., N. A. Oöl. 1857, 12.—NEWB., P. R. R. Rep. vi, 1857, 74.—HEERM., *ibid.*
x, 1859, pt. vi, 31.—DRESS., Ibis, 1865, 323 (Texas).—COUES, Pr. Phila. Acad.
1866, 42 (Arizona).—DALL & BANN., Tr. Chic. Acad. i, 1869, 270 (Alaska).—
LAWR., Ann. Lyc. N. Y. ix, 134 (Costa Rica).—STEV., U. S. Geol. Surv. Ter.
1870, 462 —SNOW, B. Kans. 1873.
Hypotriorchis (Lithofalco) columbarius, BP., Consp. Av. i, 1850, 26.
Hypotriorchis (Æsalon) columbarius, GRAY, Hand-list, i, 1869, 21, No. 193.
Æsalon columbarius, KAUP, Monog. Falc. Cont. Orn. 1850, 54.
Falco (Æsalon) lithofalco var. *columbarius,* RIDGW., Pr. Bost. Soc. 1873, 46 (but *colum-
barius* has priority).—B. B. & R., N. A. B. iii, 1874, 144.
Falco intermixtus, DAUD., Traité d'Orn. ii, 1800, 141.
Falco temerarius, AUD., Orn. Biog. i, 1831, 381, pl. 75.—NUTT., Man. i, 1832, 61.
Falco auduboni, "BLACKW., Zool. Res. 1834."
(?) *Falco (Æsalon) lithofalco* var. *suckleyi,* RIDGW.—B. B. & R., N. A. B. iii, 1874, 147
(northwest coast ; melanotic ; parallel with case of *communis* var. *pealei*).

Hab.—Generally distributed over North America. Ranging into Mexico, Central
America, and northern portions of South America. Ecuador (SCL. P. Z. S. 1858, 451).
Venezuela (SCL. & SALV., P. Z. S. 1869, 252). Cuba (D'ORBIG., La Sagra's Cuba, Ois. 23 ;
CAB., J. f. O. ii, p. lxxxiv ; GUNDL., Rep. 1865, 255). Jamaica (GOSSE, B. Jam. 1847, 17).
Late Expeditions.—60621, Green River.
In ranging this bird as a variety of the European, Mr. Ridgway has apparently over-
looked the fact that " *columbarius* " has priority over " *lithofalco*," which latter, in event
he proves correct in uniting the two, will be known as *F. columbarius* var. *lithofalco.*
Considering, however, that in this instance the fact of varietal relationship can hardly
be considered established, and that it is rarely necessary, or even expedient, to ex-
change one tentative view for another equally so, I follow the usual course in separating the two birds specifically. Upon similar considerations I retain *F. richardsoni* as
a species until its inter-gradation with *F. columbarius* is proven, although I believe
that most probably Mr. Ridgway's later view of its varietal relationship with *F. columbarius* is correct.

I have little to add to the published accounts of this elegant and
spirited Hawk, aptly styled " The Little Corporal." It is apparently
not common in the interior of the West, and even less so than has been
supposed, a part of the quoted instances of its occurrence, like Dr.
Hayden's for instance, really referring to the next species, the history
of which has only lately been disentangled from that of the true Pigeon
Hawk. Mr. Dall gives it as resident in Alaska, and notes the fact of
its even destroying Ptarmigan, birds much larger than itself—proof,
were any needed, of its audacity and prowess. According to Dr. Cooper,
it ranges over the whole of California in cold weather, but he never
observed it in summer, even in the highest mountains.

Our accounts of its nidification are defective, and sometimes conflicting. It appears to breed chiefly north of the United States, and according to Hutchins, as rendered in the Fauna Boreali-Americana, it makes
a nest on rocks and in hollow trees, of sticks and grass, lined with
feathers. Audubon describes a nest he found in Labrador in a low fir-
tree, ten or twelve feet from the ground, built of sticks, lined with moss
and feathers. The bird is unquestionably resident in Northern New
England, where Mr. Boardman says it breeds in hollow trees. No
authentic instance of its breeding further south has come to my knowledge. Mr. Samuels, indeed, in his Catalogue, gives it as resident and
breeding in Massachusetts, but this is negatived by his own subsequent

statement, in his later work, where he says he has no authentic information of its breeding in New England (p. 18). He, however, figures an egg, received from Mr. Boardman as being of this species, from Milltown, Maine. It measures only 1.50 by 1.44, and in coloration, as represented on the plate, differs materially from any authentic specimens I have seen. It may be here remarked, moreover, that the egg figured and described by Dr. Brewer proves not authentic, he having been deceived by a chain of circumstantial evidence he could not but accept as conclusive. In the uncertainty, I am the more pleased to offer an unquestionable description, derived from examination of specimens in the Smithsonian. The size varies from 1.50 by 1.30 to 1.80 by 1.30—figures also indicating the range of variation in shape, some being subspherical, others elongate-oval. Coloration ranges from a nearly uniform deep rich brown (chestnut or burnt sienna), to whitish or white only, marked with a few indistinct dots of dull grayish or drab. Such extremes are connected by every degree; a yellowish-brown ground-color, irregularly splashed with rich ruddy brown, is the usual style. The markings may be very evenly distributed, or mostly gathered in a wreath around one or the other end, or even both ends.

I may here mention a fact in oölogy, apparently not without its value. In measuring many hundred eggs, I have noticed that the variation, however great, is less in absolute bulk than in contour—in approach to, or departure from, what may be regarded as the standard of shape for the species. Now this variation in shape is produced mainly by difference in the length of the major axis, the transverse diameter being approximately constant. What additional variation in shape may occur, results from slight shifting of the point of greatest breadth toward one end or the other. Anatomical considerations bear this out. Taking the calibre of the oviduct as an approximately fixed quantity in the same species, and remembering that varying circumstances of age, season, and physical vigor, determine the amount of fluids secreted to envelope the ovum, it is evident that, while the whole capacity of the calcareous shell must vary correspondingly, the difference will be mainly in lengthening or shortening of the egg, since the contractility of the oviduct holds the transverse diameter newly fixed.

There are also few instances of greater difference in the amount, intensity, and distribution of pigmentary matter than those occurring among Hawks, and even in eggs of the same nest-complement. I think it a probable rule, that the succession of laying of the eggs can be judged by the quantity of pigment in the shell, those first extruded being generally the most heavily colored, the others growing lighter with gradual consumption of the color supply. This is strikingly illustrated in cases where the same nest has been robbed repeatedly—the later laid eggs gradually losing their coloration, as well as gradually growing smaller, with increasing exhaustion of the reproductive powers of the parent. Every poultry man is familiar with the extreme instance of this, when a hen drops an egg often no longer than a pigeon's, as the final effort before ceasing to lay.

FALCO RICHARDSONII, Ridgw.

American Merlin.

Falco æsalon, Sw. & RICH., F. B. A. ii, 1831, 37, pl. 25 (excl. syn.; *neo auct.*).—NUTT., Man. ii, 1834, 558.—TOWNS., Narr. 1839.—COOP. & SUCK., N. H. Wash. Ter. 1860, 288.—COUES, Pr. Phila. Acad. 1866, 43 (in text).
Hypotriorchis columbarius, CASS., Ill. 1854, 90 (partly).—HAYD., Rep. 1862, 152.—STEV., U. S. Geol. Surv. Ter. 1870, 462 (partly).

Falco columbarius, CASS., B. N. A. 1858, 9 (partly).
Falco (Hypotriorchis) richardsonii, RIDGW., Pr. Phila. Acad. 1870, 145 (♂ type one of Dr. Hayden's specimens).
Hypotriorchis richardsoni, SNOW, B. Kans. 1873.
Falco richardsoni, COUES, Key, 1872, 214.
Falco (Æsalon) lithofalco var. *richardsoni*, RIDGW.—B. B. & R., N. A. B. iii, 1874, 148.

Hab.—Interior of North America. United States from the Mississippi to the Rocky Mountains. Arctic America.
Lieutenant Warren's Expedition.—5170–1, mouth of Vermilion River, Dakota.
Later Expeditions.—58983, Berthoud's Pass; 60335, La Bonté Creek, Wyoming; 60617, Box Elder Creek, Utah; 60618–9, Green River, Wyoming; 60620, Sweetwater.

This species was first noticed by the authors of the Fauna Boreali-Americana, who accurately distinguished it from the common Pigeon Hawk, considering it identical with the *F. æsalon* of Europe. Subsequent writers attributed this last to North America, all apparently having the present bird in view. Mr. Cassin, with some of the specimens before him that afterward served as the basis of Mr. Ridgway's descriptions, noticed the discrepancies presented on comparison with the ordinary *F. columbarius*, but made no specific discrimination, citing *F. æsalon* of Swainson and Richardson as a synonym. I observed the same thing in 1866, remarking as follows: "In the immense series of Pigeon Hawks which I have examined from all parts of the West, I find a few specimens which constantly differ to a marked degree from any of the diverse plumages in which *F. columbarius* presents itself. These specimens are invariably much larger than any others in the series; are much lighter colored; and differ constantly in the increased number of light and dark bars on the tail. Compared with a European specimen of *F. æsalon*, they agree in every particular. I think it most probable that future careful research will demonstrate the existence of a species hitherto usually confounded with *F. columbarius*." This surmise has been verified by Mr. Ridgway, who, however, has pointed out some differences, before overlooked, between our bird and the true *æsalon*, and proposed the specific name I have adopted. The bird may prove, I still think, only a geographical race of *æsalon;* in fact Mr. Ridgway has latterly reduced it. As the species is still very little known, the description is subjoined.* It should be diligently sought for in the northwest, additional specimens being very desirable.

---

* *"Adult male:* Upper plumage, dull earth-brown, each feather grayish-umber centrally, and with a conspicuous black shaft-line. Head above, approaching ashy-white anteriorly, the black shaft-streaks being very conspicuous. Secondaries, primary-coverts, and primaries, margined terminally with dull white; the primary-coverts with two transverse series of pale ochraceous spots; primaries, with spots of the same, corresponding with those of the inner webs. Upper tail coverts, tipped and spotted beneath the surface with white. Tail, clear drab, much lighter than the primaries, but growing darker terminally, having basally a slightly ashy cast, crossed with *six* sharply defined perfectly continuous bands (the last terminal) of ashy-white. Head frontally, laterally and beneath—a collar round the nape (interrupting the brown above)—and entire lower parts, white, somewhat ochraceous, this most perceptible on the tibiæ ; cheeks and ear-coverts with sparse, fine, hair-like streaks of black; nuchal collar, jugulum, breast, abdomen, sides and flanks, with a median linear stripe of clear ochre-brown on each feather; these stripes broadest on the flanks; each stripe with a conspicuous black shaft-streak; tibiæ and lower tail-coverts with fine shaft-streaks of brown, like the broader stripes of the other portions. Chin and throat, only, immaculate. Lining of the wings spotted with ochraceous-white and brown, in about equal amount, the former in spots approaching the shaft. Inner webs of primaries with transverse broad bars of pale ochraceous—eight on the longest. Wing, 7.70; tail, 5.00; culmen, 0.50; tarsus, 1.30; middle toe, 1.25; outer, 0.85; inner, 0.70; posterior, 0.50.

"*Adult female:* Differing in coloration from the male only in the points of detail. Ground-color of the upper parts clear grayish-drab, the feathers with conspicuously black shafts; all the feathers with pairs of rather indistinct rounded ochraceous spots, these most conspicuous on the wings and scapulars. Secondaries crossed with three

This is the bird mentioned by Dr. Hayden, under name of *columbarius*, as abundant in the wooded bottoms of the Missouri region. Cne of his specimens from the Vermilion River served as the male type of Mr. Ridgway's description; another (No. 58983), taken by Mr. J. Stevenson at Berthoud's Pass of the Rocky Mountains, in Colorado, is the female type. The writer quotes a third, a young male, taken at Fort Rice, Dakota, by General Alfred Sully. Prof. Snow records it among Kansas birds, on Professor Baird's authority; whether from actual capture of specimens in the State, or upon the strength of its known distribution, I am not informed. It is not unlikely that the pale, ashy specimen noted by Dr. Cooper, as procured by him at Fort Mojave, Arizona, was an individual of this species. Dr. Richardson's bird was an old female, killed at Carlton House, on the Saskatchewan, May 14, 1827, while flying with her mate; "in the oviduct there were several full-sized white eggs, clouded at one end with a few bronze-colored spots." Another specimen is stated to have been killed at Sault St. Marie, between Lakes Huron and Superior. What little information we possess of the habits of the bird indicates nothing peculiar in comparison with those of *F. columbarius*.

FALCO SPARVERIUS, Linn.

Sparrow Hawk.

a. *sparverius*.

Falco sparverius, LINN., Syst. Nat. i, 1766, 128 (*Ac. minor*, CATES., i, 5; *Æsalon carolinensis*, BRISS., i, 386, pl. 32, f. 1).—GM., Syst. Nat. i, 1788, 284.—LATH., I. Orn. i, 1790, 42.—DAUD., Tr. Orn. ii, 1800, 142, pl. 12.—SHAW, Gen. Zool. vii, pl. 26.— WILS., Am. Orn. ii, 1810, 117, pl. 16, f. 1 (♀); iv, 57, pl. 32, f. 2 (♂).—STEPH., Gen. Zool. xiii, pt. ii, 38.—CUV., R. A. 2d ed. i, 322.—JAMES., ed. Wils. i, 56, 60.—JARD., ed. Wils. i, 262; ii, 51.—BREW., ed. Wils. 864.—BP., Syn. 1828, 27; Isis, 1832, 1136.—WAGL., Isis, 1831, 517.—SW. & RICH., F. B. A. ii, 1831, 31, pl. 24.—SW., Classif. B. ii, 1837, 212.—NUTT., Man. i, 1832, 58,—AUD., Orn. Biog. ii, 1835, 246; v, 1839, 370; pl. 142; Syn. 1839, 17; B. Am. i, 1840, 90, 22.— VIEILL., Ency. Meth. iii, 1234.—DEKAY, N. Y. Zool. 1844, 16, pl. 7, f. 16.— MAXIM., J. f. O. vi, 1858, 15.—CASS., B. N. A. 1858, 13.—COOP. & SUCK., N. H. Wash. Ter. 1860, 143.—LORD, Pr. Roy. Arty. Inst. iv, 1864, 110.—COOP., B. Cal. i, 1870, 462.—ALLEN, Bull. M. C. Z. iii, 1872, 180.—HOLD., Pr. Bost. Soc. 1872, 207.—COUES, Key, 1872, 214, fig. 142; and of most authors.
Falco (Tinnunculus) sparverius of some authors.—RIDGW., Pr. Bost. Soc. 1873, 48.—B. B. & R., N. A. B. iii, 1874, 169.
Tinnunculus sparverius, VIEILL., Ois. Am. Sept, i, 1807, 40, pl. 12.—GRAY, Gen. of B.— BP., Consp. i, 1850, 27.—WOODH., Sitgr. Rep. 1853, 60.—CASS., Ill. 1854, 92; Pr. A. N. S. 1855, 278.—BREW., N. A. Oöl. 1857, 16.—NEWB., P. R. R. Rep. vi, 1857, 74.—KENN., ibid. x, 1859, pt. iv, 19.—HEERM., ibid. pt. vi, 31.—HAYD., Rep. 1862, 152.—COUES, Pr. Phila. Acad. 1866, 42.—ALLEN, Mem. Bost. Soc. i, 1868, 499.—STEV., U. S. Geol. Surv. Ter. 1870, 462.—MERR., ibid. 1872, 696.—SNOW, B. Kans. 1873; and of many authors.
Tinnunculus (Pœcilornis) sparverius, GRAY, Hand-list, i, 1869, 23, No. 216.
Cerchneis sparverius, BOIE.—BP., Comp. List, 1838, 5.
Pœcilornis sparverius, KAUP, Monog. Falc. Cont. Orn. 1850, 53.

---

bands of deeper, more reddish-ochraceous. Bands of the tail, pure white. In other respects exactly like the male. Wing, 9.00; tail, 6.10; culmen, 0.55; tarsus, 1.40; middle toe, 1.50.

"*Young male:* Differing from the adult only in degree. Upper surface with the rusty borders of the feathers more washed over the general surface; the rusty ochraceous forming the ground-color of the head—paler anteriorly, where the black shaft-streaks are very conspicuous; spots on the primary coverts and primaries deep reddish ochraceous; tail-bands broader than in the adult and more reddish; the terminal one twice as broad as the rest (0.40 of an inch), and almost cream color. Beneath, pale ochraceous, this deepest on the breast and sides; markings as in the adult, but anal region and lower tail-coverts immaculate; the shaft-streaks on the tibiæ, also, scarcely discernible. Wing, 7.00; tail, 4.60.

b, c, d, &c.

For various races or conspecies, real or supposed, see especially R IDGW ., Pr. Phila. Acad. 1870, 147–149 ; and B. B. & R., N. A. B. iii, 1874, 166–168.

Hab.—The whole of North America, and southward.

List of specimens.

19114	67	Grosv. Fork...	♀	June 7, 1860	F. V. Hayden.	10.50	2.37	7.50

Lieutenant Warren's Expedition.—5172, 5177, Yellowstone River ; 5175, Powder River ; 5178, Fort Berthold ; ——, Farm Island, Missouri River.
Later Expeditions.—59842, Colorado ; 60336–8, Wyoming ; 60662, North Platte ; 62236–9, Idaho.

"The trees, of late so richly green, now disclose the fading tints of autumn ; the cricket becomes mute, the grasshopper withers on the fences, the mouse retreats to her winter quarters ; dismal clouds obscure the eastern horizon, the sun assumes a sickly dimness, hoar frosts cover the ground, and the long night encroaches on the domains of light. No longer are heard the feathered choristers of the woods, who throng toward more congenial climes, and in their rear rushes the Sparrow Hawk." So the great painter of Nature portrays the waning season, graphic with pen as with pencil. The dying year may bring no dismay to the intrepid little Hawk, but when its cold breath blows away the delicate creatures that afford his sustenance, perforce he follows after ; and once with us, braves all weathers and lives in plenty. Few, if any, of our birds are more widely dispersed, few are better known, and certainly no Hawk is regarded with less disfavor. Too small of frame— though stout hearted enough, I warrant—to commit depredations in the farm-yard ; subsisting on small insectivorous birds, it is true, but also destroying countless field-mice and noxious insects, he is to be held a benefactor to the agriculturist. The prettiest and jauntiest of our Hawks, and yet no prig ; a true Falcon, if a little one, with as noble mien and as much pluck as the best among his larger brethren, we can but admire him. No Hawk is more abundant in the West. Go where we may, in summer or winter, we shall before long see him hovering over the fields, or perched, erect and motionless, on his outpost, sweeping the ground below with keen, audacious eye. It is a treacherous calm ; the ardor of the Falcon grows with restraint. An unlucky Sparrow flirts in yonder bush, and gives a flippant chirp—whisk ! and it is all over. Poor, little, rollicking Sparrow ! this is no easier for *you* to bear, because it is a "law of nature," as we say. Who is ever quite ready for the last ? What pang is taken away when the cry it extorts is drowned in a sea of like lamentation ? We theorize best before the Falcon's talon strikes.

The reader has doubtless stood, as I often have, in a thicket, peering about in readiness to shoot some rare Warbler or Finch that he vainly tries to discover amid the dense foliage. And not seldom—whisk ! *something* flashes right by, twists with marvellous swiftness and address through the tangled underwood, a cry of distress is heard, along with an exultant scream, and the next moment a Sparrow Hawk glides out from the thicket on the far side, bearing his quivering victim in his claws, and makes straightway for the nearest stump or post to feast at his leisure. As eager as we were, but keen-eyed and more skilful, he snatched the prize himself, and his beak is already buried in its breast, drinking warm blood. We inwardly wish we could punish the bold robber, but the splendid exhibition of his powers almost makes amends for our loss of the specimen; and, besides, we may reflect that if the world owes us ornithology, it owes the Sparrow Hawk a living.

It is surprising what large birds the gallant little warrior will attack. I have seen it overpower and bear away a Thrasher, a bird inch for inch as long as itself, and nearly as heavy. Still, it usually preys upon humbler game, particularly such birds as those from which it derives its name. It also often picks the elegant little lizards (*Sceloporus*) off the fences. Like other Falcons, it captures its prey at a dash, or not at all. If it miss its aim, or the bird contrives to elude its clutch, it disdains to pursue, and remounts its observatory with a crest-fallen aspect, as if chagrined at its want of skill, but doubtless reflecting, "better luck next time." The difference between the true Falcons and the *Accipiters* is much like that between a tiger and a wolf. As for the Buzzards, they are bears among birds; Kites are the weasels. In the Middle districts these Hawks pair in April, and immediately go to house-keeping. As they breed in every section, from the fur countries to Mexico, the period varies in time of the year according to the state of the season. It does not appear that they ever build a nest for themselves. They generally choose the hollow of a decayed limb or tall stub; a deserted Woodpecker's hole answers every purpose, in many cases, and they are said to sometimes occupy an old Crow's nest. The skilful and industrious Woodpeckers—"carpinteros," as the Mexicans aptly call them—fit up residences for the Hawks, requiring no alteration. Five or six eggs appear to be the usual nest-full; seven are stated to have been found in one clutch. They are nearly spheroidal, measuring about 1.33 in length by 1.12 in breadth. The ground-color is usually buffy, or pale yellowish-brown; this is blotched all over with dark brown, the splashes of which are usually largest and most numerous toward the greater end, at or around which they may run into a crown or wreath. Some eggs are pale brown, minutely dotted all over with dark brown; some are white, with pale brown spots; and a few are whitish, without any markings. I have never seen the nestlings; Audubon says they are covered with whitish down. But the first true feathers are much like those of the parents, and the sexual distinctions of plumage are very early apparent.

These handsome little Hawks are often kept in confinement, and make interesting, if not entirely agreeable, pets—at least for those who like to see birds under such unfavorable circumstances. For myself, I dislike caged birds, and caged Hawks of all others; the incongruity is unpleasant, view it as we may. While I was at Columbia, in South Carolina, a neighbor had three Sparrow Hawks for some time. As they had been taken from the nest when quite young, they became in a measure reconciled to captivity. They ate any kind of meat freely, and as they grew up, began to display much of their natural spirit. When tormented in the various ingenious ways people have of "stirring up" caged birds, they would resent the indignity by snapping the bill, beating with the wings, and clutching with their talons at the offending cane or umbrella-tip. One of them was a cripple, having a broken leg very badly set, and the other two used to bully him dreadfully. One night, whether from not having been fed sufficiently, or being in unusually bad humor, they set upon him, killed him outright, and then almost devoured him before morning.

BUTEO HARLANI, "Aud."

Harlan's Buzzard; Black Warrior.

Falco harlani, AUD., Orn. Biog. i, 1831, 441; v, 1839, 380; pl. 86.—NUTT., Man. i, 1832, 105.—BREW., ed Wils. 684.
Buteo harlani, AUD., Syn. 1839, 6; B. Am. i, 1840, pl. 8.—BP., Consp. List, 1838, 3.—
DEKAY, N. Y. Zool. ii, 1844, 11.—STRICKL., Orn. Syn. 1855, 30.—LAWR., Ann. Lyc. v, 220.—CASS., Ill. 1854, 101; B. N. A. 1858, 24.—COUES, Pr. Phila. Acad. 1866, 45.—RIDGW., *ibid.* 1870, 142.—COOP., B. Cal. i, 1870, 473.—COUES, Key, 1872, 216.—SNOW, B. Kans. 1873, —, and Am. Nat. vii, 1873, 172.—B. B. & R., N. A. B. iii, 1874, 292. (Not of *Bryant.*) (Very likely not of *Audubon.*)

Hab.—"Louisiana." "New Mexico." "California." "Kansas."

I regard the claims of this species to validity as not yet established. Both Gray and Bonaparte quote it as a synonym of *B. borealis*, and it appears not improbable that it represents the complete melanism of that species, corresponding with the "*insignatus*" style of *swainsoni*. A further element of doubt is found in the fact that different authors have used the name for different species. Thus Dr. Bryant's "*harlani*" is certainly *swainsoni*, while the "*harlani*" of some of the older New England authors is almost as certainly the black state of *Archibuteo lagopus*.

The claim of the species to be embraced in the present work rests upon the capture of a specimen near Lawrence, Kansas. On being transmitted to the Smithsonian, it was pronounced by Prof. Baird and Mr. Ridgway to be *harlani*, as understood by them. I have examined this and some other specimens supposed to represent Audubon's bird, and can see all the later ascribed characters, which cause me to suspend judgment for the present, and let the bird stand on its own merits, as the differences from any known style of *borealis* are too great to be reconciled. The *Buteo cooperi* offers much the same case; additional specimens, only lately received, are just like the original type, and easily recognized. But Audubon's bird may be=*calurus*.

BUTEO BOREALIS, (Gm.) Vieill.

Red-tailed Buzzard; Hen Hawk.

a. *borealis.*

Falco borealis, GM., Syst. Nat. i, 1788, 266.—LATH., Ind. Orn. i, 1790, 25.—DAUD., Tr. Orn. ii, 1800, 157.—SHAW, Gen. Zool. vii, 112.—WILS., Am. Orn. vi, 1812, 75, pl. 52, f. 1.—
SABINE, Frankl. Journ. 670.—BP., Syn. 1828, 32; Isis, 1832, 1138.—WAGL., Isis, 1831, 517.—NUTT., Man. i, 1832, 102.—AUD., Orn. Biog. i, 1832, 265; v, 378; pl. 51.
Buteo borealis, VIEILL., Nouv. Dict. d' Hist. Nat. iv, 1816, 478; Enc. Meth. iii, 1222.—
SW. & RICH., F. B. A. ii, 1831, 50.—VIG., Zool. Journ. i, 340; Beech. Voy. 15.—
STEPH., Gen. Zool. xiii, pt. ii, 47.—LESS., Tr. Orn. 79.—JAMES., ed. Wils. i, 82, 84.—JARD., ed. Wils. ii, 280, 282.—BREW., ed. Wils. 450, 684.—BP., List, 1838, 3; Consp. i, 1850, 19.—AUD., Syn. 1839, 6; B. A. i, 1840, 32, pl. 7.—GOSSE, B. Jam. 1847, 11, pl. 2.—LEMB., Av. Cubæ, 1850, 18, pl. 1.—CASS., Ill. 1854, 97; Pr. A. N. S. 1855, 279.—WOODH., Sitgr. Rep. 1853, 59 (includes western).—PUCHER., Rev. Zool. 1850, 214.—BREW., N. A. Oöl. 1857, 21.—GAMB., J. A. N. S. i, 26.—
DEKAY, N. Y. Zool. ii, 9, pl. 8, fig. 17.—PEAB., Rep. Orn. Mass.—THOMPS., Nat. Hist. Vermont, App. 63.—PEALE, U. S. Expl. Exped. 1848, 62.—KAUP, Mus. Senck. 1845, 261.—CASS., B. N. A. 1858, 25.—MAXIM., J. f. O. vi, 1858, 17.—BD., Mex. Bound. Surv. ii, 1859, pt. ii, Birds, p. 3.—BLAK., Ibis, iii, 1861, 318.—
BRYANT, Pr. Bost. Soc. viii, 1861, 109.—HAYD., Rep. 1862, 152.—WOOD, Am. Nat. iii, 1869, 393.—ALLEN, Mem. Bost. Soc. 1868, 499; Bull. M. C. Z. ii, 1871, 322 (excl. syn. partim); iii, 1872, 180.—RIDGW., Pr. Phila. Acad. 1870, 142.—
B. B. & R., N. A. B. iii, 1874, 282.—SNOW, B. Kans. 1873.—COUES, Key, 1872, 216.
Astur borealis, CUV., R. A. 2d ed. i, 332.—SW., Classif. B. ii, 1837, 215 ("*Aster*").

Pœcilopternis borealis, KAUP, Monog. *Falc.* Cont. Orn. 1850, 76.
Buteo (Craxirex) borealis, GRAY, Hand-list i, 1869, 7, No. 46.
Falco leverianus, GM., Syst. Nat. i, 1788, 266.—LATH., Ind. Orn. i, 1790, 18.—DAUD., Tr.
    Orn. ii, 126.—SHAW, Gen. Zool. vii, 151.—WILS. Am. Orn. vi, 1812, 78, pl. 52.
Falco jamaicensis, GM., Syst. Nat. i, 1788, 266.
Falco aquilinus, BARTRAM, Trav. in Florida, 1791, 290.
Buteo ferrugineicaudus, VIEILL., Ois. Am. Sept. i, 1807, 32.—CUV., R. A. 2d ed. i, 337.
Accipiter ruficaudus, VIEILL., Ois. Am. Sept. i, 1807, 43, pl. 14*bis.*
Buteo fulvus, VIEILL., O. A. Sept. i, 1807, 84; Nouv. Dict. d' Hist. Nat. iv, 1816, 468, 472.
Buteo americanus, VIEILL., Nouv. Dict. d' Hist. Nat. iv, 1816, 477; Enc. Meth iii, 1224.

b. *calurus.*

(??) *Falco buteo*, AUD., Orn. Biog. iv, 1838, 508, pl. 372 (not of *Linnæus;* uncertain; more
    likely *swainsoni*).
(??) *Buteo vulgaris*, AUD., Syn. 1839, 5; B. Am. i, 1840, 30, pl. 6 (not of authors; same as
    Falco buteo, Audubon).
Buteo swainsoni, CASS., Ill. 1854, 98 (exclusive of the synonymy; not of *Bonaparte*, nor
    of *Cassin*, 1858).
Buteo calurus, CASS., Pr. Phila. Acad. 1855, 281.—CASS., B. N. A. 1858, 22.—BREW., N. A.
    Oöl. 1857, 32.—BD., Mex. Bound. Surv. ii, 1859, pt. ii, Birds, p. 3.—BD., P. R. R.
    Rep. x, 1859, pt. iii, p. 11, pl. 14.—COUES, Pr. Phila. Acad. 1866, 44.—COOP., B.
    Cal. i, 1870, 471.—STEV., U. S. Geol. Surv. Ter. 1870, 462.
Buteo montanus, CASS., Pr. Phila. Acad. 1856, 39.—CASS., B. N. A. 1858, 26 (but not of
    Nuttall, which is *swainsoni*).—BREW., N. A. Oöl. 1857, 26.—NEWB., P. R. R. Rep.
    vi, 1857, 75.—BD., Mex. Bound. Surv. ii, 1859, pt. ii, Birds, p. 3.—BD., P. R. R.
    Rep. x, 1859, pt. iii, 12.—KENN., *ibid.* pt. iv, 19.—HEERM., *ibid.* pt. vi, 32.—
    COOP. & SUCK., N. H. Wash. Ter. 1860, 147.—COUES, Pr. Phila. Acad. 1866,
    43.—COOP., B. Cal. i, 1870, 469.—SNOW, B. Kans. 1873.—STEV., U. S. Geol. Surv.
    Ter. 1870, 462.—MERR., *ibid.* 1872, 697.
Buteo borealis of GRAY, BRYANT, and ALLEN, partly.
Buteo borealis var. *calurus*, RIDGW.—B. B. & R., N. A. B. iii, 1874, 286.—COUES, No. 351ª.

c. *lucasanus.*

Buteo borealis var. *lucasanus*, RIDGW., Mss.—COUES, Key, 1872, 216; Check-list, 1874,
    351ᵇ.—B. B. & R., N. A. B. iii, 1874, 285.

d. *krideri.*

Buteo borealis var. *krideri*, HOOPES, Pr. Phila. Acad. 1873, 238, pl. 5 (Iowa and Wiscon-
    sin).—B. B. & R., N. A. B. iii, 1874, 284.—COUES, Check-list, 1874, No. 351ᶜ.

e. *costaricensis.*

Buteo borealis var. *costaricensis*, RIDGW.—B. B. & R., N. A. B. iii, 1874, 258, 285 (" *B.
    borealis* of Central America").

Hab.—The whole of North America. Mexico. Cuba. Jamaica.

List of specimens.

| 19118 | 6. | Wind R. Valley. | ♀ | May. 28, 1859 | F. V. Hayden. | 22.00 | 50.75 | 17.25 |

Lieutenant Warren's Expedition.—5153, Yellowstone River; 5158, Fort Randall, Dakota; 5159, L'Eau-qui-court.
    Later Expeditions.—58984, Berthoud's Pass; 60628–29, Wyoming; 60630, Uintah Moun-
tains (*melanotic*); 62231, Idaho.

    Few of our birds have caused more confusion among writers, or acquired a more in-
volved synonymy, than the Hawks of the genus *Buteo.*
    Setting aside *lineatus* and *pennsylvanicus*, as totally distinct from each other and from
the rest; ignoring for the moment "*harlani*" and "*cooperi,*" we will confine ourselves to
consideration of the two species, *borealis*, GM., and *swainsoni*, BP. These may be immediately distinguished by the emargination of *four* outer primaries in *borealis*, and
only *three* in *swainsoni.* There are other points, aside from color, which varies so greatly
in each.
    Borealis in all its variety of color is much the largest, the female averaging about
24 inches in length, with a stretch of wings over 50 inches; it is very robust, with a
comparatively short wing, and short, stout legs. In the East it remains comparatively constant in color, aside from the normal changes with age. In the West it runs
from a slightly darker, or more ferrugineous cast, into a quite fuliginous condition, the

several stages being inseparably connected. The slighter departures from the normal Eastern standard are the *montanus* of Cassin, and most later writers, but probably *not* of Nuttall; the climax is reached in *calurus*, Cassin. I adopt this name for the extreme Western variety, ignoring the intermediate stages, which have been usually designated *montanus*. In all of these birds, *when adult*, the tail becomes chestnut-red on top, which is never the case with *swainsoni*.

The *Falco buteo* or *Buteo vulgaris* of Audubon is uncertain—rather, let us say, it comprehends both the Western Red-tail and Swainson's Buzzard, being ostensibly based upon the latter, but the description and figure rather indicating the former. The *Buteo montanus* of Nuttall (1840; not in edition of 1832) is based on Audubon's "*Falco buteo*," but the description is unmistakably that of *swainsoni*. I follow Mr. Ridgway in relegating both these names to *swainsoni*, leaving *calurus* as the first distinctive name of the Western Red-tail in all its variety.

Swainsoni is the smaller species, perfectly distinct. The female is only about 21 inches long; the form is less robust; the wings are comparatively longer; the legs slenderer. This species was first noticed by Richardson and Swainson, who described and figured it accurately, calling it "*Buteo vulgaris*," under the impression that it was identical with the European bird. It was subsequently separated by Bonaparte, in 1838, under the name of *B. swainsoni*, which it should bear. Its other synonyms are noticed beyond; here, however, it may be remarked, that *B. swainsoni* of CASSIN, Ill. 1854, 98, is not this species, but the Western Red-tail, as shown conclusively by his description, although he cites the synonymy of *swainsoni*. His *swainsoni* of 1858, however, is correctly so named.

The Hen-Hawk is abundant in all parts of the West, as elsewhere in North America, and in all its variety has the same habits it shows in the East. I have obtained several specimens, of old and young, at Fort Randall, and very frequently observed the bird while I was traveling in Kansas, Iowa, and Minnesota. The fuliginous styles (extreme of *calurus*) I have never seen in the northwest, although in Arizona they were nearly as common as the others, both occurring in the same localities. These large Hawks are all heavy and rather inactive birds, ranking, in these respects, next to the species of *Archibuteo*. They are unfitted, both by their physical organization and temperament, for the daring feats that the Falcons and Hawks execute, and usually prey upon game disproportionate to their size, which they snatch as they pass along. I have, however, found nearly the whole of a rabbit in the craw. They mate early, constructing a large and bulky, though shallow, nest in a high tree, of sticks and smaller twigs, mixed toward the centre with grass, moss, or other soft material, and often a few feathers. The eggs are generally three in number, about 2.40 long by rather less than 2.00 broad. They are dull whitish in color, sometimes with only a few markings of dull brownish-gray, but oftener extensively blotched with several shades of rich brown. The young are a long time in acquiring the full plumage. They are long full grown before the red of the tail appears, and this is usually in advance of the fulvous of the under parts that the old birds display. I have seen specimens with nearly perfect red tail, yet showing pure white on the breast and the same elsewhere underneath, though marked with the usual dark-brown spots and streaks. There is a great sexual difference in size, many males being found hardly or not 20 inches long.

BUTEO LINEATUS, (Gm.) Jard.

Red-shouldered Buzzard.

a. *lineatus.*

Falco lineatus, GM., Syst. Nat. i, 1788, 268.—LATH., Ind. Orn. i, 1790, 27.—DAUD., Tr. Orn. ii, 1800, 158.—SHAW, Gen. Zool. vii, 1809, 113.—CUV., R. A. i, 2d ed. 334.— WILS., Am. Orn. vi, 1812, 86, pl. 53, f. 3.—AUD., Orn. Biog. i, 1832, 296, v, 1839, 380; pl. 56.

Butco lineatus, JARD., Am. Orn. ii, 290.—AUD., Syn. 1839, 7.—AUD., B. Am. i, 1840, 40, pl. 9.—BREW., ed. Wils. 1840, 684.—DEKAY, N. Y. Zool. 1844, pl. 6, f. 13.— KAUP, Mus. Senck. 1845, 261.—WOODH., Sitgr. Rep. 1853, 59.—MAXIM., J. f. O. vi, 1858, 19.—CASS., Ill. 1854, 99 ; B. N. A. 1858, 28.—PUTN., Pr. Ess. Inst. i, 1856, 203.—BREW., N. A. Oöl. 1857, 28.—VERR., Pr. Ess. Inst. iii, 1862, 141.— BOARDM., Pr. Bost. Soc. ix, 1862, 123.—COUES & PRENT., Smiths. Rep. 1861, 402.—ALLEN, Pr. Ess. Inst. iv, 1864, 51.—MCILWR., Pr. Ess. Inst. v, 1866, 81.— COUES, Pr. Ess. Inst. v, 1868, 256.—TURNB., B. E. Pa. 1869, 7.—ALLEN, Mem. Bost. Soc. i, 1868, 499 ; Bull. M. C. Z. ii, 1871, 329.—SNOW, B. Kans. 1873.— COUES, Key, 1872, 216.—RIDGW., Pr. Bost. Soc. xvi, 1873, 66.—B. B. & R., N. A. B. iii, 1874, 275.

Buteo (Craxirex) lineatus, GRAY, Hand-list, i, 1869, 7, No. 53.

Pœcilopternis lineatus, KAUP, Monog. *Falc.* Cont. Orn. 1850, 76.

Falco hyemalis, GM., Syst. Nat. i, 1788, 274.—LATH., Ind. Orn. i, 1790, 35.—DAUD., Tr. Orn. ii, 1800, 110.—SHAW, Gen. Zool. vii, 1809, 153.—WILS., Am. Orn. iv, 73, pl. 35, f. 1.—BP., Syn. 1828, 33 ; Isis, 1832, 1138.—NUTT., Man. i, 1832, 106.—AUD., Orn. Biog. i, 1832, 364, pl. 71.

Nisus hyemalis, CUV., R. A. 2d. ed. i, 37.

Circus hyemalis, VIEILL., Ois. Am. Sept. pl. 7.—BP., Journ. Phila. Acad. iii, 1824, 305.— JAMES., ed. Wils. i, 85, 87.

Buteo hyemalis, LESS., Tr. Orn. 81.—BP., Comp. List, 1838, 3.—DEKAY, N. Y. Zool. ii, 10, pl. 6, f. 13.

Astur hyemalis, JARD., ed. Wils. ii, 72.—VIEILL., Enc. Meth. iii, 1273.

Buteo fuscus, VIEILL., Ois. Am. Sept. pl 5.

Astur fuscus, BP., Osserv. Cuv. R. A. 37.

Falco buteoides, NUTT., Man. i, 1832, 100.—PEAB., Rep. B. Mass. 1839, 268.—LINSL., Am. Journ. Sci. 1843, 252.

Buteo "cooperi" (error), ALLEN, Am. Nat. iii, 1869, 518 (New England).

b. *elegans.*

Buteo elegans, CASS., Pr. Phila. Acad. vii, 1855, 281.—BD., B. N. A. 1858, 28.—NEWB., P. R. R. Rep. vi, 1857, 75.—KENN., *ibid.* x, 1859, pt. iv, 19.—HEERM., *ibid.* pt. vi, 32, pls. 2, 3.—COOP. & SUCK., N. H. Wash. Ter. 1860, 147.—DRESS., Ibis, 1865, 325.—COUES, Pr. Phila. Acad. 1866, 45.—SCL. P. Z. S. 1869, 344 (city of Mexico).—(?) MCILWR., Pr. Ess. Inst. v, 1866, 81 (Canada).

Buteo lineatus var. *elegans*, RIDGW.—B. B. & R., N. A. B. iii, 1874, 277.—COUES, Checklist, 1874, No. 352ª.

Hab.—United States and British Provinces (Nova Scotia, *Bland*). Var. *elegans*, western (? Canada, *McIlwraith*).

No specimens of this species were taken by either of the Expeditions, and if, indeed, the bird ranges throughout the Missouri region, it must be uncommon. The name occurs in Prof. Snow's list, but without remark. The latitudinal dispersion of the species appears to be quite restricted ; I have never heard of it from the fur countries, nor indeed anywhere beyond the United States, excepting in Canada and Nova Scotia. It reaches, however, across the continent ; examples from the limited Pacific slopes are, as might be expected, more heavily colored than ordinary, but it hardly seems necessary to recognize them by name. Southern-born birds are considerably smaller than the average, as noted by Prof. Verrill, in comparing Maine and Florida examples. In the Atlantic States it is one of the most abundant of the birds of prey. The nidification is similar to that of *B. borealis ;* the eggs, as usual, have a wide range of variation in color ; they measure from 2.00 to 2.25 in length by about 1.75 in breadth ; they number from two to four. The general habits of the species are much the same as those of allied large Hawks.

BUTEO SWAINSONI, Bp.

Swainson's Buzzard.

(??) *Falco obsoletus*, GM., Syst. Nat. i, 1788, 268.—LATH., Ind. Orn. 1790, 28.—DAUD., Tr. Orn. ii, 1800, 104.—SHAW, Gen. Zool. vii, 1809, 152 (*Strickland ;* very uncertain).

(?) *Falco buteo*, AUD., Orn. Biog. iv, 508, pl. 372

Buteo vulgaris, Sw. & Rich., F. B. A. ii, 1831, 47, pl. 27 (not of European writers).—
    Nutt., Man. ii, 1834, 539.—(?) Aud., Syn. 1839, 5; B. Am. i, 1840, 30, pl. 6
    (based on *Falco buteo* of folio ed. pl. 372).
Buteo montanus, Nutt., Man. i, 2d ed. 1840, 112 (not of authors).
Buteo swainsoni, Bp., List, 1838, 3; Cónsp. i, 1850, 19.—Strickl., Orn. Syn. 1855, 30.—
    Brew., N. A. Oöl. 1857, 24.—Cass., Baird's B. N. A. 1858, 19 (not of Cass. Ill.
    1854, 98).—Bd., P. R. R. Rep. x, 1859, pt. iii, 11, pls. 12, 13.—Hayd., Rep. 1862,
    152.—Blak., Ibis, iii, 1861, 317 (eggs).—Dress., Ibis, 1865, 324 (Texas).—
    Coues, Pr. Phila. Acad. 1866, 43 (Arizona).—Dall & Bann., Tr. Chic. Acad. i,
    1869, 272 (Alaska).—Coop., B. Cal. i, 1870, 476.—Stev., U. S. Geol. Surv. Ter.
    1870, 462.—Merr., *ibid.* 1872, 697.—Coues, Key, 1872, 217.—Snow, B. Kans.
    1873.—B. B. & R., N. A. B. iii, 1874, 263.—Coues, A. N. viii, 1874 (biography).
Buteo (Craxirex) swainsoni, Gray, Hand-list, i, 1869, 7, No. 50.
Buteo bairdii, Hoy, Pr. Phila. Acad. vi, 1853, 451 (young; Wisconsin).—Cass., Ill. 1854,
    99, 257, pl. 41.—Cass., B. N. A. 1858, 21.—Hayd., Rep. 1862, 152.—McIlwr., Pr.
    Ess. Inst. v, 1866, 81 (Canada).
Buteo insignatus, Cass., Ill. 1854, 102, 198, pl. 31 (*melanotic*; Canada).—Strickl., Orn.
    Syn. 1855, 38.—Cass., B. N. A. 1858, 23.—Brew., N. A. Oöl. 1857, 33.—Heerm.,
    P. R. R. Rep. x, 1859, pt. vi, 32.—Coues, Pr. Phila. Acad. 1866, 45.—Coop.,
    B. Cal. i, 1870, 474.—Snow, B. Kans. 1873.
Buteo swainsoni var. *insignatus*, Dall & Bann., Tr. Chic. Acad. i, 1869, 272 (Alaska).
Buteo gutturalis, Maxim., J. f. O. vi, 1858, 17 (with eggs).
Buteo oxypterus, Cass., Pr. Phila. Acad. vii, 1855, 283; B. N. A. 1858, 30 (young).—
    Strickl., Orn. Syn. 1855, 28.—Coues, Pr. Phila. Acad. 1866, 45.—Coop., B. Cal.
    i, 1870, 480.
Buteo swainsoni var. *oxypterus*, Ridgw.—B. B. & R., N. A. B. iii, 1874, 266.
Buteo fulginosus, Scl., P. Z. S. 1858, 356; Tr. Z. S. 1858, 267, pl. 62 (*melanotic*; Mexico).—
    Ridgw., Pr. Phila. Acad. 1870, 142.
Buteo "harlani, Aud.*"*—Bryant, Pr. Bost. Soc. 1861, 115 (provisional name; proposes to
    adopt *swainsoni* in the probable event that the true *harlani* is a different species).

Hab.—Chiefly Northern and Western North America. Alaska. Kansas. Wisconsin.
Canada. Massachusetts. Also Mexico, Central and parts of South America.

List of specimens.

| 19119 | 180 | Powder River . | ♂ | Sept. 24, 1859 | F. V. Hayden | 22.00 | 50.00 | 16.50 |
| 19120 | 7 | Grosventres R. | .:.. | June 3, 1860 | ......do ..... | 19.00 | 45.00 | 15.00 |

Lieutenant Warren's Expedition.—5151, 5152, Little Missouri River; 5153 (?) Loup
Fork of Platte River; 5154, mouth of Yellowstone River; 5155, Knife River; 5156,
mouth of White Earth River; 5157, Heart River.
    Later Expeditions.—54323, Wyoming; 60631–2, Sweetwater; 61765–6, Idaho; 62226–9,
Wyoming; 62230, Montana.
    As noted in a preceding article, this species may be distinguished from any style of
borealis in all its variations of color, by the emargination of only three, instead of
four, outer primaries. It is very truthfully figured by Dr. Richardson, and other plates
have been published, as above quoted, illustrating several of its plumages. "*B.
bairdii*" is now well-known to be the young bird, while "*B. insignatus*" is merely a
melanotic condition. The species appears to inhabit chiefly the western portions of
America, but has occurred several times in Canada, and once in Massachusetts. Dr.
Hayden's numerous specimens attest its abundance in the whole Missouri region. The
confusion that has arisen respecting it is deplorable—the more so that there was no
occasion for any such misunderstanding. The mal-identification of *montanus*, Nutt.,
has had much to do with causing this. It is, of course, permanently distinct from
borealis, although hastily referred to this species by Mr. Allen. In bringing "*oxypterus*"
and "*fuliginosus*" into this connection, I follow Mr. Ridgway, who is unquestionably
correct in this determination. Even the varietal distinction he attempts to maintain
in his last work is untenable, as he informs me he is now satisfied himself.

This large Hawk is very abundant in Northern Dakota, where it
came under my almost daily observation during the summer of 1873.
Excepting an occasional Rough-leg or Red-tail, it was the only buteo-
nine species observed, and the only Hawks more common were the
ubiquitous Marsh Harriers and Sparrow Hawks. The species is thoroughly distinct from its nearest ally, *B. borealis*; it never gains the red
tail, so characteristic of the latter, and differs in many other points of
coloration in its several stages of plumage, as noted beyond. Although
its linear dimensions intergrade with those of the Red-tail, it is not so

heavy nor so large a bird, and its shape differs in some points. A very tangible and convenient distinction, to which my attention was first called by Mr. Ridgway, and which I have verified in numerous instances, is found in the emargination of the primaries. As stated in my late work (Key N. A. Birds, p. 217), Swainson's Buzzard has only *three* emarginate primaries, while the Red-tail has *four;* the fourth quill of the former, like the fifth of the latter, is variously sinuate-tapering, but never shows the decided nick or emargination of the inner web.

The following measurements, taken in the flesh, illustrate the sexual difference and other variations in size: Largest adult ♀, 22 inches long, 54 in extent, the wing 16; other females, respectively, 21.50 by 51.75 by 16.25; 21.00 by 53.00 by 15.75; 20.50 by 51.00 by 15.25; 19.00 by 49.00 by 13.50—but this last one was an ungrown young. Adult ♂'s, 19.00 to 20.00 long by about 49.00 in spread of wing, the latter 15.00 or a little more. In both sexes, and at all ages, the eye is brown, but of varying shade—I have seen no approach to a yellow iris. In the old birds the feet, together with the cere, gape, and base of under mandible, are rich chrome-yellow; the rest of the bill, and the claws, being bluish-black. In the young-of-the-year these yellow parts much duller—grayish-yellow, or yellowish clay-color. Many old birds have the integument of the lower belly largely bare, yellowish in color, hardened and thickened with warty excrescences; this disease seems the rule rather than the exception. Unfledged nestlings are covered with white fluffy down; the first feathers to appear on the under parts show the characteristic color and markings of the formerly supposed species, "*bairdii.*" (The various plumages are given beyond.) A moult occurs in August and September; it is protracted, the feathers being very gradually renewed, almost one by one; the fresh heavily-colored feathers contrasting strongly with the ragged and faded ones worn during the summer. The young have no moult at this season, carrying the plumage in which they leave the nest into the winter. I have no observations upon a spring moult, which probably occurs to both old and young. I took no specimens in the melanistic state of plumage in which the bird has been described as another supposed species (*B. insignatus*)*;* and only saw one in which the entire under parts looked as dark, when the bird was sailing over me, as the pectoral band of the adult female is. This dark plumage is an individual peculiarity, not a normal stage of regular occurrence.

Swainson's Buzzard may be seen anywhere in the region mentioned— even far out on the prairie, miles away from timber, circling overhead, or perched on the bare ground. In alighting, it generally takes advantage of some little knoll commanding a view around, though it often has no more prominent place than the heap of dirt from a badger's hole, from which to cast about for some imprudent gopher* espied too far from home, or still more ignoble game. But the bird prefers timber, and, especially as its nesting is confined to trees, it is most frequently observed in the vicinity of the few wooded streams that diversify the boundless prairie. In Northern Dakota such streams cut their tortuous way pretty deeply into the ground; and the sharp edges of the banks, rising steep on one side, and on the other stretching away on a continuous level, are favorite resting-spots, where sometimes a line of several birds may be observed strung along a distance of a few yards. The Souris or Mouse River, a stream of this description, is a favorite resort,

---

* "*Gopher*": Frontier vernacular name for all the ground-squirrels (*Spermophili*) indiscriminately. *S. tridecem-lineatus* is the commonest kind here. The pouched rats are known as "pocket-gophers."

where I found the birds more numerous than elsewhere. Much of the river-bottom is well wooded with elm, oak, and other large trees; and the number of nests found in this timber—sometimes several in sight of each other—would be considered surprising by one not recollecting that conveniences for breeding are in this country practically limited to such narrow tracts.

The nests are built at varying heights, from the intricacies of heavy shrubbery, where a man may reach them from the ground, to the tops of the tallest trees. They are generally, however, placed thirty or forty feet high, in some stout crotch or on a horizontal fork. They are bulky and ragged-looking structures, from the size of sticks used for the base and outside; the interior is composed of smaller twigs more compactly arranged. The shape varies with the requirements of the location, being more or less conical in an upright crotch, flatter on a fork. The interior hollowing is slight. An average external diameter may be given as two feet, and depth half as much. I was too late for eggs in the locality above mentioned; the only nest I found with anything in it contained two half-fledged young. This was on the 15th of August—so late as to induce the belief that perhaps two broods may be reared in a season, especially as before this date I had observed many full-grown yearlings on wing. This nest was built about forty feet high, in an oak tree, was very untidy, matted with excrement and the scurfy exfoliation from the growing feathers of the youngsters, and encumbered with portions of several gophers. The nestlings were too young to make any resistance beyond a menacing hiss and a very mixed flapping when they were unceremoniously pitched out. The mother was shot near the nest with a pistol-ball, but her partner kept prudently out of the way. The young had been well cared for; their crops were full of gopher-meat at the time, and they were very fat.

In July I had a live young one in captivity, at about the age of these two; and, early in August, possessed a completely-feathered and full-grown bird of the year, probably hatched in May. This shows that either two broods are reared, or that the laying season runs through most of the summer. This grown young one made rather an acceptable prisoner for some days, as he was trim and shapely, with a fine eye and general military bearing, as well as an excellent appetite. But then he was bad-tempered, took the most civil advances unkindly, and would not even fraternize with a pair of very well-disposed and sensible Owls that were picketed with him. At last, when he so totally failed to appreciate his position as to use his claws with painful effect, he was summarily executed. Both this and the younger one before him had a peculiarly plaintive whistle to signify hunger or a sense of loneliness, a note that was almost musical in intonation. This was the only cry I heard from them; the old birds have a harsh, loud scream, much alike in all our large Hawks.

The quarry of Swainson's Buzzard is of a very humble nature. I never saw one swoop upon wild-fowl or Grouse, and, though they strike rabbits, like the Red-tails, their prey is ordinarily nothing larger than gophers. Though really strong and sufficiently fierce birds, they lack the "snap" of the Falcons and Asturs; and I scarcely think they are smart enough to catch birds very often. I saw one make the attempt on a Lark Bunting. The Hawk poised in the air, at a height of about twenty yards, for fully a minute, fell heavily, with an awkward thrust of the talons—and missed. The little bird slipped off, badly scared no doubt, but unhurt, while the enemy flapped away sulkily, very likely to prowl around a gopher-hole for his dinner, or take pot-luck at grasshoppers. They procure gophers, mice, and other small quadrupeds, both by waiting patiently at the mouth of the holes, ready to claw out the unlucky animals the moment they show their noses, and by sailing low over the ground to pick up such as they may find away from home. But I question whether, after all, insects do not furnish their principal subsistence. Those that I shot after midsummer all had their craws stuffed with grasshoppers. These insects, which appear sometimes in almost inconceivable numbers, seem to be the natural source of supply for a variety of animals. Wolves, foxes, badgers, and even rodents, like gophers, supposed vegetarians, come down to them. Sand-hill Cranes stalk over the plains to spear them by thousands. Wild fowl waddle out of the reedy pools to scoop them up. We may kill scores of Sharp-tailed Grouse, in September, to find in every one of them a mass of grasshoppers, only leavened with a few grubs, beetles, leaves, berries, and succulent tops of plants. It is amusing to see a Hawk catching grasshoppers, skipping about in an awkward way, and looking as if he were rather ashamed of being seen in such a performance. Food being abundant and easily procured, the birds become extremely fat early in the autumn, and lazy withal. Unaccustomed to the presence of man in these regions, they may be approached with little difficulty as they perch on the trees ; and they often fly unwillingly within short range. When brought down winged, they show no lack of spirit, and must be prudently dealt with, as their talons are very effective weapons of defense.

Changes of plumage with age affect more particularly the under parts, the back, wings, and tail being more nearly alike at all times.

Young-of-the-year (both sexes). Entire upper parts dark brown, everywhere varied with tawny edgings of the individual feathers. The younger the bird, the more marked is the variegation ; it corresponds in tints closely with the color of the under parts, being palest in very young examples. Under parts, including lining of wings, nearly uniform fawn-color (pale, dull yellowish-brown), thickly and sharply marked with blackish-brown. These large dark spots, for the most part circular or guttiform, crowd across the forebreast, scatter on the middle belly, enlarge to cross-bars on the flanks, become broad arrow-heads on the lower belly and tibiæ, and are wanting on the throat, which is only marked with a sharp, narrow, blackish penciling along the median line. Quills brownish-black, the outer webs with an ashy shade, the inner webs toward the base grayish, paler, and marbled with white, and also showing obscure dark cross-bars ; their shafts black on top, nearly white underneath. Tail-feathers like the quills, but more decidedly shaded with ashy or slate-gray, and tipped with whitish ; their numerous dark cross-bars show more plainly than those of the quills, but are not so evident as they are in the old birds.

Adults (either sex). Upper parts dark brown, very variable in shade according to season or wear of the feathers, varied with paler brown, or even reddish-brown edgings of the feathers, but without the clear fawn-color of the young ; the feathers of the crown showing whitish when disturbed, and usually sharp, dark shaft-lines ; the upper tail-coverts chestnut and white, with blackish bars. Quills and tail-feathers as before, but the inner webs of the former showing more decided dark cross-bars upon a lighter marbled-whitish ground, and the latter having broader and sharper, dark wavy bars. These large quills, and particularly those of the tail, vary much in shade according to wear, the new feathers being strongly slate-colored, the old ones plain dark brown. The tail, however, never shows any trace of the rich chestnut that obtains in the adult *B. borealis*. *Male:* Under parts showing a broad pectoral area of bright chestnut, usually with a glaucous cast, and displaying sharp, black shaft-lines ; this area contrasting sharply with the pure white throat. Other under parts white, more or less tinged and varied, in different specimens, with light chestnut. In some males, this chestnut is diminished to traces, chiefly in flank-bars and arrow-heads, and the white throat is immaculate ; in others, the throat shows blackish penciling, and the rest of the under parts are so much marked with chestnut, chiefly in cross-bars, that this color predominates over the white, and appears in direct continuation of the pectoral area itself. Some feathers of this area are commonly dark brown. *Female:* Much darker underneath than the male ; throat pure white, but other under parts probably never whitening decidedly. Pectoral area from rich, dark chestnut or mahogany-color, mixed with still darker feathers, to brownish-black ; and other under parts heavily marked with chestnut, chiefly in cross-bars alternating with whitish, but on the flanks, and sometimes across the belly, these markings quite blackish. The general tone of the under parts may be quite as dark as the pectoral area of the male, but it lacks uniformity, and the increased depth of color of the pectoral area in this sex suffices to preserve the strong contrast already mentioned. (About forty specimens examined.)

BUTEO PENNSYLVANICUS, (Wils.) Bp.

Broad-winged Buzzard.

Falco pennsylvanicus, WILS., Am. Orn. vi. 1812, 92, pl. 54, f. 1.—BP., Syn. 1828, 29; Isis, 1832, 1137.—NUTT., Man. i, 1832, 105.—AUD., Orn. Biog. i, 1832, 461; v, 1839, 377; pl. 91.—DEKAY, N. Y. Zool. 1844, 11, pl. 5, f. 11..
Buteo pennsylvanicus, BP., Osserv. Cuv. R. A. 55; List, 1838, 3.—AUD., Syn. 1839, 6; B. Am. i, 1840, 43, pl. 10.—CAB., J. f. O. ii, p. lxxxii (Cuba).—CASS., Ill. 1854, 100.— STRICKL., Orn. Syn. 1855, 32.—PUTN., Pr. Ess. Inst. i, 1856, 203.—BREW., N. A. Oöl. 1857, 31.—SCL., P. Z. S. 1857, 211 (Orizaba); 261 (Upper Amazon); 1858, 451 (Ecuador).—BD., B. N. A. 1858, 29.—HOY, Pr. Phila. Acad. (Wisconsin).— WHEAT., Ohio Agric. Rep. 1860, No. 11.—COUES & PRENT., Smiths. Rep. 1861, 402.—BOARDM., Pr. Bost. Soc. ix, 1862, 122.—VERR., Pr. Ess. Inst. iii, 1862, 142.— ALLEN, *ibid.* iv, 1864, 51.—MCILWR., *ibid.* v, 1866, 81.—COUES, *ibid.* v, 1868, 257.—DRESS., Ibis, 1865, 325 (Texas).—GUNDL., Rep. 1865, 223 (Cuba).—LAWR., Ann. Lyc. N. Y. vii, 1861, 288 (Panama); viii, 1866, 280; ix, 1868, 133 (Costa Rica).—TURNB., B. E. Pa. 1869, 7.—ALLEN, Bull. M. C. Z. ii, 1871, 330.—MAYN., Pr. Bost. Soc. 1872.—SNOW, B. Kans. 1873.—COUES, Key, 1872, 217.—RIDGW., Pr. Bost. Soc. xvi, 1873, 65.—B. B. & R., N. A. B. iii, 1874, 259.
Falco latissimus, WILS., Am. Orn. vi, 1812, 92, pl. 54, f. 1 (later copies).
Astur (?) *latissimus,* JARD., ed. Wils. ii, 294.
Buteo latissimus, LEMB., Av. Cubæ, 1850, 19.
Sparvius platypterus, VIEILL., Enc. Meth. iii, 1823, 1273.
Falco wilsoni, BP., Journ. Phila. Acad. iii, 1824, 348.
Buteo wilsoni, BP., Consp. Av. i, 1850, 19.
Pœcilopternis wilsoni, KAUP, Monog. *Falc.* Cont. Orn. 1850, 75.

Hab.—Temperate Eastern North America. South to Costa Rica, Panama, and Ecuador. Cuba.

This species was not noticed by either of the Expeditions, and the only indication I have found of its presence anywhere in the Missouri region is Prof. Snow's record of its occurrence in Kansas, where it is said to be not common. Its longitudinal dispersion is thus quite restricted, contrary to the rule among our birds of this family, most of which range across the continent. The Broad-winged Hawk is apparently more numerous along the Atlantic coast than elsewhere, especially in New England, where all the local writers speak of it, some giving it as the most abundant summer Hawk in certain localities, as about Umbagog Lakes. It is known to breed in various parts of New England; further south it is chiefly observed in the fall and winter, the only seasons when I saw it about Washington, D. C. I did not meet with it in either of the Carolinas, but it is given as common in Florida, known to reach southward as far at least as Ecuador, as by the above quotations, and to reside in Cuba.

The nest of this species has but seldom fallen under the notice of naturalists. Dr. Brewer describes the one that Audubon saw, and another taken by Prof. Adams, now in the museum of Middlebury College, Vermont. Mr. Samuels states that a nest he visited the 20th of May, 1864, in West Roxbury, Massachusetts, was built in the fork of a tall pine-tree, near the top, and composed of coarse sticks and twigs, lined with red cedar-bark, leaves, and feathers. It contained four eggs, measuring from 2.00 to 2.15 long, by 1.70 to 1.72 broad; "dirty yellowish-white, covered more or less thickly in the different specimens with spots and blotches of reddish-brown." Other specimens had fainter markings, while in others again the spots were finer and darker.

ARCHIBUTEO LAGOPUS var. SANCTI-JOHANNIS, (Gm.) Ridgw.

American Rough-legged Hawk.

a. *lagopus*.

Falco communis var., GM., Syst. Nat. i, 1788, 270.—LATH., Ind. Orn. i, 1790, 30 (based on
      Acc. falco leucocephalus, BRISS., Orn. i, 325; *Vultur subbuteus*, FRISCH, pl. 75).
Falco lagopus, BRÜNN., Orn. Bor. 1764, 4.—GM., Syst. Nat. i, 1788, 260.—LATH., Ind. Orn.
      i, 1790, 19.—DAUD., Tr. Orn. ii, 1800, 107.—SHAW, G. Z. vii, 1809, 145.—TEMM.,
      Man. 1815, 22.—NAUM., V. D. i, 1822, 359.—MEYER, Tasch. 37, pl. 34; and of
      most early authors.
Accipiter lagopus, PALL., Zoog. R. A. i, 1811, 360, pl. 10.
Buteo lagopus, LEACH, Cat. 1816, 10.—STEPH., G. Z. xiii, pt. ii, 47.—ROUX, Orn. Prov. i,
      41, pl. 25.—FLEM., Br. Am. 54.—JEN., Man. 87.—MACGIL., Hist. Br. B. iii, 193;
      Rap. B. Gr. B. p. —.—EYT., Cat. Br. B. 4.—KEYS. & BLAS., Wirb. Eur. 1840,
      30.—SCHL., Rev. Crit. 1844, 9.—CUV., R. A. i, 2d ed. 336.—SELBY, Ill. Br. Orn.
      i, 58.—GOULD, B. E. pl. 15.—Sw., Classif. B. ii, 1837, 211.—VIEILL., Fn. Franç.
      21, pl. 9, f. 2; Mem. Acad. Turin, xxiii, 232.—JARD., Nat. Lib. Br. B. i, 197.—
      DEGL., Orn. Eur. i, 55.—THOMPS., B. Irel. i, 76.—SELYS-L., Fn. Belg. 54.—KAUP,
      Monog. Falc. Cont. Orn. 1850, 75.
Triorchis lagopus, KAUP, Sk. Ent. Eur. Thierw. 1829, 84.
Archibuteo lagopus, GRAY, List Gen. of B. 3; Gen. of B. i, 12; List B. Br. Mus. 38; List
      Brit. B. 8.—KAUP, Classif. Säug u. Vög. 123.—STRICKL., Orn. Syn. 1855, 38.—BP.,
      Consp. i, 1850, 17.
Archibuteo lagopus var. *lagopus*, RIDGW., Pr. Bost. Soc. xvi, 1873, 72.
Butaëtes lagopus, BP., List, 1838, 3.
Falco sclavonicus, LATH., I. O. i, 1790, 26.—DAUD., Tr. ii, 1800, 166.—SHAW, G. Z. vii, 171.
Falco pennatus var., LATH., Syn. Suppl. ii, 24 (*Strickland*).—CUV., R. A. i, 1817, 323.
Falco plumipes, DAUD., Tr. Orn. ii, 163.
Butaëtes buteo, LESS., Tr. Orn. 1831, 83.
Butaëtes lessoni, A. SMITH (*Gray*).
Archibuteo planiceps et *alticeps*, BREHM, V. D. i, 46, 41.

b. *sancti-johannis*.

Falco sancti-johannis, GM., Syst. Nat. i, 1788, 273.—LATH., Ind. Orn. i, 1790, 34.—DAUD.,
      Tr. ii, 1800, 105.—SHAW, G. Z. vii, 1809, 150. (Among older quotations, com-
      pare *Rough-legged* and *Chocolate-colored Falcons* of PENNANT, Arct. Zool. pp.
      200, 201; also, *Placentia Falcon* of LATHAM, Syn. i, 76; Suppl. 19).—BP., Syn.
      1828, 32.—NUTT., Man. i, 1832, 98.—LINSL., Am. Journ. Sci. xliv, 1843.
Butaëtes sancti-johannis, BP., Comp. List, 1838, 3.
Archibuteo sancti-johannis, GRAY, Gen. of B.; Hand-list, i, 1869, 10, No. 82.—BP., Consp.
      i, 1850, 18 (excl. syn. *ferrugineus*, Licht. et *regalis*, Gray).—KAUP, Monog. Falc.
      Cont. Orn. 1850, 75.—CASS., Ill. 1854, 103.—BREW., N. Am. Oöl. 1857, 34.—BD.,
      B. N. A. 1858, 33.—BLAK., Ibis, iii, 1861, 318.—COUES, Pr. Phila. Acad. 1861,
      217.—WHEAT., Ohio Agric. Rep. 1861, No. 13.—BOARDM., Pr. Bost. Soc. ix, 1862,
      123.—VERR., Pr. Ess. Inst. iii, 1862, 143.—ALLEN, *ibid.* iv, 1864, 51.—McILWR.,
      ibid. v, 1866, 81.—COUES, *ibid.* v, 1868, 258.—LAWR., Ann. Lyc. N. Y. viii, 1866,
      280.—TURNB., B. E. Pa. 1869, 7.—COOP., B. Cal. i, 1870, 485.
Buteo sancti-johannis, SCHL. M. P.-B. 1862, *Buteones*, p. 2 (excl. syn. *ferrugineus*, LICHT.).
Archibuteo lagopus var. *sancti-johannis*, RIDGW., Pr. Phila. Acad. 1870, 142; Pr. Bost. Soc.
      1873, 72.—ALLEN, Bull. M. C. Z. iii, 1872, 181.—COUES, Key, 1872, 218.—B. B.
      & R., N. A. B. iii, 1874, 304.
Falco spadiceus, GM., Syst. Nat i, 1788, 273.—LATH., Ind. Orn. i, 1790, 27. (of PEN-
      NANT, but not *Chocolate Falcon* of FORSTER).—DAUD., Tr. ii, 1800, 109.
Buteo spadiceus, VIEILL., Ois. Am. Sept. i. 1807, 34.
Falco novæ-terræ, GM., Syst. Nat. i, 1788, 274.
Falco niger, WILS., Am. Orn. vi, 1812, 82, pl. 53, f. 1, 2.
Buteo niger, STEPH., Shaw's G. Z. xiii, pt. ii, 47.—VIG., Zool. Journ. i, 340.—JAMES., ed.
      Wils. i, 79, 80.—CUV., R. A. 2d ed. i, 336.
Falco lagopus, WILS., Am. Orn. iv, 59; v, 216; pl. 33, f. 1.—BP., Syn. 1828, 32; Isis, 1832,
      1138.—NUTT., Man. i, 1832, 97.—AUD., Orn. Biog. ii, 377; v, 217; pls. 166, 422.
Buteo lagopus, Sw. & RICH., F. B. A. ii, 1831, 52, pl. 28.—AUD., Syn. 1839, 8; B. Am. i,
      1840, 46, pl. 11.—GIR., B. L. I. 1844, 6.
Archibuteo lagopus, CASS., Ill. 1854, 104.—BREW., N. Am. Oöl. 1857, 36.—BD., B. N. A.
      1858, 32 (excl. syn.).—KENN., P. R. R. Rep. x, 1859, pt. iv, 19.—COOP. & SUCK.,
      N. H. Wash. Ter. 1860, 148.—COUES, Pr. Phila. Acad. 1866, 48.—DALL & BANN.,
      Tr. Chic. Acad. i, 1869, 272.—COOP., B. Cal. i, 1870, 483.—SNOW, B. Kans. 1873;
      and of late American writers generally.

Buteo ater, VIEILL., Nouv. Dict. d'Hist. Nat. iv, 1816, 482; Enc. Meth. iii, 1227.
(?) *Buteo* "*harlani*, AUD." (error), of the following New England writers: EMMONS, Cat. B. Mass. 1835, p. 1; PEABODY, Rep. Orn. Mass. 1839, 296; PUTNAM, Pr. Ess. Inst. i, 1856, 225. See COUES, Pr. Ess. Inst. v, 1868, 258.

Hab.—Typical *lagopus*, European. Var. *sancti-johannis* in North America at large; rather northerly. The melanotic condition chiefly observed in the Middle Atlantic States, New England, and northward.

List of specimens.

| 19123 | 261 | Fort Laramie .. | .... | Feb. °2, 1860 | F. V. Hayden. | 20.00 | 54.00 | 17.75 |

The question, long agitated, of the relationship of our "Black" and "Rough-legged" Hawks may be considered settled in favor of their specific identity, the Black Hawk being simply the melanotic condition of the Rough-legged. There is nothing either peculiar or remarkable in this, melanism being an affection common to many or most Hawks, independent of age, sex, season, or locality, and analogous to the rusty-red plumages of Owls. It is curious, if not instructive, to note, in the history of the controversy, how some authors have tried to make out two species upon wholly imaginary differences in geographical distribution and migration, nay, also, in habits, such as nidification, and even in the eggs; while other authors, admitting the identity of the two, have made each to be the old, and then the young of the other. The record is thus highly suspicious, upon *à priori* considerations; and it has been proven groundless. Specimens show every degree of melanism, from the first departure from normal *lagopus* to the complete black dress ; and this is independent of age, sex, or season.

The only qualification of these remarks that seems to be required is respecting the areas of distribution of the melanotic form. As is well known, the normal *lagopus* ranges across the country ; but, so far as I am aware, the black plumage has not been observed in any individuals from the far west. Dr. Cooper, indeed, gives "*sancti-johannis*," but with the remark that he never saw it in California. This is the more remarkable since in the West alone occur the dark ("*calurus*") forms of *borealis*, while the melanotic state of *swainsoni* ("*insignatus*") has there its chief development.

As above noted, the Black Rough-legged Hawk is chiefly found in the Middle Atlantic and New England States, and northward. According to my information, the melanism has not been observed to occur in the European *lagopus*. This brings us to consideration of the relationships of the American and European *Archibuteo*. The majority of writers have considered them identical; and it is certain that normal *lagopus* of this country cannot be specifically distinguished from the European bird. There appear to be, however, slight discrepancies of the grade of those observed in the Hawk Owls, the Marsh Hawks, and many other species common to both hemispheres, warranting the recognition of geographical races. This is the view first taken, I believe, by Mr. Ridgway, with whom I agree to separate the American bird, in all its variety, from the normal *lagopus* plumage to the perfect melanism, from the European, as a geographical race, under the name above adopted. In the foregoing synonymy, it will be observed, I unite the "*sancti-johannis*" with the various quotations of *American lagopus* alone. G. R. Gray has already done substantially the same, but he makes specific distinction. Bonaparte, in 1850 (*Conspectus*), also separated our bird under name of *sancti-johannis*, but he wrongly adduced the synonyms of *A. ferrugineus*, which is apparently a distinct species.

Since Audubon remarked, in 1834, that he had never seen this species west of the Alleghanies, its successive and repeated occurrences have entirely negatived such implied restriction of its range. It is found throughout the West—in the United States chiefly in winter, in the fur countries only in summer. Sir John Richardson remarks that it arrives in April or May, and departs in October. Its migrations appear to be quite regular and extensive—more so, perhaps, than is generally supposed—though probably it does not differ from most Hawks in this respect. Birds of this family must follow their prey, wherever this leads them, and only a few of the more powerful species, able to prey upon hares and Ptarmigan, pass the winter in our highest latitudes. The Rough-legged is a rather northerly species, rarely, if ever, breeding within the limits of the United States, and becoming rarer toward its southern terminus. On the Atlantic coast I have no authentic evidence of its appearance south of the United States, the maritime portions of which may be regarded as its winter headquarters. It is represented as being particularly numerous in the low land along the Delaware and Schuylkill Rivers. It winters thence northward into Maine at 'least, where Prof. Verrill and others have found it common at that season. It also endures the rigor of the year in parts of the Missouri region, though probably not the northernmost. Prof. Snow marks it as abundant in Kansas in winter, but at Fort Randall, in Southeast Dakota, I never saw it until April, when a fine female was secured. This was apparently a very old bird, in light-colored plumage, with very little rufous, and a complete broad abdominal zone of blackish-brown. Allen found it wintering in Wyoming. I took a single specimen at Fort Whipple, in Arizona, in the winter of 1865, and Dr. Kennerly observed the species at Zuñi, in New Mexico, in November. This brings its range almost to the Mexican border. The continuous mountain-chains probably account for its range in this longitude beyond that it completes on the Atlantic. Dr. Cooper thinks it only a winter visitor in California, where he did not observe it beyond Santa Clara Valley, but surmises it may breed in the mountains of the State, as he saw it on the Columbia in July.

Notwithstanding their size and apparent muscularity, Hawks of this genus have none of the dash and spirit of the Falcons, and indeed seem inferior to the Buteos in this respect. Their quarry, though diversified, is always humble; they prey upon various field-mice and other very small quadrupeds, lizards, and frogs, and even insects, rarely attacking birds of any kind, and then only the most defenceless. Open fields, especially in the vicinity of water, are their favorite resorts. They appear heavy and indisposed to active exertion; flying slowly and heavily, and often remaining long motionless on their perch. They show some analogy to the Owls in points of structure, as well as in their partially nocturnal habits. This has long been noticed. Sir John Richardson says: " In the softness and fullness of its plumage, its feathered legs and habits, this bird bears some resemblance to the Owls. It flies slowly, sits for a long time on the bough of a tree, watching for mice, frogs, &c., and is often seen sailing over swampy pieces of ground, and hunting for its prey by the subdued daylight, which illuminates even the midnight hours in the high parallels of latitude." Wilson observes that it habitually courses over the meadows long after the sun has set, and Audubon calls it the most nocturnal of our species.

The nest, which I have never seen, is said to be ordinarily built of sticks, &c., in a high tree; sometimes, however, on cliffs, as noted by Dr. Brewer. The eggs, three or four in number, and measuring about 2¼ by 1¾ inches, run through the usual variations, from dull whitish, scarcely or not at all marked, to drab or creamy, largely blotched with different shades of brown, sometimes mixed with purplish slate markings.

ARCHIBUTEO FERRUGINEUS, (Licht.) Gray.

Ferrugineous Buzzard, or California Squirrel Hawk.

Buteo ferrugineus, LICHT., Tr. Berlin Acad. 1838, 428.
Lagopus ferrugineus, FRASER, P. Z. S. 1844, 36.
Archibuteo ferrugineus, GRAY, Gen. of B. pl. 6 (name *A. regalis* on plate); Hand-list, i, 1869, 10, No. 83.—CASS., Ill. 1854, 104, 159, pl. 26; Pr. Phila. Acad. 1855, 277.— STRICKL., Orn. Syn. 1855, 40.—BREW., N. A. Oöl. 1857, 37.—BD., B. N. A. 1858, 34.—HEERM., P. R. R. Rep. x, 1859, pt. vi, 32.—COOP. & SUCK., N. H. Wash. Ter. 1860, 149.—HAYD., Rep. 1862, 153.—BLAK., Ibis, iii, 1861, 318 (Saskatchewan).—DRESS., Ibis, 1865, 325 (Texas).—COUES, Pr. Phila. Acad. 1866, 46 (Arizona; also, anatomical).—RIDGW., Pr. Phila. Acad. 1870, 142.—COOP., B. Cal. i, 1870, 482.—COUES, Key, 1872, 218.—B. B. & R., N. A. B. iii, 1874, 300.

Archibuteo regalis, GRAY, List B. Br. Mus. 39.
Buteo californicus, GRAYSON, Hutchin's Cal. Mag. Mar. 1857.
Archibuteo sancti-johannis (*partim*), BP., Consp. Av. i, 1850, 18.
Buteo sancti-johannis (*partim*), SCHL., M. P.-B. i, 1862, *Buteones*, p. 2.

Hab.—Western United States, chiefly from Rocky Mountains to the Pacific. Saskatchewan (*Blakiston*). Little Missouri River (*Hayden*). Platte River (*Wood*). Texas (*Kennerly* and *Dresser*).
Lieutenant Warren's Expedition.—4544, Little Missouri River, Dakota.

In uniting this species with *A. sancti-johannis*, Bonaparte subsequently received the high indorsement of Prof. Schlegel's authority; and I understand that Mr. Allen is also disinclined to allow its validity, taking it as a somewhat parallel case with that of *Buteo "elegans,"* in the increased amount of reddish colors displayed. With my present information, however, I must decide that it is a good species, and to my closet-studies of the bird I add no little experience with it in the field. It has afforded me perfectly good characters, and I have seen no indication of its grading into the ordinary form. In perfec plumage, not often seen, the under parts are entirely pure white, excepting the rich, deep chestnut legs, barred crosswise with black; the back and wings are largely ferrugineous. The young, as usual, differ materially; the under parts are white, extensively streaked and arrow-headed with dark brown, including the legs. The sexes are alike in color, but the female is larger than the male, being 23 to 24 inches long, spreading about 56, the wing about 17; tail, 10; cere, corners of mouth, and toes, yellow; claws, black; naked skin of the superciliary shield, greenish and crimson; bill, bluish-black; eye of the old birds, pale yellow; of the young, brown. Numerous anatomical features are given in my article of 1866, above quoted.

This large and handsome Hawk has been long described and nominally known, though until recently very little had been recorded of its habits, and its extensive dispersion in the West remained unsuspected. Originally described from California by Prof. Lichtenstein, in 1838, it was first brought to the notice of American ornithologists by Mr. E. M. Kern, in 1846, while attached to Colonel Frémont's Expedition. His specimens from Tulare Valley, California, came under the observation of Mr. Cassin, who, in 1854, gave us a good plate and description, accompanied by the field-notes of Dr. Heermann, who met with the bird in California. Since then it has been very generally noticed by naturalists in California, where it is the most characteristic and one of the most abundant species of its family. I frequently observed it, and procured several fine specimens at Fort Whipple, in Arizona, where it is resident and common. Dr. T. C. Henry noticed it in New Mexico, at Fort Fillmore, and Dr. Kennerly even in Texas. It has twice been observed in the Missouri region: On the Platte, by Lieutenant Bryan's party, in 1856, and on the Little Missouri River, along the western border of Dakota, adjoining Montana, by Lieutenant Warren's Expedition. These latter quotations may represent its real dispersion in those directions, as at any rate they do our knowledge in the matter.

Although belonging to a group technically said to be "ruling" Buzzards ("*Archibuteo*"), it is difficult to see where the claim to royal purple lies in this species and others of the same genus, for they certainly lack the qualities that go to make Hawks famous. Viewing their splendid presence, we wonder, as a late writer says, "that the object of such an admirable organization is nothing more important than the destruction of the smallest and most defenceless of quadrupeds or of reptiles. Yet such is apparently the case. Many of the birds of this group, though powerful in structure, and furnished with the usual apparatus of strong and sharp bill and claws, and other accompani ments of predatory habits, rarely attack any animal more formidable than a mouse or ground squirrel, or in some cases a frog or other of the weaker species of reptiles." As in some cases of conspicuous personages, become regal by the accident of a name, attributes of royalty compare unfavorably with its apparatus. The contrast between the physique of Rough-legged Hawks and their venatorial exploits, is striking, and illustrates well the fact, that muscular effectiveness is not always co-ordinate with its mass. The force of a little Falcon's onslaught is something more than that of its falling weight; this would tell to little effect, compared with the result of its weight at high velocity. Granting the heavy Buzzards commensurate courage to act with all their force, they cannot, nevertheless, acquire the requisite speed, and so fail of momentum, the product of mass and motion. Excepting during their occasional aërial evolutions, when they appear to circle lightly, they are retarded by their own weight, and are generally observed winnowing low over the ground with almost laborious movement. They pick up their prey as they pass by, dipping obliquely, and it requires no great agility to elude their clutch. Most small birds, it seems, evade capture, so that the Hawks chiefly confine themselve to less active quarry.

But we must not hastily conclude that the Ferrugineous Buzzard is spiritless because its courage is seldom conspicuous. I have seen it fight bravely at desperate odds. Riding through an open glade, I once observed a Hawk of this species perched on the top of a dead tree that stood alone. Anxious as I was to secure it, I could only ride carelessly along, for there was no cover, and the bird had already marked me. I pretended not to notice it, gradually drawing nearer without altering my horse's pace or making a movement. The ruse succeeded, and I was almost to the tree before the bird unfolded his broad wings and launched into the air. Without even drawing rein I threw up my gun, and the report echoed from the rocks beyond. But the Hawk sailed on, and I thought I had missed, till, following him with wistful eyes, I saw his course gradually lower, and at last he fell heavily to the earth, several hundred yards away. I hastened to the spot, flushed with gratification, but it was a sad sight after all. Shot had penetrated the bird's lungs, and he lay on his breast with wide-stretched wings and drooping head, breathing heavily, while the blood trickled from his beak. Thinking life almost extinct, I dismounted and came up to him, when in an instant he roused, recognized his extremity, and dared me to touch him—for with a convulsive effort he threw himself on his back, stretched out his talons defiantly, and snapped wrathfully, while the old fire flashed again in his eyes. But the effort was too much; while striking wildly, a fresh stream of blood welled up from his throat, he shivered, his eye grew filmy again, and he lay dead on the stained greensward. Who could but admire the pride that disdained to yield, even at the point of death?

This method of approaching Hawks is frequently successful, and not seldom the only one that can be employed when the birds are in exposed situations. Ten to one, when perched on a tree-top, they have already espied you before you noticed them, and are watching your movements. If you show they are observed, by attempting to work up to them, they suspect at once, and are off at their own convenience. But they appear to be less afraid of a mounted person than of one afoot, and may be often approached indirectly, with the simple precaution of not making them aware they are themselves observed. Ride until just within range, and shoot on the instant; you will have a fair snap shot, probably just as the bird spreads its wings, alarmed at your sudden stop. The same day I killed the one just spoken of, and but a few moments before, riding through the woods, I came up to a Red-tail, perched on a bough only four or five yards overhead. I did not see it myself until I was right underneath it, too near to shoot; so I rode on a few steps, wheeled suddenly, and made a successful shot as the bird flew. On another occasion a large Hawk suffered a squadron of cavalry to file past him as he cowered against the face of a rocky ledge, not fifteen yards away; and only took wing, a few seconds too late, on discovering, by my motions, that he was observed.

According to my observations in the West, the Ferrugineous Buzzards have no partiality for watery places, thus differing from the eastern Rough-legs. About Fort Whipple the birds mostly resorted to the open plains and the grassy glades intervening between patches of pine-woods. They could easily be distinguished by their size and the pure whiteness of the under parts, and were beautiful objects, especially when circling overhead. They were common, especially in winter, but were apparently resident. Their cries were loudest and most frequent in the spring, resembling the syllables *ca ca ca*, rapidly repeated in a high key. In the stomachs of those examined I found the remains of burrowing pouched-rats (*Thomomys fulvus*, Woodh.), the western wood-mouse (*Hesperomys leucopus* var. *sonoriensis*), kangaroo-mice (*Dipodomys ordii*), and some *Arvicolæ* I could not identify. I was never before aware of the existence of the latter in this locality, and would remark, in passing, how often small mammals, reptiles, and insects, which might long remain undetected, owing to their rarity or insignificance, are found in the stomachs of rapacious birds. Such examination of rapacious animals is important, on this account, as well as to learn what is the nature of their food. New species have occasionally been discovered in this way. The bellies of large snakes are often important repositories, and excellent specimens may be secured, owing to the slowness of digestion in these reptiles, and to their swallowing their prey entire.

This bird is known as the "California Squirrel Hawk" in some localities, but it is not to be inferred that they often capture the agile arboreal *Sciuri*. The name is gained from their feeding extensively, in California, upon the "ground squirrels" (*Spermophilus beecheyi*), which abound in many parts of that State. The Hawks are almost always, too, observed in the vicinity of the settlements of the *Spermophili*, standing on the ground where there are no trees, or flying low over the surface, in either case on the alert to seize any unlucky animal that may venture too far from home. They are also said to perch in wait at the entrance of the burrows, ready to clutch the first animal that shows his nose above ground.

Accounts of the nidification of this species, resting upon Dr. Heermann's testimony, have proven, I have been informed, not authentic; he had some other species, probably the western Red-tail, in view. I never saw a nest, to my knowledge; but it is not to be presumed that the mode of nidification is peculiar. Several authentic eggs examined measured from 2.50 by 2.00 to 2.00 by 1.75, and vary so much in marking that no general description will suffice. Some are whitish, with faint grayish or drab shade, the markings obsolete or entirely wanting. Others are pure white or buffy, conspicuously blotched and splashed all over with various shades of rich brown-sienna, bistre, and umber, and also a few paler markings of gray, purplish-drab, and neutral tint. They are broadly ellipsoidal in shape, with little or no appreciable difference in the contour of the opposite ends.

PANDION HALIAËTUS, (Linn.) Cuv.

Fish Hawk ; Osprey.

Aquila haliætus, BRISS., Orn. i, 440, pl. 34.—MEY., Tasch. i, 23; V. D. ii, 23.—JENYNS, Man. 81.—S.-LONGCH., Fn. Belg. 53.

Aquila (Pandion) haliæëta, SW. & RICH., F. B. A. ii, 1831, 20.

Falco haliaëtus, LINN., Fn. Suec. 22; Syst. Nat. i, 1766, 129.—GM., Syst. Nat. i, 1788, 263.—LATH., Ind. Orn. i, 1790, 17, 18.—DAUD., Tr. Orn. ii, 67.—SHAW, G. Z. vii, 82.—TEMM., Man. i, 47; iii, 25.—WILS., Am. Orn. v, 13, pl. 37, f. 1.—BP., Syn. 1828, 26; Isis, 1832, 1136.—NUTT., Man. i, 1832, 78.—AUD., Orn. Biog. i, 415; v, 362; pl. 81; Syn. 1839, 12; B. Am. i, 1840, 64, pl. 15.—GIR., B. L. I. 1844, 11.—MAXIM., Trav. Bras. 334.—NAUM., V. D. (original ed.) iv, 113, pl. 11, f. 19; (ed. of 1822), i, 241, pl. 16.—WOODH., Sitgr. Rep. 1853, 59.—WERN., Atl. Ois. Eur. pl. —.

Accipiter haliætus, PALL., Zoog. R. A. i, 1811, 355.

Pandion haliætus, CUV., R. A. i, 1817, 316.—LESS., Man. i, 86.—STEPH., G. Z. xiii, pt. ii, 12.—SW., Classif. B. ii, 1837, 207.—KAUP, Mus. Senck. 1845, 261.—MACGIL., Hist. Br. B. iii, 23.—EYT., Cat. Br. B. 2.—BP., List, 1838, 3; Cat. Ucc. 19; Consp. Av. i, 1850, 16.—KEYS. & BLAS., Wirb. Eur. 1840, 29.—SCHL., Rev. Crit. 8.—GRAY, Gen. of B. i, 1844, 17; List B. Br. Mus. 22; List Brit. B. 5.—STRICKL., Orn. Syn. 1855, 63.—TAYLOR, Ibis, 1866, 79.—COUES, Key, 1872, 219; and of authors.

Balbusardus haliætus, FLEM., Brit. B. 51 (*Balbuzard,* P. E. 414).

Falco arundinaceus, GM., Syst. Nat. i, 1788, 263.—S. G. GM., Itin. ii, 163.—DAUD., Tr. ii, 69.

Falco cayanensis, GM., Syst. Nat. i, 1788, 263.—DAUD., Tr. Orn. ii, 69.

Falco carolinensis, GM., Syst. Nat. i, 1788, 263 (*Acc. piscatorius,* CATES., Car. i, 2; *Acc. falco piscator antillarum et carolinensis,* BRISS., Orn. i, 361, 362).—DAUD., Tr. Orn. ii, 69.

Pandion carolinensis, BP., List, 1838, 3; Consp., i, 1850, 16.—DEKAY, N. Y. Zool. Birds, 6, pl. 8, fig. 18.—STRICKL., Orn. Syn. 1855, 64.—CASS., Ill. 1854, 112.—BREW., N. A. O. 1857, 53, pl. 3, f. 33, 34.—NEWB., P. R. Rep. vi, 1857, 75.—MAXIM., J. f. O. vi, 1858, 11.—CASS., B. N. A. 1858, 44.—HEERM., P. R. R. Rep. x, 1859, pt. vi, 31.—COOP. & SUCK., N. H. Wash. Ter. 1860, 153.—LORD, Pr. Arty. Inst. iv, 1864, 110.—COUES, Pr. Phila. Acad. 1866, 49.—FOWLER, Am. Nat. 1868, 192 (habits).—DALL & BANN., Tr. Chic. Acad. i, 1869, 272.—COOP., B. Cal. i, 1870, 454.—MERR., U. S. Geol. Surv. Ter. 1872, 698.—SNOW, B. Kans. 1873; and of most late United States writers.

Pandion haliætus var. *carolinensis,* RIDGW., Pr. A. N. S. 1870, 143.—B. B. & R., N. A. B. iii, 1874, 184.

Pandion fluvialis, SAVI., Descr. Egyp. i, 96.—LESS., Tr. Orn. 45, 46, pl. 9, f. 1.—VIEILL., Fn. Franç. ii, pl. 6, f. 1.—DEGL., Mem. S. S. Lille, 1831, 241.—ROUX, Ord. Prov. i, 19, pl. 11.—BAILL., Orn. Sav. i, 104.—PUCH., R. Z. 1850, 209.

Triorches fluvalis, LEACH, Cat. 1816, 10.

Aquila piscatrix, VIEILL., Ois. Am. Sept. i, pl. 4.

Aquila americana, VIEILL., Ois. Am. Sept. i, 31.

Pandion americanus, VIEILL., Gal. Ois. pl. 11.—SW., Classif. B. ii, 1837, 207.—VIG., Zool. Journ. i, 336.

Aquila balbuzardus, DUM., Dict. Sc. Nat. i, 351.

Pandion ichthyaëtus, KAUP, Class. Säug. u. Vög. 122.

Pandion indicus, HODGS., J. A. S. B. 1837, 366; Cat. Gray's Misc. 81.

Pandion leucocephalus, GOULD, Syn. B. Aust. i, 22; B. Aust. pl. 6; P. Z. S. v, 138.—GRAY, Gen. of B.—BP., Consp. i, 1850, 16.—STRICKL., Orn. Syn. 1855, 65.

Pandion haliætus var. *leucocephalus,* RIDGW.—B. B. & R., N. A. B, iii, 1874, 183.

Pandion gouldii, KAUP, Isis, 1847, —; Mon. *Falc.* Cont. Orn. 1850, 73.

Pandion alticeps et *planiceps,* BREHM, V. D. i, 33.

Pandion fasciatus, BREHM, Allg. Deut. Zeit. ii, 1856, 66 ? (St. Domingo).

Hab.—Cosmopolitan. The American and Australian, respectively, under names of *P. carolinensis* and *P. leucocephalus,* have been currently regarded as distinct races or species.

List of specimens.

19125	4	Wind River ...	♀	May 26, 1859	F. V. Hayden.	23.00	56.50	20.50

Late Expeditions.—62242, North Fork, Idaho.

The well-known Fish Hawk is abundant throughout North America, in suitable regions, especially coastwise.

AQUILA CHRYSAËTUS, Linn.

Golden Eagle.

Aquila chrysaëtos, BRISS., Orn. i, 431.—CUV., R. A. 1st ed. i, 314 ; 2d ed. i, 324.—PALL.,
  Zoog. R. A. i, 341.—STEPH., Gen. Zool. xiii, pt. ii, 15.—FLEM., Br. An. 52.—
  JENYNS, Man. 80.—SW. & RICH., F. B. Am. ii, 1831, 12.—BREHM, V. D. i, 21.—
  MACGIL., Hist. Br. B. iii, 204.—EYT., Cat. Br. B. 2.—BP., List, 1838, 2.—BENN.,
  Gard. Z. S. ii, 155, 151.—JARD., ed. Wils. ii, 304.—BAILL., Mem. Soc. Abbeville,
  1833, 56.—GOULD, B. Eur. pl. 6.—SW., Classif. B. ii, 207.—SYKES, P. Z. S. i, 79 ;
  J. A. S. B. iii, 419.—BLYTH, *ibid.* xix, 335.—GRAY, Gen. of B. i, 13, pl. 7, f. 1 ;
  Hand-list, i, 1869, 10, No. 87 ; List B. Br. Mus. 9 ; List Br. B. 3.—KEYS. & BLAS.,
  Wirb. Eur. 1840, 30.—SELBY, Br. B. i, 12, pl. 1, 1*, 2.—MUHLE, Orn. Griechl.
  20.—COUCH, Corn. Fn. 10.—JARD., Br. B. i, 165, pl. 12.—THOMPS., B. Irel. i, 1.—
  BP., Consp. i, 1850, 13.—SELYS-L., Fn. Belg. 52.—V. d. HOEV., Hdb. Dierk.
  812.—BONN., Ency. Meth. 4.—STRICKL., Orn. Syn. 1855, 55.—AUD., Syn. 1839,
  9 ; B. Am. i, 1840, 50, pl. 12.—CASS., Ill. 1854, 109.—BREW., N. A. O. 1857, 45.—
  MAXIM., J. f. O. vi, 1858, 9.—BLAS., Ber. xiv, Verz. Deut. Orn. 1862, 83.—ALLEN,
  Bull. M. C. Z. iii, 1872, 181.—COUES, Key, 1872, 219.
Aquila chrysaëtos var. *canadensis*, RIDGW.—B. B. & R., N. A. B. iii, 1874, 314.
Falco chrysaëtos, LINN., Syst. Nat. i, 1766, 125 ; Fn. Suec. 54.—GM., Syst. Nat. i, 1788,
  256.—LATH., Ind. Orn. i, 1790, 12.—SHAW, G. Z. vii, pl. 17.—DAUD., Tr. Orn. ii,
  1800, 46.—SELBY, Mem. Wern. Soc. iv, 428 ; Ill. Br. Orn. i, 4.—YARR., Br. B. i,
  7.—LUBB., Fn. Norf. 13.—AUD., Orn. Biog. ii, 464, pl. 181.
Aquila melanaëtus, BRISS., Orn. i, 434 (FRISCH, 69).—BREHM, V. D. i, 20.
Falco melanœëtos, LINN., Syst. Nat. i, 1766, 124.—GM., Syst. Nat. i, 1788, 254.—LATH.,
  Ind. Orn. i, 1790, 10.—DAUD., Tr. Orn. ii, 1800, 49.—SHAW, G. Z. vii, 174.
Aquila ——, BRISS., i, 419 ; whence—
Falco fulvus, LINN., Syst. Nat. i, 1766, 125.—GM., Syst. Nat. i, 1788, 256.—LATH., Ind.
  Orn. i, 1790, 10.—SHAW, G. Z. vii, 71.—WILS., Am. Orn. vii, 13, pl. 55, f. 1.—
  WILS., Mem. Wern. Soc. ii, 570 ; iv, 434.—CUV., R. A. 1st ed. i, 314 ; 2d ed. i,
  324.—SAVI., Descr. Egyp. i, 82.—NAUM., V. D. i, 1822, 208, pl. 8, 9.—TEMM.,
  Man. Orn. i, 38 ; iii, 19 ; Tab. Meth. 3.—BP., Syn. 1828, 24 ; Isis, 1832, 1136.—
  BAILL., Orn. Sav. i, 86.—NUTT., Man. i, 1832, 62.
Aquila fulva, MEYER, Taschenb. i, 24.—KAUP, Class. Säug. u. Vög. 121.—BREHM, V. D.
  i, 29.—SCHL., Rev. Crit. 6.—BP., Cat. Ucc. Eur. 18.—VIEILL., Fn. Franç. 7, pl·
  4, f. 1.—ROUX, Orn. Prov. i, 11, pl. 6.—KUHL, Beit. Zool. 7, 8.—TYZENH., R. Z.
  1846, 323.—PEAB., Rep. Orn. Mass. 1839, 71.
Falco fulvus var. b., *canadensis*, LINN., Syst. Nat. i, 1766, 125.—GM., Syst. Nat. i, 1788,
  256.—LATH., Ind. Orn. i, 1790, 11 (American).
Falco canadensis, LINN., Syst. Nat. i, 1758, 88.
Aquila canadensis, CASS., Baird's B. N. A. 41.—HEERM., P. R. R. Rep. x, 1859, pt. vi, 30.—
  COUES & PRENT., Smiths. Rep. 1861, 402.—COUES, Pr. Phila. Acad. 1866, 49.—
  COOP., B. Cal. i, 1870, 449.—DALL & BANN., Tr. Chic. Acad. 1869, 272.—SNOW,
  B. Kans. 1873 ; and of most late local American writers.
Falco niger, GM., Syst. Nat. i, 1788, 259.—DAUD., Tr. Orn. ii, 1800, 59.
Aquila alba, BRISS., i, 424 ; whence—
Falco albus, GM., Syst. Nat. i, 1788, 257 (*albino*).
Falco americanus, GM., Syst. Nat. i, 1788, 257 ?—LATH., Ind. Orn. i, 1790, 73 ?
Falco melanonotus, LATH., Ind. Orn. i, 1790, 16 (= *niger*, GM.).—SHAW, G. Z. vii, 86.
Falco cygneus, LATH., Ind. Orn. i, 1790, 14 (= *albus*, GM.).—SHAW, G. Z. vii, 76.
Falco aquila, DAUD., Tr. Orn. ii, 47.—BECHST., Taschenb. Deutsch.
Falco conciliator, SHAW, Gen. Zool. vii, 77.
Aquila regia, LESS., Tr. Orn. 36, pl. 8, f. 1.
Aquila nobilis, PALL., Zoog. R.-A. i, 1811, 338, pl. 8.
Aquila daphœnia, HODGS., Gray's Zool. Misc. 1844, 81 (India).
(?) *Aquila barthelemyi*, JAUB., R. M. Z. 1852, 22. See GURNEY, Ibis, 1864, 339.
  (Following are the bases of most of the above names : Golden Eagle, AUCT., *Grand
aigle*, P. E. 410 = *chrysœtos*. Black Eagle, AUCT., *Aigle noir*, BUFF., *Schwartz-braune
Adler*, FRISCH = *melanœtus*. Ring-tailed Eagle, AUCT., *Aigle commun*, P. E. 409 = *fulvus*.
White-tailed Eagle, EDW., i = *canadensis*. Black-backed Eagle, BROWN, Ill. 4, pl. 2 =
melanonotus, LATH. = *niger*, GM. White Eagle, LATH., Syn. i, 36 = *cygneus*, LATH. =
albus, GM. Royal Eagle = *regia*, Calumet Eagle, LEWIS & CLARKE, Trav. iii, 155.)

Hab.—North America northerly. South, ordinarily to about 35°. Europe. Asia.

List of specimens.

| 19124 | 200 | Deer Creek.. | .... | Nov. 22, 1859 | J. Stevenson... | 33.00 | 77.00 | 24.00 |

Although more particularly a species of boreal and alpine distribution, the Golden Eagle has an extensive dispersion in this country, greater than appears to be generally known, or, at least, recognized. It is of not infrequent and apparently regular occurrence in winter as far south, at least, as Washington, D. C., where, for several years, a specimen was taken almost every season, as already stated by Dr. Prentiss and myself. Several individuals, procured in the Washington market, are now in the Museum of the Smithsonian. Prof. Snow records its capture near Lawrence, Kansas, in January. Dr. Henry procured it at Fort Thorn, New Mexico, and I saw it in the mountains of Arizona. Mr. Allen observed it in Colorado, Wyoming, and Utah; and in California Dr. Cooper states that it is common in most parts of the State during the colder months. An account of its breeding on the Upper Missouri is given by Nuttall.

Dr. Brewer gives it as breeding in the mountainous portions of Maine, New Hampshire, Vermont, and New York, particularly instancing a nest at Franconia, New Hampshire, which was resorted to for several successive years. But its nidification is usually in such inaccessible situations, even when not in the most remote and uninhabitable regions, that its eggs were for a long time special desiderata. Even in 1857 Dr. Brewer had no American specimens for description. I have, therefore, more pleasure in describing them, from no less than a dozen examples now in the Smithsonian, where, through the liberality marking the attitude of that institution toward students of science, I have been able to examine them. The eggs are almost spherical, the degree of prolation being slight, and there being usually no appreciable difference in the shape of the opposite ends. Four selected specimens measure, respectively, 2.65 by 2.15; 2.90 by 2.40; 3.00 by 2.35; 3.10 by 2.25—figures illustrating both the difference in absolute size and the variation in shape. None are so large as the one said by Audubon to have been 3.50 by 2.50; but I can readily believe that such dimensions are sometimes reached. Among the twelve, only one is white and unmarked; this closely resembles a Bald Eagle's. The rest are whitish (white, shaded just perceptibly with neutral tint), variously spotted and splashed, without the slightest approach to uniformity in the size, number, or pattern of the markings. The color ranges from "bloody-brown" or rich sienna, to bistre and umber. There are many other spots, more or less obscure, and all apparently below the surface, showing grayish, drab, purplish, and neutral tint, by overlaying of the whitish calcareous matter in different thicknesses. Most of the markings are sharp-edged and distinct, but others shade off gradually, while many are confluent, making irregular patches. As a rule they are pretty evenly distributed, but in some specimens are chiefly gathered about one or the other end, where the coloration consequently becomes continuous.

HALIAËTUS LEUCOCEPHALUS, (Linn.) Sav.

White-headed Eagle; Bald Eagle.

Aquila leucocephalos, Briss., Orn. i, 1760, 423.—Vieill., Ois. Am. Sept. pl. 3.—Pall., Zoog. R. A. i, 1811, 347.—Sw., Classif. B. ii, 1837, 207.—Selys-L., Fn. Belg. 53.
Falco leucocephalus, Linn., Syst. Nat. i, 1766, 124 (*Aquila capite albo*, Cates., i, p. 1, pl. 1; *Aquila leucocephalos*, Briss., i, 423; *Aigle à tête blanche*, P. E. 411).—Gm., Syst. Nat. i, 1788, 255.—Lath., Ind. Orn. i, 1790, 11.—Shaw, G. Z. vii, 78.—Wils., Am. Orn. iv, 1812, 89, pl. 36, fig. -.—Bp., Syn. 1828, 26; Isis, 1832, 1136.—Nutt., Man i, 1832, 72.—Green, Am. Journ. Sci. iv, 89.—Aud., Orn. Biog. i, 1832, 160; ii, 1834, 160; v, 1839, 354; pls. 31, 126.—Brew., ed. Wils. 1840, 683.

24

Haliaëtus leucocephalus, SAVIG.—CUV., R. A. 2d ed. 326.—LESS., Tr. Orn. 40.—STEPH ,
Shaw's G. Z. xiii, pt. ii, 13.—BP., Comp. List, 1838, 3.—AUD., Syn. 1839, 10.—
AUD., B. Am. i, 1840, 57, pl. 14.—GIR., B. L. I. 1844, 9.—BP., Consp. i, 1850, 15.—
GRAY, Hand-list, i, 1869, 16, No. 145 (quotes *albicilla,* PALL.).—WOODH., Sitgr.
Rep. 1853, 59.—CASS., Ill. 1854, 111.—BREW., N. A. Oöl. 1857, 48.—CASS., B. N.
A. 1858, 43.—NEWB., P. R. R. Rep. vi, 1857, 75.—HEERM., *ibid.* x, 1859, pt. vi,
30.—COOP. & SUCK., N. H. Wash. Ter. 1860, 151.—DRESS., Ibis, 1865, 328.—
COUES, Pr Phila. Acad. 1866, 49.—DALL & BANN., Tr. Chic. Acad. 1869, 272.—
COOP., B Cal. i, 1870, 451.—TRIPPE, Pr. Ess. Inst. vi, 1871, 113.—ALLEN, Bull.
M. C. Z. ii, 1871, 333; iii, 1872, 181.—SNOW, B. Kans. 1873.—HOLD., Pr. Bost.
Soc. 1872, 207.—GILPIN, Am. Nat. vii, 1873, 429 (variation in tarsal scutella-
tion) —COUES, Key, 1872, 219.—DALL, Pr. Cal. Acad. Feb. 1873 (Aleutian
Islands).—B. B. & R., N. A. B. iii, 1874, 326; and of authors generally.
Aquila (Haliæëtus) leucocephala, SW. & RICH., F. B. A. ii, 1831, 15.
Falco pygargus, DAUD., Traité d' Orn. ii, 1800, 62 (*Le pygargue,* BUFF., i, 99).
Falco ossifragus, WILS., Am. Orn vii, 1815, 16, pl. 55, fig. 2 (juvenile).
Falco washingtoniana, AUD., London's Mag. i, 1828, 115.
Falco washingtonii, AUD., Orn. Biog. i, 1831, 58, pl. 11.—NUTT., Man. i, 1832, 67.—BREW.,
ed. Wils. 1840, 683.—JAMES., ed. Wils. iv, 261.
Haliaëtus washingtonii, BP., List, 1838, 3.—AUD., Syn. 1839, 10; B. Am. i, 1840, pl. 13.—
CASS., Ill. 1854, 110; B. N. A. 1858, 42; and of many writers, especially local.
(Examine particularly ALLEN, Bull. M. C. Z. ii, 1871, 334.)

Hab.—The whole of North America. Greenland. Casual in Europe (TEMM., Man. i,
25; GOULD, B. E. pl. 11; NAUM., Vog. pls. 344, 345).

Of frequent occurrence throughout the Missouri region, as elsewhere
in this country, although less numerous than in better watered, and
especially maritime, portions.

Breeds in suitable situations over the country at large, and resident,
except in the highest latitudes, whence the freezing of the waters forces
it to retire. Eggs dull white, unmarked, about 3 inches long by 2.50
broad.

From the circumstance that several years (at least three) are required
for the gaining of the perfect plumage, when the head and tail are entirely white, it follows that "Gray Eagles" and "Birds of Washington"
are much the more frequently met with. Those who, unpracticed in
ornithology, may be puzzled by accounts of numerous Eagles, may be
interested to know, that only *two* species have ever been found in the
United States. In any plumage they may be instantly distinguished
by the legs—feathered to the toes in *Aquila chrysaëtus,* naked on the
whole shank in *Haliaëtus leucocephalus.*

Before proceeding to an account of the Vultures, I will introduce a
notice of a vulture-like Hawk, not found in the Missouri region:

AUDUBON'S CARACARA.—POLYBORUS THARUS var. AUDUBONI, (*Cass.*) *Ridgw.*[*]

[*] The following is the synonymy of the two races of this species:

POLYBORUS THARUS, (*Molina*) Strickland.

Falco tharus, MOLINA, Chili, 1782, 234; French ed. 244.—GM., Syst. Nat. i, 1788, 254.—
LATH., Ind. Orn. i, 1790, 16.—SHAW, Gen. Zool. vii, 170.
Polyborus tharus, STRICKL., Orn. Syn. 1855, 18. (Not of *Cassin.*)
Polyborus tharus var. *tharus,* RIDGW.—B. B. & R., N. A. B. iii, 1874, 177.
Falco cheriway, JACQ., Beyt. 1784, 17, pl. 4.—GM., Syst. Nat. i, 1788, 254.—DAUD., Tr. ii, 42.
Vultur cheriway, LATH., Ind. Orn. i, 1790, 8.—SHAW, Gen. Zool. vii, 43.
Aquila cheriway, MEYEN, Nov. Act. Ak. Leop.-Carol. xvi, Suppl. p. 66.
Polyborus cheriway, SCHOMB., Guiana, 741.—NITZSCH, Pteryl. 89.—REINH., Vidd. Meddel.
1870, 64.
Falco plancus, MÜLL., Ill. pl. 17.—GM., Syst. Nat. i, 1788, 257.—DAUD., Tr. ii, 42.
Vultur plancus, LATH., Ind. Orn. i, 1790, 8.—SHAW, G. Z. vii, 41.—FORST., Descr. An. 321.
Falco brasiliensis, GM., Syst. Nat. i, 1788, 262.—LATH., Ind. Orn. i, 1790, 21.—SHAW, G.
Z. vii, 106.—DAUD., Tr. ii, 149.—MAXIM., Beit. iii, 190 (*Caracara,* AUCT.; *Circus
brasiliensis,* BRISS., i, 405).

We are not yet in position to define the geographical distribution of this variety with desirable precision. If, indeed, it were not different from the well-known bird of South America, the task would be easy; for it would be said to inhabit all of South and Central America, Mexico, parts of the West Indies, and thence to extend northward along the southern border of the United States, from one side of the republic to the other. But admitting a distinction, as recently claimed by Mr. Cassin (vide Pr. Acad. Nat. Sc. Phila. Jan. 1865, p. 2), between the United States' bird and that of regions more tropical, we have insufficient data for determination of the line along which the two varieties inosculate, as they certainly do somewhere, there being no considerable portions of country, from the southern boundaries of the United States to Cape Horn, where Caracaras are not to be found.

On the other hand, the distribution within our limits of the Vulture-eagle, or Eagle-vulture, has been accurately determined. Since its introduction into our fauna by Audubon (vide Orn. Biog. ii, p. 350, pl. 161, and B. Am. i, p. 21, pl. 4), who discovered it in Florida, it has been shown to occur thence to the Pacific coast. Thus, Mr. Wurdemann found it in Louisiana; Dr. Henry, in New Mexico; Dr. Heermann, in Arizona; Mr. Xantus, in Lower California; while almost every naturalist who has visited Texas has recorded its abundance in that State. Its northward extension is thus seen to be strictly limited; it may, in fact, be taken as a type of several subtropical species which, though known along our southern frontier, never penetrate much over the border. As a particular illustration of its general range, and in confirmation of the remark just made, we may cite its distribution in Arizona alone. There it is unknown in the northern, and even the central, mountainous regions, where the climate is temperate, but is common in the valleys of the Gila and Lower Colorado, and in the deserts of the southern portions of the Territory at large. One of the authors above mentioned has left us an interesting memorandum of his observations in this region. "I am happy," he remarks, "to be able to add this interesting species to the fauna of California, having seen it on the Colorado River, near Fort Yuma, in company with the *Cathartes aura*. The carrion of an ox

Circaëtus brasiliensis, Cuv., Règne Anim. 2d ed. i, 328.
Polyborus brasiliensis, Vig., Zool. Journ. i, 1824, 320, 336; iii, 434.—Sw., Phil. Mag. i, 1827, 366; Zool. Ill. ser. ii, pl. 2; Classif. B. ii, 1837, 209.—Bp., P. Z. S. v, 108.—Darw., Journ. Res. 64; Voy. Beag. iii, 9.—Bridges, P. Z. S. xi, 108; Ann. N. H. xiii, 499.—Gray, Gen. of B.; and of many authors, not of the United States.
Polyborus vulgaris, Spix, A. B. i, pl. 1ª.—Vieill., Gal. Ois, i, 23, pl. 7.— King, Voy. Beag. i, 532.— Vig., Zool. Voy. Beech. 15, pl. 7.—Bp., Consp. Av. i, 1850, 13.—Tschudi, Wieg. Arch. 1844, 3.
Caracara vulgaris, Less., Traité d'Orn. 34.
Pandion caracara, Griffith's Cuv. R. A. vi, 325.

Hab.—South America.

POLYBORUS THARUS var. AUDUBONI, (*Cassin*) *Ridgway*.

"(?) *Aquila maculosa*, Vieill., Ois. Am. Sept."
Polyborus vulgaris, Aud., Orn. Biog. ii, 1834, 350, pl. 161 (*nec Spix*).
Polyborus brasiliensis, Bp., List, 1838, 2.—Aud., Syn. 1839, 4; B. Am. i. 1840, 21, pl. 4.
Polyborus tharus, Cass., Ill. i, 1854, 113; Pr. A. N. S. 1855, 284; Baird's B. N. A. 1858, 45.—Brew., N. A. O. i, 1857, 58, pl. 11, figs. 18, 19.—Heerm., P. R. R. Rep. x, 1859, 31.—Scl., Ibis, i, 1859, 214 (Guatemala).—Owen, Ibis, iii, 67 (eggs).—Gurn., Cat. Rapt. B. 1864, 17.—Dress., Ibis, 1865, 329 (Texas).
Polyborus auduboni, Cass., Pr. A. N. S. 1865, 2.—Coues, ibid. 1866, 49 (Arizona).—Lawr., Ann. Lyc. N. Y. ix, 1868, 132 (Costa Rica); ibid. ix, 1869, 207 (Yucatan).—Coop., B. Cal. i, 1870, 492 (California).—Ridgw., Pr. A. N. S. 1870, 145.
Polyborus tharus var. *auduboni*, Coues, Key, 1872, 220.—B. B. & R., N. A. B. iii, 1874, 178.

Hab.—Middle America. North to the southern border of the United States. Cuba (Cab., J. f. O. ii, lxxix; Gundl., Repert. 1865, 221). (?) Trinidad (Taylor, Ibis, 1864, 79).

was covered with Turkey Buzzards, and one specimen of the Caracara Eagle was among them; but it proved so shy that I could not shoot it, although waiting in ambush fully two hours in hopes it would return. We followed this species on our survey down the Gila until we left that river, seeing one or more every day, and found it again in Texas on striking the settlements. At San Antonio, in the vicinity of slaughter-houses, it is met with in great numbers, twenty or thirty often being seen at one time. We found its nest on the Medina River, built in an oak, of coarse twigs, and lined with leaves and roots; being recently finished, it contained no eggs."

This statement in respect of the nidification of the Caracara is confirmed by other naturalists, though it may not hold good in every instance. We should rather have anticipated that it would have been found to breed on rocks, fallen logs, the ground, &c., after the fashion of Vultures. According to the distinguished naturalist, Mr. Charles Darwin, the South American bird occasionally breeds on a low cliff, or on a bush, thus evincing its vulturine affinities; and it is not to be presumed that there is any striking and constant difference in this regard between the United States and the more tropical forms of the Caracara. The situation of the nest doubtless varies with circumstances; thus, I have seen a memorandum from Mr. Xantus, stating that a nest he found at Cape Saint Lucas was placed on the top of a giant cactus. But wherever situated, the nests, like those of most *Raptores*, is a rude structure, compared with the elaborately planned and elegantly finished structures of many higher birds, being little more than a slightly hollowed platform of small sticks and twigs, lined with somewhat softer material, as dried rushes, grasses, and leaves.

It is possible, though improbable, that oölogy may eventually throw more light upon the supposed distinctions between the two forms of the *Caracara*. So Dr. Brewer intimates, in an article prepared before Mr. Cassin established *P. auduboni*. "Mr. Cassin informs me," he continues, "that his suspicions have been excited by certain variations in specimens that have fallen under his notice, and Mr. Darwin states that he met with individuals on the plains of Santa Cruz, which he and Mr. Gould were almost persuaded to be distinct species. In partial confirmation of this suspicion, I may in this connection refer to the great variations noticeable in the eggs of the Vulturine Eagle. These are neither slight nor occasional, but are constant and of so radical a character as to excite the strongest doubts of their belonging to birds of the same species, the differences affecting both their size and their ground-color. The eggs from Cuba, so far as I am aware, represent one variety exclusively, those from Brazil the other, while on the other hand, both varieties were obtained on the Rio Grande by Dr. Berlandier, who assigns them to a single species, which, in his manuscript notes, he called *Totache*." The Brazilian specimens referred to were of course of the true "*Carrancha*," as *P. tharus* is called in South America; the Cuban ones were probably those of *P. auduboni;* and the fact that both sorts were got in Mexico may serve in investigating the limits of the two birds.

In examining a large number of eggs from different localities, I found differences in size, shape, and color, to be fairly called remarkable, but still not unparalleled, I think, by those known to occur in other cases of unquestionably the same species of rapacious birds; nor did I recognize any division of the series into two distinct sets. I think it would be easy to lay them all in a row in such manner that extremes in any respect should be connected by intermediate examples. In studying these eggs, however, I was made aware of one interesting fact, namely, that some are ellipsoidal, or prolately spheroidal, having both ends of the same size and shape, while others (the greater number) are truly ovoidal, in the sense that one extremity is narrower and more pointed than the other, and that the greatest diameter consequently lies nearer one end than the other.

The eggs measure on an average a little less than $2\frac{1}{2}$ inches in length, by a little more than $1\frac{3}{4}$ in breadth; thus, one specimen was exactly 2.40 by 1.80; so much is easily affirmed. It is a difficult matter to describe the markings. Some eggs are white, almost uniform, or with numerous dots and fine points of brown evenly scattered over all the surface; others are wholly of a deep, rich, warm brown, the uniformity of which is scarcely relieved, and only by a slightly paler or darker clouding in some places. These are extremes, between which most specimens are intermediate, ranging through every degree of blotching and splashing, with various shades of dark brown upon a pale brown, buffy, fulvous, or tawny ground. The shade of these different browns varies from light sienna, almost golden or russet, to a deep red, almost blackish. Some of the most beautiful specimens are those without blotches, but artistically clouded with indeterminate hues. The various markings generally tend to aggregate together and deepen in shade around the larger end.

Audubon's biography of this species, and Heermann's noticeably similar account, present the predominant traits of the bird's character. It is nearly a Vulture, in almost every respect of mind, body, and— egg; approaching, in fact, those obscene birds so closely, that some have entertained doubts of its proper location among *Falconidæ*. It surpasses Harris' Buzzard, a not distant ally, in those traits of mind and conditions of body that develope to a maximum among *Vulturidæ*. There is a naked space on the breast, and partial denudation about the sides of the head near the bill; the tibial feathers are short, not flowing; the scutellation of the tarsus is peculiar, and there is considerable webbing between the toes. The bird is a dullard; spiritless and unambitious; it walks and leaps like a Turkey Buzzard, and stands, like that species, with its wings half spread toward the sun; its motions are sluggish and unattractive, its attitudes slouchy and negligent; finally, it feeds on carrion, and its body exhales bad odors. Altogether, this species is a rather difficult subject for the systematic naturalist, especially viewing the fact that in some structural points it comes nearest the typical Falcons.

Family CATHARTIDÆ: American Vultures.

The American Vultures are so remarkably distinguished from those of the Old World, that they should properly constitute a family apart. They are more sluggish birds, with little or none of the spirit that allies the true Vultures (*Vulturinæ*) with the typical birds of prey. The external characters, as well as those to be drawn from the internal structure, are notably different. Prominent among the former is the elevation of the hind toe above the level of the rest, betokening an interesting analogy, if not actual affinity, with the gallinaceous birds; and there is something in the general aspect of our commonest species that has given it the name of *Turkey* Buzzard. The claws are weak; the anterior toes long, with a web at their bases. The nostrils are very large and pervious, whereas those of the true Vultures are separated by an impervious septum; this is a difference probably related to the car-rion-feeding habits of our species, and believed by some to be intended to facilitate the freeing of the nostrils from the foul decomposing sub-stances in which the bird's beak is often plunged. The feathers lack aftershafts, and the oil-gland upon the rump has no circlet of feathers; these are both present in a majority of *Raptores*. There are numer-ous important anatomical, and especially osteological differences, but I will only mention one; the lower larynx is undeveloped, and as a con-sequence our birds are mute; their only voice is a curious hissing sound, apparently formed in the mouth, not in the windpipe.

It was long supposed, by savans as well as by those who might not be expected to know better, that Vultures were chiefly guided to their prey by scent; a belief that probably arose from consideration of the size of their nostrils, and the very "gamey" nature of their usual food. One of the first problems that occupied the attention of Audubon was to discover whether the birds relied mainly on sight or smell. He made a series of careful experiments, the results of which he laid before the Wernerian Society of Edinburgh, December 16, 1826, in what he called his "maiden speech," and has given a half-humorous account of the feelings with which he attempted, on that, to him, momentous occasion, to demolish the then existing beliefs, and establish the truth of what is now generally admitted—that Vultures are chiefly guided by their pierc-ing eye-sight. Another absurd belief was, and perhaps still is, that Vultures prefer putrid flesh; in support of which one might point to a group of Turkey Buzzards perched around a carcass, awaiting its de-composition. But the reason is that their beaks and claws are not strong enough to tear sound hide; they can only attack a fresh carcass at the eyes, nostrils, and vent, and when these parts are demolished, must wait until putrescence is established, or until some carnivorous bird or quadruped makes an opening.

Although the *Cathartidæ* are indolent, cowardly birds, they some-times—particularly the larger kinds—when pressed for food, attack live animals, especially sick or disabled ones, and generally overpower them in the end. Young pigs and lambs are sometimes killed by the Turkey Buzzard, which is only of medium size. But in this connection it should be remarked, that whatever damage they may thus effect is far out-weighed by their good offices as scavengers in clearing away garbage and offal. This is the true place of these foul and unseemly birds in nature's economy; they have the beauty of utility, if no other; and their usefulness is recognized in all warm countries, where they are encouraged in their familiarity with man, and rightly regarded as pub-lic benefactors.

Curious ornithologists have gone so far as to try the flavor of almost every bird. Among those not ordinarily used for food, and which are comparatively unsavory though not positively bad, may be reckoned most of the cleaner sorts of rapacious birds. Thus a young Hawk is passably good, though I believe that some such quality as that which suggested the saying, "tough as a boiled Owl," renders in the whole order. Crows and Ravens fall in the same category; so do most of the water-birds below the true wild-fowl, such as Pelicans, Cormorants, Gannetts, Gulls, Loons, and others that feed upon fish. But Vulture-meat is certainly not to be thought of. One would think that the great Israelitic law-giver hardly had need to interdict it, as he did however: "Of all clean birds ye shall eat. But these are they of which ye shall not eat: the Eagle and the Ossifrage, and the Osprey, and the Glede, and the Kite, and the Vulture after his kind." As a more modern author has remarked, " we presume this prohibition was religiously observed, so far, at least, as it related to the Vultures, from whose flesh there arises such an unsavory odor, that we question if all the sweetening processes ever invented could render it palatable to Jew, Pagan, or Christian." Certain it is, that independent of the passing contents of the alimentary canal, permanent fœtid, musky odors, exhale from the bones and muscles ; and the same stench is entangled in the web of feathers. It is retained for a long while even after the bird is killed and stuffed. So strong is it, that one author, an excellent naturalist, too, fancied it must be rather unpleasant to the birds themselves! Thus Pennant, speaking of the Vulture's habit of basking in the sun, with half-opened, drooping wings, supposed that this was done " to purify their bodies, which are most unpleasantly fœtid," as he naively remarks. It is somewhat to be wondered that, when Audubon's experiments came up, no person of an ingenious and inquiring turn advanced a theory why Vultures were deprived of the sense of smell; reasoning that if their olfactories were acute they could not bring themselves to eat carrion, and that moreover they would be continually unhappy in the noxious atmosphere emanating from their own bodies; in short, that a merciful Creator had so arranged that they might not smell themselves !

This would be about one with some of the stories that used to pass current, and not rarely found their way into books when ornithology was younger. Buffon is responsible for much absurdity of this sort. With a vivid imagination he could make, when he could not find, a way to write bird-histories; and his stories were never spoiled in the telling for want of ready language. He had, moreover, a supply of preconceived ideas regarding the habits of birds that stood him in good stead of observation, and made him a facile expounder of the way birds ought to live, if less successful in telling how they do live. Among other notions of his, a favorite one seems to have been, that American birds were apt to be found degenerate mongrels of better-breed European stock. But he has been for this and similar things already so often taken to task, that we may, without comment, give his picture of Vultures, and allow others to decide upon its faithfulness. " In every part of the globe," says Buffon, " they are voracious, slothful, offensive, and hateful ; and, like the wolves, are as noxious during their life as they are useless after death."

One excellent service that the Turkey Vultures render in warm countries, is the destruction of alligators' eggs. This was referred to over a century ago (in 1752) by Don Ulloa, whose remarks, as rendered by Mr. Ord, may be here transcribed :

"The Gallinazos are enemies of the alligators, and employ much stratagem to obtain them. During the summer the birds make it their business to watch the female alligators, for it is at that season that they deposit their eggs in the sand of the shores of the rivers which are not then overflowed. The Gallinazo conceals itself among the branches and leaves of a tree, so as to be unperceived by the alligator, and permits the eggs quietly to be laid, not even interrupting the pains she takes to conceal them. But she is no sooner under the water than the Gallinazo darts upon the nest, and with its bill, claws and wings, uncovers the eggs and gobbles them down, leaving nothing but the shells. This banquet would indeed richly reward its patience, did not a multitude of Gallinazos join the discoverer and share in the spoil."

This author has been criticised for his assertion that the Black Vultures attack live animals ; his account has been called " too improbable to merit serious refutation;" but we see nothing improbable in it. "When the Gallinazos are deprived of carrion," he says, "they are driven by hunger among the cattle of the pastures. If they see a beast with a sore on its back, they alight on it and attack the part affected; and it avails not that the poor animal throws itself on the ground and endeavors to intimidate them by its bellowing; they do not quit their hold, and by means of their bill they so enlarge the wound that the animal finally becomes their prey." It is well attested that Ravens, and even Magpies, during seasons of scarcity, alight on sore-backed animals to pick at the raw flesh and torture the creatures, if they do not actually destroy them.

The Condor of the Andes (*Sarcorhamphus gryphus*) is one of the largest, and otherwise the most distinguished, species of American Vultures. It has been attributed by Bonaparte and Nuttall to the United States, but the evidence is not good. They seemed to have relied upon the statements of Lewis and Clarke, which undoubtedly related to the Californian Vulture, not the Condor. Yet it is probable that we have a true *Sarcorhamphus* in this country, in addition to the three species of *Cathartes*. I have collected some information upon these points that I cannot refrain from presenting. We have first to notice the Sacred Vulture of Bartram (*Vultur sacra*), described by this author in his "Travels in Florida" (p. 150):

"The bill is long and straight, almost to the point, where it is hooked or bent suddenly down, and sharp; the head and neck bare of feathers nearly down to the stomach, where the feathers begin to cover the skin, and soon become long and of a soft texture, forming a ruff or tippet, in which the bird, by contracting his neck, can hide that as well as his head; the bare skin on the neck appears loose and wrinkled, which is of a bright-yellow color, intermixed with coral red; the hinder part of the neck is nearly covered with short, stiff hair, and the skin of this part of the neck is of a dun-purple color, gradually becoming red as it approaches the yellow of the sides of the forepart. The crown of the head is red; there are lobed lappets of a reddish-orange color, which lay on the base of the upper mandible. The plumage of the bird is generally white or cream color, except the quill-feathers of the wings and two or three rows of coverts, which are beautiful dark brown; the tail, which is rather large and white, is tipped with this dark brown or black; the legs and feet are of a clear white; the eye is encircled with a gold-colored iris, the pupil black." As Mr. Allen has remarked, in carefully reviewing the subject, this is probably a mythical species, some facts in connection with *Haliaëtus leucocephalus* and *Polyborus tharus* being mixed in Bartram's mind with some of his ideas respecting the King Vulture.

The King Vulture (*Sarcorhamphus papa*) is a well-known inhabitant of the warm parts of America, and has also been attributed to the United States; but accounts of its occurrence within our limits require confirmation. Nuttall gave it in his Manual (i, p. 40), but so he did, also, several other birds that we know are not found in our country. Still it is a Mexican species, that may stray into Texas, Arizona, or Southern California. I am, in fact, convinced that this, or a closely-allied species, does occur in Arizona—a large Vulture, not the Condor, nor the Californian, nor yet any of the smaller species of *Cathartes*. As the determination is a matter of prime consequence, I may be allowed to present the following considerations:

In Dr. Brewer's edition of Wilson (p. 671) the following extract is made from Clavijero's History of Mexico (Cullen's translation), i, p. 47: "The business of clearing the fields of Mexico is reserved principally for the *Zopilots*, known in South America by the name of *Gallinazzi;* in other places by that of *Aure;* and in some places, though very improperly, by that of *Ravens*. There are two different species of these birds—the one, the Zopilot, properly so called; the other, called Cozcaquanhtli; they are both bigger than the Raven. These two species resemble each other in their hooked bill and crooked claws, and by having upon their head, instead of feathers, a wrinkled membrane with some curly hairs. * * * * The two species are distinguished, however, by their size, their color, their numbers, and some other peculiarities. The Zopilots, properly so called, have black feathers, with a brown bill and feet; they go often in flocks, and roost together upon trees. This species is very numerous, and is to be found in all the different climates; while, on the contrary, the Cozcaquanhtli is far from numerous, and is peculiar to the warmer climates alone. The latter bird is larger than the Zopilot, has a red head and feet, with a beak of a deep-red color, except toward its extremity, which is white. Its feathers are brown, except on the parts about the breast, which are of a reddish-black. The wings are of an ash color upon the inside, upon the outside are variegated with black and tawny. The Cozcaquanhtli is called by the Mexicans King of the Zopilots," &c.

The "Zopilot" above mentioned is undoubtedly the Black Vulture (*C. atratus*), or some small, closely allied, species; while the "Cozcaquanhtli" is certainly the common Turkey Buzzard (*C. aura*). The paragraph is introduced to show what names these birds bore with the old authors; and particularly, that the Turkey Buzzard used to be called "King of the Zopilots." What the King Vulture really is, may presently appear. Mr. A. S. Taylor, in an article in the San Francisco Herald for April —, 1859, gives the following, also from the Abbé Clavijero's work, but interpolated and differently worded:

"The Cozqualitle is called by the Mexicans of the city and valley of Mexico the King of the Topilotés; * * * * and they say that when the two species happen to meet together, over the same carrion, the Topiloté * * * * never begins to eat until the other has tasted it. * * * * The King of the Topilotés has a red head and feet [&c.; the same as the above description]. Bonaré says that the *Aura* (pronounced Owra, for the Turkey Buzzard, by the Mexicans) is the *Cosquath* of New Spain and the *Tropilot* of the Indians, so that *Cozcaquanhtli* and *Tropilotl* are both native Mexican-Indian names for two different birds. But the bird that now goes by the name of the King of the Topilotés in New Spain, seems different from the one we are describing. This is a strong bird, of the size of a common Eagle, with stately air, strong claws, fine piercing eyes, and a beautiful *black, white, and tawny plumage*. It is remarkable, particularly, for a certain scarlet-colored fleshy substance which surrounds the neck like a collar, and comes over its head in the form of a little crown." * * * *

The above mentioned Vulture, "with a beautiful black, white, and tawny plumage," is the one we wish to determine. It is evidently no *Cathartes;* apparently a *Sarcorhamphus;* and perhaps the same bird that formed the subject of a note I gave on page 16 of my Prodrome of the Ornithology of Arizona, to the following effect: While encamped on the San Francisco River, near the mountains of the same name, in July, 1865, I saw a pair of very large rapacious birds sail over head with firm, easy, graceful flight, sustained for a long time without visible motion of the wings. They were about the size of Bald Eagles, but the shape of the wings and its mode of flight were those of Vultures. The entire under parts were *pure white*. I gazed with admiration, yet with a feeling of bitter disappointment, as the majestic birds disappeared in the distance, and with them went the opportunity of identifying them, marring the pleasure I experienced at being the first to observe the unquestionable occurrence within our limits of some Vulture, probably a *Sarcorhampus*, not recognized as an inhabitant of our country. I cannot now refer the birds to any species known to me, unless, possibly, they were *S. papa;* but this is tawny or fulvous below, not white. I desire to signalize the occurrence the more particularly, since the birds may have been of a species unknown to naturalists.

I cannot close this account without giving insertion to an article by Mr. A. S. Taylor, that appeared in the San Francisco Herald for April —, 1859. It is quite worthy of being rescued from its precarious situation in floating literature. I copy the account (somewhat abbreviated) without further comment, merely premising that, of course, there is some mistake about the "four wings":

"*The Queleli, a rare bird of Sonora.*—From the descriptions of some of our friends we are placed in possession of some curious facts relating to the habits and characteristics of this rare and highly curious bird. An intelligent Sonoraian of Oquitoa, near Alta, in Sonora, who resided in California several years, gave me the following facts at Monterey, in 1855. It inhabits particularly the Pimeria Alta and Baja, the Papagoria, the Optaria, the Apacharia, and other Indian and little-known mountain districts of Sonora, Durango, and Sinaloa to the east and south. It is called "Queleli" by the Indians, who have a great veneration for it. Its weight is from 8 to 10 lbs. The beak is hard and curved sharply down; its color, bright lemon; the iris is pink or light red. On the crown of the head it has a fleshy caruncle or comb of black and white, which forms like a cravat, and also hangs on both sides of the head, and which is bare of feathers. The skin of the chops and cheeks is mottled black and white; the neck feathers are black, with a ring of white feathers below, forming a ruff, like a circle of swan's-down on a lady's tippet; the back is striped black and white lengthwise of the bird; the ends of the wing-feathers are tipped with white; the tail feathers are striped and tipped the same as the wings; the under surfaces of the wings are barred in the same way; the wings measure from 12 to 18 inches long from the joint at the body [qu. carpus?]; the chest, belly, and lower part of the body are of lemon-colored feathers; the legs and feet are also yellow, with four toes, armed with black and very sharp claws. The female bird is of smaller size, the colors similar, but more subdued. The eggs are reddish [?] and mottled black, sharply peaked, and weigh about 2 ounces. They make their nests in the highest trees of the mountain sides and peaks, and always go in couples, and never in flocks. When they rise from the ground they make a whirring, rushing noise, moving very fast. They raise two young in a year, generally male and female; when young the plumage is yellow, black, and white. The full-grown birds are about the size of the common Turkey Buzzard. They are seen at times turning over and over in the air, in quick motions, whence the Indians have a superstition that they breed in the air. The Indians also say that the male bird breaks the egg to let the chick out. They eat dead animals, or those lately killed. The tongue is red, and has a spinous process on the under part shaped like a pen, said by the Indians to be used in making a loud whirring noise when it rises from the ground. They eat very fast, and all other carnivorous birds hold them in great fear. My informant says it is most abundant in the Alta Pimeria, of which the Gadsden purchase forms a portion. [This is now in Arizona; and compare, also, the colors of the birds as above given with those of the ones I saw; also, the facts of the young in pairs, &c.]

"But the most singular part of this bird, and which makes it such a wonder among the Sonoranians, is that it has *four wings*, or appendages for assisting flight on each side of its body; that is, a pair of wings such as other birds', each with three assistant wings or winglets, joined to the main ones, and folding under the main ones, next to the body.

"An officer of the revenue-service assured me that he had seen this bird at Guaymas in 1854, in possession of Captain Spence of that port, and that, according to his recollection, my Sonoranian informant was in the main correct. It seems to me there can be no doubt that it is a *rara avis* unknown to naturalists. A gentleman now living in Monterey, who is, like the writer, an amateur naturalist, assures me, also, that he saw a bird of this kind in Guaymas—most likely the same one—in the possession of Captain Spence, or some other foreigner there."

Mr. Taylor further states that, according to this last informant, the number of "winglets" on each side was three, not four; and their position is more particularly described. He devotes the remainder of the article to proving that the "Queleli" cannot be the small Mexican Vulture called King of the Topilotés, nor the King Vulture, nor the Sacred Vulture of Bartram.

Leaving now these uncertainties, however interesting, for something more definite, and confining attention to the genus *Cathartes*, it is to be observed that of the six or seven described species, several are not permanently distinct. The three of the United States, *C. atratus*, *C. aura* and *C. californianus*, with the South American *C. burrovianus*, are the only recognizable ones. Of these, at present, we have only to do with the following:

CATHARTES AURA, (Linn.) Ill.

Turkey Buzzard.

Vultur aura, LINN.. Syst. Nat. i, 1766, 122 (based on *Tzopilotl*, HERNAND., 331; *Urubu*, MARCG., 207; *Vultur brasiliensis*, BRISS., i, 468; *Buteo specie gallo-pavonis*, CATES., i, 6).—GM., Syst. Nat. i, 1788, 246.—LATH., Ind. Orn. i, 1790, 4.— BARTR., Trav. 1793, 285.—VIEILL., Ois. Am. Sept. i, 1807, 25; pl. 2, *bis*.—SHAW, Gen. Zool. vii, 1809, 36.—WILS., Am. Orn. ix, 1814, 96, pl. 75, f. 1.—LICHT., Verz. 1823, 63.—AUD., Edin. New Phil. Journ. ii, 172.—DARW., Journ. Res. 68.— WAGL., Isis, 1831, 517.—SELLS, P. Z. S. v, 33; Mag. Nat. Hist. 2d ser. i, 638.
Cathartes aura, ILL., Prod. 1811, 236.—CUV., R. A. i, 2d ed. 317.—SPIX, Av. Bras. i, 1825, 2.—VIG., Zool. Journ. ii, 384.—LESS., Man. i, 1828, 73; Tr. Orn. 1831, 28.—BP., Syn. 1828, 22; Isis, 1832, 1135.—MAXIM., Beit. iii, 1830, 64.—JARD., ed. Wils. iii, 226.—JAMES., ed. Wils. i, 3; iv, 245.—Sw. & RICH., F. B. A. ii, 1831, 4 (Saskatchewan).—NUTT., Man. i, 1832, 43.—Sw., Classif. B. ii, 1837, 205—AUD., Orn. Biog. ii, 1835, 296; v, 1839, 339; pl. 151; Syn. 1839, 3; B. Am. i, 1840, 15, pl. 2.—BP., List, 1838, 1; Consp. 1850, 9.—D'ORBIG., La Sagra's Cuba, 1839, 4; Voy. Am. Mérid. iv, 38.—SCHOMB., Guiana, 1840, 742.—BREW., ed. Wils. 682.— LINSL., Am. Journ. xliv, 1843, 250 (Connecticut).—DEKAY, N. Y. Zool. 1844, 2, pl. 5, f. 12.—TSCHUDI, Wieg. Arch. 1844, 262; Fn. Peru, 71.—GRAY, List B. Br. Mus. 1844, 3; Gen. of B. i, 1844, 1.—GOSSE, B. Jam. 1847, 1.—PEALE, U. S. Expl. Exped. 1848, 58.—WOODH., Sitgr. Rep. 1853, 58 (Indian Territory; New Mexico).—CASS., Ill. 1854, 57.—BREW., N. A. Oöl. 1857, 1.—NEWB., P. R. R. Rep. vi, 1857, 73.—CASS., B. N. A. 1858, 4; Pr. A. N. S. 1849, 159.—MAXIM., J. f. O. vi, 1858, 2.—HEERM., P. R. R. Rep. x, pt. vi, 59.—SCL., Ibis, i, 1859, 213 (Guatemala).— BRYANT, Pr. Bost. Soc. vii, 1859 (Bahamas).—SCL., P. Z. S. 1860, 287 (Ecuador); Ibis, ii, 1860, 222 (Honduras).—TAYL., Ibis, 1864, 78 (Trinidad).—COOP. & SUCK., N. H. Wash. Ter. 1860, 140.—HAYD., Rep. 1862, 151.—DRESS., Ibis, 1865, 322 (Texas).—COUES, Pr. Phila. Acad. 1866, 42 (Arizona).—KENN., Tr. Ill. Agric. Soc. i, 580 (breeding).—COUES & PRENT., Smiths. Rep. 1861, 401 (resident at Washington, D. C.).—WHEAT., Ohio Agric. Rep. 1860, No. 1.—BOARDM., Pr. Bost. Soc. ix, 1862, 122 (Calais, Me.; one instance).—VERR., Pr. Ess. Inst.

iii, 1862, 157 (same instance).—SAM., App. Secy's. Rep. Agric. Mass. 1863, p.
xviii (Massachusetts; two instances).—ALLEN, Pr. Ess. Inst. iv, 1864, 81 (same
instances).—GURN., Cat. Rapt. B. 1864, 42.—DRESS., Ibis, 1865, 322 (Texas).—
GUNDL., Rep. 1865, 221 (Cuba).—COUES, Pr. Ess. Inst. v, 1868, 253 (New England
instances).—MCILWR., Pr. Ess. Inst. v, 1866, 80 (Canada West).—LAWR., Ann.
Lyc. N. Y. viii, 1866, 280 (New York).—SCL., P. Z. S. 1867, 589 (Para); 1868,
569 (Peru).—COUES, Pr. Bost. Soc. 1868, 120 (South Carolina).—PELZ., Orn.
Bras. i, 1868, p. —.—ALLEN, Mem. Bost. Soc. i, 1868, 499, 526 (Iowa, and resi-
dent in Indiana).—TURNB., B. E. Pa. 1869, 5 (resident).—REINH., Vid. Med.
1870, 61 (Brazil).—COUES, Pr. Phila. Acad. 1871, 27 (North Carolina).—TRIPPE,
Pr. Ess. Inst. vi, 1871, 113 (Minnesota, breeding, and in December).—ALLEN,
Bull. M. C. Z. ii, 1871, 310 (critical); iii, 1872, 181 (Florida, Kansas, Colorado,
Wyoming, Utah).—COOP., B. Cal. i, 1870, 502.—SNOW, B. Kans. 1873.—COUES,
Key, 1872, 222.—SCOTT, Pr. Bost. Soc. xv, 1872, 229 (West Virginia).

Catharista aura, VIEILL., Gal. Ois. 1825, pl. 4.—GRAY, Hand-list, i, 1869, 3, No. 18.
Percnopterus aura, STEPH., Gen. Zool. xiii, pt. ii, 1826, 7.
Rhinogryphus aura, RIDGW.—B. B. & R., N. A. B. iii, 1874, 344.
Vultur aura, β, LATH., Ind. Orn. i, 1790, 5.
Vultur iota, MOLINA, Stor. Chili, 1782, 265.—GM., Syst. Nat. i, 1788, 247.—DAUD., Tr.
Orn. ii, 1800, 20.
Cathartes iota, BRIDG., P. Z. S. ix, 108; Ann. Nat. Hist. xiii, 498.
Cathartes ruficollis, SPIX, Av. Bras. i, 1824, 2 (quotes CATESBY).
Cathartes septentrionalis, MAXIM., Reise, i, 1839, 162.
(?) *Cathartes falklandicus*, SHARPE, Ann. Mag. Nat. Hist.

Hab.—The whole of the United States and adjoining British Possessions. South
through Central and most of South America. Much confusion has prevailed in use of
the names *aura* and *iota*, notwithstanding the perfectly distinct (perhaps even generically different) characters of the two species—a difficulty which the labors of Mr. Allen
and Mr. Ridgway have done much to remove. It is believed that the synonymy as
here collated, based upon the authors just named, as well as substantially upon Strickland's prior lists, is correct. It should be observed, that *aura* of earlier authors apparently included both species.

Lieutenant Warren's Expedition.—4603, Cedar Island, Missouri River.

Although more particularly an inhabitant of the warmer parts of
America, and most numerous in the Southern States, along with the
Black Vulture (*C. atratus*), the Turkey Buzzard is nevertheless found all
over the United States, and a little way into British America. On the
Atlantic coast its ordinary limit is Long Island; Audubon's data were
incomplete in rendering his statement that it is never seen beyond New
Jersey. It has been repeatedly observed in Southern New England,
and at least once in Maine. Its Nova Scotia record, as remarked by
Dr. Brewer, is vague and probably unfounded; and even its New England occurrences are rare, if not altogether casual. It is included in
Mr. McIlwraith's list of the birds of Hamilton, Canada West, with the
remark that it is a regular summer visitor to the extensive flats near
Chatham, and along the shores of Lake Saint Clair. In the interior, it
regularly goes further north than on the coast. Mr. Trippe found it
abundant in Minnesota, where it breeds; and Sir John Richardson's
well-known record fixes its northern limit at about latitude 53° in the
region of the Saskatchewan, where it arrives in June. The highest
point where I ever saw it myself, up to the date of present writing, was
Fort Randall, latitude 43° 11', on the Missouri. At the close of the
most terrific storm of the season of 1872–'73, memorable for its severity,
five or six birds came sailing over the fort. This was on the 15th of
April; none had been observed previously after October, and I do not
think it usually passes the inclement season at this point.

This brings us to consider the resident range of the species, as compared with its summer dispersion. It has not been observed to winter
on the Atlantic beyond New Jersey, and even in that State is more
numerous in summer than in winter. But at Washington, D. C., my
home for a number of years, where the bird is very common, I noticed
no material diminution of its numbers during the colder months. The

same is the case in both the Carolinas, where I constantly observed it during a residence of three or four years. In the interior it appears to winter higher up; thus, Mr. Trippe saw it late in October, and again in December, in Minnesota. But the last may have been an unusual occurrence; probably the parallel of 40°, or rather the isothermal corresponding to this latitude on the Atlantic coast may approximately indicate the line of its northernmost winter residence.

As is well known, the distribution of the Black Vulture, or Carrion Crow, is much more restricted than that of the Turkey Buzzard. It may not be amiss to compare the two, especially since some wholly unfounded reports are current. The most notable of these is the record, in the Fauna Boreali-Americana, of the Black Vulture's abundance in the Columbia River region and elsewhere west of the Rocky Mountains. But this rests entirely upon the statements of Mr. David Douglas, who unquestionably mistook Turkey Buzzards for Black Vultures. The fact is, that there is not a single authentic instance of the occurrence of the latter on the Pacific coast of the United States, nor anywhere west of the Rocky Mountains in this country. As Dr. Cooper suggests, in explanation of the statements of even so reliable an observer as Dr. Gambel, the *young* of the Turkey Buzzard, before acquiring the red head, may have been mistaken for the Black Vulture; and he entirely discredits the Pacific records. For the interior we have the authority of Dr. Woodhouse, which there seems to be no reason to question in this instance, for the occurrence of the Black Vulture in the Creek and Cherokee countries, and less numerously in New Mexico. Up the Mississippi Valley, it is stated to occur as far as Illinois. I find no instance of its presence in the region of the Missouri or any of its tributaries, so that I cannot formally introduce it in this work; but I should not be surprised if it were hereafter shown to occur about the mouth of the Missouri. On the Atlantic, Mr. Audubon states, it has been found as far north as Maryland, and there are several authentic instances of its straggling even into New England. But its ordinary limit is, probably, the vicinity of Wilmington, North Carolina; certainly, at most, not beyond the maritime portions of Virginia. I never saw it at Washington, D. C.; the furthest point I have traced it to being Newberne, North Carolina. At Fort Macon, on the North Carolina coast, opposite Beaufort, it regularly occurs every summer; and I once saw numbers in March at that locality (Pr. Phila. Acad. 1871, 28). But even here they are far outnumbered by the Turkey Buzzards, and it is not until we reach Charleston, South Carolina, that the reverse proportion of individuals of the two species is witnessed. They are moreover especially maritime; for, even in South Carolina, as we recede from the coast, they become less numerous, until at Columbia, South Carolina, the Turkey Buzzards are again the more plentiful of the two. In this city both species reside all the year.

No one can fail to observe with interest the great difference in the form and general appearance of the two species when he compares them sitting side by side sunning themselves upon chimney or housetop; and especially the discrepancy in their mode of flight as they wheel together overhead in endless inosculating circles. The Turkey Buzzards look larger as they fly, though really they are lighter weights; they are dingy-brown, with a gray space underneath the wing; the tail is long; the fore-border of the wing is bent at a salient angle, and there is a corresponding reëntrance in its hind outline; the tips of the longest quills spread apart and bend upward; and one may watch these splendid flyers for hours without perceiving a movement of the pinions.

Comparing now the Carrion Crows, they are seen to be more thick-set, with less sweep of wing and shorter and more rounded tail, beyond which the feet may project; the front edge of the wing is almost straight, and the back border sweeps around in a regular curve to meet it at an obtuse point, where the ends of the quills are neither spread apart nor bent upward. The birds show almost black instead of brown; in place of large gray area under the wing, there is a smaller paler-gray spot at the point of the wing. And, finally, the Carrion Crows flap their wings five or six times in rapid succession, then sail a few moments; their flight appears heavy, and even laborious, beside the stately motion of their relatives.

Turkey Buzzards are resident in the lower, hotter portions of Arizona. In the mountains I never saw them in winter. At Fort Whipple, for instance, they arrived the latter part of March and remained until November. No better opportunity could be desired of studying their habits than was afforded in this place, where they were very numerous. We had a large herd of cattle, one or more of which were daily slaughtered for the supply of the garrison; and early in the fall it was deemed advisable to "jerk" all the beef that remained on the hoof, since, in this state, it was always liable to be stolen by Apaches, and winter fodder was procurable only in limited quantity. The shambles were located in a grove of cottonwood near the fort, and day after day the meat hung drying in thin strips festooned upon ropes stretched between the trees, while bones and offal covered the ground at a little distance. These were high times for the Buzzards, Ravens, wolves, and all the dogs of the neighborhood; the place became a rendezvous for holding high carnival. The birds and beasts feasted alternately. At nightfall the coyoté-wolves and their larger relatives, the lobos, left their hiding places, emboldened by hunger and shielded by darkness, and hastened to the feast. There they fed, and fought, and caroused, yelping like things possessed, till daylight surprised them and forced them to slink away to their rocky fastnesses. Then the Buzzards and Ravens flapped lazily down from their roosting places in the tall pines round about, and took their turn. We destroyed a good many of the wolves, partly for the sake of their pelage, which was in fine order at that season; partly in revenge for the disturbance their perpetual orgies occasioned. But, of course, there was no sensible diminution of their numbers; those who lived to get away returned the next night to feed, and their ranks were continually recruited. The Buzzards were seldom molested; this and their continued surfeit made them as tame as they usually are in southern cities. They certainly did us good service, though, perhaps, no better than that rendered by the wolves themselves. Whether the birds and wolves were on good terms or not I cannot say, for they always feasted apart, at different hours; but there was evidently an understanding between the Buzzards and the dogs. They fed side by side, and quarrelled no more than selfish, gluttonous Vultures generally do. As for details of such banqueting as theirs, too much has already appeared in print for the comfort of fastidious readers.

Turkey Buzzards, like other American Vultures, are mute. Their only voice is a kind of hiss, which has been likened to the seething noise of hot iron plunged in water. Except when flying, the birds show to little advantage. The color is dull; the form uncomely; the gait is constrained, and the attitudes are negligent and slothful. They walk or hop indifferently, and sometimes move with a succession of leaps, accelerated with the wings. When about to take flight from the ground, they stoop for an instant till the breast almost touches, and then, unfolding the wings, give a vigorous spring into the air; with a few powerful, hurried flaps, they are fairly off. They soon begin their gyrations with set wings, only beating at intervals, when they are forced to rise rapidly away from some obstacle; and, circling thus, they are shortly in the upper air.

The Turkey Buzzard breeds sometimes in communities and sometimes by single pairs, depositing its eggs on the ground, on rocks, or in hollow logs and stumps. The situation is generally in thick woods; and when numbers breed together, the foulness of the resort is beyond description—vegetation may be entirely destroyed over large areas. Even single nests are offensive from their noisome deposits, not only of excrementitious matters, but of others, disgorged by the parents to feed the young. The eggs are generally two in number, often only one; they measure about 2¾ in length by 2, or rather less, in breadth, being thus notably shorter and of less capacity than those of the Black Vulture. They are creamy or yellowish-white, variously blotched and splashed with several different shades of brown, and usually showing other smaller spots of lavender and purplish-drab. The young are said to be covered at first with a whitish down, and to be fed for some time with half-digested carrion disgorged by the parents.

When wounded and captured, the Turkey Buzzard warns off its aggressor very effectually by casting up the fœtid contents of the crop, but offers no resistance. Several winged birds I have handled remained perfectly passive after this, and even seemed apathetic as they were being put to death. I learned, on one occasion, that they will simulate death. A bird that I had shot—through the lungs, as I judged from the crimson froth and blood that flowed from the beak—appeared dead soon after I picked it up, and I carried it home, some distance, holding it by the legs dangling, perfectly limp. I threw it carelessly down on the ground by my tent and turned to something else; but, in a few moments, on looking at it again, I was surprised to find the bird I had thought dead had changed its position, and I caught its bright brown eye glancing furtively around. On going up to it its eyes closed, the body relaxed, and it lay as if dead again. I compressed the chest for several minutes, till I was satisfied life was extinct, and then went to supper. But the cunning bird was still "playing possum," and, I suppose, scrambled into the bushes as soon as my back was turned; at any rate it was gone when I returned.

The remaining species of this genus are as follows:

CATHARTES BURROVIANUS, *Cassin.*

Cathartes burrovianus, Cass., Pr. Phila. Acad, ii, 1845, 212; Ill. 1854, 59 (? Mexico); B. N. A. 1858, 1.—Gray, Hand-list, i, 1869, 3, No. 19.—Coues, Key, 1872, 222.
Rhinogryphus burrovianus, Ridgw.—B. B. & R., N. A. B. iii, 1874, 344.
Cathartes urubitinga, Natt.—Pelz., Sitzb. Ak. Wien. 1861, 7; Orn. Bras. i, 1868, 1.— Gurn., Cat. Rapt. B. 1864, 46.—Scl. & Salv., P. Z. S. 1867, 589 (Amazon).— Elliot, B. N. A. ii, pl. 26.—Gray, Hand-list, i, 1869, 3, No. 20.

Hab.—Eastern Tropical America.

CATHARTES ATRATUS, *Bartram.*

Vultur brasiliensis, Ray., Syn. Meth. Av. 1713, 10.
Cathartes brasiliensis, Bp., Consp. i, 1850, 9.
Vultur atratus, Bartr., Trav. 1792, 289.—Meyer, Zool. Am. i, 1794, 290.—Brewst., Edinb. Journ. vi, 156.
Cathartes atratus, Less., Man. i, 1828, 73.—Sw. & Rich., F. B. A. ii, 1831, 6.—Temm., Tab. Meth. 1836, 1.—Sw., Classif. B. ii, 1837, 206.—Darw., Journ. Res. 1839, 68; Voy. Beagle, iii, 7.—James., ed. Wils. i, 10.—Brew., ed. Wils. 1840, 682; N. Am. Oöl. 1857, 5, pl. 1, f. 3, 4.—Aud., Syn. 1839, 3; B. Am. i, 17, pl. 3.— Bridges, P. Z. S. ix, 108; Ann. N. H. xiii, 498.—DeKay, N. Y. Zool. ii, 1844, 3.—Bp., Consp. i, 1850, 9.—Cass., Ill. 1854, 58; U. S. Astron. Exp. ii, 1855, 173;

384   CATHARTES CALIFORNIANUS.

B. N. A. 1858, 5.—Strickl., Orn. Syn. 1855, 2.—Putn., Pr. Ess. Inst. i, 1856, 223 (Swampscott, Mass., Nov. 1850, *Jillson*).—Scl., Ibis, i, 1859, 213 (Guatemala).— Scl., P. Z. S. 1860, 287 (Ecuador).—Taylor, Ibis, ii, 1860, 223 (Honduras).— Allen, Pr. Ess. Inst. iv, 1864, 81 (Massachusetts, quotes *Jillson, l. c.,* and a second specimen at Gloucester, Mass., Sept. 28, 1863, *Verrill*).—Coues, *ibid.* v, 1868, 254 (Massachusetts, quotes *Putnam* and *Allen*).—Mayn., B. Mass. 1870, 137 (same quotations).—Dress., Ibis, 1865, 322 (Texas).—Scl. & Salv., P. Z. S. 1867, 589 (Para).—Pelz., Orn. Bras. i, 1868, 1 (Rio).—Coues, Pr. Bost. Soc. xii, 1868, 120 (South Carolina, resident).—Coues, Pr. Phila. Acad. 1871, 28 (North Carolina, rare, March and November).—Allen, Bull. M. C. Z. ii, 1871, 312 (critical).— Boardm., Am. Nat. iii, 1869, 498 (Calais, Me.).—Allen, *ibid.* 646 (Hudson, Mass., in 1869; one killed, several seen).—Coues, Key, 1872, 222.
Catharista atrata, Gray, Hand-list, i, 1869, 3, No. 16 (V., Anal. 1816, 22).—B. B. & R., N. A. B. iii, 1874, 351.
Vultur aura niger, b. Kerr, Gm. 1792, 473.
Vultur aura, Daud., Tr. Orn. ii, 1800, 19 (based on P. E. 187). Not of *Linnæus*.
Cathartes aura, "Spix, Av. Spec. Nov. 1824, 2" (*Allen*). Not of authors.
Vultur urubu, Less., Tr. Orn. 1831, 27; Voy. 614.—D'Orbig., Voy. 1844, 31, pl. 1.
Percnopterus urubu, Steph., G. Z. xiii, 1826, 7, pl. 31.
Cathartes fœtens, Ill., "M. Berol."—Licht., Verz. 1823, 63.—Maxim., Beitr. iii, 1830, 58.— Schomb., Guiana, 1840, 742.—Tsch., Wiegm. Arch. 1844, 262; Fn. Peru, 71.— Hartl., Ind. Az. 1.—Gray, Gen. of B. pl. 1, f. 3.—Reinh., Vid. Med. 1870, 62.
Vultur iota, Ord, ed. Wils. ix, 1814, 104, pl. 75, f. 2 (not of *Molina, Gmelin,* or *Daudin*).— Jard., ed. Wils. iii, 236.
Cathartes iota, Bp., Syn. 1828, 23; Isis, 1832, 1135; List, 1838, 1.—Nutt., Man. i, 1832, 46.—Aud., Orn. Biog. iii, 1835, 33; v, 1839, 345; pl. 106.—Peale, U. S. Expl. Exped. 1848, 59.—King, Voy. Beagle, i, 532.
Neophron iota, Cuv., R. A. 2d ed. i, 137.

Hab.—Tropical and subtropical America. On the Atlantic coast, north regularly to North Carolina, casually to Massachusetts; resident from South Carolina southward.

CATHARTES CALIFORNIANUS, (*Shaw*) *Cuvier.*

Vultur californianus, Shaw, Nat. Misc. ix, 1797, pl. 301; Gen. Zool. vii, 1809, 10.—Lath., Ind. Orn. Suppl. 2.—Dougl., Zool. Journ. iv, 328; Isis, 1831, 110.—James., ed. Wils. iv, 259.
Cathartes californianus, Cuv., R. A. 2d ed. i, 316.—Bp., Syn. 1828, 22; Isis, 1832, 1135; List, 1838, 1; Consp. i, 1850, 9.—Nutt., Man. i, 1834, 39.—Sw., Classif. B. ii, 1837, 206.—Aud., Orn. Biog. v, 1839, 240, pl. 426; Syn. 1839, 2; B. Am. i, 1840, 12, pl. 1.—Brew., ed. Wils. 1840, 832.—Gray, Gen. of B. i, 1844, pl. 2.—DeKay, N. Y. Zool. ii, 1844, 3.—Peale, U S. Expl. Exp. 1848, 58.—Cass., Ill. 1854, 58; B. N. A. 1858, 5.—Strickl., Orn. Syn. 1855, 3.—Newb., P. R. R. Rep. vi, 1857, 73.—Heerm., *ibid.* x, 1859, pt. vi, 59.—Tay., Cal. Mag. iii, 1859, 537 (figure of eggs and young).—Coop. & Suck., N. H. Wash. Ter. 1860, 141.—Gur., Cat. Rapt. B. 1864, 39.—Coues, Pr. Phila. Acad. 1866, 42 (Fort Yuma, Ariz.).—Scl., P. Z. S. 1866, 366, fig. —; 1868, 183, fig. —.—Coop., B. Cal. i, 1870, 496.—Coues, Key, 1872, 222.
Catharista californiana, Gray, List B. Br. Mus. 1844, 4; Hand-list, i, 1869, 3, No. 17.
Sarcorhamphus californianus, Steph., Gen. Zool. xiii, 1826, 6.—Vig., Zool. Journ. ii, 375.— Sw. &. Rich., F. A. B. ii, 1831, 1.—Licht., Akad. Wissen. Berol. 424, pl. 1.
Pseudogryphus californianus, Ridgw.—B. B. & R., N. A. B. iii, 1874, 338.
Vultur columbianus, Ord, Guthrie's Geog. ii, 1815, 315.
Cathartes vulturinus, Temm., Pl. Color. 1820, 31.—Less., Man. Orn. ii, 1828, 10.

Hab.—Pacific coast of the United States, from the Columbia River to Lower California. Utah (*Henshaw*). Arizona (*Coues*).

ORDER COLUMBÆ: PIGEONS, &c.

Family COLUMBIDÆ: Pigeons.

COLUMBA FASCIATA, Say.

Band-tailed Pigeon.

Columba fasciata, SAY, Long's Exp. ii, 1823, 10.—BP., Am. Orn. i, 1825, 77, pl. —, f. 3; Syn.
1828, 119; List, 1838, 41.—WAGL., S. Av. 1827.—NUTT., Man. i, 1832, 624.—AUD.,
Orn. Biog. iv, 1838, 479, pl. 367; Syn. 1839, 191; B. Am. iv, 1842, 312, pl. 279.—
WOODH., Sitgr. Rep. 1853, 92.—NEWB., P. R. R. Rep. vi, 1857, 92.—BD., B. N. A.
1858, 597.—SCL., P. Z. S. 1858, 359 (Cordova); 1858, 304 (Oaxaca); 1859, 369
(Xalapa).—SALV., Ibis, 1860, 276 (Guatemala).—COOP. & SUCK., N. H. Wash.
Ter. 1860, 217.—COUES, Pr. Phila. Acad. 1866, 93 (Arizona).—SUMICH., Mem.
Bost. Soc. i, 1869, 562 (Vera Cruz).—COOP., B. Cal. i, 1870, 506.—COOP., Am.
Nat. iii, 1869, 80 (Montana Territory).—GRAY, Hand-list, ii, 1870, 235, No.
9269.—COUES, Key, 1872, 225.—SCHL., M. P.-B. 1873, 67.—B. B. & R., N. A.
B. iii, 1874, 358, 360, pl. 57, f. 2.
Tænioenas fasciata, REICH., Syst. Av. pl. 223, f. 1255; pl. 255, figs. 2865, 2866.
Chloroenas fasciata, BP., Consp. ii, 1854, 51.
Columba monilis, VIG., Beechey's Voy. 1839, 26, pl. 10.
Chloroenas monilis, REICH., Syst. Av. pl. 227, f. 2481.

Hab.—Rocky Mountains to the Pacific, United States, and southward to South
America.

No specimens of this bird were ever taken by the Expeditions, and
it has not yet, to my knowledge, been actually found in the Missouri
water-shed. It has occurred, however, to Dr. Cooper, near the Cœur
d'Alene Mission, in Montana, and, as a bird of the Rocky Mountains,
may not improperly be brought into the present connection. There is
no reasonable doubt of its occasional presence about the Missouri head-
waters.

It is common in many parts of the West. I was, however, disappointed in not meeting it more than once or twice in Arizona, where I
had anticipated its plentiful occurrence, at least during the migrations.
Its movements appear to be somewhat irregular; while it is abundant
in some regions, it is absent from others apparently equally favorable.
This may depend upon the precarious supply of certain favorite kinds
of food, and thus correspond somewhat to the more conspicuous case of
the Passenger Pigeon, whose notorious wanderings are mainly prompted
by the same circumstances. It appears to breed indifferently in various
parts of its range, even so far south as Santa Cruz. The accounts of its
nesting that were for some years relied upon, are not entirely correct.
Mr. Townsend's notice, which Audubon printed, is to the effect that the
bird lays on the ground without any nest whatever, the eggs being " of
a yellowish-white color, inclining to bluish-white, with minute spots at
the great end. Whereas, as in other Pigeons, the eggs are pure white,
smooth and glistening, nearly elliptical in shape, measuring 1.50 inches
long by 1.20 broad." According to other authority, the bird builds a
simple nest of twigs in a forked branch, or on a horizontal bough. But
situation of a nest is among the very variable elements of the ornithological problem, since it depends upon many fortuitous circumstances.
As is well known, the Common Dove (*Zenoedura carolinensis*) nestles
with equal readiness on the ground or in bushes. In colder countries,

25

where reptiles are few, it generally sets on the ground ; in Arizona, for instance, the paradise of snakes and lizards, it always nestles in bushes. So, also, does the Ground Dove (*Chamœpelia passerina*), in the same Territory. The nidification of the Band-tailed Pigeon may be equally variable.

According to Dr. Cooper, this Pigeon is common in all the wooded mountainous parts of California, descending to the valleys in search of grain during autumn and winter. "North of San Francisco I have seen them in flocks in the grain-fields as early as July, and along the Colum-bia River they spend the summer in the valleys as well as throughout the mountains. They are there migratory, leaving in October, but in California their wanderings are guided chiefly by want of food. I have found them breeding in the Coast Range as far south as Santa Cruz, though I did not succeed in finding any nests. I was told that they built in companies, on low bushes in unfrequented parts of the mount-ains, but Townsend found their eggs on the ground near the banks of streams in Oregon, numbers congregating together. I have myself found eggs, which I supposed to be of this bird, in a similar situation. * * * * They feed on acorns, which they swallow whole, even when very large; also on berries, especially those of the Madrona (*Arbutus*), grain, and seeds of various kinds. Being large, and delicate food, they furnish much sport for the fowler in certain districts, but soon become so watchful and shy that they are shot with difficulty, excepting when young or where they can be watched from an ambush. In Oregon they collect in flocks of thousands in the autumn, but I have never seen more than a hundred together in this State."

Dr. George Suckley, whose opportunities of investigation were excel-lent, has left us the following record : "The Band-tailed Pigeon is a very common bird in Washington Territory, especially west of the Cas-cade Mountains; I saw but one flock, containing five individuals, east of those mountains. In 1856 the first birds of this species that arrived in the spring made their appearance about May 15, which is the cus-tomary time every year for their arrival. One or two individuals are first seen, and within two or three days thereafter the main body of the migration follows. A small number remain throughout the summer and breed ; the rest retire further north. Those that remain generally make their nests in thick fir-forests, near water. They subsist during the summer on wild cherries and other berries, and later in the season, since the country has become settled, upon grain. About the first week in September large flocks congregate in stubble-fields in the vicinity of Fort Steilacoom, and for two or three weeks thereafter their numbers are daily augmented by arrivals from the North. Some flocks of these Pigeons, that I saw in September, must have contained at least one thousand individuals. I am told that in the cultivated districts on the Cowlitz River, at the same season, they are in still greater numbers. By the 5th of October, of the year 1856, all had suddenly disappeared, with the exception of a few stragglers, generally young birds. In fly-ing, the flocks, I think, are not quite so compactly crowded as those of the Passenger Pigeon. During the summer, while breeding, their cooing can be heard a long distance. The name of this bird in the Nisqually language is 'hubboh,' a good imitation of its calls. * * * * In autumn these birds are in excellent order for the table; indeed I prefer them to the Wild Pigeon of the Atlantic States."

There is another kind of Dove in the West which may yet be found in the southernmost parts of the Missouri region, but which I have no authority for introducing in the present connection. This is the White-winged Dove (*Melopelia leucoptera*)*. It has somewhat the general form and appearance of the Carolina Dove, but may be recognized by the broad, white, oblique bar on the wing. Audubon appears to have first noticed it as a bird of this country, under the name of *Columba trudeaui*, and not long afterward attention was again called to it by Colonel McCall. But it remained little known until Mr. Xantus sent a fine suite to the Smithsonian, from Cape St. Lucas, where he found it abundant. I rarely saw it in Arizona, where it reaches at least to the latitude of Fort Whipple, and breeds in that vicinity. This I ascertained by seeing a pair of squabs in a cage; they had been captured near by. Though only half-fledged, the white on the wing was already evident. The eggs of this species are 1.25 inches long by 0.95 wide, and, as usual, two in number; elliptical in shape, and of a pure, glistening white.

ECTOPISTES MIGRATORIA, (Linn.) Sw.

Wild Pigeon; Passenger Pigeon.

Columba canadensis, LINN., Syst. Nat. i, 1766, 284.—GM., Syst. Nat. i, 1788, 785.
Columba migratoria, LINN., Syst. Nat. i, 1766, 285 (*Columba americana*, FRISCH, pl. 142; KALM, It. ii, 527; (*œnas*), BRISS., i, 100; *Palumbus migratorius*, CATES., 23).— GM., Syst. Nat. i, 1788, 389.—FORST., Philos. Tr. lxii, 1772, 398.—WILS., Am. Orn. i, 1808, 102, pl. 44, fig. 1.—BP., Obs. Wils. 1825, No. 179; Syn. 1828, 120.— NUTT., i, 1832, 629.—AUD., Orn. Biog. i, 1831, 319; v, 1839, 561; pl. 62.
Ectopistes migratoria, Sw., Zool. Journ. iii, 1827, 355.—Sw. & RICH., F. B. A. ii, 1831, 363.—BP., List, 1838, 341; Consp. ii, 1854, 59.—REICH., Syst. Av. pl. 249, figs. 1377, 1379.—AUD., Syn. 1839, 174; B. Am. v, 1842, 25, pl. 285.—WOODH., Sitgr. Rep. 1853, 92.—BD., B. N. A. 1858, 600.—COOP. & SUCK., N. H. Wash. Ter. 1860, 218 (Fort Laramie, Wyo. and Milk River, Mont.).—HAYD., Rep. 1862, 171.— COOP., Am. Nat. iii, 1869, 80 (Montana).—GRAY, Hand-list, ii, 1870, 235, No. 9281.—COOP., B. Cal. i, 1870, 511 (Puget's Sound).—TRIPPE, Pr. Ess. Inst. vi, 118.—SNOW, B. Kans. 1873, —.—COUES, Key, 1872, 225, fig. 145.—B. B. & R., N. A. B. iii, 1874, 308, pl. 57, fig. 4; and of late writers generally.
Peristera migratoria, SCHL., M. P.-B. x, 1873, 142.

Hab.—The greater part of North America, but scarcely west of the Rocky Mountains (Pacific coast, near latitude 49°, *Cooper*; Nevada, *Ridgway*). Cuba (*Gundlach*, Rep. i, 1866, 102; J. f. O. ix, 112). Accidental in Europe (*Gould*, B. Eur. pl. 247; *Harting*, Man. Br. Birds, 1872, 128).

Lieutenant Warren's Expedition.—4856, 4857, mouth of Big Sioux River; 5418, above the mouth of the Yellowstone River.

There is no present occasion to particularize the general eastern range of this species by citing the authorities for its occurrence; suffice it to

---

* *Columba leucoptera*, LINN., Syst. Nat. i, 1866, 281 ("Asia," err. *Turtur indicus fuscus*, EDW., 76; *Columba indica*, BRISS., i, 105; BROWNE, Jam. 468).—GM., Syst. Nat. i, 1788, 773.—LATH., Ind. Orn. ii, 1790, 595 (White-winged Pigeon, Gen. Syn. iv, 617).—WAGL., Syst. Av. 1827, *Columba*, No. 71.—McCALL, Pr. Phila. Acad. iv, 1848, 64.
Zenaida leucoptera, GRAY, Gen. of Birds.
Turtur leucopterus, GOSSE, B. Jamaica, 1847, 304.
Melopelia leucoptera, BP., Consp. Av. ii, 1854, 81.—SCL., P. Z. S. 1856, 309 (Cordova); 1858, 305 (Oaxaca).—BD., B. N. A. 1858, 603.—XANTUS, Pr. Phila. Acad. 1859 (Cape St. Lucas).—TAYLOR, Ibis, 1860, ii, 227 (Honduras).—MARCH, Pr. Phila. Acad. 1863, 302 (Jamaica).—LAWR., Ann. Lyc. N. Y. ix, 139 (Costa Rica); 207 (Yucatan).—COUES, Pr. Phila. Acad. 1866, 93 (Arizona).—COOP., B. Cal. i, 1870, 515.—COUES, Key, 1872, 226.—SCHL., M. P.-B. x, 1873, 152.—B. B. & R., N. A. B. iii, 1874, 376.
(?) *Columba hoitotl*, GM., Syst. Nat. i, 1788, 777.—LATH., Ind. Orn. ii, 1700, 601 (White-shouldered Pigeon, Gen. Syn. iv, 654).
Columba trudeaui, AUD., B. Am. vii, 1843, 352, pl. 496.

Hab.—Southern and Lower California, Arizona, New Mexico, and Texas. South through Mexico to Central America. Also, Cuba and Jamaica.

allude to its continual wandering over the greater part of North America. But in the West its food supply is limited, and its presence corresponding\ingly restricted. Excepting along the Missouri and the principal tribu\taries of that great river, the Wild Pigeon does not ordinarily exceed the general line of *wooded* country to pass out upon the bare plains be\yond. But just as the Missouri forms for us a highway of communica\tion with the vast districts which would be otherwise almost inaccessible, so it seems to lead the Pigeons northwesterly, in great numbers, to meridians of longitude they do not gain in the southwest. I never saw or heard of one in New Mexico or Arizona, and have found no quotations from Colorado, Utah, or California. But the birds reach across Nebraska, probably following the Platte into Wyoming, and through Dakota and Montana, being even conducted to Pacific slopes along the northern border of the United States.

Many years ago Townsend mentioned the Passenger Pigeon as an in\habitant of "Oregon," but that was then so comprehensive a term that the confirmation of the occurrence, recently made by Drs. Cooper and Suck\ley, was the more acceptable. In the work above quoted these authors give the only unquestionable Pacific advices I have found. Still later Dr. Cooper contributed some interesting items to the American Natu\ralist on the occurrence of the species in Montana: "The Passenger Pigeon, like the Cat-bird, astonished me by its frequency in the Rocky Mountains, as, although I saw no very large flocks, I saw some almost every day until I passed the Spokane Falls, just north of the Columbia Plains. It thus seems to pass round to the north of that plain, and occasionally to cross the Cascade Range, as noticed by Dr. Suckley in 1853. Along the Missouri I often saw small flocks, and noticed quite a number of their nests in small trees between Forts Pierre and Berthold. I found one setting, June 7, and heard that many build farther south, near Sioux City. In the mountains they fed, in August, chiefly on the service berry (*Amelanchier alnifolia*), which, along the Hell Gate, attains a size and flavor unequaled by any I have seen elsewhere." Dr. Hayden remarks upon its abundance on the Lower Missouri, but considered it as rarer than it really is higher up the river. Still he says he has seen a hundred individuals in a season, high up on the Yellowstone, when the berries were ripe. According to Sir John Richardson, it reaches the fur countries in May and leaves in October, attaining latitudes from 58° to 62°, according to climatic conditions.

The westernmost point where I have as yet myself observed the Pas\senger Pigeon is Turtle Mountain, on the northern boundary of Dakota. It was, however, a rare bird in that locality. But a little further east, along the Red River, I observed vast flocks during the latter part of May, in all the timber of the river, for many miles from Pembina south\ward; and they doubtless extended as much further north of that point. As we steamed along the river, for several days the flocks were almost continually in view. They generally flew high, beyond gunshot range, in immense straggling flocks, or rather in successive groups, sometimes stretching as far as the eye could reach; but early in the morning and toward evening, in passing to and from their roosting places, they gen\erally flew lower, and numbers were readily procured. The woods along the river were filled with stragglers, singly or in small troops. Many nested in this region; I found females ready to lay, and nests, during the greater part of June. The nests were usually in the horizontal forks of the branches of small trees and saplings, generally ten or twelve feet from the ground. During the passage, in May of 1873, the birds were very numerous about Saint Paul, Minnesota, where hundreds were netted, to be be used instead of tame Pigeons in shooting-matches.

Some years since a great flight of Pigeons occurred near Washington, where for several days, in the fall, the woods were filled with the birds. More or fewer are usually seen there every year, and I once killed a specimen so newly from the nest as to cause me to believe that it had been hatched in the vicinity.

ZENÆDURA CAROLINENSIS, (Linn.) Bp.

Carolina Dove; Common Dove.

Columba carolinensis, LINN., Syst. Nat. i, 1766, 286 (*Turtur carolinensis*, CATES., Car. i, 24; Briss. i, 110, pl. 8, fig. 1).—GM., i, 1788, 787.—LATH., Ind. Orn. ii, 1790, 613.—WILS., Am. Orn. v, 1812, 91, pl. 43, fig. 1.—BP., Obs. Wils. 1825, No. 159; Syn. 1828, 119.—NUTT., Man. i, 1832, 626.—AUD., O. B. i, 1831, 91; v, 1839, 555; pl. 17.
Ectopistes carolinensis, RICH., List, 1837.—BP., List, 1838, 41.—AUD., Syn. 1839, 195; B. Am. v, 1842, 36, pl. 286.—WOODH., Sitgr. Rep. 1853, 92.—NEWB., P. R. R. Rep. vi, 1857, 92.—HEERM., *ibid*. x, 1859, pt. vi, 60.
Zenaidura carolinensis, BP., Consp. ii, 1854, 84.—BD., B. N. A. 1858, 604.—KENN., P. R. R. Rep. x, 1859, pt. iv, 33.—SCL., P. Z. S. 1856, 359 (Cordova); 1859, 391 (Oaxaca); Ibis, i, 1859, 222 (Guatemala).—COOP. & SUCK., N. H. Wash. Ter. 1860, 218.—TAYLOR, Ibis, 1860, 227 (Honduras).—HAYD., Rep. 1862, 172.—COUES, Pr. Phila. Acad. 1866, 93 (Arizona).—DRESS., Ibis, 1866, 24 (Texas).—BOARDM., Pr. Bost. Soc. ix, 1862, 127 (Maine, rare).—ALLEN, Pr. Ess. Inst. iv, 1864, 75 (Massachusetts, common).—GUNDL., Repert. 1866, 30 (Cuba).—MCILWR., Pr. Ess. Inst. v, 1866, 91 (Canada West).—COUES, Pr. Ess. Inst. v, 1868, 287.—LAWR., Ann. Lyc. ix, 139 (Costa Rica); ix, 207 (Yucatan).—COOP., Am. Nat. iii, 1869, 81; B. Cal. i, 1870, 512.—ALLEN, Bull. M. C. Z. iii, 1872, 181 (mountains of Colorado up to 11,000 feet).—SNOW, B. Kans. 1873.—AIKEN, Pr. Bost. Soc. 1872, 208.—STEV., U. S. Geol. Surv. Ter. 1870, 465.—COUES, Key, 1872, 226, fig. 146.—B. B. & R., N. A. B. iii, 1874, 383, pl. 58, fig. 2.
Perissura carolinensis, CAB., J. f. O. 1856, 111 (Cuba).
Chamœpelia carolinensis, GIEBEL, Nomenc. Av. i, 633.
Peristera carolinensis, SCHL., M. P.-B. x, 1873, 142.
Columba marginata, LINN., Syst. Nat. i, 1766, 286.—GM., i, 1788, 791.—WAGL., Syst. Av. 1827; Isis, 1831, 519.
Ectopistes marginata, GRAY, Hand-list, ii, 1870, 236, No. 9282.
Ectopistes marginellus, WOODH., Pr. Phila. Acad. 1852, 104; Sitgr. Rep. 1853, 93, pl. 5.—GRAY, Hand-list, No. 9283.
Zenaidura marginellus, BP., Consp. ii, 1854, 85.

Hab.—United States from Atlantic to Pacific. Canada West (*McIlwraith*). Cuba. South to Panama.
Lieutenant Warren's Expedition.—4858, Cedar Island.
Later Expeditions.—60465-66, 60770-71, Wyoming.

Unlike the last, this species is of extensive if not universal distribution in the West, as in other parts of the United States. It is more southerly, however, considering its whole range. It is not common in the Eastern States beyond Southern New England, and I note but a single instance of its occurrence in the British Provinces. The parallel of 49° is probably about its normal northern limit. Mr. Trippe does not include it among the birds of Minnesota. It is a regular migrant over about the northern half of the United States, resident elsewhere. I have found it alike abundant in all kinds of country I have visited—even in the terrible alkaline deserts of the southwest, where its presence is cheering evidence that water may be found not far off. Its nidification varies greatly with circumstances, the nest being placed indifferently on the ground, bushes, or trees; and even, according to some writers, on fences, stumps, &c. The eggs, two in number, and white, as usual in this family, measure about 1⅛ by ⅞. They are laid, according to climate, from April throughout the summer. I have found it nesting in various parts of both the Carolinas, there breeding chiefly on the ground, while in Arizona, where reptiles of the most venomous character abound, the bird seeks safety for its eggs by placing the nest on bushes. The principal bushes of some parts of the Territory are cacti and other thorny growths, so terribly prickly that snakes can scarcely climb them; indeed I have seen nests in "cholla" bushes, where it seemed scarcely possible for even a bird to alight to build without wounding its feet, there being absolutely not a smooth spot on the whole shrub. In the wooded and mountainous parts of the Territory the nidification varies. Though resident in the Territory at large, the Dove is only a summer sojourner in these higher parts, where it arrives the latter part of April and remains until the middle of October. Its coming marks the opening of spring, when the silence of the vast pine tracts, scarcely broken before but by the dismal caw of the Raven or the harsh notes of the Jays and Woodpeckers, is now enlivened by the twittering of Swallows and the agreeable songs of the birds, as well as by the cooing of the Dove, which resounds in plaintive, measured cadence, while the gentle bird is wooing his mate.

The Ground Dove, a very small and delicate species of the southern portions of the United States, has not been known to penetrate to any portion of the Missouri region. It appears to be, in some degree, a bird of our southern *coast* regions, so rarely, in the United States at least, does it stray far inland. Its usual range is limited by the Carolinas, but I have a record of the capture of a specimen, many years ago, at Washington, D. C. Audubon states that a "search for them a hundred miles inland would in all probability prove fruitless;" but against this statement I find pencilled, in a copy of his work in the State Library at Columbia, South Carolina, a note to the effect that one was shot on the Congaree River, not far from Columbia, in December, 1839. The species occurs in Southern Arizona, but not, so far as I am aware, in the region of Fort Whipple. It is also abundant at Cape Saint Lucas, and extends northward into Southern California. The nidification is not peculiar. The eggs are two, seven-eighths long by two-thirds broad. The synonymy of the species is subjoined.*

* CHAMÆPELIA PASSERINA, (*Linnæus*) *Swainson.*

Columba passerina, LINN., Syst. Nat. i, 1766, 285 (SLOANE, Jam. ii, 305, pl. 261, fig. 3; CATES., i, 26; BRISS. i, 113, pl. 9, fig. 1).—GM., Syst. Nat. i, 1788, 787.—LATH., I. Orn. ii, 1790, 611.—WILS., Am. Orn. iv, 1811, 15, pl. 46, fig. -.—WAGL., Syst. Av. *Columba*, No. 88.—BP., Syn. 1828, 120.—NUTT., Man. i, 1832, 635.—AUD., Orn. Biog. ii, 1834, 471; v, 1839, 558; pl. 182; Syn. 1839, 192; B. Am. v, 1842, 19, pl. 283.—SUND., Ofv. Vet. Akad. Forh. 1869, 586 (Saint Bartholomew).
Columba (*Goura*) *passerina*, BP., Obs. Wils. 1825, 181.
Chœmepelia passerina, Sw., Zool. Journ. iii, 1827, 361.—GRAY, Hand-list, No. 9336.
Chœmepelia passerina, Sw., Classif. Birds, ii, 1837, 349.
Chamepelia passerina, BP., List, 1838, 41.
Chamæpelia passerina, GRAY, 1841.—GOSSE, B. Jam. 1846, 311.—BP., Consp. ii, 1854, 77.— CAB., J. f. O. iv, 1856 (Cuba).—SCL., P. Z. S. 1857, 205 (Xalapa); 1859, 391 (Oaxaca); 1864, 178 (Mexico City); Ibis, i, 1859, 223 (Guatemala).—BD., B. N. A. 1858, 606.—COUES & PRENT., Smiths. Rep. 1861, 414.—MARCH, Pr. Phila. Acad. 1863, 302 (Jamaica).—COUES, Pr. Phila. Acad. 1866, 93 (Southern Arizona).—BRYANT, Pr. Bost. Soc. 1866 (Porto Rico).—LAWR., Ann. Lyc. N. Y. ix, 134 (Costa Rica); ix, 207 (Yucatan).—COOP., B. Cal. i, 1870, 516.—COUES, Key, 1872, 226.— B. B. & R., N. A. B. iii, 1874, 389, pl. 58, fig. 6.
Chamæpelia passerina var. *pallescens*, BD., Pr. Phila. Acad. 1859, 305.--COOP., B. Cal. i, 1870, 517 (Cape Saint Lucas).
Pyrgitœnas passerinus, REICH., Columbariæ.
Peristera passerina, SCHL., M. P.-B. x, 1873, 134.
Columba minuta, LINN., Syst. Nat. i, 1766, 285 (BRISS., i, 116, pl. 8, fig. 2).—GM., Syst. Nat. 1788, 788.—LATH., Ind. Orn. ii, 1790, 612 (*Passerine Turtle*, Gen. Syn. iv, 660.) *Chamæpelia granatina* et *albivitta*, BP., Consp. Av. ii, 1854, 77 (Bogota and Carthagena).
Pyrgitœnas albivitta, REICH., Columbariæ.

Hab.—Southern United States. North to about 35°. Southward through Mexico and Central America to Northern South America. Several West India Islands.

ORDER GALLINÆ: GALLINACEOUS BIRDS.

Family MELEAGRIDIDÆ: Turkeys.

These are the nearest American analogues of the true Pheasants, family *Phasianidæ*, indigenous to Asia, and are sometimes placed in that family. But the differences appear sufficient to warrant their family separation. Their next nearest allies are the Guinea Fowls, of Africa—family *Numididæ*.

MELEAGRIS GALLOPAVO var. AMERICANA, (Bartr.) Coues.

Common Wild Turkey.

a. *gallapavo*.

Meleagris gallopavo, LINN., Fn. Suec. No. 198; Syst. Nat. i, 1766, 268 (based on the domestic bird, which is most like this variety. See NEWT., Zool. Rec. v, 102. Not of authors generally, the name usually referring to the foregoing feral variety).—STEPH., Shaw's Gen. Zool. ix, pt. i, p. 156, pl. 8 (domestic).—WOODH., Sitgr. Rep. 1854, 94, in part; the paragraph on p. 93 refers to the following variety.
Meleagris mexicana, GOULD, P. Z. S. 1856, 61.—BD., B. N. A. 1858, 618; U. S. Agric. Rep. 1866, 288.—COUES, Pr. A. N. S. 1866, 93.—ELLIOT, B. N. A. pt. x, pl. 38.—DARW., Anim. and Pl. Domest. i, 292.—COOP., B. Cal. i, 1870, 523.
Meleagris gallopavo var. *mexicana*, B. B. & R., N. A. B. iii, 1874, 410.

b. *americana*.

Meleagris americana, BARTR., Trav. 1791, 290.
Meleagris gallopavo var. *americana*, COUES, Key, 1872, 232.
Meleagris gallopavo, WILS., Index, 1872, vi, p. —.—BP., Am. Orn. 1825, i, 79, pl. 9; Syn. 1828, 122; Comp. List, 1838, 42.—AUD., Orn. Biog. 1831, i, 1, pls. 1 and 6; v, 559; Syn. 1839, 197; B. Am. 1842, v, 42, pls. 287, 288.—NUTT., Man. i, 1832, 630.—REICH., Syst. Av. 1851, pl. 26; Ic. Av. pl. 289.—BD., B. N. A. 1858, 615.— MAXIM., J. f. O. vi, 1858, 426.—McILWR., Pr. Ess. Inst. v, 1866, 91.—CATON, Am. Nat. iii, pp. 28, 30; vii, 431.—ALLEN, Bull. M. C. Z. ii, 1871, 342 (origin of domestic Turkey, &c.); iii, 1872, 181 (Kansas).—SNOW, B. Kans. 1873, No. 193.—ALLEN, Mem. Bost. Soc. i, 1868, 500 (Iowa).—TRIPPE, Pr. Bost. Soc. xv, 1872, 240 (Iowa).—HATCH, Pr. Minn. Acad. i, 1874, 61 (Southwest Minnesota).— B. B. & R., N. A. B. iii, 1874, 404; and of most authors.
Meleagris sylvestris, VIEILL., Nouv. Dict. d'Hist. Nat. ix, 447.
Gallopavo sylvestris, LE CONTE, Pr. A. N. S. ix, 1857, 179.
Meleagris fera, VIEILL., Gal. Ois. ii, 1824, 10, pl. 10.—GRAY, Cat. *Gall.* Br. Mus.
Wild Turkey of authors and others.

Hab.—Of var. *americana*, the Eastern Province of the United States and portions of Canada. Of true *gallapavo*, the southern portions of the Middle Province and southward.

Dr. Hayden does not include the Wild Turkey in his report, apparently not having met with it in the Missouri region. Its occurrence, however, is sufficiently attested as far up the Missouri River as the vicinity of Yankton, if not somewhat beyond. I found no evidence of its presence in Northern Dakota; I have observed but one Minnesotian record. In these longitudes it becomes abundant further south; both the Kansas authorities above cited witness its common occurrence in the timbered districts of that State, as Mr. Trippe does in Southern Iowa. Dr. Woodhouse states, that " throughout the wooded portions of the Indian Territory and Texas this bird abounds."* The northern line of its distribution may likewise be determined with approximate accuracy, though it appears to have contracted of late years. It is scarcely now found in any part of Minnesota; but Dr. Head tells me that some thirty years ago, at old Fort Atkinson, a few miles west of Prairie du Chien, it was frequently killed, though its present northern limit cannot be far from the southern border of Minnesota. Audubon mentioned its presence in Michigan, Massachusetts, and Vermont; but in these portions of New England, at least, it appears to be nearly or quite extinct,† while I never have heard of it from Maine. According to Mr. W. Ross King (Sportsman and Naturalist in Canada, p. 135), it was still met with in various localities in Canada, in 1866–'67, and about the same time Mr. McIlwraith states that it was "common along the western frontier" of the same territory. It is not necessary to instance special regions within the boundary above sketched, its dispersion being general, and only subject to restriction by the nature of localities unsuited to its habits, or where it is exposed to persecution which it cannot withstand. Constant interference with what would otherwise be its natural distribution, gradual diminution in its numbers in many places and its final disappearance from others, are points, unfortunately, only too well assured.

Family TETRAONIDÆ : The Grouse, &c.

The Missouri region, as defined for the purposes of the present work to include the entire country drained by the great river and its tributaries, affords representatives of all the North American genera of Grouse, and, in fact, furnishes us with every North American species of Grouse, excepting only two kinds of Ptarmigan (*Lagopus albus* and *L. rupestris*). All these are game birds in strictness. In the following account, therefore, I am at pains to give the sportsman and general reader a clear and accurate idea of the whole group as represented in North America. The technicalities are, it is believed, sufficiently precise, without being unnecessarily abstruse, to enable him to determine any Grouse he may procure, and establish in his mind its relationship to its allies; while I enlarge upon the biographies of the less known species, as far as is at present practicable.

In striking contrast to the abundance and variety of Grouse in this region, may be instanced the poverty of the same country in Partridges, only one species of which is ascertained, as yet, to inhabit any portion

---

* This author's further observations on the Turkeys of New Mexico probably relate to the var. *gallapavo*, as his remarks upon those of the Gila River certainly do. I ascertained the common occurrence of this form in the mountainous portions of Arizona. It is readily distinguished from the other by its lighter general colors, and especially by the pale tips of the rump feathers, as almost invariably seen in the domestic bird. Dr. Woodhouse's note on the great size of these birds is corroborated by Lieutenant Charles Bendire, who mentioned to me a gobbler he killed weighing twenty-eight pounds. My correspondent also informed me of an interesting fact—that the males frequently lack spurs. (See Am. Nat. vii, 1873, 326.)

† "As long ago as 1839, Mr. Peabody tells us it had become very rare. At the present day (1868) it is given by some Massachusetts authorities, and not by others. Mr. Allen 'can find no authentic instance of its recent capture in this State, although it has been said to occur wild on Mounts Tom and Holyoke * * * *.' Mr. Samuels omits the species; Mr. Putnam gives it, but entirely on the authority of the older writers. It is contained in none of the Maine lists. Mr. Linsley wrote of it in 1843, 'the last Wild Turkey that I have known in Connecticut was taken * * * about thirty years since, on Letoket Mountain, in Northford.'"—(COUES, Pr. Ess. Inst. v, 1868, 288.)

of the great district under consideration. This is the familiar Eastern Partridge, "Quail," or "Bob White," as it is variously termed. None of the several elegant and interesting Partridges of the southwest have been traced even to the southern borders of the Missouri region. We may allude to them in this connection. First, we have two species of the genus *Lophortyx*, *L. californicus*, and *L. gambeli*, of California, Arizona, New Mexico, and portions of Texas, with an elegant helmet-like crest of recurved feathers. Secondly, the Mountain Partridge of California (*Oreortyx pictus*), with a long, slender, flowing crest. Thirdly, the Scaled or Blue Partridge (*Callipepla squamata*), so called from a curious appearance of the plumage; and fourthly, the Massena Partridge (*Cyrtonyx massena*), remarkable for the difference between its sexes in coloration, and the singular harlequin markings of the male. These are fully noticed beyond.

The family *Tetraonidæ*, as defined in the Key, p. 232, embraces two American subfamilies—the *Tetraoninæ* or true Grouse, and the *Odontophorinæ*, which include all the American Partridges.

Subfamily TETRAONINÆ: *Grouse.*

The Grouse will be immediately distinguished from the Partridges by the more or less complete feathering of the legs and nostrils, which, in the Partridges, are naked and scaly; by a more or less evident strip of naked, pimply skin over the eye; by a row of fringe-like scales on the side of the toes; and usually, by the presence on each side of the neck of a tuft of lengthened or otherwise modified feathers, or a patch of naked distensible skin, or both of these. I call attention, below, to the fact that the Sharp-tailed Grouse (*Pedicecetes phasianellus*) has fairly developed air-sacs on the neck, though this has usually been overlooked.

The true Grouse, or *Tetraoninæ*, are confined to the Northern Hemisphere, and reach their highest development as a group, in number and variety of forms, in North America, our species being singularly diverse in the details of structure. All the American forms are noticed in these pages, beyond. The Old World forms are the following: The Great Capercailzie, or Cock-of-the-Woods (*Tetrao urogallus*), which finds its analogue in our Sage Cock (*Centrocercus urophasianus*), though structurally nearer our species of *Tetrao*; the Black Cock of Europe (*Tetrao tetrix*), with curiously curled tail-feathers, which may be considered to represent our Dusky Grouse (*Tetrao obscurus*); the Siberian *Tetrao falcipennis*, strict analogue of our Spruce Grouse (*T. canadensis*); the *Bonasa betulina* of Europe and Asia, equally near our Ruffed Grouse; and two or three species of Ptarmigan (*Lagopus*), very closely allied to, or identical with, our own.

Any adult Grouse of our country may be readily referred to its proper genus by the following table of characters:

CENTROCERCUS. Tail equaling or exceeding the wing in length, wedge-shaped, of twenty stiff, narrowly acuminate feathers; neck with numerous bristly filaments, a patch of curious scaly feathers, and a large naked space. Tarsi fully feathered; toes naked. Size of full grown cocks, two feet or more in length; tail a foot long.

PEDIOECETES. Tail shorter than the wing, wedge-shaped, of eighteen narrowed, stiffish feathers, of which the central pair exceed the rest by an inch or more. No evidently peculiar feathers on side of neck; bare space not conspicuous. Tarsi feathered to between the roots of the toes.* Markings of under parts lengthwise.

CUPIDONIA. Tail much shorter than the wing, rounded, of eighteen broad, flat feathers. Sides of neck with tufts of a few lengthened, narrowed feathers, like little wings, beneath which is a conspicuous distensible naked skin. Tarsi barely or not feathered to the toes. Markings of under parts crosswise.

---

* In the arctic variety the feathers of the legs are sometimes so long and thick as to hide the toes, almost as in the genus *Lagopus*.

BONASA. Tail about as long as the wing, rounded, of eighteen broad feathers. Sides of neck with tufts of very numerous, broad, soft feathers. No evident naked space on the neck. Tarsi bare below.

TETRAO. Tail rather shorter than the wing, square, or little rounded, of sixteen to twenty broad feathers. No peculiar feathers on the neck, nor evident naked spaces. Tarsi feathered to the toes.

LAGOPUS. Characters as in *Tetrao*, but the whole of the toes feathered. The species turn white in winter.

TETRAO CANADENSIS var. FRANKLINI, (Dougl.) Coues.

Franklin's Spruce Grouse.

a. *canadensis* proper (Canada Grouse; Spruce Grouse).

Tetrao canadensis, LINN., Syst. Nat. i, 1766, 274 (based on EDW., *Urogallus maculatus canadensis,* 118, pl. 118, ♂, and 71, pl. 71, ♀ ; BRISS., *Bonasia freti-hudsonis,* i, p. 201).—GM., Syst. Nat. i, 1788, 749.—LATH., Ind. Orn. ii, 1790, 637.—FORST., Phil. Trans. lxii, 1772, 389.—SAB., Frankl. Journ. 683.—VIEILL., Nouv. Dict. d'Hist. Nat. —, ——, —.—BP., Syn. 1828, 127 ; Am. Orn. iii, 1830, pl. 21, fig. 1, ♀ (not pl. 20, ♂, which is var. *franklini*) ; Am. Phil. Trans. iii, 1830, 391 ; Comp. List, 1838, 44.—SW. & RICH., F. B. A. ii, 1831, 346, pl. 62, ♀.—NUTT., Man. i, 1832, 667.—AUD., Orn. Biog. ii, 1834, 437 ; v, 1839, 563 ; pl. 176 ; Syn. 1839, 203 ; B. Am. v, 1842, 83, pl. 294.—BD., B. N. A. 1858, 622.—COUES, Pr. Phila. Acad. 1861, 226.—PUTN., Pr. Ess. Inst. i, 224 (Gloucester, Mass. ; in hemlock woods, Sept. 1851).—VERR., *ibid.* iii, 1862, 153 (resident near Umbagog Lakes, Me.).—ALLEN, *ibid.* iv, 1864, 85.—MCILWR., *ibid.* v, 1866, 91.—COUES, *ibid.* v, 1868, 287.—TRIPPE, *ibid.* vi, 1871, 118 (Minnesota, abundant, breeds).—BOARDM., Pr. Bost. Soc. ix, 1862, 128 (Calais, Me. ; common, resident, breeds).—DALL & BANN., Tr. Chic. Acad. 1869, 287 (Alaska).—MAYN., Pr. Bost. Soc. xiv, 1871, p. 27 (repaged).— MAYN., Guide, 1870, 138 (Massachusetts).—FINSCH, Abh. Nat. iii, 1872, 61 (Alaska).—COUES, Key, 1872, 233.

Canace canadensis, REICH., Syst. Av. 1851, p. xxix.—BP., Comptes Rendus, xlv, 1857, 428.—ELLIOT, Pr. A. N. S. 1864, 23 ; Monog. Tetr. pl. —.—B. B. & R., N. A. B. iii, 1874, 416, pl. 59, f. 5, 6.

Tetrao canace, LINN., Syst. Nat. i, 1766, 275 (based on *Bonasia canadensis,* BRISS., Orn. i, 203, pl. 20, f. 1, 2).

Spotted Grouse, PENN., Arct. Zool. ii, 307.—LATH., Syn. iv, 735.

Spruce Partridge, Wood Partridge, Swamp Partridge, VULG.

b. *franklini.*

(?) *Tetrao fusca,* ORD, Guthrie's Geog. 2d Am. ed. ii, 1815, 317 (based on *Small Brown Pheasant,* LEWIS & CLARKE, Exp. ii, p. 182, probably this species).

Tetrao canadensis, var., BP., Am. Orn. iii, 1830, plate xx, *male.*

Tetrao franklini, DOUGL., Linn. Trans. xvi, 1829, 139 (Mounts Hood, Saint Helen, and Baker).—SW. & RICH., F. B. A. ii, 1831, 348, pl. 6, ♂ (sources of the Missouri to those of the Mackenzie).—BD., B. N. A. 1858, 623.—COOP. & SUCK., N. H. Wash. Ter. 1860, 220.—COOP., B. Cal. i, 1870, 529 (Rocky and Cascade Mountains).—LORD, Pr. Roy. Arty. Inst. iv, 1863, 123.

Canace franklini, ELLIOT, Pr. A. N. S. 1864, 23 ; Monog. Tetraonidæ, pl. —.

Tetrao canadensis var. *franklini,* COUES, Key, 1872, 233.

Canace canadensis var. *franklini,* B. B. & R., N. A. B. iii, 1874, 419, pl. 59, f. 3.

Hab.—Northern North America east of the Rocky Mountains. South somewhat beyond the northern border of the United States. Var. *franklini* from the Northern Rocky Mountains of the United States and northward ; also, Cascade Mountains.

In consequence of its boreal and alpine distribution, the Canada Grouse is apparently not so well or generally known as our other species. The cock-bird may always be recognized by the following characters: Tail of sixteen feathers, rounded, black, with a broad orange-brown terminal bar. No obviously peculiar feathers on the side of the neck. Legs feathered to between the toes. The usual naked, colored strip of skin over the eye. Prevailing color black, with numerous sharp white bars and spots on the under parts, and on the upper parts finely waved with gray or tawny. Length, about 16 inches ; wing, 7 ; tail, 5½. The female is nowhere continuously black, but much variegated with brown, tawny, and white, and is rather less in size than the male; but she has the orange-brown tail-bar, and is substantially of the same form as the male.

Var. *franklini* only differs in wanting the orange-brown tail-band, and in having the upper tail-coverts, which are plain in true *canadensis*, conspicuously spotted with white. In this lack of the terminal band on the tail there is shown an interesting parallelism with the Rocky Mountain var. *richardsoni* of *T. obscurus*.

As already observed, the Canada Grouse is chiefly a boreal bird, reaching but a little way over our border. It is common in the coniferous forests of Northern New England, but only casually seen as far south as Massachusetts. In Minnesota, where it finds congenial resorts, it is abundant; but I never observed it in Northern Dakota, where the country is too dry and open. While along the northern boundary, however, I heard of a "Black Chicken," which I suppose was this species, and there is reason to expect its occurrence on the wooded Pembina and Turtle Mountains. There is nothing to indicate that it ever comes further south in this longitude.

Var. *franklini* is the only form to be properly included among the birds of the Missouri region, and even this is only found in the mountains, about the sources of the river and some of its tributaries. Dr. Cooper, who found it abundant in the Rocky and Bitter-root Mountains, also ascertained its occurrence in the Cascade Range, where, he says, it lives among the spruces and pines, particularly in swampy tracts, feeding on the buds and leaves of various coniferæ. Dr. Suckley determined its abundance in Saint Mary's Valley of the Rocky Mountains. It does not appear to have been met with by any of the parties with which Dr. Hayden has been connected.

The eggs of Franklin's Grouse and the Canada Grouse are indistinguishable. They are less elongate than those of *T. obscurus*, broader at the butt, and more pointed—approaching the characteristic pointed shape of Partridge eggs, and being like those of Ptarmigan in size and shape. The following measurements of selected examples from a large series show the size, shape, and range of variation: 1.70 by 1.25; 1.70 by 1.20; 1.65 by 1.25; 1.65 by 1.15. High in the oviduct the egg is creamy-white, as I see by some examples in the Smithsonian stated to have been cut out of the bird. This color is washed over to a varying degree of intensity with rich chestnut-brown—generally pale, a "creamy"-brown—and is further dotted, spotted, sometimes even splashed and blotched, with a very dark, heavy shade of the same color, the markings being numerous, strong, and bold, of no determinate shape, and wholly irregularly distributed. These markings are only an intensification, in spots, of the ground-color, but are very heavy, and, in comparison with those of other Grouse, show a decided approach to the peculiarly dark and heavy pattern of Ptarmigan eggs—the nearest approach made among American Grouse.

TETRAO OBSCURUS, Say.

Dusky Grouse; Blue Grouse; Pine Grouse.

Tetrao obscurus, SAY, Long's Exped. R. Mts. ii, 1823, 14, 202 (not of *Swainson* and *Richardson*.)—BP., Syn. 1828, 127; Am. Philos. Trans. iii, 1830, 391; Am. Orn. iii, 1830, p. 189, pl. 18.—(?) NUTT., Man. i, 1832, 666.—(?) AUD., Orn. Biog. iv, 1838, 446, pl. 361; Syn. 1839, 203; B. Am. i, 1842, 89, pl. 295.—WOODH., Sitgr. Rep. 1853, 96 (Santa Fé, N. M.).—NEWB., P. R. R. Rep. vi, 1857, 93.—SCL., P. Z. S. 1858, 1.—BD., B. N. A. 1858, 620.—HEERM., P. R. R. Rep. ix, 1859, pt. vi, 61.—HAYD., Rep. 1862, 172.—COOP., B. Cal. i, 1870, 526.—ALLEN, Bull. M. C. Z. iii, 1872, 181.—HOLD., Pr. Bost. Soc. xv, 1872, 208.—COUES, Key, 1872, 233.

Canace obscura, BP., Comptes Rendus, xlv, 1857, 428.—B. B. & R., N. A. B. iii, **1874,** 422; pl. 59, f. 1, 2.
Dendragapus obscurus, ELLIOT, Pr. A. N. S. 1864, 23; Monog. *Tetr.* pl. —.

Hab.—Eastern spurs and foot-hills of the Rocky Mountains to the Pacific, in elevated and wooded (especially coniferous) regions, excepting where replaced by var. *richardsoni* or var. *fuliginosus* (see beyond). South to New Mexico.

List of specimens.

19158	257	Deer Creek, Wy.	♂	Feb. 1, 1860	G. H. Trook..	21.00	30.00	9.50
19159	256	.... do	♂	....	..... do	23.00	32.00	10.00
19160	....	.... do	♂	Feb. 21, 1860	..... do	21.00	31.00	10.00
19161	259	.... do	♂	Feb. 13, 1860	..... do	21.25	31.50	10.00
19162	258	.... do	♂	Feb. 21, 1860	..... do	21.75	30.00	9.00
19163	251	.... do	♂	Feb. 13, 1860	F. V. Hayden.	20.50	30.50	9.25
19164	252	.... do	♂	Feb. 13, 1860	..... do	20.50	30.50	10.25
19165	253	.... do	♂	Feb. 13, 1860	..... do	19.50	28.75	9.00
19166	255	.... do	♂	Feb. 13, 1860	..... do	18.00	27.00	8.25
18167	....	.... do	♂	Feb. 13, 1860	..... do	19.00	28.50	8.50

Lieutenant Warren's Expedition.—8914–20, Laramie Peak, Wyoming Territory.
Later Expeditions.—54302, 60833–37, Wyoming; 60464, Bitter Cottonwood Creek.

Dwelling in remote mountainous regions not often visited by the sportsman, the Dusky Grouse is not yet a well-known bird, and it will be well to indicate its characters. It is very large—larger than any of our Grouse, excepting the great Sage Cock, and some specimens are little inferior in size to an average bird of this species. It is dark colored; the tail is brownish-black, more or less marked with gray, and with a broad slate-gray terminal bar (characters not seen in any other species). The back and wings are dark brown, finely waved in zigzag with slate-gray, mixed with more or less ochrey-brown and some white on the scapularies. Long feathers of the sides similar to the back; other under parts a fine bluish-gray or light-slate color (much like the tail-bar), variegated with white, especially on the lower belly and under tail-coverts. Cheeks black; throat sharply speckled with black and white. Legs feathered to the toes; the usual warty, colored strip of skin over the eye. *Female* much smaller and lighter colored, being more extensively variegated with tawny and white, but showing the distinctive slate-gray on the under parts and at the end of the tail. Length, 18 to 24 inches; wing, 8 to 10; tail, 7 to 8; extent of wings, about 30.*

The eggs of the Dusky Grouse, though shaped much like those of the Canada Grouse, are rather more elongate, and, of course, much larger. Two specimens measure, respectively, 2.05 by 1.45, and 2.00 by 1.50, exhibiting the usual range of variation in shape. They are paler and more creamy in ground-color than those of *T. canadensis* usually are, and are finely speckled all over with chocolate-brown. In most specimens these markings are mere dots everywhere; a pattern that sometimes yields to

---

* Specimens from Sitka and corresponding regions, with the slate-bar on the tail, as in true *obscurus*, are very noticeably darker than even var. *richardsoni;* and the female is peculiar in the prevalence of rich rusty and chestnut-brown markings, mixed with black, comparing with the female of the other varieties much as *Bonasa* var. *sabinei* compares with the other forms of the Ruffed Grouse, and being apparently equally entitled to varietal distinction by name.

Mr. Ridgway has lately described this form as a different variety, as follows:

Tetrao obscurus, COOP. & SUCK., N. H. Wash. Ter. 1860, 219.—LORD, Pr. Roy. Arty. Inst. iv, 1864, 122 (British Columbia).—DALL & BANN., Tr. Chic. Acad. i, 1869, 287 (Alaska).—FINSCH, Abh. Nat. iii, 1872, 61 (Alaska).
Canace obscurus var. *fuliginosus*, RIDGW.—B. B. & R., N. A. B. iii, 1874, 425 (Oregon to Sitka).

I have carfully examined this form, and find it quite as worthy of recognition as the other varieties of this genus.

larger spots, though scarcely to such bold splashes as are frequently seen in the eggs of *canadensis*. The range of variation is like that seen in *Pediœcetes*, but is pushed to wider limits.

A set of eight eggs of var. *richardsoni* taken by Mr. Trook, June 23, 1860, on Clarke's Fork at the headwaters of the Missouri, are notably smaller than any examples of true *obscurus* eggs which have come under our notice, measuring only about 1.75 by 1.25 ; they are also paler and more minutely and sparsely dotted. It is not probable, however, that these distinctions would hold through a large series. The nest which contained these eggs was built on the ground, beneath a wild-cherry bush.

For an account of the habits of this large and very presentable game bird I must refer to other authors, having never yet seen it alive. Our principal authorities are Drs. Cooper and Suckley, who, apparently, en-joyed excellent opportunities of observation. The last named writes as follows in the work above cited :

"This bird, called generally in Oregon the *Blue* Grouse, and also known as the Pine Grouse, Dusky Grouse, &c., I met, for the first time, when our exploring party reached the main chain of the Rocky Mount-ains, where we found it exceedingly abundant, but not more so than in the Blue Mountains of Oregon, the Cascade Mountains, and in all the tim-bered country between the last-mentioned range and the Pacific coast. In the autumn, about November 15, they generally disappear, and it is rare, indeed, to see a single individual of the species during the interval between that period and about March 20 of the following year. Con-cerning the whereabouts of this bird during winter, there are many opinions among the settlers. Some maintain that the species is migra-tory, and that they retire to the South, while others say that they repair to the tops of the highest evergreen trees, where, in the thickest foliage of the branches, they pass the cold season in a state of semi-torpor, rarely or never descending until warm weather comes on. As they sub-sist well on the leaves of the coniferæ, and can always obtain sufficient water from the snow and rain-drops on the leaves to supply their neces-sities, I have but little doubt that this latter is the correct account, or that, if migratory, they are but partially so. I saw one bird of this species on the ground during a fall of snow in January, 1854, near the Nisqually River, Washington Territory ; and I have been told that a man, near Olympia, whose *eye-sight* is excellent, is able any day during winter to obtain several birds by searching carefully for them in the tops of the tallest and most thickly-leaved firs. This requires eye-sight of much greater power than most men possess. Even in the summer, when these birds are generally lower in the trees, it is very difficult to find them among the dense branches. They have, in addition to their sombre hues, the advantage of their habit of crowding very closely to the limbs, and of sitting almost immovably for hours.

"The first indication in the spring of their arrival? or activity? is the courting-call of the male. This is a prolonged noise, sounding much like the whirr of a rattan-cane whirled rapidly through the air. It is repeated quickly several times, and then stops abruptly for a brief inter-val. This noise is said to be produced by inflating and contracting a sac on each side of the throat, which is for the most part concealed when collapsed, and is covered with an orange-yellow, thick, corrugated, un-feathered skin. These birds, at Fort Steilacoom, are very abundant throughout the spring and early summer. They are there mostly con-fined to the forests of fir-trees (*Abies douglasii*). Late in the season, after hatching, they may be found generally at midday on the ground in search of berries, seeds, &c. When alarmed, they almost invariably seek safety in the dense foliage of the trees, instinctively appearing to understand the advantage of thus hiding. In the autumn they are more generally found on the ground feeding on sallal and other berries. One day, in October, 1856, I saw on the Nisqually plains, among fern and grass, five of these birds, full grown and in excellent order. A man killed the whole five, one by one, with a double-barreled gun, without an attempt being made by a single individual to fly. This Grouse is a very fine table bird; the little dash of *pine taste* its flesh possesses only adding to its game flavor. I have known males, in June, weighing three and a half pounds, although they rarely exceed two and three-fourths pounds. By August 1st the young are generally half grown. They are then easily killed on the wing, and are excellent for the table."

In the same work Dr. Cooper remarks that the Blue Grouse is common in most of the forests of the Territory, though less so near the coast, and continues: "As it rarely appears on the open prairie, it is difficult to find, if, as usual, it alights on a tree. So perfectly motionless does it sit, that though one may be looking straight at it, he will probably mistake it for a knot or a bunch of leaves. * * * * During May near the coast, and until August in the mountains, the low tooting of this Grouse is heard everywhere, sounding something like the cooing of a Pigeon, and in the same deep tone as the drumming of a Ruffed Grouse. It has the power of ventriloquism, so that while the bird may be sitting in a tree overhead, the sound seems to come from places quite distant. I have not seen the nest or eggs, but in June flocks of half-grown young are murdered by the Indians near Puget Sound. In winter they are so rarely seen west of the mountains, that the people think they must keep entirely in the trees. In October, 1853, I saw, however, a flock running through the snow, near the Spokane plains, and one of them was shot; but I have never seen them since then in the winter."

The same writer has some additional remarks in his later work on the Birds of California: "This fine game bird is common in Oregon and Northern California, extending in the Coast Range nearly to San Francisco Bay, and in the Sierra Nevada to about latitude 38°. They are brought to market in winter from the mountains near Napa, and are said to come down at times into the valleys, but have never been met with in California south of San Francisco. In the Sierra Nevada, latitude 39°, I found them rather scarce, and in September only above an elevation of 6,000 feet, but was informed that they went much lower down in winter, probably about as far as the snows fall, or to about 2,000 feet, in that latitude. I think their range is more dependent on the prevalence of spruce and other dense coniferous forests than on the climate, as it is much milder near Napa than at that elevation in the Sierra Nevada, and toward the north they frequent valleys. I have seen them near the Columbia River at all seasons, usually inhabiting the dense forests. They, however, come out on the borders of prairies and openings when not molested, especially in the early morning. * * * * Their food consists of various berries, nuts, and seeds, besides grain around farms. * * * * In winter they live much on the buds of trees, even those of the coniferæ."

Quotation of Dr. Newberry's notice will add to the interest of the present article: "The Dusky Grouse, among American species, is only second in size to the 'Sage Hen' (*T. urophasianus*). The cock is decidedly the handsomest of all American Grouse, and the flesh is white, and equal to that of the Ruffed Grouse or the American Partridge. This bird inhabits the evergreen forests exclusively, and is found not un-commonly in the Sierra Nevada of California, and in the wooded dis-tricts of the country lying between the Sacramento Valley and the Columbia. In the Cascade Mountains we found it associated with the Ruffed Grouse, which it resembles in habit more than any other spe-cies. When on the ground they lie very close, flying up from your feet as you approach them, and when flushed always take to a tree; while sitting on a tree, you may fire as many times as is necessary to hit the bird before you can dislodge it. In the spring the male, seated motion-less on a branch of pine or fir where it issues from the trunk, makes a booming call, which, by a remarkable ventriloquial power, serves rather to mislead than direct the sportsman, and, unless experienced in shoot-ing this kind of Grouse, he will be likely to spend much time, with nothing to show for it, in a vain search for the bird."

The habits of this species in Colorado may be elucidated by an extract from Mr. Trippe's manuscripts:

"The 'Gray Grouse,' as this species is universally called, is a rather common bird throughout the mountains, from the foot-hills up to timber-line, and, during summer, wanders at times above the woods as high as the summit of the range. Excepting for a brief period in August and September, it rarely approaches the vicinity of clearings, frequenting the dense pine forests, and showing a preference for the tops of rocky and inaccessible mountains. In its nature, in short, it is the exact counterpart of the Ruffed Grouse, having the same roving, restless dis-position; living upon the same diet of buds and berries; frequenting the same rugged, craggy mountain haunts; and, like that bird, is more or less solitary in its habits, and constantly moving from place to place on foot. Its food consists principally of the leaves and berries of vari-ous species of *Ericaceæ*, which abound in all its haunts. It is also very fond of grasshoppers and all kinds of insects, and, while the snow lies deep upon the ground, lives for the most part upon the buds and tender leaves of the pines. When the grain is cut in the valleys, the Grouse are frequently to be found, in the stubble-fields and adjacent coverts, in small flocks of from three or four up to eight or ten. They are then so tame as to be easily approached and killed, but later in the season be-come somewhat wilder, though never very shy. They never gather in large flocks, like the Pinnated and Sharp-tailed Grouse, more than a single family being rarely found together. The broods separate as soon as they are well grown, and, from the middle or close of autumn until the succeeding pairing season, the Gray Grouse is usually found alone. On being suddenly startled, this bird takes wing with great rapidity, sometimes uttering a loud cackling note, very much like that of the Prairie Hen on similar occasions, frequently alighting on the lower limb of a tree after flying a little way, and watching the intruder with out-stretched neck. Sometimes they will fly up to the top of a tall pine and remain hidden in the thick foliage for a long time; nor will they move or betray their position, although sticks and stones are thrown into the tree, or even a shot fired. Late in summer many of them ascend to the upper woods to feed upon the multitudes of grasshoppers that swarm there in August and September, in the pursuit of which they wander above timber-line, and may sometimes be met in great numbers among the copses of willows and juniper that lie above the forests.

"The flight of the Gray Grouse is rapid and powerful. Its flesh is white and tender, resembling that of the Ruffed Grouse. In all re-spects it seems to fill the same place in the mountain fauna of Colorado that is occupied by the latter bird among the mountains of New England and the Middle States. Although Allen gives the Ruffed Grouse as an inhabitant of the 'mountains of Colorado,' the most diligent search failed to discover a trace of it; while all the hunters and trappers with whom I have conversed assured me that it is never found there at all."

TETRAO OBSCURUS var. RICHARDSONI, (Dougl.) Coues.

Richardson's, or Black-tailed Grouse.

Tetrao richardsoni, DOUGL., Trans. Linn. Soc. xvi, 141.—WILS., Zool. Illust. pls. 30, 31.—
      LORD, Pr. Roy. Arty. Inst. iv, 1864, 122.—GRAY, Cat. B. Br. Mus. v, 1867, 86.—
      COOP., B. Cal. i, 1870, 528.
Dendragapus richardsoni, ELLIOT, Pr. Phila. Acad. 1864, 23 ; Monog. *Tetr.* pl. —.
Tetrao obscurus, SW. & RICH., F. B. A. ii, 1831, 344, pls. 59, 60, evidently this form. (Also
      of *Audubon* and *Baird*, partly. Not of *Say*.)
Tetrao obscurus var. *richardsoni*, COUES, Key, 1872, 233.—MERR., Rep. Geol. Surv. Ter.
      1872, 698.
Canace obscurus var. *richardsoni*, B. B. & R., N. A. B. iii, 1874, 427, pl. 59, f. 4.

Hab.—"Central Rocky Mountains, from South Pass, and northward to Fort Liard, H. B. T." (*Cooper.*)

List of specimens.

19168	....	W. side R. Mts.	....	June 5, 1860	F. V. Hayden.	19.00	28.50	9.25
19169	....	...... do	....	May 31, 1860	...... do	19.25	27.00	......
19175	....	Yellowstone R .	....	July 23, 1860	G. H. Trook..	22.50	31.50	......

Late Expeditions.—62216–22, Téton Cañon and North Fork, Idaho.

In this slight variety of the common Dusky Grouse the general colors are darker, and the terminal slate bar on the tail is reduced to a minimum, or wanting altogether. It is clearly the form described and figured by Swainson and Richardson, as above, who speak of it as inhabiting the Rocky Mountains from lat. 40° to lat. 67°, and perhaps still further, and refer it to the true *T. obscurus* of Say. These authors mention one of Mr. Douglas' specimens, in the Edinburgh Museum, as being younger, but " evidently the same species." Audubon made no distinction of the two varieties ; Baird cites " *richardsoni*" as synonymous, but noted the above characters of certain specimens. As Dr. Cooper has remarked, the apparent distribution of the variety is peculiar, it being embraced to the East, West, and South, by that of the ordinary *T. obscurus.*

CENTROCERCUS UROPHASIANUS, (Bp.) Sw.

Sage Cock; Cock of the Plains.

Tetrao urophasianus, BP., Zool. Journ. iii, 1828, 214 ; App. Syn. U. S. Birds in Ann. Lyc.
      N. Y. p. 442 ; Trans. Am. Phil. Soc. iii, 1830, 390 ; Am. Orn. iii, 1830, 212, pl. 21,
      fig. 2.—DOUG., Trans. Linn. Soc. xvi, 1829, 133, sp. 1.—WILS., Zool. Illust. 1831,
      pls. 26, 27.—NUTT., Man. i, 1832, 666.—AUD., Orn. Biog. iv, 1838, 503, pl. 371;
      Syn. 1839, 205 ; B. Am. v, 1842, 106, pl. 297.—BD., Stansbury's Rep. 1852, 319.—
      NEWB., P. R. R. Rep. vi, 1857, 95.—MAXIM., J. f. O. vi, 1858, 431.
Tetrao (*Centrocercus*) *urophasianus*, SW. & RICH., F. B. A. ii, 1831, 358, pl. 58.
Centrocercus urophasianus, JARD., Nat. Lib. Birds, 140, pl. 17.—BD., N. A. A. 1858, 624.—
      COOP. & SUCK., N. H. Wash. Ter. 1860, 222.—HAYD., Rep. 1862, 172.—COUES,
      Pr. Phila. Acad. 1866, 94 (Mojave River, Cal., latitude about 35°).—COOP., B.
      Cal. i, 1870, 536.—ALLEN, Bull. M. C. Z. iii, 1872, 181.—HOLDEN-AIKEN, Pr.
      Bost. Soc. xv, 1872, 209.—SNOW, B. Kans. 1872, No. 164 (Western Kansas).—
      COUES, Key, 1872, 233.—MERR., Rep. U. S. Geol. Surv. Ter. 1872, 699.—B. B. &
      R., N. A. B. iii, 1874, 429, pl. 60, f. 2, 4.
Cock of the Plains, LEWIS & CLARKE, ii, 180, sp. 2.

Hab.—Sage plains of the West. East to Western Kansas. South to about 35°. West and north as far as suitable surface extends. Scarcely to be found on the Missouri.

List of specimens.

19134	175	Powder River..	....	Oct. 7, 1859	G. H. Trook..	21.00	35.00	10.50
19135	215	Deer Creek	....	Dec. 29, 1859	...... do	22.00	35.00	10.00
19136	266	Platte Valley ..	....	Jan. 12, 1860	F. V. Hayden..	28.50	42.00	12.00
19137	217	Deer Creek	♂	Jan. 6, 1860	...... do	31.90	41.50	12.50
19138	....	...... do	...	....	...... do			
49139	....	...... do	♂	Jan. 5, 1860	...... do	42.25	40.50	12.50
19140	205	...... do	....	Dec. 15, 1859	...... do	21.75	33.00	10.50
19141	212	...... do	....	....	...... do	23.00	34.00	9.75
19142	218	...... do	....	Jan. 6, 1860	...... do	31.50	44.50	14.00
19143	150	...... do	....	Nov. —, 1859	...... do			
19144	221	...... do	♀	Dec. 29, 1859	...... do	22.50	35.00	10.00
19145	159	...... do	....	Nov. —, 1859	F. V. Hayden.			
19146	286	...... do	♂	Apr. 14, 1860	G. H. Trook..	31.00	40.00	12.00
19147	198	Tullock's Cr. ..	♀	Sept. 5, 1859	...... do	20.00	33.50	10.50
19148	151	Cheyenne Riv..	♂	Oct. 29, 1859	F. V. Hayden.	29.50	41.50	.....
19149	219	Deer Creek....	....	Jan. 7, 1860	...... do	23.00	38.00	11.00
19150	148	Cheyenne Riv..	♂	Oct. 27, 1859	...... do	......	42.00	13.00
19151	287	Deer Creek....	♂	....	J. Stevenson .			
19152	213	...... do	....	Jan. 12, 1860	F. V. Hayden.	29.40	39.00	11.50
19153	161	Platte River...	....	Oct. 11, 1859	G. H. Trook..	30.00	43.00	14.50
19154	172	....						
19155	152	Tongue River..	♀	Sept. 16, 1859	G. H. Trook..	24.00	36.50	11.50
19156	154	Clear Fork	♂	Sept. 17, 1859	F.V.Hayden..	22.00	34.00	12.00
19157	196	E. F. Tongue R.	♀	Sept. 16, 1859	G. H. Trook..	20.00	33.50	10.50

Lieutenant Warren's Expedition.—No. 5419, fifty miles up the Yellowstone; 8921, 8923, Cheyenne River.

Later Expeditions.—60462, Le Bonté Creek; 60826-32, Wyoming; 61096-9,.Henry's Fork; 62223-5, North Fork and Henry's Lake, Idaho.

The above extensive suite of specimens illustrates this species under the various conditions of age, sex, and season, from the downy young to the largest cocks. The measurements given show the variation in size among adult birds. Some old cocks are of great size—the birds apparently growing, in some instances, after they have attained normal dimensions. The female, as usual, is smaller than the male, averaging about one-third less. There is no occasion to describe the bird minutely in the present connection; its great size and various peculiar features will prevent mistake respecting it. The full-grown cocks average about 2½ feet in length; the hens rather under 2 feet. The tail equals, or rather exceeds, the wing in length, and consists of twenty very narrow acuminate feathers, stiffened and graduated in length from the middle pair outward. A more remarkable feature of the cock is the immense dilatable air-sac of naked yellow skin on each side of the neck, bordered by a patch of curiously stiffened, horny feathers, like fish-scales, often terminating in bristly filaments several inches long. The feet are feathered to the toes, as in most of our other Grouse. The most noticeable color-mark is a broad black area on the under parts of the adult, less extensive in the female; it contrasts with the white of the breast. The upper parts are varied with gray, black, brown, and tawny or whitish. The cocks weigh from three to six pounds, according to age and condition; the hens are correspondingly much lighter.

The history of this species is generally dated from the account by Lewis and Clarke, of a "Cock of the Plains" which they found in the Rocky Mountains, about the headwaters of the Missouri, and afterward more abundantly on the plains of the Columbia. The first technical description of the species was that of Bonaparte, who, under the name of *Tetrao urophasianus*, noticed in various periodicals, and figured in his

American Ornithology, a specimen in the Leadbeater collection. The Prince supposed this to be a female, and, comparing it with the same sex of the European Cock of the Woods (*Tetrao urogallus*), proclaimed it to be as large as the latter, which, however, is not the case. Judging from the assigned dimensions of 28 to 30 inches in length, his bird was a cock, although he does not notice the tympanum or modified scaly feathers of the neck, these, perhaps, not being evident in his immature specimen. In 1831 Swainson framed for the species the subgenus *Centrocercus*, and gave a characteristic figure. The bird being abundant, and of very marked features, it soon became generally well known, and is noticed by nearly all writers who have visited the regions it inhabits.

Not the least interesting fact in the natural history of the Sage Cock is its strict confinement to a region of peculiar character. Its dispersion over our western interior seems to be coextensive with the treeless, arid, and almost desert regions where grow the various species of *Artemisia* or wild sage, upon which it chiefly feeds, and from which it derives its name. The largest by far of the gallinaceous birds of this country, excepting the Turkey alone, and one offering attractions to the sportsman, it is, nevertheless, of the least consequence of all from an economic point of view, since the nature of its harsh and bitter food renders its flesh little acceptable—indeed unpalatable under ordinary circumstances.

As far up the Missouri as I have been (to the vicinity of Fort Stevenson, 150 miles below the mouth of the Yellowstone), I have failed to note any indication of the bird's presence; while it certainly does not occur to the northward anywhere east of longitude 103°. It is stated to be common on the plains of Western Kansas and Nebraska, as it doubtless is also in southwestern portions of Dakota, and thence westward, in suitable districts, to California and Oregon, east of the Sierra Nevada and Cascade Ranges. As above indicated, the point of ascertained southernmost range is the Mojave River, a specimen killed there having been seen by Dr. Cooper, who also found what he considered to be addditional evidence of its occurrence. I do not know the line of northward extension, and it is, apparently, not yet ascertained; it will probably be found to run, at some points at least, near the present boundary of the United States, along the 49th parallel. Sir John Richardson gives nothing to the point on this score; and the only indications I have met with are those given by Drs. Cooper and Suckley. The former mentions the Spokane plains, in Washington Territory, as a locality north of which none were seen, "the country being, apparently, too woody for them. On those plains they were common, for though level, the surface is dry, sterile, and elevated near 1,000 feet above the sea." Dr. Suckley writes that they are found "on the sage barrens of the Yakima and Simcoe Valleys, in Washington Territory, about latitude 46° and 47° north." He also speaks of shooting it on the Milk River, Montana, about 200 miles west of Fort Union, the most northeastern point at present on record to my knowledge. The same gentleman refers to their food in the following terms:

"I have dissected these Grouse in situations where there was abundance of grass seeds, wild grain, grasshoppers, and other kinds of food that a person would imagine would be readily eaten by them, yet I have failed to obtain a single particle of any other food in their full stomachs than the leaves of the artemisia. This food must be either highly preferred, or else be essential to their existence. They seem to have the faculty of doing for a long time without water, as I have found them habitually in dry desert situations, during severe droughts, a long distance from water. The flesh of this bird is rather strong and bitter, from the nature of its food, and it quickly decomposes after death."

Dr. Suckley's account of the diet of these birds is, however, too exclusive. They certainly eat various insects, especially grasshoppers, and an indiscriminate variety of vegetable substances. Mr. Ridgway informs me of an interesting fact : that the gizzard of the Sage Cock is a slightly muscular membranous bag, quite different from the strong, dense "grist-mill" of ordinary *Gallinæ*. The point has been recorded in the following terms :

"A peculiarity of this species, which I have not seen noticed, is that its stomach, instead of being hard and very muscular as in other *Gallinacea*, is soft and membraneous, like that of the birds of prey. This was first told me by hunters in Nevada, and I afterward satisfied myself of the truth of their statement that the Sage Hen "has no gizzard," by dissecting a sufficient number of individuals. This bird is never known to eat grain, but subsists almost entirely upon green leaves of artemisia and on grasshoppers."—(*Am. Nat.* viii, 1874.)

The same feature is also noticed by a late writer in *Forest and Stream*, in the following article, which I reproduce, somewhat abbreviated :

"A measurement of the picture gives length of bill and head 3 inches, neck 7, body 14, and tail 10 inches; total, 34 inches. Its actual weight in feather was seven pounds, and it was a fair specimen of a full-grown male bird, the female being about two pounds less. The attitude is characteristic, half crouching as it steals off when alarmed. The color is also true to life, black and brown, mottled with white, except the breast, where white predominates. You will perceive, also, that the legs are slightly feathered. A remarkable feature of the bird is, that it has no gizzard; and in hundreds examined, no seeds, grain, or insects were ever found in the craw, or rather paunch, which is very large. This lack of a gizzard indicates it to be a browser, and not a grain eater. Its food is principally the artemisia or wild sage, though indications of the leaves and buds of the grease-wood and various grasses were sometimes found. I have never met with it where the wild sage did not abound.

"I notice that some of your correspondents state that it is scarcely eatable on account of the bitter taste caused by the artemisia. Here is the remedy : Immediately after killing, draw the bird, thoroughly removing the intestines and their contents, but all other dressing can be delayed till camp is reached. Treated in this manner it has no disagreeable taste. This is what we should expect, when it is recollected that in all animals the peculiarities of food pass off by secretions through the natural channels. The milk and butter of a cow feeding upon wild garlic, cabbage, rag-weed, &c., will be tainted with their peculiar qualities, but the flesh is not. So when the bird is dead the operations of the body cease, absorption commences, and the contents of the intestines begin to affect the flesh. The power of life to resist absorption and decay are as wonderful as mysterious. A live fish in salt water continues fresh. The rubbing of salt upon a live hog's back would hardly cure the meat, but when slaughtered, it takes up the salt through skin and flesh alike. But perhaps too much upon this familiar principle, unless it serves to redeem this magnificent bird from its unlucky reputation. The flesh is quite dark and rather dry, but when the bird is about two-thirds grown, with the bitter taste prevented in the manner I have described, it is not easy for a hungry man to find fault with it, especially in camp. I notice also that a correspondent says that it does not lie well before a dog ; I have not found it so under favorable circumstances. When there is reasonable cover, its conduct in that respect is better than that of the Pinnated Grouse. But the peculiarities of its habitat do not give the dog a fair chance to work, or do himself or the game justice. The artemisia grows only upon barren prairies, from 4,000 to 10,000 feet above the level of the ocean, where the soil is composed of dry sand, alkaline clay, granite rocks, &c., with little other vegetation but stunted shrubs, cactus, and an occasional clump of wild grass, where rains rarely occur, and there is little moisture in the air or upon the ground. It is a tough, sprawling, crooked evergreen, or rather ever-gray shrub, from six inches to six feet high, partly deciduous in appear-ance, much like the garden sage, and when thick, very difficult for man, horse or dog, to get through.

"The Sage Cock is a good skulker and runner, and not easily flushed if it can hide. It gets up heavily, like the Wild Turkey, laboring hard with the wings until a proper height is reached and speed is obtained, when it sails rapidly away, and, if alarmed, often goes from half a mile to a mile before dropping.

"The packs are smaller than any other variety of Grouse, rarely ex-ceeding ten. They never alight upon trees, and, indeed, I have never seen them among timber. They are rarely found east of Fort Laramie or of the range of Black Hills, which constitutes the first step or shelf of the Rocky Mountains going west. The mountain deserts constitute their home. I have met them in the Laramie plains, on the upper waters of the North Platte, on Sweetwater River, on the headwaters of Green River (the Colorado of the West), on Lewis' Fork of the Colum-bia, and on Wind River, but nowhere so numerous as on the latter stream and its tributaries, where scores would be often seen in a mile's ride.

"The Sage Cock is also said to be common north nearly or quite to the British line, and west to California, but in these observations I have confined myself to the sections I have personally visited. It would be safe to presume that they would be found wherever there was a barren prairie stocked with artemisia.

"I have heard it said that the Sage Cock migrates, but this is not so, as I have seen them at all seasons of the year on the same ground. In this respect their habits are the same as other varieties of Grouse, never moving far from the spot where hatched, unless compelled to do so. The idea no doubt arises from the fact that they are rarely seen moving in the severe weather and terrible storms of this region, their habit being to lie close in ravines and hollows, and dense thickets of artemisia, where they can have food and shelter."

Dr. Newberry's account, which I extract almost entire as no less interesting to the sportsman than to the naturalist, will bring this great "Bustard" vividly to mind:

"Coming into camp at evening, I had been attracted by a white chalk-like bluff, some two miles to the right of our trail, which I visited and examined. Near it was a warm spring, which came out of the hill-side, and, spreading over the prairie, kept a few acres green and fresh, strongly contrasting with the universal brown of the landscape. In this little oasis I found some, to me, new flowers, many reptiles, and a considerable number of Sharp-tailed Grouse, of which I killed several, the whole presenting attractions sufficiently strong—as we were to re-main in camp one day—to take me over there next morning. I had filled my plant-case with flowers, had obtained frogs, and snakes, and chalky infusorial earth enough to load down the boy who accompanied me, and had enjoyed a fine morning's sport, dropping as many Grouse on the prairies as we could conveniently carry. Following up the little stream toward the spring on the hill-side, a dry, treeless surface, with patches of ' sage brush " (*Artemisia tridentata*), I was suddenly startled by a great flutter and rush, and a dark bird, that appeared to me as large as a Turkey, rose from the ground near me, and, uttering a hoarse *hēk hēk*, flew off with an irregular, but remarkably well-sustained, course.

" I was just then stooping to drink from the little stream, and quite unprepared for game of any kind, least of all for such a bird, evidently a Grouse, but so big and black, so far exceeding all reasonable dimensions, that I did not think of shooting him, but stood with open eyes, and, doubtless, open mouth, eagerly watching his flight to mark him down. But stop he did not—so long as I could see him, now flapping, now sailing, he kept on his course till he disappeared behind a hill a mile away.

" I was, of course, greatly chagrined by his escape, but knowing that, given one Grouse, it is usually not difficult to find another, I commenced looking about for the mate of the one I had lost. My search was not a long one; almost immediately she rose from under a sage brush with a noise like a whirl-wind, not to fly a mile before stopping to look around, as the cock had done, but, by a fortunate shot, falling helpless to the ground. No deer-stalker ever felt more triumphant enthusiasm while standing over the prostrate body of a buck, or fisherman when the silvery sides of a salmon sparkled in his landing-net, than I felt as I picked up this great, and to me unknown, bird. I afterward ranged the hill-sides for hours, with more or less success, waging a war on these birds, which I found to be quite abundant, but very strong-winged and difficult to kill. I repeatedly flushed them not ten yards from me, and, as they rose, poured my whole charge, right and left, into them, knocking out feathers, perhaps, but not killing the bird, which, in defiance of all my hopes and expectations, would carry off my shot to such a distance that I would not follow him, even did I know he would never rise again. Here, as elsewhere, I found these birds confined to the vicinity of the ' sage bushes,' from under which they usually spring.

" A few days later, on the shores of Wright and Rhett Lakes, we found them very abundant, and killed all we cared to. A very fine male which I killed there was passed by nearly the whole party, within thirty feet, in open ground. I noticed him as soon, perhaps, as he saw us, and waited to watch his movements. As the train approached he sank down on the ground, depressing his head, and lying as motionless as a stick or root, which he greatly resembled. After the party had passed I moved toward him, when he depressed his head till it rested on the ground, and evidently made himself as small as possible. He did not move till I had approached within fifteen feet of him, when he arose, and I shot him. He was in fine plumage, and weighed over five pounds. We continued to meet with the Sage Hen, whenever we crossed sage plains, till we reached the Columbia.

" To the westward of the Cascade Range this bird probably does not exist, as all its habits and preferences seem to fit it for the occupancy of the sterile and anhydrous region of the central desert. Its flesh is dark and, particularly in old birds, highly flavored with worm-wood, which, to most persons, is no proof of excellence. The young bird, if parboiled and stewed, is very good; but, as a whole, this is inferior for the table to any other species of American Grouse."

In the paper above cited, Mr. Holden remarks a habit of this Grouse probably known to few. "They roost in circles on the ground," he says; "I have seen a patch of ground, fifteen feet in diameter, completely covered with their excrement. I think they resort to the same place many nights in succession, unless disturbed."

Some of those habits of the Sage Cock which are peculiar to the pairing season were described by one of the earlier writers, doubtless with substantial accuracy, and are quoted in the Fauna Boreali-Americana. "They pair in March and April. Small eminences on the banks of streams are the places usually selected for celebrating the weddings, the time generally about sunrise. The wings of the male are lowered, buzzing on the ground; the tail, spread like a fan, somewhat erect; the bare, yellow œsophagus inflated to a prodigious size—fully half as large as his body, and, from its soft, membranous substance, being well contrasted with the scale-like feathers below it on the breast, and the flexible, silky feathers on the neck, which on these occasions stand erect. In this grotesque form he displays, in the presence of his intended mate, a variety of attitudes. His love-song is a confused, prating, but not offensively disagreeable, tone—something that we can imitate, but have difficulty in expressing—*hurr–hurr–hurr–r·r·r–hoo*, ending in·a deep, hollow tone, not unlike the sound produced by blowing into a large reed."

Even those who are familiar with the appearance of the "drums" of the common Pinnated Grouse when fully inflated, may fail, without actual inspection, to form a fair idea of the enormous yellow air-sacs of the Sage Cock in their condition of greatest distension. Instead of being regularly hemispherical, like half a small orange, they are immense, bulging masses of irregular contour, seeming to meet in front, and singularly distorting the figure of the bird—surmounted with a fringe of filaments depending from the mass of erect white feathers, and ending below in a solid set of white scaly plumes. Perhaps no bird of our country presents a more remarkable aspect than the Sage Cock under the circumstances just noted; while at all times his presence and bearing are sufficiently striking. The mode of flight is most like that of the Sharp-tailed Grouse—indeed, what resemblances the Sage Cock bears to any other of our birds, are closest, in all respects, with this species. There is the same complete spread of the wing, when the ends of the outer quills show spaces between them—the same heavy yet swift and steady course, accomplished with an alternation of a few energetic strokes, and a period of sailing with stiffly motionless wings, until the impulse is spent. A point in which the Sage Grouse differs from the Sharp-tailed, if not also from every other one of our Grouse, is that it never takes to the trees, its exclusively terrestrial habits being, indeed, a necessity arising in the nature of the country it inhabits.

The egg of the Sage Fowl may be recognized at a glance by its size and elongated shape; it is comparatively narrower and more pointed than that of any other Grouse of this country, and our specimens, selected from a great number in the Smithsonian collection, measure, respectively, 2.25 by 1.50; 2.10 by 1.60; 2.10 by 1.50; 2.05 by 1.50. The shell first forms pale grayish-white, with a faint greenish shade, and subsequently becomes a grayish or greenish-drab by acquiring more or less of a brown tint; this is spotted with chocolate-brown, mostly in specks and minute dots, pretty evenly and rather thickly distributed, sometimes very sparsely so marked, and occasionally with larger spots (size of a split pea) tending to a circular shape, with sharp edges. The same circularity may be observed in the case of the smaller markings.

An interesting law affecting egg-coloration may be deduced from examination of eggs which, like those of all our Grouse and many other birds, are colorless, or of uniform color at first, yet variously marked when laid. In such cases, probably without exception, the markings are *entirely upon the surface*, and consequently appear of the same color, only varying in intensity according to the depth of the pigment deposited. The shell being entirely formed in an upper portion of the oviduct, where there are no cells for the elaboration of special pigments, these various colorations are never obscured by being overlaid with shell substance; whereas in those cases where special coloring matter is early laid down, during the formation of the shell, we have different sets of spots, some *in* the shell, others on its surface, the former being those so often conventionally described as "lilac," "lavender," &c., but being in reality the various browns and reds, like those of the surface, only overlaid with the white or whitish calcareous substance.

The young Sage Fowl shows features parallel with those of the young Sharp-tailed, as might be expected from the affinity of the two. We find the same sharp, white shaft-lines in various places on the upper parts, and the same brown speckling of the plumage of the breast. We find, at a very early age, indication of the future black abdominal area in a dark brown patch on the belly.

PEDIŒCETES PHASIANELLUS var. COLUMBIANUS, (Ord,) Cs.

Southern Sharp-tailed Grouse.

a. *phasianellus* proper.

Tetrao phasianellus, LINN., Syst. Nat. i, 10th ed. 1758, 160 (*T. urogallus B., phasianellus,* of 12th ed. p. 273).—FORST., Philos. Tr. lxii, 1772, pp. 394, 495.—GM., Syst. Nat. i, 1788, 747.—LATH., Ind. Orn. ii, 1790, 635.—SAB., App. Frank. Journ. p. 680.—BP., Am. Orn. iii, 1828, 37; text of ♂ from Arctic America, but *not* the plate.
Tetrao (Centrocercus) phasianellus, SW. & RICH., F. B. A. ii, 1831, 361 (relates chiefly to the present, though including the following variety).
Pediocaetes phasianellus, ELLIOT, Pr. Phila. Acad. 1862, 403 (not of United States writers).—MUR., Edinb. Journ. 1859.—GRAY, Cat. B. Br. Mus. v, 1867, 88.—DALL & BANN., Tr. Chic. Acad. i, 1869, 287 (Yukon).
Pediœcetes phasianellus, COUES, Key, 1872, 234.—B. B. & R., N. A. B. iii, 1874, 434, pl. 69, f. 3.
Pediocœtes kennicottii, SUCK., Pr. Phila. Acad. 1861, p. 361.
Long-tailed Grouse (Urogallus minor), EDW., iii, 117.
Sharp-tailed Grouse, PENN., Arct. Zool. ii, 306.

b. *columbianus.*

Phasianus columbianus, ORD, Guthrie's Geog. 2d Am. ed. 1815, 317 (based on Columbian Pheasant of *Lewis* and *Clarke*, ii, 180).
Pediocaetes columbianus, ELLIOT, Pr. Phila. Acad. 1862, 403; Monog. *Tetr.* pl.—HOLD.-AIKEN, Pr. Bost. Soc. xv, 1872, 208.
Pediœcetes columbianus, COOP., B. Cal. i, 1870, 532.
Pediœcetes phasianellus var. *columbianus*, COUES, Key, 1872, 234.—ALLEN, Bull. M. C. Z. iii, 1872, 181.—B. B. & R., N. A. B. iii, 1874, 436, pl. 60, f. 1.
Tetrao phasianellus, ORD, Guthrie's Geog. 2d Am. ed. 1815, 317 ?—BP., Syn. 1828, 127; Am. Orn. iii, 1828, 37, pl. 19 (not description of ♂, which was from Arctic America).—NUTT., Man. i, 1832, 669.—AUD., Orn. Biog. iv, 1838, 569, pl. 382; Syn. 1839, 205; B. Am. v, 1842, 110, pl. 298.—NEWB., P. R. R. Rep. vi, 1857, 94.—MAXIM., J. f. O. vi, 1858, 435.—TRIPPE, Pr. E. Inst. 1871, 118 (Minnesota).
Pediocaetes phasianellus, BD., B. N. A. 1858, 626.—COOP. & SUCK., N. H. Wash. Ter. 1860, 223.—LORD, Pr. Roy. Arty. Inst. iv, 1864, 123.—SNOW, B. Kans. 1873.—TRIPPE, Pr. Bost. Soc. xv, 1872, 240.
Pediœcetes phasianellus, HAYD., Rep. 1862, 172.—MERR., Rep. U. S. G. S. Ter. 1872, 699.
Tetrao urophasianellus, DOUGL., Tr. Linn. Soc. xvi, 1829, 136.

Hab.—Of the northern variety, or true *phasianellus*, the interior of British America, east to Hudson's Bay, north and west to Fort Yukon, south nearly to the United States boundary, where it shades into var. *columbianus.* The latter inhabits the western portions of Minnesota and Iowa, all of Dakota, thence diagonally across Nebraska and Kansas to Colorado, thence in suitable districts across the country to the Sierra Nevada and Cascade Ranges.

List of specimens.

19173	195	Rosebud Creek.	♀	Sept.	8, 1861	G. H. Trook..	16.50	25.50	9.00
19174	225	Deer Creek	♀	Jan.	5, 1860	F. V. Hayden.	17.00	25.00	8.00
19175	223	.......do	♀	Jan.	1, 1860	.......do	....	....	....
19176	224	.......do	....	Jan.	7, 1860	G. H. Trook .	19.00	29.00	9.00
19177	204	.......do	♀	Dec.	29, 1859	.......do	....	....	....
19178	220	.......do	....	Jan.	11, 1860	F. V. Hayden.	19.00	29.00	9.50

Lieutenant Warren's Expedition.—5420, Fort Union; 5421, 5422, mouth of Vermilion River; 5442, 5443, Fort Pierre.

Later Expeditions.—54326, Wyoming; 60463, Le Bouté Creek; 61792–3, Port Neuf River, Idaho.

The nomenclature of the Sharp-tailed Grouse became somewhat involved when it was found necessary to distinguish by name the two geographical races which constitute the species. Prior to 1861 there was supposed to be but a single kind, the *Tetrao phasianellus* of authors. At that time examination of numerous specimens from Arctic America, and their comparison with the ordinary bird of the United States, showed the existence of two forms of Sharp-tailed Grouse, and the northern variety was published by Dr. Suckley as a new species under the name of *Pediocaetes kennicottii.* The following year, however, Mr. Elliot showed that this northern form was really the one upon which Linnæus originally based the name of *Tetrao phasianellus*, and that it was the southern one, therefore, that required to be distinguished by a separate name. He very properly adopted for the latter the term *columbianus*, after Ord, whose bird was the "Columbian Pheasant" of Lewis and Clarke, unquestionably our common Sharp-tailed Grouse. Dr. Suckley and Mr. Elliot, alike right in distinguishing the two varieties, went too far in supposing them to be different species; for, as stated in the "Key," p. 234, they are simply geographical races shading into each other, as I shall point out more particularly in this article. To the northern, British American, form belongs the name *Tetrao phasianellus* of Linnæus, and of those early writers who drew their inspiration from him, as well as the *Pediocætes phasianellus* of those late writers whose notices are based upon the same bird. To the southern form, var. *columbianus*, belongs the name *Tetrao phasianellus*, or *Pediœcetes phasianellus*, of those writers who refer to the United States bird. Certain authors, however, obviously include *both* forms in their articles; thus Bonaparte, in the American Ornithology, describes the male from Arctic America, and figures the female var. *columbianus* from the United States; while Richardson, whose account relates, of course, chiefly to the northern bird, includes the southern in his statement that the species is found down to latitude 41° on the Missouri.

But such bibliographical points, the establishing of which is a part of the drudgery the closet naturalist must perform, have little or no general interest, and we willingly turn to a more inviting aspect of our subject, the proper natural history of the Sharp-tailed Grouse. While some descriptions of the colors of the bird have been minute even to tediousness, no one, as it seems to me, has been sufficiently explicit in regard to certain points of structure which can only be satisfactorily ascertained in examining the freshly-killed bird, or respecting the changes of plumage. If, as I shall presently show, the *egg-shell*, which exists but a few days, is very differently colored at different periods of its existence, what variation may we not expect to find in the coloration of the bird itself, which lives for several years? We will begin by noting those differences which, owing to the operation of climatic influences, subsist between the average bird of Arctic America and that of the United States prairies. That these two are not distinct species, but only geographical varieties of the same species, will be as evident to the sportsman and amateur naturalist from their points of view as it is to the technical scientist from his.

The northern variety, or true *phasianellus*, is much darker* and more heavily colored than its southern representative, var. *columbianus.*

---

* The *eggs* of this northern form differ from those of the southern in a manner analogous to the difference in plumage, averaging decidedly darker and browner drab, sometimes attaining a chocolate-brown color, and showing greater tendency to spotting.

There is much less of the buff, tawny, or brownish-yellow variegation, so conspicuous in the latter. The general colors might be called brownish-black and white in the former, the markings disposed in a pattern common to both varieties, yet the fulvous of var. *columbianus* assuming a dark brown cast. In the northern bird the angular dark-markings on the white ground of the under parts are almost black, and acutely arrow-head shaped for the most part; in the southern, these markings are much lighter brown, and, excepting generally the hinder ones, have a more rounded outline. In the northern bird the throat is white, speckled with blackish; in the southern it is tawny, and nearly or quite unmarked. Now these are the prominent characteristics, as they obtain in the more strongly marked examples. But it must be remembered that they are mixed and obscured in every degree in the complete and gentle intergradation which obtains between the two varieties, proving them to be but a single species. Along the United States northern boundary, and rather to the northward, specimens are more or less perfectly intermediate between the two extremes above noted. There is, moreover, in both forms, such a difference between the breeding and the autumnal plumages (the latter being the lighter), as to further prove the impossibility of specific distinctions being established. Birds that I killed in June and July along the northern border of Dakota, decidedly approached the dark northern form; their offspring, shot in the same locality the following September, when they were full grown, very clearly pertained to the southern. They were all, indeed, much lighter than the heaviest colored arctic birds; but the old ones had the white and speckled instead of buff throat, and so had the young ones through the summer; they only assumed the buff throat, and thus distinctively showed their relationship with the southern form, after the September moult. Speaking geographically, as well as zoologically, it is impossible to assign limits to the two forms. All the United States specimens I have seen, however, are unquestionably var. *columbianus*; and we may as well conventionally fix its limit along our present political boundary, although the other variety only attains its special characteristics in all their purity considerably further north.

The northern line of distribution of var. *columbianus* being thus determined, we have to note its dispersion in other directions. Its eastern limit offers interesting considerations of a different character; for in this direction we find the bird to have been affected, not by climatic influence modifying its physical characters, but by less obscure agencies operating to gradually restrict its range. These agencies are directly consequent upon the advance of civilization, which, very singularly, pushes the Sharp-tailed Grouse continually westward, and at the same time carries along with it the Pinnated Grouse. There is abundant evidence that the Sharp-tailed once ranged much further east than it does now; and so rapidly is it being driven westward that a decided change has been affected within the memory of those now living. How far eastward it may have once ranged is uncertain. We have in the earlier accounts some vague and evidently not reliable allusions to the Sharp-tailed Grouse as an inhabitant of Virginia. This may or may not have been the case, most probably it was an entire mistake; and yet there is no *à priori* reason against it. The Sharp-tailed is no more exclusively a prairie-bird than the Pinnated, which we know once ranged across the whole country, and lingers to this day in certain isolated localities in the Middle States and even New England. Under later and more authentic dates we find the Sharp-tailed Grouse mentioned by Audubon, in 1838, as "accidental in the northern parts of

Illinois." This leads to the inference that not long previously the bird inhabited all suitable prairie land of Michigan,[*] Minnesota, and Iowa, intervening between the point indicated and its present *habitat*. What this now is I am able to show with accuracy, thanks to the kindness of several friends, who have noted, in Minnesota, a gradual restriction of the Sharp-tailed and corresponding advance of the Pinnated. My friend, Surgeon J. F. Head, United States Army, writes me that General H. H. Sibley, a keen sportsman and pretty accurate scientific observer, who lived at the mouth of the Minnesota River long before St. Paul was settled, states that formerly the Sharp-tailed Grouse was the prevailing, if not the only, species there, and that it has been replaced by *T. cupido* within his own memory. A paper which Dr. Head prepared in 1853, gave *T. cupido* as the Grouse about Fort Ripley, Minnesota, but he lately told me that this was a mistake, the bird of that vicinity being then the Sharp-tailed, and the Pinnated being only just now approaching that locality. For in September, 1873, the Doctor, with some friends, shot a young but full-grown solitary *T. cupido*—" so far as I know," he writes, "the first instance of its occurrence in this vicinity. The place was remote from any cultivated ground; and within a few minutes several individuals of the Sharp-tailed Grouse were shot." In another communication kindly offered me, Dr. Head states further: "The Sharp tailed Grouse is found in great abundance from the Mississippi to the Red River of the North; * * * * the Grouse now inhabiting the region about St. Paul is the *T. cupido*—a few of the Sharp-tailed are still found near White Bear Lake, about twelve miles north of this city. The dividing line between *T. cupido* and *T. phasianellus* runs probably not more than fifteen or twenty miles north of the Falls of St. Anthony, bending thence to the southwest, or in the direction of Yankton. *T. cupido* appears to replace the other as the *wheat-fields* advance."

The accuracy of this line determined by Dr. Head is verified by other observations. Its south*west* trend is confirmed by Mr. Trippe, as above cited, who believes that the Sharp-tailed scarcely[†] comes into Iowa; and more particularly by my own observations, between Fort Randall and Yankton. In this stretch of seventy-five miles along the Missouri the normal dividing-line runs somewhere—the two species interdigitating, however, to such an extent that it cannot be precisely fixed. How many Sharp-tailed, if any, are still found about Yankton, I cannot say; but there the Pinnated is the prevailing form, and so numerous that I have known them to be trapped and used instead of tame Pigeons in a shooting-match. Starting up the river they accompany us part of the day, till suddenly one of the "White-bellies" whirs up from the roadside, and we are soon fairly among them. At Fort Randall they are the prevailing species; so nearly exclusively, that in the course of my six months' residence there, I never became aware of the occurrence of the other, excepting in three instances, although officers and others, beside myself, did a good deal of shooting. The *Cupidones* are unquestionably creeping up the Missouri, just as the Quail have already done, although they have not, apparently, as yet progressed quite so far; and with their advance, the Sharp-tailed are probably receding along this line as elsewhere. There may be some antagonism, or other incompatibility, between the two species; but more probably the different conditions of environment, induced by the settling of the country, are the

---

[*] Fort William, on the northern shore of Lake Superior, is among the earlier localities cited.

[†] But I am reliably informed of its occurrence, with *Cupidonia*, in northwestern portions of Iowa.

main cause of the change—what the Pinnated likes best being not to the taste of the other. Just as the Quail is a " home bird," loving the stubble-field and hay-rick near the owner's house, so the Pinnated prefers to glean over cultivated fields, while the wilder Sharp-tailed clings to its native heath. The railroad will take the former along and warn away the latter.

Proceeding now nearly due south, we find the line of distribution (however it may lead to the right or left, according to the nature of special locality) gives over the greater portion of Nebraska to this species, and passes nearly through the middle of Kansas to the vicinity of Fort Hays, where the bird was found by Mr. Allen. This is the easternmost point in this latitude that I have ascertained, and may represent the southernmost limit of distribution, or nearly so—about 38°. From the line above sketched the species reaches across the entire country, in suitable regions, to the east side of the Sierra Nevada of California, and of the continuation of the same range into Oregon and Washington—the Cascades. It does not, apparently, cross this range into the valleys on the west side; nor has it been found in California quite so far south as in Kansas and Colorado—not quite to latitude 40°. In fact it has only lately been included in the fauna of that State. Dr. Newberry saw it about fifty miles northeast of Fort Reading, near Canoe Creek, on the prairie near Pitt River, about the Klamath Lakes, and in the Des Chutes basin to the Dalles. In Washington Territory Dr. Cooper says it is found only in the low alluvial prairies of the streams emptying into the Columbia east of the Cascade Mountains; but this restriction probably requires to be removed. He mentions an interesting fact in contrast of the present bird and the Blue Grouse (*Tetrao obscurus*): " They shun high grounds and forests entirely; and within a distance of half a mile I have seen both these and the Blue Grouse (which avoids open plains altogether) as I passed from prairie to forest." Dr. Suckley noticed the "exceeding abundance" of the species from the mouth of the Yellowstone to the Cascades, wherever there is open country and a sufficiency of food. The bird is probably nowhere more numerous than in the regions where I have had opportunity of studying it, namely, in the vicinity of Fort Randall on the Missouri, from October to May; at Fort Pembina, on the Red River, in June, and at various points along the Souris or Mouse River, Dakota, during the rest of the year.

We may begin with the egg, and will take it a little earlier in its history than usual. High up the oviduct, when the shell first forms, it is of a uniform pale, dull *green* color. The first one I ever saw was of this description; it was brought to me as having been "cut out of a Prairie Chicken," which I could scarely credit, though I could not help believing my informant; and as the egg had been boiled, I set it down to this having somehow changed the color. Soon after, however, I killed a hen off her nest, and found in her a duplicate of the first specimen. As the egg passes down it acquires a deposit of brown pigment, which, mingled with the green, or overlying it, produces the characteristic olive or drab tint of the mature egg. When this brown is in less quantity, a pale, dull drab, nearly uniform, results; when in excess, the tint is a darker olive, and in most specimens, further deposit of brown, not fairly mixed with the original green, produces a minutely dotted egg, the dark brown being picked into the shell, as it were, in points. These markings are rarely, if ever, aggregated into spots of any considerable size (any larger than a pin's head), and are uniformly distributed; at least I have seen no specimens otherwise marked.

During incubation they usually acquire a variety of scratches or other abrasions, in which the pale underlying color appears. The eggs are shaped like those of the common hen (though more pointed, and nearer a perfect oval), and vary as much, in size and shape, as those of the same breed of domestic fowl commonly do. They are always quite different from those of the Pinnated Grouse. They measure from 1.60 to 1.80 inches in length by 1.20 to 1.30 in breadth, averaging about 1.75 by 1.25. (Thirty specimens measured.) The clutch varies greatly, as usual in the cases of those birds which lay many eggs. The largest number I ever found in a nest was thirteen, but I suppose a few more may sometimes be laid. The fewest I have noticed, after incubation had commenced, showing that no more would have been laid, was five. In the latitude of Pembina they are laid late in May and through part of June*—probably a little earlier farther south.

But we have come to speak of the eggs without reference as yet to the preliminaries needful for their production. The Grouse revive from the stolid and apathetic mood in which they pass the winter early in the spring—often previous to the severe snow-storms and cold that may prevail in April in part of the regions they inhabit, and the earliest indication of their renewed activity is their sexual excitement. I shall never forget the first time their strange booming fell upon my ear—a new experience to me, though I had for months been familiar with the birds under the influence of their winter *régime.* It was on the 1st of April, and I think that had the birds awakened sooner, the fact would not have escaped me. It was in the vicinity of Fort Randall. I was miles away from the fort or any other human habitation, whither I had gone into lonely bivouac the night before to make sure of securing some wild fowl at the break of day. Awakened before it was light by the sonorous cries of the wild fowl making for the reedy lake where I had encamped, I arose—there was no need to dress—pushed off into the expanse of reeds in a light canoe I had brought with me, and with my gun across my knees, sat quietly waiting for light to come. The sense of loneliness was oppressive in the stillness that preceded morning, broken only by the quack or plash of the Wild Duck, and the distant honking of a train of Wild Geese winnowing their sinuous way afar. I felt desolate—almost lost—and thought how utterly insignificant man is in comparison with his self-assertion. The grand bluffs of the Missouri, rising past each other interminably, were before me in shadowy outline, that seemed to change and threaten to roll upon me; all around stretched the waste of reeds, secret, treacherous, limitless—unmoved, yet whispering to the water about their roots with a strange trickling. But the light came on; the distant hills took shape and settled in firm gray outline against the sky, and a breath of fresher, purer air, messenger of morning, passed over the lake, dispelling the vapors that hung reluctant, and causing the reeds to sway in graceful salute to the coming sun. A Sparrow chirped from her perch with joy; a Field Lark rose from her bed in the grass; tuning her limpid pipe to a song of gladness; and the wild fowl plashed about right heartily, when the highest hill-top was touched with gold, and another and another, till the scene was illumined to the very bosom of the lake. The feathered orchestra sounds never so impressive as when it ushers in the day;

---

* Says Dr. Suckley: "At Fort Dalles, on the 1st of April, 1855, a young bird, scarcely two days old, was brought to me. This early incubation would lead us to suspect that the species, in favorable situations, has two or more broods during the season." But this is certainly not the case in any locality I have observed the birds—they have all they can do to get *one* brood off their hands by the end of the summer.

never so fine and complete as when familiar voices sing the higher notes to the strange deep bass of the Grouse; heard for the first time, as it was on this occasion, the effect is indescribable. No one could say whence the sound proceeded, nor how many birds, if more than one, produced it; the hollow reverberations filled the air, more like the lessening echoes of some great instrument far away, than the voice of a bird at hand. I listened to this grand concert, absorbed in the reflections it stirred within me, no longer alone, but in company I love, till the booming fell less frequently upon my ear, and then ceased—it was broad day; the various birds were about their homely avocations, and I must betake myself to practical concerns.

Thus, in no faltering accents of timid expectancy, but in the bold tone of assured success, the Grouse calls upon his intended mate to forget the shyness that will no longer serve their purpose; nor does the invitation lack defiance to a rival who may presume to dispute his rights. At the rallying cry the birds assemble, in numbers of both sexes, at some favorable spot, and a singular scene ensues as the courtship progresses. There is a regular "walk-around," as ludicrous, to the disinterested observer, as some of the performances on the comic stage. The birds run about in a circle, some to the right, others to the left, crossing each other's path, passing and repassing in stilted attitudes, stopping to bow and squat in extravagant postures, and resuming their course, till one would think their heads as well as their hearts were lost. But this is simply their way, and they amuse themselves in such fashion till the affair is settled. The cocks have bristled and swelled, strutted and fought, till some have proven their claims to first choice, and others have concluded to take what they can get. Their subsequent history, I am sorry to state, is neither particularly creditable to themselves nor of absorbing interest to us. Leaving them to go about their business in their usual humdrum way, let us look to what now occupies their mates.

A nest will soon be required for her eggs, and the hen has to select suitable premises, though, being an architect of only the humblest order, she has little building work to do; and, moreover, not being fastidious, her choice is made without difficulty. I have found the nests in such various locations that I can hardly determine what her preference is, if, indeed, she have any. I suppose the site depends much upon circumstances. She will enter a tract overgrown with the low, scrubby willow bushes, so abundant in our higher latitudes, and settle beneath one of these; she will ramble along the edge of a wooded stream and hide in a patch of tall weeds; she will stroll out on the boundless, bare prairie, and take a tuft of grass at random. But wherever she makes down her bed she is solicitous to conceal it, not only from the rude glances of men, but from the equally cruel eye of her many four-footed enemies. Her method of concealment is most artful—perfected by its witlessness. With admirable instinct, she will avoid a place that offers such chances of concealment as to invite curious search; her willow bush is the duplicate of a thousand others at hand; her tuft of grass on the prairie is the counterpart of a million others around; her nest will be found by accident oftener than by design. And when, stooping over a warm nest on the prairie, whence she has just fluttered in dismay, we note how exposed it seems, now that it is found; we wonder how the dozen blades of grass that overarch the eggs, or the rank weed that shadows them, could have hidden the home so effectually that we nearly trod upon the bird before we saw her. She is now but a few yards off, in plain view, amid the scrubby prairie herbage, perhaps squatting, but more likely moving away with a swaying motion of the head at each step. We will not combine murder with the robbery we are about to commit, and let us hope she will be consoled in time. Lifting up the eggs carefully, one by one, we find the nest to be merely a few spears of grass, pressed down and somewhat circularly arranged with, in all probability, a few feathers that appear to have rather been mechanically detached from the mother bird than laid down by design. If the place is near our northern border, and early in June, we shall probably find the eggs quite fresh; but by the third week of that month they will be about hatching. At this period should we, for any sufficient reason, destroy the setting bird, we should find her in sad plight— her plumage, harsh and worn, entirely gone from a large space on her belly; her flesh thin and flabby, and her crop containing only a few buds of some weed that grows close by her nest, with some grasshoppers or other insects.

No bird is a more faithful mother than this Grouse; no one clings to her eggs more steadfastly, or guards her young with more sedulous care. In proof of how close she will set while incubating, let me mention two instances that came under my observation. One poor bird was actually trodden upon and killed, and some of her eggs smashed. On another occasion, I drove a large four-mule ambulance over a nest; the animals shied as they stepped over it, when the bird fluttered out from between their legs. Stopping instantly, I discovered the nest just between the hinder wheels. The Grouse lies hard and close, never relinquishing hope of escaping observation until the last moment.

The young, as usual among gallinaceous birds, run about almost as soon as they are hatched; and it is interesting to witness the watchful solicitude with which they are cherished by the parent when she first leads them from the nest in quest of food, glancing in every direction, in her intense anxiety, lest harm befall them. She clucks matronly to bring them to brood under her wings, or to call them together to scramble for a choice morsel of food she has found. Should danger threaten, a different note alarms them; they scatter in every direction, running, like little mice, through the grass till each finds a hiding place; meanwhile, she exposes herself to attract attention, till, satisfied of the safety of the brood, she whirrs away and awaits the time when she may reassemble her family. In the region where I observed the birds in June and July, they almost invariably betook themselves to the dense, resistent underbrush, which extends for some distance outward from the wooded streams, seeking safety in this all but impenetrable cover, where it was nearly impossible to catch the young ones, or even to see them, until they began to top the bushes in their early short flights. The wing and tail-feathers sprout in a few days, and are quite well grown before feathers appear among the down of the body. The first coveys seen able to rise on wing were noticed early in July; but by the middle of this month most of them fly smartly for short distances, being about as large as Quails. Others, however, may be observed through August, little, if any, larger than this, showing a wide range of time of hatching, though scarcely warranting the inference of two broods in a season.

Returning to the newly-hatched chicks, we will note their characteristics as they progress toward maturity. The down in which they are clothed when hatched is rather dingy yellow, mottled on the crown, back, and wings with warm brown and black; it extends to the toes, but leaves a bare strip along the hind edge of the tarsus; the bill and feet are light brown. They are about as large as Bantam chickens of the same age, and very pretty little things, indeed. They are very quick in their movements, scrambling to squat and hide, on the least alarm, even at this early age.

The first feathers—those of the wings—are light brown, with broken black bars, and strong shaft-lines of pure white, as well as edging of the same. The tail sprouts next. Then some brown feathers appear on the crown. Next, two broad strips of white feathers, with circular brown spots, appear on each side of the breast, coalescing and gradually extending down the side; meanwhile the scapular and dorsal feathers appear, and the feathering finishes with the neck, when the birds are about one-third grown. With the final disappearance of the down the birds are in a plumage which differs materially from that of the adults, and may be thus described: Crown, warm rich brown, variegated with black. White shaft-lines of the upper plumage persistent, making sharp, white, lengthwise stripes, which, together with a black area on each feather, contrast with the fine gray and brown mottling of the upper parts. Wing-coverts and inner quills somewhat like the back, on their outer webs at least, but with whitish spots along the edge. Several inner tail-feathers with a shaft-line of white, and otherwise mottled blackish and brown. Lower throat and breast with a buffy suffusion, and with numberless dark brown spots; sides, similar, but the markings lengthened into streaks. Bill, brown above, light-colored below.

This plumage lasts through the greater part of September, and is one of several distinctive evidences of immaturity. Sometime during this month a moult occurs, and the perfect plumage of the fall and winter is gained with its completion. By the time of the moult the birds are well grown—sometimes full grown—and delicate for table; but it is hardly fair to shoot them before the change is completed. Though they fly well enough, they lack spirit and vigor, drop at a touch of small shot, and, altogether, try the qualities of the sportsman little more than gunning in a hen-yard would. They should be let alone till they are stronger, warier, and clothed in the fresh, crisp plumage they are about to assume, and which, when completed, makes a bird like this:

Neck without obviously peculiar feathers, like those of either of the Pinnated or Ruffed Grouse or Sage Cock, but with a hidden, definitely circumscribed space on each side of reddish, vascular, and distensible skin, constituting an undeveloped tympanum, over which lies a lateral series of slightly enlarged feathers. *Head* lightly crested, the longest feathers of the crown falling on the occiput; a crescentic naked patch over each eye of numerous orange or chrome-yellow fringe-like processes, in several parallel curved rows. *Bill* and *wings* of an ordinary gallinaceous character. *Feet* full-feathered to between the bases of the toes, with long, hair-like plumage reaching to or beyond the end of the hind claw. *Toes above* with one row of broad, transverse scutella, a row on each side of smaller rounded scales, and a conspicuous fringe of horny processes; *below*, bossed and scabrous. *Tail* much shorter than the wings, normally of eighteen true rectrices, of which the central pair are soft, parallel-edged, and square-tipped, projecting an inch or two beyond the next pair; the rest rapidly graduated, stiffish, and crisp (making a creaking sound when rubbed together), and, though at first about straight-edged, soon becoming club-shaped (with a constriction near the apex) by mutual attrition. *Sexes* similar, but cock rather larger and darker than the hen, with more prominent supraciliary papillæ. *Length*, 18 or 20 inches; extent, 24 to 30; wing, 8 to 9; middle tail-feathers, 4 to 6; shortest tail-feathers (outermost), about $1\frac{1}{2}$; tarsi, 2 inches; middle toe and claw, about the same; culmen of bill, about $\frac{2}{3}$; gape of bill, 1 to $1\frac{1}{4}$; depth of bill at base, $\frac{1}{2}$, or rather less. *Colors :* Upper parts closely and pretty evenly variegated with blackish-brown, reddish-brown, and grayish-brown, the pattern smallest on the rump and lower back, where the blackish is mostly in sharp-angled stars; the reddish most conspicuous on the upper back, and both the lighter colors everywhere finely sprinkled with blackish.   Wing-coverts like the upper back, but with numerous conspicuous rounded white spots, one on the end of each feather.   Crown and back of neck nearly like the back, but in smaller pattern, and the markings mostly transverse.   An illy-defined white area on each side of the neck, over the tympanum, and slight, whitish stripe behind the eye.   Throat, fine light buff, usually immaculate, but sometimes finely speckled quite across. Under parts white, more or less tinted with buff toward the throat; the breast with numerous regular dark-brown U-shaped spots, one on each feather; similar but smaller, sharper, and fewer such spots thence scattered over most of the under parts, only the middle of the belly being left unmarked.   Long feathers of the sides under the wings matching the upper wing-coverts nearly; under wing-coverts and axillaries pure white, not marked; flanks with bars or U-spots of dark brown.   Legs grayish-white, unmarked.   Quills of the wings fuscous; outer webs of the secondaries with equidistant, squarish, white or tawny spots, the secondaries tipped and imperfectly twice or thriced barred with white, and gradually becoming sprinkled with the varied colors of the back, so that the innermost of them are almost precisely like the greater coverts.   Four middle tail-feathers variegated, much like the back; others white, or grayish-white, on the inner web, the outer web being mottled; a few under tail-coverts spotted, the rest white; upper tail-coverts nearly like the rump.   Iris, light brown; bill, dark horn-color; part of under mandible, flesh-colored; claws, like the bill; toes on top, light horn-color, the soles darker.

As already intimated, this rich plumage of the fall and winter differs a good deal from that of the breeding season.   In summer there is much less of the rusty tinges, the colors being nearly blackish, gray, and white.   The throat is more nearly white and speckled.   I have shot (September) birds moulting in which the old feathers of the throat were of this character, mixed with new ones of a rich, pure buff.   There are other characters; the bare stripe over the eye is more conspicuous, more pimply, and more brightly colored.   The legs are very much less heavily clothed; in fact, scarcely more feathered than those of the Pinnated Grouse.   The tail of this bird is among its peculiarities, and has occasioned comment.   The long central pair of feathers appear to belong to the coverts, as stated in my work, p. 233, from examination of dried skins alone; but this is not so.   They are true tail-feathers, implanted fairly in line with the others, as any one can satisfy himself on examination of a fresh-killed bird; the longest coverts belong to a different set, as shown by their site as well as form.   It is not easy to describe the *shape* of the tail-feathers, since they are continually changing their form by wearing away in rubbing against each other.   Before the September moult, these feathers in the young-of-the-year are rather short and indeterminate in shape, and they are all shed nearly simultaneously; I have shot birds without any tail at all.   The new ones are generally as above described, but constantly wear; by June following they often become mere shafts with ragged edges.   The decided tympanum that this species possess has not received sufficient attention.   In both sexes during winter, and in the female at all times, it is not conspicuous, but during the breeding season becomes much enlarged in the cock, and susceptible of very considerable distension.   Thus, it shows plainly in a poorly-prepared dried skin now before me.   In investigating the nature of these air-sacs I was unable, after several trials, to find any direct communication with the wind-pipe, and came to the conclusion that air was admitted from the lung through an opening similar to those by which air gains access to others of the various air-cells in birds' bodies; that, therefore, the tympanum is simply an exaggerated cervical cavity, belonging to the general system of pneumatic cells. On introducing a blow-pipe into the trachea, I could fully distend the air-sacs, but only coincidently with the general inflation of the body which ensued.

To return to the habits of this interesting bird. Throughout the region of the Red, Pembina, and Souris or Mouse Rivers, where I observed the birds during the summer, I found them mostly in the underbrush along the streams, which they seemed to seek instinctively as affording the best shelter and protection, as well as plenty of food. Where they were most abundant I frequently observed the "scratching holes" in the bare earth among the bushes, where they resorted to dust themselves, and most probably, in the instances of ungrown coveys, to roost. Late in the summer and in September, those who cared to shoot the tender young found them to lie well to a dog; in fact, to lie so close that they were flushed with difficulty without one. No game birds could be tamer or more readily destroyed. Except when temporarily scattered by molestation, the coveys kept close together, and only occasionally left the covert to stray on the adjoining prairie. They appeared to be feeding chiefly on wild-rose seeds, and those of another kind of plant equally abundant along the river-bottoms. The majority of these birds were ungrown up to September, and scarcely any had at that date begun to assume their new plumage. Up to this time I do not recollect that I ever saw one alight in a tree; and they were still, for the most part, under charge of the parent, as separate families, rather than as the indiscriminate packs in which they afterward associate. With the advance of the month these family associations seemed to break up, the change of plumage was finished, the birds grew strong of wing, and able in all respects to look after themselves. No longer solicitous of shelter, they haunted the innumerable ravines that make down to the streams, and strolled in company far out on the prairie. In this region, at least, they showed little wariness all through the month. I could generally walk up to a covey in fair view on the bare prairie, even to within a few feet, before they would fly, and they seldom went far before re-alighting. Their appearance when not obscured by the herbage is characteristically peculiar. They seem to stand remarkably high on their legs, and generally carry their short, pointed tail somewhat elevated; the singularity is increased when the long neck is outstretched, as it generally is when they are on the lookout. On alighting after being flushed, if not much alarmed, they often stand motionless at full height, but if badly scared, squat closely, and are then difficult to find if not exactly marked down. If without a dog, one may pass and repass among them without finding one, unless he happen to stumble on them; and often, going away after such want of success, one may look back to find the heads of the whole lot raised above the grass, intently regarding his retreat. It is astonishing how closely they can squat—even laying the head flat upon the ground, and appearing scarcely half their natural size. At this season their food appears to be chiefly grasshoppers. I have opened numbers to find their crops crammed with these insects, only varied with a few flowers, weed-tops, succulent leaves, and an occasional beetle or spider.

By the first of October the Sharp-tailed Grouse have mostly finished the renewal of their plumage, are all full grown and strong of wing; their habits are considerably modified. They grow wary and watchful,

27

flushing often at long distances to fly clear out of sight, and running far on the ground. They also begin to alight on trees, a habit, however, not confirmed until somewhat later, when with the advance of cold weather and the failure of former supplies of food, they assume the routine of their winter life. The close coveys of the earlier season are for the most part broken up, and the birds wander often alone in search of food. They haunt the interminable ravines along the Missouri, making away from the river-bottoms in search of food, but mostly returning at evening to roost in the trees. Early in the morning they may be seen leaving their perches in straggling troops, flying high and swiftly to other feeding grounds ; and again in the evening, if one loiter beneath the immense cottonwoods where, during the day, scarcely a chicken was to be seen, he will observe their return, till the trees are almost covered, and the air resounds with the hoarse *kuk-kuk-k-k-k.* Frequently, in very cold and especially in falling weather, the Grouse will not leave their perches during the day, but may be seen at any hour roosting quietly in the tops of the tallest cottonwoods. They are decidedly not graceful objects under these circumstances. They look very large, sharply defined among the bare straggling branches against the gray sky, and assume ungainly attitudes, particularly when standing erect on their long legs, with outstretched necks and upturned tails. Their behavior under these circumstances varies in a manner to me inexplicable. Sometimes a group thus scattered among the tree-tops will permit the closest approach desired, and more than one may be brought down before the rest are off in alarm ; not seldom one may fire twice or thrice at the same bird without dislodging it, or kill several without stirring from his tracks. But ordinarily the chickens' wits serve them to better purpose than this. As we approach, when just beyond range, the crackling of the underbrush attracts the attention of one of the birds, which before had been squatting "like a bump on a log"; he rises on his feet and twists his neck around to have a look. The rest follow his example. A moment more, the warning *kuk-kuk-k* sounds, and the nearest bird leaves his perch—the cry is taken up by the rest, and the whole are off to settle again a few hundred yards away, and tempt renewed pursuit that is likely to end as unsuccessfully. From the sportsman's standpoint, the arrangement is wholly unsatisfactory when the birds behave so; nor when they are tame is it much more attractive ; for, unless a supply of meat be the only point, dropping chickens from the trees is no more exciting than robbing a hen-roost. Killed under these circumstances, the food of the Grouse is readily ascertained ; in the dead of winter it consists chiefly of the berries of the cedar, and buds of the poplar or cottonwood and willow, still closely sealed, awaiting the coming of spring. I have taken from one crop a double-handful of such food, almost as dry as when swallowed. This diet does not improve the quality of the flesh ; a chicken at this season is quite a different thing from one killed earlier in the season. The rating of the Grouse as an article of food necessarily varies, not only with circumstances, but according to individual preferences. I myself do not esteem it very highly. A tender young Grouse, early in the season, is not to be despised, but all such specially-flavored meat is likely to soon become distasteful, especially if, on one or two occasions, a person has been forced upon a surfeit of it. Confined to Grouse for a few days, most persons, I should judge, would find relief in mess-pork.

The mode of flight of this species is not peculiar; it rises with a startling whirr from the ground, till it attains a certain elevation—its straight, steady course, performed with great velocity by alternate sailing and flapping, are points it shares with its relatives. The wing-beats are rapid and energetic, giving it an impulse that enables it to sail long distances, when the wings are held stiffly expanded to their full extent, somewhat decurved, and with the points of the quill-feathers separated. The bird's voice is highly characteristic. It is so almost invariably uttered during flight, at particular moments with reference to the delivery of the wing-strokes, that for some time after my first acquaintance with the birds I was in doubt whether the sound were mechanical or vocal; nor was the uncertainty removed until I had heard it from the birds at rest. The ordinary note of alarm is almost invariably sounded just before the bird takes wing, whether from the ground or from a tree, and is usually repeated with each succeeding set of wing-beats, seeming to be jerked out of the bird by its muscular efforts. But we hear it also when, the bird being at rest, it becomes alarmed, yet not sufficiently to fly away; and when a bird is passing at full speed, sufficiently near, we may clearly distinguish the mechanical whirring sound of its wings, as well as, sometimes, the creaking rustle of its tail-feathers as it turns its flight. When roosting at ease among the trees, and probably at other times, the Grouse have a different set of notes—a sociable cackling or clucking, with which they entertain each other.

In conversation with Captain Hartley, of the Twenty-second Regiment, an accomplished sportsman, well acquainted with the ways of our game birds, I was informed of an interesting point of difference in the habits of this bird and the Pinnated Grouse. In entering a cultivated field the latter goes on foot, and may consequently be readily trailed by a dog, while the Sharp-tailed flies in, and is only likely to be overhauled by the dog's winding it, or coming accidentally upon it. The same gentleman has noted the preference of this species for the skirts of woods, brush, and broken places generally, in contrast to the entirely open places which the Pinnated Grouse frequents.

CUPIDONIA CUPIDO, (Linn.) Bd.

Pinnated Grouse; Prairie Hen.

a. cupido.

Tetrao cupido, LINN., Syst. Nat. i, 1766, 274 (based on CATES., iii, 1, pl. 1; BRISS. i, 212).—GM., Syst. Nat. i, 1788, 751.—LATH., Ind. Orn. ii, 1790, 638.—WILS., Am. Orn. iii, 1811, 104, pl. 27.—BP., Obs. Wils. 1825, No. 183; Syn. 1828, 126; Monog. *Tetrao*, in Am. Phil. Trans. iii, 1830, 392.—NUTT., Man. i, 1832, 662.—AUD., Orn. Biog. ii, 1834, 490; v, 1839, 559; pl. 186; Syn. 1839, 204; B. Am. v, 1842, 23, pl. 296.—EMMONS, Cat. B. Mass. 1835, 4.—KOCH, Wieg. Archiv, 1836, 159.—PEAB., Rep. Orn. Mass. 1839, 355.—CABOT, Pr. Bost. Soc. v, 1855, 154 (Long Island).—LINSL., Cat. B. Conn., Am. Journ. 1843, 264.—DEKAY, N. Y. Fauna, 1844, 205.—PUTN., Pr. Ess. Inst. i, 1856, 229 (Massachusetts).—WOODH., Sitgr. Rep. 1853, 96 (Arkansas and Eastern Texas).—MAXIM., J. f. O. vi, 1858, 439.
Bonasa cupido, STEPH., Shaw's Gen. Zool. xi, 299.—GRAY, Cat. *Gall.* Br. Mus. 1867, 88.
Cupidonia cupido, BD., B. N. A. 1858, 628.—WHEAT., Ohio Agric. Rep. 1860, No. 178 (Ohio, few remaining in northwest portions).—HAYD., Rep. 1862, 172 (up the Missouri to the Niobrara).—SAM., App. Secy's Rep., Cat. B. Mass. 1864, p. 11 (Martha's Vineyard and Naushon).—ALLEN, Cat. B. Mass., Pr. Ess. Inst. iv, 1864, 8. (nearly extinct in Massachusetts).—LAWR., Ann. Lyc. N. Y. viii, 1866, 291.—COUES, Pr. Ess. Inst. vi, 1868, 287.—TURNB., B. E. Pa. 1869, 27 (now very rare; few still in Monroe and Northampton Counties, Pa., and New Jersey Plains).—ALLEN, Mem. Bost. Soc. i, 1868, 500 (Western Iowa, abundant).—ALLEN, Bull. M. C. Z. iii, 1872, 181 (Middle and Western Kansas).—SNOW, B. Kans. 1873, 9.—TRIPPE, Pr. Bost. Soc. xv, 1872, 240 (Iowa).—MAYN., Guide, 1870, 138 (Massachusetts).—COUES, Key, 1872, 234, fig. 148.—B. B. & R., N. A. B. iii, 1874, 440, pl. 61, figs. 1, 7.
Cupidonia americana, REICH., Syst. Av. 1850, p. xxix.—BP., Comptes Rend. xlv, 1857, 428.

b ? *pallidicinctus.*

Cupidonia cupido var. *pallidicinctus*, RIDGW.—B. B. & R., N. A. B. iii, 1874, 446 (Texas).

Hab.—Fertile prairie country of the United States, nearly to eastern foot-hills of the Rocky Mountains in some latitudes—especially Illinois, Iowa, Missouri, eastern half of Minnesota, Southeastern Dakota, Middle and Eastern Kansas and Nebraska, Arkansas and Eastern Texas. Var. *pallidicinctus* from Western Texas. Still lingers in certain localities in the Middle States and New England.

Lieutenant Warren's Expedition.—4540–41, Big Sioux River; 5423, Mouth of Niobrara.

It is well known that formerly the Pinnated Grouse inhabited various Eastern regions where it has been almost entirely extirpated. The principal localities where it still lingers are cited above. At present its centre of abundance is the Upper Mississippi Valley, for a considerable distance on either side of the river. Our notice of the distribution of the Sharp-tailed Grouse involved some particulars respecting the western limits of the present species. I have no reason to believe that it occurs at all in Northwestern Minnesota or Northern Dakota, where the other species is so abundant. Its progress upon the Missouri River has been traced by Dr. Hayden further than by myself—to the Niobrara; and this writer adds that it *may* proceed to the White River. Lower down, as at Council Bluffs, he speaks of its occurrence "in myriads." Mr. Allen notes its westward spread from Middle Kansas; but I have found no record of its reaching, as yet, either Colorado or Wyoming. Southward it reaches Texas and Louisiana. I have met with no indication of its occurrence north of the United States boundary.

It is unnecessary to renew an account of the habits of this abundant and well-known game bird. The eggs are usually distinguished from those of the Sharp-tailed Grouse by being shorter and rounder, as well as rather smaller, though some of the more elongate samples cannot be recognized with certainty. Two specimens will show the greater range of variation in shape—1.82 by 1.20; 1.58 by 1.25. The color is a peculiar, very pale, greenish-gray, usually unmarked, though often with uniform, fine, brown dotting. The variation is much as in *Pediœcetes*, but the tendency to spotting is not so strong. Eggs of both these birds sometimes show a peculiar glaucous cast, something like the "bloom" on a grape.

BONASA UMBELLUS, (Linn.) Steph.

Ruffed Grouse.

a. *umbellus* proper (Brown Ruffed Grouse, called "Partridge" in the Northern States, and "Pheasant" in the Southern).

Tetrao umbellus, LINN., Syst. Nat. i, 1766, 275 (based on EDW., p. 79, pl. 248, and BRISS., p. 214).—GM., Syst. Nat. i, 1788, 782.—LATH., Ind. Orn. ii, 1790, 638.—WILS., Am. Orn. vi, 1812, 46, pl. 49.—BP., Obs. Wils. 1825, 132; Syn. 1828, 136; Am. Philos. Trans. iii, 1830, 389.—NUTT., Man. i, 1832, 657.—SABINE, App. Frankl. Journ. 679.—DOUGHTY, Cab. N. H. i, 1830, 13, pl. 2.—SW. & RICH., F. B. A. ii, 1831, 342 ?—AUD., Orn. Biog. i, 1831, 211 ; v, 1839, 560; pl. 41; Syn. 1839, 202; B. Am. v, 1842, 72, pl. 293.—PUTN., Pr. Ess. Inst. i, 1856, 215.—TRIPPE, Pr. Ess. Inst. vi, 1871, 118 (Minnesota) ; and of earlier authors generally.

Bonasa umbellus, STEPH., Shaw's Gen. Zool. xi, 1824, 300.—BP., Comp. & Geog. List, 1838, 43; Comptes Rendus, xlv, 1857, 428.—BD., B. N. A. 1858, 630.—ELLIOT, Monog. *Tetraonidæ.*—MCILWR., Pr. Ess. Inst. v, 1866, 91 (Canada West).— FOWLER, Am. Nat. iii, 1869, 365 (biography).—ALLEN, Mem. Bost. Soc. i, 1868, 501 (Iowa).—DALL & BANN., Tr. Chic. Acad. i, 1869, 287 (Nulato, Alaska).—SNOW, B. Kans. 1873, 9 (very rare).—TRIPPE, Pr. Bost. Soc. xv, 1872, 240 (Iowa).— COUES, Key, 1872, 235, fig. 149.—B. B. & R., N. A. B. iii, 1874, 448, pl. 61, figs. 3, 9; and of later authors generally.

Tetrao togatus, FORST., Phil. Trans. lxii, 1772, 393.—LINN., Syst. Nat. i, 1766, 275.

Ruffed Grouse of authors and others.

b. var. *umbelloides* (Gray Ruffed Grouse).

Tetrao umbelloides, DOUGL., Tr. Linn. Soc. xvi, 1829, 148.
Bonasa umbellus var. *umbelloides*, BD., B. N. A. 1858, 925.—COUES, Key, 1872, 235.—MERR.,
    Rep. U. S. Geol. Surv. Ter. 1872, 699.—B. B. & R., N. A. B. iii, 1874, 453, pl. 61, f. 10.
Bonasa umbellus, ALLEN, Bull. M. C. Z. iii, 1872, 181 (Rocky Mountains).

c. var. *sabinii* (Red Ruffed Grouse).

Tetrao sabinii, DOUGL., Tr. Linn. Soc. xvi, 1829, 137.—SW. & RICH., F. B. A. ii, 1831, 343,
    foot-note.
Bonasa sabinii, BD., B. N. A. 1858, 631.—COOP. & SUCK., N. H. Wash. Ter. 1860, 224.—
    LORD, Pr. Arty. Inst. 1864, 123.—ELLIOT, Monog. *Tetr.* pl. —.—COOP., B. Cal. i,
    1870, 540.—DALL & BANN., Tr. Chic. Acad. i, 1869, 287 (Sitka).
Bonasa umbellus var. *sabinei*, COUES, Key, 1872, 235.—B. B. & R., N. A. B. iii, 1874, 454.
Tetrao umbellus, NEWB., P. R. R. Rep. vi, 1857, 94 (Oregon).

Hab.—Of the typical form, the United States to the high central plains, in wooded districts. Canada, and interior of the fur countries, to Nulato, Alaska (*Dall*). (But I am informed by Mr. Ridgway that the British American—even Canadian—specimens are all more or less referable to var. *umbelloides*, being grayer than those of the United States.) Of var. *umbelloides*, the Rocky Mountain region. Of var. *sabinii*, the Pacific province, from the northern border of California to Sitka.

The Ruffed Grouse occurs over only a very limited portion of the Missouri region, by far the greater part of the country not fulfilling its requirements, which are those of an exclusively woodland bird. Dr. Hayden does not mention the species at all, and I never saw it in the Missouri region. It apparently occurs only toward the mouth of the river and in the adjacent country. I have seen no Nebraskan record. In Kansas Mr. Snow says it is "very rare," and it is, no doubt, confined to the eastern part of the State, where it probably breeds. It is given as abundant in Southern Iowa by Mr. Trippe, and occurs in various parts of Missouri. At the other extreme of the Missouri region it is represented by var. *umbelloides*, as noted beyond.

It is somewhat singular that a misapprehension should subsist, even among well-informed persons, in regard to this species. The confusion in the minds of some is, doubtless, partly due to the fact that the bird goes under different names in different parts of the country; and we are often asked, is it a Partridge, or is it a Pheasant? to which reply may be made that it is *neither*, but a Grouse. "Pheasant" is a name of a variety of birds of the family *Phasianidæ*, indigenous to Southern Asia, and not represented in this country at all. The best known species is that one long ago introduced into England, and there thoroughly naturalized. (The nearest American representative of the Pheasants is the *Wild Turkey*, which is sometimes included in the family *Phasianidæ*.) "Partridge" is the name of a group of small gallinaceous birds, which, like the *Phasianidæ*, belong exclusively to the Old World, our American Partridges, so called, being quite a different set of birds. A poverty of our language in the matter of names of various American birds has caused them to become known by some term really belonging only to their (real or supposed) nearest European relatives. It would simplify matters much to discard altogether the terms "Pheasant" and "Partridge," by which this species is known in, respectively, the Northern and Southern States, and call it by its proper name of "Ruffed Grouse." The bird itself is unmistakable; no other species has the conspicuous ruffle of lengthened, broad, soft, silky feathers on the neck; and the only other species with any feathery neck-appendages is the Pinnated Grouse, where the appendages are like little wings of narrow, straight, pointed feathers. The Ruffed Grouse may be confounded by some with the Canada Grouse, or "Spruce Partridge" (*Tetrao canadensis*); but this has no lengthened feathers on the neck, and is otherwise entirely different. Nor need any one misunderstand the subject through observing that three kinds of Ruffed Grouse (*Bonasa umbellus*) are here presented. They are Ruffed Grouse, each and all of them, and he may ignore the varieties unless he desires to be very precise. They are merely geographical races of the same bird, differing a little in color according to certain climatic influences to which they are respectively subjected.

The habits of the Ruffed Grouse are perfectly well known to those who have been interested in the matter. The eggs are very character-istic—cream-colored—from a creamy-white to a rich creamy-brown, usually immaculate, or scarcely dotted in minute points, but sometimes with small round spots of pale chocolate, irregularly and sparsely set in among numerous uniform dots. In shape they are very near those of Partridges, approaching the pyriform contour, very broad and blunt at one end and pointed at the other.* They measure about 1.66 inches long by 1.20 broad.

The "drumming" of the Ruffed Grouse has always excited interest, and furnished occasion for various speculations upon the way in which the peculiar noise is made. It was at first supposed to be a vocal effort, and, in fact, the name *Bonasa* was given on this score ("*bonasus*," a bull, in allusion to the bellowing). This, of course, is entirely errone-ous, the sound being produced with the wings. An account is given by Mr. Ridgway, in a late number of the "American Sportsman," which I transcribe entire, as it furnishes a *résumé* of various earlier views of ornithologists:

"I send you a few facts bearing upon the subject of why does the Ruffed Grouse drum, which I have been able to gather from some of our best authorities, and supplement them by the opinions of some reliable sportsmen of my acquaintance. As regards my own views, I have none, since my opportunities for observing this species in a state of nature have been very limited, in consequence of its scarcity in the portions of the country where I have hunted.

"The question of *why* the Ruffed Grouse drums is, perhaps, more easily answered than that of *how* this sound is produced; and, since the latter has been very erroneously described by our highest authorities on ornithology, I impose upon your space by considering both questions together. Audubon's account of the drumming of the Ruffed Grouse is as follows:

"'Early in April the Ruffed Grouse begins to *drum* immediately after dawn, and again toward the close of the day. As the season advances, the drumming is repeated more frequently at all hours of the day; and where these birds are abundant, this curious sound is heard from all parts of the woods in which they reside. The drumming is performed in the following manner: The male bird, standing erect on a prostrate, decayed trunk, raises the feathers of its body in the manner of the Turkey-cock, draws its head toward its tail, erecting the feathers of the latter at the same time, and raising its ruff around the neck, suffers its wings to droop, and struts about on the log. A few moments elapse, when it draws the whole of its feathers close to the body, and, stretch-ing itself out, beats its sides with its wings in the manner of the do-mestic cock, but more loudly, and with such rapidity of motion, after a few of the first strokes, as to cause a tremor in the air, not unlike the rumbling of distant thunder.' (Birds of America, octavo edition, vol. v, pp. 77 and 78.)

---

* The egg of one of our Partridges (*Oreortyx pictus*) is a perfect miniature of that of the Ruffed Grouse, and only distinguishable from the unmarked specimens of the latter by its smaller size—1.45 by 1.10

" Wilson's account is substantially the same, though he does not say that the bird *beats the body* with its wings. We quote his own words:

" 'The drumming, as it is called, of the Pheasant is another singularity of this species. This is performed by the male alone. This drumming is most common in the spring, *and is the call of the cock to his favorite female.* It is produced in the following manner: The bird, standing on an old, prostrate log, generally in a retired and sheltered situation, contracts his throat, erects his expanded tail, elevates the two tufts of feathers on his neck, and inflates his whole body, something in the manner of the Turkey-cock, strutting and wheeling about with great stateliness. After a few manœuvres of this kind, he begins to strike with his stiffened wings in short and quick strokes, which become more and more rapid until they run into each other, as has been already described.' (American Ornithology, Wilson and Bonaparte, vol. ii, pp. 266 and 267.)

" Nuttall describes it more in the manner of Audubon, and is more satisfactory in his conjectures as to *why* this sound is produced. Accordingly we quote his account in full:

" 'In the month of April the Ruffed Grouse begins to be recognized by his peculiar *drumming,* heard soon after dawn and toward the close of evening. At length, as the season of pairing approaches, it is heard louder and more frequent till a later hour of the day, and commences again toward the close of the afternoon. This sonorous, crepitating sound, strongly resembling a low peal of distant thunder, is produced by the male, who, as a preliminary to the operation, stands upright on a prostrate log, parading with erected tail and ruff, and with drooping wings, in the manner of the Turkey. After swelling out his feathers and strutting forth for a few moments, at a sudden impulse, like the motions of a crowing-cock, he draws down his elevated plumes, and, stretching himself forward, loudly beats his sides with his wings with such accelerating motion, after the first few strokes, as to cause the tremor described, which may be heard reverberating, in a still morning, to the distance of from a quarter to a half a mile. This curious signal is repeated at intervals of six or eight minutes. The same sound is also heard in autumn as well as in the spring, and is given by the caged bird as well as the free, *being, at times, merely an instinctive expression of hilarity and vigor.* The drumming parade of the male is often likewise the signal for a quarrel; and when they happen to meet each other in the vicinity of their usual and stated walks, obstinate battles, like those of our domestic fowls for the sovereignty of the dung-hill, but too commonly succeed.' (Manual of Ornithology, Land Birds, second edition, pp. 96 and 97.)

" Most writers follow Audubon and Nuttall in saying that the drumming is produced by striking the wings against the body; but, from the accounts given me by reliable sportsmen, there is no doubt that the above high authorities are in error. Wilson, as will be seen above, does not say that the wings are struck against the body, though it is somewhat uncertain whether he meant to say so or not, since the rest of his description is, substantially, that of Audubon and Nuttall.

" My esteemed friend, Mr. H. W. Henshaw, of Cambridge, Massachusetts, has furnished me with what I believe to be a reliable account of the manner in which the drumming is produced. His authorities are his father and Mr. William Brewster, of Cambridge—the latter an accomplished sportsman, whose statements I can vouch for myself. Mr. Henshaw describes the drumming process as follows:

" The bird sits crosswise upon the log, resting upon the back of the tarsi (not standing erect, as described by some writers), its tail projecting nearly horizontally behind (not erected) and spread; the head is drawn back, the feathers pressed close to the body. The wings are then raised and stiffened, and drumming commences by a slow, hard stroke with both wings, downward and forward; but they are stopped before they touch the body. The rapidity of this motion is increased after the first few beats, when the wings move so fast that only a semi-circular haze over the bird is visible, this rapid vibration causing the rolling noise with which the sound terminates. The movements of the wings, and the rumbling thereby produced, are entirely analogous to those produced by the Humming-bird when hovering over a flower. This I believe to be the true description of the *manner* of drumming, and, I am happy to add, that my father, who has often crawled up to within twenty feet of the bird at such times, corroborates it in every particular. There are, doubtless, among those who read the 'Sportsman,' many who have had opportunities to watch the operations of the Ruffed Grouse when engaged in drumming, and the experience of each one would be a very acceptable contribution to our knowledge of the habits of this very interesting species.

"The fact that the drumming of the Ruffed Grouse is heard as often in autumn as in spring, has raised the question of *why* this sound is produced. In regard to this, Nuttall is probably correct in saying that it is often 'an instinctive expression of hilarity and vigor,' as well as the call-note of the male during the breeding season."

To this article Mr. J. H. Batty replies in the following terms:

"In No. 21 of the 'Sportsman' I find an article of my friend, Mr. Ridgway, 'Why and how does the Ruffed Grouse drum?' I solved the mystery, to my own satisfaction, some five years ago, when living at Springfield, Massachusetts. The peculiar noise made by the Ruffed Grouse is caused by the backs or exterior sides of the wings *striking each other* as they are forcibly raised over the back of the bird. I have seen the Grouse drum, within a few yards of me, a number of times. On one occasion I was sitting on a log in the woods, by a stone wall, eating my lunch. While thus engaged, a Ruffed Grouse mounted the wall, about fifty yards from my position, and commenced walking on it directly toward me. I immediately laid down behind the log on which I had been sitting, and awaited the approach of the bird. When it had reached a point opposite me it mounted a large elevated stone on the top of the wall and commenced drumming, after a series of struttings backward and forward on the wall, as described by Audubon, Wilson, and others. When the bird was drumming its back was toward me, and I had an unobstructed view of it against the sky. The Grouse first struck its wings together slowly and strongly, then gradually increased these strokes until the single strokes could not be detected. During the more rapid beating of the wings the 'semi-circular haze' caused by the wings was observable, as stated by Mr. Henshaw. The wings of the Grouse were stiffened and the strokes given from the shoulder (if I may so speak), and the wings did not appear to touch the bird's sides.

"This occurred in October. Later in the season, when going the round of my mink and muskrat traps, I found a male Ruffed Grouse caught in one of them by the leg. The bird had evidently been caught but a short time before my arrival, and, as the trap which held it was a small and weak one, and the jaws were filled with leaves, the bird's leg had not been broken. I carried the Grouse home and put it in a large feed-box, which was standing in the open air under the shade of an apple-tree. When returning from a hunting excursion one day, one of my neighbors said, 'Your Partridge has been drumming.' I put an old stump in the box of my captive and it had the desired results, for the next morning it was drumming loudly. I observed its motions when drumming, through a hole in the box, and I am confident that the noise was caused by the wings coming forcibly in contact with each other. Let any person take the wings of a dead Grouse in his hands and beat them quickly together, over the bird's back, and they will see at once that the peculiar sounds made by the Ruffed Grouse, and called drumming, is naturally produced. The 'young-of-the-year' of the male Grouse drum in the autumn more frequently than the adult males, as I have ascertained by shooting them when in the act. I have found great difficulty in stalking the Grouse at their drumming-posts, and have often failed in my attempts to do it. The male birds fight hard battles in the spring, and I once caught an old cock by the legs in a snare that had its head cut and bruised very badly, and portions of its neck almost destitute of feathers, the effects of fighting."

I have myself never witnessed the act; but my present view is, that the noise is made by beating the air simply—not by striking the wings either together or against the body, or any hard object.

BONASA UMBELLUS var. UMBELLOIDES, (Dougl.) Bd.

Gray Ruffed Grouse.

(For synonymy and habitat of this variety, see preceding article.)

List of specimens.

19170	36	Grosv. Fork ...	....	June 2, 1860	F. V. Hayden.	17.75	21.00	7.25
19171	83	.... do	....	June 2, 1860	..... do	16.00	21.25	5.00
19172	69	.... do	....	June 3, 1860	..... do	16.50	20.00	7.00
19374	....	Pryor's Fork ...	♀	June 19, 1860	G. H. Trook..	17.00	23.00	7.00

Not obtained by Lieutenant Warren's Expedition.
Later Expeditions.—60823-5, Uintah Mountains ; 62353-7, Idaho and Wyoming.

The preceding article presents the synonymy of this variety in connection with that of the typical *umbellus* and of the Pacific Province var. *sabinii*. Its varietal character lies chiefly in the prevalence of slate-gray color ; it is one extreme (of paleness), of which the reddish-brown var. *sabinii* is the other. This bird has only been noted from the Rocky Mountain region, and occurs about the sources of the Missouri and some of its principal tributaries. Mr. C. H. Merriam found it in Idaho and Wyoming, and states that, although not abundant, it was found throughout the pine forests from Téton Cañon to the Yellowstone. As already noticed, all the British-American Ruffed Grouse, excepting those of var. *sabinii*, are grayer than the ordinary bird of the United States, more or less nearly approaching var. *umbelloides*. Its habits are, beyond doubt, substantially the same as those of the common bird.

LAGOPUS LEUCURUS, Sw.

White-tailed Ptarmigan.

Tetrao (Lagopus) leucurus, Sw. & RICH., F. B. A. ii, 1831, 356, pl. 63.—NUTT., Man. ii, 1834, 612 ; 2d ed. 1840, 820.—AUD., Orn. Biog. v, 1839, 200, pl. 418.
Lagopus leucurus, AUD., Syn. 1839, 208 ; B. Am. v, 1842, 125, pl. 302.—BD., B. N. A. 1858, 636.—COUES, Pr. A. N. S. Phila. 1866, 94 (Canton Burgwyn, N. M., latitude 37°).—ELLIOT, Mon. *Tetraonidæ,* pl. —.—COOP., B. Cal. i, 1870, 542.—ALLEN, Bull. M. C. Z. iii, 1872, 164 (common in mountains of Colorado, above timber-

line).—AIKEN, Pr. Bost. Soc. xv, 1872, 209 (Snowy Range of Colorado).—COUES, Key N. A. B. 1872, 236.—B. B. & R., N. A. B. iii, 1874, 464, pl. 62, f. 6.

Hab.—Rocky Mountains, from the Arctic Ocean to latitude 37°. Higher mountains of Washington Territory and British Columbia.

Ptarmigan may be said to be simply Grouse which turn white in winter. They are the only members of this family of birds in which such a remarkable seasonal change of plumage occurs. All the Ptarmigan are Grouse of boreal or alpine distribution, only reaching sea-level in the higher latitudes, elsewhere confined to mountains. There are five or six species of the Northern Hemisphere, three of which inhabit North America. The present species is immediately distinguished from the rest by having the tail white at all seasons, as implied in its name; this member, in both our other species, being wholly black, and being at least in part black in the species of the Old World. In size, form, and general aspect, the Ptarmigan come nearest the Spruce Partridge (*Tetrao canadensis*); like this species lacking any peculiar feathers on the neck; their most notable characteristic is the dense feathering of the feet, in adaptation to the boreal regions they inhabit. The feathers reach quite to the claws, and cause the bird's feet to look something like a rabbit's—a similarity that suggested the technical term *Lagopus*, or "hare-foot." The same thing occurs in the Snowy Owl, to the same purpose. In winter this Ptarmigan is entirely snow-white; in summer the plumage is variegated with ochrey and tawny, in finely undulated pattern, much of the under parts, however, and wings, remaining white. It shows little or nothing of the rich brown and chocolate colors that the other Ptarmigan display.

This is the only Ptarmigan of regular occurrence in the United States (exclusive of Alaska). Another species, the Willow Ptarmigan (*Lagopus albus*), is occasional in northernmost New England, but in winter only. Audubon, indeed, gives it from the "Rocky Mountains," but there is nothing to show that he means that portion of the mountains within the United States. The White-tailed Ptarmigan is found on the highest mountains of the main chain, as far south as latitude 37°, and on the peaks of Washington Territory and British Columbia. Little has been recorded of its habits, which, however, are probably not materially different from those of its better-known allies. Mr. Aiken, as above quoted, states that it is said to be common on the Snowy Range of Colorado, and gives a description of the nest, upon a miner's authority, as composed of leaves and grass, placed on the ground, among bushes on a side-hill. "Eggs fourteen in number, light bluish-brown, spotted with dark brown." The following description of the egg, furnished by Mr. Allen, who took it on the Coloradan Mountains, above timber-line, where he found the bird common, is more precise: "The only egg of this species I have seen, was an imperfect one presented to me at Montgomery, Colorado Territory, by Mr. A. G. Mead, who obtained it a few days before on Mount Lincoln. It is thickly sprinkled with small, bright reddish-brown spots, on a chocolate-colored ground, and measures about 2.00 inches in length by 1.20 inches in diameter. The White-tailed Ptarmigan breeds above timber-line, probably throughout the snow-capped range of the Rocky Mountains, descending into the timbered valleys in winter, when many are killed for food by the miners."

The following interesting communication was prepared for this work by Mr. Trippe, from his observations in Clear Creek County, Colorado:

"The White-tailed Ptarmigan is a very abundant bird on the main range, living entirely above timber-line the year round, except during the severest part of winter, when it descends into the timber for shelter and food, occasionally straggling as low as 10,000 feet. It begins to change color about the middle of March, when a few specks of blackish-brown begin to appear in the plumage of the oldest males; but the change is very slow, and it is late in April before there is much black visible, and the close of May, or early in June, before the summer plumage is perfect. The Ptarmigan builds its nest in the latter part of June, and commences hatching toward the close of the month or early in July. The nest—which is almost always placed on or near the summit of a ridge or spur, many hundred feet above timber-line—is merely a depression in the ground, lined with a few straws and white feathers from the mother's breast. The eggs are eight in number, of a light buff brown, thickly sprinkled with spots of dark chocolate-brown, somewhat thicker at the larger end. While on her nest, the bird is very tame. Once, while walking near the summit of the range, I chanced to look down, and saw a Ptarmigan in the grass, at my very feet; at the next step I should have trodden upon her. Seeing that she did not appear frightened, I sat down gently, stroked her on the back, and finally, putting both hands beneath her, raised her gently off the nest and set her down on the grass, while she scolded and pecked my hands like a setting hen; and on being released, merely flew off a few yards and settled on a rock, from which she watched me till I had gone away. Late in July I came across a brood of young ones, apparently not more than four or five days old. They were striped with broad bands of white and blackish-brown, and looked precisely like little game chickens. The mother flew in my face and hit me with her wings, using all the little artifices that the Quail and Partridge know so well how to employ, to draw me away; while her brood, seven or eight in number, nimbly ran and hid themselves in the dense grass and among the stones. On another excursion above timber-line, toward the close of August, I found most of the young ones nearly grown and strong on the wing; but one brood was of the size of Quails, showing that some birds must begin breeding much later than others, or that they occasionally raise two broods. These little ones were colored much like the older birds, having blackish-brown bodies and pure white tails. About the first of September the Ptarmigan begins to change color again; but, as in the spring, the process is very gradual, white feathers appearing, one by one, and taking the place of the dark ones. The white on the lower parts enlarges first; then the white areas on the wing; and next, white specks appear on the upper parts, becoming larger and more numerous as the season wears on; but so gradual is the change, that a month after it begins there is not much difference in the plumage perceptible, the general aspect being that of summer. There is much more of the light rufous, however, and the appearance is lighter and grayer, as though bleached. The dark areas predominate, however, throughout October; and, as I have been informed by persons who have killed them throughout the year, it is late in December or January before they become pure white, some few birds showing occasional dark spots even throughout the latter month.

"The Ptarmigan feeds upon the leaves and stalks of various alpine plants, being particularly fond of those of a species of *Cassia*(?), the flowers of which I have frequently taken from its crop. It also lives largely upon insects, and in winter is said to subsist on the buds and leaves of the pines and firs. Its flesh is light colored, though not as white as that of the Gray Grouse, to which it is usually considered inferior for the table. In localities where it is seldom molested it is very tame, and I have been informed by persons whose word is worthy of belief, that they have frequently killed it with sticks. But when

persistently persecuted, it soon becomes wild, and leaves the range of
a shot-gun with surprising quickness. After hunting several large
flocks for three or four days, they grew so shy that it was difficult to
approach within gunshot, although at first they had been comparatively
tame. Nimble of foot, the Ptarmigan frequently prefers to run away,
on the approach of danger, rather than take wing, running over the
rocks and leaping from point to point with great agility, stopping every
little while to look at the object of alarm. I have sometimes chased
them half a mile or more, over the rocky, craggy ridges of the main
range, without being able to get within gunshot, or force them to take
wing. The flight of the Ptarmigan is strong, rapid, and at times sustained for a considerable distance, though usually they fly but a few hundred yards before alighting again. It resembles that of the Prairie
Hen, consisting of rapid flappings of the wings, alternating with the
sailing flight of the latter bird. The note is a loud cackle, somewhat
like the Prairie Hen's, yet quite different; and when uttered by a large
flock together, reminds one of the confused murmur and gabble of a
flock of shore-birds about to take wing. It is a gregarious bird, associating in flocks throughout the year, except in the breeding season.
The different broods gather together as soon as they are nearly grown,
forming large flocks, sometimes of a hundred or more. The colors of
this bird closely resemble those of the surrounding objects, at all seasons
of the year. In its summer plumage of speckled black and gray, it is
very difficult to detect while sitting motionless among the gray and
lichen-covered rocks. The Ptarmigan is apparently well aware of this,
and often squats and remains quiet while one is walking past, trusting
to its resemblance to the surrounding rocks to escape observation. So
perfect is this resemblance that, sometimes on seeing one alight at a
certain spot and withdrawing my eyes from it a moment, I have been
unable to find it again, although I knew the exact place where it sat,
until a movement on the part of the bird betrayed its position. In
summer the white areas of the plumage are completely hidden while
the bird is squatting, although plainly visible while on the wing; in
winter, the first appearing black specks are concealed beneath the white
feathers; and at this period, as I am informed, is almost indistinguishable from the snow. On being pursued, it will dive into the snow and
reappear at a considerable distance."

In further illustration of the history of this species, I reproduce the
following interesting communication from Mr. J. H. Batty, of Dr. Hayden's survey. It appeared in "Forest and Stream," of January 29,
1874. That the bird never lays more than four eggs is, however, open
to question.

"The *Lagopus leucurus* is the smallest of its genus, and inhabits the
highest ranges of the Rocky Mountains. It was first taken by Douglas
and presented to the Zoological Society of London. Since then, specimens of it have been taken by the United States expeditions, and during
the last summer I collected several adults and one young chick while in
the Sierra Madre Mountains with the United States Geological Survey
under Dr. F. V. Hayden. The White-tailed Ptarmigan is the only one
of its family that is found in the Southern Rocky Mountains. During
the summer months they are found in pairs near the snow-banks on the
bare tops of the mountains. Their nests I have seen on several occasions, all of which had been deserted by the young. They are generally
placed in some little cavity among the loose rocks, and are constructed
of dried grasses. The nests are small in proportion to those of the
different species of Grouse, and scantily built. In fact, they select just

such places for their nest in the rocks of the mountains as the *Uria grylle* (Black Guillemot) would on the rocky islands of the Atlantic Ocean. I do not think the *Lagopus leucurus* ever has more than three or four young at a brood, as I have seen pairs of old birds with their young on several occasions, and at such times have never observed more than four chicks in a family. It is barely possible that their numbers may have been lessened by being devoured by Hawks or by the cold rains, which may have chilled and killed them. It is a well-known fact to most naturalists that large numbers of the young Ruffed Grouse often perish from exposure during late springs accompanied by cold rains. I have several times found them dead and in a dying state, caused by exposure in the woods near Springfield, Massachusetts. I do not think that is the case with the young Ptarmigans, however, as they are hatched late in the season, and last spring was a favorable one for their propagation. Neither do I think they are destroyed by Hawks, as there are none where the Ptarmigans breed, with the exception of a few straggling Sparrow Hawks, which are rarely seen. Therefore I think the *Lagopus leucurus* has but three or four eggs at a sitting, and but one brood in a season. They have a continued moult which lasts during the summer months, and the variation in their plumage is so great that it is almost impossible to find two individuals in the same plumage. During the months from April to September their plumage is very scant and ragged; but when in their full winter plumage their feathers are heavy and compact, which gives them a much larger appearance than when seen in the summer dress, mottled with brown and grayish-white. The tail at all times is pure white. They are generally known in Colorado as White and Mountain Quails by the hunters, miners, and ranchmen. When with their young they will fight the ornithological robber, flying so near as to hit one with their wings, in their endeavor to protect their chickens. Both male and female are equally courageous, and will defend their young. In the summer they are very tame, and when approached will run among the rocks or in the dwarf willows, a few yards from the hunter, and squat, and will not continue their retreat until the hunter is upon them. When raised they fly in a straight line for seventy-five or a hundred yards, and alight on some elevated rock, stretching out the neck its full length to see if they are followed, and if nothing is seen to excite their suspicion they walk off from the rocks and commence to feed as usual. During deep snows in the winter the Ptarmigan descend from the mountains and feed in the edges of the timber and on the hill-sides. Last winter some were seen as far east as South Park, Colorado, feeding on the foot-hills. They are gregarious in winter. The White-tailed Ptarmigan is 26.25 inches in extent, and 14.50 inches long; eye, hazel; superciliary membrane, red; toes, feathered half their length in summer, and entirely covered with hair-like feathers in the winter; claws, blackish, lighter at their tips, long, broad and strong, rounded above, concave beneath, arched, edges sharp; and in some individuals the claws are notched on the sides."

NOTE.—The only North American *Tetraoninæ* not treated of in the foregoing pages are two species of Ptarmigan, the synonymy of which is given in the accompanying foot-note, to complete a view of the subfamily.*

* 1. LAGOPUS ALBUS, (*Gmelin*), *Audubon.*

Tetrao albus, GM., Syst. Nat. i, 1788, 750.—LATH., Ind. Orn. ii, 1790, 639 (*Lagopède de la Baie d'Hudson*, BUFF., ii, 276; *White Partridge*, EDW., 72; *White Grous*, PENN., Arct. Zool. ii, No. 183; LATH.; Gen. Syn. iv, 743).
Lagopus albus, AUD., Syn. 1839, 207; B. Am. v, 1842, 114.—BP., List, 1838, 44.—NUTT., Man. i, 2d ed. 1840, 816.—COUES, Pr. A. N. S. 1861, 227 (Labrador).—VERR., Pr.

Subfamily ODONTOPHORINÆ : *American Partridges.*

As previously remarked, the Partridges are distinguished from the Grouse by the nakedness of the feet and nostrils, and other characters. They average much smaller—the largest of our species is smaller than the least of our Grouse. The American Partridges have been separated as a subfamily from those of the Old World, but this division, however convenient and geographically distinctive, does not appear to rest upon structural peculiarities of any considerable moment. They are stated to be peculiar in the presence of a tooth or notch on the edge of the under mandible, but this character is often obscure and sometimes inappreciable. There may be, however, some anatomical differences not yet fully elaborated. The group is represented by numerous species, some of great beauty, of Central and South America, and several others which reach over our southern border. The familiar and well-known Partridge of the Southern States—and Quail of the Northern—is one of the most attractive game birds of this country. The several United States genera may readily be distinguished, as follows :

ORTYX. An inconspicuous crest, scarcely visible except in life. Tail about two-thirds as long as the wing. Coloration everywhere variegated. (One species).

CALLIPEPLA. A short, soft, full crest. Tail nearly as long as the wing. Coloration much the same all over, showing curious semicircular markings. (One species).

OREORTYX. A long slender arrowy crest, two or three inches long, of two narrowly linear feathers. Tail two-thirds (rather less) as long as the wing. Parti-colored, but the coloration chiefly in masses. (One species).

LOPHORTYX. A long, recurved, helmet-like crest, of several imbricated plumes, enlarged at the extremity. Tail about as long as the wing. Coloration chiefly in masses. (Two species).

CYRTONYX. A short, soft, full crest. Tail scarcely half as long as the wing. Coloration peculiar. (One species).

As all these genera have each but a single species in this country, excepting *Lophortyx*, the foregoing is nearly equivalent to a determination of the species.

Ess. Inst. iii, 1862, 158 (Maine).—COUES, Pr. Ess. Inst. v, 1868, 289 (Northern New England).—GRAY, Cat. *Gallinæ* Br. Mus. 1867, 80.—DALL & BANN., Tr. Chic. Acad. i, 1869, 287 (Alaska).—FINSCH, Abh. Nat. iii, 1872, 62 (Alaska).— COUES, Key, 1872, 235.—B. B. & R., N. A. B. iii, 1874, 457, pl. 62, f. 1, 2, 3.

Tetrao saliceti, TEMM., Man. ii, 471.—SAB., App. Frank. Journ. 681.—RICH., App. Parry's 2d Voy. 347.—AUD., Orn. Biog. ii, 1834, 528, pl. 191.

Tetrao (Lagopus) saliceti, SW. & RICH., F. B. A. ii, 1831, 351.

(?) *Tetrao lagopus*, FORST., Philos. Tr. lxii, 1772, 390.

Tetrao lapponicus, GM., Syst. Nat. i, 1788, 751.—LATH., Ind. Orn. ii, 1790, 640.

"*Tetrao rehusak*, TEMM., Pig. et Gall. iii, 225."

Lagopus subalpinus, NILS., Orn. Suec. i, 307.

Lagopus brachydactylus, TEMM., Man. Orn. iii, 328.—GOULD, B. E. pl. 256.

Hab.—Northern North America, into the northernmost States.

2. LAGOPUS RUPESTRIS, (*Gmelin*), Leach.

Tetrao rupestris, GM., Syst. Nat. i, 1788, 751.—LATH., Ind. Orn. ii, 1790, 640 (*Rock Grous*, PENN., Arct. Zool. ii, No. 184 ; LATH., Syn. Suppl. 217).—SAB., Suppl. Parry's 1st Voy. p. cxcv.—RICH., App. Parry's 2d Voy. 348.—AUD., Orn. Biog. iv, 1838, 483, pl. 368.

Tetrao (Lagopus) rupestris, SW. & RICH., F. B. A. ii, 1831, 354, pl. 64.

Lagopus rupestris, LEACH, Zool. Misc. ii, 290.—BP., List, 1838, 44.—AUD., Syn. 1839, 208 ; B. Am. v, 1842, 122, pl. 301.—BD., B. N. A. 1858, 635.—COUES, Key, 1872, 235.

Attagen rupestris, REICH., Syst. Av. 1851, p. xxix.

Tetrao (Lagopus) mutus, SW. & RICH., F. B. A. ii, 1831, 350 (quote *Tetrao lagopus*, SAB., Suppl. Parry's 1st Voy. p. cxcvii ; SAB., Frank. Journ. 682 ; RICH., App. Parry's 2d Voy. 350).

Tetrao mutus, AUD., Orn. Biog. v, 1839, 196.

Lagopus mutus, BP., List, 1838, 44.—GRAY, Cat. *Gall.* Br. Mus. 1867, 91.

Lagopus mutus var. *rupestris*, B. B. & R., N. A. B. iii, 1874, 462, pl. 62, f. 4, 5.

Lagopus americanus, AUD., Syn. 1839, 207 ; B. Am. v, 1842, 119, pl. 300.

Lagopus islandorum, FABER, Prod. Isl. Orn. 6.

Lagopus reinhardtii et *grœnlandicus*, BREHM.

Hab.—Arctic America.

ORTYX VIRGINIANUS, (Linn.) Bp.

Virginia Partridge, or Quail; Bob White.

a. *virginianus.*

Tetrao virginianus, LINN., Syst. Nat. i, 1766, 277 (based on *Perdix virginiana*, CATES., Car. i, 12, pl. 12; BRISS., Orn. i, 230).—GM., Syst. Nat. i, 1788, 761.
Perdix virginiana, LATH., Ind. Orn. ii, 1790, 650.—WILS., Am. Orn. vi, 1812, 21, pl. 47.—
    BP., Syn. 1828, 124 (subg. *Ortyx*).—DOUGH., Cab. Nat. Hist. i, 1830, 37, pl. 4.—
    BP., Journ. Phila. Acad. iv, 1825, 268, No. 203.—AUD., Orn. Biog. i, 1831, 388;
    v, 1839, 564; pl. 76.—NUTT., Man. i, 1832, 646.
Ortyx virginianus, JARD., Nat. Lib. Birds, iv, 101, pl. 10.—BP., List, 1838, 43.—AUD.,
    Syn. 1839, 199; B. Am. v, 1842, 59, pl. 289.—GOULD, Monog. *Odontophorinæ*, pl.
    1.—WOODH., Sitgr. Rep. 1853, 94 (Indian Territory and Texas).—BD., B. N. A.
    1858, 640.—HAYD., Rep. 1862, 173 (Missouri River to White River).—ALLEN,
    Bull. M. C. Z. ii, 1871, 352 (critical); iii, 1872, 181 (Kansas).—TRIPPE, Pr. Ess.
    Inst. vi, 1871, 118 (Minnesota); Pr. Bost. Soc. xv, 1872, 240 (Iowa).—SNOW, B.
    Kans. 1873, 9, No. 197 (Eastern and Middle Kansas).—COUES, Key, 1872, 236.—
    B. B. & R., N. A. B. iii, 1874, 468, pl. 63, f. 1, 2; and of authors generally.
Tetrao marilandicus, LINN., Syst. Nat. i, 1766, 277 (based on *Perdix novæ angliæ*, BRISS.,
    i, 229).—GM., Syst. Nat. i, 1788, 761.
Perdix marilandica, LATH., Ind. Orn. ii, 1790, 650.
Tetrao minor, BARTR., Trav. in Fla. 1791, 290*bis.*
Perdix borealis, VIEILL., Nouv. Dict. d'Hist. Nat.; Gal. ii, 44, pl. 214.
Ortyx borealis, STEPH., Shaw's Gen. Zool. xi, 1819, 377.—JARD. & SELBY. Ill.
Perdrix (Ortyx) mexicanus, LESS., Tr. 507 (quotes GM., and P. E. 149).
(?) *Ortyx castaneus*, GOULD, P. Z. S. x, 182; Monog. *Odont.* pl. 3 (*melanotic?*).

b. *texanus.*

Ortyx texanus, LAWR., Ann. Lyc. N. Y. vi, 1853, 1.—BD., B. N. A. 1858, 641; Mex. Bound.
    Surv. ii, 1859, pt. ii, p. 22, pl. 24.
Ortyx virginianus var. *texanus*, COUES, Key, 1872, 237.—B. B. & R., N. A. B. iii, 1874, 474,
    pl. 63, f. 3, 4.

c. *floridanus.*

Ortyx virginianus var. *floridanus*, COUES, Key, 1872, 237.—B. B. & R., N. A. B. iii, 1874, 522.

d. *cubanensis.*

Ortyx cubanensis, GOULD, Monog. *Odont.* pl. 2.—GRAY, Gen. of B. iii, 514.
Ortyx virginianus var. *cubanensis*, B. B. & R., N. A. B. iii, 1874, 468.

Hab.—Eastern United States. North to Massachusetts and slightly beyond; Canada West; Minnesota. West to high central plains. Up the Missouri to White River (*Hayden*). Salt Lake Valley, introduced (*Allen*). Var. *texanus* in Texas. Var. *floridanus* in Florida, and very similar specimens up the Mississippi Valley to Southern Illinois (*Ridgway*). Introduced in Bahamas (*Bryant*) and Santa Cruz (*Newton*).
Lieutenant Warren's Expedition.—4859, Iowa Point.
Not obtained by Captain Raynolds' Expedition.

I find no record of the Quails in New England beyond Massachusetts, and it does not go much further north. In Minnesota it is abundant in southern portions of the State, and appears to be spreading with the advance of the settlements, like the Pinnated Grouse. I found no indication of its presence along the Red River, or anywhere in Northern Dakota. Along the Missouri River it is abundant up to Fort Randall, where I have enjoyed as fine Quail shooting as I have found anywhere; and, according to Dr. Hayden, it has followed up the course of the river to the White River. In this region, according to my observation, they are strictly confined to the wooded and brushy portions of the river-bottoms, which form an interrupted series of natural "preserves," in every way adapted to the shelter of the bird, and the affording of a supply of food. Even in this rigorous climate, where the thermometer falls every winter to 20° or 30° below zero, the birds show no disposition to migrate, and generally succeed in braving such severe cold, although I have authentic information of instances in which a whole covey has been found frozen to death, huddled together in the vain attempt to preserve their warmth. At Fort Randall, a place where the river flows nearly due east, I observed that the Quail were all on the north bank, although the other afforded equally attractive resorts; this may be accounted for by a suggestion ·of Captain Hartley's, that they choose the sunny side of the river, the south side being overshadowed by the bold bluffs.

SUPPLEMENTARY ACCOUNT OF ODONTOPHORINÆ.

As the Missouri region furnishes but a single species of this interesting group, I will illustrate it further with an account of all the remaining species of the United States, derived chiefly from my observations in New Mexico, Arizona, and California. The distinctive characters of the *genera* have already been given.

PLUMED QUAIL.—LOPHORTYX GAMBELI,* *Nutt.*

As the principal game bird of Arizona, and in fact the only one found all over the Territory since the Turkeys and water-fowl are necessarily of partial distribution, the Plumed Quail claims the special attention of the sportsman, as well as naturalist, and has charms for both. It is resident in all parts of the Territory, and always at hand to furnish healthful and agreeable sport, no less than to contribute a dainty to larders that are rarely overstocked.

The geographical distribution of this species has been determined with precision, thanks to the observations of several naturalists besides myself, who have recorded their experiences in different localities. In general terms, the Territories of New Mexico and Arizona may be called its *habitat;* but this indication may be given with more exactitude. To the eastward the bird has been found as far as the Rio Pecos, in Texas, a region that seems to be its limit in this direction, the Massena replacing it beyond. The Colorado nearly defines it western extension, but this statement requires the qualification given below. The conditions of the Quails existence are fulfilled throughout the broad region between the rivers just named; while to the northward enough is now known of its extension to make it certain that it reaches somewhat further than the limits Colonel McCall assigned in his extremely interesting contribution to Mr. Cassin's work. This gentleman gives the *habitat* as lying between the 31st and 34th parallels; but I found it abundant at Fort Whipple, a little north of 35°, and think the limit should not be fixed lower than 36° at least. But its numbers dwindle as we approach its northern confines, and the broken mountain portions of Northern Arizona appear less suited to its wants than the plains and

<hr>

* The following is the synonymy of this species:

Lophortyx gambeli, "NUTT."—GAMB., Pr. A. N. S. i, 1843, 260; Journ. A. N. S. i, 219.—
    McCALL, Pr. A. N. S. 1851, 221.—BD., B N. A. 1858, 645.—KENN., P. R. R.
    Rep. x, 1859, Whipple's Route, Birds, 33.—HEERM., *ibid.* Parke's Route, Birds,
    19.—BD., Mex. B. Surv. ii, 1859, Birds, 23.—COUES, Ibis, 1866, 46 (biography).—COUES, Pr. Phila. Acad. 1866, 94.—DRESS., Ibis, 1866, 23.—COOP., B.
    Cal. i, 1870, 553.—COUES, Key, 1872, 236.—B. B. & R., N. A. B. iii, 1874, 482, pl.
    64, f. 4, 5.
Callipepla gambeli, GOULD, Monog. *Odont.* 1850, pl. 17.—CASS., Ill. i, 1853, 45, pl. 9.—
    HEERM., P. R. R. Rep. x, 1859, Williamson's Route, Birds, 60.
Callipepla venusta, GOULD, P. Z. S. xiv, 1846, 70.
Lophortyx "*californicus,*" COUES, Ibis, 1865, 165 (error).

deserts further south. We may without hesitation fix upon the valleys of the Gila and Colorado as its centres of abundance; about Fort Yuma, for example, there were more Quails to the square mile than I ever saw elsewhere, and, indeed, I could scarcely see how many more could well have been accommodated with food and hiding-places. The numbers diminish but little up the river to Fort Mojave, but they soon after decrease. Quail being so abundant at Fort Whipple, I regarded it as a little singular that I saw none at all in approaching that locality from the eastward, along the same parallel; but such was the case. Numerous observers, however, attest its presence at various points along the Rio Grande. Southward the Quail passes beyond the United States, and spreads over contiguous portions of Mexico.

An interesting fact in the distribution of this species is the effect of the Colorado desert in shutting it off from the fertile portions of California. This dreary, sterile waste offers a barrier to its westward extension that is only exceptionally overcome. Although the birds enter the desert a little way, they rarely reach far enough to mix with the representative species of California (*L. californicus*). The strip of country that mostly assists in their occasional passage westward is along the Mojave River, a stream arising in the San Bernardino Mountains, and flowing eastward toward the Colorado, from which it is shut off by a range of hills, and consequently sinks in the desert at Soda Lake. Among other birds, the two kinds of Plumed Quail—Gambel's and the Californian—meet along this comparatively fertile thoroughfare, upon neutral ground, as Drs. Heermann and Cooper, as well as myself, have witnessed. Much further south, Colonel McCall found birds at Alamo Mucho, forty-four miles west of the Colorado; but still the desert is in effect the barrier I have represented, and the two Quails, speaking generally, do not meet. One wonders the less at this who has any good idea of the Colorado desert, such as may be gained, for example, from the following passage from Colonel McCall's article, which remains associated in my mind with the Plumed Quails with all the freshness of first impressions. Speaking of the Alamo, where he shot a pair, "Here is in truth a desert!" exclaims the Colonel. "Figure to yourself, if you can, a portion of this fair earth, where, for some hundreds of miles, the whole crust seems to have been reduced to ashes by the action of internal fires; behold a vast plain of desolation surrounded, and at intervals intersected, by abrupt mountain ranges, which are little better than gigantic heaps of scoria; imagine this scenery to be actually glowing under the direct rays of a midsummer sun, and you may have some idea of the prospect that meets the eye of the traveler who looks out upon the desert from the well of the Alamo. You may perceive in his rear a few stunted cottonwood-trees scattered along the edge of a channel, in which, apparently, water once *was*, but now is not; while around him, here and there, is a light-leafed mezquite, that stretches forth its slender arms and appears to invite him to a shade that is but a mockery. Here it was that I first heard the plaintive voice of this bird as he strove to cheer his mate while occupied in the tedious task of incubation." And singularly enough, the bird is almost equally hemmed in by desert to the eastward as well; for according to the same writer's accounts, "a sandy desert, between the Pecos and Devil's River, is the barrier beyond which the species under consideration has not extended its range."

Such a glimpse of the haunts of the Plumed Quail make one wonder how it ever became a game bird at all; how sportsmen could be able to make game of it, without being themselves rather made game of!

28

But great as are the natural disadvantages of the surroundings, the bird's attractions are still greater, and partly so from this very fact. But Arizona is a large place, and one need not always endure desert in his Quail-shooting. There is a much brighter side to the picture; we have just seen only the darkest possible. Perhaps no Territory rivals Arizona in *variety* of climate, physical geography, and natural productions. Between rugged mountains that lift snow-capped peaks among the clouds lie hidden pleasant green valleys, whose fresh verdure contrasts with surrounding desolation. Vast primæval forests stretch for leagues, or are only interrupted by oak and cedar openings. Bright fringes of cottonwoods and willows mark the devious course of streams, where walnut and cherry are scattered, and grape-vines cling to them, and roses bloom beneath leafy boughs. Here is plenty at least, if not peace. Nothing mars the pleasures of the chase, but the chances of being chased. Were it not for Indians, we should have here the acmé of Quail-shooting.

Gambel's Quail may be looked for in every kind of cover. Where they abound it is almost impossible to miss them, and coveys may often be seen on exposed sand-heaps, along open roads, or in the cleared patches around settlers' cabins. If they have any aversion, it is for thick high pine-woods, without any undergrowth; there they only casually stray. They are particularly fond of the low, tangled brush along creeks, the dense groves of young willows that grow in similar places, and the close-set chaparral of hillocks or mountain ravines. I have often found them, also, among huge granitic boulders and masses of lava, where there was little or no vegetation, except some straggling weeds; and have flushed them from the dryer knolls in the midst of a reedy swamp. Along the Gila and Colorado they live in such brakes as I described in speaking of Abert's Finch; and they frequent the groves of mezquite and mimosa, that form so conspicuous a feature of the scenery in those places. These scrubby trees form dense interlacing copses, only to be penetrated with the utmost difficulty, but beneath their spreading scrawny branches are open intersecting ways, along which the Quail roams at will, enjoying the slight shade. In the most sterile regions they are apt to come together in numbers about the few water-holes or moist spots that may be found, and remain in the vicinity, so that they become almost as good indication of the presence of water as the Doves themselves. A noteworthy fact in their history, is their ability to bear, without apparent inconvenience, great extremes of temperature. They are seemingly at ease among the burning sands of the desert, where, for months, the thermometer daily marks a hundred, and may reach a hundred and forty, " in the best shade that could be procured," as Colonel McCall says; and they are equally at home the year round among the mountains, where snow lies on the ground in winter.

The Quail's food is made up of various substances. Like the rest of its tribe, it is chiefly granivorous, eating seeds of every description; but fruits and insects form a large portion of its fare. It devours insects of such sorts as it can capture, and particularly those kinds that infest plants. In the fall it gathers cherries and grapes, and other "fruits" properly speaking, as well as the various berries not usually so called. It visits patches of prickly-pear (*Opuntia*) to feed upon the soft juicy "tunas," that are eaten by everything in Arizona, from men and bears, to beetles. In the spring it shows fondness for the buds of different plants, particularly mezquite and willow; birds shot at this time are frequently found with sticky bits of the buds about their bills. But though they thus feed so extensively upon this substance, containing salicine, I never noticed that the flesh acquired a bitter taste. There is as yet little cultivated grain in Arizona; but doubtless some future historian will have to add our cereals to the bird's list, and speak of Gambel's Quail as frequenting old corn and wheat-fields, and the neighborhood of hay-ricks, where a large share of its food is to be gleaned. Like other *Gallinæ*, it swallows quantities of sand and gravel to facilitate, it is supposed, the trituration in the gizzard of the harder kinds of food.

I believe that the Quail moults at least twice a year; but the spring change is apparently less complete, and certainly more gradual than that of the fall, the birds seeming rather to furbish up a part of their plumage than to furnish themselves with entirely new attire. By the latter part of summer* the plumage is faded and worn with incubation and the care of the young, and the renewal begins as soon as the latest brood is reared. The process is a long one, and birds are rarely found at any season in such poor condition as to be unfit for preservation, nor are they ever deprived of flight. No crest is occasionally found for a short time in early autumn; but new feathers generally sprout before all the old ones are dropped. I think they are shed from behind forward, so that the front ones are lost the last. The fully-developed crest is a striking and beautiful ornament, hardly to be surpassed in stylishness and jaunty effect. It averages an inch and a half in length, and sometimes reaches two inches in the most vigorous males; in the females it is rarely over an inch. The male's is glossy jet-black; the female's has a brownish cast. The number of feathers composing it is variable; five or six is usual, but there may be ten. They all spring from a single point on the top of the head—just behind the transverse white line that crosses the crown from eye to eye. The feathers are club-shaped, enlarged at the tip, and curling over forward, together forming a helmet-shaped bundle. The webs are loose; they bend backward from the shaft, so that this forms the front border of the feather. Each feather is thus folded or imbricated over the next succeeding, and the whole are packed into a single fascicle in this manner. The crest is freely movable, and its motions are subject to voluntary control. It is usually carried erect, but sometimes drops forward, or obliquely over one eye; and occasionally is allowed to hang backward, though it cannot be made to lie close over the occiput. The crest sprouts when the chicks are only a few days old, about the time that the first true feathers appear upon the wings and tail. It then consists of three or four feathers, forming a short tuft, brown instead of black, not club-shaped, nor recurved, nor imbricated. Even in the adult female, though the crest has the same general characters as that of the male, it is only slightly, if at all, recurved, and is always shorter, as we have seen.

The hen may easily be distinguished from the cock by other differences; she is smaller, averaging an inch less in length; she has no pure black, white, or chestnut about the head, and wants the great black spot upon the belly. Similar in other respects, there is still a general dullness and want of tone about all her colors, as well as less sharpness of definition of the several differently colored areas. The sexual characters are evident before the birds are half grown. The chicks in the downy state, a few days old, do not in the least resemble either parent. They are very prettily marked; in fact they are more attractive before they have any feathers than afterward, until mature; just as little

---

* I speak of observations as made at Fort Whipple, unless the contrary is stated.

children and grown folks are about equally agreeable, while half-fledged people are apt to be more or less offensive. The bill is bright-reddish, with the under mandible nearly white; the feet are flesh-colored; the head yellowish-white, with a pure brown spot on the nape, and a few black feathers on the crown, each streaked with white; the upper parts tawny or brownish-gray, mottled and clouded with black, and conspicuously streaked with long, narrow, sharply-penciled whited-white lines; the primaries dusky, marbled with lighter and darker colors on the outer webs; throat whitish; all other under parts with narrow, blended, transverse bars of black and yellowish-white. The little things, in this condition, are about $3\frac{1}{2}$ inches long, and may be found up to the last of August, though by this time most of the summer's brood are partly grown. When the chicks are six or seven inches long the general color is dull, leaden-gray, becoming ochraceous on the scapulars and wing-coverts, which are still mottled, as just described; the chin and belly are nearly whitish; the breast still has a few longitudinal white lines, but is mostly waved across with dark shades of gray; the flanks become tinged with brown, and the sides with fulvous, though, as yet, without distinct white and chestnut stripes; there is a broad white superciliary line; the crest is brown, half an inch long. Progressing from this stage to one nearly complete, birds occur, in September, October, and part of November, with the bill black and feet dark colored; the crest an inch long, and beginning to recurve; the white lines about the head of the young males now apparent; the sides rusty-brown, with traces of definite white stripes; black becoming evident on the abdomen; on the breast, clear plumbeous feathers, mixed with light gray waved ones; the upper parts mostly clear plumbeous, but still somewhat waved and marbled with pale gray.

All Quail are *Præcoces*, as already explained; and the chicks of this species are certainly precocious little things, if we may judge by their actions when they are disturbed. They run about as soon as they are hatched, though probably not "with half shell on their backs," as some one has said. In a few days they become very nimble, and so expert in hiding that it is difficult either to see or catch them. When the mother bird is surprised with her young brood, she gives a sharp warning cry, that is well understood to mean danger, and then generally flies a little distance to some concealed spot, where she crouches, anxiously watching. The fledglings, by an instinct that seems strange when we consider how short a time they have had any ideas at all, instantly scatter in all directions, and squat to hide as soon as they think they have found a safe place, remaining motionless until the reassuring notes of the mother call them together again, with an intimation that the alarm is over. Then they huddle close around her, and she carefully leads them off to some other spot, where she looks for greater security in the enjoyment of her hopes and pleasing cares. As long as they require the parent's attention they keep close together, and are averse to flying. Even after becoming able to use their wings well, they prefer to run and hide, or squat where they may be, when alarmed. If then forced up, the young covey flies off, without separating, to a little distance, often realighting on the lower limbs of trees or in bushes, rather than on the ground. As they grow older and strong of wing, they fly further, separate more readily, and more rarely take to trees; and sometimes, before they are fully grown, they are found to have already become wary and difficult of approach. As one draws near where a covey is feeding, a quick, sharp cry from the bird who first notices the approach alarms the whole, and is quickly repeated by the rest, as they start to run, betraying their course by the rustling of dried leaves. Let him step nearer, and they rise with a whirr, scattering in every direction.

Newly-hatched birds may be found all summer; and incubation goes on from; say, early in May until the middle of August. Not that any single pair are engaged so long, but that different broods may be hatched during all this time. The greater number of old birds pair in April, and hatch their first brood some time during the following month. Most of them doubtless raise another. Others appear to defer incubation for a month or two, and have but one brood. The first chicks that I saw in the summer of 1865 were hatched in May; and I found others, the same year, only a few days old in August; but by this month almost all the birds of the year were well grown, and by September were in condition to afford legitimate sport. In October a few are found not yet ready to be shot; but the great majority are as large as the parents, and nearly as strong of wing. The season may, therefore, be said to begin in October and continue into March, but birds should not be pursued later than the middle of this month. For although few birds, if any, actually mate before April, it is cruel as well as injudicious to disturb them while they are preparing to do so. The beginning of the pairing season may be known to be at hand when certain peculiar cries, different from any usually emitted during the fall and winter, are heard.

These notes are a sign that the coveys are breaking up and mating about to commence. They are analogous to the "bob-white" of the Eastern Quail (*Ortyx virginianus*), and are uttered, as with that species, more particularly in the breeding season. The note is a loud, energetic, two-syllabled whistle, delivered in a clear, ringing tone. It is difficult to write down intelligently, but, once heard, is not likely to be afterward mistaken, except for one of the cries of the Black-headed Grosbeak. It sounds, to my ears, something like the forcible pronunciation of the syllables "*killink, killink*," indefinitely repeated, sometimes with a rising, sometimes a falling, intonation. The old cocks, if they can be seen so engaged, are found strutting along some fallen log, or gesticulating from the top of some broad rock, or stepping with dignified air along a pathway under the bushes; sometimes even perched in a tree or bush, without other motion than the heaving of the chest. But, wherever they may be, they have one mind in common; their only thought, to secure the admiration and then the favor of birds more modest if not more fair.

A beautiful sight it is to see the enamored birds pressing suit with all the pomp and circumstance of their brilliant courtships. The firm and stately tread; with body erect and comely shape displayed to best advantage; the quivering wings; the motion of the plumes, that wave like the standard of knights-errant; the flashing eyes—bespeak proud consciousness of masculine vigor. The beautiful bird glances defiance and challenges loudly, eager for a rival; but none disputes, and he may retire, his rights proven. Only a gentler bird is near, hidden in a leafy bower, whence she watches, admiring his bearing, fascinated by the courage she sees displayed, hoping every moment that the next will bring him, dreading lest it may. As their eyes meet, she trembles and would turn to fly, but cannot; his glow again, but with a different light, even more intense than before. With an exultant cry, he flies straight to her, and, like the true knight he is, for just one instant bends till his breast touches the ground, and is then erect again. He leans toward her, half-spreads his wing over her, and pleads in under-tone. She listens, but draws away; she listens, but only stands irresolute; she listens, and, listening, yields.

They must prepare for new duties. With deep sense of responsibility and earnest solicitude, the pair now cast about for a suitable spot for their home. They search through the tall, rank herbage alongside the stream, through the willow-copses, among fallen moss-covered logs that are scattered around the glen, and at length make up their minds. Little more is needed than to fix upon the spot, for the nest is a simple affair, the work of a few hours perhaps, scratching a suitable depression and lining it with a few dried grasses pressed together. Day by day eggs are laid, till a dozen or more fill the nest. They cannot be distinguished from those of the California Quail. They measure an inch and a quarter in length by an inch in breadth, and are almost pyramidal in shape, the larger end flattish and very broad, the other narrow and pointed. The color is a buff or rich creamy, dotted and spotted all over with bright brown, and splashed here and there with large blotches of the same. When the female is not pressed to lay, the pair ramble about together, in close company, until the complement is finished. Then she gives up all recreation, grown already quite sober and maternal, and resolutely sets about her long tour of duty. But she is not forgotten because she can no longer share the idle pleasures of her lord. Mounted on a stump or bush near by, he stands watch, and continually solaces her with the best music he can make. It is not very harmonious, to be sure; in fact his ditty at such times is a medley of odd notes, sounding rather lugubrious than hilarious, but it is presumably satisfactory to the one most concerned. So the long days pass for two weeks or more, till feeble cries come from the nest; the mother dries and cuddles the curious little things, and the delighted birds, brimful of joy, lead their family off in search of food.

From the number of eggs sometimes found in a nest, it becomes a question whether birds, hard pressed, may not occasionally deposit in nests not their own. We have no positive evidence that it may occur, but observation has rendered it highly probable that such is the case with some other birds, as the Rails, and, I think, the Virginia Quail. However this may be, it is pretty certain that broods of young sometimes coalesce, at a varying time after hatching. I do not remember to have myself seen a covey of more than twenty; but it is currently reported, upon good authority, that troops numbering as many as fifty partly-grown birds, and including several old ones, may be met with. This raises, of course, the question of polygamy, so common in birds of this order; and something may be said in favor of the view. The same surmise has been made in the case of *L. californicus*, but I believe it remains to be proven. I am bound to observe, that I have never witnessed anything supporting this view; had I done so, what has just gone before would not have been written.

In an article communicated some years since to the "Ibis," I used the following language, which I have since found no reason to modify:

"Compared with the Eastern Quail (*O. virginianus*), from the sportsman's stand-point, Gambel's Plumed Quail is more difficult to kill. Not that it rises with more startling suddenness. or flies faster, for I noticed no material difference in these respects. But when a bevy is flushed and one, or at most two, birds secured, it is exceedingly difficult, and usually only by chance, that other shots are obtained. For, except under certain circumstances, they lie very badly; and when they drop, after being for the first time started, it is usually not to squat and remain hid, but to run as fast and far as possible; so that if found at all, it will be dozens of yards from where they were marked down. This propensity to run, which is also a great obstacle to their being flushed within proper distance, is exceedingly troublesome both to the sportsman and his dog; so much so, that the best trained dogs can often be of little or no service. It is true that this habit of running affords many shots on the ground, and often places the whole bevy directly under fire; but no true sportsman would thus ingloriously fill his bag by 'potting' a bevy of such noble game birds. Like all their tribe, their flight is exceedingly rapid and vigorous; but it is always even and direct, so that it only requires a very quick hand and eye, and the usual intuitive calculation for cross shots, to kill them readily. Notwithstanding all I have heard to the contrary, I consider them far from being tough birds, and No. 8 shot is abundantly large enough for them. The fault in most cases, I presume, is with the shooter rather than the shot. I may add, that many of the places in which bevies are found would compare unfavorably with the worst Woodcock-brake of the Eastern States, as regards facilities for obtaining a fair shot. I have had a bevy flushed all around me, and hardly caught a glimpse of a feather. But these and all other difficulties should only increase one's ardor, and confer additional value on the lovely birds when obtained."

Man is, I suppose, the Quail's worst enemy; what the White does with dog and gun the Red accomplishes with ingenious snares. The Indians take great numbers alive in this way, for food or to trade with the whites along the Colorado; and they use the crests for a variety of purposes that they consider ornamental. I saw a squaw once who had at least a hundred of them strung on a piece of rope-yarn for a necklace. But the birds have other foes: the larger Hawks prey upon them, so also do the wolves, as I had good evidence upon one occasion, when hunting in a precipitous, rocky place near Fort Whipple. I heard a covey whispering about me as they started to run off in the weeds, and followed them up to get a shot. They passed around a huge boulder that projected from the hill-side, and then, to my surprise, suddenly scattered on wing in every direction, some flying almost in my face. At the same instant a wolf leaped up from the grass, where he had been hiding, a few feet off, intending to waylay the covey, and looking very much disappointed, not to say digusted, at the sudden flight. We had marked the covey together, and were hunting it up from opposite sides, and neither of us could account for their flushing so unexpectedly; then he caught sight of me, and it was a question which of us was most surprised. However, I felt that I owed him a private grudge for getting in the way of the birds and spoiling my shot; so I fired both barrels in quick succession. With nothing but mustard-seed in my gun, I hardly expected to more than frighten the beast, but he was so near that he rolled over quite handsomely, his hind-quarters paralyzed with a charge that took effect in the small of the back. I kept his skin as a trophy, and since that time have had unlimited confidence in small shot!

VALLEY QUAIL OF CALIFORNIA.—LOPHORTYX CALIFORNICA,* Bp.

This species is readily distinguished from the last. In place of the large black area on the belly, there is a tract of rich golden-brown or

---

* *Tetrao californicus.* SHAW, Nat. Misc. pl. 345.
Perdix californicus, LATH., Ind. Orn. Suppl. 1801, p. lxii.—AUD., Orn. Biog. v, 1839, 152, pl. 413.—BP., Syn. 1828, 125 (subg. *Ortyx*).—HUTCHIN's Cal. Mag. ii, 1857, 241.
Ortyx californica, STEPH., Shaw's Gen. Zool. xi, 1819, 384.—JARD., Nat. Lib. iv, 104, pl. 11.—CUV., R. A. (illust. ed.) Ois. pl. 64.—BENNETT, Gard. & Men. Z. S. ii, 29, fig. —.—AUD., Syn. 1839, 199; B. Am. v, 1842, 67, pl. 290.
Callipepla californica, GOULD, Monog. *Odont.* 18, pl. 16.—REICH., Syst. Av. 1850, pl. 27.—NEWB., P. R. R. Rep. vi, 1857, 92.—HEERM., *ibid.* x, 1859, pt. vi, 60.

orange-chestnut, where the feathers are sharply edged with black. The forehead is whitish, with black lines, instead of black with whitish lines; the occiput is smoky-brown, instead of chestnut-brown; there is a small white loral stripe; the vent, flanks and crissum are tawny, with dark stripes; the long feathers of the sides are like the back, with sharp, white stripes. In the hen bird the belly is whitish, or tawny, with black semicircles, as in the cock; while in the hen of *gambeli* the same parts are whitish, with lengthwise dark marks.

This species replaces the last in the Pacific coast region, from Washington Territory southward. It is abundant from the Columbia River to Cape Saint Lucas, on the plains and in the valleys. In California they are mostly restricted to the regions west of the Sierra Nevada, which, with the Great Colorado Desert, form a barrier to their spread eastward. But they do reach nearly to the Colorado River, following along the course of the Mojave River to the spot where it sinks in the desert, there meeting the western extension of the range of *L. gambeli*. Up the mountains it does not appear to reach a higher altitude than three or four thousand feet, beyond which it is replaced by the *Oreortyx pictus*. In its general habits it is the counterpart of Gambel's Quail.

MOUNTAIN QUAIL OF CALIFORNIA.—Oreortyx pictus,* Bd.

This is a magnificent species, much the largest and handsomest Quail of this country. Its distribution is limited and rather peculiar, as it inhabits almost exclusively the mountain ranges of Oregon and California. Having never yet seen the bird alive, I can say nothing from personal observation of its habits. Dr. Cooper furnishes the following account:

"This bird, one of the most beautiful of its family, is common in the higher ranges of California and Oregon, and I think a few are found north of the Columbia. South of San Francisco they are unknown near the coast, unless some birds seen by members of the Survey, in the Mount Diablo range, at an elevation of over 3,000 feet, were of this species. In the Sierra Nevada they have been obtained at Fort Tejon, at about 4,000 feet elevation, and were seen at Cajon Pass, in winter, about the same elevation, and in latitude 34°. They probably extend further south in the mountains. At latitude 39° they descend in winter to about 3,000 feet, and are found lower toward the north, until, in Oregon, they frequent the borders of the Willamette Valley, but little above the sea-level. They are not common anywhere within the range of the gunners who supply the San Francisco market; all those I have seen there having been brought alive from the Sierra Nevada. They abound in summer up to 7,000 feet in that range, where I found them in September, the young not quite full grown and the old birds moulting. In habits and flight they have considerable resemblance to our

Lophortyx californica, Bp., List, 1838, 42.—Nutt., Man. i, 2d ed. 1840, 789.—Bd., B. N. A. 1858, 644.—Coop. & Suck., N. H. Wash. Ter. 1860, 225.—Coop., B. Cal. i, 1870, 549.—Coues, Key, 1872, 238.—B. B. & R., N. A B. iii, 1874, 479, pl. 64, figs. 1, 2.

* *Ortyx picta*, Dougl., Tr. Linn. Soc. xvi, 1829, 143.
Callipepla picta, Gould, Monog. *Odont.* 1850, 18, pl. xv.—Newb., P. R. R. Rep. vi, 93.— Heerm., *ibid.* x, 1859, Williamson's Route, Birds, 61.
Oreortyx pictus, Bd., B. N. A. 1858, 642.—Coop. & Suck., N. H. Wash. Ter. 1860, 225.— Coop., B. Cal. i, 1870, 546.—Coues, Key, 1872, 237.—B. B. & R., N. A. B. iii, 1874, 475, pl. 63, fig. 5.
Ortyx plumifera, Gould, P. Z. S. v, 1837, 42.—Aud., Syn. 1839, 200; B. Am; v, 1842, 69, pl. 291. (May represent a slight variety.)
Perdix plumifera, Aud., Orn. Biog. v, 1839, 220, pl. 422.
Lophortyx plumifera, Nutt., Man. i, 2d ed. 1840, 791.

other Quail, but their cries are quite different. Their note of alarm is a rather faint chirp, scarcely warning the sportsman of their presence before they fly. They scatter in all directions when flushed, and then call each other together by a whistle, very much like that of a man calling his dog. According to Newberry the hen has a cluck, much like that of the common hen, when calling together her young brood, about the first of August. The chickens also utter a piping note, scattering and concealing themselves in the grass. * * * * They do not seem anywhere to associate in flocks of more than fifteen or twenty, and from the rugged, shrubby character of the country they inhabit, they are not easily shot, except in the early morning, when they come out into the roads and openings to feed. They live on seeds, berries, and insects, and are very good for the table. As with the other species (*L. californicus*), more are taken in traps than with the gun. When hunted in thick brush they generally run some distance before flying, and then rise singly, scattering so that only one can usually be killed at a shot. I have never seen them perch in trees, like the other species."

BLUE QUAIL.—CALLIPEPLA SQUAMATA,* (*Vig.*) *Gray.*

As we have already referred the three Arizonian Quails to as many genera, we may briefly notice some of the points of their structure. That of the *Blue* Quail is most like Gambel's in bill, wings, tail, and feet, but entirely different in the crest, which, instead of being helmet-like, of club-shaped, recurved feathers, is short, soft, and full, and, though capable of erection in a conspicuous manner, can be laid quite flat, out of sight. The Blue is also called the Scaled Quail, from the peculiar appearance of the plumage of the under parts, which is seemingly abnormal in texture or disposition; but this is merely an optical effect of the singular coloration of the feathers, simulating imbricated scales or tiles. A corresponding result is said to appear, from the same cause, in the plumage of the under parts of young Gannets. The *Massena* Quail has the crest in general similar to that of the Blue, but differs from this species, as well as from Gambel's, in the structure of the wings and tail. These are both short; the wing-coverts and tertials are remarkably enlarged, hiding the primaries when the wing is closed, and the tail-coverts are so long as to conceal the true tail-feathers, which are soft and weak. The Massena is of striking and elegant colors, having sharply contrasted round spots upon a rich ground, and other peculiarities; both it and Gambel's are singularly, almost fantastically, striped about the head; the Blue is of plainer, though scarcely less-pleasing tints. Thus each species shows some marked features with one of the other two, but none of consequence with both; and each has peculiarities of its own not shared by either of the others.

The Blue Quail has another peculiarity, of a different sort; the two sexes differ but little in appearance. As a general rule the sexual differences among gallinaceous birds are very striking—more so, perhaps, than in any other group. Contrary to the rule in our own species, the male is gaudily attired, while the female is of plain and homely appear-

* *Ortyx squamata*, VIG., Zool. Journ. 1830, 275.—ABERT, Pr. A. N. S. iii, 1847, 221.
Callipepla squamata, GRAY, Gen. of B. iii, 1846, 514.—GOULD, Monog. *Odont.* 1850, pl. 19.—
    McCALL, Pr. A. N. S. v, 1851, 222.—CASS., Ill. i, 1854, 129, pl. 19.—BD., B. N. A.
    1858, 646.—COOP., B. Cal. i, 1870, 556.—COUES, Pr. A. N. S. 1866, 95.—COUES,
    Key, 1872, 238.—B. B. & R., N. A. B. iii, 1874, 487, pl. 63, fig. 6.
Callipepla strenua, WAGL., Isis, xxv, 1832, 278.
Tetrao cristata, DE LA LLAVE, Registro Trimestre, i, 1832, 144.

ance, as well illustrated by the domestic Cock and Hen, and especially by the Peafowls. Among Arizonian *Gallinæ*, the Massena differs most in sexual distinctions of color, for the female is quite subdued in her dress, while the male is showy in coloration. The Blue presents the other extreme, as if, with tender gallantry, he were unwilling to outshine.

This species is a bird of noticeably terrestrial habits, rarely taking to trees or bushes unless hard pressed in one of those extremities into which some people are fond of forcing any birds large enough to be worth a charge of shot, and wary enough to make it exciting sport to penetrate their poor bodies with it. It generally trusts to its legs rather than its wings, though these are not at all deficient in size or strength. On level ground it glides along with marvellous celerity, and makes good progress over the most rocky and difficult places. As a consequence it is rather difficult to shoot fairly, though it may be "potted" in great style by one so disposed; and it will probably require several generations in training before it can be taught to lie well to a dog. I am inclined to think, indeed, that the lying of Quail, an essential feature for the chase in its perfection, is almost as much a result of education as the "pointing" that the intelligent brute who helps us kill them has learned. In a primitive and strictly natural condition, Quail, as a general rule, rather use their legs to escape pursuit than squat and attempt to hide. That the reverse is the case with the Virginia Quail I am perfectly aware, but this proves nothing to the contrary, and I am inclined to think its crouching, till almost trodden upon, to be an acquired trick. This would surely be a poor way of escape from any of its natural enemies—any carnivorous bird or mammal; yet they found it to succeed so well against their chief persecutor, that he has had to call in the aid of a sharper-sighted, sharper-nosed brute than himself, else he might stumble over stubble-fields all day without seeing a bird, except by accident. I presume that Virginia Quail, in the days of Captain Smith and Pocahontas, were very much in the social status of the Arizonian to-day; and these certainly trust to their legs and wings rather than to the artifice of thrusting their heads in tussock of grass, and then fancying they are safe.

Like our other southwestern species, the Blue Quail has a rather restricted range in the United States. The valley of the Rio Grande at large may be given as its especial habitat; it is said to be more abundant there than I have found it to be in other regions. Colonel McCall, with that accuracy for which he has well-deserved name, states that this valley, "though comparatively narrow, contains a country of great extent from north to south, and embraces, in its stretch between the Rocky Mountains and the Gulf of Mexico, every variety of climate, from the extreme of cold to that of tropical heat. This entire region, not even excepting the narrow mountain valleys, covered in winter with deep snows, is inhabited by the species under consideration. I have met with it on the Rio Grande and its affluents from the 25th to the 38th degree of north latitude—that is to say, from below Monterey, in Mexico, along the borders of the San Juan River to its junction with the Rio Grande; and at different points on the latter as high up as the Taos and other northern branches which gush from the mountain sides. I have also found it, though less frequently, near the head of the Riado Creek, which likewise rises in the Rocky Mountains and flows eastward to the Canadian." I did not meet with the bird near Taos, and we have no knowledge of its occurrence so far north, except that afforded by Colonel McCall's observations; I presume this must be the extreme limit of its range. The only naturalist of the Railroad Surveys who appears to have met with it was Dr. Heermann, who found it on the San Pedro, a branch of the Gila, east of Tucson, and thence to Limpia Springs. Those of the Mexican Boundary Survey, however, all observed it, and Dr. Kennerly makes the summary statement, that it was "found everywhere where there was permanent water, from Limpia Creek, Texas, to San Bernardino, Sonora." Lieutenant Couch records it from "about sixty leagues west of Matamoras; not until free from prairie and bottomland;" an observation confirmed by Mr. Clarke, who states that it "does not occur on the grassy prairies near the coast." I was rather surprised to find no Blue Quail about Fort Whipple, since it seemed that that locality was in their ordinary range; and probably my observations, or rather want of observations in this particular, represent the actual truth, as I was repeatedly assured that none live there. In Arizona they appear really to be confined to what is called the "lower country," that is, to the valleys of the Gila and Colorado, in a restricted sense. On the latter river it must ascend at least as high as Fort Mojave; and to the eastward, to the country about the Hassayampa.

The egg of the Blue Quail differs in color from that of the Californian or Gambel's, though of the same size and shape. A specimen measures 1.20 by 1.00; it is buffy-white, or with the faintest possible brownish-yellow tinge, and is very regularly and thickly dotted with minute specks of light brown. The usual large number are laid for each setting.

MASSENA QUAIL.—Cyrtonyx massena,* (*Less.*) *Gould.*

I found no Massena Quail about Fort Whipple until a few days before my final departure. A pair were then procured, setting at rest the doubts I had all along entertained regarding the veracity of reports I had often received, of the occurrence there of Quail different from Gambel's. But the species must certainly be rare in that region, since I could not otherwise have overlooked it for so long a time.

This remarkable Quail was described about forty years ago by several writers, nearly simultaneously. For a long while it was only known as a Mexican species. It remained for American naturalists and, I may add, officers of the Army to show its existence in our country, and give us something definite about its habits. In Colonel McCall's observations upon Texan and New Mexican birds, published in the Philadelphia Academy's proceedings for 1851, we find the following interesting account:

"The species was not seen before crossing the San Pedro, but it was not long before it made its appearance in the waste and rocky region into which we then entered. And from that time until we reached the Rio Pecos, a distance of one hundred and forty miles (westwardly by the route we traveled), it was frequently seen, though I should not say

---

* *Ortyx massena*, Less., Cent. Zool. 1830, 189.—Finsch, Abh. Nat. Bremen, 1870, 357 (Guadalaxara).
Cyrtonyx massena, Gould, Monog. *Odont.* 1850, 15, pl. 7.—McCall, Pr. A. N. S. v, 1851, 221.—Cass., Ill. i, 1853, 21, pl. 21.—Reich., Syst. Av. 1850, pl. 27.—Bd., B. N. A. 1858, 647; Mex. B. Surv. ii, 1859, Birds, 23.—Coues, Pr. Phila. Acad. 1866, 95.—Dress., Ibis, 1866, 29.—Gray, Cat. *Gallinæ* Br. Mus. 1867, 74.—Coop., B. Cal. i, 1870, 558.—Coues, Key, 1872, 239.—B. B. & R., N. A. B. iii, 1874, 492, pl. 64, f. 3, 6.
Ortyx montezumæ, Vig., Zool. Journ. v, 1830, 275.—Jard. & Selby, Ill. pl. 126.
Odontophorus meleagris, Wagl., Isis, xxv, 1832, 279.
Tetrao guttata, De La Llave, Registro Trimestre, i, 1832, 145.
"*Perdix perspicillata*, Licht."

it was very common. This region is a desert of great length from north to south, our trail crossing it at nearly right angles. The general face of the country is level, and consists of either a crumbling argillaceous limestone, or a coarse, gray sand, producing nothing but a sparse growth of sand plants. Water is found only at long intervals, and, except at those points, there is little cover for game, and apparently less food—the principal growth being *Cacti*, of which the most common is *Cactus arborescens ;* yet here, among projecting rocks, or on the borders of dry gullies or in loose scrub, I found the Massena Partridge in all the beauty of his rich and varied plumage.

"The habits of this species are different from those of any other species of Partridge that I have met with. They were in coveys of from eight to twelve individuals, and appeared to be extremely simple and affectionate in disposition. In feeding they separated but little, keeping up a social *"cluck"* all the time. They were so gentle as to evince little or no alarm on the appearance of man, scarcely moving out of his way as he passed, and only running off or flying a few yards, when perhaps half their number were laid low by a shot. This inclined me to think that they might with little difficulty be domesticated, although I found them here in a barren, boundless waste, and nowhere near the habitation of man. This trait of gentleness is the very opposite of those manifested by the Scaly Partridge (*Callipepla squamata*), which I always observed to be, though found perchance in grounds as little frequented as these, remarkably vigilant, shy, and difficult to approach. The call or signal note of this species is peculiar. I never saw it after crossing the Pecos."

This account of the gentle and confiding disposition of the Massena Quail, so at variance with the character of nearly all the other species, agrees entirely with the representations which were made to me at Fort Whipple; and the same trait has also been noticed by other writers. Don Pablo de la Llave noticed it in his original account of the birds in the following terms, which I copy from Mr. Cassin's translation of his article: "—— and in everything it shows an amiability, and, so to speak, a kindness of character (*una bondad de caracter*) which is not found in any other species of this genus, and it is naturally so tame and domestic as to permit itself to be caught with the hand." So, also, Dr. Woodhouse, in the following paragraph from Sitgreave's Report:

"My attention was first called to this beautiful bird a few miles beyond the head of the Rio San Pedro, where we started three of them, and Major Backus succeeded in procuring a female specimen, which is now in my collection. This was the only time that I observed this bird. Captain S. G. French, Assistant-Quartermaster United States Army, informs me that in the year 1849, when he first passed over this road, he met with these birds in a number of localities—at the head of the San Pedro, Howard's Springs, and also at the Eagle Springs—showing evidently that it has a range over the country lying between the Rio Grande and San Pedro Rivers. He also stated that he had never met with it near the settlements, but always among the wild, rocky, and almost barren hills of this country. They are more sociable and not so shy as others of the same family. Their food appears to be principally insects."

To give, as nearly as possible, a complete view of what has been put on record concerning the habits of the beautiful Massena, I continue with the following quotations from the notes made by the naturalists of the Mexican Boundary Survey. It will be noticed that Mr. Clark's account is considerably at variance with those just presented:

"Once, on flushing a covey of *Ortyx texana*, my attention was attracted by a bird which remained behind, showing no inclination to follow the rest. It attempted to hide in the grass, but not to fly, and on being shot proved to be a male *Massena*. It occurs in pairs or flocks, and when flushed it flies further than the Virginia Quail; and does not lie so close. They may be approached within a few feet, and followed up, particularly when in pairs, running along before you like so many domestic fowls. It is quiet as well as retired; a subdued though sharp note is the only noise I ever heard it make, and that only when frightened. I have seen it pursued, and all the barrels of a six-shooter fired at it without giving it alarm, and finally forced to fly only by an attack of stones and clubs. It was first met in the neighborhood of San Antonio, and thence sparsely distributed, as an inhabitant of both prairies and mountains, as far westward as Sonora. It is a much wilder bird than the *squamata* ; less conspicuous, as also less noisy, and never seen in flocks, living about old camps, as is often the case with the latter. Its haunts are far removed from the habitation of man, and the indifference it sometimes manifests to his presence is due to its ignorance of his power and attributes. Though distributed over the same country as the *squamata*, it is not found in such barren regions as the latter frequently is, preferring those regions most luxuriantly covered with vegetation."—*J. H. Clark.*

"First seen in the Cañon Guapuco, twelve leagues south of Monterey. Though rather shy, it seemed quite at home in the cultivated fields and stubbles of the ranches."—*D. N. Couch.*

"This bird I have never seen further south in Texas than Turkey Creek. In this vicinity it was very common, and also at various points thence to the Rio Grande. In the valley of this river it is very rarely seen, giving way apparently to the Scaly and Gambel's Partridges.' West of the river it was very common as far as we traveled, wherever there was fresh and permanent water. In the valley of the Santa Cruz River, and among the adjacent hills, it was extremely abundant. In the months of June and July it was observed there, always in pairs, while in Texas, in the months of October and November, it was found in very large flocks, sometimes of various ages, from the very small and partly fledged to the full grown bird. When hunted it hides itself very closely in the grass, and I have often known Mexican soldiers in Sonora to kill them with their lances, by striking them either while on the ground or just as they rise. Some of these men are very expert in this business, and will kill many in the course of a day's travel."—*C. B. R. Kennerly.*

It is not difficult to gain from these accounts a pretty definite idea of the range of the species in the United States, though we do not know how far south it penetrates in Mexico, which is really its native country. We have no record of it as yet as a bird of California. To the indications of its range in Texas and New Mexico, I have only to add, as just now done, its occurrence in Arizona at Fort Whipple, a locality at some distance from those previously recorded, and further north, as well as west, than any before known. There it is rare, as stated, nor do I think that the species can be very abundant even in the southern portions of the Territory, unless it be at the southeast corner.

We see that none of the fragmentary published accounts are more than isolated facts of an imperfect history ; yet they do good service as contributions toward a biography. The bird is mentioned as an inhabitant of the most barren, desolate, and unfrequented regions, as well as the vicinity of cultivated ranches; as very unusually tame, or quite wild; as occurring in pairs or in flocks: each account being circumstantial and limited. But this very diversity of statement helps to a knowledge of the bird; and here, as elsewhere, I cannot refrain from pressing the importance of the record of any facts whatever, however isolated, that may be gleaned by personal observation upon the habits and manners of birds, no matter how small and unpromising the field, or how often it has been gone over before. Any information, so be it that it is accurate, is better than none; though still it should be remembered that *ex parte* statements are liable to mislead, particularly when used in generalizations, the inductive not being in natural history, as it is in the more exact sciences, always a safe method of reasoning.

There are two points in the history of this species to which attention may profitably be directed. One is the bird's remarkable unsophistication. Living in what we should consider lonely desolation, but which is to it a happy home, the bird has not yet learned to throw aside the gentle, confiding disposition its Maker gave. No contact with the lords of the universe, guardians of civilization and progress, jobbers in ethics and æsthetics, has yet begotten in its ingenious nature the wholesome change that the requirements of self-preservation will some day demand, and which it will instinctively adopt. Birds that live in populous districts have had a lesson to learn of bitter experience, and its fruits have been instilled through generation after generation, till a second nature replaces the first, and a shrewd distrust of the whole human race is instilled. It is a nauseous dose that these Quail, like innocent children, have to swallow; but the medicine acts vigorously and beneficially, heart-longings and soul-breathings, and the like, giving way to something more substantial and sensible. Some day a fine old Cock Massena shall say to his family, "*timeo Danaos et dona ferentes;*" the newly-born wisdom shall take well, and become gospel to succeeding generations, to outlive in the code of Quail ethics the memory of the Æneid in the minds of men.

We are familiar with the structural peculiarities of the Massena Quail, and it is not likely that these deviations from a common standard are not reflected in some way in the bird's habits and manners; but how, we are still ignorant. Nothing accounting for these peculiarities has yet been learned; and yet there must be some traits that, for their proper exhibition, require the special modification that we find. These individualizing traits offer an inviting field for investigation. Mr. Cassin has, perhaps, taken the initiative toward such discovery, in an observation founded upon consideration of the bird's colors. "The circular spots," he says, "which are numerous on the inferior parts of the body in this Partridge, appear to indicate as a character an analogy to the Guinea-fowls, which is further sustained by its habit of uttering its note continually when in company with its fellows, or when feeding."

Adult male: Bill convex, very stout, the under mandible doubly toothed; legs large and strong, toes very short, claws long, strong, much curved; wings moderate, the tertials and coverts highly developed; tail very short and soft, not reaching beyond the thick, long coverts; a short, full crest. Under parts pure velvety black, with a broad longitudinal band of deep chestnut, the black parts on the sides beautifully marked with distinct, rounded white spots, several on each feather; upper parts varying shades of yellowish or tawny white, and most of them with narrow transverse bars of blackish, changing into spots on the wing-coverts; primaries dusky, barred with reddish or yellowish-white; crown variegated with black, brownish, and yellowish; the crest yellowish, nearly white behind; other parts of the head white, or ashy, fantastically edged and striped with black; chin black, separated by a white stripe from a maxillary black line, this latter by white from a triangular black patch below the eye; a black stripe from the nostrils over the side of the crown, separated by a white line from the central black on the forehead. Iris, brown; bill, deep bluish horn-color; legs, pale dull bluish. Length, 9½ inches; extent, 18; wing, 5; tail, 2; bill, 0.70; tarsus, 1¼.

Adult female: Like the male on the upper parts, but wanting the distinct markings on the head; colors of the under parts entirely different; the crest less developed; the size of the whole bird less; no black about the head; chin yellowish or tawny white; whole under parts plain, pale brownish-white, inconspicuously marked with a few little black spots. Bill, light horn-color; upper mandible with a tinge of reddish, lower nearly white; iris, brownish-olive; legs and feet, livid bluish-white, with a yellowish tinge behind. Length, 9 inches; extent, 17; wing, 4¼; tail, 2; tarsus, 1.20.

Young, scarcely fledged: Bill, reddish-brown above, whitish below; feet, dull brownish. General plumage of the upper parts light, warm brown, variegated with black, and very boldly striped with white—each feather having a broad, sharp, white shaft-line, hammer-headed or transversely enlarged at apex, bordered on either side by the areas that cause the variegation. A few of the inner wing-quills like the back; the rest dusky, with whitish shafts, and interruptedly barred, chiefly on the outer webs, with light, dull buffy-brown, or whitish. Feathers of under parts white, with a slight buffy suffusion, boldly marked with innumerable spots of brownish-black, paired on each feather, quite circular and sharp on the breast, further back widening into transverse bars. The head of the specimen is still in the down, except a feather or two just sprouted on the vertex; these feathers are like the back; there is a triangular chestnut-brown area on the crown; the head is otherwise light grayish-brown, fading into white on the chin and throat, and with a dusky auricular mark. Length of the specimen about 3½ inches.

For opportunity of describing this early stage, hitherto unpublished, so far as I know, and quite new to me, I am indebted to Lieutenant G. M. Wheeler, Corps of Engineers, the accomplished officer in charge of the Explorations and Surveys west of the 100th meridian, which are doing so much to develop the resources of the West. I was kindly shown, by Dr. H. C. Yarrow, the well-known naturalist in charge of the Natural History Department, several specimens of the species from Arizona, forming part of the collection made during the season of 1873 by H. W. Henshaw—one of the largest, best prepared, and most valuable suites of bird-skins ever brought from our Western Territories.

NOTE.—The foregoing account of *Gallinæ* includes all the species known to inhabit North America, north of Mexico.

ORDER GRALLATORES: WADING BIRDS.

SUBORDER LIMICOLÆ: SHORE BIRDS.

These two groups, represented by a great variety of forms, are sufficiently defined for our present purposes in the Key, p. 239. The *Limicolæ*, or Shore Birds (as distinguished from the other two groups of the order, *Herodiones*, or the Herons and their allies, and *Alectorides*, or the Cranes, Rails, and their allies), comprehend all kinds of Plover, Snipe, Woodcock, and birds collectively known as "Bay Snipe," as well as Phalaropes, Avocets, Stilts, Turnstones, and Oyster-catchers.

Family CHARADRIIDÆ: Plover.

Subfamily CHARADRIINÆ: *True Plover.*

Besides the birds properly so called, several others are loosely designated as Plovers by unscientific experts in ornithology. The principal of these is the so-called "Upland Plover," which is a true Tattler of the family *Scolopacidæ*, its proper name being the Bartramian Tattler (*Actiturus bartramius*)—see under this head. Our true Plover may be recognized by the shortness and stoutness of the bill, as compared with this member in the *Scolopacidæ*, and especially by having only *three* toes. The only American exceptions to this last statement are the Black-bellied Plover, or Bull-head (*Squatarola helvetica*), in which there is a rudimentary hind toe, and the curious Surf Bird of the Pacific coast (*Aphriza virgata*), in which the hind toe is as well developed as is usual in the *Scolopacidæ* (where perhaps it belongs). The only three-toed American bird of the family *Scolopacidæ* is the Stilt (*Himantopus nigricollis*).

SQUATAROLA HELVETICA, (Linn.) Brehm.

Black-bellied Plover.

Tringa helvetica, LINN., Syst. Nat. i, 1766, 250 (based on *Vanellus helveticus* of BRISS., v, 106, pl. 10, f. 1).—FORST., Phil. Trans. lxii, 1772, 412; Pl. Enlum. 853, 854, 923.
Squatarola helvetica, BREHM, V. D. 554.—BP., Comp. List, 1838, 46; K. & B., Wirb. Eur. 207.—GRAY, Gen. of B. iii, 543; and of most late authors.—CASS., Pr. Phila. Acad. 1858, 195 (Japan); *ibid.* 1860, 195 (Carthagena).—CAB., J. f. O. iv, 1856, 423 (Cuba).—BRY., Pr. Bost. Soc. vii, 1859 (Bahamas).—REINH., Ibis, iii, 1861, 9 (Greenland).—DRESS., Ibis, 1866, 34 (Texas).—SALV., Ibis, 1866, 196 (Guatemala).—LAWR., Ann. Lyc. N. Y. ix, 1210 (Yucatan).—PELZ., Orn. Braz. iii, 296 (Brazil).—BD, B. N. A. 1858, 697.—COOP. & SUCK., N. H. Wash. Ter. 1860, 232.—DALL & BANN., Tr. Chic. Acad. i, 1869, 290.—COUES, Key, 1872, 243, fig. 154.—SNOW, B. Kans. 1873, 10, No. 212 (Kansas).—GRAY, Hand-list, iii, 1871, Nos. 9980, 9981.—SH. & DRESS., B. E. pt. vi, Aug. 1871.
Vanellus helveticus, VIEILL., Ency. Meth. iii, 1823, 1077.
Charadrius helveticus, LICHT., Verzeich. 1823, No. 728.—BP., Syn. 1828, 298, No. 221.—NUTT., Man. ii, 1834, 26.—AUD., Orn. Biog. iv, 1838, 280, pl. 334; Syn. 1839, 221; B. Am. v, 1842, 199, pl. 315.—KJÆRB., Naum. 1850, 6.
Charadrius (Squatarola) helvetica, RIDGW., Ann. Lyc. N. Y. x, 1874, 383.
Tringa varia, LINN., Syst. Nat. i, 1766, 252 (based on *Vanellus varius*, BRISS., v, 103).
Charadrius varius, FINSCH & HARTL., Vög. Ost. Afr. 1871, 644.
Pluvialis varius, SCHL., Mus. P.-B., *Cursores*, 1865, 53.—DEAL. & GERBE, O. E. 1867, 127.
Tringa squatarola, LINN., Syst. Nat. i, 1766, 252 (based on *Pluvialis cinerea* of various authors, and *Vanellus griseus* of BRISS., v, 100, pl. 9, f. 1).
Pluvialis squatarola, MACGIL., Man. N. H. Orn. ii, 48; Hist. Br. B. iv, 1852, 86.
Charadrius squatarola, NAUM., Vög. Deutschl. vii, 1834, 265, pl. 178.
Vanellus squatarola, SCHL., Rev. Crit. 1864, 84.
Squatarola cinerea, FLEMING, Br. Anim., 1828, 111.—EYT., Cat. Br. B. 34.
Charadrius hypomelanus, PALL., Reise, iii, 1773, 699; Zoog. R.-A. ii, 1811, 138, pl. 59.
Charadrius pardela, PALL., Zoog. R.-A. ii, 1811, 142.
Squatarola grisea, LEACH, Cat. B. Br. Mus. 1816, 29.—STEPH., Shaw's Gen. Zool. xi, p. 505.
Vanellus griseus, JENYNS, Man. Br. Vert. 181.

Vanellus melanogaster, BECHSTEIN, Naturg. Deut. 1809, 356.—TEMM., Man. 1815, 345; ii, 547.—SAB., App. Frank. Journ. 684.—RICH., App. Parry's 2d Voy. 352.—Sw. & RICH., F. B. A. ii, 1831, 370.
Squatarola melanogaster, MALH., Fn. Orn. Sicil. 1840, 166.
Charadrius apricarius, WILS., Am. Orn. vii, 1813, 41, pl. 57, f. 4.
Squatarola wilsoni, LICHT., Nomencl. Av. 1854, 95.
Charadrius longirostris, BREHM, J. f. O. 1854, 79.
Squatarola australis, BONAPARTE.
Squatarola rhynchomega, BP., Compt. Rend. 1856, 417.
Squatarola megarhynchus, BREHM, Vollst. Vogelf. 1855, 284.
Figured.—Sw., Cat. of B. fig. 321; GRAY, Gen. of B. iii, 542, pl. 145, f. 9.—REICH., Syst. Av. pl. 18—GOULD, B. E. pl. 290; B.\Aust. vi, pl. 12.—NAUM., Vög. pl. 178.
Black-bellied, Gray and Swiss Plover. Beetle-head, Bull-head Plover. Oxeye, and a variety of other names.
Hab.—Nearly cosmopolitan.

With a close general resemblance to the Golden Plover, especially when in fall plumage, this species will be immediately recognized by the presence of a small hind toe, no trace of which occurs in any of our other Plovers. There are also additional characters.

In the United States—in fact in most parts of North America—the Black-bellied Plover is less abundant than the Golden Plover, and such is particularly the case in the Missouri region, where I never observed it, and where, so far as I have determined, it is recorded only by one writer. Although stated by Audubon and others to breed from Virginia and the Middle States northward, no such instances have come to my knowledge; and in the United States the species is only known with certainty to occur now during the migrations. In the extensive journeys it performs it gives evident preference for coast-lines of travel, being decidedly more numerous along either of our coasts than in the interior. Nevertheless Dr. Suckley states that he found it "moderately abundant" in Minnesota (where it was not observed by Mr. Trippe or myself). Dr. Cooper remarks that it seems to be a resident bird near the mouth of the Columbia, as he there shot young birds in July; this, however, is not proof that they were actually bred in the vicinity.

Eggs of this species in the Smithsonian cabinet, collected by R. MacFarlane, esq., on the Arctic coast, east of Anderson River, July 4, 1864, afford the following description: Size, 2.10 by 1.40, to 1.90 by 1.40, in a set of four. Color, brownish-drab, or rather dark brownish-clay color, very thickly marked at and around the larger end, for nearly half the length of the egg, with irregularly sized and shaped spots and blotches of brownish-black, and over the rest of the surface thinly spotted with smaller marks of the same color. The larger markings around the butt are to a great extent confluent, producing an imperfect wreath. A very few paler shell markings are noted on close scrutiny. The nest was a depression of the ground on the side of a slight eminence, lined with a few dried grasses. Another set of four from the same source average more elongated, the most pointed one being 2.30 long by 1.45 broad; the markings are much more evenly distributed over the whole egg, are smaller, and tending to a confused, scratchy pattern, as well as rather lighter in tone. A third set of four, collected by Mr. MacFarlane, at Franklin Bay, are intermediate between the other two in these respects, though most like the first described.

CHARADRIUS FULVUS var. VIRGINICUS, (Bork.) Coues.

American Golden Plover.

a. *fulvus*.

Charadrius fulvus, GM., Syst. Nat. i, 1788, 687 ; and of authors.
Pluvialis fulvus, BP., C. R. 1856, 417.—SCHL., M. P.-B. 1864, 50.

Charadrius pluvialis, HORSF., Linn. Tr. xiii, 1822, 187.—PEALE, U. S. Expl. Ex. 1848, 239.
Charadrius xanthocheilus, WAGL., S. A. 1827.—GOULD, B. A. vi, pl. 13.—CASS., Expl. Ex. 325.
Pluvialis xanthocheilus, BP., C. R. 1856, 417.
Charadrius taitensis, LESS., Man. ii, 1828, 321.
Pluvialis taitensis, BP., C. R. 1856, 417.
Charadrius virginianus, JARD. & SELB., Ill. ii, pl. 85.—HARTL., Wieg. Arch. 1852, 134.
Charadrius glaucopus, FORST., Descr. An. ed. Licht. 1844, 176.
Charadrius virginicus, BLYTH, Cat. B. Mus. As. Soc. 1849, 262.
Charadrius longipes, "TEMM., Mus. Lugdun."
Pluvialis longipes, BP., C. R. 1856, 417.
Charadrius auratus orientalis, TEMM. & SCHL., Fn. Japon. pl. 62.
Charadrius auratus, SCHRENCK, Reise Amur, 1860, 410.

b. *virginicus.*

Charadrius dominicus, MÜLLER, Syst. Nat. 1776, 116.—CASS., Pr. Phila. Acad. 1864, 241.
Charadrius pluvialis, WILS., Am. Orn. vii, 1813, 71, pl. 59, f. 5.—SAB., Suppl. Parry's 1st
    Voy. p. cxcix; Frank. Journ. 683.—BP., Syn. 1828, No. 220.—SW. & RICH., F.
    B. A. ii, 1831, 369.—NUTT., Man. ii, 1834, 16.—AUD., Orn. Biog. iii, 1835, 623;
    not of *Linnæus*, nor of European writers.
Charadrius pluvialis var. *virginicus*, RIDGW., Ann. Lyc. x, 1874, 383.
Charadrius virginicus, "BORK., Mus. Berol."—LICHT., Verzeichniss, 1823. No. 729.—
    MEYEN, Nova Acta K. C. L. Acad. xvi, Suppl. 1834, 106, pl. 18.—NEWB., P. R.
    R. Rep. vi, 1857, 97.—BD., B. N. A. 1858, 690.—COOP. & SUCK., N. H. Wash.
    Ter. 1860, 229.—HAYD., Rep. 1862, 173.—DRESS., Ibis, 1866, 33 (Texas).—DALL
    & BANN., Tr. Chic. Acad. i, 1869, 289.—REINH., B. of Greenland, 9, No. 40 (*cf.*
    Comptes Rendus, xliii, p. 1019).—STEV., Rep. U. S. Geol. Surv. Ter. 1870, 465,
    No. 96.—SNOW, B. Kans. 1873, 9, No. 207.—TRIPPE, Pr. Bost. Soc. xv, 1872,
    240 ; and of nearly all the late local lists.—(See HART., P. Z. S. 1871, 116 ; critical.)
Pluvialis virginicus, BP., C. R. 1856, 417.
Charadrius marmoratus, WAGL., Syst. Av. 1827, No. 42.—AUD., Orn. Biog. v, 1839, 575,
    pl. 300 ; Syn. 1839, 222 ; B. Am. v, 1842, 203, pl. 316.—PUTN., Pr. Ess. Inst. i,
    1856, 216.
(?) *Charadrius pectoralis*, VIEILL., Nouv. Dict. d'Hist. Nat. xxvii, 1819, 145.
Pluvialis fulvus americanus, SCHL., M. P.-B. 1865, Cursores, 53.
Charadrius fulvus var. *virginicus*, COUES, Key, 1872, 243, fig. 155.

    Extralimital quotations.—CAB., J. f. O. iv, 1856, 432 (Cuba).—NEWT., Ibis, i, 1859,
255 (Santa Cruz).—LAWR., Ann. Lyc. N. Y. viii, 1864, 99 (Sombrero).—SUND., Öfv. Vet.
Ak. 1869, 588 (St. Bartholomew).—FINSCH, P. Z. S. 1870, 587 (Trinidad).—SCL., Ibis,
1859, 227 (Guatemala).—BURM., Reise, 501 (La Plata).—DARW., Voy. Beagle, 126.—
SCL. & SALV., P. Z. S. 1866, 567 (Ucayali) ; 1867, 331 (Chili) ; 1869, 598 (Peru).—LAWR.,
Ann. Lyc. ix, 1868, 141 (Costa Rica).—PHILIPPI, Cat. 69 (Chili).—PELZ., Orn. Bras. 297
(Brazil).—REINH., Vid. Med. Nat. For. 1870, 34 (Brazil).

    Hab.—Var. *fulvus*, Asia and Pacific regions generally. Prybilov Islands (*Elliot*).
Var. *virginicus*, all of North America. Greenland. Accidental in Europe. (Heligoland,
Mus. Gætke, *fide Blasius*, List B. Eur. 1862, 17.)
    Lieutenant Warren's Expedition.—4551, 5425, at and near Saint Pierre ; 5426, Fort
Berthold ; 5427, "Nebraska."
    Later Expeditions.—61100–2, Camp Dawes, on Rock Creek, Wyoming.
    Not obtained by Captain Raynolds' Expedition.

    Presenting the extensive and somewhat intricate synonymy of the
typical *fulvus*,* I also give the principal references to the North American variety. Our Golden Plover is distinct from that of Europe, *C.
apricarius* or *pluvialis* of authors, to both of which it has been referred ;
for, although very similar, it may always be distinguished by the color

---

    * I have at length the pleasure of announcing the true *Ch. fulvus* as an inhabitant
of North America, a specimen having been lately transmitted to the Smithsonian from
the Prybilov Islands, collected May 2, 1873, on Saint Paul Island, by Mr. H. W. Elliot,
who has so ably elucidated the birds of that group of the Aleutians. Examining this
specimen, I was at once struck with a peculiarity of its general appearance, and on
comparing it with Chinese, Japanese, Fiji Island, and other specimens in the National
Museum, I found it to be identical. It is smaller than var. *virginicus*—length, about
9.50 ; wing, 6.40 ; tail, 2.60 ; tarsus, 1.60 ; middle toe and claw, 1.10 ; culmen, 0.95.
There is a yellowish suffusion about the head, and especially along the supraciliary
stripe, hardly to be noticed in the ordinary North American bird in corresponding
plumage. (*Cf.* COUES, Elliot's Prybilov Islands, App. 1873, p. —.)

of the lining of the wings, which is pure white in the European, and ashy-gray in the American species. It cannot, however, be specifically separated from the *C. fulvus* of Asia, the *C. xanthocheilus, longipes*, or *taitensis* of various Pacific regions—being only varietally distinguishable by its somewhat superior size and usually a slight disproportion in the lengths of the tarsi and toes. My view of the relationships of these several forms is at present substantially the same as that of Prof. Schlegel.

The Golden Plover migrates through Dakota in large numbers. While traveling over the prairie between Fort Randall and Yankton, early in May, I was delighted to meet with flock after flock of the birds, in more nearly perfect nuptial attire than I had before seen them anywhere in the United States, the under parts appearing, at a little distance, perfectly black. I noticed them particularly in the early morning, feeding at their leisure in scattered parties over the prairie, in company with Bartramian Tattlers and Esquimaux Curlew. They were not at all shy, and numbers might have been procured had I been so disposed. They ran rapidly and lightly in search of food, flew with a mellow, whistling note, and settled again with a momentary graceful poise of the upturned wings. Their stay at this season is brief compared with their loitering in the fall, when I again saw them at various points along the Mouse River and the Missouri, in the vicinity of Fort Stevenson, where they reappeared late in September. At this season they coursed over the prairie, often in extensive flocks, feeding on grasshoppers, and often frequented the pools, forming part of the varied company of waders that flocked to the same resorts. Their favorite associates were the Red-breasted Snipe, with which they mingled on the most intimate terms. Both of these birds, when not too much molested, are gentle and unsuspicious—excellent company for each other, and equally attractive to the sportsman. The earlier arrivals were not in particularly good condition, after the journey from their distant breeding places, but food was abundant and easily procured, so that in a short time the birds became exceedingly fat—some of them weighing five or six ounces. Being in such excellent order and so easily procurable, the savory morsels often varied our hard fare.

The Golden Plover breeds only far northward, and is not ordinarily seen in the United States in the advanced breeding plumage above noted. It appears to have no special lines of migration, but passes over the country at large, sometimes in vast flocks, its autumnal progress being more leisurely than its advance in the spring. It reaches its breeding grounds late in May—the Barren Grounds of British America, and the coasts and islands of the Arctic Ocean. It is found throughout Alaska, according to Mr. Dall, and is common all along the Yukon. The same writer states that the nests are made in a hillock of grass, of the same material, and frequently a few feathers, the eggs being generally only two in number; this, however, is not the rule, the eggs being, as usual in this family, oftenest four in number. They are of the ordinary pyriform shape, pointed at one end and very obtuse at the other. The following measurements may indicate extremes of variation in shape—2.00 by 1.35; 1.80 by 1.40. They are distinguished from those of *S. helvetica* by their decided average smaller size; and though the general pattern of coloration is similar, the shade is not quite the same. The ground-color is rather a pale, brownish-clay color, than a drab, in most specimens, although some shade quite closely into the drab of *helvetica*. A few specimens in the large series before me have the ground-color extremely pale grayish-white, nearly dead white. On all the eggs the markings are exceedingly bold, dark and numerous; it is impossible to describe adequately the endless variations in precise pattern. The average egg is heavily marked about the butt with blackish-brown, in large irregular spots and blotches; while similar smaller spots are sparsely distributed over the rest of the surface. Sometimes the markings are much lighter brown, a rich, dark sienna, and they are sometimes distributed over the whole surface with approximate uniformity, but the decided tendency is to aggregate around the butt in semi-confluent masses, or a wreath. Various labels of the collection before me state that the nest is a mere depression in the ground, lined with a few dried grasses or leaves.

Some of the birds begin to work southward almost as soon as they are full grown, though others linger till driven away by the cold.

ÆGIALITIS VOCIFERA, (Linn.) Bp.

Killdeer Plover.

Charadrius vociferus, LINN., Syst. Nat. i, 1766, 253 (based on *Pluvialis vociferus*, CATES., Car. i, 71, pl. 71 ; *P. virginiana torquata*, BRISS., Orn. v, 68).—GM., Syst. Nat. i, 1788, p. 685.—LATH., Ind Orn. ii, 1790, 742.—WILS., Am. Orn. vii, 1813, 73, pl. 59, f. 6.—BP., Syn. 1828, No. 219.—VIG., Zool. Journ. xii, 448.—Sw. & RICH., F. B. A. ii, 1831, 368.—NUTT., Man. ii, 1834, 22.—AUD., Orn. Biog. iii, 1835, 191 ; v, 1839, 577, pl. 225 ; Syn. 1839, 222 ; B. Am. v, 1842, 207, pl. 317.—SOHL., Mus. Pays-Bas, 1865, *Cursores*, 23.—WOODH., Sitgr. Rep. 1853, 96.—NEWB., P. R. R. Rep. vi, 1857, 97.—PUTN., Pr. Ess. Inst. i, 1856, 216.—TRIPPE, *ibid.* vi, 1871, 119 ; and of earlier authors generally.
Ægialitis vociferus, BP., Comp. List, 1838, 45.—CAB., J. f. O. iv, 1856, 424 (Cuba).— BD., B. N. A. 1858, 692.—SCL., P. Z. S. 1859, 393 (Oaxaca).—SCL., Ibis, i, 1859, 227 (Guatemala).—BRY., Pr. Bost. Soc. vii, 1859 (Bahamas).—COOP. & SUCK., N. H. Wash. Ter. 1860, 230.—TAYLOR, Ibis, 1860, 313 (Tigre Island).—DRESS., Ibis, 1866, 33 (Texas).—LAWR., Ann. Lyc. ix, 1868, 209 (Yucatan).—HAYD., Rep. 1862, 173.—SCL., P. Z. S. 1864, 178 (Mexico) ; 1868, 176 (Islay).—SALV., *ibid.* 1870, 219 (Veragua).—ALLEN, Mem. Bost. Soc. 1868, 501 ; Bull. M. C. Z. iii, 1872, 181.—HOLD.-AIKEN, Pr. Bost. Soc. xv, 1872, 209.—TRIPPE, *ibid.* xv, 1872, 240.—STEV., U. S. Geol. Surv. Ter. 1870, 466.—MERR., *ibid.* 1872, 699.—COUES, Key, 1872, 244, fig. 156 ; and of most late writers.
Oxyechus vociferus, REICH., Syst. Av. 1853, p. —.
Charadrius torquatus, LINN., Syst. Nat. i, 1766, 255 (based on *Pluvialis dominicensis torquata*, BRISS., v, 70, pl. 6, f. 2).
Charadrius jamaicensis, GM., Syst. Nat. i, 1788, 685 (based on SLOAN, 318, pl. 265, f. 3).

Hab.—All of temperate North America. West Indies. Central and South America in winter. Accidental in Europe. (See SCL., Ibis, 1862, 275 ; HART., Br. Birds, 1872, 134.)
Lieutenant Warren's Expedition.—4646, White River ; 5428, Yellowstone ; 6591, Cedar Creek.
Later Expeditions.—60377-81, Camp Carling, Wyoming ; 60789, Fort Bridger ; 61645, Salt Lake, Utah ; 62362, Lower Geyser Basin, Wyoming.
Not noticed by Captain Raynolds' Expedition.

Abundant throughout the Missouri region, as elsewhere in suitable localities in North America. The Killdeer is conspicuous among the few waders that breed at large through the United States, the great majority of these birds passing further northward for this purpose. Being, also, one of the most numerous and widely diffused, few birds are more familiarly known. It must not be inferred, however, from its general dispersion at various seasons that it is non-migratory. On the contrary, it performs extensive journeys, reaching even to South America. I think it migrates chiefly by night. As I sit at midnight penning these pages, in the town of Columbia, South Carolina, in February, I continually hear their well-known piercing notes, as they pass rapidly on through the darkness.

The eggs of the Killdeer measure about an inch and a half in length by one and one-eighth in breadth, and are of a creamy clay-color, variously but usually thickly marked with blackish-brown. The marks are usually of small size, tending to speckles and scratches rather than full spots, only a few specimens of the large series before me being boldly spotted around and at the butt. The markings tend to aggregate about the larger end, but are usually quite numerously distributed all over. The ground-color sometimes tends to a brownish-drab rather than the color above mentioned.

ÆGIALITIS SEMIPALMATA, (Bp.) Cab.

Semipalmated or Ring Plover.

Tringa hiaticula, WILS., Am. Orn. vii, 1813, 65, pl. 59, f. 3.
Charadrius hiaticula, ORD, ed. Wils. vii, 69.—SAB., Frankl. Journ. 684.—RICH., Parry's
    2d Voy. 351.
Charadrius (Ægialitis) hiaticula var. *semipalmatus*, RIDGW., Ann. Lyc. N. Y. x, 1874, 383.
Charadrius semipalmatus, BP., Obs. Wils. 1825, No. 219; Syn. 1828, 296; Am. Orn. iv,
    1832, 92, pl. 25.—KAUP, Isis, 1825, 1375, pl. 14.—WAGL., Syst. Av. 1827, No. 23.—
    SW. & RICH., F. B. A. ii, 1831, 367.—NUTT., Man. ii, .1834, 24.—AUD., Orn. Biog.
    iv, 1838, 256; v, 579; pl. 330; Syn. 1839, 224; B. Am. v, 1842, 218, pl. 320.—
    PUTN., Pr. Ess. Inst. i, 1856, 216.—SCHL., M. P.-B. 1865, *Cursores*, 30.—GRAY,
    Hand-list, iii, 1871, 16, No. 10009.
Ægialitis semipalmatus, BP., Comp. List, 1838, 45.—CAB., J. f. O. 1856, 428.—BD., B. N.
    A. 1858, 694.—COOP. & SUCK., N. H. Wash. Ter. 1860, 231.—COUES, Pr. Phila.
    Acad. 1861, 228.—COUES & PRENT., Smiths. Rep. 1861, 415.—WHEAT., Ohio
    Agric. Rep. 1860, No. 193.—VERR., Pr. Ess. Inst. iii, 1862, 22.—BOARDM., Pr. Bost.
    Soc. ix, 1862, 128.—DRESS., Ibis, 1866, 347 (Texas, wintering).—COUES, Pr.
    Phila. Ac. 1866, 96.—COUES, Pr. Bost. Soc. xii, 1868, 122.—McILWR., Pr. Ess. Inst.
    v, 1866, 92.—COUES, *ibid.* v, 1868, 291.—DALL & BANN., Tr. Chic. Acad. i, 1869,
    290.—TURNB., B. E. Pa. 1869, 29.—MAYN., Nat. Guide, 1870, 139.—ALLEN, Bull.
    M. C. Z. ii, 1871, 355.—COUES, Pr. Phila. Acad. 1871, 28.—SNOW, B. Kans. 1873,
    9.—COUES, Key, 1872, 244.
Ægialeus semipalmatus, REICH., Syst. Av. 1853.—ALLEN, Mem. Bost. Soc. i, 1868, 501;
    Pr. Ess. Inst. iv, 1864, 77.
Charadrius brevirostris, MAXIM., Beitr. iv, 769 (Brazil).—SCHOMB., Guiana, iii, 750.—
    BURM., Ueb. iii, 359.
" *Charadrius collaris*, LICHT. *nec* VIEILL.″ (*Schlegel*.)

Extralimital quotations.—CAB., J. f. O. iv, 1856, 428 (Cuba).—BRY., Pr. Bost. Soc. vii,
1859 (Bahamas).—SUND., Ofv. Ak. 1869, 588 (St. Bartholomew).—LAWR., Ann. Lyc. N.
Y. viii, 1864, 101 (Sombrero); ix, 238 (Puna Island).—SCL., Ibis, 1866, 197 (Guatemala).—PELZ., Orn. Braz. 297 (Brazil).—DARW., Voy. Beagle, 128 (Galapagos).

Hab.—Continent of North America, breeding chiefly in higher latitudes, wintering
from our southern border to Brazil.*

The American Semipalmated or Ring Plover—" Ringneck," as it is familiarly called—is at once distinguished from its European congener, as well as from any species of this country, by the extent of the basal webbing of the toes. The web between the middle and outer toe is larger than in any other, while that between the middle and inner (rudimentary in our other species) is as large as that between the outer and middle toes of the rest. A glance at these two decided webs is sufficient to determine the species.

As noted above, its dispersion is more than coextensive with the continent of North America ; for, in winter, although many individuals pass that season on our southern coasts, others penetrate far into South America. In the Middle States it is chiefly a bird of passage, and it is only known to breed regularly † in higher latitudes. Along the coast of North Carolina it appears in great numbers in April, and remains

---

* Dr. Schlegel cites a specimen from Brazil, type of the Prince of Wied's *C. brevirostris.*
† The breeding of a pair on Muskeget Island, off the Massachusetts coast, in June,
1866, is noticed by Mr. Samuels, Orn. New England, p. 420.

through May, after which none are to be observed until late in August following, they being engaged to the northward in the duties of reproduction. Before their departure from our coasts in the spring, they assume the perfect breeding dress, with brightly-colored bill, feet, and eye-lids, and perfect black bars. Returning in August, in limited numbers, the great body come after in September, thronging the beaches in company with various Sandpipers. In Labrador, where I found them breeding abundantly, they remained, apparently as plenty as ever, up to the first week in September, frequenting both the sea-beaches and the mud-flats, with Bonaparte's and the Semipalmated Sandpipers, in scattering troops, eagerly searching for food. Here they were more than ordinarily gentle and unsuspicious, especially the young ones, wholly unaccustomed to the presence of man. Subsequently, after persecution by the boys and pot-hunters, to whom they are objects of wanton pursuit, they seem to acquire a little wisdom by experience, though they cannot be regarded as wary under any circumstances. Their call-note is a mellow whistle, much like that of their allies, yet distinguishable. In the interior of our country the Plovers are nowhere so numerous, according to my observations, as they are along the coasts; yet they migrate in considerable numbers along the main water-courses, and are of regular occurrence each season, in April and May, September and October. Such is more particularly the case in the better-watered eastern portions of the Missouri region than in the dryer districts westward. I have, however, met with it on the Colorado River, which penetrates hundreds of miles into the desert.

The nesting of the Semipalmated Plover is not peculiar, the arrangements being the same as those made by most birds of the family. The eggs are laid in a depression of the ground, in a grassy or mossy spot, lined with a few blades of the same substances. The eggs vary in number from two* to four, the fewer being laid, it would appear, in the higher latitudes. They are hardly or not distinguishable from Killdeer eggs excepting by their smaller size, having the same ground-color and tone of the markings. The ground ranges from quite olivaceous-drab to pale clay-color, or even grayish-white, some of these lightest and least

---

* There are numerous exceptions to the rule of four eggs among the limicoline birds. Wilson's Plover is another instance, the more unexpected in that the bird breeds in comparatively low latitudes of the Middle and Southern States, along the coast. In none of the many nests I found on the sea-shore of North Carolina were there more than three eggs. They offer the following characters: Length, 1.22 to 1.45; breadth, 1.00 to 1.05; ground-color, pale olive-drab, more inclining to green in some cases, to brown in others, but always very pale, thickly marked all over with blackish-brown in irregular, sharply-defined spots, small splashes, and fine dots. "In some specimens the markings show a tendency to run into fine lines, and in these are the smallest, darkest, most numerous [most evenly distributed], and most sharply outlined; but ordinarily the distinctive speckled character is maintained. Commonly the markings are rather larger, and consequently more thickly set, on the larger part of the egg, where there is also some tendency to run together, though scarcely to form a ring around the butt; but in none of the specimens examined was the pointed end free from spots. Here and there may usually be observed a few pale, obsolete spots, but they are not conspicuous; in fact, hardly to be detected without close scrutiny." (COUES, Am. Nat. iii, 1869, p. 348.)

Comparing the eggs of all the species of *Ægialitis* mentioned in this work, as they lie before me in large series (excepting those of *Æ. montanus*, of which I have only three), we see that the Kildeer's and Ringneck's are essentially alike, only of different sizes. Wilson's and the Piping Plover's are approximately similar, both averaging lighter in ground-color and of fewer markings, but the latter are very appreciably paler and less marked than the former; and the egg of *Æ. montanus* stands somewhat alone, not only in its dark-olive ground-color and nearly even, fine speckling, but also in in its shape, which is notably less pyriform than that of the others, or than that of Plovers in general.

marked specimens resembling the egg of _Æ. meloda_. Compared with Killdeer's eggs, the markings are more definite, averaging larger and bolder, with little of the scratchiness observable in the latter. The largest Ringneck's egg does not equal the smallest Killdeer's, being only 1.40 by 0.95, and thence running down to 1.20 by 0.90. A few obscure shell-markings may usually be observed.

ÆGIALITIS MELODA var. CIRCUMCINCTA, Ridgw.

Piping Plover; Ring Plover.

a. _meloda_.

Charadrius hiaticula var., WILS., Am. Orn. v, 1812, 30, pl. 37, f. 2.
Charadrius melodus, ORD, ed. Wils. vii, 1824, 71.—BP., Am. Orn. iv, 1832, 74, pl. 24.—
    NUTT., Man. ii, 1834, 18.—AUD., Orn. Biog. iii, 1835, 154; v, 1839, 578; pl. 220;
    B. Am. v, 1842, 223, pl. 321.—PUTN., Pr. Ess. Inst. i, 1856, 216.—SCHL., M. P.-B.
    1865, _Cursores_, 29.—GRAY, Hand-list, 1871, 16, No. 10010.—FINSCH, Abh. Nat. iii,
    1872, 62 (Alaska).
Charadrius (Ægialitis) melodus, RIDGW., Ann. Lyc. N. Y. x, 1874, 383 (Illinois).
Ægialitis melodus, BP., Comp. List, 1838, 45.—CAB., J. f. O. iv, 1856, 424 (Cuba).—BD.,
    B. N. A. 1858, 695.—BRYANT, Pr. Bost. Soc. vii, 1859 (Bahamas).—SCL., P. Z. S.
    1861, 80 (Jamaica).—HAYD., Rep. 1862, 173.—WHEAT., Ohio Agric. Rep. 1860,
    No. 194.—VERR., Pr. Ess. Inst. iii, 1862, 22 (coast of Maine, breeding).—BOARDM.,
    Pr. Bost. Soc. ix, 1862, 123 ('breeds).—COUES, Pr. Bost. Soc. 1868, 122.—MCILWR.,
    Pr. Ess. Inst. v, 1866, 92.—COUES, _ibid._ v, 1868, 292.—TURNB., B. E. Pa. 1869,
    29.—MAYN., Nat. Guide, 1870, 39.—ALLEN, Bull. M. C. Z. ii, 1871, 355.—COUES,
    Pr. Phila. Acad. 1871, 28.—SNOW, B. Kans. 1873, 10.—COUES, Key, 1872, 244.
Ægialeus melodus, ALLEN, Pr. Ess. Inst. iv, 1864, 86.
Charadrius okeni, WAGL., Syst. Av. 1827.

b. _circumcincta_.

Ægialitis melodus var. _circumcinctus_, RIDGW., Am. Nat. viii, 1874, 109.—COUES, Check-
    list, App. p. 133, No. 400ᵃ.

Hab.—United States and British Provinces, east of the Rocky Mountains (beyond which apparently replaced by _Æ. cantiana_). Abundant along the Atlantic coast of the United States, breeding north to the St. Lawrence, and wintering from the Carolinas southward. Cuba. Bahamas. Jamaica. Var. _circumcincta_ from the Missouri region.
    Lieutenant Warren's Expedition.—9038, 9034-5, 9038-9, Fork of the Platte (types of var. _circumcincta_).
    Not obtained by Captain Raynolds' Expedition or the later ones.

As observed sometime since by Mr. Cassin, Dr. Hayden's specimens are in full breeding dress, with the black pectoral band complete, instead of forming, as in most instances, an area on either side of the breast, This is the basis of Mr. Ridgway's new variety. This condition, and the date of collection (July 8), warrant the inference that the species breeds in Nebraska—a surmise not yet confirmed, but strengthened by the general facts of the distribution of the species. For, unlike its near relative (_Æ. semipalmata_), the Piping Plover does not proceed to high latitudes to breed, being quite unknown in the fur countries, and, indeed, in British America, excepting the portions immediately bordering the United States. It is content to find its summer home in the northern half of the United States, especially along the Atlantic coast from New Jersey to the St. Lawrence. I think that though some breed so far south as the Carolinas, the fact escaped me during the two years I spent on the coast, at Fort Macon, paying much attention to the ornithology of the locality. There the Piping Plovers were chiefly migrants, coming and going with the Semipalmated, and were not nearly so abundant. It is noted as a common summer bird of the New England coast, and is said to breed in abundance along the shores of Maine. The nest, which I have not myself observed, is stated to be made preferably along the sea-beach of the main land and adjoining islands, and to be merely a slight hollow of the sand, lined or not with a few grasses or bits of sea-weed. This is somewhat different from the nidification of the Semipalmated Plover, which selects a mossy or grassy spot away from the beach; and entirely like the Wilsonian Plover.
    The eggs of the Piping Plover may be distinguished at a glance from those of the Ringneck by their light color and fine, sparse speckling. The ground is clay-color, or palest possible creamy-brown, marked nearly uniformly all over, but sparsely, with

small blackish-brown dots and specks, but no spots of any size nor scratchy lines; the largest markings observed scarcely exceed a pin's head. The dotting is sometimes extremely fine, mere points, and with it appear to be always mingled a few obscure shell-markings of lilac or lavender. The egg appears to be about of the same size (capacity) as that of the Ringneck, but is rather less elongate and pointed. Several specimens measure: 1.30 by 1.00; 1.25 by 0.95; 1.25 by 1.00; 1.20 by 0.95,* &c.

The following North American species of this genus have not been found in the Missouri region:

ÆGIALITIS WILSONIA, (Ord,) Cassin.

Charadrius wilsonius, ORD, ed. Wils. ix, 1825, 77, pl. 73, fig. 5.—BP., Syn. 296.—NUTT., Man. ii, 1834, 21.—AUD., O. B. iii, 1835, 73; v, 1839, 577; pl. 284; Syn. 1839, 223; B. Am. v, 1842, 214, pl. 319.—GIR., B. L. I. 1844, 216.—PEAB., Rep. Orn. Mass. 1839, 360 ("Nahant, Aug. 1838").—LINSL., Am. Journ. Sci. xliv, 1843, 265 (Connecticut).—PUTN., Pr. Ess. Inst. i, 1856, 224 (quotes *Peabody*).
Ægialites wilsonius, BP., List, 1838, 45.
Ochthodromus wilsonius, REICH., Syst. Av. 1853, p. xviii.—ALLEN, Pr. Ess. Inst. iv, 1864, 86 (Massachusetts; quotes *Peabody*).—ALLEN, Am. Nat. iii, 1870, 637.
Ægialitis wilsonius, CASS., Baird's B. N. A. 1858, 693.—SAM., Descr. Cat. B. Mass. ii, ("common, spring and fall"?).—DRESS., Ibis, 1866, 34 (Texas).—LAWR., Ann. Lyc. N. Y. viii, 1866, 294 (Long Island).—COUES, Pr. Ess. Inst. v, 1868, 291 (Connecticut, *Linsley*, and (?) Massachusetts, *Peabody*, *Samuels*—a mistake?).—COUES, Pr. Bost. Soc. xii, 1868, 122 (South Carolina).—TURNB., B. E. Pa. 1869, 28 (New Jersey, rather rare).—COUES, Am. Nat. iii, 1869, 337 (biography and eggs).—ALLEN, Bull. M. C. Z. ii, 1871, 355 (Florida, wintering).—COUES, Key, 1872, 244.
Charadrius crassirostris, SPIX, Av. Bras. ii, 1825, 77, pl. 94 (cf. PELZ., Orn. Bras. 1870, 297).

Hab.—Atlantic and Gulf coasts, United States. North to Long Island and Connecticut, probably to Massachusetts, but rare beyond New Jersey. Also on the Pacific side to California (?). Middle and South America and West Indies (Cuba, CAB., J. f. O. iv, 424; Bahamas, BRY., Pr. Bost. Soc. vii, 1859; Saint Thomas, CASS., Pr. Phila. Acad. 1860, 378; Guatemala and Honduras, SALV., Ibis, 1866, 197; Venezuela, SCL. & SALV., P. Z. S. 1868, 169; Brazil, SPIX; PELZ., Orn. Bras. 297).

ÆGIALITIS CANTIANA var. NIVOSA, (Cassin,) Ridgway.

Ægialitis (Leucopolius) nivosa, CASS., Baird's B. N. A. 1858, 696 (San Francisco, Cal.).—COUES, Ibis, 1866, 274 (San Pedro, Cal.).—(?) SALV., Ibis, 1866, 196 (Chiapam).—SCL. & SALV., P. Z. S. 1868, 176 (Islay, Peru).—LAWR., Ann. Lyc. N. Y. ix, 1868, 209 (Yucatan).
Charadrius cantianus, HEERM., P. R. R. Rep. x, 1859, pt. vi, 64.
Ægialitis cantianus, COUES, Key, 1872, 245.
Ægialitis cantianus var. *nivosus*, RIDGW., Am. Nat. viii, 1874, 109.—COUES, Check-list, App. No. 401.

Hab.—Coast of California, and southward to Peru. East probably to the Rocky Mountains. Utah, breeding (*Ridgway*).

ÆGIALITIS MICRORHYNCHA, Ridgway.

Ægialitis microrhynchus, RIDGW., Am. Nat. viii, 1874, 109 (San Francisco).—COUES, Check-list, No. 400*bis*.

Hab.—Coast of California.

EUDROMIAS MONTANUS, (Towns.) Harting.

Mountain Plover.

Charadrius montanus, TOWNS., Journ. A. N. S. vii, 1837, 192; Narr. 1839, 349.—AUD., Orn. Biog. iv, 1838, 362, pl. 350; Syn. 1839, 223; B. Am. v, 1842, 213, pl. 318.

---

* The eggs of the Snowy Plover (*A. nivosa* of Cassin) are much like those of *A. meloda*, being of about the same size, and having the same light ground and fine markings. The markings, however, are more numerous and scratchy, comparing with those of *meloda* in this respect, much as the eggs of the Killdeer do with those of the Ringneck. The coloration is very nearly as in *wilsonia*, though the size is much less. Two eggs measure each 1.20 by 0.90; these were from a set of three taken by Dr. Cooper, May 23, 1862, at San Pedro, Southern California, where, as I found the species in November, it is probably resident. Another egg, in the Smithsonian collection, was procured by Mr. Hepburn at San Francisco.

Ægialitis montanus, BD., B. N. A. 1858, 693.—COOP. & SUCK., N. H. Wash. Ter. 1860,
    231.—HAYD., Rep. 1862, 173.—DRESS., Ibis, 1866, 33 (San Antonio, Texas).—
    ALLEN, Bull. M. C. Z. iii, 1872, 181.—AIKEN, Pr. Bost. Soc. xv, 1872, 209.—
    SNOW, B. Kans. 1873, 9, No. 209.
Podasocys montanus, COUES, Pr. Phila. Acad. 1866, 96.—ELLIOT, B. N. A. ii, pl. 39.
Charadrius (Podasocys) montanus, GRAY, Hand-list, iii, 1871, 15, No. 9997.
Ægialitis asiaticus var.* *montanus*, COUES, Key, 1872, 245.
Eudromias montanus, HARTING.—COUES, Check-list, App. No. 402.

Hab.—Western United States, from the plains of Middle Kansas and Nebraska, and
Western Dakota, to the Pacific. Texas (*Dresser*). Also, Florida (*Maynard*).

List of specimens.

19301	....	....	....	....	....	......	......	.....
19302	32	Otter Creek ...	....	May 29, 1860	F. V. Hayden	......	......	.....
19303	92	Smith's Fork ..	♀	July 7, 1860	...... do	9.00	18.75	6.75

Lieutenant Warren's Expedition.—9043–44, Loup Fork of the Platte.
Later Expeditions.—59866, Middle Park, Colorado (*Stevenson*).

Although this beautiful and interesting bird is strictly a western
species, still its range is more extensive than was formerly supposed,
both in latitude and longitude. No one has found it, so far as I am
aware, north of the United States boundary, but it probably penetrates
some little way, at least, into the British possessions, while, on the other
hand, it enters Mexico, and may even, as Mr. Cassin surmises, migrate
into South America in winter. But this is not yet determined. Its
Eastern limit is pretty nearly ascertained. The farthest point recorded
is the vicinity of Fort Hays, near the centre of Kansas, where Mr. Allen
found it "moderately common," and it is known to occur in Nebraska
in a corresponding longitude. Further north, however, its range seems
to trend somewhat westward, for I never saw it in the eastern half of
Dakota, over much of which I have traveled, nor in the northern part
east of 103°. We have, nevertheless, a record of its occurrence and
breeding in Southwestern Dakota, in the vicinity of the Black Hills.
From the region thus indicated it may be found, in suitable situations,
to the Pacific coast.

The name of "Mountain Plover" does not appear to be well chosen,
further than as an expression of very general import. Though found
on highly elevated plateaux, it is not a bird of the mountains, but of
the plains. While most other Plovers haunt the vicinity of water, to
which some are almost confined, the present species is not in the least
degree of aquatic habits, but, on the contrary, resorts to plains as dry
and sterile as any of our country—sometimes the grassy prairies, with
Shore Larks and Titlarks, various Ground Sparrows, and the Burrowing
Owl; sometimes sandy deserts, where the sage brush and the "chamizo,"
the prickly pear and the Spanish bayonet, grow in full luxuriance. It
approaches the Pacific, but will never be found on the beach itself, with
maritime birds, nor even on the adjoining mud-flats or marshes, preferring the firm, grassy fields further back from the water.

---

* It appears from Mr. Harting's recent critical article on *Charadrius asiaticus* (Ibis,
1870, 201, pl. 5), that I may have too hastily united our *montana* with that species—a
course in which I relied upon Prof. Schlegel's authority, not having the opportunity of
a direct comparison of specimens. As mentioned in the Check-list, the bird should
probably stand as *Eudromias montanus*. (Compare, however, FINSCH, Ibis, 1872, p. 144.)
    I have only recently had an opportunity of examining the species in perfect dress.
There is *no* pectoral band of black, but a broad, transverse, coronal, black bar of varying width (sometimes occupying half the pileum, sometimes a mere line), and another
sharp, black, loral line separating the white forehead and superciliary stripe from the
white of the chin and throat. There is a little ochraceous edging of the feathers of the
upper parts, and a similar shade suffuses the breast.

In the desert region of New Mexico, between the Rio Grande and the base of the mountains to the westward, I found these Plovers abundant, late in June, together with the Long-billed Curlews, and presume that they breed there, although I found no nests. The old birds that I shot were in poor condition and worn plumage. A few were seen in Arizona, at various seasons, but they did not again occur to me in abundance until I reached Southern California, in November of the following year. In the vicinity of Los Angeles I found them in large flocks on the dry plain which stretches down to the ocean. They were not difficult of approach, and I had no difficulty in securing as many as I desired. On being disturbed by too near approach, they lower the head, run rapidly a few steps in a light, easy way, and then stop abruptly, drawing themselves up to their full height and looking around with timid yet unsuspicious glances. Their notes are rather peculiar, as compared with those of our other Plovers, and vary a good deal, according to circumstances. When the birds are feeding at their leisure, and in no way apprehensive of danger, they utter a low and rather pleasing whistle, though in a somewhat drawling or rather lisping tone; but the note changes to a louder and higher one, sometimes sounding harshly. When forced to fly by persistent annoyance, they rise rapidly with quick wing-beats, and then proceed with alternate sailing and flapping, during the former action holding the wings decurved. They generally fly low over the ground, and soon realight, taking a few mincing steps as they touch the ground; they then either squat low, in hopes of hiding, or stand on tiptoe, as it were, for a better view of what alarmed them.

The Mountain Plover's food consists principally, if not wholly, of insects. I examined the stomachs of a great many with reference to this matter, finding in them nothing whatever but insects, excepting, as usual, a little sand or gravel. Grasshoppers, in their season, seem to be the bird's main reliance, though numerous other insects, as crickets and beetles, are also eaten; and I suppose that worms and small land-molluscs would not come amiss. In the fall, when food is plenty, the birds become very fat, tender and juicy, affording excellent eating.

No previous writer upon this bird has said anything of its nest and eggs, which remained until lately unknown. In the Key I gave a brief description of the eggs, which I can now make more extended, adding an item regarding the nest. The two eggs I described were, as I am informed by Mr. Stevenson, of Dr. Hayden's party, who took them himself, only half of the nest-complement, the other two having been accidentally destroyed. They were discovered July 13, 1859, on the North Fork of the Platte, about one hundred and twenty miles west of Fort Kearney, and contained large embryos. They differ in size and shape, though from the same nest, one being more pointed and longer than the other. The measurements are: 1.50 by 1.10, and 1.40 by 1.10. The form is notably less pointed than usual in this genus, and altogether the eggs are peculiar. In color they are about alike, olive-drab, with a decided shade of brown, thickly marked all over, but especially at the larger end, with blackish, very dark brown, and neutral tint. All the spots are small—in fact, mere dots and specks—the largest scarcely exceeding a pin's head. They show no tendency to aggregate into splashes, and the edges of the markings are sharp. Mr. Stevenson tells me that the nest was a mere depression in the bare ground, lined with a few grass-blades. The eggs would probably have hatched in another week. Another egg, in the Smithsonian, is nearly a duplicate of these, but rather browner, with rather smaller and more numerous markings. It is also more pointed; size, 1.48 by 1.12. Mr. Allen saw newly-hatched young, and others full grown, the 27th and 28th of July, in South Park, Colorado, showing that the time of laying varies. Yet the range thus indicated is nothing unusual; I have observed much the same thing with regard to the Bartramian Sandpiper and other species which I have had an opportunity of observing closely.

Mr. Allen communicates the following notes: "The Mountain Plover (*Ægialitis montana*), though scarcely to be regarded as an abundant species, occurs with considerable frequency throughout the plains from Middle and perhaps Eastern Kansas westward. In the breeding season it is generally seen in isolated pairs, usually in the driest situations, and is silent and unsuspicious. Later in the season it occurs occasionally in small parties, composed of one or two broods of young, accompanied by their parents. Newly-hatched young were observed at intervals throughout the month of July. This species was also often met with in South Park, as well as on the high table-lands that occur at intervals thence eastward to the plains."

The Turnstone has not, to my knowledge, been found in the Missouri region, but is reported from Lake Erie and Minnesota. Following is its synonymy :

STREPSILAS INTERPRES, (*Linnæus*,) *Illiger*.

a. *interpres*.

Tringa interpres, LINN., Fn. Suec. 63 ; Syst. Nat. i, 1766, 248 (based on *Arenaria*, BRISS., v, 132; *Morinellus marinus*, WILLUG., 231, pl. 58; *M. canadensis*, EDW., Av. 141).— GM., Syst. Nat. i, 1788, 671.—LATH., Ind. Orn. ii, 1790, 738.—WILS., Am. Orn. viii, 1813, 32, pl. 57, f. 1.
Strepsilas interpres, ILL., Prod. 1811, 263.—LEACH, Cat. 1816, 29.—STEPH., G. Z. xi, 520.— BP., Syn. 1828, 299; List, 1838, 46.—Sw. & RICH., F. B. A. ii, 1831, 371.—NUTT., Man. ii, 1834, 30.—FLEM., Br. An. 110.—NAUM., V. D. vii, 1834, 303, pl. 160.— JENYNS, Man. 1835, 182.—EYT., Cat. Br. B. 43.—KEYS. & BLAS., Wirb. Eur. 1840, 71.—MACGIL., Man. ii, 57.—SCHL., Rev. Crit. 1844, 85.—AUD., Orn. Biog. iv, 1838, 31, pl. 304 ; Syn. 1839, 227 ; B. Am. v, 1842, 231, pl. 323.—CASS., in Bd. B. N. A. 1858, 701.—WHEAT., Ohio Agric. Rep. 1860, No. 196 (Lake Erie).— COOP. & SUCK., N. H. Wash. Ter. 1860, 233.—COUES, Pr. Phila. Acad. 1861 128 (Labrador) ; 1871, 29 (Carolina).—COUES, Pr. Ess. Inst. v, 1868, 292 (New England).—DALL & BANN., Tr. Chic. Acad. i, 1869, 290 (Alaska).—FINSCH, Abh. Nat. iii, 1872, 62 (Alaska).—COUES, Key, 1872, 246.—NEWT., Ibis, i, 1859, 256 (Santa Cruz).—CAB., J. f. O. iv, 1856, 423 (Cuba).—SWINH., Ibis, 1863, 414 (Formosa).—DARW., Voy. Beagle, 132 (Peru and Galapagos).—LAWR., Ann. Lyc. N. Y. viii, 1864, 101 (Sombrero).—NEWT., Ibis, 1865, 505 (Spitzbergen).— SALV., Ibis, 1866, 198 (Guatemala).—HARTL., P. Z. S. 1867, 831 (Pelew Islands).— HARTING, P. Z. S. 1868, 118 (Pelew Islands).—PHILIPPI, Cat. 33 (Chili).—SUND., Ofv. Vet. Akad. 1869, 588 (St. Bartholomew).—PELZ., Orn. Braz. 1870, 297 (Brazil).—HATCH, Bull. Minnesota Acad. i, 1874, 63 (Minnesota).—RIDGW., Ann. Lyc. N. Y. x, 1874, 383 (Lake Michigan).
Cinclus interpres, GRAY, Gen. of B. iii, 1849, 549 ; List Br. B. 1863, 143.
Tringa morinella, LINN., Syst. Nat. i, 1766, 248 (*Morinellus marinus*, CATES., i, 72 ; *Arenaria cinerea*, BRISS., v, 137, pl. 11, f. 2).—GM., Syst. Nat. i, 1788, 671.
Cinclus morinellus, GRAY, List of Gen. of B. 1841, 87.
Tringa hudsonica, MÜLL., Syst. Nat. Suppl. 1776, 114.—CASS., Pr. Phila. Acad. 1864, 246.
Morinella collaris, MEYER, Vög. Liv. u. Esthl. 210.
Strepsilas collaris, TEMM., Man. 1815, 349; ii, 553.—BREHM, V. D. 558.—SAB., Suppl. Parry's 1st Voy. p. cc.—SAB., Frankl. Journ. 684.—RICH., App. Parry's 2d Voy. 352.
Charadrius cinclus, PALL., Zoog. R.-A. ii, 1811, 148.
Tringa oahuensis, "BLOX., Voy. 251." (*Gray*.)
Strepsilas borealis et *littoralis*, BREHM, V. D. 558, 560.

Hab.—Sea-coasts of nearly all countries. Less frequent in the interior.

b. *melanocephalus*.

Strepsilas melanocephalus, VIG., Z. J. iv, 1829, 356 ; Voy. Bloss. 1839, 29.—GAMB., J. A. N. S. Pa. 2d ser. 1849, 220.—CASS., Baird's N. A. B. 1858, 702.—HEERM., P. R. R. Rep. x, 1859, pt. vi, pl. 7.—COOP. & SUCK., N. H. Wash. Ter. 1860, 234—DALL & BANN., Tr. Chic. Acad. i, 1869, 290.
Strepsilas interpres var. *melanocephalus*, COUES, Key, 1872, 246.

Hab.—Pacific coast, North America.

Family RECURVIROSTRIDÆ: Avocets.

RECURVIROSTRA AMERICANA, Gm.

Avocet.

Recurvirostra americana, GM., Syst. Nat. i, 1788, 693.—LATH., Ind. Orn. ii, 1790, 787.—
WILS., Am. Orn. vii, 1813, 126, pl. 63, f. 2.—BP., Syn. 1828, No. 280.—SW. &
RICH., F. B. A. ii, 1831, 375.—NUTT., Man. ii, 1834, 75.—BP., List, 1838, 54.—AUD.,
O. Biog. iv, 1838, 168, pl. 318; Syn. 1839, 252; B. Am. vi, 1843, 24, pl. 353.—EMM.,
Cat. B. Mass. 1835, 5.—GIR., B. L. I. 1844, 269.—WOODH., Sitgr. Rep. 1853, 100
(Indian Territory and New Mexico).—PUTN., Pr. Ess. Inst. i, 1856, 230.—CAB.,
J. f. O. iv, 1856, 422 (Cuba).—BD., B. N. A. 1858, 703.—COOP. & SUCK., N. H.
Wash. Ter. 1860, 234.—WHEAT., Ohio Agric. Rep. 1860, No. 197.—HAYD., Rep.
1862, 173 (Yellowstone).—VERR., Pr. Ess. Inst. iii, 1862, 158 (coast of Maine, one
instance).—BOARDM., Pr. Bost. Soc. ix, 1862, 128 (same instance).—ALLEN, Pr.
Ess. Inst. iv, 1864, 86.—LAWR., Ann. Lyc. N. Y. viii, 1866, 295.—COUES, Pr.
Phila. Acad. 1866, 97 (Arizona).—MCILWR., Pr. Ess. Inst. v, 1866, 92 (Toronto).—
DRESS., Ibis, 1866, 35 (Texas).—SALV., Ibis, 1866, 198 (Guatemala).—COUES,
Pr. Bost. Soc. xii, 1868, 124 (South Carolina).—COUES, Pr. Ess. Inst. v, 1868,
292 (New England, rare or accidental).—TURNB., B. E. Pa. 1869, 28 (rather
rare).—MAYN., Guide, 1870, 143.—STEV. ,U. S. Geol. Surv. Ter. 1870, 466 (North
Platte).—COUES, Pr. Phila. Acad. 1871, 33.—ALLEN, Bull. M. C. Z. ii, 1871, 357
(Florida, in winter); iii, 1872, 182 (Great Salt Lake).—MERR., U. S. Geol. Surv.
Ter. 1872, 701 (Great Salt Lake).—AIKEN, Pr. Bost. Soc. xv, 1872, 209 (Arkansas
River).—SNOW, B. Kans. 1873, 10, No. 213.—GRAY, Hand-list, iii, 1871, 47, No.
10288.—COUES, Key, 1872, 147, fig. 159.—RIDGW., Ann. Lyc. N. Y. x, 1874, 385
(Illinois).

Recurvirostra occidentalis, VIG., Zool. Journ. iv, 1829, 356; Zool. Voy. Blossom, 1839, 28,
pl. 12.—WAGL., Isis, 1831, 520.—GRAY, Gen. of B. pl. 155.—BD., Stansbury's
Rep. 1852, 334.—CASS., Ill. 1855, 232, pl. 40.—NEWB., P. R. R. Rep. vi, 1857,
99. (*Young.*)

American Avosit, PENN., Arct. Zool. ii, 502, pl. 21.—LATH., Syn. v. pl. 93.

Hab.—United States and British Provinces. North to the Saskatchewan and Great
Slave Lake. Rare or casual in New England. Breeds throughout. Winters on our
southern border and beyond (to Guatemala).

List of specimens.

19376	....	Fort Randall...	....	Sept. 12, 1860	G. H. Trook..	......	......	....

Lieutenant Warren's Expedition.—5446, Yellowstone River.
Later Expeditions.—59872-3, Colorado; 60775, North Platte; 61641-2, Great Salt Lake.

The Avocet is irregularly distributed over nearly all of temperate
North America; that is, from rather high latitudes in British America
to Mexico and the Gulf, and from one ocean to the other. Nevertheless, there are large tracts of country that it scarcely ever visits; thus,
it is little more than a straggler in New England, though not rare
southward on the Atlantic coast. It is, perhaps, more abundant than
elsewhere in the interior of the United States, along the Mississippi
Valley, and thence westward, in all suitable localities, to the Rocky
Mountains. Several observers state that they have never met with it
on the Pacific coast; and Dr. Suckley records that a single specimen he
procured in Washington seemed to be astray, and was unknown to the
settlers. This writer speaks of its abundance in Dakota, and notes the
fact, perhaps not generally known, that it frequented the banks of running brooks as well as the margins of still pools. These latter, however, together with swampy places throughout the interior, and marshy
places along the coast, are its favorite resorts. Some have asserted that
it gives preference to salt or brackish waters, as would seem to be indicated by its abundance at Great Salt Lake, in Utah, and about the alkaline
waters of Dakota, as just noticed; but it is found to be equally abundant upon fresh lakes and rivers throughout the interior.

In the United States and northward the Avocet is chiefly a summer visitor, entering our limits from the South in spring, though many winter along our border. A part of the birds scatter over the United States, and others go further north, to breed; for they raise their young with equal facility from the latitude of the Middle States—or even further south, especially in the West—to that, for instance, of Great Slave Lake. Their wide distribution in the West, during the breeding season, is evidenced, among other things, by the number of localities whence we have records of the "White-necked Avocet" (*R. occidentalis*), which is, in reality, only the young of this species. It was first described by Mr. Vigors, the distinguished English naturalist, in 1829, and has only recently been determined to be the same bird in immature plumage. Mr. Cassin gives a handsome plate of it in his "Illustrations."

My first acquaintance with Avocets was made on the plains, early in June, 1864. I found plenty of the birds in some shallow reedy ponds, near the Arkansas River, in company with several other waders, among them Wilson's Phalaropes and some Gulls (*Chrœcocephalus franklini*); while on the dry ground near by were great numbers of the Burrowing Owls, living, as usual, in a prairie-dog town. The Avocets were in full plumage, with the head and neck cinnamon color; and, from their actions, I had no doubt they had nests somewhere about the ponds. They were quite gentle and familiar, and not at all disturbed by my approach, displaying a characteristic of theirs during the breeding season, at least in regions where they are not often molested, and have, therefore, not learned a wholesome dread of man. They walked leisurely about, up to the belly in the water, with graceful, deliberate steps, each of which was accompanied by a swaying of the head and neck, as usual with birds of similar form. When approached too closely, they rose lightly from the water, uttering their peculiar cries, flapped leisurely to a little distance, and again alighted to pursue their peaceful search for food, forgetting, or at least not heeding, their recent alarm. As they rose from the water, their singular, long legs were suffered to dangle for a few moments, but were afterward stretched stiffly backward, as a counterpoise to their long necks; and, thus balanced, their lithe bodies were supported with greatest ease by their ample wings. When about to realight, they sailed without flapping for a little distance, just clearing the water, their legs again hanging loosely; as they touched the ground, their long wings were held almost upright for an instant, then deliberately folded and settled in place with a few slight motions. Contrary to what I had expected, they showed no sympathetic concern, and, indeed, only moderate alarm, when some of their number were killed; for I must confess that after learning something of their ways by observing them alive, I was anxious for a still closer acquaintance, and therefore destroyed several individuals. In one of the poor birds I found an egg almost ready to be laid, confirming my supposition that the birds were then in the place where they hoped and fully intended to raise their families. Though there were a great many of them associating together, those that were already paired kept closer by each other, I thought, than the rest of the flocks. Some isolated pairs, that I subsequently observed on a pond near Fort Larned, kept side by side during the whole time that I watched them.

Contrary to my expectations I saw no Avocets on the Rio Grande, though the Stilts—birds very closely allied and often found with the Avocets—were plenty. On the Colorado, in the fall of 1865, I saw both kinds flocking on the sand-bars and hard, dry flats. This was in September, when all the Avocets that I noticed were white-necked, showing that they were young birds, either bred in that vicinity or else then on their southward migration from some distant birth-place.

Avocets and Stilts correspond with each other in habits as closely as they do in form. One of the most marked physical differences is found in the structure of the feet. Avocets have a hind toe, which the Stilts have not, and their feet are almost completely webbed, so that they are among the best swimmers of the long-legged fraternity. Stilts, on the contrary, scarcely swim at all, and never except on an emergency. When the Avocets are wading about, it often happens that they get beyond their depth, when, instead of rising on wing, they keep on as if nothing had happened to take them off their feet. If they are wounded, they sometimes escape by diving as well as swimming.

It is scarcely necessary to proceed further with the history of a bird whose general habits are already known through several earlier biographies. Wilson has written an excellent account, upon which Nuttall's is in a great measure modeled. Audubon's history is specially good; at once complete, accurate, and full of interest. Nothing so good as his model piece of biography, chiefly taken up with an account of a pair of birds he watched near Vincennes, Indiana, has been written on this subject.

An egg which I took from the oviduct of an Avocet killed near Fort Lyons, on the Arkansas, is the shortest and comparatively thickest of a dozen now before me, measuring only 1.80 by 1.37. It was, however, perfectly formed and just ready to be laid, as shown by the perfection of the markings. Other specimens run up to 2.10 in length by 1.44 in breadth. One of the longest specimens is also the narrowest—2.10 by only 1.25. This is one of a set of three taken by Mr. Ridgway at Soda Lake, near Carson Desert, June 28, 1873. They were deposited in a depression of the alkaline incrustation of the ground. The ground-color of this series ranges from a dark olive through a lighter olivaceous-drab to brownish-drab, and thence to a fine creamy-brown or buff, nearly as in the Shanghai breed of fowls. The eggs are nearly uniformly marked all over with spots of several shades of chocolate-brown, all on the surface, and others of neutral tint in the shell. In only one of the specimens is there any decided tendency to aggregation about the larger end or confluence of the spots anywhere. The spots are of small to moderate size and indeterminate shape, none being blotches of any considerable dimensions. All the markings are sharp. Those of the buff eggs are the most numerous and finest, while the spots of the darkest, olivaceous eggs are the boldest.

The young Avocet has the head and neck white, with an ashy or plumbeous shade, instead of chestnut or cinnamon-red. In this condition it constitutes the *R. occidentalis* of authors. Of the adult, the bill is black; the iris, bright red; the legs and feet, clear, pale blue, with part of the webs flesh-colored. The plumage is white, changing to cinnamon or chestnut on the neck and head; the back, wing-coverts, and primaries black, contrasting with the white of the scapulars and rump. In size the bird is extremely variable; perhaps seventeen inches in total length by thirty in extent represents average measurements. Contrary to the rule among waders, the female is smaller than the male.

HIMANTOPUS NIGRICOLLIS, Vieill.

Black-necked Stilt.

a. *nigricollis*.

Charadrius mexicanus, MÜLLER, Syst. Nat. 1776, 117.—CASS., Pr. Phila. Acad. 1864, 246.
Himantopus mexicanus, ORD, ed. Wils. vii, 1824, 52.—MAXIM., Beitr. iv, 741.—BURM., Syst. Ueb. iii, 367.—WAGL., Isis, 1831, 520.—BP., Comp. List, 1838, 54.
Charadrius himantopus, LATH., Ind. Orn. ii, 1790, 741 (in part; includes the American species, quoting Arct. Zool. ii, No. 405, &c.).

Recurvirostra himantopus, WILS., Am. Orn. vii, 1813, 48, pl. 58, f. 2.
Himantopus nigricollis, VIEILL., Nouv. Dict. d'Hist. Nat. x, 1817, 42; Enc. Meth. 340;
   Gal. Ois. ii, 1834, 85, pl. 229.—BP., Syn. 1828, 322; List, 1838, 54.—NUTT., Man.
   ii, 1834, 8.—AUD., Orn. Biog. iv, 1838, 247, pl. 328; Syn. 1839, 253; B. Am. vi, 1843,
   31, pl. 354.—EMM., Cat. B. Mass. 1835, 5.—PEAB., Rep. Orn. Mass. 1839, 358.—GIR.,
   B. L. I. 1844, 270.—PUTN., Pr. Ess. Inst. i, 1856, 230.—NEWB., P. R. R. Rep. vi,
   1857, 99 (California to the Columbia River).—SALLÉ, P. Z. S. 1857, 237.—SCL.,
   Ibis, i, 1859, 228 (Guatemala).—NEWT., *ibid.* 260 (Santa Cruz).—DRESS., *ibid.*
   1866, 33 (Texas) —BRY., Pr. Bost. Soc. vii, 1859 (Bahamas).—SCL., P. Z. S. 1857,
   206; *ibid.* 1864, 178 (Mexico); *ibid.* 1860, 290 (Ecuador); 1866, 567 (Ucayali);
   1867, 591 (Mexiana); 1870, 323; 1873, 310, 453 (Peru).—BD., B. N. A. 1858, 704.—
   WHEAT., Ohio Agric. Rep. 1860, No. 198.—VERR., Pr. Ess. Inst. iii, 158 (coast
   of Maine, one instance).—BOARDM., Pr. Bost. Soc. ix, 1862, 128 (same instance).—
   ALLEN, Pr. Ess. Inst. iv, 1864, 86.—LAWR., Ann. Lyc. N. Y. viii, 1863-'66, 295
   (Panama and New York).—COUES, Pr. Phila. Acad. 1866, 91 (Arizona).—COUES,
   Pr. Bost. Soc. xii, 1868, 124 (South Carolina).—COUES, Pr. Ess. Inst. v, 1868,
   292 (New England, rare or accidental).—ALLEN, Am. Nat. iii, 1869, 638 (Mas-
   sachusetts).—TURNB., B. E. Pa. 1869, 29 (rather rare, breeding).—MAYN., Guide,
   1870, 143.—ALLEN, Bull. M. C. Z. ii, 1871, 356 (Florida, in winter); iii, 1872,
   172 (Great Salt Lake).—MERR., U. S. Geol. Surv. Ter. 1872, 702 (Great Salt
   Lake).—GRAY, Hand-list, iii, 1871, 48, No. 10294.—COUES, Key, 1872, 247, fig.
   160.—RIDGW., Ann. Lyc. N. Y. x, 1874, 385 (Illinois).
Hypsibates nigricollis, CAB., Schomburgk's Reise, iii, 758.
Macrotarsus nigricollis, GUNDL., J. f. O. iv, 1856, 422.

b ? brasiliensis.

Himantopus melanurus, VIEILL., Nouv. Dict. d'Hist. Nat. x, 1817, 42; Ency. Meth. 340
   (from *Zancudo*, Az., Apunt. iii, 299?).
Himantopus leucurus, VIEILL. (*Gray.*)
Himantopus mexicanus, HARTL., Ind. Azara, 25 (not of authors).
Himantopus nigricollis, GAY (*Sclater*).—CASS., Gillis's Exp. ii, 196.—BURM., Reise, ii, 502
   (La Plata).—DARW., Beagle, 130 (La Plata).—SCL., P. Z. S. 1867, 339 (Chili).—
   SCL. & SALV., P. Z. S. 1868, 144 (Buenos Ayres).
Himantopus brasiliensis, BREHM, Vög. Deutschl. 1831, 684.—SCL. & SALV., P. Z. S. 1873,
   454 (figures of heads of the two varieties).

   Hab.—The typical form from the United States generally, Mexico, part of West Indies, Central America, and South America to Peru and Brazil. Var. *brasiliensis* from
South Brazil, Argentine Republic, and Chili.
   Respecting the var. *brasiliensis*, Mr. J. E. Harting, in a letter to Prof. Baird, which has
been sent to me, states: "The difference in the measurements of the two species is
very striking; the wing, tibia and tarsus in the southern *brasiliensis* being all, respectively, about an inch longer than in the northern *nigricollis.*" A point not given in
Messrs. Sclater and Salvin's paper is, that the disposition of the colors of the upper
parts also differs, the black of the neck being cut off from that of the back by a white
interval; this being, Mr. Harting remarks, a resemblance to the *H. leucocephalus* of
Australia and New Zealand. The form may prove to be specifically distinct.
   Not obtained by either of the earlier Expeditions.
   Later Expeditions.—61643-4, June 19, 1872, Great Salt Lake, Utah (*Merriam*).

   Some of the vagaries that from time to time have found their way
into print, representing sober opinions of naturalists who, from the most
superficial observation of Stilts and Avocets, might have learned better,
are extremely curious. The slight upward curvature of the Avocet's
bill has served whereon to hang fables and theories too absurd to de-
serve a moment's serious consideration; and it has been repeatedly
caricatured in illustrations. The imagination has also been stretched
out of all due proportion to treat of the really very long legs of the Stilts,
and drawn upon to support hypotheses even more feeble and tottering
than the gait which some authors attribute to the bird. It is easy to
see how such notions had their origin. Descriptions and figures were
at first taken from stuffed specimens, awkward preparation of which, or
else the unavoidable shrinkage of the delicate and vascular bill, resulted
in a false shape. It would be hard to find the bill of a live Avocet of
the shape represented by Wilson and Nuttall; Audubon's figure is the
most accurate one I have seen. The other fallacy, respecting the gait

of the Stilt, probably grew out of some such statement as that of Wilson, which, while perfectly true, has been improperly taken. "As they frequently alight on the bare marsh," says the author, referring to Stilts, "they drop their wings, stand with their legs half bent and trembling, as if unable to sustain the burden of their bodies. In this ridiculous posture they will sometimes stand for several minutes, uttering a curring sound, while from the corresponding quiverings of their wings and long legs they seem to balance themselves with great difficulty." Now Wilson generally wrote whereof he had seen and knew, and it is safe to accept his statements for facts, whatever we may think of his opinions. But a sensational or meretricious writer could easily make a sufficiently-startling story out of the above, to the effect that the Stilt's legs are not strong enough to support its body. We may, however, turn aside from such stories as these, assured that, sooner or later, like curses and chickens, they will come home to roost with their authors.

Palpable fabrications aside, there are still some questions to be settled, one of which is respecting the construction of the nests. Wilson says they are at first slightly built of grasses, and afterward elevated and strengthened, as the birds lay and set, by the addition of dry twigs and various other materials; to which statement Audubon takes exception, and, in fact, is evidently inclined to discredit the whole story. It is certainly unusual for nests to be worked upon after incubation has commenced, and probably those that Wilson describes were not then fitted for the reception of the eggs. But we know, also, that the stress the mother bird may be under to deposit an egg may sometimes demand hasty dropping, even before her nest is as elaborately finished as it would otherwise have been. The conflicting statements are probably to be reconciled in this way. Writers are also largely at variance respecting the degree of swimming power that these birds possess; doubtless a result of varying facilities they have enjoyed for forming an opinion. And in general I think that it may be safely asserted that different circumstances of observation play as active a part in producing discrepant statements as all other causes combined. The degree to which many or most birds differ in habits, according to circumstances, is not sufficiently recognized. Partial statements, based upon imperfect or insufficient observation, are usually neither entirely true nor wholly false, but become the more fruitful sources of error from the very admixture of truth that is in them. Error is never so captivating as when truthfully dressed. The fact in this case is, that the Stilts are wretchedly poor swimmers, as might have been expected from the condition of their legs and absence of webs. As waders they are a great success; but when out of their depth, which is rarely, if ever, the case from choice, they only make shift to keep their heads above water, and progress in the most helpless and uncertain way. The Avocets, on the contrary, are fair swimmers.

Though Audubon's statement, that the Stilt is rarely found at any great distance from the sea-shore, may apply on the Atlantic coast, it is manifestly correct in any general application. Thus, Dr. Henry has taken it at Fort Thorne, New Mexico; Mr. Xantus at Fort Tejon, California; Dr. Newberry at Rhett Lake; and, not to multiply previous instances, I found it abundant on the Rio Grande near Albuquerque, and again on the Colorado. It occurs, in fact, on most of the lakes and rivers of the West, hundreds of miles from the ocean. It is also found occasionally in some dry localities, where one would hardly expect to meet with any wader. On the plains it appears to be of unusual occurrence, and I am not aware that it proceeds north of the United States.

Except in this last respect, its range may be said, in general terms, to be nearly the same as that of the Avocet, with which it often associates. It breeds wherever found in summer, and is a migratory bird, departing for the South in autumn, to spend the winter.

While at Los Pinos, New Mexico, late in June, 1864, I had an excellent opportunity of studying the habits of the Stilts. There are large shallow "lagunas" near this place, whose muddy flats and reedy margins are well adapted to the wants of these birds, as well as other waders, particularly Avocets, and a few Ducks, chiefly Mallards. The Stilts had evidently bred there, though I found no nests or very young birds. They were in flocks of twenty or thirty, keeping closely together. All those I shot appeared to be in perfect plumage, with greenish-black backs, this color running in full intensity up the back of the neck, black bills, crimson eyes, and carmine or lake-red legs. They offered a very striking and pleasing effect, wheeling in easy flight, the flock appearing one moment black, the next white, as they showed alternately the upper and under parts, with the long bright-tinted legs heightening the contrast of color. Although not heedless or unduly familiar, they were not very shy, and I secured as many as I wished without much trouble. Besides being almost unacquainted with the danger that may lie in man's approach, they appeared of a gentle, unsuspicious nature, the more noticeable in contrast with the restlessness and watchfulness of most waders. Thus I remember to have approached, on one occasion, within a dozen paces of a large flock, with no other artifice than stooping a little and walking quietly and slowly. The birds had observed me, of course, as the grass was only a few inches high and the ground perfectly flat, but they stood motionless, looking with more of curiosity than fear. It was a picturesque group; still as statues the birds stood in the water, raised only a little above it, on their firm, though so slender, supports, their trim bodies drawn up to full height, and their large, soft eyes dilated in wonder. In an instant, however, as if they had but one mind in common, a thought occurred, and quick as the thought they were off. A flash—a report—the leaden pellets followed after; the thinned ranks kept on, with piteous cries, while the stricken ones dropped heavily into the water and lay motionless, or fluttered helpless with broken wings, vainly essaying to dive. I had to wade into the water to secure the specimens, which, however, was of little consequence, as I was already wet and muddy to the waist; picked up the dead ones from the crimsoned water, and had an exciting chase after the wounded. It was painful to witness their struggles, and I almost wished they could be restored to the health and pleasure they had enjoyed up to the last moment. But the mischief was not to be undone, and it was the part of mercy then to put those still living out of their pain. This I did, and, resolving to use all my specimens to the best advantage and take no more innocent lives, I left the Stilts to their peaceful occupations.

The wings of the Stilt are very long and pointed, as well as ample in width ; its flight, in consequence, is firm, vigorous, and swift. When folded they reach beyond the tip of the tail, and as the under-coverts reach to the end, the bird tapers off behind to a fine point. The black shorter quills and secondaries meet across the back, hiding the white rump and tail. On the ground, whether walking or wading, the bird moves gracefully, with measured steps ; the long legs are much bent at each step (only at the joint, however !), and planted firmly, perfectly straight ; except under certain circumstances, as those Wilson narrates, there is nothing vacillating, feeble or unsteady, either in the attitudes or movements of the birds. When feeding, the legs are bent backward

30

with an acute angle at the heel-joint, to bring the body lower; the latter is tilted forward and downward over the centre of equilibrium, where the feet rest, and the long neck and bill reach the rest of the distance to the ground. Its food consists of aquatic insects of all sorts, probably also of the ova or smallest fry of fish, and various kinds of lacustrine vegetation ; in seeking it, the whole head is frequently immersed in the water. The eggs appear very large for the size of the bird ; they are pyriform in shape, broad at one end and pointed at the other; four constitute a nest-full. But both size and shape vary a good deal. Two specimens I selected as representing the extremes in a large series, measured, respectively, 1.85 by 1.15, and 1.70 by 1.25; the former being long and narrow, the latter short and comparatively blunt. The color is dark ochraceous, or pale brownish-olive, blotched all over with spots and splashes of brown and blackish-brown, of irregular size and shape. The exact time required for hatching is not known. Both sexes are said to incubate; and the young birds, though able to run about as soon as hatched, are assiduously cared for by the parents for some time.

Family PHALAROPODIDÆ : Phalaropes.

Several wading birds, properly so classed, furnish exceptions to the rule that these birds have but slight powers of swimming, only exercised in an emergency. The Avocet is a fair swimmer, the toes being nearly full webbed ; still better swimmers are the Coots and Phalaropes, birds not very closely allied, yet alike fitted for highly aquatic life and habitual swimming by the presence of broad lobes on the toes. Phalaropes are swimming Sandpipers—with the modification of the feet just mentioned, a thin shank to cut the water, a depressed boat-shaped body to rest upon it, and thickened duck-like under plumage to prevent wetting of the body. Not one of the waders surpasses the Phalaropes in ease and variety of movement, grace and elegance of form, or beauty of color when in perfect plumage. Like other peculiar or somewhat exceptional groups of birds, the family is a small one, of not more than three well-ascertained species, all of which occur in this country; two, if not also three, inhabiting the Missouri region. I shall bring them all into the present account. Wilson's Phalarope is indigenous only in America ; the other two are dispersed over the Northern Hemisphere. The following is an analysis of the technical characters of the three genera, or rather subgenera, which the three species have taken to represent :

STEGANOPUS, *Vieillot*, 1825 (type *P. wilsoni ; Holopodius, Bp.*, 1828; (?) *Amblyrhynchus, Nutt.*, 1834, *nec Leach*, 1814). Bill long, equaling the tarsus, exceeding the head, extremely slender, terete and acute. Culmen and gonys broad and depressed. Lateral grooves long and narrow, reaching nearly to tip of bill. Interramal space narrow and very short, extending only half way to the end of the bill. Nostrils at the extreme base of the bill. Wings of moderate length. Tail short, deeply, doubly emarginate ; legs greatly elongated ; tibiæ bare for a considerable distance ; tarsus exceeding the middle toe. Toes long and slender, broadly margined with an even, unscolloped membrane, united but for a brief space basally. Claws moderately long, arched, and acute.

LOBIPES, *Cuvier*, 1817 (type *Tringa hyperborea, Linn.*). Bill generally as in *Steganopus*, but shorter, basally stouter, and tapering to a very acute, compressed tip ; ridge of culmen and gonys less depressed ; interramal space longer and broader. Wings long. Tail short, greatly rounded. Legs and feet short ; tibiæ denuded for but a brief space ; tarsus not longer than the middle toe. Toes very broadly margined with a membrane which is scolloped or indented at each phalangeal joint, and united basally as far as the second joint between the outer and middle toe, and as far as the first joint between the inner and middle toe. The feet are thus semipalmated. Claws very small and short.

PHALAROPUS, *Brisson*, 1760 (type *Tringa fulicaria, Linn.; Crymophilus, Vieill.*, 1816). Bill scarcely longer than the head or tarsus; very stout for this family ; much depressed ; so broad as to be almost spatulate, the tip only moderately acute. Upper mandible with the ridge broad and flattened, its apex arched and decurved, its lateral grooves wide and shallow. Interramal space broad and very long, extending nearly to the end of the bill. Nostrils subbasal, at some distance from the root of the bill. Wings long and pointed. Tail long, rounded, the central rectrices projecting, rather acuminate. The legs and feet are much as in *Lobipes*, but the semipalmation is of less extent.

STEGANOPUS WILSONI, (Sab.) Coues.

Wilson's Phalarope.

(?) *Tringa glacialis,** GM., Syst. Nat. i, 1788, 675 (based on *Plain Phalarope* of PENN., Arct. Zool. ii, 495, No. 415, and LATH., Syn. v, 173.
(?) *Phalaropus glacialis,* LATH., Ind. Orn. 1790, 776 (same basis).
(?) *Amblyrhynchus glacialis,* NUTT., Man. ii, 1834, 247 (same basis).
Phalaropus lobatus, ORD, ed. WILS., Am. Orn. ix, 1825, 72, pl. 73, fig. 3. (Not of *Linnæus.*)
Phalaropus wilsoni, SAB., App. Frank. Journ. 1823, 691.—SW. & RICH., F. B. A. ii, 1831, 405, pl. 69 (north to the Saskatchewan, latitude 54°).—NUTT., Man. ii, 1834, 245.—AUD., Orn. Biog. iii, 1835, 400, pl. 254.—GRAY, Gen. of B. iii, pl. 158.—BD., B. N. A. 1858, 705.—WHEAT., Ohio Agric. Rep. 1860, No. 199—HAYD., Rep. 1862, 174 (Lower Missouri, abundant).—SCL., P. Z. S. 1864, 179 (city of Mexico, in breeding plumage).—ALLEN, Pr. Ess. Inst. iv, 1864, 86 (Massachusetts).—DRESS., Ibis, 1866, 35 (Texas).—SALV., Ibis, 1866, 198 (Guatemala).—ALLEN, Bull. M. C. Z. iii, 1872, 182 (Great Salt Lake).—LAWR., Ann. Lyc. N. Y. viii, 1866, 295 (New York).—SCHL., Mus. Pays-Bas, *Scolopaces,* 60.—STEV., U. S. Geol. Surv. Ter. 1870, 466 (Wyoming).—SNOW, B. Kans. 1873, 10 (Kansas).—PELZ., Orn. 313 (Brazil).
Phalaropus (Holopodius) wilsoni, BP., Syn. 1828, 342, No. 279 ; A. O. iv, 1832, 59, pls. 24, 25.
Holopodius wilsoni, BP., Comp. & Geog. List, 1838, 54.—LESS., Tr. Orn. 1831, 563.
Lobipes wilsoni, AUD., Syn. 1839, 241 ; B. Am. v, 1842, 299, pl. 341.—GIR., B. L. I. 1844, 246.—PUTN., Pr. Ess. Inst. i, 1856, 217.
Phalaropus (Steganopus) wilsoni, GRAY, Hand-list, iii, 1871, 55, No. 10362.
Steganopus wilsoni, COUES, Ibis, Apr. 1865 ; Pr. Phila. Acad. 1866, 97 (Colorado River) ; Pr. Ess. Inst. v, 1868, 292 (New England, rare or casual).—ALLEN, Mem. Bost. Soc. i, 1868, 501 (Western Iowa).—COUES, Key, 1872, 248, fig. 161 (head).
Phalaropus frenatus, VIEILL., Gal. Ois. ii, 1825, 178, pl. 271.
Phalaropus stenodactylus, WAGL., Oken's Isis, 1831, 523.
Phalaropus fimbriatus, TEMM., Planches Coloriées, v, pl. 270.
Lobipes incanus, JARD. & SELBY, Ill. Orn. i, pl. 16.
Steganopus tricolor, VIEILL.
Lobipes antarcticus, LESS.—(See FRAZER, P. Z. S. 1843, 118 ; SCI., *ibid.* 1867, 332.—PELZ., Novara Reise, Aves, 132).—PHILIPPI, Cat. 37.

Hab.—United States and British Provinces, generally. North to the Saskatchewan. Rare or casual in the Eastern United States. Common in the Mississippi Valley and westward. Breeds in Western United States and in the interior of the fur countries in the lower latitudes. Mexico, Central and South America, in winter.

Lieutenant Warren's Expedition.—4876-80, Omaha and Council Bluffs ; 5444-5, Medicine Creek.

Later Expeditions.—60376, Camp Carling, Wyoming.

Not procured by Captain Raynolds' Expedition.

Adult in breeding dress: Bill, legs, and feet, pure black ; crown of head, pale ash, passing into white along a narrow strip on the nape. A narrow, distinct, pure white line over the eye. Sides of neck intense purplish-chestnut, or dark wine-red ; anteriorly deepening upon the auriculars into velvety black ; posteriorly continued, somewhat duller in tint, as a stripe along each side of the back to the tips of the scapulars. Other upper parts pearly-ash, blanching on the rump and upper tail-coverts. Wings pale, dull grayish-brown ; the coverts slightly white-tipped, the primaries dusky-brown, their shafts brownish-white, except at tip. Tail marbled with pearly-gray and white. All the under parts pure white, but the forepart and sides of the breast washed with pale chestnut-brown, as if with a weak solution of the rich color on the neck, and a faint tinge of the same along the sides of the body to the flanks. The female is identical with the male in color.

Specimens just fully fledged are in a plumage not generally known, and one of which I have seen no adequate description : Bill, blackish, about 1.10 long ; legs, dull yellow (tarsus, 1.20 ; middle toe and claw, 1.05). Upper parts, including crown and upper surface of wings, brownish-black, each feather edged with rusty-brown, very conspicu-

---

* I do not agree with those authors who unhesitatingly refer the "*Plain Phalarope*" of Pennant and Latham to *P. fulicarius,* as I am by no means satisfied it was not a *young* Wilson's Phalarope. The diagnosis given corresponds quite as well to the latter as to the former, and in one item, namely, "toes bordered with a plain or unscolloped membrane," is applicable only to the latter. I therefore range *Tringa* or *Phalaropus glacialis* here, with a query. It is also quite possible that some of the older synonyms adduced under *P. hyperboreus* may really belong to *P. wilsoni ;* but they are so uncertain, and different accounts are so involved, that it would probably not be now possible to determine the point, even were it particularly desirable to do so.

ous on the long inner secondaries, and giving a general aspect like that of a Sandpiper of the genus *Actodromas*. Upper tail-coverts pure white. Tail clear ash, edged and much marbled with white, the ash darker at its line of demarcation from the white. Line over eye, and whole under parts white, the breast with a faint rusty tinge, and the sides slightly marbled with gray. Quills dusky, the secondaries white-edged, and the shafts of the primaries whitish.—This stage is of extremely brief duration, beginning to give way, almost as soon as the bird is full grown, to the clear uniform ashy of the upper parts of the fall and winter condition. The change, in some specimens shot early in August, is already very evident, clear ashy feathers being mixed, on the crown and all the upper parts, with such as just described. Size of the smallest specimen only 8.25 in length by 14.50 in extent; the wing 4.60.

In full plumage this is the handsomest of the three Phalaropes, as well as the largest, and one of the most elegant birds of the entire group of waders. It was apparently first noticed by the gifted naturalist to whom it was subsequently dedicated, under the previously occupied name of *P. lobatus*. To those familiar with Wilson's writings, which portray his own character with the same fidelity that the birds it was his passion to depict are rendered, his name brings sadness to the mind, and tempts a question of the wisdom of a dispensation that took him away, while countless useless and hurtful lives were spared. His friend and admirer, Thomas Nuttall, expresses thoughts that find an echo in our own hearts: "Hurried to the tomb from amidst his unfinished and ill-requited labors, his favorite Orpheus and Woodthrush pour out their melody in vain. The Bluebird, which hastens to inform us of the return of spring, delights no longer the favorite of their song. Like his own beautiful and strange bird now before us, his transient visit, which delighted us, has ended; but his migration, no longer to be postponed, has exceeded the bounds of the earth, and spring and autumn, with their wandering hosts of flitting birds, may still return; while he, translated to Elysian groves, will only be remembered in the thrill of the plaintive Nightingale! * * *"

Wilson's Phalarope is of very general distribution and common occurrence in the United States from the Mississippi Valley westward, but apparently rare, or even exceptional, in most of the Eastern States. Our New England and Middle States' records are comparatively few, and agree in attesting the rarity of the species in those sections. I never saw it in Maryland, Virginia, or either of the Carolinas—all places where my protracted collecting would doubtless have brought it to my notice had it been of regular occurrence. Its line of migration appears to be mainly the Mississippi Valley, and thence to the Rocky Mountains, and in this region it may be called common. It does not go far north to breed; in this being strikingly contrasted with the other two. Latitude 54° is stated to be the limit, in the region of the Saskatchewan, while the greater proportion of individuals nest within our limits—in Dakota, Minnesota, Iowa, Nebraska, Idaho, Utah, Kansas, and even Illinois, from all of which places we have authentic advices. Perfectly dressed specimens are taken even so far south as Texas. I am under the belief that I found it breeding along the Arkansas River, between Forts Larned and Lyons, on some of the many pools that dot the prairie. There were many water birds here, among them Franklin's Gull, the Black Tern, and the Avocet, the latter certainly breeding. My specimens of the Phalarope were in full plumage, and appeared, by their actions, to have established themselves for the summer, although I found no eggs. This was in June. The same month, nine years subsequently, I found the Phalaropes breeding on reedy pools, together with Godwits, Curlew, Black Terns and Coots, and various Ducks, along that portion of the Red River of the North which separates Minnesota from Dakota; and later, in the beginning of August, I took newly-fledged young on the Mouse River, in Dakota, near Turtle Mountain. These young were specially interesting to me, as showing a plumage with which I had up to that time been unacquainted. It is described above. In all such breeding localities, where the birds feel at home, and have none of the restlessness they show when migrating, their habits may be studied to the best advantage. I had excellent opportunity of seeing how gentle and confiding the birds become when not molested, and how surprisingly graceful they are, either pacing the brink of their favorite pool, or swimming buoyantly upon its surface. I had no heart to destroy any of the beautiful creatures, much as I desired some for my cabinet, after a scene I had witnessed when I had secured some Avocets. Three Phalaropes came in great concern and alighted on the water where a dead Avocet was floating, swimming back and forth and almost caressing it with their bill. The Avocet's mate himself, who was not long in reaching the spot, showed no more agitation than his little friends and neighbors, the Phalaropes, did ; and though it was only birds "of a low order of beings" who thus exhibited sympathy and grief, who could look on such a scene unmoved ?

The eggs of Wilson's Phalarope are from 1.20 to 1.35 inches long, by about 0.90 broad, thus being of an elongate as well as pyriform shape. The ground ranges from a clay color to a brownish-drab ; it is very heavily overlaid with the markings, sometimes to such extent that the ground struggles to appear amid the almost continous overlying color, and an egg like a Ptarmigan's results. Ordinarily the markings consist of numerous large, heavy splashes and sizable spots of indeterminate contour, mixed with numberless specks and fine scratches ; occasional eggs are much more lightly and sparsely speckled in finer pattern. The color of the markings is a varying shade of dark bistre-brown, sometimes chocolate. Shell-markings are not ordinarily noticeable.

LOBIPES HYPERBOREUS, (Linn.) Cuv.

Northern Phalarope.

Tringa hyperborea, LINN., Syst. Nat. i, 1766, 249 (based on Fn. Suec. 179 ; EDW., 143 ; WILL., 270 ; RAY, 132 ; *Phalaropus cinereus*, BRISS., vi, 15).—BRÜNN., Orn. Bor. 1764, 172.—FABR., Fn. Groen. 1780, No. 75.—GM., Syst. Nat., i, 1788, 675.
Phalaropus hyperboreus, ♂, LATH., Ind. Orn. ii, 1790, 775 (excl. syn. of supposed female= *P. fulicarius*) ; Planch. Enlum. 766.—TEMM., Man. 1815, 457 ; ii, 1820, 709.— SAB., Frankl. Journ. 690.—BP., Syn. 1828, 342.—NUTT., Man. ii, 1834, 239.— AUD., Orn. Biog. iii, 1835, 118 ; v, 1839, 595 ; pl. 215.—NEWB., P. R. R. Rep. vi, 1857, 98 (Des Chutes River, in summer).—BD., B. N. A. 1858, 706.—SCL. & SALV., Ibis, ii, 1860, 277 (Guatemala).—SWIN., Ibis, 1863, 415 (Formosa).— COOP. & SUCK., N. H. Wash. Ter. 1860, 236.—WHEAT., Ohio Agric. Rep. 1860, No. 200.—VERR., Pr. Ess. Inst. iii, 1862, 158 (Maine, possibly breeding).— (?)BOARDM., Pr. Bost. Soc. ix, 1862, 128 (Bay of Fundy).—LAWR., Ann. Lyc. N. Y. viii, 1866, 295 (New York).—ALLEN, Pr. Ess. Inst. iv, 1864, 86 (Massachusetts).— MCILWR., Pr. Ess. Inst. v, 1866, 92 (Canada West).— SCHL., Mus. Pays-Bas, *Scolopaces*, 58.—TURNB., B. E. Pa. 1869, 29 (May and September).—STEV., U. S. Geol. Surv. Ter. 1870, 466 (Wyoming).
Phalaropus (Lobipes) hyperboreus, GRAY, Hand-list, iii, 1871, 55, No. 10861.
Lobipes hyperboreus, CUV., Régne Anim. i, 1829, 532.—STEPH., Gen. Zool. xii, 169, pl. 21.— FLEM., Br. An. 100.—BREHM, V. D. 676, pl. 35, f. 4.—JEN., Man. Br. Vert. 214.— EYT., Cat. Br. B. 43.—MACGIL., Man. N. H. Orn. ii, 84.—BP., List, 1838, 54.— AUD., Syn. 1839, 240 ; B. Am. v, 1842, 295, pl. 340.—GIR., B. L. I. 1844, 248.— COUES, Pr. Ess. Inst. vi, 1868, 292 (migratory along the coast, perhaps breeding).—DALL & BANN., Tr. Chic. Acad. i, 1869, 290 (Alaska).—COUES, Key, 1872, 248, fig. 161 (foot).—RIDGW., Ann. Lyc. N. Y. x, 1874, 385 (Illinois).
(?) *Tringa lobata*, LINN., Syst. Nat. i, 1766, 249 (based on Fn. Suec. No. 179 ; *Tringa grisea*, BRISS., ii, 206, pl. 20s ; Phil. Trans. vol. l, 255, pl. 6 ; EDW., pl. 308 ; *Phalaropus*, BRISS., vi, p. 12).—BRÜNN., Orn. Bor. 1764, 51.—MÜLLER, No. 195.— FABR., Fn. Groen. 1780, No. 75.—GM., Syst. Nat. i, 1788, 674.

(?) *Phalaropus lobatus*, LATH., Ind. Orn. ii, 1790, 776.
Tringa fusca, GM., Syst. Nat. i, 1788, 675.
Phalaropus fuscus, LATH., Ind. Orn. ii, 1790, 776 (BRISS., vi, 18).
Phalaropus ruficollis, PALL., Zoog. R.-A. ii, 1811, 203.
Phalaropus cinerascens, PALL., Zoog. R.-A. ii, 1811, 204.
Phalaropus cinereus, MEY. & WOLF, Tasch. ii, 417.—KEYS. & BLAS., Wirb. Eur. 73.—
    SCHL., Rev. Crit. 94.—FINSCH, Abh. Nat. iii, 1872, 65 (Alaska).
Phalaropus angustirostris, NAUM., Vög. Deutschl. viii, 1836, 240, pl. 205.
Phalaropus australis, TEMM. & BP. (*Schlegel.*)
Phalaropus williamsii, SIMM., Linn. Trans. viii, 264.

Hab.—Northern Hemisphere, penetrating to very high latitudes to breed, migratory sometimes into the tropics in winter. Generally distributed, but more particularly maritime.

Not noticed by Captain Raynolds' or Lieutenant Warren's Expedition.

Later Expeditions.—59867, Middle Park, Colorado; 60796, Big Sandy River, Wyoming.

Specimens of the Northern Phalarope, just from the egg, were lately procured by Mr. Henry W. Elliott, on St. Paul Island, one of the Prybilov group, outliers of the Aleutians. They are very pretty little creatures indeed. The whole head and upper parts are clear, warm, brownish-yellow, or rich buff, variegated with black; the under parts, from neck to rump, are white with a slight silvery-gray cast. The black variegation occupies a triangular area on the crown (where it is mixed with buff), forms a long stripe down the back, bounded by a streak over each hip and a spot on each shoulder, and terminates by a cross-bar on the rump. The bill is only a third of an inch long, and no larger than a dressing-pin; the total length of the bird is about 2¾ inches. As with others of the family, the changes of plumage with age, and especially with season, are very great; but in any condition the species may be recognized by its small size and scolloped toe-membranes, in comparison with *P. wilsoni*, and by its slender, subulate bill, as compared with the broad, flattened one of *P. fulicarius*.

In the interior of the United States the Northern Phalarope is nowhere so abundant as Wilson's, and appears to be of less general dispersion, though it occurs, sometimes in large flocks, in particular localities. It is oftener seen flocking along either coast. On the Atlantic I have not been able to trace it beyond the Middle States, although it certainly winters along the Gulf of Mexico. Mr. Giraud quotes a letter of Prof. Baird's, dated Carlisle, Pennsylvania, October 10, 1842, in regard to its occurrence in that locality; and Dr. Turnbull states that it is "rare; arriving early in May, and again in September; being more frequent in the autumn." On the coast of New England it is more abundant and of regular occurrence during the migrations, some apparently breeding among the islands in the Bay of Fundy. It appears to migrate mainly off the coast, in flocks of considerable size, and doubtless many of the occasions of its capture along our coast are the result of storms driving it inshore. On the Pacific side, says Dr. Cooper, "the Lobefoot passes in spring and fall through Washington Territory in small flocks, which associate sometimes with the Sandpipers, but appear to prefer wetter feeding-grounds, wading in the shallow creeks at low tide, and even swimming on the ocean, several miles off shore. In August, 1853, I saw a pair, either of this or the next species, swimming on a small lake on the summit of the Cascade Mountains, where they probably had a nest. The young birds appear near the mouth of the Columbia early in July." Dr. Suckley also found them about Puget Sound in August, becoming quite abundant during the month, and keeping principally among beds of kelp and floating patches of sea-weed. Dr. Bannister mentions eggs brought from the vicinity of Unalaklik, Alaska, and Mr. Dall states that the bird is very common all along the Yukon River, as well as at its mouth. " I observed it," he continues, "running among stranded blocks of ice on the muddy beach at Nulato, stopping and glancing around every few steps; the pure white of the breast more conspicuous by the black mud over which it passed. Two eggs, in a small, round nest, lined with grass, were found at Pastolik."

A very large series of eggs of this Phalarope has been received at the Smithsonian, collected by Messrs. Kennicott and Macfarlane, and others, in the Anderson and Yukon River regions. They show such a range of variation in color that it is scarcely possible to describe them intelligibly. The ground varies from dark greenish-olive or brownish-olive, through various lighter drab-tints, nearly to a buffy-brown, and in one instance to a light grayish-drab. The markings are usually very bold and heavy, consisting of large spots and the still larger splashes produced by their confluence, mingled with dots and scratches in interminable confusion. The markings are, in general, pretty evenly distributed, sometimes aggregated about the butt, and in rarer instances forming a complete, definite circle. In a few instances all the markings are mere dots. In general, the heaviness and size of the markings bear some proportion to the intensity of the ground-color. The color of the markings is dark bistre, chocolate, and sometimes still lighter browns. The longest and narrowest egg measures 1.30 inches by only 0.75; a short and thick one only 1.10 by 0.82; average, about 1.20 by 0.80. The eggs are three or four, oftenest four, and are laid in June— more frequently in the latter half of the month—in a depression of the ground, variously lined with withered vegetation.

PHALAROPUS FULCARIUS, (Linn.) Bp.

Red Phalarope.

Tringa fulicaria, LINN., Syst. Nat. i, 1766, 249 (based on *Phalaropus rufuscens*, BRISS., vi. 20, and EDW., pl. 142).—FABR., Fn. Grœn. 1780, No. 76.—GM., S. N. i, 1788, 676.
Phalaropus hyperboreus, ♀, LATH., Ind. Orn. ii, 1790, 775 (excl. syn. of supposed male).— WILS., Am. Orn. ix, 75, pl. 73, f. 4.
Phalaropus fulicarius, BP., Journ. Phila. Acad. iv, 1825, 232; Syn. 1828, 341; List, 1838, 54.—Sw. & RICH., F. B. A. ii, 1831, 407.—NUTT., Man. ii, 1834, 236.—AUD., Orn. Biog. iii, 1835, 404, pl. 255; Syn. 1839, 239; B. Am. v, 1842, 291, pl. 339.—GIR., B. L. I. 1844, 245.—GRAY, Gen. of B. iii, 1849, 586.—NEWB., P. R. R. Rep. vi, 1857, 98 (off California coast).—BD., B. N. A. 1858, 707.—COOP. & SUCK., N. H. Wash. Ter. 1860, 236.—WHEAT., Ohio Agric. Rep. 1860, No. 201.—COUES, Pr. Phila. Acad. 1861, 228 (Labrador).—ALLEN, Pr. Ess. Inst. iv, 1864, 86.—NEWT., Ibis, 1865, 505 (Spitzbergen).—LAWR., Ann. Lyc. N. Y. viii, 1866, 295.—COUES, Pr. Ess. Inst. vi, 1868, 292 (migratory along the coast).—DALL & BANN., Trans. Chic. Acad. i, 1869, 291 (Alaska).—SCHL., Mus. Pays-Bas, 1865, *Scolopaces*, p. 58.—NEWT., P. Z. S. 1867, 165, pl. 15, f. 1 (egg).—GRAY, Hand-list, iii, 1871, 55, No. 10360.—COUES, Key, 1872, 248.—RIDGW., Ann. Lyc. N. Y. x, 1874, 385 (Illinois).
Phalaropus rufus, PALL., Zoog. R.-A. ii, 1811, 205, pl. 63.—BECHST., Naturg. Deut. iv, 381.—BREHM, V. D. 678, pl. 35. f. 3.
Crymophilus rufus, VIEILL., Nouv. Dict. Nat. d'Hist. viii, 521.
Phalaropus platyrhynchus, TEMM., Man. 1815, 459; ii, 712.—BREHM, V. D. 679.—NAUM., V. D. viii, 1836, 255, pl. 206.—SAB., Greenl. Birds, 536 ; Suppl. Parry's 1st Voy. p. cci.—RICH., App. Parry's 2d Voy. 335.—ERRA, Atti Soc. Ital. 1860, ii, 58.
Phalaropus rufescens, BRISS., vi, 20.—KEYS. & BLAS., Wirb. Eur. 73.—SCHL., Rev. Crit. 94.
Phalaropus griseus, LEACH, Cat. Mam. and B. Br. Mus. 34.

Hab.—Essentially the same as that of *L. hyperboreus*.
This species was not noticed by any of the Expeditions.

I introduce this species, although it has not yet been found in the Missouri region, as one which unquestionably occurs at times, and in order to complete an account of the family. It is more particularly a maritime bird, yet we have accounts of its occurrence in the interior of the United States. It is mentioned by Mr. Wheaton among the birds of Ohio, and by Mr. Ridgway among those of Illinois.

The nidification of this species is the same as that of the preceding, and the eggs are so similar that they cannot be distinguished with certainty in any given instance. Several specimens are in the collection from Franklin Bay, on the Arctic coast, east of Anderson River. They were taken early in July, by Mr. MacFarlane, who states that they are deposited in a depression of the ground lined with withered leaves. Their average capacity is greater than those of *L. hyperboreus*. The longest specimen measures 1.30 by 0.90; the shortest, 1.15 by 0.90; another, 1.25 by 0.85.

Family SCOLOPACIDÆ: Snipe, &c.

The great number of birds belonging to this family which claim the attention of the sportsman, the epicure, and the amateur ornithologist, renders it especially an interesting one. Here are classed nearly all the "long-billed fraternity," as these birds are called, somewhat facetiously, but nevertheless with technical accuracy—the Woodcock and the true Snipe, the Sandpipers in all their variety, the Godwits, Curlews and Willets, the Yellowlegs, and all the numerous birds that pass under the loose name of "Bay Snipe." They may be distinguished from any kind of Plover by the slenderness and sensitiveness of the bill, as well as, usually, by its length, which for the most part exceeds the head, and absence of any constriction between the nasal and terminal parts. It is always furnished with long, deep grooves on both mandibles, and may be either straight, curved down, or a little recurved. The gape of the mouth is usually very much contracted. The *Scolopacidæ* are probably without exception migratory, and some of them pass to the highest latitudes where birds can live, to breed, nesting always on the ground, and laying three or four eggs, placed with the small ends together in a slight nest or on the bare ground. The North American species are numerous, and nearly all occur in the Missouri region. For convenience of reference we here bring them together in the several natural groups in which they fall:

A. Woodcock, Wilson's Snipe, and Redbreasted Snipe.
B. Godwits, of four species, large, with the bill a little turned up.
C. Sandpipers, numerous species, all but one with short, straight bill; going in large flocks on the beaches and elsewhere.
D. Tattlers, various species of different sizes, with rather long bill, harder than in the foregoing, straight or very slightly turned up. Here belong some species improperly called "Plover," as the "Upland Plover," "Yellowshank Plover," &c., together with Willets, or "Stone Snipe," "Teeter-tails," &c.
E. Curlew, distinguished from all the others by the downward curve of the long and slender bill.

PHILOHELA MINOR, (Gm.) Gray.

American Woodcock.

Scolopax minor, GM., Syst. Nat. i, 1788, 661.—LATH., Ind. Orn. ii, 1790, 714 (based on "*Little Woodcock*" of LATH., Syn. v, 131, and PENN., Arct. Zool. ii, 463, No. 365, pl. 19).—WILS., Am. Orn. vi, 1812, 40, pl. 48, f. 2.—BP., Syn. 1828, 331.—AUD., Orn. Biog. iii, 1835, 474, pl. 268; also of various sporting authorities.
Rusticola minor, VIEILL., Anal. 1816; Gal. Ois, ii, 1834, 112, pl. 142.—BP., List, 1838, 52.
Rusticola (Microptera) minor, NUTT., Man. ii, 1834, 194.
Philohela minor, GRAY, Gen. of B. 1849.—WOODH., Sitgr. Rep. 1853, 101 (Indian Territory, rare).—BD., B. N. A. 1858, 709.—HAYD., Rep. 1862, 174 (Loup Fork).—McILWR., Pr. Ess. Inst. v, 1866, 92 (Hamilton, C. W.; summer, common).—ALLEN, Mem. Bost. Soc. i, 1868, 501 (Western Iowa).—SCOTT, Pr. Bost. Soc. xv, 1872, 227 (West Virginia, breeding).—SNOW, B. Kans. 1873, 10 (Kansas, rare).—COUES, Key, 1872, 251, fig. 162; and of most late authors.
Microptera americana, AUD., Syn. 1839, 250; B. Am. vi, 1843, 15, pl. 352.—GIR., B. L. I. 1844, 266.

Hab.—Eastern United States and British Provinces. North to Nova Scotia (*Audubon*) and Canada (*McIlwraith*). Northwest to Fort Rice, Dakota (*Coues*). West to Kansas (*Snow*) and Nebraska (*Hayden*). *No extralimital record.*

Lieutenant Warren's Expedition.—9140, Loup Fork of the Platte.
Not obtained by Captain Raynolds' Expedition.

The restriction of the range of the Woodcock is a singular circumstance in the history of a family of birds noted for their wide dispersion and extensive migrations.   It is only known to inhabit the United States and immediately adjoining portions of the British possessions, while in the West its extension is equally limited.   To Dr. Hayden's instance of its occurrence in Nebraska, hitherto the westernmost on record, I am enabled to add another, which somewhat extends the range.   While I was at Fort Randall I was assured by several officers, and particularly Captain Hartley and Lieutenant Campbell, that a Woodcock had been shot considerably further up the river, at Fort Rice.   It would appear that the bird is creeping up the river, like the Quail, though it is still rare.   Mr. Trippe did not meet with it anywhere in Minnesota; but in a list of the game birds found about Saint Paul, kindly furnished by Dr. A. Heger, United States Army, I find it included as a summer resident, and until the end of September.   Its time of arrival was not noticed.   Mr. Allen states that it is common in Western Iowa, where, however, Mr. Trippe did not observe it; and according to Prof. Snow it occurs, though rarely, in Kansas, where it breeds.   Dr. Woodhouse found it rare in the Indian Territory.   These references probably fully exhibit the limit of its western extension.   I myself never saw it anywhere in Dakota.

There is no occasion at present to enter into the history of the Woodcock, which is well known to those who are interested in the subject; in fact, most competent sportsmen are more familiar with the bird than some who have written about it appear to be.   I wish, however, to call attention to a point of nomenclature, in which some of the best field naturalists are often at fault.   It is a common practice of untechnical observers to use the term " *Scolopax*" as a designation of various American birds of the family *Scolopacidæ*, to no one of which can it be properly applied in strictness.   This term belongs to the European Woodcock, quite a different bird from ours, and still more different from the other scolopacine species.   Our Woodcock might be called *Scolopax minor*, as it used to be, without violent stretching of the significance of the term; but the name *Scolopax* had much better be left where it belongs—to the European species.   Ours differs from that one, beside being smaller and somewhat differently shaped and colored, in having the first three quills of the wing very narrow and scythe-shaped.   This is a structural peculiarity, important enough, in connection with some other points, to warrant our putting the bird in a different genus, and calling it *Philohela minor*.

Accounts sometimes reach us of an extraordinarily big Woodcock killed in this country—say about a third larger and heavier than the ordinary bird.   It is probable that in every such instance the specimen was a European Woodcock that had somehow straggled to this country. The point can always be decided, independently of size, by the above character of the quill-feathers.   The European Woodcock (*Scolopax rusticola*) is perfectly authentic as a casual inhabitant of this country, having been found in Newfoundland, Long Island, and New Jersey. Dr. Lewis, author of the admirable volume, "The American Sportsman," speaks of a bird which was undoubtedly of this sort, in the footnote on p. 169 of the edition of 1868; and other unquestionable instances, in which the specimen was examined by a competent ornithologist, have come to our knowledge.   (See *Lawrence*, Ann. Lyc. N. Y. 1866, 292; *Baird*, Amer. Journ. Sci. xli, 1866, 25.)   The species was formally introduced to our fauna in 1872, in my late work, where these and other technical points are presented.   Such occurrences of stragglers from another continent are very interesting, and should be published without delay by any one who is fortunate enough to observe them.

Of all sportsmen who habitually enjoy cock-shooting, know every trick of the bird's, just where to find them at any time, and how to bring them to bag, how many have seen a nest or eggs? Yet the bird breeds, in greater or less abundance, over nearly all of its range, and especially in the Middle and Eastern States. One reason doubtless is, that of course sportsmen are not after Woodcock in the breeding season; and another, that, were they so disposed, they might search long and fruitlessly for the nest, so careful are the birds, in general, to conceal it in the most secluded resorts. It is placed in low, thick, swampy woods or brakes, on the ground, at the foot of a bush or tussock, or on some fallen log or decayed stump, and it is formed of a few dried leaves or a little grass, just enough to keep the eggs from the cold or moist ground. The Woodcock is an early layer, generally in April, but even, according to Audubon, in March or February at the South—the period varying a month or more according to latitude. The eggs may be recognized by the following description, as they are quite unlike those of any of their allies, not only the coloration, but also the shape, being peculiar: Instead of a pointedly pyriform egg, such as most waders lay, we find a bluntly-rounded form, the diameter being comparatively great for the length. The shortest and broadest egg of a dozen before me measures only 1.40 by fully 1.20; a long, narrow specimen is 1.55 by 1.15; an average is about 1.50 by 1.15. This rotund shape corresponds to the plump figure of the bird, as compared with other slenderer waders. The ground-color is a light clay, with more or less of a brownish cast, sometimes quite buffy-brown, sometimes merely grayish-white. The spots are mostly small and not very bold; they consist of numerous chocolate-brown surface markings, with many other pale, stone-gray shell spots. The size and intensity of the markings generally correspond with the depth of the ground-color.

As the habits of the Woodcock during the mating season are very little known, the following account is copied from Audubon as one of interest: "At this season its curious spiral gyrations, while ascending or descending along a space of fifty or more yards of height, when it utters a note somewhat resembling the word *kwank*, are performed every evening and morning for nearly a fortnight. When on the ground, at this season as well as in autumn, the male not unfrequently repeats this sound, as if he were calling to others in his neighborhood, and on hearing it answered he immediately flies to meet the other bird, which in the same manner advances toward him. On observing the Woodcock while in the act of emitting these notes, you would imagine he exerted himself to the utmost to produce them, the head and bill being inclined toward the ground, and a strong forward movement of the body taking place at the moment the *kwank* reaches your ear. This over, the bird jerks its half-spread tail, then erects itself, and stands as if listening for a few moments, when, if the cry is not answered, it repeats it. I feel pretty confident that, in the spring, the female, attracted by these sounds, flies to the male; for on several occasions I observed the bird that had uttered the call immediately caress the one that had just arrived, and which I knew from its greater size to be a female. I am not, however, quite certain that this is always the case, for on other occasions I have seen a male fly off and alight near another, when they would immediately begin to fight, tugging and pushing at each other with their bills, in the most curious manner imaginable."

The Woodcock is by no means so exclusively an inhabitant of bog and brake as those who are not entirely familiar with it may suppose. It frequently visits corn-fields and other cultivated tracts in the vicinity of swampy grounds, and often betakes itself to the woods, where it rustles among the dry leaves, turning them over to search for food. It is erratic, or rather capricious, in its resorts as well as in its general movements north and south. A few linger, unless the season be very severe, in the Middle districts all winter, but they are generally off for the South with the freezing of the ground. A cold snap will suddenly drive them away altogether from places where, a few hours before, they had been found in numbers. The general and regular movement occurs chiefly in March and October. Some reside in the South, but the greater number pass north, to return again in the fall. None appear to winter, except casually, beyond our Middle districts.

GALLINAGO WILSONI, (Temm.) Bp.

American Snipe; Wilson's Snipe.

Scolopax gallinago, WILS., Am. Orn. vi, 1812, 18, pl. 47, fig. 1.
Scolopax wilsoni, TEMM., Pl. Color. v, *livr.* lxviii (in text).—BP., Syn. 1828, 330.—Sw. & RICH., F. B. A. ii, 1831, 401.—NUTT., Man. ii, 1834, 185.—AUD., Orn. Biog. iii, 1835, 322; v, 1839, 583; pl. 243; Syn. 1839, 248; B. Am. v, 1842, 339; pl. 350.— GIR., B. L. I. 1844, 261.—TRIPPE, Pr. Ess. Inst. vi, 1871, 119 (Minnesota); and of many earlier authors.
Gallinago wilsoni, BP., Comp. List, 1838, 52.—SCL., P. Z. S. 1856, 310 (Cordova).—BD., B. N. A. 1858, 710.—SALV., Ibis, 1859 (Honduras).—NEWT., *ibid.* 258 (Santa Cruz).—TAYLOR, *ibid.* 1860, 314.—DRESS., *ibid.* 1866, 36.—CAB. J. f. O. iv, 350 (Cuba).—BRYANT, Pr. Bost. Soc. vii, 1859 (Bahamas).—COOP. & SUCK., N. H. Wash. Ter. 1860, 237.—HAYD., Rep. 1862, 174 (Loup Fork and Black Hills).— SCL., P. Z. S. 1861, 80 (Jamaica); 1864, 178 (Mexico); 1867, 280 (Mosquito Coast).— SALV., *ibid.* 1870, 219 (Veragua).—BOARDM., Pr. Bost. Soc. ix, 1862, 128 (Maine, breeds).—COUES, Pr. Phila. Acad. 1866, 97 (Arizona).—DALL & BANN., Tr. Chic. Acad. i, 1869, 291 (Alaska).—ALLEN, Mem. Bost. Soc. i, 1868, 501 (Iowa); Bull. M. C. Z. iii, 1872, 181 (Utah).—LAWR., Ann. Lyc. ix, 141 (Costa Rica).—SUND., Ofv. Kong. Vet. Ak. 587 (St. Bartholomew).—TRIPPE, Pr. Bost. Soc. xv, 1872, 240 (Iowa).—AIKEN, *ibid.* 209 (Colorado, wintering).—STEV., U. S. Geol. Surv. Ter. 1870, 466 (Wyoming).—MERR., *ibid.* 1872, 700 (Montana).—SNOW, B. Kans. 1873, 10.—COUES, Key, 1872, 262, fig. 163; and of authors.
Gallinago gallinaria var. *wilsoni*, RIDGW., Ann. Lyc. N. Y. x, 1874, 383.
Gallinago brehmii, BP., Obs. Nomen. Wils. 1825, No. 204. (Not of *Kaup*.)
Scolopax delicatula, ORD, ed. Wils. ix, 1825, 218.
Scolopax drummondii, Sw. & RICH., F. B. A. ii, 1831, 400.—NUTT., Man. ii, 1834, 190.— AUD., Orn. Biog. v, 1839, 319; Syn. 1839, 249; B. Am. vi, 1843, 9.
Gallinago drummondii, BP., List, 1838, 52.
Scolopax douglasii, Sw. & RICH., F. B. A. ii, 1831, 400.—NUTT., Man. ii, 1834, 191.
(?) *Scolopax leucurus*, Sw. & RICH., F. B. A. ii, 1831, 501.—NUTT., Man. ii, 1834, 617.
(?) *Gallinago leucurus*, GRAY, Genera of Birds, pl. 157.

Hab.—The whole of North America, and southward to South America. Mexico. West Indies. (?) Accidental in England (HART., Br. Birds, 1872, 143). Breeds from Northern New England northward.
Lieutenant Warren's Expedition.—4874, Mouth of Bighorn River; 9041-42, Black Hills.
Later Expeditions.—61103, Fort Sanders, Wyoming; 62370, Fort Ellis, Montana; 61157, Wyoming.
Not obtained by Captain Raynolds' Expedition.

The name of "English" Snipe, of common but erroneous application to this bird, is wholly a misnomer, the bird being entirely different from that of England, as any one may perceive on comparing the two. It is another of the deplorable instances in which paucity of language has caused American birds to be called by the name of their nearest European relative, real or supposed—a circumstance tending to promulgate error and confusion. We should do our best to suppress such wrong names in every instance, even without such an example as the well-nigh hopeless muddle about our Bob White before us. "Jack Snipe" is another soubriquet of this bird, of no obvious application, indeed, but not particularly bad, though the same term is also used to designate the Pectoral Sandpiper (*Actodromas maculata*).

Throughout the greater part of the United States the Snipe is found only during the migrations, and in winter. It breeds, however, in Northern New England, and may do so along other portions of our northern border, although I have not so determined. Mr. Trippe speaks of its common occurrence in Minnesota, from April to the close of October, but adds that he did not observe it to breed. In Northern Dakota, likewise, where I enjoyed excellent Snipe-shooting late in September, I found nothing to indicate its summer residence there. It is almost exclusively a migrant through the Missouri region, though some probably winter in the southern portions. Its migrations are pushed, at that season, even to South America, and it also occurs in Mexico, Central America, and the West Indies, according to numerous extralimital quotations. The eggs of Wilson's Snipe are moderately pyriform, and measure about 1.60 by 1.12 ; some, however, being so small as 1.50 by 1.05. The ground color is a grayish-olive, with more or less brownish shade in different specimens. The markings are numerous, generally heavy, and often massed, though, as a rule, distinct; they may appear all over the surface, but are always thickest and largest on the major half of the egg. The color is umber-brown, of varying shade, according to the depth or quantity of pigment. With these surface markings are associated some paler or obscure shell spots, not ordinarily so noticeable, however, as in some other species. And over all we find, in occasional specimens, curious sharp, straggling lines of what appears to be pure black. The other markings have the ordinary splashed or blotched character. The nest-complement is three or four. A set of eggs in the Smithsonian is labeled Oneida County, New York. The nest is a mere depression in the grass or moss of a boggy meadow; the down of the newly-hatched young is mottled with white, ashy, ochrey, and dark brown.

MACRORHAMPHUS GRISEUS, (Gm.) Leach.

Red-breasted Snipe; Gray Snipe.

Scolopax grisea, GM., Syst. Nat. i, 1788, 658.—LATH., Ind. Orn. ii, 1790, 724 (based on *Brown Snipe*, PENN., Arct. Zool. ii, 464, No. 369; LATH., Syn. v, 154).—TEMM., Man. ii, 1820, 679.—FLEM., Br. An 106.—JENYNS, Man. Brit. Vert. 207.—SCHL., Rev. Crit. Ois. Eur. 86.
Scolopax (Macrorhamphus) grisea, BP., Syn. 1828, 330, No. 267.—NUTT., Man. ii, 1834, 181.
Macrorhamphus griseus, LEACH, Cat. Brit. Mus. 1816, 31.—STEPH., Shaw's Gen. Zool. xii, 1824, 61.—EYT., Cat. Br. B. 40.—KEYS. & BLAS., Wirb. Eur. 75.—MACGIL., Man. Orn. ii, 100.—GRAY, Gen. of B. iii, 1849, 582.—BP., Am. Orn. iv, 1832, 51, pl. 23, fig. 3; List, 1838, 52.—GUNDL., J. f. O. iv, 1856, 350 (Cuba).—BD., B. N. A. 1858, 712.—COOP. & SUCK., N. H. Wash. Ter. 1860, 238 (May, perhaps breeding.)—SALV., Ibis, 1860, 277; 1865, 191 (Guatemala).—WHEAT., Ohio Agric. Rep. 1860, No. 204.—REINH., Ibis, iii, 1861, 11 (Greenland).—BLAS., B. Eur. ed. Newt. 1862, 18 (England; quotes YARR., ii, 621).—BOARDM., Pr. Bost. Soc. ix, 1862, 128 (Maine, summer visitant).—VERR., Pr. Ess. Inst. iii, 1862, 159 (Maine, coast in summer).—ALLEN, *ibid.* iv, 1864, 86.—McILWR., *ibid.* v, 1866, 92 (rare in spring; Hamilton, C. W.).—COUES. *ibid.* v, 1868, 293 (New England, chiefly migratory).—LAWR., Ann. Lyc. N. Y. vii, 274 (Cuba); 479 (Panama); viii, 1864, 101 (Sombrero); viii, 1866, 293.—DRESS., Ibis, 1866, 36 (Matamoras).—DALL & BANN., Tr. Chic. Acad. i, 1869, 291 (Alaska, breeding).—TURNB., B. E. Pa. 1869, 30 (April and August).—COUES, Pr. Bost. Soc. xii, 1868, 122 (South Carolina); Pr. Phila. Acad. 1861, 229 (Labrador); 1866, 97 (Arizona); 1871, 30 (North Carolina).—ALLEN, Bull. M. C. Z. iii, 1872, 181 (Utah).—TRIPPE, Pr. Bost. Soc. xv, 1872, 241 (Iowa).—MAYN., Guide, 1870, 139 (Massachusetts, migratory).—COUES,

Key, 1872, 253, fig. 164.—SNOW, B. Kans. 1873, 10 (Kansas, migratory).—PELZ.,
  Orn. Bras. 313 (Para).—SCL. & SALV., P. Z. S. 1873, 455.
Limosa grisea, SCHL., Mus. Pays-Bas, *Scolop.* p. 26.
Scolopax noveboracensis, GM., Syst. Nat. i, 1788, 658.—LATH., Ind. Orn. ii, 1790, 723 (based
  on *Red-breasted Snipe*, PENN., Arct. Zool. ii, 464, No. 368; LATH., Syn. v, 154).—
  WILS., Am. Orn. vii, 1813, 45, pl. 58, fig. 1.—SW. & RICH., F. B. A. ii, 1831, 398.—
  AUD., Orn. Biog. iv, 1838, 288, pl. 399; Syn. 1839, 249; B. Am. vi, 1843, 10, pl.
  351.—GIR., B. L. I. 1844, 263.—PUTN., Pr. Ess. Inst. i, 1856, 218 (Massachusetts).
Totanus noveboracensis, SABINE, Franklin's Journ. 687.
Limosa scolopacea, SAY, Long's Exp. Rocky Mountains, ii, 1823, 170.
Macrorhamphus scolopaceus, LAWR., Ann. Lyc. N. Y. v, 1852, 4, pl. 1; *ibid.* vii, 273 (Cuba);
  ibid. viii, 1866, 293; *ibid.* ix, 1868, 142 (Costa Rica).—BD., B. N. A. 1858, 712.—
  ELLIOT, B. N. A. pl. 40.—COUES, Ibis, 1866, 271 (California).—DALL & BANN.,
  Tr. Chic. Acad. i, 1869, 291 (Alaska, breeding).—SNOW, B. Kans. 1873, 10 (Kansas).
Scolopax longirostris, BELL, Ann. Lyc. v, 1852, 3.
Scolopax paykullii, NILSSON, Orn. Suec. ii, 106.
" *Scolopax leucophœa* et *ferrugineicollis*, VIEILL." (*Gray.*)

Hab.—The whole of North America. Greenland. Mexico. West Indies. Central
America. Much of South America. Brazil (PELZ., Orn. 313); Chili (PHIL., Cat. 36).
Breeds in high latitudes. Chiefly migratory in the United States. Winters in the
South, and beyond, as above. Of frequent casual occurrence in Europe. (See HART.,
Br. Birds, 1872, 144; fifteen occurrences in Great Britain recorded, with references.
GOULD, B. Eur. pl. 323).

  Lieutenant Warren's Expedition.—4871, Omaha City. (Omitted from Hayden's Report.)
Not obtained by Captain Raynolds' or later Expeditions.

  This Snipe is about as large as Wilson's, and the bill is exactly as in that species. It
is distinguished by the greater length of the legs, the whole naked portion being 3½ to
4 inches long, of which the bare part of the tibia is three-quarters of an inch or more;
by a web between the outer and middle toes; by 12 instead of 16 tail feathers, and
many points of coloration. Tail and its coverts, with lining of wings and axillars,
beautifully barred with black and white or tawny; shaft of first primary white. In
breeding plumage, brownish-black above, variegated with bay; reddish-brown below,
variegated with dusky; a tawny superciliary and dusky loral stripe. At other seasons,
dark gray above, the feathers with dusky centres and pale gray or whitish edges;
lower back pure white; superciliary line and spot on under eye-lid white; below, white,
the jugulum, fore-breast, and sides heavily shaded with gray, leaving chin whitish; the
flanks and crissum with wavy, dusky spots or bars. Length, 10.25 to 12.50; extent,
17.50 to 20.25; wing, 5.40 to 6.10; bill, 2.20 to 3.25; whole naked leg, 3.40 to 4.15.
Weight, 2 oz. 7 dr. to 4 oz. 4 dr., according to condition.

  The supposed species (*M. scolopaceus*), based on larger size and larger bill, is not even
entitled to rank as a variety. Almost any flock contains a per cent. of such individuals.
The difference in these respects is merely the normal individual variation. The following fresh measurements of nine individuals, shot out of the same flock, exhibit the extremes connected by imperceptible gradations, and will convince those most skeptical
of the identity of the two supposed species:

Total length	10.25	10.50	11.00	11.25	11.50	11.75	11.90	12.25	12.50
Extent of wings	17.50	18.00	18.50	19.25	19.00	19.50	19.75	20.25	19.50
Wing	5.40	5.50	5.65	5.80	5.75	5.90	6.00	6.10	5.85
Whole naked leg	3.40	3.40	3.40	3.35	4.00	4.10	4.00	4.10	4.15
Bill	2.20	2.40	2.50	2.85	2.90	2.90	2.95	3.05	3.25

  These nine specimens are graded according to length of bill, with which it will be
seen other dimensions grade approximately, though not corresponding in every instance. The length of bill varies over an inch, or about .34 per cent. of the mean
length, which is 2.77 inches; that is to say, its variation is about one-third of the
whole length. The variation is next greatest in the length of leg. There is nothing
peculiar in this variation. The bill of *Ereunetes pusillus*, of *Numenius longirostris*, and
doubtless of other waders, is quite as variable.

  This species has a very extensive distribution in the Western Hemisphere, and is one of those most frequently occurring as a straggler in
the Old World. Its regular migrations are of immense extent, and are
performed with great expedition. Passing the Middle districts in April,
the birds wend their way to the far North, where they breed, and are
again among us before the end of August. The line of migration seems
immaterial; many pass along either coast, while as great numbers fly

over the interior, along our larger water-courses. The spring passage is performed with greater celerity than the return in the autumn, when they linger leisurely over suitable feeding grounds all the way along. Many winter in the southern portions of the Union, though others reach South America, even Brazil and Chili. I have found them in November in Southern California and the Carolinas, in both of which regions some probably winter. In the spring passage many are found in nearly or quite perfect dress, like the Golden Plovers, but in the fall the gray plumage is mostly assumed before they reach the United States, the change doubtless occurring as soon as the duties of incubation are completed, though traces of the summer vesture, in a few black, bay-edged feathers of the upper parts, and a slight rufescence of the under plumage, may frequently be observed until October. The earliest period when I have seen the birds anywhere in the United States was the first week in August, in Northern Dakota, and I was led to infer, from the evident youth of the specimens then secured, that they were bred there, or not far off. We have, however, no more unquestionable instance of the breeding within our limits. Writers upon Maine birds speak of the species as a "summer visitor," and Dr. Suckley, in Washington Territory, refers to a May specimen he supposed to be breeding. So little has hitherto been made known of the breeding of the species, that I have the more pleasure in giving an account. Mr. Dall found it nesting in Alaska, and the eggs are in the Smithsonian. "I found a nest of this species," he says, "on the 3d of June, and on the 6th secured the parent bird with the eggs. The nest was a simple hollow in the ground, in a grassy hummock, in the centre of a marshy spot, with scarcely any lining whatever—nothing in the shape of a nest to bring away. The female, when startled from the nest, shuffled off with great rapidity among the grassy hummocks, making a very difficult mark to shoot at." Very little has been recorded of the breeding resorts of the *Macrorhamphus*, while the eggs are almost unknown. Several sets are in the Smithsonian Institution, collected by the indefatigable MacFarlane, at the Anderson River Fort, and on the Arctic coast, east of that river. They were taken late in June, at which season they appear to have been fresh, or nearly so. The labels state that the eggs were placed on a few dried leaves, in or around a marshy tract. One set contains four eggs, another three, another only two; but we must presume that four is the regular nest-complement. The eggs are not peculiar among their allies in any respect, and probably no description would suffice for their positive identification. The following measurements indicate the size and shape: 1.75 by 1.15 (unusually long, narrow, and pointed); 1.70 by 1.15; 1.62 by 1.12 (about an average); 1.68 by 1.10; 1.55 by 1.10 (very short). The ground-color is the same as in *Gallinago*, with all its variation, while the general character of the markings is identical, even to the occasional occurrence of sharp, black tracery over the ordinary spots and blotches. One of the eggs has the markings rather chocolate than umber-brown, and much smaller and more diffuse than they are in any of the examples of *Gallinago* which happen to be before me.

On the sand-bars, muddy flats, and marshy meadows of the North Carolina coast I found the Gray-backs very common, in flocks, all through the fall, associated with Godwits, Telltales, and various Sandpipers. But nowhere have I seen them so abundant as in Dakota during the fall passage—everywhere on the ponds, and especially in the saline pools of the alkali region along the Upper Missouri. There the birds were loitering in great flocks, wading in water so loaded with alkali that it looked sea-green and blew off a white cloud with the slightest breeze, while the edges for several yards all around were snow-white with solid efflorescence. Gazing only at the pool, one would fancy himself on an ice-bound Arctic region, while the surrounding country was desolate to match. Around such pools, the water of which was utterly undrinkable for man or beast, were numerous Ducks and waders, especially Teal, Plover, and these Snipe, swimming, wading, or dozing in troops on the banks in the yellow light of autumn, all in excellent order for the table. They were loaded with fat, though it seemed incredible that they could thrive in such bitterly nauseating and purgative waters.

The Red-breasted Snipe is a gentle and unsuspicious creature by nature, most sociably disposed to its own kind, as well as toward its relatives among the Ducks and waders. In the western regions, where they are not often molested, no birds are more confiding, though none more timid. They gather in such close flocks, moreover, that the most cruel slaughter may be effected with ease by one intent only on filling his bag. As we approach a pool we see numbers of the gentle birds wandering along the margin, or wading up to the belly in the shallow parts, probing here and there as they advance, sticking the bill perpendicularly into the mud to its full length with a quick, dexterous movement, and sometimes even submerging the whole head for a second or two. All the while they chat with each other in a low, pleasing tone, entirely oblivious of our dangerous proximity. With the explosion that too often happens, the next moment some stretch dead or dying along the strand, others limp or flutter with broken legs or wings, while the survivors, with a startled *weet*, take wing. Not, however, to fly to a place of safety; in a compact body they skim away, then circle back, approaching again the fatal spot with a low, wayward, gliding motion, and often realight in the midst of their dead or disabled companions. No birds fly more compactly, or group together more closely in alighting; it seems as if the timid creatures, aware of their defenceless condition, sought safety, or at least reassurance, in each other's company. Thus it happens that a whole flock may be secured by successive discharges, if the gunner will seize the times when they stand motionless, in mute alarm, closely huddled together. In a little while, however, if no new appearance disturbs them, they cast off fear and move about separately, resuming their busy probing for the various water-bugs, leeches, worms, and soft molluscs, which form their food, as well as the seeds of various aquatic plants. When in good order, they are excellent eating.

Being partly web-footed, this Snipe swims tolerably well for a little distance in an emergency, as when it may get for a moment beyond its depth in wading about, or when it may fall, broken-winged, on the water. On such an occasion as this last, I have seen one swim bravely for twenty or thirty yards, with a curious bobbing motion of the head and corresponding jerking of the tail, to a hiding place in the rank grass across the pool. When thus hidden they keep perfectly still, and may be picked up without resistance, except a weak flutter, and perhaps a low, pleading cry for pity on their pain and helplessness. When feeding at their ease, in consciousness of peace and security, few birds are of more pleasing appearance. Their movements are graceful and their attitudes often beautifully statuesque.

MICROPALAMA HIMANTOPUS, (Bp.) Bd.

Stilt Sandpiper.

Tringa himantopus, BP., Ann. Lyc. N. Y. ii, 1826, 157.—LESS., Man. ii, 1828, 284.—SW. &
   RICH., F. B. A. ii, 1831, 380.—BP., Am. Orn. iv, 1833, 89, pl. 25, f. 3.—AUD., Orn.
   Biog. iv, 1838, 332, pl. 334 ; Syn. 1839, 235 ; B. Am. v, 1842, 271, pl. 334.—GIR.,
   B. L. I. 1844, 232.—SCHL., M. P.-B. *Scolopaces*, 54.
Tringa (Hemipalama) himantopus, BP., Specc. Comp. 1827, 61 ; Syn. 1828, 316.—NUTT., Man.
   ii, 1834, 138.
Hemipalama himantopus, BP., List, 1838, 49.—DEKAY, N. Y. Zool. 1844, 235, pl. 86, fig. 196.
Totanus himantopus, LEMB., Av. Cuba, 1850, 95.
Micropalama himantopus, BD., B. N. A. 1858, 726.—SALV., Ibis, i, 1859, 229 (Guatemala).—
   WHEAT., Ohio Agric. Rep. 1860, No. 213 (Ohio).—COUES, Pr. Phila. Acad. 1861,
   174.—LAWR., Ann. Lyc. N. Y. viii, 1866, 294 ; viii, 1864, 101 (Sombrero).—COUES,
   Pr. Ess. Inst. v, 1868, 294.—COUES, Pr. Bost. Soc. xii, 1868, 122 (South Caro-
   lina).—SCL., P. Z. S. 1860, 290 (Ecuador).—DRESS., Ibis, 1866, 37 (Texas).—
   SCL. & SALV., P. Z. S. 1866, 199 (Peru).—TURNB., B. E. Pa. 1869, 31 (New Jer-
   sey ; May and Aug.).—ALLEN, Am. Nat. iii, 1870, 639 (Massachusetts and New
   Hampshire).—STEV., U. S. Geol. Surv. Ter. 1870, 466 (Fort Bridger).—MAYN.,
   Guide, 1870, 140 (New Hampshire).—BREWST., Am. Nat. vi, 1872, 307 (Massa-
   chusetts and New Hampshire).—COUES, Key, 1872, 253.—SCL. & SALV., P. Z.
   S. 1873, 309 (Peru).—RIDGW., Ann. Lyc. N. Y. x, 1874, 383 (Illinois).
Ereunetes himantopus, SUND., Ofv. Kongl. Vet. Ak. Forh. 1869, 587, 602 (St. Bartholo-
   mew and Porto Rico).
Micropelama himantopus, GRAY, Hand-list, iii, 1871, 48, No. 10298.
Tringa multifasciata, LICHT.   (*Gray.*)
Hemipalama multistriata, GRAY, G. of B. iii, 1849, 578, pl. 156, f. 2.—PELZ., O. Bras. iii, 311.
Tringa douglasii, SW. & RICH., F. B. A. ii, 1831, 379, pl. 66.
Eringa (Hemipalama) douglasii, NUTT., Man. ii, 1834, 141.
Tringa (Hemipalama) auduboni, NUTT., Man. ii, 1834, 140.

Hab.—North America generally. Not observed west of the Rocky Mountains. Rare
in the United States. West Indies, Central America, and most of South America.
Not obtained by Captain Raynolds' or Lieutenant Warren's Expedition.

Later Expeditions.—60790, Fort Bridger, Wyoming (*Stevenson*).

This is a very remarkable Sandpiper, connecting this group with the true Snipe by
means of *Macrorhamphus*, with which its relationships are very close. Its pattern of
coloration and changes of plumage are much as in *M. griseus*. The bill is quite snipe-
like, though shorter ; the legs are very long, relatively exceeding those of *Macrorhamphus*, and there are two basal webs to the toes, as in *Ereunetes*. Full descriptions appear
in my Monograph above cited, and in the Key.

I have never yet seen the Stilt Sandpiper alive, and it appears to be
rather rare in the United States, through which it passes during the
migration, some probably wintering toward the South. It occurs both
along the coast and in the interior. Its range is probably much the same
as that of *Macrorhamphus griseus ;* like this species, it is extensively dispersed over the West Indies, in Central and part of South America
during the winter. It is only known to breed in high latitudes, beyond
our border. Several collectors have lately taken it during the migration along the New England coast, where, however, like *Tringa bairdii*,
it appears to be of rare occurrence, as elsewhere on the Atlantic coast.
I placed it in my South Carolina list on Prof. Gibbes' authority. Mr.
Stevenson procured it at Fort Bridger. It undoubtedly migrates generally through the Missouri region.

Two sets of eggs, purporting to be of this species, are in the Smithsonian ; but it does not appear that the parent was secured, or, at least,
received, and I question the identification, believing the eggs to be
those of *Tryngites rufescens*. At any rate, if they are not the latter,
they are absolutely identical with them in every respect, as fully described further on.

EREUNETES PUSILLUS, (Linn.) Cass.

Semipalmated Sandpiper.

Tringa pusilla, LINN., Syst. Nat. i, 1766, 252 (based on *Tringa cinclus dominicensis minor*,
   BRISS., v, 222, pl. 25, f. 2.   Not of *Meyer*, nor of *Bechstein*, nor of *Wilson*).—
   GM., Syst. Nat. i, 1788, 681.—LATH., Ind. Orn. ii, 1790, 737.—(?) VIEILL., Nouv.
   Dict. d'Hist. Nat. xxxiv, 1819, 452.—SCHL., M. P.-B. *Scolopaces*, 55.
Ereunetes pusillus, CASS., Pr. Phila. Acad. xiii, 1860, 195 (Carthagena).—COUES, *ibid.*
   1861, 177, 233.—COUES & PRENT., Smiths. Rep. 1861, 416.—BOARDM., Pr. Bost.
   Soc. ix, 1862, 129.—VERR., Pr. Ess. Inst. iii, 1862, 159.—ALLEN, *ibid.* iv, 1864,
   87.—MCILWR., *ibid.* v, 1866, 93.—COUES, *ibid.* v, 1868, 294.—LAWR., Ann. Lyc.
   N. Y. viii, 1864, 101 (Sombrero) ; viii, 1866, 294.—DALL & BANN., Tr. Chic.
   Acad. i, 1869, 292.—SUND., Ofv. Vet. Ak. 1869, 587, 602 (St. Bartholomew
   and Porto Rico).—MAYN., Guide, 1870, 140.—COUES, Pr. Phila. Acad. 1866, 97;
   1871, 31.—ALLEN, Mem. Bost. Soc. i, 1868, 501.—ALLEN, Bull. M. C. Z. ii, 1871,
   355 ; iii, 1872, 182.—COUES, Key, 1872, 254, fig. 165.—RIDGW., Ann. Lyc. N. Y.
   x, 1874, 384.
Ereunetes petrificatus, ILL., Prod. 1811, 262 (Bahia).—CASS., Baird's B. N. A. 1858, 724.—
   WHEAT., Ohio Agric. Rep. 1860, No. 212.—HAYD., Rep. 1862, 174.—TURNB., B.
   E. Pa. 1869, 31.—TRIPPE, Pr. Bost. Soc. xv, 1872, 241.—SNOW, B. Kans. 1873, 10.
Tringa semipalmata, WILS., Am. Orn. vii, 1813, 131, pl. 63, f. 3 ; Ord's ed. iii, 1829, 132;
   Brewer's ed. 1840, 542, fig. 225 ; Syn. 725.—VIEILL., Nouv. Dict. d'Hist. Nat.
   xxxiv, 1819, 462.—SW. & RICH., F. B. A. ii, 1831, 381.—AUD., Orn. Biog. v, 1839,
   iii, pl. 408 ; Syn. 1839, 236 ; B. Am. v, 1842, 277, pl. 336.—GIR., B. L. I, 1844,
   239.—PUTN., Pr. Ess. Inst. i, 1856, 217.—NEWB., P. R. R. Rep. vi, 1857, 100.—
   FINSCH, Abh. Nat. iii, 1872, 65.
Tringa (Hemipalama) semipalmata, BP., Obs. Wils. 1825, No. 212 ; Specc. Comp. 1827, 62.
Hemipalama semipalmata, LEMB., Av. Cuba, 1850, 96.
Tringa (Heteropoda) semipalmata, NUTT., Man. ii, 1834, 136.
Heteropoda semipalmata, BP., List, 1838, 49.—DEKAY, N. Y. Zool. 1844, 236, pl. 86, fig.
   195.—GRAY, Gen. of B. iii, 1849, 580, pl. 156, f. 1.
Ereunetes semipalmata, CAB., Schomb. Reise, iii, 758; J. f. O. 1856, 419.—BP., Comptes
   Rendus, xliii, 1856, p. —.
Tringa brevirostris, SPIX, Av. Bras. ii, 1825, 76, pl. 93.
Pelidna brissoni, LESS., Man. ii, 1828, 277 (" *T. pusilla* L.").
Heteropoda mauri, BP., List, 1838, 49.—GUNDL., J. f. O. 1856, 419 (Cuba).
Hemipalama minor, LEMB., Av. Cuba, 1850, 97.
Ereunetes occidentalis, LAWR., Pr. Phila. Acad. 1864, 107 (var. ? Pacific coast).

   Quotations additional to the above are : SALV., Ibis, i, 1859, 229 (Guatemala); NEWT.,
ibid. 258 (Santa Cruz) ; BRY., Pr. Bost. Soc. vii, 1859, p. — (Bahamas) ; SCL. & SALV.,
P. Z. S. 1867, 592 (Amazon); PELZ., Orn. Bras. 311 (Brazil ; March and April).

   Hab.—The whole of North and Central, and most of South America. West Indies.
   Lieutenant Warren's Expedition.—4870, Bijoux Hills ; 9045, 9047, 9048, Loup Fork.
   Not procured by either of the later Expeditions. (The bird so quoted by *Stevenson*,
p. 466, is *Tringa minutilla*.)

   This abundant and well-known little bird occurs throughout the
Missouri region, in suitable places, during the migration, as elsewhere
in the United States.
   A very large series of the eggs of *Ereunetes* shows the variations
probably always observable when great numbers of any limicoline
wader's eggs are examined. Some of them are nearly like the Buff-
breasted Sandpiper's eggs described beyond, and such appears to be the
normal pattern. Others, however, are quite different. One variation
affects the ground-color, which, instead of being clay-colored (very pale
grayish or greenish-drab), is decidedly olivaceous; and in these eggs
the markings are correspondingly heavy, rather umber-brown than
chocolate. In another decided variety the markings, instead of being
bold blotching, massed at the large end, are exceedingly fine dotting,
uniform over the whole egg, drawn like a veil, as it were, over the
ground, giving the predominant complexion to the egg. The following
are several measurements : 1.22 by 0.84; 1.24 by 0.83; 1.20 by 0.85.
The sets, complete, contain three or four eggs; those with one or two

31

are presumably incomplete. They were mostly collected late in June
and early in July, by Mr. MacFarlane, in the Anderson River region,
the Barren Grounds, and the Arctic coast, at Franklin Bay. Others
are from Hudson's Bay. According to the labels, the nests are, as
usual, a depression of the ground, lined with a few dried grasses or
leaves, and are generally situate in or near marshy tracts.

TRINGA MINUTILLA, Vieill.

Least Sandpiper.

Tringa minutilla, VIEILL., Nouv. Dict. d'Hist. Nat. xxxiv, 1819, 452.—GRAY, Gen. of B.
    iii, 1849, 579.—SCHL., Mus. Pays-Bas, *Scolopaces*, p. 48.—SHARPE & DRESSER,
    B. Eur. pt. xii, Aug. 1872.—COUES, Key, 1872, 254.—FINSCH, Abh. Nat. iii, 1872,
    65.—SCL. & SALV., P. Z. S. 1873, 456 (Peru).
Actodromus minutilla, BP., Comptes Rendus, 1856.
Actodromas minutilla, COUES, Pr. Phila. Acad. 1861, 191, 230.—COUES, Pr. Phila. Acad.
    1866, 97 ; *ibid*. 1871, 30.—COUES, Ibis, 1866, 269.—COUES, Pr. Bost. Soc. xii,
    1868, 122.—COUES, Pr. Ess. Inst. v, 1868, 294.—DRESS., Ibis, 1866, 37 (Texas).—
    COUES & PRENT., Smiths. Rep. 1861, 415.—LAWR., Ann. Lyc. viii, 1866, 294.—
    ALLEN, Pr. Ess. Inst. iv, 1864, 77.—ALLEN, Bull. M. C. Z. ii, 1871, 356 ; iii, 1872,
    182.—ALLEN, Mem. Bost. Soc. i, 1868, 501.—VERR., Pr. Ess. Inst. iii, 1862, 159.—
    BOARDM., Pr. Bost. Soc. ix, 1862, 128.—VERR., *ibid*. 138.—NEWT., P. Z. S. 1867,
    165, pl. 15, f. 4 (egg).—DALL & BANN., Tr. Chic. Acad. i, 1869, 292 (Alaska).—
    MAYN., Guide, 1870, 140.—DALL, Pr. Cal. Acad. Feb. 1873 (Aleutian Islands).—
    RIDGW., Ann. Lyc. N. Y. x, 1874, 384.
Tringa pusilla, WILS., Am. Orn. v, 1813, 32, pl. 37, f. 4 (not of *Linnœus* and European
    writers).—ORD, ed. Wils. iii, 1829, 134.—BREW., ed. Wils. 1840, 347, fig. 161.—
    BP., Comp. Specc. 1827, 237 ; Syn. 1828, 319.—SW. & RICH., F. B. A. ii, 1831,
    386.—AUD., Orn. Biog. iv, 1838, 180, pl. 320 ; Syn. 1839, 237 ; B. Am. v, 1842,
    280, pl. 337.—GIR., B. L. I. 1844, 240.—WOODH., Sitgr. Rep. 1853, 100.—PUTN.,
    Pr. Ess. Inst. i, 1856, 217.—HOY, Smiths. Rep. 1864, 438.—HART., Br. Birds,
    1872, 143 (European).
Pelidna pusilla, BP., List, 1838, 50.—GOSSE, B. Jam. 1847, 348.
Tringa wilsoni, NUTT., Man. ii, 1834, 121.—BD., B. N. A. 1858, 721.—COOP. & SUCK., N.
    H. Wash. Ter. 1860, 240.—CASS., Pr. Phila. Acad. xiii, 1860, 196 (Carthagena).—
    WHEAT., Ohio Agric. Rep. 1860, No. 209.—TURNB., B. E. Pa. 1869, 31.—TRIPPE,
    Pr. Bost. Soc. xv, 1872, 241.
Actodromus wilsoni, BP., Comptes Rendus, 1856.
(?)*Tringa campestris*, LICHT., Verz. Doubl. 1823, 74 (may be *bairdii* or *bonapartii*).
Tringa nana, LICHT., Nomen. Av. 1854, 92.
Tringa georgica, LICHT. (*Gray*.)
    Extralimital quotations.—SCL., P. Z. S. 1856, 311 (Cordova) ; SCL., Ibis, 1859, 229
(Guatemala) ; NEWT., *ibid*. 258 (Santa Cruz) ; CAB., J. f. O. iv, 422 (Cuba) ; BRY., Pr.
Bost. Soc. vii, 1859 (Bahamas) ; SCL., P. Z. S. 1860, 263 (Orizaba) ; 1861, 80 (Jamaica) ;
LAWR., Ann. Lyc. N. Y. 1861, 334 (Panama) ; DARW., Voy. Beagle, Birds, 131 (Gala-
pagos) ; SCL., P. Z. S. 1864, 178 (Mexico) ; SCL. & SALV., P. Z. S. 1867, 591 (Amazon) ;
PELZ., Orn. 311 (Brazil).

Hab.—North, Central and South America, and West Indies. Accidental in Europe
(Cornwall, RODD, Zool. 1854, 4297 ; Devon, ID., *ibid*. 1869, 1920 ; *fide* HARTING).
    Lieutenant Warren's Expedition.—9046, Loup Fork.
    Later Expeditions.—60792, North Platte.
    Not obtained by Captain Raynolds' Expedition.

Abundant in the Missouri region during the migrations, as everywhere else, in suitable places, throughout the United States. Finding
it in July, in the Red River region, I am led to believe it may sometimes nest so far south, but of this I am not certain.

This little bird is one of several species that collectively inhabit all
the world, and resemble each other so closely that naturalists have
difficulty in telling them apart. Perhaps they all sprung from the pair
that Noah kept, but this is doubtful. Difference of species aside, I
should be afraid to say how many millions of the little creatures run
about the sand and mud of this world to-day ; and in thinking of any
single one of them, a grain of sand comes to mind. We remember the

pretty fable of the drop of water that, complaining to the gods of its utter uselessness and insignificance, evaporated into mist, and, distilled as a dew-drop, fell into the open shell of an oyster, to become a pearl that flashed in the coronet of kings. Such exaltation of the little bird as this may never be; it would be a difficult task, indeed, to select any one of the species and distinguish it from, still less above, the others. Yet who knows just how much even a single one of the birds may feel?

Fogs hang low and heavy over rock-girdled Labrador. Angry waves, palled with rage, exhaust themselves to encroach upon the stern shores, and baffled, sink back howling into the depths. Winds shriek as they course from crag to crag in mad career, till the humble mosses that clothe the rocks crouch lower still in fear. Overhead the Sea Gulls scream as they winnow, and the Murres, all silent, ply eager oars to escape the blast. What is here to entice the steps of the delicate birds? Yet they have come, urged by resistless impulse, and have made a nest on the ground in some half-sheltered nook. The material was ready at hand, in the mossy covering of the earth, and little care or thought was needed to fashion a little bunch into a little home. Four eggs are laid (they are buffy-yellow, thickly spotted over with brown and drab), with the points together, that they may take up less room and be more warmly covered; there is need of this, such large eggs belonging to so small a bird. As we draw near the mother sees us, and nestles closer still over her treasures, quite hiding them in the covering of her breast, and watches us with timid eyes, all anxiety for the safety of what is dearer to her than her own life. Her mate stands motionless, but not unmoved, hard by, not venturing even to chirp the note of encouragement and sympathy she loves to hear. Alas! hope fades and dies out, leaving only fear; there is no further concealment—we are almost upon the nest—almost trodden upon she springs up with a piteous cry and flies a little distance, realighting, almost beside herself with grief; for she knows only too well what is to be feared at such a time. If there were hope for her that her nest were undiscovered, she might dissimulate, and try to entice us away by those touching deceits that maternal love inspires. But we are actually bending over her treasures, and deception would be in vain; her grief is too great to be witnessed unmoved, still less portrayed; nor can we, deaf to her beseeching, change it into despair. We have seen and admired the home—there is no excuse for making it desolate; we have not so much as touched one of the precious eggs, and will leave them to her renewed and patient care.

This is one verse in the little Sand-bird's life, with the wolf at the door of what would seem the perfect security of an humble home. Now later in the season, when the young birds are grown strong of wing, family joins family, and the gathering goes to the sea-beach. Stretches of sand, or pebbly shingle, or weed-loaded rocks, or muddy flats bestrewn with wrack, invite, and are visited in turn; and each yields abundant sustenance. The unsuspecting birds ramble and play heedlessly in the very front of man, unmindful of, because unknowing, danger; they have a sad lesson to learn the coming winter, when they are tormented without stint, and a part of their number slaughtered in more civilized countries for mere sport, or for the morsel of food their bodies may afford. Blasts fiercer than they ever knew before come out of the north; autumn is upon them, and they must not wait. Flocks rise on wing, and it is not long before the beaches and the marshes of the States are thronged.

But except from ourselves, the birds have little to fear. Their enemies are few, they lead a merry, contented life, and it is no wonder they increase and multiply till they become like armies as to numbers. Besides being gregarious among themselves, they are sociable with other birds, and there is hardly a gathering of waders of any sort any where that the Peep family is not represented in. Gadabouts, perhaps, they are, but no scandal mongers; ubiquitous, turning up everywhere when least expected, but never looked ill upon; bustling little busy bodies, but minding their own business strictly. Besides environing a continent on three sides at least (and perhaps on the Arctic shores as well), not a river or lake, not a creek or pond, the banks of which are not populated at one season or another; the track of their tiny feet, imprinted on the sand of the sea-shore and the soil of the inland water, shows where they have gone. Their numbers swell in no small degree the great tide of birds that ceaselessly ebbs and flows once a year in the direction of the polar star; they taken away, a feature of the land would be lost. Altogether, they become imposing, though singly insignificant. If we do not know just what part is given out to them in the grand play of Nature, at least we may be assured they have a part that is faithfully and well performed.

TRINGA BAIRDII, Coues.

Baird's Sandpiper.

(?) *Tringa melanotos*, VIEILL. (based on *Chorlito lomo negro* of AZARA.)
(?) *Tringa pectoralis*, CASS., Gilliss' Exp. ii, 1855, 195.
Tringa schinzii, WOODH., Sitgr. Rep. 1853, 100 (excl. syn.; *nec Brehm*).
Tringa bonapartii, CASS., Baird's B. N. A. 1858, 722 (*partim; nec Schlegel*).—HAYD., Rep. 1862, 174 (error).—ELLIOT, Introd. B. N. A. (*partim*).
Tringa maculata, SCHL., M. P.-B. *Scolopaces*, 1864, 39 (*partim*).
Actodromas bairdii, COUES, Pr. Phila. Acad. 1861, 194; 1866, 97.—SCL., P. Z. S. 1862, 369 (Mexico).—DALL & BANN., Tr. Chic. Acad. i, 1869, 292 (Alaska).—STEV., U. S. Geol. Surv. Ter. 1870, 466 (Wyoming).—ALLEN, Bull. M. C. Z. iii, 1872, 182 (Colorado).—BREWST., Am. Nat. vi, 1872, 306 (Boston, Mass.).—SNOW, B. Kans. 1873, 10.
Tringa bairdii, SCL., P. Z. S. 1867, 332 (Chili).—SCL. & SALV., *ibid.* 1868, 144 (Conchitas).— HART., Ibis, 1870, 152 (Panama, New Granada, and Peru).—NEWT., P. Z. S. 1871, 577 (egg).—ANDER., B. Damaraland, 1872, 308 (Walwich Bay, South Africa).—MERR., U. S. Geol. Surv. Ter. 1872, 700 (Wyoming).—COUES, Key, 1872, 255.—SCL. & SALV., P. Z. S. 1873, 455.—RIDGW., Ann. Lyc. x, 1874, 384 (Illinois).
Tringa (Heteropygia) bairdii, GRAY, Hand-list, iii, 1871, 49, No. 10308.

Hab.—North America, chiefly in the Interior. Rare on the Atlantic coast. Mexico, Central and South America. Accidental in Africa.
Lieutenant Warren's Expedition.—4869, Omaha City; 5442, Yellowstone River; 5443, Cedar Creek.
Later Expeditions.—54327, 61154, Wyoming; 60791, 60793-5, North Platte and Little Sandy; 62361, Lower Geyser Basin, Wyoming.
Not obtained by Captain Raynolds' Expedition.

Erroneously given in Dr. Hayden's Report as "*Tringa bonapartii*," upon Mr. Cassin's identification, who, in 1858, gave these three specimens as *bonapartii*, together with two others, Nos. 8800, 8769, of the Smithsonian Register, taken by Dr. Cooper, while *en route* from Fort Kearney to Fort Laramie. Dr. Woodhouse's specimens, from Zuñi, New Mexico, as above cited, are this species, though given as "*T. schinzii*" in his report.
It is not a little singular that this perfectly distinct species should ever have been confounded with *T. fuscicollis*, to which it bears only a superficial resemblance. It is really much nearer both *T. maculata* and *T. minutilla*, between which it stands exactly intermediate, though readily distinguished from either. Of its characters I have nothing to add to the perfectly accurate account given in my works above quoted, and here partly reproduced in substance. As Dr. Sclater has shown, since the species has been ascertained to inhabit Central and South as well as North America, the name *bairdii* is quite probably anticipated by at least one other; but this point has not been determined.

Adult ♂.—Bill wholly black, small and slender, slightly shorter than the head, just as long as the tarsus or as the middle toe and claw, slightly expanded or lancet-shaped at the end, the point acute; grooves long, narrow, deep; feathers on side of lower mandible evidently reaching further than those on upper. Upper parts brownish-black (deepest on the rump and middle upper tail-coverts, and lightest on the neck behind), each feather bordered and tipped with pale brownish-yellow, the tipping of the scapulars broadest and nearly white, their margining broad and brightest in tint, making several deep scollops toward the shafts of the feathers. Only the outer series of upper tail-coverts on each side varied with whitish. Middle tail-feathers brownish-black, the others plain gray, with paler margins. Jugulum tinged with light, dull yellowish-brown, spotted and streaked with illy-defined blackish markings, as are also the sides under the wings. Throat and the other under parts white, unmarked. Feet black, like the bill. Length, 7¼: extent, 15¼; wing, 4⁹⁄₁₀; bill, 0.85; tarsus, and middle toe and claw, the same. The ♀ is entirely similar, but slightly larger. The *young* have the upper parts wholly light brownish-ash, darker on the rump, and all the feathers with a dark field, and pale or whitish edging; waves of brownish-black on the scapulars. Jugulum and breast suffused with dull, light reddish-brown; the spotting small, sparse, and very indistinct.

T. fuscicollis is a little larger, on an average; the bill noticeably stouter, flesh-colored at base below; the feathers on the sides of the lower mandible do not extend noticeably beyond those on the upper; the scapular edging is bright chestnut; the jugulum is white, or barely perceptibly ashy with numerous narrow, distinct streaks; and the upper tail-coverts are white. *T. bairdii* is exactly intermediate in size between *T. maculata* and *T. minutilla*, and is almost identical with the latter in pattern of coloration, but the markings upon the breast are not thick and heavy, and the edgings of the scapulars not bright chestnut. The species scarcely requires comparison with *maculata;* the latter is much larger; it differs in the colors and proportions of the bill; the pattern (plain, unscolloped) of coloration of the scapular edgings; the abrupt transition from the color of the crown to that of the hind neck; the heavy pectoral markings, &c. *T. bairdii*, like all its allies, is subject to a partially melanotic condition of plumage.

Dr. Hayden's specimens, above enumerated, were the first I saw of this species; they were in autumnal or otherwise imperfect plumage, as were also Dr. Woodhouse's. Some time afterward a fine and extensive suite, in breeding plumage, was procured in Arctic America, by Mr. Kennicott and Mr. Ross, in the vicinity of Fort Resolution, Great Slave Lake. It has since been found in various localities in Alaska, where it also breeds; and is very generally dispersed through the interior of North America, east of the Rocky Mountains. Until recently, we had no evidence of its occurrence on the Atlantic coast, where it was lately taken by Mr. Henshaw, the specimen being forwarded to me for identification. The extralimital quotations are numerous and varied, demonstrating a range in general coincident with that of other small waders of this country. Its line of migration seems to be chiefly in the interior, between the Rocky Mountains and the Pacific. During the passage it is generally distributed over the Missouri region, and is rather common. It enters the United States as early as August, spreading during the following month, when I have found it at various points in Dakota, in small flocks, associating with several other small species, such as the Red-breasted Snipe and Wilson's Phalarope, along the sandy margins of small streams, and around muddy sloughs. It has a soft, mellow pipe, like others of its genus, and appeared very innocent and confiding. In its general habits and manners I noticed nothing peculiar.

Mr. Trippe informs me that during the latter part of August he found large flocks of this species near the summit of Mount Evans, Colorado, between 13,000 and 14,000 feet above sea-level, feeding upon grasshoppers.

The egg of this species was first described by Professor Newton from a defective specimen, not permitting a complete account. The Smithsonian has several full sets, of three or four eggs each, all taken by Mr. MacFarlane, on the barren grounds of the Anderson River region, and on the Arctic coast, east of that river. They were collected in 1865, late in June, and were the first, if not the only, specimens which have reached naturalists. The labels give no items of the nidification, but this is undoubtedly not peculiar in any respect. The shape and coloration conform to the usual styles of the restricted group *Actodromas*. The ground of the egg of *bairdii* is clay-colored, tending in some cases to gray, in others to buffy. The spotting is of rich umber and chocolate browns of varying shade or depth, with the usual paler shell-markings. In most instances the markings are fine and innumerable, of indefinite small size and shape, and though thickest and largest at the greater end, only occasionally mass there into great blotches. Some specimens show a little black tracery over all at the large end. Several specimens measure as follows : 1.30 by 0.90 inches ; 1.35 by 0.94 ; 1.28 by 0.92. Some were taken early in July, at which date they contained advanced embryos.

TRINGA MACULATA, Vieill.

Pectoral Sandpiper; Grass Snipe; Jack Snipe.

Tringa maculata, VIEILL., N. D. xxxiv, 1819, 465.—WHEAT., Ohio Agric. Rep. 1860, No. 208.—SCHLEG., M. P.-B. *Scolopaces*, 39.—BLAS., List B. Eur. 1862, 18.—TURNB., B. E. Pa. 1869, 31.—TRIPPE, Pr. Bost. Soc. 1872, 241.—DRESS., Ibis, 1866, 36.— SNOW, B. Kans. 1873, 10.—SUND., Ofv. Vet. Ak. 1869, 587 (St. Bartholomew).— HART., Br. Birds, 1872, 140.—COUES, Key, 1872, 255.—SCL. & SALV., P. Z. S. 1873, 455.
Tringa (Actodromas) maculata, CASS., B. N. A. 720.—RIDGW., Ann. Lyc. N. Y. x, 1874, 384.
Tringa (Limnocinclus) maculata, GRAY, Hand-list, iii, 1871, 49, No. 10303.
Pelidna maculata, PARZ., Cat. Ois. Eur. 1856, 15.
Actodromas maculata, COUES, Pr. Phila. Acad. 1861, 197 and 230.—COUES & PRENT., Smiths. Rep. 1861, 415.—COUES, Pr. Ess. Inst. v, 1868, 294.—MCILWR., *ibid.* 1866, 93.—ALLEN, Pr. Ess. Inst. iv, 1864, 77.—VERR., *ibid.* iii, 1862, 153.—BOARDM., Pr. Bost. Soc. ix, 1862, 128.—LAWR., Ann Lyc. N. Y. viii, 1866, 294.—COOP., Pr. Cal. Acad. 1868.—ALLEN, Mem. Bost. Soc. i. 1868, 501.—COUES, Pr. Bost. Soc. xii, 1868, 122.—DALL & BANN., Tr. Chic. Acad. i, 1869, 292.—MAYN., Guide, 1870, 140.—ALLEN, Bull. M. C. Z. iii, 1872, 182.
Pelidna pectoralis, BP., Comp. List, 1838, 50 ; Cat. Meth. 1842, 60.—(?) CASS., U. S. Ast. Exp. ii, 1855, 195 (may be *bairdii*).
Tringa pectoralis, SAY, Long's Exp. R. Mts. i, 1823, 171.—BP., Am. Orn. iv, 1833, 43, pl. 23 ; Syn. 1828, 318.—NUTT., Man. ii, 1834, 111.—JEN., Man. 1835, 210.—YARR., Br. Birds, ii, 654 ; iii, 82.—EYT., Cat. Br. Birds, 41.—KEYS. & BLAS., Wirb. Eur. 77.—AUD., Orn. Biog. iii, 1835, 601 ; v, 1839, 582 ; pl. 294 ; Syn. 1839, 232 ; B. Am. v, 1842, 259, pl. 329.—MACGIL., Man. Br. Birds, ii, 1842, 69.—TEMM., Man. iv, 1840, 397.—GIR., B. L. I. 1844, 233.—DeKAY, N. Y. Zool, 1844. 242, pl. 85, f. 193.—SCHL., Rev. Crit. Ois. Eur. 1844, 89.—GRAY, Gen. of B. iii, 1849, 579.— LEMBEYE, Av. Cuba, 1850, 98.—WOODH., Sitgr. Rep. 1853, 100.—MEYER, Br. Birds, v, 1857, 89.—PUTN., Pr. Ess. Inst. i, 1856, 216.—HOY, Smiths. Rep. 1864, 438.—REINH., Ibis, iii, 1859, 10 (Greenland).—SUND., Ofv. Vet. Ak. 1869, 602 (Porto Rico).
Tringa dominicensis, DEGL., Orn. Eur. ii, 1849, 232.
(?) "*Tringa campestris*, LICHT., Verz. 1823, 74." (*Gray*.)

Among the extralimital quotations are : SCL., P. Z. S. 1856, 310 (Cordova); *ibid.* 1858, 566 (Ecuador) ; *ibid.* 1866, 189 (Peru); *ibid.* 1867, 754 (Huallajo); *ibid.* 1869, 598 (Peru).— SCL., Ibis, i, 229 (Guatemala).—NEWT., Ibis, i, 258 (Santa Cruz).—LAWR., Pr. Bost. Soc. 1867, 69 (Bahamas).—LAWR., Ann. Lyc. N. Y. viii, 63 (Panama).—CAB., J. f. O. iv, 421 (Cuba).—PELZ., Orn. Bras. 311 (Brazil).—GOULD, B. Eur. pl. 327.—HARTING gives sixteen British instances, with references.

Hab.—North, Central, and South America. West Indies. Greenland. Europe. Not obtained by any of the Expeditions.

Under the various names above given, and also under that of "Meadow Snipe," the Pectoral Sandpiper is well known to sportsmen and others, and is frequently sought after, as its somewhat game-like habits of lying to a dog and flushing correctly from the grass, like a true Snipe, render it an attractive object of pursuit; beside which, in the fall it becomes very fat, and it is then excellent eating. Unlike most Sandpipers, it does not flock, at least to any extent, being oftenest found scattered singly or in pairs. In the United States it is chiefly, if not wholly, a bird of passage; for, though some may winter along our southern border and others breed along the northern tier of States, such probabilities require to be confirmed. As may be gathered from the above quotations, its winter range is very extensive, yet some individuals may be found in the Middle States as late as November. I found it in July along the forty-ninth parallel, where it probably breeds, though I did not ascertain the fact. It occurred sparingly about pools on Turtle Mountain, in company with *T. minutilla*. It is a very abundant bird in summer in Labrador, where it frequents low, muddy flats, laid bare by the tide, and the salt-marshes adjoining. When they arise from the grass to alight again at a little distance, they fly in silence or with a single *tweet*, holding the wings deeply incurved; but when suddenly startled and much alarmed, they spring quickly, with loud, repeated cries, and make off in a zigzag, much like the common Snipe. Sometimes, gaining a considerable elevation, they circle for several minutes in silence overhead, flying with great velocity, perhaps to pitch down again nearly perpendicularly to the same spot they sprang from. The southward migration begins in August, and is usually completed by the following month.

TRINGA FUSCICOLLIS, Vieill.

Bonaparte's Sandpiper; White-rumped Sandpiper.

Tringa fuscicollis, VIEILL., Nouv. Dict. d'Hist. Nat. xxxiv, 1819, 461 (based on *Chorlito pestorejo pardo*, AZARA, Apunt. iii, 1785, 322 (Paraguay).—DRESS., B. Eur. pt. xx, Aug. 1873 (Europe).—(?) TSCHUDI, Fn. Peru. 1844, 51 (Peru; uncertain; quotes *minutilla*, VIEILL., and *campestris*, LICHT.).
Tringa cinclus, var., SAY, Long's Exp. R. Mts. i, 1823, 172.
Tringa schinzii, BP., Syn. 1828, 249.—BP., Am. Orn. iv, 1833, 69, pl. 24, f. 2.—NUTT., Man. ii, 1834, 109.—SW. & RICH., F. B. A. ii, 1831, 384.—AUD., Orn. Biog. iii, 1833, 529, pl. 278.—AUD., Syn. 1839, 236.—AUD., B. Am. v, 1842, 275, pl. 335.—(?) NAUM., Vög. Deutsch. vii, 1834, 453.—EYT., Ann. Mag. N. H. ii, 53.—MACGIL., Man. Orn. ii, 72.—GRAY, Gen. of B. iii, 579.—GIR., B. L. I. 1844, 241.—DEKAY., Zool. N. Y. 1844, 241, pl. 84, f. 191.—PUTN., Pr. Ess. Inst. i, 1856, 217.—REINH., Ibis, iii, 1861, 10 (*Greenland*). (Not of *Brehm*.)
Pelidna schinzii, BP., List, 1838, 50.—BP., Cat. Met. 1842, 60.
Tringa bonapartii, SCHL., Rev. Crit. Ois. Eur. 1844, 89.—SCHL., M. P.-B. *Scolopaces*, 42.— CASS., B. N. A. 1858, 722, *partim* (of the specimens there enumerated only one, No. 3451, is of this species; the others belong to *T. bairdii*). (Not of HAYD., Rep. 1862, which actually refers to *T. bairdii*.)—WHEAT., Ohio Agric. Rep. 1860.— GRAY, List Br. Birds, 1863, 167.—TURNB., B. E. Pa. 1869, 31.—COUES, Key, 1872, 255.—SCL. & SALV., P. Z. S. 1872, 455 (Panama to Falkland).—RIDGW., Ann. Lyc. N. Y. x, 1874, 384.
Actodromas (Heteropygia) bonapartii, COUES, Pr. Phil. Acad. 1861, 199; *ibid*. 1861, 232.
Tringa (Heteropygia) bonapartei, GRAY, Hand-list, iii, 1871, 49, No. 10307.
Actodromas bonapartii, COUES, Pr. Phila. Acad. 1871, 30.—COUES, Pr. Bost. Soc. xii, 1868, 162.—COUES, Ibis, Apr. 1865, p. —.—COUES, Am. Nat. v, 1871, 197.—COUES, Pr. Ess. Inst. v, 1868, 294.—ALLEN, Bull. M. C. Z. ii, 1871, 356.—ALLEN, Pr. Ess. Inst. iv, 1864, 87.—LAWR., Ann. Lyc. viii, 1866, 294.—BOARDM., Pr. Bost. Soc. ix, 1862, 129.—VERR., *ibid*. 139; Pr. Ess. Inst. iii, 1862, 159.—MAYN., Guide, 1870, 140.
Tringa melanotus, BLAS., List B. Eur. 1862, 19 (accidental in Europe). (*Nec Vieill*.)
Actodromus melanotos, BP., R. and M. Z. ix, 1857, 59 (Europe).
Pelidna melanotos, DEGLAND-GERBE, Ois. Eur. ii, 202.—BP. Comp. Rend. 1856, 596.
Tringa dorsalis, LICHT., Nomenc. Av. 1854, 92 (*fide Dresser*).

Hab.—North America, east of the Rocky Mountains. Not observed in Alaska. Breeds in the far North. Migratory through the United States, in the Eastern Province. Winters in the Southern States. Greenland. West Indies (Cuba, LEMBEYE, Aves, 1850, 98; CAB., J. f. O. iv, 421; Jamaica, SCL., P. Z. S. 1861, 80). Central and South America (Amazon, SCL. & SALV., P. Z. S. 1867, 591; Falklands, *ibid*. 1860, 387; Buenos Ayres, *ibid.* 1868, 144; Brazil, PELZ., 311).   Europe, rarely (GOULD, B. E. pl. 330; SCHL., *l. c.*; DEGL., Orn. Eur. ii, 1849, 231; MEYER., Brit. B. v, 1857, 96; HART., Man. Brit. B. 1872, 142; this author enumerates fourteen British instances, with the references). Not obtained by either Expedition.

Dr. Hayden's quotation of *Tringa bonapartii*, p. 174 of his Report, is erroneous, being based, as stated in the last article, upon *Tringa bairdii*. The claim of *fuscicollis* to a place among the Missouri birds rests, therefore, upon my discovery of it in Kansas, where I found it, migrating northward in flocks. May 22, 1864, on the Republican Fork of the Kansas River.   As Dr. Richardson cites an example from the Saskatchewan, we may be sure it ranges over the intermediate ground.   It is a very abundant bird along the whole Atlantic coast from Labrador to Florida, occurring in most of the States during the migration only, being found in Labrador in July, August, and September, and wintering far southward.

Mr. Dall did not, it appears, meet with it in Alaska, where, however, I presume it will be at length found.   During the migrations it associates freely with other small allies along the sea-shore and in the muddy flats back of the beaches.   Its general habits are much those of its allies, though it has some traits of its own, among them a peculiarly low, soft "*tweet*," and a remarkable familiarity, or, rather, heedlessness.   It may be distinguished, even at a distance, by its white upper tail-coverts, which show conspicuously when not covered by the folded wings.   A full account of its technical characters, as well as other items, may be found among my various papers above cited, and Sharpe & Dresser's great work on the Birds of Europe, in which country, it seems, the species is of comparatively frequent, although only casual, occurrence.

To judge from the only two sets I have examined, said to be of Bonaparte's Sandpiper, the egg is altogether peculiar and unmistakable. But the eggs resemble those of the Sanderling (*Calidris*) so very closely that I fear the identification is not beyond question.   The label states that the female was shot, but it was not received at the Smithsonian with the other collections of 1865, made by MacFarlane on the Arctic coast and Anderson River region.   These eggs being somewhat suspicious, I will not describe them further than may be implied in the remark that they are absolutely indistinguishable from an unquestionable set of *Calidris arenaria* procured in the same region.

TRINGA MARITIMA, Brünn.

Purple Sandpiper.

Tringa maritima, BRÜNN., Orn. Bor. 1764, 54.—GM., Syst. Nat. i, 1788, 678.—LATH., Ind. Orn. ii, 1790, 731.—VIEILL., Nouv. Dict. d'Hist. Nat. xxxiv, 1819, 471.—TEMM., Man. ii, 1820, 619.—LESS., Man. ii, 1828, 283.—SAB., B. Greenl. 532; App. Parry's 1st Voy. p. cci.— RICH., Parry's 2d Voy. 354.—SW. & RICH., F. B. A. ii, 1831, 382.— BP., Syn. 1828, 318.—NUTT., Man. ii, 1834, 115.—NAUM., Vög. Deuts. vii, 1834, 467, pl. 188.—JENYNS, Man. 1835, 211.—AUD., Orn. Biog. iii, 1835, 558, pl. 284; Syn. 1839, 233; B. Am. v, 1842, 261, pl. 330.—KEYS. & BLAS., Wirb. Eur. 1840, 76.—MACGIL., Br. Birds, ii, 1842, 67.—SCHINZ, Eur. Fn. i, 1840, 324.— SCHL., Rev. Crit. 1844, 88; M. P.-B. *Scolop.* 30.—GIR., B. L. I. 1844, 236.—DE-KAY, N. Y. Zool. ii, 1844, 237, pl. 87, f. 98.—HOLB., Fn. Groen. 1846, 39.—DEGL., Orn. Eur. ii, 1849, 222.—GRAY, Gen. of B. iii, 1849, 579.—PARZ., Cat. Ois. Eur. 1856, 14.—MEYER, Br. Birds, v, 1857, 80.—NILSS., Scand. Fn. ii, 1858, 235.— REINH., Ibis, iii, 1861, 11.—NEWT., *ibid.* 1865, 505.—GOULD, B. Eur. pl. 344.— HOY, Smiths. Rep. 1864, 438 (Western Missouri).—PUTN., Pr. Ess. Inst. i, 1856, 216.—WHEAT., Ohio. Agric. Rep. 1860, No. 206.—TURNB., B. E. Pa. 1869, 30 (rare).—DALL & BANN., Tr. Chic. Acad. i, 1869, 291.—COUES, Key, 1872, 255.— FINSCH, Abh. Nat. iii, 1872, 65.

Tringa (Arquatella) maritima, BD., B. N. A. 1858, 717.—GRAY, Hand-list, iii, 1871, 49,
    No. 10302.—RIDGW., Ann. Lyc. N. Y. x, 1874, 384 (Illinois).
Arquatella maritima, COUES, Pr. Phila. Acad. 1861, 183.—BOARDM., Pr. Bost. Soc. ix,
    1862, 128.—VERR., Pr. Ess. Inst. iii, 1862, 159.—ALLEN, *ibid.* iv, 1864, 87.—
    COUES, *ibid.* v, 1868, 293.—LAWR., Ann. Lyc. N. Y. viii, 1866, 294.—MAYN.,
    Guide, 1870, 140.
Tringa (Pelidna) maritima, DALL, Pr. Cal. Acad. Feb. 1873 (Aleutians).
Pelidna maritima, BP., List, 1838, 49 ; Cat. Met. 1842, 60 ; Rev. Crit. 1850, 185.
Totanus maritimus, STEPH., Gen. Zool. xii, 1824, 146.
(?) *Tringa striata*, LINN., Syst. Nat. i, 1766, 248.—GM., *ibid.* 1788, 672.—FAB., Fn. Groen.
    1789, No. 73.—LATH., Ind. Orn. ii, 1790, 733 (*Striated Sandpiper*, PENN., Arct.
    Zool. ii, 1785, 472).—FLEM., Brit. An. 110.
Tringa undata, BRÜNN., Orn. Bor. 1764, 55.—GM., Syst. Nat. i, 1788, 678.—LATH., Ind.
    Orn. ii, 1790, 732.—VIEILL., Nouv. Dict. d'Hist. Nat. xxxiv, 1819, 470.
Tringa nigricans, MONT., Linn. Tr. iv, 1796, 40.—LEACH, Cat. 1816, 30.—BREHM, V. D. 652.
Trynga arquatella, PALL., Zoog. R.-A. ii, 1811, 190.
Tringa canadensis, LATH., Ind. Orn. Suppl. 65.—VIEILL., N. D. d'H. Nat. xxxiv, 1819, 453.
(?) *Tringa lincolniensis*, LATH., I. Orn. ii, 1790, 734 (*Black Sandpiper*, Br. Zool. ii, No. 197).
Tringa littoralis, BREHM, Vög. Deutschl. 652.

Hab.—North America, northerly and chiefly coastwise. South to the Middle States
in winter. Great Lakes. Greenland. Europe. Asia.
    Not noticed by the Expeditions.

This species is included in the present work on the strength of its
occurrence in Western Missouri, attested by Dr. P. R. Hoy, as above
cited. Its presence, however, may be regarded exceptional. As its scientific name implies, it is chiefly a coastwise bird, though also occurring
on the larger inland waters. It is said to be common on the shores of
Lake Michigan. It is eminently a boreal bird, breeding very far to the
northward, and only rarely reaching the coast of the Middle States in
winter, beyond which its occurrence is open to question. It is rather
plenty along the New England coast in autumn, winter and spring, when
it frequents chiefly rocky shores covered with sea-weed, rather than the
bare sandy beaches.

The egg of *Tringa maritima* is of the usual pyriform shape, and
measures about 1.40 by 1.00. The ground is clay color, shaded with
olivaceous; the markings are large, numerous and distinct, of rich umber-
brown of different depths and intensity, occurring all over the shell,
but being most numerous as well as largest on the major half. With
these spots are associated shell-markings of pale purplish-gray and light
neutral tint.

TRINGA ALPINA var. AMERICANA, Cass.

American Dunlin ; Black-bellied or Red-breasted Sandpiper.

a. *alpina.*

Tringa alpina, LINN., Fn. Suec. 64 ; Syst. Nat. i, 1766, 249 (*Cinclus torquatus*, BRISS., v,
    216, pl. 19, f. 2).—LEACH, Cat. 1816, 30.—BOIE, Isis, 1822, 561.—FLEM., Br. B.
    108.—NAUM., V. D. vii, 1834, 427, pl. 186.—GRAY, List Br. B. 1863, 167.
Pelidna alpina, BOIE.—BREHM, V. D. 661.
Tringa cinclus, LINN., Syst. Nat. i, 1766, 251 (BRISS., v, 211, pl. 19, f. 1).—LEACH, Cat.
    1816, 30.—KEYS. & BLAS., Wirb. Eur. 1840, 76.—SCHL., Rev. Crit. 1844, 89.—
    MACGIL., Man. Orn. ii, 70.—GRAY, Gen. of B. iii, 1849, 579.
Pelidna cinclus, BP., List, 1838, 50.
"*Tringa pusilla*, GM., Syst. Nat. i, 1788, 663," according to *Gray;* but very dubious.
Tringa ruficollis, PALL., Reis. iii, 700.
Numenius variabilis, BECHST., Naturg. Deutschl. iv, 141.
Tringa variabilis, MEYER, Tasch. ii, 397.—TEMM., Man. i, 1815, 395.—JENYNS, Man.
    Br. Vert. 209.
Pelidna variabilis, STEPH., Gen. Zool. xii, 98.—BREHM, V. D. 662.
Pelidna schinzii, BREHM. (Var.?) Not of American writers.

b. *americana*.

Tringa alpina, WILS., Am. Orn. vii, 1813, 25, pl. 56, f. 2.—ORD, ed. Wils. iii, 1829, 126.—
    BREW., ed. Wils. 1840, 475, fig. 220.—BP., Obs. Wils. 1825; Syn. 1828, 317.—SW.
    & RICH., F. B. A. ii, 1831, 383.—NUTT., Man. ii, 1834, 106.—AUD., Orn. Biog.
    iii, 1835, 580, pl. 290 ; Syn. 1839, 234 ; B. Am. v, 1842, 266, pl. 332.—GIR., B. L.
    I. 1844, 228.—NEWB., P. R. R. Rep. vi, 1857, 100.—PUTN., Pr. Ess. Inst. i, 1856,
    217.—WHEAT., Ohio Agric. Rep. 1860, No. 207.
Tringa (Schœniclus) alpina var. *americana*, CASS., Baird's B. N. A. 1858, 719.
Tringa (Pelidna) alpina var. *americana*, RIDGW., Ann. Lyc. N. Y. x, 1874, 384.
Tringa alpina var. *americana*, COOP. & SUCK., N. H. Wash. Ter. 1860, 239.—TURNB., B.
    E. Pa. 1869, 30.—COUES, Key, 1872, 256, fig. 166.—SNOW, B. Kans. 1873, 10.
Pelidna alpina var. *americana*, ALLEN, Bull. M. C. Z. iii, 1872, 182.—DALL & BANN., Tr.
    Chic. Acad. i, 1869, 291.
Pelidna americana, COUES, Pr. Phila. Acad. 1861, 188.—VERR., Pr. Ess. Inst. iii, 1862,
    159.—ALLEN, ibid. iv, 1864, 77.—COUES, ibid. v, 1868, 294.—BOARDM., Pr. Bost.
    Soc. ix, 1862, 128.—LAWR., Ann. Lyc. viii, 1866, 294.—COUES, Pr. Bost. Soc. xii,
    1868, 122.—COUES, Pr. Phila. Acad. 1871, 30.—MAYN., Guide, 1870, 140.—ALLEN,
    Bull. M. C. Z. ii, 1871, 355.
Tringa variabilis, SAB., Suppl. Parry's 1st Voy. p. cc.—SAB., Frankl. Journ. 686.—RICH.,
    Parry's 2d Voy. 353.
Tringa cinclus, WILS., Am Orn. vii, 1813, 39, pl. 57, f. 3.—ORD, ed. Wils. iii, 1829, 138.—
    BREW., ed. Wils. 1840, 484, fig. 225.—DeKAY, N. Y. Zool. ii, 1844, 84, fig. 292.
Pelidna cinclus, BP., List, 1838, 50.
Pelidna pacifica, COUES, Pr. Phila. Acad. 1861, 189 (in text).

Hab.—North America, especially coastwise. Migratory and wintering in the
United States. Breeding in high latitudes only.
    Not noticed by either of the Expeditions.

The Dunlin has only been observed by Mr. Allen, so far as I am aware,
in the Missouri region, he finding it near Leavenworth. Like the preceding and following species, it is especially a coast bird, migrating in
abundance along both our shores in spring and fall, when it occurs often
in large flocks. I found them very plentiful along the Carolina coast in
April and May, and in October. Some of them obtain a perfect dress
before leaving in the spring, although they have far to go before
reaching their breeding grounds. These are only in high boreal regions,
as along the Arctic coast and the Yukon River region. The vernal
change begins early in April, during the migration ; in the fall many
retain the summer plumage until they reach the Southern States, though
most come in plain gray attire.

TRINGA CANUTUS, Linn.

Red-breasted Sandpiper ; Robin Snipe ; Knot.

Tringa canutus, LINN., Syst. Nat. i, 1766, 251.—GM., Syst. Nat. i, 1788, 679.—LATH., Ind.
    Orn. ii, 1790, 738.—BRÜNN., Orn. Bor., 1764, No. 182.—PALL., Zoog. R.-A. ii,
    1811, 197.—VIEILL., Nouv. Dict. d'Hist. Nat. xxxiv, 1819.—TEMM., Man. Orn.
    ii, 1820, 627.—FLEM., Brit. An. 109.—JEN., Man., 1835, 213.—EYT., Cat. Br. Birds,
    41.—KEYS. & BLAS., Wirb. Eur. 76.—BP., List, 1838, 49.—SCHINZ, Eur. Fn. i,
    1840, 326.—MACGIL., Man. Br. Birds, ii, 1842, 67.—DeKAY, N. Y. Zool. ii, 1844,
    243, pl. 85, fig. 194; pl. 97, fig. 218.—SCHL., Rev. Crit. Ois. Eur. 1844, 88.—GRAY,
    Gen. iii, 1849, 579.—DEGL., Orn. Eur. ii, 1849, 219.—BP., Cat. Met. 1842, 61 ; Rev.
    Crit. 1850, 185.—MEY., Br. B. v, 1857, 67.—NAUM., Vog. pl. 183.—GOULD, B. Eur.
    pl. 324.—SCHL., M. P.-B. *Scolop.* p. 29.—CASS., B. N. A. 1858, 715.—COUES, Pr.
    Phila. Acad., 1861, 180, and 229.—WHEAT., Ohio Agric. Rep., 1860, No. 205.—
    BOARDM., Pr. Bost. Soc. ix, 1862, 128.—VERR., Pr. Ess. Inst. iii, 1862, 159.—
    ALLEN, ibid. iv, 1864, 86.—COUES, ibid. v, 1868, 293.—McILWR., ibid. v, 1866, 93.—
    LAWR., Ann. Lyc. N. Y. viii, 1866, 294.—MAYN., Guide, 1870, 140.—COUES, Pr.
    Bost. Soc. xii, 1868, 122.—DALL & BANN., Tr. Chic. Acad. i, 1869, 291.—COUES,
    Key, 1872, 256.—SNOW, B. Kans. 1873, 10 (Kansas, common).—RIDGW., Ann.
    Lyc. N. Y. x, 1874, 384 (Illinois).
Tringa cinerea, BRÜNN., Orn. Bor. 1764, 53.—GM., Syst. Nat. i, 1788, 673.—LATH., Ind.
    Orn. ii, 1790, 733.—WILS., Am. Orn. vii, 1813, 36, pl. 57, f. 2.—BOIE, Isis, 1822,
    560.- -ORD, ed. Wils. iii, 1829, 142.—BREW., ed. Wils., 1840, 482, fig. 224 ; Syn.

725.—LICHT., Verz. 1823, 72.—LESS., Man. ii, 1828, 283.—Sw. & RICH., F. B. A.
ii, 1831, 387.—NUTT., Man. ii, 1834, 125.
Canutus cinereus, BREHM, Vog. Deutschl. 655, pl. 34, f. 2.
Tringa islandica, GM., Syst. Nat. i, 1788, 682.—LATH., Ind. Orn. ii, 1790, 737.—BP., Specc.
Comp. 1827, 62; Syn. 1828, 350.—AUD., Orn. Biog. iv, 1838, 130, pl. 315; Syn.
1839, 232; B. Am. v, 1842, 254, pl. 328.—GIR., B. L. I. 1844, 224.—HOLB., Fn.
Groen. 1846, 38.—NILSS., Scand. Fn. ii, 1858, 252.—NAUM., Vög. Deut. vii, 1834,
372, pl. 183.—PUTN., Pr. Ess. Inst. i, 1856, 216.
Canutus islandicus, BREHM, Vög. Deutschl. 654.
Tringa nævia, GM., Syst. Nat. i, 1788, 681.—LATH., Ind. Orn. ii, 1790, 732.
Tringa grisea, GM., Syst. Nat. i, 1788, 681.—LATH., Ind. Orn. ii, 1790, 733.
(?) *Tringa australis*, GM., Syst. Nat. i, 1788, 679.—LATH., Ind. Orn. ii, 1790, 737.
(?) *Tringa ferruginea*, BRÜNN., Orn. Bor. 1764, 53.—VIEILL., Nouv. Dict. d'Hist. Nat.
xxxiv, 1819, 466.—MEYER, Tasch. ii, 395.
Tringa rufa, WILS., Am. Orn. vii, 1813, 43, pl. 57, f. 5.—ORD, ed. Wils. iii, 1829, 140.—
BREW., ed. Wils. 1840, 487, fig. 227; Syn. 725.—BP., Obs. Wils. 1825, 93.
" *Tringa calidris*, LINN., Syst. Nat. i, 1766, 253."
" *Tringa utopiensis*, MÜLLER."
" *Tringa lomatina*, LICHT."

Hab.—Northern Hemisphere. Australia. New Zealand. South America (CAB.,
MAXIM., and BURM.; see SCL. & SALV. P. Z. S. 1873, 456.)
Not obtained by the Expeditions.

This species is introduced on the authority of Prof. Snow, who states
that it is " common" in Kansas. It is also given by Mr. Wheaton as
occurring in Ohio, and may not be rare on our larger inland waters,
though, like the two preceding species, it is more particularly maritime.
It occurs along the whole Atlantic coast during the migrations or in
winter, and is plentiful. Its breeding resorts are far beyond our limits.

NOTE.—As completing an account of the North American Sandpipers, I introduce
the following species, which are not known to occur in the Missouri region:

BLACK-BREASTED SANDPIPER.—TRINGA PTILOCNEMIS, *Coues.*

Tringa crassirostris, DALL, Am. Nat. viii, 1873, 635 (St. Paul's Island).—COUES, App.
Rep. Prybilov Isl. 1873 (not paged); Check-list, 1874, 85, No. 426*bis* (same local
ity). (Not of *Temm.* and *Schl.*)
Tringa ptilocnemis, COUES, *op. et loc. cit.*, 1873 (based on same specimens).
" *Tringa gracilis*, HARTING, P. Z. S. 1874" (in press; *fide Hart. epist.*)

Hab.—Prybilov Islands. (The large suite of specimens brought in by Mr. H. W.
Elliot, the same as formerly identified with *T. crassirostris* by Mr. Harting, are fully
discussed in my work above cited, where the species is named *T. ptilocnemis.*)

COOPER'S SANDPIPER.—TRINGA COOPERI, *Baird.*

Tringa cooperi, BD., B. N. A. 1858, 716, pl. 89, f. 1.
Tringa (Actodromas) cooperi, COUES, Key, 1872, 255.
Actodromas (Heteropygia) cooperi, COUES, Pr. A. N. S. 1861, 202.
Tringa (Heteropygia) cooperi, GRAY, Hand-list, iii, 1871, 49, No. 10309.

Hab.—Long Island. The type specimen remains unique.

CURLEW SANDPIPER.—TRINGA SUBARQUATA, (*Guld.*) *Temm.*

Scolopax subarquata, GULD., Nov. Comm. Petrop. xix, 1775, 471, pl. 18.—GM., Syst. Nat.
i, 1788, 658.
" *Numenius subarquata*, BECHST., Naturg. Deutschl. iv, 135." (Not of authors.)
Tringa subarquata, TEMM., Man. i, 1815, 393; ii, 1820, 609.—VIEILL., Nouv. Dict. d'Hist.
Nat. xxxiv, 1819, 454.—BOIE, Isis, 1822, 560.—BP., Specc. Comp. 1827, 62.—
FLEM., Br. An. 107.—JEN., Man. Br. Vert. 1835, 208.—EYT., Cat. Br. B. 42.—
NAUM., V. D. viii, 1834, 408, pl. 185.—NUTT., Man. ii, 1834, 104.—AUD., Orn. Biog.
1835, 444; Syn. 1839, 234; B. Am. v, 1842, 269, pl. 333.—KEYS. & BLAS., Wirb.
Eur. 1840, 76.—SCHINZ, Eur. Fn. i, 1840, 320.—MACGIL., Man. Br. Orn. ii, 1842,
71.—SCHL., Rev. Crit. Ois. Eur. 1844, 88.—GIR., B. L. I. 1844, 237.—DEKAY, N.
Y. Fn. 1844, 239, pl. 95, fig. 213.—GRAY, Gen. of B. iii, 1849, 579.—DEGL., Orn.
Eur. ii, 1849, 225.—MEYER, Br. Birds, v, 1857, 91.—NILSSON, Scand. Fn. ii, 1858,
239.—SCHL., M. P.-B. vi, *Scolopaces*, p. 31.—TURNB., B. E. Pa. 1869, 44 (occasion-
ally shot at Egg Harbor); and of authors generally.
Tringa (Ancylocheilus) subarquata, BP., Cat. Met. 1842, 60.—GRAY, List Br. Birds, 169;
Hand-list, iii, 1871, 50, No. 10319.—COUES, Key, 1872, 256.

Tringa (Erolia) subarquata, CASS., in Baird's B. N. A. 1858, 718.
Pelidna subarquata, CUV., R. A.—BREHM, V. D. 657.—BP., List, 1838, 50.
Ancylocheilus subarquata, KAUP, Sk. Ent. Eur. Thierw. 1829, 50.—COUES, Pr. Phila. Acad.
   1861, 185.—BOARDM., Pr. Bost. Soc. ix, 1862, 128 (Maine).—VERR., Pr. Ess. Inst.
   iii, 1862, 159 (Maine).—LAWR., Ann. Lyc. N. Y. viii, 1866, 294.—ALLEN, Pr. Ess.
   Inst. iv, 1864, 87.—COUES, Pr. Ess. Inst. v, 1868, 293 (New England, rare).—
   COUES, Pr. Bost. Soc. xii, 1868, 122 (South Carolina, *fide Gibbes*).
Scolopax africanus, GM., Syst. Nat. i, 1788, 655.
Numenius africanus, LATH., Ind. Orn. ii, 1790, 712 (Cape Curlew, Gen. Syn. v, 126).
Numenius pygmœus, BECHST., Naturg. Deutschl. iv, 148.
Tringa pygmœa, LEACH, Cat. 1816, 30.   (Not of authors.)
(?) *Tringa islandica*, RETZ., Fn. Suec. 192.
(?) *Tringa ferruginea*, BRÜNN., Orn. Bor. 1764, No. 180.
Numenius ferrugineus, MEYER & WOLF, Tasch. Deutschl. Vög. ii, 356.
Trynga falcinella, PALL., Zoog. R.-A. ii, 188.
Pelidna macrorhyncha, BREHM, V. D. 658.
Erolia variegata, VIEILL., Anal. 1816, 55 ; Nouv. Dict. d'Hist. Nat. 1817, 409.—LESS., Man.
   ii, 1828, 302.
Ærolia varia, VIEILL., Gal. Ois. ii, 1834, 89, pl. 231 (=*Erolia variegata*).
Scolopax dethardingii, SIEMSSEN.   (*Gray.*)
" *Falcinellus cursorius*, TEMM."
   Other names of this species, according to Gray, are : *caffra*, FORST. ; *longirostra*,
GRABA ; *griseus*, LESS. ; *chinensis*, GR. ; *cuvieri*, BP.; *subarcuata*, FINSCH & HARTL. It is
figured, besides as above, in P. E. 851 ; P. C. 510 ; GOULD, B. E. pl. 328 ; B. A. vi, pl. 32.

Hab.—The greater part of the Old World. In America, rare and scarcely more than
a straggler along the Atlantic coast.

SANDERLING.—CALIDRIS ARENARIA, (*Linnæus*) *Illiger*.

Tringa arenaria, LINN., Syst. Nat. i, 1766, 251.—SCHL., Rev. Crit. 1844, 90.—AUD., Orn.
   Biog. iii, 1835, 231 ; v, 1839, 582 ; pls. 285, 230 ; Syn. 1839, 237 ; B. Am. v, 1842,
   287, pl. 338.—SCHL., Mus. P.-B. ; *Scolopaces*, p. 55.—PHIL., Cat. 36 (Chili).
Calidris arenaria, ILL., Prod. 1811, 249.—LEACH, Cat. 1816, 28.—TEMM., Man. ii, 524.—
   LICHT., Verz. 1823, 72.—BP., Obs. Wils. 1825, 105; Syn. 1828.—FLEM., Br. An.
   112.—BREHM., V. D. 673.—Sw. & RICH., F. B. A. ii, 1831, 366.—NUTT., Man. ii,
   1834, 4.—NAUM., V. D. vii, 1834, 353, pl. 182.—JEN., Man. 1835, 183.—EYT., Cat.
   Br. B. 42.—BP., List, 1838, 50 ; Cat. Met. 1842, 61.—MACGIL., Man. Brit. Orn. ii,
   1842, 65.—KEYS. & BLAS., Wirb. Eur. 1840, 75.—GIR., B. L. I. 1844, 243.—GRAY, G.
   of B. iii, 1849, 581.—BP., Rev. Crit. 1850, 184.—CASS.,U. S. Astron. Exped. ii, 1855,
   194 ; Baird's B. N. A. 1858, 723 ; Pr. Phila. Acad. 1860, 195 (Carthagena).—
   NILSS., Scand. Faun. ii, 1858, 255.—COOP. & SUCK., N. H. Wash. Ter. 1860, 241.—
   LAWR., Ann. Lyc. ix, 1868, 210 (Yucatan).—SCL. & SALV., P. Z. S. 1868, 176
   (Peru).—PELZ., Orn. Bras. 312 (Brazil).—DALL & BANN., Tr. Chic. Acad. i,
   1869, 292 (Alaska).—FINSCH, Abb. Nat. iii, 1872, 65 (Alaska).—COUES, Pr. Phila.
   Acad. 1861, 181 (critical) ; *ibid.* 1871, 31 (North Carolina, wintering); Pr. Ess.
   Inst. v, 1868, 293 ; Key, 1872, 257, fig. 167.—RIDGW., Ann. Lyc. N. Y. x, 1874,
   384 (Illinois); and of authors generally.
Charadrius calidris, LINN., Syst. Nat. i, 1766, 255.—WILS., Am. Orn. vii, 1813, 68, pl. 59. f.
   4 ; Ord's ed. iii, 1829, 167 ; Brewer's ed. 1840, 503.
Arenaria calidris, MEYER, Tasch. Deutschl. Vög. 68, pl. 59, f. 4.—DEGL., Orn. Eur. ii,
   1849, 240.—LEMB., Av. Cuba, 1850, 100.
Charadrius rubidus, GM., Syst. Nat. i, 1788, 688.—WILS., Am. Orn. vii, 1813, 129, pl. 58, f.
   3 ; Ord's ed. iii, 1829, 170 ; Brewer's ed. 1840, 541.
Arenaria vulgaris, BECHST., Tasch. Deutschl. ii, 462.—TEMM., Man. Orn. ii, 1815, 334.—
   STEPH., Gen. Zool. xi, 490, pl. 35.
Arenaria grisea, BECHST., Naturg. Deutschl. iv, 368.
Calidris grisea, BREHM, Vög. Deutschl. 674.
Trynga tridactyla, PALL., Zoog. R.-A. ii, 1811, 198.
Calidris tringoides, VIEILL., Gal. Ois. ii, 1834, 95, pl. 234.
Calidris americana, BREHM, Vög. Deutschl. 1831, 695.—BREHM, Naumannia, 1850, 68.
Calidris nigellus, VIEILL.

Hab.—Sea-coasts of nearly all countries.

LIMOSA FEDOA, (Linn.) Ord.

Great Marbled Godwit.

Scolopax fedoa, LINN., Syst. Nat. i, 1766, 244 (based on *Fedoa americana*, EDW., 137, and
   Limosa americana rufa, BRISS., v, 287).—GM., Syst. Nat. i, 1788, 663.—LATH.,

Ind. Orn. ii, 1790, 718 (*American Godwit*, Arct. Zool. ii, 465, No. 371; LATH., Syn. v, 142).—WILS., Am. Orn. vii, 1813, 30, pl. 56, f. 4.

Limicula fedoa, VIEILL., Analyse, 1816.

Limosa fedoa, ORD, ed. Wils. vii, 1825, —.—BP., Obs. Wils. 1825; Syn. 1828, 328; List, 1838, 52.—SAB., Frankl. Journ. 689.—SW. & RICH., F. B. A. ii, 1831, 395.—NUTT., Man. ii, 1834, 173.—AUD., Orn. Biog. iii, 1835, 287; v, 590; pl. 238; Syn. 1839, 246; B. Am. v, 1842, 331, pl. 348.—GIR., B. L. I. 1844, 259.—PUTN., Pr. Ess. Inst. i, 1856, 217.—NEWB., P. R. R. Rep. vi, 1857, 100.—CASS., B. N. A. 1858, 740.— HEERM., P. R. R. Rep. x, 1859, pt. vi, 65.—COOP. & SUCK., N. H. Wash. Ter. 1860, 245.—CAB., J. f. O. iv, 350 (Cuba).—SCL., Ibis i, 1859, 230 (Belize).— LEYL., P. Z. S. 1859, 64 (Honduras).—SALV., Ibis, 1865, 190 (Guatemala).— DRESS., Ibis, 1866, 39 (Texas).—LAWR., Ann. Lyc. N. Y. viii, 1866, 294; ix, 210 (Yucatan).—WHEAT., Ohio Agric. Rep. 1860, No. 221.—HAYD., Rep. 1862, 175.—HOY, Smiths. Rep. 1864, 438 (Missouri).—VERR., Pr. Ess. Inst. iii, 1862, 159.—ALLEN, *ibid.* iv, 1864, 87.—McILWR., *ibid.* v, 1866, 93.—COUES, *ibid.* v, 1868, 296.—TRIPPE, *ibid.* vi, 1871, 119 (Minnesota).—COUES, Pr. Bost. Soc. xii, 1868, 123.—TURNB., B. E. Pa. 1868, 32.—MAYN., Guide, 1870, 142.—COUES, Pr. Phila. Acad. 1871, 32.—ALLEN, Bull. M. C. Z. ii, 1871, 356 (Florida, in winter).—TRIPPE, Pr. Bost. Soc. xv, 1872, 241 (Iowa).—COUES, Key, 1872, 257.—SNOW, B. Kans. 1873, 10.— RIDGW., Ann. Lyc. N. Y. x, 1874, 384.

Scolopax marmorata, LATH., Ind. Orn. ii, 1790, 720.

Limicula marmorata, VIEILL., Nouv. Dict. d'Hist. Nat.; Gal. Ois. ii, 1825, 115, pl. 243.

Limosa americana, STEPH., Shaw's Gen. Zool.

Limosa adspersa, LICHT.

Hab.—Entire temperate North America; Central and South America. West Indies. Breeds in the Missouri and Upper Mississippi regions, and thence to the Saskatchewan. Winters in the Southern States and southward.

Lieutenant Warren's Expedition.—4884, Kanesville; 5450, Fort Union.

Not observed by Captain Raynolds' Expedition, nor by the later ones.

Comparatively little has been learned of the breeding resorts and habits of this Godwit, though it is such a common and generally distributed bird during its migrations and in winter. Audubon surmises that it may breed in South Carolina and perhaps also in Texas, where, as Mr. Dresser found it in summer, it probably does. Occurring in abundance along most of the Atlantic coast, it nevertheless appears less common north of Massachusetts, and has not, it would appear, been observed much, if any, beyond New England in that longitude. The centre of its abundance in summer, and its main breeding ground, is, apparently, the Northern Mississippi and Eastern Missouri regions, and thence to the Saskatchewan; for, unlike its relative (*L. hudsonica*), it does not proceed very far north to nest. It breeds in Iowa, and in Minnesota and Eastern Dakota, where I observed it in June, and where the eggs have been procured. I found it on the plains bordering the Red River, in company with Long-billed Curlews and great numbers of the Bartramian Sandpipers, nesting, like these species, on the prairie near the river and about the adjoining pools, but not necessarily by the water's edge. In its habits at this season it most nearly resembles the Curlew, and the two species, of much the same size and general appearance, might be readily mistaken at a distance where the difference in the bill might not be perceived. On intrusion near the nest, the birds mount in the air with loud, piercing cries, hovering slowly around with labored flight in evident distress, and approaching sometimes within a few feet of the observer.

The only perfect set of eggs of the Godwit I have seen were taken June 1, 1871, fifty miles northwest of Saint Paul, Minnesota; both parents were secured and deposited in the Saint Paul Academy, where I examined them; so that the identification is unquestionable. There are three eggs in this set, measuring 2.30 by 1.60, 2.28 by 1.56, and 2.25 by 1.62. The color is a clear, light olivaceous-drab; the markings are small and numerous, but not very strongly pronounced—there is nothing (in this set) of the heavy blotching and marking usually seen in waders' eggs. The spots are pretty evenly distributed, though rather larger in two instances, and more numerous in the other instance, about the butt than elsewhere. These markings are of various umber-brown shades, with the usual stone-gray shell spots.

LIMOSA HUDSONICA, (Lath.) Sw.

Hudsonian or Black-tailed Godwit.

Scolopax alba et *candida*, LINN., Syst. Nat. i, 1766, 247 (based on *Fedoa canadensis*, EDW., pl. 139; *Limosa candida*, BRISS., v, 290; *Totanus canadensis*, EDW., pl. 139, f. 1; *Totanus candidus*, BRISS., v, 207: whence also *Limosa edwardsii*, SW. & RICH., F. B. A. ii, 1831, 398).
Scolopax lapponica, var. β, GM., Syst. Nat. i, 1788.
Scolopax hudsonica, LATH., Ind. Orn. ii, 1790, 720.
Limosa hudsonica, SW. & RICH., F. B. A. ii, 1831 (EDW., pl. 138).—NUTT., ii, 1834, 175.—
AUD., Orn. Biog. iii, 1835, 426; v, 592; pl. 258; Syn. 1839, 247; B. A. v, 1842,
335, pl. 349.—BP., List, 1838, 52.—GIR., B. L. I. 1844, 260.—PUTN., Pr. Ess. Inst.
i, 1856, 217.—BD., B. N. A. 1858, 741.—SCL., P. Z. S. 1860, 387 (Falklands).—
CAB., J. f. O. iv, 350 (Cuba).—DARW., Voy. Beagle, Birds, 129 (Chiloe).—PELZ.,
Novara Reise, Vög. 128 (Chiloe).—PHIL., Cat. 35 (Chili).—SCL. & SALV., P. Z.
S. 1869, 252 (Venezuela).—SCL., P. Z. S. 1860, 387 (Magellan Straits and Falk-
lands).—PELZ., Orn. Bras. 308 (Brazil).—WHEAT., Ohio Agric. Rep. 1860, No.
222.—BOARDM., Pr. Bost. Soc. ix, 1862, 129 (Maine, migratory).—VERR., Pr. Ess.
Inst. iii, 1862, 159.—ALLEN, *ibid.* iv, 1864, 87.—MCIWR., *ibid.* v, 1866, 93.—COUES,
ibid. v, 1868, 296.—COUES, Pr. Bost. Soc. xii, 1868, 123.—DALL & BANN., Tr.
Chic. Acad. i, 1869, 293.—TURNB., B. E. Pa. 1869, 32.—MAYN., Guide, 1870, 142.—
COUES, Key, 1872, 258.—SNOW, B. Kans. 1873, 10.—SCL., P. Z. S. 1873, 456 (South
America).—RIDGW., Ann. Lyc. N. Y. x, 1874, 385 (Illinois).
Limosa melanura, BP., Specchio Comp. 1827, No. 204; not of authors.
Limosa ægocephala, BP., Syn. 1828, 327; not of authors.
Limosa australis, GRAY, Cat. Br. Mus. 1844, 95. (*Sclater*.)

Hab.—Northern and Eastern North America. West Indies. South America. Breeds far northward. Not noted west of the Rocky Mountains. Rare along the Atlantic. Observed by none of the Expeditions.

This Godwit is much less abundant in the United States than the preceding, and appears to range chiefly along the Atlantic coast. It is, however, included by Prof. Snow among the birds of Kansas on Prof. Baird's authority. I have never seen it alive. Its breeding resorts are entirely beyond our limits, in hyperborean regions. A set of four eggs of *Limosa hudsonica* is in the Smithsonian, from Anderson River, where they were secured by Mr. MacFarlane, June 9. They measure 2.15 to 2.20 in length by about 1.40 in breadth. The ground is a very heavily-shaded olive-drab, much darker (almost as in a Loon's or Jäger's egg) in two of the specimens than in the other. In these darker specimens the markings are almost lost in the general heavy color, merely appearing a little darker; they are chiefly evident at the greater end. In the other the markings, of the same general character, are, however, much more conspicuous, owing to the lighter ground.

TOTANUS SEMIPALMATUS, (Gm.) Temm.

Semipalmated Tattler; Willet; Stone Snipe.

Scolopax semipalmata, GM., Syst. Nat. i, 1788, 659.—LATH., Ind. Orn. ii, 1790, 722 (Arct.
Zool. ii, No. 380, pl. 20, f. 2; LATH., Syn. v, 152).—WILS., Am. Orn. vii, 1813, 27,
pl. 56, f. 3.
Totanus semipalmatus, TEMM., Man. Orn. ii, 637.—BP., Obs. Wils. 1825, No. 206.—SW. &
RICH., F. B. A. ii, 1831, 388, pl. 67 (north to 56°).—AUD., Orn. Biog. iii, 1835,
510; v, 1839, 585; pl. 274; Syn. 1839, 245; B. Am. v, 1842, 324, pl. 347.—GIR., B.
L. I. 1844, 254.—WOODH., Sitgr. Rep. 1853, 99 (New Mexico).—PUTN., Pr. Ess.
Inst. i, 1856, 217.—HEERM., P. R. R. Rep. x, 1859, pt. vi, 65.—COUES, Key, 258.
Totanus (Catoptrophorus) semipalmatus, BP., Syn. 1828, 328.—NUTT., Man. ii, 1834, 144.

Catoptrophorus semipalmatus, BP., List, 1838, 51.—BLAS., List B. Eur. 1862, 18 (Sweden).
Glottis semipalmata, NILSSON, Fn. Suec. 1817.
Hodites semipalmata, KAUP, Sk. Ent. Eur. 1829.
Symphemia semipalmata, HARTL., R. Z. 1845, 342.—BD., B. N. A. 1858, 729.—BRY., Pr.
    Bost. Soc. vii, 1859 (Bahamas).—CAB., J. f. O. iv, 351 (Cuba).—SCL., P. Z. S.
    1860, 253 (Orizaba).—CASS., Pr. Phila. Acad. 1860, 195 (Carthagena).—COOP. &
    SUCK., N. H. Wash. Ter. 1860, 240.—WHEAT., Ohio Agric. Rep. 1860, No. 214.—
    COUES & PRENT., Smiths. Rep. 1861, 416.—BOARDM., Pr. Bost. Soc. ix, 1862, 129
    (Maine, breeds).—COUES, *ibid.* xii, 1868, 122 (South Carolina, resident).—VERR.,
    Pr. Ess. Inst. iii, 1862, 159.—ALLEN, *ibid.* iv, 1864, 77 (Massachusetts, perhaps
    breeding).—COUES, *ibid.* v, 1868, 295 (New England, in summer).—DRESS.,
    Ibis, 1866, 37 (Texas).—SALV., Ibis, 1866, 178 (Guatemala).—LAWR., Ann. Lyc.
    N. Y. vii, 272 (Cuba); viii, 1866, 294; ix, 210 (Yucatan).—TURNB., B. E. Pa.
    1868, 31 (in summer).—MAYN., Guide, 1870, 141.—ALLEN., Bull. M. C. Z. ii, 1871,
    356 (Florida, resident).—COUES, Pr. Phila. Acad. 1866, 97 (Arizona); 1871, 32
    (North Carolina, breeding and resident).—SNOW, B. Kans. 1873, 10.—MERR., U.
    S. Geol. Surv. Ter. 1872, 700 (Utah and Idaho).—RIDGW., Ann. Lyc. N. Y. x,
    1874, 384 (Illinois).
Totanus crassirostris, VIEILL., Nouv. Dict. d'Hist. Nat. 1816, 406.
Symphemia atlantica, RAFINESQUE, Journ. Phys. lxxxviii, 1819, 417.
(?) *Totanus speculiferus*, CUV., R. A. i, 1817, 351.—PUCH., R. and M. Z. iii, 1851, 569.

Hab.—Temperate North America, north to 56°, but chiefly United States. Breeds
throughout its United States range. Resident in the Southern States. Common in
the interior, but more so along the coast. West Indies. Central and South America
(PELZ., Orn. Bras. 309). Accidental in Europe (GOULD, B. Eur. pl. 311).
    Lieutenant Warren's Expedition.—5434, Medicine Creek; 8998, —— (no label).
    Later Expeditions.—59870, Colorado; 61638-9, Salt Lake, Utah; 62358, N. Fork, Idaho.
    Not obtained by Captain Raynolds' Expedition.

The Willet is distributed across North America; but, unlike many of
its allies, its northern dispersion is restricted, and it breeds anywhere
in the United States in suitable resorts. I have found it wherever I
have been in the United States. There were a few on the Upper Rio
Grande when I crossed that river in June, 1864, and during the same
month I saw many more westward, in New Mexico, especially along the
Zuñi River, where I am sure they were breeding. Some resided in a
marshy tract near Fort Whipple, in Arizona. Others occurred to me
in June and July in Eastern Dakota. On the North Carolina coast I
found the bird breeding in great numbers in the marshy flats just back
of the beach in May and June.

The nest is placed near the water of some secluded pool, or in the
midst of a marsh, whether fresh or salt, in a tussock of grass or rushes.
It is a rude structure, of the simplest materials, raised a little way from
the ground, and with a shallow indentation. The eggs are very variable in all respects. As to size and shape, the following measurements
show the differences: 1.90 by 1.45; 1.95 by 1.50; 2.00 by 1.50; 2.05 by
1.55; 2.12 by 1.50; averaging about 2.00 by 1.50. They are less pointedly pyriform than the eggs of the smaller Tattlers and Sandpipers.
The ground is sometimes brownish-olive, or drab, or clay-color; sometimes, again, quite buffy-brown; in a few cases greenish or grayish-
white. The spotting is bold and distinct, but little massed even at the
greater end, where, though the spots are largest and most numerous,
they generally remain distinct. The spots are mostly clean-edged and
sharp, of moderate size, but sometimes quite fine and scratchy. They
are of various umber-brown shades, and accompanied with the usual
obsolete shell-markings.

Under ordinary circumstances Willets are notoriously restless, wary,
and noisy birds; but their nature is changed, or, at any rate, held in
abeyance, during and for a short time after incubation. They cease
their cries, grow less uneasy, become gentle, if still suspicious, and may
generally be seen stalking quietly about the nest. When Willets are
found in that humor—absent-minded, as it were, absorbed in reflection

upon their engrossing duties, and unlikely to observe anything not directly in front of their bill—it is pretty good evidence that they have a nest hard by. It is the same with Avocets, and probably many other waders. During incubation the bird that is "off duty" (both parents are said to take turns at this) almost always indulges in revery, doubtless rose tinted, and becomes in a corresponding degree oblivious to outward things. If then they are not set upon in a manner entirely too rude and boisterous, the inquiring ornithologist could desire no better opportunity than he will have to observe their every motion and attitude. But once let them become thoroughly alarmed by too open approach, particularly if the setting bird be driven from her nest, and the scene quickly shifts; there is a great outcry, violent protest and tumult, where was quietude. Other pairs, nesting near by, join their cries till the confusion becomes general. But now, again, their actions are not those they would show at other times; for, instead of flying off with the instinct of self-preservation, to put distance between them and danger, they are held by some fascination to the spot, and hover around, wheeling about, flying in circles a little ways to return again, with unremitting clamor. They may be only too easily destroyed under such circumstances, provided the ornithologist can lay aside his scruples and steel himself against sympathy.

The half-webbing of the toes renders this species something of a swimmer, if necessity arise; but it only takes to water beyond its depth under urgent circumstances. In size as well as in plumage it is very variable; the length of the legs, particularly, varies in different individuals to a surprising degree.

TOTANUS MELANOLEUCUS, (Gm.) Vieill.

Greater Telltale; Greater Yellowshanks; Tattler.

Scolopax melanoleuca, GM., Syst. Nat. i, 1788, 659.—LATH., Ind. Orn. ii, 1790, 723.
Totanus melanoleucus, VIEILL., Nouv. Dict. d'Hist. Nat. 1816.—LICHT., Verz. 1823, No. 750.—BP., Syn. 1828, 324; List, 1838, 51.—AUD., Orn. Biog. iv, 1838, 68, pl. 308.—WOODH., Sitgr. Rep. 1853, 99.—NEWB., P. R. R. Rep. vi, 1857, 98.— HEERM., *ibid.* x, 1859, pt. vi, 65.—COUES, Key, 1872, 258.—FINSCH, Abh. Nat. iii, 1872, 63.—RIDGW., Ann. Lyc. N. Y. x, 1874, 384.
Gambetta melanoleuca, BP., Comptes Rendus, 1856, p. —.—BD., B. N. A. 1858, 731.— COOP. & SUCK., N. H. Wash. Ter. 1860, 242.—WHEAT., Ohio Agric. Rep. 1860, No. 215.—COUES & PRENT., Smiths. Rep. 1861, 416.—HAYD., Rep. 1862, 174.— BOARDM., Pr. Bost. Soc. ix, 1862, 129.—VERR., Pr. Ess. Inst. iii, 1862, 153 (Maine, in summer).—ALLEN, *ibid.* iv, 1864, 77.—McILWR., *ibid.* v, 1866, 93.— COUES, *ibid.* v, 1868, 295.—COUES, Pr. Phila. Acad. 1861, 234 (Labrador); 1866, 98 (Arizona); 1871, 32 (North Carolina).—DRESS., Ibis, 1866, 38 (Texas).— COUES, Pr. Bost. Soc. xii, 1868, 122.—LAWR., Ann. Lyc. viii, 1866, 294; ix, 1868, 141 (Costa Rica).—TURNB., B. E. Pa. 1869, 31.—DALL & BANN., Tr. Chic. Acad. i, 1869, 292 (Alaska).—MAYN., Guide, 1870, 141.—ALLEN, Bull. M. C. Z. ii, 1871, 356 (Florida); iii, 1872, 182.—STEV., U. S. Geol. Surv. Ter. 1870, 466.—MERR., *ibid.* 1872, 700 (Wyoming).—MAYN., Pr. Bost. Soc. 1871.—TRIPPE, Pr. Bost. Soc. 1872, 241.—SNOW, B. Kans. 1873, 10.
Scolopax vociferus, WILS., Am. Orn. vii, 1813, 57, pl. 58, f. 5.
Totanus vociferus, SAB., Frank. Journ. 687.—Sw. & RICH., F. B. A. ii, 1831, 389.—NUTT., Man. ii, 1834, 148.—AUD., Syn. 1839, 244; B. Am. v, 1842, 316, pl. 345.—GIR., B. L. I. 1844, 252.—PUTN., Pr. Ess. Inst. i, 1856, 217.—TRIPPE, *ibid.* vi, 1871, 119.—HOY, Smiths. Rep. 1864, 438.
Totanus sasashew, VIEILL., Nouv. Dict. d'Hist. Nat. 1816.
Totanus chilensis, PHILIPPI.

Extralimital quotations are: *Ecuador*, SCL., P. Z. S. 1858, 461; *Guatemala*, SCL., Ibis, i, 1859, 229; *Carthagena*, CASS., Pr. Phila. Acad. 1860, 195; *Cuba*, CAB., J. f. O. iv, 351; *Orizaba*, SCL., P. Z. S. 1860, 253; *Jamaica*, SCL., P. Z. S. 1861, 80; *La Plata*, BURM., Reise, 503; *Chili*, PELZ., Novara Reise, 131; PHIL., Cat. 35; *Bahamas*, BRY., Pr. Bost.

Soc. 1867, 69; *Buenos Ayres*, SCL. & SALV., P. Z. S. 1868, 144; *Peru*, SCL. & SALV., P. Z. S. 1869, 156; *Saint Bartholomew*, SUND., Ofv. Vet. 1869, 588; *Brazil*, PELZ., Orn. 308.

Hab.—The Western Hemisphere. In the United States, chiefly migratory, and in winter. Breeds mostly in high latitudes. Abundant.

List of specimens.

| 19305 | 194 | Big Sandy Fork. | .... | Sept. 30, 1860 | G. H. Trook. | 15.00 | 25.00 | 8.00 |

Lieutenant Warren's Expedition.—4860, Saint Joseph's, Missouri; 5435, Fort Berthold, Dakota.
Later Expeditions.—60362-3; 60776-84, 61104-6, 62360, various Wyoming localities.

Occurs wherever there is water throughout the Missouri region; especially numerous during the migration, and in some places one of the most abundant of all the waders. The eggs I have never seen.

TOTANUS FLAVIPES, (Gm.) Vieill.

Lesser Telltale; Lesser Yellowshanks.

Scolopax flavipes, GM., Syst. Nat. i, 1788, 659.—LATH., Ind. Orn. ii, 1790, 723.- WILS., Am. Orn. vii, 1813, 55, pl. 58, 4.
Totanus flavipes, VIEILL., Nouv. Dict. d'Hist. Nat. 1816, 400.—BP., Syn. 1828, 324; List, 1838, 51.—SAB., Frank. Journ. 688.—SW. & RICH., F. B. A. ii, 1831, 390.—NUTT., Man. ii, 1834, 152.—AUD., Orn. Biog. iii, 1835, 573; v, 586; pl. 228; Syn. 1839, 243; B. Am. v, 1842, 313, pl. 344.—GIR., B. L. I. 1844, 250.—WOODH., Sitgr. Rep. 1853, 99.—MOSCHL., J. f. O. 1856, 335 (Greenland).—PUTN., Pr. Ess. Inst. i, 1856, 217.—REINH., Ibis, iii, 1861 (Greenland).—YARR., Br. Birds, ii, 637 (England).—NEWB., P. R. R. Rep. vi, 1857, 98 (California and Oregon).—MILNER, Zool. 1858, p. 5958 (England).—HOY, Smiths. Rep. 1864, 438.—NEWT., P. Z. S. 1867, 166, pl. 15, f. 5 (egg).—TRIPPE, Pr. Ess. Inst. vi, 1871, 119.—RODD, Zool. 1871, 2807 (England).—COUES, Key, 1872, 259.—RIDGW., Ann. Lyc. N. Y. x, 1874, 384.
Gambetta flavipes, BP., C. R. 1856.—BD., B. N. A. 1858, 732.—WHEAT., Ohio Agric. Rep. 1860, No. 216.—COUES & PRENT., Smiths. Rep. 1861, 416.—BOARDM., Pr. Bost. Soc. ix, 1862, 129.—VERR., Pr. Ess. Inst. iii, 1862, 153 (Maine, perhaps breeding).—ALLEN, *ibid.* iv, 1864, 77.—McILWR., *ibid.* v, 1866, 93.—COUES, *ibid.* v, 1868, 295.—DRESS., Ibis, 1866, 38 (Texas).—COUES, Pr. Bost. Soc. xii, 1868, 122.—COUES, Pr. Phila. Acad. 1871, 32.—LAWR., Ann. Lyc. 1861, 334 (Panama); viii, 1864, 101 (Sombrero); viii, 1866, 294 (New York); ix, 1868, 141 (Costa Rica); *ibid.* 210 (Yucatan).—TURNB., B. E. Pa. 1869, 32.—DALL & BANN., Tr. Chic. Acad. i, 1869, 292 (Alaska).—MAYN., Guide, 1870, 141.—ALLEN, Bull M. C. Z. ii, 1871, 356 (Florida); iii, 1872, 182 (Colorado and Utah).—STEV., U. S. Geol. Surv. Ter. 1870, 466 (Wyoming).—MAYN., Pr. Bost. Soc. 1871.—TRIPPE, Pr. Bost. Soc. 1872, 241 (Iowa).—SNOW, B. Kans. 1873, 10.
Totanus natator et fuscocapillus, VIEILL., Nouv. Dict. d'Hist. Nat. 1816.
" ―――― *leucopyga*, ILLGER." (*Gray.*)

Extralimital quotations are: *Oaxaca*, SCL., P. Z. S. 1859, 393; *Guatemala*, SCL., Ibis, i, 1859, 229; *Santa Cruz*, NEWT., *ibid.* 251; *Carthagena*, CASS., Pr. Phila. Acad. 1860, 195; *Cuba*, CAB., J. f. O. iv, 352; *Ecuador*, SCL., P. Z. S. 1860, 290; *Brazil*, REINH., Viddensk. Meddel. 1870, 37; *La Plata*, BURM., Reise, 503; *Bahamas*, BRY., Pr. Bost. Soc. 1867, 69; *Mexiana*, SCL. & SALV., P. Z. S. 1867, 592; *Buenos Ayres, ibid.* 1868, 144; *Chili*, PHIL., Cat. 35; *Saint Bartholomew*, SUND., Ofv. Vet. Acad. 1869, 588; *Great Britain*, HART., Br. Birds, 1872, 137; *Peru*, SCL. & SALV., P. Z. S. 1873, 310.

Hab.—Western Hemisphere. Breeds from the Northern States northward. Many winter in the Southern States. Accidental in Europe.
Lieutenant Warren's Expedition.—4861, Council Bluffs (omitted from Hayden's Report).
Later Expeditions.—59869, Soda Springs, Colorado; 60304-9, Bitter Cottonwood and La Bonté Creek; 60785, North Platte.
Not obtained by Captain Raynolds' Expedition.

Occurs with the preceding, under similar conditions, and in equal abundance.

This species appears to be more numerous and generally distributed east of the Rocky Mountains than on the Pacific side, where, however, a doubt of its occurrence is no longer entertained.

32

The Yellowshank, so far as known, nests only in high latitudes. The eggs are deposited on the ground, in a little depression, lined with a few dried leaves or grasses. They are three or four in number, narrowly and pointedly pyriform, measuring from 1.58 by 1.18, to 1.78 by 1.15; the longest eggs not being always also the broadest. The ground is a clean clay-color, sometimes tending more to buffy or creamy, sometimes rather to light brown. The marking is bold and heavy, but presents the customary great diversity, some eggs being very heavily splashed with blotches confluent about the larger end, while others have smaller clean-edged spots all over the surface. The markings are rich umber-brown, often tending to chocolate, sometimes almost blackish. The paler shell-markings are usually numerous and noticeable. An occasional " albino " egg is seen, whitish, with scarcely any markings. All the many eggs examined are from Arctic America.

TOTANUS SOLITARIUS, (Wils.) Aud.

Solitary Tattler; Wood Tattler.

Tringa ochropus var. β, LATH., Ind. Orn. ii, 1790, 730.
Tringa solitaria, WILS., Am. Orn. vii, 1813, 53, pl. 58, f. 3.
Totanus solitarius, AUD., Syn. 1839, 242 ; B. Am. v, 1842, 309, pl. 343.—GIR., B. L. I. 1844, 256.—PUTN., Pr. Ess. Inst. i, 1856, 216.—TRIPPE, Pr. Ess. Inst. vi, 1871, 119.—HOY, Smiths. Rep. 1864, 438.—SCHL., M. P.-B. *Scolop.* 1862, p. 73.—GRAY, Ibis, 1870, 292 ; B. West Scotland, 295.—HART., Br. Birds, 1872, 137.—COUES, Key, 1872, 259.
Rhyacophilus solitarius, CASS., Baird's B. N. A. 1858, 733.—WHEAT., Ohio Agric. Rep. 1860, No. 217.—COUES & PRENT., Smiths. Rep. 1861, 416.—HAYD., Rep. 1862, 174.—BOARDM., Pr. Bost. Soc. ix, 1862, 129.—VERR., Pr. Ess. Inst. iii, 1862, 153.—ALLEN, *ibid.* iv, 1864, 77.—COUES, *ibid.* v, 1868, 295.—COUES, Pr. Bost. Soc. xii, 1868, 122.—COUES, Pr. Phila. Acad. 1866, 98 (Arizona) ; 1871, 32 (North Carolina).—TURNB., B. E. Pa. 1869, 32 (May to Sept.).—DRESS., Ibis, 1866, 38 (Matamoras, summer).—LAWR., Ann. Lyc. 1861, 334 (Panama) ; viii, 1866, 294 ; ix, 1868, 141 (Costa Rica).—DALL & BANN., Tr. Chic. Acad. i, 1869, 292 (Alaska).—ALLEN, Bull. M. C. Z. iii, 1872, 182 (Kansas, Colorado, and Wyoming).—TRIPPE, Pr. Bost. Soc. xv, 1872, 241 (Iowa).—MAYN., Guide, 1870, 141 ; Pr. Bost. Soc. 1871 (New Hampshire, breeding).—SNOW, B. Kans. 1873, 10 (Kansas, rare).—STEV., U. S. Geol. Surv. Ter. 1870, 466 (Wyoming).
Totanus chloropus var. *solitarius*, RIDGW., Ann. Lyc. N. Y. x, 1874, 384.
Totanus chloropygius, VIEILL., Nouv. Dict. d'Hist. Nat. vi, 1816, 401.—BP., Obs. Wils. 1825, No. 210 ; Syn. 1828, 325 ; List, 1838, 51.—SW. & RICH., F. B. A. ii, 1831, 393.—WAGL., Isis, 1831, 521.—NUTT., Man. ii, 1834, 159.—AUD., Orn. Biog. iii, 1835, 576 ; v, 583 ; pl. 289.
Rhyacophilus chloropygius, BP., Comptes Rendus, 1856.
Totanus glareola, ORD, ed. Wils. vii, 1825, 57.
Totanus macroptera, SPIX, Av. Bras. ii, 1825, 76, 92.
" (?) *Totanus caligatus*, LICHT." (*Gray*.)
" *Totanus guttatus*, ILLIGER." (*Gray*.)
Additional quotations.—CAB., J. f. O. iv, 352 (Cuba).—SCL., P. Z. S. 1861, 80 (Jamaica).—NEWT., Ibis, i, 1859, 257 (Santa Cruz).—SUND., Ofv. Vet. Ak. 1869, 587 (Saint Bartholomew).—SCL., P. Z. S. 1856, 310 (Cordova) ; 1860, 254 (Orizaba) ; 1864, 178 (city of Mexico) ; 1867, 592 (Mexiana).—SCL., P. Z. S. 1858, 461 (Ecuador).—SCL., Ibis, i, 1859, 229 (Guatemala).—SCL. & SALV. P. Z. S. 1868, 199 (Eastern Peru) ; 1867, 979 ; 1868, 169 (Venezuela) ; 1869, 598 (Peru) ; 1872, 309 (Peru).—PELZ., Orn. Bras. 309.

Hab.—Western Hemisphere. Accidental in Europe. North to Alaska. Breeds in Northern United States and northward, if not also throughout most of its United States range. Abundant. Migratory. Winters chiefly or altogether beyond our limits, in Mexico, Central and South America, and West Indies.
Lieutenant Warren's Expedition.—4866, Omaha ; 5437, Fort Union ; 8992–4, Upper Missouri.
Later Expeditions.—60370–3, 60773, Camp Raynolds and Fort Fetterman, Wyoming. Not obtained by Captain Raynolds' Expedition.

In most of the United States this is a bird of passage, chiefly observed in the spring and fall, but I am satisfied that it breeds, in suitable places, over a much more extensive area than is generally supposed. Indeed little has been put on record, or apparently known, respecting its breeding resorts. Wilson says that it breeds on mountains in Pennsylvania, and such is undoubtedly the case. In Maryland and Virginia, and in nearly correspondent latitudes in the West, I have shot birds in August so young as to leave no doubt in my mind that they were bred in the vicinity. Mr. Maynard makes substantially the same observation about the Franconia Mountains, in New Hampshire; and I have found young birds in July in Northern Dakota, about the pools of Turtle Mountain. In the Carolinas I only observed it during the migration, though Professor Gibbes marks it as resident. It seems to be very retiring and secretive in its habits during the breeding season, which may, perhaps, in part, account for the lack of observations respecting it at this season. At the same time it is not to be inferred that it is restricted in its northern dispersion, for it occurs on the Yukon, where, according to Mr. Dall, it arrives early in May. Other writers give it from various portions of the fur countries.

The only eggs supposed to be of the Solitary Tattler I have seen, are two in the Smithsonian collection from Cleveland, Ohio (Dr. Kirtland). The size is 1.50 by 1.05; the shape ordinarily pyriform. The ground is clay-colored, without olivaceous or other shade. The markings are heavy and numerous on the larger half of the egg, smaller and fewer elsewhere. They are very dark—quite blackish-brown—lacking the slightest shade of the rich umber or chocolate which most waders show more or less evidently. The shell-spots are similarly of a darker neutral tint than usual. The identification of these eggs, however, is open to question: they may be those of the Killdeer.

About Washington, D. C., the Solitary Tattler is very common indeed at certain seasons. It arrives from the South late in April, and for two weeks or so is to be found in all suitable situations; then none are to be seen, except a few straggling young just at the end of summer, until late in September; when, after an equally late sojourn, the birds pass on. In the Carolinas I have seen them nearly a month earlier in the spring. They differ from most of their relatives in their choice of feeding-grounds, or of places where they usually alight to rest while migrating; a difference accompanied, I suppose, by a corresponding modification in diet. Their favorite resorts are the margins of small, stagnant pools, fringed with rank grass and weeds; the miry, tide-water ditches that intersect marshes; and the soft, oozy depressions in low meadows and watery savannas. They frequent, also, the interior of woods not too thick, and collect there about the rain-puddles, the water of which is delayed in sinking by the matted layer of decaying leaves that covers the ground. After heavy rains I have seen them running about like Grass Plovers, on open, level commons, covered only with short turf. They also have a fancy, shared by few birds except the Titlarks, for the pools of liquid manure usually found in some out of the way place upon the thrifty farmer's premises. They find abundant food in all these places; aquatic insects of all sorts, and especially their curious larvæ, worms, grubs, and perhaps the smallest sorts of molluscs; with all these, they also take into their gizzards a quantity of sand and gravel, to help along the grinding process. With food to be had in such plenty with little labor, the birds become, particularly in the fall, extremely fat.

They cannot be said with entire propriety to be "solitary," though this name is well enough to indicate less social propensities than most of the waders possess. I generally found from two or three to half a dozen together; frequently only one at a time; occasionally, but not often, upwards of a score, that seemed, however, to be drawn together by their common tastes in the matter of feeding-grounds, rather than by any gregarious instinct. They are, moreover, pretty exclusive in their own set; rather declining than encouraging familiarity on the part of other waders; though the Peetweets and others sometimes intrude hoydenish society upon the more sedate and aristocratic members of the long-legged circle. They should rightly, however, rather embrace, than merely endure such company, for they are of easy-going, contemplative natures, and their sharper-eyed associates often do them good service in sounding alarms.

These Tattlers indulge on all occasions a propensity for nodding, like Lord Burleigh or the Chinese mandarins in front of tea shops; and when they see something they cannot quite make out, seem to reason with themselves, and finally come to a conclusion in this way; impressing themselves heavily with a sense of their own logic. They go through the bowing exercise with a gravity that may quite upset that of a disinterested spectator, and yet all through the performance, so ludicrous in itself, contrive to preserve something of the passive sedateness that marks all their movements. This bobbing of the head and foreparts is the correspondent and counterpart of the still more curious actions of the Spotted Tattlers, or "Tip-ups," as they are aptly called, from this circumstance; a queer balancing of the body upon the legs, constituting an amusement of which these last-named birds are extremely fond. As often as the Tip-up, or "Teeter-tail," as it is also called, stops in its pursuit of insects, the fore part of the body is lowered a little, the head drawn in, the legs slightly bent, whilst the hinder parts and tail are alternately hoisted with a peculiar jerk, and drawn down again, with the regularity of clock-work. The movement is more conspicuous in the upward than in the downward part of the performance; as if the tail were spring-hinged, in constant danger of flying up, and needing constant presence of mind to keep it down. It is amusing to see an old male in the breeding season busy with this operation. Upon some rock jutting out of the water he stands, swelling with amorous pride and self-sufficiency, puffing out his plumage till he looks twice as big as natural, facing about on his narrow pedestal, and bowing with his hinder parts to all points of the compass. A sensitive and fastidious person might see something derisive, if not actually insulting, in this, and feel as Crusoe may be presumed to have felt when the savages who attacked his ship in canoes showed the signs of contumaceous scorn that DeFoe records. But it would not be worth while to feel offended, since this is only the entirely original and peculiar way the Tip-up has of conducting his courtships. Ornithologists are not agreed upon the useful purpose subserved in this way, and have as yet failed to account for the extraordinary performance. The Solitary Tattlers, that we have lost sight of for a moment, are fond of standing motionless in the water when they have satisfied their hunger, or of wading about, up to their bellies, with slow, measured steps. If startled at such times, they rise easily and lightly on wing, fly rather slowly a little distance with dangling legs and outstretched neck, to soon realight and look about with a dazed expression. Just as their feet touch the ground, the long, pointed wings are lifted, till their tips nearly meet above, and are then deliberately folded. The Esquimaux Curlews and some other birds have the same habit. The Tattlers are unusually silent birds; but when suddenly alarmed, they utter a low and rather pleasing whistle as they fly off, or even without moving.

These birds seem rather delicate of body, and may be killed with a touch of shot. I have frequently brought them down, particularly when they were on wing, with the sides of the body therefore unprotected by strong feathers, at very long range, and with shot so fine that it would not have mutilated a Warbler at half the distance. I think they differ noticeably in this respect from the majority of waders, which require to be pretty hard hit; .the Peetweets, in particular, are rather tough birds for their size. Neither do they attempt to escape, when wounded, by diving, at which the last-named is expert under similar circumstances. At least such has been my experience, which I am the more careful to give, since others have stated just the contrary. I think them gentle birds, almost like Doves among their kind. They yield captives without a struggle. They show concern and sympathy for a dead or wounded comrade. I have seen them gather around to gaze upon one of their number that had fallen, so taken up with whatever their emotions were that they quite forgot they were in like danger. Though under some circumstances rather watchful, they sometimes show a curious *insouciance* that borders on what might be called stupidity, and is quite a different thing from the reckless familiarity of such birds, for example, as the timid yet confiding little Sandpeeps. An illustration may stand in good stead of further explanation. Once coming up to a fence that went past a little pool, and peeping through the slats, I saw eight Tattlers of this species wading about in the shallow water, searching for food. I pulled trigger on one; the others set up a simultaneous outcry, and I expected them, of course, to fly off, but they presently quieted down and began feeding again. Without moving from my place, I fired three times more, killing a single bird at each discharge; still no effect upon the survivors, except as before. Then I climbed over the fence, and stood in full view of the four remaining birds; they merely flapped to the further side of the pool, and stood still looking at me, nodding away, as if agreed that the whole thing was very singular. I stood and deliberately loaded and fired three times more, taking one bird each time; and it was only as I was ramming another charge, that the sole surviving bird concluded to make off, which he did, I will add in justice to his wits, in a great hurry. The seven birds were all killed with mustard seed, at from twelve to twenty paces.

TRINGOIDES MACULARIUS, (Linn.) Gray.

Spotted Sandpiper.

Tringa macularia, LINN., Syst. Nat. i, 1766, 249 (based on *Tringa maculata*, EDW., ii, 139, pl. 277, fig. 2; *Turdus aquaticus*, BRISS., v, 255).—GM., Syst. Nat. 1788, 672.—LATH., Ind. Orn. ii, 1790, 734 (*Spotted Sandpiper* of Arct. Zool. ii, No. 385; Gen. Syn. v, 179).—WILS., Am. Orn. vii, 1813, 60, pl. 59, fig. 1.
Totanus macularius, TEMM., Man. 1815, 422; ii, 1820, 656.—BOIE, Isis, 1822, 560.—FLEM., Br. An. 103.—JENYNS, Man. 199.—EYT., Cat. Br. B. 44.—BREHM, V. D. 646.—BP., Obs. Wils. 1825, No. 211; Syn. 1828, 325.—NUTT., Man. ii, 1834, 162.—AUD., Orn. Biog. iv, 1838, 81, pl. 310; Syn. 1839, 242; B. Am. v, 1842, 303, pl. 342.—GIR., B. L. I. 1844, 257.—PUTN., Pr. Ess. Inst. i, 1856, 217.—HOY, Smith's Rep. 1864, 438.—TRIPPE, Pr. Ess. Inst. vi, 1871, 119.
Actitis macularius, BOIE, Isis, 1826, 979.—NAUM., V. D. viii, 1836, 34, pl. 195.—BP., List, 1838, 51.—KEYS. & BLAS., Wirb. Eur. 73.—SCHL., M. P.-B. *Scolopaces*, 83.—FINSCH, Abh. Nat. iii, 1872, 63.
Tringoides macularius, GRAY, Gen. of B. iii, 1849, 574.—WOODH., Sitgr. Rep. 1853, 99.—BD., B. N. A. 1858, 735.—COOP. & SUCK., N. H. Wash. Ter. 1860, 244.—COUES, Pr. Phila. Acad. 1861, 235 (Labrador, breeding); 1866, 98 (Arizona).—HAYD., Rep. 1862, 174.—DRESS., Ibis, 1866, 38 (Texas).—DALL & BANN., Tr. Chic. Acad. 1869, 293 (Alaska).—MAYN., Guide, 1870, 139.—ALLEN, Bull. M. C. Z. ii, 1871, 356; iii, 1872, 182 (mountains of Colorado, up to 13,000 feet).—STEV., U. S.

Geol. Surv. Ter. 1870, 466.—Merr., *ibid.* 1872, 701.—Trippe, Pr. Bost. Soc. xv, 1872, 241.—Aiken, *ibid.* 210.—Snow, B. Kans. 1873, 10.—Coues, Key, 1872, 260, fig. 172; and of most late United States writers.
Tringoides hypoleucus var. *macularius*, Ridgw., Ann. Lyc. x, 1874, 384.
Tringites macularius, Scl. & Salv., P. Z. S. 1873, 309 (Peru).
Tringa notata, Illiger. (*Gray.*)
Actitis notata et *wiedi*, Bp. (*Gray.*)

Other quotations.—Scl., P. Z. S. 1858, 460 (Ecuador, winter); 1860, 254 (Orizaba); 1867, 592 (Mexiana); 1868, 629 (Venezuela); Ibis, i, 1859, 230 (Guatemala).—Lawr., Ann. Lyc. 1861, 334 (Panama); *ibid.* 1868, 142 (Costa Rica).—Cab., J. f. O. iv, 417 (Cuba).—Newt., Ibis, i, 1859, 257 (Santa Cruz).—Bry., Pr. Bost. Soc. 1866 (Porto Rico).—Scl., P. Z. S. 1861, 80 (Jamaica).—Taylor, Ibis, 1864, 93 (Trinidad).—Sund., Ofv. Vet. Ak. 1869, 587 (St. Bartholomew).—Pelz., Orn. Bras. 309 (Brazil).—Gould, B. Eur. pl. 317 (Europe).—Naum., Vög. pl. 195 (Europe).—Hart., Br. Birds, 139 (Great Britain, numerous instances, with the references).

Hab.—North America at large. Breeds nearly throughout its North American range. Winters in the Southern States and beyond. Central and South America, to Brazil. West Indies. Casual in Europe. (No Greenland record.)

List of specimens.

| 19304 | 26 | Wind River ... | ♀ | May 26, 1860 | F. V. Hayden. | 7.50 | 13.50 | 4.25 |

Lieutenant Warren's Expedition.—8995, Loup Fork; 5439, Knife River; 5440, mouth Powder River.
Later Expeditions.—59868, Middle Park, Colorado; 60374-75, Fort Fetterman; 60788, North Platte; 61160, Wyoming; 62359, Idaho.

Although reaching high latitudes, such as that of the Yukon, this little species, unlike most of its allies, breeds with equal readiness almost throughout the country, and is one of the best known and most abundant of its tribe. It nests in a field or orchard, generally near water, laying four creamy or clay-colored eggs, blotched with blackish-brown and neutral tint. From the Southern States, where it spends the winter, as it also does much further south, it reaches the Middle districts about the 15th of April, and is found along the streams and ponds of the interior, as well as on the coast. Many stop to breed all along the line of migration, while others pass on at least to Labrador. Eggs may be found all through June and July, according to latitude, and perhaps in some cases more than one brood may be raised.

According to Mr. Trippe, in the mountains of Colorado this is the only species of its family that is abundant throughout the summer. It arrives at Idaho Springs early in May, leaving in September. It pushes up all the larger streams to an altitude of 8,000 or 9,000 feet, and even, occasionally, to the shores of the lakes near the timber-line.

ACTITURUS BARTRAMIUS, (Wils.) Bp.

Bartramian Sandpiper or Tattler; Upland Plover.

Tringa bartramia, Wils., Am. Orn. vii, 1813, 63, pl. 59, fig. 2.—Aud., Syn. 1839, 231; B. Am. v, 1842, 248, pl. 327.—Gir., B. L. I. 1844, 226 (breeding in Pennsylvania and Illinois).—Putn., Pr. Ess. Inst. i, 1856, 216.—Trippe, *ibid.* vi, 1871, 119 (Minnesota, abundant).
Tringa (Euliga) bartramia, Nutt., Man. ii, 1834, 168.
Totanus bartramius, Temm., Man. ii, 1820, 650.—Bp., Obs. Wils. 1825, No. 209; Syn. 1828, 262.—Sw. & Rich., F. B. A. ii, 1831, 391 (Saskatchewan).—Aud., Orn. Biog. iv, 1838, 24, pl. 303.—Hoy, Smiths. Rep. 1864, 438 (Missouri).
Actiturus bartramius, Bp., Saggio, 1831; List, 1838, 51.—Bd., B. N. A. 1858, 737.—Wheat., Ohio Agric. Rep. No. 219.—Coues & Prent., Smiths. Rep. 1861, 416 (Washington, summer).—Hayd., Rep. 1862, 174.—Boardm., Pr. Bost. Soc. ix, 1862, 129 (Maine, summer).—Verr., Pr. Ess. Inst. iii, 1862, 153 (Maine, breeding).—Allen, *ibid.* iv, 1864, 78 (Massachusetts, breeding.)—Coues, *ibid.* v, 1868, 295 (New England, summer).—McIlwr., *ibid.* v, 1866, 93 (Canada West, uncom-

mon).—LAWR., Ann. Lyc. 1861, 334 (Panama); 1868, 141 (Costa Rica); viii, 1866, 294 (New York).—SCL., Ibis, i, 1859, 230 (Guatemala).—DRESS., *ibid.* 1866, 38 (Texas).—CAB., J. f. O. iv, 418 (Cuba).—SCL., P. Z. S. 1860, 253 (Orizaba); 1866, 567 (Ucayali River); 1867, 979 (Peru); 1868, 169 (Venezuela); 1869, 598 (Peru).— LORD, Pr. Roy. Arty. Inst. iv, 124 (Colville Bay).—REINH., Vid. Med. Nat. For. 1870, 38 (Brazil).—BURM., Reise, 503 (La Plata).—COUES, Pr. Bost. Soc. xii, 1868, 123 (South Carolina, migratory).—ALLEN, Mem. Bost. Soc. i, 1868, 501 (Iowa).—DALL & BANN., Tr. Chic. Acad. i, 1869, 293 (Fort Yukon).—TURNB., B. E. Pa. 1869, 32 (April to September).—MAYN., Guide, 1870, 141 (Massachusetts, breeding).—ALLEN, Bull. M. C. Z. iii, 1872, 182 (Kansas and Colorado).— TRIPPE, Pr. Bost. Soc. xv, 1872, 241 (Iowa, breeding).—SNOW, B. Kans. 1873, 10 (Kansas, breeding).—HART., Br. Birds, 1872, 137 (Great Britain, four instances).— COUES, Key, 1872, 260.—SCL. & SALV., P. Z. S. 1873, 309 (Peru).—RIDGW., Ann. Lyc. N. Y. x, 1874, 384 (Illinois).

Tringoides bartramius, GRAY, Gen. of B. iii, 1849, —.—WOODH. Sitgr. Rep. 1853, 99 (Arkansas).—PELZ., Orn. Bras. 310 (Brazil).
Tringoides (Bartramia) bartramius, GRAY, Hand-list, iii, 1871, 46, No. 10281.
Actitis bartramius, SCHL., M. P.-B. *Scolopaces,* 78.
Tringa longicauda, "BECHST., Vög. Deutschl.—NAUM., Nachtrage, pl. 38."
Actiturus longicaudus, BLAS., List. B. Eur. ed. Newton, 1862, 18 (Germany and England).
Bartramius longicaudus, BP., R. and M. Z. 1857.
"*Totanus melanopygius et campestris?* VIEILL., Nouv. Dict."
Totanus variegatus, VIEILL., Nouv. Dict. vi, 1816, 317; Gal. Ois. ii, 1825, 107, pl. 239.
Bartramia laticauda, LESS., Traité d'Orn. 1831, 553.

Hab.—North America. North to the Yukon. Not observed in the United States west of the Rocky Mountains. Atlantic coast to Nova Scotia. Breeds from the Middle districts northward. Winters in Mexico, West Indies, Central and South America, to Brazil. Casual in Europe (Sweden, *Nilsson;* Germany, NAUM., V. D. viii, 51; GOULD, B. Eur. pl. 313; Great Britain, REID, Zool. 1852, 3330; GURNEY, *ibid.* 3388; MORE, *ibid.* 1854, 4254; BALLMORE, *ibid.* 1866, 37; Cornish Fn. 31; YARR., Br. Birds, ii, 633; TEARLE, Ill. Lond. News, Jan. 20, 1855, with figure; MORRIS, Br. Birds, iv, 296; See *Harting, l. c.*). Australia (GOULD, B. Aust. Suppl. iv, 1867).

Lieutenant Warren's Expedition.—4629, Fort Pierre; 4633, Fort Union; 4868, Loup Fork; 5432, Medicine Hill, 8988–91, Loup Fork and Platte River.
Not obtained by Captain Raynolds' or by the later Expeditions.

Bartram's Tattler, or the "Upland Plover," as it is generally called by sportsmen, is a bird of wide and general dispersion in the Western Hemisphere, while its casual occurrence in Europe is attested, and it is even stated to have been found in Australia. It inhabits at different seasons nearly all of North America, and in winter pushes its migration even to Central and South America, as well as into the West Indies. But it has not, to my knowledge, been found in the United States west of the Rocky Mountains. It occurs in summer as far north as the Yukon, though thousands of the birds also breed within the limits of the United States.

On its presence and movements in the East I have made few observations, and know nothing beyond the general items familiar to all sportsmen who, with good reason, consider the Upland Plover, or Grass Plover, as a prime game bird, wild and difficult to secure, best hunted from a carriage, and capital for the table. It is said to breed from the Middle districts, as in Illinois and Pennsylvania, northward. The principal shooting is done in August and September, as the birds move southward by the end of the latter month.

In most parts of the West, between the Mississippi and the Rocky Mountains, this Tattler, commonly known as the "Prairie Pigeon," is exceedingly abundant during the migrations—more so than I can suppose it to be in settled portions of the country. In Texas, I am told, it occurs in flocks "of thousands." In Kansas, during the month of May, it migrates in great numbers, being scattered over the prairies everywhere, and it is so tame that it may be destroyed without the slightest artifice; I have seen it just escape being caught with the crack of a coach-whip. Passing northward, it enters Dakota, Iowa, and Minnesota

the same month. About the middle of May it reaches the latitude of
Fort Randall, with great numbers of Golden Plover and Esquimaux
Curlew, flecking the prairies everywhere. Its breeding habits may be
studied with perfect success in Northern Dakota, where it is the most
abundant of all the waders. We can scarcely cross a piece of prairie,
or travel a mile along the roads anywhere, without seeing it. Its gentle
and unsuspicious ways, its slender and graceful shape, and the beauty
of its markings, are all alike attractive, while the excellence of its flesh
is another point not less interesting, but less favorable for the bird.
Too many are destroyed at this season when they are pairing, for few
can resist the tempting shots, as the birds step along the road-side or
stand erect in the scanty grass, gazing at the passing vehicle with mis-
placed confidence. By the end of May those that are to breed further
north have passed on, while the remainder have paired and are about to
nest.

As soon as they are mated the pairs keep close company, being rarely
beyond each other's call, and are oftenest seen rambling together through
the grass. At such times they seem very slender, as indeed they are,
overtopping the scanty herbage with their long, thin necks, swaying
continually in graceful motion. Their ordinary note at this, as at other
seasons, is a long-drawn, soft, mellow whistle, of a peculiarly clear, resonant quality; but beside this, they have a note peculiar, I believe, to
this period of their lives. This is a very loud, prolonged cry, sounding
more like the whistling of the wind than a bird's voice; the wild sound,
which is strangely mournful, is generally uttered when the bird, just
alighted, holds its wings for a moment perpendicularly, before adjusting
them over its back. It is frequently heard in the night, all through the
breeding season, and is, I think, one of the most remarkable outcries I
ever heard. There is yet another note that the Tattler utters, chiefly
when disturbed breeding; this is a harsh scream, quickly and often
repeated, much like that given by other waders under the same circumstances.

In Northern Dakota the eggs are mostly laid by the second week in
June; the time is quite constant; and, so far as I know, only one brood
is raised each year. The nest, like that of other birds breeding on the
open prairie, is hard to find, as there is nothing whatever to guide a
search, and the herbage of the prairie, flimsy as it usually is at this
season, is sufficient to hide the variegated eggs which assimilate with
the colors of their surroundings. The nesting is quite similar to that
of the Curlews and Godwits. I have found nests on the open prairie
without landmarks; but, perhaps, oftener they are placed in the vicinity
of pools and sloughs, or along the edge of a piece of woods—always,
however, in an open spot. The female is a close setter, and will suffer herself to be almost trodden upon before she will quit her charge—indeed
nests are oftenest found by the fluttering of the female from under
one's feet. Early in incubation she generally flies to a little distance
and realights, walking leisurely about the grass; but if the eggs be far
advanced she is more solicitous, and will feign lameness, in hope of
drawing attention from the nest. The male soon joins her, and the pair
hover low of the ground, flying slowly around with incurved wings,
uttering their cries of distress; and as several pairs are usually nesting
within hearing, they, too, become alarmed, and the general clamor is
continued until the intruder withdraws. The scene is much the same
as when the breeding places of the Curlews, Willets, or Godwits are
invaded.

The nest is flimsy—merely a few straws to keep the eggs from the ground, in a slight depression. The eggs are ordinarily four in num-ber, as usual among Waders. The numerous specimens I have collected are somewhat notably constant in characters, both of size and coloration. In dimensions they range from 1.90 by 1.30 inches, to 1.70 by 1.25, averaging about 1.75 by 1.28. The ground is pale clay-color, or a very light drab—sometimes the palest possible creamy-brown—with scarcely a shade of olivaceous. They are spotted all over, but much more thickly at the larger end, with rather small, sharp, surface markings of umber-brown, overlaying a smaller number of purplish-gray shell-markings. However thickly they may be sprinkled, the spots are rarely, if ever, confluent into masses of any size, the largest I have seen not exceeding the diameter of a pea. These larger blotches are irregular in contour, but the smaller ones are mostly rounded.

Young birds are abroad late in June—curious little creatures, timid and weak, led about by their anxious parents, solicitous for their well-fare, and ready to engage in the most unequal contests in their behalf. When half grown, but still in the down, the little creatures have a curiously clumsy, top-heavy look; their legs look disproportionately large, like those of a young colt or calf; and they may be caught with little difficulty, as they do not run very well. I once happened upon a brood, perhaps two weeks old, rambling with their mother over the prairie. She sounded the alarm, to scatter her brood, but not before I had secured one of them in my hand. I never saw a braver defence attempted than was made by this strong-hearted though powerless bird, who, after exhausting her artifices to draw me in pursuit of herself, by tumbling about as if desperately wounded, and lying panting with out-stretched wings on the grass, gave up hope of saving her young in this way, and then almost attacked me, dashing close up and retreating again to renew her useless onslaught. She was evidently incited to unusual courage by the sight of her little one struggling in my hand. At this downy stage the young birds are white below, finely mottled with black, white, and rich brown above; the feet and under mandible are light colored; the upper mandible is blackish.

Although these Tattlers are generally dispersed over the prairies dur-ing the summer, yet they affect particular spots by preference. Away from the river valleys, such spots are the numerous depressions of rolling prairie, often of great extent, which are moist or even watery at some seasons, and where the vegetation is most luxuriant. Here they gather almost into colonies. Riding into some such spot in July, when the young birds are being led about by their parents, some old bird more watchful than the rest, or nearest to the person approaching, gives the alarm with a loud outcry, the young scatter and hide, and all the old birds are soon on wing; hovering in the air, often at a great height, crossing each other's path, and ceaselessly vociferating their displeasure. I have often seen a dozen or twenty overhead at once, all from a little spot only a few acres in extent. Later in the season, when all the summer's broods are on wing, they make up into flocks, often of great extent, and old and young together assume the ordinary routine of their lives. They leave these northern regions early. I saw none after the forepart of September.

The food of this Tattler is mainly insects, especially grasshoppers, of which they must devour enormous quantities in the aggregate. They also feed on other small animal substances, as well as upon various berries. I have found them very well conditioned even in the spring, and in the fall they grow surprisingly fat. They are a tender and well-flavored bird. Being so delicate, they are easily killed, dropping to a touch of the finest shot.

There is but little difference in the plumage of these birds at any season, and their size is also quite constant. The sexes are not distinguishable by any outward marks (though the female *averages* slightly larger than the male), and the young closely resemble the parents upon their first complete feathering. In measuring a great number of fresh specimens, I found the length to vary only from 11.50 to 12.75; the extent, 21.50 to 23.00; the wing, 6.25 to 7.00; the tail is about 3.60; the tarsus about 1.75; the bill, 1.00 to 1.25, measured along the culmen.

TRYNGITES RUFESCENS, (Vieill.) Cab.

Buff-breasted Sandpiper.

Tringa rufescens, VIEILL., Nouv. Dict. d'Hist. Nat. xxxiv, 1819, 470 (Louisiana); Ency. Meth. ii, 1823, 1050; Gal. Ois. ii, 1825, 105, pl. 238.—NUTT., Man. ii, 1834, 113.—BP., List, 1838, 50.—TEMM., Man. Orn. iv, 1840, 408.—AUD., Orn. Biog. iii, 1835, 451, pl. 265; Syn. 1839, 235; B. Am. v, 1842, 264, pl. 331.—GIR., B. L. I. 1844, 230.—KEYS. & BLAS., Wirb. Eur. 77.—JENYNS, Man. 214.—EYT.,' Cat. Br. B. 41.—MACGIL., Man. ii, 68.—GRAY, Gen. of B. iii, 1849, 579.—JARD., Br. Birds, iii, 235.—YARR., Tr. Linn. Soc. xvi, 1819, pl. 11; Br. Birds, iii, 60 (European).—PUTN., Pr. Ess. Inst. i, 1856, 217 (autumn, rare).

Actiturus rufescens, BP.—BLAS., List B. Eur. 1862, 18 (England and Heligoland).

Tryngites rufescens, CAB., J. f. O. iv, 418 (Cuba).—BD., B. N. A. 1858, 739.—COOP. & SUCK., N. H. Wash. Ter. 1860, 244 (Shoalwater Bay, migratory).—WHEAT., Ohio Agr. Rep. 1860, No. 220.—ALLEN, Pr. Ess. Inst. iv, 1864, 78 (migratory, rare).—COUES, *ibid.* v, 1868, 296.—DRESS., Ibis, 1866, 39 (Texas).—LAWR., Ann. Lyc. N. Y. viii, 1866, 294.—SCL. & SALV., P. Z. S. 1866, 199 (Ucayali, Eastern Peru); 1866, 567; 1867, 754, 979.—COUES, Pr. Bost. Soc. xii, 1868, 123 (South Carolina, migratory).—TURNB., B. E. Pa. 1869, 32 (autumn, rare).—DALL & BANN., Tr. Chic. Acad. i, 1869, 293 (Nulato and Sitka; breeding abundantly in the Anderson River region).—MAYN., Guide, 1870, 142 (Massachusetts, migratory, rare).—COUES, Key, 1872, 260, fig. 173.—SNOW, B. Kans. 1873, 10 (occasional).—SCL. & SALV., P. Z. S. 1873, 309 (Peru).—RIDGW., Ann. Lyc. N. Y. x, 1874, 385 (Illinois).

Actitis rufescens, SCHL., Rev. Crit. Ois. Eur. 92; M. P.-B. *Scolopaces*, 79.

Tringoides rufescens, PELZ., Orn. Bras. 310 (Brazil, October to April).

Tringoides (Tryngites) rufescens, GRAY, Hand-list, iii, 1871, 46, No. 10283.

Tringa subruficollis, VIEILLOT. (*Gray* and *Schlegel*.)

Tringa brevirostris, LICHTENSTEIN. (*Gray* and *Schlegel*.)

Actidurus nævius, HEERM., Pr. Phila. Acad. vii, 1854, 179; P. R. R. Rep. x, pt. vi, 1859, 20, pl. 6 (Texas).

Hab.—The whole of North America. Migratory in the United States. Rather uncommon along the eastern coast. Breeds in the interior of the fur countries, and in Alaska. South America. Montevideo (DARWIN, Voy. Beagle, Birds, 130; and as above). Europe (GOULD, B. E. pl. 331; HARTING, Br. Birds, 1872, 138; numerous British instances, with references).

[NOTE.—Examining the types of *Tringa parvirostris*, PEALE, which has been referred to *T. rufescens*, with a query, by Dr. Schlegel, and made a variety of the same by Bonaparte, I find that not only is it an entirely different bird, specifically, but that it is scarcely congeneric. Having the extremely small bill of *T. rufescens*, this organ is smaller still, slenderer, and without the peculiar forward outline of the feathers at its base, which characterizes *T. rufescens*. In the mounted specimens, the wings fall far short of the end of the tail instead of reaching rather beyond. There is none of the peculiar mottling of the primaries, which is such a strong feature of *T. rufescens*; the tail is barred transversely, and there are other differences in coloration. Should it be deemed worthy of subgeneric separation, it may be called *Æchmorhynchus parvirostris.*] Not obtained by any of the Expeditions.

Though usually classed as a Sandpiper in the genus *Tringa*, mainly, it would seem, on account of its short, straight bill, this remarkably interesting little bird is really a Tattler, and its nearest relative, among our species, is the Bartramian Tattler, *Actiturus bartramius*. Its aspect is peculiar; no other species very closely resembles it. The bill is very short and small, and appears still more so by the great forward extension of the feathers on its base—to the nostrils on the upper mandible, still further on the sides of the lower mandible, and all the way into the interramal space. In any plumage it may be recognized by the unique coloration of the primaries, which are silvery-gray or white on the inner webs, beautifully and curiously mottled with fine, wavy, black tracery. It has many names, both generic and specific, but appears to have been first described by the voluminous French ornithologist above cited.

This species I have never yet seen alive. Its habits, as described, appear to be most like those of the Bartramian, in its preference for dry fields and plains, where it feeds upon grasshoppers and other insects. In the United States, where it is only known as a migrant, it appears to be nowhere very abundant, and this is particularly the case along the Atlantic coast. But great numbers nest in the Anderson River region, as shown by the large series of eggs in the Smithsonian, and these must pass through the United States along some line of migration, where the species may yet be found in abundance. Dr. Cooper calls it "common" at Shoalwater Bay, during the migration. According to Mr. Giraud, "the Buff-breasted Sandpiper is not a very common bird, though its occurrence is by no means unusual. Almost every season a few are observed along the southern shores of Long Island, and during autumn we occasionally find it in our markets. * * * * In August, 1841, Mr. Brasher met with a party of five on the shore of Gowannus Bay, which number is larger than I have seen in one group. He informs me that they appeared very gentle, allowing him to advance within shooting distance without seeming to notice his presence. At the first discharge of his gun (which procured him three), the surviving two made a short flight over the water, returning in a few minutes to the shore, at a short distance from where they had previously taken wing, which gave him an opportunity of securing the whole number."

Of the very rare and scarcely known eggs of the Buff-breasted Sandpiper I have examined about a dozen sets in the Smithsonian, all collected by Mr. MacFarlane in the Anderson River region and along the Arctic coast to the eastward. They are very pointedly pyriform. The following measurements indicate the size, shape, and limits of variation: 1.50 by 1.03; 1.48 by 1.10; 1.45 by 1.02; 1.40 by 1.04. The ground is clay, sometimes with a slight olivaceous or drab shade, oftener with a clear grayish cast, of rather peculiar shade. The markings are extremely bold and sharp, though not heavier than usual. Taking a specimen in which the markings are most distinct, we find heavy blotches and spots of indeterminate size and shape all over the egg, but largest and most numerous on the major half of the egg, of rich umber-brown, deeper or lighter according to the quantity of pigment. Nearest these blotched varieties come the splashed ones, in which the markings mass more heavily about the larger end, and are elsewhere splattered over in rather small markings. This is the more frequent pattern; and in some cases the splashing hides the ground-color at the large end. Other examples are spotted with rather narrow markings that seem to radiate from the large end, becoming largest and thickest around the greatest diameter of the egg, and being much smaller elsewhere. All the eggs have the usual neutral or stone-gray shell-markings, and in most of them there are at the large end a few spots or scrawls of blackish over all the other markings. According to the labels, the nidification is not peculiar, the nest being a slight depression of the ground, lined with a few dried grasses or leaves. The eggs are four in a majority of instances.

NUMENIUS LONGIROSTRIS, Wils.

Long-billed Curlew.

Scolopax arquata var. β, GM., Syst. Nat. i, 1788, 656.
Numenius arquata var. B, LATH., Ind. Orn. ii, 1790, 710.
Numenius longirostris, WILS., Am. Orn. viii, 1814, 24, pl. 64, f. 4.—BP., Obs. Wils. 1825,
    No. 200; Syn. 1828, 314; List, 1838, 49.—SW. & RICH., F. B. A. ii, 1831, 376.—
    NUTT., Man. ii, 1834, 94.—AUD., Orn. Biog. iii, 1835, 240; v, 1839, 587; pl. 231;
    Syn. 1839, 254; B. Am. vi, 1843, 35, pl. 355.—GIR., B. L. I. 1844, 271.—WOODH.,
    Sitgr. Rep. 1853, 98.—PUTN., Pr. Ess. Inst. i, 1856, 218.—NEWB., P. R. R. Rep.
    vi, 1857, 99 (California).—HEERM., *ibid.* x, 1859, pt. vi, 66 (California).—BD.,
    B. N. A. 1858, 743.—LORD, Pr. Roy. Arty. Inst. iv, 125.—COOP. & SUCK., N. H.
    Wash. Ter. 1860, 245.—COUES, Pr. Phila. Acad. 1861, 235.—BOARDM., Pr. Bost.
    Soc. 1862, ix, 129 (Maine, migratory).—VERR., Pr. Ess. Inst. iii, 1862, 159.—ALLEN,
    ibid. iv, 1864, 87.—MCILWR., *ibid.* v, 1866, 93 (Canada West, rare).—COUES, *ibid.*
    v, 1868, 296 (New England).—TRIPPE, *ibid.* ix, 1871, 119 (Minnesota).—COUES,
    Pr. Phila. Acad. 1866, 98 (Arizona).—COUES, Pr. Bost. Soc. xii, 1868, 123 (South
    Carolina).—HOY, Smiths. Rep. 1864, 438 (Missouri).—CAB., J. f. O. iv, 349
    (Cuba).—SCL., P. Z. S. 1864, 78 (Mexico).—DRESS, Ibis, 1866, 40 (Matamoras).—
    SALV., Ibis, 1866, 197 (Guatemala).—LAWR., Ann. Lyc. N. Y. viii, 1866, 294.—
    TURNB., B. E. Pa. 1869, 32.—ALLEN, Mem. Bost. i, 1868, 501 (Iowa).—MAYN.,
    Guide, 1870, 142.—ALLEN, Bull. M. C. Z. ii, 1871, 356 (Florida); iii, 1872, 182
    (Kansas).—COUES, Pr. Phila. Acad. 1871, 32 (North Carolina, resident).—MERR.,
    U. S. Geol. Surv. 1872, 701 (Utah).—TRIPPE, Pr. Bost. Soc. xv, 1872, 241 (Iowa,
    breeding).—FINSCH, Abh. Nat. iii, 1870, 363 (Mazatlan).—COUES, Key, 1872,
    262, fig. 174.—SNOW, B. Kans. 1873, 10.—RIDGW., Ann. Lyc. N. Y. x, 1874, 385
    (Illinois).
Numenius rufus, VIEILL., Galerie Ois. ii, 1825, 118, pl. 245 (in part).
Numenius occidentalis, WOODH., Pr. Phila. Acad. vi, 1852, 194; Sitgr. Rep. 1853, 98, pl. 6
    (Young; Albuquerque, New Mexico).
(?) *Numenius melanopus*, VIEILL.
(?) *N. brasiliensis*, MAXIM. (Brazil.) (*Gray*.)

Hab.—United States and British Provinces. Breeds nearly throughout its range,
and resident in the South.   South to Mexico.   Guatemala (? to Brazil).   Cuba.
Not obtained by Captain Raynolds' Expedition.
Later Expeditions.—59871, Colorado; 61649, Utah.

The Curlew issues from the egg clothed in whitish down, thickly blotched above
with brownish-black, and with the bill straight, about an inch long. This member
rapidly grows to a length of three or four inches, and becomes decurved. Up to the
time when the bill is still no longer than that of *N. hudsonicus*, it may readily be distinguished from that species by the strong rufescence of the under parts, nearly clear of
the hastate or sagittate dark markings which occur in *N. hudsonicus;* by its rather
larger size, even at an early age, and the usual evidences of immaturity in the texture
of the plumage. *N. occidentalis* of Woodhouse is a bird apparently of this sort.

Unlike our other two species of Curlew, the Long-billed is perfectly
at home in most parts of the United States, rearing its young even
down to our southern border. Its northern range is restricted, apparently, by the region of the Saskatchewan, as intimated by Richardson,
and the length of the British Provinces adjoining the United States. I
was, however, assured of its occurrence in Labrador, though I did not
see it myself. In New England it appears to be rather uncommon, according to all accounts, and I have found no record of its nesting in that
quarter. I found it resident on the North Carolina coast, where it undoubtedly breeds. I found it breeding with Godwits and Bartramian
Tattlers on the prairies of Minnesota and Eastern Dakota, and likewise
observed it in June, apparently breeding, in New Mexico, near Fort Wingate, just west of the Rio Grande. I procured it at Fort Whipple toward the close of summer. Dr. Woodhouse saw large flocks on the
prairies of Texas and the Indian Territory. According to the authors
above quoted, it breeds in Kansas and Iowa, as well as about Great Salt
Lake, in Utah.
It is by no means confined to the vicinity of the water, but, on the

contrary, is often seen on extensive dry plains, where it feeds on various molluscs, insects, and berries, which it deftly secures with its extra- ordinarily long bill. The length and curve of this member, measuring sometimes eight or nine inches in length, gives the bird a singular and unmistakable appearance, either in flight or when gathering its food. Its voice is sonorous and not at all musical. During the breeding sea- son, in particular, its harsh cries of alarm resound when the safety of its nest or young is threatened. In the fall, when food is plenty, it be- comes very fat, and affords delicate eating.

Dr. Newberry found the Curlew quite abundant in the vicinity of San Francisco, and throughout the Sacramento Valley during the autumn and winter, though there were comparatively few in the summer before the rainy season. " In our march," he adds, " through the Sacramento Valley and northward, we did not meet with it until we came down into the plains bordering Pitt River, above the upper cañon. Here we found them in immense numbers, and they formed a valuable addition to our bill of fare. This prairie is entirely covered with water during the wet season, as is proven by the myriads of aquatic shells (*Planorbis*, *Physa*, &c.) scattered over the ground in the grass, and as it does not dry up so completely as the other valleys, the Curlews apparently pass the sum- mer there. Around the Klamath Lakes and others of that group they were abundant in August, and we found them associated with the Geese and other water-birds, which were congregated in countless numbers on the low lands bordering the Columbia, in October."

The eggs of the Long-billed Curlew are not often so pyriform as among the smaller waders, being in shape not unlike a hen's eggs. Different specimens measure: 2.45 by 1.85; 2.60 by 1.80; 2.65 by 1.80; 2.70 by 1.90; 2.80 by 1.90. They are clay-colored, with more or less olivaceous in some instances, and in others decidedly buffy shade. The spotting is generally pretty uniformly distributed and of small pattern, though in many cases there is larger blotching and even massing about the great end. The color of the markings is sepia or umber, of different shades in the buffy-tinged specimens, rather tending to chocolate. The shell-markings are commonly numerous and evident.

NUMENIUS HUDSONICUS, Lath.

Hudsonian Curlew.

Scolopax borealis, GM., Syst. Nat. i, 1788, 654 (not of *Forster*, 1772).—WILS., Am. Orn. vii, 1813, 22, pl. 56, fig. 1.
Numenius borealis, ORD, ed. Wils. 1825.—BREW., ed. Wils. 1840, 473 (excluding the syn- onymy which, with part of the account, belongs to true *borealis;* description, with most of the account, is of *hudsonicus*).
Numenius hudsonicus, LATH., Ind. Orn. ii, 1790, 712 (based on *Esquimaux Curlew*, Arct. Zool. ii, 461, No. 364, pl. 19, and *Hudsonian Curlew*, LATH., Syn. Suppl. vii, 243).— BP., Obs. Wils. 1825, No. 201; Syn. 1828, 314; List, 1838, 49.—SW. & RICH., F. B. A. ii, 1831, 377.—NUTT., Man. ii, 1834, 97.—AUD., Orn. Biog. iii, 1835, 283; v, 589, pl. 237; Syn. 1839, 254; B. Am. vi, 1843, 42, pl. 356.—GIR., B. L. I. 1844, 272.—BD., B. N. A. 1858, 744.—TAYLOR, Ibis, ii, 1860, 313 (Fonseca Bay).—REINH., Ibis, iii, 1861, 10 (Greenland).—DRESS., *ibid.* 1866, 40 (Texas).—SALV., *ibid.* 197 (Chiapam, Guat.).—WHEAT., Ohio Agric. Rep. 1860, No. 224.—COUES, Pr. Phila. Acad. 1861, 235 (Labrador).—BOARDM., Pr. Bost. Soc. ix, 1862, 129 (Maine, mi- gratory, rare).—COUES, *ibid.* xii, 1868, 123 (South Carolina, wintering).—VERR., Pr. Ess. Inst. iii, 1862, 159 (Maine, migratory, not common).—ALLEN, *ibid.* iv, 1864, 87 (Massachusetts, migratory, rare).—COUES, *ibid.* v, 1868, 296 (New En- gland, migratory, rare).—MCILWR., *ibid.* v, 1866, 93 (Canada West).—LAWR., Ann. Lyc. N. Y. viii, 1864, 101 (Sombrero); 1866, 294.—SCL. & SALV., P. Z. S. 1867, 333 (Chili); 1868, 176 (Islay).—DARW., Voy. Beagle, 129 (Chiloe).—PELZ., Novara Reise, 128 (Chiloe).—PHIL., Cat. 34 (Chili).—TURNB., B. E. Pa. 1869, 32 (New Jersey, "plentiful ").—DALL & BANN., Tr. Chic. i, 1869, 293 (Alaska).—

MAYN., Guide, 1870, 142 (Massachusetts, migratory, rare).—FINSCH, Abh. Nat.
    iii, 1870, 363 (Mazatlan).—NEWT., P. Z. S. 1871, 57, pl. 4, fig. 3 (egg).—ALLEN,
    Bull. M. C. Z. ii, 1871, 356 (Florida, winter).—COUES, Key, 1872, 262.—SNOW,
    B. Kans. 1873, 10.—SCL. & SALV., P. Z. S. 1873, 456.—RIDGW., Ann. Lyc. N. Y.
    x, 1874, 385 (Illinois).
Numenius intermedius, NUTT., Man. ii, 1834, 100.
Numenius rufiventris, VIG., Zool. Journ. iv, 1829, 356; Voy. Bloss. 1839, 28.
Numenius phæopus, CAB., Schomb. Guiana, iii, 757.—PELZ., Orn. Bras. 308.
Numenius brasiliensis, MAXIM. et BURM. (*Sclater*.)
    Hab.—North America. Greenland. Central and South America. No West Indian
record. Breeds in high latitudes. Migratory through the United States, wintering in
the Southern States and far beyond.
    Not obtained by any of the Expeditions.

The Hudsonian appears to be much less abundant everywhere in the
United States than either of the others, although generally distributed,
and moving over much the same area as the Esquimax Curlew. I found
it sparingly in Labrador, amid the countless thousands of *N. borealis*
that throng those shores in August and September. According to all
observers it is rare in New England, but more common on the New Jersey coast. It is included among the birds of Kansas, on Prof. Baird's
authority. The extent of its southern dispersion in winter is as great
as that of *N. borealis*, and, like the latter, it breeds only in high latitudes. I am not at all familiar with its habits, concerning which very
little has been recorded.
    The eggs are always larger than those of *N. borealis*, but cannot be
otherwise distinguished with certainty, for both show the great range
of variation indicated in my description of the latter. The size is from
2.12 to 2.30 in length, by about 1.60 in width.

NUMENIUS BOREALIS, (Forst.) Lath.

Esquimaux Curlew.

Scolopax borealis, FORST., Philos. Trans. lxii, 1772, 411 (not of *Wilson*).
Numenius borealis, LATH., Ind. Orn. ii, 1790, 712.—BP., Syn. 1828, 314.—BP., Am. Orn. iv,
    118, pl. 26, fig. 3.—BP., List, 1838, 49.—SW. & RICH., F. B. A. ii, 1831, 378, pl.
    65.—NUTT., ii, 1834, 101.—AUD., Orn. Biog. iii, 1835, 69; v, 1839, 590; pl. 208.—
    AUD., Syn. 1839, 255.—AUD., B. Am. vi, 1843, 45, pl. 357.—GIR., B. L. I. 1844,
    274.—PUTN., Pr. Ess. Inst. i, 1856, 218 (Massachusetts, migratory, rare).—BD.,
    B. N. A. 1858, 744.—COUES, Pr. Phila. Acad. 1861, 236 (Labrador, migratory,
    abundant).—HAYD., Rep. 1862, 175 (Upper Missouri, not uncommon).—VERR.,
    Pr. Ess. Inst. iii, 1862, 159.—BOARDM., Pr. Bost. Bost. ix, 1862, 129 (Calais, Me., rare,
    migratory).—ALLEN, Pr. Ess. Inst. iv, 1864, 87 (Massachusetts, rare, spring and
    fall; "*occasional in winter*"(! ?).—REINH., Ibis, iii, 1861, 10 (Greenland).—SALV.,
    ibid. 356 (Central America).—DRESS., *ibid.* 1866, 40 (Texas).—SCL., P. Z. S. 1867,
    333 (Chili).—LAWR., Ann. Lyc. N. Y. viii, 1868, 294.—COUES, Pr. Ess. Inst. v,
    1868, 296 (New England, migratory, not common).—COUES, Pr. Bost. Soc. xii,
    1868, 123 (South Carolina, winter (?).—TURNB., B. E. Pa. 1869, 33 (May and
    September, rather rare).—DALL & BANN., Tr. Chic. Acad. i, 1869, 293 (Alaska).—
    MAYN., Guide, 1870, 142 (Massachusetts, migratory, not uncommon).—NEWT.,
    P. Z. S., 1871, 56, pl. 4, fig. 1 (egg).—ALLEN, Bull. M. C. Z. 1871, 356 (Florida,
    winter (?).—ALLEN, *ibid.* iii, 1872, 182 (Kansas, in June).—COUES, Key, 1872,
    262.—SNOW, B. Kans. 1873, 10.—SCL. & SALV., P. Z. S. 1873, 456.—RIDGW., Ann.
    Lyc. N. Y. x, 1874, 385 (Illinois).—DRESS., B. Eur. pt. xvi, 1873 (Europe).
Numenius brevirostris, LICHT., Verz., 1823, 75.—DARW., Voy. Beagle, iii, 129 (Buenos
    Ayres).—PELZ., Orn. Bras. 308 (Brazil).
Numenius microrhynchus, PHIL. & LANDB., Wieg. Arch. 1866, 129 (Chili); Cat. 35.
    Hab.—North and Middle America. Not recorded west of the Rocky Mountains.
Alaska. Breeds within the Artic circle. Migratory through the United States, where
rarely if ever observed to winter, never to breed. Extraordinarily abundant in Lab-
rador in August. Winters in Middle and South America. No West Indian record.
Accidental in Europe (Great Britain, four instances, HART., Man. Br. Birds, 1872, 145).
    Lieutenant Warren's Expedition.—4881, 5572, Upper Missouri River.
    Not obtained by Captain Raynolds' Expedition, nor by the later ones.

The Esquimaux Curlew migrates through the Missouri region, in immense numbers, in May. During the second week of that month I saw numerous flocks of fifty to several hundred on the prairies along the road between Fort Randall and Yankton. Snow, many feet in depth, still filled the ravines, where it had accumulated from the memorable storm of April 15–17, but the hills and flat prairie were bare, soft, and oozy, and about springing into the life of the new season. The Curlews were scattered everywhere, dotting the prairie with the Bartramian Sandpipers and Golden Plovers, in large, loose flocks, which, as they fed, kept up a continuous, low, piping noise, as if conversing with each other. Their return in the fall along this line of migration, I have not remarked; but my observations in Labrador, in 1860, were extended. I quote from my article in the Philadelphia Proceedings, above cited:

"The Curlews associate in flocks of every size, from three to as many thousand, but they generally fly in so loose and straggling a manner that it is rare to kill more than half a dozen at a shot. When they wheel, however, in any of their many beautiful evolutions, they close together in a more compact body, and offer a more favorable opportunity to the gunner. Their flight is firm, direct, very swift, when necessary much protracted, and is performed with regular, rapid beats. They never sail, except when about to alight, when the wings are much incurved downward, in the manner of most waders. As their feet touch the ground, their long, pointed wings are raised over the back, until the tips almost touch, and then deliberately folded, much in the manner of the Solitary Sandpiper (*Rhyacophilus solitarius*). Their note is an often-repeated, soft, mellow, though clear, whistle, which may be easily imitated. By this means they can readily be decoyed within shot, if the imitation is good and the gunner is careful to keep concealed. The smaller the flock the more easily are they allured, and a single individual rarely fails to turn his course toward the spot whence the sound proceeds. When in very extensive flocks, they have a note which, when uttered by the whole number, I can compare to nothing but the chattering of a flock of Blackbirds. When wounded and taken in hand, they emit a very loud, harsh scream, like that of a common hen under similar circumstances, which cry they also utter when pursued.

"Their food consists almost entirely of the crow-berry (*Empetrum nigrum*), which grows on all the hill-sides in astonishing profusion. It is also called the 'bear-berry' and 'curlew-berry.' It is a small berry, of a deep purple color, almost black, growing upon a procumbent, running kind of heath, the foliage of which has a peculiar moss-like appearance. This is their principal and favorite food, and the whole intestine, the vent, the legs, the bill, throat, and even the plumage, are more or less stained with the deep purple juice. They are also very fond of a species of small snail that adheres to the rock in immense quantities, to procure which they frequent the land-washes at low tide. Food being so abundant, and so easily obtained, they become excessively fat. In this condition they are most delicious eating, being tender, juicy, and finely flavored; but, as might be expected, they prove a very difficult job for the taxidermist.

"Although the Curlews were in such vast numbers, I did not find them so tame as might be expected, and as I had been led to suppose by previous representations. I was never able to walk openly within shooting distance of a flock, though I was told it was often done. The most successful method of obtaining them is to take such a position as they will probably fly over in passing from one feeding ground to another. They may then be shot with ease, as they rarely fly high at such times. The pertenacity with which they cling to certain feeding grounds, even when much molested, I saw strikingly illustrated on one occasion. The tide was rising and about to flood a muddy flat, of perhaps an acre in extent, where their favorite snails were in great quantities. Although six or eight gunners were stationed upon the spot, and kept up a continual round of firing upon the poor birds, they continued to fly distractedly about over our heads, notwithstanding the numbers that every moment fell. They seemed in terror lest they should lose their accustomed fare of snails that day. On another occasion, when the birds had been so harassed for several hours as to deprive them of all opportunity of feeding, great numbers of them retired to a very small island, or rather a large pile of rocks, a few hundred yards from the shore, covered with sea-weed and, of course, with snails. Flock after flock alighted on it, till it was completely covered with the birds, which there, in perfect safety, obtained their morning meal."

Some of these Curlews may winter on our southern border, but I am not aware that such is the case. The great extent of their southward movement at this season into Central and South America may be gathered from the above citations, which attest their presence in Brazil, Chili, and Buenos Ayres. For their summer resorts we must turn to the far North, where the species breeds in numbers commensurate with the hordes that pass regularly through the United States. They occur on the Yukon River, though they are not yet known to take up a line of migration along the Pacific side of the Rocky Mountains. (Compare, however, *Heerm.*, P. R. R. Rep. x, pt. vi, 66.) We learn of extensive breeding-grounds from the series of eggs transmitted to the Smithsonian, by Mr. MacFarlane, from the Arctic coast, east of Anderson River.

This species breeds in great numbers in the Anderson River region, usually making up its nest-complement of four eggs by the third week in June. The nest is generally in an open plain, and is a mere depression of the ground, lined with a few dried leaves or grasses. The eggs vary to the great extent usually witnessed among waders. The ground is olive-drab, tending either to green, gray, or brown in different instances, The markings, always large, numerous and bold, are of different depths of dark chocolate, bistre, and sepia brown, with the ordinary stone-gray shell spots. They always tend to aggregate at the larger end, or, at least, are more numerous on the major half of the egg; though in a few instances the distribution is nearly uniform. Occasionally the butt end of the egg is almost completely occupied by confluence of very dark markings. Eggs vary from 1.90 by 1.40 to 2.12 by 1.33, averaging about 2.00 by 1.45.

SUBORDER HERODIONES: HERONS AND THEIR ALLIES.

Family TANTALIDÆ: Ibises, &c.

Ibises inhabit the warmer parts of both hemispheres. They are nearly related to Herons, but differ in the shape of the bill, sometimes thick and heavy, or even spoon-shaped, sometimes very long, slender, and decurved, like a Curlew's; in the more or less extensive baldness of the head, absence of pectination of the middle claw, and other characteristics. We have several species, the Wood, Glossy or Bay, White, and Red Ibis, and the Spoonbill, which also belongs here. The Jabiru of tropical America (*Mycteria americana*), may be brought under this family, though generally referred to the Storks (*Ciconiidæ*). This singular bird was once taken in Texas, though the fact is known to few, the bird having been but lately introduced to our fauna (COUES, Check-list, 1874, App. 135, No. 448*bis*).

Two species of Ibis, the Wood and Bay, are known to occur so near the Missouri region, that I shall introduce them here, confident that they have a place about the mouth of the river, though not yet actually detected there.

Subfamily TANTALINÆ: *Wood Ibises.*

TANTALUS LOCULATOR, Linn.

Wood Ibis.

Tantalus loculator, LINN., Syst. Nat. i, 1766, 240 (CATES., i, 81; BRISS., v, 335).—GM., Syst. Nat. i, 1788, 647.—LATH., Ind. Orn. ii, 1790 (*Wood Ibis*, Arct. Zool. ii, No. 360; Gen. Syn. v, 104; Pl. Enl. 868).—WILS., Am. Orn. viii, 1814, 39, pl. 66, f. 1.— BP., Obs. Wils. 1825, No. 197; Syn. 1828, 310; List, 1838, 48; Consp. ii, 1855, 149.—WAGL., Isis, 1831, 530.—NUTT., Man. ii, 1834, 82.—AUD., Orn. Biog. iii, 1835, 128, pl. 216; Syn. 1839, 259; B. Am. vi, 1843, 64, pl. 361.—KENN., Pr. Phila. Acad. v, 1856, 391 (Southern Illinois).—GUND., J. f. O. iv, 1856, 348 (Cuba).—BD., B. N. A. 1858, 682.—SCL., Ibis, i, 1859, 227 (Guatemala).—SCL., P. Z. S. 1860, 253 (Orizaba); *ibid.* 290 (Ecuador).—LAWR., Ann. Lyc. 1861, 334 (Panama).—DRESS., Ibis, 1866, 32 (Texas).—SCL. & SALV., P. Z. S. 1866, 199; 1873, 305 (Ucayali, Peru).—WHEAT., Ohio Agric. Rep. 1860, p. 21 of reprint (quotes Illinois and Wisconsin).—COUES, Pr. Phila. Acad. 1866, 96 (Colorado River up to Fort Mojave).—COUES, Pr. Bost. Soc. xii, 1868, 123 (South Carolina).—ALLEN, Bull. M. C. Z. ii, 1871, 360 (Florida).—PELZ., Orn. Bras. 305 (Brazil).—REINH., Vid. Med. Nat. Forh. 1870, 23 (Brazil).—COUES, Key, 1872, 262, fig. 175.—RIDGW., Ann. Lyc. N. Y. x, 1874, 385 (Illinois).
Tantalus plumicollis, SPIX, Av. Bras. pl. 85.
"*Ibis nandasson; I. nandapoa*, VIEILL." (*Gray & Bp.*)

Hab.—South Atlantic and Gulf States, and across in corresponding latitudes to the Colorado River. North to Ohio, Illinois, and the Carolinas (accidentally to Pennsylvania, Chester County; *Vincent Barnard*, in letter to *Prof. Baird*). Cuba. Mexico. Central and South America. La Plata (*Burmeister*).

The Wood Ibis is a remarkable and interesting bird. In its general size, shape and color, it might be likened to a Crane, being about four feet long, and standing still higher when erect; white in color, with black-tipped wings and black tail. The head is peculiar, being entirely bald in the adult bird, and having an enormously thick, heavy bill, tapering and a little decurved at the end. In Florida it is sometimes called the "Gannet"; on the Colorado it is known as the Water Turkey.

Mr. Allen found the birds common in the Upper Saint John's, in Florida. "In March they were undergoing their spring moult, and were consequently in poor plumage. According to Dr. Bryant, who, so far as I am aware, is the first and only writer who has minutely described their eggs and breeding habits, incubation is generally commenced by

the first of April.   Dr. Bryant visited two of their breeding places, one
of which was between New Smyrna and Enterprise, in a large cypress
swamp on the border of Lake Ashby.   He estimated that a thousand
pairs were breeding there.   There is a singular discrepancy in the
accounts of authors in respect to the habits of this bird.   Bartram
mentions it as solitary in its habits, not associating in flocks.   Audubon, always finding it in large flocks, calls attention to this remark of
Bartram's as being wholly erroneous.   Dr. Bryant fully corroborates
Bartram's account, and censures Audubon for not remembering that
birds vary in their habits at different times and places.   He says he
never saw it in flocks except at its breeding places, and that they
usually went off and returned either singly or in pairs.   I almost invariably saw them in flocks, both at their feeding grounds and flying in
the air, they varying in number from a dozen to a hundred.   While
more or less gregarious at all times, they often doubtless also separate
into pairs, or wander singly."   My experience agrees with Mr. Allen's,
as the following account will show.

While I would not advise the reader to visit such an uncomfortable
place as Fort Yuma, from any great distance, merely to study the habits of this bird, yet, if he should by any unfortunate chance find himself at the "Botany Bay of America" (as I have heard it called in the
Army), he will have an excellent opportunity of doing so; for the Water
Turkeys are very common there.   Meanwhile, let my experience answer
the purpose.

We will walk abroad, in imagination, this fine September morning.
We leave camp as soon as it is light enough to see, for when the sun is
two or three hours high, we shall be glad enough to return to the shelter of the verandah.   Just now it is pleasant and comparatively cool,
for since midnight the thermometer has fallen below 90°; it was 115°
in the shade yesterday afternoon, and will mark 100°, perhaps, to-day,
at breakfast time, when we return with an Ibis or two.   No wonder we
prefer early rising.

The Colorado makes a broad bend around the bluff we stand on, a
promontory with a neck of low land, and the water on either side.   The
Ibises will very likely be found in this swampy covert, into which we
descend by a steep, well-worn path, and are at once lost in the bushes.
Certainly, it is hard work to push along; the bushes are thick and
determined enough to hold us back, even were they such well-disposed
and respectable members of the vegetable kingdom as grow in civilized
countries.   But in Arizona, "no bush without a thorn;" even the oaks
have prickly leaves.   Wide-spreading mimosas stretch out their skinny
arms and clutch us, and the claws of straggling acacias and mezquites
take hold.   Lesser shrubs rattle prickly seeds around us; we are con-
fronted with great piles of driftwood, and hedged about with compact
heaps of twigs and rushes, stranded by the last overflow.   But fortunately the place is intersected with cattle-paths, along which we can
thread a devious way; and though no Ibises are yet in sight, plenty of
other birds whistle and chirp encouragement.   Coveys of Plumed Quail
are trooping along half-covered ways, clinking in merry concert; Abert's
Finches rustle in every tangle; in the green willow clumps Orange-
crowned Warblers are disporting, and sipping dew from leafy, scroll-
like cups.   Now the path grows soft and oozy—we must take care, and
leap from log to log, or we shall sink up to the knees; while here and
there the shallow, stagnant pools we are searching for appear.   It is
to be hoped some Ibises are feeding around them; let us creep now as
quietly as we can, and, if inclined to curse the twigs that crackle under

foot, let us do it in an undertone. We peer now through a thick fringe
of arrow-wood, but only in time to see a flock of Ibises hurrying over
the tops of the copse beyond, croaking dismally, it seems to us, though
doubtless in exultation. Never mind! we are used to this sort of thing,
and know that neither pet nor wild birds always do just as we would
have them—but what is this? "Croak, croak, croak!" right overhead;
a pair of birds, flapping along from the direction we have come, doubtless to join the feasting party they expected to find here. That was a
good shot! so was that! An Ibis each time, at forty or fifty yards.
There lie the birds, one quite dead, floating on the slimy pool, the
other winged, with a pellet in his brain, too, perhaps, he tumbles so
wildly over the mud, soiling his snowy plumage. How the birds for
half a mile around are croaking! there'll be no more shooting at this
particular spot; we may as well go home to breakfast. It is eight
o'clock, and already the sun glares fiercely.

We have skinned and put away the dead Ibises, after careful measurements, and noting the colors of the parts that fade in drying. The
usual question arises, how to worry through with the day, as we loiter,
sweating, half-undressed, under the verandah on the shady side of the
house. To go out after birds at noon-day is impossible; will not some
birds kindly come to us? Fulfilment we have, even in the expression
of the wish; there are birds to lend wings to leaden hours even during
the sun's reign of terror at Fort Yuma. A long white line, dimly seen at
first in the distance, issues out of the gray-green woods. It is a troop
of Wood Ibises, leaving their heated covert for what seems the still
less endurable glare of day, yet reckoning well, for they have before enjoyed the cooler currents of the upper air, unheated by reflection from
the parched and shrinking sands. They come nearer, rising higher as
they come, till they are directly over head, in the bright blue. Flapping heavily until they had cleared all obstacles, then mounting faster
with strong, regular beats of their broad wings, now they sail in circles
with wide-spread, motionless pinions, supported as if by magic. A
score or more cross each other's paths in interminable spirals, their
snowy bodies tipped at the wing-points with jetty black, clear cut
against the sky; they become specks in the air, and finally pass from
view.

I am not aware that the Ibises circle about as I have described at
particular hours of the day, but I generally saw them so occupied in the
forenoon. The habit is constant with them, and quite characteristic.
They are often joined by numbers of Turkey Buzzards—birds that have
the same custom. Those familiar with the aërial gyrations of these birds,
when, away from their loathsome feasts, they career high over head,
will have, by adding to the Buzzard's movements the beauty of plumage
that the Ibises possess, a good idea of the pleasing appearance of the
latter. Audubon says that their evolutions are performed when digestion is going on, and continued until they again feel the cravings of
hunger. He has so well described their mode of feeding, that I cannot
do better than quote his paragraph. "The Wood Ibis," he says, "feeds
entirely upon fish and aquatic reptiles, of which it destroys an enormous
quantity, in fact more than it eats; for if they have been killing fish for
half an hour, and gorged themselves, they suffer the rest to lie on the
water untouched, to become food for alligators, Crows, and Vultures.
To procure its food, the Wood Ibis walks through shallow, muddy lakes,
or bayous, in numbers. As soon as they have discovered a place abound-
ing in fish, they dance, as it were, all through it, until the water becomes
thick with the mud stirred from the bottom with their feet. The fishes,

on rising to the surface, are instantly struck by the beak of the Ibises, and on being deprived of life they turn over and so remain. In the course of ten or fifteen minutes, hundreds of fishes, frogs, young alligators, and water-snakes, cover the surface, and the birds greedily swallow them until they are completely gorged, after which they walk to the nearest margins, place themselves in long rows, with their breasts all turned toward the sun, in the manner of Pelicans and Vultures, and thus remain for an hour or so."

The great abundance of the Wood Ibis on the Colorado, especially the lower portions of the river, as at Fort Yuma, has not been generally recognized until of late years. It is probably as numerous there as anywhere in the United States, though I have never seen flocks "composed of several thousands," such as Audubon speaks of. Oftenest the numbers together would fall short of an hundred, and single birds were very frequently seen flapping overhead or wading in the shallow pools. But they are like all of their great tribe, gregarious birds, spending most of their time in each other's society. I doubt that any are found on the Colorado higher than Fort Mojave. They probably occur along the greater part of the Gila, but how far up I am unable to say. I have not noticed them in Arizona except on these two rivers. Wherever found in the Territory they are permanent residents, as elsewhere in most parts of the United States. In the Eastern province they reach to the Carolinas. They are said to ascend the Mississippi to Ohio; but the swampy tracts and bayous of Louisiana, Mississippi, Alabama, and Florida, are, with the lagoons of the lower Colorado, their favorite homes. I do not know of them in California, except as along the river just named.

The carriage of the Wood Ibis is firm and sedate, almost stately; each leg is slowly lifted and planted with deliberate precision, before the other is moved, when the birds walk unsuspicious of danger. I never saw one run rapidly, since on all the occasions when I have been the cause of alarm, the bird took wing directly. It springs powerfully from the ground, bending low to gather strength, and for a little distance flaps hurriedly with dangling legs, as if it was much exertion to lift so heavy a body. But fairly on wing, clear of all obstacles, the flight is firm, strong, and direct, performed with continuous moderately rapid beats of the wing, except when the birds are sailing in circles as above noted. When proceeding in a straight line the feet are stretched horizontally backward, but the head is not drawn closely in upon the breast, as is the case with Herons, so that the bird presents what may be called a top-heavy appearance, increased by the thick large bill.

The eggs of the Wood Ibis are like Heron's, in being nearly ellipsoidal, but differ from these, as well as from those of the Bay Ibis, in color, which is uniform dull white, without markings. The shell is rather rough to the touch, with a coating of softish, flaky, calcareous substance. A specimen that I measured was exactly $2\frac{3}{4}$ inches in length by $1\frac{3}{4}$ in breadth. Two or three are said to be a nest-complement. According to Audubon the young are entirely dusky-gray, with brownish-black wings and bill. The head is at first covered, but becomes partially bare after the first moult. Four years are said to be required for the bird to attain its full plumage, though it may breed at two or three years of age, and is largely white or whitish after the first moult. The head and upper part of the neck of the adult are wholly bare, and of a livid bluish color, tinged with yellowish on the forehead. The bill is yellowish; the legs blue, becoming blackish on the toes, and tinged with yellow on the webs. The female is considerably smaller than the male.

Subfamily IBIDINÆ : *True Ibises.*

IBIS FALCINELLUS var. ORDII (Bp.) Coues.

Glossy or Bay Ibis.

Tantalus mexicanus, ORD, Journ. Phila. Acad. i, 1817, 53 (New Jersey).
Ibis falcinellus, BP., Obs. Wils. 1825, No. 199 ; Am. Orn. iv, 1831, 23, pl. 23, f. 1 ; Syn. 1828,
    312.—NUTT., Man. ii, 1834, 88.—AUD., Orn. Biog. iv, 1838, 608, pl. 387 ; Syn.
    257 ; B. Am. vi, 1843, 50, pl. 358.—EMM., Cat. B. Mass. 1835, 5.—PEAB., Rep. B.
    Mass. 1839, 365.—LINSL., Am. Journ. Sci. xliv, 1843, 266 (Connecticut).—PUTN.,
    Pr. Ess. Inst. i, 1856, 230 (Massachusetts).—CABOT, Pr. Bost. Soc. iii, 313, 333,
    355 ; iv, 346.—ALLEN, Bull. M. C. Z. ii, 1871, 361 (Florida).—HUDSON, P. Z. S.
    1870, 799 (biography).—RIDGW., Ann. Lyc. N. Y. x, 1874, 386 (Illinois).
Ibis falcinellus var. *ordii*, COUES, Key, 1872, 263.
Ibis ordii, BP., List, 1838, 49.—BD., B. N. A., 1858, 635.—WHEAT., Ohio Agric. Rep. 1860,
    No. 190 (one or two occasions).—ALLEN, Pr. Ess. Inst. iv, 1864, 86 (Massachu-
    setts, occasional, irregular).—LAWR., Ann. Lyc. N. Y. viii, 1866, 292 (New York,
    rare).—COUES, Pr. Ess. Inst. iv, 1868, 290 (Massachusetts, exceptionally).—
    COUES, Pr. Bost. Soc. xii, 1868, 123 (South Carolina, summer).—TURN., B. E. Pa.
    1819, 44 (New Jersey, occasional).—MAYN., Guide, 1870, 145 (Massachusetts).—
    ALLEN, Am. Nat. iii, 1870, 637 (Massachusetts and New Hampshire).
Falcinellus ordii, BP., Consp. ii, 1855, 159.—COUES, Pr. Phila. Acad. 1866, 96 (Arizona).
    In the present uncertainty attending the discrimination of species, I only quote the
references to the ordinary North American bird.

Hab.—United States, southerly, straying north to Massachusetts and Ohio.

The Glossy Ibis is not figured in Wilson's Ornithology, and remained
an unknown inhabitant of the United States up to the termination of
that author's labors.   In 1817 a specimen was taken in New Jersey, and
announced by Mr. Ord under the name of *Tantalus mexicanus.*   Since
that time it has been found at irregular intervals along our coast, chiefly
in the Southern and Middle districts, but occasionally as far north as
Massachusetts ; where, however, its occurrence must be considered as
accidental.   Audubon says that he found it in flocks in Texas, but gives
only a meagre account of its habits.   Nuttall's article is mainly an account of Ibises in general, devoted principally to mention of ancient,
and particularly Egyptian, chronicles and superstitions regarding them.
The United States species was first separated under the name of *ordii*
by Bonaparte, 1838.

The eggs of Ibises are very different from those of Herons.   The shell
is heavier, rougher, and more granular, the difference in texture being
very apparent ; and are ovoidal, not ellipsoidal, with considerable difference in the degree of convexity of the two ends.   Those of the Glossy
Ibis measure from 1.90 by 1.45 to 2.10 by 1.50, and are of a dull greenish-
blue color, without markings.   The number usually deposited is believed
to be three.

Family ARDEIDÆ: Herons.

Subfamily ARDEINÆ : *True Herons.*

ARDEA HERODIAS, Linn.

Great Blue Heron.

Ardea herodias, LINN., Syst. Nat. i, 1766, 237 (based on CATES., iii, 10, and BRISS., v,
    416).—GM., Syst. Nat. 1788, 630.—LATH., Ind. Orn. ii, 1790, 692 (Arct. Zool. ii,
    234; Gen. Syn. v, 85).—WILS., Am. Orn. viii, 1814, 28, pl. 65, fig. 5.—TEMM., Man.
    ii, 1820, 566.—BP., Obs. Wils. 1825, No. 188 ; Syn. 1828, 304; List, 1838, 47 ; Consp.
    ii, 1855, 112.—SW. & RICH., F. B. A. ii, 1831, 373 (Hudson's Bay).—NUTT., Man.
    ii, 1834, 42.—AUD., Orn. Biog. iii, 1835, 87 ; v, 599 ; pl. 211 ; Syn. 1839, 265 ; B.

Am. vi, 1843, 122, pl. 369.—GIR., B. L. I. 1844, 276.—DARW., Voy. Beagle. 128 (Galapagos).—WOODH., Sitgr. Rep. 1853, 97 (Arkansas, Texas, and New Mexico).—PUTN., Pr. Ess. Inst. i, 1856, 218 (Massachusetts, summer).—GUNDL., J. f. O. iv, 1856, 340 (Cuba, breeds).—NEWB., P. R. R. Rep. vi, 1857, 97 (California, common).—BD., B. N. A. 1858, 668.—SCL., Ibis, i, 1859, 220 (Guatemala).—NEWT., *ibid.* 263 (Santa Cruz).—BRY., Pr. Bost. Soc. 1859 (Bahamas).—HEERM., P. R. R. Rep. x, 1859, pt. vi, 63 (California).—COOP. & SUCK., N. H. Wash. Ter. 1860, 228 (Puget Sound).—HAYD., Rep. 1862, 173.—WHEAT., Ohio Agric. Rep. 1860, No. 185.—CASS., Pr. Phila. Acad. 1860, 196 (Atrato).—COUES & PRENT., Smiths. Rep. 2861, 415 (Washington, summer).—SCL., P. Z. S. 1861, 81 (Jamaica).— BOARDM., Pr. Bost. Soc. ix, 1862, 128 (Maine, breeds, common).—VERR., Pr. Ess. Inst. iii, 1862, 153 (Maine, breeds).—ALLEN, *ibid.* iv, 1864, 76 (Massachusetts, breeding).—MCILWR., *ibid.* 1866, 91 (Canada West).—COUES, *ibid.* v, 1868, 289.— LAWR., Ann. Lyc. N. Y. viii, 1863 (Panama); viii, 1864, 99 (Sombrero); ix, 1868, 152 (Costa Rica); 210 (Yucatan); viii, 1866, 292.—COUES, Pr. Bost. Soc. xii, 1868, 123 (South Carolina, resident.)—COUES, Pr. Phila. Acad. 1866, 95 (Arizona, breeding); 1871, 33 (North Carolina).—SUND., Ofv. Vet. Ak. Forh. 1869, 589 (St. Bartholomew).—ALLEN, Mem. Bost. Soc. i, 1865, 501 (Iowa).—DALL & BANN., Tr. Chic. Acad. 1869, 283 (Sitka, Alaska).—TURNB., B. E. Pa. 1869, 29 (summer).—ALLEN, Bull. M. C. Z. ii, 1871, 358 (Florida); iii, 1872, 182 (Kansas and Utah).—MAYN., Guide, 1870, 143 (Massachusetts); Pr. Bost. Soc. 1871 (New Hampshire).—TRIPPE, Pr. Bost. Soc. xv, 1872, 240 (Iowa).—COUES, Key, 1872, 267.—SNOW, B. Kans. 1873, 9.—RIDGW., Ann. Lyc. N. Y. x, 1874, 386 (Illinois).
Ardea hudsonias, LINN., Syst. Nat. i, 1766, 338 (EDW., pl. 135; BRISS., v, 407).—GM., Syst. Nat. i, 1788, 631.—LATH., I. O. ii, 1790, 693 (Arct. Zool. ii, No. 342; Gen. Syn. v, 86).

Hab.—North America, to Hudson's Bay and Sitka. South to Guatemala and Galapagos. West Indies. Breeds throughout its range, and winters in the South.
Lieutenant Warren's Expedition.—5454, near Big Sioux River.
Not obtained by Captain Raynolds' Expedition, nor by the later ones.

No species of Heron has a wider distribution in North America, and only the Bittern equals it in the extent of its dispersion. It appears to be more common, however, in the United States than further north, and is resident south of the Middle districts. Herons, as a group, are rather southern birds; only these two just named proceed beyond the United States, and most, if not all, are more abundant in the southern portions of the Union. They are particularly numerous in the South Atlantic and Gulf States, where they breed by thousands, and in which districts several species occur that are not found in corresponding latitudes in the West. On the Pacific side we have no peculiar species, all that occur there being of wide distribution.

The breeding places of the Great Blue Heron on the Colorado River offer no such scenes as those of the same bird do in Florida, for instance. There may, indeed, be places along this river overgrown with low, dense woods, simulating a cypress swamp, where the birds may resort to breed, along with the Wood Ibises; but, for the most part, the Herons that wend their way along the Colorado are only screened by low, straggling mezquite, that scarcely hides them, or patches of arrow-wood (*Tessaria borealis*), that they can overlook. Where the river flows deepest and swiftest, cutting its way through bold cañons that rise frowning on either hand like the battlements of giant castles—where the fervid rays of the sun heat the rocks till they almost crack, and the sand blisters the feet—there the Herons fix their nests, overhanging the element whence they draw subsistence. The face of the cliffs in many places is covered with singular nests of the Eave Swallow, breeding by thousands; while on the flat projecting shelves of rock we find, here and there, the bulky platforms of twigs and sticks, and perhaps see the sedate bird herself, setting motionless on the nest, hopefully biding her time, cheered during her long waiting by the joyous troops of the Swallows that flutter incessantly around.

Wherever placed, on tree, bush, or rock, the nest of the Heron is a large bed of twigs, more or less matted together with grasses and weeds, some two feet in diameter and about one-third as high. Two or three eggs are laid, probably never more; they measure about 2.50 by 1.50, and are rather narrowly elliptical, with both ends of about the same shape; the color is a pale, dull, greenish-blue, varying in shade in different specimens, but always uniform over the same egg.

I have not observed the breeding of the Heron in the Missouri region, but have noticed the bird high up the river as late as the end of October.

ARDEA EGRETTA, (Gm.) Gray.

Great White Egret; White Heron.

Ardea egretta, GM., Syst. Nat. i, 1788, 629.—LATH., Ind. Orn. ii, 1790, 694.—WILS., Am. Orn. vii, 1813, 106, pl. 61, f. 4.—NUTT., Man. ii, 1834, 47.—AUD., Orn. Biog. iv, 1838, 600, pl. 386; Syn. 1839, 265; B. Am. vi, 1843, 132, pl. 370.—WOODH., Sitgr. Rep. 1853, 97 (Texas and Indian Territory).—PUTN., Pr. Ess. Inst. i, 1856, 218 (Massachusetts, very rare).—TURNB., B. E. Pa. 1869, 27 (rather rare).—COUES, Key, 1872, 267.
Herodias egretta, GRAY, Gen. of B. iii, 1849.—BD., B. N. A. 1858, 666.—WHEAT., Ohio Agric. Rep. 1860, No. 184 (not very uncommon).—COUES & PRENT., Smiths. Rep. 1861, 415 (Washington, occasional).—ALLEN, Pr. Ess. Inst. iv, 1864, 86 (Boston).—COUES, *ibid.* v, 1868, 290 (New England, to Massachusetts).—MCILWR., *ibid.* v. 1866, 91 (Hamilton, C. W.; rare).—DRESS., Ibis, 1866, 31 (Texas).—LAWR., Ann. Lyc. N. Y. viii, 1866, 292 (New York).—COUES, Pr. Bost. Soc. xii, 1868, 123 (South Carolina, summer, common).—COUES, Pr. Phila. Acad. 1866, 95 (Colorado River, common); *ibid.* 1871, 33 (North Carolina, common).—MAYN., Guide, 1870, 143 (Massachusetts, casual).—JONES, Trans. Nova Scotia Inst. ii, 1868, 72 (Nova Scotia).—ALLEN, Am. Nat. iii, 1870, 637 (Massachusetts).—ALLEN, Bull. M. C. Z. ii, 1871, 358 (Florida, abundant, breeding).—SNOW, B. Kans. 1873, 9 (Kansas, one instance).—HATCH, Bull. Minnesota Acad. i, 1874, 62 (Minnesota).
Herodias alba var. *egretta,* RIDGWAY, Ann. Lyc. N. Y. x, 1874, 386 (Illinois).
Herodias egretta var. *californica,* BAIRD, B. N. A. 1856, 667 (larger).
Ardea leuce, ILLIGER.—LICHTENSTEIN, Verz. 1823, No. 793.
Egretta leuce, BONAPARTE, List, 1838, 47; Consp. ii, 1855, 114.
Herodias leuce, BREHM, Hand-buch, 1831, 585.
Ardea alba, BONAPARTE, Obs. Wils. 1825, No. 189; Syn. 1828, 304 (not of *Linnæus*).
Ardea " occidentalis," NEWB., P. R. R. Rep. vi, 1857, 27 (California). (Not of *Audubon*).

Extralimital quotations.—GUNDL., J. f. O. iv, 1856, 341 (Cuba).—BRY., Pr. Bost. Soc. vii, 1859 (Bahamas).—SCL., P. Z. S. 1861, 80 (Jamaica).—SCL., P. Z. S. 1860, 253 (Orizaba); 290 (Ecuador).—SCL. & SALV., P. Z. S. 1866, 199 (Peru); 1867, 334 (Chili); 1869, 156 (Peru); 1873, 305 (Peru).—SCL., Ibis, 1859, 226 (Central America).—TAYLOR, Ibis, 1860, 312 (Tigre Island, Honduras).—LAWR., Ann. Lyc. viii, 63 (Panama); ix, 142 (Costa Rica).—PELZ., Orn. Bras. 300 (resident).—PHIL., Cat. 33 (Chili).—DARW., Voy. Beagle, 128 (Maldonado and Patagonia).

Hab.— United States, southerly, straggling northward to Nova Scotia (*Jones*), Massachusetts, Canada West, and Minnesota. West Indies; Mexico; Central and S. America. Not obtained by any of the Expeditions.

The only instance of the occurrence of this species in the Missouri region which has come to my knowledge is that of a specimen taken at Lawrence, Kansas, August 15, 1872, as stated by Prof. Snow. It must be, however, of at least occasional occurrence on the Lower Missouri.

This fine bird may be immediately recognized by its color—pure white at all seasons, with yellow bill and black legs, with its large size—about three feet in length. The head is not adorned with a crest, but in the breeding season the back has a magnificent train drooping beyond the tail. The Little White Egret is much smaller, only about two feet long, and has a recurved crest, lengthened breast-feathers, and a recurved train, in the breeding season. An erroneous impression prevails that an "Egret" is something different from a Heron; but all Egrets are Herons, although all Herons are not Egrets. It is a term applied to certain Herons, especially white ones, that have long plumes (*aigrettes*); but the distinction is entirely arbitrary. The Reddish Egret, for instance, and the Louisianan, are not white; while the small Green Heron has long, flowing dorsal plumes.

Audubon has a paragraph upon this species susceptible of extensive application, and expressing a favorite idea of mine, strengthened into conviction by repeated observation. Speaking of finding Egrets much wilder in early spring than after they had settled to their duties of reproduction, he says: "I have supposed this to be caused by the change of their *thoughts* on such occasions, and am of opinion that birds of all kinds become more careless of themselves. As the strength of their attachment toward their mates or progeny increases through the process of time, as is the case with the better part of our own species, lovers and parents perform acts of heroism which individuals having no such attachment to each other would never dare to contemplate. In these birds the impulse of affection is so great that, when they have young, they allow themselves to be approached so as often to fall victims to the rapacity of man, who, boasting of reason and benevolence, ought at such a time to respect their devotion." No one unfamiliar with birds' natures, as exhibited at different seasons of the year, and at varying ages, can have adequate conception of the opposite traits they display. Even Doves, those meekest of birds—the emblems of "peace on earth and good-will"—fight furiously when the *furor amantium* is on them; the wariest birds forget to consider personal danger in defence of their young; suspicious birds sometimes grow impudently familiar; knowing birds appear stupid; dull birds become frisky, and frisky birds beside themselves, when in love; silent birds cry out, and singing birds sing all the time.

Another point may be mentioned here. The *young*, even of birds by nature shy and suspicious, require some time to get over their early verdancy and acquire a wholesome degree of caution. Instincts of this sort are undoubtedly hereditary, and sufficiently well marked to enable us to predicate it, in a certain greater or less degree, of all birds; and circumstances of subsequent experience, moreover, have much control over its development and exhibition. But, beyond these variations, it is unquestionable that, other things being equal, young birds are for a while less wary than their parents, as certainly as in the case of our own species. The White Egret is an illustration in point. We are familiar with the difficulty that Audubon records of his experience in attempting to shoot these birds; and those of us who have tried can attest the same thing. But such strategy is not always required, late in the summer and early in the fall, to obtain birds of the year. At Fort Yuma, where the birds were very common, I had frequent occasion to wonder at their want of shyness in the fall, not to say their absolute stupidity. On one occassion that I remember I came upon a young bird that was quietly feeding at a little pool. Notwithstanding that I was on horseback and had come clattering along, the bird, not frightened at the noise and sudden appearance, merely drew itself up at full height to look a moment, and then bent its long neck again to resume its meal, within fifteen steps of me. It was to have been hoped that it could have lived long enough to learn better. Speaking in general terms, and without considering the artificial frame of mind brought about by man's interference, the shyness of any Heron corresponds exactly to its size; and it is so with many o'her birds, particularly Gulls— the larger the species, the more wary. The smaller kinds, as the Green Heron and the Least Bittern, show little concern at being approached. It would almost seem as if the greater birds were aware how likely to attract harmful attention their imposing appearance made them, and as if the little ones trusted to their insignificance for protection. It is only another interpretation of La Fontaine's crowned rats. The gradation in size among Herons calls up one other point. Such species as the Great Blue and the Great White are certainly to be considered of dignified bearing, and their motions have something of grace and beauty as well. But, though the Green, and the Least, and others have almost exactly the same form and the same attitudes and movements, they would never be called dignified or elegant birds. Analyzing this difference in the way the birds impress us, I cannot see that anything but *size* is in question. This is the real secret; the large Blue Heron is dignified by its size alone; the little Green Heron, that copies every posture and action of the other, only succeeds in being grotesque, if not actually ridiculous—the more so from the very fact of its imitation. The parallel that may be drawn is a broad and long one.

The White Egret is rather a delicate bird, preferring warm weather, and consequently restricted in geographical distribution. In New England it is only a rare visitor, and is not known to breed. I may here observe that a certain *northward* migration of some southerly birds at this season is nowhere more noticeable than among the Herons and their allies, the migrants consisting chiefly of birds hatched that year, which unaccountably stray in what seems to us the wrong direction. Massachusetts is the northernmost record of the species in New England. It is rather decidedly a maritime bird, like its smaller relative (*Ardea candidissima*), and seldom penetrates any distance inland except along our largest rivers—the Mississippi, Rio Grande, and Colorado. I never saw it in the interior of the Carolinas, along the coasts of which I found it very abundant, and throughout the low, flat, marshy or swampy districts. On the Pacific coast it is not recorded north of California. I met with it frequently in Southern California near the coast, and on a few occasions on the Mojave River, not far from Soda Lake, perhaps rather an exceptional inland locality, as the desert environing on all sides but one must be a great barrier. The Arizonian birds are gathered chiefly along the Colorado, particularly its lower portions.

ARDEA CANDIDISSIMA, Gm.

Little White Egret; Snowy Heron.

Ardea nivea, JACQ., Beitr. 1784.—LATH., Ind. Orn. ii, 1790, 696 (*partim*).—LICHT., Verz. 1823, No. 795. (Name preoccupied.)

Egretta nivea, CAB. (*nec auct.*). (*Bp.*)

Ardea candidissima, GM., Syst. Nat. i, 1788, 633.—WILS., Am. Orn. vii, 1813, 120, pl. 62. f. 4.—BP., Obs. Wils. 1825, No. 174; Syn. 1828, 305.—NUTT., Man. ii, 1834, 49.—, AUD., Orn. Biog. iii, 1835, 317; v, 1839, 606; pl. 242; Syn. 1839, 267; B. Am. vi, 1843, 163, pl. 374.—GIR., B. L. I, 1844, 283.—WOODH., Sitgr. Rep. 1853, 97 (Indian Territory and Texas).—PUTN., Pr. Ess. Inst. i, 1856, 218 (Massachusetts, very rare).—HEERM., P. R. R. Rep. x, 1859, pt. vi, 63 (California).—PELZ., Orn. Bras. 300 (resident).—COUES, Key, 267.—SCL. & SALV., P. Z. S. 1873, 305 (E. Peru).

Egretta candidissima, BP., List, 1838, 47.—GOSSE, B. Jam. 1847, 336.

Herodias candidissima, GRAY, Gen. of B. iii, 1849.—GUNDL, J. f. O. iv, 1856, 342.

Garzetta candidissima, BP., Consp. Av. ii, 1855, 119.—BD., B. N. A. 1858, 665.—CASS., Pr. Phila. Acad. 1860, 196 (Carthagena, Darien).—WHEAT., Ohio Agric. Rep. 1860, No. 183 (very rare).—COUES & PRENT., Smiths. Rep. 1861, 415 (not uncommon).—ALLEN, Pr. Ess. Inst. iv, 1864, 86 (Massachusetts, accidental).—COUES, *ibid.* v, 1868, 290.—DRESS., Ibis, 1866, 31 (Texas).—SCL. & SALV., P. Z. S. 1866, 199 (Eastern Peru).—COUES, Pr. Phila. Acad. 1866, 95 (Colorado River, abundant); 1871, 31 (North Carolina).—COUES, Pr. Bost. Soc. xii, 1868, 123 (South Carolina).—LAWR., Ann. Lyc. N. Y. viii, 1866, 292 (New York); ix, 1868, 142 (Costa Rica); 210 (Yucatan).—JONES, Tr. Nova Scotia Inst. ii, 1868, 72 (Nova Scotia).—ALLEN, Am. Nat. iii, 1870, 637 (Massachusetts); Bull. M. C. Z. ii, 1871, 356 (Florida).—TURNB., B. E. Pa. 1869, 27 (not uncommon).—MAYN., Guide, 1870, 143 (Massachusetts).—SNOW, B. Kans. 1873, 9.—RIDGW., Ann. Lyc. N. Y. x, 1874, 386 (Illinois).

Ardea carolinensis, ORD, ed. Wils. vii, 1825, 125.
   Additional extralimital quotations.—SCL., P. Z. S. 1861, 81 (Jamaica); 1864, 179 (Mexico); 1867, 334 (Chili).—SCL. & SALV., *ibid.* 1867, 280 (Mosquito Coast).—SCL., Ibis, i, 1859, 226 (Central America).—BRY., Pr. Bost. Soc. vii, 1859 (Bahamas).—PELZ., Novara Reise, Vög. 118 (Chili).—PHIL., Cat. 33 (Chili).

Hab.—United States, southerly. North regularly to the Middle States, casually to Massachusetts, and even Nova Scotia (*Jones*). Kansas (*Snow*). Mexico. West Indies. Central and South America to Chili. Breeds throughout its regular United States range, and resident in the Gulf States and further south.
   Obtained by none of the Expeditions.

Among the American Herons this species is only liable to be confounded with the *young* of the Little Blue Heron (*A. cœrulea*), which is white for a time, and of about the same size. It is recognized, however, by certain differences in the proportions and color of the bill, legs, and feet ; and it never shows any trace of bluish or ashy, as is usually the case with the young *A. cœrulea.*
The introduction of this species into the present connection rests on its occurrence in Kansas, as recorded by Prof. Snow, *l. c.* (Topeka, July 25, 1872). The range of the last species and of this smaller but equally elegant and showy one, appear to be nearly or quite coincident, and their habits are much the same.

The Little Blue Heron (*A. cœrulea*) will probably be found about the Lower Missouri, but at present I have no authority for introducing it here.

ARDEA VIRESCENS, Linn.

Green Heron; Poke.

Ardea virescens, LINN., Syst. Nat. i, 1766, 238 (based on *Ardea minor*, CATES., Car. i, 80 ;
   Cancrophagus viridis, BRISS., v, 486, pl. 38, f. 1).—GM., Syst. Nat. i, 1788, 635.—
   LATH., Ind. Orn. ii, 1790, 684 (*Green Heron*, Arct. Zool. ii, 447 ; Gen. Syn. v,
   68).—WILS., Am. Orn. vii, 1813, 97, pl. 61, f. 1 ; ORD'S ed. 102.—BP., Obs. Wils.
   No. 190.—WAGL., Syst. Av. 1827, No. 36.—NUTT., Man. ii, 1834, 63.—AUD., Orn.
   Biog. iv, 1838, 247, pl. 333 ; Syn. 1839, 264 ; B. Am. vi, 1843, 105, pl. 367.—GIR.,
   B. L. I. 1844, 284.—WOODH., Sitgr. Rep. 1853, 97.—PUTN., Pr. Ess. Inst. i, 1856,
   218.—SUND., Ofv. Vet. Ak. 1869, 589 (St. Bartholomew).—HEERM., P. R. R. Rep.
   x, 1859, pt. vi, 63 (California).—TRIPPE, Pr. Ess. Inst. vi, 1871, 119 (Minne-
   sota).—COUES, Key, 1872, 268.
Ardea (Botaurus) virescens, BP., Specc. Comp. 1827, No. 180 ; Syn. 1828, 307.
Herodias virescens, BOIE.—BP., List, 1838, 47.—GOSSE, B. Jam. 1847, 340.
Egretta virescens, SW., 2¼ Cent. 1838, No. 156.
Agamia virescens, REICH., Icones Avium ; Syst. Av. pl. 131, figs. 489, 490.
Ocniscus virescens, GUNDL., J. f. O. iv, 1856, 343 (Cuba).
Butorides virescens, BP., Consp. Av. ii, 1855, 128.—SCL., P. Z. S. 1856, 310 (Cordova).—
   SCL. & SALV., *ibid.* 1867, 250 (Mosquito Coast) ; 1869, 252 (Venezuela).—SALV.,
   ibid. 1870, 218 (Veragua).—BD., B. N. A. 1858, 676.—SCL., Ibis, i, 1859, 227
   (Guatemala).—NEWT., *ibid.* 261 (Santa Cruz).—TAYL., *ibid.* 1864, 93 (Trinidad) ;
   171 (Porto Rico).—BRY., Pr. Bost. Soc. vii, 1859 (Bahamas).—WHEAT., Ohio
   Agric. Rep. 1860, No. 188.—COUES & PRENT., Smiths. Rep. 1861, 415 (summer,
   abundant).—BOARDM., Pr. Bost. Soc. ix, 1862, 128 (Maine, common, breeds).—
   COUES, *ibid.* xii, 1868, 123 (South Carolina).—SCOTT, *ibid.* 1872, 227 (Virginia).—
   TRIPPE, *ibid.* 240 (Iowa).—VERR., Pr. Ess. Inst. iii, 1862, 158 (Maine).—ALLEN,
   ibid. iv, 1864, 76.—McILWR., *ibid.* v, 1866, 91 (Canada West, rare).—COUES, *ibid.*
   vi, 1868, 290.—COUES, Pr. Phila. Acad, 1866, 95 (Arizona) ; 1871, 33 (North Carolina).—LAWR., Ann. Lyc. N. Y. viii, 1866, 292 ; ix, 1868, 142 (Costa Rica).—
   TURNB., B. E. Pa. 1869, 28.—MAYN., Guide, 1870, 144.—ALLEN, Bull. M. C. Z. ii,
   1871, 359 (Florida) ; iii, 1872, 182 (Kansas).—ALLEN, Mem. Bost. Soc. i, 1868,
   501, 507, 520, 526 (Iowa, Illinois, Indiana).—SNOW, B. Kans. 1873, 9.—RIDGW.,
   Ann. Lyc. N. Y. x, 1874, 386 (Illinois).
Ardea ludoviciana, GM., Syst. Nat. i, 1788, 630 (not of *Wilson*).—LATH., I. O. ii, 1790, 690.
Ardea torquata, MILL., Ill. pl. 60. (*Gray.*)
Ardea chloroptera et *maculata*, BODD. ; P. E. 909, 912. (*Gray.*)

Hab.—United States generally, breeding throughout, and wintering in the South. Canada West (*McIlwraith*). Mexico. West Indies. Central America to Venezuela.
   Not noticed by the Expeditions.

Occurs chiefly in the southern and eastern portions of the Missouri region.

NYCTIARDEA GRISEA var. NÆVIA, (Bodd.) Allen.

American Night Heron.

Botaurus nævius, BRISS., Orn. v, 1760, 462.
Ardea nævia, BODD., Planch. Enlum. Tabl. 1784, pl. 939 (young). (*Gray.*)
Nyctiardea nævia, GRAY, Hand-list, iii, 1871, 33, No. 10175.
Nycticorax nævia, GRAY, G. of B. iii, 558.—SCL. & SALV., P. Z. S. 1873, 305 (Eastern Peru).
Nyctiardea grisea var. *nævia*, ALLEN, Bull. M. C. Z. iii, 1872, 182.—COUES, Key, 1872, 269.
Nycticorax griseus, REINH., Vid. Nat. For. 1870, 25 (Brazil).—ALLEN, Bull. M. Z. C. ii, 359.
(?) *Ardea jamaicensis*, GM., Syst. Nat. i, 1788, 625.—LATH., Ind. Orn. ii, 1790, 679 (*Jamaica Night Heron* of Gen. Syn. v, 54; rather *A. violaceus*).
Ardea hoactli, GM., Syst. Nat. i, 1788, 630.—LATH., Ind. Orn. ii, 1790, 700 (*A. mexicana cristata*, BRISS. v, 218; *Day Heron* of Gen. Syn. v, 100).
Ardea gardeni, GM., Syst. Nat. i, 1788, 645.—LATH., Ind. Orn. ii, 1790, 685 (*Gardenian and Spotted Heron*, Gen. Syn. 70, 71; Arct. Zool, No. 355).
Nycticorax gardeni, JARD., Notes Wils. Orn.—BP., C. A. ii, 1855, 141.—GUNDL., J. f. O. iv, 1856, 346.—SCL. P. Z. S. 1860, 387.—SCL. & SALV. P. Z. S., 1866, 199 (E. Peru).
Nyctiardea gardeni, BD., B N A. 1858, 678.—COOP. & SUCK., N. H. Wash Ter. 1860, 223.—WHEAT., Ohio Agric. Rep. 1860, No. 189 (rare).—COUES & PRENT., S. I. Rep. 1861, 415 (occasional).—BOARDM., Pr. Bost. Soc. ix, 1862, 128.—VERR., Pr. Ess. Inst. iii, 1862, 158 (Maine. breeding).—ALLEN, ibid. (Maine. breeding).—COUES, ibid. v, 1868, 290.—MCILWR., ibid. v, 1866, 92 (common).—COUES, Pr. Phila. Acad. 1866, 95 (Arizona).—LAWR., Ann. Lyc. N. Y. viii, 1866, 292.—COUES, Pr. Bost. Soc. xii, 1868, 123 (South Carolina)—TURNB., B. E. Pa. 1869, 28.—ALLEN, Mem. Bost. Soc. i, 1868, 507 (Illinois).—MAYN., Guide, 1870, 144.—SNOW, B. Kans. 1873, 9.
Nyctiardea grisea var. *gardeni*, RIDGW., Ann. Lyc. N. Y. x, 1874, 386 (Illinois).
Ardea nycticorax, WILS., Am. Orn. vii, 1813, 101, pl. 61, f. 2 (not of *Linnæus*).—BP., Obs. Wils. 1825, No. 193; Syn. 1828, 306.—AUD., Orn. Biog. iii, 1835, 275; v, 1839, 600; pl. 236; Syn. 1839, 261; B. Am. vi, 1843, 82, pl. 363.
Ardea maculata, FRISCH, Av. ii, pl. 9.
Ardea discors, NUTT., Man. ii, 1834, 54.
Nycticorax americanus, BP., List, 1838, 48.—TSCH., Fn. Peru, 50.—GOSSE, B. Jam. 1847, 344.

Hab.—United States and British Provinces. Breeds abundantly in New England. Winters in the South and beyond. Part of the West Indies. Mexico. Central America. South America (Peru, *Tschudi, Sclater & Salvin;* Chili, *Darwin;* Brazil, *Pelzeln;* Falkland, *Sclater*). (Compare *A. obscura, Lichtenstein.*)
Not obtained by the Expeditions.

Observed by me on the Red River of the North, near Pembina, Dakota, in May. Like the *A. herodias* and *Botaurus minor*, this species goes quite far north—a little beyond the limits of the United States. It breeds in suitable places throughout its range, in colonies, sometimes of great extent; and is resident in the South.

BOTAURUS MINOR, (Gm.) Boie.

American Bittern.

Botaurus freti-hudsonis, BRISS, Orn. v, 449, pl. 37, f. 1.—DEGL., Orn. ii, 309.
Ardea freti-hudsonis, SCHLEGEL, Mus. Pays-Bas; *Ardeæ*, p. 49.
Ardea hudsonias, MERR., Ersch. Grub. Ency. v. 175.
Ardea stellaris var., FORST., Phil. Trans. lxii, 1772, 410.
Ardeo. stellaris var. β, *Botaurus freti-hudsonis*, LATH., Ind. Orn. ii, 1790, 680 (EDW., pl. 136; Gen. Syn. v, 58; Arct. Zool, ii, 451.)
Ardea stellaris var. B, *minor*, GM., Syst. Nat. i, 1788, 635.
Ardea minor, WILS., Am. Orn. viii, 1814, 35, pl. 65, f. 3.—BP., Obs. Wils. 1825, No. 186.—AUD., Orn. Biog. iv, 1838, 296, pl. 337.—NEWB., P. R. R. Rep. vi, 1857, 96 (California and Oregon).
Botaurus minor, BOIE, Isis, 1826, 979.—BP , List, 1838, 48; Consp. ii, 1855, 136.—GUNDL., J. f. O. iv, 1856, 346 (Cuba).—GRAY, Hand-list, iii, 1871, 32, No. 10163.—COUES, Key, 1872, 269.
Ardea lentiginosa, MONT., Orn. Dict. Suppl. 1813.—JEN., Man. 191.—LEACH, Cat. 33.—TEMM., Man. Orn. iv, 381.—FLEM., Brit. An. 96.—EYT., Brit. B. 37.—KEYS. & BLAS., Wirb. Eur. 80.—SAB., Frankl. Journ. 683.—SW. & RICH., F. B. A. ii, 1831,

374.—NUTT., Man. ii, 1834, 60.—AUD., Syn. 1839, 263; B. Am. vi, 1843, 94, pl 365.—GIR., B. L. I. 1844, 285.—PUTN., Pr. Ess. Inst. i, 1856, 218.—TRIPPE, *ibid.* vi, 1871, 119.

Botaurus lentiginosus, STEPH., Shaw's Gen. Zool. xi, 1819, 596.—MACGIL., Man. ii, 124.— GRAY, Gen. of B. iii, 557.—BD., B. N. A. 1858, 674; Mex. Bound. Surv. ii, pt. ii, 1859, 24 (Matamoras).—HEERM., P. R. R. Rep. x, 1859, pt. vi, 63 (California.)— COOP. & SUCK., N. H. Wash. Ter. 1860, 228.—WHEAT., Ohio Agric. Rep. 1860, No. 187.—COUES, Pr. Phila. Acad. 1861, 227 (Labrador); 1866, 95 (Arizona); 1871, 34 (North Carolina).—COUES & PRENT., Smiths. Rep. 1861, 415 (resident).— HAYD., Rep. 1862, 173.—CASS., Pr. Phila. Acad. 1862, 321 (California).—BOARDM., Pr. Bost. Soc. ix, 1862, 128 (Maine, common, breeds).—COUES, *ibid.* xii, 1868, 123 (South Carolina, resident).—MAYN., *ibid.* 1871 (New Hampshire).—AIKEN, *ibid.* 1872, 209 (Colorado).—TRIPPE, *ibid.* 1872, 240 (Iowa, abundant, breeds).—VERR., Pr. Ess. Inst. iii, 1862, 153 (Maine, breeds).—ALLEN, *ibid.* iv, 1864, 76.—McILWR., *ibid.* v, 1866, 91 (Canada West, abundant, summer).—COUES, *ibid.* v, 1868, 290.— HOY, Smiths. Rep. 1864, 438 (Missouri).—LAWR., Ann. Lyc. N. Y. viii, 1866, 292.— DRESS., Ibis, 1866, 32 (Texas).—SALV., Ibis, 1866, 196 (Guatemala).—ALLEN, Mem. Bost. Soc. i, 1868, 501, 507, 520 (Iowa and Illinois).—ALLEN, Bull. M. C. Z. ii, 1871, 359 (Florida); iii, 1872, 182 (Kansas and Utah).—TURNB., B. E. Pa. 1869, 28.—MAYN., Guide, 1870, 144 (Massachusetts, April to October).—ENDI-COTT, Am. Nat. iii, 1869, 169 (best biography).—STEV., U. S. Geol. Surv. Ter. 1870, 465 (Wyoming).—SNOW, B. Kans. 1873, 9.—RIDGW., Ann. Lyc. N. Y. x, 1874, 386 (Illinois).

Butor lentiginosus, JARD., Br. Birds, iii, 147.
Butor americana, SWAINS., Classif. B. ii, 1837, 354.
Ardea mokoko, VIEILL., Nouv. Dict. d'Hist. Nat. xiv, 440.—WAGL., Syst. Av. 1827, No. 29.
Ardea adspersa, LICHT., "Mus. Berol."
Botaurus adspersus, CAB. (*Bp.*)

Hab.—Entire temperate North America (up to 58° or 60°). Cuba. South to Guatemala. Breeds chiefly from the Middle districts northward, wintering thence southward. Regularly migratory. Accidental in Europe (GOULD, B. Eur. pl. 281.—THOMP., Ann. Mag. N. H. xvii, 1846, 91.—HART., Brit. B. 1872, 150; numerous instances).

Lieutenant Warren's Expedition.—5455, Vermilion River; 8911, Platte River.
Later Expeditions.—60774, Sweetwater.
Not obtained by Captain Raynolds' Expedition.

The very great variation in size of this species has not usually been recognized. I have measured individuals from 23 to 34 inches in length, with an extent of wing from 32 to 43 inches; the wing 9½ to 13, and other measurements to correspond. The coloration varies interminably; even the characteristic velvety black spot on the side of the neck is sometimes obsolete.

Audubon has given accounts of nearly all our Herons, with which he was very familiar, in a series of admirable biographies, leaving little to be desired. He was less fortunate in the case of the Bittern, admitting that he never had a good opportunity of observing all its habits. This being the case with "the American Woodsman," it is less singular that no other writer has completed the history of the species. Latterly, however, Mr. Endicott has gone far toward supplying the deficiency, in his excellent article above cited; and Mr. Samuels gives some interesting particulars. Every one knows the Bittern by sight, and has a general, if vague, idea of its character, but few have become familiar with its ways. Wilson conveys but little information, and that not entirely to the point. Richardson fixes its northern limit at 58°, but has little more to say. Nuttall's account is chiefly a compilation from these two sources. Although I am tolerably familiar with the bird, I have never seen its nest, or found it where I could suppose it was breeding. According to the best accounts, its peculiarities in respect of nidification are, that it does not assemble in communities, at any rate of large extent, to breed, and that the nest is usually placed on the ground. Mr. Samuels says: "It breeds in communities, sometimes as many as a dozen pairs nesting within the area of a few rods. The nests are placed on low bushes, or thick tufts of grass, sometimes in low, thickly-wooded trees; and are composed of coarse grasses, twigs, and a few leaves. I know of no other place in New England where these birds breed in such abundance as in the neighborhood of Richardson's Lakes, in Maine· There, in some of the tangled, boggy, almost impenetrable swamps, these birds have several heronies, which they have inhabited for years." It will be observed that this account is directly contradictory of a statement of Audubon's: "Although in a particular place, apparently favorable, some dozens of these birds may be found to-day, yet, perhaps, on visiting it to-morrow, you will not find one remaining, and districts resorted to one season or year, will be found deserted by them the next."

With these accounts we may compare Mr. Endicott's observations: "Some speak of finding the Bittern breeding in colonies in trees. Good observers say so, and I believe them; but I think that all such cases are owing to accidental circumstances, such as the inundation of their marshes. Certain it is, that I have never found them so associated. 'Le butor,' says M. Holandre, 'est très sauvage, farouche, solitaire.' One tiger's den to a jungle, one eyry to a mountain, and one pair of Bitterns to a bog, seems to be the rule. In the place where I have found them there is retired feeding ground for a thousand; dense cedar swamps, extensive enough for as many nests, if they only chose to congregate, like their sociable cousins, the Herons; and yet two by two they live, their next neighbors nobody knows how far away—not in the same swamp at any rate; and on the ground, the bare ground, they lay their four or five eggs, among low laurel, tufts of grass, or, as in the case of the first nest I ever found, at the foot of a swamp huckleberry, from which the callow young, unable yet to stand, tried to drive me away by repeated tumbling charges, menacing me by clumping their soft mandibles, and by sending angry hisses from their wide-yawning yellow throats."

Mr. Endicott remarks very pointedly upon the general uncertainty that pervades ornithological writings respecting the color of the Bittern's eggs, "finding the enumerated authorities determined that the eggs should have green on them of some shade or other." He calls them "a dark drab"; Mr. Samuels says "a rich drab, with sometimes an olive tinge." The color of the several sets before me may be called a brownish-drab, with a shade of gray. It is a difficult color to name, and doubtless varies in tint in different specimens; but it is probably never anything like the clear, pale greenish of the eggs of ordinary Herons. Specimens measure 1.90 by 1.50, to 2.00 by 1.50; the nest-complement is three to five.

The "booming of the Bittern" is an expression, alliterative if not accurate, which generally gets into writings upon this bird. I have never heard any sound from our species which could be called booming, bleating, bellowing, or even neighing—all of which words, among others, have been used to suggest the queer, uncouth voice of the bird. On this subject I will again have recourse to Mr. Endicott for an extract. "Mudie speaks as follows of the European Bittern's voice: 'Anon a burst of savage laughter breaks upon you, gratingly loud, and so unwonted and odd that it sounds as if the voices of a bull and a horse were combined; the former breaking down his bellow to suit the neigh of the latter, in mocking you from the sky.' 'When the Bittern booms and bleats overhead, one certainly feels as if the earth were shaking. * * * * Chaucer speaks as follows in *The Wife of Bath's Tale*:

'And as a bitore bumbleth in the mire,
She laid hire mouth into the water doun,
Bewray me not, thou water, with they soun',
Quod she, to the I tell it, and no mo,
Min husband hath long asses eres two.'

Another notion was that the bill was put inside a reed to increase the sound; the truth is, of course, that the bird uses no means to produce its bellow but its own organs of voice. Our own Bittern has no such roar, but, as its name in most parts of the country denotes, makes a noise very much like driving a stake with an axe. It has also a hollow croak at the moment of alarm." This is exactly true. The curious noise is spoken of in Audubon as a "hoarse croaking, as if the throat were filled with water." Nuttall makes a successful attempt to suggest the sound by the syllables *'pump-aŭ-gah.* But I prefer, on the whole, Mr. Samuels' rendering. "In the mating season," he says, "and during the first part of the period of incubation, the male has a peculiar love-note, that almost exactly resembles the stroke of a mallet on a stake; something like the syllables *chunk-a-lunk–chunk, quank chunk-a-lunk–chunk.* I have often, when in the forests of Northern Maine, been deceived by this note into believing that some woodsman or settler was in my neighborhood, and discovered my mistake only after toiling through swamp and morass for perhaps half a mile." Besides this peculiar call-note, the bird has another, its ordinary cry, when its breast is not in the least swelling with the tender passion. This is a single, abrupt, explosive syllable, something like *quark,* or *hauk,* delivered with a rough, guttural intonation. It is always uttered when the bird is surprised while feeding, or when its haunts are invaded. As it lives so much among reeds and rushes, very often the first intimation one has of its presence is the energetic utterance of this note, to be followed in an instant by the heavy form of the bird itself, as it tops the tall weeds. Ordinarily, however, the Bittern is decidedly a silent bird, as it were mistrusting its vocal ability; besides, noisiness is not altogether compatible with its sedate ways and contemplative turn of mind.

We might expect to find in the wind-pipe some peculiarity to account for such vocal efforts. In such instances as those of the Trumpeter Swan, and Whooping Crane, for instance, the remarkable notes emitted depend evidently upon the peculiarly convoluted structure of the trachea. But ordinarily, little connection can be traced between quality of voice and tracheal structure. The curious cartilaginous or osseous bulbs at the lower larynx of most Ducks seem to have no influence on the voice. Who would suspect the marvellous musical ability of a Mocking Bird, from comparison of its vocal organ with that of a Crow for instance, a bird which anatomically considered, is truly *oscine,* for all that its croak is so harsh. The conformation of the Bittern's windpipe is not remarkable, according to descriptions; there is no dilation into a membranous or gristly tympanum, nor any convolution, nor is the muscular arrangement remarkable. The calibre of the tube is perhaps greater, proportionately, than is usual in Herons, with laterally compressed walls, narrow rings, and wide spaces, but for all that we can discover by examination of the organs, the voice of the Bittern is likely to remain its own secret.

The Bittern is migratory, and its movements are regular. Excepting the Great Blue Heron, no bird of its tribe in this country is so extensively dispersed. It reaches the Northern States in March, or early in April, and may pass still further north. I ascertained its occurrence at Rigolet, in Labrador, and it is stated to reach 58° or 60° in the interior. It has frequently been shot in Europe, though not recorded from Greenland. It reaches across our continent. To the south, its movements extend to Guatemala, although it winters in the Southern States as well, and also, I am inclined to think, even in the Middle States, as I have procured it in January at Washington. It visits some of the West Indian Islands. In September I found it migratory through Dakota in comparative plenty. It may breed in almost any portion of its range, but nests preferably toward the North.

The Bittern, as has been said, is essentially " wild, shy, and solitary." We oftener start one from his lonely vigils in the bog, than find several, or even a pair together, excepting in the breeding season. No doubt he enjoys life after his own fashion, but his notions of happiness are peculiar. He prefers solitude, and leads the eccentric life of a recluse, " forgetting the world, and by the world forgot." To see him at his ordinary occupation, one might fancy him shouldering some heavy responsibility, oppressed with a secret, or laboring in the solution of a problem of vital consequence. He stands motionless, with his head drawn in upon his shoulders, and half-closed eyes, in profound meditation, or steps about in a devious way, with an absent-minded air ; for greater seclusion, he will even hide in a thick brush-clump for hours together. Startled in his retreat whilst his thinking-cap is on, he seems dazed, like one suddenly aroused from a deep sleep ; but as soon as he collects his wits, remembering unpleasantly that the outside world exists, he shows common sense enough to beat a hasty retreat from a scene of altogether too much action for him. Some such traits have doubtless led to the belief that he is chiefly a nocturnal bird ; but such is not the case. He may migrate by night, but so does the Killdeer, and the Bobolink, and many other birds not in the least nocturnal. Nor is the Bittern either lazy or stupid, as some may suppose. He is simply what we call a shady character—one of those non-committal creatures whom we may invest, if we please, with various attributes, and perhaps consider very deep, without sufficient reason ; the fact being, that we make the mystery about him. There is nothing remarkable in the fact that he prefers his own company, and dislikes to be bored. He lives in the bog, where he finds plenty to eat that he likes best, and is satisfied to be simply let alone.

When the Bittern is disturbed at his meditation, he gives a vigorous spring, croaks at the moment in a manner highly expressive of his disgust, and flies off as fast as he can, though in rather a loose, lumbering way. For some distance he flaps heavily with dangling legs and outstretched neck ; but when settled on his course he proceeds more smoothly, with regular measured wing-beats, the head drawn in closely and the legs stretched straight out behind together, like a rudder. He is very easily shot on the wing—easily hit, and dropping at a touch even of fine shot. When winged, he croaks painfully as he drops, and no sooner does he touch the ground than he gathers himself in defensive attitude to resent aggression as best he can. He fights well, and with more spirit and determination than he might be expected to show— like many other quiet inoffensive creatures when quite sure they have a grievance and are pushed to desperation. He has a very ugly way of pointing his resistance with quick thrusts of his spear-like bill, capable of inflicting no slight wound on an incautious hand. But it avails little ; a kick from a cowhide boot, or a thump with the butt of a gun, generally decides the unequal contest.

The food of this bird consists of various kinds of small aquatic animals. In its stomach may be found different molluscs, crawfish, frogs, lizards, small snakes and fishes, as well as insects. Such prey is captured with great address, by spearing, as the bird walks or wades stealthily along. The thrust of the bill is marvellously quick and skilful—more action is displayed on such occasions than probably under any other circumstance. As an article of food itself, the Bittern is not a success, notwithstanding eminent authority to the contrary. I have several times seen it brought to table, under favorable culinary circumstances; but in each instance it furnished occasion for a joke at some one's expense, as little relished, apparently, as the meat itself.

ARDETTA EXILIS, (Gm.) Gray.

Least Bittern.

Ardea exilis, GM., Syst. Nat. i, 1788, 645.—LATH., Ind. Orn. ii, 1790, 683 (based on *Minute Bittern*, of Gen. Syn. v, 66).—WILS., Am. Orn. viii, 1814, 37, pl. 65, f. 4.—WAGL., Syst. Av. 1827, *Ardea* No. 36.—NUTT., Man. ii, 1834, 66.—AUD., Orn. Biog. iii, 1835, 77 ; v, 1839, 606; pl. 210 ; Syn. 1839, 263 ; B. Am. vi, 1843, 100, pl. 366.—GIR., B. L. I. 1844, 287.—PUTN., Pr. Ess. Inst. i, 1856, 210 (Massachusetts).—NEWB., P. R. R. Rep. vi, 1857, 98 (Sacramento Valley, Cal.).
Ardea (Ardeola) exilis, BP., Obs. Wils. 1825, No. 191; Syn. 1828, 308.
Ardeola exilis, BP., List, 1838, 47 ; C. A. ii, 1855, 134.—GOSSE, B. Jam. 1847, 343.—HOY, Smiths. Rep. 1864, 438 (Missouri).
Butor exilis, SW., Classif. of Birds, ii, 1837, 354.
Ardetta exilis, GRAY, Gen. of B. iii, 1849 ; Hand-list, iii, 1871, 31, No. 10150 (subgenus).—GUND., J. f. O. iv, 1856, 345 (Cuba).—BD., B. N. A. 1858, 673.—WHEAT., Ohio Agric. Rep. 1860, No. 186.—SCL., P. Z. S. 1861, 81 (Jamaica).—COUES & PRENT., Smiths. Rep. 1861, 415.—VERR., Pr. Ess. Inst. iii, 1862, 158 (Maine, rare).—ALLEN, *ibid.* iv, 1864, 76 (Massachusetts, very rare).—McILWR., *ibid.* v, 1866, 91 (Canada West, common summer resident).—COUES, *ibid.* v, 1868, 290.—LAWR., Ann. Lyc. N. Y. viii, 1863 (Panama) ; 1866, 292.—COUES, Pr. Phila. Acad. 1866, 95 (Arizona).—COUES, Pr. Bost. Soc. xii, 1868, 123 (South Carolina).—DRESS., Ibis, 1866, 32 (Texas).—BRY., Pr. Bost. Soc. 1866 (Porto Rico).—SALV., Ibis, 1866 196 (Guatemala).—ALLEN, Mem. Bost. Soc. i, 1868, 520 (Illinois).—TURNB., B. E. Pa. 1869, 28.—ALLEN, Bull. M. C. Z. ii, 1871, 359 (Florida, not common); iii, 1872, 182 (Eastern Kansas).—MAYN., Guide, 1870, 144 (Massachusetts, very rare).—COUES, Key, 1872, 270.—SNOW, B. Kans. 1873, 9.—RIDGW., Ann. Lyc. N. Y. x, 1874, 386 (Illinois).

Hab.—United States and British Provinces. Breeds throughout its United States range, wintering in the South. Cuba. Jamaica. Central America. (?) South America. Not obtained by any of the Expeditions.

Although very generally distributed, this curious little Heron does not appear to be anywhere abundant. I have seen it alive but few times, and am not very familiar with its habits. I have invariably found it in reedy swamps—just such places as the Rails frequent—where, when startled, it flies up in a manner reminding one of a Rail. Like the Bittern, it is regularly migratory, passing northward in April, and returning in September. It is said to reside in the Gulf States, and to be more numerous there than elsewhere. It does not appear to gather in communities to breed, like most of the Herons, but is oftenest found singly, in pairs, or at most, three or four pairs. It is also an exception to the general rule among Herons that the sexes are alike in color. It bears a curious likeness, or rather analogy, in several respects to the Rails.

The nest I have never seen. According to Audubon, it is " sometimes placed on the ground, amid the rankest grasses, but more frequently it is attached to the stems several inches above it. It is flat, composed of dried or rotten weeds, and in shape resembles that of the Louisiana Heron, though this latter employs nothing but sticks. * *

* In two instances I found the nests of the Least Bittern about three feet above the ground in a thick cluster of smilax and other briary plants. In the first, two nests were placed in the same bush, within a few yards of each other. In the other instances there was only one

nest of this bird, but several of the Boat-tailed Grakle, and one of the Green Heron, the occupants of all of which seemed to be on friendly terms. When startled from the nest, the old birds emit a few notes resembling the syllable *quā*, alight a few yards off, and watch all your movements. If you go toward them, you may sometimes take the female with the hand, but rarely the male, who generally flies off, or makes his way through the woods. * * * * * The food of this bird consists of snails, slugs, tadpoles, or young frogs and water-lizards. In several instances, however, I have found small shrews and field-mice in their stomachs."

The eggs, three to five in number, are elliptical, or equal at both ends, from 1.20 by 0.90, to 1.25 by 0.95 in size, and white, with the faintest bluish tint. They look very much like pigeon's eggs, except in the equality of the ends

34

SUBORDER ALECTORIDES: CRANES, RAILS, &c.

Family GRUIDÆ : Cranes.

GRUS AMERICANA, (Linn.) Temm.

White or Whooping Crane.

Ardea americana, LINN., Syst. Nat. i, 1776, 234 (based on EDW., pl. 132; CATES., pl. 75; BRISS., v, 382).—GM., Syst. Nat. i, 1788, 621.—FORST., Phil. Trans. lxii, 1772, 382 (York Fort).—LATH., Ind, Orn. ii, 1790, 675 (Arct. Zool. ii, 442; Gen Syn. v, 42, Planch. Enlum. 889).—WILS., Am. Orn. viii, 1814, 20, pl. 64, f. 3.
Grus americana, TEMM., Analyse.—ORD, ed. Wils. viii, 1825.—BP., Obs. Wils. 1825, No. 195; Syn. 1828, — ; List, 1838, 46; Consp. ii, 1855, 99.—Sw. & RICH., F. B. A. ii, 1831, 372 ("every part of the Fur Countries").—NUTT., Man. ii, 1834, 34.— AUD., Orn. Biog. iii, 1835, 202, pl. 226; Syn. 1839, 219; B. A. v, 1842, 188, pl. 313.—BRY., Pr. Bost. Soc. iv, 1853, 303 (critical).—PUTN., Pr. Ess. Inst. i, 1856, 229 (Massachusetts, very doubtful; based on Emmons, Cat. B. Mass. 135; see COUES, Pr. Ess. Inst. v, 1868, 289).—BD., B. N. A. 1858, 654.—MAXIM, J. f. O. vii, 1859, 82 (immature).—WHEAT., Ohio Agric. Rep. 1860, No. 181 (Ohio, occasional).—DRESS., Ibis, 1866, 30 (Lower Rio Grande).—COUES, Pr. Bost. Soc. xii, 1868, 123 (South Carolina in winter, doubtful; on authority of *Prof. Gibbes*, probably referring back to *Audubon*, who did not distinguish between this and *G. canadensis*).—TURNB., B. E. Pa. 1869, 43 ("now very rare;" three at Beesley's Point, in 1851).—TRIPPE., Pr. Ess. Inst. vi, 1871, 118 (Minnesota, "quite common at certain seasons, occasionally breeding").—TRIPPE, Pr. Bost. Soc. xv, 1872, 240 (Decatur County, Iowa, "quite a number").—AIKEN, Pr. Bost. Soc. xv, 1872, 209 (Colorado, migratory, occasional).—ALLEN, Bull. M. C. Z. iii, 1872, 182 (Kansas).—SNOW, B. Kans. 1873, 9 (rare in migration).—COUES, Key, 1872, 271.—RIDGW., Ann. Lyc. N. Y. x, 1874, 387 (Illinois).
Grus clamator, BARTRAM, Trav. in E. Fla. 1791.
Grus struthio, WAGLER, Syst. Av. 1827, *Grus* No. 6.
Grus hoyanus, DUDLEY, Pr. Phila. Acad. vii, 1854, 64.—HARTL., J. f. O. iii, 1855, 336, 427.—(See STIMPSON, Mem. Chic. Acad. i, 1868, 129, pl. 19.)

Hab.—Interior of North America. Up the Mississippi Valley, spreading through the Fur Countries. Texas to Florida, and occasionally up the coast to the Middle States. Not obtained by any of the Expeditions.

It is unnecessary, at this late day, to argue the question of the distinctness of this species and its formerly supposed young, *G. canadensis*. But a very remarkable anatomical difference between the two species may be presented, as a structural character of *G. americana* not generally recognized, if indeed it be not altogether unknown. In *G. canadensis* the trachea is stated to be simple; in *G. americana* it is remarkably convoluted within the sternum, to a degree perhaps not surpassed by any bird whatever, and certainly equaled by few. This is an instance of an anatomical peculiarity like that of the Trumpeter Swan (*Cygnus buccinator*), in comparison with some allied species, and it appears to exercise a similar direct influence upon the voice, in each case.

My attention was first directed to this peculiarity by Dr. R. O. Sweeny, of Saint Paul, when visiting the Museum of the Academy of Natural Sciences in that city, where I was shown a beautiful preparation of the sternum and trachea, exhibiting the entire course of the windpipe inside the keel of the bone. The sternal keel is broad and tumid, and is entirely excavated. The greater part of the excavation is occupied by the singular duplications of the trachea, to be presently described; but there are two—an anterior and a posterior—large empty air cells in the bone, with smooth walls, and two other air cells—one superior and one along the edge of the keel—filled with light, bony meshwork. Excepting these cancellated portions, the whole keel is hollow, and is occupied by the folds of the windpipe, as follows: Coming down the throat, the trachea enters the sternal keel at its anterior inferior apex, and runs along the lower edge of the keel, inside, almost to the very posterior angle; curving abruptly upward and forward, at about 45°, it runs along the top of the keel just under the body of the bone to the very front, where it appears; curving next downward, it reënters the keel just alongside its original entrance, passes about a third way to the posterior end of the bone, then coils upward with a strong curve, folding on itself, to reëmerge from the bone close alongside its first entrance; and thence passes up to the bronchi with a strong curve.   In fewer words, the trachea, entering the apex of the keel, traverses the whole contour of the keel in a long vertical coil, emerges at the front upper corner of the keel, enters again at the lower corner of the keel and makes a smaller vertical coil in the center, emerging again where it went in.   On looking at the object from the front, we see three parallel vertical coils, side by side; the middle one is the trachea coming down from the neck above; on the left hand is the bulge of the first great coil; on the right is the windpipe passing to the lungs after it has made its second coil inside. Measuring loosely, with a thread laid along the track of the folds, I find there are about *twenty eight inches* of windpipe coiled away in the breast-bone—certainly over two feet; from upper larynx to the entrance is about twenty-two inches, and there are about eight inches more of the tube from its exit from the bone to the forks of the bronchi; altogether, *fifty-eight inches.* The Whooping Crane has a windpipe between four and five feet long—quite as long as the bird itself.

The distribution of the Whooping Crane appears to be somewhat peculiar, as may be gathered from the foregoing indications.   It is said to be found throughout the Fur Countries; but in the United States its dispersion is limited, and there is a difficulty in determining from the accounts, since several authors have confounded it with the Sandhill Crane.   I find no satisfactory evidence of its occurrence in New England, and Mr. Lawrence omits it from his New York list.   Dr. Turnbull gives it as now very rare, but remarks that in Wilson's time it bred at Cape May, New Jersey.   It is said to be common in Florida, where, however, Mr. Allen "saw no White Cranes."   It occurs in Texas.   I have never seen it alive excepting in Northern Dakota, where I observed it in August, September, and October, and where, probably, it breeds.   Its principal line of migration appears to be the Mississippi Valley at large; accounts of its presence all along this belt, from Texas to Minnesota, for a considerable breadth, are unanimous and conclusive.   Here it seems to be chiefly migratory, but there is every reason to believe that it breeds in Minnesota and, as just said, in Dakota, as it also does further north.

Two eggs of the Whooping Crane are in the Smithsonian from Great Slave Lake, where they were taken by Mr. J. Lockhart.   Though from the same nest, one is noticeably more elongated than the other, measuring about 3.90 by 2.65, the other being about 3.60 only, with the same width.   The shell is much roughened with numerous elevations, like little warts, and is, moreover, punctulate all over.   The ground is a light brownish-drab; the markings are rather sparse, except at the great end; they are large irregular spots of a pale dull chocolate-brown, with still more obscure or nearly obsolete shell-markings.   A queried, but probably correct set of eggs is in the collection from Dubuque, Iowa

This tall and stately white bird, of the most imposing appearance of any of this country, I have only seen on the broad prairie, or soaring on motionless pinion in spiral curves high overhead. Its immense stature is sometimes singularly exaggerated by that quality of the prairie air which magnifies distant objects on the horizon, transforming sometimes a weed into a man, or making a Wild Turkey excite suspicion of a buffalo. The most fabulous accounts of a Crane's size might readily arise without intentional deception. I have known a person to mistake a Sandhill Crane for one of his stray mules, and go in search; and another enthusiastic teamster once declared that some he saw were "bigger than his six-mule team." Once, while antelope-shooting on the prairie, my companion—a good hunter—and myself saw what we took to be an antelope standing quietly feeding with his broad, white stern toward us, and only about five hundred yards off. We attempted, for at least fifteen minutes, to "flag" the creature up to us, waving a handkerchief on a ramrod in the most approved style. This proving unavailing, my friend proceed to stalk the game, and crawled on his belly for about half the distance before the "antelope" unfolded his broad black-tipped wings and flapped off, revealed at length as a Whooping Crane.

GRUS CANADENSIS, (Linn.) Temm.

Brown or Sandhill Crane.

Ardea canadensis, LINN., Syst. Nat. i, 1766, 234 (EDW., i, 33; BRISS., v, 385).—FORST., Philos. Trans. lxii, 1772, 382, 409 (Severn River).—GM., Syst. Nat. i, 1788, 620.— LATH., Ind. Orn. ii, 1790, 675 (Arct. Zool. ii, 443; Gen. Syn. v, 43).
Grus canadensis, TEMM., Anal. p. c.—BP., Syn. 1828, No. 225; Consp. ii, 1855, 98.—SAB., Frankl. Journ. 685.—RICH., Parry's 2d Voy. 353.—SW. & RICH., F. B. A. ii, 1831, 373.—NUTT., Man. ii, 1834, 38.—BRY., Pr. Bost. Soc. iv, 1853, 303 (critical); vii, 1859, p. 14.—WOODH., Sitgr. Rep. 1853, 96 (New Mexico and Arizona).—GUNDL., J. f. O. iv, 1856, 339 (Cuba, breeding).—NEWB., P. R. R. Rep. vi, 1857, 97 (Pacific coast).—BD., B. N. A. 1858, 655.—HEERM., P. R. R. Rep. x, 1859, pt. vi, 62 (California).—MAXIM., J. f. O. vii, 1859, 84.—COOP. & SUCK., N. H. Wash. Ter. 1860, 227.—WHEAT., Ohio Agric. Rep. 1860, No. 182.—HAYD., Rep. 1862, 173 (Nebraska).—HOY, Smiths. Rep. 1864, 438 (Western Missouri).—DRESS., Ibis, 1866, 30 (Texas).—COUES, Pr. Phila. Acad. 1866, 95 (Colorado and Gila Rivers, abundant).—ALLEN, Mem. Bost. Soc. i, 1868, 501 (Iowa, migratory and breeding).— DALL & BANN., Tr. Chic. Acad. i, 1869, 289 (Alaska, common, breeding).—ALLEN, Bull. M. C. Z. ii, 1871, 357 (Florida, abundant).—TRIPPE, Pr. Ess. Inst. vi, 1871, 118 (Minnesota, very common, breeding); Pr. Bost. Soc. xv, 1872, 240 (Iowa, "vast numbers in migration").—AIKEN, *ibid.* 209 (Colorado, common in migration).—MERR., U. S. Geol. Surv. Ter. 1872, 702 (Idaho).—COUES, Key, 1872, 271.—SNOW, B. Kans. 1873, 9 (abundant in migrations).—RIDGW., Ann. Lyc. N. Y. x, 1874, 387 (Illinois).
Ardea canadensis var. β, LATH., Ind. Orn. ii, 1790, 676 (Mexico).
Grus mexicana, MÜLLER (Briss., v, 380).
Grus pratensis, BARTR., Trav. in Florida, 1791, p. —.
Grus fusca, VIEILL., Nouv. Dict. d'Hist. Nat. vii, 548.
Grus poliophœa, WAGLER, Syst. Av. 1827, *Grus* No. 7.
Grus americana, AUD., Orn. Biog. iii, 1835, 441 (in part), pl. 261; Syn. 1839, 219 (in part); B. Am. v, 1842, 188 (in part); pl. 314 (supposed young).
Grus fraterculus, CASS., Baird's B. N. A. 1858, 656 (New Mexico).
Compare *Grus longirostris*, BP., C. A. ii, 1854, 98 (Fn. Japon. pl. 72.)

Hab.—United States, from Florida and the Mississippi Valley to the Pacific, and interior of the Fur Countries. North to the Yukon (*Dall*) and west coast of Baffin's Bay (latitude 72°; Ibis, ii, 167). Breeds apparently nearly throughout its range. Cuba.
Lieutenant Warren's Expedition.—8914, Sand Hills, Nebraska (erroneously given as *G. americana* in Dr. Hayden's earlier report).
Later Expeditions.—62369, North Fork, Idaho.
Not obtained by Captain Raynolds' Expedition, nor by the later ones.

I find no indication of the occurrence of this species anywhere in the Eastern or Middle States, nor indeed east of the Mississippi and its tributaries, excepting in Florida. There it is abundant, according to several observers. Dr. Bryant refers to its breeding, stating that two eggs are laid, from early in February until about the middle of April. I have met with it in various parts of the West, finding it breeding in Northern Dakota, quite plentifully, on the broad prairie. Newly-hatched young were secured in July, near Turtle Mountain. Late in September and early in October numbers of this species and *G. americana* together were migrating through the same region; they appeared to journey chiefly by night. Often, as we lay encamped on the Mouse River, the stillness of midnight would be broken by the hoarse, rattling croaks of Cranes coming overhead, the noise finally dying in the distance, to be succeeded by the shrill pipe of numberless waders, the honking of Geese, and the whistle of the pinions of myriads of wild fowl that shot past, sounding to sleepy ears like the rushing sound of a far away locomotive.

We have accounts of the Sandhill Cranes from the whole extent of the Mississippi Valley (in the broad sense of the term), and of their breeding in Iowa and Minnesota, as well as in Dakota. In Alaska, Mr. Dall says, it is a common bird at St. Michael's and around the mouth of the Yukon, but less so in the interior, as at Nulato. "The eggs, obtained June 17, on the Yukon River, are laid in a small depression on the sandy beach, without any attempt at a nest." He adds that the fibula is a favorite pipe-stem with the Indians, who, also, are fond of domesticating the young; the birds eating up vermin and insects, as well as refuse scraps of food about the settlements. Further south, on the Pacific coast, says Dr. Suckley, Sandhill Cranes are very abundant at Puget Sound, on the Nisqually plains, in autumn. "They there commence to arrive from the summer breeding grounds about the last week in September, from which time until about the 10th of November they are quite plentiful. After this they disappear, probably retiring to warmer latitudes during the cold months. In the fall they are found on all the prairies near Fort Steilacoom, but are not indifferent to choice of certain spots. These are generally old 'stubble-fields,' or spots of ground that have been ploughed. They rise heavily and slowly from the ground on being disturbed, and, flying in circles, at length acquire the desired elevation. When proceeding from one favorite resort to another, or when migrating, the flight is high, and not unfrequently their approach is heralded, before they are in sight, by their incessant, whooping clamor. While feeding they are generally silent." To this account Dr. Cooper adds that the Brown Cranes are common *summer* residents in Washington Territory, "arriving at the Straits of Fuca in large flocks, in April, and there dispersing in pairs over the interior prairies to build their nests, which are placed amid the tall fern on the highest and most open ground, where they can see the approach of danger. They frequent, at this season, the mountains to the height of 6,000 feet above the sea. The young are often raised from the nest by the Indians for food."

"In the autumn and winter," Dr. Newberry observes, "it is abundant on the prairies of California, and is always for sale in the markets of San Francisco, where it is highly esteemed as an article of food. In August we frequently saw them about the Klamath Lakes, and early in September, while in the Cascade Mountains, in Oregon, the Cranes were a constant feature of the scenery of the beautiful but lonely mountain meadows in which we encamped. We found them always exceedingly shy and difficult of approach, but not unfrequently the files of their tall forms stretching above the prairie grass, or their discordant and far-sounding screams, suggested the presence of the human inhabitants of the region, whose territory was now, for the first time, invaded by the white man. The Cranes nest in these alpine meadows, and retreat to the milder climate of the valleys of California on the approach of winter. In Oregon they begin to move southward in October."

Thousands of Sandhill Cranes repair each year to the Colorado River Valley, flock succeeding flock along the course of the great stream, from their arrival in September until their departure the following spring. Taller than the Wood Ibises or the largest Herons with which they are associated, the stately birds stand in the foreground of the scenery of the valley, the water now reflecting the shadow of their broad wings, then the clear blue sky exhibiting in outline their commanding forms. Such ponderous bodies, moving with slowly-beating wings, give a great idea of momentum from mere weight—of force of motion without swiftness; for they plod along heavily, seeming to need every inch of their ample wings to sustain themselves. One would think they must soon alight fatigued with such exertion, but the raucous cries continue, and the birds fly on for miles along the tortuous stream, in Indian file, under some trusty leader, who croaks his hoarse orders, implicitly obeyed. Each bird keeps his place in the ranks; the advancing column now rises higher over some suspected spot, now falls along an open, sandy reach, swaying meanwhile to the right or left. As it passes on, the individual birds are blended in the hazy distance, till, just before lost to view, the line becomes like an immense serpent gliding mysteriously through the air. When about to alight, fearful lest the shadows of the woods harbor unseen danger, the Cranes pass by the leafy intricacies where the Ibises and other less suspicious birds feed, and choose a spot for the advantage it may offer of uninterrupted vision. By nature one of the most wary and discreet of birds, his experience has taught the Crane to value this gift and put it to the best use. His vigilance is rarely relaxed, even when he is feeding where less thoughtful birds would feel perfectly secure. After almost every bending of his long neck to the ground, he rises erect again, and at full length glances keenly on every side. He may resume his repast, but should so much as a speck he cannot account for appear to view, he stands motionless, all attention. Now let the least sound or movement betray an unwelcome visitor—he bends his muscular thighs, spreads his ample wings, and springs heavily into the air, croaking dismally in warning to all his kind within the far-reaching sound of his voice.

The eggs of the Sandhill Crane are of the same general character as those of *G. americana*, in texture of shell, its color, and markings, but, to judge from limited comparisons, are usually more elongate, if not also somewhat less capacious—3.80 by 2.60; 3.90 by 2.60; 4.10 by 2.40 (long and narrow); 3.65 by 2.10; the latter remarkably small, as well as unusually narrow. Eggs are in the collection from Liverpool Bay, on the Arctic coast; from Great Slave Lake; from Washington Territory; Fort Crook, California; Lake Simpson, Utah; Iowa, Florida, and Cuba, They cannot be positively distinguished, in any given instance, from those of *G. americana*.

Family RALLIDÆ: Rails.

Subfamily RALLINÆ: *True Rails.*

The Rails inhabit all temperate countries; they are remarkably distinguished by the extreme narrowness or compression of the body, which enables them to thread a way through the closest reeds and rushes of the marshes where they always live. Instead of long, flat, pointed, narrow wings, with flowing tertials, characteristic of the great Plover-snipe group, they have short, concave, rounded wings, and their flight is consequently of a different sort. They are neither swift nor vigorous on wing. When flushed, a matter of some difficulty, they fly in so feeble and vague a way that it is not very easy to understand how they make the extensive migrations for which, nevertheless, they are noted. The legs, as well as more particularly the feet, are large and strong; the thighs extremely muscular; they trust rather to these members than to their wings in avoiding pursuit or escaping danger; probably no birds are more accomplished pedestrians than they are. There is generally, if not always, a slight membrane between the base of the toes, but nothing amounting even to semipalmation; nevertheless, some of the species swim short distances with ease. While not exactly gregarious, since they do not go in flocks that are actuated by a common impulse and the instinct of socialism, nevertheless they frequent, through community of tastes and wants, the marshes in immense numbers; where they breed, and where they appear during the migration, particularly the autumnal, the marshes appear full-stocked with them. Their cries are loud, dry, and harsh; in the spring time the marshes resound. They scream piteously when wounded and caught, and fight as well as they can with their strong claws. Their food consists of all sorts of aquatic animals small enough to be swallowed—little crabs, snails, and other small molluscs, grubs, worms, and insects. They probably all live at times, and in a measure at least, upon the seeds and tender shoots of aquatic plants. They lay many white or whitish, much-spotted, oval or elliptical eggs, in a rude flat nest, built of sticks, rush-stalks, and grasses, upon the ground. The young, of which more than one brood may be annually raised, are generally black in the downy state, whatever the color of the adults. They appear to be of somewhat nocturnal habits, and probably migrate mostly by night. The flesh of some of our species is esteemed good eating, and great numbers are annually destroyed for the table, in the fall, when they are generally very fat.

RALLUS ELEGANS, Aud.

King Rail; Fresh-water Marsh Hen.

a. *elegans.*

Rallus crepitans, WILS., Am. Orn. vii, 1813, pl. 62, f. 2 (figure, but not the description. Not of authors).
Rallus elegans, AUD., Orn. Biog. iii, 1835, 27, pl. 203; Syn. 1839, 215; B. Am. v, 1842, 160, pl. 309.—BP., List, 1838, 53.—LINSL., Am. Journ. Sci. xliv, 1843, 267 (Connecticut).—GIR., B. L. I. 1834, 209.—GUNDL., J. f. O. iv, 1856, 427 (Cuba, breeding); Reperto. i, 360.—NEWB., P. R. R. Rep. vi, 1857, 96 (California).—BD., B. N. A. 1858, 746.—HEERM., P. R. R. Rep. x, 1859, pt. vi, 62 (California).—COOP. & SUCK., N. H. Wash. Ter. 1860, 246.—WHEAT., Ohio Agric. Rep. 1860, No. 226.—COUES & PRENT., Smiths. Rep. 1861, 416.—HOY, Smiths. Rep. 1864, 438 (Missouri).—LAWR., Ann. Lyc. N. Y. viii, 1866, 295.—COUES, Pr. Ess. Inst. v, 1868, 296 (Connecticut).—COUES, Pr. Bost. Soc. xii, 124 (South Carolina, resident).—SCL. & SALV., P. Z. S. 1868, 444 (critical).—TURNB., B. E. Pa. 1869, 33.—ALLEN, Bull. M. C. Z. ii, 1871, 357 (Florida.)—COUES, Key, 1872, 273.—SNOW, B. Kans. 1873, 10 (rare).—RIDGW., Ann. Lyc. N. Y. x, 1874, 387 (Illinois).
Aramus (Pardirallus) elegans, GRAY, Hand-list, iii, 1871, 59, No. 10417.
Rallus longirostris, SCL., P. Z. S. 1864, 179 (error). (Mexico.)

b. *obsoletus.*

Rallus elegans var. *obsoletus*, RIDGW., Am. Nat. viii, 1874, 111.—COUES, Check-list, App. 1874, 137, No. 466ª (California).

Hab.—United States, rather southerly. North on the Atlantic coast regularly to the Middle States, casually to Connecticut; in the interior to Kansas and Missouri at least; on the Pacific side to Oregon or Washington. Cuba. Mexico. Winters in the Southern States.
Not obtained by any of the Expeditions.

The King Rail is more limited in dispersion than any other one of our species of the family. The extralimital quotations are few, and to the northward its range is likewise restricted. None of the later New England writers mention it except myself, and I have only the authority of Mr. Linsley for its occurrence near Stratford, Connecticut. According to Mr. Turnbull it is "rather scarce" along the New Jersey coast. In the District of Columbia it is often observed early in the fall, when

the common Sora is so abundant in the marshes bordering on the Potomac. On the Pacific side it is stated to be common in California as far
as San Francisco, and to reach Humboldt Bay. In the interior it has
only been traced to Kansas and Missouri.

What little has been placed on record respecting its habits does not
indicate anything peculiar. The eggs are precisely like those of *R.
crepitans*, of which I have the following account, in substance, in the
American Naturalist, iii, 601 : Sizes: 1.80 by 1.10; 1.70 by 1.20; 1.66 by
1.00; 1.60 by 1.16; 1.50 by 1.15; 1.50 by 1.05; average about 1.66 by
1.10. Ground-color, from dull white to creamy or pale buff. Markings,
either sparse or plentiful, evenly or very irregularly distributed, varying from mere dots to large splashes, on the same or different eggs, but
usually largest at or around the great end, where they are apt to become confluent. The markings are reddish-brown of variable shade,
but never pure brown; with these are always a number of shell-spots
of lilac, lavender or pale-purplish.

I am not aware that the Clapper Rail (*R. longirostris*) has yet been
observed anywhere on the Missouri. It is chiefly confined to *salt*
marshes, along the coasts, but has been noted also in the interior, as at
Great Salt Lake, and may not improbably be detected in some of the
alkaline portions of the Missouri region. The accompanying foot-note
gives a portion of the synonomy of the species.*

RALLUS VIRGINIANUS, Linn.

Virginia Rail.

Rallus virginianus, LINN., Syst. Nat. i, 1766, 263 (based on CATES., 70, and BRISS., v,
175).—GM., Syst. Nat. i, 1688, 716.—WILS., Am. Orn. vii, 1813, 109, pl. 62, f. 1.—
BP., Obs. Wils. 1825, No. 210; Syn. 1828, 334; List, 1838, 53.—NUTT., Man. ii,
1834, 205.—AUD., Orn. Biog. iii, 41; v, 1839, 573; pl. 205; Syn. 1839, 216; B.
Am. v, 1842, 174, pl. 311.—GIR., B. L. I. 1844, 208.—WOODH., Sitgr. Rep. 1853,
101 (Rio Laguna).—GUNDL., J. f. O. iv, 1856, 427 (Cuba); Rep. Fis. i, 361.—
NEWB., P. R. R. Rep. vi, 1857, 96 (California).—HEERM., P. R. R. Rep. x, 1859,
pt. vi, 62 (California).—BD., B. N. A. 1858, 748.—COOP. & SUCK., N. H. Wash.
Ter. 1860, 247.—SCL. & SALV., Ibis, 1860, 277 (Guatemala).—DRESS., *ibid.* 1866, 40
(Texas).—SCL. & SALV., Exot. Orn. i, 196 (diagnosis); P. Z. S. 1868, 445.—SCHL.,
M. P.-B. *Ralli*, p. 11.—ALLEN, Mem. Bost. Soc. i, 1868, 501 (Iowa).—HOY, Smiths.
Rep. 1864, 438 (Missouri).—COUES, Pr. Phila. Acad. 1866, 98 (Arizona).—COUES,
Pr. Ess. Inst. v, 1868, 297 (breeding north to Maine).—COUES, Pr. Bost. Soc. xii,
1868, 124 (South Carolina).—COUES & PRENT., Smiths. Rep. 1861, 416.—PUTN.,
Pr. Ess. Inst. i, 1856, 216 (Massachusett, in summer).—VERR., *ibid.* iii, 1862, 159
(Maine, breeds).)—ALLEN, *ibid.* iv, 1864, 78 (Massachusetts, breeding).—MC-

---

* *Rallus longirostris*, BODD., Tabl. Planch. Enlum. 1784, pl. 489.—BURM., Syst. Ueb. iii,
381 (Bahia).—NEWT., Ibis, 1859, 260 (Santa Cruz).—GOSSE, B. Jam. 1847, 364.—
LÉOT., Ois. Trinidad, 491.—CASS., Pr. Phila. Acad. 1860, 378 (St. Thomas).—
SCL. & SALV., P. Z. S. 1868, 444 (critical).—COUES, Key, 1872, 273, fig. 178.
Aramus (Pardiralus) longirostris, GRAY, Hand-list, iii, 1871, 59, No. 10418.
Rallus crepitans, GM., Syst. Nat. i, 1788, 713.—WILS., Am. Orn. vii, 1813, 112 (not the
plate).—BP., Obs. Wils. 1825; Syn. 1828, 334; List, 1838, 53.—NUTT., Man. ii,
1834, 201.—AUD., Orn. Biog. iii, 1835, 331, pl. 214; Syn. 1839, 215; B. Am. v,
1842, 165, pl. 310.—GIR., B. L. I. 1844, 206.—GUNDL., J. f. O. 1856, 427 (Cuba);
Rep. Fis. Nat. i, 491.—BD., B. N. A. 1858, 747.—CAB., Schomb. Guiana, iii. 76.—
SCL., P. Z. S. 1861, 81 (Jamaica).—BRY., Pr. Bost. Soc. vii, 1859 (Bahamas).—
COUES, Pr. Ess. Inst. v, 1868, 296 (Massachusetts).—PUTN., Pr. Ess. Inst. i, 1856,
229.—ALLEN, Pr. Ess. Inst. iv, 1864, 87.—CABOT, Pr. Bost. Soc. iii, 326.—LAWR.,
Ann. Lyc. N. Y. viii, 1866, 295.—MCILWR., Pr. Ess. Inst. v, 1866, 93 (Canada
West).—TURNB., B. E. Pa. 1869, 33.—COUES, Pr. Bost. Soc. xii, 1868, 124.—
COUES, Am. Nat. iii, 1870, 600 (biography).—MAYN., Guide, 1870, 145 (Massa-
chusetts).—ALLEN, Bull. M. C. Z. ii, 357 (Florida); iii, 1872 (Salt Lake, Utah).

Hab.—Atlantic coast from Massachusetts to Brazil. Canada West (*McIlwraith*).
Great Salt Lake (*Allen*).

ILWR., *ibid.* v, 1866, 92 (Hamilton, C. W.).—TRIPPE, *ibid.* vi, 1871, 118 (Minnesota, breeds).—LAWR., Ann. Lyc. N. Y. viii, 1866, 295.—TURNB., B. E. Pa. 1869, 33 (not uncommon).—MAYN., Guide, 1870, 145.—ALLEN, Bull. M. C. Z. ii, 1871, 357 (Florida); iii, 1872, 182 (Kansas).—AIKEN, Pr. Bost. Soc. xv, 1872, 210 (Colorado, breeding).—COUES, Key, 1872, 273.—SNOW, B. Kans. 1873, 11.—RIDGW., Ann. Lyc. N. Y. x, 1874, 387 (Illinois).
Aramus (Pardirallus) virginianus, GRAY, Hand-list, iii, 1871, 59, No. 10419.
Rallus aquaticus var. β, LATH., Ind. Orn. ii, 1790, 755.
Rallus limicola, VIEILL., Ency. Meth. 1823, p. 1059.

Hab.—Entire United States and British Provinces. Breeds commonly in New England. Winters in the Southern States and beyond. South to Guatemala. Cuba. Not obtained by the Expeditions.

A night at Soda Lake, the *débouchure* of that singular river, the Mojave, was one of the strangest, as well as most uncomfortable, I ever passed. It was late in October, and the full moon threw a pale, uncertain light upon a scene of desolation and of death. On one side stretched the interminable desert of shifting sand, broken here and there by clumps of the foul creasote plant, straggling patches of grease-wood and bitter sage, and scattered, sentinel-like, Spanish bayonet. Along the road just traversed were strewn bleached skeletons of beasts that had fallen in their tracks beneath the scorching rays of the sun. At the foot of some cliffs near by lay whitening the heads and horns of the argali (*Ovis montana*), shot by previous travelers. The bare bones looked of double size and fantastic shape in the uncertain moonlight. Before us lay a dead-white sea of salty efflorescence, where the lake had evaporated or sunk in the sand, leaving its saline matter. It was dry, except toward the middle, where dark green masses of Tulé reeds, contrasting with the snowy whiteness all around, showed that a little water was left. Our animals, like ourselves, were exhausted; one poor creature, cruelly over-tasked, had given birth to a foal, and lay groaning by the wayside, unable to rise. The water was too nauseous to drink, and hardly answered to cook with. After a poor meal, we lay down with gloomy thoughts. But sleep was impossible, though wrapped never so closely, head and all, in our blankets. We contended with a bloodthirsty swarm of mosquitoes, wafted like a cloud from the stagnant pools. Every breath of air seemed to vibrate to the continuous hum of the insects; it was open onslaught, as well as stealthy attack, with them, as we huddled around the camp-fire, on the side to which the smoke was wafted, enveloped in blankets, and impatiently waiting the day. We were bitten on every exposed point; for days afterward our hands and faces were sore and swollen, inflamed by the tiny drops of poison instilled into each wound.

But even under such circumstances I was gratified by the presence of feathered friends. At nightfall some Mallard and Teal settled into the rushes, gabbling curious vespers as they went to rest. A few Marsh Wrens had appeared on the edge of the reeds, queerly balancing themselves on the thread-like leaves, see-sawing to their own quaint music. Then they were hushed, and as darkness settled down, the dull, heavy croaking of the frogs played bass to the shrill falsetto of the insects. Suddenly they too were hushed in turn, frightened, may be, into silence; and from the heart of the bullrushes, "*crik–crik–rik–k–k–k,*" lustily shouted some wide-awake Rail, to be answered by another and another, till the reeds resounded. Then all was silent again till the most courageous frog renewed his pipes. The Rail are, partially at least, nocturnal. During such moonlight nights as this they are on the alert, patrolling the marshes through the countless covered ways among the reeds, stopping to cry "all's well" as they pass on, or to answer the challenge of a distant watchman. That they feed by night, as well as by day, cannot be doubted. Their habit of skulking and hiding in the almost inaccessible places they frequent renders them difficult of observation, and they are usually considered rarer than they really are. During the spring migration they seem to pass more swiftly and secretly than in the fall, when, their ranks recruited by the summer's broods, they become more noticeable. Some, like the Clapper Rail (*R. longirostris*), are almost exclusively maritime, and never quit the salt-marshes; others, as the Fresh-water Marsh Hen (*R. elegans* of Audubon), of which the present species is a perfect miniature in size, are generally distributed in the interior. The Virginia Rail extends across the continent; it is strictly a bird of passage, proceeding to and somewhat beyond our northernmost States, and returning in the fall. At the approach of cold weather it retires still further southward. Still, numbers breed in various latitudes within our limits. I have not myself met with the nest of this species. It is described as a slightly hollowed platform of matted grass and reeds, placed in a tussock of grass or directly on the ground, in the interior of secluded bogs and morasses. The eggs, of which a large number are before me, are eight or ten in number. They are exactly like those of the Elegant and Clapper Rails, only much smaller, measuring about 1.25 by 0.95. The ground-color distinguishes them from those of the Sora, which, of about the same size and shape, always show a shade of soiled greenish or olive-drab.

PORZANA CAROLINA, (Linn.) Cab.

Carolina Rail; Sora; "Ortolan."

Rallus carolinus, LINN., Syst. Nat. i, 1766, 263.—GM., Syst. Nat. i, 1788, 715.—BP., Syn. 1828, No. 272.—DOUGH., Cab. N. H. i, 1830, 206, pl. 18.—SW. & RICH., F. B. A. ii, 1831, 403.—AUD., Orn. Biog. iii, 1835, 251; v, 1839, 572; pl. 233.
Rallus (Crex) carolinus, BP., Obs. Wils. 1825, No. 230.—NUTT., Man. ii, 1834, 209.
Gallinula carolina, LATH., Ind. Orn. ii, 1790, 771 (EDW., 144; BRISS., v, 541; CATES., i, pl. 70; Arct. Zool. ii, 491; Gen. Syn. v, 262).—SAB., Frank. Journ. 690.
Ortygometra carolina, BP., List, 1838, 53.—AUD., Syn. 1839, 213; B. Am. v, 1842, 145, pl. 306.—GOSSE, B. Jam. 1847, 371.—GIR., B. L. I. 1844, 201.—LÉOT., Ois. Trinidad, 493.—WOODH., Sitgr. Rep. 1853, 101.—PUTN., Pr. Ess. Inst. i, 1856, 216.—REINH., Ibis, iii, 1861, 12 (Greenland).
Porzana carolina, BD., B. N. A. 1858, 749; and of all late U. S. writers.—GUNDL., J. f. O. iv, 1856, 428 (Cuba).—SCL., Ibis, i, 1859, 230 (Guatemala).—NEWT., *ibid.* 260 (Santa Cruz).—DRESS., *ibid.* 1866, 40 (Texas).—HAYD., Rep. 1862, 175 (Niobrara).—SCL., P. Z. S. 1861, 81 (Jamaica).—SCL. & SALV., P. Z. S. 1864, 179, 372 (Mexico); 1868, 450 (critical); 1869, 252 (Venezuela); 1870, 219 (Veragua).—BRY., Pr. Bost. Soc. 1866 (Porto Rico).—LAWR., Ann. Lyc. N. Y. vii, 479 (Panama).—SUND., Ofv. Vet. Ak. 587 (St. Bartholomew).—COUES, Key, 273.
Aramides (Muste\-lirallus) carolina, GRAY, Hand-list, iii, 1871, 61, No. 10431.
Crex carolina, HART., Br. Birds, 1872, 152 (accidental in Great Britain; *cf.* NEWT., P. Z. S. 1865, 196; EYRE, Zool. 1865, 9540; KENNEDY, B. of Berks and Bucks, 196).
Rallus stolidus, VIEILL., Ency. Meth. 1823, p. 1071.

Hab.—Entire temperate North America; especially abundant along the Atlantic coast during the migrations. Breeds from the Middle districts northward. Winters in the Southern States and beyond. South to Venezuela. Various West Indian Islands. Greenland. Accidental in Europe.
Lieutenant Warren's Expedition.—4875, Yankton Camp.
Later Expeditions.—61646, Ogden, Utah.
Not obtained by Captain Raynolds' Expedition.

The Sora does not appear to occur anywhere in the Missouri region in such numbers as it does along the Atlantic coast, probably on account of lack of the peculiar resorts best suited to its wants. I observed it migrating southward in September, along the Mouse River, in Northern Dakota, but it was not very abundant. It has not been much noticed in the West, nor by any means throughout that portion of our country. Mr. Allen found it in Utah, about Great Salt Lake, and I in Arizona. I have also taken it, in the breeding season, in Montana.

The eggs of *Porzana carolina* are spotted just like those of the fore-going *Ralli*, but are readily distinguished by their strong drab ground-color, instead of the white or creamy and pale buffy of the former. They are rather smaller than those of *R. virginianus*, and perhaps more ob-tuse, measuring about 1.20 by 0.90.

PORZANA NOVEBORACENSIS, (Gm.) Cass.

Little Yellow Rail.

Fulica noveboracensis, GM., Syst. Nat. i, 1788, 701.
Gallinula noveboracensis, LATH., Ind. Orn. ii, 1790, 771 (Arct. Zool. ii, 491; G. S. v, 262).
Ortygometra noveboracensis, STEPH., Shaw's Gen. Zool. xii, 1824.—BP., List, 1838, 53.—
    AUD., Syn. 1839, 213; B. Am. v, 1842, 152, pl. 307.—LINSL., Am. Journ. Sci. xliv,
    1843, 268 (Connecticut).—GIR., B. L. I. 1844, 204.—PUTN., Pr. Ess. Inst. i, 1856,
    229 (Massachusetts; compare PEAB., Rep. Orn. Mass. 375; EMMONS, Cat. 6).
Rallus noveboracensis, BP., Specc. Comp. 1827, 212; Syn. 1828, 335; Am. Orn. iv, 1832,
    136, pl. 27, f. 2.—NUTT., Man. ii, 1834,'215.—Sw. & RICH., F. B. A. ii, 1831, 402
    (Hudson's Bay).—AUD., Orn. Biog. iv, 1838, 251, pl. 329.
Coturnicops noveboracensis, BP., Ann. Sc. Nat. i, 1854, 46.
Porzana noveboracensis, CASS., Baird's B. N. A. 1858, 750.—WHEAT., Ohio Agric. Rep.
    1860, No. 229.—COUES & PRENT., Smiths. Rep. 1861, 416.—ALLEN, Pr. Ess. Inst.
    iv, 1864, 87 (Massachusetts, rare).—COUES, *ibid.* v, 1868, 297.—DRESS., Ibis,
    1866, 40 (Texas).—COUES, Pr. Bost. Soc. xii, 1868, 124 (South Carolina, migra-
    tory).—SCL. & SALV., P. Z. S. 1868, 457.—LAWR., Ann. Lyc. viii, 1866, 295.—
    TURNB., B. E. Pa. 1869, 33 (rare).—ALLEN, Bull. M. C. Z. ii, 1871, 357 (winter-
    ing in Florida, common).—MAYN., Guide, 1870, 146 (Massachusetts, migratory,
    rare, perhaps breeding).—ALLEN, Am. Nat. iii, 1870, 639 (Massachusetts).—
    COUES, Pr. Phila. Acad. 1871, 35 (North Carolina).—COUES, Key, 1872, 274.—
    HATCH, Bull. Minn. Acad. Sci. i, 1874, 65 (Minnesota).—RIDGW., Ann. Lyc.
    N. Y. x, 1874, 387 (Illinois).
Aramides (*Coturnicops*) *noveboracensis*, GRAY, Hand-list, iii, 1871, 61, No. 10448.
Perdix hudsonica, LATH., Ind. Orn. ii, 1790, 655.
Rallus ruficollis, VIEILL., Nouv. Dict. d'Hist. Nat. xxviii, 556; Enc. Meth. 1070; Gal.
    Ois. ii, 168, pl. 266.

Hab.—Eastern North America. North to Hudson's Bay, but in New England not observed beyond Massachusetts. Apparently nowhere abundant. Winters in the Southern States. (No extralimital record).

The Smithsonian has a set of six eggs of *P. noveboracensis*, taken May 17, at Winnebago, Illinois. They are the only ones I have seen, and differ from all those of *P. carolina* in the color of the ground, which is a rich, warm buffy-brown, marked at the great end with a cluster of reddish-chocolate dots and spots. Size 1.15 by 0.85, to 1.05 by 0.80; shape as in the foregoing.

PORZANA JAMAICENSIS, (Gm.) Cass.

Little Black Rail.

a. *jamaicensis*.

Rallus jamaicensis, GM., Syst. Nat. i, 1788, 718. –LATH., Ind. Orn. ii, 1790, 761 (BRISS.,
    Suppl. 140; EDW., pl. 278; BROWNE, Jam. 479; Gen. Syn. v, 239).—AUD., Orn.
    Biog. iv, 1838, 359, pl. 349.
Ortygometra jamaicensis, STEPH., Shaw's Gen. Zool.—BP., List, 1838, 53.—AUD., Syn.
    1839, 214; B. Am. v, 1842, 157, pl. 308.—GOSSE, B. Jam. 1847, 375.—BP., Comptes
    Rendus, xliii, 599.—SALV., Ibis, 1866, 198 (Dueñas, Guat.).
Creciscus jamaicensis, CAB., J. f. O. iv, 1856, 428 (Cuba).—GUNDL., Rep. Fis. i, 362 (Cuba)
Porzana jamaicensis, CASS., Baird's B. N. A. 1858, 749.—COUES & PRENT., Smiths. Rep.
    1861, 416 (Washington, D. C., accidental).—SCL., P. Z. S. 1861, 81 (Jamaica);
    1867, 333, 343 (Lima, Peru).—SCL. & SALV., P. Z. S. 1868, 455 (critical).—SCHL.,
    M. P.-B. *Ralli*, p. 67.—COUES Pr. Bost. Soc. xii, 1868, 124 South Carolina).—

TURNB., B. E. Pa. 1869, 33 (breeding in marshes of Cape May County, N. J.).—
COUES, Key, 1872, 274.—SNOW, B. Kans. 1873, 11 (Kansas, one specimen,
Allen).—RIDGW., Ann. Lyc. N. Y. x, 1874, 387 (Illinois, summer).
Aramides (Creciscus) jamaicensis, GRAY, Hand-list, iii, 1871, 61, No. 10444.
'*Crex pygmæa*, BLACKWELL, Brewster's Journ. vi, 1832, 77.
'*Ortygometra chilensis*, BP., Comptes Rendus, xliii, 599.
[*Rallus salinasi*, PHIL., Wiegen. Archiv, 1867, 262.
'" *Gallinula salinasi*, PHIL., Cat. 1869, 38."

b. *coturniculus.*

,*Porzana jamaicensis* var. *coturniculus*, BD., MSS.—RIDGW., Am. Nat. viii, 1874, 111.—
COUES, Check-list, 1874, App. p. 137, No. 470ª.

Hab.—South America to Chili. Central America. West Indies. In North America
to New Jersey and Kansas, rare. Var. *coturniculus*, Farallone Islands (*Gruber*, Mus.
Smiths. Inst.; types of the variety).

The introduction into the present connection of the Black Rail, which
appears to be very rare everywhere in North America, rests upon the
authority of Mr. Allen, who found a specimen in Kansas. Several of
the rare eggs of the Little Black Rail are in the Smithsonian from New
Jersey. They are altogether different, again, from those of the Sora, or
the Red-breasted, being creamy-white, sprinkled all over with fine dots
of rich, bright reddish-brown, and with a few spots of some little size
at the great end. They are most like the more finely speckled examples of the eggs of the large *Ralli.* Dimensions, 1.05 by 0.80.

Subfamily FULICINÆ: *Gallinules and Coots.*

The birds of this group will be immediately recognized by the presence of a broad,
horny plate (an expansion of the bill), which covers the forehead. In the structure of
the feet the Gallinules are much like ordinary Rails, having little or no marginal fringe
on the toes; but the Coots are conspicuously lobe-footed, the toes being furnished with
a series of broad, semi-circular flaps.

GALLINULA GALEATA, (Licht.) Bp.

Florida Gallinule.

Crex galeata, LICHT., Verz. Doubl. 1823, 80, No. 826.
Gallinula galeata, BP., Am. Orn. iv, 1832, 128; List, 1838, 53.—NUTT., Man. ii, 1834,
221.—MAXIM., Beitr. iv, 1833, 807.— SCHOMB., Guiana, iii, 760.—TSCH., Fn. Peru,
302.—BURM., Syst. Ueb. iii, 389; La Plata Reise, ii, 505.—GAY, Fn. Chilen.
437.—GOSSE, B. Jam. 1847, 381.—GUNDL., J. f. O. iv, 1856, 428; Rep. Fis. 362
(Cuba).—SALLÉ, P. Z. S. 1857, 237 (St. Domingo).—NEWB., P. R. R. Rep. vi,
1857, 96 (San Francisco).—BD., B. N. A. 1858, 752.—HEERM., P. R. R. Rep. x,
1859, pt. vi, 61 (California).—NEWT., Ibis, i, 1859, 260 (Santa Cruz, breeding).—
BRY., Pr. Bost. Soc. vii, 1859 (Bahamas).—WHEAT., Ohio Agric. Rep. 1860, No.
231 (occasional; north to Lake Erie).—TAYLOR, Ibis, 1860, 314 (Honduras).—
SCL., P. Z. S. 1861, 81 (Jamaica); 1867, 339 (Chili).—SCL. & SALV., P. Z. S.
1868, 176 (Islay, Peru); *ibid.* 462 (critical).—SALV., Ibis, 1866, 198 (Guatemala).—MCILWR., Pr. Ess. Inst. v, 1866, 93 (Canada West, common).—LAWR.,
Ann. Lyc. N. Y. viii, 185 (Nicaragua); *ibid.* 295 (New York).— BRY., Pr. Bost.
Soc. xi, 1866, 97 (Porto Rico).—ALLEN, Pr. Ess. Inst. iv, 1864, 87 (Massachusetts).—EULER, J. f. O. 1867, 419 (Brazil, egg).—COUES, Pr. Ess. Inst. v, 1868,
297 (Massachusetts).—COUES, Pr. Bost. Soc. xii, 1868, 124 (South Carolina,
resident).—TURNB., B. E. Pa. 1869, 34 (New Jersey, rare, May to Oct.).—ALLEN,
Am. Nat. iii, 1870, 639 (Massachusetts, breeding).—MAYN., Guide, 1870, 146
(Massachusetts, accidental, probably breeds).—SALV., Ibis, 1870, 115 (Costa
Rica).— REINH., Ved. Med. Nat. For. 1870, 40 (Brazil).—LÉOT., Ois. Trinidad,
503.—PHIL., Cat. 39 (Chili).—PELZ., Orn. Bras. 318 (Brazil).—ALLEN, Bull.
M. C. Z. ii, 1871, 357 (Florida, wintering).—COUES, Key, 1872, 275.—SNOW, B.
Kans. 1873, 11 (Kansas, *Baird*).—HATCH, Bull. Minnesota Acad. i, 1874, 63
(Minnesota).
Gallinula chloropus, BP., Syn. 1828, 336.—AUD., Orn. Biog. iii, 1835, 330, pl. 224; Syn.
1839, 210; B. Am. v, 1842, 132, pl. 304.—GIR., B. L. I. 1844, 197.
Gallinula chloropus, var. *galeata*, HARTL. & FINSCH.—RIDGW., Ann. Lyc. N. Y. x, 1874,
387 (Illinois).

Hab.—United States, southerly. Resident in the Southern States. Northward to Massachusetts rarely, to Canada West, Kansas, Minnesota, and San Francisco. West Indies. Central America. South America to Chili.

Not obtained by the Expeditions.

I have not taken occasion to institute direct comparison of specimens, but believe that our bird will be found to be merely a variety of the European *G. chloropus*, as held by Drs. Hartlaub and Finsch, and as indicated in my work above cited.

Included in the present connection on the strength of its occurrence in Kansas, as by the foregoing authority. Its dispersion in tropical America is general and very extensive. In the United States it appears to extend regularly only to the Middle districts, though apparently breeding occasionally in Massachusetts, and recorded as "common" about Hamilton, Canada West, as well as occurring in Minnesota. It winters in the South Atlantic and Gulf States.

FULICA AMERICANA, Gm.

American Coot; Mud Hen.

Fulica americana, GM., Syst. Nat. i, 1788, 704.—LATH., Ind. Orn. ii, 1790, 779 (*Cinereous Coot* of Gen. Syn. v, 279).—BP., Obs. Wils. 1825, No. 234 ; Syn. 1828, 338 ; List, 1838, 53.—Sw. & RICH., F. B. A. ii, 1831, 404.—SAB., Frank. Journ. 690.—NUTT., Man. ii, 1834, 229.—AUD., Orn. Biog. iii, 1835, 291 ; v, 1839, 568 ; pl. 239 ; Syn. 1839, 212 ; B. Am. v, 1842, 138, pl. 305.—BD., B. N. A. 1858, 751.—COUES, Key, 1872, 275 ; and of all late American writers.—HARTL., J. f. O. i, 1854, extra-h. 87 ; 1855, 99.—GUNDL., J. f. O. iv, 1856, 430 (Cuba).—BRY., Pr. Bost. Soc. vii, 1859 (Bahamas).—GOSSE, B. Jam. 1847, 304 (Jamaica).—LÉOT., Ois. Trinidad, 504 (casually).—GUNDL., Rep. Fis. i, 363 (Cuba).—SCL., Ibis, i, 1859, 230 (Guatemala).—NEWT., *ibid.* 260 (Santa Cruz).—SCL., P. Z. S. 1857, 206 ; 1859, 369.— MOORE, P. Z. S. 1859, 64.—SCL., P. Z. S. 1861, 81 (Jamaica); 1866, 179 (Mexico).— REINH., Ibis, iii, 1861, 12 (Greenland).—LAWR., Ann. Lyc. N. Y. viii, 1864, 101 (Sombrero).—SCL. & SALV., P. Z. S. 1868, 468, f. 10.—SUND., Ofv. Vet. Ak. 1869, 587 (St. Bartholomew).—SALV., P. Z. S. 1870, 219 (Veragua).—DALL & BANN., Tr. Chic. Acad. i, 1869, 293 (Alaska).—RIDGW., Ann. Lyc. N. Y. x, 1874, 387 (Illinois).

Fulica wilsoni, STEPH., Shaw's Gen. Zool. xii, 1824, 236.

Fulica atra, WILS., Am. Orn. ix, 1825, 61, pl. 73, f. 1.

Hab.—Entire temperate North America. Alaska (*Dall*). Greenland (*Reinhardt*). Mexico. West Indies. Central America. In South America replaced by an allied form.

List of specimens.

| 19377 | .... | M'th G. Bull C'k. | ♀ | June 5, 1860 | G. H. Trook.. | ...... | ...... | ...... |

Lieutenant Warren's Expedition.—8906, Upper Missouri ; 8907, Loup Fork of Platte.
Later Expeditions.—59874-6, Colorado ; 60773, North Platte.

Not only is the Coot extensively and very generally dispersed over North America, but, unlike most water-birds, its breeding range is almost equally wide. It has been observed to nest in various parts of British America, in New England, in the Missouri region, along the Pacific coast, and in the Gulf States. There is, nevertheless, a regular migration in the spring and fall, when, in company with other water-fowl, most of the Coots pass through on their way to or from the rather northerly regions where they especially breed, only a few lingering in suitable places along the route to nest. It appears that the whole body of the birds leave the British Provinces and even the northern tier of States in the fall to winter in the Southern States and beyond ; some penetrating into Mexico, the West Indies, and Central America.

During the migrations, and especially that of the fall, the species is frequently exposed for sale in our markets, and I have observed the bird in every portion of our country where I have been, at one season or another. I found it breeding along the Red River of the North, about Pembina, in the reedy pools bordering the river, and in the prairie sloughs, there as well as elsewhere in Nortern Montana and Dakota. Eggs procured at Pembina, June 19th, contained young nearly ready to hatch; and during the following month I frequently saw newly hatched young swimming about with their parents. They are very pretty and curious little creatures, covered with sooty-blackish down, fantastically striped with rich orange-red, and with vermilion bill, tipped with black. The nidification of the Coot is not the least interesting portion of its history. The mode of nesting is most like that of the Grebes. The nest is said to be sometimes a floating one, moored to the stems of reeds, rising and falling with the tide. One author, in illustration of the insecurity of the bird's home, has related that once during a storm a nest became detached from its moorings by a rise of the water, and drifted about, the parent nevertheless remaining at her post of duty, and safely hatching out her brood during the cruise. This may or may not have been a strict statement of fact. Among many Coots' nests I have found, one was built in a clump of reeds where the water was about knee-deep; it was a bulky affair, resting securely on a mass of reedy *debris*. The nest itself was built of the same materials, heaped up and little hollowed; it was about fifteen inches in diameter, and half as high. The reed-stems appeared to have been bitten by the bird into short pieces; there was no special lining. This nest was a floating one, in the sense that the platform of broken-down reeds upon which it was built rested on the water; but it was perfectly secure, raised out of the wet, and though loosely constructed, could be lifted up intact. It contained eleven eggs nearly ready to hatch. They measured from 1.75 to 2.00 in length, by 1.20 to 1.35 in breadth, exhibiting the usual variation in contour as well as in absolute size. The shape is much like that of an average hen's egg—perhaps rather more pointed. The ground is clear clay-color, uniformly and minutely dotted all over with innumerable specks of dark brown; a few of the bolder markings are of the size of a pin's head, but the greater number are mere points. But the eggs are not always so uniformly and finely dotted as those of this set were; sometimes the spots being aggregated into blotches of some size, or tending chiefly to wreath around the larger end. Various other nests examined contained an average of ten eggs; some were built just like the one described, while others were on the ground, in comparatively dry spots around the margin of the pools, hidden in rank grass; in all the materials and mode of construction were much the same.

In the southwest, where the Coots are apparently resident, I frequently observed them, and they are probably more abundant than one might suppose; for, like their allies the Rails, they are naturally much withdrawn from general observation by their habits, and by the intricate character of their resorts. While steaming along the Colorado River, in September, Coots frequently appeared for a moment in places where the banks were fringed with reeds, to croak a note or two at sight of the boat, and then paddle out of sight again. The most satisfactory observations I ever made upon them was at a point on the Mojave River, in California, where the stream became a broken chain of reedy lagoons, alternating with half-submerged tracts of oozy marsh, grown up to short crisp grass. There were great numbers of Ducks here, in October, along with Hutchins' and Snow Geese, Herons, and a variety of small waders. While wading about waist-deep, in default of any more elegant or less fatiguing method of duck-shooting, I continually heard the gabbling of the Coots among the rushes, where they were disporting in flocks of a dozen or more, and noisy enough to be quite troublesome, since I was in urgent need of more desirable game for the table. But with all their clamor and apparent heedlessness, they were shy birds, and it was only by stratagem that, after securing all the wild-fowl I desired, I got an opportunity of watching them at my leisure. Standing motionless just within the edge of a clump of reeds bordering an open space, and perfectly concealed, I could see the birds, after what appeared to be a council as to the expediency of their proposed move, come out of the rushes on the other side, swimming silently at first and glancing stealthily around to make sure the coast was clear before commencing their gambols. They swam with ease and gracefully; the head now drawn back and held upright over their plump bodies, that floated lightly and changed their course at a movement of their broad paddles, now stretched out to full length as the birds hurried about, throwing off the ripples from their half-submerged breasts, crossing and recrossing each others path, in wanton sport, or attracted by some delicacy floating at a little distance. They were as gay and careless a crew as one could wish to see—yet not altogether given up to sport, for on the slightest movement on my part, their suspicions were aroused, and off they scurried into the impenetrable masses of vegetation that effectually hid them from view and precluded pursuit. I have several times since met with the birds under somewhat similar circumstances, in ponds near the sea-coast of Southern California, and in Dakota, always finding them much the same when not breeding. Though as shy as Ducks, they have not the wariness and wildness of those birds, to teach them to fly from danger; but perhaps the nature of the resorts to which they trust for concealment serves as well for their protection. I do not recollect when, if ever, I have seen Coots fly up into the air and away. If they are surprised too far from their retreats to gain them in an instant, they splatter along just over the water, half-flying—a habit which has gained for them in some districts the name of "Shufflers" or "Fluster-ers." They are generally, however, called Mud Hens—a name shared by some Grebes—as well as *Poules-d'eau*, White-bills, and other local designations. As an article of food they may take fair rank, though they are to be considered, on the whole as inferior to most Ducks.

ORDER LAMELLIROSTRES: ANSERINE BIRDS

Family ANATIDÆ: Swan, Geese, and Ducks.

Subfamily CYGNINÆ: *Swan.*

CYGNUS BUCCINATOR, Rich.

Trumpeter Swan.

Cygnus buccinator, RICH., F. B. A. ii, 1831, 464 (Hudson's Bay).—YARRELL, Trans. Linn.
Soc. xvii, 1834 (anatomy of trachea, &c.).—WYMAN, Pr. Bost. Soc. (sternum).—
NUTT., Man. ii, 1834, 370.—BP., List, 1838, 55.—AUD., Orn. Biog. iv, 1838, 536;
v, 1839, 114; pls. 376, 406; Syn. 1839, 274; B. Am. vi, 1843, 219, pls. 382, 383.—
EYT., Monog. Anat. 1838, 100.—NEWB., P. R. R. Rep. vi, 1857 (California and
Oregon).—BD., B. N. A. 1858, 758.—MAXIM., J. f. O. vii, 1859, 162.—COOP. &
SUCK., N. H. Wash. Ter. 1860, 248.—WHEAT., Ohio Agric. Rep. 1860, No. 234
(to Lake Erie).—HAYD., Rep. 1862, 175 (breeding about the Yellowstone).—
DALL & BANN., Tr. Chic. Acad. i, 1869, 294 (breeding on Frazer River and the
Yukon).—TURNB., B. E. Pa. 1869, 45 (Chesapeake Bay, casual).—TRIPPE,
Pr. Ess. Inst. vi, 1871, 119 (Minnesota, not common).—MERR., U. S. Geol. Surv.
Ter. 1872, 703 (Wyoming).—COUES, Key, 1872, 281.—SNOW, B. Kans. 1873, 11
(migratory; breeds in Iowa).—RIDGW., Ann. Lyc. N. Y. x, 1874, 388 (Illinois).
Olor buccinator, WAGL., Isis, 1832, 1234.—BP., Comp. Rend. xliii, 1856, p. —.
Cygnus passmorei, HINCKS, Pr. Linn. viii, 1864, 1 (Toronto); P. Z. S. 1868, 211 (see
MOORE, P. Z. S. 1867, 8).

Hab.—Chiefly from the Mississippi Valley, and northward, to the Pacific. Hudson's
Bay. Canada. Casually on the Atlantic coast. Breeds from Iowa and Dakota north-
ward. In winter, south to the Gulf. Said to have occurred in England; see HARTING,
Br. Birds, 155.
Lieutenant Warren's Expedition.—5476, Yellowstone River.
Later Expeditions.—62367-8, Snake River, Wyoming.
Not obtained by Captain Raynolds' Expedition.

The vocal apparatus of this species is peculiar, causing its remarkably raucous voice.
Richardson simply states that "a fold of the windpipe enters a protuberance on the
dorsal or interior aspect of the sternum at its upper part, which is wanting in both
Cygnus ferus and *bewickii.*" Mr. Yarrell, as above, has made the organ the subject of a
more extended article. In *C. americanus,* according to Audubon, the trachea " reaches
the curve of the furcula, bends a little upward, and enters a cavity formed on the sternum, along which it passes to the length of six inches, bends upon itself horizontally,
returns, passes up between the crura of the furcula, bends backward and enters the
thorax." The external distinctions are the (usually) twenty-four-feathered tail of
buccinator, and wholly black bill rather larger than the head, with the nostrils fairly in
its basal half; in *C. americanus* the tail having usually only twenty feathers, and there
being a yellow spot on the bill, which is shorter than the head, with the nostrils at its
middle. The superior size of *C. buccinator* is another mark, though one not always
reliable. Audubon mentions one nearly ten feet in alar expanse, and weighing above
thirty-eight pounds.

I have observed the Trumpeter Swan on but few occasions, in Dakota
only, late in September and during the first half of October, when the
birds were migrating southward with great numbers of Canada and Snow
Geese and various Wild Ducks. Their loud and strange—almost startling—notes were oftenest heard during the night, as the birds passed
overhead; bnt I also saw some Swans flying in the day time near Fort
Stevenson, on the Upper Missouri. According to Dr. Hayden, the
birds breed in the Yellowstone region, as they also do, according to
other writers, in Minnesota and Iowa. We have other accounts of their
breeding in Alaska; and Dr. Richardson, who gives it as the common-

est species in the interior of the fur countries, states that it nests " principally within the Arctic Circle." In the fall, the birds proceed along the whole course of the Mississippi; Audubon states that they make their appearance on the lower waters of the Ohio about the end of October, and that they are frequently exposed for sale in the New Orleans market, being procured on the ponds of the interior, and on the great lakes leading to the Gulf of Mexico. The record of the bird east of the Mississippi is not so satisfactory. Mr. Wheaton mentions its occasional presence on Lake Erie; in Mr. Turnbull's List the species " is included on the authority of reliable sportsmen who have shot it on the Chesapeake, as also on Delaware Bay." The so-called *C. passmorei* furnishes a Canadian instance.

On the West Coast, according to Dr. Newberry, " the Trumpeter Swan visits California with its congeners, the Ducks and Geese, in their annual migrations, but, compared with the myriads of other water birds which congregate at that season in the bays and rivers of the West, it is always rare. Before we left the Columbia, early in November, the Swans had begun to arrive from the north, and frequently, while at Fort Vancouver, their trumpeting drew our attention to the long converging lines of these magnificent birds, so large and so snowy white, as they came from their northern nesting places, and, screaming their delight at the appearance of the broad expanse of water, perhaps their winter home, descended into the Columbia."

CYGNUS AMERICANUS, Sharp.

American or Whistling Swan.

Cygnus musicus, BP., Syn. 1828, 379, *nec auct.*—LINSL., Am. Journ. xliv, 1843, 268.
Cygnus bewickii, SW. & RICH., F. B. A. ii, 1831, 465, *nec auct.*—NUTT., Man. ii, 1834, 372.
Cygnus ferus, NUTT., Man. ii, 1834, 366, *nec auct.*
Cygnus americanus, SHARP., Doughty's Cab. N. H. i, 1830, 185, pl. 16; Am. Journ. Sci.
xxii, 1831, 83.—MACGIL., Man. Orn. ii, 157 (Scotland).—AUD., Orn. Biog. v, 1839,
133, pl. 411; Syn. 1839, 274; B. Am. vi, 1843, 226, pl. 384.—GIR., B. L. I. 1844,
298.—NEWB., P. R. R. Rep. vi, 1857, 100.—COOP. & SUCK., N. H. Wash. Ter.
1860, 248.—BD., B. N. A. 1858, 758.—WHEAT., Ohio Agric. Rep. 1860, No. 223.—
COUES & PRENT., Smiths. Rep. 1861, 417 (Washington, D. C.).—COUES, Pr.
Phila. Acad. 1866, 98 (Colorado River).—COUES, Pr. Ess. Inst. v, 1868, 297 (New
England, rare or irregular).—COUES, Pr. Bost. Soc. xii, 1868, 124 (South Carolina, in winter).—McILWR., Pr. Ess. Inst. v, 1866, 94 (Canada West, migratory).—LAWR., Ann. Lyc. N. Y. viii, 1866, 295.—TURNB., B. E. Pa. 1869, 34
(frequent on Chesapeake Bay, during the migrations and in winter).—DALL &
BANN., Tr. Chic. Acad. i, 1869, 293 (common, and breeding all along the Yukon).—MAYN., Guide, 1870, 146 (Massachusetts, very rare, in winter).—COUES,
Key, 1872, 281, fig. 182.—SNOW, B. Kans. 1873, 11 (rare).—RIDGW., Ann. Lyc.
N. Y. x, 1874, 388 (Illinois).
Olor americanus, BP., Comptes Rendus, xliii, 1856, p. —.

Hab.—Continent of North America; breeding only in the far North; wintering in the United States. Accidental in Scotland (MACGIL., Hist. Br. B. 682; Man. Br. B. 157; HART., Br. B. 154).
Not noticed by either of the Expeditions.

Excepting Sir John Richardson's short note of the breeding of this species within the Arctic Circle, nothing appears to have been definitely ascertained in the matter until Mr. Dall made his observations in Alaska. The Swan, he observes, is " common all along the Yukon. Arrives with the Geese about May 1, but in a contrary direction, coming down instead of up the Yukon. Breeds in the great marshes near the Yukon mouth. The eggs, two in number, vary from pure white to fulvous, as do the parents on the head and neck, apparently without regard to age. The eggs are usually in a tussock quite surrounded with water, so that the female must sometimes set with her feet in the water. They are usually laid about May 21 at Nulato, but later at the Yukon mouth. In July the Swans moult and cannot fly, and the Indians have great sport spearing them with bone tridents. They are very shy birds, and usually shot on the wing or with a bullet. This species, if hung long enough, is tender, well-flavored, and excellent eating."

This Swan is only seen in the United States during the migrations, and in winter. It does not proceed much beyond the Middle districts, being apparently unknown in the Gulf States, although reaching our southern border on the Pacific side. One of its favorite resorts is Chesa-peake Bay, where it is comparatively abundant from November, as attested by its constant exhibition at restaurants of Philadelphia, Baltimore and Washington. It appears to come inland from the North, for it is very rare or merely casual in New England, where it has not been traced, so far as I am aware, beyond Massachusetts. In the Mississippi Valley it is apparently rare, at least in comparison with the Trumpeter, but it is much more plentiful along the Pacific coast, where it winters.

The eggs of the Swan vary in size from about $4\frac{1}{2}$ inches in length by $2\frac{3}{4}$ in breadth, down to 4 by $2\frac{1}{2}$, and are nearly ellipsoidal in shape. The shell is more or less roughened, and is dull, dirty white, with a wholly indeterminate amount of brownish discoloration. The eggs of the Trumpeter may average a little larger, but cannot be distinguished. The largest number I have known of in a nest is five. Numerous specimens are examined from various points in British and Russian America.

The yellow spot on the bill is not constant; in young birds, especially, often no trace can be observed. In such cases the species would be distinguishable from *C. buccinator* by the smaller size, fewer tail-feathers, and shorter, differently shaped bill. The proper name of this species is, most probably, *Cygnus columbianus*, after *Anas columbianus* of Ord (Guthrie's Geog. 2d Am. ed. 1815, 319), based on the Whistling Swan of Lewis & Clarke (ii, 192), who correctly distinguish the two species.

Subfamily ANSERINÆ : *Geese.*

ANSER ALBIFRONS var. GAMBELI, (Hart.) Coues.

White-fronted Goose; Speckle-belly.

a. *albifrons.*

Anas albifrons, GM., Syst. Nat. 1, 1788, 509.—TEMM., Man. 1815, 529.
Anser albifrons, BECHST., Naturg. iv, 898.—LEACH, Cat. 1816, 36.—BOIE, Isis, 1822, 563.—
    STEPH., Gen. Zool. xii, 25.—BREHM, V. D. 843.—BP., List, 1838, 55.—JENYNS,
    Man. 222.—KEYS. & BLAS., Wirb. Eur. 1840, 83.—NAUM., V. D. xi, 1842, 352,
    pl. 289.—MACGIL., Man. ii, 1842, 149.—SCHL., Rev. Crit. Ois. Eur. 1844, 110.—
    NEWT., P. Z. S. 1861, 99 (critical).
Anser erythropus, FLEM., Br. An. 127.—GRAY, Gen. of B. iii, 1849, 607.—SCHL., M. P.-B.
    ix, *Anseres* 110. (According to NEWTON, this is not *erythropus* of *Linnœus,*
    which is *temminckii, Boie,* and *minutus, Naumann.*)
" Anas casarca, GM."
(?) *" Anser intermedius,* NAUM."
(?) *" Anser medius,* TEMM."
(?) *" Anser pallidipes,* SELYS."

b. *gambeli.*

Anser albifrons, BP., Syn. 1828, 376.—SW. & RICH., F. B. A. ii, 1831, 466 (Mackenzie
    River region north of 67°, and Arctic coast, breeding; Hudson's Bay).—NUTT.,
    Man. ii, 1834, 346.—AUD., Orn. Biog., iii, 1835, 568, pl. 286; Syn. 1839, 272; B. Am.
    vi, 1843, 209, pl. 380.—GIR., B. L. I. 1844, 296.—HENRY, Pr. Phila. Acad. 1855,

316.—MAXIM., J. f. O. vii, 1859, 166.—HEERM., P. R. R. Rep. x, 1859, pt. vi, 68 (California).—HOY, Smiths. Rep. 1864, 438 (Missouri).—TRIPPE, Pr. Ess. Inst. vi, 1871, 119 (Minnesota, common).
Anser gambeli, HART., R. M. Z. 1852, 7.—CAB., J. f. O. v, 1857, 226 (Cuba).—BD., B. N. A. 1858, 761.—COOP. & SUCK., N. H. Wash. Ter. 1860, 249.—WHEAT., Ohio Agric. Rep. 1860, No. 236.—ALLEN, Pr. Ess. Inst. iv, 1864, 87 (Massachusetts).—COUES, *ibid*. v, 1868, 298 (New England, very rare or accidental).—COUES, Pr. Phila. Acad. 1866, 98 (Arizona).—COUES, Pr. Bost. Soc. xii, 1868, 124 (South Carolina).—DRESS., Ibis, 1866, 42 (Texas).—COUES, Ibis, 1866, 269.—BROWN, Ibis, 1868, 425.—DALL & BANN., Tr. Chic. Acad. i, 1869, 294 (Yukon, breeding).—TURNB., B. E. Pa. 1869, 35 (rare).—BANN., Pr. Phila. Acad. 1870, 131 (critical).—SNOW, B. Kans. 1873, 11 (two instances).
Anser albifrons var. *gambeli*, COUES, Key, 1872, 282.—RIDGW., Ann. Lyc. N. Y. x, 1874, 388 (Illinois).
Anser erythropus, BD., Stansbury's Rep. 1852, 321.—WOODH., Sitgr. Rep. 1853, 102.—NEWB., P. R. R. Rep. vi, 1857, 101.
Anser frontalis, BD., B. N. A. 1858, 562 (New Mexico).—HENRY, Pr. Phila. Acad. 1859, 109.—MCILWR., Pr. Ess. Inst. v, 1866, 94 (Canada.) (*Young*.)

Hab.—Continent of North America; breeding in the far North; wintering in the United States. Cuba.

Not noticed by the Expeditions.

As Audubon suggests, this bird may, in highest breeding-plumage, be entirely black below. The amount of black blotching in United States (winter) specimens is extremely variable; sometimes there are only a few scattered and isolated black feathers, and sometimes the uniformity of the black is only here and there interrupted by a few gray or whitish feathers. While the species is distinguishable on sight from all other North American ones, it is so closely allied to the European *A. albifrons* as to be only with difficulty separated in a satisfactory manner. It apparently only differs in the larger bill; that of *albifrons* is said to measure 1½ inches along the culmen, and that of *gambeli* 2 inches; but I suspect that so great a difference does not always obtain. Audubon's measurement of our bird's bill is 1⅞; Baird's are 1.86 and 2.00. Dr. H. Schlegel gives for the adult European bird 19 to 22 lines (twelfths of an inch), and for the young 17 to 18. These observations indicate that the ordinary variation in either case is as great as the difference supposed to distinguish the two species, and that, moreover, the bills of some American specimens are no longer than those of some European ones. A slight *average* discrepancy, therefore, is probably all that can fairly be said to exist.

Many thousands of the White-fronted Geese inhabit California during the winter, at which season they are distributed over the United States at large, though not in such prodigious numbers in the East and interior as along the Pacific coast and slope. It leaves its northern breeding-grounds generally in September, and accomplishes its migration during the following month. From the numbers that pass the winter with us it is to be inferred that its southward extension is generally not much, if any, beyond our limits. Some remain in California in April, but the great body depart the month before. None, to our knowledge, breed in the United States; a statement that also holds good with reference to all our other species, except the Canadian.

The " Speckle-bellies," as they are called in California, associate freely at all times with both the Snow and Hutchins' Geese, and appear to have the same general habits, as well as to subsist upon the same kinds of food. Their flesh is equally good for the table. As is the case with the other species, they are often hunted, in regions where they have become too wild to be otherwise successfully approached, by means of bullocks trained for the purpose. Though they may have learned to distrust the approach of a horse, and to make off with commendable discretion from what they have found to be a dangerous companion of that animal, they have not yet come to the same view with respect to horned cattle, and great numbers are slaughtered annually by taking advantage of their ignorance. The bullock is taught to feed quietly along toward a flock, the gunner meanwhile keeping himself screened from the birds' view by the body of the animal until within range. Though I have not myself witnessed this method of hunting, I should judge the gunners killed a great many Geese, since they talk of its "raining geese" after a double discharge of the tremendous guns they are in the habit of using. Man's ingenuity overreaches any bird's sagacity, no doubt, yet the very fact that the Geese, which would fly from a horse, do not yet fear an ox, argues for them powers of discrimination that command our admiration.

The White-fronted Goose is said to leave the United States at the same time as the Snow, and a little before the Canadian, and to migrate apart from other kinds. According to Richardson, it breeds in woody districts north of the 67th parallel, and thence to the Arctic Ocean. Mr. Dall says it is extremely common on the Yukon, arriving at Nulato about May 6 to 10, and breeding all along the river, from Fort Yukon to the sea, gregariously, laying from six to ten eggs in a depression in the sand, without any kind of nest or lining. A set of eggs in the Smithsonian, selected for description, contains seven; the accompanying label states that the nest was lined with down and feathers. There are considerable differences in the seven in respect of size and shape; the greatest variation was between two that measured respectively 3.30 by 2.10 and 2.90 by 2.10. This constancy of the minor axis, with the variation of the major, results in a great discrepancy in shape. In general the eggs are nearly elliptical, one end being scarcely larger than the other. The shell is perfectly smooth, and dull yellowish in color, with a shade of greenish, obscurely marked in places with a darker tint, as if soiled, or with an oily discoloration. Out of a large number examined, I found none so small as to correspond with Audubon's measurements, viz: 2¾ by 1¾; he may have had an egg of another species before him, but the color is as he says.

As attested by observers along the Pacific coast, the numbers of White-fronted Geese wintering there are out of all proportion to those which visit other parts of the United States. They are particularly rare on the Atlantic coast, where they have not to my knowledge been traced beyond Massachusetts. In the interior, according to Audubon, they are often and regularly seen, even reaching New Orleans. He states that in Kentucky they generally arrive and depart before the Canada Goose, along with the Snow Goose, but in separate flocks. I have myself never recognized them in the Mississippi or Missouri regions, nor seen them anywhere further eastward.

ANSER HYPERBOREUS, Pall.

Snow Goose; White Brant.

a. *hyperboreus.*

Anser hyperboreus, PALL., Spic. Zool. viii, 1767, 80, 25, pl. 65; Zoog. R.-A. ii, 1811, 227.—
    VIEILL., Enc. Meth. 1823, 112.—STEPH., Gen. Zool. xii, pt. ii, 1824, 33.—BP.,
    Syn. 1828, 376.—Sw. & RICH., F. B. A. ii, 1831, 467.—NUTT., Man. ii, 1834, 344.—
    Sw., Classif. B. ii, 1837, 365.—AUD., Orn. Biog. iv, 1838, 562, pl. 381; Syn. 1839,
    273; B. Am. vi, 1843, 212, pl. 381.—EYT., Mon. Anat. 1839, 92.—TEMM., Man.
    iv, 1840, 516.—NAUM., V. D. xi, 1842, 213, pl. 284.—GIR., B. L. I. 1844, 297.—
    DEKAY, N. Y. Zool. 1844, ii, 350.—SCHL., Rev. Crit. 1844, 109; M. P.-B. viii, 1865,
    107.—GRAY, Gen. of B. iii, 1849, 401.—LEMB., Av. Cub. 1850, 111.—WOODH., Sitgr.
    Rep. 1853, 101.— PUTN., Pr. Ess. Inst. i, 1856, 219 (Massachusetts, rare).—CASS.,
    Pr. Phila. Acad. 1856, 11; 1861, 72.—CAB., J. f. O. v, 1857, 225 (Cuba).—NEWB.,
    P. R. R. Rep. vi, 1857, 101 (California).—HEERM., *ibid*. x, 1859, 68.—BD., B. N. A.
    1858, 760.—WHEAT., Ohio Agric. Rep. 1860, No. 235.—COOP. & SUCK., N. H.
    Wash. Ter. 1860, 249.—REINH., Ibis, iii, 1861, 12 (Greenland).—BLAK., Ibis,
    1863, 139.—BOARDM., Pr. Bost. Soc. ix, 1862, 129 (Maine, rare).—ROSS, Canad.
    Nat. vii, Apr. 1862, p. —.—BREE, B. Eur. iv, 1863, 126, pl. —.—VERR., Pr. Ess.

Inst. iii, 1862, 159 (Maine, winter, rare).—ALLEN, *ibid.* iv, 1864, 87.—MCILWR.,
ibid. v, 1866, 94 (Canada West, frequent).—COUES, *ibid.* v, 1868, 297.—TRIPPE,
ibid. vi, 1871, 119 (Minnesota, common).—SWINH., P. Z. S. 1863, 323 (China).—
DRESS., Ibis, 1866, 41 (Texas).—LAWR., Ann. Lyc. N. Y. viii, 1866, 295.—COUES,
Pr. Phila. Acad. 1866, 98 (Arizona, common).—COUES, Pr. Bost. Soc. xii, 1868, 123
(South Carolina).—BROWN, Ibis, 1868, 425.—TURNB., B. E. Pa. 1869, 34 (rather
rare).—DALL & BANN., Tr. Chic. Acad. i, 1869, 294 (Alaska, breeding).—BANN.,
Pr. Phil. Acad. 1870, 131.—MAYN., Guide, 1870, 147.—ALLEN, Bull. M. C. Z. iii,
1872, 183 (Utah).—TRIPPE, Pr. Bost. Soc. xv, 1872, 241 (Iowa, migratory, com-
mon).—COUES, Key, 1872, 282.—SNOW, B. Kans. 1873, 11.—RIDGW., Am. Nat.
viii, Feb. 1874 (semi-domestic).—RIDGW., Ann. Lyc. N. Y. x, 1874, 388 (Illinois).
Anas hyperboreus, GM., Syst. Nat. i, 1788, 504.—LATH., Ind. Orn. ii, 1790, 837.—WILS.,
Am. Orn. viii, 1814, 76, pl. 68, f. 3.—RICH., App. Parry's 2nd Voy. 365.—TEMM.,
Man. 1835, 816.
Chen hyperboreus, BOIE, Isis, 1822, 563; 1826, 981.—BP., List, 1838, 55; Compt. Rend.
Sept. 1856.—GOSSE, B. Jam. 1847, 408.—BLAS., List, 1862, 20 (Europe).—GUNDL.,
Cat. Aves Cuban. 1866, 387.—DEGL.-GERBE, Orn. Eur. ii, 1867, 493.
Chionochen hyperborea, REICH., Syst. Av. 1852, 9.
Anas nivalis, FORST., Phil. Trans. lxii, 1772, 413.
Anser niveus, BRISS., Orn. vi, 288.—BREHM, Eur. Vög. 1823, 766.
Tadorna nivea, BREHM, Vög. Deutschl. 1831, 854.
White Brant, LAWSON, Car. 147.—LEWIS & CLARKE, ii, 58.
Snow Goose, PENN., Arct. Zool. ii, No. 479.—LATH., Gen. Syn. vi, 445.

b. *albatus.*

Anser albatus, CASS., Pr. Phila. Acad. 1856, 41; 1861, 73.—BD., B. N. A. 1858, 925.—
TURNB., B. E. Pa. 1869, 45 (casual).—SAUND., P. Z. S. 1872, 519 (Ireland).—
HART., Br. Birds, 1872, 155 (same instance).
Chen albatus, ELLIOT, B. Am. ii, pl. 42.
Anser hyperboreus var. albatus, COUES, Key, 1872, 282.

Hab.—The whole of North America. Breeds in high latitudes, migrating and wintering in the United States; abundant in the interior and along the Pacific coast, rare on
the Atlantic. Greenland, transient. Cuba. Rare or casual in Europe (NAUM., V. D.
xi, 221, p. 924; GOULD, B. Eur. pl. 346).

On the question of the relationships of the lesser Snow Goose, var. *albatus,* there is
little to be noted beyond the fact of smaller size on an average. The variety appears
to bear much the same relationship to *hyperboreus* that *Branta hutchinsii* does to *canadensis.* Measurements of a pair lately taken in Wexford, Ireland, as given by Mr.
Howard Saunders: 2⅗ to 3 for tarsus, and 2 to 2½ for bill.

Dispersed over all of North America, the Snow Goose is nowhere a
permanent resident; its migrations are extensive, and performed with
the utmost regularity; the maximum variation, depending upon the
advance or retardation of the season—less strictly speaking, upon the
weather—is slight. It is never seen in the United States in summer,
for it returns to high latitudes to breed. Along the Atlantic coast, and
indeed through the whole Eastern Province, it may be called rare, at
least in comparison with its great abundance in various parts of the
West. Those found in Texas, and anywhere about the Gulf of Mexico,
undoubtedly migrate inland, following the course of the larger rivers;
while those that pass along the Atlantic seaboard generally hug the
coast, and are hardly to be met with beyond maritime districts. In
Arizona, this Goose is abundant in the winter; it arrives at the Colorado
Basin in October, with hordes of other water-fowl, and remains until
spring opens. Some disperse over all the permanent waters of the
Territory, but these are few in number compared with the assemblages
on the Colorado. Thus I saw some, and took one, in October, on the San
Francisco River, not far from Fort Whipple; on the Mojave River, in
California, the same month of the following year, I met with great
numbers, in some reedy lagoons. Though they could not have been
much molested there, they were shy, and none would have been procured were it not that the nature of the locality offered good opportunities of unseen approach. On the Pacific coast itself, particularly that

of California, the birds are probably more abundant, in winter, than anywhere else. Upon their arrival in October, they are generally lean and poorly flavored, doubtless with the fatigue of a long journey; but they find abundance of suitable food, and soon recuperate. At San Pedro, in Southern California, in November, I saw them every day, and in all sorts of situations—some on the grassy plain, others among the reeds of a little stream or the marshy borders of the bay, others on the bare mud-flats or the beach itself. Being much harassed, they had grown exceedingly wary, and were suspicious of an approach nearer than several hundred yards. Yet with all their sagacity and watchfulness—traits for which their tribe has been celebrated ever since the original and classic flock saved Rome, as it is said—they are sometimes outwitted by very shallow stratagem—the same that I mentioned in speaking of the Speckle-bellies. It is strange, too, that the noise and general appearance of a carriage should not be enough to frighten them, but such is the case. I have driven in a buggy, along the open beach, directly into a flock of Snow Geese, that stood staring agape, "grinning" the while, till they were almost under the horse's hoofs; the laziest flock of tame Geese that were ever almost run over in a country by-road were in no less hurry to get out of the way. Advantage is often taken of this ignorance to shoot them from a buggy; and, though they have not yet learned that anything is to be dreaded when the rattling affair approaches, yet no doubt experience will prove a good teacher, and its acquirements be transmitted until they become inherent. A wild Goose of any species is a good example of wariness in birds, as distinguished from timidity. A timid bird is frightened at any unusual or unexpected appearance, particularly if it be accompanied by noise; while a wary one only flies from what it has learned to distrust or fear, through its acquired perceptions or inherited instincts. Audubon has a paragraph to the point, and one also showing that birds can and do communicate to each other their individual experiences.

"When the young Snow Geese first arrive in Kentucky, about Henderson, for instance, they are unsuspicious, and therefore easily procured. In a half-dry, half-wet pond, running across a large tract of land, on the other side of the river, in the State of Indiana, and which was once my property, I was in the habit of shooting six or seven in a day. This, however, rendered the rest so wild, that the cunning of any 'Red-skin' might have been exercised without success upon them; and I was sorry to find that they had the power of communicating their sense of danger to the other flocks that arrived. On varying my operations, however, and persevering for some time, I found that even the wildest of them suffered; for having taken it into my head to catch them in large traps, I tried this method, and several were procured before the rest had learned to seize the bait in a judicious manner."

Dr. Heermann's notice of this species gives an idea of the immense numbers of the birds in some localities, besides relating a novel method of hunting them. He says they "often cover so densely with their masses the plains in the vicinity of the marshes, as to give the ground the appearance of being clothed in snow. Easily approached on horseback, the natives sometimes near them in this manner, then suddenly putting spurs to their animals, gallop into the flock, striking to the right and left, with short clubs, and trampling them beneath their horses' feet. I have known a native to procure seventeen birds in a single charge of this kind, through a flock covering several acres."

In Alaska, Mr. Dall states, the Snow Goose is common in the spring, arriving about May 9th, flying up the river from the south, and leaving usually by the end of the month. "They do not breed in the vicinity of the Yukon, nor do they return in the fall by the way they came; they only stop to feed and rest on the marshes, during the dusky twilight of the night, and are off again with the early light of an arctic spring." Sir John Richardson, in the Fauna Boreali-Americana, after noting the abundance of the birds, continues: "The eggs, of a yellowish-white color, and regularly ovate form, are a little larger than those of an Eider Duck, their length being three inches, and their greatest breadth two. The young fly in August, and by the middle of September all have departed to the southward. The Snow Goose feeds on rushes, insects, and in autumn on berries, particularly those of the *Empetrum nigrum*. When well fed it is a very excellent bird, far superior to the Canada Goose in juiciness and flavor. It is said the young do not attain their full plumage before their fourth year, and until that period they appear to keep in separate flocks. They are numerous at Albany Fort, in the southern part of Hudson's Bay, where the old birds are rarely seen; and on the other hand, the old birds in their migrations visit York Factory in great abundance, but are seldom accompanied by the young. The Snow Geese make their appearance in spring a few days later than the Canada Geese, and pass in large flocks both through the interior and on the coast." Examples of the eggs in the Smithsonian agree exactly with the above description, but show the usual variation in size, some being noticeably less than three inches in length by over two in breadth.

In the Territory of Dakota I have observed the movements of the Geese during both seasons. They reach the southern portions of the Territory, as the vicinity of Fort Randall, for example, very early in April, or even during the latter part of March, but may be observed during the greater part of the former month. On the 1st of April I saw many in flocks on a reedy lake near Randall, and they were still flying up to the 20th of that month. Higher up on the Missouri, in the vicinity of Fort Stevenson, and also in the neighborhood of Fort Wadsworth, I again saw numerous flocks during the first half of October, frequenting the saline pools which occupy much of that portion of the Territory. In this region they are universally known as White Brant. I can say nothing from personal observation of the bird's movements along the Atlantic coast. According to Dr. Turnbull they are rather rare in New Jersey, arriving in November, and again late in February.

I was lately shown, by Mr. Ridgway, a fine specimen of the Snow Goose, which had voluntarily become semi-domesticated. He has given the following account in the Naturalist: "On the 6th of October, 1873, I shot at Mount Carmel, Illinois, a fine adult male *Anser hyberboreus*, which had been living with a flock of tame Geese for nearly a year. The bird had been crippled in the wing the preceding fall, but the wound, which was merely in the muscles, soon healed, and it escaped by flight. It flew about half a mile, and, observing a flock of tame Geese upon the grassy 'commons' between the town and the river, alighted among them. It continued to stay with them, going home with the flock regularly every evening, to be fed and inclosed in the barn-yard. My attention was attracted to this bird by its owner, Mr. Thomas Hoskinson, from whom I got the above facts, and who kindly told me that if I would shoot the bird he was willing to have it sacrificed to science. Accordingly, I repaired to the 'commons,' and found the flock at a locality designated. After some little search the 'White Brant' was discovered, being distinguished by its black quill-feathers, rather smaller size, shorter neck, black instead of bluish eyes, and the black space along the commissures of the bill. When unmolested this bird was as unmindful of a person as the tame Geese, and it required chase to make it endeavor to escape, which it always did by rising easily from the ground, and flying to the river—sometimes half a mile distant. The specimen was in fine plumage and excellent condition, and made a very clean, perfect specimen, when prepared. It measured as follows: Length, 27 inches; extent, 57; wing, 17; culmen, 2.25; tarsus, 2; middle toe, 1.75. Its weight was $5\frac{1}{4}$ lbs. Bill deep flesh-color, the upper mandible with a salmon-colored tinge, and the lower with a rosy-pink flush; the terminal unguis nearly white; the commissures inclose an elongate oval space of deep black; iris very dark brown; eyelids greenish-white; tarsi and toes purple-lake, the soles of the feet dingy Naples-yellow. A remarkable feature of this specimen is that one or two of the primaries are entirely pure white, while most of the remaining ones have longitudinal spaces, of greater or less extent, on the inner webs. The question arises, whether this is merely a case of partial albinism, or a change produced by the modified condition of its food and mode of life."

"The bill of this bird," says Wilson, "is singularly curious. The edges of the upper and lower gibbosities have each twenty-three indentations, or strong teeth, on each side; the inside, or concavity of the upper mandible, has also seven lateral rows of strong projecting teeth, and the tongue, which is horny at the extremity, is armed on each side with thirteen long and sharp, bony teeth, placed like those of a saw, with their points directed backward; the tongue, turned up and viewed on its lower side, looks very much like a human finger with its nail. This conformation of the mandibles, exposing two rows of strong teeth, has probably given rise to the epithet 'Laughing,' bestowed on one of its varieties, though it might, with as much propriety, be named the 'Grinning Goose.'" No one familiar with the appearance of the Snow Goose will fail to recognize the aptness of the suggestion with which Wilson concludes his truthful, if not quite technically accurate, description, conveying an idea of the bird's queer physiognomy. The design and use of the conspicuous corneous lamellæ (common to other Geese, but remarkably developed in this one) are evident, when we know the bird's food and its manner of procuring it. It feeds upon reeds, grasses, and other herbs, which it forcibly pulls up by the roots, or twitches in two. The shape and singular armature of the bill admirably adapt it for seizing and retaining firm hold of yielding plant-stems. The bird's "horrible smile," then, so far from being a sign of vapid and inane character, is at once the mark and the means of the praiseworthy industry by which it gains an honest livelihood.

Various kinds of ordinary grass form a large part of this bird's food, at least during their winter residence in the United States. They gather it precisely as tame Geese are wont to do. Flocks alight upon a meadow or plain, and pass over the ground in broken array, cropping to either side as they go, with the peculiar tweak of the bill and quick jerk of the neck familiar to all who have watched the barn-yard birds when similarly engaged. The short, turfy grasses appear to be highly relished; and this explains the frequent presence of the birds in fields at a distance from water. They also eat the bulbous roots and soft succulent culms of aquatic plants, and in securing these the tooth-like processes of the bill are brought into special service. Wilson again says that, when thus feeding upon reeds, "they tear them up like hogs;" a questionable comparison, however, for the birds *pull* up the plants instead of *pushing* or "rooting" them up. The Geese, I think, also feed largely upon aquatic insects, small molluscs, and marine invertebrates of various kinds; for they are often observed on mud-flats and rocky places by the sea-side, where there is no vegetation whatever; and it is probable that when they pass over meadows they do not spare the grasshoppers. Audubon relates, that in Louisiana he has often seen the Geese feeding in wheat-fields, where they plucked up the young plants entire.

ANSER ROSSII, Bd.

Horned Wavy; Ross' Goose.

Horned Wavy of HEARNE.
Anser rossi, BD., MSS.—CASS., Pr. Phila. Acad. 1861, 73.—COUES, Key, 1872, 282.
Exanthemops rossi, ELLIOTT, B. N. A. pt. ix, pl. 44.

Hab.—Arctic America. South to San Francisco in winter.

This curious little *Chen*, in which a long-lost species is perfectly recognized, is an inhabitant chiefly of Arctic America, but, like the Snow Goose, is now known to migrate into the United States in winter. It has been taken at San Francisco. With exactly the coloration and form of *A. hyperboreus*, it is immediately recognized by its small size, being no larger than a Mallard, less exposure of the teeth of the bill, corrugation of the base of the bill, and the nearly straight instead of strongly convex outline of the feathers at the sides.

ANSER CŒRULESCENS, (Linn.) Vieill.

Blue Goose.

Anas cœrulescens, LINN., Syst. Nat. i, 1766, 198.—GM., Syst. Nat. i, 1788, 513.—LATH.,
    Ind. Orn. ii, 1790, 836.
Anser cœrulescens, VIEILL., Ency. Meth. i, 1823, 115.—CASS., Pr. Phila. Acad. 1856, 42;
    1861, 73.—BREE, B. Eur. iv, 1863, 132.—COUES, Key, 1872, 282.—RIDGW., Ann.
    Lyc. N. Y. x, 1874, 388 (Illinois).
Anser hyperboreus, *juv.* of some authors.

Hab.—North America generally.

This proves to be a perfectly distinct species from *A. hyperboreus*, the young of which, however much resembling it, is quite different. In adult plumage it bears a curious superficial resemblance to *Philacte canagica*, the distribution of the colors being much the same. Specimens are in the Smithsonian from Chicago, and various localities in North America, where its distribution is apparently general.

BRANTA CANADENSIS, (Linn.) Gray.

Canada Goose; Common Wild Goose.

a. *canadensis*.

Anas canadensis, LINN., Syst. Nat. i, 1766, 198.—GM., Syst. Nat. i, 1788, 514.—FORST.,
    Phil. Trans. lxii, 1772, 414.—LATH., Ind. Orn. ii, 1790, 838.—WILS., Am. Orn.
    viii, 1814, 52, pl. 67, f. 4; and of all earlier authors.
Anser canadensis, VIEILL., Nouv. Dict. d'Hist. Nat.; Ency. Meth. i, 1823, 114.—FLEM., Brit.
    An. 128.—KEYS. & BLAS., Wirb. Eur. 82.—BP., Syn. 1828, 377; List, 1838, 55.—
    SW. & RICH., F. B. A. ii, 1831, 468.—NUTT., Man. ii, 1834, 349.—AUD., Orn. Biog.
    iii, 1835, 1; v, 1839, 607; pl. 201; Syn. 1839, 270; B. Am. vi, 1843, 178, pl. 376.—
    EYT., Mon. *Anat.* 1838.—DEKAY, N. Y. Zool. ii, 1844, 348.—GOSSE, B. Jam. 1847,
    408.—GIR., B. L. I. 1844, 289.—BD., Stansbury's Rep. 1852, 321.—MAXIM., J. f.
    O. vii, 1859, 164.—SCHL., M. P.-B. ix, 1865, *Ansers*, 105.
Cygnus canadensis, STEPH., Shaw's Gen. Zool. xii, 1824, 19.—EYT., Cat. Br. Birds, 65.—
    JEN., Man. 1835, 227.

Bernicla canadensis, BOIE, Isis, 1826, 921.—GRAY, Gen. of B. iii, 1849, 608.—WOODH.,
Sitgr. Rep. 1853, 102.—BP., Compt. Rend. Sept. 1856.—NEWB., P. R. R. Rep.
vi, 1857, 100.—HEERM., *ibid.* x, 1859, pt. vi, 66.—COOP. & SUCK., N. H. Wash.
Ter. 1860,250.—MUR., Edin. New Phil. Journ. 1859, 225.—COUES, Pr. A. N. S. 1861,
238 ; 1866, 62.—ROSS, Canad. Nat. 1862.—HAYD., Rep. 1862, 175 (some breeding
on the Yellowstone).—VERR., Pr. Ess. Inst. iii, 1862, 153.—BOARDM., Pr. Bost.
Soc. iv, 1862, 139.—BLAK., Ibis, 1862, 9.—REINH., Vid. Med. f. 1864, 1865, 246
(Disco, Greenland).—HOY, Smiths. Rep. 1864, 438 (Missouri).—DRESS., Ibis,
1866, 42.—COUES, Pr. Ess. Inst. vi, 1868, 298.—BROWN, Ibis, 1868, 425.—DALL
& BANN., Tr. Chic. Acad. i, 1869, 295 (Alaska).—COUES, Pr. Phila. Acad. 1871,
35 (North Carolina, probably breeding).—STEV., U. S. Geol. Surv. Ter. 1870,
466 (Wyoming).—SNOW, B. Kans. 1873, 11 ; and of most late authors.
Branta canadensis, GRAY.—BANN., Pr. Phila. Acad. 1870, 131.—COUES, Key, 283, fig. 185ᵃ.
Bernicla (*Leucoblepharon*) *canadensis*, BD., B. N. A. 1858, pp. xlix, 764.
Branta (*Leucoblepharon*) *canadensis*, GRAY, Hand-list, iii, 1871, 76, No. 10578.
" *Cygnopsis canadensis*, BRANDT." (*Gray.*)
Anser parvipes, CASS., Pr. Phila. Acad. 1852, 138 (Vera Cruz).
Bernicla barnstoni, ROSS, Canad. Nat. vii, Apr. 1862.

b. *leucopareia*.

Anser canadensis, PALL., Zoog. R.-A. ii, 1811, 230.
Anser leucopareius, BRANDT, Bull. Sc. Acad. St. Peters. i, 1836, 37 (Aleutians); Descr. et
Ic. Av. 1836, 13, pl. 2.
Bernicla leucopareia, CASS., Ill. 272, pl. 45.—DALL & BANN., Tr. Chic. Acad. i, 1869, 295.
Bernicla (*Leucoblepharon*) *leucopareia*, BD., B. N. A. 1858, pp. xlix, 765.
Branta (*Leucoblepharon*) *leucopareia*, GRAY, Hand-list, iii, 1871, 76, No. 10580.
Branta canadensis var. *leucopareia*, COUES, Key, 1872, 284, fig. 185ᵇ.
Bernicla occidentalis, BD., B. N. A. 1858, 766, in text.
Bernicla canadensis var. *occidentalis*, DALL & BANN., Tr. Chic. Acad. i, 1869, 295.
(?) *Bernicla leucolœma*, MUR., Edinb. Phil. Journ. Apr. 1859, 226, pl. 4, f. 1.

c. *hutchinsii*.

Anas bernicla var. *b*, RICH., App. Parry's 2d Voy. 368.
Anser hutchinsii, SW. & RICH., F. B. A. ii, 1831, 470.—NUTT., Man. ii, 1834, 362.—AUD.,
Orn. Biog. iii,1835, 226, pl. 277 ; Syn. 1839, 271 ; B. Am. vi, 1843, 198, pl. 377.—
BP., List, 1838, 55.—LINSL., Am. Journ. xliv, 1843, 249 (Connecticut).—GIR., B.
L. I. 1844, 292.—PUTN., Pr. Ess. Inst. i, 1856, 219 (Massachusetts).
Bernicla hutchinsii, WOODH., Sitgr. Rep. 1823, 102 (California).—NEWB., P. R. R. Rep.
vi, 1857, 101 (California).—HEERM., *ibid.* x, 1859, pt. vi, 67 (California).—COOP.
& SUCK., N. H. Wash. Ter. 1860, 251.—MUR., Edinb. Phil. Journ. xi, 1859, 228,
pl. 4, fig. 2.—ALLEN, Pr. Ess. Inst. iv, 1864, 87 (Massachusetts, rare).—COUES,
ibid. v, 1868, 298.—LAWR., Ann. Lyc. viii, 1866, 296.—TURNB., B. E. Pa. 1869, 45
(occasional).—DALL & BANN., Tr. Chic. Acad. i, 1869, 295 (Alaska).—SNOW, B.
Kans. 1873, 11.
Bernicla (*Leucoblepharon*) *hutchinsii*, BD., B. N. A. 1858, pp. xlix, 766.
Branta (*Leucoblepharon*) *hutchinsii*, GRAY, Hand-list, iii, 1871, 76, No. 10579.
Branta hutchinsii, BANN., Pr. Phila. Acad. 1870, 131.
Branta canadensis var. *hutchinsii*, COUES, Key, 1872, 284.
Anser (*Branta*) *canadensis* var. *hutchinsii*, RIDGW., Ann. Lyc. N. Y. x, 1874, 388 (Illinois).

Hab.—The whole of North America, breeding in the United States, as well as
further north. Accidental in Europe (see above quotations). Var. *hutchinsii* with
nearly coincident range; especially abundant on the west coast in winter. Var. *leucopareia* from the northwest coast.
Lieutenant Warren's Expedition.—5471, Yellowstone River.
Later Expeditions.—00000-0, Sweetwater River.
Not obtained by Captain Raynolds' Expedition.

Both Hutchins' and the Common Wild Goose I have found migrating
through Dakota, in April and October, in considerable numbers, and
Dr. Hayden states that the latter breeds on the Yellowstone. That it
occasionally nests at large through the United States is abundantly attested. While in North Carolina I had reason to believe that it did so
in the vicinity of Fort Macon, as stated in my article above quoted.
But the most interesting information of its breeding that I have to
offer is that it nests in various parts of the Upper Missouri and Yellowstone regions, *in trees.* This fact of arboreal nidification is probably little known, and might even be doubted by some ; but, although

I have not myself seen the nests in trees, I am perfectly satisfied of the reliability of the accounts furnished me by various persons, among whom I need only mention Mr. J. Stevenson, of Dr. Hayden's party. While I was in Montana I found the circumstance to be a matter of common information among residents of that Territory, who expressed surprise that it was not more generally known. The birds are stated to build in the heavy timber along the larger streams, and to transport the young to the water in their bills. This corresponds with the habit of the Wood Duck; while the exceptional mode of nesting is paralleled in the case of the Herring Gull, which, according to Audubon, has been found breeding in communities in trees, though, as is well known, it ordinarily nests on the ground.

While ascending the Missouri in June, 1874, I saw broods of young geese on several occasions, apparently two or three weeks old, swimming in the river near the bank. Later in the same season, along the northern border of Montana, many geese were observed breeding in small lakes. At one of these, several dozen were killed with clubs by some members of the Survey. The old birds being then in moult, were consequently unable to fly, while the young were also still deprived of the power of flight. At this point one of the birds furnished an instance of voluntary semi-domestication much like that narrated by Mr. Ridgway in the case of the tame Snow Goose; it entered camp, as if to escape the sad destruction that was carried on, became perfectly tame, and at last accounts was being carried along by the party as a pet.

Hutchins' Goose has not, to my knowledge, been known to nest within our limits. A set of four eggs before me, collected on the Arctic coast east of Anderson River, July 4, 1863, are larger than as described by previous writers, measuring 3.40 by 2.25; they are almost perfectly ellipsoidal, and, while appearing to have been originally white, are now tinged with dirty-yellowish, as if soiled or discolored. Mr. Dall states that in Alaska, where it is the most common of all the Geese, breeding at Saint Michael's and Pastolik, as well as all along the Yukon, it lays six or eight eggs on the beaches, like *A. gambeli*, with which species it arrives in the spring, departing about the end of October. Along our Atlantic coast this variety appears to be rare, and not to proceed further than the Middle districts; but its great resemblance to the common variety may cause it to be overlooked in a measure. But, as Audubon surmised, its regular occurrence has been established. "I had occasion to allude," he continues, "to a small species, called by the gunners of Maine the Winter or Flight Goose, which they described to me as resembling the large common kind in almost every particular except its size." Both Mr. Lawrence and Mr. Turnbull include it in their lists, as do various New England writers. We must, however, visit the regions west of the Rocky Mountains to find the Hutchins' Goose plentiful in its favorite winter residences, and observe it under the most favorable circumstances. On river, lake and marsh, and particularly along the sea-coast, it is found in vast numbers, being probably the most abundant representative of its family. It enters the United States early in October, or sometimes a little earlier, according to the weather, and in the course of that month becomes dispersed over all its winter feeding grounds. It is generally in poor condition on its arrival, after the severe journey, perhaps extending from the uttermost Arctic land; but it finds abundance of food, and is soon in high flesh again. During the rainy season in California the plains and valleys, before brown and dry, become clothed in rich verdure, and the nourishing grasses afford sustenance to incredible numbers of these and other Geese. Three kinds, the

Snow, the White-fronted, and the present species, have almost precisely the same habits and the same food during their stay with us, and associate so intimately together that many, if not most, of the flocks contain representatives of all three.   At least, after considerable study of the Geese in Arizona and Southern California, I have been unable to recognize any notable differences in choice of feeding grounds.

The following extract on Hutchins' Goose, from Dr. Heermann's Report, will be found interesting: "While hunting during a space of two months in the Suisun Valley I observed them, with other species of Geese, at dawn, high in the air, winging their way toward the prairies and hilly slopes, where the tender young wild oats and grapes offer a tempting pasturage.   Their early flight lasted about two hours, and as far as the eye could reach the sky was spotted with flock after flock, closely following in each other's wake, till it seemed as though all the Geese of California had given rendezvous at this particular point.   Between 10 and 11 o'clock they would leave the prairies, first in small squads, then in large masses, settling in the marshes and collecting around the ponds and sloughs thickly edged with heavy reeds.   Here, swimming in the water, bathing and pluming themselves, they keep up a continual but not unmusical clatter.   This proves the most propitious time of the day for the hunter, who, under cover of the tall reeds and guided by their continual cackling, approaches closely enough to deal havoc among them.   Discharging one load as they sit on the water and another as they rise, I have thus seen twenty-three Geese gathered from two shots, while many more, wounded and maimed, fluttered away and were lost. About 1 o'clock they leave the marshes and return to feed on the prairies, flying low, and affording the sportsman again an opportunity to stop their career.   In the afternoon, about 5 o'clock, they finally leave the prairies, and, rising high up in the air, wend their way to the roosting places whence they came in the morning.   These were often at a great distance, as I have followed them in their evening flight until they were lost to view.   Many, however, roost in the marshes.   Our boat, sailing one night down the sloughs leading to Suisun Bay, having come among them, the noise they made as they rose in advance of us, emitting their cry of alarm (their disordered masses being so serried that we could hear their pinions strike each other as they flew), impressed us with the idea that we must have disturbed thousands.   Such are the habits of the Geese during the winter.   Toward spring they separate into smaller flocks, and gradually disappear from the country, some few only remaining, probably crippled and unable to follow the more vigorous in their northern migration."

BRANTA BERNICLA, (Linn.) Scop.

Brant Goose; Black Brant.

a. bernicla.

Anas bernicla, LINN., Syst. Nat. i, 1766, 198.—GM., Syst. Nat. i, 1788, 513.—LATH., Ind. Orn. ii, 1790, 844.—WILS., Am. Orn. viii, 1814, pl. 72, f. 1.—TEMM., Man. 1815, 531; ii, 1835, 824.—LESS., Man. ii, 1828, 408.
Branta bernicla, SCOP., Bemerk. Naturg. 1770, 73.—GRAY, Hand-list, iii, 1871, 76, No. 10575.—BANN., Pr. Phila. Acad. 1870, 131.—COUES, Key, 1872, 284, f. 184a.
Anser bernicla, ILL., Prod. 1811, 277.—VIEILL., Enc. Meth. i, 1823, 121.—BP., Syn. 1828, 378.—SW. & RICH., F. B. A. ii, 1831, 469.—NUTT., Man. ii, 1834, 359.—TEMM., Man. iv, 1840, 522.—AUD., Orn. Biog. v, 1839, 24, 610, pl. 391; Syn. 1839, 272; B. Am. vi, 1843, 203, pl. 379.—SW., Classif. B. ii, 1837, 365.—SELYS-L., Fn. Belg. i, 1842, 139.—GIR., B. L. I. 1844, 293.—DEKAY, N. Y. Zool. 1844, 351.—SCHL., Rev. Crit. 1844, 100; M. P.-B. vii, 1865, 105.—DEGL., Orn. Eur. ii, 1849, 404.— PUTN., Pr. Ess. Inst. i, 1856, 219.

Anser brenta, PALL., Zoog. R.-A. ii, 1811, 229.—LEACH, Cat. 1816, 37.—FLEM., Br. An. 127.—KEYS. & BLAS., Wirb. Eur. 1840, 83.—SWINH., P. Z. S. 1863, 323 (China).
Bernicla brenta, STEPH., Gen. Zool. xii, pt. ii, 1824, 46.—EYT., Cat. Br. B. 62; Mon. *Anat.* 1838, 85.—BP., List, 1838, 56; C. R. Sept. 1856.—GRAY, Gen. of B. iii, 1849, 607; Cat. Br. B. 1863, 184.—REICH., Syst. Av. 1852, ix, —.—WOODH., Sitgr. Rep. 1853, 102.—BD., B. N. A. 1858, 767.—REINH., Ibis, iii, 1861, 12 (Greenland).—ROSS, Canad. Nat. vii, Apr. 1862.—VERR., Pr. Ess. Inst. 1862, 153.—BLAK., Ibis, 1862, 145.—MALMG., J. f. O. 1865, 209 (Spitzbergen).— DRESS., Ibis, 1866, 42 (Texas).— DEGL.-GERBE, Orn. Eur. ii, 1867, 489.—COUES, Pr. Ess. Inst. vi, 1868, 298; Pr. Phila. Acad. 1871, 36 (North Carolina).
Anser torquata, FRISCH, Vög. Deutschl. ii, pl. 156.—BREHM, Eur. Vög. 1823, 777.—NILSS., Orn. Suec. 117.—JEN., Man. 1835, 224.—NAUM., V. D. xi, 1842, 391, pl. 292.
Bernicla torquata, BOIE, Isis, 1822, 563.—BREHM, V. D. 851.
Bernicla melanopsis, MACGIL., Man. Orn. ii, 1842, 151.
Bernicla glaucogaster, micropus, platyurus, collaris, BREHM., V. D. 849–851.

b. *nigricans.*

Anser nigricans, LAWR., Ann. Lyc. N. Y. iv, 1846, 171, pl. —.
Bernicla nigricans, CASS., Ill. 1853, 52, pl. 10.—BD., B. N. A. 1858, 767.—COOP. & SUCK., N. H. Wash. Ter. 1860, 252.—LAWR., Ann. Lyc. N. Y. viii, 1866, 296 (Long Island).—BROWN, Ibis, 1868, 425.—DALL & BANN., Tr. Chic. Acad. i, 1869, 295 (Alaska).—TURNB., B. E. Pa. 1849, 46 (rare).
Branta nigricans, BANN., Pr. Phila. Acad. 1870, 131.
Branta bernicla var. *nigricans*, COUES, Key, 1872, 284, fig. 184b.

Hab.—Europe. North America; rare or casual on the Pacific. Var. *nigricans*, rare or casual on the Atlantic.
Not obtained by the Expeditions.

While ascending the Missouri in October, 1872, I observed vast numbers of the Common Brant in flocks on the banks and mud-bars of the river. It is generally dispersed over the continent, but chiefly in its eastern portions, where var. *nigricans* is rare. The latter almost entirely replaces the common form on the Pacific side.

In the paper by Messrs. Dall and Bannister, above quoted, the following passages relating to the Black Brant occur: "This Goose arrives in immense flocks, in the spring, along the sea-coast, but is rarely seen on the Yukon. 1 killed one, May 29, 1868, at Nulato, which was said to be a very rare visitor. They pass Fort Yukon in the spring, as they do at Saint Michael's, being present but a few days, and breeding on the shores of the Arctic Ocean. I was informed at Fort Yukon that it is not seen there in the fall. Unlike the White Geese, they return to Norton Sound in small numbers in the fall. * * * * The few that appear at Norton Sound in the fall are the last Geese excepting the *canagica.* A few of this species were killed at Saint Michael's the season I was there; it was said to be altogether less abundant that spring than ordinarily. It arrives there about the 12th of May, almost the last of all the migratory birds. They were observed in the fall of 1865 (September 23), on their return. Usually the Black Brant is said to come in immense flocks, and to afford more profitable sport for a few days than all the other species put together. The flight of the main body of these migratory birds seems to me to be along the western edge of Saint Michael's Island, touching Stewart's Island, and then directly northward, across the open sea, to Golownin Sound. I saw no such large flocks passing the fort as I saw down the canal flying toward Cape Stephens." According to Dr. Suckley these Brant are extremely abundant about the Straits of Fuca in winter, preferring the vicinity of the coast, and subsisting by choice upon sedge-grass growing near salt water. On the Atlantic coast I have noticed the common variety as far as the Carolinas.

The following *Anserinæ* of North America have not been found in the Missouri region:

BRANTA LEUCOPSIS (*Boie*). *Barnacle Goose.*

(?) "*Anas erythropus*, GM., Syst. Nat. i, 1788, 513.—DEGL., Orn. Eur. ii, 1849, 402."
Bernicla erythropus, STEPH., Gen. Zool. xii, 1824, 49.
Anas leucopsis, TEMM., Man. 1815, 531 ; ii, 1835, 823.
Anser leucopsis, BECHST., Tasch. ii, 1810, 557 ; Naturg. iv, 921.—BP., Syn. 1828, 377.—
    NUTT., Man. Orn. ii, 1834, 355.—JEN., Man. 1835, 224.—KEYS. & BLAS., Wirb.
    Eur. 1840, 83.—NAUM., V. D. xi, 1842, 378, pl. 291.—SCHL., Rev. Crit. 1844, 109.—
    AUD., Orn. Biog. iii, 1835, 609, pl. 296 ; Syn. 1839, 271 ; B. A. vi, 200, pl. 378.
Bernicla leucopsis, BOIE, Isis, 1822, 563.—KAUP, Sk. Ent. Eur. Thierw. 1829, 25.—BREHM,
    V. D. 847.—EYT., Cat. Br. B. 18—, 62.—MACG., Man. ii, 1842, 150.—GRAY, G. of
    B. iii, 1849, 607 ; List Br. B. 1863, 184.—BD., B. N. A. 1858, 768.—REINH., Ibis,
    iii, 1861, 12 (Greenland).
Branta leucopsis, BANN., Pr. Phila. Acad. 1870, 131.—GRAY, Hand-list, iii, 1871, —, No.
    —.—COUES, Key, 1872, 283.
Anser bernicla, LEACH, Cat. 1816, 37.—FLEM., Br. An. 127.—PALL., Zoog. R.-A. ii, 230.

    Hab.—Europe. Very rare or casual in North America (Hudson's Bay, BD., Am. Nat.
ii, 49; North Carolina, LAWR., *ibid.* v, 1871, 10).

PHILACTE CANAGICA, *Bann.* *Emperor Goose.*

Anas canagica, SEVAST., N. Act. Petrop. xiii, 1800, 346, pl. 10.
Anser canagicus, BRANDT, Bull. Acad. Sc. St. Petersb. i, 1836, 37 ; Descr. An. i, 1836, 7,
    pl. 1.—SCHL., M. P.-B. viii, 1865, 113.—FINSCH, Abh. Nat. iii, 1872, 66.
Bernicla canagica, GRAY, G. of B. iii, 1849, 607.—DEGL.-GERBE, O. E. 1867, 492.
Chloëphaga canagica, BP., C. R. xlii, Sept. 1856.—BD., B. N. A. 1858, 768.—ELLIOT, B. N.
    A. pl. 45.—DALL & BANN., Tr. Chic. Acad. i, 1869, 296.
Philacte canagica, BANN., Pr. Phila. Acad. 1870, 131.—COUES, Key, 1873, 283, f. 183.—
    COUES, in Elliott's Prybilov Islands, App. p. —.

    Hab.—Northwest coast of America.

DENDROCYGNA AUTUMNALIS (*Linn.*) *Eyton.*

Anas autumnalis, LINN., Syst. Nat. i, 1766, 176.—GM., Syst. Nat. i, 1788, 537.—LATH.,
    Ind. Orn. ii, 1790, 852.—VIEILL., E. M. 1823, 140.—LICHT., Verz. 1823, 84.—
    STEPH., G. Z. xii, pt. ii, 1824, 99.—BURM., Th. Bras. iii, 1856, 436.
Dendronessa autumnalis, WAGL., Isis, 1832, 282.
Dendrocygna autumnalis, EYT., Mon. Anat. 1838.—GRAY, Cat. Br. M. 1844, 131 ; G. of B.
    iii, 1849, 612 --GOSSE, B. Jam. 1847, 398.—LAWR., Ann. Lyc. N. Y. 1851, 117.—
    BD., Stansbury's Rep. 1852, 334 ; B. N. A. 1858, 770 ; 1860, pl. 63, f. 2; Mex. B.
    Surv. 1859, ii, pt. ii, 26, pl. 25 (Texas).—BP., Compt. Rend. 1856, 648.—SCL., P.
    Z. S. 1858, 360 (Honduras) ; 1864, 299 (Guatemala).—SCL. & SALV., P. Z. S. 1864,
    372 ; 1866, 200 (Peru).—CASS., Pr. Phila. Acad. 1860, 197 (Darien).—TAYLOR,
    Ibis, 1864, 172 (Porto Rico) ; 1860, 315 (Honduras).—DRESSER, Ibis, 1866, 42
    (Texas).—LAWR., Ann. Lyc. N. Y. viii, 63 (Panama) ; ix, 1869, 143 (Costa
    Rica).—PELZ., Orn. Bras. 320 (Brazil).—COUES, Key, 1872, 284.

    Hab.—Central and South America. Southwestern United States. West Indies.

DENDROCYGNA FULVA (*Gm.*) *Burm.*

"*Penelope mexicana*, BRISS."
Anas fulva, GM., Syst. Nat. i, 1788, 530.—LATH., Ind. Orn. ii, 1790, 863.—VIEILL., Nouv.
    Dict. d'Hist. Nat. v, 1816, 127 ; E. M. 1823, 137.—STEPH., G. Z. xii, 1819, 204.—
    WAGL., Isis, 1831, 532.—BURM., Thier. Bras. iii, 1856, 435.
Fuligula fulva, STEPH., Gen. Zool. xii, pt. ii, 1824, 204.
Dendronessa fulva, WAGL., Isis, 1832, 281.
Dendrocygna fulva, BURM, Reise La Plata, 515.—BD., B. N. A. 1858, 770 (California).—
    PELZ., Orn. Bras. 319.—XANTUS, Pr. Phila. Acad. 1859, 192 (Fort Tejon).—
    DRESS., Ibis, 1866, 42 (Texas).—COUES, Pr. Phila. Acad. 1866, 98 (Arizona).—
    MOORE, Am. Nat. —, (New Orleans, Louisiana).—SCHL., M. P.-B. *Anseres* p. 87.
Anas virgata, MAXIM., Beit. Nat. Bras. iv, 918 ; Reise Bras. i, 322.
"*Anas sinuata*, LICHT., Mus. Berol."
"*Anas bicolor*, VIEILL., Nouv. Dict. d'Hist. Nat. v, 136."
"*Anas collaris*, MERREM."

    Hab.—Central and South America. North to Arizona and California.

    The following species of *Dendrocygna* may yet be detected in North America:

DENDROCYGNA ARBOREA (*Linn.*) *Sw.*

Anas arborea, LINN., Syst. Nat. i, 1766, 176.—GM., Syst. Nat. i, 1788, 540.—LATH., Ind.
    Orn. ii, 1790, 852.—VIEILL., E. M. 1823, 141.—STEPH., G. Z. xii, pt. ii, 1824, 98.—
    BURM, Thier. Bras. iii, 1856, 436.
Dendronessa arborea, WAGL., Isis, 1832, 282.

Dendrocygna arborea, Sw., Classif. B. ii, 1837, 365.—EYT., Mon. *Anat.* 1838, 110.—GOSSE,
B. Jam. 1847, 395.—GRAY, G. of B. iii, 1849, 612.—REICH., Syst. Av. 1852, 10.—
BD., Stansbury's Rep. 1852, 334.—BP., Compt. Rend. xlii, 1852, 648.—BRY., Pr.
Bost. Soc. viii, 1859; 1867, 70 (Bahamas).—SCL., P. Z. S. 1864, 300 (Jamaica).—
NEWT., Ibis, 1859, 366 (Santa Cruz).—SCHL., M. P.-B. viii, 1865, *Anseres* 84.—
GUNDL., Av. Cub. 1866, 387.

DENDROCYGNA VIDUATA (*Linn.*) *Eyt.*

Anas viduata, LINN., Syst. Nat, i, 1766, 205.—GM., Syst. Nat. i, 1788, 536.—LATH. Ind.
Orn. ii, 1790, 858.—STEPH., G. Z. xii, pt. ii, 1824, 102.—MAXIM., Beit. Bras. iv,
1833, 921.—BURM., Thier. Bras iii, 1856, 434.
Dendrocygna viduata, EYT., Mon. *Anat.* 1838, 109.—TSCH., Fn. Peru. 54.—GRAY, G. of B.
iii, 1849, 612.—LAWR., Ann. Lyc. N. Y. vii, May, 1860, 274 (Cuba).—SCL. P. Z.
S. 1864, 299 (Guiana, Brazil, &c.).—SCL. & SALV., P. Z. S. 1865, 200.—SCHL.,
M. P.-B. viii, 1865, *Anseres* 90.—GUNDL., Av. Cub. 1866, 388.—PELZ., Orn. Bras.
319.—REINH., Vid. Meddel. 1870, 21 (Brazil).

The following is the synonymy of the Musk Duck, domesticated in this country :

HYONETTA MOSCHATA, (*Linn.*) *Sund.*

Anas moschata, LINN., Fn. Suec. 41; Syst. Nat. i, 1766, 199.—GM., Syst. Nat. i, 1788,
515.—LATH., Ind. Orn. ii, 1790, 846.—VIEILL., Ency. Meth. 1823, 129 ; Nouv. Dict.
d'Hist. Nat. v, 1816, 129.—LICHT., Verz. 1823, 84.—MAXIM., Naturg. Bras. iv,
1833, 910.—DEGL., Orn. Eur. ii, 1849, 421.—SCHL., M. P.-B. viii, 1865, 73.
Anas (Moschatus) moschata, LESS., Man. Orn. ii, 1828, 416.
Anas (Gymnathus) moschata, NUTT., Man. ii, 1834, 403.
Branta moschata, SCOP., Bemerk. Naturg. 1770, 74.
Cairina moschata, FLEM., Br. Anim. 1828, 122.—JEN., Man. 1835, 230.—EYT., Cat. Br. B.
65 ; Monog. Anat. 1838, p. —.—KEYS. & BLAS., Wirb. Eur. 1840, 85.—GOSSE, B.
Jam. 1847, 408.—GRAY, Gen. of B. iii, 1849, 618 ; Cat. Br. B. 1863, 198.—REICH.,
Syst. Av. 1852, 10.—BURM., Th. Bras. iii, 1856, 440.—BP., Compt. Rend. xlii,
1856, 649.—SCL. & SALV., Ibis, i, 1859, 232 (Central America).—TAYL., Ibis,
1860, 315 (Honduras).—SCL. & SALV., P. Z. S. 1864, 373 ; 1865, 200 (Ucayali).—
LAWR., Ann. Lyc. N. Y. April, 1863.—PELZ., Orn. Bras. 320 (Brazil).—REINH.,
Viddensk. Meddel. Forh. 1870, 21 (Brazil).
Hyonetta moschata, SUND., Meth. Av. Nat. Disp. Tent. 1873, 146.
Cairina sylvestris, STEPH., Gen. Zool. xii, pt. ii, 1824, 79.

For synonymy of hybrids of this species with *A. boschas*, see that species. A description of the usual hybrid condition is given by COUES, *Forest and Stream*, Feb. 19, 1874.

Subfamily ANATINÆ : *River Ducks.*

ANAS BOSCHAS, Linn.

Mallard.

Anas boschas, LINN., Syst. Nat. i, 1766, 205.—SCOP., Bemerk. Naturg. 1770, 68.—FORST.,
Phil. Trans. lxii, 1772, 383.—GM., Syst. Nat. i, 1788, 538.—LATH., Ind. Orn. ii,
1790, 850.—PALL., Zoog. R. A. ii, 1811, 255.—WILS., Am. Orn. viii, 1814, 112, pl.
70, f. 7.—BOIE, Isis, 1822, 564.—LICHT., Verz. 1823, 84.—STEPH., Gen. Zool. xii,
pt. ii, 1824, 84.—BP., Syn. 1828, 383; List, 1838, 56.—BREHM, V. D. 1831, 862.—
WAGL., Isis, 1831, 531.—TEMM., Man. ii, 1835, 855 ; iv, 1840, 531.—EYT., Mon.
Anat. 1838, p. —.—VIG., Zool. Beech. Voy. 1839, 30.—AUD., Orn. Biog. iii, 1835,
164, pl. 221 ; Syn. 1839, 276 ; B. Am. vi, 1843, 236, pl. 385.—KEYS. & BLAS.,
Wirb. Eur. 1840, 85.—MACGIL., Man. ii, 1842, 165.—SELYS-L., Fn. Belg. i, 1842,
140.—NAUM., V. D. xi, 1842, 575, pl. 300.—GRAY, Cat. B. Br. Mus. 1844, 135 ; G. of
B. iii, 1849, 615 ; List Br. B. 1863, 193.—DEKAY, N. Y. Zool. ii, 1844, 347.—GIR.,
B. L. I. 1844, 299.—SCHL., Rev. Crit. Ois. Eur. 1844, 113 ; M. P.-B. 1865, 40.—
GOSSE, B. Jam. 1847, 408.—DEGL., Orn. Eur. ii, 1849, 425.—CASS., U. S. Expl.
Ex. 1858, 340.—REICH., Syst. Av. 1852, 10.—BD., B. N. A. 1858, 774.—WOODH.,
Sitgr. Rep. 1853, 103.—NEWB., P. R. R. Rep. vi, 1857, 102.—MUR., New Edinb.
Phil. Journ. 1859, 229.—COOP. & SUCK., N. H. Wash. Ter. 1860, 253.—COUES,
Phila. Acad. 1861, 238; 1866, 98; Pr. Ess. Inst. 1868, 298.—VERR., Pr. Ess. Inst. iii,
1862, 153.—ROSS, Canad. Nat. vii, Apr. 1862.—HAYD., Rep. 1862, 175.—SWINH.,
P. Z. S. 1863, 324.—JERD., B. India, iii, 1864, 798.—LAWR., Ann. Lyc. N. Y. Apr.
1863.—GUNDL., Av. Cuban. 1866, 388.—DEGL.-GREBE, Orn. Eur. 1867, 506.—
STEV., U. S. Geol. Surv. Ter. 1870, 466.—MERR., *ibid.* 1872, 703.—COUES, Key,
1872, 285; and of authors generally.

Anas adunca, LINN., Syst. Nat. i, 1766, 206.—GM., Syst. Nat. i, 1788, 538.—JEN., Man. 234.—DONOVAN, Br. Birds, ix, pl. 218.
Anas domestica, GM., Syst. Nat. i, 1788, 538.
Anas (Boschas) domestica, Sw. & RICH., F. B. A. ii, 1831, 442.—NUTT., Man. ii, 1834, 378.
Anas curvirostra, PALL. (*Gray.*)
Anas freycineti, BP. (*Gray.*)
Anas fera, BRISS.—LEACH, Cat. M. and B. Br. Mus. 1816, 39.
Anas archiboschas, subboschas, conboschas, BREHM, V. D. 862, 864, 865.

Among hybrids, proven or presumed, of the Mallard with other Ducks, are the following:
Anas purpureoviridis, SCHINZ. (*Muscovy?*)
Anas maxima, GOSSE, B. Jam. 1847, 399. (*Muscovy?*)
Anas bicolor, DONOVAN, Br. Birds, ix, pl. 212. (*Muscovy?*)
Anas breweri, AUD., Orn. Biog. iv, 1838, 302, pl. 338 (("*glocitans*")); Syn. 1839, 277 ; B. Am. vi, 1843, 252, pl. 387. (*Gadwall?* or *Canvasback?*)
Anas auduboni, BP., List, 1838, 56 ("*bimaculata*"). (Same as *breweri*.)
Fuligula viola, BELL, Ann. Lyc. N. Y. v, 1852, 219. (*Muscovy?*)
Anas iopareia, PHIL., Arch. Naturg. i, 1860, 25 ; P. Z. S. 1866, 531. (*Muscovy*.)

Hab.—Nearly cosmopolitan, and nearly everywhere domesticated. Wild throughout the whole of North America, breeding sparingly throughout the United States, as well as further north. Very rare and scarcely found in New England beyond Massachusetts, where apparently replaced by the Dusky Duck. Greenland (REINH., Ibis, iii, 1861, 13). Cuba (CAB. J. f. O. v, 1857, 229). Bahamas (BRY., Pr. Bost. Soc. viii, 1859). Panama (LAWR., Ann. Lyc. N. Y. viii, 63).

List of specimens.

19306	289	Deer Creek	♂	Apr. 13, 1860	F. V. Hayden.	20.00	37.25	10.75
19507	288	.... do	♀	Apr. 13, 1860	.... do	15.50	33.25	9.25
19308	169	Rosebud.......	♀	Sept. 15, 1860	G. H. Trook..	21.25	34.90	11.50

Lieutenant Warren's Expedition.—No. 9691, Upper Missouri.
Later Expeditions.—59877, Colorado; 60853-7, Sweetwater and North Platte; 61107-7, Bass Creek and Green River; 62464-5, North Fork, Idaho.

Abundant throughout the Missouri region, in suitable situations, especially during the migrations. Many breed in various places, and during the fall movement Mallards are conspicuous among the hordes of wild fowl that throng the waters of this part of the continent.

ANAS OBSCURA, Gmelin.

Dusky Duck; Black Duck.

a. *obscura.*

Anas obscura, GM., Syst. Nat. i, 1788, 541.—LATH., Ind. Orn. ii, 1790, 871.—WILS., Am. Orn. viii, 1814, 141, pl. 72, f. 5; Ord's ed. viii, 155.—VIEILL., Nouv. Dict. v, 1816, 131; Enc. Meth. i, 1823, 146.—STEPH., Gen. Zool. xii, 1824, 104.—BP., Obs. Wils. 1825, No. 260; Syn. 1828, 234; List, 1838, 56; C. R. 1856, 649.—NUTT., Man. ii, 1834, 392.—GRAY, List B. Br. Mus. 1844, 135; Gen. of B. iii, 1849, 615.—AUD., Orn. Biog. iv, 1838, 15, pl. 302; Syn. 1839, 276; B. Am. vi, 1843, 244, pl. 386.— EYT., Mon. Anat. 1838, 140.—GIR., B. L. I. 1844, 301.—DEKAY, N. Y. Zool. ii, 1844, 344.—CAB., J. f. O. v, 1857, 229 (Cuba).—BD., B. N. A. 1858, 775.—PUTN., Pr. Ess. Inst. i, 1856, 219.—VERR., *ibid.* iii, 1862, 154 (Maine, breeding).—ALLEN, *ibid.* iv, 1864, 78 (Massachusetts, breeds).—MCILWR., *ibid.* v, 1866, 94 (Canada West).—COUES, *ibid.* v, 1868, 298.—WHEAT., Ohio Agric. Rep. 1860, No. 241.— COUES, Pr. Phila. Acad. 1861, 238 (Labrador, breeding).—COUES & PRENT., Smiths. Rep. 1861, 417 (winter).—BOARDM., Pr. Bost. Soc. ix, 1862, 129 (Maine, resident).—BLAK., Ibis, 1863, 146.—SCHL., Mus. P.-B. viii, 1815, 41.—LAWR., Ann. Lyc. N. Y. viii, 1866, 296.—DRESS., Ibis, 1866, 42 (Texas).—COUES, Pr. Bost. Soc. xii, 1868, 724 (South Carolina, winter).—ALLEN, Mem. Bost. Soc. i, 1868, 502 (Iowa, in summer).—TURNB., B. E. Pa. 1869, 35.—MAYN., Guide, 1870, 147 (Massachusetts, breeding); Pr. Bost. Soc. 1871.—ALLEN, Bull. M. C. Z. ii, 1871, 363 (Florida).—COUES, Pr. Phila. Acad. 1871, 36 (North Carolina).— COUES, Key, 1872, 285.—SNOW, B. Kans. 1873, 11 (Kansas).

b. *fulvigula.*

Anas obscura var. *fulvigula*, RIDGW., Am. Nat. viii, 1874, p.—.—COUES, Check-list, App.
p.—.

Hab.—Eastern North America, especially along the Atlantic coast, from Labrador to Texas. Iowa and Kansas. Cuba. Var. *fulvigula*, resident in Florida.

The Dusky Duck is peculiar among our species for its partial distribution, being confined to the Eastern Province. It was not noticed by either of the Expeditions, and probably only reaches the border of the Missouri region. Its occurrence in Iowa and Kansas is sufficiently attested. I never saw it, to my knowledge, in Dakota. In 1860 I found it abundant in Labrador, where it was breeding, in pools back of the coast, though occasionally seen also on the islands where the Eiders were nesting. It moults there in July, when the young are able to take care of themselves, and is for a time unable to fly owing to loss of the quills. It also breeds plentifully in New England, especially in Maine, being there, as in Labrador, one of the most abundant and characteristic Ducks during the summer. I have traced it along the Atlantic coast as far as the Carolinas; it is found still further, in Florida and Texas, as well as, according to Cabanis, in Cuba; and, during the winter, is one of the common market ducks of our Atlantic cities. The northward migration appears to be incomplete, many individuals nesting on our Southern coasts; Audubon states that it breeds in Texas "and throughout the United States." The eggs, of which eight or ten are laid, are not distinguishable from those of the Mallard, being pale, dirty yellowish-drab, averaging about 2⅓ inches in length by 1¾ in breadth. The nest is quite compactly and carefully built of weeds and grass, with a slight hollow lined with the parent's feathers.

DAFILA ACUTA, (Linn.)

Pintail; Sprigtail.

Anas acuta, LINN., Syst. Nat. i, 1766, 202.—GM., Syst. Nat. 1788, 258.—LATH., Ind. Orn. ii, 1790, 864.—TEMM., Man. 1815, 540.—BOIE, Isis, 1822, 564.—LICHT., Verz. 1823, 84.—LESS., Man. ii, 1828, 417.—FLEM., Br. An. 124.—BREHM, V. D. 1831, 866.—WAGL., Isis, 1831, 531.—JEN., Man. 232.—TEMM., Man. ii, 1835, 838; iv, 1840, 532.—KEYS. & BLAS., Wirb. Eur. 85.—NAUM., V. D. xi, 1842, 638, pl. 301.— DEGL., Orn. Eur. ii, 1849, 428.—SCHL., Rev. Crit. Ois. Eur. 115; M. P.-B. 1865, 37.—SELYS-L., Fn. Belg. i, 1842, 142.—WILS., Am. Orn. viii, 1814, pl. 68, f. 3.— BP., Obs. Wils. 1825, No. 258; Syn. 1828, 383; List, 1838, 56.—NUTT., Man. ii, 1834, 386.—AUD., Orn. Biog. iii, 1835, 214; v, 1839, 615; pl. 227; Syn. 1839, 279; B. A. vi, 1843, 266, pl. 390.—VIG., Zool. Beechey's Voy. 1839, 31.—GIR., B. L. I. 1844, 310.—DEKAY, N. Y. Zool. ii, 1844, 341.—LEMB., Av. Cub. 1850, 113.— FINSCH, Abh. Nat. iii, 1872, 66.—SW., P. Z. S. 1863, 324.
Trachelonetta acuta, KAUP, Natur. Syst. 1829, 115.
Phasianurus acutus, WAGL., Isis, 1832, 1235.
Dafila acuta, BP., List, 1-38, 56.—GRAY, List. B. Br. Mus. 1844, 134; G. of B. iii, 1849, 615; List Br. B. 1863, 192.—GOSSE, B. Jam. 1847, 402.—REICH., Syst. Av. 1852, x.—CASS, Orn. U. S. Expl. Exped. 1858, 431.—BD., Stanbury's Rep. 1852, 323.—WOODH., Sitgr. Rep. 1853, 103 (New Mexico and California).—NEWB., P. R. R. Rep. vi, 1857, 102 (California and Oregon).—CAB., J. f. O. v, 1857, 229 (Cuba).—BD., B. N. A. 1858, 776.—SCL., Ibis, i, 1859, 231 (Honduras).—HEERM., P. R. R. Rep. x, 1859, pt. vi, 69 (California).—MUR., Edinb. N. Phil. Journ. 1859, 229.—COOP. & SUCK., N. H. Wash. Ter. 1860, 252 (Oregon and Washington).— NEWT., P. Z. S. 1861, plate 68 (hybrid with Mallard).—HAYD., Rep. 1862, 175 (Nebraska).—ROSS, Canad. Nat. Apr. 1862.—JERD., B. India, 1864, 803. — GUNDL., Av. Cub. 1866, 388.—COUES, Pr. Phila. Acad. 1866, 98 (Arizona).— LAWR., Ann. Lyc. N. Y. viii, 1866, 163 (Panama); ix, 1869, 14 (Costa Rica).— DRESS., Ibis, 1862, 42 (Texas).—COUES, Pr. Ess. Inst. v, 1868, 298.—VERR., Pr. Ess. Inst. iii, 1862, 158.—DALL & BANN., Tr. Chic. Acad. i, 1869, 297 (Alaska, breeding).—DEGL.-GERBE, Orn. Eur. 1867, 515.—ALLEN, Bull. M. C. Z. iii,

1872, 183 (Utah).—AIKEN, Pr. Bost. Soc. xv, 1872, 210 (Colorado).—TRIPPE, ibid. 241 (Iowa).—STEV., U. S. Geol. Surv. Ter. 1870, 466 (Wyoming).—MERR., ibid. 1872, 703 (Wyoming).—COUES, Key, 1872, 286, fig. 186.—SNOW, B. Kans. 1873, 11; and of authors generally.
Querquedula acuta, SELBY, Brit. Orn. ii, 311.
Anas alandica, SPARRMANN, Mus. Carls. iii, pl. 60.
Anas sparrmanni, LATH., Ind. Orn. ii, 1790, 876.
Anas caudacuta, PALL., Zoog. R.-A. ii, 1811, 280.—LEACH, Cat. M. & B. Br. Mus. 1816, 38.
Dafila caudacuta, STEPH., Shaw's Gen. Zool. xii, 1824, 127, pl. 49.—JARD., Br. Birds, iv, 120.—EYT., Mon. Anatidæ, 1838, 113.
Daphila caudacuta, Sw., Classif. B. ii, 1837, 367.
Anas (Dafila) caudacuta, Sw. & RICH., F. B. A. ii, 1831, 441.
Querquedula caudacuta, MACGILL., Man. Orn. ii, 1842, 170.
Anas longicauda, BRISS., Orn. vi, 366, pl. 34, f. 1, 2.—BREHM, Vög. Deutschl. 868.
Anas caudata, BREHM, Vög. Deutschl. 869.
Dafila acuta var. americana, BP., Compt. Rend. xlii, 1856.

Hab.—North America and Europe. Breeds chiefly in high latitudes. In winter south to Panama. Cuba.
Lieutenant Warren's Expedition.—8910, "Nebraska."
Later Expeditions.—61109, Rock Creek, Wyoming. 62366, Shoshone Lake, Wyoming. Not obtained by Captain Raynolds' Expedition.

The Pintail is emphatically a "river" Duck, being far more abundant on the pools and streams of the interior than along either coast. It is one of the earlier arrivals in the United States, passing our northern boundary early in September, with the Teal, and becoming generally distributed during the following month. It is one of the most elegant and graceful of our Ducks, either on the land or water, walking and swiming with the long pointed tail elevated, and the thin sinuous neck swaying in all directions. It is shy and vigilant, but owing to its habit of clustering close in groups about the margins of pools where the reeds or brush-wood favor approach, it is sometimes slaughtered in numbers with ease; and if the gunner be ready with another barrel, additional birds may usually be procured, as they fly off in a compact flock.

Few Ducks exceed the Pintail in extent and regularity of migration. In the spring it withdraws altogether from most parts of the United States to high latitudes to breed, and in winter pushes its migration even to Panama. While its general habits when with us are well known, little has been ascertained respecting its breeding in this country; and I have therefore greater pleasure in being able to attest its nesting within our limits. Although I have not recognized it in the Missouri region proper during the breeding season, yet I found it to be one of the commonest of the various ducks that nest in the country drained by the Milk River and its tributaries, throughout most of the northern parts of Montana. In traveling through that country in July, I found it on all the prairie pools and alkaline lakes. At this date the young were just beginning to fly, in most instances, while the old birds were for the most part deprived of flight by moulting of the quills. Many of the former were killed with sticks, or captured by hand, and afforded welcome variation of our hard fare. On invasion of the grassy or reedy pools where the ducks were, they generally crawled shyly out upon the prairie around, and there squatted to hide; so that we procured more from the dry grass surrounding than in the pools themselves. I have sometimes stumbled thus upon several together, crouching as close as possible, and caught them all in my hands.

The following note from Mr. Dall continues this subject: "Extremely common in all parts of the Yukon, and on the marshes near the sea coast. In the early spring, arriving about May 1 at Nulato, it is gregarious; but as soon as it commences to breed, about May 20, or later, they are generally found solitary or in pairs. Their nest is usually in the sedge, lined with dry grass, and, in the absence of both parents, is covered with dry leaves and feathers. * * * * They lay from six to ten, or even twelve eggs, and as soon as the young are hatched, they withdraw from the river to the small creeks and rivulets, where they remain until the ducklings are fully able to fly, when all repair to the great marshes, where, on the roots of the horsetail (*Equisetum*), they grow so fat that frequently they cannot raise themselves above the water."

A nest-complement of seven eggs, from the Yukon, now in the Smithsonian, furnishes the following characters: size, 2.10 by 1.50, to 2.30 by 1.55; shape, rather elongate ellipsoidal; color, uniform dull grayish-olive, without any buff or creamy shade.

Hybrids of this species with the Mallard are of comparatively frequent occurrence; and in at least one instance (that recorded by Prof. A. Newton, as above cited) these have proved fertile *inter se*. Those that I have examined show unmistakably the characters of both parents in about equal proportions.

CHAULELASMUS STREPERUS, (Linn.) Gray.

Gadwall; Gray Duck.

Anas strepera, LINN, Syst. Nat. i, 1776, 200.—GM., Syst. Nat. i, 1788, 520.—LATH., Ind. Orn. ii, 1790, 849.—WILS., Am. Orn. viii, 1814, 120, pl. 71.—TEMM., Man. 1815, 539; ii, 1835, 837; iv, 1840, 532.—BOIE, Isis, 1832, 564.—BP., Obs. Wils. 1825, No. 257; Syn. 1828, 383.—STEPH., Gen. Zool. xii, 1824, 103.—FLEM, Br. An. 1828, 124.—BREHM, Vög. Deutsch. 1831, 870.—NUTT., Man. ii, 1834, 383.—AUD. Orn. Biog. iv, 1838, 353, pl. 348; Syn. 1839, 378; B. Am. vi, 1843, 254, pl. 388.—NAUM., Vög. Deutsch. xi, 1842, 659, pl. 302.—KEYS. & BLAS., Wirb. Eur. 1840, 85.—SELYS-L., Fn. Belg. i, 1842, 141.—GIR., B. L. I. 1844, 304.—DEKAY, N. Y. Zool. ii, 1844, 343.—SCHL., Rev. Crit. 1844, 115; M. P.-B. viii, 1865, 48.—DEGL., Orn. Eur. ii, 1849, 430.—NEWB., P. R. R. Rep. vi, 1857, 102.—SWIN., P. Z. S. 1863, 124; and of most earlier authors.
Anas (Chauliodus) strepera, SW. & RICH., F. B. A. ii, 1831, 440.—JEN., Man. 1835, 231.—Sw., Classif. B. ii, 1837, 360.
Chauliodus strepera, Sw., Journ. Roy. Inst. ii, 19.—EYT., Cat. Br. B. 1836, 60.
Ktinorhynchus strepera, EYT., Monog. Anat. 1838, 137.
Chaulelasmus streperus, GRAY, 1838; List B, Br. Mus. 1844, 139; List of Gen. of B. 1840, 74; Gen. of B. iii, 1849, 617; List Br. B. 1863, 196.—BP., List, 1838, 56.—GOSSE, B. Jam. 1847, 408.—REICH., Syst. Av. 1852, 10.—WOODH., Sitg. Rep. 1853, 104. BD., B. N. A. 1858, 782.—COOP. & SUCK., N. H. Wash. Ter. 1860, 256.—HEERM., P. R. R. Rep. x, 1859, pt. vi, 69.—GUNDL., Av. Cub. 1866, 389.—JERD, B. India, iii, 1864, 892.—COUES, Pr. Phila. Acad. 1866, 99 (Arizona).—DEGL.-GERBE, Orn. Eur. ii, 1867, 516.—DRESS., Ibis, 1866, 43 (Texas).—DALL & BANN., Tr. Chic. Acad. i, 1869, 298.—MERR., U. S. Geol. Surv. Ter. 1872, 704 (Idaho).—ALLEN, Bull. M. C. Z. iii, 1872, 183 (Colorado).—AIKEN, Pr. Bost. Soc. xv, 1872, 240 (Colorado).—COUES, Key, 1872, 286.—SNOW, B. Kans. 1873, 11; and of authors generally.
Querquedula strepera, MACGIL., Man. Orn. ii, 1842, 169.
Anas strepera americana, MAXIM., J. f. O. vii, 1859, 169.
Chaulelasmus americana, BP. (Gray.)
Anas cinerea et subulata, S. G. GMELIN. (Gray.)
Anas kekuschka, GM., Syst. Nat. i, 1788, 531.—LATH., Ind. Orn. ii, 1790, 877.
Anas mail, HODGSON. (Gray.)
Anas capensis, SWAINSON. (Gray.)

Hab.—North America generally. Europe. Asia. Africa. Generally distributed in this country.
Not obtained by Captain Raynolds' or Lieutenant Warren's Expedition.
Later Expeditions.—62363, Idaho.

The Gadwall breeds in various parts of the United States, and does not appear to proceed to the extreme North like some other species. Mr. Dall mentions a British Columbian specimen, with merely the probability that the species reaches as far as Sitka. Audubon notes the breeding in Texas, and in the Middle States and New England, while I have seen eggs from Sacramento, California. These are of the usual shape, of a uniform creamy-buff color, and measure a trifle over 2 inches in length by about 1.50 in breadth.

I found Gadwalls quite common in September, in Northern Dakota, with Mallard, Teal, and Widgeon; some doubtless had bred in the vicinity, as the species certainly does in Montana, along the Milk River and its tributaries. I found unfledged young late in August.

MARECA AMERICANA, (Gm.) Steph.

American Widgeon; Baldpate.

Anas americana, GM., Syst. Nat. i, 1788, 526.—LATH., Ind. Orn. ii, 1790, 861.—WILS., Am. Orn. viii, 1814, 86, pl. 69, f. 1.—BP., Obs. Wils. 1825, No. 259; Syn. 1828, 384.—NUTT., Man. ii, 1834, 389.—AUD., Orn. Biog. iv, 1838, 337, pl. 345; Syn. 1839, 279; B. Am. vi, 1843, 259, pl. 389.—GIR., B. L. I. 1844, 306.—SCHL., Rev. Crit. 114; M. P.-B. viii, 1865, 45.—FINSCH, Abh. Nat. iii, 1872, 66 (Alaska).— DEKAY, N. Y. Zool. ii, 1844, 345.

Mareca americana, STEPH., Shaw's Gen. Zool. xii, 1824, 135.—SW. & RICH., F. B. A. ii, 1831, 445.—SW., Classif. of B. ii, 1837, 366.—BP., List, 1838, 56; C. R. xlii, 1856, 650.—EYT., Mon. Anat. 1838, 116.—THOMP., Ann. Mag. N. H. 1845, 310.—GRAY, Gen. of B. iii, 1849, 613; Cat. Br. B. 1863, 192.—GOSSE, B. Jam. 1847, 408.—BD., Stansbury's Rep. 1852, 322.—WOODH., Sitgr. Rep. 1853, 102.—CAB., J. f. O. v, 1857, 227 (Cuba).—NEWB., P. R. R. Rep. vi, 1857, 102.—HEERM., *ibid.* x, 1859, pt. vi, 68.—BD., B. N. A. 1858, 783; Mex. B. Surv. ii, 1859, Birds, p. 27.—CASS., U. S. N. Astr. Exp. 1858, 432.—SCL., Ibis, i, 1859, 231 (Guatemala).—MUR., Edinb. N. Philos. Journ. 1859, 229.—COOP. & SUCK., N. H. Wash. Ter. 1860, 256.—ROSS, Canad. Nat. April, 1862.—VERR., Pr. Ess. Inst. iii, 1862, 158.— HAYD., Rep. 1862, 176.—BLAK., Ibis, 1863, 147.—DRESS., Ibis, 1866, 43 (Texas).— BROWN, Ibis, 1868, 426.—GUND., Av. Cub. 1866, 388.—COUES, Pr. Phila. Acad. 1866, 99 (Arizona).—COUES, Pr. Ess. Inst. v, 1868, 299.—DALL & BANN., Tr. Chic. Acad. i, 1869, 298 (Yukon).—STEV., U. S. Geol. Surv. Ter. 1870, 466 (Wyoming).—ALLEN, Bull. M. C. Z. iii, 1872, 183 (Utah).—COUES, Key, 1872, 286.—SNOW, B. Kans. 1873, 11.—HART., Br. Birds, 1872, 159 (Great Britain, several instances).

Mareca penelope, b, BLAS., List B. Eur. 1862, 21.

Hab.—North America. South to Guatemala. Breeds in various parts of the United States. Cuba. Accidental in Europe. (DEGL.-GERBE, Orn. Eur. 1867, 514.)

Not obtained by Captain Raynolds' Expedition.

Lieutenant Warren's Expedition.—5453, Bijoux Hills.

Later Expeditions.—61110, Pass Creek, Wyoming.

The Widgeon breeds in abundance in Northern Dakota and Montana along the banks of the streams and pools. Some such places which I visited, the resort of many pairs of various Ducks during the breeding season, and of innumerable flocks during the migrations, resemble the duck-yard of a farm, in the quantities of moulted feathers and amount of ordure scattered everywhere. I was surprised to find young Widgeons, still unable to fly, even as late as the middle of September, at a time when all the other Ducks observed were well on the wing. Although this bird passes far north, many nest in various parts of the United States. Audubon notices its breeding in Texas, and others in the Middle States, about the Great Lakes, and in Oregon. Mr. Dall found it nesting along the Yukon, with the Pintail.

The Widgeon's eggs are eight to twelve in number, about 2 inches long by 1½ broad, of a dull, pale buff color.

Obs.—The European Widgeon (*Mareca penelope*) is said to have occurred in Wisconsin (*Kumlein*), and in Illinois; its casual presence in the Missouri region is to be anticipated. Following is its synonymy:

MARECA PENELOPE, (*Linn.*) Selby.

Anas penelope, LINN., Syst. Nat. i, 1766, 202.—GM., Syst. Nat. i, 1788, 527.—LATH., Ind. Orn. ii, 1790, 860.—PALL., Zoog. R.-A. ii, 1811, 251.—LEACH, Cat. 1816, 37.—BOIE, Isis, 1822, 564.—VIEILL., Enc. Meth. 1823, 141.—LICHT., Verz. 1823, 84.—BREHM,

Eur. Vög. 1823, 798.—FLEM., Br. An. 124.—BREHM, V. D. 1831, 874.—TEMM., Man. ii, 1835, 840; iv, 1840, 532.—KEYS. & BLAS., Wirb. Eur. 1840, 84.—NAUM., V. D. xi, 1842, 724, pl. 305.—SELYS-L., Fn. Belg. 1842, 142.—SCHL., Rev. Crit. 1844, 114; M. P.-B. viii, 1865, 44.—DEKAY, N. Y. Zool. ii, 1844, 346.—GIR., B. L. I. 1844, 307.—DEGL., Orn. Eur. ii, 1849, 431.—REINH., Ibis, iii, 1861, 13 (Greenland).—SWINH., P. Z. S. 1863, 324.—WRIGHT, Ibis, 1864, 155.

Mareca penelope, SELBY, Br. Orn. ii, 324.—JEN., Man. 1835, 236.—BP., List, 1838, 56; C. R. xlii, 1856, 650.—MACG., Man. ii, 1842, 174.—GRAY, List B. Br. Mus. 1844, 133; Gen. of B. iii, 1849, 614; List Br. B. 1863, 191.—REICH., Syst. Av. 1852, ix.—BD., B. N. A. 1858, 784.—SWINH., Ibis, 1861, 345.—JERD., B. Ind. iii, 1864, 804.—DEGL.-GERBE, Orn. Eur. 1867, 512.—COUES, Pr. Ess. Inst. v, 1868, 299 (New England).—COUES, Key, 1872, 268.

Anas kagolka, GM., Syst. Nat. i, 1788, 527.—BREHM, V. D. 872.

Mareca fistularis, STEPH., G. Z. xii, pt. ii, 1824, 131, pl. 50.—EYT., Mon. Anat. 1838, 118.

Anas fistularis, BREHM, V. D. 874.

QUERQUEDULA CAROLINENSIS, (Gm.) Steph.

Green-winged Teal.

Anas crecca, var., FORST., Philos. Tr. lxii, 1772, 383, 419.

Anas (Boschas) crecca, var., SW. & RICH., F. B. A. ii, 1831, 443.—NUTT., Man. ii, 1834, 400.

Anas crecca, WILS., Am. Orn. viii, 1814, 101, pl. 60, f. 1.—BP., Obs. Wils. 1825, No. 263; Syn. 1828, 386.—AUD., Orn. Biog. iii, 1835, 218; v, 1839, 616, pl. 228.

Anas carolinensis, GM., Syst. Nat. i, 1788, 533.—LATH., Ind. Orn. ii, 1790, 874.—AUD., Syn. 1839, 281; B. Am. vi, 1843, 281, pl. 392.—GIR., B. L. I. 1844, 314.—DEKAY, N. Y. Zool. ii, 1844, 340.—LEMB., Av. Cub. 1850, 114.—REINH., Vid. Med. 1853, (1854) 84; Ibis, iii, 1861, 13 (Greenland).—MAXIM., J. f. O. vii, 1859, 172.—TRIPPE, Pr. Ess. Inst. vi, 1871, 119 (Minnesota).

Querquedula carolinensis, STEPH., Shaw's Gen. Zool. xii, 1824, 128.—EYT., Mon. Anat. 1838.—BP., List, 1838, 57; C. R. 1856, 650.—GRAY, Cat. B. Br. Mus. 1844, 137; Gen. of B. iii, 1849, 616.—BD., Stansbury's Rep. 1852, 322.—WOODH., Sitgr. Rep. 1853, 103.—CASS., U. S. N. Astr. Exp. 1858, 342.—NEWB., P. R. R. Rep. vi, 1857, 102.—HEERM., *ibid.* x, 1859, pt. vi, 69.—SCL., P. Z. S. 1859, 237, 369; 1860, 254.—SCL. & SALV., Ibis, i, 1859, 231.—COUES, Key, 1872, 287.

Nettion carolinensis, BD., B. N. A. 1858, 777; Mex. B. Surv. ii, pt. ii, Birds, 26.—COOP. & SUCK., N. H. Wash. Ter. 1860, 254.—COUES, Pr. A. N. S. Phila. 1861, 208 (Labrador).—HAYD., Rep. 1862, 175.—MOORE, P. Z. S. 1859, 65 (Honduras).—CAB., J. f. O. v, 1857, 229 (Cuba).—Ross, Canad. Nat. 1862.—BLAK., Ibis, 1862, 9; 1863, 146.—BRY., Pr. Bost. Soc. vii, 1859 (Bahamas).—SCL., P. Z. S. 1860, 254 (Orizaba).—COUES, Pr. Phila. Acad. 1866, 98 (Arizona).—DRESS., Ibis, 1866, 43 (Texas).—GUNDL., Cat. Av. Cub. 1866, 389.—BROWN, Ibis, 1868, 426.—DALL & BANN., Tr. Chic. Acad. i, 1869, 297 (Alaska, breeding).—STEV., U. S. Geol. Surv. Ter. 1870, 466 (Wyoming).—ALLEN, Bull. M. C. Z. iii, 1872, 183 (Kansas and Utah).—TRIPPE, Pr. Bost. Soc. xv, 1872, 241 (Iowa).—AIKEN, *ibid.* 210 (Colorado; and of late American writers generally.

Anas americana, VIEILL., Enc. Meth. 1823, 155.

Querquedula americana, MUR., Edinb. New Philos. Journ. v, 1859, 230.

" *Anas sylvatica*, VIEILL. ?" (*Gray*.)

Hab.—The whole of North America. Greenland. Mexico. Cuba. South to Honduras. Breeds from the northern border of the United States northward.

List of specimens.

19314	....	Rosebud	....	....	G. H. Trook..	14.00	27.00	7.50
19315	159	...... do	....	Sept. 10, 1860	Dr. Hines....	14.50	24.00	7.50
19316	142	....	....	Oct. 20, 1860	F. V. Hayden..	13.00	23.00	6.00
19317	190	Deer Creek	....	..... do	..... do	16.50	25.00	8.00

Lieutenant Warren's Expedition.—5461, Blackfoot Country; 5462, Big Bend, Missouri River.

Later Expeditions.—59878–80, 60842–50, various Wyoming localities; 61112–15, Green River.

The Green-winged Teal enters the Missouri region from the north in August, among the earliest arrivals of the water-fowl, and soon becomes extremely abundant over all the pools and water-courses. It may breed in Northern Dakota; but I have not satisfied myself of the fact; and I am still uncertain whether some eggs of Teal taken along the Milk River, in Montana, were of this or the succeeding species. According to Mr. Dall it breeds in Alaska, about the 20th of May. The eggs are about eight in number, of a pale, dull, greenish color, measuring from 1.75 to 1.90 in length, by 1.20 to 1.30 in breadth. The nest is built on the ground, of grass and weeds, lined with feathers.

NOTE.—The European Green-winged Teal, which occurs as a straggler to this country, has the following synonymy:

QUERQUEDULA CRECCA, (*Linn.*) *Steph.*

Anas crecia, LINN., Fn. Suec. 45.
Anas crecca, LINN., Syst. Nat. i, 1766, 204.—GM., Syst. Nat. i, 1788, 532.—LATH., Ind. Orn. ii, 1790, 872.—PALL., Zoog. R.-A. ii, 1811, 263.—TEMM., Man. 1815, 547.—BOIE, Isis, 1822, 564.—LICHT., Verz. 1823, 84.—FLEM., Br. An. 1828, 125.—BREHM, V. D. 1831, 884.—JEN., Man. 1835, 235.—TEMM., Man. ii, 1835, 846; iv, 1840, 539.—KEYS. & BLAS., Wirb. Eur. 1840, 85.—SELYS-L., Fn. Belg. i, 1842, 142.—NAUM., V. D. xi, 1842, 701, pl. 304.—SCHL., Rev. Crit. 1844, 113; M. P.-B. viii, 1865, 52.—DEGL., Orn. Eur. ii, 1849, 438.—SWINH., P. Z. S. 1863, 324 (China).—JERD., B. Ind. iii, 1864, 806.
Querquedula crecca, STEPH., Shaw's Gen. Zool. xii, pt. ii, 1824, 146.—EYT., Mon. Anat. 1838.—BP., List, 1838, 57.—MACG., Man. ii, 1842, 167.—GRAY, Cat. Br. Mus. 1844, 137; Gen. of B. iii, 1849, 616; List Br. B. 1863, 194.—REICH., Syst. Av. 1852, ix.—DEGL.-GERBE, Orn. Eur. ii, 1867, 521.—COUES, Key, 1872, 287.
Nettion crecca, KAUP, Sk. Ent. Eur. Th. 1829, 95.—BD., B. N. A. 1858, 778.—COUES, Pr. Phila. Acad. 1861, 238 (Labrador).—COUES, Pr. Ess. Inst. v, 1868, 298.
Querquedula subcrecca et *creccoides,* BREHM, V. D. 885, 886.

QUERQUEDULA DISCORS, (Linn.) Steph.

Blue-winged Teal.

Anas discors, LINN., Syst. Nat. i, 1766, 205 (quotes *Querq. amer. variegata,* CATES., 100; BRISS., vi, 452, and *Querq. an er. fusca,* CATES., 99, and *Querq. virginiana,* BRISS., vi, 455).—GM., Syst. Nat. i, 1788, 535.—LATH., Ind. Orn. ii, 1790, 854.—WILS., Am. Orn. viii, 1814, 74, pl. 68, f. 4.—VIEILL., Enc. Meth. 1823, 156.—BP., Obs. Wils. 1825, No. 262; Syn. 1828, 385.—WAGL., Isis, 1831, 531.—AUD., Orn. Biog. iv, 1838, 111, pl. 313; Svn. 1839, 282; B. Am. vi, 1843, 287, pl. 393.—GIR., B. L. I. 1844, 315.—DeKAY, N. Y. Zool. ii, 1844, 339.—TRIPPE, Pr. Ess. Inst. vi, 1871, 119 (Minnesota).—SCHL., M. P.-B. viii, 1865, 50.
Anas (Boschas) discors, SW. & RICH., F. B. A. ii, 1831, 444.—NUTT., Man. ii, 1834, 397.
Querquedula discors, STEPH., Shaw's Gen. Zool. xii, 1824, 149.—GRAY, Cat. B. Br. Mus. 1844, 138.—BD., B. N. A. 1858, 779; Mex. B. Surv. 1859, 26.—CAB., J. f. O. v, 1857, 228 (Cuba).—MOORE, P. Z. S. 1859, 64 (Honduras).—SCL., *ibid.* 393 (Oaxaca); 1860, 83 (Ecuador); 1860, 254 (Orizaba); 1861, 82 (Jamaica).—SCL., & SALV., *ibid.* 1869, 252 (Venezuela).—SCL. & SALV., Ibis, i, 1859, 231 (Guatemala).—TAYL., *ibid.* 1860, 315 (Tigre Island).—BLAK., *ibid.* iv, 1862, 9; v, 1863, 146.—DRESS., *ibid.* 1866, 43 (Texas, breeding).—ROSS., Canad. Nat. April, 1862.—VERR., Pr. Ess. Inst. iii, 1862, 153.—BRY., Pr. Bost. Soc. vii, 1859 (Bahamas).—LAWR., Ann. Lyc. viii, 1864, 102 (Sombrero); 1869, 143 (Costa Rica).—SUND., Ofv. Vid. Med. 1869, 591 (St. Bartholomew).—DEGL.-GERBE, Orn. Eur. 1867, 520.—COUES, Pr. Ess. Inst. v, 1868, 299.—DALL & BANN., Tr. Chic. Acad. i, 1869, 297 (Alaska, breeding).—HAYD., Rep. 1862, 176.—COOP. & SUCK., N. H. Wash. Ter. 1860, 254.—ALLEN, Bull. M. C. Z. iii, 1872, 183 (Kansas).—AIKEN, Pr. Bost. Soc. xv, 1872, 210 (Colorado).—TRIPPE, *ibid.* 241 (Iowa).—COUES, Key, 1872, 287.—SNOW, B. Kans. 1873, 11.
Cyanopterus discors, EYT., Mon. Anat. 1838.—BP., List, 1838, 57.—GOSSE, B. Jam. 1847, 101.—BLAS., B. Eur. 1862, 21 (France).
Pterocyanea discors, BP., Comptes Rendus, xlii, 1856, 650.—GRAY, Gen. of B. iii, 1849, 617.—WOODH., Sitgr., Rep. 1853, 103.—NEWB., P. R. R. Rep. vi, 1857, 103? (California and Oregon; may rather refer to *Q. cyanoptera*).

Hab.—North America, chiefly east of the Rocky Mountains. To the Pacific coast in Alaska. West Indies. Mexico. Central and South America to Ecuador. Accidental in Europe (France, Revue Zool. 1857, 62).

List of specimens.

| 19313 | 189 | Rosebud........ | ♀ | Sept. 9, 1860. | G. H. Trook.. | 14.50 | 24.00 | 7.50 |
| 19378 | .... | Bighorn .... | ♂ | June 5, 1860. | ..... do...... | ...... | ...... | ..... |

Lieutenant Warren's Expedition.—5464, Vermilion River ; 5465, Iowa River.
Not obtained by the later Expeditions.

This Teal is very abundant in the Missouri region during the migrations, and doubtless also breeds there, as it does in various parts of the United States, as well as farther north. It is the species most frequently noticed by extralimital writers, as occurring in tropical America, though it also winters in the Southern States. It is one of the few Ducks apparently not equally abundant on both sides of the continent, and, in fact, its presence on the Pacific coast, south of Alaska, is still questionable. Dr. Newberry can hardly be right in stating that it is common throughout California and Oregon, having probably confounded it with the next species.

The eggs are of the same size and shape as those of the Green-winged Teal, but rather lighter colored. A nest, believed to be of this species, containing eight eggs with advanced embryos was found on the Milk River early in July; it was built on dry prairie many yards from the nearest water, of dried grasses and weeds, carefully finished with the parents' down.

QUERQUEDULA CYANOPTERA, (Vieill.) Cassin.

Cinnamon Teal; Red-breasted Teal.

Anas cyanoptera, VIEILL., Nouv. Dict. d'H. N. v, 1816, 104.—SCHL., M. P.-B. viii, 1865, 51.
Querquedula cyanoptera, CASS., U. S. N. Astr. Exp. ii, 1855, 202; Ill. 1855, 82, pl. 15
(Utah, California, Louisiana, Chili).—SCL., P. Z. S. 1855, 104; 1859, 237.—
BD., B. N. A. 1858, p. 780 (Rocky Mountains to Pacific) ; Mex. B. Surv. ii, pt.
ii, 1859, Birds, p. 26 (Texas).—KENN., P. R. R. Rep. x, 1859, Whipple's Route,
Birds, p. 35 (Arizona and California).—HEERM., ibid. Williamson's Route,
Birds, p. 69 (New Mexico and California).—COOP. & SUCK., ibid. xii, 1860, p.
255 (Oregon).—ABBOTT, Ibis, 1861, 161.—COUES, Pr. Phila. Acad. 1866, 62
(Arizona).—SCL., P. Z. S. 1860, 389 (Falklands) ; 1867, 335 (Chili).—SCL. &
SALV., ibid. 1869, 160 (Buenos Ayres).—SCL. & SALV., Ibis, 1869, 189.—BURM.,
Reise, 577 (La Plata).—STEV., U. S. Geol. Surv. Ter. 1870, 466 (Wyoming).—
MERR., ibid. 1872, 703 (Idaho, breeding).—AIKEN, Pr. Bost. Soc. xv, 1872, 210
(Colorado).—ALLEN, Bull. M. C. Z. iii, 1872, 183 (Utah).—COUES, Key, 1872, 288.
Anas rafflesii, KING, Zoöl. Journ. iv, 1828, p. 87 ; Suppl. pl. 29 (Magellan Straits).—
CASS., Journ. A. N. S. Phila. iv, 1848, p. 195 (Louisiana).
Cyanoptera rafflesi, EYT., Mon. Anat. 1838.
Pterocyanea rafflesii, BD., Stansbury's Rep. 1852, p. 322 (Great Salt Lake).
Pterocyanea coeruleata, ("LICHT").—GRAY, Gen. Birds, iii, 1849, p. 617.—LAWR., Ann.
Lyc. Nat. Hist. N. Y. v, 1852, p. 220.—WOODH., Sitgr. Rep. 1853, p. 103 (Texas,
New Mexico, California).—BP., C. R. 1856, 650.—NEWB., P. R. R. Rep. vi, 1857,
p. 103 (Southern California).—PHIL., Cat. 1869, 42 (Chili).
Querquedula coeruleata, BRIDGES, P. Z. S. 1842, 118.—GRAY, Cat. B. Br. Mus. i, 1844, 138.—
GAY, Fn. Chilen. i, 1847, 452.—GOULD, P. Z. S. 1859, 96.
Hab.—South America, westerly. In North America, from the Rocky Mountains to the Pacific, north to the Columbia. Louisiana. Florida??? (*Maynard*).

List of specimens.

19310	5	....	♂	....	F. V. Hayden	13.50	......	6.50
19311	....	....	♂		..... do.....	......	......	.....
19312	5	Popoagie Cr'k.	♀	May 22, 1860	G. H. Trook..	14.50	22.75	6.50

Not obtained by Lieutenant Warren's Expedition.
Later Expeditions.—60838-41, Sweet Water and Platte Rivers; 61648-9, Utah.

It has not often occurred that an abundant bird of North America has been first made generally known from the extreme point of South America, and for a long time recognized only as an inhabitant of that continent. Yet this species furnishes such a case, having been early named by King *Anas rafflesi*, from a specimen taken in the Straits of Magellan. It is, moreover, a singular fact, that it was first discovered in the United States in a locality where it is of very unusual and probably only accidental occurrence. It has not, to my knowledge, been found in Louisiana since its discovery in that State, at Opelousas, in 1849. Mr. Cassin notices this occurrence, in the journal cited above, as that of a bird new to our fauna, and subsequently makes the following remarks in his "Illustrations," &c.: "In a communication to us, accompanying one of the first specimens obtained by him [Dr. E. Pilaté], and intended for the collection of the Philadelphia Academy, that gentleman mentions having occasionally seen it in company with other species of ducks, but regards its appearance as unusual in Louisiana." Our next notice, after Mr. Cassin's original one, is Prof. Baird's, of 1852, also above cited. This author observes: "This beautiful species is now for the second time presented as an inhabitant of North America. * * It appears to be a common bird in Utah." The same year it is also given by Mr. Lawrence; the following one, Dr. Woodhouse recorded it as "very abundant throughout Western Texas, New Mexico and California." In 1855, Mr. Cassin, in the work just mentioned, describes and figures the species, alluding to previous discoveries, and to the occurrence of the bird in Chili, as shown by the collections of the United States Astronomical Expedition. By this time, it had become known as a bird of Western North America at large, numerous fragmentary accounts having been given by the naturalists attached to the various Pacific Railroad Surveys, who observed it in many different localities. Among these, Dr. Suckley's is of special interest. "I myself," he says, alluding to its previously noticed occurrences, "have carried its recorded habitat as far north as the Columbia River, where, at Fort Dalles, I obtained several specimens. Fort Dalles is situated about latitude 46° 45′ north. I presume this forms the northernmost limit of the species, excepting, perhaps, a narrow point of the same general geographic region which, crossing the Columbia, extends north of Fort Dalles about 100 miles. This is the culmination northwards of the great wedge-shaped northern prolongation of the Southern fauna, occuring in the arid interior of Oregon and Washington Territories. Near Fort Dalles this Teal seems to be an annual summer resident, where it breeds on the lagoons of the Columbia, and near the small lakes and pond-holes in the basaltic trap of the vicinity."

The Cinnamon Teal was found breeding in Idaho by Mr. Merriam, who took a set of nine eggs, containing large embryos, on the 29th of June, on Marsh Creek. The nest was in swamp grass, and lined with down. The eggs of this bird are strictly oval in shape, one end being much smaller than the other—more so than is usual in this family. They are creamy-white or pale buff, not shaded perceptibly with the grayish or olive-drab so commonly observable in Ducks' eggs. Two specimens, selected as extremes, measured 1.75 by 1.30 and 1.90 by 1.35, respectively; the set to which they belonged, now in the Smithsonian, was taken at Fort Crook, California, by Mr. J. Feilner. I do not think that the bird breeds in Arizona; at least, I have not been able to determine satisfactorily that it does so, as it always appeared to me to come in the fall, in September and October, with other species of wild-fowl, and to leave in the spring with them. But its movements are not yet clearly defined, especially since we have to take into consideration those of the South American representatives of the species. It has not yet been determined whether these are coincident in migration or not; but the supposition that they are so is the more improbable one. It is also a question whether the species was indigenous to both or only one of the divisions of the hemisphere; and if the latter, which one, and at what time did the migration into the other occur. Some may incline to the opinion that it was originally a bird of South America that only recently extended into our country, arguing from the extreme improbability of so conspicuous a bird as it now is remaining so long undiscovered. It being first detected in Louisiana, where it is now scarcely or not at all to be found, strengthens the belief that the Louisiana birds were among the first to apper in the country, at a time before the species determined for itself the habitat that it subsequently found best suited to its new conditions.

There appears to be nothing in the habits of this Teal noticeably different from those of its well-known ally, the Blue-winged, and probably little need be said on this score. But I never think of the bird without recalling scenes in which it was a prominent figure. I have in mind a picture of the headwaters of the Rio Verde, in November, just before winter had fairly set in, although frosts had already touched the foliage and dressed every tree and bush in gorgeous colors. The atmosphere showed a faint yellow haze, and was heavy with odors— souvenirs of departing flowers. The sap of the trees coursed sluggishly, no longer lending elastic vigor to the limbs, that now cracked and broke when forced apart; the leaves loosened their hold, for want of the same mysterious tie, and fell in showers where the Quail rustled over their withering forms. Woodpeckers rattled with exultation against the resounding bark, and seemed to know of the greater store for them now in the nerveless, drowsy trees, that resisted the chisel less stoutly than when they were full of juicy life. Ground squirrels worked hard, gathering the last seeds and nuts to increase their winter's store, and cold-blooded reptiles dragged their stiffening joints to bask in sunny spots, and stimulate the slow current of circulation, before they should withdraw and sink into torpor. Wild fowl came flocking from their northern breeding places—among them thousands of Teal, hurtling overhead and plashing in the waters they were to enliven and adorn all winter.

The upper parts of both forks of the Verde are filled with beavers, that have dammed the streams at short intervals, and transformed them, in some places, into a succession of pools, where the Teal swim in still water. Other wild fowl join them, such as Mallards, Pintails, and Green-wings, disporting together. The approach to the open waters is difficult in most places, from the rank growths, first of shrubbery, and next of reeds, that fringe the open banks; in other places, where the stream narrows in precipitous gorges, from the almost inaccessible rocks. But these difficulties overcome, it is a pleasant sight to see the birds before us—perhaps within a few paces, if we have very carefully crawled through the rushes to the verge—fancying themselves perfectly secure. Some may be quietly paddling in and out of the sedge on the other side, daintily picking up the floating seeds that were shaken down when the wind rustled through, stretching up to gather those still hanging, or to pick of little creatures from the seared stalks. Perhaps a flock is floating idly in midstream, some asleep, with the head resting close on the back and the bill buried in the plumage. Some others swim vigorously along, with breasts deeply immersed, tasting the water as they go, straining it through their bills, to net minute insects, and gabbling to each other their sense of perfect enjoyment. But let them appear never so careless, they are quick to catch the sound of coming danger and take alarm; they are alert in an instant; the next incautious movement, or snapping of a twig, startles them; a chorus of quacks, a splashing of feet, a whistling of wings, and the whole company is off. He is a good sportsman who stops them then, for the stream twists about, the reeds confuse, and the birds are out of sight almost as soon as seen.

Much as elsewhere, I presume, the Duck hunter has to keep his wits about him, and be ready to act at very short notice; but there is double necessity on the Verde. The only passages along the stream are Indian trails, here always war paths. In retaliation for real or fancied wrongs— or partly, at least, from inherent disposition—these savages spend most of their time in wandering about, in hopes of plunder and murder; this, too, against each other, so long as the tribes are not leagued in common cause against a common enemy. On the day I have in mind more particularly, we passed a spot where lay the bodies of several Apachés; from the arrows still sticking in them we judged, afterwards, that they had been killed by a stray band of Navajos. But this was not what we thought most about at the time; we were only four together, and this was close by the place we designed to spend the day in hunting and fishing. Contemplation of the decaying Indians was not calculated to raise our spirits; for though, of course, we knew the danger beforehand, and meant to take our chances, it was not pleasant to have the thing brought up in such a way. We kept on through the cañon a little more cautiously, talked a little more seriously, and concluded to look for game in places where there was the least likelihood of an ambuscade. I confess that the day's sport was rather too highly spiced to be altogether enjoyable, and suspect that others shared my uncomfortable conviction of foolhardiness. However, the day passed without further intimation of danger; game was plenty, and the shooting good. Out of the woods, and with a good bag, we were disposed, and could better afford, to laugh at each other's fears.

SPATULA CLYPEATA, (Linn.) Boie.

Shoveller; Spoonbill Duck.

Anas clypeata, LINN., Syst. Nat. i, 1766, 200.—SCOPOLI, Bemerk. Naturg. 1770, 63.—GM., Syst. Nat. i, 1788, 518.—LATH, Ind. Orn. ii, 1790, 856.—ILL., Prod. 1811, 276.— PALL., Zoog. ii, 1811, 282.—VIEILL., Enc. Meth. 1823, 150.—BREHM., Eur. Vög. 1823, 788.—LICHT., Verz. 1823, 84.—WILS., Am. Orn. viii, 1814, 65, pl. 67, f. 7.— TEMM., Man. Orn. 1815, 544.—BP., Obs. Wils. 1825, No. 255; Syn. 1828, 382.— WAGL., Isis, 1831, 531.—SW. & RICH., F. B. A. ii, 1831, 439.—NUTT., Man. ii, 1834, 375.—JEN., Man. 1835, 230.—TEMM., Man. ii, 1835, 842; iv, 1840, 540.— SW., Classif. B. ii, 1837, 367.—AUD., Orn. Biog. iv, 1838, 241, pl. 327; Syn. 283; B. Am. vi, 1843, 293, pl. 394.—NAUM., Vög. Deutschl. xi, 1842, 747, pl. 306.—GIR., B. L. I. 1844, 317.—DEKAY, N. Y. Zool. ii, 1844, 342.—SCHL., Rev. Crit. 1844, 115; Mus. Pays-Bas, 1865, 33.—DEGL., Orn. Eur. ii, 1849, 423.—LEMB., Av. Cub. 1850, 115.—SWINH., P. Z. S. 1863, 324.—WRIGHT, Ibis, 1864, 155; and of earlier authors generally.

Spatula clypeata, BOIE, Isis, 1822, 564; 1826, 980.—GRAY., List B. Br. Mus. 1844, 139; Gen. of B. iii, 1849, 618; List Br. B. 1863, 197.—WOODH., Sitgr. Rep. 1853, 104.—CASS., Orn. U. S. N. Astr. Exp. 343.—BD., B. N. A. 1858, 781; Mex. B. Surv. 1859, 27.—HEERM., P. R. R. Rep. x, 1859, pt. vi, 69.—SCL., Ibis, i, 1859, 231 (Guatemala).—CAB., J. f. O. v, 228 (Cuba).—SCL., P. Z. S. 1861, 82 (Jamaica).— COOP. & SUCK., N. H. Wash. Ter. 1860, 255.—HAYD., Rep. 1862, 176.—LAWR., Ann. Lyc. 1860, 28.—SWINH., Ibis, 1863, 434.—BLAK., Ibis, 1862, 9; 1863, 146.— ROSS, Canad. Nat. 1862.—COUES, Pr. Phila. Acad. 1866, 99 (Arizona).—COUES, Pr. Ess. Inst. v, 1868, 299.—VERR., *ibid.* iii, 1862, 158.—DALL & BANN., Tr. Chic. Acad. i, 1869, 297 (Alaska).—JERD., B. India, iii, 1864, 796.—GUNDL., Cat. Av. Cub. 1866, 389.—DEGL.-GERBE, Orn. Eur. 1867, 503.—STEV., U. S. Geol. Surv.

Ter. 1870, 466 (Wyoming).—ALLEN, Bull. M. C. Z. iii, 1872, 183 (Utah).—COUES,
Key, 1872, 288.—SNOW, B. Kans. 1873, 11; and of most late writers.
Spathulea clypeata, FLEM., Br. Anim. 1828, 123.
Rhynchaspis clypeata, LEACH.—STEPH., Gen. Zool. xii, pt. ii, 1824, 115, pl. 48.—BP., List,
1838, 57; Comp. Rend. 1856.—VIG., Zool. Beechey's Voy. 1839, 31.—SELYS-L.,
Fn. Belg. i, 1842, 143.—MACG., Man. ii, 1842, 172.—GOSSE, B. Jam. 1847, 408.—
EYT., Cat. Br. B. 61; Mon. Anat. 1838, 134.—KEYS. & BLAS., Wirb. Eur. 85.—
NEWB., P. R. R. Rep. vi, 1857, 103.—MUR., Edinb. New Phil. Journ. 1859, 229.
Anas rubens, GM., Syst. Nat. i, 1788, 419.—LATH., Ind. Orn. ii, 1790, 857.
(?) *Anas mexicana*, LATH., Ind. Orn. ii, 1790, 857.
Clypeata macrorhynchus, platyrhynchus, brachyrhynchus, pomarina, BREHM, Vog. Deutschl.
876, 877, 878, 879.

Hab.—North America. Europe. Asia. Australia. In this country throughout the
continent, breeding from Texas to Alaska, and wintering abundantly from the Middle
districts southward to Guatemala, Mexico, Cuba, and Jamaica. Replaced in South
America by a nearly allied species, *A. platalea*, VIEILLOT.

List of specimens.

| 17309 | | | | G. H. Trook.. | 20 00 | 34.50 | 10.00 |

Lieutenant Warren's Expedition.—No. 5452, Ayoway River.
Later Expeditions.—60851–'2, Sweetwater; 61111, Green River.

I have found the Shoveller to be abundant in season in all parts of
the West, and determined its breeding in Northern Dakota, where I
found young still unable to fly in August, on the Mouse River; and in
Montana, along the Milk River and its tributaries, where the bird is
common through the summer. The eggs have not, so far as I know,
been described from American specimens. They measure on an average 2.10 in length, by 1.50 in breadth; the shape is as usual in the
family; the color a uniform dull, pale, greenish-gray, sometimes with a
faint bluish tinge. These eggs were taken on the Yukon; the nest complement was eight. Others from the region last mentioned are entirely
similar.

AIX SPONSA, (Linn.) Boie.

Summer Duck; Wood Duck.

Anas sponsa, LINN., Syst. Nat. i, 1766, 207.—GM., Syst. Nat. i, 1788, 539.—LATH., Ind.
Orn. ii, 1790, 876.—WILS., Am. Orn. viii, 1814, 97, pl. 70, f. 3.—VIEILL., Ency.
Meth. 1823, 130.—LICHT., Verz. 1823, 85.—STEPH., Gen. Zool. xii, pt. ii, 1824,
96.—BP., Obs. Wils. 1825, No. 261.—NUTT., Man. ii, 1834, 394.—AUD., Orn. Biog.
iii, 1835, 52; v, 1839, 618; pl. 206; Syn. 1839, 280; B. Am. vi, 1843, 271, pl. 391.—
VIG., Zool. Beechey's Voy. 1839, 30.—GIR., B. L. I. 1844, 312.—KEYS. & BLAS.,
Wirb. Eur. 84.—DEKAY, N. Y. Zool. ii, 1844, 338.—DEGL., Orn. Eur. ii, 1849,
440.—MAX., J. f. Orn. vii, 1859, 170, pl. 2, f. 1. 2 (anatomical).
Aix sponsa, BOIE, Isis, 1826, 329.—EYT., Mon. Anat. 1838, 120 ("*Aia*").—BP., List, 1838,
57; Comp. Rend. 1856.—GRAY, Gen. of B. iii, 1849, 614; Cat. Br. B. 1863, 196.—
GOSSE, B. Jam. 1847, 408.—WOODH., Sitgr. Rep. 1853, 102.—CAB., J. f. O. v, 226
(Cuba).—NEWB., P. R. R. Rep. vi, 1857, 102.—BD., B. N. A. 1858, 785.—HEERM.,
P. R. R. Rep. x, 1859, pt. vi, 68.—COOP. & SUCK., N. H. Wash. Ter. 1860, 256.—
VERR., Pr. Ess. Inst. iii, 1862, 153.—COUES, *ibid*, 1868, 299.—HAYD., Rep. 1862,
176.—GUNDL., Cat. Av. Cub. 1866, 389.—DRESS., Ibis, 866, 43.—CARUS, Hand-
buch, i, 1868, 352.—COUES, Key, 1872, 288; and of most late writers.
Dendronessa sponsa, SW. &. RICH., F. B. A. ii, 1831, 446.
Lampronessa sponsa, WAGL., Isis, 1832, 282.
Cosmonessa sponsa, REICH., Syst. Av. 1852, x.

Hab.—North America, especially United States, breeding throughout in suitable
places, and wintering chiefly in the south. Cuba.
Lieutenant Warren's Expedition.—5456, 5460, Vermilion River; 5457, Heart River; 5458,
Nishnalitra; 5459, Ioway River.
Not obtained by Captain Raynolds' or the later Expeditions.

The beautiful Wood Duck breeds more generally throughout the

United States than any other, and is further notable for furnishing a conspicuous exception to the general rule that Ducks nest on the ground; for it breeds in trees. The following account of Audubon's of the nidification of the species, its most interesting peculiarity, leaves little to be desired:

"The Wood Duck breeds in the Middle States about the beginning of April, in Massachusetts a month later, and in Nova Scotia, or on our northern lakes, seldom before the first days of June. In Louisiana and Kentucky, where I have had better opportunities of studying their habits in this respect, they generally pair about the first of March, sometimes a fortnight earlier. I never knew one of these birds to form a nest on the ground, or on the branches of a tree. They appear at all times to prefer the hollow, broken portion of some large branch, the hole of our large Woodpecker (*Picus principalis*), or the deserted retreat of the fox squirrel; and I have frequently been surprised to see them go in and out of a hole of any one of these, when their bodies while on wing seemed to be nearly half as large again as the aperture within which they had deposited their eggs. Once only I found a nest (with ten eggs) in the fissure of a rock, on the Kentucky River, a few miles below Frankfort. Generally, however, the holes to which they betake themselves are either over deep swamps, above cane-brakes, or on broken branches of high sycamores, seldom more than forty or fifty feet from the water. They are much attached to their breeding-places, and for three successive years I found a pair near Henderson, in Kentucky, with the eggs, in the beginning of April, in the abandoned nest of the Ivory-billed Woodpecker. The eggs, which are from six to fifteen, according to the age of the bird, are placed on dry plants, feathers, and a scanty portion of down, which I believe is mostly plucked from the breast of the female. They are perfectly smooth, nearly elliptical, of a light color, between buff and pale green, two inches in length by one and a half in diameter.

"No sooner has the female completed her set of eggs than she is abandoned by her mate, who now joins others, which form themselves into considerable flocks, and thus remain apart till the young are able to fly, when old and young of both sexes come together, and so remain until the commencement of the next breeding season. In all the nests I have examined I have been rather surprised to find a quantity of feathers belonging to birds of other species, even those of the domestic fowls, and particularly those of the Wild Goose and Wild Turkey. On coming on a nest with eggs when the bird was absent in search of food, I have always found the eggs covered over with feathers and down, although quite out of sight, in the depth of a Woodpecker's or squirrel's hole. On the contrary, when the nest was placed on the broken branch of a tree, it could easily be observed from the ground, on account of the feathers, dead sticks, and withered grasses about it. If the nest is placed immediately over the water, the young, the moment they are hatched, scramble to the mouth of the hole, launch into the air with their little wings and feet spread out, and drop into their favorite element; but whenever their birth-place is some distance from it, the mother carries them to it one by one in her bill, holding them so as not to injure their yet tender frame. On several occasions, however, when the hole was thirty, forty, or more yards from a bayou or other piece of water, I observed that the mother suffered the young to fall on the grasses and dried leaves beneath the tree, and afterward led them directly to the nearest edge of the next pool or creek. At this early age, the young answer to their parents' call with a mellow *pee, pee, pee-e,* often and rapidly repeated. The call of the mother at such times is low, soft, and prolonged, resembling the syllables *pe-ēē*, *pē-ēē*. The watch-note of the male, which resembles *hoe-ēēk*, is never uttered by the female; indeed, the male himself seldom uses it, unless alarmed by some uncommon sound, or the sight of a distant enemy, or when intent on calling passing birds of his own species."

Subfamily FULIGULINÆ: *Sea Ducks.*

FULIGULA MARILA, (Linn.) Steph.

Greater Scaup Duck; Big Black-head; Blue-bill; Broad-bill; Shuffler.

Anas marila, LINN., Syst. Nat. i, 1766, 196.—GM., i, 1788, 599.—LATH., Ind. Orn. ii, 1790, 853.—PALL., Zoog. R.-A. ii, 1811, 248.—TEMM., Man. Orn. 1815, 562.—LEACH, Cat. 1815, 39.—VIEILL., Nouv. Dict. d'Hist. Nat. 1816, 127; Enc. Meth. i, 1823, 152.—LICHT., Verz. 1823, 85.—TEMM., Man. ii, 1835, 865; iv, 840, 545.—SCHL., Rev. Crit. 1844, 120.—NAUM., V. D. xii, 1844, 84, pl. 311.—? WILS., Am. Orn. viii, 1814, 84, pl. 69, f. 3 (may rather be the next species).
Fuligula marila, STEPH., Gen. Zool. xii, pt. ii, 1824, 198.—BP., Syn. 1828, 392; List, 1838, 58.—Sw. & RICH., F. B. A. ii, 1831, 453 (includes *affinis*).—NUTT., Man. ii, 1834, 437 (includes *affinis*).—JEN., Man. 1835, 243.—EYT., Mon. Anat. 1838, 156.—VIG., Zool. Beech. Voy. 1839, —.—KEYS. & BLAS., Wirb. Eur. 1840, 87.—SELYS-L., Fn. Belg. 1842, 145.—MACGIL., Man. ii, 1842, 188.—AUD., B. Am. vii, 1843, 355, pl. 498 (not of vi, 1843, 316, pl. 397, nor of his earlier works).—GIR., B. L. I. 1844, 321.—DeKAY, N. Y. Zool. ii, 1844, 323.—GRAY, List B. Br. Mus. 1844, 143; Gen. of B. iii, 1849, 621; List Br. B. 1863, 199.—DEGL., Orn. Eur. ii, 1849, 453.—CASS., Orn. U. S. Expl. Exped. 1858, 343.—SWINH., Ibis, 1860, 67; 1863, 324.—REINH., Ibis, iii, 1861, 13.—JERD., B. India, iii, 1864, 814.—SCHL., Mus. P.-B. viii, 1865, 26.—DEGL.-GERBE, Orn. Eur. ii, 1867, 536.—COUES, Key, 1872, 289.
Nyroca marila, FLEM., Br. Anim. 122.
Aythya marila, BOIE, Isis, 1822, 564.—BREHM, V. D. 912.—BP., List B. Eur. 1842.
Fulix marila, BD., B. N. A. 1858, 791.—BRY., Pr. Bost. Soc. vii, 1859 (Bahamas).—COOP. & SUCK., N. H. Wash. Ter. 1860, 258.—Ross, Canad. Nat. 1862.—BLAK., Ibis, 1863, 147.—DRESS., Ibis, 1866, 43.—BROWN, Ibis, 1868, 426.—DALL & BANN., Tr. Chic. Acad. i, 1869, 298.—ALLEN, Bull. M. C. Z. iii, 1872, 183 (Kansas and Utah).—SNOW, B. Kans. 1873, 11.
Anas frenata, SPARRM., Mus. Carls. 1786, pl. 38.
Marila frenata, BP., Comptes Rendus, xlii, 1856.
Fuligula gesneri, EYT., Cat. Br. Birds, 58.—JARD., Br. Birds, iv, 138, pl. 5.

Hab.—The whole of North America. Greenland. Europe. Asia.
Not obtained by the Expeditions.

I frequently saw Black heads in Dakota and Montana, especially during the migrations, but whether this species was with the succeeding was not determined. It is abundant in summer in Alaska, where Mr. Dall procured eggs, early in June, at the mouth of the Yukon. The nest was " very rude, a mere excavation with a few sticks about it."

FULIGULA AFFINIS, Eyton.

Lesser Scaup Duck; Little Black-head; Blue-bill; Broad-bill.

"*Anas marila*, FORST., Phil. Trans. lxii, 1772, No. 44."
Fuligula marila, AUD., Orn. Biog. iii, 1835, 226; v, 1839, 614; pl. 229; Syn. 1839, 286; B. Am. vi, 1843, 316, pl. 397.
Fuligula affinis, EYT., Monog. Anat. 1838, 157.—GOSSE, B. Jam. 1847, p. —.—TURNB., B. B. E. Pa. 1869, 36.—COUES, Key, 1872, 289.
Marila affinis, BP., Comptes Rendus, xlii, 1856.
Fulix affinis, BD., B. N. A. 1858, 791.—SCL., Ibis, i, 1859, 231 (Guatemala).—LAWR., Ann. Lyc. ix, 1869, 143 (Costa Rica); 210 (Yucatan).—DRESS., Ibis, 1866, 43 (Texas).—SALV., P. Z. S. 1870, 219 (Veragua).—NEWT., *ibid.* 1867, 167 (egg).—DALL & BANN., Tr. Chic. Acad. i, 1869, 298 (Yukon, breeding).—WHEAT., Ohio Agric. Rep. 1860, No. 250.—COUES & PRENT., Smiths. Rep. 1861, 417.—BOARDM., Pr. Bost. Soc. iv, 1862, 129.—VERR., Pr. Ess. Inst. iii, 1862, 159.—ALLEN, *ibid.* iv, 1864, 88.—COUES, *ibid.* v, 1868, 299.—McILWR., *ibid.* v, 1866, —.—COUES, Pr.

Bost. Soc. xii, 1868, 129.—ALLEN, Bull. M. C. Z. ii, 1871, 363 (includes the pre-
ceding).—MAYN., Guide, 1870, 148.—COUES, Pr. Phila. Acad. 1871, 37.—AIKEN,
Pr. Bost. Soc. xv, 1872, 210.—SNOW, B. Kans. 1873, 11.
Fuligula mariloides, VIG., Zool. Voy. Blossom, 1839, 31.
Fuligula minor, GIR., B. L. I. 1844, 323.—BELL, Pr. Phila. Acad. i, 1842, 141.

Hab.—The whole of North America, and south to Guatemala in winter. Breeds in
high latitudes and southward at least to the United States border. Part of the West
Indies.
Not obtained by the Expeditions.

Authors are at variance concerning the relationship of the bird to the
preceding, and the question is not yet settled. For myself, I am rather
inclined to keep the two apart, notwithstanding their very close resemblance, and admitting the probability that intermediate examples may
be found. There appears to be something different in their range, the
F. affinis being the more southerly. Not that it does not, in the breeding season, reach as high latitudes as the other, but that its autumnal
movement is pushed to the West Indies and Central America, where
the true *F. marila* is not recorded as occurring. It is improbable that
two varieties, if they be really such, should preserve this difference.
Good observers have also noted some differences in habits and resorts,
and gunners, practically very familiar with both birds, recognize a distinction. The Lesser Black-head seems to be more generally distributed
in the interior of the United States than the other, and probably most
of the "Scaups" from such regions are of this kind. All of the
numerous Scaups that I found breeding along the Upper Missouri and
Milk River appeared to be of this species, as were the several specimens
examined. In some places they seemed more abundant than any other
species, and they were the principal representatives of the *Fuligulinæ*,
the Buffle-head itself not excepted.

FULIGULA COLLARIS, (Donov.) Bp.

Ring-necked Duck.

Anas collaris, DONOV., Br. Birds, vi, pl. 147 (England).
Fuligula collaris, BP., List Eur. Birds, 1842.—GRAY, List B. Br. Mus. 1844, 142; Gen. of
B. iii, 1849, 621; List Br. B. 1863, 199.—BLAS., List B. Eur. 1862, 21 (England;
quotes *De Selys*, Mem. Liege, iv, 9).—SCHL., M. P. B. viii, 1865, 26.—DEGL.-
GERBE, Orn. Eur. 1867, 535.—TURNB., B. E. Pa. 1869, 36.—COUES, Key, 1872, 289.
Fulix collaris, BD., B. N. A. 1858, 792; Mex. Bound. Surv. 1859, Birds, 27.—BRY., Pr.
Bost. Soc. vii, 1859 (Bahamas).—ROSS, Canad. Nat. 1862.—VERR., Pr. Ess. Inst.
iii, 1862, 153.—COUES, *ibid.* v, 1868, 299.—SALV., Ibis, ii, 1860, 277 (Guatemala).—
DRESS., *ibid.* 1866, 43 (Texas).—BLAK., *ibid.* 1863, 148.—BROWN, *ibid.* 1868, 426.—
GUNDL., Av. Cub. 1866, 390.—STEV., U. S. Geol. Surv. Ter. 1870, 466.—AIKEN, Pr.
Bost. Soc. xv, 1872, 210 (Colorado).—TRIPPE, *ibid.* 241 (Iowa).—SNOW, B. Kans.
1873, 11; and of most United States writers.
Marila collaris, BP., Comptes Rendus, 1856, 651.
Anas fuligula, WILS., Am. Orn. viii, 1814, 66, pl. 67, f. 5 (not of *Linnæus*).—TEMM., Man.
ii, 1835, 873; iv, 1840, 549.
Anas (Fuligula) rufitorques, BP., Journ. Phila. Acad. iii, 1824, 381.
Anas rufitorques, ORD, ed. Wils. viii, 1825, 61.—SCHL., Rev. Crit. 1844, 119.
Fuligula rufitorques, BP., Syn. 1828, 393; List, 1838, 58.—SW. & RICH., F. B. A. ii,
1831, 454.—NUTT., Man. ii, 1834, 439.—AUD., Orn. Biog. iii, 1835, 259, pl. 234;
Syn. 1839, 287; B. Am. vi, 1843, 320, pl. 398.—EYT., Mon. Anat. 1838, 158.—GIR.,
B. L. I. 1844, 324.—DEKAY, N. Y. Zool. 1844, 325.—GOSSE, B. Jam. 1847, 408.—
LEMB., Av. Cub. 1850, 117.—CASS., Orn. U. S. Expl. Exped. 1858, 343.—MAXIM.,
J. f. O. 1859, 176.

Hab.—The whole of North América, breeding far north, wintering in the United
States and beyond. South to Guatemala. Cuba. Jamaica. Accidental in Europe.
Not obtained by either of the earlier Expeditions.
Later Expeditions.—61116, Green River, Wyoming.

FULIGULA FERINA var. AMERICANA, (Eyt.) Coues.

American Pochard; Red-head.

Anas ferina, WILS., Am. Orn. viii, 1814, †10, pl. 70, f. 6.—DOUGH., Cab. N. H. ii, 1832.
    40. (Not of European writers.)
Anas (Fuligula) ferina, BP., Obs. Wils. 1825, No. 270.
Fuligula ferina, BP., Syn. 1828, 392.—SW. & RICH., F. B. A. ii, 1831, 452.—NUTT., Man.
    ii, 1834, 434.—AUD., Orn. Biog. iv, 1838, 198; pl. 322; Syn. 1839, 287; B. Am. vi,
    1843, 311, pl. 396.—GIR., B. L. I. 1844, 320.
Nyroca ferina, WOODH., Sitgr. Rep. 1853, 104.
Aythya ferina var. *americana*, ALLEN, Bull. M. C. Z. iii, 1872, 183.
Fuligula ferina var. *americana*, COUES, Key, 1872, 289.
Aythya erythrocephala, BP., List, 1838, 58.—NEWB., P. R. R. Rep. vi, 1857, 103.
Nyroca erythrocephala, HEERM., P. R. R. Rep. x, 1859, vi, 70.
Fuligula americana, EYT., Monog. Anat. 1838, 155.—GOSSE, B. Jam. 1847.—TURNB., B.
    E. Pa. 1869, 36.—MAXIM., J. f. O. vii, 1859, 175.
Nyroca americana, GRAY, Gen. of B. iii, 1849.
Aythya americana, BP., Comptes Rendus, 1856.—BD., B. N. A. 1858, 793; and of most late
    United States writers.

Hab.—Whole of North America, but more particularly Eastern North America.
Breeds in the Fur Countries. Bahamas (*Bryant*).

List of specimens.

| 19218 | 35 | Otter Creek.... | .... | Mar. 27, 1860 | F. V. Hayden. | 20.00 | 31.50 | 7.50 |

Not obtained by Lieutenant Warren's Expedition, nor by the later ones.

FULIGULA VALLISNERIA, (Wils.) Steph.

Canvas-back Duck.

Anas vallisneria, WILS., Am. Orn. viii, 1814, 103, pl. 7, f. 3.—DOUGH., Cab. N. H. ii,
    1832, 36, pl. 4.
Fuligula vallisneria, STEPH., Shaw's Gen. Zool. xii, pt. ii, 1824, 196.—BP., Syn. 1828,
    392.—SW. & RICH, F. B. A. ii, 1831, 451.—NUTT., Man. ii, 1834, 430.—EYT., Mon.
    Anat. 1838.—AUD., Orn. Biog. iv, 1838, 1; pl. 301; Syn. 1839, 285; B. Am. vi, 1843,
    299, pl. 395.—GIR., B. L. I. 1844, 318.—DEKAY, N. Y. Zool. ii, 1844, 321.—SCHL.,
    M. P.-B. viii, 1865, 25.—TURNB. B. E. Pa. 1869, 36.—COUES, Key, 1872, 290.
Aythya vallisneria, BOIE, Isis, 1826, 980.—BP., List, 1838, 58; Compt. Rend. 1856, 651.—
    NEWB., P. R. R. Rep., vi, 1857, 103.—BD., B. N. A. 1858, 794.—COOP. & SUCK.,
    N. H. Wash. Ter. 1860, 258.—Ross, Canad. Nat. Apr. 1862.—BLAK., Ibis, 1862,
    10; 1863, 148.—DRESS., Ibis, 1866, 43 (Texas).—SALV., *ibid.* 1866, 198 (Guate-
    mala).—BROWN, Ibis, 1868, 426.—DALL & BANN., Tr. Chic. Acad. i, 1869, 298
    (Alaska).—AIKEN, Pr. Bost. Soc. xv, 1872, 210.—SNOW, B. Kans. 1873, 11; and
    of most late writers.
Nyroca vallisneria, GRAY, List B. Br. Mus. 1844, 43; Gen. of B. iii, 1849, 621.—WOODH.,
    Sitgr. Rep. 1853, 104.—HEERM., P. R. R. Rep. x, 1859, pt. vi, 70.
Aristonetta vallisneria, BD., B. N. A. 1868, 793 (in text).
Anas vallisneriana, SABINE, App. Frankl. Jour. 699.

Hab.—The whole of North America. Breeds from the Northern States northward.
Winters from the Middle States southward to Guatemala.
Not procured by the Expeditions.

Some persons experience difficulty in discriminating between the
Canvas-back and Red-head, but there is no occasion for this, at least
in the case of males. In the Red-head, the whole head is clear chestnut-red, with coppery or bronzy reflections, and the bill is clear pale
grayish-blue, with a dark tip. In the Canvas-back, nearly all the head
is obscured with blackish-brown, and the bill is dusky throughout.
There is also a marked difference in the shape of the head and bill; in
the Red-head, the head is puffy and globose, sloping abruptly down to
the base of the bill; in the Canvas-back, the head is longer and narrower, and slopes gradually down to the bill, which rises high on the

forehead. These distinctions of form hold with the females, though less evident in that sex. In the Canvas-back, moreover, the back has much more light than dark color, instead of an equal amount or less, the fine black lines being very narrow and mostly broken up into minute dots.

The Canvas-back does not appear to nest anywhere in the Eastern States, but does so in the West. I found younglings, unable to fly, in July, on Turtle Mountains, latitude 49°, and others attest its breeding in the Rocky Mountains even further south, and in Upper California. Dr. Newberry states : "During the summer we found them more numerous than any other Ducks in the lakes and streams of the Cascade Mountains. In those solitudes they nest and rear their young, as we frequently saw broods there, though the period of incubation had passed." The breeding range extends from these regions very far North; Mr. Dall found Canvas-backs breeding in abundance on the Yukon. In most of the Missouri region, the Canvas-back is not so common as the Red-head; still it is found throughout, in suitable places.

BUCEPHALA CLANGULA, (Linn.) Coues.

Golden-eye; Whistle-wing; Garrot.

Anas clangula, LINN., Syst. Nat. i, 1766, 201.—SCOP., Bemerk. 1770, 64.—FORST., Phil.
    Trans. lxii, 1772, 365, 417.—GM., Syst. Nat. i, 1788, 523.—LATH., Ind. Orn. ii,
    1790, 867.—ILL., Prod. 1811, 276.—WILS., Am. Orn. viii, 1814, 62, pl. 67, f. 6.—
    TEMM., Man. 1815, 566.—LEACH, Cat. 1816, 37.—VIEILL., Nouv. Dict. d'Hist Nat.
    v, 1816, 117; Enc. Meth. i, 1823, 138.—DOUGH., Cab. N. H. i, 1830, 110, pl. 10.—
    TEMM., Man. ii, 1835, 870; iv, 1840, 555.—NAUM., V. D. xii, 1844, 162, pl. 316.—
    SCHL., Rev. Crit. 1844, 118; M. P.-B. viii, 1865, 20.—SWINH., Ibis, 1863, 324.
Clangula clangula, BOIE, Isis, 1822, 564.
Glaucion clangula, KAUP, Sk. Ent. Eur. Thierw. 1829, 53.—KEYS. & BLAS., Wirb. 1840, 86.
Fuligula clangula, BP., Syn. 1828, 393.—NUTT., Man. ii, 1834, 441.—AUD., Orn. Biog. iv,
    1838, 318, pl. 342; Syn. 1839, 292; B. A. vi, 1843, 362, pl. 406 (includes *island-
    ica*).—GIR., B. L. I. 1844, 334.—DEGL., Orn. Eur. ii, 1849, 443.—MAXIM., J. f. O.
    vii, 1859, 178.—TURNB., B. E. Pa. 1869, 86.—FINSCH, Abh. Nat. iii, 1872, 66.
Bucephala clangula, COUES, Key, 1872, 290.
Anas glaucion, LINN., Syst. Nat. i, 1766, 201.—GM., Syst. Nat. i, 1788, 525.—LATH., Ind.
    Orn. ii, 1790, 868.
Clangula glaucion, BP., List, 1838, 58.—GRAY, List B. Br. Mus. 1844, 140; Gen. of B. iii,
    1849, 622; List Br. B. 1863, 202; Hand-list, No. —.
Anas peregrina, S. G. GMELIN. (*Gray.*)
Anas hyemalis, PALL., Zoog. R.-A. ii, 1811, 270.
Clangula vulgaris, FLEM., Br. An. 120.—SW. & RICH., F. B. A. ii, 1831, 456.—SW., Classif.
    B. ii, 1837, 369.—EYT., Mon. Anat. 1838.
Clangula chrysophthalmus, STEPH., G. Z. xii, pt. ii, 1824, 182, pl. 56.—JEN., Man. 1835,
    246.—MACGIL., Man. Orn. ii, 1842, 183.
Clangula americana, BP., List, 1838, 58 ; Compt. Rend. 1856.—EYT., Mon. Anat. 1838.—
    GRAY, Gen. of B. iii, 1849, 622.—NEWB., P. R. R. Rep. vi, 1857, 104.
Bucephala americana, BD., B. N. A. 1858, 796.—COOP. & SUCK., N. H. Wash. Ter. 1860,
    259.—ROSS, Canad. Nat. Apr. 1862.—VERR., Pr. Ess. Inst. iii, 1862, 153.—COUES,
    ibid. v, 1868, 200.—BLAK., Ibis, 1862, 10 ; 1863, 148.—BROWN, Ibis, 1868, 426.
Clangula leucomelas, peregrina, glaucion, BREHM, V. D. 927, 929, 929.

Hab.—All of North America. Cuba. Europe.
Not obtained by any of the Expeditions.

I have not myself observed the Golden-eye in any portion of the Missouri region, nor was it brought in by any of the Expeditions; and we may conclude that it is rare in this part of the country, where its little congener, the *B. albeola*, is very common. This Duck is only known to breed far to the North. Mr. Dall records its early arrival on the Yukon in the beginning of May; it is common there, and the eggs were obtained from the Pastolik Marshes.

BUCEPHALA ISLANDICA, (Gm.) Bd.

Barrow's Golden-eye; Rocky Mountain Garrot.

Anas islandica, GM., Syst. Nat. i, 1788, 541.—LATH., Ind. Orn. ii, 1790, 871.—VIEILL., Nouv. Dict. d'Hist. Nat. v, 1816, 121; Enc. Meth. i, 1823, 133.—NAUM., V. D. xii, 1842, 186, pl. 317.
Clangula islandica, BP., List B. Eur. 1842; Compt. Rend. 1856, 651.—GRAY, List B. Br. Mus. 1844, 145; Gen. of B. iii, 1849, 622.—REINH., Ibis, iii, 1861,14 (Greenland, breeding).—DEGL.-GERBE, Orn. Eur. 1867, 544.
Bucephala islandica, BD., B. N. A. 1858, 796.—ELLIOT, Ann. Lyc. N. Y. vii, Jan. 1862 (critical); B. N. A. ii, pl. 46.—BOARDM., Pr.'Bost. Soc. ix, 1862, 129 (Maine).— BLAK, Ibis, 1863, 148.—COUES, Pr. Ess. Inst. v, 1868, 300 (New England).—DALL & BANN., Tr. Chic. Acad. i, 298 (Sitka and the Yukon).—COUES, Key, 290.
Fuligula islandica, SCHL., M. P.-B. viii, 1865, 121.—FINSCH, Abh. Nat. iii, 1872 (Alaska).
Clangula barrovii, SW. & RICH., F. B. A. ii, 1831, 456, pl. 70.—SW., An. in Menag. 1838, 271.—BP., List. 1838, 58.—EYT., Mon. Anat. 1838, 165.
Fuligula barrovii, NUTT., Man. ii, 1834, 444.—SELYS-L., Fn. Belg. 1842, 146.—DEGL., Orn. Eur. ii, 1849, 446.—PREYER, Reise, 1862, 409.—BREE, B. Eur. iv, 1863, 164.
Clangula scapularis , BREHM, Vög. Deutschl. 1831, 931.
Fuligula clangula, var., AUD., Orn. Biog. v, 1839, 105, pl. 403 ; Syn. 1839, 292 (in part); B. A. vii, 1843, 362 (in part; describes the species as supposed summer plumage of *B. clangula*).

Hab.—North America, northerly; south to New York and Utah. Greenland. Iceland. Europe (GOULD, B. E. pl. 380 ; NAUM., pl. 317). Probably breeds in the Rocky Mountains of the United States.
Not procured by the Expeditions.

Barrow's Golden-eye, upon which some doubt has been cast by myself, among others, appears, nevertheless, to be a valid species; the differences pointed out in the Key, and in other works above cited, being apparently constant as well as appreciable, and there being, moreover, certain anatomical peculiarities in the form of the skull, of which I have only lately become aware. Originally described in 1788, and subsequently renamed and figured in 1831, the species was ignored by Audubon, who mistook it for the summer plumage of the common Golden-eye. It is the most northerly species of the genus, having apparently a circumpolar distribution, breeding only (?) in high latitudes, and penetrating but a limited distance south in winter. Its claim to a place in the present connection rests upon its occurrence in the Rocky Mountains, and as far south as Utah, where it was lately procured by Mr. H. W. Henshaw. On the Eastern Coast it occurs as far south, in winter, as New York.

BUCEPHALA ALBEOLA, (Linn.) Bd.

Buffle-head; Butter-ball; Dipper; Spirit Duck.

Anas albeola, LINN., Syst. Nat. i, 1766, 199.— FORST., Phil. Trans. lxii, 1772, 383,.416.— GM., Syst. Nat. i, 1788, 517.—LATH., Ind. Orn. ii, 1790, 866.—WILS., Am. Orn. viii, 1814, 51, pl. 62, f. 2, 3.—SCHL., Rev. Crit. 1844, 119.
Fuligula albeola, BP., Syn. 1828, 394.—NUTT., Man. ii, 1834, 445.—AUD., Orn. Biog. iv, 1838, 217 ; pl. 225 ; Syn. 1839, 293 ; B. Am. vi, 1843, 369, pl. 408.—GIR., B. L. I. 1844, 335—DEKAY, N. Y. Zool. ii, 1844, 329.—SCHL., M. Pays-Bas, viii, 1865, 22.
Clangula albeola, STEPH., Gen. Zool. xii, pt. ii, 1824, 184.—BOIE, Isis, 1836, 980.—SW. & RICH., F. B. A. ii, 1831, 458.—JEN., Man. 1835, 246.—EYT., Mon. Anat. 1838, 164.— BP., List, 1838, 58.—VIG., Zool. Beech. Voy. 1839, 32.—GRAY, List B. Br. Mus. 1844, 144 ; Gen. of B. iii, 1849, 622 ; List Br. B. 1863, 203.—BD., Stansbury's Rep. 1852; 324.—NEWB., P. R. R. Rep. vi, 1857, 104.—MURR., Ed. N. Phil. Journ. 1859, 230.—HEERM., P. R. R. Rep. x, 1859, pt. vi, 70.—REINH., Ibis, 1861, 14.—DEGL.-GERBE, Orn. Eur. ii, 1867, 545.—NEWT., P. Z. S. 1871, 57 (egg).—HART., Man. Br. Birds, 1872, 161 (Great Britain).
Bucephala albeola, BD., B. N. A. 1858, 797.—COOP. & SUCK., N. H. Wash. Ter. 1860, 259.—DRESS., Ibis, 1866, 44 (Texas).—COUES, Pr. Phila. Ac. 1836, 99 (Arizona).— DALL & BANN., Tr. Chic. Acad. i, 1869, 298 (Alaska, breeding).—STEV., U. S.

37

Geol. Surv. Ter. 1870, 466 (Wyoming).—AIKEN, Pr. Bost. Soc. xv, 1872, 210 (Colorado).—COUES, Key, 1872, 290.—SNOW, B. Kans. 1873, 11; and of most late writers.
Anas bucephala, LINN., Syst. Nat. i, 1766, 200 (♂).—GM., Syst. Nat. i, 1788, 521.
Anas rustica, LINN., Syst. Nat. i, 1766, 201 (♀).—GM., Syst. Nat. i, 1788, 524.

Hab.—North America. Mexico. Cuba (CAB., J. f. O. v, 230). Greenland. Accidental in England (HART., *l. c.*, several instances).
Not procured by the earlier Expeditions.
Later Expeditions.—61118, Fort Sanders, Wyoming.

I have reason to believe that this Duck, not hitherto reported as breeding in the United States, nests in Northern Dakota, as it certainly does in the same latitude in Montana, along Milk River and its tributaries. I found very young birds, in July, about Turtle Mountain, on the boundary line, but they were all able to fly, and may have been hatched a little further north. In the autumn, winter, and spring, the species is very abundant on the waters of the Missouri, much as elsewhere in suitable places throughout the United States. Some individuals reach Mexico and Cuba; further south than this I have no records.

The Buffle-head is not often seen in the United States, except from fall to spring; as it usually retires to high latitudes to breed, as along the Yukon and elsewhere in boreal America, its nidification is consequently not generally known. A set of fourteen eggs taken, the accompanying label states, from a feathery nest in a dead poplar, some distance from the ground, furnishes the following description: Shape, perfectly ellipsoidal; size, slightly over 2 inches in length by $1\frac{1}{2}$ in breadth; color, a peculiar tint, just between rich creamy-white and grayish-olive, unvaried by markings. Other eggs are described as being about $1\frac{2}{3}$ long by $1\frac{1}{4}$ broad, and buff-colored.

HISTRIONICUS TORQUATUS, (Linn.) Bp.

Harlequin Duck.

Anas histrionica, LINN., Syst. Nat. i, 1766, 204.—FORST., Phil. Trans. lxii, 1772, 383, 419.—GM., Syst. Nat. i, 1788, 534.—LATH., Ind. Orn. ii, 1790, 849.—BRÜNN., Orn. Bor. 1764, 84.—PALL., Zoog. R. A. ii, 1811, 273.—WILS., Am. Orn. viii, 1814. 139, pl. 72, f. 4.—TEMM., Man. 1815, 574; ii, 1835, 878; iv, 1840, 549.—NAUM., V. D. xii, 1844, 199, pl. 318.—SCHL., Rev. Crit. 119.—SWINH., Ibis, 1863, 324.
Anas (Fuligula) histrionica, BP., Obs. Wils. 1825, No. 277.
Fuligula (Clangula) histrionica, BP., Syn. 1828, 394.—NUTT., Man. ii, 1834, 448.
Fuligula histrionica, AUD., Orn. Biog. iii, 1835, 612; v, 1839, 617; Syn. 1839, 294; B. Am. vi, 1843, 374, pl. 409.—SELYS-L., Fn. Belg. 1842, 147.—DEKAY, N. Y. Zool. ii, 1844, 331.—GIR., B. L. I. 1844, 336.—DEGL., Orn. Eur. ii, 1849, 451.—SCHL., M. Pays-Bas, viii, 1865, 23.
Cosmonessa histrionica, KAUP, Sk. Ent. Eur. Th. 1829, 40.
Clangula histrionica, BOIE, Isis, 1822, 564.—STEPH., Gen. Zool. xii, 1824, 180, pl. 57.—FLEM., Br. Anim. 120.—JEN., Man. Br. Vert. 246.—SW. & RICH., F. B. A. ii, 1831, 459.—EYT., Mon. Anat. 1838, 163.—MACGIL., Man. ii, 184.—GRAY, Gen. of B. iii, 1869, 622.—BP., List, 1838, 58.—REINH., Ibis, iii, 1861, 14 (Greenland).
Harelda histrionica, KEYS. & BLAS., Wirb. Eur. 1840, 87.—BP., List Eur. Birds, 1842.—FINSCH, Abh. Nat. iii, 1872, 67 (Alaska).
Phylaconetta histrionica, BRANDT, Mem. Acad. St. Petersburg, vi, 1849, 9.
Bucephala (Histrionicus) histrionica, GRAY, Hand-list, iii, 1871, 87, No. 10700.
Histrionicus torquatus, BP., Comptes Rendus, xliii, 1856.—BD., B. N. A. 1858, 798.—COOP. & SUCK., N. H. Wash. Ter. 1860, 260.—WHEAT., Ohio Agric. Rep. 1860, No. 256.—ROSS, Canad. Nat. 1862.—VERR., Pr. Ess. Inst. iii, 1862, 158.—DALL & BANN., Tr. Chic. Acad. 1869, 298 (Yukon, breeding).—BOARDM., Pr. Bost. Soc. ix, 1862, 130 (breeding, rarely, in Bay of Fundy).—COUES, Pr. Ess. Inst. v, 1868, 300 (New England).—LAWR., Ann. Lyc. N. Y. viii, 1866, 297.—TURNB., B. E. Pa. 1868, 46 (very rare).—COUES, Key, 1872, 291.—RIDGW., Ann. Lyc. N. Y. x, 1874, 390 (Lake Michigan).—COUES, Am. Nat. 1874 (breeding in Rocky Mountains of the United States).
Anas minuta, LINN., Syst. Nat. i, 1766, 204 (♀).

Hab.—North America, northerly and chiefly coastwise. South in winter to the Middle States and California. Rocky Mountains of the United States, *breeding.*

List of specimens.

| 19320 | 9 | Mount. Stream. | ♂ | May 31, 1860 | F. V. Hayden | 17.50 | 25.50 | 7.50 |
| 19321 | 7 | ...... do .... | ♀ | May 31, 1860 | ..... do ...... | 25.50 | 25.50 | 7.50 |

This species is included on the strength of the above-named specimens; it is doubtless of rare occurrence, being chiefly a maritime and more northerly bird. In the female was found an egg nearly ready for extrusion. It breeds in the Northern Rocky Mountains of the United States. In August, 1874, I found broods, still unable to fly, swimming in the clear streams which empty into Chief Mountain Lake.

Several of the maritime and boreal species have occurred on the Great Lakes, and may be hereafter added to the Missouri region. These, with the other *Fuligulinæ* of North America, are as follows :

HARELDA GLACIALIS, (*Linnæus*) *Leach.*

Anas glacialis, LINN., Syst. Nat. i, 1766, 203.—FORST., Linn. Trans. lxii, 1772, 418.—GM., Syst. Nat. i, 1788, 529.—LATH., Ind. Orn. ii, 1790, 864.—PALL., Zoog. R.-A. ii, 1811, 276.—WILS., Am. Orn. viii, 1814, 93, 96, pl. 70.—VIEILL., Enc. Meth. i, 1823, 129.—LICHT., Verz. i, 1823, 85.—TEMM., Man. i, 1815, 558 ; ii, 1835, 860 ; iv, 1840, 553.—NAUM., V. D. xii, 1844, 210, pl. 319.—SCHL., Rev. Crit. 1844, 117.
Anas (Fuligula) glacialis, BP., Obs. Wils. 1825, No. 275.
Clangula glacialis, BOIE, Isis, 1822, 569.—FLEM., Br. An. 1828, 121.—BREHM, V. D. 937.
Platypus glacialis, BREHM, Eur. Vög. 1823, 840.
Pagonetta glacialis, KAUP, Sk. Ent. Eur. Thierw. 1829, 66.
Harelda glacialis, "LEACH."—STEPH., Gen. Zool. xii, pt. ii, 1824, 175, pl. 58.—SW. & RICH., F. B. A. ii, 1831, 460.—JEN., Man. 1835, 247.—EYT., Mon. 1838, 162.—SW., Classif. B. ii, 1837, 369.—BP., List, 1838, 59.—KEYS. & BLAS., Wirb. Eur. 1844, 87.—GRAY, List B. Br. Mus. 1844, 145 ; Gen. of B. iii, 1849, 622 ; List Br. B. 1863, 203.—REICH., Syst. Av. viii, 1852.—BP., Comp. Rend. 1856.—NEWB., P. R. R. Rep. vi, 1857, 104.—BD., B. N. A. 1858, 800.—MURR., Edinb. N. Phil. Journ. 1859, 230.—COOP. & SUCK., N. H. Wash. Ter. 1860, 261.—REINH., Ibis, iii, 1831, 14.—ROSS, Canad. Nat. Apr. 1862.—VERR., Pr. Ess. Inst. iii, 1862, 153.—BOARDM., Pr. Bost. Soc. ix, 1862, 139.—BLAK., Ibis, 1863, 149.—NEWT., Ibis, 1865, 515.—DEGL.-GERBE, Orn. Eur. 1867, 549.—COUES, Pr. Ess. Inst. v, 1868, 206.—CARUS, Hand-buch Zool. i, 1868, 352.—BROWN, Ibis, 1868, 426.—DALL & BANN., Tr. Chic. Acad. i, 1869, 298.—FINSCH, Abh. Nat. iii, 1872, 67.—COUES, Key, 1872, 291.—RIDGW., Ann. Lyc. x, 1874, 390 (Lake Michigan).
Fuligula (Clangula) glacialis, BP., Syn. 1828, 395.
Fuligula (Harelda) glacialis, NUTT., Man. ii, 453.—BRANDT, M. Ac. St. Petersb. vi, 1849, 8.
Fuligula glacialis, AUD., Orn Biog. iv, 1838, 403, pl. 312 ; Syn. 1839, 295 ; B. Am. vi, 1843, 379, pl. 410.—SELYS-L., Fn. Belg. i, 1842, 146.—DEKAY, N. Y. Zool. 1844, 328.—GIR., B. L. I. 1844, 337.—DEGL., Orn. Eur. ii, 1849, 447.—SCHL., Mus. Pays-Bas, viii, 1865, 23.
Crymonessa glacialis, MACGIL., Man. Orn. ii, 1842, 186.
Anas hyemalis, LINN., Fn. Suec. 44.—SCOP., Bemerk. 1770, 66.—GM., Syst. Nat. i, 1788, 529.
Clangula hiemalis, BREHM, Vög. Deutschl. 933.
Anas miclonia, BODD. (*Gray.*)
Anas leucocephalus, BECHST. (*Gray.*)
Anas brachyrhynchus, BESEKE. (*Gray.*)
Clangula faberi, megauros, musica, brachyrhynchas, BREHM, V. D. 935, 936, 937, 938.

Hab.—Northern Hemisphere. Chiefly maritime. Also on the Great Lakes.

CAMPTOLÆMUS LABRADORIUS, (*Gmelin*) *Gray.*

Anas labradora, GM., Syst. Nat. i, 1788, 587.—LATH., Ind. Orn, ii, 1790, 859.—WILS., Am. Orn. viii, 1814, 91, pl. 69.—VIEILL., N. D. v, 1816, 132 ; Enc. Meth. i, 1823, 132.
Anas (Fuligula) labradora, BP., Obs. Wils. 1835, No. 276.
Fuligula labradora, BP., Syn. 1828, 391.—NUTT., Man. ii, 1834, 428.—AUD., Orn. Biog. iv, 1838, 271, pl. 332 ; Syn. 1839, 288 ; B. Am. vi, 1843, 329, pl. 400.—DEKAY, N. Y. Zool. ii, 1844, 326.—GIR., B. L. I. 1844, 337.—SCHL., Mus. P.-Bas, viii, 1865, 19.
Rhynchaspis labradora, STEPH., Gen. Zool. xii, pt. ii, 1824, 121.
Kamptorhynchus labradorius, EYT., Monog. 1838, 151.—BP., List, 1838, 58.
Camptolæmus labradorius, GRAY, List Gen. of B. 1840 ; List B. Br. Mus. 1844, 141 ; Gen. of B. iii, 1849, 623.—REICH., Syst. Av. 1852, 8.—BP., Compt. Rend. Sept. 1856,

651.—BD., B. N. A. 1858, 803.—COUES, Pr. A. N. S. Phil. 1861, 239.—VERR., Pr. Ess. Inst. iii, 1862, 158.—COUES, *ibid.* v, 1868, 200.—TURNB., B. E. Pa. 1869, 37 (rare).—COUES, Key, 1872, 291.

Hab.—Northeastern coast of North America, rarely south to New Jersey.

SOMATERIA STELLERI, *(Pall.) Jard.*

Anas stelleri, PALL., Spic. Zool. vi, 1765, 35, pl. 5 ; Zoog. R.-A. ii, 1811, 208.—GM., Syst. Nat. i, 1788, 518.—SCHL., Rev. Crit. 1844, 116.—SWINH., P. Z. S. 1863, 324 (China).
Clangula stelleri, BOIE, Isis, 1822, 564.—MACGIL., Man. Orn. ii, 1842, 183.
Fuligula (Clangula) stelleri, BP., Syn. 1828, 394.
Fuligula (Macropus) stelleri, NUTT., Man. ii, 1834, 451.
Fuligula (Polysticta) stelleri, BRANDT, Mem. Acad. St. Petersb. vi, 1849, 7.
Fuligula stelleri, DEGL., Orn. Eur. ii, 1869, 469.
Polysticta stelleri, EYT., Cat. Br. B. 58 ; Mon. Anat. 1838, 150.—BD., B. N. A. 1858, 801.— DALL & BANN., Tr. Chic. Acad. i, 1869, 299.
Eniconetta stelleri, GRAY, List Gen. of B. 1840, 95 ; Gen. of B. iii, 1849, 624 ; List Br. B. 1863, 204.—DEGL.-GERBE, Orn. Eur. ii, 1867, 553.
Heniconetta stelleri, AG., Ind. Univ. 1846, 178.
Harelda stelleri, KEYS. & BLAS., Wirb. Eur. 1840, 87.
Somateria stelleri, JARD., Br. B. iv, 173.—NEWT., P. Z. S. 1861, 400 (eggs).—DRESS., B. Eur. pt. —, pl. —.—COUES, Key, 1872, 291 ; Elliott's Prybilov Islands, App. —.
Anas dispar, SPARRM., Mus. Carls. 1786, pls. 7, 8.—GM., Syst. Nat. i, 1788, 535.—LATH., Ind. Orn. ii, 1790, 866.—VIEILL., Enc. Meth. i, 1823, 145.—TEMM., Man. iv, 1840, 547.—NAUM., V. D. xii, 1844, 240, pl. 320.
Fuligula dispar, STEPH., Gen. Zool. xii, pt. ii, 1824, 206.—JEN., Man. 1835, 243.—AUD., Orn. Biog. v, 1839, 253, pl. 430 ; Syn. 1839, 293 ; B. Am. vi, 1843, 368, pl. 407.— DEKAY, N. Y. Zool. ii, 1844, 334.—SCHL., Mus. Pays-Bas, viii, 1865, 15.
Stelleria dispar, BP., List, 1838, 57 ; Compt. Rend. Sept. 1856, 650.
Anas occidua, SHAW, Nat. Misc. pl. 34.—VIEILL., Enc. Meth. i, 1823, 130.
(?) *Anas beringii,* GM., Syst. Nat. i, 1788, 508.

Hab.—Arctic and high northern coasts of both hemispheres.

SOMATERIA FISCHERI, *(Brandt) Coues.*

Fuligula (Lampronetta) fischeri, BRANDT, Mem. Ac. St. Peter. vi, 1849, 6, 10, 14, pl. 1, f. 1-4.
Lampronetta fischeri, BD., B. N. A. 1858, 803.—ELLIOT, B. N. A. pt. v, pl. 47.—DALL & BANN., Tr. Chic. Acad. i, 1869, 299.
Arctonetta fischeri, GRAY, P. Z. S. 1855, 212, pl. 108.
Somateria fischeri, COUES, Key, 1872, 292.

Hab.—Northwest coast.

SOMATERIA MOLLISSIMA var.(?) DRESSERI, *Sharpe.*

a.(?) *mollissima.*

Anas mollissima, LINN., Syst. Nat. i, 1766, 198.—GM., Syst. Nat. i, 1788, 514.—LATH., Ind. Orn. ii, 1790, 845.—LICHT., Verz. 1823, 85.—VIEILL., Nouv. Dict. d'Hist. Nat. v, 1816, 112.—TEMM., Man. 1815, 549 ; ii, 1835, 848 ; iv, 1840, 541.—NAUM., V. D. xii, 1844, 252, pls. 321, 322.—SCHL., Ois. Eur. Rev. Crit 1844, 116.
Somateria mollissima, BOIE, Isis, 1822, 564.—STEPH., Gen. Zool. xii, pt. ii, 1824, 224, pl. 60.—JEN., Man. 1835, 227.—Sw., Classif. B. ii, 1837, 368.—BP., List, 1838, 57 ; Comptes Rend. 1856.—MACGIL., Man. ii, 1842, 177.—GRAY, Cat. B. Br. Mus. 1844, 141 ; Gen. of B. iii, 1849, 624 ; List Br. B. 1863, 205.—REICH., Syst. Av. 1852, viii.—(?) MALMG., J. f. O. 1865, 214.—NEWT., Ibis, 1865, 515.—DEGL.-GERBE, Orn. Eur. ii, 1867, 555 ; and of authors generally.
Anser mollissimus, VIEILL., Ency. Meth. i, 1823, 119.
Platypus mollissimus, BREHM, Eur. Vög. 1823, 809.
Fuligula mollissima, SELYS-L., Fn. Belg. i, 1842, 143.—DEGL., Orn. Eur. ii, 1849, 463.— SCHL., Mus. P.-B. viii, 1865, 14.
Anas cuthberti, PALL., Zoog. R.-A. ii, 1811, 235.
Somateria st. cuthberti, EYT., Cat. Br. B. 58 ; Mon. Anat. 1838, 149.
Anser lanuginosus, LEACH, Cat. 1816, 37. (*Gray.*)
(?) *Somateria thulensis,* MALMG., Kongl. Vet. Ak. Ofv. 1864, 380 ; J. f. O. 1865, 396 (Spitzbergen).
Somateria danica, norwegica, platyuros, faroensis, megauros, islandica, borealis, lcisleri, planifrons, BREHM, V. D. 890, 891, 892, 893, 894, 895, 896, 897.

b.(?) *dresseri.*

Anas mollissima, WILS., Am. Orn. viii, 1814, 122, pl. 71.
Anas (Fuligula) mollissima, BP., Obs. Wils. 1825, No. 244.
Fuligula (Somateria) mollissima, BP., Syn. 1828, 388.—NUTT., Man. ii, 1834, 407.—BRANDT, Mem. Acad. St. Petersb. vi, 1849, 5.
Fuligula mollissima, AUD., Orn. Biog. iii, 1835, 344 ; v, 1839, 611 ; pl. 246 ; Syn. 1839, 291 ; B. Am. vi, 1843, 349, pl. 405.—DEKAY, N. Y. Zool. ii, 1844, 332.—GIR., B. L. I. 331.

Somateria mollissima, BP., List, 1838, 57.—BD., B. N. A. 1858, 809.—REIN., Ibis, iii, 14.—
COUES, Pr. Phila. Acad. 1861, 239.—BRY., Pr. Bost. Soc. viii, 1861, 66.— BOARDM.,
Pr. Bost. Soc. ix, 1862, 139.—VERR., Pr. Ess. Inst. iii, 1862, 159.—COUES, *ibid.*
v, 1868, 200.—BLAK., Ibis, 1863, 150.—LAWR., Ann. Lyc. N. Y. viii, 1866, 297.—
TURNB., B. E. Pa. 1869, 46 (New Jersey).—COUES, Key, 1872, 293.
Somateria dresseri, SHARPE, Ann. Mag. N. H. July, 1871, p. —, figs. 1, 2.

    Hab.—Atlantic and Arctic coasts.

SOMATERIA V-NIGRA, *Gray.*
Somateria v-nigra, GRAY, P. Z. S. 1855, 212, pl. 107.—BP., Comptes Rend. 1856, 650.—BD.,
B. N. A. 1858, 810.—MUR., Edinb. N. Phil. Journ. 1859, 229.—Ross, Canadian
Nat. Apr. 1862.—BLAK., Ibis, 1863, 150.—ELLIOT, B. N. A. pl. 48.—DALL & BANN.,
Tr. Chic. Acad. i, 1869, 300.—COUES, Key, 1872, 293.

    Hab.—Northwest coast. Great Slave Lake.

SOMATERIA SPECTABILIS, (*Linn.*) *Boie.*
Anas spectabilis, LINN., Fn. Suec. 39 ; Syst. Nat. i, 1766, 195.—GM., Syst. Nat. i, 1788,
507.—LATH., Ind. Orn. ii, 1790, 845.—PALL., Zoog. R.-A. ii, 1811, 236.—VIEILL.,
Ency. Meth. i, 1823, 125.—TEMM., Man. ii, 1835, 851 ; iv, 1840, 541.—NAUM., V.
D. xii, 1844, 285, pl. 322, f. 1 ; pl. 323.—SCHL., Rev. Crit. Ois. Eur. 1844, 115.—
SWINH., P. Z. S. 1863, 324 (China).
Somateria spectabilis, BOIE, Isis, 1822, 564 ; 1826, 980.—STEPH., Gen. Zool. xii, pt. ii, 1824,
229.—SW. & RICH., F. B. A. ii, 1831, 447.—JEN., Man. 1835, 238.—SW., Classif.
B. ii, 1837, 368.—EYT., Mon. Anat. 1838, 148.—BP., List, 1838, 57 ; Compt. Rend.
1856.—KEYS. & BLAS., Wirb. Eur. 1840, 86.—MACGIL., Man. ii, 1842, 178.—
GRAY, List B. Br. Mus. 1844, 141 ; Gen. of B. iii, 1849, 624 ; List Br. B. 1863,
206.—BD., B. N. A. 1858, 810.—REINH., Ibis, iii, 1861, 14.—VERR., Pr. Ess. Inst.
iii, 1862, 159.—BOARDM., Pr. Bost. Soc. ix, 1862, 140.—BLAK., Ibis, 1863, 150.—
NEWT., Ibis, 1865, 516 (Spitzbergen).—DEGL.-GERBE, Orn. Eur. ii, 1867, 557.—
COUES, Pr. Ess. Inst. v, 1868, 201.—LAWR., Ann. Lyc. N. Y. viii, 1866, 298.—
DALL & BANN., Tr. Chic. Acad. i, 1869, 301.—TURNB., B. E. Pa. 1869, 46 (New
Jersey, in severe winters).—WHEAT., Ohio Agric. Rep. 1860, No. 259 (Lake
Erie!)—HARTING, P. Z. S. 1871, 118 (figs. of heads).—COUES, Key, 1872, 293.
Platypus spectabilis, BREHM, Eur. Vög. 1823, 809.
Fuligula (Somateria) spectabilis, BP., Syn. 1828, 389.—NUTT., Man. ii, 1834, 414.—BRANDT,
Mem. Acad. St. Petersb. vi, 1849, 5.
Fuligula spectabilis, AUD., Orn. Biog. iii. 1835, 523, pl. 276 ; Syn. 1839, 291 ; B. Am. vi,
1843, 347, pl. 404.—SELYS-L., Fn. Belg. i, 1842, 143.—DEKAY, N. Y. Zool. 1844,
334.—GIR., B. L. I. 1844, 333.—SCHL., Mus. P.-B. viii, 1865, 13.—DEGL., Orn.
Eur. ii, 1849, 466.

    Hab.—Northern North America and Europe. Chiefly coastwise. South to New Jer-
sey. In the interior to Lake Erie.

ŒDEMIA AMERICANA, (*Wils.*) *Sw.*
Anas nigra, WILS., Am. Orn. viii, 1814, 135, pl. 72 (not of *Linnæus*).
Anas (Fuligula) nigra, BP., Obs. Wils. 1825, No. 267.
Fuligula (Oidemia) nigra, BP., Syn. 1828, 390.
Œdemia nigra var. *americana*, RIDGW., Ann. Lyc. N. Y. x, 1874, 390 (Lake Michigan).
Oidemia americana, SW. & RICH., F. B. A. ii, 1831, 450 —BP., List, 1838, 53 ; Compt. Rend.
Sept. 1856, 650.—GRAY, List B. Br. Mus. 1844, 140 ; Gen. of B. iii, 1849, 625.—
NEWB., P. R. R. Rep. vi, 1857, 104.—BD., B. N. A. 1858, 807.—MUR., Edinb.
N. Phil. Journ. 1859, 231.—COOP. & SUCK., N. H. Wash. Ter. 1860, 263.—VERR.,
Pr. Ess. Inst. iii, 1862, 159.—BLAK., Ibis, 1863, 149.—? SWINH., P. Z. S. 1863,
324.—COUES, Pr. Ess. Inst. v, 1868, 201 ; Pr. Bost. Soc. xii, 1868, 125 ; Pr. Phila.
Acad. 1871, 27.—TURNB., B. E. Pa. 1869, 37.—LAWR., Ann. Lyc. N. Y. viii, 1866,
297.—BROWN, Ibis, 1868, 426.—FINSCH, Abh. Nat. iii, 1872, 68.—COUES, Key, 1872, 293.
Fuligula (Oidemia) americana, NUTT., Man. ii, 1834, 422.
Melanitta americana, EYT., Mon. Anat. 1838, 144.
Fuligula americana, AUD., Orn. Biog. v, 1839, 117, pl. 408 ; Syn. 1839, 290 ; B. Am. vi,
1843, 343, pl. 403.—DEKAY, N. Y. Zool. ii, 1844, 336.—GIR., B. L. I. 1844, 330.—
SCHL., Mus. P.-B. viii, 1865, 19.

    Hab.—North America, both coasts, and larger inland waters.

ŒDEMIA FUSCA, (var?).

a.(?) *fusca.*

Anas fusca, LINN., Fn. Suec. 39 ; Syst. Nat. i, 1766, 196.—GM., Syst. Nat. i, 1788, 507.—
LATH., Ind. Orn. ii, 1790, 848.—TEMM., Man. 1815, 552.—SCHL., Rev. Crit. 1844,
117.—NAUM., V. D. xii, 1844, 123, pl. 313.
Melanitta fusca, BOIE, Isis, 1822, 564.—BREHM, V. D. 905.

Oidemia fusca, FLEM., Phil. of Zool. ii, 1823, 260.—STEPH., Gen. Zool. xii, pt. ii, 216.—
     FLEM., Br. An. 1828, 119.—JEN., Man. 1835, 239.—BP., List, 1838, 57.—EYT.,
     Cat. Br. B. 58.—KEYS. & BLAS., Wirb. Eur. 1840, 86.—MACGIL., Man. ii, 1842,
     180.—GRAY, Gen. of B. iii, 1849, 625 ; List Br. B. 1863, 206.
Anas fuliginosa, BECHST., Naturg. iv, 962, pl. 36.
Anas carbo, PALL., Zoog. R.-A. ii, 1811, 244.
Melanitta hornschuchii, megapus, platyrhynchus, BREHM, V. D. 904, 906, 907.

b.(?) *velvetina.*

Anas fusca, WILS., Am. Orn. viii, 1814, 137, pl. 72.
Anas (Fuligula) fusca, BP., Obs. Wils. 1825, No. 266.
Fuligula (Oidemia) fusca, BP., Syn. 1828, 390.—NUTT., Man. ii, 1834, 419.
Oidemia fusca, SW. & RICH., ii, 1831, 449.—TURNB. B. E. Pa. 1869, 37.—COUES, Key, 294.
Fuligula fusca, AUD., Orn. Biog. iii, 1835, 454, pl. 247 ; Syn. 1839, 280 ; B. Am. vi, 1843,
     332, pl. 401.—DEKAY, N. Y. Zool. ii, 1844, —.—GIR., B. L. I. 1844, 328.
Fuligula bimaculata, HERBERT, Field Sports, 2d ed. ii, 1848, 366, fig. — (immature).
Oidemia (Pelionetta) bimaculata, BD., B. N. A. 1858, 808.
Oidemia velvetina, CASS., Pr. Phila. Acad. v, 1850, 126.—FINSCH, Abh. Nat. iii, 1872, 68.
Melanetta velvetina, BD., B. N. A. 1858, 805.—COOP. & SUCK., N. H. Wash. Ter. 1860,
     262.—COUES, Pr. Phila. Acad. 1861, 239.—WHEAT., Ohio Agric. Rep. 1860, No.
     258 (Lake Erie).—VERR., Pr. Ess. Inst. iii, 1862, 153.—BOARDM., Pr. Bost. Soc.
     ix, 1862, 130.—LAWR., Ann. Lyc. N. Y. viii, 1866, 297.—COUES, Pr. Ess. Inst. v,
     1868, 200.—COUES, Pr. Bost. Soc. xii, 1868, 125.—DALL & BANN., Tr. Chic. Acad.
     1869, 300.—RIDGW., Ann. Lyc. N. Y. x, 1874, 390 (Lake Michigan).
Oidemia deglandii, BP., Rev. Crit. Degland, 1850, 108 ; Compt. Rend. 1854.
Melanetta deglandii, BP., Compt. Rend. Sept. 1856.

Hab.—Europe and America, chiefly maritime, but also on the inland waters. The
assigned characters of the American bird are very slight, certainly not warranting specific distinction, and scarcely affording grounds for varietal recognition.

ŒDEMIA PERSPICILLATA, *(Linn.) Steph.*

a. *perspicillata.*

Anas perspicillata, LINN., Syst. Nat. i, 1766, 201.—FORST., Phil. Trans. lxii, 1772, 417.—
     GM., Syst. Nat. i, 1788, 524.—LATH., Ind. Orn. ii, 1790, 847.—WILS., Am. Orn.
     viii, 1814, 49, pl. 67.—TEMM., Man. Orn. ii, 1835, 853; iv, 1840, 542.—VIEILL.,
     Ency. Meth. i, 1823, 138.—NAUM., V. D. xii, 1844, 140, pl. 314.—SCHL., Rev. Crit.
     Ois. Eur. 1844, 117.
Anas (Fuligula) perspicillata, BP., Obs. Wils. 1825, No. 265.
Anas (Macrorhamphus) perspicillata, LESS., Man. ii, 1828, 414.
Fuligula (Oidemia) perspicillata, BP., Syn. 1828, 389.—NUTT., Man. ii, 1834, 416.
Melanitta perspicillata, BOIE, Isis, 1822, 564.—EYT., Mon. Anat. 1838, 146.
Platypus perspicillatus, BREHM, Eur. Vög. 1823, 823.
Oidemia perspicillata, STEPH., Gen. Zool. xii, pt. ii, 1824, 219.—FLEM., Br. An. 1828,
     119.—SW. & RICH., F. B. A. ii, 1831, 449.—JEN., Man. 1835, 240.—SW., Classif.
     B. ii, 1837, 368.—BP., List, 1838, 57.—KEYS. & BLAS., Wirb. Eur. 1840, 86.—
     MACGIL., Man. ii, 1842, 181.—GRAY, List B. Br. Mus. 1844, 141 ; Gen. of B. iii,
     1849, 625 ; List Br. B. 1863, 207.—GOSSE, B. Jam. 1847, 408.—NEWB., P. R. R.
     Rep. vi, 1857, 104.—CASS., Orn. U. S. Expl. Exp. 1858, 344.—MURR., Edinb. N.
     Phil. Journ. 1859, 230.—REINH., Ibis, 1861, 14.—DEGL.-GERBE, Orn. Eur. 1867,
     563.—TURNB., B. E. Pa. 1869, 37.—NEWT., P. Z. S. 1867, 167 (egg).—COUES,
     Pr. Phila. Acad. 1871, 27.—HART., Br. B. 1872, 162 (Great Britain, many in-
     stances).—COUES, Key, 1872, 294.
Pelionetta perspicillata, KAUP, Sk. Ent. Eur. Thierw. 1829, 107.—REICH., Syst. Av. 1852,
     x.—BP., Compt. Rend. Sept. 1856.—BD., B. N. A. 1858, 806.—COOP. & SUCK., N.
     H. Wash. Ter. 1860, 262.—COUES, Pr. Phila. Acad. 1861, 239 ; Pr. Ess. Inst. v,
     1868, 200 ; Pr. Bost. Soc. xii, 1868, 125.—Ross, Canad. Nat. 1862.—VERR., Pr.
     Ess. Inst. iii, 1862, 153.—BOARDM., Pr. Bost. Soc. ix, 1862, 130.—BLAK., Ibis,
     1863, 149.—LAWR., Ann. Lyc. N. Y. viii, 1866, 297.—BROWN, Ibis, 1868, 426.—
     DALL & BANN., Tr. Chic. Acad. i, 1869, 300.
Fuligula perspicillata, AUD., Orn. Biog. iv, 1838, 161, pl. 317 ; Syn. 1839, 289 ; B. Am. vi,
     1843, 337, pl. 402.—SELYS-L., Fn. Belg. i, 1842, 143.—DEKAY, N. Y. Zool. ii, 1844,
     335.—GIR., B. L. I. 1844, 329.—DEGL., Orn. Eur. ii, 1849, 474.

b. *trowbridgei.*

Pelionetta trowbridgii, BD., B. N. A. 1858, 806.—ELLIOT, B. N. A. pl. —.
Œdemia perspicillata var. *trowbridgei*, COUES, Key, 1872, 295.

Hab.—North America, coastwise. Jamaica. Europe, rare : GOULD, B. Eur. pl. 377 ;
RODD, Zool. 1865, p. 9794. Var. *trowbridgei* on the coast of California.

ERISMATURA RUBIDA, (Wils.) Bp.

Ruddy Duck.

Anas rubida, WILS., Am. Orn. viii, 1814, 128, 130, pl. 71, f. 5, 6.—SAB., Frankl. Journ. 700.
Anas (Fuligula) rubida, BP., Obs. Wils. 1825, No. 268.
Fuligula (Oxyura) rubida, BP., Syn. 1828, 390.
Fuligula (Gymnura) rubida, NUTT., Man. ii, 1834, 426.
Fuligula rubida, SW. & RICH., F. B. A. ii, 1831, 455.—AUD., Orn. Biog. iv, 1838, 326; pl.
    343; Syn. 1839, 288; B. Am. vi, 1843, 324, pl. 399.—GIR., B. L. I. 1844, 326.—
    DEKAY, N. Y. Zool. ii, 1844, 327.—LEMB., Av. Cub. 1850, 118.
Cerconectes rubida, WAGL., Isis, 1832, 282.
Erismatura rubida, BP., List, 1838, 59; Compt. Rend. Sept. 1856, 652.—EYT., Mon. Anat.
    1838, 171.—GRAY, List B. Br. Mus. 1844, 146; Gen. of B. iii, 1849, 627.—BD., B.
    N. A. 1858, 811.—SCL., P. Z.·S. 1859, 393 (Oaxaca); Ibis, i, 1859, 232 (Guate-
    mala, breeding).—HEERM., P. R, R. Rep. x, 1859, pt. vi, 70 (California).—Ross,
    Canad. Nat. 1862.—HAYD., Rep. 1862, 176.—BLAK., Ibis, 1862, 150.—VERR., Pr.
    Ess. Inst. iii, 1862, 159.—COUES, *ibid.* v, 1868, 201.—GUNDL., Av. Cuba, 1866,
    390.—STEV., U. S. Geol. Surv. Ter. 1870, 466.—COUES, Key, 1872, 295; Am. Nat.
    viii, 1874, p. —.
Biziura rubida, SCHL., Mus. P.-B. viii, 1865, 11.—GIEBEL, Nomencl. Av. i, 1872, p. —.
Anas jamaicensis, ORD, ed. Wils. viii, 1825, 138.
*Erismatura "dominica"** (err.), HOLDEN, Pr. Bost. Soc. xv, 1872, 210.

Hab.—North America at large. South to Guatemala, where found breeding at Due-
ñas. Cuba (CAB., J. f. O. v, 1857, 230).
Lieutenant Warren's Expedition.—5472, Mouth of the Platte.
Later Expeditions.—60862, Pacific Creek, Wyoming.

This species occurs throughout the Missouri region in suitable situations, during the migrations, and also breeds within such limits. I
found it nesting in numbers in the pools about Turtle Mountain, Dakota, where the young were swimming in July. It was also observed
during the breeding season in Montana, along the Milk River and its
northern tributaries.

Subfamily MERGINÆ: *Mergansers.*

MERGUS MERGANSER, Linn.

Merganser; Goosander; Sheldrake; Fishing Duck.

Mergus merganser, LINN., Syst. Nat. i, 1766, 208.—GM., Syst. Nat. i, 1788, 544.—LATH.,
    Ind. Orn. ii, 1790, 828.—WILS., Am. Orn. viii, 1814, 68, pl. 68.—TEMM., Man.
    1820, 575.—BP., Obs. Wils. 1825, No. 248; Syn. 1828, 397.—DOUGHTY, Cab. N.
    H. i, 1830, 109, pl. 10.—FLEM., Br. An. 128.—JEN., Man. 249.—SW. & RICH., F.
    B. A. ii, 1831, 461.—NUTT., Man. ii, 1834, 461.—AUD., Orn. Biog. iv, 1838, 261,
    pl. 331; Syn. 1839, 297; B. Am. vi, 1843, 387, pl. 411.—GIR., B. L. I. 1844, 339.—
    NAUM., V. D. xii, 1844, 356, pl. 326.—SCHL., Rev. Crit. 121.—MAX., J. f. O. vii,
    1859, 241.—ALLEN, Bull. M. C. Z. iii, 1872, 183.—COUES, Key, 1872, 296; and of
    authors generally.

---

* The synonymy of *E. dominica* is as follows:
Anas dominica, LINN., Syst. Nat. i, 1766, 201.—GM., Syst. Nat. i, 1788, 521.—LATH., Ind.
    Orn. ii, 1790, 874.—VIEILL., Ency. Meth. i, 1823, 157.—MAXIM., Naturg. Bras.
    iv, pt. ii, 1833, 938.—BURM., Th. Bras. iii, 1856, 439.
Fuligula dominica, STEPH., Gen. Zool. xii, pt. ii, 1824, 203.
Erismatura dominica, EYT., Mon. Anat. 1838, —.—GRAY, Cat. B. Br. Mus. 1844, 146; Gen.
    of B. iii, 1849, 627.—BP., Compt. Rend. 1856, 652.—CAB., J. f. O. v, 1857, 231.—
    NEWT., Ibis, 1859, 367.—SCL., P. Z. S. 1860, 254.—GUNDL., Av. Cuba, 1866, 391.—
    REINH., Vid. Med. 1870, 20.—COUES, Key, 1872, 295.
Biziura dominica, SCHL., Mus. P.-B. viii, 1865, 9.
Anas spinosa, GM., Syst. Nat. i, 1788, 522.—LATH., Ind. Orn. ii, 1790, 874.—BURM., Th.
    Bras. iii, 1856, 440.
Cerconectes spinosa, WAGL., Isis, 1832, 282.
Erismatura spinosa, GOSSE, B. Jam. 1847, 404.
Erismatura ortygoides, GOSSE, B. Jam. 1847, 407.—BP., Compt. Rend. 1856, 652.

Hab.—West Indies and South America. Accidental in North America. (Lake Cham-
plain, CABOT, Pr. Bost. Soc. vi, 375, and Wisconsin, *ibid.* xiv, 154, and Am. Nat. v, 441.)

Mergus castor, LINN., Syst. Nat. i, 1766, 209.—GM., Syst. Nat. i, 1788, 545.—LATH., Ind.
    Orn. ii, 1790, 829.—KEYS. & BLAS., Wirb. Eur. 88.—GRAY, Gen. of B. iii, 629.
Merganser castor, BP., Comp. List, 1838, 59.—MACGIL., Man. Orn. ii, 194.
Merganser castor var. *americanus*, BP., Compt. Rend. xliii, 1856.
Merganser raii, LEACH, Syst. Cat. M. and B. Br. Mus. 36.
Merganser gulo, STEPH., Gen. Zool. xii, 161, pl. 53.—LEACH, *l. c.*
Mergus americanus, CASS., Pr. Phila. Acad. 1853, 187.—BD., B. N. A. 1858, 813.—COOP. &
    SUCK., N. H. Wash. Ter. 1860, 263.—HAYD., Rep. 1862, 176.—DRESS., Ibis, 1866,
    44 (Texas).—STEV., U. S. Geol. Surv. Ter. 1870, 466.—DALL, Pr. Cal. Acad. 1873
    (Aleutians).—DALL & BANN., Tr. Chic. Acad. i, 1869, 301 (Alaska).—FINSCH,
    Abh. Nat. iii, 1872, 70.—SNOW, B. Kans. 1873, 11 ; and of many late United
    States writers.

Hab.—North America. Europe. Asia.

List of specimens.

19322	293	Deer Creek	♂	May 3, 1860	G. H. Trook..	26.00	36.00	11.00
19323	....	.......do........	♀	May 18, 1860	..... do	26.50	37.00	11.50
19324	156	Powder River..	....	May 19, 1860	..... do	25.50	35.50	10.00
19325	177	.......do........	....	May 18, 1860	..... do	22.00	36.00	......
19326	170	......do........	....	Sept. 19, 1860	.... do	26.00	36.00	......
19327	171	..... do........	....	Sept. 19, 1860	..... do	......	......	......

Lieutenant Warren's Expedition.—No. 5473, Yellowstone River.
Later Expeditions.—60858-60, Fort Bridger and Sweetwater.

MERGUS SERRATOR, Linn.

Red-breasted Merganser; Fishing Duck.

Mergus serrator, LINN., Syst. Nat. i, 1766, 208.—GM., Syst. Nat. 1788, 546.—LATH., Ind.
    Orn. ii, 1790, 829.—PALL., Zoog. R.-A. ii, 1811, 287.—ILL., Prod. 1811, 278.—
    WILS., Am. Orn. viii, 1814, 81, pl. 69.—TEMM., Man. 1815, 579 ; ii, 1835, 884 ;
    iv, 1840, 556.—BOIE, Isis, 1822, 564.—LICHT., Verz. 1823, 85.—BREHM, Eur. Vög.
    1823, 855.—BP., Obs. Wils. 1825, No. 249 ; Syn. 1828, 397.—FLEM., Br. An. 1828,
    129.—SW. & RICH., F. B. A. ii, 1831, 462.—NUTT., Man. ii, 1834, 463.—JEN., Man.
    1835, 249.—EYT., Mon. *Anat.* 1838, 175.—AUD., Orn. Biog. v, 1839, 92, pl. 401 ;
    Syn. 1839, 298 ; B. Am. vi, 1843, 395, pl. 412.—KEYS. & BLAS., Wirb. Eur. 1840,
    88.—SELYS-L., Fn. Belg. i, 1842, 147.—MACGIL., Man. ii, 1842, 194.—NAUM., V.
    D. xii, 1844, 333, pl. 325.—GRAY, List B. Br. Mus. 1844, 147 ; Gen. of B. iii, 1849,
    629 ; List Br. B. 1863, 209.—DEKAY, N. Y. Zool. ii, 1844, 319.—GIR., B. L. I. 1844,
    342.—SCHL., Rev. Crit. 1844, 121 ; Mus. P.-B. viii, 1865, 3.—DEGL., Orn. Eur. ii,
    1849, 480.—REICH., Syst. Av. 1852, ix.—BP., Compt. Rend. Sept. 1856.—NEWB.,
    P. R. R. Rep. vi, 1857, 104.—BD., B. N. A. 1858, 814.—MURR., Edinb. N. Journ.
    1859, 231.—MAXIM., J. f. O. vii, 1859, 242.—COOP. & SUCK., N. H. Wash. Ter.
    1860, 264.—SWINH., Ibis, ii, 1860, 67 ; iii, 1861, 344 ; v, 1863, 434 ; P. Z. S. 1863,
    323.—REINH., Ibis, iii, 1861, 14.—COUES, Pr. Phila. Acad. 1861, 241 ; Pr. Bost.
    Soc. xii, 1868, 125 ; Pr. Ess. Inst. v, 1868, 201 ; Pr. Phila. Acad. 1871, 27 ; Key,
    1872, 296.—ROSS, Canad. Nat. Apr. 1862.—VERR., Pr. Ess. Inst. iii, 1862, 153.—
    BOARDM., Pr. Bost. Soc. ix, 1862, 140.—BLAK., Ibis, 1863, 150.—WRIGHT, Ibis,
    1864, 156.—DEGL.-GERBE, Orn. Eur. 1867, 570.—DALL & BANN., Tr. Chic. Acad.
    1869, 201.—TURNB., B. E. Pa. 1869, 37.—FINSCH, Abh. Nat. iii, 1872, 72.—SNOW,
    B. Kans. 1873, 11.
Merganser serrator, VIEILL., Ency. Meth. i, 1823, 102.—STEPH., Gen. Zool. xii, 1824, 165
    (" *serrata*").—BP., List, 1838, 59.
Mergus niger, GM., Syst. Nat. i, 1788, 546.
Mergus cristatus, BRÜNN., Orn. Bor. 1764, No. 95.
Mergus leucomelas, BREHM, V. D. 1831, 947.

Hab.—Northern hemisphere.

MERGUS CUCULLATUS, Linn.

Hooded Merganser.

Mergus cucullatus, LINN., Syst. Nat. i, 1766, 207.—GM., Syst. Nat. i, 1788, 544.—LATH.,
    Ind. Orn. ii, 1790, 830.—BP., Obs. Wils. 1825, No. 251 ; Syn. 1828, 397.—SW. &
    RICH., F. B. A. ii, 1831, 463.—NUTT., Man. ii, 1834, 465.—JEN., Man. 1835, 249.—

AUD., Orn. Biog. iii, 1835, 246, pl. 233; Syn. 1839, 299; B. Am. vi, 1843, 402, pl.
413.—EYT., Mon. *Anat.* 1838, 177.—KEYS. & BLAS., Wirb. Eur. 1840, 88.—TEMM.,
Man. iv, 1840, 557.—GRAY, List B. Br. Mus. 1844, 147; Gen. of B. iii, 1849, 629;
List Br. B. 1863, 209.—SCHL., Rev. Crit. 1844, 121; Mus. P.-B. viii, 1865, 5.—
DEKAY, N. Y. Zool. ii, 1844, 320.—GIR., B. L. I. 1844, 341.—DEGL., Orn. Eur. ii,
1849, 483.—NEWB., P. R. R. Rep. vi, 1857, 104.—CASS., U. S. Expl. Exp. 1858,
345.—MURR., Edinb. N. Phil. Journ. 1859, 231.—SCL., P. Z. S. 1859, 237.—DEGL.-
GERBE, Orn. Eur. ii, 1867, 572.—COUES, Key, 1872, 296.
Merganser cucullatus, STEPH., Gen. Zool. xii, pt. ii, 1824, 168.—BP., List, 1838, 59.—
MACGIL., Man. Orn. ii, 1842, 196.
Lophodytes cucullatus, REICH., Syst. Av. 1852, ix.—BP., Comptes Rend. xliii, 1856.—
BD., B. N. A. 1858, 816.—SCL., P. Z. S. 1859, 369.—COOP. & SUCK., N. H. Wash.
Ter. 1860, 265.—HAYD., Rep. 1862, 176.—VERR., Pr. Ess. Inst. iii, 1862, 159.—
COUES, *ibid.* v, 1868, 201.—GUNDL., Av. Cuba, 1866, 391.—DRESS., Ibis, 1866,
144.—DALL & BANN., Tr. Chic. Acad. i, 1869, 202.—STEV., U. S. Geol. Surv.
Ter. 1870, 466.—SNOW, B. Kans. 1873, 12.—ALLEN, Bull. M. C. Z. iii, 1872, 183;
and of many writers.

Hab.—The whole of North America. Europe: for occurrences, see authors above
quoted. Cuba (CAB., J. f. O. v, 1857, 231).
Lieutenant Warren's Expedition.—5475, Yellowstone River.
Later Expeditions.—60861, Green River.

The Hooded Merganser is the most abundant one of the three in the
Missouri region. *M. serrator* is the rarest; I have not myself met with
it. *M. cucullatus* breeds in Northern Dakota, and also on the Upper
Missouri and Milk Rivers.

ORDER STEGANOPODES: TOTIPALMATE BIRDS.

Family PELECANIDÆ: Pelicans.

PELECANUS TRACHYRHYNCHUS, Lath.

White Pelican.

Pelecanus erythrorhynchus, GM., Syst. Nat. i, 1788, 571.—DONND., Beytr. Orn. ii, 850.—
BONN., Ency. Meth. 1791, 44.—SCHL., Mus. P.-B. livr. iv, 35.—BD., B. N. A. 1858,
868.—COOP. & SUCK., N. H. Wash. Ter. 1860, 265.—WHEAT., Ohio Agric. Rep.
1860, No. 278 (rare).—ELLIOT, P. Z. S. 1869, 588 (monographic).—COUES, Ibis,
1866, 271 (coast of California).—DRESS., Ibis, 1866, 45 (Texas, in winter, common).—COUES, Pr. Phila. Acad. 1866, 100 (Arizona).—BOARDM., Pr. Bost. Soc.
ix, 1862, 130 (Calais, Maine, accidental).—VERR., Pr. Ess. Inst. iii, 1862, 160
(same).—ALLEN, *ibid.* iv, 1864, 89 (same).—COUES, *ibid.* v, 1868, 302 (same).—
MCILWR., *ibid.* v, 1866, 95 (Canada West, two instances).—ALLEN, Bull. M. C.
Z. ii, 1871, 364 (Florida, winter, common, and said to breed); iii, 1872, 183
(Utah).—COUES, Pr. Bost. Soc. xii, 1868, 125 (South Carolina).—TURNB., B. E.
Pa. 1869, 46 (rare).—LAWR., Ann. Lyc. N. Y. viii, 1866, 298 (New York).—
TRIPPE, Pr. Bost. Soc. xv, 1872, 241 (Iowa).—GILMAN, Am. Nat. iv, 1871, 758
(Lake Huron).—? MAYN., Guide, 1870, 149 (Nantucket).—CLARKE, Am. Nat. v,
1871, 252 (Lake Michigan).—SNOW, B. Kans. 1873, 11.—RIDGW., Ann. Lyc. N.
Y. x, 1874, 390 (Illinois).
Pelecanus trachyrhynchus, LATH., Ind. Orn. ii, 1790, 884 (based on *Rough-billed Pelican* of
Gen. Syn. vi, 586).—STEPH., Shaw's G. Z. xiii, 1825, 117.—LICHT., Abb. Akad.
Berl. 1838, pl. 3, f. 5.—BP., List, 1838, 60.—GRAY, Gen. of B. iii, 1849, 309.—SCL.,
P. Z. S. 1868, 269; Ibis, i, 1859, 233 (Western Central America).—NEWB., P. R.
R. Rep. vi, 1857, 109.—HEERM., *ibid.* x, 1859, pt. vi, 72.—MAXIM., J. f. O. vii,
1859, 259.—BD., Stansbury's Rep. 1852, 324.—WOODH., Sitgr. Rep. 1853, 105.—
COUES, Key, 1872, 300.
Cyrtopelicanus trachyrhynchus, REICH.—BP., Consp. Av. ii, 1855, 163.
Pelecanus onocrotalus var., FORST., Phil. Trans. lxii, 1772.
Pelecanus onocrotalus, BP., Syn. 1828, 400.—SW. & RICH., F. B. A. ii, 1831, 472 (north to
61°).—NUTT., Man. ii, 1834, 471. (Not of European writers.)
Pelecanus americanus, AUD., Orn. Biog. iv, 1838, 88, pl. 311; Syn. 1839, 309; B. Am. vii,
1844, 20, pl. 422.—TRIPPE, Pr. Ess. Inst. vi, 1871, 119 (Minnesota, common, mi-
gratory).
" *Pelecanus brachydactylus*, LICHT. ?"
(?) *Pelecanus occipitalis*, RIDGW., "American Sportsman," iv, 1874, 297 (Nevada).

Hab.—North America, up to lat. 61° at least. Rare or casual in the Middle States
and New England. Abundant in the interior, especially west of the Mississippi. Texas
and Florida. South to Central America.

The geographical distribution of the White Pelican may be clearly
traced from the above quotations. Its occurrence in New England at
the present time is wholly fortuitous, though it has been observed in
Maine and Massachusetts. But Mr. Allen's record of a flock at Nantucket (*Am. Nat.* iii, 640) is erroneous, as he subsequently pointed out
(*ibid.* iv, 68), *P. fuscus* having been mistaken for it. It is of scarcely
oftener occurrence in the Middle States and most portions east of the
Mississippi, but is said to be common in Florida. In the West I have
found it in many localities—on the Red River of the North and some of
its affluents, on the Colorado of the West, and on the coast of Southern
California. It formerly bred in immense numbers about Great Salt
Lake, where it has decreased in abundance of late. Mr. Ridgway tells
me of vast bands now nesting about Pyramid Lake in Nevada, where
he took over a hundred eggs from as many nests; these were merely a

heap of eartn scraped up to the height of a few inches. He has also shown that the curious horny comb or crest of the bill, being deciduous, is regularly shed in a manner somewhat analogous to the casting of deers' horns. The breeding range of the species is very extensive, apparently determined less by latitude than by the occurrence of suitable places anywhere within the general range of the species. I have not noted any breeding resorts within the Missouri region, though doubtless there are such. The large numbers of Pelicans I observed, however, in Northern Dakota, at various times in the summer, leads me to presume that they nest in that region, especially about the Lake River, a short expansive affluent of the Mouse River, more like a great prairie slough than an ordinary river. In May, 1873, I took a female on the Red River, near Pembina; the specimen was in very poor flesh, with worn, harsh plumage, which was attributable to a disease of the pouch. On the inside of this organ were fastened in clusters great numbers of a louse-like parasite, which produced an induration, ulceration, and, finally, perforation of the membrane in several places, so that the bird must have had difficulty in feeding. The intestines were loaded with some kind of *ascarides*. In the stomach were found about fifty crawfish (*Astacus*).

Family PHALACROCORACIDÆ: Cormorants.

GRACULUS DILOPHUS, (Sw.) Gray.

Double-crested Cormorant; Shag.

a. *dilophus.*

Pelecanus (Carbo) dilophus, Sw. & Rich., F. B. A. ii, 1831, 473.
Carbo dilophus, Gamb., Journ. Phila. Acad, i, 1849, 227.
Phalacrocorax dilophus, Nutt., Man. ii, 1834, 483.—Bp., List, 1838, 60.—Aud., Orn. Biog.
    iii, 1835, 420; v, 1839, 629; pl. 257; Syn. 1839, 302; B. A. vi. 1844, 423, pl. 416.—
    Gir., B. L. I. 1844, 344.—Bd., Stansbury's Rep. 1852, 324 (Great Salt Lake).—
    Putn., Pr. Ess. Inst. i, 1856, 221.—Bry., Pr. Bost. Soc. viii, 1861, 71 (Gulf of
    Saint Lawrence, breeding).—Turnb., B. E. Pa. 1869, 38 (winter, rare).
Graculus dilophus, Gray, Gen. of B. iii, 1849, —.—Bp., Consp. Av. ii, 1855, 172; Compt.
    Rend. 1856, 766.—Bd., B. N. A. 1858, 877; Pr. Phila. Acad. Nov. 1859 (Cape
    Saint Lucas).—Coop. & Suck., N. H. Wash. Ter. 1860, 267.—Coues, Pr. Phila.
    Acad. 1861, 241 (Labrador); 1866, 100 (California); 1871, 38 (North Carolina,
    common in winter).—Boardm., Pr. Bost. Soc. ix, 1862, 130 (Maine, in winter).—
    Coues, *ibid.* xii, 1868, 126 (South Carolina, in winter).—Allen, Pr. Ess. Inst.
    iv, 1864, 89 (New England coast, in winter).—Verr., *ibid.* iii, 1862, 160 (the
    same).—Coues, *ibid.* v, 1868, 302 (the same).—Lawr., Ann. Lyc. N. Y. viii, 1866,
    298.—Dall & Bann., Tr. Chic. Acad. i, 1869, 302 (Alaska).—Allen, Bull. M. C.
    Z. iii, 1872, 183 (Great Salt Lake).—Snow, B. Kans. 1873, 11 (migratory).—
    Coues, Key, 1872, 303.—Ridgw., Ann. Lyc. N. Y. x, 1874, 390 (Illinois).
Phalacrocorax floridanus, Maxim., J. f. O. vii, 1859, 260 (Missouri).
Graculus floridanus, McIlwr., Pr. Ess. Inst. vi, 1871, 95 (Canada).

b. *floridanus.*

Phalacrocorax floridanus, Aud., Orn. Biog. iii, 1835, 387; v, 1839, 632; pl. 251; Syn. 1839,
    303; B. Am. vi, 1843, 430, pl. 417.
Graculus floridanus, Bp., Consp. Av. ii, 1855, 172; Compt. Rend. lxii, 1856, 766.—Lawr.,
    B. N. A. 1858, 879.—Bry., Pr. Bost. Soc. vii, 1859.—Schl., Mus. P.-B. livr. iv,
    1863, 23 (in part; includes *mexicanus* and " *townsendii*")—Allen, Bull. M. C. Z.
    ii, 1871, 365.—Coues, Pr. Phila. Acad. 1871, 38 (north to North Carolina).
Graculus dilophus, Gray, Gen. of B. iii (in part).
Graculus dilophus var. *floridanus,* Coues, Key, 1872, 303.—Ridgw., Ann. Lyc. N. Y. x,
    1874, 390 (Illinois).
Phalacrocorax brasiliensis, Bp., Comp. List, 1838, 60. (Whether of authors? If found

not specifically distinct from *dilophus*, the name will take priority for this species. Schlegel unites the two.)

Hab.—North America at large, in the interior as well as coastwise. Var. *floridanus* from the South Atlantic and Gulf States, ranging north to the Ohio (*Audubon*) and to North Carolina (*Coues*).

This is the only species of Cormorant known to range generally throughout the interior. Most of the several species attributed to North America occur on the Pacific coast alone, *G. carbo* being the Atlantic-coast species, and *G. mexicanus* being from the Gulf and someways up the Mississippi Valley.

I am credibly informed of breeding places of this species on the Missouri, where, however, I never recognized the bird myself, though I saw it on the Red River of the North in May. It was first described by Swainson from the Saskatchewan, and it ranges southward through the Missouri region. It has been found to breed in Labrador and the Gulf of Saint Lawrence, whence it migrates southward in the fall, wintering along the coast from Maine to the Carolinas. Its occurrence at Great Salt Lake and various points on the Pacific coast, from Sitka to Cape Saint Lucas, has been noted.

GRACULUS MEXICANUS, (Brandt) Bp.

Mexican Cormorant.

Carbo mexicanus, BRANDT, Bull. Sc. Acad. St. Petersb. iii, 1837, 56.
Graculus mexicanus, BP., Consp. Av. ii, 1855, 173.—LAWR., B. N. A. 1858, 879.—SNOW, B.
    Kans. 1873, 12 (specimen near Lawrence, Kansas, April, 1872.—COUES, Key, 203.
Graculus "floridanus et" mexicanus, SCHL., Mus. P.-B. livr. iv, 1863, 24 (excl. syn. "*town-
    sendii*, AUD.")
" *Carbo graculus, ex parte*, TEMM." (*Schlegel.*)
" *Phalacrocorax lacustris*, GUNDL., Mss." (*Lawrence.*)
" *Phalacrocorax resplendens* (*ad.*), et *townsendii* (*juv.*), LEMB., Aves de Cuba."

Hab.—Southern United States and southward. Up the Mississippi Valley to Illinois (*Ridgway*) and Kansas (*Snow*). Texas. New Mexico (*Henry*). Matamoras (*Dresser, Ibis*, 1866, 45). Honduras (*Taylor*, Ibis, 1860, 315). Cuba (*Lawrence, Gundlach, Lembeye*).

In my present judgment, this species is entirely distinct from *G. dilophus*, though nearly allied. Dr. Schlegel is certainly wrong in identifying it with the *P. floridanus* of Audubon, and in citing as synonymous *P. townsendii*; the latter belongs to *penicillatus*.

The claim of this species to a place in the present work rests upon the announcement of its occurrence in Kansas, by Prof. Snow, as above.

Of the five remaining families of North American birds (*Procellariidæ, Laridæ, Colymbidæ, Podicipidæ, Alcidæ*), the first and fifth are marine, and have no representatives in the Missouri region. They will, therefore, not be considered in this volume, my material on *Procellariidæ* and *Alcidæ* being reserved for elaboration in another connection. The other three families will here be treated monographically, to include all the known North American species, biographical items of those found in the Missouri region being added, in correspondence with the general plan of this work.

MONOGRAPH OF THE NORTH AMERICAN

LARIDÆ.

Several years have passed since the writer began to pay special attention to this interesting and difficult group. He has already published, in the Proceedings of the Philadelphia Academy of 1862–'63, revisions of the North American forms of the principal subfamilies, preliminary to the present more complete work. This memoir has lain in Mss. since 1864, being retouched from time to time, as additional material offered. Final revision has been made within the present year, bringing the subject up to date. Since the earlier papers were published, my views of what constitutes a species have been modified, while a few mistakes in those articles have been corrected; but I find comparatively little to alter. The article on *Laridæ*, in the "Key to North American Birds" (1872), expresses very nearly my present views, though one or two hasty steps in that portion of the work require to be retraced.

Containing the richest collection of American *Laridæ* in the world, the Smithsonian Museum offers great facilities for this study—facilities of which the liberality of the policy of the Institution has permitted me to fully avail myself. I have also examined the specimens in other of our large public collections, while many have been furnished me from private sources. For favors of this kind I am particularly indebted to my friend Mr. Lawrence. I have aimed to make the present article strong enough to bear the term "monograph." It embraces all the species known to occur in North America. These are treated in full, with frequent reference to extralimital allies. As will be observed, extensive synonymical lists have been prepared, embracing, it is believed, nearly all the names which have been proposed, with many additional references for geographical distribution, &c. Most of the quotations have been personally made or verified; in cases in which this was impracticable, the authority is generally added. No one need be reminded how difficult it is to get such lists of thousands of *figures* printed correctly, there being, of course, no guiding context for the compositor. I can only hope that, as elsewhere in this volume, references to dates, volumes, pages, and plates, will be found generally correct. Most points of synonymy are freely discussed, without the slightest personal bias. The matter of geographical distribution receives special attention. Seasonal changes of plumage, and those dependent on age—great in this family, and frequently perplexing—as well as individual variations in size and coloration, are given in full, so far as I am acquainted with them. The chief anatomical peculiarities of the subfamilies and leading genera are presented from original dissections.

A beautiful series of colored illustrations of the head, wing, and other characteristic parts, prepared for this memoir by a competent artist, will be presented in the concluding volume of Prof. Baird's work, now publishing, it being impracticable to print them here.

It is unnecessary to advert to various classifications of the *Laridine* birds which have been proposed and received more or less support. Authors differ even as to the limitations of the group, while no two are entirely in accord as to its subdivisions. Prof. Huxley unites the *Laridæ* and *Procellariidæ* with the *Alcidæ*, &c., in a group *Cecomorphæ*. Respecting the *Laridæ* alone, most authors make them a family with either two or four subfamilies. The genera which have been proposed are altogether too many. There are but four leading genera, corresponding to the four subfamilies; and but few others need or even permit recognition. I subdivided too much in my earlier papers, and now throw most of the so-called genera under *Larus* and *Sterna* respectively.

Disclaiming any desire to institute comparisons between this and other memoirs on the subject, a few leading ones may be noticed. One of the earliest special papers of any considerable merit, is Macgillivray's, in the Wernerian Society's Memoirs; it is very good, as far as it goes. The same cannot be said of certain later articles. Bruch and Bonaparte, it is believed, have been signally unsuccessful in handling these birds. Bruch's work of 1853 required in 1855 altogether too many changes to leave much to be said in its favor; while his later paper itself might be very harshly criticized. The character of Bonaparte's general work just before his death, which occurred while the article on *Laridæ* was printing in the "Conspectus," is too well known to require comment. Prof. Schlegel's articles in the "Museum Pays-Bas" are much more satisfactory, though some species are rejected which he might have retained had he seen them. Mr. Lawrence's contribution to Prof. Baird's work of 1858 is an important advance from the Audubonian period, as far as the North American species are concerned. Dr. Blasius's review of the family (J. f. O. 1865-'66) is a very important contribution, as is also Messrs. Sclater and Salvin's paper, in the Proceedings of the Zoological Society of 1871, on the Neotropical forms.

Determination of species in this family is difficult. Without reference to the abstract questions involved of the nature of species, it is practically impossible to recognize or define a considerable number of species which authors holding such views as Bruch and Bonaparte do, have sought to maintain. The same laws of variation under latitude, climate, and other physical influences which have been proven elsewhere, hold here, requiring recognition of various geographical races, rather than species, many forms being found to grade into each other. Further difficulty arises in the circumstance that while the sexes, as a rule if not without exception, of *Laridæ* are alike, the individual differences in size and plumage, according to age and season, are at a high rate, requiring large allowances. Characters must be decided to furnish grounds for species in this group; and, although very nice distinctions frequently subsist (among *Sterninæ* particularly), it must be confessed that every large collection contains doubtful specimens. The shade of the "gull-blue" of the mantle of most species of this family varies within wide limits, according to age and wear of the feathers, season, locality, and even as a purely fortuitous circumstance. The pattern of the primaries when marked, as is usual, with black and white in certain areas, is only approximately constant for the same age of individual feathers; for the rest, it is subject to nearly *continuous* progressive changes with age and "wear" of the quills. In their progress toward maturity, young *Laridæ* are usually subject to a series of changes affecting the color of the plumage and of the bill and feet very materially, as well as the stature. There are also, among the Jaegers, special states of plumage. The moult appears to be always double, vernal and autumnal; from this result the seasonal changes which are over and above the others referred to; these are almost always strongly pronounced. The moulting of the wing-quills is always gradually successive, almost feather by feather, so that the birds are at no time deprived of flight. The change may be advantageously studied in the Terns, from the heavily-silvered fresh quill to the worn dusky-brown one. The *white* areas on the quills of Gulls and Terns appear to have less vitality than those parts which are loaded with pigment, for we frequently find the quills worn away according to the pattern of their markings. Some rules of change in plumage are these: Young birds have their own livery; at first darker than that of the adults, or at least mottled with dark colors; there may be several different stages. Sexes are alike. Winter and summer vestures are different; black on the head, and rosy on the under parts, are greatly restricted or wanting in winter; even a black body may be changed to light. In white-headed species, dusky variegation of the head and neck occurs. Ordinarily more than a year is consumed in the progress to maturity; such is particularly the case with the larger Gulls and Jaegers.

Anatomical characters are very constant throughout the family. The osteology is almost the same throughout, excepting the skull of *Rhynchops;* minor skeletal features are given under several heads beyond. Other peculiarities are nearly confined to details of the digestive system. Of the pterylosis it may be observed, after Nitzsch, that the general character is perfectly scolopacine; that the tracts and spaces are narrowed in *Sterninæ*, and somewhat peculiar in *Lestridinæ*, there approaching the *Procellariidæ*. It is a curious rule (subject, however, to exceptions) that three of the four subfamilies are distinguished by shape of tail—cuneate in *Lestridinæ*, square in *Larinæ*, forked in *Sterninæ* and *Rhynchopinæ*.

The bibliography of the family is extensive and involved, though perhaps not unusually so, and certainly not more so than would be expected in a group where it is difficult to discriminate the species even upon examination of specimens, let alone descriptions. I have done my best in this matter, following the law of priority in the selection of names, excepting only when earlier ones would, if used, supersede those Linnæus, and taking this author at 1758.

More or fewer (in some cases scores) of specimens of all the North American *Laridæ* have been personally examined, excepting these: *Rhodostethia rosea* and *Xema furcatum*. The available material includes a large proportion of types, among them those of Audubon, Richardson, Peale, Gambel, Cassin, Lawrence, Baird.

Family LARIDÆ.

Ch. NATATORES *longipennes, naribus perviis, lateralibus, halluce libro.*

The preceding brief diagnosis distinguishes the *Laridæ* from other families of the *Natatores. Anseres* and *Pygopodes* differ in their short wings, &c.; the *Steganopodes*, which are longipennine, are separated by their totipalmated feet; while the *Procellariidæ*, the associates of *Laridæ* under *Longipennes*, are recognized by the peculiarities of the nostrils, beside some anatomical features. The family, thus separated from other *Natatores*, may be fully defined as follows:

Bill of moderate length, entire, or furnished with a cere, the upper mandible longer than, as long as, or shorter than the under; the culmen convex; the commissure very large, the cutting edges without lamellæ, the symphysis of the inferior mandibular rami complete for a considerable distance, an eminence being formed at their junction. No gular sac. Feathers usually extending further on the sides of the upper mandible than on the culmen, and further between the rami than on the sides of the under mandible.

Nostrils linear or oval; direct, pervious, lateral, opening on the basal half of the bill.
Eyes of moderate size, placed about over the angle of the mouth.
Wings long, broad, strong, pointed, with little or no concavity. Primaries very long, more or less acute, the first longest, the rest rapidly graduated. Secondaries numerous, short, broad, with rounded or excised tips. Tertials of moderate length, straight, rather stiff.
Legs placed well forward on the abdomen, more or less perfectly ambulatorial. Thighs entirely covered and concealed.
Tibiæ projecting; feathered above; a considerable portion below naked, covered with more or less dense, sometimes reticulated, skin.
Tarsi of moderate length or rather short; compressed; rather slender; anteriorly transversely scutellate, posteriorly and laterally reticulate.
Anteror toes of moderate length, the middle usually about equal to the tarsus; the outer shorter than the middle, intermediate between it and the inner; scutellate superiorly; all of normal number of segments (3, 4, 5).
Hallux present; very small, short, elevated above the plane of the other toes; entirely free and disconnected; of the normal number of segments, (2)—except in *Rissa*.
Webs broad and full, extending to the claws; their surfaces finely reticulated, their edges usually more or less incised, sometimes rounded.
Claws fully developed, compressed, curved, more or less acute, the edge of the middle dilated, but not serrated.
Tail very variable. *Body* generally rather full, and sometimes slender. *Neck* rather long. *Head* of moderate size. *Plumage* soft, close, thick; its *colors* simple—white, black, brown, or pearl-blue predominating; bright tints hardly found, except on the bill or feet, or as a temporary condition; the *sexes* alike in color, but the plumage varying greatly with age and season. Eggs generally *three*, light-colored, with numerous heavy dark blotches. Nidification normally terrestrial; reproduction altrical; young ptilopædic.
Palate with a median and two lateral ridges, papillate. *Nasal aperture* long, linear, its edges papillate. Opening of *Eustachian tube* conspicuous. *Tongue* fully formed, fleshy, apically more or less corneous and bifurcate, posteriorly bipartite, papillate. *Mouth* capacious.
Œsophagus capacious, muscular, very distensible, but straight, without permanent dilatations, its mucous membrane longitudinally plicate. *Proventriculus* directly continuous with œsophagus, saccular; its glands simple follicles, forming a complete zone. *Gigerium* nearly directly continuous with the proventriculus; moderately muscular, its cuticular lining dense, hard, rugose. No fully-formed pyloric valves. Duodenal fold of ordinary character. *Intestines* of moderate length and calibre. *Colon* very short. *Cœca coli* always present, but extremely variable in length. A capacious globular cloaca. A more or less perfectly developed *urinary bursa*.
Lobes of *liver* unequal, connected loosely superiorly. No *lobulus spigelii*. *Pancreas* well developed. Hepatic and pancreatic ducts opening usually close together, at the termination of the duodenal fold. *Gall-bladder* and *spleen* usually if not always present; the latter small, elongated.
Kidneys more or less completely divided into lobules, especially in *Sterninæ*. Openings of ureters and vasa deferentia upon minute papillæ, side by side, on the fold of mucous membrane separating the two portions of the cloaca. No intromittent male organ.
Opening of the *glottis* rather large, linear, its edges papillate. *Superior larynx* with a median longitudinal internal crest. *Trachea* straight, simple, without folds or dilatations; flattened above, cylindrical and smaller in calibre below; its rings cartilaginous, numerous, closely apposed; each varying in width from right to left successively. *Inferior larynx* small and simple. *Bronchi* of moderate and about equal length; anteriorly with numerous rings, of unvarying width; posteriorly entirely membranous.
General osteology closely correspondent with that of *Pygopodes*. No basipterygoids(?), nor accessory ossicles in the elbow, nor tibial apophysis; no long bones flattened as in *Sphenisci*.
The above characters define a natural group of birds found in every part of the world. Regarding the value of the group, however, and of its subdivisions, authors are greatly at variance. It has usually been held to be of family rank, and to comprise four subfamilies, with numerous genera. Again, it has been divided into two

groups, *Lari* and *Sternæ*; the former comprising *Lestris* and *Larus*; the latter, *Sterna* and *Rhynchops*. Yet, once more, some recent ornithologists have judged that the Jaegers, Gulls, Terns, and Skimmers each represent a distinct family. Not to mention other classifications of the group, I am in favor of the first of these modes of subdivision. The value of the characters which separate the *Laridæ* from the *Procellariidæ* is the same as of those distinguishing other families of *Natatores*; the line dividing them is trenchant; and there are no aberrant forms in either.*

The four subfamilies of the *Laridæ*, while equally well defined, have yet genera upon their confines which serve to connect them with each other and with other families. Witness the cered bill of *Stercorarius*, by which it approaches the *Procellariidæ*, but is in nearly every other particular essentially a Gull. Such subgenera as *Xema* and *Creagrus* among *Larinæ* change the Larine very gradually to the Sternine form, meeting, on the confines of the latter subfamily, such a subgenus as the thick-billed, short-tailed *Gelochelidon*, to render the transition still less abrupt. And the *Rhynchopinæ* are in every respect true Terns, except in the feature of the unique bill. Examination of the internal as well as the external characters of the four subfamilies (*Lestridinæ, Larinæ, Sterninæ*, and *Rhynchopinæ*) demonstrates that the first and second and the third and fourth are more nearly related to each other than are the second and third.

With these brief remarks upon the family in question, I proceed to give a detailed account of its osteology, the skeletons of the four subfamilies being so similar that I have thought it best to consider them collectively, indicating subfamily discrepancies. The splanchnology of the four differs more extensively; and I have, therefore, considered the viscera of each under the head of its typical species, except as regards those of the *Rhynchopinæ*, which are so similar to those of the *Sterninæ* that I have omitted them altogether. Other minor points of splanchnic details I have presented when considering the more marked species. I had hoped to have given the myology of the family in detail, but want of time and space forbade.

OSTEOLOGY.

CRANIA.—The skull of the *Rhynchopinæ* differs in so many and so essential respects from that of the other three subfamilies that it has been deemed advisable to describe it separately. The others may be most conveniently described together, in connection with the general osteology of the family, any differences of importance being, as is the case with the rest of the skeleton, pointed out. The skulls selected for description are those of *Stercorarius pomatorhinus, Larus argentatus*, and *Sterna hirundo*, each being considered as typical of its respective subfamily. In this case I use ordinary anatomical terms, for the most part, without reference to any theory of the composition of the skull.

The general shape of the skull, as in by far the majority of *Aves*, is that of an elongated pyramid with a tetragonal base. Its greatest length is from the occipital protuberance to the apex of the intermaxillary bone; its greatest depth from the middle of the parietal anchylosis directly downward to the base of the sphenoid; its greatest width is from one tympano-zygomatic articulation to the other. This pyramid is shortest and broadest in *Stercorarius*, narrowest and most elongated in *Sterna*.

On the base of the pyramid the superior curved line of the occiput is well marked; the perpendicular spine less developed; the surrounding surfaces of bone are only slightly depressed. The foramen magnum is rather large, and of a nearly circular shape. The occipital condyle is small, but stands out as a prominent very convex hemisphere. There are well developed "mastoid" processes.

The temporal fossa on either side of the superior aspect of the skull is not very deep, indicating a rather small aggregate of temporal and masseter muscles. It is incompletely divisible into two portions—a posterior, which stretches toward the median line just anterior to the occipital ridge; and an anterior, which constitutes the depression just behind the posterior orbital processes. This division is most marked in *Larus*, and is hardly apparent in *Stercorarius*. In neither of the subfamilies do these fossæ approach very near to the median line, and there is thus left a much more extensive, elevated, smooth portion on the vertex than exists in other natatorial genera, as *Puffinus, Colymbus*, &c., where the broad and deep fossæ are only separated by a narrow ridge. The vertex is marked by a smooth longitudinal depression denoting the bi-parietal suture. The anterior and posterior orbital processes are well developed, the former especially, which project directly outward and *backward*, with no downward obliquity. The posterior ones incline at a considerable angle downward. The outline of the orbital ridge included between them differs in each subfamily, owing to the difference in the shape and position of the "nasal" glands. In *Larus* these glands are almost wholly contained, except just at their anterior termination, in very deep, well-marked fossæ, so that they project but little over the real bony margin of the orbit. In *Sterna*, on the contrary, the concavity of the outline of the orbital ridges is very great, the skull being exceedingly narrow at that point, and therefore the glands

---

* Audubon has, indeed, included the Jaegers among the *Procellariidæ*, on the strength of their unentire bill. The error of such a procedure, however, needs no comment.

lie rather in grooves along the edges of the orbital ridges than in true fossæ, and consequently project so as to form more of the roof of the orbit than is afforded by its bony parietes. *Stercorarius* is intermediate between the two, but much nearest to *Larus*. In all three of the subfamilies, however, the internal or convex borders of these supra-orbital fossæ meet on the median line, where they are merely separated by a longitudinal ridge; and the fossæ are so deficient anteriorly that the ducts of the glands do not pass through a foramen in the roof of the orbit as in some genera of brachypterous *Natatores*, but pass directly beneath the anterior orbital processes.

The forehead is rather broad and flat, with a slight concavity both longitudinally and transversely. It is bounded posteriorly by the broad and prominent anterior orbital processes; anteriorly by the fronto-maxillary suture. This suture is only very moderately moveable (very different in this respect from that of *Rhynchops*), and is somewhat concave from the projecting backward of the articulation of the nasal bones behind that of the intermaxillary. In the most adult skulls the nasal bones may be distinctly traced, lying on either side of and closely apposed to the intermaxillary bone at its base, running forward for a short distance, and then becoming perfectly anchylosed with the latter. Just external to the nasal bones, on either side, is the "nasal process of the superior maxillary," running upward and backward from the superior maxillary, to join the frontal bone at its edge just anterior to the orbital process. This bone, which forms the posterior boundary of the anterior nasal fossæ, is usually called the "maxillary or descending ramus of the nasal bone;" and such is its true character, as appears even in such a nearly allied genus as *Puffinus*. But here this bone seems quite disconnected with the nasal bone proper, and at the same time to be completely consolidated with the superior maxillary. The separation is well marked in the three subfamilies, especially in *Sterna*.

The chief difference in the intermaxillary bones of the three subfamilies is, that in *Larinæ* and *Lestridinæ* the apex is decurved at a considerable angle over the apex of the inferior maxilla; while in *Sterninæ* there is no such deflection. The coalescence of the two mandibular with the superior mesial process is also here more extended than in the other subfamilies, and consequently the bony margin of the nasal aperture is of less extent. In all, the mesial process is thin and depressed, flat beneath, transversely convex above, rising gradually to the fronto-maxillary suture; and there is but a slight angle between the planes of the frontal and intermaxillary bone, very different from what obtains in *Rhynchops*. This mesial process always retains more or less distinctly marked the longitudinal line denoting its original separation into two halves. The mandibular processes, as usual, are weaker and slenderer than the mesial, though not greatly so; they diverge from it, and from each other, at a very slight angle. They are horizontal and quite straight, and lie nearly in a direct line with the zygomatic bones.

The orbits, as usual among the *Natatores*, are large and irregularly shaped, being deficient as to their bony parietes. Beside the difference in their roofs, already detailed, each of the subfamilies varies as to the character of the ethmoidal plate which forms the inter-orbital septum. In *Larus** this plate is perfect, and the two orbits are completely separated by bone. In *Stercorarius* the moderate-sized oval foramen exists in the centre of the plate, while in *Sterna* there can hardly be said to be a bony septum at all, beyond a slight backward projection of the ethmoidal plate from the middle of the anterior walls of the orbit. The septum between the orbits and the interior of the cranium is also exceedingly defective in *Sterna*, all the anterior nerves escaping by *one* large orifice, which extends from the roof to the floor of the cavity. There is seen, however, an indication of the more complete foramina which exist in the other subfamilies, in processes which project inward from the edges of this large orifice. They do not, however, meet each other, nor yet meet the process of the ethmoidal plate which extends backward. Even the olfactory nerves have not distinct foramina of egress, but escape by the common orifice. In all the subfamilies the course of the olfactory nerve is indicated by a distinct deep groove along the roof of the orbit. In the skulls of *Larus* and *Stercorarius* before me, the foramen, or rather canal, which conducts this nerve from the orbit into the nasal passages, is large and conspicuous; in *Sterna* it is much more contracted. The anterior parietes of the orbits, which separate them from the nasal passages, is very deficient below, but superiorly it is more complete, and there pierced by two foramina; one, just described, for the olfactory nerve; the other for the duct of the nasal gland. The extremity of this bony septum is acute, and extends downward nearly to the level of the zygoma in *Larus* and in *Sterna*; in *Stercorarius* it is much shorter and more obtuse.

The skull presents on its inferior aspect the shape of an almost perfect isosceles triangle. The base of this triangle is a little wider in the *Lestridinæ* than in the other two subfamilies, in consequence of the greater divergence of the mandibular processes of the intermaxillary bone, and, beyond them, of the malar bones. These last form, as usual, with the thin flat rami of the inferior mandible the lateral boundaries of this

* Skulls may vary in this respect. I describe the three subfamilies from the samples I have before me.

aspect of the skull. Along the median line the stout, broad edge of the conjoined bases of the occipital and sphenoid, and further on of the sphenoid and ethmoid, extend about as far as opposite the fronto-maxillary suture; there they terminate in a small acutely-pointed process.

The palate bones are rather widely separated anteriorly; but posteriorly, by an increase of their width, they are brought into close apposition, and nearly meet together over the ridge of the sphenoid. They are exceedingly thin and delicate; their external borders straight; their posterior extremity more or less abruptly rounded or truncated, bearing at its internal angle the usual small projecting process for the pterygoid articulation. They are completely anchylosed with the superior maxillary, so that all traces of their union are lost. They vary slightly in shape and in comparative length, in the different subfamilies, but not to any notable degree. The inferior surface in all of them is more or less concave in a transverse direction, from the curving downward of the margins.

The internal or mesial edge of the palate bone has joined to it, along its anterior moiety, the *vomer*. This is small and light, projecting forward from between the divergence of the palatals, on the median line, to divide the nasal passages into two. This bone is bifid for about its third, when the two sides become firmly united, presenting inferiorly a sharp, narrow edge; superiorly a broader margin, which is deeply grooved for nearly its whole length, to enable it to ride over the ridge of the ethmoid. The bone is thin and delicate throughout, terminating anteriorly in an extremely attenuated apex.

The malar bones, or "zygomatic arches," are long and slender, having a considerable outward convexity. They are thin and compressed throughout their length, except just where they fuse with the superior maxillary, when they become perpendicularly depressed instead of laterally compressed, so that they may yield by their elasticity to an upward motion of the facial bones.

The malar process of the os pedicellatum is elongated and well developed, carrying the head of the zygoma far outward and downward. The articulation is of the ordinary character. The orbital process of the tympanic bone is moderately long, and compressed and broad, and with a wide, truncated, somewhat nodulated, extremity. The body of the bone is short and thin, being compressed in a lateral direction, but, like the orbital and malar processes, its other processes are all largely developed and quite strong. Its articulation with the os temporale proper is by two very convex, rounded eminences on either side of the articulating head of the bone, separated by a deep notch, which is deprived of a smooth articulating surface. The proper articulation of the pterygoid bone is merely a very small prominent convex condyle, which is received into a corresponding cavity in the head of the pterygoid bone. The head of the latter, however, is rather wide, and is in apposition with the edge of the pedicellatum for a greater extent than is apparent on a slight inspection. In consequence of the development of the malar and pterygoid eminences of the pedicellatum, the articulating surface for the inferior maxilla is much elongated transversely, and very narrow antero-posteriorly. Its surface, as usual, is irregular.

The pterygoid bones are of moderate length, nearly straight, their superior borders thin and sharp; their anterior extremities slightly curved, and with something of a groove to play along the edge of the basilar process of the sphenoid. Their articulation with the palate bones is of the ordinary character.

Lack of basipterygoids may prove a diagnostic feature of *Laridæ* as compared with *Procellariidæ;* for they are certainly present in many of the *Cecomorphæ*, contrary to the original definition of that group. A late writer has shown that they occur perhaps throughout *Procellariidæ*, and has proposed upon this basis to separate the latter under the name of *Nectriomorphæ.*

The superior maxillary bones are small and inconspicuous. They are so wedged between the intermaxillary, malar, and palatal, that, if we except that process which perhaps belongs to them, which forms the posterior boundary to the nasal aperture, they are only apparent internal and superior to the palatal bones, where they form on either side a broad, thin concavo-convex dilation, the concavity of which presents outward and downward. The inferior curled margins of this, their dilation, may be seen on the inferior aspect of the skull, just within and between the palatals, on either side of the vomer, commencing about opposite its extremity.

The inferior maxillary bone retains at all ages, as usual among *Natatores*, very evident traces of the original elements of which it was composed. The suture by which the symphyseal elements are united to the supposed conjoined angular and supra-angular is specially noticeable, and the splenial element may be distinctly traced on the inside of the ramus of the jaw. This splenial element is very short (especially in *Stercorarius*), and has but little of a forward obliquity. The union of the other pieces of the jaw is complete in adult life. The rami are united at the symphysis for an exceedingly short distance in *Larus* and *Stercorarius*, more extensively in *Sterna*. The coronoid process is moderately arched, but the convexity is very gradual, and has no sharp apex. The angle on the lower margin of the jaw, just at the gomphosal suture, is pretty prominent. The outline of the tomial edge of the rami is nearly straight to the tip, where it is considerably decurved, in *Larus* and *Stercorarius ;* in *Sterna* no such deflection exists. The articulating surface has, as usual, an internal deep concavity, and an external more shallow portion, both being bounded posteriorly by a raised border. The internal process of the articulating surface is well developed and rather acute ; and from the external edges of the articulation there proceeds downward and forward on the edge of the jaw a raised line, for muscular attachments, most conspicuous in *Larus*. The surface of bone just posterior to the articulation, for the attachment of the digastricus, is of a triangular shape, and its face presents backward and downward instead of backward and upward, as in some other natatorial genera.

The tomial edges of the inferior maxilla are thin, sharp, and erect ; while those of the mandibular processes of the intermaxillary are broad and flat, without sharp edges.

§ *Table showing the comparative proportions, and relative sizes of the skulls of the four sub-families of Laridæ.*

Dimensions.	Stercorarius pomatorhinus.	Larus argentatus.	S. hirundo.	Rhynchops nigra.
Length from apex of intermaxillary to occipital protub...	*3.60	5.00	2.85	5.10
Length from apex of intermaxillary to fronto-max. suture.	2.00	2.70	1.50	3.20
Length from apex of intermaxillary to occipital condyle..	3.25	4.55	2.50	4.75
Length from apex of intermaxillary to end of palatals....	2.55	3.55	2.00	4.10
Length from apex of intermaxillary to end of malar......	3.00	4.35	2.40	4.65
Length from apex of intermaxillary to post-orbital proc's.	2.95	4.20	2.35	4.50
Length from apex of intermaxillary to ante-orbital proc's.	2.20	3.25	1.75	3.85
Length of malar bones..	1.25	1.85	1.00	1.55
Length of vomer	1.05	1.15	0.55	0.70
Length of pterygoid bones...................................	0.48	0.79	0.34	0.56
Length of ossa pedicellata (greatest)......................	0.55	0.78	0.34	0.66
Width of skull across tympano-zygomatic articulation ...	1.45	1.95	0.90	1.50
Width of skull across mastoid processes	0.75	0.95	0.55	0.75
Width of skull across post-orbital processes..............	1.40	1.70	0.85	1.10!
Width of skull across ante-orbital processes	1.00	1.20	0.68	1.10!
Width of skull across fronto-maxillary suture............	0.40	0.58	0.25	0.60
Width of skull across narrowest point of orbital roof.....	0.31	0.58	0.20	0.58
From ante to post-orbital processes......................	0.80	1.00	0.68	0.78
Length of nasal aperture	1.45	1.90	0.80	......
Diameter of foramen magnum (antero-post.)..............	0.22	0.30	0.20	......
Greatest width of both palatals	0.60	0.70	0.30	0.70
Length of symphysis of rami of intermaxillary...........	0.50	0.85	0.74	2.25!
Length of fossa for nasal gland	0.85	1.00	0.60	0.50!
Length of inferior maxilla (total).......................	3.00	4.35	2.40	4.60
Depth of inferior maxilla (greatest)	†0.45	0.70	0.22	0.55
Length of symphysis of inferior maxilla.................	0.28	0.45	0.58	2.90!
Width of articulating surface of inferior maxilla.........	0.63	0.48	0.20	0.55

* Inches and hundredths.

† The greatest depth in *Larinæ, Lestridinæ,* and *Sterninæ* is opposite the coronoid process. In *Rhynchopinæ* the depth just anterior to the symphysis exceeds this, the depth at the coronoid process being only 0.45.

SPINAL COLUMN.—The number of vertebræ throughout the four subfamilies is nearly constant, varying at most by one or two vertebræ, if at all. The *Sterninæ* appear to have one less vertebra in the sacrum, *i. e.,* eleven instead of twelve; but this is the only difference that I have been able to discover. The following table exhibits the number of vertebræ belonging to the different spinal regions in three of the four groups:

Species.	Cervical.	Dorsal.	Sacral.	Coccygeal.	Total.
Stercorarius pomatorhinus..............................	14	8	12	8	42
Larus argentatus	14	8	12	8	42
Sterna hirundo......................................	14	8	11	8	41

The above table differs from those given by OWEN, Todd's Cyclop. Anat. and Phys., Art. *Aves*, and by EYTON, Osteol. Avium. Prof. Owen's figures are : " *Catarractes*," 13— 9—13—8 ; " *Gull*," 18—8—11—8 ; " *Tern*," 14—8—10—8. Mr. Eyton gives : *Larus ridibundus*, 14—7—12—7 ; *Sterna arctica*, 13—6—12—6 ; *Rhynchops nigra*, 13—6—12—8. It is to be expected that discrepant statements should occur in the enumeration of the sacral vertebræ, as the composition of that most complex of all bones is difficult to interpret. In the other instances we may presume that there is actually a variation with the species in number of vertebræ of the several regions. I give the numbers as determined by myself in the specimens of the three species above mentioned, adding the formulæ of Owen and Eyton for comparison.

The peculiarities of the several regions, and of the different vertebræ composing them, may be briefly noticed :

CERVICAL VERTEBRÆ.—The *atlas* is little more than a simple ring, its foramen slightly flattened inferiorly. Its "body" is merely a slight projection on the inferior edge of its circumference ; bearing, cephalad, a perfectly circular facet for articulation with the occipital condyle ; and caudad, and upon its superior margin, a deep longitudinal channel, so deep as almost to amount to a canal for the reception and retention of the axial odontoid process. Superiorly on each side are indications of transverse processes ; inferiorly there is the rudiment of a " ventral spine."

AXIS.—This is of a somewhat peculiar shape. The spinous and transverse processes, both of which are quite well developed, seem to lie considerably posterior to the body of the vertebra, in consequence of an obliquity backward of the neural arch from the centrum. The ventral spine is well developed, thin, with an anteriorly convex, posteriorly concave margin ; oblique in direction, projecting backward as well as downward. The body of the vertebra proper consists of little more than a base for the support of the odontoid process, which latter is acute, well developed, semicylindrical, its surface toward the spinal canal being flattened. The transverse articulating facets are small, subcircular, slightly concave, situated beneath the processes, at their bases. The other articulation is elongated, compressed, vertically concave, horizontally convex. The motion between the atlas and the third vertebra is very free in a vertical direction, less so in a horizontal, while rotation is greatly restricted.

The third and fourth vertebræ somewhat resemble the axis in having a broad, thin, longitudinal lamina of bone extending between the anterior and posterior articular processes. They are also very short and broad. The other vertebræ all differ somewhat, but the difference is so gradual that they may most conveniently be described collectively. The lowest or dorsal vertebræ are the largest and broadest, but comparatively the shortest. Their posterior articular processes are short and slightly divaricating ; as we proceed up the neck they become longer, more attenuated, and more widely diverging. This attenuation is greatest on about the fifth vertebra. The transverse processes are very wide below, and extend directly outward from the median line. Further up the neck they are less prominent, and have also an anterior obliquity. This process on the last vertebra does not form a canal for the passage of the artery ; the canal commences on the twelfth, as a simple foramen, becoming narrower in diameter, but at the same time more and more lengthened and canal-like, up to the atlas.

Superior spinous processes, or the "neural spines," are well developed on the first five vertebræ, but they diminish in size from the third to the sixth, when they become quite obsolete, and do not reappear. Inferior or ventral spinous processes are found very well developed on the first four vertebræ, being largest on the atlas ; they then entirely disappear, and are not found again until about the eleventh vertebra, where they are slightly elevated, longitudinal, vertical lamellæ. Styloid processes are found throughout the whole length of this portion of the spine, except the atlas and axis, and, usually, the last vertebra. They commence on the third vertebra, elongate on each successively to the sixth or seventh, where they are longest and thinnest, measuring two-thirds the length of the body of the vertebra. They then regularly grow shorter and more obtuse till they are hardly perceptible on the thirteenth and quite obsolete on the fourteenth or last cervical.

Air is admitted into the vertebræ by numerous foramina on the sides of the bodies, about the roots of the transverse processes and in the canal for the artery.

There is the ordinary difference in the calibre of the spinal canal in the centre and at the extremities of each vertebra. The planes of the articular surface are, as usual, so disposed as to produce, in the most natural position of the head and neck, the ordinary sigmoid flexure. When the neck is extended there is on the dorsal surface a large diamond-shaped space between each vertebra and the next covered in only by ligamentous tissue.

DORSAL VERTEBRÆ.—If we regard the presence of a rib as characteristic of the vertebræ of this region of the spine, we shall have eight as the total number of dorsal vertebræ. But the two last of these are perfectly consolidated with and continuous with the first sacral ; and their transverse and spinous processes also have a lateral and superior anchylosis with the iliac bones. At the same time there is a perfect articulation between these two last vertebræ and the one just before them, producing a somewhat moveable joint, never so firmly consolidated as are the other dorsal vertebræ with each other. But for the fact that they are costiferous, therefore, the two last vertebræ might be considered as a portion of the sacrum.

On the first dorsal there commence abruptly prominent subrectangular spinous processes, which are a distinguishing feature of this portion of the column. These processes of any two contiguous vertebræ are in contact for their whole extent, and more er less completely consolidated. Scleroskeletal tendons extend backward from the posterior apices of each of them. The transverse processes are all broad, thin, flat, horizontal, stretching outward and a little backward, strengthened by a prop, which proceeds from the sides of the bodies of the vertebræ to the apices of these processes. Their apices bear the ordinary facet for the articulation of the rib, and from each there stretches backward an osseous tendon.

The bodies of the vertebræ are not so deep vertically nor so compressed as usual. Anteriorly, indeed, they are wider than deep; their free ventral surface broad and roughened, either with or without tubercles, as far as the fourth, for the attachment of the longus colli. The other posterior vertebræ are thinner, being especially compressed at their centres.

Although the vertebræ of this region cannot be said to be anchylosed, except perhaps in very old birds, yet they enjoy but very little motion upon each other, particularly the more central ones. The first is usually moveable to a degree, while some little motion is permitted between the sixth and seventh.

SACRAL VERTEBRÆ.—It is difficult to ascertain the number of vertebræ in the sacrum, but, as well as can be made out, the *Sterninæ* have one less than the other subfamilies. The elements of the sacrum are completely consolidated into one piece, together with the last two dorsal; so that it is only by counting the number of transverse processes which stretch outward to abut against the innominate bones that their number can be estimated. The body of the sacrum is thickest in the middle, tapering somewhat toward both extremities; the tapering, however, of the anterior extremity is only apparent, since it makes up by increased depth for decreased width. The body is decidedly curved, giving a notable degree of antero-posterior concavity to the dorsum of the pelvis. Anteriorly the iliac bones unite on the median line, and the united spinous processes of the sacrum are completely anchylosed with them as well as the transverse. About the middle of the sacrum the elevated longitudinal ridge formed by the united spinous processes disappears, and the median line of the bone is smooth and flat. There are no signs of inferior or ventral spinous processes on any part of the length of the sacrum. The transverse processes of the first three vertebræ are conspicuous, and project directly outward to be consolidated with the middle of the under surface of the ilia; the next three are short and inconspicuous, very little more than ridges on the body of the sacrum. The seventh pair, however, suddenly become the longest of all, running far outward, reaching even quite to the margins of the acetabula, and they are strengthened by a thin vertical plate of bone, which stretches down from them to the dorsum of the ilia. The succeeding transverse processes are well developed, projecting obliquely outward and backward to join the margin of the ischia.

COCCYGEAL VERTEBRÆ.—The coccyx has constantly eight segments. These are chiefly noticeable for the length and width of their transverse processes. In *Stercorarius* they are larger than elsewhere, being all of nearly the same length, whereas in other genera the anterior ones are more or less shortened, and do not reach their full development until the fourth or fifth vertebra. These processes become very small on the sixth, and are obsolete on the seventh. Superior spines are present, moderately well developed, but short. Ventral spines are wanting on the first three, but quite largely developed on the last five vertebræ. They are much the largest in *Stercorarius*, and bifid at their extremity.

The pygostyle is large, of an irregularly trihedral shape; its superior margin convex, its inferior a little concave; its base thickened for articulation with the seventh. Its two superior angles are thin and rounded; the inferior is prolonged into a thick, stout nodulated apex.

RIBS.—The ribs are eight in number. Of these all are articulated with the spine, there being none disconnected with it, as in some other genera of *Natatores*. Six have a sternal attachment as well as a spinal, while five possess retrocedent processes. The first is an exceedingly slender elongated spiculum of bone, tapering to a very acute apex, which is free. It extends to about opposite the process on the second rib. The next five ribs have both vertebral and sternal portions movably articulated. Of these the former are greatly the longest, and elongate rapidly with each successive rib. The sternal portions are very much shorter, but also lengthen rapidly from before backward. The splints which stretch backward and inward between one rib and another are well developed. In the unexpanded thorax they reach quite across two intercostal spaces. The " sacral ribs" are very long and extremely slender. Tho first articulates with the sternum; the last one does not, although it has a sternal rib attached to it. Neither of them shows traces of posterior oblique processes.

STERNUM.—The *sternum* varies more in the different subfamilies than any other portion of the skeleton except the skull. It will, therefore, be necessary to institute comparisons between the four types, although a general description may still be made for either of the groups. I describe it held upside down.

The body of the bone is pretty regularly rectangular, and about twice as long as broad across the middle. In *Lestridinæ* and *Sterninæ* the lateral borders are nearly straight or but slightly concave, while in *Larinæ* the outline is very concave from the protrusion of the costal processes. This much greater development of the costal processes in *Larus* gives a greater breadth anteriorly, and detracts from the more perfectly rectangular shape which obtains in the other subfamilies. Just posterior to the costal processes are the six articulating facets for the sternal ribs. These are simply linear perpendicular eminences, separated by curved sulci from each other. They extend but little more than half the length of the sternum, the remaining portion of the border being thin and plain.

The anterior border is very convex, running forward a considerable distance from the costal processes, having on the median line a large semicircular, well-developed manubrial process. The outer half of this border is thin, corresponding with the costal processes; the inner very thick, and deeply grooved to form the coracoid facets. These facets are of a shape somewhat peculiar, as they curl downward and inward toward each other, to meet on the median line beneath the manubrium, which consequently overhangs them. In the middle of their course they are very shallow, but again, at their outer extremity, become sulci by means of a short, stout process of bone which overhangs them.

The posterior border differs in the *Lestridinæ* from the other subfamilies. It has but a single long, slender incurved process, forming with the xiphoid cartilage a single deep oval excavation. In the other subfamilies the outer process is not so long and slender, it projecting but little if any beyond the extremity of the xiphoid; and there is, in addition, a second small, short, slender process midway between the external one and the xiphoid, which divides the single membranous space of the *Lestridinæ* into two small spaces, each of a more or less oval shape.

The dorsum of the sternum is strongly vaulted, both transversely and longitudinally. The amount of convexity both ways is greatest in *Lestridinæ*, least in *Sterninæ*. In *Lestridinæ*, also, the convexity is very much the greatest anteriorly, while in the other subfamilies the whole dorsum is more equally vaulted. The most noticeable feature of the dorsum is the prominent ridge which extends from the osseous projection at the extremity of the coracoid facets obliquely backward and inward to meet the keel near its posterior extremity. This ridge limits the attachment of the *pectoralis medius* muscle to the sternum. It is proportionally shortest in the *Lestridinæ*.

The keel is remarkably well developed, rising high above the dorsum. Its height is equal to half the average width of the bone. Its ridge is very convex, and does not lose itself in the dorsum until it has quite reached the end of the bone. Its anterior border curves forward with a strong, wide, and deeply concave margin, being terminated by a well developed and greatly projecting though not very acute apex.

The xiphoid process is broad, rounded, and flattened in *Lestridinæ*, and extends a little way beyond the subsidence of the keel. In *Larinæ* it is narrow and more acute, and the keel is continued to its very tip, while in *Sterninæ* it is so compressed as to appear simply like the termination of the keel, slightly broadened.

The pneumatic foramina are very numerous. They are situated along the whole length of the median line of the inner surface; at the base of the anterior border of the keel; in the sulci between the costal facets, &c.

The *coracoids* are of moderate length and stoutness. The shaft of the bone centrally is subcylindrical, but at either extremity is greatly expanded in various directions. The basal articulating surface, besides being deeply concave, is twisted upon itself in a peculiar manner to adapt it to the shape of the sternal facet. The inner margin of the bone is thick and rounded, the outer thin and sharp, and expanded into a well marked rounded process. The head of the bone presents a large irregular expansion, generally convex in its outer aspect, but made exceedingly thin by a deep concavity or excavation on its inner side. A prominent process at the inner and inferior border of the head supports the tip of the furculum. Between this projection and the process which supports the head of the scapula is a deep groove, which extends some distance along the shaft. It is nearly bridged over and converted into a canal by an overhanging projection of the scapular process. A dense ligament completes that portion of the canal which wants osseous parietes, and through it plays the tendon of the pectoralis medius.

On the outer aspect of the head of the bone is the depression which contributes to form the glenoid fossa. Neither it, however, nor the scapula itself, present any peculiarities worthy of special notice.

The *clavicles* have, as usual, a scapular as well as a coracoid articulation. The former is, however, merely the apposition of the extreme tip of the bone with the inner side of the head of the scapula. There is a well developed tubercle and articulating facet for the head of the coracoid. The bones are not connected except ligamentously with the sternum. They unite at about the same angle, and have much the same amount of longitudinal curvature in all the subfamilies. The symphysis is perhaps a little broader and stronger in the *Lestridinæ* than in the others. There is a well developed projecting process at the symphysis, most marked in the *Sterninæ*. The bones curve greatly downward and backward toward the sternum, and then approach each other with a still greater amount of inclination; so that while the angle the shafts of the bone make with each other is small, the real angle of the union of the two is very obtuse. This gives the bones the requisite amount of power in preventing the approximation of the heads of the coracoids.

HUMERUS.—This bone presents several interesting features. The superior or anterior crest is short but very high; it rises abruptly from the shaft, and from the upper extremity of the head of the bone, with perfectly plane, smooth sides The inferior or posterior crest, on the other hand, is broadly convex both longitudinally and transversely on its outer aspect; its longitudinal convexity gives the head of the bone nearly all of its obliquity with reference to the axis of the shaft. It arches over the posterior aspect of the end of the shaft, this vaulting being formed by a deep excavation or concavity on its posterior aspect. This excavation is complete and open in *Larinæ* and *Sterninæ*, and is divided in two by a prominent longitudinal ridge; while in the *Lestridinæ* the excavation is partially closed in by a plane prolongation of the shaft, which leaves only a rather small oval foramen to open into the excavation. The apex of the crest has a considerable prolongation backward, separated from the articular head by a deep notch. Its convex surface is marked near the head of the bone by two deep grooves, one parallel with, the other perpendicular to, the axis of the shaft. The articular head of the bone is narrowly oval, but very convex, its long axis lying between the extremities of the two crests. A prominent ridge of bone arises from the shaft, and runs up between the two crests to the head. The greater part of the expansion about the head of the bone is rough, for the attachment of ligaments and tendons.

The most notable feature of the lower extremity of the bone is the presence on its outer edge, just above the radial tubercle, of a prominent, well developed, acute "styloid" process. This projects directly from the side of the bone, and at right angles with it. It serves for the origin of the tendon of the *extensor carpi radialis longior*. On the opposite side of the bone, just above the ulnar tubercle, there is a slight prominence, but nothing deserving the name of a process. I have observed none of the supplementary bones lately described by Prof. Reinhardt as occurring in a majority of the *Procellariidæ*, and do not think any such exist.

The elongation and obliquity of the radial facet are well marked, but present nothing unusual in shape or size, as is the case with the rounded ulnar tubercle. There is a very large and deep coronoid fossa on the anterior aspect of the bone just above the condyles, most extensive in the *Larinæ*, shallowest in the *Lestridinæ*. There is no olecranoid depression, but in place of it the extremity of the bone posteriorly presents a deep longitudinal groove on the ulnar side, which conducts the extensor tendon. This groove is bounded internally by a well developed ulnar condyle; externally by a slight ridge, which separates it from a narrow, shallow groove that runs over the radial side of the extremity of the bone.

BONES OF THE FOREARM.—The ulna is considerably longer than the humerus, and very stout and strong. It is considerably curved on its axis, the convexity presenting backward. Its posterior aspect is marked with two or three rows of slight roughened eminences, denoting the attachment of feathers. The head is large and stout, its articulating facets presenting forward. The inner of these is a perfectly circular cup-shaped depression, the anterior margin of which forms what there is of a coronoid process, while a considerable projection posteriorly to it constitutes the olecranon. Just beside this facet there is on the radial side of the head of the bone the smooth concavo-convex depression, which forms, together with the head of the radius, the elongated oblique facet for articulation with the radial tubercle of the humerus. The distal extremity of the bone presents the usual curved surface on its radial aspect, over which the expanded and deflected extremity of the radius is applied. Below and posterior to this is an elongated, smooth, longitudinally convex and transversely concave trochlear surface.

The radius is, as usual, very slender and cylindrical. Its head is rather oval than round, but its facet is nearly circular. Its distal extremity is laterally expanded and deflected, to overlie the extremity of the ulna. It is marked with a slight longitudinal groove along which plays the tendon of the extensor.

The radio-carpal bone is comparatively very small, being much less than the "pisiform." It is of an indescribably irregular form. It has three smooth articulating surfaces; a deep, oval transverse one for the radius; a very small, shallow one beside it for the ulna; and on the opposite side a larger, somewhat crescentic, concavo-convex one for the head of the metacarpus. Its superior non-articular surface is grooved for the passage of the extensor tendon.

The ulnar carpal or so-called pisiform bone is very large. The notch on its metacarpal aspect is exceedingly broad and deep ; so much so that the bone is saddled, as it were, on the inner ridge of the metacarpal articulating surface, along which it rides freely. The inner prong of the bifurcation is greatly elongated ; the outer is shorter and stouter ; and it is by the extremity of this that the bone chiefly articulates with the metacarpus. The ulnar articulating surface is merely a slight oval depression. The apex of the bone is tolerably acute, and rough for the attachment of tendons.

The composition and movements of the wrist-joint, as well as those of the elbow, afford an interesting study ; but as there is nothing in them peculiar to the group under consideration, I pass them over with the foregoing brief description.

The metacarpal segment of the arm is about half the length of the antibrachium. The two principal bones of which it is composed are entirely separate, except at their extremities, where they are firmly consolidated. Of these the radial one is much the largest, the ulnar being merely a delicate cylindrical shaft, somewhat broadened and flattened toward its proximal extremity. The main shaft of the bone is rather flattened than cylindrical. The superior edge of the proximal extremity bears a short but unusually prominent and well-developed crest, with a tuberculated apex, for the attachment of the extensor tendon. Its distal extremity is abruptly truncated, for the articulation of the pollex. Just at its base, on the inner or under aspect of the bone, is a small osseous projection, either for the attachment of a tendon or the confining of some that go to the digits. The articulating face of the bone is very long, extending from the superior border over the head, and some distance along the inferior aspect. It is transversely deeply concave, having raised borders, the inner and most prominent of which is received in the bifurcation of the " pisiform " bone.

The pollex is simply a small, slender, straight, compressed spiculum of bone, moveably articulated with, and projecting directly from, the truncated extremity of the metacarpal crest. The "ulnar finger" in like manner projects from the extremity of the ulnar segment of the metacarpus, being closely bound to the under surface of the first phalanx of the radial finger.

The radial finger, or the proper continuation of the limb, consists of two phalanges only, each rather more than half as long as the metacarpus. The first of these somewhat resembles the metacarpus, in being wide, thin, and compressed, and partially divided into two longitudinal parallel segments. The distal is simply a straight, slender, tapering and acutely-pointed spiculum, articulating with the preceding by a somewhat enlarged head.

OSSA INNOMINATA.—The pelvis has, for a natatorial family, considerable depth and concavity. Anteriorly it is flat, its parietes very deficient ; but posteriorly the large ischia project downward and backward, forming extensive and solid walls ; while medially there is a subrectangular deep fossa formed by the vaulting of the innominate bones for the reception of the renal organs.

The ilia are rather small and thin bones projecting as far forward as the seventh dorsal vertebra. The dorsum is slightly concave in every direction ; the venter is about flat ; the external margins deeply concave ; the anterior broadly convex ; the internal meeting and being anchylosed with its fellow and with the superior sacral spines over the median line. It receives the transverse processes of the sacrum against its inferior surface and inner margin. Toward the posterior border, and opposite the acetabulum, the bone spreads out and becomes much arched and expanded, to form with a similar enlargement on the anterior portion of the ischia, the chief part of the concavity proper of the pelvis, that which contains the kidneys.

The ischia stretch downward, backward, and outward, as broad, thin planes, flat, except at the commencement near the acetabulum, where they are vaulted. The proper "tuber ischii" is merely a small projection on the posterior margin of the bones ; what is properly the "ascending ramus" continues directly onward and forms the real extremity of the bone, which is remarkably elongated and tapering. The ischiadic notch is, as usual, converted into a foramen, in this case very large, subcircular, situated just posterior to the acetabulum.

The pubis is merely a long, thin, flexible, nearly straight spiculum of bone, a little curved inward, and dilated at its floating extremity. It commences at the acetabulum, which, as usual, it contributes to form, and runs backward, outward, and downward, lying parallel to the anterior edge of the ischium and abutting against, but being quite disconnected with its extremity. Thus the obturator foramen is converted into an exceedingly long, deep, narrow notch, resulting from the concavity of the border of the ischium being applied against the straight edge of the pubis. Perhaps, however, the real obturator is to be found in a small oval or subcircular dilatation at the apex of the notch, which is wider than the notch itself, partly shut off from it by ligaments, and, with its edges, thickened and smooth.

The acetabulum is situated at the confluence of the three pelvic bones, just at the middle of the inferior border. As usual, it is a simple ring, entirely deficient internally, with smooth, thickened, elevated edges, and a prominent overhanging articulating facet on its supero-posterior border, for the trochanter major of the femur to rest upon.

FEMUR.—This bone is exceedingly short, but quite straight (differing greatly in this respect from *Puffinus*), and only moderately stout. The shaft is nearly cylindrical, inclining above slightly inward toward the median line of the body, its lower extremity presenting somewhat backward. Superiorly the bone expands into a large, thick, stout trochanter, much elevated, and with a well-marked margin, which rises high above, curves toward and slightly overhangs the head of the bone. From the inner side of this trochanter the head projects directly inward; there is no constriction of the "neck," except to a very slight degree below; above, the articular head of the bone is directly continuous with a smooth concavo-convex space between it and the crest of the trochanter. The shape of the articulating surface is such that it permits the head to sink but slightly into the acetabular ring, the chief weight of the bird being borne by the superior aspect of the trochanteric prominence, which is accurately coaptated to the overhanging abutment which projects from the superior margin of the acetabulum. The fossa for the ligamentum teres is directly on the superior aspect of the head. The whole outer aspect of the trochanter is rough for tendinous and ligamentous attachments.

The femoral condyles differ markedly in size and shape. The outer is the longest, and very much the largest. The two are widely separated by a deep groove, which runs up a considerable distance on the anterior face of the bone, and on the posterior is continuous with the popliteal depression. The outer projects much the furthest outward, downward, and especially backward. Its face, posteriorly, is divided by a longitudinal groove. This groove receives the antero-posteriorly elongated head of the fibula, forming the chief part of the femoro-fibular articulation; while the ridge which bounds the groove internally dips down into the space between the heads of the fibula and tibia. The inner condyle has a broad, flat, oval face, which is applied directly to the plane head of the tibia.

The two tibial crests are peculiar in shape and situation. The anterior of these is short, but very high, rising as a thin, vertical lamina to quite an apex; being triangular, and nearly as high as long at the base. It is exceedingly thin, its sides perfectly plane and vertical. The other crest is at right angles with the first; looking directly outward instead of forward, and having its side instead of base applied to the bone. Its base is nearly identical with the base of the first, but is at right angles with it. The superior margins of these crests unite at their termination, and both rise above the level of the head of the bone. The lateral crest being transverse to the line of motion in the joint, forms a protecting wall or face in front of the joint, between the margins of which, and the head of the bone proper, there is a gentle and regular concavity. The inner edge of the true head of the bone is directly continuous with the base of the anterior crest; but between the outer edge and the extremity of the lateral crest there is a deep notch.

The head of the fibula is on the same plane with, and at the inner edge of, the head of the tibia. It is narrowly oval, almost crescentic, its long axis antero-posterior. It is only ligamentously connected with the tibia; below, after a short space, it becomes more or less completely anchylosed; becomes again detached from the tibia, to finally disappear a little below the middle of the bone.

The tibial condyles, as usual, project further forward than backward. They are much of the same size and shape, and on the same plane; the inner, however, is less stout and projects more, both inward and forward. Posteriorly the condyles subside into two acute ridges, having between them a smooth, laterally concave surface, over which pass the extensor tendons. Above and between the two condyles on the anterior surface of the bone, there is the ordinary fossa, partially converted by a bridge of bone into a canal for the confinement of the tendon of the *extensor digitorum*.

The metatarsus is moderately long, contained 1⅓ times in the tibia. Its shaft is compressed into a pretty regular quadrilateral shape, the lateral sides, however, remaining a little convex. The tendons that go to the toes are mostly aggregated upon the anterior and posterior aspects of the bone. Above, the bone expands into a large, irregular head, widened laterally for the reception of the two condyles, and posteriorly by a short, high crest, into which is inserted the gastrocnemial tendon. This crest has also several longitudinal grooves, deep and distinct, which conduct tendons to the toes. The facets for the reception of the tibial condyles are merely two small subcircular depressions near the edge of the bone, not differing much from each other in size or shape. They are separated by a prominent process on the edge of the bone anteriorly on the median line. The end of the bone is, as usual, divided into three heads, separated by narrow but very deep sulci. Of these heads the middle is the largest, and directly in the line of the bone; the outer is placed a little higher up, but nearly in the same plane. The inner, however, beside being much higher up, is placed far around toward the posterior aspect of the bone. The articular faces of these heads present in a high degree of perfection the peculiar shape by which extension of the toes at the same time *abducts* them, and *vice versâ*.

The four toes have all the normal number of segments : 2, 3, 4, 5. They present nothing of special interest, being of the ordinary size and shape. The hallux, and its accessory metatarsal bone, may, however, be here described. It does not differ appreciably throughout the family, except in the genus *Rissa* of *Larinæ*, for the characters of which, see under the head of the genus.

Were it not for analogy, the *os metatarsale accessorium* might be considered as a phalangeal rather than metatarsal segment. It is nearly or quite as long as the first true phalangeal bone. It is obliquely flattened, and somewhat twisted upon itself, tapering to a thin, rather acute, apex. Its distal extremity is broadened and oval, bearing a slightly convex articulating surface, which is coaptated with that of the first phalanx. There is no eminence or depression of any consequence for its attachment with the metatarsus ; it is only loosely connected by ligaments, and enjoys all the freedom of motion which the hallux itself possess. Its essentially metatarsal character is nevertheless demonstrated by its irregular and peculiar shape ; by the formation of its two extremities ; and by the want of a proper articulation (capsulated and with a synovial membrane) with the metatarsus.

This bone in the *Lestridinæ* differs from that of the other subfamilies in being shorter, stouter, with a broader metatarsal extremity, and having a constriction about its middle.

The proximal phalangeal segment is a very short, stout, straight bone, irregularly cylindrical, with slightly enlarged extremities. These have subcircular articulating facets, the proximal concave, the distal convex. The distal segment is merely a minute, irregularly shaped, osseous nodule, supporting the claw.

Subfamily LESTRIDINÆ.

DIAG. LARIDÆ *rostro cerâ instructo, rectricibus mediis elongatis, unguibus validissimis.*

CH. Tip of the upper mandible overhanging that of the lower. Covering of upper mandible not continuous, the basal half being furnished with a corneous cere, beneath the edges of which the nostrils open. Culmen at first about straight, then rapidly convex. Commissure slightly sinuate, declinato-convex on the terminal portion. Gonys short, about straight. Rami widely divaricating, their outline about straight. Eminentia symphysis well marked. Nostrils lateral, pervious, somewhat club-shaped, being widest at their distal extremity. Wings long, strong, pointed ; the primaries broad and rigid, more or less rounded at the tips. Tail square, or nearly so, the central feathers projecting to a greater or less distance beyond the others ; either rounded at their tips, or attenuated and filiform. Legs decidedly ambulatorial, placed well forward, supporting the body in a horizontal posture. Tibiæ denuded of feathers on the lower third. Tarsi rather stout, anteriorly transversely reticulated, pósteriorly and laterally reticulated, the plates more or less elevated and acutely pointed. Proportions of toes, and their segments, as in other *Laridæ*. Webs broad and full, their margins rounded, not excised. Claws large, strong, curved and acute. Of moderate and large size. The body full, the general organization strong and powerful. The changes of plumage in most of the species, with age and season, very great.

The anatomical characters of this subfamily are fully given under one of its most common and typical species, the *Stercorarius pomatorhinus.*

§. *Analytical table of the subgenera and species of North American Lestridinæ.*

I. Staturâ maximus, et formâ robustissimus ; pedibus et rostro validis ;
　　tarso medio digito cum ungue breviore ; caudâ brevi, rectricibus
　　mediis latis, vix ultrâ cæteras porrectis .... *Buphagus.*

　　a. Rostri longit. 2.00 poll. et ultrâ ; altitudo 0.75 ; ab oris angulo
　　　　ad apicem 3.00...................................... *B. skua.*

II. Staturâ minores, et formâ graciliores ; pedibus et rostro gracilioribus ; tarso medio digito cum ungue non breviore ; caudâ elongatâ, rectricibus mediis valdè ultrâ cæteras porrectis........... *Stercorarius.*

　　a. Tarsis posticè asperrimis ; rectricibus mediis latis in apices
　　　　ipsas, flexibilibus, cæteris 4 pollices longioribus .... *S. pomatorhinus.*

　　b. Tarsis posticè subasperis ; rectricibus mediis acuminatis, rigidis, cæteris 4 pollices longioribus .... *S. parasiticus.*

　　c. Tarsis posticè subasperis ; rectricibus mediis longissimis,
　　　　flexibilibus, cæteris 8 ad 10 pollices longioribus.......... *S. buffoni.*

Subgenus BUPHAGUS, (*Moeh.*) Coues.

= *Buphagus*,* MOEH., Gen. Av. 1752, No. 71 ; typus *Larus catarractes*, Linn.—COUES, Rev.
  Lestridinæ, in Pr. A. N. S. Phila. May 1863, p. 120.
< *Stercorarius*, " BRISS. ;" VIEILL., Nouv. Dict. d'Hist. Nat. 1817, 153 ; typus idem. (Sed
  non verus *Stercorarius*, Briss. ; cujus typus *Larus parasiticus*, Linn.).—GRAY,
  Gen. of B. iii, 1849, 651.—DEGL., Orn. Eur. 1849, ii, 287.—BP., Consp. Av. 1856,
  206.—LAWR., Baird's Birds N. A. 1858, 838.
≶ *Catharacta*, BRÜNN., Orn. Bor. 1764, 32 ; typus *Catharacta skua*, Brünn.
≶ *Cataracta*, BP., Comp. List, 1838, 63.
≶ *Larus* (partim), LINN., Syst. Nat. i, 1766.—GMEL., Syst. Nat. 1788.—LATH., Ind. Orn.
  1790 —MEY. & WOLF, Tasch. 1810.
< *Catarractes*, PALL., Zoog. Rosso-As. ii, 1811, 308 ; typus *C. skua*.—STEPH., Shaw's Gen.
  Zool. xiii, 1825, 214.
< *Lestris*, " ILL. ;" TEMM, Man. Orn. 1820-'40 ; typus *L. catarractes* (Sed non verus
  Lestris, Ill. ; cujus typus *L. parasitica*, Linn.).—FABER, Pr. Isl. Orn. 1822.—
  LESS., Traité d'Ornith. 1831.—KEYS. & BLAS., Wirb. Eur. i, 1840, 239 ; et auct. al.
= *Megalestris*, BP., Consp. Av. ii, 1856, p. 206 ; typus *Larus catarractes*, Linn.

GEN. CHAR. Bill shorter than the middle toe without the claw ; exceedingly robust ;
width at base about equal to the height, which is a third of the length of culmen.
Striæ and sulci numerous and well marked. Encroachment of feathers on bill moderate, and nearly the same on both mandibles. Occiput scarcely crested. Wings only
moderately long for this subfamily ; the primaries very broad, and rounded at their
tips. Tail very short, broad, nearly even, the feathers truncated ; central pair projecting but little, and broad to their very tips, which are also truncated. Feet large
and stout ; tarsi shorter than the middle toe and claw. Size large ; form robust and
heavy ; general organization very powerful. Colors much the same over the whole
body ; not subject to any very remarkable changes with age, sex, or season.

The essential characters lie in the large size and strong form, exceedingly robust
bill and feet, the middle toe of which latter is longer than the tarsus ; and in the very
short truncated tail, the broad central rectrices of which project but slightly beyond
the tips of the others. A discrepancy between it and *Stercorarius* is found in the changes
of plumage to which it is subject. These are slight, being chiefly of intensity, and have
little in common with the widely varying stages for which the species of *Stercorarius*
are noted. Its species when adult are of nearly uniform colors, presenting no indications of the trenchant lines of division of light and dark areas which are found in
Stercorarius. North America contains a single representative of the genus, *B. skua*,
referred by most authors to *Stercorarius*.

The synonyms of this subgenus require to be considered at length and with care, to
avoid confounding them with those of the succeeding, with which they always have been
to a greater or less degree mingled. The first distinctive appellation of the genus in question appears to be *Buphagus*, Moeh. 1752. This is unquestionably based upon the *Larus
catarractes* of Linnæus, and the diagnosis of the genus (vide infrà†) is as definite and
pertinent as perhaps any one throughout Moehring's work. This being the case, it is
a little singular that the name has not come into general employ, along with such genera as *Philomachus*, *Collyrio*, *Trogon*, &c., which have, by Gray, Baird, Cassin, Bryant,
and other authors, been accorded that precedence to which their early date entitles
them. The rule generally acknowledged by authors, which would cause the adoption
of the genera of Moehring and other pre-Linnæan writers, provided they are identified
and do not conflict with Linnæus' titles, does not appear to have been adhered to in
this instance. But if we are to be guided by the law of *priority*, and are to accord justice to a pre-Linnæan writer, we cannot avoid the adoption of Moehring's name ; since
there is no Linnæan appellation with which it conflicts, as the latter author ranged all
the Jaegers known to him under *Larus*. Moehring's not being a binomalist, or rather
his not dealing at all with species, can have no weight in the question of the adoption

* In the synonymy of this article I use the convenient signs introduced by Strickland to indicate the relative value of the various generic names quoted. Being not in
general use, they will require explanation. The sign of equality signifies that the
word before which it stands was originally employed in the same sense as here meant ;
thus, *Buphagus* and *Megalestris* are based upon the same type as *Buphagus* of the present paper, and are therefore coequal with it. The sign < indicates that the name before which it stands was originally used in a more extended sense than is here meant,
and must consequently be restricted to become completely synonymous. Thus, *Catharacta* of Brünnich, included, besides *C. skua*, *pomarinus* and *parasiticus*. The sign >
is the converse of the last.

† *Moehring, Genera avium*, 1752, page 66, No. 71. " *Rostrum* postice rectum, membrana
callosa ad nares usque tectum, versus apicem incurvum, lateribus compressis. *Femora*
extra abdomen. Digiti antici tres membrana intermedia toti cohærentes, posticus liber."

of his *genera*. Guided by these considerations, in the Proceedings of the Philadelphia Academy, as above, I revived the name *Buphagus*, and gave it that precedence over other appellations to which it is entitled.

"*Stercorarius*, Briss., 1760," is the name which has lately been most frequently employed for this subgenus. But this is clearly an error ; for the type of *Stercorarius*, as is evident by Brisson's elaborate description, is the *Larus parasiticus* of Linnæus, and not the *catarrhactes*. Regarding this latter species, it is surprising that Brisson should have been so far at fault in his estimation of its affinities as to separate it from its congeners, and range it with the true Gulls under the name of *Larus fuscus*. If *Stercorarius* is to be used at all, it must be for the group of which *parasiticus* is typical.

Catharacta of Brünnich (1764) has as its type *catarrhactes*, though all the other species known to that author are included in it. But this name, besides being antedated by *Buphagus*, is also anticipated by *Catarractes* of Moehring, a name applied to a pygopodous genus, of which *Uria troile* is the type, and which has been accepted and employed by late writers, as Cassin, Bryant, and others. This is in effect the same word as Brünnich's *Catharacta*, both having the same root, viz, κατα and ξηγνυμι, whence καταρρακτης, "a robber or despoiler." Brünnich's spelling of the word might perhaps lead us to suppose it derived from καθαιρω, "to cleanse or purify ;" but this is evidently not the case—the latinization of the word formed from the latter root giving us *cathartes*, Illiger's genus of American Vultures. Therefore, unless we allow a varying orthography of the same word to stand for two different genera, Brünnich's name must be superseded. Besides the above spelling we also find *cataracta, cataractes, catarracta, catarrhacta*, and *catarrhactes*. The last is the proper orthography, as is evident from the etymology of the word.

Lestris of Illiger (1811) is based upon *parasitica*, and, although used subsequently by many authors for the present subgenus, has really no connection with it.

Megalestris, Bonaparte (1856), is based upon the *catarrhactes*, and is strictly its only synonym. The choice is therefore between *Megalestris* and *Buphagus*. Of these I prefer the latter, which I shall continue to use as heretofore.

BUPHAGUS SKUA, (Brünn.) Coues.

The Skua.

a. *skua*.

Catarracta aldrovandi, WILL., Orn. 265.
Skua hojeri, RAY, Syn. Av. 128.
Larus fuscus, BRISS., Orn. vi, 1760, 165.—SCOP., Bemerk. Nat. 1770, 90.
Catarracta fusca, LEACH, Syst. Cat. 1816, 40.
Larus varius sive skua, BRISS., Orn. vi, 1760, 167 (juv.).
Larus catarractes, SCHAEFF., Mus. Orn. 1779, 63, pl. 39.
Catharacta skua, BRÜNN., Orn. Bor. 1764, 33.
Catarracta skua, RETZ., Fn. Suec. 1800, 161.—BP., Cat. Meth. Ucc. 79; Rev. Crit. 1850, 202.
Catarractes skua, PALL., Zoog. R.-A. ii, 1811, 309.—STEPH., Gen. Zool. xiii, 1825, 215.
Cataractes skua, MACGIL., Man. ii, 1842, 255.
Cataracta skua, BP., List, 1838, 63.
Lestris skua, BREHM, Vög. Deutschl. 1831, 716.
Buphagus skua, COUES, Pr. Phila. Acad. 1863, 125 ; Pr. Ess. Inst. v, 1868, 305.
Stercorarius (Buphagus) skua, COUES, Key, 1872, 309.
Cataractes vulgaris, FLEM., Brit. Anim. —, 137.
Larus catarractes, LINN., Syst. Nat. i, 1766, 226 (based on WILL., RAY & BRISS., *suprà ;* EDW., 149, &c.).—GM., Syst. Nat. i, 1788, 603.—LATH., Ind. Orn. ii, 1790, 818.
Lestris catarractes, ILL., Prod. 1811, 272.—TEMM., Man. 1815, 511 ; ii, 1820, 792 ; iv, 1840, 494.—FAB., Prod. Isl. Orn. 1822, 102.—BOIE, Isis, 1822, 562.—JEN., Man. 1835, 280.—EYT., Cat. Br. B. 51.—BP., Syn. 1828, No. 304.—NUTT., Man. ii, 1834, 312.—KEYS. & BLAS., Wirb. Eur. 1840, 239.—NAUM., V. D. x, 1840, 470, pl. 270.—SCHL., Rev. Crit. 1844, 84.
Lestris catharactes, BREHM, Naturg. Eur. Vög. 1823, 739.
Lestris catharactes, SCHINZ, Eur. Fn. i, 1840, 387.
Lestris catarrhactes, KAUP, Sk. Ent. Eur. Thierw. 1829, 64.
Stercorarius catarrhactes, VIEILL., Nouv. Dict. d'Hist. Nat. iv, 1817, 154; Fn. Franç. 1838, 385.—GRAY, Gen. of B. iii, 1849, 652: Cat. Br. B. 1863, 227.—DEGL., Orn. Eur. ii, 1849, 289.—BLAS., J. f. O. 1865, 384.
Stercorarius catarractes, BP., Consp. Av. ii, 1856, 206 ; Tabl. Longip. Compt. Rend. xlii, 770.—LAWR., Baird's B. N. A. 1858, 838.—SCHL., M. P.-B. iv, 1863, 45.—ELLIOT, B. N. A. i, pl. 56.
Stercorarius cataractes, SELYS-L., Fn. Belg. 1842, 155.
Stercorius catharactes, DES MURS, Traité Oöl. 1860, 551.

Stercorarius pomarinus, VIEILL., Gal. Ois. ii, 1834, 220, *nec Auct.*
Larus keeask, LATH., Ind. Orn. ii, 1790, 818.

b. antarcticus.*

Lestris catarractes, QUOY et GAIM., Voy. Uran. Ois. 38.
Stercorarius catarractes, SCHL., Mus. P.-B. iv, 1863, *Lari*, p. 45.
Lestris antarcticus, LESS., Tr. Orn. 1831, 606.—SCL., P. Z. S. 1860, 390.—ABBOTT, Ibis,
    1861, 165.—SCL. & SALV., Ibis, 1869, 284; P. Z. S. 1871, 579.—PHIL. & LANDB.,
    Cat. Av. Chili, 47.—HUTTON, B. N. Z. 1871, 39.
Stercorarius antarcticus, BP., Consp. ii, 1856, 207.—PELZ., Orn. Novara, 150.
Buphagus antarcticus, COUES, Pr. Phila. Acad. 1863, 127.

DIAG. *B. maximus, robustissimus, tarso breviore digitis mediis cum ungue; rectricibus mediis
latis vix ultrà cœteras porrectis. Rostri longit.* 2¼ *poll. Ang.*

Hab.—Seas and sea-coasts of the Northern Hemisphere, chiefly in the more arctic
regions. Var. *antarcticus*, Southern seas.

Adult, breeding plumage.—Bill about as long as or a little shorter than the head, shorter
than the tarsus, robust, somewhat broader than high at the base, compressed from the
middle, its sides bulging; culmen broad, flattened, very slightly concave, or nearly
straight on the ceral portion, the concavity increased by the great convexity of the
unguis, which rises higher than the ceral portion; unguis smooth, broad, rounded,
so decurved that the apex overhangs the tip of the lower mandible nearly perpendicularly. Outline of rami and gonys both slightly concave, the former very long. Eminentia symphysis well marked. Divarication of rami very slight. Tomia of upper
mandible sinuate, at first ascending, then deflected, then again gradually ascending
to beyond the nostrils, where it curves sharply downward. Ceral longer than the
ungual portion of the bill, its anterior extremity projecting further on the sides than
on the culmen, so that a <-shaped recess is formed; its inferior edge curving gradually upward from the base, to give passage to the nostrils; provided at the base with
several striæ. Nostrils lateral, pervious, somewhat club-shaped, broadest anteriorly;
a sulcus on the unguis leads into them from before. Several oblique striæ on the
inferior maxilla. Feathers extend on the sides of the superior mandible in a rather
acute angle, leaving a deep recess on the culmen; retreating on the sides of the bill
so nearly parallel with the tomia as to leave the edges of the superior mandible exposed nearly to the angle of the mouth. Their extent on the lower madible is less, but
is broader, and with a rounded extremity. Between the rami the feathers reach two-
thirds the way to the symphysis, the remainder being naked integument. Eye of
moderate dimensions, placed directly over the angle of the mouth. Wings rather short
for the subfamily; the primaries regularly graduated, very broad, with rounded apices;
rachis stiff and strong; secondaries short, broad, flexible, with broad rounded tips,
formed entirely by the inner web. Tertials in the folded wing ending about 3¼ inches
from apex of first primary. Tail short, broad, strong, even, or nearly so; the feathers
rather broad, with square, almost truncated extremities. Central pair much the same
in shape as the lateral; of equal breadth, projecting one or two inches. Superior and
inferior tectrices very long and thick, the latter reaching quite to the end of the tail.
Feet large and strong; the tarsi as long as the middle toe without the claw. Tibiæ
nude for nearly an inch. That part of the tibia which is bare, the tibio-tarsal articulation all around, and the sides and posterior aspects of the tarsus, and both surfaces
of the webs, covered with small, irregular polyhedral plates; these plates largest and
most regular (being hexagonal) on the sides of the tarsus; very small and numerous
on the webs; elevated, rough, and conical on the joints and inner surfaces of the toes.
Anteriorly the tarsus and toes are covered with imbricated scutella, regular and
transverse on the toes, but with exceedingly oblique edges on the tarsus, on the upper
third of which they bifurcate into two rows. Toes very long; middle longest; outer
but little less; inner only two-thirds the middle; hallux exceedingly abbreviated.
Claws all large, strong, much arched, very acute, the middle one dilated on its inner
edge, but not serrated. Membranes long, broad, full, unincised. Dorsal feathers broad,
rounded, rigid, closely imbricated, not very thick. Inferiorly the plumage is exceedingly long, thick, compact, almost mollipilose. Latero-nuchal feathers elongated,
rigid, with long disconnected fibrillæ. Above blackish-brown, more or less variegated
with chestnut and whitish; each feather being dark-colored, with a spot of chestnut
toward its extremity, which in turn fades into whitish along the shaft toward the tip
of each feather. On the latero-nuchal region and across the throat the chestnut light-
ens into a decided reddish-yellow, the white being as a well-defined, narrow, longitudinal streak on each feather. The crown, post-ocular, and mental region have but little
whitish. Inferiorly the plumage is of a blended fusco-rufous, lighter than on the
dorsum, with a peculiar indefinite plumbeous shade. The wings and tail are black-

* The only discrepancy I find, in examination of several from Southern seas, is the
shorter, stouter, and more obtuse bill.

ish ; their rhachides white, except toward the apices; the remiges and rectrices white for some distance from the bases. This white on the tail is concealed by the long tail-coverts, but appears on the outer primaries as a conspicuous spot. The bill and claws are blackish horn ; the feet pure black. Bill, from base to tip, 2.10; to end of cere, 1.20 ; gape, 3.00 ; height at base, 0.75; width a little less; rami, 1.60; gonys, 0.50; wing, 16.00 ; tail, 6.00 ; tarsus, 2.70 ; middle toe and claw, 3.10.

Young-of-the-year (Spec. No. 22266, Mus. S. I. from Iceland, shot September 1, 1839).— The size is much less than that of the adults; the bill every way weaker and slenderer; the cere illy developed ; striæ are not yet apparent, and its ridges and angles all want sharpness of definition ; the gonys is extremely short. Wings exceedingly short and rounded, the quills having very different proportional length from those of the adults; the second being longest, the third next and but little shorter ; the first about equal to the fourth. The inner or longest secondaries reach, when the wing is folded, to within an inch or so of the tip of the longest primary. The central retrices are, if anything, a little shorter than the next. The colors generally are as in the adult, but everywhere duller and more blended, having few or no white spots; and though the reddish spots are numerous and occupy a large space on each feather, yet in color they are very dark and dull. These dull reddish spots are especially numerous along the edge of the forearm and on the least and lesser coverts. On the under parts the colors are lighter, duller, and still more blended than above. The prevailing tint is a light, dull rufous, most marked on the abdomen ; but there and elsewhere more or less obscured with an ashy or plumbeous hue. The primaries, secondaries, and tertials, together with the rectrices, are dull brownish-black; their shafts yellowish-white, darker terminally. At the bases of the primaries there exists the ordinary large white space, but it is more restricted than in the adults, and so much hidden by the bastard quills that it is hardly apparent on the outside of the wing, though very conspicuous on the inferior surface. The legs and feet are parti-colored—brownish-black, variegated with yellowish. Bill, along culmen, 1.75; along gape, 2.75; height at base, 0.50 ; length of gonys, 0.35 ; tarsus, 2.60 ; middle toe and claw the same. Wing, from the flexure, 12.25. Tail, 5.75.

This species requires comparison with no other of North America. *B. antarcticus*, from the sea-coasts of the Southern Hemisphere, differs somewhat in the shape of the bill. This is shorter, deeper, and more obtuse at the tip.

Although this species is burthened with an extensive synonymy, yet in consequence of its marked character the list is pretty definite. It is one of the very oldest species, being well known to pre-Linnean writers. It is well described by both Brisson and Brünnich, the former considering it as a Gull, the latter making it the type of his genus *Catharacta*. The *Larus keeask* of Latham is stated to be 22 inches, with a bill of 3 inches, and its habitat is given as " Hudson's Bay." There is no one of the *Lestridinæ* inhabiting North America but the present which is of such large dimensions. The plate which Vieillot (Galerie des Oiseaux) gives of his *Stercorarius pomarinus* shows conspicuously the large white alar spot, which is diagnostic of the present species. Vieillot had previously recognized the characters of the species with precision.

Subgenus STERCORARIUS, *Briss.*

= *Stercorarius*, BRISS., Orn. v, 1760, 149. (Type *Larus parasiticus*, Linn.).—COUES, Pr. Phila. Acad. 1863, 128 ; and of many authors.
< *Catharacta*, BRÜNN., Orn. Bor. 1764, 32.
< *Larus*, p. LINN., Syst. Nat. 1766. Also of Gm., Lath., Meyer.
= *Lestris*, ILL., Prod. 1811, 272. (Type *L. parasiticus*, Linn.). And of most authors.
= *Prædatrix*, VIEILL., Anal. 1816, 62.
= *Labbus*, RAF., 1816.
> *Coprotheres*, REICH., 1850.

GEN. CHAR.—Bill equal to middle toe without the claw, moderately robust, the height at base more than a third the length of the culmen ; striæ and sulci few and slightly marked. Encroachment of feathers on bill very great, especially on the upper mandible, where it greatly exceeds that on the lower, and is of a different outline from that of *Buphagus*. Occiput decidedly subcrested. Wings exceedingly long, the primaries narrow, tapering, with quite acute tips. Tail long; the lateral feathers more or less graduated ; the central pair considerably, sometimes excessively, elongated, tapering, and acuminate. Feet rather slender, the tarsi equal to or slightly longer than the middle toe and claw. Size moderate or small. Form less robust, general organization much less powerful than in *Buphagus*. Nearly bicolor when adult; passing through various states of plumage before arriving at maturity.

The preceding paragraph expresses the chief diagnostic features of this subgenus. A comparison with *Buphagus* has already been instituted, and an analytical table of its species given on a preceding page. It only remains to notice its bibliography.

The first distinctive name was proposed by Brisson in 1760. This has as type the *S. parasitica*, and may include all the species of the subfamily excepting *Buphagus skua*. I accept and employ it exactly as it was constituted by its author. *Lestris*, Illiger (1811); *Prædatrix*, Vieillot (1816); *Labbus*, Rafinesque (1816); and *Coprotheres*, Reichenbach (1850), are all based upon species of the subgenus as here restricted, and are therefore synonymous with, and must be superseded by, *Stercorarius*. *Catharracta*, Brünnich, has already been treated of. By Linnæus, Gmelin, and Latham the species were arranged under *Larus*, which thus becomes a partial synonym.

STERCORARIUS POMATORHINUS, (Temm.) Vieill.

The Pomarine Jaeger.

Stercorarius striatus, BRISS., Orn. vi, 1760, 152, pl. 13, f. 2 (juv.).
Lestris striatus, EYTON, Cat. Br. B. 1836, 51.
Larus parasiticus, MEYER, Tasch. Deutsch. ii, 1810, 490 ; not of authors.
(?) *Larus crepidatus*, GM., Syst. Nat. i, 1788, 602.—LATH., Ind. Orn. ii, 1790, 819 (juv.).
Lestris pomarinus, TEMM., Man. 1815, 514 ; ii, 1820, 793 ; iv, 1840, 495.—FABER, Prod. Isl.
       Orn. 1822, 104.—BOIE, Isis, 1822, 562.—BREHM, Eur. Vog. 1823, 741.—BP., Syn.
       1828, No. 305 ; List, 1838, 63.—LESS., Man. ii, 1828, 388.—KAUP, Sk. Ent. Eur.
       Thierw. 1829, 64.—SW. & RICH., F. B. A. ii, 1831, 429.—NUTT., Man. ii, 1834,
       315.—AUD., Orn. Biog. iii, 1835, 396 ; Syn. 1839, 332 ; B. Am. vii, 1844, 186, pl.
       451.—KEYS. & BLAS., Wirb. Eur. 1840, 240.—SCHINZ, Eur. Fn. i, 1840, 388.—
       NAUM., V. D. x, 1840, 470, pl. 270.—BP., Cat. Met. Ucc. 1842, 80 ; Rev. Crit. 1850,
       202.—SCHL., Rev. Crit. 1844, 84 ; Mus. Pays-Bas, iv, 1865, 47.—DEKAY, N. Y.
       Zool. ii, 1844, 316, pl. 133, f. 292.—GIR., B. L. I. 1844, —.—THOMP., Nat. Hist.
       Irel. iii, 1851, 392.—MIDD., Sib. Reise, ii, 1853, 240.—BP., Consp. Av. ii, 1856,
       207.—DES MURS, Traité d'Oöl. 1860, 551.—BLAS., List B. Eur. 1862, 23 (subge-
       nus *Coprotheres*).—NEWT., P. Z. S. 1861, 401 (eggs).
Stercorarius pomarinus, VIEILL., Nouv. Dict. d'Hist. Nat. xxxii, 1819, 158 ; Fn. Franç.
       1828, 387.—SELYS-L., Fn. Belg. 1842, 155.—DEGL., Orn. Eur. ii, 1849, 291.—
       GRAY, Gen. of B. iii, 1849, 652 ; List Br. B. 1863, 227.—LAWR., B. N. A. 1858,
       838.—REINH., Ibis, iii, 1861, 16.—COUES, Pr. Phila. Acad. 1861, 243 ; *ibid.* 1863,
       129.—BOARDM., Pr. Bost. Soc. ix, 1862, 130.—VERR., Pr. Ess. Inst. iii, 1862, 160.—
       ALLEN, *ibid.* iv, 1864, 90.—COUES, *ibid.* v, 1868, 305.—TURNB., B. E. Pa. 1869, 47.
Cataractes pomarinus, STEPH., G. Z. xiii, 1826, 216, pl. 24.—MACGIL., Man. ii, 1842, 256.
Coprotheres pomarinus, REICH., Syst. Av. 1850, 52.—BP., Comp. Rend. xlii, 1856, 770.—
       BLAS., J. f. O. 1865, 384.
Stercorarius pomatorhinus, NEWT., Ibis, 1865, 509.—LAWR., Ann. Lyc. N. Y. viii, 1866,
       298.—COUES, Key, 1872, 309.—COUES, Elliot's Prybilov Islands, 1874, p. —.
Cataractes parasita var. *camtschatica*, PALL., Zoog. R.-A. ii, 1811, 312.
Lestris sphœriuros, BREHM, V. D. 1831, 718.

DIAG. *S. tarsis posticè asperrimis ; rectricibus mediis latis in apices ipsas, ultrà cœteras* 4 *pollices porrectis.*

Hab.—Seas and sea-coasts of Europe, Asia, and America. Interior of North America.

Adult, breeding plumage (No. 23215, Smithsonian Museum).—Bill shorter than the head, or three-fourths the tarsus, about two and one-half times its own height at the base ; width about the same as the height ; horn-colored, growing black at the tip. Feet black. Tail somewhat less than half the wing. First primary but little surpassing the second. Occiput subcrested. Feathers of the neck rather rigid and acuminate, their fibrillæ disconnected. Caudal feathers, including the central, broad quite to their tips, which are truncated, the rhachis projecting as a small mucro. The central pair project about 3 inches ; are broad to near the tip, where they form an angle of 45° with the rhachis. Their fibrillæ exceedingly long (2¾ inches), while those of the lateral feathers are only 1¾. Tail slightly graduated. Inferior tectrices reach within ½ inch of end of tail. Tibiæ bare for ¾ of an inch, scutellate for ½ inch. Tarsi very rough ; anteriorly covered with a single row of scutella, except toward the tibio-tarsal articulation, where these scutella gradually degenerate into small, irregular polygonal plates, with which the whole of the rest of the tarsus is reticulated. These plates are largest on the sides of the tarsus externally ; on the heel-joint, and posterior aspect of the tarsus generally, they become raised into small conical pyramids, acutely pointed. The scutella of the anterior portion of the tarsus is continuous with the superior surface of the toes, while the polygonal reticulation occupies both surfaces of the webs, and the inferior surface of the toes. Hallux extremely short, its nail stout, conical at the base, acute, little curved. Anterior claws all very strong and sharp ; inner most so ; the middle expanded on its inferior edge, not serrated. Webs broad, full, unincised, their free margins a little convex.

The "cere" has a straight, smooth, convex culmen ; its inferior border curves gently upward to give passage to the nostrils. The union of the two lateral halves leaves a well-marked acutely-angular recess over the culmen. There is a well-marked lateral longitudinal groove, denoting the union of that part of the cere which is attached to the culmen, with that part which depends over the nasal fossal. Curve of nail regular, gradual. Commissure straight to the nostrils, then gradually declinato-convex. Rami of both mandibles divaricate at a considerable angle, making the base of the bill very broad. Eminentia symphysis slightly marked ; commissure long, gonys short, a little concave, gape wide. Outline of feathers on the bill much as in the *Larinæ*, but supero-laterally they do not run so far forward, nor with so acute an angle. Nostrils placed far forward, lateral, linear, direct, pervious, their opening a little club-shaped. Bill horn, deepening into black ; feet black. Pileum and occipital crest brownish-black ; this color extending much below the eyes, and occupying the feathers on the ramus of the inferior maxilla. Acuminate feathers of the neck light yellow. Back, wings, tail, upper wing-coverts, under tail-coverts as far as the flanks, deep blackish-brown. Under parts, from chin to abdomen, and neck all round (except the acuminate feathers), *pure white*. (A state of plumage not often met with. The var. "C" of Temminck.)

Nearly adult.—Generally as in the preceding, but with a row of brown spots across the breast ; the sides under the wings transversely barred with white and brown ; the purity of the dark color of the abdomen interrupted by some touches of white. The legs wholly black, and the tail feathers projecting as much as in the fully adult. (A very common state of plumage, described by most authors as fully adult. Temminck's var. "B.")

Intermediate stage.—The band of dark spots across the breast has widened and enlarged, so that the whole breast appears brown, mottled with white ; the sides under the wings are conspicuously barred with white and brown ; the white of the under parts is continued down over the abdomen to the under tail-coverts ; the pure brown of these parts which obtains in the adult, now only appearing as transverse bars among the white. The upper tail-coverts and some of the wing-coverts are barred with white. The bases of the primaries are inferiorly white. The centrail tail feathers now only project an inch. The tarsi are quite changed in color ; they are now irregularly blotched with chrome-yellow—the hind toe and nail being of this color. (A very common stage, corresponding to var. "A" of Temminck.)

Dusky stage.—The bird is very nearly *unicolor ;* blackish-brown all over ; this color deepening into quite black on the pileum ; lightening into fuliginous brown on the abdomen, with a slight gilding of the black on the sides of the neck. The whitish bases of the primaries exist. The feet are in the chromo-variegated condition. The central tail feathers scarcely project half an inch. (Var. "D" of Temminck.)

Young-of-the-year.—Bill much smaller and weaker than in the adult, light colored to beyond the nostrils, when it becomes brownish-black. Feet and toes mostly *bright yellow*, the terminal portions of the latter black. The whole body is everywhere transversely waved with dull rufous. On the head, neck, and under parts, this rufous forms the predominating color ; and the bands are exceedingly numerous, of about the same width as the intervening dark color. On the flanks and under tail-coverts the bars become wider, and almost white in color. On the back and wing-coverts the brownish-black is the predominating color ; and if any rufous is present, it is merely as a narrow edging to the feathers   The under wing-coverts have irregularly-angular transverse waves of brownish-black and white. The remiges and rectrices are brownish-black, darker at their tips ; fading into whitish toward the bases of the inner vanes. On the nead and neck the light rufous decidedly predominates, and seems indistinctly but thickly nebulated with dusky ; this dusky forming a conspicuous spot just at the anterior canthus of the eye. (In this plumage the bird is the *Stercorarius striatus* of Brisson, and probably the *Larus crepidatus* of Gmelin and Latham.)

The above stages are gradual, and merge into each other, so that one can without difficulty be traced into another. As a brief exposition of the mode in which the change from the young bird, in the variegated state of plumage and with particolored feet, it may be stated that the light and dark colors, at first everywhere intermingled, gradually grow more and more distinct, being separated by lines becoming more and more trenchant, until the two colors occupy entirely different regions of the body, and are wholly separated from each other. The feet gradually lose their yellow blotches and become black.

If we examine Temminck's Manual of 1840, page 491, we find that he presents four "varieties" of this species. Comparison of his diagnosis of these supposed varieties with the four stages of plumage characterized above, it will be seen that they correspond. The adult plumage above described is his variety "C," of which he correctly says, that it is not very often met with. Our "nearly adult" is his variety "B;" our third intermediate stage is about his variety "A;" while the fusco-unicolor state corresponds to his "D." He early maintained the opinion that this dusky stage is entirely independent of sex ; but he subsequently gives as his mature opinion that the white-bellied birds are males, the others females. This view is combatted by most ornithologists; and some even of those who admit that the difference in color is a sexual peculiarity, say that it is the males and not the females that are dusky all over. This diversity of opinion I consider as strong evidence that *sex* does not determine the plumage. I think that the four "varieties" which Temminck characterises are really the progressive stages of the same individual—stages which every Jaeger must pass through or attain to in arriving at maturity. The birds which are in the unicolor state, so different from that of the adults, all have weaker bills, less elongated central rectrices, *particolored tarsi*, and are generally smaller and less robust than the adults, all of which points indicate immaturity. As regards the other conditions, the fact of our being able to trace one directly from another, seems to me proof that they are not permanent during the life of any single individual. (See continuation of the discussion of this question under head of *S. parasiticus.*)

Anatomical characters.—The mouth is capacious. It is quite narrow at the tip of the bill, but by the rapid divergence of the rami of the mandibles, quickly becomes very broad. The palate is not arched nor vaulted at all, but quite flat; but the integument, and membranes forming the floor of the mouth are very loose, and capable of considerable distension. The membrane at the angle of the mouth is loose and full; and a longitudinal elevation of it on the lower mandible is received into a corresponding depression in the upper.

The palate is quite soft and easily movable. On it there is a central very prominent longitudinal ridge, which commences at the very apex of the bill. There it is exceedingly narrow, but it widens and becomes less prominent as it goes backward. About half way to the nasal aperture there are a few reversed papillæ. Somewhat less than an inch and a half from the tip of the bill this ridge bifurcates, being longitudinally divided by the slit forming the opening of the nares. The edges of this slit, accurately coaptated, are about three-fourths of an inch long, and beset with reversed acute papillæ, which are especially large at the posterior extremity of the sides of the slit. By the approximation of these straight edges the nasal aperture can be perfectly closed; but posterior to where they terminate, the nares remain permanently open.

On either side of this central ridge is another, quite high and prominent, which, however, subsides an inch from the tip of the bill. Posteriorly this ridge also is beset with fine reversed setæ. The space between this and the median ridge is quite smooth and flat for some distance further back, where it is terminated by a single fringe of long, slender papillæ.

The membrane of the floor of the mouth is loose, flaccid, and, in the undistended state, longitudinally wrinkled. The tongue is stout; tapers but little, and is fleshy quite to the tip itself, which is scarcely at all horny, but bifid. The dorsum of the tongue is longitudinally channelled for its entire length; its sharp sides rising up from the longitudinal central depression. The base is square and terminated by a fringe of papillæ pointing outward and backward. The tip is quite deeply notched, the base emarginate, with a lateral projecting papillated cornu on either side.

About half an inch behind the base of the tongue the rima glottidis is found. As usual, it is a simple slit; about half an inch long in this species. The elevation over the larynx, in the centre of which the glottis opens, is on its posterior half, thickly beset with stout, rapidly tapering, conical papillæ.

The basi-hyal element of the hyoid bone is about a third of an inch long; flattened, subrectangular, tapering anteriorly to an obtuse, nodulated, deflected extremity, which supports the glosso-hyals. It articulates moveably with the glosso- and apo-hyals, immoveably with the uro-hyal. The glosso-hyal elements are chiefly cartilaginous; they lie side by side imbedded in the substance of the tongue, being articulated with the basi-hyal by their under surfaces, so that their posterior extremities project backward beyond their articulation, as two prominent cornua, which support the posterior extremity of the tongue. The uro-hyal is consolidated with the basi-hyal. It is osseous for about a fourth of an inch, when it becomes cartilaginous and tapers gradually to a very acute apex.

The apo-hyals are about one and a third inches long. They are nearly straight, entirely osseous, cylindrical, enjoying free motion at their basi-hyal articulation. From their extremities the cerato-hyals, chiefly cartilaginous, curve upward and outward for about an inch.

The *œsophagus* measures about ten inches from the glottis to the cardiac orifice of the gizzard. It is very capacious, and capable of being exceedingly dilated. In the undistended state the lining mucous membrane is thrown up into numerous very prominent longitudinal rugæ, which of course disappear upon dilatation. These rugæ are perfectly straight in the lower three-fourths of the canal, but toward the fauces they become wavy and zigzag. The contractile power of the tube is very great, as is evidenced by the thickness of the planes of muscular fibres by which it is enveloped. These fibres are both longitudinal and circular, and increase in volume toward the proventriculus.

The normal diameter of the canal seems to vary but slightly throughout its whole extent. At the proventriculus it is somewhat enlarged, but the dilatation is by no means very marked, and there is no change in the direction of the tube. The belt of gastric glands in the proventriculus is about an inch in uniform breadth, and forms a complete uninterrupted zone. The line of demarcation between it and the simple mucous membrane of the œsophagus is very distinct and quite straight. The color is quite different, being of a slaty tinge, while that of the œsophagus is rather reddish ; and it has a peculiar soft velvety feel. The openings of the gastric tubules may be readily seen with the naked eye, scattered thickly and evenly over the whole surface. On making an incision into the proventricular walls, the follicles themselves are plainly discernably lying imbedded in the tissue side by side. As well as can be made out with an ordinary magnifying glass, they seem to be simple, straight, cylindrical tubes, of a nearly uniform diameter, commencing by a free, rounded, closed extremity ; and proceeding directly to open on the surface of the gastric mucous membrane. Their length is but little less than the thickness of the proventricular parietes. The zone of glands is directly continuous with the lining membrane of the gizzard.

The gizzard is situated behind and somewhat posterior to the left lobe of the liver, lying far back in the abdomen, opposite the space between the last rib and the ramus of the pubis. It is a regular flattened oval in shape, one and three quarters of an inch long by one and a quarter wide, and three quarters thick. It continues in a direct line from the proventriculus. The central tendons are of rather small extent, most of the parietes being muscular ; but the bulk of the muscular fibre seems small, when we reflect that fishes, &c., are swallowed almost entire, and that consequently the bones require trituration. The thickest part of the muscular walls of the gizzard in its uncontracted state, is only about a fourth of an inch.

The cuticular lining of the gizzard is thrown up into rugæ and folds, which, on the sides, are tolerably regularly arranged longitudinally ; but at the bottom of the cul-de-sac, and about the cardiac and pyloric orifice, are irregularly reticulated. This membrane is of a dark or reddish color, and very strong and tough ; but it is of uniform width, presenting little or no thickening opposite the bellies of the lateral muscles. It terminates abruptly at the two orifices of the gizzard by a simple free extremity.

There is hardly any constriction of the proventriculus at the commencement of the gizzard, so that the cardiac orifice is nearly as large as the proventriculus itself. The pyloric orifice, on the contrary, is quite small. There does not appear to be any valve protecting it, other than the puckering of the membrane surrounding it.

The intestinal canal is between twenty-eight and thirty inches in length, from the pylorus to the anus. The duodenal fold begins almost immediately from the pylorus, curling around the right side of the gigerium to get behind and below it, and not ascending very high ; it is about two inches and a half in length, as usual containing in its concavity the pancreas. Just beyond the termination of the fold are the openings for the hepatic and pancreatic ducts, in very close proximity to each other.

The cœca are present and well developed, being quite long, when we consider the piscivorous character of the bird. They arise about two and a half inches from the anus, and measure two and three quarter inches in total length. They are throughout apposed to the intestine ; they increase in calibre from their origin to the extremities, which are free and club-shaped. The large intestine is thus very short and straight, and does not differ materially in size from the other portion of the intestines. The rectum terminates in a large globular cloaca.

The spleen is a small, narrow, elongated organ, about half an inch in length, of a slightly elliptical shape, rounded extremities, and of a light, dull-reddish color. Its situation in the specimens examined was, as nearly as could be determined, behind and to the right of the proventriculus, between it and the corresponding hepatic lobe.

The liver is of moderate size, consisting of two unequal lobes ; of these the right one is much larger than the left, measuring two and a quarter inches in length, while the other is less than two inches. Both are of about the same width, measuring nearly an inch, and are of an irregularly triangular shape on a transverse section. The right is more elongated, with sharper edges and thinner extremities than the left. They are quite separated from each other except superiorly, where rather a thin but broad band of glandular substance stretches between and unites them. There is no indication of a third posterior lobe—a "lobulus Spigelii." I have failed in detecting a gall-bladder. The two lobes lie in close apposition, except abo.e, where they divaricate for the reception of the apex of the heart.

The kidneys commence opposite to the interspace between the penultimate and the antepenultimate ribs, immediately below the termination of the lungs, and extend to the end of the sacrum. They are, as usual, accurately moulded to the bony depressions and elevations in their course, their anterior surfaces being more smooth and rounded. They are divided into only two pretty distinct and nearly disconnected portions. The superior of these is much the larger and is broader, with more decidedly convex borders.

The cloaca is very capacious and of a nearly globular shape, inclining somewhat to the conoidal from the stretching up of its fundus to join the rectum. The division into the large anterior cavity, the cloaca proper, and the posterior dilatation is un-usually well marked by a very prominent projecting ridge or fold of mucous membrane. Just anterior to this ridge, on either side, open the ureters, and in the male, in close proximity to them, the orifices of the vasa deferentia. The papillæ denoting the terminations of these tubes, as well as the orifices themselves, are exceedingly minute and require careful search for their discovery. The posterior dilatation of the cloacal parietes leads through a very narrow canal—a fourth of an inch or there-about in length—into a well-developed *bursa*. This pouch is quite capacious, measur-ing nearly a third of an inch in length by a fourth in breadth. It is of a flattened oval shape, with a rounded free extremity, and *in situ* lies pretty closely opposed to the posterior wall of the cloaca.

The superior larynx is small and very simple in structure, being, as usual, merely a flattened conical cavity formed by the plane thyroid cartilage inferiorly, supporting at its anterior extremity the arytenoid cartilages which form the rima glottidis on the superior aspect of the larynx. This aperture is commanded by the ordinary con-strictor and dilator muscles.

The trachea measures five inches in length from the superior to the inferior larynx. It is, as usual, flattened antero-posteriorly. The compression is more marked near the anterior extremity; the tube becomes more rounded and narrower toward the lower larynx. It is composed of about ninety rings. But few of these rings are of uniform width for the whole of their circumference. They are mostly broader at one point than at another, the narrow part of one being opposite a correspondingly broadened portion of the one next succeeding, so that the inequalities of any two rings mutually correct each other. Along each side of the trachea a quite distinct band of muscular fibres runs the whole length of the tube.

The cartilage composing the lower larynx is much firmer and denser than that of the upper. The rings of which this portion of the air passage was originally composed are on its posterior aspect still distinctly traceable, but anteriorly the marks of sepa-ration are quite lost, and the surface of the larynx is quite smooth. The shape of the larynx is that of a truncated pyramid, with a subtriangular base, whose posterior plane has a concave indentation, and whose anterior edge has become obsolete. Above, the opening of the larynx is a simple flattened oval, similar in shape to the trachea. Be-low it is divided in two by a cartilaginous trabeculum, which is thrown across from the posterior side to the anterior apex of the base of the pyramid. The shape of this septum is such that it forms of the lower aperture of the larynx two oval openings—the commencements of the two bronchi.

The bronchi consist of about twenty half rings, their posterior parietes being en-tirely membranous. These rings are slender and of uniform width, the membrane connecting them, and completing the canal posteriorly, being delicate and elastic. They are of about equal length.

Synonymy.—The account of *Stercorarius striatus* is one of the earliest and an accurate description of this species. The *Larus crepidatus* of Gmelin and Latham is in all prob-ability based upon the young; and, if so, has of course priority over *pomatorhinus*. But the description is short, unsatisfactory, and not diagnostic; while, being based upon an immature state of plumage, which the Pomarine Jaeger shares with *parasiticus*, I do not think it advisable to supersede a long and well-known name. The *Stercorarius crepidatus* of Vieillot is, however, the true *parasiticus*, as is also the *Lestris crepidata* of Degland, and of Schinz; but the *Lestris crepidata* of Brehm refers to *S. buffoni*. (*Vide* synonyms of these two species.) The only instance I have found of the application of the name *parasiticus* to this species is that of Meyer and Wolf. The rest of the synon-ymy does not require special notice. For a discussion of *Catharacta cepphus* of Brün-nich see remarks under *S. buffoni.*

STERCORARIUS PARASITICUS, (*Brünn.*)

Parasitic Jaeger.

Larus parasiticus, LINN., Fn. Suec. 55; Syst. Nat. i, 1766, 226.—GM., Syst. Nat. i, 1788, 601.—LATH., Ind. Orn. ii, 1790, 819.
Catharacta parasitica, BRÜNN., Orn. Bor. 1764, 37.
Cataracta parasitica, RETZ., Fn. Suec. 1800, 160.
Catarractes parasiticus, FLEM., Br. An. 138.
Lestris parasitica, ILL., Prod. 1811, 273.—TEMM., Man. ii, 1820, 796 (includes next spe-cies).—FABER, Prod. Isl. Orn. 1822, 105 (both species?).—BOIE, Isis, 1822, 562.—BREHM, Eur. Vög. 1823, 744.—KAUP, Sk. Ent. Eur. Thierw. 1829, 47.—LESS., Tr. Orn. 1831, 616.—SCHINZ., Eur. Fn. i, 1840, 390.—NAUM., V. D. x, 1840, 510, pls. 272, 273.—BP., Consp. ii, 1856, 208; Compt. Rend. xlii, 1856, 770.—BLAS., J. f. O. 1865, 384.
Lestris parasitica var. *coprotheres*, BP., Consp. Av. ii, 1856, 209.

Stercorarius parasiticus, SCHÆFF., Mus. Orn. 1779, 62, pl. 37 (*fuscus*).—SELYS-L., Fn. Belg. 1842, 155.—GRAY, Gen. of B. iii, 1849, 653; List Br. B. 1863, 228.—LAWR., B. N. A. 1858, 839; Ann. Lyc. N. Y. viii, 1866, 299.—COUES, Pr. Phila. Acad. 1861, 243; *ibid.* 1863, 132; Pr. Ess. Inst. v, 1868, 305; Key, 1872, 309; Elliot's Prybilov Is. 1874.—MALM., J. f. O. 1865, 205.—NEWT., Ibis, 1865, 570.—SCHL., Mus. P.-B. iv, 1863, 47.—DALL & BANN., Tr. Chic. Acad. i, 1869, 303.—TURNB., B. E. Pa. 1869, 47.
Catharacta coprotheres, BRÜNN., Orn. Bor. 1764, 38.
Lestris coprotheres, DES MURS, Tr. Oöl. 1860, 551.
Catarractes parasita, PALL., Zoog. R.-A. ii, 1811, 310.
Lestris parasita, KEYS. & BLAS., Wirb. Eur. 1840, 95.—BP., Cat. Met. Ucc. 1842, 80; Rev. Crit. 1850, 202.—SCHL., Rev. Crit. 1844, 85.—MIDD., Sib. Reise, ii, 1853, 241.
Cataracta cepphus, LEACH., Syst. Cat. 1816, 39.
Stercorarius cepphus, STEPH., Gen. Zool. xiii, 1826, 211, pl. 23.—SW. & RICH., F. B. A. ii, 1831, 432.—DEGL., Orn. Eur. ii, 1849, 295. (Not of authors.)
Stercorarius crepidatus, VIEILL., Nouv. Dict. d'Hist. nat. 1819, 155. (Nec *Gm.*, *Lath.* ?)
Lestris crepidata, TEMM., Man. 1815, 515.—DEGL., Mem. Soc. Roy. Lille, 1838, 108.— SCHINZ, Eur. Fn. 1840, 390. (Juv.).
Lestris richardsoni, SW. & RICH., F. B. A. ii, 1831, 433, pl. 73.—NUTT., Man. ii, 1834, 319.— BP., List, 1838, 63.—EYT., Cat. Br. B. 1836, 51.—AUD., Orn. Biog. iii, 1835, 503; Syn. 1839, 332; B. Am. vii, 1844, 190, pl. 452.—TEMM., Man. iv, 1840, 499.— SCHINZ, Eur. Fn. i, 1840, 392.—GIR., B. L. I. 1844, 367.—THOMPS., Nat. Hist. Ireland, iii, 1851, 394.
Cataractes richardsonii, MACGIL., Man. ii, 1842, 257.
Stercorarius richardsoni, COUES, Rev. *Lestrid.* Pr. Phila. Acad. 1863, 135.
Lestris boji, schleepii, benickii, BREHM, V. D. 719, 720, 723.
(?) *Lestris hardyi, spinicauda*, BP., Consp. ii, 1856, 210. (*Blasius* puts these under *buffoni*.)

DIAG. *St. rectricibus mediis rigidis, acuminatis, ultrà cœteras 4-pollices porrectis ; tarsis subasperis.*

Hab.—North Atlantic Ocean, and sea-coasts of Europe and America. Interior of Arctic America.

Adult, breeding plumage (No. 16802, Mus. Smithson.).—Bill much shorter than the head or tarsus; as high as broad at the base; basally rounded, compressed from nostrils to tip; rather robust, the sides converging from base to apex. Culmen broad, flattened, scarcely appreciably convex to the unguis, which rises slightly above the level of the cere, is moderately convex, tip not very strongly deflexed. Rami very long; gonys very short; both somewhat concave in outline. Eminentia symphysis small but well marked. Tomia of superior mandible at first ascending and a little concave; then descending and a little convex; again, very decidedly concave as it decurves toward the tip. Cere without oblique striæ; with a straight longitudinal sulcus on each side of the culmen. Feathers extending far forward on superior mandible, with a curved free outline, so broad that the feathers of the sides meet over the culmen. Feathers on inferior mandible also project considerably, almost filling the triangular sulcus on the side as well as the angular space between the rami. Middle of eye just over angle of mouth. Wings moderately long, strong, pointed; first primary much the longest; rest regularly and rapidly graduated; all rather narrow and tapering to an acute apex, somewhat rigid and falcate. Secondaries short and inconspicuous; broad, the tips of the outer ones nearly square, of the inner obliquely incised, the apex being formed by the inner web alone. Tertials long, soft, flexible. Tail moderately long, contained not quite two and a half times in the wing; very slightly rounded, the graduation being only half an inch. Feathers moderately broad quite to their tips, which are truncated. The central pair project three to four inches. They begin to taper about four inches from their apices, and regularly converge to a very acute tip. Upper tail coverts moderately long; the inferior still longer, but neither as long as in *skua*. Feet rather short and quite slender; tarsi as long as the middle toe and claw. Tibia naked half an inch above the joint. The scutellation and reticulation is the same as that already described, but the nails are weaker and less arched, though fully as acute. A decided occipital crest and a calotte. Nuchal region with the feathers acuminate and rigid, with loosened fibrillæ. Pileum, occipital crest, and whole upper parts deep brownish-black, with a somewhat slaty tinge, and a slight but appreciable metallic shade; this color deepening into quite black on the wings and tail. Rhachides of primaries and rectrices whitish, except at their tips; the inner vanes albescent basointernally. Chin, throat, sides of head, neck all round, and under parts to the vent, pure white; the feathers of the latero-nuchal region rigid, acuminate, with disconnected fibrillæ, light yellow. Under tail coverts like the upper parts, but somewhat of a fuliginous tint; the line of demarcation from the white of the abdomen very trenchant.

Nearly mature (No. 20144).—Size and form of the adult. Pileum and latero-nuchal region, and whole upper parts, as in the adult. The under parts white (as in the adult), but clouded everywhere with dusky patches, most marked across the breast, on the sides, the flanks, and under tail coverts, and leaving the middle of the belly and throat nearly pure. Varying degrees of this dusky nubilation approach in some specimens nearly to the uniform dusky below characterized; in others fade almost into the pure white of the adult, connecting the two ages perfectly. The tarsi of the most dusky specimens have small yellow blotches; the others not.

Dusky stage (No. 20362).—With the size and proportions of the adult. Wholly deep dusky; darker and more plumbeous superiorly; lighter, and with a fuliginous tinge, inferiorly; the pileum quite black; the latero-nuchal region yellow; the remiges and rectrices quite black; feet black.

Immature (No. 18652).—Size and general proportions nearly those of the adult. Bill and cere perfectly formed; feet mostly black, but with some yellow blotches. The upper parts are unadulterated with any rufous bars; the deep brownish-black pileum has appeared, and the sides of the neck have obtained their yellow shade, which contrasts conspicuously with the fuliginous back-ground. Evidences of immaturity, however, are found on the under parts, where the dark color is mixed with the illy-defined transverse bars of ochraceous. Rufous is also found at the bend of the wing and on the under wing and tail coverts. The primaries are still whitish at the outside, as are also the rectrices. The central rectrices project 2½ inches, and have the tapering form of those of the adults.

Younger (No. 2754).—The juvenility of the specimen is attested by its small size, delicate bill and feet, little projection of the central rectrices, general mollipilose condition of plumage, &c. The rufous of the very young bird, instead of giving way everywhere to dusky, yields to this color only on the upper parts and crown; on the sides of the head, neck, and the whole under parts, whitish being the predominating color; the continuity of this last being interrupted by indistinctly marked dusky bars. The yellow of the sides of the neck has not yet appeared. There is the same white space on the bases of the wings and tail that exists on the very young. The central tail feathers only project about 2½ inches.

Young-of-the-year in August.—Size considerably less than that of the adult, form every way more delicate. Wings more than an inch shorter; bill and feet much slenderer and weaker. Bill in some specimens light bluish-horn; in others greenish-olive, the terminal portion brownish-black. Tarsi and greater part of the toes yellow. The bird is everywhere rayed and barred with rufous and brownish-black. On the head and neck the rufous has a very light ochraceous tinge, and is by far the predominating color, dark only appearing as a delicate line along the shaft of each feather. There is an aggregation of the brown into a spot at the anterior canthus of the eye. Proceeding down the neck to the back, the longitudinal lines become larger, and gradually spread wider and wider, until between the shoulders they occupy the whole of each feather, except a narrow border of rufous, which latter is of a deeper tint than on the head. Passing down the throat to the breast, the rufous becomes decidedly lighter—almost whitish—while the brown, which on the throat exists only as a light longitudinal line, changes on each feather to transverse bars of about equal width with the light rufous bars with which it alternates. This pattern prevails over the whole under parts, the transverse bands being broadest on the flanks and under tail and wing coverts, narrowest in the middle of the belly. The primaries are brownish-black, narrowly tipped with rufous, their shafts yellowish, their inner webs fading basally into white. The tail has the same coloration as the wings. The central feathers project about three-fourths of an inch.

In this species we can favorably study the changes of plumage which are characteristic of all the species. I am enabled by the extensive series at my command to trace the various stages of the present species.

Beginning with the stage last described, that of the young-of-the-year, we find it characterized essentially by the presence of *rufous* or *ochraceous*, disposed chiefly in *transverse bars*, or spots, or waves, which alternate with similarly shaped dusky or brownish-black markings. The birds are much smaller than the adults, the bill and feet more delicate. As the bird grows older the bill and feet become stouter, the cere better developed, and the rufous everywhere grows first lighter and then more restricted, giving way to an encroachment of the blackish. This increase of the darker color is particularly rapid on the upper parts, which become uniformly dusky before the under parts do. When this has taken place the bird is in the plumage of No. 18652. The tarsi and feet are still mostly yellow; there is still the white space at the bases of the primaries; the central rectrices still have only a partial development. By the time the rufous mentioned in No. 18652 as existing on the alar coverts, under parts, &c., has entirely disappeared, the bird has become half-grown, and is now in that peculiar state of plumage characterized in the description of No. 20362. This is a definite stage. But some few specimens in the collection do not seem to pass through this dusky epoch in arriving at maturity. The rufous yields to black only on the upper parts; on the under parts the blackish bars as well as the rufous ones become changed to white; so that the bird tends at once to assume the bicolor plumage of the adults without going through the dusky-unicolor stage. This is one of the perplexing facts we encounter in studying the question. We find that the very immature plumage of the young birds in August can be traced through one series directly into the fusco-unicolor stage; through another into a state which seems to pass directly into that of the normally-colored, fully adult bird. Various explanations have been offered to account for the dusky stage of plumage. Some authors consider it as a sexual feature, regarding it as the normal adult plumage of one sex (according to some the male; to others the female!) Others look upon it as a seasonal feature, attained at a certain time in each year, and regularly recurring each successive season. Still others, again, consider it as a distinct *variety*, accidental and irregular according to some, permanent according to others. With regard to the question of the *sexual* nature of this state, I think the evidence is decidedly against such a belief. The very fact that those authors who contend for this opinion differ as to *which* sex—some affirming that they found testicles and others that they saw ovaries in the dusky birds they dissected—seems to me conclusive evidence that the state of plumage in question is common to both sexes. I cannot admit the hypothesis that this state constitutes a permanent or accidental variety. I do not think it possible that normally-colored adult birds can have young which attain at once this dusky state and retain it during their lives; still less that they can transmit their abnormal characters to their offspring, as would be necessary to constitute a permanent variety. The supposition that it is a purely accidental variety—*i. e.*, that certain individuals, without any cause, by a freak of nature as it were, become thus colored and remain so for their whole lives—seems still less worthy of credence. Examples of this condition of plumage are too numerous, and bear altogether too definite relations with certain other stages, not to be brought about by and dependent upon some definite law. The preceding suppositions being untenable, I think there can be no reasonable doubt as to the true character of the stage of plumage in question, from the amount of evidence which we have tending to prove it dependent upon *age* and *season*. I do not hesitate, therefore, to express the decided opinion that this unicolor state is a transient, immature stage of plumage, perfectly normal, and universal, or nearly so, independently of sex, which every Jäger—or at least the great majority of individuals—passes through in its progress toward maturity, after leaving the plumage it first assumed, and before it arrives at the plumage which is indicative of maturity. The only question is, exactly *what* age this plumage is indicative of, and whether, after once having attained to this fully mature condition, the adults do or do not return to this unicolor state at certain season of each year. My opinion is, that it supervenes, ordinarily at least, directly upon the disappearance of the rufous, which is characteristic of the very young bird, and therefore is probably assumed after the first moult and retained until the second. I do not think it *probable* that the adults which have passed through this state ever return to it; for, as remarked under head of *S. pomatorhinus*, we nearly always find these unicolor birds possessed of of smaller, weaker bills, and slenderer, generally particolored, feet; all of which characters are invariably indicative of the immature bird.

Synonymy.—It is difficult, perhaps impossible, to say whether the names and descriptions of authors before 1800 really refer to this species or to the *buffoni*. It is most probable, however, that the former is really the species meant, both because it is the most abundant and well known, and because Retzius, in his edition of the Fn. Suec. (in which work the species is definitely settled by giving the exact length of the central rectrices *), cites as synonymous nearly all the names and descriptions in question. He errs, however, in adducing *S. longicaudatus*, Brisson, which is the *buffoni*. *Catharacta parasitica* of Brünnich and the *Larus parasiticus* of Linnæus, Gmelin, and Latham in all probability really refer to this species, and it is from the former of these authors that the specific name is accepted. But *Larus parasiticus* of Latham (1790) may have been based upon the long tailed species, for the reason that the length of his bird is given as 21 inches—a dimension never attained by *parasiticus*. The synonyms of the two species are indiscriminately cited.

The *Catharacta coprotheres* of Brünnich is this species in its fusco-unicolor stage. On its very first introduction, in 1764, Brünnich himself doubts its validity as a species, and says of it: "*An precedenti—parasiticus—sexu vel specie diversa*"? Yet down to the present time it has always been held by some authors as distinct. Thus, in 1856, Bonaparte gives a variety (*coprotheres*), and still later, in 1860, Des Murs presents a species (*Lestris coprotheres*).

An early, detailed, and unmistakable description of this species is that of Brisson, in 1760, who gives an accurate account of it under the mononomial appellation *stercorarius*. The species serves as the type of his genus.

The *Stercorarius crepidatus* of Vieillot (ut suprà) is based upon this species, although his specific name is taken from Gmelin and Latham, who probably based their descriptions of *crepidatus* upon the young *pomatorhinus*. So, also, the *Lestris crepidata* of

---

* Fn. Suec. p. 180: "Rectrices 6, 6 (*i. e.*, the central pair) cæteris 4 poll. longiores."

Degland (1838), and, following his authority, Schinz (1840) are both synonyms of the young of the present species, according to Degland's subsequent admission.

The name *cephus* has been applied to this species by very few writers, the principal of which I have given in the synonymy. Those writers who use this name for the present species apply to the long-tailed species either *parasitica*, or *longicaudata*, or *buffoni*. For the discussion of the names of those authors who thus interchange *cephus* and *parasiticus*, see remarks under head of *buffoni*.

The *Lestris parasitica* of Temminck (1820) is a mixture of the present species and the long-tailed one, as is shown by his list of authorities cited as well as by his description. This error Temminck soon afterward became aware of, and in subsequent editions corrected by contradistinguishing the two species. The same combination probably exists in Faber's description of his *Lestris parasiticus*.

In 1863 I indorsed the validity of *S. richardsoni* as different from *parasiticus*, but not without hesitation, and I am now of opinion that it is inseparable. It is, it is true, larger in all its parts, and the specimens I have examined have a longer and apparently more rounded tail than usual, with broader rectrices ; but with increased knowledge of the range of individual variability in this genus, I scarcely think the name tenable even as that of a variety.

The name has been quite generally employed, especially by American writers, for the true *parasiticus* (to which it belongs, but is of course antedated). How this came about is readily explained. The two species of Jägers—the Common and the Long-tailed—were generally confounded by authors (except Brisson) down to a comparatively recent date, or at least the two names " *parasiticus* " and " *cephus*," were used indiscriminately for either species by those even who recognized two. Thus, in 1820, Temminck, then perhaps the best authority on the subject, gives but a single species, under the name of " *parasiticus*, Brünnich," which, according to his description and synonymy, is a combination of both. He soon after, however, became aware of his error, and acknowledges it in 1840, saying that " comme notre article du *Stercoraire parasite* ou labbe, renferme * * * les synonymes de deux espèces destinctes * * * il est nécessaire de refaire en totalité toutes les indications," &c. But in the mean time Swainson's *richardsoni* had been described and figured, and Temminck, looking for a name under which to present the Common Jäger (for he considered the name " *parasitica* " as referring to the Long-tailed species), adopted Swainson's appellation for it. His example has been followed by Audubon and other American as well as by some European writers.

STERCORARIUS BUFFONI, (Boie) Coues.

Buffon's or the Long-tailed Jaeger.

Stercorarius longicaudatus, BRISS., Orn. vi, 1760, 155.—VIEILL., Nouv. Dict. d'Hist. Nat. xxxii, 1819, 157.—DEGL., Orn. Eur. ii, 1849, 298.—SELYS-L., Fn. Belg. 1842, 156.—SCHL., Mus. P.-B. iv, 1863, 49.
Lestris longicaudatus, THOMPS., N. H. Irel. iii, 1851, 399.
Cataractes longecauda, MACGIL., Man. ii, 1842, 258.
Stercorarius longicauda, NEWT., Ibis, 1865, 571.
(?) *Catharacta cephus*, BRÜNN., Orn. Bor. 1764, 36.
Lestris cephus, KEYS. & BLAS., Wirb. Eur. 1840, 240.—BP., Cat. Met. Ucc. 1842, 80 ; Rev. Crit. 1850, 202 ; Consp. ii, 1856, 209.—DES MURS, Tr. Oöl. 1860, 551.—BLAS., J. f. O. 1865, 384.
Stercorarius cephus, GRAY, Gen. of B. iii, 1849, 653 ; List Br. B. 1863, 229.—LAWR., B. N. A. 1858, 840.—COUES, Pr. Phila. Acad. 1861, 243.—SCHL., Mus. P.-B. iv, 1863, 49.—BOARDM., Pr. Bost. Soc. ix, 1862, 131.—VERR., Pr. Ess. Inst. iii, 1862, 160.— ALLEN, *ibid*. iv, 1864, 90.
(?) *Larus parasiticus*, LATH., Ind. Orn. ii, 1790, 819. Uncertain.
Cataractes parasiticus, PALL., Zoog. R.-A. ii, 1811, 310.—MACGIL., Br. B. v, —.
Lestris parasitica, TEMM., Man. Orn. iv, 1840, 502.—LESSON, Man. ii, 1828, 388 —SW. & RICH., F. B. A. ii, 1831, 430.—NUTT., Man. ii, 1834, —.—JEN., Man. 1835, 283.— EYT., Cat. 1836, 52.—AUD., Orn. Biog. iii, 1835, 470 ; Syn. 1839, 333 ; B. Am. vii, 1844, 192, pl. 452.—GIR., B. L. I. 1844, 364.
Lestris buffoni, BOIE, " in Meyer's Tasch. iii, 1810, 212 ;" Isis, 1822, 562.—BP., Syn. 1828, No. 306 ; List, 1838, 63.—KAUP, Sk. Ent. Eur. Thierw. 1829, 47.—LESS., Tr. Orn. 1831, 616.—SCHINZ, Eur. Fn. i, 1840, 391.—SCHL., Rev. Crit. 1844, 135.—DEKAY, N. Y. Zool. ii, 1844, 315, pl. 133, f. 291.—MIDD., Sib. Reise, ii, 1853, 241.
Stercorarius buffoni, COUES, Pr. Phila. Acad. 1863, 136 ; Pr. Ess. Inst. v, 1868, 305 ; Key 1872, 309 ; Prybilov Isl. 1874, —.—MALMG., J. f. O. 1865, 206.—LAWR., Ann. Lyc. N. Y. viii, 1866, 299.—DALL & BANN., Tr. Chic. Acad. i, 1869, 304.
Lestris crepidata, BREHM, Eur. Vog. 1823, 747 ; V. D. 724.—NAUM., V. D. x, 534, pl. 274.
Lestris lessoni, DEGL., Mem. Acad. Roy. Lille, 1838.—SCHINZ, Eur. Fn. 1840, 392. (*Young*.)
" *Lestris brachyrhynchus, microrhynchus*, BREHM."

DIAG. *S. rectricibus mediis ultrà cœteras* 8 *ad* 10 *poll. porrectis.*

Hab.—Coasts of North America and Europe, chiefly in higher latitudes. Interior of Arctic America.

Adult, breeding plumage.—Bill shorter than the head, less than the middle toe without the claw ; stout, compressed, higher than broad at the base, its sides regularly converging. Ceral portion of culmen broad, flat, depressed, slightly concave in outline; ungual portion very decidedly declinato-convex to the greatly overhanging tip; narrower than the ceral. Tomia of superior mandible sinuate; at first concave and ascending; then convex and descending; again very concave as they decurve toward the deflected tip, just posterior to which there is an imperfect notch. Tomia of inferior maxilla nearly straight to the tip, where they are decurved. Gonys very short, slightly concave in outline. Eminentia symphysis acute, but not very large; rami very long as compared with the gonys, but absolutely rather short, from the encroachment of the feathers. Cere very short, being scarcely if at all longer than the unguis; its lower border curving upward to give passage to the nostrils. The encroachment of the feathers on the bill is greater than that of any other species ; on the upper mandible they extend within half an inch of the distal end of the cere, having a broad, rounded termination, the feathers of the two sides meeting on and covering the culmen some distance from its real base. The feathers on the sides of the lower mandible extend nearly as far as on the upper, and those between the rami quite to the symphysis. Wings exceedingly long; first primary much the longest; rest rapidly graduated ; all rather narrow, tapering, falcate, actually pointed, their rhachides stiff and strong. Secondaries short and inconspicuous ; rather broad; their apices as in the other species. Tertials moderately long, very straight, flexible, rounded at their extremities, the edges of their vanes convoluted. Tail very long ; longer, both absolutely and relatively, than in any other North American species, being half as long as the wings; graduated, the lateral feather being three-fourths of an inch shorter than the next to central pair ; all the feathers moderately broad, converging somewhat to their rather broad, rounded tips. Central rectrices extremely lengthened, exceeding the wings ; projecting 8 to 10 inches beyond the tips of the lateral ones. They are extremely rigid at the base, being there much stiffer than the other feathers, but gradually become flexible, and at length filamentous in character, but preserve great elasticity throughout. They are about the same as the other feathers at their bases; thence taper uniformly to their exceedingly acute tips. Their edges are sinuate Superior tectrices moderately long; the inferior reaching nearly to the tips of the rectrices. Feet quite slender ; tarsus equal to middle toe and claw. Tibiæ bare of feathers for three-fourths of an inch. The reticulation of the feet is identical with that already described under other species. The scutella of the anterior face of the tarsus, however, show a tendency to degenerate into minute plates near the tibio-tarsal joint. Proportions of the toes as in other species, but the claws are comparatively small and weak, and but moderately curved and acute.

Occiput decidedly subcrested. The latero-nuchal region has its feathers lengthened, with disconnected fibrillæ, but they are hardly acuminate or rigid. The plumage about the bill is short, thick, and compact; that of the upper parts is soft and flexible, only moderately imbricated and compact; that of the under parts is long, soft, and very thick.

Bill dusky, its nail almost black. Tarsi deep leaden-blue ; tibiæ, phalanges, interdigital membranes, and claws black. Occiput subcrested, more decidedly than in any other species, forming a calotte of brownish-black, which color extends downward on the cheeks, the feathers before and below the eye and on the sides of the bill being of this color. Neck all round, but especially the sides of the head and the peculiarly-formed feathers on the latero-nuchal region, light straw-yellow. Whole upper parts, with upper wing and tail coverts, deep slate, which, on the primaries, secondaries, lateral tail feathers, and distal half of central pair, deepens into a lustrous brownish-black. Under surface of wings and tail deeper slate than the black, but not so deep as the upper surfaces. Chin, throat, and upper breast white, gradually becoming obscured with dusky-plumbeous, which deepens posteriorly, so that the abdomen and under tail coverts are nearly as dark as the back. Rhachides of first two or three primaries pure white, deepening into brownish-black at their tips ; of the other primaries, and of the tail feathers (including the central pair), brown, except just at the base, blackening terminally. Under surfaces of all the rhachides are white for nearly their whole length.

Dimensions.—Length of culmen, 1.15 inches; gape, 1.70; cere, 0.60; unguis about the same ; gonys, 0.30; from feathers on sides of bill to tip, 0.90 ; wing, 12.50 ; tail, 6.25 ; central pair, 14.00 to 16.00 ; the projection, 8.00 to 10.00 inches; tibiæ bare, 0.75 ; tarsus, 1.60 ; middle toe without claw, 1.40.

The changes of plumage of this species being exactly like those of *S. parasiticus*, it is unnecessary to repeat them.

Synonymy.—As already remarked, while speaking of *S. parasiticus*, it is exceedingly difficult to determine to which of the two species of Jäger the names " *parasiticus* " and

" *cepphus*" really refer. This difficulty results partly from the brevity and vague character of the diagnoses given, and partly from the fact that the two species were really confounded (except by Brisson) until a comparatively recent date. From this it results that many of the older names and citations may without difficulty be referred to either species. This has been done; some authors considering Brünnich's or Linnæus' " *parasiticus* " to refer to the Long-tailed, and others thinking that it was based upon the common species, until the identification of this name has become almost a matter of choice, or rather of tacit understanding. A glance at the synonyms of the two species will show that authors are about equally divided on this point. Before the introduction of " *richardsoni*" by Swainson, the Common Jäger usually received the appellation of *parasiticus*, but after the adoption of Swainson's name for this species by Temminck and others, the name *parasiticus* was for some years almost universally applied to the Long-tailed Jäger. Within the last few years, however, the name has again reverted to the common species, and Buffon's Jäger has usually been called " *cepphus*." This identification of Brünnich's name is sanctioned by Gray, Bonaparte, and other writers. The following are my reasons for rather referring it to the young *pomarinus :*

It is apparent, from almost every sentence of Brünnich's description of *cepphus*, that he had in view a young bird of the year, in the state in which it is transversely waved with rufous and dusky, &c. The only point to determine is, what species it is the young of. Regarding its size, Brünnich compares it with his *Catharacta skua*, saying that it is much smaller than that species, and the size of *parasitica*. The young-of-the-year of *pomatorhinus* is more nearly the size of the adult *parasiticus* than is the young of the Long-tailed Jäger. The account of the colors, proportions, &c., which follows, agrees precisely with those of the young *pomatorhinus ;* and when we remember that at that time the differences between the Common and Buffon's Jäger were not appreciated, it seems by no means certain that Brünnich had the latter in view in drawing up his description. He would in that case have doubtless compared it with the *parasiticus*. Moreover, authors who wrote but shortly after Brünnich's time, considered his *cepphus* to be the *pomatorhimus :* thus, *e. g.*, Latham places it as a synonym of that species. I by no means insist upon its reference to *pomatorhimus*, but merely wish to show that it very possibly belongs there, and that it is altogether too indefinite to be employed in either connection.

The name *longicaudatus* of Brisson (1760) is the very first one accompanied by a sufficiently definite description to enable the species to be identified. As Brisson is no authority for species, the name *buffoni*, proposed by Boie, is the first tenable specific designation.

I have already given my reasons for referring the *Larus parasiticus*, Latham, to this species, rather than to the *parasiticus* of Brünnich.

The *Lestris lessoni* of Degland (1838) is, according to that author's own admission, based upon the youg *buffoni*. This same immature plumage of this species has served as the basis of *Lestris crepidata* of Brehm (1823).

Subfamily LARINÆ.

DIAG. *Laridæ rostro integro, maxillæ superioris apice aduncá, inferiorem excedente.*

CH. Bill entire ; the apex of the upper mandible overhanging the tip of the lower. General shape of the bill as in *Lestridinæ.* Eminentia symphysis always prominent. Rami of inferior mandible divaricating at an acute angle. Submental space partially feathered. Feathers of forehead extending further on the sides than on the culmen of upper mandible. Nostrils direct, linear-oval, somewhat club-shaped, pervious, situated on the side of the upper mandible near its base. Wings long, strong, and acutely pointed, the first primary usually longest. Tail usually square, or very slightly emarginate ; sometimes forked ; in *Rhodostethia* cuneate. Legs ambulatorial, of moderate length, placed far forward. Tibiæ denuded for a greater or less space below ; moderately stout, anteriorly scutellate, posteriorly smoothly reticulate. Toes as in the other subfamilies. Webs moderately full, always more or less emarginate. Hind toe always fully developed, except in *Rissa.* Of very variable size, from the largest of the family to nearly the smallest. Plumage full and thick, especially beneath ; varying in color greatly with age and season, hardly, if at all, with sex. Sexes of nearly equal size, female usually a little the largest.

Anatomical characters.—For these see the account of the anatomy of *L. argentatus* (*smithsonianus*), a typical species well illustrating the internal structure of the whole subfamily.

The numerous species of this cosmopolitan group have been unwarrantably subdivided into a large number of genera, so-called by modern systematists. It may not be possible, even were it judged expedient, to define these genera as such ; for with the exception of the cuneate-tailed *Rhodostethia*, and the fork-tailed *Xema*, no characters are observed beyond those of pattern of coloration, by which the groups can be trenchantly separated, as the species are all variously interrelated.* Among the North American forms we may distinguish three genera, one of them with several sections, as follows:

Analytical table of the North American genera and sections of Larinæ.

I. Tail square... LARUS.
   A. Head never hooded; under parts never rosy-tinted; Size medium and large; bill stout.
      a. Hallux well developed, with perfect claw.
         1. Adult white, with a colored mantle................ *Larus.*
         2. Adult dark, with white head...................... *Blasipus.*
         3. Adult entirely white............................ *Pagophila.*
      b. Hallux usually defective............................. *Rissa.*
   B. Head in summer hooded, and under parts rosy-tinted; size medium and small; bill slender....................... *Chrœcocephalus.*
II. Tail wedge-shaped; neck collared; small.................... RHODOSTETHIA.
III. Tail forked; small; hooded and collared..................... XEMA.
         large; hooded, not collared..................... *Creagrus.*

Subgenus LARUS, *Linn.*

< *Larus*, LINN., Syst. Nat. 1735–1766; *et auct.*
< *Gavia*, MOEHR., Gen. Av. 1752.
> *Leucus*, KAUP, Sk. Ent. Eur. Thierw. 1829, 86. (*L. marinus.*)
> *Laroides*, BREHM, 1830.—BP., Consp. ii, 1850, 217. (*L. argentatus.*)
> *Plautus*, REICH., 1853. (*L. argentatus.*)
> *Glaucus*, BRUCH, J. f. O. 1853, 101. (*L. glaucus.*)
> *Dominicanus*, BRUCH, J. f. O. 1853, 100. (*L. marinus.*)
> *Laroides*, BRUCH, J. f. O. 1855, 281. (*L. glaucus.*)
> *Gavina*, BP., Consp. Av. 1856, 222. (*L. audouini.*)
> *Leucus*, BP., Consp. Av. ii, 1856, 215. (*L. glaucus.*)
> *Clupeilarus*, BP., Consp. Av. ii, 1856, 220. (*L. fuscus.*)
> *Gabianus*, BP., Consp. Av. ii, 1856, 212. (*L. pacificus.*)

GEN. CHAR. Bill shorter than the head or tarsus, large, strong, more or less robust, usually very stout, deep at the base, higher than broad, compressed throughout, the apex not very acute and never much attenuated or decurved. Culmen about straight to beyond the nostrils, then convex, the amount of curvature increasing toward the end, varying in different species. Commissure slightly sinuate at its extreme base, then about straight to near the end, where it is more or less arcuato-declinate. Eminentia symphysis always large, prominent, and well defined, rather obtuse, seldom acute. Nostrils placed rather far forward in a well-defined nasal fossa, lateral, longitudinal, pervious, rather broader anteriorly than posteriorly. Feathers of forehead extending considerably farther on the sides of the upper mandible than on its culmen, but falling considerably short of the nostrils. Wings when folded reaching beyond the tail, the remiges strong, not very acute, first longest, second but little shorter, rest rapidly graduated. Tail of moderate length, always even, never forked nor rounded. Legs rather slender, of moderate length; tibiæ bare for a considerable distance above the joint, the naked part smooth. Tarsi about equal to or a little longer than the middle toe and claw, varying but slightly in proportions among the different species; anteriorly scutellate, posteriorly and laterally reticulate. Hallux fully developed and always present. Anterior claws stout, strong, little curved, rather obtuse, the inner edge of the middle one dilated. Webs full and broad, scarcely incised.

Of very large or medium size, never very small. Robust and powerful. Comprising the largest species of the subfamily and those typical of it. White, with a darker mantle, without a hood; the head and neck in winter streaked with dusky.

The preceding paragraphs express the essential characters of the subgenus *Larus*, as it is here accepted. I take as my type of the section the old Linnæan *L. canus*, and consider as congeneric with that species all the true Gulls which are white, with yellowish bills, with a darker mantle, without hoods, and with the head and neck streaked with dusky in winter, and which have squarely truncated tails and perfectly developed

---

* The character of defective hallux, supposed to distinguish *Rissa*, does not always hold; for in a North Pacific form, not specifically distinguishable from *R. tridactyla*, the hind toe is perfectly formed. *Pagophila* has stout, roughish tarsi. The species of "Hooded Gulls" (*Chrœcocephalus*, &c.) are generally small and delicate slender-billed species; but one, at least, is among the largest of the Gulls, while from the slender, tern-like form of the bill, seen in *C. minutus* and *philadelphia*, the transition is gradual and unbroken to species with a very stout hooked bill.

halluces. It will be seen that the definition excludes all the *Xemœ*, which seem to form a very natural section by themselves, and, among the *Larecæ* proper, excludes *Rissa*, with its usually imperfect hallux ; *Pagophila*, with its entirely white color and some peculiarities of form ; and the whole group of dark colored, usually red-billed, Gulls, comprising *Leucophœus, Blasipus, Adelarus,* &c.

The old genus, *Larus*, has been, to an entirely unwarrantable extent, subdivided by some late systematists. There being scarcely *any* appreciable differences of form among most of the *Lari*, these authors have based generic characters upon the *color of the mantle and primaries*. But between two extremes of color, *e. g. L. marinus* and *glaucus* (from slaty black to the lightest of pearly or whitish blue), there is found every shade, and such features as these should not be made grounds for generic divisions. If it be admitted that the "genera" of *Lari typici* are quite arbitrary, established to facilitate the determination and recollection of species, somewhat after the fashion of an index, in which subjects are arranged after some fixed and previously agreed upon order of sequence, their usefulness cannot be questioned, but I do not think that they are natural genera.

We find among the *Lari* three, perhaps four, groups, the species of each of which are more closely allied among themselves than are those of the different groups. They may be thus arranged and defined :

A. "*White-winged Gulls*."—Of large size, inhabiting exclusively the higher latitudes of the Northern Hemisphere ; with exceedingly light-bluish, sometimes almost white, mantles, and white or bluish primaries, without any black on them; light yellow bills; flesh-colored legs. This group constitutes the genus *Glaucus* of Bruch (1853); *Laroides* of Bruch (1855); *Leucus* of Bonaparte (1856). All the well-accredited species are represented in North America. They are three in number—*glaucus, leucopterus,* and *glaucescens.*

B. "*Black-backed Gulls*."—Of the very largest and medium size, cosmopolitan ; with slaty-black mantles ; primaries crossed with black ; yellowish bills, flesh-colored legs. They again are of two types—a larger, embracing the most powerful known Gulls (*marinus,* &c.), upon which is founded Bruch's genus *Dominicanus ;* and a smaller, comprising *L. fuscus* and its representative species from various parts of the world, serving as the type of Bonaparte's genus *Clupeilarus.*

C. "*Herring Gulls*."—Of rather large and medium size, cosmopolite; the quite numerous species all having the bill yellowish, with a spot of red at the eminentia; the legs flesh-colored ; the mantle some shade of blue ; the primaries crossed with black. Upon the type of this section is based *Laroides* of Brehm. The type is the European Herring Gull—*argentatus* of Brünnich; intimately allied species or varieties are, *smithsonianus,* Coues ; *michahellesii,* Bruch ; *occidentalis,* Audubon ; (?) *borealis,* Brandt. *Californicus,* Lawrence, is exactly intermediate between this and the succeeding section.

D. "*Mew Gulls*."—Of medium and small size, inhabiting the Northern Hemisphere ; greenish-yellow bill, not very robust ; bluish mantles ; primaries crossed with black ; legs greenish-yellow, instead of flesh-color. Typical *Larus* of Linnæus, comprising *delawarensis,* Ord ; *canus,* Linnæus ; *brachyrhynchus,* Richardson ; and other representative species and varieties.

The North American species may be tabulated as follows :

Analysis of the North American Lari.

A. Large and robust: mantle whitish or pale-pearly ; no black on
    primaries at any age.
    a. Mantle very pale ; primaries the same, fading insensibly
        into white far from the tips.
        1. Larger: length, about 30 inches; wing, 18.00 or
            more; bill and tarsus, each, about 3.00.......   GLAUCUS.
        2. Smaller: length, about 24 inches; wing, 17 or
            less; bill, about 2; tarsus, 2.25 ....   LEUCOPTERUS.
    b. Mantle light blue ; primaries the same, with definite
        white tips ....   GLAUCESCENS.
B. Very large: mantle slaty-blackish ; primaries crossed with
    black ; size of the first...............................   MARINUS.
C. Large: mantle some shade of blue, darker than in A, lighter
    than in B ; primaries crossed with black ; feet flesh-colored.
    1. Mantle grayish-blue; bill moderately ro-
       bust ....ARGENTATUS var. *smithsonianus.*
    2. Mantle slaty-blue; bill very robust..ARGENTATUS var. *occidentalis.*
D. Medium and small : primaries crossed with black ; feet dark ;
    webs yellow.
    1. Tarsus obviously longer than the middle toe
       and claw ; bill of adult greenish-yellow, en-
       circled with a black band; first primary
       usually with a sub-apical white spot;
       length, about 18—20 inches ....   DELAWARENSIS.

1ª. Tarsus little if any longer than middle toe
and claw ; bill with a red spot, but an imperfect black band, if any; first primary
usually with the end broadly white; length,
about 20—22 inches ............DELAWARENSIS var. *californicus.*
2. Tarsus little if any longer than the middle
toe and claw ; bill slender, without a black
band or red spot ; size, very small; length,
16 or—inches ....CANUS var. *brachyrhynchus.*

LARUS GLAUCUS, Brünn.

Glaucous Gull; Burgomaster.

Larus glaucus, BRÜNN., Orn. Bor. 1764, 44.—SAB., Linn. Trans. xii, 757.—TEMM., Man. ii,
1820, 757.—BOIE, Isis, 1822, 562.—STEPH., Gen. Zool. xiii, 1826, 189.—FLEM., Br.
Anim. 1828, 139.—BP., Syn. 1828, 361 ; List, 1838, 63.—SW. & RICH., F. B. A. ii,
1831, 416.—NUTT., Man. ii, 1834, 306.—JEN., Man. 1835, 279.—EYT., Cat. Br. B.
1836, 53.—BREHM, V. D. 1831, 733.—AUD., Orn. Biog. v, 1839, 59, pl. 396 ; Syn.
1839, 329 ; B. Am. vii, 1844, 170, pl. 449.—NAUM., V. D. x, 1840, 350, pl. 264.—
KEYS. & BLAS., Wirb. Eur. 1840, 96.—MACGIL., Man. ii, 1842, 247.—GIR., B. L.
I. 1844, 363.—SCHL., Rev. Crit. 1844, 525.—GRAY, Gen. of B. iii, 1849, 654 ; List
Br. B. 1863, 230.—MIDD., Sib. Reise, ii, 1853, 241.—LAWR., B. N. A. 1858, 842.—
REINH., Ibis, iii, 1861, 16.—COUES, Pr. A. N. S. 1861, 243 ; 1862, 294 ; Pr. Ess.
Inst. v, 1868, 306 ; Key, 1872, 311.—NEWT., Ibis, 1865, 509.—SCHL., Mus. P.-B.
iv, 1863, *Lari,* 4.—LAWR., Ann. Lyc. N. Y. viii, 1866, 299.—DALL & BANN., Tr.
Chic. Acad. i, 1869, 304.—ELLIOT, introd. B. N. A. fig. —.—RADDE, Reisen, ii,
1863, 382 (Siberia).—BLAS., J. f. O. 1865, 381.
Leucus glaucus, KAUP, Sk. Ent. Eur. Thierw. 1829, 86.—BP., Consp. Av. ii, 1856, 215 ;
Compt. Rend. xlii, 1856, 770.
Plautus glaucus, REICH., Syst. Av. pl. 47, figs. 316-17-18.
Laroides glaucus, BRUCH, J. f. O. 1855, 281.
Larus glacialis, BENICKEN.—MACGIL., Mem. Wern. Soc. v, 1824, 270.—BREHM, V. D. 732.
Glaucus glacialis, BRUCH, J. f. 1853, 101, pl. 2, f. 14 (Schlegel says this =*leucopterus*).
Laroides glacialis, BRUCH, J. f. O. 1855, 282.
" *Larus giganteus,* BENICKEN."
Larus consul, BOIE, " Wied. Zool. Mag. i, 757."—BREHM, V. D. 1831, 735.
Glaucus consul, BRUCH, J. f. O. 1853, 101.
Larus islandicus, EDMONSTON, Mem. Wern. Soc. iv, 1822, pp. 176, 182 ; not of EDMON-
STON, *ibid.* 1823, which =*leucopterus.*
Larus hutchinsii, RICH., F. B. Am. ii, 1831, 419.—CASS., Pr. Phila. Acad. 1862, 290.—
COUES, *ibid.* 294.—LAWR., Ann. Lyc. N. Y. viii, 1866, 299.—COUES, Pr. Ess. Inst.
v, 306.—ELLIOT, B. N. A. ii, pl. 53.—DALL & BANN., Tr. Chic. Acad. i, 1869, 304.
(?) *Leucus arcticus,* BP., Consp. ii, 1856, 216.
" *Larus leuceretes,* SCHLEEP."
" *Larus leuconotus,* AUCT."—(BP.) (But what authors ?)

DIAG. *L. pallio albido aut diluté perlaceo, primariis similibus versus apices sensim nec statim
albis, staturá inter maximos. Long.* 30 *poll., rostr. et tars.* 3 + *poll.*

Hab.—Northern and Arctic Seas, circumpolar; south in winter on the Atlantic coast
of North America to Long Island.

Adult summer plumage.—Very large, nearly or quite equaling *L. marinus.* Bill large
and strong ; very wide, but not so deep at the angle nor so much arched toward the
termination of the culmen as in *marinus.* Bill about as long as the middle toe and
claw. Second primary nearly equaling the first. Bill chrome-yellow, with a tinge of
olivaceous, the tip diaphanous, the sides of the symphyseal eminence with a small spot
of vermilion. Mantle very light pearl-blue (or bluish-white). Primaries a shade
lighter than back, fading insensibly into pure white a considerable distance from their
tips. Shafts of primaries straw-yellow. Legs and feet pale flesh-color. Otherwise
wholly white.
Adult in winter.—The head and neck are streaked with pale brownish-gray.
Young-of-the-year.—" Streaked longitudinally on the neck with pale wood-brown ;
the upper plumage barred transversely with ashy-gray and grayish-yellow ; the tail
irregularly spotted. The shafts of the primaries white, and the spots on the webs
much paler than in the young of *L. marinus* and *argentatus.* The bill horn-colored at
the base ; brownish-black at the tip. Feet flesh-colored."—[*Rich.*]
Dimensions of adult.—Length, 30 inches ; extent of wings, 62 ; wing from carpus,

18.50 ; bill along culmen, 2.75 to 3.00 ; along rictus, 3.75 ; depth opposite nostrils, 0.80 ; at angle, 0.85 ; tarsus, 3.00 ; middle toe and claw, 2.75.

One of the largest and most powerful of the subfamily, nearly equaling in these respects the *L. marinus*. The combination of the large size and the extremely light colors render it perfectly easy to distinguish it at a glance. The well-defined, rounded, white apical spots of the primaries of *glaucescens* at once separate that species. The differences of *leucopterus*, as shown by the dimensions, may be seen by comparing the measurements given.

All authors are agreed as to the great variation in size which this species presents. Sabine found one to measure 32 by 65 inches, with a tarsus 3.50 and a bill upward of 4 inches long. The dimensions given are, it is believed, about the average.

NOTE.—" *Larus hutchinsii*."—In earlier papers I recognized this as a species distinct from *L. glaucus*, basing characters as follows :

Adult(???)—Entire plumage pure white; shafts of primaries straw-yellow. Bill flesh-colored, blackish on the terminal third. Feet flesh-colored.

Young.—Head, neck, and upper parts white, mottled with light reddish-brown, appearing on the back as irregular patches, and on the rump as more or less regular transverse bars. Under parts nearly uniform, very pale reddish-brown ; the under tail coverts barred with white. Wings and tail pure white, with yellow shafts.

Dimensions.—Length, 27.50 ; extent, 60.00 ; wing, 17.75 ; bill along culmen, 2.40 ; along gape, 3.20 ; height at nostrils, 0.70 ; tarsus, 3.40 ; middle toe and claw, 3.50.

The particular coloration of the bill, however, is against the supposition that the bird is adult, as this coloration is the ordinary style in young birds of this group. I am now disinclined to allow that the bird is anything more than some stage of *L. glaucus*, although it is difficult to account for the absence of any shade of pearly-blue on the mantle. In the foregoing synonymy I assign it to *glaucus*, with this explanation ; and in further elucidation of the question I present the following remarks, just as I find them in my Mss. prepared in 1863 :

" Under the above name, and by the foregoing description, I wish to indicate a form of Gull as large, or almost as large, as *glaucus*, differing from this species mainly in being pure white all over, and in having a differently colored bill. It looks, indeed, like an albino *glaucus* ; but, as other species of Gulls are equally liable to albinism, we should not find so many albinos of *glaucus* to so few, if any, of other species. *Glaucus*, as is well known, grows lighter with age, but is never wholly pure white ; at least I have seen none such, nor have I found descriptions of such a condition. And, moreover, the bill of an old *glaucus* is never of the color of what I call *hutchinsii*. In this respect the bird is like young *glaucus, leucopterus*, &c. This fact excites suspicion that the bird may be an immature, if not an abnormal, *glaucus* ; yet I have no more authority for saying so than for denying that it is so. I do not know that I clearly recognize, or could separate, specimens of young *hutchinsii* (supposing it to be distinct) from young *glaucus*, but the adults are not to be mistaken for each other.

" I revived this overlooked species in the ' Proceedings,' as above. We have now several specimens in the Smithsonian, from widely separated localities. One of them was taken in winter in New York State. Other specimens are in Captain Rodgers' collections, from the North Pacific, where the bird is represented to be common. These are noticed by Mr. Cassin, as above quoted. There is a New England specimen in the Museum of the Peabody Academy, at Salem, Massachusetts, mentioned by me, as above, in the Essex Institute Proceedings. In selecting a name for this bird I have been perplexed, rather from not knowing which one to choose than from any dearth of names. Ornithologists differ as to the synonymy. Bonaparte (Consp. Av.) calls it ' arcticus,' Macgill.' and puts ' argentatus, Sabine,' as a synonym. Both of these authors speak of their subjects as having a notable amount of blue on the back—the latter writer especially dwelling on this character (' back pure pearl-gray, with a good deal of blue,' &c.) Their descriptions, beyond question, refer to *leucopterus*, as, indeed, one of them (Macgillivray) subsequently affirmed. Sabine gives (Mem. B. Greenland, Trans. Linn. Soc. xii, 1818), under head of *L. glaucus*, a full and accurate description of *hutchinsii*, which he considers as a variety of *glaucus*, ' caused by sickness or a scarcity of supply of food. I have not been able to examine the original notice of *L. glacialis*, Benicken ;' but Bruch, who adopts that name, speaks of the gull-blue of the upper parts. The name is therefore not to be used in this connection. Bonaparte gives as a synonym ' leuconotus,' Auct.', though what authors he refers to I have not been able to determine. This name would seem to belong here. I do not know whether or not it antedates *hutchinsii*, proposed in 1831, for a bird that can be no other than the one now under discussion. Bonaparte's Conspectus Gaviarum differs much from his Conspectus Avium with regard to this species. In the latter he admits it as valid, assigning specific characters and synonymy. In the former he discards it, and scatters the synonymy indiscriminately among several species."

LARUS LEUCOPTERUS, Faber.

White-winged Gull.

Larus argentatus, SABINE, Linn. Trans. xii, 1818, 546. Not of authors.
Larus argentatus, var., TEMM., Man. ii, 764.
Larus leucopterus, FABER, Prod. Isl. Orn. 1822, 91.—BP., Syn. 1828, 361; List, 1838, 63.—
    SW. & RICH., F. B. Am. ii, 1831, 418.—NUTT., Man. ii, 1834, 305.—AUD., Orn.
    Biog. iii, 1835, 553, pl. 282; Syn. 1839, 327; B. Am. vii, 1844, —, pl. —.—EYT.,
    Cat. Br. B. 1836, 53.—TEMM., Man. iv, 1840, 467.—NAUM., V. D. x, 1840, 367, pl.
    265.—KEYS. & BLAS., Wirb. Eur. 1840, 96.—MACGIL., Man. ii, 1842, 247.—SCHL.,
    Rev. Crit. Ois. Eur. 1844, 125.—GRAY, Gen. of B. iii, 1849, 654; List Br. B. 1863,
    230.—MIDD., Sib. Reise, ii, 1853, 242.—LAWR., B. N. A. 1858, 843; Ann. Lyc. N.
    Y. viii, 1866, 299.—COUES, Pr. Phila. Acad. 1862, 294; Pr. Ess. Inst. v, 1868,
    306; Key, 1872, 311.—RIDGW., Ann. Lyc. N. Y. x, 1874, 393 (Ohio, *Wheaton*).—
    VERR., Pr. Ess. Inst. iii, 1862, 160.—ALLEN, *ibid.* iv, 1864, 90.—DALL & BANN.,
    Tr. Chic. Acad. 1869, 304.—SCHL., Mus. P.-B. ix, 1863, *Lari*, 5.—BLAS., J. f. O.
    1865, 382.
Plautus leucopterus, REICH.
Glaucus leucopterus, BRUCH, J. f. O. 1853, 101.—BP., Consp. ii, 1856, 217.
Laroides leucopterus, BRUCH, J. f. O. 1855, 281.—BREHM, V. D. 1831, 745.
Larus arcticus, MACGIL., Mem. Wern. Soc. v, 268.
Larus glaucoides, "TEMM."—BOIE, Isis, 1822, 562.—TEMM., Man. iv, 1840, 469.
Laroides glaucoides, BREHM, V. D. 744.
Larus islandicus, EDMONST., Mem. Wern. Soc. iv, 1823, 503; not of EDMONST., 1822.—
    FLEM., Br. An. 1828, 139.—JEN., Man. 1835, 279.
Laroides minor, BREHM, V. D. 1831, 736, pl. 37, f. 2.
Laroides subleucopterus, BREHM, V. D. 746.

DIAG. *L. glauco omnino similis, sed minor. Long. bipedalis ; rostr.* 2.00 *poll., tars.* 2. 25.

Hab.—With the preceding.

Adult in summer.—Bill rather small, the symphyseal eminence very largely developed; the depth at the angle but little more than at the nostrils. First primary longest. Tarsus not longer than the middle toe and claw. Bill greenish-yellow, chrome along the tomia and toward the extremity ; the tip diaphanous ; the vermilion spot on the lower mandible rather small. Mantle and wings light pearl-blue, this color toward the tips of the primaries, secondaries, and tertials fading insensibly into white. Bases of the primaries the same color as the body of the feather ; without well-defined, rounded white apices, their rhachides straw-yellow. Legs and feet flesh-colored.
Adult in winter.—As in summer, but the head and neck narrowly streaked with dusky-gray.
Young.—"Pale, dusky cinereous, with a few slightly darker spots ; the primaries somewhat darker at their tips."—[*Bp.*]
Dimensions.—Length, 24 inches ; wing, 16.75 ; bill along culmen, 1.80 ; along rictus, 2.80 ; depth at angle, 0.65 ; tarsus, 2.25 ; middle toe and claw the same.
    This species is a perfect counterpart of *L. glaucus :* but, although quite identical in colors, may be readily distinguished by its greatly inferior size. Beside this there are some differences of proportion. The specimens before me have disproportionately weaker bills than has the adult *glaucus ;* the tarsus is not longer than the middle toe and claw, and the first primary is decidedly longest. The rather larger size, darker primaries, and their *their well-defined, round, apical spots* readily distinguish the *glaucescens*.
    There is a remarkable discrepancy in the statements of authors concerning the dimensions of this species. Thus, Bonaparte gives 20 inches, while Richardson says 26 ! The specimens before me average about 24 inches, as above given.
    The discussion of the synonyms "*argentatus*, Sabine," and " *arcticus*, Macgill." is presented under the head of *L. hutchinsii.* Macgillivray's name is certainly a synonym of *leucopterus*, Faber, as he himself subsequently admits ; notwithstanding which, Bonaparte, in his Conspectus, adopts it for what I call *hutchinsii*, upon what grounds does not appear. Temminck at first considered this species as a variety of the common Herring Gull (*L. argentatus*). He subsequently, however, became convinced of his error, and named it *L. glaucoides*—an appropriate title, but antedated. In 1823 Edmonston (*op. cit*) applies the name *islandicus* to this species, only a year after he had so named the *L. glaucus.*

LARUS GLAUCESCENS, Licht.

Glaucous-winged Gull.

Larus glaucescens, LICHT.—LAWR., B. N. A. 1858, 842.—COUES, Pr. Phila. Acad, 1862,
    295 ; Key, 1872, 311.—COOP. & SUCK., N. H. Wash. Ter. 1860, 270.—ELLIOT, B.

N. A. Introd. fig. of primaries (with labels of this and the accompanying figure transposed).—DALL & BANN., Tr. Chic. Acad. 1869, 304.—FINSCH, Abh. Nat. iii, 1872, 83.

Glaucus glaucescens, BRUCH, J. f. O. 1853, 101.
Laroides glaucescens, BRUCH, J. f. O. 1855, 281.
Leucus glaucescens, BP., Consp. Av. ii, 1856, 216; Compt. Rend. xlii, 1856, 770.
Larus glaucopterus, "KITTLITZ."
Glaucus glaucopterus, BRUCH, J. f. O. 1853, 101.
Laroides chalcopterus, BRUCH, J. f. O. 1855, 282.
Leucus chalcopterus, BP., Consp. Av. ii, 1856, 216; Compt. Rend. xlii, 1856, 770.
Larus chalcopterus, LAWR., B. N. A. 1858, 843.—COUES, Pr. Phila. Acad. 1862, 295.

DIAG. *L. pallio cœruleo-perlaceo fere ut in L. argentato, primariis dorso concoloribus, apicibus statim nec sensim albis.*

(The shade of the mantle is almost exactly as in *argentatus*, and the primaries are pictured exactly as in that species, the black of *argentatus* being replaced by a pearly-blue like the mantle.)

SP. CH.—Bill long and rather weak, the upper mandible acute and projecting considerably beyond tip of the under, the convexity near the end comparatively slight; angle pretty well defined, the outline between it and the tip about straight. First primary longest; the tarsus rather longer than the middle toe and claw.

Adult in summer.—Bill light yellow, an orange spot at the angle of the lower mandible, and a dusky one just above. Mandible pearl-blue, much the same shade as in *argentatus*. Primaries scarcely darker than the back, all with well-defined, rounded apical spots of white. First, the base not appreciably lighter than the body of the feather, with a well-defined white spot on both webs near the end, separated from the white tip by a transverse band of the color of the body of the feather; second, third, and fourth, basal portions notably lighter than the terminal, fading into pure white at their juncture with the latter, without spots except at the apex; fifth, sixth, basal portions the color of the back, fading into white near the end, separated from the white apices by a band, narrowest on the sixth, of the color of the outer primaries. Inner primaries like the secondaries, with plain broadly white ends. Feet light flesh-color.

Adult in winter.—Head, neck, and breast thickly nebulated with light grayish-dusky, the throat mostly immaculate.

Approaching maturity.—Bill dark-colored, yellowish along the culmen and gonys. Wings and tail light grayish-ashy, the former without sharply-defined white tips or spots. Under parts generally marked with dusky, the wing coverts marked with dusky and white. Feathers of the back narrowly edged with gray.

Intermediate.—Bill flesh-colored, the terminal portion black. Wings and tail darker than in the preceding, especially on the outer webs of the former. Everywhere dusky-gray, more or less mottled with white, the gull-blue of the upper parts appearing as mottling of greater or less extent.

Young-of-the-year.—Bill black. Everywhere deep grayish-dusky, somewhat mottled with whitish; the feathers of the back, wings, and upper tail coverts edged, tipped, and crossed with more or less regular transverse bars of grayish-white.

Nestling, nearly fledged.—Dark gray; under parts, wings, and tail transversely waved with rufous; under parts nearly pure dark ashy-gray; bill and feet black.

Nestling, unfledged.—Bill and feet black; head and neck all whitish, irregularly spotted with blackish; upper parts spotted with grayish-black and grayish-white; under parts more uniform gray, the abdomen fading into white.

Dimensions.—Length, about 27 inches; wing, 16.75; bill above, 2.25; gape, 3.25; height at angle, 0.70; tarsus, 2.60; middle toe and claw, 2.50.

Hab.—Pacific coast of North America.

The present is a well characterized species. The most striking peculiarity of form is in the bill, in the very slight comparative convexity of the culmen near the end, the tip being slender and acute and projecting considerably over the tip of the lower mandible. This form of bill is recognizable even in the young-of-the-year, in which the bill is every way much smaller than in the adult. The color of the upper parts is much that of *L. argentatus*. The terminal spots of the primaries are as well defined as in the species with black primaries, and are much and regularly rounded. The shafts of the quill-feathers are much the color of the webs. The dusky of the young birds is very light, and, except in the early stages, is much mottled with grayish-white. The upper parts soon become very light-colored by the broad whitish margins of the feathers. The primaries early acquire notably lighter tips, but do not obtain the well-defined white terminal apexes, nor the spot on the first primaries, till maturity. The primaries of the youngest birds have a shade of silvery-gray, which is quite peculiar, and very different from the color of those parts in the young of the Gulls with black primaries.

Larus glaucescens may be considered a well-established species. As already noted, it is when adult almost exactly like an *argentatus* with the black of the primaries replaced by a pearly gray-blue shade like that of the mantle. Young birds in all stages are paler and grayer than the corresponding stages of *argentatus*. Agreeing with *leucopterus* in respect of size, *glaucescens* may be immediately known by the pattern of the primaries; the pearly-blue color continuing undiminished in intensity to the tips of the feathers, instead of fading gradually into white as in *glaucus* and *leucopterus*.

I have never seen a specimen purporting to be "*chalcopterus*," which Mr. Lawrence admitted in 1858. As described, it is "exactly like *leucopterus*, except on the primaries, which are ashy-gray, with rounded white apical spots"—which is precisely the character of *glaucescens*. The young are said to be "dark gray, as in *glaucopterus*" (of Kittlitz, = *glaucescens*, Licht.) There is not the slightest likelihood that it is anything more than *glaucescens*, probably in somewhat immature condition.

LARUS MARINUS, Linn.

Great Black-backed Gull.

Larus marinus, LINN., Syst. Nat. i, 1766, 225.—GM., Syst. Nat. i, 1788, 598.—LATH., Ind. Orn. ii, 1790, 813.—TEMM., Man. 1815, 490.—BOIE, Isis, 1822, 562.—STEPH., Gen. Zool. xiii, 1826, 186.—FLEM., Br. An. 1828, 140.—BP., Syn. 1828, — ; List, 1838, 63.—NUTT., Man. ii, 1834, 308.—BREHM., V. D. 1831, 731.—JEN., Man, 1835, 278.—EYT., Cat. 1836, 53.—AUD., Orn. Biog. iii, 1835, 305 ; v, 1839, 636; pl. 241 ; Syn. 1839, 329 ; B. Am. vii, 1844, 172, pl. 450.—NAUM., V. D. x, 1840, 439, pls. 268, 269.—KEYS. & BLAS., Wirb. Eur. 1840, 97.—MACGIL., Man. Orn. ii, 1842, 244.—GIR., B. L. I. 1844, 361.—SCHL., Rev. Crit. 1844, 124 ; Mus. P.-B. ix, 1863, *Lari*, p. —.—GRAY, Gen. of B. iii, 1849, 654 ; List Br. B. 1863, 231.—LAWR., B. N. A. 1858, 844 ; Ann. Lyc. N. Y. viii, 1866, 299.—BRY., Pr. Bost. Soc. viii, 1861, 72.—COUES, Pr. Phila. Acad. 1861, 244 ; *ibid.* 1862, 295 ; Pr. Ess. Inst. v, 1868, 306 ; Key, 1872, 312.—BOARDM., Pr. Bost. Soc. ix, 1862, 131.—VERR., Pr. Ess. Inst. iii, 1862, 160.—ALLEN, *ibid.* iv, 1864, 90.—SHARPE & DRESS., B. Eur. pt. xv, Dec. 1872.—RIDGW., Ann. Lyc. x, 391 (Lake Michigan, *Velie*); and of authors.
Leucus marinus, KAUP, Sk. Ent. Eur. Thierw. 1829, 86.
Dominicanus marinus, BRUCH., J. f. O. 1853, 100 ; 1855, 280.—BP., Consp. Av. ii, 1856, 213; Compt. Rend. xlii, 1856, 770.
Larus niger, BRISS., Orn. vi, 1760, 158.
Larus nævius, LINN., Syst. Nat. i, 1766, 225.—GM., Syst. Nat. i, 1788, 598.—LATH., Ind. Orn. ii, 1790, 814.
Larus albus, MÜLL., Syst. Nat. Suppl. 1776, 108.
Larus maculatus, BODD., Tabl. P. E. 1783, 16.
Larus maximus, LEACH, Cat. 1816, 40.—BREHM, V. D. 1831, 728.
Larus mulleri et *fabricii*, BREHM, V. D. 1831, 729, 730.

DIAG. *L. staturâ maximus, pallio schistaceo-nigro. Long. 30.00 poll.*

Hab.—American and European coasts of the Atlantic. South in winter to Long Island (to Florida, *Aud.*). Great Lakes and the Mississippi (*Aud.*).

Adult, breeding plumage.—Size very large ; general form strong, compact, and powerful. Bill very stout, deep at the angle, rather short for its height ; culmen toward the end exceedingly convex, so much so as to make a tangent to it at the point where the tip of the lower mandible touches it perpendicular to the commissure. Symphyseal eminence very large and prominent ; tarsus but little if any longer than the middle toe and claw, compressed, rather slender for the size of the bird. Interdigital membranes broad, scarcely emarginate. Bill bright chrome, the tip of both mandibles diaphanous. A large bright vermilion spot occupies the terminal half of the lower mandible and encroaches a little on the upper. Edges of jaws bright vermilion. Palate and tongue pale orange-red. Eyelids vermilion. Iris pale lemon-yellow. Legs and feet pale flesh-color. Mantle intense slate-color, nearly black, with a purplish reflection. The secondaries and tertials broadly tipped with white, the line of demarcation distinct. Primaries : *first*, black, scarcely lighter at its base, its tip white for 2¼ inches, its shaft white inferiorly, and superiorly along the white portion of the feather ; *second*, like the first, but its base lighter, the white tip less extensive, and interrupted by a narrow bar of black on one or both webs ; *third, fourth, fifth*, broadly tipped with white, their bases of a lighter shade of slate than the second, and fading into white at the junction with the broad black subterminal band.

Adult in winter.—As in summer, but the head and neck streaked with dusky.

Young-of-the-year.—As large as the adult ; the bill as large, but not so strong, nor the eminence so well developed ; wholly *black*. Upper parts wholly dusky chocolate-brown, mottled with whitish and light rufous, the latter on the back and wings, the feathers being tipped and the wing coverts deeply indented with this color. Under parts mottled with white or rufous-white and dusky, the throat mostly immaculate.

Primaries and tail deep brownish-black, the former tipped, subterminally barred, and its outer feather mottled, with whitish.

Dimensions.—Lenth, 30.00 inches; extent, 65.00; wing from the carpus, 18.50; bill above, 2.50; rictus, 3.50; height at nostril, 0.85; at angle, 0.95; tarsus, 3.00; middle toe and claw slightly less.

The very large size of this bird and its dark colors at once separate it from any other of North America, and render comparisons unnecessary.

I cannot understand the following statement of Audubon (B. Am. vii, p. 178): "The most remarkable circumstance relative to these birds is, that they either associate with another species, giving rise to a hybrid breed, or that when very old they lose the dark color of the back, which is then of the same tint as that of *L. argentatus*, or even lighter." It is difficult to understand how Audubon could have entertained such an opinion. That the *marinus* should accidentally hybridize with *argentatus* or *glaucus* is not impossible, though improbable; but to suppose that it regularly does so, or that it "grows gray" with the advancing years, seems unreasonable. Audubon's statement that the *Larus argentatus* (*smithsonianus*) is not found on the Labrador coast, is equally erroneous.

Both Bonaparte and Bruch give several species of *Dominicanus*, all more or less closely allied with the present. The species found in North America is the true *marinus* of Linnæus, whatever may be said of the relationships of the others.

For so long known a species the present has remarkably few synonyms, owing to the many distinctive characters presented by it. *Nævius* of Gmelin, and also probably *maculatus* of Boddært, are based upon the immature bird. *Maculatus* of Brünnich, however, cannot be this species, since it is said to be of the same size as *L. canus*. As usual, several nominal species have been instituted by Brehm.

LARUS ARGENTATUS, Brünn.

Herring Gull.

a. *argentatus*.

Larus cinereus, BRISS., Orn. vi, 1760, 160, pl. 14.
Larus argentatus, BRÜNN., Orn. Bor. 1764, 44.—GM., Syst. Nat. i, 1788, 600.—TEMM., Man. 1820, 764; iv, 1840, 470.—BOIE, Isis, 1822, 562.—WOLF & MEY., Zusät. Tasch. 1822, 195.—STEPH., Gen. Zool. xiii, 1826, 191.—FLEM., Br. An. 1828, 140.—JEN., Man. 1835, 276.—EYT., Cat. 1836, 52.—BP., List, 1838, 63.—KEYS. & BLAS., Wirb. Eur. i, 1840, 96.—MACGIL., Man. ii, 1842, 246.—SCHL., Rev. Crit. 1844, 124.—DEGL., Orn. Eur. ii, 1849, 306.—GRAY, Gen. of B. iii, 1849, 654; List Br. B. 1862, 232.—HARTL., Syst. Orn. W. Afr. 1857, 251.—SCHL., Mus. P.-B. iv, 1863, *Lari*, 16 (includes the other varieties).—BOCAGE, Jorn. Sc. Lisbon, 1868, 149, 330.—BLAS., J. f. O. 1865, 380 (unites *leucophæus*, *michahellesii*, and *cachinnans*).—DRESS., B. Eur. pt. —, pl. —.
Laroides argentatus, BREHM, V. D. 1831, 740.—BRUCH, J. f. O. 1855, 282.—BP., Consp. ii, 1856, 218; Naum. 1854, 212.
Glaucus argentatus, BRUCH, J. f. O. 1853, 101.
Larus fuscus, PENN., Brit. Zool. ii, 1768, 131.—*Nec* AUCTT.—MONT., Orn. Dict. 1802.
Goëland à manteau gris, BUFF., Hist. Nat. Ois. viii, 1781, 406, pl. 32.—P. E. 253.
Larus marinus, var. *β.*, LATH., Ind. Orn. ii, 1790, 814.
Larus glaucus, RETZ., Fn. Suec. i, 1800, 156.—WOLF & MEY., Tasch. ii, 1810, 471.—BENICK., Ann. Wett. Ges. Nat. iii, 1812, 138.—TEMM., Man. 1815, 493 (partly).—*Nec* AUCTT.
Larus argenteus, BREHM, Beit. Vögelk. iii, 1822, 781, 799.
Laroides argenteus, BREHM, V. D. 1831, 741.
Larus argentatoides, BREHM, Beit. Vögelk. 1822, 791, 799 (partly).
Laroides argentatoides, BREHM, V. D. 1831, 742.
Laroides argentatoides, THOMPS., P. Z. S. 1835, 83 (Ireland).
Laroides major, BREHM, V. D. 1831, 738.
Laroides argentaceus, BREHM, V. D. 1831, 742.—BP., Consp. ii, 1856, 218.

b. *smithsonianus*.

Larus argentatoides, BREHM, Beitr. Vögelk. 1822, 791, 799 (in part; "Germany and America.")--(?) BP., Syn. 1828, 360, No. 299 (may be *delawarensis*).—(?) SW. & RICH., F. B. A. ii, 1831, 417 (may be *californicus*).—SCHINZ, Eur. Fn. i, 1840, 380 ("North America").—BP., Rev. Zool. 1855, 16 ("North America").
Glaucus argentatoides, BRUCH, J. f. O. 1853, 101 ("North America").
Laroides argentatoides, BP., Naum. 1854, 212 ("North America"); Consp. ii, 1856, 218.—BRUCH, J. f. O. 1855, 282 ("North America").

40

Larus argentatus, BP., Syn. 1828, 360, No. 300.—NUTT., Man. ii, 1834, 304.—AUD., Orn.
Biog. iii, 1835, 588; v, 1839, 638; pl. —; Syn. 1839, 328; B. Am. vii, 1844, 163,
pl. 448.—DEKAY, N. Y Zool. ii, 1844, 306, pl. 122, f. 270; pl. 129, fig. 284; pl.
130, fig. 286.—GIR., B. L. I. 1844, —.—CAB., J. f. O. v, 236 (Cuba).—LAWR., B. N.
A. 1858, 844; Ann. Lyc. vii, 275.—REINH., Ibis, iii, 1861, 17 (Greenland, rare).—
COUES, Pr. Phila. Acad. 1861, 245.—BRY., Pr. Bost. Soc. viii, 1861, 72.—WHEAT.,
Ohio Agric. Rep. 1860, No. 266.—BOARDM., Pr. Bost. Soc. ix, 1862, 131.—VERR.,
Pr. Ess. Inst. iii, 1862, 154.—TURNB., B. E. Pa. 1869, 38.—DALL & BANN., Tr.
Chic. Acad. i, 1869, 305.—SCL. & SALV., P. Z. S. 1871, 576.—COUES, Key, 1872, 312.
(?) *Larus americanus*, BRHEM, V. D. 1831, 743 (= *argentatoides*, BR.).
(?) *Larus affinis*, REINH., Vid. Med. 1853, 78; J. f. O. 1854, 433; Ibis, iii, 17 (Greenland).
Larus smithsonianus, COUES, Pr. Phila. Acad. 1862, 296.—COUES & PRENT., Smiths. Rep.
1861, 418.—ALLEN, Pr. Ess. Inst. iv, 1864, 80.—LAWR., Ann. Lyc. N. Y. viii, 1866,
299.—COUES, Pr. Ess. Inst. v, 1868, 306.—COUES, Pr. Phila. Acad. 1871, 39.—
GUNDL., Rep. Fn. Nat. i, 391 (Cuba).
Larus argentatus var. *smithsonianus*, COUES, Check-list, 1874, 103, No. 547ᵇ.—RIDGW.,
Ann. Lyc. N. Y. x, 1874, 391 (Illinois).

c. *occidentalis.*

Larus occidentalis, AUD., Orn. Biog. v, 1839, 320; Syn. 1839, 328; B. Am. vii, 1844, 161.—
LAWR., B. N. A. 1858, 845.—HEERM., P. R. R. Rep. x, 1859, pt. vi, 73.—COOP. &
SUCK., N. H. Wash. Ter. 1860, 271.—ELLIOT, B. N. A. ii, pl. 52.—COUES, Pr. A. N.
S. 1862, 296.—SCHL., Mus. P.-B. iv, 1863, *Lari*, p. 15.—(?) SWINH., P. Z. S. 1863,
326 (China).—BLAS., J. f. O. 1865, 379.
Glaucus occidentalis, BRUCH, J. f. O. 1853, 101.
Laroides occidentalis, BRUCH, J. f. O. 1855, 282.—BP., Consp. ii, 1856, 219.
Larus argentatus var. *occidentalis*, COUES, Key, 1872, 312.

d. *borealis.*

Larus borealis, BRANDT.—DALL & BANN., Tr. Chic. Acad. i, 1869, 305.—BD., *ibid.* 324.
Laroides borealis, BP., Consp. Av. ii, 1856, 219.
(?) *Larus cachinnans*, PALL., Zoog. R.-A. ii, 1811, 318.
(?) *Larus argentatus*, MIDD., Sib. Reise, ii, 242.—RADDE, Reisen, ii, 1863, 383.
(?) *Larus argentatus* var. *cachinnans*, SCHRENK, Reise, i, 504.

e (?). *leucophœus.*

Larus argentatus, BP., Ic. Fn. Ital. Ucc. 1832-41, p. —.—CARA, Ornit. Sard. 1842, 172
(Sardinia).—COSTA, Fn. Napoli, Ucc. 1857, 73.—HEUGL., Syst. Uebers. 1855,
69.—SCHL., Mus. P.-B. iv, 1863, *Lari*, p. 17 (partim).—BLAS., J. f. O. 1865, 380
(partim).—HUME, Lahore to Yarkand, 1873, 299; Stray Feathers, 1873, 270
(Kashmir and Scinde).
Laroides argentatus, BP., Cat. Met. Ucc. 1842, 79 (partim).
Larus cachinnans, "PALL."—MUHLE, Orn. Griech. 1842, 143 (Greece; nec PALL.)—MEVES,
Ofv. K. Vet. Ak. Förh. 1871, 786 (Cholmogory).
Glaucus leucophœus, ("LICHT.")—BRUCH., J. f. O. 1853, 101 (Red Sea).
Larus leucophœus, LICHT., Nom. Av. Mus. Berol. 1853, 99 (Arabia; descr. nulla).—BP.,
R. M. Z. 1855, 16.—SALVAD., Cat. Ucc. Sardegna, 1864, 129.—FINSCH & HARTL.,
Vog. Ost.-Afr. 1870, 818.—DRESS., B. Eur. pt. —, pl. —.
Laroides leucophœus, BP., Naum. 1854, 212; C. Rend. xlii, 1856, 644; Consp. ii, 1856, 219.
Glaucus michahellesii, BRUCH, J. f. O. 1853, 101.
Larus michahellesii, BP., R. M. Z. 1855, 16.
Laroides michahellesii, BRUCH, J. f. O. 1855, 282.—BP., Compt. Rend. xlii, 1856, 644; Consp.
ii, 1856, 219.

NOTE.—The foregoing synonymy includes the several races of this species I consider it necessary to adopt. I bring *L. leucophœus* into this connection with some hesitation, but I do not observe any ascribed characters which may not be accounted for
upon a supposition of merely varietal distinction. As, however, I have had no opportunity of studying this supposed species satisfactorily, my present view must be
regarded as tentative. Most of its synonymy is adapted from Mr. Dresser's work, as
prepared by Lord Walden. Without further reference to this form or to typical *argentatus* of Europe, I proceed to consider the North American representative:

Var. SMITHSONIANUS, *Coues.*

DIAG. *L. argentato vero simillimus, sed major, alis caudâque longioribus, rostro pedibusque
validioribus, remige primo sœpius maculâ alba subapicali, rarius laté albo-terminato. Long.*
25.00 *poll. ala,* 18.00; *rostr.* 2.25; *tars.* 2.50.

Hab.—North America, generally; especially along the Atlantic coast. Cuba to Labrador; breeding from New England northward. Also in the interior, and occasionally on the Pacific coast.

Adult.—Bill rather less than the tarsus, shorter than the head; robust, its height at the angle slightly more than at the base. Culmen nearly straight at the nostrils; then rapidly convex to the stout, deflected, overhanging apex. Outline of rami slightly concave; gonys about straight; eminence at symphysis large and prominent, but its apex not very acute. Wings long-pointed; the first primary always longest. Tail even. Feet of moderate size; tarsi compressed, anteriorly scutellate, laterally and posteriorly reticulate. Membranes full and broad, scarcely incised. Claws obtuse, but little arched; the inner edge of the middle one dilated, but not serrated.

Breeding plumage.—Bill bright chrome, its tip diaphanous; a vermilion spot at the angle, with sometimes a small black one just anterior to it. Legs and feet pale flesh-color; the claws blackish. Mantle typical "gull-blue," much lighter than in *occidentalis;* lighter than in *brachyrhynchus;* of much the same shade as in *delawarensis* or *glaucescens;* darker than in *glaucus* or *leucopterus.* The bases of the primaries are the same as the back, or very slightly lighter, not so light, nor of so great extent (being exceedingly short on the first primary), nor so broad at the end, as in *californicus.* On the *first* primary this light basal portion is very short, hardly reaching within six or seven inches of the tip of the primary. It is not lighter at its junction with the black, nor does it extend further on the central portion than on the edge of the feather. On the *second, third,* and *fourth* primaries the bluish of the basal portions of the feather extends about the same distance on each (within four inches of the tip of the second), and runs up further on the centres of the feathers than on their edges, and grows nearly white at its junction with the black portion of the feathers. *First* primary *with a subapical white spot near its tip;* small, rounded, not much over an inch in diameter; generally not longer on the outer vane than on the inner; sometimes wanting on the former; in oldest birds this spot enlarging to coalesce with the white tip of the feather, but such state rarely observed; second primary usually without a subapical spot, or if one is present it is very small. All the primaries with small rounded white apices, and black from these apical spots to their bluish-white bases; this band of black growing narrower from the first toward the seventh, where it is a mere point.

Winter plumage.—The head and neck are streaked with dusky. The bill is less brightly colored. Otherwise as in summer.

Immature.—The feathers of the back have gray margins, and the upper wing coverts are mottled with dusky gray. An imperfect subterminal bar of dusky on the tail.

Young of first winter.- Head, neck, and whole under parts more or less thickly mottled with dusky, as are the wing-coverts, secondaries, and tertials. The gull-blue of the upper parts appears in irregular patches, mixed with gray. Remiges and rectrices brownish-black, with very narrow whitish tips, the former wanting both apical and subapical white spots. Bill flesh-color, its terminal third black. Feet dull flesh-color.

Younger.—Entirely a deep dull brownish; the throat lightly streaked and the rump transversely barred with whitish; the feathers of the back with yellowish or grayish-white edges; wings and tail black; bill black; legs and feet dusky flesh-color.

Dimensions of adult.—Length, 24 to 25 inches; extent, 54 to 58; wing, 17.25 to 18.00; bill along culmen, 2.40; height at nostril, 0.75; at angle, 0.80; tarsus, 2.75; middle toe and claw the same. Female a little and young considerably less than the above.

Other variations.—These are very considerable as regards size and proportions. The bill along the culmen varies from 2.55 to 2.20 inches, being, however, in adult birds, generally very near the former measurement. The tarsus will vary more than a fourth of an inch—from 2.75, its usual length, to about 2.40. The difference in the length of the wings is slight for so large a Gull, only about an inch. The younger the bird the smaller it is, the weaker and shorter its bill, and the slenderer its feet. Very old birds sometimes become almost abnormally big, as is the case with *L. glaucus* and others.

Between the time of leaving the nest and of assuming the complete plumage of the adult bird the changes are very great. While the uniform dusky of the body is turning to pure white and clear blue, and while the black tail is whitening and the black primaries are assuming their peculiar characteristic markings, the variations *in degree and extent* of all the colors are endless. It is hardly possible to characterize any definite stages, as they glide insensibly into each other. But in adult birds, which have attained their second or third summer, the colors of the whole body and the markings of the primaries are so constant that, taken in connection with the size, form, and other particulars, they afford fair varietal characters. I do not mean to assert that there is no variation in these points, but that adult birds generally preserve a certain definite pattern of coloration of the primaries.

In this species this "pattern" may be summed up, briefly, as: The presence of a black band on the first seven primaries, which takes in nearly the whole of the first, and rapidly narrows until on the seventh it is a mere spot; bluish bases to all the primaries, of a width inversely as that of the black portion; small white apical spots on all the primaries;* and a large rounded subapical white spot on the first (rarely becoming confluent with the white apical spot), with or without a smaller one on the second.

---

* These may be absent, being worn off from very old feathers, just before the moult.

The characters afforded by the markings of the primaries—and especially of their bases—have been usually disregarded or lightly passed over by some in the preparation of diagnoses. Others, myself probably included, have inclined to lay too much stress upon these features, which are to be found varying to a great degree in different examples of the same species, as a consequence of immaturity. Birds of this family may be of full size, possessing powers of reproduction, before they have attained the ultimate, and then unvarying, picture of the primaries. Take a case susceptible of demonstration. Mr. Lawrence describes *californicus* as having the white apical space on the first primary crossed by a black subterminal bar. So it is in his type-specimen now lying before me. But this expression does not characterize the adult of the species. If his type had lived longer the subterminal bar would have broken in two, become first a spot and then a mere scollop on each web, and finally disappeared, leaving the broad white apical space on the first primary, which is characteristic of the species, as attested by a multitude of specimens taken in the highest stage of spring plumage.

It must also be borne in mind that the expression "immature" may also be applied to the primaries themselves as well as to the age of the bird. For it is most probable that at each successive moult, after the bird itself is fully adult, the new primaries, when they first sprout, have a *pictura* somewhat different from that finally attained when they are of full length; but the perfect feather has practically characteristics often distinctive of species.

Mr. Audubon always maintained an opinion of the continual variability of the primaries : " From the examination of individuals of this species [" *argentatus* "] it would appear that little reliance can be placed on the markings of the quills as affording a specific character" (B. N. Amer. vii, p. 169). Let us examine the facts he adduces in support of his views. He continues: " Four undoubted specimens of *Larus argentatus* now before me have a white spot, varying in length from one to two inches and including both webs, near the end of the first quill. One has no spot on the second quill. Another has a spot on both webs of the second quill of one wing, and a smaller spot on part of the inner web of the same quill of the other wing. The third has a very small spot on part of the inner web of the same quill of both wings. The fourth has a large circular spot on the inner web of that quill of both wings." Although these paragraphs seem to indicate material discrepancies, yet such is not really the case. The white subapical spot on the first primary existed in all his specimens, only varying somewhat in size; and the same is the case with the spot on the second primary, which so often makes its appearance with increasing age, though in perhaps the majority of specimens it is wanting. In all his specimens the differences were only in the minor details of a certain pattern which was not departed from.

In examining the Herring Gulls contained in all the large collections of the Eastern United States I have met with two specimens—one in the Cambridge Museum, and the other in Mr. Lawrence's private cabinet—which present the distinctive characters of the European bird. They are smaller than the average of *smithsonianus*, and have the apex of the first primary broadly white. Prof. Baird's opinion on these specimens, in which I coincide, is that they are probably stragglers from Europe. The fact that these specimens could be distinguished under circumstances so prone to cause doubt and confusion renders them quite the reverse of counter-arguments to the separation of the two varieties.

It was with some hesitation that I separated, some years since, the American from the European Herring Gull, fully anticipating the adverse criticism which such a procedure would call forth. A recent and more thorough reëxamination of the whole subject confirms my general conclusions, though I by no means insist upon or even admit specific distinction. Provided the specimens before me exhibit typically the characters of the European bird, which there is no reason to doubt, certain slight differences do exist almost throughout extensive series compared. These points are the following :

First. The American bird *averages* larger in all its dimensions than the European. The difference in length of wing of the two averages from one to two inches. The feet, including both tarsus and toes, are about half an inch longer and proportionally stouter. The bill, especially, is longer and stouter, particularly at the base.

Second. There is generally preserved, in adult birds, a somewhat different pattern of coloration of the primaries. In that of Europe the first primary has a white terminal space * two inches long ; the second primary a large, rounded, subterminal white spot, usually occupying both vanes. The first primary of the American bird usually has a rounded white subapical spot on the first primary (much like that on the second primary of the European), almost always separated from the white apex ; and if a spot is present on the second primary, it is small. By these features together, the American bird may usually be recognized as a variety, which should not be wholly ignored.

There is another consideration to be taken in connection with the points already

---

* This is precisely as in *californicus ;* and, as in the latter species, the feather when imperfect has a narrow, transverse, subterminal bar of black, which gradually resolves into two spots or scollops, and finally disappears.

detailed heightening the probability of the varietal distinction of *L. smithsonianus*. The Herring Gulls of both continents differ from such species as *glaucus, leucopterus,* &c., in not being truly boreal birds. They migrate northward only to breed, and return south as soon as the duties of incubation are accomplished. The American species, at least, rarely passes beyond Labrador, and is more abundant in its southern than its northern portions. It is well known that the nearer to either pole is the habitat of a species the more likely it is to range indiscriminately on both hemispheres; and, conversely, the more tropical a species the more likely it is, *cœteris paribus,* to be specifically distinct from its transoceanic representative. We can see here a reason why *smithsonianus* may be somewhat different, while *L. glaucus, leucopterus,* and *P. eburnea* are identical. This fact is adduced merely to show why we may expect to find the differences which do exist in var. *smithsonianus* and are absent in *glaucus;* though, at the same time, I separate the variety upon its physical characters alone, irrespective of any preconceived theory of geographical distribution.

Synonymy.—*Laroides argentatoides,* Brehm, appears to include both the European and American bird. His *americanus* indicates a bird smaller and less robust than European *argentatus,* and may be consequently inapplicable here. It corresponds more nearly with "*californicus.*" The *argentatoides* of Bonaparte's Synopsis, represented as common along the Atlantic coast, may really refer to *delawarensis. L. affinis* of Reinhardt, of Greenland, I have not been able to identify.

Anatomical characters.—The mouth, in capacity, is intermediate between that of *Stercorarius* and of *Sterna;* the angle of divergence of the mandibular rami being less than in the former, but greater than in the latter. The palate is quite flat both transversely and longitudinally, being not at all vaulted and scarcely concave, except toward the tip of the bill, where it curves downward with a considerable degree of convexity. The palate is soft and vascular to within about an inch of the tip, where it becomes corneous and divided by five or six longitudinal striæ. At the commencement of the more vascular part of the palate there begins a median elevation, quite broad and without a central ridge, which continues back for more than two inches. This is everywhere beset with stout, reversed papillæ, the largest of which are along the median line. The central elevation is bifurcated for nearly its posterior half, to form the opening of the posterior nares, the edges of which fissure are thickly papillate, as are the posterior extremities of the elevation itself. This median longitudinal prominence is separated on each side by a deep sulcus from a lateral ridge. This lateral ridge anteriorly sinks insensibly into the common level of the palate; posteriorly it rises up very broad and thick, and, together with its extremity, is papillate. Just external to these ridges are the deep depressions in which the tomia of the lower mandible are received.

Posterior to that portion of the palate just described, there is a large, vaulted, subtriangular space, extending quite to the extremity of the palate. This space is bounded anteriorly by the termination of the central median elevation already described; laterally by the continuation backward of the lateral ridges; more posteriorly, where the sides of the triangle come together to form the apex, by a very perfect fringe formed by a single thick-set row of slender, acute papillæ, placed obliquely, their posterior extremities divaricating, their anterior meeting on the median line. The place thus inclosed is quite smooth, being free from sulci or rugæ, and presents the orifice of the Eustachian tube. It is fissured along the median line by the posterior continuation of the nasal aperture. The edges of the fissure cannot be accurately coaptated, as can that portion of it more anterior, the portion of the posterior nares consequently remaining always more or less patent. The edges of the opening terminate each in a soft papilla. On separating them, the vomer is seen nearly for its whole length, dividing the nasal aperture into a right and left. Posterior to the termination of the nasal fissure is the usual median, longitudinally oval foramen, the opening of the Eustachian tube; measuring in this species a full fourth of an inch. All around this central smooth portion the mucous membrane of the mouth is thrown up into more or less irregular rugæ, mostly longitudinal, and continuous with the ordinary œsophageal folds.

The floor of the mouth is of a very regularly triangular shape, the sides being scarcely at all concave. The rising up of the tomia of the mandible on either side gives it a very considerable depth and almost perpendicular sides, especially anteriorly. The muscular and other layers composing the floor, are very distensible and elastic. The mucous membrane, in its undilated condition, is everywhere thrown up into rugæ, chiefly longitudinal, except just over the larynx. The muscular layers are well marked, but present nothing peculiar either in shape or distribution. The tongue is just two inches long. It is stout and fleshy almost to the tip, which is obtuse, flattened, slightly bifid. Its dorsum is longitudinally channeled; its under surface transversely convex; its posterior extremity prolonged into two short, obtuse cornua, which are thickly papillate. The triangular, smooth eminence which is borne upon the surface of the larynx, measures about an inch in extent by half as much in breadth. The opening of the glottis divides it longitudinally for its whole length. The rima is quite smooth, except just at its termination, where the mucous membrane is prolonged into long, acute papillæ ; and from this, as a centre, extends on either side a triangular bed of large, acute, reversed papillæ, stretching quite to the borders of the laryngeal elevation.

The œsophagus is, as in all the family, very capacious, and capable of great distension. In its undilated state its mucous membrane is thrown up into exceedingly prominent longitudinal striæ, nearly all of which run the whole length of the tube. The muscular layers, both circular and longitudinal, are also extremely thick and powerful. The œsophagus itself is quite straight and of pretty uniform calibre. At the proventriculus it dilates a little, and at the same time bulges a little to the left. The gizzard, also, is not in a direct line with the œsophagus, but its greatest convexity inclines considerably to the right.

Just at the proventriculus the straight longitudinal œsophageal folds become convoluted (in the undilated state of the organ), and then gradually lose themselves in the irregular eminences of the soft, very vascular, proventricular mucous membrane. This portion of the tube is, when contracted, divided into six or eight large prominent folds, divided by deep narrow sulci, corresponding to similar elevations and depressions in the cuticular lining of the gigerium. The solvent glands form a perfect uninterrupted zone, quite around the tube, which has a well-defined and straight termination in the ordinary œsophageal mucous membrane. The sensible differences of this portion of the canal are the absence of longitudinal rugæ, the substitution for them of irregular eminences and depressions, its grayer color, soft velvety feel, greater vascularity and thickness, and the presence of minute puncta, which are scattered thickly over its entire surface—the mouths of the solvent glands. In cutting into the walls of the proventriculus these glands may be seen with an ordinary lens, or even with the naked eye, as simple follicles, with a somewhat bulging outline, proceeding straight from their blind extremities to their opening in the mucous membrane. They lie side by side imbedded in the tissue of the walls of the proventriculus, and are of a length but little less than the thickness of the parietes itself.

The gigerium, in situ, is far back in the abdomen, its middle about opposite the last rib and to the left side, lying nearly apposed to the abdominal parietes. It is in shape a somewhat irregular and flattened ovoid ; its walls comparatively thicker and more powerful than in the other subfamilies. The musculi laterales, at their thickest portions, measure a third of an inch or more in thickness. If we consider the gizzard as extending upward as far as the cuticular lining extends, i. e., to where the zone of gastric glands begins, it is divisible into two portions : a lower, with strong, thick, muscular walls, and very convex outline ; and an upper, narrower, more constricted portion, with much thinner and less powerfully contractile parietes. The hard cuticle lines both these portions uninterruptedly, extending quite to the glandular zone. It presents the ordinary rugæ and convolutions.

The duodenal fold is rather short, scarcely two inches in length. After forming this fold, the intestine proceeds in a pretty straight course to make a second fold, longer than the first, and quite disconnected with it. After that the intestine forms a mass of closely aggregated convolutions. Between six and seven inches from the cœca the intestine returns toward the duodenum, near the gizzard, and forms a definite fold, much of the same character as, and closely apposed to, the first duodenal fold, with which it is connected for the greater part of its course. There are only slight convolutions between this last fold and the cœca, beyond which the intestine proceeds in a nearly straight course to the cloaca.

The intestines measure, from the pylorus to the anus, a little over forty inches. There is but little difference in calibre throughout their length until we reach the cloaca ; the duodenum being, however, if anything, a little the largest. A little beyond the termination of the duodenal fold, just four and a half inches from the pylorus, the hepatic duct opens ; one inch further down the cystic duct is received by the intestine ; and just half way between the two is the orifice of the pancreatic duct. These three ducts, which convey the hepatic and pancreatic secretions into the intestine, open nearly on a line with each other on the mesenteric edge of the intestine.

The cœca resemble those of *Sterninæ*, and differ greatly from those of *Lestridinæ*. They arise within an inch and a quarter of the large globular cloaca, and are very short, measuring only about a fourth of an inch in total length.

The "large" intestine is very short and perfectly straight. Its calibre is a little greater than that of the ileum just anterior to the cœca, but it is not as large in circumference as is the duodenum. It differs from the other portions of the intestine in the thickness of its muscular walls, the increased amount of muscular tissue being quite appreciable to the eye.

After but a little more than an inch of length the colon terminates in the cloaca. This is exceedingly capacious and distensible, measuring, when fully inflated, an inch and three quarters in length by one and a half in breadth. It is of a nearly globular shape ; its superior portion, however, being somewhat conical and tapering where it contracts into the rectum. It is very slightly and incompletely divided into two unequal portions by a crescentic fold or reduplication of mucous membrane. The anterior or internal of this is the cloaca proper, and is greatly the largest ; the posterior or external forms the "*bursa Fabricii*," and consists merely of a bulging or unequal dilation of that portion of the cloacal parietes that is beyond the curved fold of mucous membrane already mentioned. Just beside this fold, about a fourth of an inch on either side of the median line, on the posterior aspect of the cloaca, are two small papillæ, placed side by side and in close contact. On the summits of these papillæ terminate the ureters and vasa deferentia, the excretory ducts of the sexual and urinary organs.

The pancreas occupies the whole length of the concavity of the duodenal fold. It is therefore of an elongated shape, and is somewhat triangular on a cross-section. The rounded free extremity of the gland is rather larger than the other end, the whole organ being somewhat club-shaped. Its long slender duct opens into the duodenum between the hepatic and cystic ducts. The two lobes of the liver are of very unequal size, the right being much the largest. It measures about three inches in length, while the left is only a little over two. Their internal or apposing surfaces are flat, and in contact for the greater part of their length, only separating above to admit the apex of the heart between them. They are both somewhat of a triangular shape on a cross-section ; rising up high, and thick in the middle ; tapering toward both extremities ; the right being the most elongated and attenuated. They are somewhat loosely connected by a thin, flat band of hepatic substance. The surface of both presents several eminences and depressions, produced by the impact of neighboring organs and parts.

The hepatic duct proceeds from the middle of the under surface of the left lobe, near the commissure ; has a length of about two inches, and opens into the duodenum, as already described.

The gall-bladder lies in a depression on the under surface of the right lobe, and is well developed. It is of an ovoid shape, tapering toward its proximal extremity ; more obtuse at its distal. The cyst-hepatic duct is very short, opening directly into the base of the bladder. The cystic duct arises about midway between the two extremities of the bladder, on its posterior aspect. It is larger, but shorter than the hepatic duct, and opens into the duodenum an inch further down.

The kidneys measure about two and a fourth inches in total length, but are of very varying breadth at different points along their extent. They are irregularly divided into several lobes, which are not, however, of regular shape, and closely adapted to each other, as in *Sterna ;* nor do they appear to be constant as to their mode of subdivision. The upper lobe of each is the largest, and has the most convex outline. The next is very narrow, serving as a connection between the anterior and posterior extremities, and is sometimes almost divided into two. The posterior lobe is nearly rectangular in shape ; about twice as long as broad ; and has a deep, longitudinal sulcus upon its surface, in which is received the ureter.

The sexual organs lie superimposed upon the superior lobes of the kidneys, closely bound down to them. Their efferent ducts run along in close apposition with the ureters, and terminate in the cloaca side by side with the orifices of the urinary ducts, as has been already described.

The superior larynx is composed of four principal elements : A thyroid cartilage, two arytenoid, and a cricoid, the latter divided into three separate portions. The thyroid is much the largest of these, forming all of the anterior or inferior portion of the organ. It is of a tapering, subconical form, with an ovoid truncated extremity, and an obtuse tip. Its lateral edges curl over upward, especially posteriorly, where it supports the cricoid, forming all of the cartilaginous lateral parietes which the larynx possesses. Its inferior surface is marked with a longitudinal groove ; its internal with a well-developed eminence, situate on the median line, not distantly resembling the crista galli of the human ethmoid bone. Anteriorly the thyroid extends forward as a mere flat lamina, with scarcely any convexity. The posterior portions of the thyroid support the two lateral elements of the cricoid. These are quite broad at their base ; curl over toward the median line ; growing narrower as they approach each other, till they complete the circle of the larynx posteriorly by uniting with the central azygoid element. This is a small, irregular, cartilaginous nodule, situate on the median line, having, posteriorly, two surfaces for the reception of the lateral cricoid elements ; more anteriorly two others for the articulation of the two arytenoid cartilages. These latter are of denser consistency than the rest of the larynx, being sometimes almost osseous. They are four-tenths of an inch long. Their base presents on their inner surfaces the facet for the articulation with the azygos element of the cricoid. They are so twisted or curled upon their own axes, that their lateral edges, at first horizontal, are afterward perpendicular, rising above the level of the rest of the larynx, and lying parallel to each other, thus forming the rima glottidis. These several cartilaginous pieces of the larynx are all connected by a delicate, elastic, fibro-cellular tissue. The motion which they possess is limited almost entirely to the opening and shutting of the arytenoid cartilages, effected by the muscles attached to them ; the motion being chiefly at the aryteno-cricoid articulation. These proper muscles of the larynx are the thyro-arytenoid or *dilatores glottidis*, and the *constrictores glottidis*, having the ordinary form and disposition.

The larynx thus composed is a flattened, tapering organ, situate between the apo-hyals, near the base of the hyoid, supported by the uro-hyal, which runs along its infe-rior surface. It measures seven-tenths of an inch in length by about half an inch in breadth at its widest part posteriorly. It is connected with surrounding parts by con-densed cellular tissue; by the prolongation into it of the mucous membrane of the mouth, and by various muscles.

The trachea measures nine inches in length. It is not of uniform width throughout, but superiorly it is broad and flattened, having much the shape of a transverse section of the larynx; while as it proceeds downward it becomes smaller and almost perfectly cylindrical. The rings are there also much denser and more resisting, so that the tube is much less compressible below than above. The tracheal rings are about one hun-dred and forty in number. As usual, they are alternately broader from right to left; the increased width on the right of one ring being compensated for by the narrowness of the next, at the same point of its circumference.

The *sterno-tracheal* muscles arise from the sternum, just above the sterno-coracoid ar-ticulation; reach the trachea an inch or so above the inferior larynx, and run as narrow, flattened bands, one on each side of the windpipe, quite to the thyroid cartilage; being then continued on to the hyoid bone, forming the thyro-hyoids. These muscular bands are well developed. Small fibrous offsets proceed from the supra-clavicular fascia to the trachea at its termination, and, with others from the intra-clavicular air-cell, pro-ceeding to the posterior part of the lower larynx, aid to hold the parts in situ.

The lower larynx does not differ in any essential points from that of *Stercorarius*, already described in sufficient detail. The bronchial half rings are twenty-four in number. They are all of equal width at all points of their circumference, and thin and delicate, except the first one, which is larger and stouter, and bears to the lower larynx much the relation that the cricoid does to the upper.

My earlier experiences with this Gull were along the coast of Labra-dor, in 1860; it is there the most abundant representative of its family, spending the summer and breeding plentifully on the mossy islands, and retiring southward in September. On approaching one of the breeding-grounds where, from a distance, numerous birds could be observed sitting on their nests, or walking leisurely about, we soon gave an alarm, when all would rise on wing, with loud screams, and circle high over head. The nests were found scattered irregularly over the ground, with little choice as to situation, except that the birds seemed to rather prefer moss-covered rocky places, and dry, bare spots; the grassy patches being generally appropriated by Eider Ducks. The numbers of Ducks and Gulls on any island were usually complementary, there being more of the latter than of the former on the bare islands, and conversely. The Gulls' nests were large and bulky, composed of dry grass, moss, and lichens, gathered into a heap, with a slight cavity, as if merely result-ing from the weight of the birds. The eggs, in all the instances that came under my observation, were three in number; in other respects they showed the great variation customary in this family. They aver-aged about 2.80 in length by about 1.90 in width. Some were light bluish or greenish, others deep brownish-olive; while the dark markings were of every size and shape, very irregularly distributed. Early in July eggs were found in every stage of development, though in most instances the embryos were advanced. At the same time many newly-hatched birds were caught skulking beneath stones or scrambling over the luxuriant moss. These downy nestlings are curious objects, like soiled carded wool, variegated with angular, dusky markings. On being caught they would squeal loudly, and fight with spirit. Placed on water they swam easily, and seemed quite at home. They fed freely from the first on fish and pork scraps.

Terrestrial nidification is the rule with this species, as it is throughout the family; yet there are authentic accounts—as that given by Audu-bon—of their nesting in colonies in trees. During the summer, in Lab-rador, the principal food appears to be the lance-fish (*Mallotus villosus*), which schools in myriads along the coast, affording the fishermen almost their only bait for cod. The breeding range is chiefly from New England to Labrador. Birds occasionally reach Greenland, yet Labrador is the regular terminus. When the fall migration occurs they are spread along our whole Atlantic coast, but principally from New England to the Carolinas, where many winter. I observed them constantly at Fort Macon, North Carolina, from September through May. In winter they are very abundant, being, in fact, the characteristic and only common bird of the family. There is little falling off in their numbers during March; most wend their way north early in April, when the Terns and Hooded Gulls make their appearance, but some linger through May. In the fall some arrive in September, but they are not plentiful until the latter part of October. Being here rarely molested, they get quite tame, often mixing with the domestic Geese around the fort, and sometimes permitting an approach within a few feet, though in general they show an appreciation of the limits of gunshot range. Most of the mature birds gain their nuptial livery before leaving. They are nearly silent during the winter, except when quarreling over their food; but they grow noisy in April, at the approach of the breeding season, and before they finally depart the air fairly resounds with their harsh cries.

A great part of their food at this season consisted of the refuse from the fort; they were always hovering over the spot where the garbage was thrown, contending for the booty with Turkey-buzzards and Fish Crows. At ebb-tide they frequently strung along the beach, at the water's edge, gathering various animal and vegetable substances stranded by the receding waves. A favorite resort was the large sand spots and muddy flats of the harbor, where they gathered soft molluscs, ascidians, and other matters. They seemed particularly fond of a kind of bivalve there, the *Cytharea gigantea*. Holding the shell under their feet, as a Hawk would its quarry, they hammered with the beak until the shell was broken in, and feasted on the contents. They managed the *Pectens* (*P. dislocatus*) in the same manner, but the quahogs were too much for them. I once found remains of a marsh hare in the stomach of one of these Gulls.

In the interior, I have found this species on the Upper Missouri, and we have authentic advices of its occurrence in several of the States, particularly those in the region of the Great Lakes. I have also seen specimens from the Pacific coast.

Var. OCCIDENTALIS, (*Aud.*) *Coues.*

DIAG. *L. argentato similis, sed pallio valde obscuriore (intensè plumbeo) et rostro brevi, altiore, robustissimo.*

Hab.—Pacific coast of North America (and Asia?)

Bill large, very stout and deep; the culmen convex at the end; the angle strongly developed, making the under outline doubly concave. Feet large and stout; the tarsus equal to the middle toe and claw.

Adult, summer plumage.—Bill bright chrome-yellow; a vermilion spot, more or less extensive, at the angle. Mantle dark bluish-ash, almost slate-color; the tips of the secondaries and tertials white; the line of demarcation distinct. Primaries: first three black throughout their exposed portions, the outer white for some distance at the tip (1.75 inches), crossed near the end with an irregular black bar, the shafts entirely black; second, without a white spot, but its tip, and the tips of all the others, white. Legs and feet flesh-color.

Approaching maturity.—As in the preceding, but the upper parts rather lighter, and the tail with an imperfect subterminal bar.

Intermediate.—Bill much as in the adult. White of the head, neck, and under parts, more or less mottled with dusky; "gull-blue" of the upper parts appearing in irregular patches; most of the feathers tipped with light gray. Primaries and tail uniform deep blackish-brown, with scarcely lighter tips, the former without spots.

Young-of-the-year.—Bill entirely black, rather shorter than in the adults, but at the same time with great comparative depth at the angle. Everywhere a deep black-ish-brown, mottled with grayish-white, the feathers of the upper parts being tipped and edged with that color. Rump and upper tail-coverts barred with whitish and dusky. Wings and tail as in the preceding.

Winter plumage.—This species seems to form an exception to the rule which obtains so extensively among large Gulls, since in winter the head and neck behind are not, ordinarily at least, streaked with dusky. I do not mean to assert that such a plumage is never acquired; but many hundred individuals which I have observed, under peculiarly favorable circumstances, at this season, all had the head and neck immaculately white, as in summer. The fact was brought more prominently into my notice from the fact that these Gulls were usually seen in company with three other species, every individual of which latter were, as usual, streaked on the head and neck.

Dimensions.—Length, 24 inches; extent, 55; wing, 15.50; bill above, 2.30; along gape, 3.10; height at nostril, 0.75; width, 0.40; height at angle, 0.85; tarsus, and middle toe and claw, 2.75.

This is a strongly-marked variety. Its most striking peculiarity of form lies in the rather short and remarkably robust bill, the depth at the angle being very great. It is about the size of *argentatus*, but, in addition to the stout bill, may be distinguished from that species by its very dark upper parts (a slate, approaching that of *marinus* in intensity), and the black, or nearly black, bases of the three first primaries. The species hardly requires comparison with *californicus;* its superior size, very robust bill, dark mantle and bases of the primaries, and restricted character of the subterminal spots, readily distinguish it. With one specimen, however (No. 22020, a bird of the year), we are in a little doubt. In size and general very dark colors it agrees with specimens of undoubted *occidentalis;* but the bill is small, perhaps less than the average of adult *californicus*, and with comparatively little depth at the angle. Although the young *occidentalis* has the depth of bill at the angle, compared with that at the nostrils, fully as great as in the adult, yet it is according to analogy with the feature presented by most Gulls, that the bill should be smaller every way in the young; and we therefore do not consider the discrepancy as irreconcilable to the species.

The specimens before us do not seem to indicate so great a diversity in size as exists among some large Gulls. The difference in the length of the longest and shortest wings amounts to scarcely an inch. The bill, however, varies greatly in size and proportions. The character of the changes of plumage is much that of *argentatus*, but the two birds may be distinguished by their bills. Without an undoubted young *californicus*, we cannot institute a comparison; but the differences will doubtless be those of smaller size, much weaker bill, and, probably, lighter colors generally.

Bruch is greatly in error in saying that this species is "not larger than *L. zonorhynchus.*" We see little grounds for the assertion of Bonaparte, that it is "intermediate between *Laroides argentatoides* and *Larus zonorhynchus.*" Bonaparte's diagnosis is otherwise very accurate.

I have quoted with a query, as synonyms of this species, the names of the large, dark Asiatic bird, considered as distinct by Bonaparte, but which Schlegel unhesitatingly assigns here. I have never had an opportunity of examining a specimen from that locality; but judging from descriptions, the bird is exceedingly closely related to, if not identical with, the present.

LARUS CALIFORNICUS, Lawr.

Californian Gull.

(?) *Larus argentatoides*, BP., Syn. 1828, 360.—RICH., F. B. A. ii, 1831, 417.
Larus californicus, LAWR., Ann. Lyc. N. Y. vi, 1854, 79; B. N. A. 1858, 846.—BP., Compt. Rendus, 1856, 770.—COOP. & SUCK., N. H. Wash. Ter. 1860, 273.—COUES, Pr. A. N. S. 1862, 300.
Laroides californicus, BP., Consp. Av. ii, 1856, 226.
Larus delawarensis var. *californicus*, COUES, Key, 1872, 313.

DIAG. *Larus pedibus fusco-olivaceis, remige primo lato spatio apicali albo.*

Hab.—Pacific coast of North America. California. Interior of Arctic America, on the great lakes and rivers.

NOTE.—Believing that I may have been hasty in reducing this supposed species, in the Key, to a variety of *delawarensis*, I shall here treat it as distinct, at the same time urging the probability that it will be found to intergrade completely with that species.

Bill moderately stout and strong, the angle well developed; varying considerably in size, larger than in *delawarensis*, sometimes nearly equaling that of *argentatus* in size. Tarsus equal to or slightly longer than the middle toe and claw.

Adult, summer plumage.—Bill chrome-yellow, tinged with greenish; a vermilion spot on lower mandible at angle; a black spot just above, forming, with a very small black spot on the upper mandible, an imperfect transverse band. Feet dusky bluish-green, the webs lighter. Mantle pearl-blue, much as in *brachyrhynchus*, lighter than in *canus* (Linn), perhaps slightly darker than in *argentatus*. Primaries: bases of all light bluish-white, internally almost white, especially on the outer, and of great extent on all; first with a white space at the end for about two inches, rather further on the outer than inner web, the shaft white along the white portion of the feather; second with a white spot near the end on the whole of the inner and most of the outer web, divided by the black shaft; tips of all white; black forming merely a narrow subterminal band on the sixth. Tips of inner primaries white, as are also the tips of the secondaries and tertials, the line of demarcation between the white and the blue of the mantle pretty distinct.

Adult, breeding plumage.—Eyelids bright saffron-yellow. Upper mandible bright chrome, the greater part of the lower vermilion, the rest chrome. Gape of mouth deep crimson.

Adult, winter plumage.—Bill dully colored. Head and neck behind streaked and mottled with dusky.

Nearly mature.—As in the preceding. Tail with an imperfect subterminal black bar. Some of the feathers of the upper parts edged with gray. White space at end of first primary crossed by a transverse black bar; no spot on second primary.

Young.—Bill yellowish flesh-color, black on the terminal half. Head, neck, rump, wing-coverts, tertials and secondaries, mottled with dusky. Primaries and tail uniformly brownish-black, scarcely lighter at the tips. Back as in the adults, but the feathers with grayish edges.

Dimensions.—Length, 20 inches; wing, 15 to 16; bill, 1.60 to 1.90; depth at eminentia symphysis, 0.56; tarsus, 2 to 2.25; middle toe and claw, about the same.

A very full series of this species in the collection, embracing specimens in every stage of plumage, except that of the young-of-the-year, enables us to give full diagnoses of the different ages, and to present its variations. The latter, as regards size, and especially the size and shape of the bill, are very great, equaling, if not exceeding, those of any other species. In the smallest specimen before me the wing, bill, and tarsus, measure, respectively, 14.25, 1.65, and 2.15; in the largest, 16.75, 2.20, and 2.60, making the difference in these parts 2.50, 0.55, and 0.40 inches, respectively. Yet with these variations it is not difficult to recognize the species. The bill is larger than in *delawarensis* or variety *Bruchii*, and has seldom or never the perfect black band near the tip; the upper parts are darker than in either, and the character of the primaries is quite different, in the long, white space on the first, instead of a white subterminal spot. From *occidentalis* it may always be known by its much less robust and deep bill, with lighter upper parts, and the light bases of the primaries. Though usually considerably smaller, with a smaller, weaker bill than in *argentatus*, mature birds from high latitudes sometimes approach or nearly equal the latter in size, and one specimen before us has actually a larger bill than in one undoubted *argentatus*. But the darker upper parts of *californicus*, and the very different character of the primaries, both basally and terminally, separate the two without difficulty.

The first primary of this species, though white for about two inches in mature birds, has, perhaps usually, a narrow, irregular, black band across one or both webs, near the end, dividing the white into a subterminal spot and broad tip. The shaft is always white along the white portion of the feather. The spot on the second primary sometimes extends only on the inner webs; the shaft is always wholly black. The shafts of all the primaries are white at the white tips. The orange eyelids and crimson gape are retained only for a short time during the breeding season. In winter the head and neck are streaked with dusky.

The type-specimen of *californicus*, kindly furnished for examination by Mr. Lawrence, is moulting, and some of the primaries are not fully grown out. The white apical space on the first primary is crossed by a narrow, transverse, black bar. A large series of skins, however, demonstrates that the black bar is soon resolved into two spots, or indentations, on the edges of the feather, and then quite disappears, leaving the primary purely and uninterruptedly white at its tip for about two inches.

Synonymy.—I incline to the opinion that *californicus* is not the first designation of this species, believing that *argentatoides* of Richardson (1831) was based upon it. Very numerous specimens of a Gull from the interior of Arctic America are doubtless of the species which Richardson calls *argentatoides*. Their size is somewhat greater than that of typical examples from California, though no more so than might be expected from their more northern habitat; and they are a shade lighter in the color of the mantle, but otherwise so entirely similar to *californicus* proper that they were unhesitatingly referred to the latter species by both Prof. Baird and myself. The only real discrepancy to be reconciled in Richardson's description is the statement that the legs are "flesh-colored," those of the true *californicus* being of a dusky olivaceous, with chrome-yellow webs, much as in *delawarensis*. In this respect, as well as in a less powerful organization, weaker bill, &c., it shows an evident approach to the "Mew-Gulls" (*delawarensis, canus*, &c.), and apparently connects the latter group with larger Herring-Gulls with flesh-colored feet. But the liability to error in giving the colors of the feet, &c., of water birds, is very great; Mr. Lawrence himself (B. N. A. p. 846) stating that the legs are "flesh-colored," although their tint was correctly given by him when introducing the species.

For a more extensive discussion of the point, I refer to my paper in the Philadelphia Academy "Proceedings." While it is probable that Richardson's name refers to the species described by Mr. Lawrence, I by no means insist upon this identification, nor would wish to supersede the name *californicus*.

Comparison of L. californicus with the European L. argentatus.—The terminal markings of the primaries of the two are identical, and in size the species are not very dissimilar. The color of the feet is strikingly diverse (dusky greenish in *californicus ;* flesh-colored in *argentatus*); and the picture of the *bases* of the primaries very different, as follows : In *californicus* the bluish color is very light in tint, in fact almost white terminally; extends very far along the feathers (especially on the first quill), its edge parallel with the rhachis for nearly its whole length, and then it turns suddenly off at an acute angle, running up nearly as far on the edge as in the centre of the inner vane of the feather. In *argentatus* the color is but little, if any, lighter than the mantle; it extends along the feather with an outline oblique to the shaft ; runs up much further in the centre of the inner web than along its edge, along which latter the black descends a little way as a narrow marginal line. In *californicus* the line of demarcation of the two colors is much more trenchantly marked than it is in *argentatus*.

LARUS DELAWARENSIS, Ord.

Ring-billed Gull.

Larus delawarensis, ORD, Guthrie's Geog. 2d Am. ed. ii, 1815, 319.—LAWR., B. N. A. 1858, 846; Ann. Lyc. N. Y. viii, 1866, 299.—COOP. & SUCK., N. H. Wash Ter. 1860, 273.—WHEAT., Ohio Agric. Rep. 1860, No. 267.—COUES, Pr. Phila. Acad. 1861, 246 ; 1862, 302.—COUES, Smiths. Rep. 1861, 418.—VERR., Pr. Ess. Inst. iii, 1862, 160.—BOARDM., Pr. Bost. Soc. ix, 1862, 131.—SCHL., Mus. P.-B. iv, 1863, *Lari*, p. 22.—ALLEN, Pr. Ess. Inst. iv, 1864, 80.—COUES, Pr. Bost. Soc. xii, 1868, 126.—TURNB., B. E. Pa. 1869, 38.—COUES, Pr. Phila. Acad. 1871, 39.—COUES, Key, 1872, 313.—RIDGW., Ann. Lyc. N. Y. x, 1874, 38 (Illinois).
Larus canus, BP., Syn. 1828, 259. Not of authors.
Larus zonorhynchus, RICH., F. B. A. ii, 1831, 421.—NUTT., Man. ii, 1834, 300.—AUD., Orn. Biog. iii, 1835, 98 ; v, 1839, 638 ; pl. 212 ; Syn. 1839, 327 ; B. Am. vii, 1844, 152, pl. 446.—GIR., B. L. I. 1844, 360.—BP., Comptes Rendus, 1856, 771 ; Consp. Av. ii, 1856, 224.—BLAS., J. f. O. 1865, 330.
Larus zonorhynchus var. *bruchii*, BP., Consp. ii, 1856, 224.
Larus zonorhynchus var. *mexicanus*, BP., Consp. ii, 1856, 224.
Glaucus zonorhynchus, BRUCH, J. f. O. 1853, 102.
Gavina zonorhyncha, BP., Naum. iv, 1854, 202.—BRUCH, J. f. O. 1855, 282.
Gavina bruchii, BP., Naum. iv, 1854, 202.—BRUCH, J. f. O. 1855, 283.

DIAG. *L. rostro nigrocincto, pallio cœruleo-perlaceo, remige primo spatio subapicali albo, tarso digito medio longiore.*

Hab.—North America generally; throughout the interior as well as coastwise. Cuba (CAB., J. f. O. v, 236).

Adult in summer.—Bill rather stout, as long as the middle toe and claw ; the upper mandible considerably convex at the end ; under mandible much thickened at the angle, which is prominent ; the outline from base to angle, and from angle to tip, both concave. Middle toe and claw scarcely more than three-fourths the tarsus. Bill greenish-yellow, at tip chrome, encircled at the angle with a broad band of black. Legs and feet dusky bluish-green. Mantle light pearl-blue, fading into white at the ends of the secondaries and tertials, the line of demarcation indistinct. Primaries : first black, the basal portion of the inner web very light bluish-white, almost pure, with a spot of white about 1.25 inches long near the end, of equal extent on both webs, divided by the black shaft ; second with a small white spot on the inner web, and the inner web whitish at base for a longer distance ; the whitish of the bases of the primaries regularly increases inward and the black decreases, until on the sixth it is merely a transverse bar. Apex of first primary black, of others white, the spot being very minute on the second, and gradually increasing ; seventh and innermost primaries without any black, like the secondaries.
Adult in winter.—As in summer, but the head and neck behind spotted (not streaked nor nebulated) with dusky.
Young, first winter.—Upper parts irregularly mottled with dusky brown and the pearl-

blue of the adults, the wing coverts being almost entirely dusky, with lighter margins to the feathers. Head, neck, and under parts, mottled with white and dusky. Primaries uniformly black; secondaries with a patch of brownish-black near the ends; tertials wholly brownish-black, narrowly tipped with whitish. Tail with a broad, subterminal band of black, narrowly tipped with white. Terminal half of bill black, the extreme tip yellowish.

Young-of-the-year in August.—Everywhere mottled thickly with brownish-black, on the upper parts the feathers with yellowish-white edges, the pearl-blue of the adults scarcely apparent, except on the wing-coverts. Terminal two-thirds of bill with the tip black, the rest light flesh-color. Other parts as in the preceding.

Dimensions.—Length, 19.75; extent, 48.50; wing, 14.75; bill above, 1.70; gape, 2.30; height at nostril, 0.45; at angle, 0.50; tarsus, 2.05; middle toe, 1.80.

The *anatomical characters* of this species do not differ in any notable degree from those of *L. smithsonianus,* already fully described.

Although of about the same size as *L. canus,* this species may readily be distinguished from it. It is rather larger; the bill, somewhat longer, is much more robust, the angle much more strongly developed, and are both mandibles crossed by a well-defined bar near the angle, wanting in *canus.* The upper parts are very decidedly lighter, being a very light pale blue, instead of darker bluish-gray. The characters of the primaries are quite different. In *delawarensis* the bases of the primaries are very light bluish-white, on the first almost pure white, and extending to within three inches of the tip of the second. In *canus* the light bases of the feathers are very much more restricted, the difference especially conspicuous on the second primary, the color of the bases bluish-gray, scarcely lighter than the back. The subterminal spots on the first and second primaries in *delawarensis* are small, divided by the black shaft, and not longer on the outer than on the inner vane, while in *canus* the spots are nearly twice as large; that on the first longer on the outer than on the inner vane, and not divided by the black shaft. *Canus* has, moreover, a spot on the third primary, wanting in *delawarensis.*

The relationship of this species to the *L. brachyrhynchus* of Richardson will be found discussed under the head of the latter. There is no other North American Gull with which the present requires comparison.

This species, in common with others of the genus, varies very considerably in size. The difference in the length of wing and tarsus of the largest and smallest specimen before us amounts to a full inch in the former, and 0.35 of an inch in the latter. The longest tarsus measures 2.25, the shortest 1.90. The difference in the bills is considerable. The smallest specimen before me is an adult female from Laramie River; the largest a young bird of the year from Labrador. Both Bonaparte and Bruch present a species or variety in their monographs, distinguished from *zonorhynchus* by its larger size, more robust bill, &c. An adult winter specimen before me, from Nebraska, differs in these and some other respects from the ordinary standard. The bill is every way larger and stouter, the culmen terminally more convex, the eminentia symphysis perhaps less strongly developed. The head and neck are streaked rather than spotted with dusky, and the first primary has a more decidedly white apex. The chord of the culmen measures 1.75; height of bill at nostrils, 0.53; at eminentia symphysis, hardly greater. The wing is 15.25 inches from the carpal joint. The feet are not larger nor stouter than average of *delawarensis.* A second specimen, from the interior of Arctic America, a little surpasses these measurements, being so large that it would be taken at first sight for *californicus,* but for the ring around the bill and the different pattern of the primaries. Without feeling assured that these specimens constitute even a decided variety, I present the above considerations to show how greatly the species may vary in size, and to indicate exactly in what consists this species or variety of the authors quoted.

Although the present is a marked and well-characterized species, there has been considerable confusion respecting it, occasioned by its being confounded by some authors with the European *canus,* and by others, and the greater majority, with the *canus* of Richardson, which is the succeeding species. It may therefore be well to trace its history from the beginning.

In 1815 a "Tooth-billed Gull" (*L. delawarensis*) is characterized by Ord, in Guthrie's Geography, as above. This, as Mr. Lawrence has shown, can be no other than the present bird. "His account of the measurements and coloration agrees precisely with the adult *L. zonorhynchus,* the only character to reconcile is the toothed bill. This I consider as a possible malformation, or probably an accidental toothing, caused by its being worn in some particular mode of feeding."—(LAWR.) In an adult and very old bird before us, the culmen along its entire length is jagged and irregularly serrate. This same feature along the commissure would produce precisely the "Tooth-billed Gull" of Ord. Moreover, this malformation actually exists along the commissure of a *Larus occidentalis,* now before us, thus proving that the character is entirely accidental and not confined to a single species, and fully confirming the position assumed by Lawrence. *Delawarensis* being undoubtedly, therefore, the present species, is the first distinctive appellation, and must take priority over the more usual name of *zonorhynchus* Richardson.

Bonaparte, in his Synopsis, presents the species under the name of "*L. canus* Linnæus." The description is that of an immature bird, in which the primaries have not yet attained their white tips. The measurement, "tarsus a little more than two inches," excludes the *brachyrhynchus* Richardson, to which the description might otherwise apply.

The species was definitely characterized by Richardson in 1831, under the name *zonorhynchus*, and separated from the *brachyrhynchus* of that author. This name was in almost universal employ, until Mr. Lawrence showed that it had not rightful priority. But authors have greatly erred in assigning as synonyms of this species *canus* and *brachyrhynchus* of Richardson, the former being the adult and the latter the young of a very different species. Neither is this species the "*L. canus* from North America of authors," as stated by Bonaparte, which citation is only referable to the succeeding species. A fuller elucidation of these names will be found under head of *L. brachyrhynchus.*

The Ring-billed Gull is more generally distributed throughout the interior than the Herring Gull, occurring on the larger waters of the Missouri region, and elsewhere. It migrates through the interior, up the Mississippi, as well as along the coast. Prof. Snow does not give it in his Kansas List, but in my copy received from him I find a penciled note of its occurrence at Lawrence in April, 1873. This was the Gull I oftenest observed in Northern Dakota; I found it in large numbers in September, on Lake River, a tributary of the Souris; and again in September of the following year on the Upper Missouri, in company with Herring Gulls. They were mostly young birds, apparently hatched not far off. Along the Atlantic coast I have traced the bird from Labrador to the Carolinas, finding it numerous in the former locality in summer, with Herrings and Black-backs. It winters abundantly on the coast of the Middle States; I saw it constantly during two winters over the harbor of Baltimore, where it flies among the shipping with Bonaparte's Gull and several kinds of Terns.

LARUS CANUS var. BRACHYRHYNCHUS, (Rich.) Coues.

American Mew Gull.

a. *canus.*

Larus canus, LINN., Syst. Nat. i, 1766, 224.—GM., Syst. Nat. i, 1788, 596.—LATH., Ind. Orn. ii, 1790, 815.—TEMM., Man. 1815, 499.—LEACH, Cat. 1816, 40.—BOIE, Isis, 1822, 563.—STEPH., Gen. Zool. xiii, 1826, 198.—FLEM., Br. An. 1828, 140.—JEN., Man. 1835, 275.—EYT., Cat. 1836, 52.—KEYS. & BLAS., Wirb. Eur. 1840, 96.— NAUM., V. D. x, 1840, 301, pl. 261.—MACGIL., Man. ii, 1842, 248.—SCHL., Rev. Crit. 1844, 125.—BP., Consp. ii, 1856, 223.—SCHL., Mus. P.-B. iv, 1863, *Lari*, p. 23.—GRAY, List Br. B. 1863, 233.—BLAS., J. f. O. 1865, 380.—SHARPE & DRESS., B. Eur. pt. xvii, Apr. 1873.
Laroides canus, BREHM, V. D. 1831, 751.
Gavina cana et *Glaucus canus*, BRUCH.
Larus cinereus, SCOP., Ann. Hist. Nat. i, 1768, 80.
Larus hybernus, GM., Syst. Nat. i, 1788, 596 (*Gavia hyberna*, BRISS., Orn. 1760, 189, pl. 16, f. 2).—GRAY, Gen. of B. iii, 1849, 654.—BP., Consp. ii, 1856, 223.
Larus cyanorhynchus, MEY. & WOLF, Tasch. ii, 1810, 480.
"*Larus cyanopus*, BECHST."
Larus procellosus (partim), BECHST., Orn. Tasch. 1802, 373; Naturg. Deut. iv, 647.
Laroides procellosus, BREHM, V. D. 1831, 750.
Laroides canescens, BREHM, V. D. 1831, 753.

b. *niveus.*

Larus niveus, PALL., Zoog. R.-A. ii, 1811, 320, pl. 76.—BP., Consp. ii, 1856, 224.
Larus canus var. major, MIDD., Sib. Reise, ii, 1853, 243, pl. 24, f. 4.—SCHL., Mus. P.-B. iv, 1863, *Lari*, p. 26.
Larus heinei, HOMEYER, Naum. 1853, 129.
"*Gavina heinii*, BRUCH, J. f. O. 1855, 283 (*partim*)."
Larus canus, BP., Consp. ii, 1856, 223 (*partim*).—SCHR., Reise, 511.
Larus kamtschatkensis, BP., R. and M. Z. vii, 1855, 16.
Gavina citrirostris, BRUCH, (*partim*).

c. *brachyrhynchus.*

Larus canus, RICH., F. B. A. ii, 1831, 420 (adult); not of authors.—NUTT., Man. ii, 1834, 300.
Larus brachyrhynchus, RICH., F. B. A. ii, 1831, 421 (juvenile).—NUTT., Man. ii, 1834, 301.—
COUES, Pr. A. N. S. 1862, 302.— ELLIOT, B. N. A. ii, pl. 53.—DALL & BANN., Tr. Chic. Acad. 1869, 305.—FINSCH, Abh. Nat. iii, 1872, 84.
Larus canus var. *brachyrhynchus,* COUES, Key, 1872, 313.
Larus suckleyi, LAWR., Ann. Lyc. N. Y. 1854, 264; B. N. A. 1858, 847 (young).— COOP. &
SUCK., N. H. Wash. Ter. 1860, 274.—SCHL., Mus. P.-B. iv, 1863, Lari, p. 27.—
BLAS., J. f. O. 1865, 381.
Rissa septentrionalis, LAWR., Ann. Lyc. N. Y. 1854; B. N. A. 1858, 854.—COOP. & SUCK., N. H. Wash. Ter. 1860, 277.

NOTE.—The foregoing synonymy is based upon the consideration that there are three recognizable varieties, but not species, of the *canus* group: 1. The typical European bird. 2. The larger and perhaps otherwise distinguished bird of Asia, *L. canus major* of Middendorff and Schlegel (see BLAS., J. f. O. 1865, 330). 3. The North American bird, of which the adult as *canus,* and the young as *brachyrhynchus,* were described by Richardson, and subsequently as *Rissa septentrionalis* (adult) and *L. suckleyi* (juvenile) by Lawrence. We have here only to do with the latter.

Var. BRACHYRHYNCHUS, *(Rich.) Coues.*

DIAG. *L. cano (Europæ) similis ; minor, rostro breviore, culmine magis convexo, pallio dilutiore, tarso vix longiore quam digitum medium cum ungue.*

HAB.—Interior of Arctic America, and Pacific coast generally. Not authenticated as occurring on the Atlantic coast.

SP. CH. Bill small, somewhat stout for its length, much shorter than the head or tarsus. Upper mandible straight to the end of the nostriis, moderately convex to the tip, rather more so than in *canus.* Angle of lower mandible pretty well developed, comparatively more so than in *canus;* the lower outline considerably concave posterior to it, somewhat so before it. Commissure about straight to near the tip. Tarsus and middle toe and claw about equal, the former but little if any longer than the latter.

Adult in summer.—Bill bluish-green, its terminal third bright yellow. Legs and feet dusky bluish-green, the webs yellowish. Mantle light grayish-blue or dark pearl-blue, a shade lighter than in *canus,* much darker than in *delawarensis.* Primaries: the bluish-gray bases rather lighter than in *canus,* much darker than in *delawarensis,* but fading into nearly pure white on all but the first at the juncture with the black portion ; these bluish-gray bases of the feathers extend toward the ends much further than in *canus,* as far as in *delawarensis,* and, as in that species, on the second, third, and fourth, extend further along the central portions of the inner web than at the edges, so that they are bordered for some distance with the black of the terminal portions of the feathers. The black takes in the outer web of the first primary and nearly the whole of the inner, but rapidly becomes narrower, till it is merely a subterminal transverse bar on the sixth. The seventh has frequently a spot of black on one or both webs. First, with a large white spot near the end two inches long, longer on the outer than on the inner web, not divided by the black shaft, the tip of the feather black ; second, with a similar spot, but smaller, not longer on the outer than on the inner web, and divided by the black shaft ; the extreme apex white, as are the apices of all the other primaries except the first.

Adult, high breeding plumage.—Eyelids, ocular region, and gape of mouth, bright orange-yellow, which color extends over the tip and cutting edges of the bill. The green of the bill with a peculiar hoary glaucescence. Legs and feet bluish-green, the webs bright gamboge-yellow. Otherwise as in the preceding stage.

Adult in winter.—The head and neck all round, with the upper part of the breast, mottled with dusky.

Approaching maturity.—Head and neck faintly mottled. Primaries brownish-black, without decided white tips ; the spots on the first and second restricted. Tertials with a dusky spot on each web near the end. Tail with a more or less perfect subterminal band.

Young, first winter.—Bill, basally, flesh-color ; black on the terminal half. Legs and feet light yellowish. Head, neck, rump, and whole under parts, mottled irregularly with dusky. Back as in the adult, but the feathers with grayish edgings. Wing-coverts, secondaries, and tertials, dusky ; darkest on the latter ; all with light edgings. Primaries uniform brownish-black, without white spots, tips, or lighter bases. Tail almost entirely brownish-black, with a narrow border of white.

Young in August.—Bill and legs as in the preceding. Everywhere whitish-gray ; the white of the under parts appearing as mottling, and the blue of the upper parts as irregular patches. Otherwise as in the preceding.

Dimensions.—Length, 17.50; extent, 42; wing, 13.75; bill above, 1.40; gape, 2 ; width at nostrils, 0.25; height, 0.35; height at angle, 0.35; tarsus, and middle toe and claw, 1.80.

The variations in size presented by this species, though considerable, are not greater than those of others of the genus. The difference in the lengths of the wing, tarsus, and bill, of the largest and smallest specimens before me, amounts to, respectively, 1.80, 0.30, and 0.20 inches. There is a considerable difference also in general size, which, however, is not always accompanied with corresponding discrepancies in length of bill and feet, small birds having sometimes longer bills and tarsi than those which surpass them in total length; the indefinite character of these variations showing pretty conclusively that they are those of a single species. As might be expected, adult birds, as a general rule, are larger, with longer and stouter bills than the young. As will be seen in the diagnosis, during the breeding season the bill, mouth, eyelids, and feet, become very highly colored, although the bright tints are retained for only a short time. There may also be sometimes detected a faint rosy blush on the under parts during this season. In adult birds the markings of the primaries are very constantly preserved. The relative proportions of the tarsus and toes vary a little, but the former never greatly exceeds the latter in length, as is always the case with *canus* and *zonorhynchus*.

I have before me the type-specimen of Richardson's *Larus brachyrhynchus*—the original of his description in the Faun. Bor. Am.—"a female, killed on the 23d of May, 1826, at Great Bear Lake." "Some brown markings on the tertials, primary coverts, and bastard wing, with an imperfect subterminal bar on the tail, point it out as a young bird, most probably commencing its second spring." The specimen in question is labeled in a handwriting unknown to me, "♀, May 23, 1826, Great Bear Lake," and corresponds in every detail with Richardson's description, so there can be no doubt of its identity. This author, in drawing up his diagnosis of the species from a young bird, fell into the error of saying "remigibus apicè concoloribus," whereas in the adult the primaries are as broadly white tipped as in other species. In this type-specimen the bill is very small, bearing perhaps less than the average even of young birds, but in other specimens before me it is quite as short.

This is the North American representative of the European *canus*, but is varietally distinct in the following features: The tarsus little if any longer than the middle toe and claw, instead of being a fourth longer. The bill is shorter and smaller in all its proportions, with a rather more convex culmen and less developed eminentia. The bluish bases of the primaries are much lighter, fading nearly into white at their junction with the black portion; extend for a greater distance along the feathers, and run up further in the centre than along the edge of the inner vane. The average size of the bird is less, and the color of the mantle rather lighter.

The differences between this species and *delawarensis*, the only other American species which it at all resembles, are so palpable that a detailed comparison is scarcely necessary.

Synonymy.—Much confusion prevails in the synonymy of this species, for which there is really no occasion, as it is perhaps the most thoroughly marked of all our North American species. Most authors present it as a synonym of *zonorhynchus* (*delawarensis*); and in addition several nominal species must be referred to it. The difficulty doubtless originated in the reference by some of *Larus canus* "Linn." of Richardson to the true European *canus*, and by others to the *zonorhynchus* Richardson. *Brachyrhynchus* Richardson being founded upon an immature bird naturally excited suspicion as to its validity, heightened by the fact that Richardson himself expresses doubts of its distinction from his *canus*.

The proper location of *Larus niveus* Pallas is a point upon which authors widely differ. Bonaparte considers it as a valid species. Cassin queries it as a synonym of *occidentalis* Audubon. Bruch, and following him Lawrence, consider it as a *Rissa*, identifying it with *brachyrhyncha** Gould (not of Richardson). I see nothing in Pallas' description or plate which renders its reference to the large Asiatic form of *canus* inadmissible. The plate, it is true, shows no subterminal spots on the primaries, but this is contradicted by the text, which says that the bird is in this respect "entirely like the preceding," which is L. *cachinnans* Pallas, a species the description of whose primaries shows it to be not essentially diverse from *brachyrhynchus* Richardson. The measurements given are those of an adult *brachyrhynchus*. The doubt involved appears to be this. Pallas' bird is from Kamtschatka, and is doubtless the species described by Middendorff as L. *canus major* (Siberische Reise, Birds, p. 213). The question then really hinges upon the identity or distinction of the Asiatic and American bird. The former, according to Middendorff, is larger than *canus*, and has a bigger bill, while the American bird is as much smaller and weaker billed. But it appears that there is in Siberia, &c., a distinct variety, larger than the standard European *canus*, just as there is in North America one smaller than the latter. In view of these considerations there seems to be no doubt that *niveus* Pallas is the larger form, which I recognize as L. *canus* var. *niveus*.

---

* For discussion of this view see below, under head of *Rissa brachyrhyncha*.

Bonaparte, in his Conspectus, places his own *Gavina* or *Larus kamtschatkensis* as a synonym of *niveus* Pallas, and also quotes with a query the *Gavina citrirostris* Bruch, a species founded upon *Larus citrirostris* Schimper. Bruch says that *camtschatkensis* is an "undoubted synonym" of his [Bruch's] *citrirostris*. Upon the authority, then, of these writers, their species are reduced to the *niveus* Pallas.

In 1831 Richardson gives as species of North American "Mew Gulls," *canus* "Linn.," and *zonorhynchus* and *brachyrhynchus* Richardson. The error here is in giving *canus* as identical with that of Europe, and in separating *brachyrhynchus* from it; a mistake magnified by nearly all authors, considering all three names as referring to a single species, *zonorhynchus*. *Canus* of Nuttall's Manual (1834) is the same as that of Richardson; *canus* of Bonaparte's Synopsis (1828) is the *delawarensis*.

Examination of the type-specimens of *Larus suckleyi* and *Rissa septentrionalis* of Lawrence, and comparison of them with the type of *L. brachyrhynchus* Richardson, shows all three to be identical. Most of the specimens of "*suckleyi*" are immature, and agree in the minutest particulars with Richardson's type. The type of *Rissa septentrionalis* is quite mature, and agrees entirely with the large series of skins from the interior of Arctic America, representing what Richardson called "*canus*." In this connection it is due to Mr. Lawrence to state that at the time of the founding of his species he had not Richardson's type to guide him; and as "*brachyrhynchus* Rich." had always been quoted (though erroneously) as the young *zonorhynchus*, he was obliged to take for granted existing opinions on the subject.

It is probable that the species sometimes reaches the Missouri region, but I have never seen it there, nor indeed anywhere, alive.

Subgenus BLASIPUS, *Bp.*

= *Larus*, CASS., Ill. 1853, 28. (*L. heermanni.*)
= *Blasipus*, BP., MSS.—BRUCH, J. f. O. 1853, 108 (see BP., R. Z. 1855, 21; SCL. & SALV., P. Z. S. 1871, 573).—BP., Consp. ii, 1856, 211 (type *B. heermanni*).—LAWR., B. N. A. 1858, 848.—COUES, Pr. Phila. Acad. 1862, 204.
= *Adelarus*, BRUCH, J. f. O. 1853, 106; 1855, 278.
= *Leucophæus*, BP., Consp. ii, 1856, 231 (type *scoresbyi*, Traill).

Bill shorter than head or tarsus, rather slender, moderately compressed, the tip rather acute; its color red in part in the adult. Folded wings reaching beyond the tail. Tail of moderate length, even, slightly emarginate in the young. Feet rather large. Tarsus equal to the middle toe and claw. General colors dark; tail mostly blackish.

This section scarcely differs in form from *Larus* proper, and is only worth recognition as a convenient means of grouping certain species which differ from ordinary *Lari* in the pattern of coloration, being mostly dark colored, with black or largely dark tail, and not showing the usual "mantle" contrasted with pure white.

Bonaparte's Conspectus recognizes three species of *Blasipus* as restricted: *heermanni* (type), *bridgesi* (*modestus* Tschudi), and *crassirostris*. He, however, has another "genus" *Leucophæus*, in which he places *scoresbyi* Traill (*hæmatorhynchus* King), *fuliginosus* Gould, and *belcheri* Vigors. The first two of these I have never seen; the first is said to be peculiar in the depth of its bill; *belcheri* has a bill much stouter than that of *heermanni*.

LARUS (BLASIPUS) HEERMANNI, Cass.

Heermann's White-headed Gull.

Larus heermanni, CASS., Pr. Phila. Acad. vi, 1852, 187; Ill. 1853, 28, pl. 5 (adult and juvenile).—HEERM., P. R. R. Rep. x, 1859, pt. vi, 74.
Larus (Blasipus) heermanni, SCL. & SALV., P. Z. S. 1871, 574, *cum fig.*
Blasipus heermanni, BP., Consp. Av. ii, 1856, 211; Compt. Rend. 1856, 770.—LAWR., B. N. A. 1858, 848.—COOP. & SUCK., N. H. Wash. Ter. 1860, 275.—COUES, Pr. Phila. Acad. 1862, 304; Ibis, 1864, 388.—SALV., *ibid.* 1866, 198.
Adelarus heermanni, BRUCH, J. f. O. 1853, 107; 1855, 279.
Larus belcheri, SCHL., Mus. P.-B. Lari, p. 9, *partim.* (Unites several species.)
Larus (Blasipus) belcheri, COUES, Key, 1872, 314, excl. syn. *fuliginosus* Gould. (*Nec* Vig.)

DIAG. *Adultus plumbeo-schistaceus subtus dilutior, capite sensim albo, caudâ totâ nigricante, albo-terminatâ, tectricibus superioribus albicantibus ; remigibus caudâ concoloribus, primariis interioribus secondariisque albo-terminatis, rostro plerumque rubro, pedibus rubronigricantibus. Long. tot. sesquiped. ; al. 14 poll. ; caud. 5 ; rostri culm. 1.75 ; tars. 2.25. Junior : sat similis, sed obscurior, capite fusco-variegato, rostro vix incarnato, apice nigro. Juvenis : minor ; corpore toto cum capite fuliginoso, plus minusve albido variegato, remigibus et rectricibus vix albo-terminatis, rostro magnâ ex parte nigro.*

Hab.—Pacific coast of North America, British Columbia to Panama.

Adult, breeding plumage.—Bill bright vermilion red, black for its terminal third, sometimes wholly red; a red ring around eye. Head white; this color gradually merging
41

on the neck into plumbeous ash, which extends over the whole under parts, being lighter on the abdomen and under tail-coverts than elsewhere. The back is deep plumbeous slate, lighter on the rump. Upper tail-coverts clear ashy. Upper surfaces of wings like the back; the primaries black; the tips of all, except the two or three outer ones, narrowly white. Tail black, narrowly tipped with white. Legs and feet reddish-black.

Young-of-the-year.—Smaller than the adult. Bill and feet brownish-black. Entire plumage deep sooty or fuliginous blackish; all the feathers, but especially those of the back and upper wing-coverts, edged with grayish-white. Primaries and secondaries black, as in the adults, with only traces of white tips on the former. Tail black, very narrowly tipped with dull white.

Immature.—Considerably larger than the above-described adult, the length being from 18 to 21 inches. Bill as in the adult. Head all round, and the throat, mottled with brownish-black and dull white, the latter color predominating on the forehead and throat. Upper tail-coverts lighter than in the adult, and the white tips of the tail-feathers broader; otherwise generally as in the adult, but with all the colors rather deeper.

Dimensions.—"Length, about 17.50; wing, 13.50; tail, 5.50." (No. 58797, Isabella Island, adult): Length of skin, 18.50; wing, 14; tail, 5.75; bill along culmen, 1.80; along gape, 2.40; depth at base, 0.55; at angle, about the same; tarsus, 2.20; middle toe and claw, a little less. (No. 30848, Guatemala, young): Wing, 12.25; tail, 4.75; bill along culmen, 1.60; depth at base, 0.50; at angle, 0.45; tarsus, 1.90. Length of some skins up to about 20 inches.

This species varies materially in size, though not beyond the usual limits in this family. The figures above given are near the extremes I have observed. At first the bird is a nearly uniform smoky-brown all over, with blackish quills and tail-feathers, usually varied with whitish edgings of the feathers of the upper parts, particularly those of the scapulars and wing-coverts. The bill is pale, with a dark tip. This stage gives way to a slaty plumage, paler below, with the ends of the secondaries and the upper tail-coverts growing more and more pale ashy, the tail acquiring a whitish tip, the head mottled with fuscous or whitish, and the bill reddening. With the clearing of all these colors, the head grows pure white, gradually shading into the slaty-ash of the fore-parts. The feet appear to be always blackish. The first and final stages are excellently well represented in Mr. Cassin's plate, above cited.

This species seems to me to be thoroughly established. Soon after its original description Mr. Lawrence noted some similarity of its characters to the description of *Larus belcheri*, Vigors, and likewise of *Larus fuliginosus*, Gould, suggesting a probable identity. Prof. Schlegel went further, unhesitatingly uniting the three, an error that I unfortunately adopted in the "Key," being at that time without the means of satisfying myself. Latterly Messrs. Sclater and Salvin have unraveled the synonymy of these and some allied species, showing that they are perfectly distinct. I have lately gone over the Smithsonian series, in company with Mr. Salvin, finding the specimens, as far as they go, to verify all the points given in the paper just referred to. *L. fuliginosus*, said to be only from the Galapagos, I have not seen; the specimens before me are of *modestus, heermanni*, and *belcheri*. The latter are labeled by Mr. Cassin "*L. fuliginosus* Gould," and are those referred to in his Ornithology of the United States Exploring Expedition, 1858, p. 378, under such name. An older label on each of the same specimens says "*hæmatorhynchus* King," apparently Mr. Peale's original identification; whereas Mr. Salvin points out to me that the birds are neither *fuliginosus* nor *hæmatorhynchus* (= *scoresbyi* Traill), but are *belcheri* Vigors. This wrong labeling, which I had no reason to suspect, was what threw me off the scent altogether. Granting these specimens to be *belcheri*, they are altogether different from *heermanni*, as claimed by Messrs. Sclater and Salvin. They are much larger; the bill and feet, in particular, are very much larger and stouter; the mantle, instead of being slaty-gray, is of a blackish-slate, much as in *L. dominicanus*. Most of the under parts, and the upper tail-coverts and ends of the secondaries, are ashy white. The tail, instead of being black, white-tipped, may be better described as white, with a broad, black subterminal bar—indeed the outer web of the outer feather is entirely white; the black bar on the inter web of this feather is only about an inch broad, and on the middle feathers is only about half as broad as the tail is long. The bird is not a "white-headed" Gull at all, having a dark hood like the mantle. I also verify the curious restriction of the frontal antiæ, as figured by the authors just mentioned. Wing, 14.25; tail, 5.50; bill along culmen, 2; its depth at angle, 0.70; the angle well defined, the tip obtuse, the whole bill very stout; depth at base, about the same as at angle; tarsus, 2.40. The bill in its present state is light colored, with a dark subterminal zone, and the tarsi are rather light, but the bird has been dried many years (described from No. 15693 Callao, Peru). No. 15692, from the same locality, is altogether similar. No. 15513, from Orange Bay, Terra del Fuego, is a very young bird, in the smoky-brown state of plumage, like that of *heermanni*, but very extensively varied with whitish on the upper parts; and although so young, the tail is already whitening at the base. These three specimens are the basis of "*hæmatorhynchus* Peale, 1848, *nec* King," and of "*fuliginosus* Cassin, 1858, *nec* Gould."

As just stated, I have not seen the true *fuliginosus* Gould from the Galapagos. Sclater and Salvin describe the adult as "nearly uniform cinereous, with a well-marked blackish hood ; the wing-primaries black ; the tail cinereous, like the body, with the upper coverts grayish-white and the under coverts still paler ; the legs and feet black ; the bill black, with the point of the upper mandible reddish." These features are strongly at variance with those of *heermanni* or *belcheri*. The young *fuliginosus* is stated to be "uniform brown, very similar to the corresponding stage of *L. heermanni*, but immediately recognizable by its much stouter bill."

Nor have I seen the *L. scoresbyi* (= *hæmatorhynchus* King), from Chiloe and southward, which the authors mentioned place in a different genus *Leucophæus*, on account of the singular short, stout, obtuse and curiously wrinkled bill. It is stated to have a brown hood, when young, like *L. belcheri*, but to lose this when old. I should not be surprised if *L. belcheri* finally lost this hood, and in fact I consider the indications to be that way ; but this would not invalidate its specific characters.

A fifth species of this group is the *L. modestus* of Tschudi (= *bridgesi* Fraser), from Peru and Chili. Of this I have before me a good example, No. 31977, from Chili, the basis of Mr. Cassin's notice in Gillis's U. S. Astron. Exped. p. 205. This is a "white-headed" Gull, with a general superficial resemblance to *heermanni*, though perfectly distinct, as it also is, according to Sclater and Salvin, who examined the type of "*bridgesi*," from *L. fuliginosus*. The head is white, shading into the clear, light plumbeous of the whole body (much lighter than in *heermanni*), and nearly uniform above and below. The tail and its coverts are like the body, with a rather narrow and not sharply-marked subterminal black bar. The primaries are black, with the innermost whitish tipped, and the secondaries are broadly white tipped. The bill and feet are wholly reddish-black. The bill is different in shape from that of any of the species here discussed, being much compressed, very slender, less deep at angle than at base, with an attenuated, decurved, and acute tip, bringing the point down to the level of the gonydeal angle. This is very peculiar, and reminds one of the shape in *Chœcocephalus atricilla* or *Rissa tridactyla*. Wing, 13 ; tail, 5 ; tarsus, 1.95 ; middle toe and claw, decidedly less ; bill along culmen, 1.75 ; depth at base, 0.50 ; at angle, 0.40.

The following determinations, it will be observed, of the five species discussed, are substantially the same as those of Messrs. Sclater and Salvin, P. Z. S. 1871, 573 *et seq.*

1. L. MODESTUS, *Tschudi*, Wieg. Arch. 1843, 389 ; Fn. Peru. 306, pl. 35.—*L. bridgesi*, FRAS., P. Z. S. 1845, 16 ; Zool. Typ. pl. 69 ; CASS., U. S. Naval Exp. 205.—*Blasipus bridgesi*, BP., R. Z. 1855, 21 ; Consp. ii, 212.

Hab.—Peru ; Chili.

2. L. FULIGINOSUS, *Gould*, Zool. Voy. Beagle, iii, 141 ; SCL. & SALV., P. Z. S. 1870, 323 ; 1871, 573 (not of *Cassin*, 1858).—*Leucophæus fuliginosus*, BP., Consp. ii, 232 ; Comptes Rendus, 1856, 771.—"*Adelarus neptunus*, BP."

Hab.—Galapagos.

3. L. HEERMANNI, *Cassin*, as above.

Hab.—Pacific coast of America to British Columbia. Panama.

4. L. BELCHERI, *Vigors*, Zool. Journ. iv, 1829, 358 ; Beechey's Voy. 39 ; SCL. & SALV., P. Z. S. 1867, 991 ; 1871, 575 (not of COUES, Key, 1872, which = *heermanni*) ; SCHLEG., Mus. P.-B., *Lari*, p. 9 (*partim ;* excl. syn. *heermanni* et *fuliginosus*).—*Adelarus belcheri*, BRUCH, J. f. O. 1853, 107 ; 1855, 279.—*Leucophæus belcheri*, BP., Consp. ii, 232 ; Comptes Rendus, 1856, 771 (quotes BP., Rev. Zool. 1855, 20 ; NAUM., 1854, 17).—*Larus* "*hæmatorhynchus*, KING," PEALE, U. S. Expl. Exped. 1848, — (*nec* KING ; *testibus specc. ipsis*).—*Larus* "*fuliginosus*, GOULD," CASS., U. S. Expl. Exped. 1858, 378) *nec* GOULD ; *testibus specc. ipsis*).—*Larus frobeeni*, PH. & LANDB., Wieg. Arch. 1861, 292 ; Cat. Av. Chil. 48 (*fide* S. & S.).

Hab.—Peru to Straits of Magellan.

5. L. SCORESBYI, *Traill*, Mem. Wern. Soc. iv, 1823, 514 ; PELZ., Orn. Nov. Exp. 151 ; ABBOTT, Ibis, 1861, 165 ; SCL., P. Z. S. 1860, 391.—*Leucophæus scoresbii*, BLAS., J. f. O. 1865, 378 ; SCL. & SALV., P. Z. S. 1871, 579.—*Larus hæmatorhynchus*, KING, Zool. Journ. iv, 1828, 105 ; JARD. & SELBY, Ill. Orn. pl. 106 ; DARW., Voy. Beagle, iii, 142 (not of PEALE, 1848, which = *belcheri*).—*Leucophæus hæmatorhynchus*, BRUCH, J. f. O. 1853, 108 ; 1855, 287.

Hab.—Chiloe. Patagonia. Falklands.

Subgenus RISSA, Leach.

< *Larus*, LINN., Syst. Nat. 1758. (*Gray*.)
= *Gavia*, BOIE, Isis, 1822, 563.
= *Rissa*, LEACH, Stephen's Gen. Zool. xiii, 1825, 180 (*Larus rissa*, BRÜNN).
= *Cheimonea*, KAUP, Sk. Ent. Eur. Thierw. 1829, 84 (same type).
= *Pulocondora*, REICHENBACH. (*Bp*.)

GEN. CHAR. Of medium size. Bill rather short, stout, and little compressed at the base, shorter than the head, equal to middle toe without the claw, longer than the tarsus; the tip decurved and attenuated; the convexity of culmen regular and gradual from base to tip; gonys concave, in consequence of the great deflexion of the apex of lower mandible; outline of rami slightly concave; eminentia symphysis well marked and acute, but not large. Wings very long, pointed, reaching beyond the tail; the primaries pointed, first longest. Tail moderately long, even; slightly emarginate in the young. Legs stout and short. Tarsus shorter than middle toe alone; anterior toes all long, and united by broad, full webs with unincised margins. Hallux rudimentary, or not well formed, the ungual phalanx being generally obsolete.

Anatomical characters.—Generally as in *Larus*, except those of the hallux.

A small genus, differing from *Larus* in few particulars: the attenuated, decurved shape of the bill and concave gonys; the short tarsi; the pattern of coloration of the long, pointed wings; the full, rounded interdigital membranes; and especially the rudimentary character of the hallux of the typical species, readily distinguish it from *Larus*. The markings of the primary quills are different. The changes of plumage of the young, and the winter vesture, are also characteristic.

In *Larus tridactylus* the two bones composing the hallux are very small, both together forming merely a knob on the metatarsus. The accessory metatarsal is a small, flat bone, scarcely longer than wide, with a rounded, thin, proximal extremity, lying in apposition, but loosely connected with the side of the metatarsus, and freely movable, being held only ligamentously. Its distal extremity is somewhat enlarged, and has a convex facet for articulation with the phalangeal segment. The latter is a short, irregularly-cylindrical ossicle, movably articulated by a circular, concave facet, with the accessory metatarsal. It tapers somewhat to a rather acute, free, distal extremity, over which the metatarsal skin is stretched. The ungual phalanx is obsolete in most instances, yet we occasionally find it bearing a well-formed claw.

There are but two species of this group satisfactorily determined. One is the common bird of the North Atlantic, which has a varietal representative in the North Pacific; the other is a very distinct species, confined to the last-mentioned region. They may be thus tabulated:

1. Feet dark; bill clouded with olivaceous. Bill, about 1.50 long; wing, 12.00.
    a. Hallux rudimentary, without a claw-bearing terminal phalanx.. TRIDACTYLUS.
    b. Hallux better formed, bearing a claw .... var. *kotzebui*.
2. Feet coral red (drying yellow); bill clear yellow. Bill, about 1.20; wing, 13.00 .... BREVIROSTRIS.

It may be proper here to remark upon the bibliography of the species collectively, a point much needing of critical consideration. The synonymy of *R. tridactyla* is definite enough; we have only to do with the two northwest *Rissæ*.

A great mistake of authors, I hope I have been able to prove, is in considering the *Larus niveus* of Pallas as a *Rissa*, and deducing therefrom a *Rissa nivea* to antedate and take the place of *Rissa brachyrhyncha* or Brandt's *R. brevirostris*. Then from the fact of the characters and relationships of these two very distinct northwestern species not being clearly understood, different authors have indiscriminately adduced the synonyms of both species for either of them, others often giving the synonyms of *Kotzebui* for what, according to their description, is the *brevirostris*, and *vice versâ*. Quite recently the subject has been further complicated by the introduction of a *Rissa septentrionalis*, which is no *Rissa*, but a true *Larus*, and nothing more nor less than the lesser American Mew-Gull, the adult of which was described by Richardson in 1831 as *L. canus*, and the young as *L. brachyrhynchus*.

The whole matter may thus be summed up: There are on the northwest coast of North America two forms of *Rissa* (neither of which is *L. niveus* Pallas). The first of these is the representative of *R. tridactyla*, the proper name of which is (probably) *Kotzebui*. The other is a very different species, with a short, bright yellow bill, coral-red or orange-yellow feet; described by Brandt as *L. brevirostris*, and by Gould as *Larus brachyrhynchus*.

This is the gist of my views on the subject. The matter is more fully discussed under the heads of the two species.

LARUS (RISSA) TRIDACTYLUS, Linn.

The Common Kittiwake.

Larus rissa, BRÜNN., Orn. Bor. 1764, 42.—LINN., Syst. Nat. i, 1766, 224.—GM., Syst. Nat. i, 1788, 594.—LEACH, Cat. 1816, 40.—FLEM., Br. An. 1828, 141.
Laroides rissa, BREHM, V. D. 1831, 755, pl. 37, f. 3.
Larus riga, GM., Syst. Nat. i, 1788, 594.—LESS., Tr. Orn. 1831, 619.

Larus tridactylus, LINN., Fn. Suec. 55; Syst. Nat. i, 1766, 224.—GM., Syst. Nat. i, 1788,
595.—LATH., Ind. Orn. ii, 790, 818.—RETZ., Fn. Suec. 1800, 154.—NILSS., Fn.
Suec. ii, 174.—SCHÆFF., Mus. Orn. 1779, 64.—MEY. & WOLF, Tasch. Deuts. ii,
1810, 486.—TEMM., Man. 1815, 502; ii, 1820, 774.—VIEILL., Nouv. Dict. xxi, 1818,
503; Fn. Franç. 39.—FABER, Prod. Isl. Orn. 1820, —.—BREHM, Eur. Vög. 1823.
705.—BP., Syn, 1828. 359.—SW. & RICH., F. B. A. ii, 1831, 423.—NUTT., Man. ii,
1834, 298.—JEN., Man. 1835, 274.—AUD., Orn. Biog. iii, 1835, 186, pl. 224; Syn.
1839, 326; B. A. vii, 1844, 146, pl. 444.—SCHINZ. Eur. Fn. 1840, 385.—NAUM., V.
D. x, 1840, 322, pl. 262.—KEYS. & BLAS., Wirb. Eur. 1840, 95.—SCHL., Rev. Crit.
1844, 126.—DeKAY, N. Y. Fauna, ii, 1844, 313.—GIR., B. L. I. 1844, 361.—SCHL.,
Mus. P.-B. iv, 1863, *Lari*, p. 30.—COUES, Key, 1872, 314.
Gavia tridactyla, BOIE, Isis, 1822, 563.
Cheimonea tridactyla, KAUP, Sk. Ent. Eur. Thierw. 1829, 84.
Laroides tridactyla, BREHM, V. D. 1831, 754.
Rissa tridactyla, BP., List, 1838, 62; Consp. Av. ii, 1856, 225; Compt. Rend. 1856, 770.—
MACGIL., Man. ii, 1842, 250.—GRAY, Gen. of B. iii, 1849, 655.—BRUCH, J. f. O.
1853, —; 1855, 284.—LAWR., B. N. A. 1858, 854.—COUES, Pr. Phila. Acad. 1861,
247; *ibid* 1862, 304.—WHEAT., Ohio Agric. Rep. 1860, No. 270 (Lake Michi-
gan).—RIDGW., Ann. Lyc. N. Y. x, 1874, 393 (the same).—BOARDM., Pr. Bost.
Soc. ix, 1862, 131.—VERR., Pr. Ess. Inst. iii, 1862, 161.—ALLEN, *ibid.* iv, 1864,
90.—COUES, *ibid.* v, 1868, 306.—LAWR., Ann. Lyc. N. Y. viii, 1866, 299.—MALMG.,
J. f. O. 1865, 202.—NEWT., Ibis, 1865, 508.—DALL & BANN., Tr. Chic. Acad. 1869,
305 (? *Kotzebui*).—TURNB., B. E. Pa. 1869, 38.—FINSCH, Abh. Nat. iii, 1872
(? *Kotzebui*).—BLAS., J. f. O. 1865, 384.
Larus nævius, SCHÆFF., Mus. Orn. 1779, 64.
Larus torquatus, "*canus*" et *gavia*, PALL., Zoog. R. A. ii, 1811, 328, 329, 330.
Rissa brünnichii, LEACH, Steph. Gen. Zool. xiii, 181, pl. 21.
Rissa cinerea, EYT., Cat. Br. B. 1836, 52.
Laroides minor, BREHM, V. D. 1831, 756.

DIAG. *L. pedibus sub-tridactylis, fuscis, rostro flavo-virescente .*

Hab.—Arctic regions of both hemispheres. South in winter on the Atlantic coast to
the Middle States.

Bill rather longer than the tarsus, about equal to the middle toe without the claw,
stout at the base, tapering toward the tip, which is attenuated, acute, and decurved.
Convexity of culmen regular from the base to the apex. Eminentia symphysis moderately developed, but acute. Gonys concave, as are also the rami. Nostrils rather far
forward, lateral, linear, direct. Feathers encroach far on the upper mandible, within a
tenth of an inch of the nostrils, and meet over the culmen some distance in front of
the base. Their extent on the sides of the lower mandible is much less, but between
the rami they reach to the apex of the mental space, which is narrow and acute anteriorly. The formation of the palate as in *Larus* generally, but the ridges all broad and
distinct, more thickly covered with larger papillæ than in most species. Tongue large,
fleshy, corneous only for its anterior half. Wings very long and acute; first primary
largest, second nearly equal to it, rest rapidly graduated. Tail rather long for this
subfamily, perfectly square. Feet short and stout, the tarsus little compressed; the
reticulations on its posterior aspect, as well as on the inferior surface of the toes,
roughened and elevated into small conical papillæ. The scutellation of the tarsus anteriorly breaks up into small polygonal reticulations some distance below the tibio-
tarsal joint. Anterior toes all long; the interdigital webs broad, full, with unincised
margins. Hallux typical of the genus. Claws short, stout, little arched, not very
acute, absent on the hallux.

Adult, breeding plumage.—Color of bill light yellow, clouded with olivaceous. Head
and neck all round, under parts and tail, pure white. Mantle rather dark bluish or
nereous-blue, the tertiaries and secondaries of the same color nearly to their tips,
.uch are white. Primaries: the first very light bluish-white, without white apex, its
ter web, and its inner web for about two inches from the tip, black; second like the
st, but without the black outer web, its tip being black for nearly the same distance
the first, its apex with a minute white spot; on the third and fourth the black tips
ow shorter, while the apices are more broadly white; this lessening of the black on
.h feather is exactly proportional to the shortening of the successive quills, causing
the bases of all the black tips to be in the same straight line. A sub-apical black spot
is usually present on one or both webs, but is sometimes absent. Legs and feet dusky
olive.

Adult in winter.—Occiput, nape behind, and sides of the breast, clouded over with
the color of the back, deepening into slate over the auriculars. A very small but well-
defined ante-ocular lunula. Otherwise as in summer.

Young.—Bill black; an ante-ocular lunula, and a post-ocular spot, dusky slate. A
broad transverse bar across the neck behind, the whole of the lesser and median wing-
coverts, the bastard quills, the tertiaries, except at their edges, and a terminal bar on

the tail, black. The outer four primaries with their outer webs, outer half of inner webs, and tips for some distance, black, the rest of the feathers pearly white. Tips only of the fifth and sixth black, their extreme apices with a white speck.

Dimensions.—Wing, 12.25 ; bill above, 1.40 to 1.50 ; along rictus, 2.10; height at base, 0.59 ; at angle, 0.40 ; tarsus, 1.30 ; middle toe and claw, 1.80.

Regarding so long and well known a species as the present, any further remarks upon its characters and relationships are unnecessary. Its principal synonyms are given in the preceding list. The relationships of the other North American species will be found discussed under their respective heads.

LARUS TRIDACTYLUS var. KOTZEBUI, (*Bp.*) *Coues.*

(?) *Rissa brachyrhyncha*, BRUCH, J. f. O. 1853, 103, sp. 31.
Rissa nivea, BRUCH, J. f. O. 1855, 285, sp. 36 (excl. syn.).   Not *Larus niveus*, PALL.
Rissa kotzebui, BP., Consp. Av. ii, 1856, 226.—BP., Compt. Rend. 1856, 771.—COUES, Pr. A. N S. Phila. 1862, 305.—CASS., Pr. A. N. S. Phila. 1862, 325.—ELLIOT, B. N. A. pl. 54.
" *Rissa brevirostris*, BRANDT," LAWR., B. N. A. 1858, 855, *partim.* Sed non Brandtii, quæ species sequens.
Larus tridactylus var. *kotzebui*, COUES, Key, 1872, 314 (see COUES, Pr. Phila. Acad. 1869, 207, foot-note).—COUES, Elliot's Prybilov Islands, 1874, App. p. —.

DIAG. *Rissæ tridactylæ simillimus ; nonnisi halluce magis explicato differt.*

Hab.—The North Pacific, American and Asiatic.

There is no occasion to describe this form, because it is exactly the same as *R. tridactyla*, except in the singular character given in the diagnosis.

I have now a great number (f specimens, enabling me to speak confidently of the bird. A part of the Kittiwakes from the North Pacific are not distinguished *in any way* from the common North Atlantic bird. Others have the hind toe as perfectly formed and proportionally as large as it is in any species of *Larus !* And there is a gradation up to this feature.

A specimen (No. 50197, September, 1867, Plover Bay) exhibits the extreme of this variation. The hallux is two-tenths of an inch long, and bears a perfect claw. In fact this bird is not "*Rissa*," but *Larus*, in respect of its feet.

It is certainly a singular fact, that while the Atlantic bird is not known to vary in this respect, the race inhabiting the North Pacific should exhibit the anomaly.

No comparison of this form with the succeeding species is required.

Synonymy.—In the next article some points will be discussed that have a bearing here also. I have now only to speak of the above-cited names. *R. brachyrhyncha*, Bruch, 1853, is to me doubtful ; I scarcely know where to locate it ; probably it comes here, rather than under the next head. Bruch's *Rissa nivea* (of 1855) must fall here, because he says that it has the hind toe better developed ; whereas it is his other species whereof he says "feet coral-red" (*i. e. brevirostris*). His species 36 therefore being thus *kotzebui*, he is wrong in adducing " *brachyrhyncha* Gould" as a synonym. Still, if reference to authors is allowed to override description as an index, *R. nivea* Bruch is the next species. *R. kotzebui* Bonaparte is diagnosticated much as above ; no questions have arisen about it ; Cassin and I have used it in precisely its author's acceptation. The " *R. brevirostris* Brandt" of Lawrence is partly this species, partly the succeeding, as evident from his brief diagnosis ("hind toe better formed"=*kotzebui ;* "feet coral-red"=*brevirostris*). But *R. brevirostris* Brandt is really the next species. I rather think that almost all, if not all, the various *Rissa* synonyms really go to the next species, and that Bonaparte alone, in his *R. kotzebui*, has exactly hit off the bird I am now defining ; at any rate no description that speaks of red or yellow legs—no matter what is said of the hind toe— can come here.

It will thus be seen that the views I printed in 1862, with an expressed doubt as to their entire accuracy, meet with confirmation ; the only modification I offer is not believing in the permanent distinction of *kotzebui* and *tridactyla*, examination of many specimens having shown that but one of the supposed and accredited differences has any special significance, and that this one is inconstant.

LARUS (RISSA) BREVIROSTRIS, (Brandt) Coues.

Red-legged Kittiwake.

(?) *Rissa nivea*, GRAY, Gen. of B. 1849, iii (sed non *Larus niveus*, PALL.).—BP., Compt. Rend. xlii, 1856, 771.—LAWR., B. N. A. 1858, 855 (descriptionem *Lari brachyrhynchi* Gouldii transcripta est).—ELLIOT, Birds N. Am. pl. 54.
Larus brachyrhynchus, GOULD, Pr. Zool. Soc. July, 1843, 106.—GOULD, Zool. Voy. Sulphur, 50, pl. 34. (Not of Richardson.)

(?) *Rissa brachyrhyncha*, BRUCH, J. f. O. 1853, 103.
Rissa brachyrhyncha, BP., Consp. Av. ii, 1856, 226.—COUES, Pr. A. N. S. Phila. 1862, 306.
Rissa brevirostris, "BRANDT."—BRUCH, J. f. O. 1855, 285.—LAWR., B. N. A. 1858, 855
   (*partim*).—DALL & BANN., Tr. Chic. Acad. i, 1869, 305.
Larus brevirostris, COUES, Key, 1872, 315 ; Elliot's Prybilov Islands (biography, &c.).
(?) *Larus warneckii*, COMDE, R. M. Z. 1860, 401.

DIAG. *L. albus, pallio cinereo, pagonio exteriore et apice remigis* 1^{mi} *nigris, remigibus* 2do,
3^{tio}, *et* 4to *notâ apicali cinereâ*, 5to *vittâ nigrâ et apice cinereo ; rostro brevi, flavissimo, pedibus rubroflavis.*

Hab.—North Pacific, both Asiatic and American.

SP. CH. *Adult, breeding plumage.*—(No. 24296, Smithsonian Museum ; from Kamtschatka; received from Mr. Gould.) Bill very short, stout, wide at the base, the upper mandible much curved, though not attenuated nor very acute. *Convexity of culmen very great toward the tip ;* the culmen being, from the nostrils to the apex, almost the arc of a circle, whose centre is the symphyseal eminence. Outline of rami of under mandible and gonys both somewhat concave ; the eminentia symphysis but slightly developed. Tarsus *very short,* hardly more than two-thirds the middle toe and claw. Wings exceedingly long, reaching, when folded, far beyond the tail. Tail of moderate length; even.

Bill a uniform clear light straw-yellow, with no tinge of olivaceous (some specimens, however, are thus tinged). Head and neck all round, under parts and tail, pure white. Mantle deep leaden or bluish-gray, much darker than in *R. tridactyla ;* the color on the wings extending to within half an inch of the apices of the secondaries, which terminal half inch is white. Primaries: the *first* has its shaft and outer vane black, but has on its inner vane a space of dull gray (*not white*), which at the base of the feather occupies nearly all the vane, but gradually grows narrower until it ends by a well-defined rounded termination half as broad as the vane itself, about 2½ inches from the tip of the feather, these 2½ inches being black, like the outer vane. *Second :* The outer vane is of the same leaden gray as the back, to within 4 inches of the tip; the inner vane is of a rather lighter shade of the same color, to within 3 inches of the tip, the gray ending abruptly, being in fact almost truncated. *Third :* Like the second, but the gray extends further, leaving only a space of 2 inches black ; and the tip has also a minute *apical* gray spot. *Fourth :* Wholly bluish-gray to within 1½ inches of the tip, which has a larger gray apical spot than has the third, so that the black is less than 1½ inches long. *Fifth :* The gray extends so far that it is separated from the well-defined white apical spot by a band of black less than 1½ inch wide. *Sixth :* Gray, fading into white at the tip, and with the black reduced to a small subapical spot on one or both webs; other primaries like the sixth, minus the black spot. (This "gray" of the primaries is the color of the mantle.) Legs and feet in the dried specimen clear straw-yellow (in life coral-red, especially the toes and webs; the tarsi themselves not quite so bright). Claws black.

Dimensions.—Bill, along culmen, 1.20 inches ; along rictus, about 1.70 ; from nostril to tip, 0.60 ; depth at base, 0.50 ; width, 0.42 ; depth at symphyseal eminence, 0.42 ; wing, 13 ; tail, about 5 ; tarsus, 1.25 ; middle toe and claw, nearly 2 ; length of the whole bird, apparently about 14 inches.

In the above specimen the feet are plain yellow ; in one more recently obtained (No. 54695, St. George's Island, August 15, 1868—*W. H. Dall*) the toes and webs are coral, almost vermilion red; the tarsi nearly yellow, but apparently already faded somewhat. This bird agrees minutely with Gould's typical specimen ; the bill, however, is a little more attenuated toward the tip, with less convexity of the culmen, and is clouded with olivaceous. It appears to be perfectly mature. I have since examined scores of specimens from the Prybilov Islands—they are all alike red-legged.

I know of no species that resembles this one so intimately that detailed comparison is required for the separation of the present. The species is in fact one of the more strongly marked of the subfamily: The shape and color of the bill ; the relative proportions and color of the feet ; the dark mantle and peculiar pictura of the primaries. stamp it with an individuality not easily overlooked or misunderstood.

Young birds I have not seen ; but I presume that the changes of plumage will be found correspondent with those of *R. tridactyla*. The bill may be black, very likely ; there may be a bar of black on the wings, and another across the back of the neck ; but this, it must be cautioned, is merely suppositious on my part. Of the color of the feet of the young I prefer not to conjecture.

So much has been said of the hind toe of Pacific *Rissæ* that it is incumbent upon me to add my testimony in respect of this species in this particular. The hallux of *R. brevirostris* is not appreciably *larger* than that of *tridactyla ;* it bears a minute, abortive black claw—a mere speck of corneous, as distinguished from cuticular, tissue. I should, not on this account, say that the hind toe was better developed than in *R. tridactyla ;* but some authors may have done so, thus further entangling the *Rissa* question ; for it is to such a condition of the hallux as I have described under *R. kotzebui* that such expression properly applies.

Synonymy.—I might discourse at great length on this subject, but it would scarcely be profitable ; and I will therefore confine myself to the more definite among the many things that might be said. In the first place, I throw *Larus niveus* Pallas entirely out of the present consideration (see elsewhere in this memoir, and also my discussion of the point in Pr. A. N. S. Phila. 1862, p. 307). Nevertheless other writers have come to different conclusions, and taking up the name, give us *Rissa nivea* for the bird, as shown in the above synonymy. But Bruch's *Rissa nivea* of 1855 is, I take it, from his description, rather *R. kotzebui* than this species. *Rissa brevirostris* of Brandt (whose original notice I have not seen) is, by both Bruch and Bonaparte, located here ; I presume that there is no reasonable doubt on this score. Bruch's *brevirostris* is certainly this species. Lawrence's *brevirostris* is mixed ; his expression, feet "coral-red," brings it here ; the rest of his brief diagnosis carries it elsewhere ; but I have no doubt he meant this species rather than *kotzebui*.

This is *Larus brachyrhynchus* Gould, above quoted, just as described and figured by him. It is to be carefully distinguished from *Larus brachyrhynchus* Richardson, which is simply the American form of *canus*.

Some authors have here located *Larus citrirostris*, Schimper (see, however, BLASIUS, J. f. O. 1866, 73).

Subgenus PAGOPHILA, *Kaup.*

< *Gavia*, BOIE, Isis, 1822, 563.
= *Pagophila*, KAUP, Sk. Ent. Eur. Thierw. 1829, 69.
= *Cetosparactes*, MACGILLIVRAY, Man. Br. Orn. ii, 1842, 251 (by err. *Catosparactes*, GRAY).

GEN. CHAR. Bill very short, much less than the head, about equal to the greatly abbreviated tarsus, very stout, but little compressed. Nasal sinus deep, the nostrils placed far forward. Legs and feet very short and stout, the scales of the tarsus and toes large and rough. Tibia feathered to near the joint; tarsus about equal to the middle toe without the claw ; claws all large, stout, and much curved. Interdigital webs narrow and deeply incised. Wings very long, the primaries more or less falcate and attenuated. Size moderate ; general form stout ; color entirely white.

Pagophila differs from other *Larinæ* in its short, stout, obtuse bill ; much abbreviated, very stout and roughened tarsus and toes ; feathered tibia, deeply excised webs, &c. ; and constitutes one of the better-marked subgenera of the subfamily. The habits of the species composing the genus also differ notably from those of other Gulls, as attested by all observers.

Cetosparactes of Macgillivray (1842), based upon the *Larus eburneus*, is antedated by *Pagophila* of Kaup (1829) with the same type. *Gavia*, applied by Boie to this group, was first used by Mœhring in a different connection.

LARUS (PAGOPHILA) EBURNEUS, Gm.

Ivory Gull.

Larus eburneus, GM., Syst. Nat. i, 1788, 596.—LATH., Ind. Orn. ii, 1790, 816.—TEMM., Man. 1815, 498 ; ii, 1820, 769.—VIEILL., Nouv. Dict. 1818, 494 ; Fn. Franç. 1828, 389.— NILSS., Orn. Suec. ii, 1823, 171.—STEPH., Gen. Zool. xiii, 195.—LESS., Tr. Orn. 1831, 618.—BP., Syn. 1828, No. 297.—NUTT., Man. ii, 1834, 301.—JEN., Man. 1835, 276.—AUD., Orn. Biog. iii, 1835, 571 ; Syn. 1839, 326 ; B. Am. vii, 1844, 150, pl. 445.—KEYS. & BLAS., Wirb. 1840, 96.—NAUM., V. D. x, 1840, 341, pl. 263.—SCHL., Rev. Crit. 1844, 126 ; Mus. P.-B. iv, 1863, *Lari*, p. 5.—COUES, Key, 1872, 313.
Gavia eburnea, BOIE, Isis, 1822, 563.—BREHM, V. D. 1831, 765.—BP., List, 1838, 62.
Pagophila eburnea, KAUP, Sk. Ent. Eur. Thierw. 1829, 69.—GRAY, Gen. of B. iii, 1849, 655 ; List Br. B. 1863, 237.—LAWR., B. N. A. 1858, 836.—BP., Consp. ii, 1856, 230 ; Compt. Rend. 1856, 771.—NEWT., P. Z. S. 1861, 400 (eggs) ; Ibis, 1865, 507.—COUES, Pr. Phila. Acad. 1862, 308.—MALMG., J. f. O. 1865, 200.—BLAS., J. f. O. 1865, 384.
Cetosparactes eburneus, MACGIL., Man. ii, 1842, 252 ; Hist. Br. B. v, ——, ——.
Larus albus, SCHÆFF., Mus. Orn. 1779, 65, pl. 42.
Larus candidus, FABR., Fn. Groenl. 1780.—FLEM., Br. An. 142.
Larus niveus, MART., Spitzb. 77, pl. 4, f. A. (nec auct.).
Gavia nivea, BREHM, V. D. 1831, 766, pl. 38, f. 1.
Pagophila nivea, BP., Consp. Av. ii, 1856, 230 ; Compt. Rend. 1856, 771.
Larus brachytarsus, HOLB., Fn. Groenl. 1846, 52.
Pagophila brachytarsus, BRUCH, J. f. O. 1855, 287.—LAWR., B. N. A. 1858, 856.—COUES, Pr. Phila. Acad. 1862, 309.

DIAG. *L. corpore toto albo, rhachidibus remigum flavis, pedibus nigris, rostro virescente-flavo.*

Hab.—Arctic seas, coming southward in winter.

Adult, breeding plumage.—Culmen straight to the nostrils, then regularly convex; commissure gently curved to the tip, where it is considerably decurved; gonys straight to near the angle, which is well defined, the outline from angle to tip perfectly straight. Feathers extending between the rami nearly to the angle. Wings long and pointed, reaching beyond the tail; primaries gradually attenuated to the tip.

Entirely pure white, the shafts of the primaries straw-yellow. Bill dusky greenish, yellow at tip and along the cutting edges. Legs and feet black.

Young.—Front, chin, and sides of the head, grayish dusky; the upper part of the neck, all round, irregularly spotted with the same. Scapulars, and upper and under wing-coverts, spotted with brownish-black, the spots most numerous along the lesser coverts. Tips of the primaries and tail feathers with a dusky spot. Otherwise as in the preceding.

Dimensions.—Length, 19.50; wing, 13.25; bill above, 1.40; along gape, 2.10; height at nostrils, 0.45; tarsus, about 1.45; middle toe and claw, 1.75.

The bill of this species, in five specimens before me, varies greatly in size. The difference in shape is also quite notable. But it is in the tarsus that the greatest variations are found. The shortest tarsus before me measures but 1.20. This would nearly do for the *Larus brachytarsus* of Holböll, but the other characters do n t correspond with those given by that author. This specimen is from Mr. Audubon's collection, and corresponds minutely with his plate.

The present being a bird of such marked character, there are no questions of doubtful synonymy which here need special mention. The quotations "*albus* Schæffer, 1799," and *candidus* Fabricius, as well as *niveus* Martens, are all undoubtedly referable to the present species. The other synonyms of the species arise chiefly from the various genera to which the bird has been referred. There is no reasonable doubt that the supposed "*L. brachytarsus*" is the same bird; the description gives no tangible characters.

Subgenus CHRŒCOCEPHALUS, *Eyton.*

= *Xema*, BOIE, Isis, 1822, 563, nec LEACH.
> *Gavia*, KAUP, Sk. Ent. Eur. Thierw. 1829, 99 (*L. ridibundus*), nec MÖHR.
> *Ichthyaëtus*, KAUP, op. cit. 99 (*L. ichthyætus*, PALL.).
> *Hydrocoloeus*, KAUP, op. cit. 99 (*L. minutus*, PALL.).
= *Chroicocephalus*, EYT., Cat. Br. B. 1836, 53 (*L. capistratus*, TEMM.).—LAWR., B. N. A. 1858, 850.—COUES, Pr. Phila. Acad. 1862, 309.
× *Gavia*, MACGIL., Man. Orn. ii, 1842, 239, nec MÖHR.
> *Atricilla*, BP., 1854 (*A. catesbœi*, BP.).
> *Melagavia*, BP., 1854 (*L. franklini*).
> *Cirrhocephalus*, BRUCH, J. f. O. 1855, 288 (*L. cirrhocephalus*, VIEILL.).
= *Chrœcocephalus*, STRICKL.—COUES.
= *Chroocephalus*, SCL. & SALV.

CHAR. Form as in *Larus* proper, but general organization less robust (with some exceptions) and the bill usually weaker, slenderer and more acute, and less hooked. Head enveloped in a hood in the breeding season, and white of under parts then usually rosy-tinted. Tail square, or nearly so.

There are no marked peculiarities in form of this group, the pattern of coloration being mainly its basis. The species average smaller than those of *Larus* proper, though the *C. ichthyaëtus* is among the largest of the subfamily. The group approximates to *Xema* and *Rhodostethia* in nearly all respects, but the tail is neither forked nor cuneate. Its subdivision, as indicated in the above synonymy, is entirely unrequired.

There are but three established North American species; the *C. cucullatus* proving to be the same as *C. franklini*, while *C. minutus* is not proven to inhabit this country. These species may be tabulated as follows:

Analysis of species.

a. Tarsus longer than the middle toe and claw.
　1. Bill reddish, feet the same .... ATRICILLA.
b. Tarsus not longer than the middle toe and claw.
　2. Bill reddish, feet the same .... FRANKLINI.
　3. Bill black, feet red or yellow........................ PHILADELPHIA.
c. Tarsus shorter than the middle toe without claw.
　4. Wings underneath, dark plumbeous..................... MINUTUS.

LARUS (CHRŒCOCEPHALUS) ATRICILLA, Linn.

Laughing Gull.

Larus atricilla, LINN.; Syst. Nat. i, 1766, 225 (*L. major*, CATES., i, 89, but also includes
      the European species).—TEMM., Man. ii, 1820, 779.—STEPH., Gen. Zool. xiii,
      1825, 205.—FLEM., Br. An. 1828, 142.—BP., Syn. 1828, 359.—NUTT., Man. ii, 1834,
      291.—JEN., Man. 1835, 273.—AUD., Orn. Biog. iv, 1838, 118, pl. 314; Syn. 1839,
      324; B. Am. vii, 1844, 136, pl. 443.—KEYS. & BLAS., Wirb. Eur. 1840, 96.—GIR.,
      B. L. I. 1844, 358.—DEKAY, N. Y. Zool. ii, 1844, ——, ——.—SCHL., Rev. Crit.
      1844, 127.—GRAY, Gen. of B. iii, 1849, 654.—PUTN., Pr. Ess. Inst. 1856, 221
      (Massachusetts).—TURNB., B. E. Pa. 1869, 38.—PELZ., Orn. Bras. 323.—SCHL.,
      Mus. P.-B. iv, 1863, *Lari*, p. 44.—GRAY, List Br. B. 1864, 234.—TAYLOR, Ibis,
      1864, 172 (Porto Rico).—SUND., Ofv. K. Vet. Ak. 1869, 590 (St. Bartholomew).—
      SCL. & SALV., P. Z. S. 1871, 576.—HARTING, Br. B. 1872, 175.—COUES, Key,
      1872, 315.—RIDGW., Ann. Lyc. N. Y. x, 1874, 391 (Illinois).
Xema atricilla, BOIE, Isis, 1822, 563.—BP., List, 1838, 62.—CAB., Schomb. Guiana, iii, 761.
Gavia atricilla, MACGIL., Man. Orn. ii, 1842, 240.—BLAS., J. f. O. 1865, 378.
Chroicocephalus atricilla, LAWR., B. N. A. 1858, 850.—SCL., Ibis, i, 1859, 223 (Belize).—
      NEWT., Ibis, i, 1859, 372 (St. Thomas).—BRY., Pr. Bost. Soc. vii, 1859, 134 (Ba-
      hamas).—WHEAT., Ohio Agric. Rep. 1860, No. 268.—COUES & PRENT., Smiths.
      Rep. 1861, 418 (Washington, D. C.).—COUES, Pr. Phila. Acad. 1862, 310.—SCL.,
      P. Z. S. 1864, 179 (Mexico).—LAWR., Ann. Lyc. viii, 1864, 104 (Sombrero); viii,
      1866, 299 (New York).—BOARDM., Pr. Bost. Soc. ix, 1862, 131 (Maine).—VERR.,
      Pr. Ess. Inst. iii, 1862, 160 (Maine).—ALLEN, *ibid*. iv, 1864, 90 (Massachusetts "in
      winter;" an error).—COUES, *ibid*. v, 1868, 307 (New England, "winters;"
      error).—COUES, Ibis, 1864, 388 (Central America, both coasts).—COUES, Pr.
      Phila. Acad. 1866, 99 (Colorado River).—DRESS., Ibis, 1866, 44 (Texas).—GUNDL.,
      Rep. Fis. Nat. i, 391 (Cuba).—COUES, Pr. Bost. Soc. xii, 1868, 126 (South Caro-
      lina).—COUES, Pr. Phila. Acad. 1871, 40 (North Carolina).—HATCH, Bull. Minn.
      Acad. i, 1874, 67 (? Minnesota).
Larus ridibundus, WILS., Am. Orn. ix, 89, pl. 74.—LEOT., Ois. Trin. 532.
"*Larus plumbiceps*, BREHM, Lehrb. 722." (*Gray*.)
Atricilla catesbœi, BP., Compt. Rend. 1856, 771.—BRUCH, J. f. O. 1855, 287.
Atricilla micropterus, BRUCH, J. f. O. 1855, 287.
Atricilla minor et *macroptera*, BP., Compt. Rend. 1856, 771.

DIAG. *L. tarso medium digitum superante, rostro nigrescente-rubro apice acuminato, remigibus nigris, albo-terminatis.*

Hab.—Tropical and temperate America. In the United States north on the Atlantic
in summer to Maine; in the interior to Ohio; on the Pacific to California. Central
America, both coasts, and various West Indies. In South America to the Lower Amazon. Casual in Europe.

Bill longer than the middle toe and claw, shorter than the tarsus or head, moderately
compressed, rather stout for this genus. Culmen and commissure both decurved at the
end, the latter somewhat sinuate at the base. Gonys considerably concave in front of
the angle, somewhat so between the angle and tip; although the angle is well defined,
the tip of the bill is so decurved that a chord from tip to base does not touch it. Middle toe barely three-fourths the tarsus.

Adult in summer.—Bill deep carmine; legs and feet brownish-red. Hood deep plumbeous grayish-black, extending further on the throat than on the nape. Eyelids white
posteriorly. Neck all round, rump, tail, broad tips of secondaries and tertials, and
whole under parts, white, the latter with a rosy tinge. Mantle grayish-plumbeous.
Outer six primaries black, their extreme tips white; their bases for a very short distance on the first, and only in the inner web, and for a successively increasing distance
on both webs of the others, are of the color of the back.

Adult in winter.—Under parts simply white, not rosy; hood lost, the head being
white, intermixed with blackish. Bill and feet more dull in color. Otherwise as in
summer.

Immature.—Bill and feet brownish-black, tinged with red. Plumbeous of the upper
parts more or less mixed with irregular patches of light grayish-brown. Primaries
wholly deep brownish-black, fading at the tip. Secondaries brownish-black on the
outer web. Tail feathers more or less tinged with plumbeous, and with a broad terminal band of brownish-black, the extreme tips of the feathers white. Upper tail-
coverts white.

Young-of-the-year.—Entire upper parts, and neck all round, light brownish-gray; the
feathers tipped with grayish or rufous white, broadly on the scapulars and tertials, the
blue of the adults appearing on the wing-coverts. Eyelids whitish; a dusky space
about the eye. Forehead, throat, and under parts, dull whitish, more or less clouded

with gray, especially on the breast, where this is the prevailing color. Wings and tail as in the preceding.

Dimensions.—Length, 16.50 inches; wing, 13; tail, about 5; bill above, 1.75; along gape, 2.25; height at nostril, 0.45; tarsus, 2; middle toe and claw, 1.50.

This is the largest species of the group inhabiting North America, and one not easily confounded with any other. The bill is large and stout for a *Chrœcocephalus*, but the tip is attenuated and much decurved, the convexity of the culmen regular and gradual. The most striking peculiarity of form lies in the proportions of the tarsus and toes, the former being fully a fourth longer than the middle toe and claw. The hood is lighter than that of the other North American species of the genus. The rosy of the under parts is retained in greater or less degree until the autumnal moult is accomplished (September to October).

Bonaparte and Bruch recognize a genus *Atricilla* upon the proportions of tarsus and toes, with the *A. catesbœi*, Bonaparte, as type. In this genus are comprised, according to Bonaparte (Comptes Rendus, 1856, xlii, p. 771), three species, viz : the type and common species of North America, and two others—one, *Atricilla macroptera*, Bonaparte (with *serranus* and *megalopterus* of Bruch as synonyms), which is larger than the type; and the other, *Atricilla minor*, Bonaparte (with *micropterus*, Bruch, and (?)*poliocephalus*, Temm., as synonyms), which differs in its smaller size. Whether these two "species" be anything more than races, I am unable to say; but I have seen undoubted specimens of *Chrœcocephalus atricilla* as much larger and as much smaller than the average, as are these supposed species of Bonaparte's and Bruch's. A difference of half an inch or more in the wing of a bird as large as the present, is by no means an unusual discrepancy. Southern birds will, I think, be found usually smallest.

An immature *Chrœcocephalus*, from the Pacific coast of Mexico, differs from the usual type of *atricilla* in being decidedly smaller, with somewhat unusual proportions of the tarsi and toes. The latter are nearly as long as those of an average *atricilla*, while the tarsus is disproportionately shorter. The bird being so young, it is difficult to say what the markings of the adult would have been; but in these features just detailed there is an approach to *franklini*.

This species was erroneously referred by Wilson to the *ridibundus* of Europe. Bonaparte, in taking the specific name for the genus, dedicated the species to Catesby, who had described it under the name of *Larus major*. According to Bruch, the *L. poliocephalus* of Temminck appears to be the same bird. The other synonyms I quote refer to larger and smaller races, which, however, I do not think to be constant, nor yet to mark distinct geographical areas, although as a general rule southern birds may be found smaller.

This species is given by Dr. Hatch among the birds of Minnesota, but the observation may perhaps require confirmation. It is essentially a southern species, and more particularly one of the Gulf and South Atlantic States, though its summer range extends to New England. On the coast of North Carolina, which is therefore an intermediate point, it is, according to my observations, mainly, if not wholly, a migrant. It appears early in April, and remains through the greater part of May; in fact I have seen some so late in the spring that I thought they could not proceed very far to breed; but I am not aware that any nest south of the Middle Districts. It returns in September, and thousands spend this month and the next on the coast, retiring further south at the approach of real cold weather, though a few linger in November. It is no exaggeration to say, that a flock I have seen rise on wing simultaneously from a sand-bar, where they had been resting, must have contained a thousand individuals. These were mostly gray young birds. Some old ones, shot in September, were then moulting, and still showed traces of the rosy on the under plumage. This species is among our more especially maritime ones, and does not often go inland beyond tide-water; but there are some notable exceptions to this rule. While at Fort Wingate, New Mexico, in June, I was shown a specimen captured there, many miles from the nearest water of consequence. This was evidently a stray bird in that particular locality; but its occurrence shows that it must have come up the Rio Grande. I think that I also saw it on the Colorado, but cannot be sure, owing to the circumstances of observation. None of the naturalists of the Pacific Railroad surveys mention it as a bird of the Pacific slope or coast; and until quite recently it was supposed not to inhabit that side of the continent. The contrary, however, was proven by Mr. Xantus, as I satisfied myself by examination of specimens in his collections from the California coast. In the general interior of the United States the bird may be said to be still almost unknown.

A distinguishing feature of birds of the genus *Chrœcocephalus* is the dark-colored hood that ornaments both sexes at times; this envelopes the head and descends some distance on the nape or throat; it is usually relieved by some white spots about the eyes. It is assumed with the vernal moult, worn all summer, and then lost with the autumnal change, the only winter traces being a few dark feathers scattered over the head, or gathered in a patch over the nape and ear-coverts. Another change heightens the beauty of the birds when they are to be decked for their nuptials in full attire; they gain a rich rosy tint over all the white plumage of the under part; then few birds are of more delicate hues than these. Nature blushes, filling the bird's breast with amorous imagery, till the feathers catch a glow and reflect the blush. Burning with inward fire, the whole frame thrills with the enthusiasm of sexual vigor. The dark glittering eye is encircled with a fiery ring; now it flashes defiance at a rival; now tenderly melts at sight of his mate, soon to be sacrificed to masculine zeal. The breath of desire seems to influence the mouth till it shares the carmine hue that tinges other parts. The birds speed on high with vigorous pinion, making haste to the wedding with joyful cries till the shores resound. But such ardor is too consuming to last; with the touch of a moment, the life-current flies like an electric shock, lighting a fire in another organism, only to be subdued in the travail of maternity. Not only once, but often, till the tide ebbs that at its flood transfigured the bird. Its force all spent, the change comes; the red mouth pales again; the glowing plumage fades to white; the bird is but the shadow of his former self, dull colored, ragged, without ambition beyond the satisfaction of a gluttonous appetite. He loiters southward, recruiting an enervated frame with plenteous fare in this season of idleness, till the warm rays of another spring restore him.

Audubon mentions some interesting facts that show the dependence of the plumage upon the sexual condition. "At the approach of the breeding season, or, as I like to term it, the love season," he says, "this species becomes first hooded, and the white feathers of its breast, and those of the under surface of its wings, assume a rich blush of roseate tint. If the birds procured at that time are several years old, and perfect in their powers of reproduction, their primary quills show little or no white at their extremities, and their hood descends about three quarters of an inch lower on the throat than on the hind part of the head, provided the bird be a male. But should they be barren birds, *the hood will be wanting*, that portion of their plumage remaining as during winter; and although the primaries will be black, or nearly so, each one of them will be broadly tipped, or marked at the end, with a white spot, which in some instances will be found to be half an inch in size; yet the tail of these birds, as if to prove that they are adults, is as purely white to its extreme tip as in those that are breeding; but neither the breast nor the under wing coverts will exhibit the rosy tint of one in the full perfection of its powers." Upon the same subject Audubon continues with an observation in which he is alone, so far as I know: "Previously to my visit to that interesting peninsula [Florida] I had not unfrequently noticed indications of strong amatory propensities in several species of Gulls, but never to the extent exhibited by the present species, many of which I saw copulating in the latter part of autumn, and in winter, fully three months before the usual time of depositing their eggs in that country. * * * On some such occasions, when I was at St. Augustine, in the month of December, I have observed four or five males of the present species paying their addresses to one female, who received their courtesies with evident welcome. Yet the females in the country did not deposit until the 20th day of April." These facts are curious. That males should in and out of season attempt to prevail with the opposite sex is not at all singular; but that the females should accept attentions so offered, at a time, too, when there was no chance of profiting by their misdeeds, in the substantial matter of eggs, is unusual, to say the least. As is well known, birds are among the most truly periodic of animals as to their reproductive functions, having neither appetite nor potency during the greater part of the year.

From personal observation, I only know of this bird breeding north of the Carolinas; but it is said to breed from Texas to Massachusetts. Its Pacific breeding grounds, if there are any, have not been brought to light. Its nesting is a simple process; it builds upon the ground, near the sea, generally gathering for this purpose into large communities. The nests, of which there may be many close together, are formed with little art, being mere hollowed heaps of sea-weed, eel-grass, or other vegetable substances, two or three inches high, and thrice as wide. The eggs are mostly three in number, never more, and occasionally only two. Their ground color is some shade of olive, ranging from dull grayish to deeper greenish; this is thickly marked all over with spots and splashes of brown, blackish, dull reddish, and pale purplish; but sometimes the markings are mostly collected in an irregular band about the larger end of the egg.

One noticeable habit of this bird is its incessant persecution of the Pelicans, to obtain food that may drop from the capacious pouch of these forced purveyors. I have seen the same thing in the case of the White-headed Gull of California (*Blasipus heermanni*), which makes a business of harassing the Brown Pelicans. Both these Gulls are as truly "parasitic" as the Jaegers themselves.

LARUS (CHRŒCOCEPHALUS) FRANKLINI, Rich.

Franklin's Rosy Gull.

"*Larus atricilla*, FRANKLIN."
Larus franklini, RICH , F. B. A. ii, 1831, 424, pl. 71.—AUD., Orn. Biog. v, 1839, 324 (not
    figured); Syn. 1839, 325; B. Am. vii, 1844, 145.—SCHL., Mus. P.-B. iv, 1863,
    Lari, p. 36.—SUND., Ofv. Vet. Akad. 1860, 590 (St. Bartholomew).—NEWT., P.
    Z. S. 1871, 57, pl. 4, f. 4 (Manitoba; breeding, with description of egg).—SCL.
    & SALV., P. Z. S. 1871, 577.—COUES, Key, 1872, 316.—RIDGW., Ann. Lyc. N. Y.
    x, 1874, 39 (Illinois).
Xema franklini, BP., List, 1838, 62.
Chrœcocephalus franklini, BRUCH, J. f. O. 1855, 289.—LAWR., B. N. A. 1858, 851.—HAYD.,
    Rep. 1862, 176.—COUES, Pr. Ph. Ac. 1862, 310.—SNOW, B. Kans. 1873, 12 (Kansas).
Gavia (Melagavia) franklini, BP., Compt. Rend. 1856, 771.
Gavia franklini, BLAS., J. f. O. 1865, 371.
Larus pipixcan, WAGL., Isis, 1831, 515 (*fide Salvin*).
Larus cucullatus, LICHT., Nomencl. 98 (*descr. nulla*); see BLAS., J. f. O. 1865, 371.
Chroicocephalus cucullatus, BRUCH, J. f. O. 1855, 290.—LAWR., B. N. A. 1858, 851.—COUES,
    Pr. Phila. Acad. 1862, 309 —COUES, Ibis, 1864, 388 (Chiapam).—SALV., Ibis,
    1866, 198.
Larus cinereo-caudatus, PHIL. & LANDB., Wieg. Arch. 1861, 293.
(?) *Chrœcocephalus kittlitzii*, BRUCH, J. f. O. 1853, 104.
(?) *Chrœcocephalus subulirostris*, BP.; BRUCH, J. f. O. 1853, pl. 3, f. 44. (Schlegel.) (*Cf.*
    BLAS., J. f. O. 1865, 371.)

DIAG. *L. rostro rubro, cucullo schistaceo-nigro, pallio griseo-cœruleo, caudâ perlaceâ, remigibus primis sex nigro-cinctis latè albo-terminatis, rhachidibus albis, pogonio externo primi nigro nisi in apicem. Long. tot. 14.00 poll. ; al. 11.25 ; tars. 1.60.*

Hab.—North America to high latitudes, but only in the interior (observed on neither coast). Mexico. Part of the West Indies. Central and South America to Chili.

Lieutenant Warren's Expedition.—4897, Nebraska.
Later Expeditions.—58981, Upper Missouri.

Adult, breeding plumage.—Bill rather slender, attenuated and a little decurved at the tip, which is acute ; outline of both rami and gonys concave. Bill shorter than head; tarsus equal to middle toe and claw. Bill red (carmine, lake, or vermilion), crossed with black near the end. Legs dusky reddish. Edges of eyelids orange. Eyelids white, this color also reaching a little behind the eye. Hood deep slaty or plumbeous black, encircling the upper part of the neck as well as the head, and extending further on the throat than on the nape. Mantle not quite so dark as in *atricilla* (more blue), darker than in *philadelphia*. First primary with the outer vane black to within an inch of the tip ; the inner pearly white, crossed an inch or more from the tip by an isolated black bar an inch broad, thus leaving the feather white on both webs for an inch or more from the tip. The next five primaries are basally of the color of the back, paler on the inner web, and both webs fading toward their tips into white ; each is crossed by a black bar near the end, two inches wide on the second primary, narrowing on successive feathers to a small bar or pair of little spots on the sixth ; the tips of all these primaries pure white. Other primaries, with secondaries and tertials, colored like the back, fading at the tips into white ; shafts white, sometimes black along the black portion of the feather. Tail very pale pearly blue, the three lateral pairs of rectrices white—or rather tail white, lightly washed with pearly on the six central feathers. Neck all around, rump, broad tips of secondaries and tertials, and whole under parts, white, the latter rosy.

Younger, that is to say, in summer plumage, and with a perfect hood, red bill, &c., but the primaries not yet having attained their perfect pattern :—General coloration exactly as before. Shafts of first three primaries black, of the rest gray, except along the black portion of the feathers; first primary with the outer web wholly black, the inner web pearly gray, much like the back but lighter, to within two or three inches of the tip, then black for the rest of its extent ; second like the first, but the base of the outer web like the inner ; on the third, fourth, and fifth, successively, the black decreases in extent, till on the sixth it is merely a little bar, or pair of spots ; tips of all the primaries white ; that of the first primary smallest, that of the others successively increasing in size.

The bird in this plumage just described, is what Mr. Lawrence and myself have been calling "*cucullatus* Licht." for some years. It has all the marks of being an adult bird, and so we were misled—the more easily, because the original specimen (No. 4320, Mus. Smiths., Calcasieu Pass, La.), type of pl. 93, fig. 1, Atlas B. N. A., identified as *cucullatus,* has an unusually small, short bill,* a small hood, and certain other marks a little different from anything we had then seen in *franklini.* There are now, however, in the Institution plenty of specimens showing that our *cucullatus* is only a state of *franklini,* just before absolute maturity. In No. 4320 the hood is a good deal speckled with white, but I have seen others (*e. g.* No. 27621) with perfectly black hood, and the primaries identical with those of 4320. Without going into any further explanations, I may simply state that this identity of the supposed two species is established.

With this reduction, a number of names range as synonyms of *franklini.* I have not been able, of course, to verify Lichtenstein's *cucullatus* as appertaining to what Lawrence and I have been calling *cucullatus,* but I presume there is no doubt on that score. There are some other names, as *pipixcan* Wagler, and that go wherever *cucullatus* does. In fact, any known *Chroicocephalus* in North America or Mexico, that is not *atricilla* nor *philadelphia,* must be *franklini ;* for it is certain that we have only these three distinct species, as far as known.

To resume description of *franklini :* A specimen (No. 45688, Selkirk settlement) shows exactly how the *pictura* of the primaries changes from that last described (the formerly considered *cucullatus*) to the perfect condition. It is just half way between. The terminal black on the first primary is disappearing, to leave the tip pure white for an inch or more, but a remnant of it is left. This bird is otherwise mature (black hood, red bill, &c.).

Winter plumage.—As in summer ; the hood wanting or indicated by a few slaty feathers about the eyes, on the auriculars and nape ; the rosy wanting ; the bill and feet dull colored. I have no winter specimens that have attained their perfect picture of the primaries, but presume that the primaries will be found, in adult birds, to be colored as in summer.

---

* As an example of extreme variation of this species in size and shape of bill, I give these measurements : No. 4320, along culmen, 1.20 ; height opposite nostril, 0.35. No. 27621, along culmen, 1.40 ; height at nostril, only 0.35, as before.

Young.—Bill black; feet dusky. Traces of a hood or nape, largely slaty, &c., according to precise age. Outer five or six primaries wholly black in their continuity, rather lighter and somewhat slaty at base, with or without a minute white speck at the tip. Mantle gray or brown, more or less mixed with blue, according to age. Tail ashy white, with a broad, black subterminal bar. Under parts white. This appears to be the usual plumage of birds of the first autumn.

Dimensions.—Length, about 14 inches; extent, 35; wing, 11.25; tail, about 4.50; bill, along culmen, 1.30; along gape, 1.75; height at nostril, 0.35; tarsus, 1.60; middle toe and claw, about the same. The young are a little smaller, with the bill especially shorter and smaller.

This beautiful bird requires no special comparison with any other. The case of "*cucullatus*" being disposed of, there remains little to be said on points of synonymy. A *Larus melanorhynchus* of Temminck (of which I know nothing) has been adduced by some authors among the synonyms of "*cucullatus;*" Schlegel puts it under *philadelphia;* Messrs. Sclater and Salvin do not enumerate it in their late paper. These authors query the *Ch. kittlitzii* of Bruch, which Schlegel, without hesitation, assigns to *franklini.* The last-named author adduces *Ch. subulirostris* of Bonaparte and Bruch. According to Messrs. Sclater and Salvin, the *L. cinereo-caudatus* of Philippi and Landbeck belongs here.

In North America, as far as is known, this Gull is confined to the interior, west of the Mississippi. I have met with it on several occasions; in Kansas, during the spring migration, and in Northern Dakota, where, at Turtle Mountain, I took in July a bird so young that I felt satisfied it had been hatched not far off. It breeds in the adjoining British province of Manitoba, as attested by eggs in the Smithsonian, one of which was lately described by Prof. Newton, as above cited. The egg is 2⅛ inches long, 1⅔ broad, and closely resembles that of the Esquimaux Curlew in size, shape, and color, though the dark splashes are more evenly distributed over the surface. The very young bird, just mentioned, measured 13.75 × 33.75 × 9.75; tail, 4; bill, 1.10; tarsus, and middle toe and claw, each, 1.65. The bill was livid blackish, with pale base of under mandible; the feet were flesh-colored. The habits of the species are essentially the same as those of its congeners; its extensive dispersion through Middle and South America is perceived from the foregoing quotations.

LARUS (CHRŒCOCEPHALUS) PHILADELPHIA, (Ord) Gray.

Bonaparte's Gull.

Sterna philadelphia, ORD, Guthrie's Geog. 2d Am. ed. ii, 1815, 319.
Chrœcocephalus philadelphia, LAWR., B. N. A. 1858, 852; Ann. Lyc. N. Y. viii, 1866, 299.—
    COOP. & SUCK., N. H. Wash. Ter. 1860, 276.—WHEAT., Ohio. Agric. Rep. 1860,
    No. 269.—COUES & PRENT., Smiths. Rep. 1861, 418 (Washington, D. C.).—COUES,
    Pr. Phila. Acad. 1861, 247 (Labrador); *ibid.* 1862, 310 (critical); *ibid.* 1866, 99
    (Arizona); *ibid.* 1871, 41 (North Carolina).—COUES, Pr. Ess. Inst. v, 1868, 307
    (New England).—COUES, Pr. Bost. Soc. xii, 1868, 126 (South Carolina).—VERR.,
    Pr. Ess. Inst. iii, 1862, 155 (Maine).—BOARDM., Pr. Bost. Soc. ix, 1862, 131
    (Maine).—ALLEN, Pr. Ess. Inst. iv, 1864, 80 (Massachusetts).—DALL & BANN.,
    Tr. Chic. Ac. 1869, 305 (Alaska).—MAYN., N. Guide, 1870, 151 (Massachusetts).—
    NEWT., P. Z. S. 1871, 57, pl. 4, f. 6 (egg).
Larus philadelphia, GRAY, List Br. B. 1863, 235 (Great Britain).—HART., Br. B. 1872, 172
    (Great Britain; six instances).—COUES, Key, 1872, 316; Check-list, 1874, No.
    556.—RIDGW., Ann. Lyc. N. Y. x, 1874, 391 (Illinois).
Larus philadelphicus, TURNB., B. E. Pa. 1869, 38.
Larus capistratus, BP., Am. Orn. iv, ——; Syn. 1828, 358. (Not of authors.)
Larus bonapartei, RICH., F. B. A. ii, 1831, 425, pl. 72.—NUTT., Man. ii, 1834, 294.—AUD.,
    Orn. Biog. iv, 212, pl. 324; Syn. 1839, 323; B. Am. vii, 1844, 131, pl. 452.—GIR.,
    B. L. I. 1844, 359.—PUTN., Pr. Ess. Inst. i, 1856, 221.—SCHL., Mus. P.-B. iv, 1863,
    Lari, p. 41. (Not of SCL. & SALV., P. Z. S. 1868, 178 (Peru), which is *L. serranus;* see *ibid.* 1871, 577.)
Xema bonapartei, BP., List, 1838, 62.
Chroicocephalus bonapartei, BRUCH, J. f. O. 1855, 292.
Gavia bonapartei, BP., Compt. Rend. 1856, 771.—BLAS., J. f. O. 1865, 371.
(?) *Larus minutus,* SAB., Frankl. Journ. 693.—RICH., F. B. A. ii, 1831, 426 (most probably).
(?) "*Larus melanurus,* ORD." (*Fide Bp.*) (Where?)
(?) "*Larus melanorhynchus,* TEMM, Mus. Lugd." (*Fide Schl.*) (*Cf.* BLAS., J. f. O. 1865, 371.)

DIAG. *L. inter mimimos, rostro sternino, nigro, pedibus flavis, rhachidibus remigum primariorum quinque albis apicibus nigris.*

Hab.—Continent of North America, (?)Mexico and Middle America (but no valid reference seen). Casual in Europe (Great Britain). In addition to the above quotations note: THOMP., Ann. Mag. N. H. 1848, 192; Zool. 1849, 2069.—LEITH, Zool. 1851, 3117; 1867, 966.—YARR., Br. B. iii, 555.—POWYS, Zool. 1855, 4762.—KNOX, Zool. 1866, 306.—RODD, Zool. 1865, 9501; *fide Harting).*

Adult, breeding plumage.—Bill shorter than the head or tarsus, much compressed, very slender and sternine; both mandibles with a slight but distinct notch near the tip. Convexity of culmen slight, gradual from base to apex.' Rami slightly concave; gonys about straight. Nostrils lateral, linear, direct, pervious, extremely narrow. Tarsus equal to middle toe and claw, with the ordinary scutellation and reticulation. Webs moderately broad, somewhat incised. Wings and tail of ordinary characters, the latter somewhat emarginate in the young. Bill black. Mouth and eyelids carmine. Legs and feet coral-red, tinged with vermilion. Webs bright vermilion. Hood plumbeous slate, not so deep as in *franklini,* enveloping the head and upper part of the neck, reaching further before than behind. White patches on eyelids narrow, and half posterior to the eye. Mantle pearl-blue, much lighter than in *franklini,* not so light as in *minutus.* Ends of the tertials and scapulars scarcely lighter than the back. Primaries: shafts of the first five or six white, except at their extreme tips, the others dark colored; first, outer web and extreme tip black, rest white; second, white, its tip black for a greater distance than the first, and on one or both webs, for a greater or less distance (sometimes half way down the feather) narrowly bordered with black; third, fourth, fifth, sixth, black at the ends for about the same distance on each, the black bordering the inner web much further than the outer; the inner webs of the third and fourth, and both webs of the fifth and sixth, of a rather lighter shade of the color of the back. Other primaries like the back, the seventh and eighth with a touch of black on one or both webs near the tip. The third to sixth primaries with a white or pearly-white speck at extreme tip. As is not the case with either of our other species of the genus, the primary wing-coverts, bastard quills, &c., are wholly or in great part white (much as in *cirrhocephalus* or *albipennis* of South America), which causes the whole wing to be bordered with white as far as the carpus. Neck all around, and under parts, including under wing-coverts, pure white; the belly, &c., rosy in breeding time. There is no difference in color between the sexes.

Adult, winter plumage.—Bill light colored at base below; feet flesh-color. Crescent before the eye, and patch below the auriculars, deep slate. Crown and occiput mottled with grayish-black and white. Back of neck washed over with the color of the mantle. Forehead, sides of the head and throat, white, continuous with the white of the under parts. Otherwise as in summer.

Young, first winter.—Bill dusky flesh-color, except toward the end; legs and feet light flesh-color. Without the slaty mottling of the crown. Auricular patch distinct. Lesser wing-coverts and tertials dusky brown, lighter along their edges. Secondaries with a patch of dusky near the end, which on the innermost three or four becomes restricted to the outer web. First primary, with about half the inner web along the shaft, black; second and third with the outer webs wholly black, and a narrow line of black on the inner, along the shaft. Tail with a subterminal brownish-black bar.

Very young.—Bill flesh-color, dusky on the terminal half. Crown of head, and neck behind to the interscapulars, clouded with dusky bluish-gray, heightening on the sides of the neck into light grayish-ochrous. Scapulars and middle of the back light gull-blue, as in the adult, but the feathers so broadly (for ⅓ inch) tipped with grayish-brown, fading into dull white at tip, that the original color is nearly lost. Lesser wing-coverts and tertials brownish-black, the latter edged with the color of the edgings of the back. Bastard quills and feathers along the edge of the wing variegated with black and white. Primaries black; the outer two-thirds of the inner vane of the first four bluish-white to near the end; both vanes of the others of that color for a little distance; the extreme tips of all but the two first, white. Secondaries light gull-blue, each with a large terminal blackish spot continuous with the black ends of the inner primaries. Tail with a broad terminal bar of black, and very narrowly tipped with dull white.

Dimensions.—Length, 14 inches; extent, 32; wing, 10.25; bill above, 1.20; gape, 1.75; height at nostrils, 0.25; tarsus, or middle toe and claw, 1.40.

Anatomical characters.—The median palatal ridge is well defined, broad, beginning six-tenths of an inch from the tip. Just at its centre the aperture of the posterior nares begins. Anteriorly it is thickly papillate along its median line; posteriorly there are papillæ only on its edges and terminally. The two lateral palatal ridges, separated from the median by a rather illy-defined sulcus, do not, as usual, terminate abruptly in a papillated raised extremity, but gradually lose themselves in a fold of mucous membrane at the angle of the mouth. The posterior vaulted space is well defined; bounded posteriorly by a quadrant of well-developed slender acute papillæ. Tongue measures a little more than an inch, of the ordinary shape and consistency. Nasal aperture 0.80 long.

The specimen examined was shot while feeding, and the whole digestive apparatus was in full play. *Œsophagus* measures between six and seven inches in length, presenting the usual characteristics of muscularity and dilatability. It was contracted and longitudinally plicate to within an inch of the proventriculus, where it was distended with an enormous wad of coleopterous and hymenopterous insects; this part of the canal being, of course, devoid of rugæ, and its walls thin and tense. The difference in appearance of the proventricular portion of the tube was very marked. Its color was gray; the mucous membrane soft velvety to the touch, without rugæ, marked everywhere with thickly aggregated puncta. The solvent follicles were *counted*, and found to amount to 1,643. The gastric zone was 0.6 broad. The insects in this portion of the canal were in a perfect state of integrity, as in the *œsophagus*, but were much softened. Gizzard of proportionate size, and with the general characteristics of the *Larinæ*.

Intestine 24 inches from pylorus to anus. Besides the ordinary duodenal fold, there is another which commences 4 or 5 inches from the cœca, and runs up behind the gizzard as high as the œsophagus, and then descends in a pretty straight line to the cœca. The cœca are hardly 0.12 long, but are broad and capacious, with rounded free extremities. They lie closely apposed to the gut, 0.75 of an inch from the cloaca. Cloaca, as usual, large, capacious, globular. Its posterior division is small, but marked by a well-developed ridge of mucous membrane. Orifices of urinary and seminal ducts in the usual position.

Lobes of liver of nearly equal size, 1.75 inches long; the right is a little the most attenuated, left the thickest. They are connected by a broad, thin band of glandular substance.

Kidneys chiefly divided into three lobes, of which the superior is the largest and most convex; the inferior smallest; the central connecting lobe irregular in outline.

Trachea 4 inches long, flattened above, tapering and cylindrical below; its rings weak and cartilaginous, numbering about 120. The sterno-trachealis inserted only 0.3 above the lower larynx. A single pair of inferior laryngeal inserted into the first bronchial half ring. Bronchial rings abut 22.

Very numerous specimens of this species now before me exhibit little variation in colors other than those dependent on age and season; though, as will be seen from the preceding paragraphs, its normal changes of plumage are very great. The differences are chiefly in the amount of the narrow edging of the black of the tips of the primaries, which runs along to their bases; in the amount of black on the seventh and eighth primaries; and in the size of the white apices of all of them. The difference in size is more notable; the specimens being marked according to collectors' measurements as from 12 to 14.50 in total length, though I think that so great a discrepancy may be accounted for by supposing slightly different methods of measurement, and errors of carelessness and otherwise. I have never seen a specimen so large as is indicated by Richardson, viz, 15.60 inches. The bills differ somewhat in stoutness; in the young they are always slenderer and weaker. The notch toward the extremities of the tomia is always quite distinct.

By both Audubon and Bonaparte the female of the present species is said to have a brown instead of a black head; and Audubon's plate shows an entirely different color of the hood of the female from that of the male. This statement is at variance with Richardson's account and with the experience of authors, except those two above mentioned, which has invariably shown the hoods of the two sexes to be colored alike. I have never seen any brown-headed examples; and as the species is so abundant that the difference, if it really existed, would have been readily detected, I think it is safe to assert that it does not. Still it is difficult to see how both Audubon and Bonaparte fell into such an error, and I can offer no explanation of the matter.

Bibliography.—The first specific name of this species is, as proven by Mr. Lawrence, *philadelphia* of Ord. "The slender and tern-like form of the bill probably induced Mr. Ord to put it in *Sterna.*" Until the name of Mr. Ord's was revived by Mr. Lawrence, the species almost universally received the appellation of *bonapartei*, imposed upon it by Richardson in 1831. It was referred to the genus *Chrœcocephalus*, by Bruch, in 1855. Bonaparte in his American Ornithology, and in his Synopsis of 1828, before the introduction of Richardson's specific name, referred the bird very erroneously to the *capistratus* of Temminck, which is quite another thing. In his subsequent works he adopts the name bestowed in honor of himself, referring the bird to the genera *Xema* and *Gavia*. I quote "*Larus melanurus* Ord" as a synonym of the young, on the authority of Bonaparte. The *Larus melanorhynchus* of Temminck is, by Dr. Schlegel, considered as referring to this species. By other authors it is placed as a synonym of "*cucullatus.*" *L. subulirostris* may belong here rather than to *franklini.*

No one of our species is more widely dispersed than this. Go where we may in North America, the pretty bird may be seen at one or another season, if we are not too far from any considerable body of water. The Gull holds its own from the Labrador crags, against which the waves of an angered ocean ceaselessly beat, to the low, sandy shores of the Gulf, caressed by the soothing billows of a tropical sea. It follows the sinuosities of the two coasts with wonderful pertinacity, making excursions up every bay and estuary, and threads the course of all our three great rivers, while performing its remarkably extensive migrations. Considering in what high latitudes it breeds, it is astonishing how early toward the fall it again appears among us after its brief absence. The last birds have not all left the United States in May; some time in August the young come straggling back, though they are not numerous until the autumn has fairly set in. Perhaps some breed in the United States; of this, however, I have no personal knowledge, and at any rate, they only do so along our northern tier of States. Very little is recorded of its nidification and special breeding habits, and this is not so definite as could be wished. Audubon says, at second hand, that it breeds on the islands off Grand Menan; I only know of its nesting in British America, and this too merely from the labels of specimens examined. But I saw a great many in Labrador, and about the mouth of the St. Lawrence, at such time that rendered it pretty certain they had not bred far off.

While in North Carolina I made some observation on the vernal migration, that I thought interesting. There these Gulls are simply birds of passage, none wintering or breeding. They appear early in April, or with the first genial weather, and may be seen through part or most of May; then they go off, to return in September, and stay a month or so. But in spring it was a succession of birds passing, rather than the same individuals remaining so long. Thus from the first of April to the twenty-second, in 1869, great numbers were over the bay, with a decided preponderance of full-plumaged individuals. Then, without any marked change in the weather or other apparent reason, none were to be seen for a week or ten days. The first week in May, however, they became more numerous than ever, and, what seemed singular, this last lot was almost entirely composed of young birds—that is, birds only a year old, as was shown by the plumage, lacking the hood, having the black bar on the tail, and the upper parts imperfectly blue, variegated with gray and brown. Evidently the old birds, hurrying north to breed, led the van; and the young, with no such important business on hand, came trooping leisurely in the rear. The question was, what would these young birds do the ensuing summer? Would they reach the boreal regions to which the great majority of the perfect fertile birds repair, after loitering so late on the Carolina coast? or did they only propose to go part way, spend the summer frolicking, and return with soberer intentions for another year? I doubt that any breed until they are full plumaged.

NOTE.—The *Chrœcocephalus minutus*, by some included among North American birds, has no grounded claim to be so considered. I therefore omit the species, which I cannot recognize as an inhabitant of this country until some conclusive evidence is brought forward. The whole claim may be seen to rest upon an identification of Sabine's, who, in all probability, mistook *philadelphia* for *minutus*.

Genus RHODOSTETHIA, *Macgil.*

Larus, MACGIL., 1824; RICH., 1825 (*nec* LINN.).
Rossia, BP., Comp. List, 1838, 62 (*nec* OWEN).
Rhodostethia, MACGIL., Man. Orn. ii, 1842, 253 (type *Larus roseus*, MACGIL.).—LAWR., B. N. A. 1858, 856.—COUES, Pr. A. N. S. Phila. 1862, 311.—GRAY, List Br. B. 1863, 229.

GEN. CHAR. "Body moderate; neck rather short; head ovate; bill short, rather slender; upper mandible with the dorsal line straight for half its length, arcuate-decurvate toward the end; lower mandible with the intercrural space narrow, the knot slight, the dorsal line concave, the tip narrow; legs short; tibiæ bare for a very short space; tarsus rather stout, anteriorly scutellate, rough behind; first toe short, with a large curved claw; anterior toes moderate, with their webs entire; claws rather large, arched, compressed, acute; plumage soft and full; wings long, rather narrow, pointed; tail cuneate, of twelve feathers, of which the central are much larger than the lateral."

Never having seen a specimen of the type of this genus, I have borrowed my diagnosis from Macgillivray. It's essential character lies in the cuneate tail, which is a peculiarity not shared by any other species of the subfamily. The pattern of coloration too is peculiar.

The type of the genus was first named under, and for some years referred to, the genus *Larus*. In 1838 Bonaparte first separated it generically under the name of *Rossia*. This name, however, had previously been applied by Prof. Owen to a genus of cephalopods. *Rhodostethia* of Macgillivray is based upon the same type, and is the proper name to be employed. The only known species of the genus is an inhabitant of the arctic regions of North America, and corresponding latitudes in the Old World.

RHODOSTETHIA ROSEA, Macgil.

Wedge-tailed Gull.

Larus roseus, MACGIL., Mem. Wern. Soc. v, 1824, 249.—JARD. & SELBY, Ill. Br. Orn. 1828, pl. 14.—KEYS. & BLAS., Wirb. Eur. 1840, 95.
Rossia rosea, BP., List, 1838, 62.
Rhodostethia rosea, "BP." (?Naum. 1854, 212; ? Rev. Zool. Guer. 1855, 278).—BRUCH, J. f. O. 1853, 106.—BRUCH, J. f. O. 1855, 278.—BP., Consp. ii, 1856, 230.— LAWR., B. N. A. 1858, 856.—COUES, Pr. Phila. Acad. 1862, 311; Key, 1872, 316; Check-list, 1874, No. 557.
Larus rossii, RICH., App. Parry's 2d Voy. 1825, 359; F. B. A. ii, 1831, 427.—WILS., Ill. 1831, pl. 3.—NUTT., Man. ii, 1834, ——.—AUD., Orn. Biog. v, 1839, 324; Syn. 1839, 323; B. Am. vii, 1844, 130 (not figured).—SCHL., Rev. Crit. 1844, 128.— NAUM., V. D. xiii, 1844, pl. 388, f. 3, 4.—MILN., Zool. 1847, 1694.—CHARLESW., Zool. 1847, 1782.—DEGL., Orn. Eur. ii, 1849, 332.—HART., Br. B. 1872, 173 (British instances).
Rhodostethia rossii, MACGIL., Man. Orn. ii, 1842, 253; Br. B. v, 618.—GRAY, Gen. of B. iii, 1849, 653; List Br. B. 1863, 229.—BP., Compt. Rend. 1856, 771.—BLAS., J. f. O. 1865, 370.
"*Larus richardsoni*, WILS." (*Fide* BP.) (Where?)

DIAG. *R. caudâ cuneatâ, torque collari nigro, rostro nigro, pedibus rubris.*

Hab.—Arctic regions. No United States record. Europe. Great Britain (see GRAY & HARTING, *l. c.*). Heligoland; Ibis, 1865, 103.

SP. CH. "*Color.*—Scapulars, interscapulars, and both surfaces of the wings, clear pearl-gray; outer web of the first quill blackish-brown to its tip, which is gray; tips of the scapulars and lesser quills whitish; some small feathers near the eye, and a collar round the middle of the neck, pitch-black, rest of the plumage white; the neck above, and whole *under plumage*, deeply tinged with peach-blossom red in recent specimens; *bill* black; its rictus, and the edges of the eyelids, reddish-orange; *legs* and *feet* vermilion-red; nails blackish.

"*Form.*—Bill slender, weak, with a scarcely perceptible salient angle beneath; the upper mandible slightly arched and compressed toward the point; the commissure slightly curved at the tip. *Wings* an inch longer than the decidedly cuneiform *tail;* the central feathers are an inch longer than the outer ones. Tarsi rather stout; the thumb very distinct, armed with a nail as large as that of the outer toe.

"*Dimensions.*—Length, 14 inches; wing, 10.50; tail, 5.50; bill above, 0.75, along gape, 1.25; tarsus, 1$\frac{1}{12}$." [RICH., F. B. A. ii, 1831, 427.]

The Smithsonian Institution contains no specimens of this exquisite Gull; and having been unable to examine an individual elsewhere, I have been obliged to copy Richardson's description, as given in the Fauna Boreali-Americana. There is little danger that in the accounts by American authors of this species there will be found material discrepancies, since I have not met with a single one who has not taken his description wholly or in part from the same source.

There are no specimens in America, to my knowledge. According to the editor of the Ibis (1865), no more than five specimens were then known: the one from Melville peninsula, June, 1823, in the University Museum, Edinburgh; another in the Derby Museum, believed to be from the same source; one at Mayence, from Kamtschatka; one in the Gætke collection, from Heligoland; and one in possession of Herr Benzon, of Copenhagen, obtained on the Færoes in February, 1863. Mr. Harting cites an example recorded (Zool. as above) from Yorkshire, but adds that accounts differ as to locality and date of capture.

Discussion of synonymy.—This Gull had the misfortune to be ushered into ornithological literature under trying circumstances, which caused pointed personalities. I think, however, that its proper name is not doubtful, as may be made evident. The bird was first mentioned by Macgillivray in the Memoirs of the Wernerian Society for January, 1824, under the name of *Larus roseus*. This author does not, it is true, give a formal description of the species; and also acknowledges in his subsequent works, that his name was only a "provisional" appellation. In the following year Richardson, in the Appendix to Parry's Second Voyage, named the bird *Larus rossii*, and accompanies his name with a description; and although this latter author admits that the bird was called *roseus* before he named it *rossii*, yet he claims precedence for his name, on the grounds that his was the first published description. The priority of Macgillivray's *roseus* being clearly established, and his name indisputably referring to the species under consideration, the only question is whether it is to be set aside because it was only a "provisional" designation given by one not "commissioned" to describe the object. I think that no valid reason can be given for changing the name. Rules of nomenclature require the adoption in every instance of the *first* published name when it is by any means identifiable. The first identifiable name to go on record, no matter how it gets there, must be used if it be not antedated in the same genus, and not wholly inept; and an author has no more right to change a name of his own than any one else's. Furthermore, no one can introduce a "provisional" name without becoming bound by it. I am ignorant of what the "personal" or "official" circumstances of this case were; but according to the record, Macgillivray's only fault was in not standing by the name he originally bestowed.

Genus XEMA, *Leach.*

= *Larus*, SAB., Linn. Trans. xii, 1818, 520 (*L. sabinei*).
= *Larus*, PREV. & DES MURS, Voy. Venus, 1855, 277 (*L. furcatus*).
> *Xema*, LEACH, Ross's Voy. App. 1825, p. lvii (*L. sabinei*).
= *Xema*, BRUCH. J. f. O. 1853, 103.
< *Gavia*, MACGIL., Man. ii, 1842, 241 (*L. sabinei*).
> *Creagrus*, BP., "1854" (*L. furcatus*).

GEN. CHAR. Tail forked (here only in *Larinæ*). Head hooded, with a more or less evident darker collar. Bill black, with light tip. Size moderate and small.

With a general bearing toward *Chræcocephalus*, in the hooded head and other features, the genus is distinguished from this or any group of *Larinæ* by the sternine character of forked tail. The name is generally restricted to the type, a "genus" *Creagrus* being employed for the second known species; but the latter is apparently a true *Xema*. The two are readlily distinguished, as follows:

Small: Wing, 11 inches or less; tail, lightly forked; a definite black collar bounding the hood; feet, black ---------------------------------- SABINEI.
Large: Wing, 16 inches or more; tail, deeply forked; black collar inconconspicuous; feet, red -------------------------------------- FURCATUM.

XEMA SABINEI, (Sab.) Leach.

Fork-tailed Gull.

Larus sabinei, J. SAB., Linn. Trans. xii, 1818, 522, pl. 29.—JEN., Man. 1828, 270.—WILS., Ill. Zool. 1831, pl. 8.—Sw. & RICH., F. B. A. ii, 1831, 428.—NUTT., Man. Orn. ii, 1834, 295.—AUD., Orn. Biog. iii, 1835, 561, pl. 285; Syn. 1839, 323; B. Am. vii, 1844, 127, pl. 441.—KEYS. & BLAS., Wirb. Eur. 1840, 95.—TEMM., Man. iv, 1840, 488.—NAUM., V. D. xiii, 1844, pl. 388, f. 1, 2.—SCHL., Rev. Crit. 1844, 128; Mus. P.-B. iv, 1863, *Lari*, p. 44.—DEGL., Orn. Eur. ii, 1849, 332.—MIDD., Sib. Reise, ii, 1853, 244, pl. 24, f. 5, pl. 25, f. 1 (*pullus et ovum*).—HART., Br. B. 1872, 171 (Great Britain, numerous instances).
Xema sabinei, LEACH, App. Ross's Voy. 1825, p. lvii, fig. —; Gen. Zool. xiii, 1826, 177, pl. 20.—EYT., Cat. Br. B. 1836, 54.—BP., List, 1838, 62; Comptes Rendus, 1856, 771.—GRAY, Gen. of B. iii, 1849, 655; List Br. B. 1863, 236.—BRUCH, J. f. O. 1855, 292.—BLAS., *ibid.* 1865, 370.—LAWR., B. N. A. 1858, 857.—NEWT., P. Z. S. 1861, 401; 1871, 57, pl. 4, f. 5 (egg).—COUES, Pr. Phila. Acad. 1862, 311.—LAWR., Ann. Lyc. N. Y. viii, 1866, 299 (New York).—COUES, Pr. Ess. Inst. v, 1868, 307.— DALL & BANN., Tr. Chic. Acad. 1869, 306 (Alaska).—ALLEN, Bull. M. C. Z. iii, 1872, 183 (Great Salt Lake).—COUES, Key, 1872, 317; Check-list, No. 558.
Gavia sabini, MACGIL., Man. Orn. ii, 1842, 241.
"*Larus collaris*, SAB." (*Fide* BP.) (Where?)
"*Xema collaris*, LEACH." (*Fide* GRAY.) (Where?)

Diag. *X. minor, caudâ emarginatâ, capite cucullato, collo torquato, rostro nigro apice flavo, pedibus nigris. Long. tot.* 14.00 *poll.*

Hab.—Arctic regions of both hemispheres. Spitzbergen. In America, south in winter to New York, and Great Salt Lake, Utah.

Adult, breeding plumage.—Bill black to the angle, abruptly bright chrome from angle to tip. Mouth bright orange; eyelids orange; legs and feet black. Hood uniform clear deep slate, bounded inferiorly by a ring, narrowest on the nape, of deep velvety black. Lower part of neck all round, tail and its coverts, four inner primaries, secondaries, greater part of greater coverts, tips of tertials, except the innermost, and whole under parts, pure white. Mantle slate-blue, extending quite to the tips of the inner tertials. Edge of wing, from the carpal joint with the bastard wing, black. First five primaries, with their shafts, black; their extreme tips, and the outer half of the inner webs, to near the end, white. Other primaries white, the sixth with a touch of black on the outer web. Emargination of tail 1.25 inches.

Dimensions.—Length, 13.75; wing, 10.75; bill, 1; along gape, 1.50; height at angle, 0.30; tarsus, 1.25; middle toe and claw, same.

Young-of-the-year.—(No. 50182, Plover Bay, Sept. 1867.) Tail forked, nearly as in the adult. Bill small and weak, flesh-color and dusky. Legs apparently flesh-colored. No hood nor collar. Most of the head, the back of the neck, and upper parts in general, slaty-gray, transversely waved with brownish-white; each feather being tipped with this color. Under parts white. Tail white, with a broad terminal bar of black, an inch wide on the central rectrices, growing narrower on the others successively; on the outermost sometimes invading only one web. This black bar very narrowly edged with white. Wings surprisingly similar to those of the adult, but the white on the inner webs more restricted, and the white tips very small or wanting altogether. Dimensions a little less than those of the adult.

The pictura of the primaries in the above-described specimen is remarkably like the adult's, considering how young the specimen is; but I presume the condition is constant, or at least usual. As the bird advances toward maturity the primaries gain more decided white tips; the black bar disappears from the tail; the upper parts become first mottled with the clear pearl-blue of the adults, then lose altogether the feathers of the present hue and pattern. Exactly at what time the hood and collar are assumed I cannot say; I should judge not till the second year.

The yellow tip of the bill varies greatly in size. Half of the bill may be yellow; or the yellow may be reduced to *nil;* but birds with an entirely black bill are not often seen. The adult winter plumage I have not seen, and cannot say whether the hood is lost or not; but I should judge, from analogy, that it is not retained. The species varies less than most Gulls; in fact I have little to add to the above on this score. The bill varies, as usual, in length and stoutness. Young birds look something like young *Cnrœocephalus philadelphia,* but I believe the tail is always at least emarginate.

This species was first introduced in 1818 by Capt. J. Sabine as *Larus sabinei,* but its peculiarities were almost immediately made the basis for generic separation by Leach. Macgillivray referred it to the genus *Gavia.* I have not been able to verify Bonaparte's quotation of "*Larus collaris* Sabine." The same author incorrectly gives Leach as authority for the specific name.

XEMA FURCATUM, (Neb.) Bruch.

Swallow-tailed Gull.

Mouette à queue fourchue, NEBOUX, Rev. Zool. iii, 1840, 290.
Larus furcatus, PREV. & DES MURS, Zool. Voy. Venus, Ois. 1855, 277, pl. 10.
Xema furcatum, BRUCH, J. f. O. 1853, 103.—COUES, Key, 1872, 317; Check-list, No. 559.
Creagrus furcatus, BP., "1854."—BRUCH, J. f. O. 1855, 292.—BP., Compt. Rend. 1856, 771.—LAWR., B. N. A. 1858, 857.—COUES, Pr. Phila. Acad. 1862, 312.—BLAS., J. f. O. 1865, 370.

DIAG. "*L. suprà cineraceus, capite colloque fuliginosè nigrescentibus; subtus albus; strigâ post-oculari et basi frontali albis; palpebris aurantiis, tarsis palmisque rubris.*"

Hab.—Coast of California. (?) Also, Arctic regions.

Adult.—Bill of moderate robustness, much bent at the tip, black at its base, white toward its apex, with "a small rounded white spot on either side of the base of the upper mandible." Tarsi, toes, and interdigital membranes, red; the claws black. Irides red the [edges of the] eyelids orange. Head, and greater part of the neck all round, black ["*gris brun*," NEBOUX; "*fuliginosè nigrescentibus,*" PREVOST and DES MURS]. Mantle light gray ["*blanc gris,*" NEBOUX]. Breast, belly, under surfaces of the wings, and the tail, pure white. The folded wings reach —— inches beyond the tail. Primaries bordered both internally and externally with black. Middle wing-coverts white ; greater coverts slaty-gray [*ardoisée*], bordered with white. Tail deeply forked ; the external pair of rectrices having an elongation not met with in any other species of the subfamily.

I regret exceedingly that I have had no opportunity of examining a specimen of this rare and remarkable Gull. The Smithsonian has never received an example, and I am not aware of the existence of one in any American collection. This is the more to be regretted since the original description by Neboux, which has served as the basis of nearly all subsequent accounts, both of American and European ornithologists, is brief, deficient, and unsatisfactory. Fortunately, however, the species is one presenting such peculiar features, that no confusion has arisen concerning it. I have taken my diagnosis from the Zoology of the Voyage of the Venus, and compiled the above outline description from Neboux's original account. I transcribe the further remarks of MM. Prévost and Des Murs :

" In spite of the great difficulty usually experienced in determining the species composing the genus *Larus*, on account of their close resemblance to each other, and the many variations in colors which each presents, the one in question may be distinguished at a glance by its orange eyelids and red legs and webs, and particularly by the two white spots which ornament the forehead at the upper mandible ; though the red feet are indeed shared by several other species, e. g., *L. hœmatorhynchus* King, and *bonapartei* Richardson. We lay no stress upon the semicircular white spot on the under eyelid, because this also exists in the *franklini* and *bonapartei* of Richardson. The two other most striking and remarkable features of the species lie in the decurved bill, which is a little like that of *Larus modestus* Tschudi ; and in the deeply forked shape of the tail, which is elsewhere only found among typical *Sterninæ.*"

Bibliography.—The species was first introduced by Neboux, as above, in 1840, under the appellation of " La mouette à queue fourchue," no Latin binomial designation being given. Upon this name and description MM. Prévost and Des Murs founded in 1855 their *Larus furcatus.* In consequence, doubtless, of its forked tail, it was in 1853 referred by Bruch to the genus *Xema.* A distinct genus was first framed for it by Bonaparte in 1854.

Since the foregoing was penned I have been favored, through the courtesy of Howard Saunders, esq., with an original description of a specimen in the British Museum. Under date of March 6, 1873, Mr. Saunders writes me that the bird is a true *Xema,* and has the appearance of being an Arctic species. " Head, neck, and throat, of a sootier color than in *X. sabinei,* darkening toward the base of the hood, but not forming a distinct black collar, as in this species ; a white frontal band ; under parts and tail pure white, the latter more deeply forked than in *sabinei ;* mantle pale pearl-gray, somewhat darker on the wing-coverts ; primaries blackish-brown on outer webs and continuation of inner webs, thence white, except at tip ; secondaries white, tinged with gray at their tips ; bill blackish, tipped with horn-yellow from the angle. Wing, 16.50 inches ; tarsi, nearly 2 inches ; middle toe the same ; hind toe very small, but bearing a well-developed claw."

Subfamily STERNINÆ.

DIAG. *Laridæ rostro integro, paragnatho.*

CH. Bill entire, its upper and under mandible of equal length ; always compressed, and higher than broad. Curve of culmen gentle and gradual from base to apex. Commissure gently declinato-convex, sometimes slightly sinuate at base. Symphysis of inferior mandibular rami much more extensive than in *Lestridinæ* or *Larinæ,* but the eminentia symphysis less marked. Interramal space narrow. Encroachment of feathers on the bill as in *Larinæ.* Nostrils linear-oblong, lateral, direct, pervious, varying with genera as regards degree of approximation to the base of the bill. Wings extremely lengthened, narrow, and acute, the first primary much the longest, the rest rapidly graduated. Secondaries short and inconspicuous. Tail usually much elongated and deeply forked, the lateral feathers being more or less attenuated and filiform ; only occasionally short and broad (*Gelochelidon*), or graduated (*Anous,* &c.). Legs placed rather further back, and less decidedly ambulatorial than in *Larinæ.* Tibia denuded for a varying distance. Tarsi short and usually slender ; scutellate and reticulate, as in *Larinæ.* Toes of moderate length, and of the usual relative proportions. Webs rather narrow, and (except in *Anous,* &c.) more or less excised. Claws small, compressed, but much curved and acute. Size moderate, or very small. General form slender and delicate. Plumage as in other subfamilies, but the pterylæ narrow, the sexes hardly differing in coloration, but the variations with age and season very great. For anatomical peculiarities of the subfamily, see under head of *Sterna hirundo.*

The generic and subgeneric groups of the *Sterninæ* are rather better marked than those of the *Larinæ.* They are in number about thirteen. Of these more than half (seven) are represented in North America. *Phæthusa, Gygis,* and several subgenera near *Anous* are extralimital. The North American forms may readily be distinguished by the following analysis. *Hydrochelidon* and *Anous* may be regarded as genera, the remainder being subgenera of *Sterna.*

Analysis of the North American forms of Sterninæ.

A. Nostrils sub-basal. Frontal antiæ prominent, embracing base of culmen. Tail more or less forked. Tarsus not shorter than middle toe without the claw. Lateral toes much shorter than the middle. Webs excised .... *Group* STERNEÆ.

   a. Webs moderately incised. Tail well formed, generally more than half as long as the wing. Under parts white or light.

      a′. Upper parts pearl-gray. Cap in summer black, or a black bar through eye.

         1. Bill short and very stout, somewhat, gull-like, black. Tarsi much longer than the toes, black. Tail lightly forked. Medium size .... *Gelochelidon.*

         2. Bill long, large, bright colored, or with yellow tip. An occipital crest. Feet black. Forking of tail variable. Of large size.. *Thalasseus.*

         3. Bill moderate, slender, usually bright colored, like the feet. No crest. Tail long, deeply forked. Size medium and small.. STERNA.

      b′. Upper parts dusky. Cap like the back.

         4. Bill and feet black. A white frontal crescent .... *Haliplana.*

   b. Webs deeply incised (feet little more than semipalmate). Tail merely emarginate, hardly or not half as long as the wing. Under parts in summer black.............. HYDROCHELIDON.

B. Nostrils nearly median. No frontal antiæ, the feathers extending further on culmen than at the sides. Tail double-rounded. Tarsi very short. Toes lengthened, the lateral nearly as long as the middle, with full webs .... *Group* ANOEÆ.

   Color fuliginous.. ANOUS.

Subgenus GELOCHELIDON, *Brehm.*

< *Sterna,* MONT., Orn. Dict. Suppl. 1813. (*S. anglica.*)
× *Thalasseus,* BOIE, Isis, 1822, 563 (not of LEACH).
× *Viralva,* STEPH., Gen. Zool. xiii, 1826, 174 (not of LEACH).
= *Gelochelidon,* BREHM, Naturg. Vög. Deutsch. 1831, p. —. (*S. anglica.*)
= *Laropis,* WAGL., Isis, 1832, 1225. (*S. anglica.*)

CHAR. Bill rather shorter than the head, exceedingly robust, not very acute, compressed ; the culmen nearly straight to beyond the nostrils, then very declinato-convex to the tip, rather broad and rounded for its whole length ; the gonys about straight; rami slightly concave; symphyseal eminence well marked ; tomia of lower mandible inflected ; commissure gently curved. Height of bill at base, a third of total length. Nasal groove exceedingly short and broad, not deep ; nostrils short, widely oval, placed very near the base of the bill, just beyond the termination of the feathers. Wings exceedingly long and acute, each primary surpassing the next by a full inch ; the secondaries short, soft, obliquely incurved at their extremities. Tail rather short, contained 2¼ times in the wing from the carpus ; deeply emarginate, but its lateral feathers not elongated nor attenuated. Feet long and stout for this subfamily. Tarsus shorter than the bill, longer than the middle toe and claw. Hind toe remarkably developed, being unusually long for this subfamily ; inner shorter than outer ; interdigital membranes moderately broad, deeply incised, especially the inner. Tibia naked for half an inch. Claws slender, slightly arched, acute. Scutella as in *Sterninæ* generally. Size moderate. Tail and rump concolor with the back. Anatomical characters those of *Sterninæ* generally.

The above diagnosis is of a group which differs chiefly from other *Sterninæ*, in the robust and obtuse bill, though other characters may be noted. The bill not distantly resembles that of *Larinæ*, and the group may be looked upon as the connecting link between the two subfamilies. It differs in pattern of coloration from most other Terns, in having the color of the mantle continued uninterruptedly on to the tail. Anatomical differences between it and *Sterna* proper are hardly to be appreciated, except, of course, those characters of the bones upon which the proportions of the bill and feet depend.

Of the several accredited species supposed to compose the genus, North America possesses but one, which is identical with that of Europe.

The genus has but few synonyms, the species comprised in it having been ordinarily referred to *Sterna.* Wagler's synonym (*Laropis*) is antedated by *Gelochelidon* of Brehm, which latter is the first distinctive name.

STERNA (GELOCHELIDON) ANGLICA, Mont.

Gull-billed Tern.

Sterna anglica, MONT., Orn. Dict. Suppl. 1813, p. —.—LEACH, Cat. 1816, 41.—TEMM., Man.
Orn. ii, 1820, 745.—FLEM., Br. An. 1828, 143.—NUTT., Man. ii, 1834, 269.—JEN.,
Man. 1835, 269.—EYT., Cat. Br. B. 1836, 54.—AUD., Orn. Biog. v, 1839, 127, pl.
410 ; Syn. 1839, 316 ; B. Am. vii, 1844, 81, pl. 430.—KEYS. & BLAS., Wirb. Eur.
1840, 98.—SCHINZ, Eur. Fn. 1840, 374.—DEKAY, N. Y. Zool. 1844, 301, pl. 127, f.
270.—GIR., B. L. I. 1844, 353.—SCHL., Rev. Crit. Ois. Eur. 1844, 130.—GRAY, G.
of B. iii, 1849, 659 ; List Br. B. 1863, 241.—DEGL., Orn. Eur. ii, 1849, 336.—PUTN.,
Pr. Ess. Inst. i, 1856, 230 (quotes EMM., B. Mass. p. 6).—TURNB., B. E. Pa. 1869,
38.—MAXIM., Beit. iv, 867 (Brazil).—RADDE, Reise, ii, 1863, 388 (Siberia).—
COUES, Key, 1872, 319.—RIDGW., Ann. Lyc. N. Y. x, 1874, 391 (Illinois).
Thalasseus anglicus, BOIE, Isis, 1822, 563.
Viralva anglica, STEPH., Gen. Zool. xiii, 1826, 174.
Laropis anglica, WAGL., Isis, 1832, 1225.
Gelochelidon anglica, BP., List, 1838, 61 ; Compt. Rend. 1856, 772.—BOIE, Isis, 1844, 187.—
COUES, Pr. Phila. Acad. 1862, 536 (critical).—COUES, Ibis, 1864, 389 (Guate-
mala).—SALV., Ibis, 1866, 199 (Guatemala).—COUES, Pr. Ess. Inst. v, 1868, 308.—
LAWR., Ann. Lyc. N. Y. viii, 1866, 299 (New York).—COUES, Pr. Bost. Soc. xii,
1868, 126 (S. Carolina).—GUNDL., Rep. F. N. i, 392 (Cuba ; CAB., J. f. O. v, 234).—
SCL. & SALV., P. Z. S. 1871, 572 (Tropical America).—BLAS., J. f. O. 1866, 82.
Sterna stubberica, OTTO, "Deuts. Übers. Buffon."
Sterna aranea, WILS., Am. Orn., viii, 1814, 143, pl. 72, f, 6.— VIEILL., Nouv. Dict. d'Hist.
Nat. 1819, 169 ; Fn. Franç. 1828, 398.—BP., Syn. 1828, 354.—LAWR., B. N. A.
1858, 859.—WHEAT., Ohio Agric. Rep. 1860, No. 272.—COUES & PRENT., Smiths.
Rep. 1861, 418.—ALLEN, Pr. Ess. Inst. iv, 1864, 90.—DRESS., Ibis, 1866, 44
(Texas).—PELZ., Orn. Bras. 325 (Brazil).—BURM., Syst. Uebers. iii, 452.
Gelochelidon aranea, BP., List, 1838, 61.
Sterna risoria, BREHM, Lehrb. 1823, 683 ; "Beitr. iii, 650."
Sterna macrotarsa, GOULD.
Sterna affinis, HORSF. (*fide* BLAS.).
Gelochelidon palustris, MACGIL., Man. ii, 1842, 237 ; Br. B. v, —.
Gelochelidon balthica, agraria, meridionalis, BREHM, V. D. 772, 773, 774.

DIAG. *S. rostro brevi, robusto ; rostro pedibusque nigris ; pallio cœrulescente-perlaceo, uropygio concolore, caudâ emarginatâ.*

Hab.—Nearly cosmopolitan. In North America, chiefly Eastern United States ; not
detected on the Pacific side. Patagonia (DARWIN, Voy. Beag. 145).

Adult in summer.—Bill with the culmen regularly declinato-convex from near the
base to the tip ; the culmen broad and flattened, especially basally. Outline of rami a
little concave ; gonys very long, its outline about straight. Depth of bill at base a
third of total length ; its width very much less than its height. Both mandibles
marked with numerous longitudinal striæ. Angle between the rami moderately acute ;
the symphyseal eminence well marked ; the tip not very acute. Nasal groove exceedingly short, wide, of somewhat triangular shape, not deep. Nostrils unusually wide,
broadly oval, short, lateral, pervious, placed very far back, only just anterior to the
termination of the feathers. The feathers extend on the side of the bill but little further than on the culmen, the re-entrant angle formed there being very obtuse. Those
on the side of the lower mandible do not extend so far as on the upper. Submental
space feathered almost to the symphysis. Head of ordinary sternine aspect ; body
rather stout, full, and thick set. Wing lengthened, as long as the whole body and tail.
Primaries exceedingly long, narrowing regularly from base to tip, which latter is attenuated and acute. The first surpasses the second by a full inch ; the rest are rapidly
graduated. Secondaries short and inconspicuous. Tertials rather long, broad, and
flowing. Tail quite short for this subfamily, contained 2½ times, or more, on the wing
from the carpus. The emargination is moderate, amounting to about 1¾ inches. The
middle pair of feathers are broad almost to their very tips, which are rounded, with
only a slightly acute apex just at the tip of the rhachis ; the lateral ones grow successively more elongated and tapering ; the outer pair maintains its breadth until within
about an inch of the tip, when it rather suddenly narrows and grows acute. The feet
are rather long ; the tarsus considerably exceeding the middle toe and claw. The tibiæ
are long, naked for half an inch, but have no feathers inserted into them for three-
fourths of an inch, and are perfectly smooth, with no scutellæ or reticulations. The
tarsus is compressed, moderately smooth, anteriorly defended by the ordinary row of
scutella, which break up toward the tibio-tarsal joint into two or more rows ; posteriorly and laterally it is reticulated with small, smooth, very regular polygonal (chiefly
hexagonal) scales. Anterior toes of ordinary relative length ; but the hallux is remark-

ably developed for this subfamily, and is inserted rather low down. Webs only moderately broad, and deeply incised, especially the outer one. Claws exceedingly slender, little arched, very acute, the inner edge of the middle one moderately dilated, not serrated.

Crown and long occipital crest deep glossy greenish-black. This pileum extends on each side to a level with the lower border of the eye, and leaves only a very narrow line of white to run along the edge of the feathers on the sides of the upper mandible; and it grows even wider on the latero-nuchal regions behind the eyes. Neck all round. and under parts, white. Mantle light pearl-blue, this color extending on the rump to the tail, and quite to the tips of the rectrices. The tail feathers indeed are deepest colored at their tips, fading into nearly pure white toward their bases, on that portion of each feather which is covered with the next one. The color of the mantle extends quite to the tips of the tertials, but dilutes a little toward the apices of the secondaries. Shafts of primaries yellowish-white. Primaries all grayish-black, deepest on the outer vane of the first; but this color is so heavily silvered as to be really much lighter in appearance. All the primaries have on their inner webs a space of white, which extends toward their apices for a varying distance on each. On the first the white is largest, purest, and extends furthest; is distinctly defined from the black, and has not a margin of black along its inner border, except just at its apex. The amount of the white diminishes in length and breadth with each successive primary, until on the last one it is inconspicuous; still it is quite perceptible on all. The bill is black, with or without a minute yellowish tip. The legs and feet are greenish-black.

Adult, winter plumage.—The winter plumage of this species, as usual among *Sterninæ*, hardly differs, except in the character of the pileum. The black usually becomes restricted chiefly to the occiput and nape, extending forward over the auricular and temporal regions to the eye, and sometimes almost entirely disappearing, leaving the whole head pure white, except a slight dusky trace through the eye and on the auriculars. There is the usual ante-ocular lunula. The forehead is entirely pure white; on the crown this color decreases in amount, becoming mixed with blackish-brown, and on the occiput almost entirely disappears. The general tint of the upper parts is perhaps rather lighter than in summer. For a while after the autumnal moult the primaries are also rather lighter than in summer, but toward spring they become fully as dark.

Young-of-the-year.—The bill is blackish-brown, lighter toward its tip, dusky yellowish or dull flesh-color toward the base of the under mandible. Legs and feet dull brownish, the claws blackish-brown. The general color of the upper parts is light pearl-blue, as in the adults, extending over the whole back from the neck to the upper tail-coverts, and including the median and greater coverts, and the tertials. The continuity of this color, however, is interrupted by numerous more or less distinct crescentic or hastate spots of dull brownish. Each feather bears a spot toward its extremity; its extreme tip, however, being yellowish or ochraceous-white, much lighter than the ground color of the upper parts. Along the edge of the fore-arm there is the ordinary band of brownish-black on the least coverts. The forehead and greater part of the vertex is white; but this color is interrupted on the latter by narrow lines of black along the shaft of each feather; these lines growing larger and wider toward the occiput and nape, where the white nearly disappears. An ante-ocular crescent and post-ocular space of brownish-black. The neck all round, and the whole under parts, including the inner wing-coverts and upper as well as under tail-coverts, pure white. Primaries much as in the adults; their shafts white. Secondaries as in the adults. The tail is less deeply forked; the rectrices much as in the adults, but fading into pure or yellowish-white at their tips, each having a more or less distinct hastate subterminal spot of brownish. The general proportions are somewhat less than in the adult, especially as regards the length of the bill and of the lateral rectrices.

Dimensions.—Length, 13 to 14.50 inches; extent of wings, 33 to 35; bill, 1.40; the gape, 2; gonys, 0.60; height at base, 0.45; tibiæ naked ¼ inch, no feathers inserted for ¾ inch; tarsus (average), 1.30; middle toe and claw, 1.10; hallux, with its claw, 0.40; wing, from carpus, 11.75 to 12.25; tail, to end of outer feather, 5.50; depth of emargination, 1.50 to 1.75 inches. "Average weight 6¾ oz. avoird." Female usually, but not always, smaller than the male.

The *anatomical* characters of the species do not present any special peculiarities, and therefore it has not been deemed necessary to introduce a description of them.

This strongly marked and well-known species requires no further description than the above. The chief variations to which it is subject appear to be those of dimensions. In the above paragraph I have given what will, I think, be found to be the average. The amount of variation is well displayed in the table given by Audubon. Most authors assert that the female is the smaller; but although this seems usually to be the case, it does not always hold. The amount of emargination of the tail in adult birds seems to be pretty constant, being, comparatively, free from both accidental or sexual variation.

The comparisons I have made of *S. anglica* with *S.* "*aranea*" have convinced me that there is not the slightest grounds on which to found a species distinct from the Europ-

ean. I have been unable to detect any discrepancies, nor do I think that any characters have ever been assigned to our bird. Wilson, in his description, does not compare
it with the European, doubtless for the best of reasons—that he did not know it. His
name, however, has been generally adopted for our bird since the time of its use in that
connection by Bonaparte, in 1838.

Synonymy.—The name *anglica* is rather an unfortunate one, since the bird, though
then described from specimens shot in England, seems to be much less abundant in that
country than in most other places where found. As, however, there is implied in the
name no actual geographical error, it is unnecessary to change it, as was done by
Macgillivray. Several names, additional to those above cited, appear to belong here,
but as I have made no critical examination of these supposed species, I do not here
consider them. Schlegel unites a number of current species, and is probably right in
so doing.

Subgenus THALASSEUS, *Boie.*

< *Sterna*, PALL., Nov. Comm. Petrop. xiv.
< *Thalasseus*, BOIE, Isis, 1822, 563 (type *S. caspia*, PALL.).—COUES, Rev. *Sterninæ* N. A.
  Pr. A. N. S. Phila. Dec. 1862, 536.
> *Hydroprogne*, KAUP, Sk. Ent. Eur. Thierw. 1829, 91. (*S. caspia.*)
> *Sylochelidon*, BREHM, Vög. Deutsch. 1831, 770. (*S. caspia.*)
> *Helopus*, WAGL., Isis, 1832, 1224. (*S. caspia.*)
> *Actochelidon*, KAUP, Sk. Ent. Eur. Thierw. 1829, 31. (*Sterna cantiaca.*)

GEN. CHAR. Bill as long as, or longer than, the head ; robust ; its height at the base
a fourth to a third of its length along culmen. Culmen variable in amount of curvature, from nearly straight to very convex. Gonys of variable length. Wings only
moderately long for this subfamily ; pointed, but the first primary not surpassing the
second by as much as the second does the third. Tail moderate or very short, in the
type of the genus greatly abbreviated, being contained three times in the wing from
the carpus, and but moderately emarginate. In other species more elongated and quite
deeply forked, contained about twice in the wing. Feet stout, of moderate length ;
tarsi usually about two-thirds the bill ; as long as, or somewhat exceeding, the middle
toe and claw. Hallux exceedingly short. Webs moderately broad, quite deeply incised,
especially the inner one. Of variable size, from the largest of the subfamily to quite
moderate. General form always more or less robust. A decided occipital crest. Under
parts always white. Feet black.

The essential characters of the subgenus, as compared with *Sterna* proper, are found in
the very large size and robust form ; in the depth and stoutness of the bills ; in the
stouter feet ; and in the shorter tail, which is usually rather emarginate than forked,
and never so deeply forked as in *Sterna*. The pattern of coloration is different in some
respects, and there is a decided occipital crest. *Gelochelidon* is apparently the most
closely allied, but this differs remarkably in the bill ; there is no occipital crest, the
wings are longer, the interdigital webs more deeply incised.

I have been obliged, in the preceding diagnosis of this group, to define it with considerable latitude, in consequence of the somewhat dissimilar types which I have referred to it. I have not, however, felt assured of the propriety of dividing it, as now
limited, into two or more groups, in consequence of the close connection which the different extremes of form present through intermediate species. Thus the *Thalasseus
caspius* and *T. cantiacus* differ considerably in such features as shape and robustness of
bill, length and emargination of tail. If we examine, however, other species, such as
T. regius and *elegans* of North America, *velox* of Europe, &c., we shall find some characters of form which are different in nearly every species, as *e. g.*, proportions of tarsus
and toes in *regius* and *elegans ;* and we shall moreover be able to trace gradual transitions in every respect, from one species to another. I prefer to retain all these large
species under the same subgeneric designation, as they all possess strong points of similarity among themselves, and recognizable discrepancies from *Sterna* in its restricted
sense.

Thalasseus is the first distinctive name which was proposed for this group, and is the
one now in most general employ. It is based upon *Sterna caspia*, as are also all the other
synonyms quoted at the head of this article, with the exception of *Actochelidon*, which
has *Sterna cantiaca* as type.

Analysis of the North American species of THALASSEUS.

A. Of large size and robust form. Bill entirely bright colored, feet black.
Tail slightly forked, with little or no attenuation of the outer
feathers.

    a. Tail merely emarginate. Primaries concolor on both webs (with-
    out white stripe on inner web). Bill red. Largest : Wing
    about 16 inches ; tail only 5 to 6 ; bill nearly 3 .... *caspia.*

b. Tail forked. Primaries with white stripe.

   1. Bill orange, stout, 2.25 to 2.75 long, 0.50 to 0.66 deep at base ; gonys only about 1 long ; wing, 14 to 15 ; tarsus, about 1.25, decidedly not longer than middle toe and claw .... *regiœ.*

   2. Bill orange, comparatively slender, about 2.50 long, less than 0.50 deep at base ; gonys, about 1.50 long ; wing, 12 to 13 ; tarsus, about 1, decidedly longer than middle toe and claw... *galericulata.*

B. Smaller and less robust. Bill black, tipped with yellow. Tail deeply forked, with narrow outer feathers .... *cantiaca.*

STERNA (THALASSEUS) CASPIA, Pall.

Caspian Tern.

Sterna caspia, PALL., Nov. Comm. Petrop. xiv, 1770, 582 ("Mus. Carls. fasc. iii, pl. 62").—GM., Syst. Nat. i, 1788, 603.—LATH., Ind. Orn. ii, 1790, 803.—RETZ., Fn. Suec. 1800, 164.—TEMM., Man. 1815, 476 ; ii, 1820, 733.—NILSS., Orn. Suec. ii, 1821, 155.—BREHM, Eur. Vög. 1823, 680.—STEPH., Gen. Zool. xiii, 145.—JEN., Man. 1835, 264.—KEYS. & BLAS., Wirb. Eur. 1840, 97.—NAUM., V. D. x, 1840, 18, pl. 248.—MACGIL., Man. ii, 1842, 230 ; Brit. B. v, ——.—SCHL., Rev. Crit. Ois. Eur. 1844, 128.—DEGL., Orn. Eur. ii, 1849, 337.—GRAY, Gen. of B. iii, 1849, 658 ; List Br. B. 1863, 238.—LAWR., B. N. A. 1858, 859.—TURNB., B. F. Pa. 1869, 47 (New Jersey).—RADDE, Reise, ii, 1863, 388 (Siberia).—COUES, Key, 1872, 319.

Thalasseus caspius, BOIE, Isis, 1822, 563.—COUES, Pr. Phila. Acad. 1862, 537.—VERR., Pr. Ess. Inst. iii, 1862, 161 (Maine).—COUES, *ibid.* v, 1868, 308.—LAWR., Ann. Lyc. N. Y. viii, 1866, 299.—ELLIOT, B. N. A. pl. 56.

Thalasseus caspius var. *imperator,* COUES, Pr. Phila. Acad. 1862, 538 (in text).—RIDGW., Ann. Lyc. N. Y. x, 1874, 391 (Illinois).

Hydroprogne caspia, KAUP, Sk. Ent. Eur. Thierw. 1829, 91.

Helopus caspius, WAGL., Isis, 1832, 1224.

Sylochelidon caspia, BREHM, V. D. 1831, 770.—BP., List, 1838, 62 ; Compt. Rend. 1856, 772.—LAWR., Ann. Lyc. N. Y. v, 1850, 37.—BLAS., J. f. O. 1866, 82

Sterna tschegrava, LEPECH., Nov. Comm. Petrop. xiv, 1770, 500, pl. 13, f. 2.

Sterna megarhynchos, MEYER, Tasch. Deut. Vög. ii, 457.

Sterna strenna, GOULD,

Thalassites melanotis, Sw. (*Fide* BLAS.)

Sylochelidon balthica et *schillingii,* BREHM, V. D. 769, 770.

(?) *Sylochelidon cayanensis,* BP., Compt. Rend. 1856, 772 (gives *regia* also).

Hab.—The Northern hemisphere. Arctic America, and south along the Atlantic coast to New Jersey.

Adult, breeding plumage.—(No. 17978. Mus. S. I., from Hudson's Bay.) Bill about the length of the head, very much longer than the tarsus, exceedingly robust, much compressed, deep at base, its tip not very acute. The culmen is broad and flattened at the base, more compressed and narrow anteriorly ; very regularly declinate convex throughout its whole length. The commissure is curved from the angle of the mouth to the tip, the amount of declination increasing toward the tip. The outline of the mandibular crura is slightly concave ; the gonys is about straight ; the symphyseal eminence only tolerably well marked. The nasal groove is short and wide, and becomes quite obsolete before it reaches the tomia. The nostrils are of the ordinary shape and size, or slightly widened, placed at the anterior extremity of the nasal fossa. Several striæ proceed out from them on the upper mandible, but the lower is quite smooth. The submental space is tolerably broad, bare of feathers for about half its length. The outline of the feathers on the upper mandible is as in *Sterna* generally, but those on the side are rather broad and rounded.

The palate is antero-posteriorly very concave, but transversely it is very flat and little arched or vaulted. For three inches from the tip the roof of the mouth is quite smooth, with only slight indications of a median ridge ; but there is on each side a deep groove, just along the edge, for the reception of the inferior mandible. The nasal aperture begins 2¾ inches from the tip, and is rather more than an inch long. The two lateral ridges are short, beginning only slightly in advance of the nasal aperture ; but they are greatly elevated, very conspicuous, and their ridges so largely papillate as to appear almost serrated.

Wings of ordinary length and shape for this subfamily. The primaries are quite broad at their bases, but about two or three inches from their tips become rapidly narrower, and taper to their slender rounded apices. The first surpasses the second by fully as much as the latter surpasses the third. The tail is of peculiar shape; it is short, the emargination being only 1½ inches. The middle feathers are broad to their very ends, which are rounded; the lateral ones become successively more lengthened and acute, till the external pair narrows rapidly to a fine point; but this pair has nothing of the slender and filamentous character common to most of the species.

The feet are short, and of moderate robustness. The tibiæ are bare for only about ¾ of an inch, or rather less than in *regia*, which is a much smaller bird. The tarsus is peculiar in having the scutella on its anterior aspect replaced by polygonal plates of a similar character to those of the lateral aspect, but larger, smoother, more regular. The toes superiorly have something of this reticulation. The tarsus is elsewhere covered with small, rough, elevated plates of irregular shape, as is also the superior surface of the webs. The middle toe is a little less than the tarsus; the outer is nearly as long, the tip of its claw reaching beyond the base of the middle claw; the inner is very short, its claw not reaching the base of the middle one. The hallux is extremely abbreviated. The claws are all short, stout, little curved or acute. The interdigital membranes are rather narrow and deeply incised, especially the inner one, the emargination of which reaches to between the second and third joints of the median digit.

Bill dark vermilion red, growing lighter and somewhat "diaphanous" toward the tip. Pileum and occipital crest glossy greenish-black, extending to below the lower level of the eyes, and occupying the termination of the feathers on the side of the mandible to the exclusion of the white. The lower eyelid is white, forming a noticeable spot on the greenish. A white streak along the sides of the upper mandible, *not*, however, extending to the end of the feathers. Mantle pearl-blue, the line of demarcation between it and the white rather indefinite, both on the nape of the neck and on the rump; most of the tail feathers, and especially the central ones, retaining a more or less notable pearly tint. The rhachides of the primaries are yellowish-white; the primaries themselves grayish-black, but when new, so heavily silvered over as to appear of a light hoary gray, especially on their superior aspects. On the inner web of all there is a central light field; this is very narrow, even on the first primary, although it runs for some considerable distance, and on the others it rapidly grows less; and it has no trenchant line of division on any of the primaries from the darker portions of the feather. The whole inner web of the secondaries is pure white, the outer pearl-blue. Legs and feet, with their soles, black.

Adult, winter plumage.—The winter plumage of this species, as is the case with other Terns, is chiefly distinguished by a diminution in the brightness of the colors of the bill, and by a change in the character of the pileum. The vermilion is replaced by light orange-red, growing still yellower toward the tip of the bill and along the tomia. The forehead is white, usually quite pure; the crown white, with small, narrow, distinct streaks of brownish-black along the shaft of each feather. On the sides of the head, before and behind the eyes, and over the auriculars, the black is more largely intermixed with the white; and on the nape of the neck, that is toward the termination of the occipital crest, the black is the predominating color, being only slightly variegated with white. There is no essential difference in the amount of emargination of the tail, but it has ordinarily at this season more of a pearl-blue tinge than in summer.

Young-of-the-year.—Every way much smaller than the adult, the bill especially smaller, shorter and weaker, and of a duller red, more inclining to orange. Upper parts as in the adult, but the pearl-blue everywhere spotted with very numerous rather small roundish or hastate spots of brownish-black, largest on the tertials. Forehead grayish-white; vertex speckled unto grayish-white and black, the latter color increasing in amount until it becomes nearly or quite pure on the short occipital crest. Wings much as in the adult. Tail much shorter and less forked; the rectrices with brownish spaces near their tips, chiefly on their inner webs. Under parts dull white. Legs and feet rather shorter and weaker than those of the adult, but of much the same color.

A series of American skins, compared with a fully adult bird from Europe, differ in size and proportion, as shown by the following table of comparative measurements:

Comparative measurements of American and European birds.

	Amer.	Eur.
Length of bill along culmen	2.75	2.40
Length of bill along gape	4.00	3.55
Height of bill at base	0.90	0.75
Width of bill opposite nostrils	0.50	0.50
Length of wing from flexure	16.50	15.00
Length of tarsus	1.75	1.65
Length of middle toe and claw	1.65	1.55
Length of tail	5.75	5.25

From these measurements it is apparent that the American bird is decidedly larger than the European. The bill is nearly a third of an inch longer, and at the same time is especially remarkable for its great comparative depth at the base, the width at the base being no greater than that of the skins from Europe. This gives to the bill quite a different shape. The next most striking discrepancy is found in the length of the wing from the carpal joint, in which dimension the American bird surpasses the European by fully 1½ inches. The greatest variation I have found in specimens from the same continent is only about ⅓ an inch. Indeed the wing of the adult European hardly exceeds that of a young American bird of the year. But there are no other discrepancies, and as it is probable that a larger suite of skins than that examined would show a wider range of individual variation, it may not be necessary to recognize var. *imperator*.

STERNA (THALASSEUS) REGIA, Gamb.

Royal Tern.

(?) *Grande Hirondelle de mer de Cayenne*, BUFF., viii, 346; whence *Sterna maxima*, BODD., P. E. 988; *S. cayennensis*, GM., Syst. Nat. i, 1788, 604; *Cayenne Tern*, LATH., Syn. vi, 352; *S. cayana*, LATH., Ind. Orn. ii, 1790, 804. (Doubtful.)
Sterna maxima, SCL. & SALV., P. Z. S. 1871, 567 (Middle and South America).
Sterna cayennensis, LEÓT., Ois. Trinidad, 535.
Sterna cayana, BP., Syn. 1828, 353.—NUTT., Man. ii, 1834, 268.—AUD., Orn. Biog. iii, 1835, 505; v, 1839, 639; pl. 273; Syn. 1839, 316; B. Am. vii, 1844, 76, pl. 429.—DE-KAY, N. Y. Fauna, ii, 1844, 299, pl. 127, f. 277.—GIR., B. L. I. 1844, 355.
Thalasseus cayanus, BP., List, 1838, 61.—GOSSE, B. Jam. 1847, 431.
Sterna regia, GAMB., Pr. Phila. Acad. iv, 1848, 228.—LAWR., B. N. A. 1858, 859.—NEWT., Ibis, i, 1859, 371 (Santa Cruz).—CAB., J. f. O. v, 234 (Cuba).—BRY., Pr. Bost. Soc. vii, 1859, 134 (Bahamas).—SCL., P. Z. S. 1861, 82 (Jamaica).—DRESS., Ibis, 1866, 44 (Texas).—TURNB., B. E. Pa. 1869, 47 (New Jersey).—COUES, Key, 1872, 319.—RIDGW., Rep. Surv. 40th parallel (in press; Nevada, breeding).—RIDGW., Ann. Lyc. N. Y. x, 1874, 391 (Illinois).
Thalasseus regius, GAMB., Journ. Phila. Acad. i, 2d series, 1849, 228.—COUES, Pr. Phila. Acad. 1862, 539.—COUES, Ibis, 1864, 388 (Guatemala).—SALV., Ibis, 1866, 199 (Guatemala).—LAWR., Ann. Lyc. N. Y. viii, 1864, 104 (Sombrero); viii, 1866, 299 (New York); ix, 1868, 210 (Yucatan).—GUNDL., Repert. 1866, 392 (Cuba).—COUES, Pr. Bost. Soc. xii, 1868, 126 (South Carolina).—COUES, Pr. Phila. Acad. 1871, 42 (North Carolina; biography).
Phætusa regia, BP., Compt. Rend. 1856, 772.
(?) "*Sterna erythrorhynchus*, MAXIM., Beit. iv, 857.—TSCHUDI, F. N. Peru. *Aves*, 305.—BURM., Syst. Übers. iii, 450" (SCL. & SALV.).
"*Sterna galericulata*, PELZ., Orn. Bras." (error for this species, *sec.* SCL. & SALV., P. Z. S. 1871, 565).
(??) *Sterna chloripoda*, VIEILL., Nouv. Dict. xxxii, 171; E. M. 349 (*Haté cogote obscuro*, Az., Apunt. iii, 372). (Very uncertain.)

Hab.—More southern portions of the Atlantic coast; north to Long Island. Gulf of Mexico. On the Pacific side north to California. Nevada, breeding (*Ridgway*). Southward into the Antilles and Central America.* South America to Brazil and Peru.
Adult, spring plumage.—Bill about as long as that of *T. caspius*, but of very different shape, being much slenderer, its height at base being only from a fourth to a fifth of its total length. Culmen gradually declinato-convex from base to tip, the amount of curvature increasing but slightly toward the apex, which is not very acute. Commissure somewhat sinuate basally, regularly declinato-convex for the rest of its length. Rami decidedly a little concave along their edges. Gonys straight, shorter than the rami, the prominence between the two illy developed. Wings of ordinary length, the primaries of the usual shape and relative lengths. The tibiæ are bare for a considerable distance (0.90 of an inch). The tarsus is not longer than the middle toe and claw. Its anterior aspect shows a tendency toward reticulations instead of transverse scutella, but there are usually some scales which extend quite across it. The lateral and posterior aspects are thickly reticulated, as in *caspius*, but the plates are not so rough nor elevated. The toes have the usual relative length for this genus. The interdigital membranes are as described under *caspius*, but the emargination is not quite so great. The tail is long for this genus, and quite deeply forked. The central feathers are broad to their very tips, which are rounded; the lateral ones grow successively more elongated and narrower toward their tips, the external pair being slender and quite filamentous for some distance from their narrow rounded apices.

---

* Audubon says that these birds are found in *Labrador*. This is certainly an error; and the birds that he observed there, and mistook for this species, must have been individuals of the *S. caspius*.

The glossy greenish-black pileum does not extend below the eyes, and is so narrow on the sides of the upper mandible that it allows a broad white streak to extend along the edge of the mandible to the extreme tip of the feathers. The mantle is exceedingly light pearl-blue, fading imperceptibly into white on the rump and toward the extremities of the tertials. The tail is white, with a faint tinge of pearly, especially on the central feathers and inner webs of the others. The secondaries are pure white for their whole length, except a small space on the outer web near the tip, which is grayish-blue, deeper than the mantle. The outer web of the first primary is grayish-black; the inner web of the same has a space of black extending the whole length of the feather, very narrow at the base, widening as it runs toward the tip, within 1½ inches of which it occupies the whole web, to the exclusion of the white portion; the rest of the web is white, separated from the black by a straight distinctly-defined trenchant line of division. The second, third, fourth, and fifth primaries have the same general characteristics, but the white space rapidly grows narrower and shorter, and runs up further in the centre along the edge of the web, so that for a little way from its end it has a border of blackish along its outer margin. The other primaries have no grayish-black, but are wholly pearl-blue, their inner webs margined with white. The bill is coral or orange-red, with a slightly lighter tip. The feet are blackish, their soles dull yellowish.

Winter plumage.—Bill less brightly colored than in summer, its apex and tomia dull yellowish. Front white; crown variegated with black and white, the former color increasing on the occiput and nuchal crest, which latter, though shorter than in summer, is almost or quite unmixed with white. This black extends forward on the sides of the head to the eye, which it includes. The tail is not pure white, as in summer, but is glossed over with the bluish of the mantle, which deepens toward the tips of the feathers into dusky plumbeous. It is also considerably less deeply forked, the lateral feathers having little or nothing of a filamentous character. Otherwise as in summer.

Young-of-the-year in August.—Bill considerably smaller and shorter than in the adult; its tip less acute, and its angles and ridges less sharply defined; mostly reddish-yellow, but light yellowish at tip. Crown much as in the adults in winter, but the occipital crest scarcely recognizable as such. Upper parts mostly white; but the pearl-gray of the adults appearing in irregular patches, and the whole back marked with small, irregularly shaped, but well-defined spots of brown. On the tertials the brown occupies nearly the whole of each feather, a narrow edge only remaining white. Lesser wing-coverts dusky plumbeous. Primaries much as in the adults, but the line of demarcation of the black and white wanting sharpness of definition. Tail basally white, but soon becoming plumbeous, then decidedly brownish, the extreme tips of the feathers again markedly white. Otherwise as in the adults.

Dimensions of the adults.—Length, 18 to 20 inches; extent of wings, 42 to 44; wing, from carpal joint, 14 to 15; tail, 6 to 8; the depth of forking, about 3 to 4; bill, along culmen, 2.50 to 2.75; along commissure, 3.75; its height at base, 0.70; its width, 0.50; gonys, 1 to 1.25; tibiæ base, 0.90; tarsus, 1.37; middle toe and claw, 1.40.*

Other variations.— For so large a species, and one of this family, the variations are not very great. When found, they consist chiefly in differences of dimensions, as usual, and in a less degree in the shape and size of the bill. The measurements indicated above are, I believe, about the average. There seems to be no difference in the sexes. The young are invariably smaller, with weaker bill and feet, and only slightly forked tail. The relative proportions of the tarsus and tail of the adults, as well as the absolute length of these parts, seem to be very constant, and always preserve the radical difference from those of *elegans*, which is noticed below.

Immature birds, of course, exhibit every gradation between the state of plumage above described, and that of the adults. When very young, however, they preserve pretty constantly the pattern of coloration given. The adults, in winter, vary a good deal as to the exact amount of black remaining in the pileum; but the essential characters of white front, spotted vertex, nearly black occiput, and variegated lateral stripe along the sides of the head, are always found. In the plumage of adult summer birds I have found no variations worth noticing.

Comparison with allied species.—The species is liable to be confounded with only one other of North America—*galericulata*. While the bill is nearly or quite as long as is that of *caspius*, it is of a very different shape, being every way weaker, with a straighter culmen. Besides, the coloration of the primaries of *caspius* is peculiar in lacking the white stripe on the inner webs of the primaries. *S. galericulata* is more nearly allied; but it is considerably smaller, with the bill, though as long or nearly so, much slenderer and differently shaped (compare descriptions), with a different proportionate length of tarsus and toes, a rich rosy blush in the breeding season, &c.

Bibliography.—While I agree with Messrs. Sclater and Salvin that *S. maxima* Bodd. (=*cayennensis* Gm., *cayana* Lath.) is not improbably this species, I cannot make the identification satisfactorily. The description (of a young bird) is too short and vague to be determined positively. It might have been based on *Phaetusa magnirostris.* The

---

* Audubon's measurements, "tarsus, 3$\frac{2}{12}$; middle toe, 1; its claw, $\frac{1}{2}$;" are so glaringly erroneous, that they must be either typographical or clerical mistakes.

name had better rest, at least until it is certain there is no other large species of Trop
ical America to which it can apply. Besides, the name *maxima* involves an inaccuracy
Gamble's name, *regia*, is perfectly definite. I quote *S. erythrorhynchos* as doubtless conspecific with *regia*, but should not be surprised if some varietal distinctions were found
in this case. *S. chloripoda* Vieill. I can make nothing of.

My personal observations on this species are confined to the coast of
North Carolina; on a former occasion I gave the following account:
This Tern certainly breeds somewhere in the vicinity of Fort Macon;
for, although I did not find any nests, I saw it constantly through two
summers, and occasionally noticed birds so young that they were still
receiving attentions from their parents; while in June and July small
flocks were often noticed pursuing so straight a course for long distances,
that I had no doubt they were passing directly between their nests and
their feeding-places. It commonly arrives from the south early in April,
and through this and the next month is more abundant than at other
times until the fall—a part, I presume, passing further north. It
becomes numerous again in September, and so continues until the end
of November. I cannot say whether or not any remain all winter, but
think that, if observed at that season, it will be an exceptional case. It
is more wary than any of the other Terns, and is always the first to rise
among the miscellaneous troops that fleck the sand-bars. It is conspicuous by its size and bright red bill; and the young are easily distinguished
by the smaller size, yellow instead of red bill, and spotted plumage.
The old birds lose the black pileum in September, the crown then
becoming white, bordered behind by the long, loose blackish feathers of
the occiput, and a few other dark ones on the sides of the head. The
bill in winter is not so vivid in color as in summer, and much shorter.
All the changes of the old are finished by October; but the young
remain blotched, and with mere traces of the pearl-blue mantle, all the
fall. I took one old bird with the feet curiously mottled with yellowish
and black, and yellow claws—probably a pathological state, although
the bird appeared perfectly healthy. These are vigorous, spirited birds,
showing good fight when captured, and strong enough to bite pretty
severely. Their voice is loud and raucous, though still without the deep
guttural intonation of that of the Shearwaters.

STERNA (THALASSEUS) GALERICULATA, Licht.

Elegant Tern.

Sterna galericulata, LICHT., Verz. 1823, 81 (Brazil).—SCHL., Mus. P.-B. *Sternæ*, p. 7.—
        FINSCH, Abh. Nat. 1870, 359 (Mazatlan).—SCL. & SALV., P. Z. S. 1871, 568.—
        COUES, Key, 1872, 319.
(?) *Thalasseus galericulatus*, BLAS., J. f. O. 1866, 82.
Sterna elegans, GAMB., Pr. Phila. Acad. iv, 1848, 129 (immature).—LAWR., B. N. A. 1858,
        860.—BD., B. N. A. 1860, pl. 94.—LEÓT., Ois. Trinidad, 542.
Thalasseus elegans, GAMB., Journ. Phila. Acad. i, 2d series, 1849, 228.—BP., Compt. Rend.
        1856, 772.—COUES, Pr. Phila. Acad. 1862, 540.—COUES, Ibis, 1864, 389 (San
        Salvador).—SALV., Ibis, 1866, 198.
Sterna comata, PHIL. & LANDB., Wieg. Arch. 1868, 126 (*Scl. & Salv.*).
"*Sterna cayennensis*, PELZ., O. B." (err. for this spec. *fide* SCL. & SALV., P. Z. S. 1871, 565).
(?) "*Sterna cristata*, Sw."

Hab.—Middle and South America. Up the Pacific coast from Peru (*Frobeen*) to California (*Gambel*). Tehuantepec (*Sumichrast*). Trinidad (*Leótaud*). Brazil (*Lichtenstein*).
Not observed on the Gulf or Atlantic coast of the United States.

Adult, winter plumage.—(No. 24281, Mus. Smith. Inst., from San Francisco, Cal.; the
type of the above-cited plate.) Bill much longer than the head, exceeding the tarsus,
middle toe and claw together; much compressed, very slender, its tip attenuated.
Culmen quite straight to beyond the nostrils, then slightly and equably convex for the
rest of its length; broad basally, more compressed and transversely convex anteriorly.
Commissure declinato-convex for nearly its whole length. Mandibular rami very short,
decidedly concave in outline, their angle of divergence very acute. .Gonys extremely

long, exceeding the crura of the mandible, its outline straight. Tomia of both mandibles sharp and much inflected. Nasal groove long, fully half the culmen, narrow, not deep, directed obliquely downward and forward toward the tomia ; but it becomes obsolete, however, before reaching them. A few oblique indistinct striæ on both mandibles. The outline of the feathers on the bill is as usual. The bill is orange-red, insensibly fading into yellow on the tip and cutting edges.

The naked portions of the tibiæ, the tarsus and the toes, with the claws, are black ; the soles of the feet mostly yellowish. The most striking peculiarity of the feet is the length of the tarsus, as compared with the toes. The former is very much longer than the middle toe alone, and slightly exceeds the middle toe and claw together.* The feet are of the ordinary shape and stoutness, with the usual extent of the tibiæ bare. The outer toe, without its claw, is very long, being but very slightly shorter than the middle ; while the extremity of the claw of the inner toe falls short of the base of the claw of the middle. Hallux of usual dimensions. Claws all moderately long, arched, acute ; the inner edge of the middle very much thinned and dilated, and usually more or less serrate. The emargination of the webs is moderate, that of the inner only reaching to the third joint of the middle toe. The wings present no special peculiarities of form or color, being in both these respects quite similar to *regius*, already fully described. The markings of the primaries are quite identical. The tail also has the form of that of *regius*. In the winter skin before me, it has considerably less elongated tail feathers than it will have in summer. All the feathers are also washed over with a very notable amount of grayish-blue, most conspicuous in their outer webs. The lateral feathers in this specimen have little or none of this bluish tinge, and still preserve a considerably elongated and tapering shape. The forehead, and feathers on the side of the bill, are pure white ; on the vertex this white becomes variegated with rounded, rather illy-defined spots of grayish-black, which all have pure black centres along the shaft. On the occiput the black preponderates largely over the white, which is only left as a slight tip to each feather. The long-flowing nuchal crest is glossy greenish and black, unadulterated with white ; and this color extends forward on the sides of the head as a well-defined band, passing through and a little beyond the eyes. Even in this winter specimen the rosy hue of the under parts is perceptible.

Dimensions of same specimen.—Culmen, 2.60 ; rictus, 3.75 ; gonys, 1.40 ; height of bill at base, 0.50 ; width, 0.45 ; "length, 17 ;" wing, 12.25 ; tail, 4.75 ; depth of fork, 2.25 ; tarsus, 1.25 ; middle toe, 0.85 ; its claw, 0.30.

The above is taken from a perfect winter specimen (the original of the figure in the Atlas of Birds N. A.), which does not differ materially from Gambel's type. The following gives the perfect summer plumage :

Adult.—Bill bright red, salmon-colored toward tip. Feet black ; soles and under surfaces of claws slightly flavescent. Crown of head, including long-flowing occipital crest, pure black, reaching down on the sides of the head to a straight line just on a level with the lower border of the eye ; the white of the cheeks, &c., accompanying the black to the foremost point of extension of the feathers in the nasal fossæ. All the under parts rosy-white, with satin gloss. Tail entirely pure white, longer and more deeply forked than in winter. Back and wings pale pearl-blue ; the usual pattern of coloration of the primaries. "Length, 19 ; extent, 48" (label) ; culmen, 2.75 ; wing, as before ; tail, 7.50 ; depth of fork, 3.50 ; tarsus, 1.25 ; middle toe and claw, the same.

This species scarcely requires comparison with any other. The following measurements give the difference in size and shape between it and *regia*—the only North American species with which it is likely to be confounded :

S. regia : Bill along culmen, 2.60 (average) ; depth at base, 0.75 (or about 0.333 its length) ; gonys 1.25, about equal to rami of lower mandible, measured from the feathers on the side ; wing, 14.50 to 15 ; tibiæ, bare, 0.90 ; middle toe and claw, 1.30 to 1.40 ; tarsus, 1.25.

S. galericulata : Bill along culmen, 2.60 (average) ; depth at base, 0.50 (or about 0.2 of its length) ; gonys 1.40, or rather longer than rami, measured as above ; wing, 12.25 to 12.50 ; tibiæ, bare, 0.65 ; middle toe and claw, about 1.15 ; tarsus, 1.25.

Compare also Gambel's original description and remarks. *Galericulata* is a smaller bird than *regia*, yet with bill, tail, and tarsi as long ; the bill much slenderer ; the toes shorter ; the under parts colored as they never are in *regia*.

I now follow several European ornithologists in referring the species generally known as "*elegans*" to *S. galericulata* of Lichtenstein—a name which had escaped me in my earlier studies of this group. Messrs. Sclater and Salvin say that *comata* Phil. & Landb. is the same bird.

---

* The species may always be diagnosed from *S. regia* by the measurements of these parts, the toes being in *galericulata* considerably shorter, compared with the tarsus, than in *regia*. In *regia* the middle toe and claw are somewhat longer than the tarsus ; in *galericulata* the two are of about the same length. The tarsus of *regia* but very slightly surpasses the middle toe without its claw ; the tarsus of *galericulata* is nearly a fourth of its own length longer than the middle toe without its claw.

STERNA (THALASSEUS) CANTIACA, Gm.

Sandwich Tern.

Sterna cantiaca, GM., Syst. Nat. i, 1788, 606.—TEMM., Man. 1815, 479.—STEPH., Gen. Zool.
xiii, 147.—JEN., Man. 1835, 265.—EYT., Cat. Br. B. 1836, 54.—KEYS. & BLAS.,
Wirb. Eur. 1840, 97.—NAUM., V. D. x, 1840, 51, pl. 250.—SCHL., Rev. Crit. 1844,
129 ; Mus. P.-B. *Sternæ*, p. 5.—GRAY, Gen. of B. iii, 1849, 658 ; List Br. B. 1863,
239.—AUD., Orn. Biog. iii, 1835, 531, pl. 279 ; Syn. 1839, 317 ; B. Am. vii, 1844,
87, pl. 431.—DEKAY, N. Y. F. ii, 1844, 303, pl. 124, f. 274.—TURNB., B. E. Pa.
1869, 47 (New Jersey ; straggler).—SCL. & SALV., P. Z. S. 1871, 569.—ALLEN.,
Am. Nat. iii, 1870, 644 (Massachusetts).—COUES, Key, 1872, 320.—PELZ., Orn.
Bras. 324 (Brazil).
Thalasseus cantiacus, BOIE, Isis, 1822, 563.—BP., List, 1838, 61.—BLAS., J. f. O. 1866, 81
(locates *nubilosa*, SPARRM., here).
Actochelidon cantiacus, KAUP, Sk. Ent. Eur. Thierw. 1829, 31.
(?) *Sterna africana*, GM., Syst. Nat. i, 1788, 605.—LATH., Ind. Orn. ii, 1790, 805 (uncertain).
(?) *Sterna striata*, GM., Syst. Nat. i, 1788, 609.—LATH., Ind. Orn. ii, 1790, 807 (uncertain).
Sterna boysii, LATH., Ind. Orn. ii, 1790, 806 (=*cantiaca*, GM.).—LEACH, Cat. 1816, 41.—
FLEM., Br. An. 1828, 142.—NUTT., Man. ii, 1834, 276.—MACGIL., Man. ii, 1842, 230.
Sterna columbina, SCHRK. (*Fide* BLAS.)
" *Sterna nævia*, BEWICK, Br. B. ii, 1804, 207." (*Gray*.)
Sterna stuberica, BECHST., Naturg. Deut. iv, 679.
Sterna canescens, MEYER, Tasch. Deut. Vög. ii, 458.
Thalasseus canescens et *caudicans*, BREHM, V. D. 1831, 776, 777.
Sterna acuflavida, CAB., Pr. Bost. Soc. ii, 1847, 257.—LAWR., B. N. A. 1858, 860.—BRY.,
Pr. Bost. Soc. vii, 1859, 134 (Bahamas).
Thalasseus acuflavidus, COUES, Pr. Phila. Acad. 1862, 540.—COUES, Ibis, 1864, 389 (Central
America).—SALV., Ibis, 1866, 198 (the same).—GUNDL., Repert, 1866, 392.—
LAWR., Ann. Lyc. N. Y. viii, 1866, 299 (New York) ; ix, 210 (Yucatan).—COUES,
Pr. Ess. Inst. v, 1868, 60 (New England).—COUES, Pr. Bost. Soc. xii, 1868, 126
(South Carolina).—COUES, Pr. Phila. Acad. 1871, 42 (North Carolina).

Hab.—Atlantic coast of North America to Southern New England. Bahamas ; Cuba ;
Jamaica ; ranging into Central America (both coasts). Honduras, breeding (*Salvin*).
South into Brazil (*Pelzeln*).

Adult, breeding plumage.—Bill much longer than the head, exceeding in length the
tarsus, middle toe and claw together ; quite slender and attenuated for this genus, the
tip excessively acute. The convexity of the culmen, from tip to base, is regular, but
very slight. The commissure is gradually declinato-convex throughout its whole
length. The outline of the mandibular crura is decidedly concave ; that of the gonys
about straight. An eminentia symphysis is hardly appreciable. The submental or
intercrural space is very short and extremely narrow, the feathers only covering its
posterior half. Nasal groove very long, narrow, not deep, extending more than half
the length of the bill, and subsiding at the tomia. Both mandibles are marked with
oblique longitudinal striæ. The outline of the feathers on the bill is as usual in this
subfamily. Wings of moderate length, of ordinary shape ; the primaries quite broad
to within a short distance of their rounded, not very narrow nor acute, tips. The
formation of the tail is exactly as in *regia*. The feet are quite slender, moderately
compressed, anteriorly scutellate, laterally and posteriorly reticulate, as usual in the
subfamily. Webs moderately incised for this genus ; relative proportions of the toes
as in other species. Claws all long, strong, arched, acute, the inner edge of the middle
one greatly dilated.

Bill black ; the tip for ¼ to ¾ of an inch bright yellow, sharply defined against the
black ; "inside of mouth deep blue." Feet dull black. Pileum and occipital crest
glossy black, with a tinge of green ; the color extending just below the eyes, but leaving a space along the side of the mandible white to the extremity of the feathers. The
mantle is exceedingly light pearl-blue, fading on the rump and upper tail-coverts into
pure white ; but the rectrices themselves have a slight shade of pearly bluish. The
primaries are colored exactly as in *regia*. On the inner web of the first the black space
is broad and deep in color ; when about 1½ inches from the apex of the quill it quite
suddenly grows wider, so as to exclude the white portion from the tip altogether. The
second, third, and fourth primaries have the same general pattern, but the white runs
up further on the central portion than on the edge of the web, so that toward its end
it receives a narrow edging of blackish. The other primaries have no blackish, but
are simply pearl-blue, with broad white margins along the whole length of their inner
webs. The outer primaries are all heavily silvered when the quills are new.

Dimensions of the adult.—Length, 15 to 16 inches ; extent, ——— ; wing, from the carpus,
12.50 ; tail, 6 ; depth of emargination, 2.35 ; bill, along culmen, 2.25 ; along gape, 3 ;
its height at base, 0.48 ; width, ditto, 0.37 ; length of rami from feathers on side of

43

lower mandible, 1; gonys, 1.20 (longer than rami); tarsus, 1; middle toe and claw, very slightly longer.

Adult, winter plumage.—The yellow tip of the bill decreases in extent and intensity of color; the front is white, either pure or speckled with black; the crown variegated with black and white, the former color consisting of small, narrow, distinct streaks along the shaft of each feather; but the long occipital crest, which does not entirely disappear at this season, usually remains of an unmixed brownish-black. The lateral tail feathers are shorter than in summer.

Young-of-the-year in August.—Considerably smaller than the adult, as is usual in this subfamily, the wing being a full half inch shorter. The bill is shorter and weaker, and is without any very sharply-defined angles and ridges. It is brownish-black, the extreme point only yellowish. The crown, front, and occiput, are brownish-black, variegated with white; the white touches very small on the forehead. The upper parts are as in the adult, but everywhere marked with irregularly-shaped but well-defined spots and transverse bars of decided brownish-black. There is no well-formed occipital crest until after the first moult. The primaries are like those of the adults. The tail, however, is very different. The feathers for three-fourths their length are of the color of the back; this color gradually deepens, until toward the tips it becomes brownish-black, each feather having a terminal irregular edge left whitish. The tail, in shape, is simply deeply emarginate, the outer feathers being but slightly longer than the second.

Other variations.—The yellow tip of the bill varies greatly in extent, and has also a varying outline and distinctness of definition from the black. The length of this yellow tip appears to depend in a good measure upon the age of the bird, while the intensity of the color is apparently affected most by the season of the year. The difference between the longest and shortest tips that have come under my observation is full half an inch (varying from $\frac{1}{4}$ to $\frac{3}{4}$). The length of the tarsus and toes seems very constant, as are the markings of the primaries in their extent and distribution. The difference in length of wing from the carpus is only about one-half an inch in adult birds. The forking of the tail varies somewhat, but never equals that of the species of *Sterna* proper.

A series of winter skins from *Jamaica* in, probably, their first moult (if they really belong to this species), differ from adult examples from various points on the Atlantic coast in being every way considerably smaller. The bills are about a third of an inch shorter than the average; and other parts differ proportionally.

European : White margin of inner web of outer three or four primaries wide, extending quite to tip, which it wholly occupies. Breadth of white portion one and a half inches from tip of first primary, 0.25 of an inch.

American : White margin of inner web of three or four outer primaries narrow, falling short of tip, which is wholly occupied by the black portion. Breadth of white margin one and a half inch from tip of first primary, 0.10 of an inch.

The foregoing expresses certain points of difference I have found to subsist between the American and European birds, but I do not now attach to them any importance, since they may depend mainly upon age of the individual quills. Whether or not I can agree with my friends, Dr. Sclater and Mr. Salvin, "that Dr. Coues has ably discussed the subject," I am ready to concede that he "has succeeded in reducing the differences to a minimum which is too small to warrant specific separation !"

Subgenus STERNA, *Linn.*

< *Sterna*, LINN., Syst. Nat. 1748, et auct. (Type *S. hirundo*, LINN.)
> *Thalassea*, KAUP, Sk. Ent. Eur. Thierw. 1829, 97. (Type *S. paradisea*, BRÜNN.)
> *Hydrocecropis*, BOIE, Isis, 1844, 178. (Same type.)
> *Sternula*, BOIE, Isis, 1822, 563. (Type *S. minuta*, LINN.)

GEN. CHAR. Bill about as long as, or a little shorter than, the head, much longer than the tarsus; variable in stoutness, but generally quite slender, compressed, very acute; the culmen declinato-convex, gradually and regularly curved from base to apex; the commissure gently curved; the outline of the rami straight, or a little concave; the gonys quite straight, slightly ascending; the eminentia symphysis well marked, but not very prominent. Wings long and pointed, typical of the subfamily. Tail long, forked; varying in these respects; but the lateral feathers always elongated, tapering, and filamentous, and the depth of the forfication very considerable. Tarsus slender, compressed, a little shorter than the middle toe and claw, slightly longer than the middle toe alone, much shorter than the bill, about as long as the ramus of the inferior maxilla. Toes moderately long. Webs moderately broad and incised; varying in this respect, but never so deeply cut out as in *Hydrochelidon*. Size moderate, or very small; general form slender and graceful. Head without a decided occipital crest. A black pileum; the back some shade of blue; the primaries variegated with black and white, and silvery; the under parts white, with or without a plumbeous or rosy tinge.

The genus *Sterna*, as restricted by most later ornithologists, includes the numerous species which are closely allied to *S. hirundo*. They agree very closely in size, general form and proportion, and pattern of coloration, as well as in seasonal changes of plumage. So closely is this resemblance maintained, that it is with some difficulty that the group can be divided into sections. Specific characters likewise are sometimes a little obscure, especially when we have to deal with immature specimens.

In winter the species lose the bright color of the bill and tarsi, to a greater or less degree, and also the black pileum, which is mostly restricted to an occipital patch, and a fascia on each side of the head. The long-forked tail is shortened; the lateral feathers have little of the elongated filamentous character they possess in summer. The young-of-the-year resemble the adults in winter in most points, but are generally variegated on the upper parts with brown markings.

Of the many species of the genus, nine or ten are known to inhabit North America. Of these, three (*hirundo*, *macrura*, and *paradisea*) are common to Europe and America, while of those remaining, two have a wide tropical dispersion. They may be recognized by the following brief diagnoses:

Analysis of North American species of STERNA.

A. Mantle pearl-gray.
    I. No black cap.
        Head whitish, with black bar through eye ; under parts like the
        mantle .... *trudeaui.*
    II. A black cap.
        a. No white frontal crescent.
            a'. Bill wholly or mostly red or reddish.
                Bill red, blackening at end. Feet coral-red. Outer
                web of outer tail feather, white ; inner, gray or
                dark. Tarsus 0.90, or more........................ *forsteri.*
                Bill red, blackening at end. Feet coral-red. Outer
                web of outer tail feather, gray or dark ; inner,
                white. Tarsus about 0.75. Under parts decidedly
                paler than upper .... *hirundo.*
                Bill wholly red. Feet vermilion. Tail feather as in
                the last. Tarsus 0.65, or less. Under parts nearly
                like upper .... *macrura.*
            b'. Bill black, often red at the base. Feet reddish........ *paradisea.*
        b. A white frontal crescent.
            Bill yellow, tipped with black. Feet yellow............ *superciliaris.*
            Bill and feet black.. *aleutica.*
B. Mantle dusky. A white frontal crescent. Bill black.
    Mantle blackish-brown ; crown the same........................... *fuliginosa.*
    Mantle smoky gray ; crown much darker........................... *anosthæta.*

NOTE.—The above analysis is based upon adult summer birds, and is not available for the young in which the characters, especially of color of the bill and feet, may be materially different. These, especially of Sec. II, can only be determined by reference to the detailed descriptions. *S. portlandica* is not presented here.

STERNA TRUDEAUI, Aud.

Trudeau's Tern.

Sterna trudeaui, AUD., Orn. Biog. v, 1839, 125, pl. 409 ; Syn. 1839, 319 ; B. Am. vii, 1844,
    105, pl. 435 (New Jersey and Long Island).—GIR., B. L. I. 1844, 354.—LAWR.,
    B. N. A. 1858, 861.—COUES, Pr. Phila. Acad. 1862, 542.—SCHL., Mus. P.-B. *Sternæ*,
    p. 29.—SCL. & SALV., P. Z. S. 1871, 570.—COUES, Key, 1872, 322.
Thalasseus trudeaui, BP., Comptes Rendus, 1856, 772.
Phoëtusa trudeaui, BLAS., J. f. O. 1866, 73.
Sterna frobeeni, PHIL. & LANDB., Wieg. Arch. 1863, 125 ; Cat. Av. Chil. 49. (*Scl. & Salv.*)

DIAG. *S. corpore perlaceo, capite et tectricibus alarum inferioribus albis, vittâ transoculari nigrâ, rostro rubescente, nigro-cincto, apice flavicante.*

Hab.—South America. Brazil (*Scl. & Salv.*). Chili (*Phil. & Landb. ; Leybold*). Buenos Ayres (*Mus. S. I.*). Atlantic coast of United States (*Audubon & Trudeau*).

Adult, perfect plumage.—The bill is noticeably stout for its length, especially deep at the base. The culmen is regularly curved; the outline of the rami is a little concave, that of the gonys straight and ascending; the gape follows nearly the curve of the culmen. In shape the bill, in fact, almost repeats *forsteri*, and averages the same in length. The tip is broadly straw-yellow; at the base it appears to have been bright colored (probably reddish); a broad band of black intervenes. The whole head is pure white, including all the parts about the base of the bill; this deepens insensibly into the pearly color all around. There is a narrow distinct bar of slaty-black on the side of the head, passing through the eye from a point just in advance of the auriculars, where the fascia widens and bends down a little. All the rest of the plumage, below as well as above, is of a uniform lustrous pale pearly, with the following exceptions: The under surfaces of the wings are pure white; the tail, with its coverts and the rump, are white, but still with an appreciable pearly tint; the tips, and part of the inner vanes of the secondaries and tertials, are white; the primaries have the picture common to most Terns, with a white space on the inner webs; their darker portions are beautifully silvered over with hoary gray, which makes them appear paler than usual; the shafts are white above and below, except at the extreme tips; the feet appear to have been reddish or yellowish, certainly of some bright color.

Dimensions.—Wing, 10.25; tail, 6.50; depth of the fork, 2.75; bill, along culmen, 1.50; its depth at base, 0.38; length of gonys, 1.75; tarsus, 0.90; middle toe and claw, 1.05.

A specimen belonging to J. P. Giraud, esq., believed to be the original of Audubon's plate and description, agrees minutely with the one from which the foregoing description was taken from Buenos Ayres (No. 45801, Mus. Smiths.). In my above-quoted article I discussed the relationships of Audubon's type to *S. forsteri* rather elaborately, but not very satisfactorily, in as far as considering it as possibly that species is concerned. I was deceived by the great similarity in its size and proportions to *forsteri*, and was under the wrong impression that it might gain a black cap. It is clear to me that *trudeaui* is perfectly distinct from all other North American species, and that it never gains a black cap; it is, in fact, one of the most remarkable of all the Terns. I am under the impression that *trudeaui* is not its first name, believing it to be one of Vieillot's species; but I cannot now make a determination.

The species requires comparison with no other, its coloration being peculiar if not unique. In addition to the two specimens above referred to, I have, if my memory be not at fault, seen another in the La Fresnaye collection, now in Boston, labeled with a Vieillotian name.

The only question is regarding the propriety of introducing the species among North American birds. For myself, I doubt that it was ever actually taken within our limits; but I have no means of disproving one author's positive assertion to that effect.

STERNA FORSTERI, Nutt.

Forster's Tern.

Sterna hirundo, Sw. & RICH., F. B. A. ii, 1831, 412; not of authors.
Sterna forsteri, NUTT., Man. ii, 1834, 274 (foot-note); based on *S. hirundo*, Sw. & RICH.).—
    LAWR., Ann. Lyc. N. Y. v, 1852, 222.—BP., Compt. Rend. 1856, 772.—LAWR., B.
    N. A. 1828, 862.—COUES, Pr. Phila. Acad. 1862, 544.—ELLIOT, B. N. A. Introd.
    (figure of tail).—COUES, Ibis, 1864, 390 (Guatemala).—SALV., Ibis, 1866, 199
    (the same).—BLAS., J. f. O. 1866, 74, 78.—LAWR., Ann. Lyc. N. Y. viii, 1866, 299
    (Long Island).—COUES, Pr. Phila. Acad. 1866, 99 (Arizona).—COUES, Pr. Ess.
    Inst. v, 1868, 308 (New England).—SCL. & SALV., P. Z. S. 1871, 569 (Guatemala
    and Brazil).—COUES, Pr. Phila. Acad. 1871, 44 (North Carolina).—COUES, Key,
    1872, 321.—SNOW, B. Kans. 1873, 12.—RIDGW., A. Lyc. N. Y. x, 1874, 391 (Illinois).
Sterna havelli, AUD., Orn. Biog. v, 1839, 122, pl. 409, f. 1; Syn. 1839, 318; B. Am. viii,
    1844, 103, pl. 434 (young or winter plumage).—LAWR., B. N. Am. 1858, 861.—
    COUES, Pr. Phila. Acad. 1862, 543 (refers it to *forsteri*).
Gelochelidon havelli, BP., Comptes Rendus, 1856, 772.

DIAG. *S. Sternæ hirundini similis, sed major, caudâ longiore, magis forficata, alis brevioribus, rostro robustiore, tarsis longioribus, pogonio interno rectricis exterioris griseo, externo albo, gastræo albido.*

Hab.—North America at large. Middle America. South America to Brazil. Only known to breed in the higher latitudes.

Adult, spring plumage.—Bill orange-yellow, black for nearly its terminal half, the extreme points of both mandibles yellowish; robust, deep at the base; culmen markedly declinato-convex, eminence at symphysis well developed; in total length from $\frac{7}{10}$ to $\frac{9}{10}$ of an inch longer than that of *S. hirundo*. The black pileum does not extend so far down on the sides of the head as it does in *hirundo*, barely embracing the eye (the lower lid of which is white), and leaving a considerably wider white space between the eye and commissural edge of superior maxilla than in *hirundo*. The color of the back hardly differs appreciably from that species; it is perhaps a shade lighter. The wings are comparatively considerably shorter than those of *hirundo*, being absolutely a little shorter, though *forsteri* is a larger bird. They are very light colored, being strongly silvered with the peculiar hoariness common to most of the species of the genus, this light color being very observable even on the coverts. The outer web of the first primary is not black, but silvery like the others; all the primaries want the very decided white space on the inner webs which exists in *hirundo* and *macrura;* there are indications of it, indeed, on the three or four outer primaries, but the others are a nearly uniform dusky gray, moderately hoary. The entire under parts are white, with scarcely a trace of the plumbeous which is so evident in *hirundo*, and amounts to so decided a color in *macrura*. The tail is a slightly lighter shade of the color of the mantle, separated from the latter for a short space by the decidedly white rump. The lateral feathers are much more lengthened than in *hirundo*, the elongation generally quite equaling that of *macrura*, and sometimes even exceeding it. These two lateral feathers are white on the outer web, dusky gray on the inner. This being exactly the reverse of *hirundo*, and a very noticeable feature, was the first to draw attention to the bird; and this character being so tangible and convenient, writers have perhaps laid too much stress upon it, to the exclusion of others quite as evident and more important. The feet are bright orange, tinged with vermilion; the tarsus shorter than the middle toe and claw; the feet longer and stouter by over 0.10 of an inch than the same parts in *hirundo*.

Adult, winter plumage.—The black of the terminal portion of the bill increases so much in extent that nearly the whole bill becomes dusky, except a small space at the base of the under mandible, and a terminal space of varying extent. The feet lose their vermilion tinge and become dusky yellowish. The black pileum is more or less variegated with white on the forehead to the almost complete exclusion of the black; but there is always considerable black left on the nape, and a more or less broad and distinct bar always extends along the sides of the head, embracing the eyes. The lateral tail feathers have not the elongation and attenuation of those of summer, being but little, if any, longer than those of *hirundo* during the breeding season. The color of the inner web is usually somewhat darker, and sometimes extends on the outer as well as the inner, especially toward the tip of the feather.

At the time of the moult the old primaries lose their silvering and become plain brown and white, their shafts being of a decided yellow. The inner webs at this season have white spaces, with nearly as distinctly-defined margins as are found in *hirundo* and *macrura*.

Young.—Bill in all its proportions considerably smaller and weaker than that of the adults, and wanting its very acute tip and sharply-defined ridges and angles; brownish-black, fading into dull flesh-color at the base of the under mandible. Front white, but the crown and nape show considerable traces of the black that is to appear, which is now mixed with a good deal of light brown. The pearl-blue of the back and wing-coverts is everywhere interrupted by irregular patches of light grayish-brown, showing a tendency to become transverse bars; this grayish-brown on the tertials deepens into brownish-black, and occupies nearly the whole extent of each feather. The primaries differ from those of the adult in having less of the silvery gloss, and the inner white spaces are more marked, being in fact like those of the adult *hirundo*. The rump and under parts are pure white. The tail intensifies, so to speak, its adult characters as regards color; and, independently of any other feature, will always serve to identify the species. It is deeply emarginate, but the lateral feather is not greatly produced, surpassing the second by scarcely more than the latter surpasses the third. Its inner web, for an inch or so from the tip, and both webs of the other feathers, are quite decidedly grayish-black; the intensity of this color, and also its extent, decreasing successively on each feather from without inward, so that the central pair scarcely deepen their color at the tips. The outer web of the lateral feather generally stays pretty uninterruptedly white, but sometimes is just at the tip invaded by the darker color of its inner web.

The foregoing descriptions embrace all the stages of plumage of this species which are well characterized. Between them, of course, there will be found every gradation. The number of immature specimens of this species which are found in collections, as compared with the adults, is surprising. Fully one-half of all the examples before me are in the *"havelli"* state of plumage, having white fronts and the ordinary ocular fascia. This is doubtless owing to the northern localities in which the bird breeds. Few, if any, United States specimens are to be taken, except in winter.

Sterna forsteri affords a good illustration of a species bearing so intimate a general resemblance to another as to be confounded with it at first glance, and yet when carefully examined proving to be totally distinct. It is perfectly easy to separate it from the *hirundo* by its characters of bill, wings, tail or feet, either of which, *taken alone*, would identify it. The following table will exhibit at a glance the distinctive features of our three most intimately allied species.

Differential diagnoses of S. forsteri, hirundo, and macrura.

S. forsteri : Bill (average), 1.60 along culmen ; depth at base, 0.40 ; robust. Bill orange-yellow, nearly its terminal half black. White space between eye and cutting edge of upper mandible broad. Under parts white. Outer web of first primary silvery ; the inner webs also of the others strongly hoary, without well-defined white spaces. Tail bluish-pearl, like the back, its lateral feather greatly produced (average nearly 7 inches in length); its outer web white, inner the color of the rest of the tail. Legs long and stout. Length of tarsus (average) rather over 0.90 of an inch ; orange-yellow, tinged with vermilion. Length of tarsus, middle toe and claw, 2 inches.

S. hirundo : Bill (average), 1.45 along culmen ; depth at base, 0.33 ; moderate. Bill vermilion-red, its terminal third black. White space between eye and cutting edge of upper mandible narrower than in *forsteri.* Under parts lightly washed with plumbeous, fading into white on the throat and abdomen. Outer web of first primary black ; inner webs of the others somewhat hoary, with well-defined white spaces. Tail white, different from the back, its lateral feather moderately produced (average 6 inches in length); its outer web grayish dusky, inner white. Legs moderate. Length of tarsus about 0.80 of an inch ; light vermilion-red. Length of tarsus, middle toe and claw, 1.75 inches.

S. macrura : Bill (average), 1.30 along culmen ; depth at base, 0.30 ; slender. Bill wholly deep carmine-red. White space between eye and cutting edge of upper mandible narrower than in *hirundo.* Under parts decidedly plumbeous, extending from vent to throat, both of which become abruptly white. Primaries as in *hirundo.* Tail with the elongation of *forsteri*, or rather exceeding it (average 7.50 inches), and the color of *hirundo.* Legs very short and slender. Length of tarsus (average) 0.65 of an inch ; deep vermilion, almost lake. Length of tarsus, middle toe and claw, about 1.50 inches.

Comparison of the young-of-the-year of S. forsteri and hirundo.—The bill and feet constantly present differences proportional to those which exist in the adults, as regards length and stoutness. The bill of *hirundo* is more decidedly yellowish at the base of the lower mandible than in that of *forsteri*, and the feet are clear yellow instead of being tinged with dusky. The mottled and variegated crown and upper parts are much the same in both, and the markings of the quills quite identical. The tail, however, differs remarkably. In *hirundo* the outer webs of all the feathers are dusky gray. In *forsteri* the reverse is the case. The difference is even more marked than in the adults.

Synonymy.—This species was first indicated by Swainson and Richardson, as above, under the name of *Sterna hirundo*, these authors, however, appreciating and commenting upon the differences from that species. Nuttall was the first to give it a specific name, based upon the indications afforded by the authors above mentioned. To Mr. G. N. Lawrence, however, is really due the credit of first establishing the species by giving complete descriptions, and of showing its relationships to *S. hirundo.* This misapplication of Linnæus' name by Swainson and Richardson is, I believe, the only specific synonym (excepting Audubon's "*havelli*"), unless the *Sterna nuttalli* of Nuttall's work (from Audubon's Mss.) is to be referred here, as is probably the case. In Bonaparte's Table of Longipennes (C. R. xlii, 1856, p. 768) not only is *havelli* separated specifically from *forsteri*, but it is placed in a different genus (*Gelochelidon*), while *trudeaui* is made a *Thalasseus.* It is difficult to account for such a misapprehension of their affinities, but vagaries of this sort are too often found in the latest works of this illustrious author. It is unnecessary to reproduce here the argument by which I showed (Pr. A. N. S. Phil. 1862, p. 543) the identity of *havelli* and *forsteri*, for the fact is fully established.

I append the measurements of several specimens of *forsteri*, showing the limits of its variation in size :

Smithsonian Cat. No.	Locality.	Sex.	Wing.	Tail length.	Depth of fork.	Bill length.	Height at base.	Tarsus.	Middle toe and claw.
24274	New Jersey	♂	10.00	6.90	4.00	1.65	0.40	0.94	1.15
12692	....do	×	9.50	7.70	5.00	1.58	0.40	0.91	1.10
11624	....do	×	10.10	6.75	3.60	1.64	0.40	0.90	1.15
4928	Florida	♀	10.30	5.00	2.30	1.50	0.35	0.95	1.14
......	....do	×	9.75	7.00	4.10	1.60	0.40	0.95	1.05
9973	Sac Valley	♂	9.70	6.90	4.00	1.56	0.40	0.90	1.10
13473	Utah	×	9.70	7.70	4.70	1.56	0.49	0.93	1.08
......	California	×	10.30	7.20	3.70	1.55	0.38	0.99	1.15
4317	Louisiana	♂	10.20	6.60	3.55	1.54	0.35	0.90	1.08

The history of Forster's Tern is interesting. It is singular that so common and widely-distributed a species.should have remained unrecognized as long as it did. Swainson and Richardson described it as the Common Tern; Wilson did not know it at all, and Audubon only became aware of it in the imperfect plumage which he described as "*havelli*." Nuttall doubtingly gave it a name upon the strength of Richardson's description. Mr. Lawrence, in 1858, was the first to elucidate its characters satisfactorily, while it was not until the appearance of my paper that its changes of plumage became known. It bears, indeed, a close resemblance to Wilson's Tern, yet is perfectly distinct, the curious difference in the colors of the two webs of the outer tail feathers being only one of several strong characters. In fact, I learned to distinguish the two species at gun-shot range, when they are, in winter dress, so different are they at that season. Forster's then has the crown white, the occiput blackish, and a remarkably distinct black transocular fascia, better marked than in any other species of ours. The bill is nearly as in summer, but not so bright; the feet are orange instead of red. This plumage was finished in all of a number of old birds shot the second week in September. The young-of-the-year have the whole head white, faintly washed with brownish, except the transocular fascia, which is pure black, and very sharply defined; but nearly all the feathers of the crown have dusky bases, that will increase during the fall and coming winter until the condition above noticed is attained. The eye-stripe is 1¼ inch long and about ½ an inch wide, reaching from the lores through the eyes to and over the auriculars. The blue mantle only partly appears at this time, being lightly washed over with gray and clear brown; the rectrices are heavily dusky, as in *hirundo* at the same season, but the dark color is on opposite webs in the two species. The wing-feathers are new and perfect, and more hoary-silvery than those of *hirundo* of the same age; but the pattern of coloration is exactly duplicated. The feet are yellow, more or less obscured with dusky.

No Tern of this country is more widely and generally distributed than this one. It may be found in every part of the country, at one season or another, and in the interior, especially, almost replaces *hirundo*, being in fact the most characteristic of the species. Doubtless some of the local quotations of "*hirundo*" from interior States really refer to this species. It appears to be hardier than some of its allies, as it winters on our Atlantic coast north of Long Island, while most others proceed further south at this season. It is the commonest Tern, in winter and during the migrations, in the harbor of Baltimore. Nevertheless, its wanderings at this season are pushed to South America. On the Carolina coast it is chiefly a migrant, but also a winter resident. Comparing it with *hirundo*, it is there seen to be the more northerly species of the two, migrating earlier in the spring and later in the fall, besides wintering where *S. hirundo* does not. A few of Forster's Terns come back to the Carolinas in August; they become abundant the following month, and there is little or no decrease of their numbers until December, when a part go further south, to return the latter part of March, and the rest remain. It is one of the most plentiful Terns on the harbor of Beaufort in October and November, when it may be distinguished at any reasonable distance with ease, Wilson's Tern being the only one at all resembling it, and this being differently marked about the head at this season. Quite early in the spring it leaves for its northern breeding-grounds, generally acquiring its complete plumage before it leaves the United States. It breeds in the interior of British America, and very abundantly, to judge from the great number of eggs from that region I have seen. It may yet be found to nest on or near the northern tier of States. Of its general habits there is little to be said, as they agree entirely with those of its well-known allies.

STERNA HIRUNDO, Auct.

Common Tern.

Sterna hirundo, (?) LINN., Fn. Suec. 158; Syst. Nat. i, 227 (*S. major*, BRISS., Orn. vi, 203, pl. 19, f. 1; "*rostrum pedesque rubri*"—may have been *macrura*). (Not of Brünnich, Fabricius, Faber, or Richardson.)—SCHÆFF., Mus. Orn. 1779, 65.—GM., Syst. Nat. i, 1788, 606.—LATH., Ind. Orn. ii, 1790, 807.—BECHST., Naturg. iv. 1802, 682.—MEY. & WOLF, Tasch. ii, 1810, 459.—WILS., Am. Orn. vii, 1813, 76, pl. 60, f. 1.—TEMM., Man. 1815, 481.—LEACH, Cat. 1816, 41.—VIEILL., N. D. xxxii, 1819, 172.—TEMM., Man. ii, 1820, 740.—NILSS., Orn. Suec. ii, 1821, 156.—BOIE, Isis, 1822, 563.—STEPH., G. Z. xii, 150, pl. 18.—VIEILL., Fn. Franç. 1828, 401.—BP., Syn. 1828, 354.—FLEM., Br. An. 1828, 143.—KAUP, Sk. Ent. Eur. Thierw. 1829, 26.—BREHM, V. D. 1831, 781.—LESS., Tr. Orn. 1831, 621.—NUTT., Man. ii, 1834, 271.—JEN., Man. 1835, 266.—BP., List, 1838, 61.—AUD., Orn. Biog. iv, 1838, 74, pl. 309; Syn. 1839, 318; B. Am. vii, 1844, 97, pl. 433.—KEYS. & BLAS., Wirb. Eur. 1840, 97.—SCHINZ, Eur. Fn. 1840, 373.—NAUM., V. D. x, 1840, 89, pl. 252.—MACGIL., Man. Orn. ii, 1842, 231.—SCHL., Rev. Crit. Ois. Eur. 1844, 129.—DE KAY, N. Y. Fn. ii, 1844, 298, pl. 125, figs. 275, 276.—GIR., B. L. I. 1844, 347.—DEGL., Orn. Eur. ii, 1849, 342.—GRAY, Gen. of B. iii, 1849, 659; List Br. B. 1863, 240.—THOMPS., Nat. Hist. Irel. iii, 1851, 281.—PUTN., Pr. Ess. Inst. i, 1856, 221.—COUES, Pr. Phila. Acad. 1862, 547.—VERR., Pr. Ess. Inst. iii, 1862, 161 (Maine).—BLAS., J. f. O. 1866, 78.—LAWR., Ann. Lyc. N. Y. viii, 1866, 299 (New York).—ALLEN, Pr. Ess. Inst. iv, 1864, 90 (New England).—COUES, *ibid.* v, 1868, 308 (the same).—COUES, Pr. Bost. Soc. xii, 1868, 126 (South Carolina).—ALLEN, Am. Nat. iii, 1870, 641.—TURNB., B. E. Pa. 1869, 39.—COUES, Pr. Phila. Acad. 1871, 43 (North Carolina, migratory.)—COUES, Key, 1872, 320.—COUES, Check-list, No. 565.—ALLEN, Bull. M. C. Z. ii, 1871 (Florida, winter).—MAYN., Guide, 1870, 152.—RIDGW., Ann. Lyc. N. Y. x, 1874, 391 (Illinois).

Hydrocecropis hirundo, BOIE, Isis, 1844, 179.
Sterna nilotica, HASSELQ. (*Fide Blas.*)
Sterna fluviatilis, NAUM., Isis, 1820, p. —.—BREHM, V. D. 1831, 779.—BP., Compt. Rend. 1856, 772.—GRAY, Hand-list, iii, 1871, 118, No. 11021.
Sterna pomarina, BREHM, V. D. 1841, 781.
Sterna blasii, BREHM. (*Gray*)
(?) *Sterna marina*, EYT., Cat. Br. B. 1836, 55 (by some assigned to *macrura*).
Sterna wilsoni, BP., List, 1838, 61.—LAWR., B. N. A. 1858, 861.—BRY., Pr. Bost. Soc. vii, 1859, 134 (Bahamas).—WHEAT., Ohio Agric. Rep. 1860, No. 273.—COUES, Pr. Phila. Acad. 1861, 247 (Labrador).—COUES & PRENT., Smiths. Rep. 1861, 418 (Washington, D. C.).—BOARDM., Pr. Bost. Soc. ix, 1862, 131 (Maine).—DRESS., Ibis, 1865, 44 (Texas, breeds).—SNOW, B. Kans. 1873, 12 (Kansas, rare).

DIAG. *S. rostro rubro, in apicem nigricante, pedibus rubris, pileo nigro, pallio perlaceo, gastræo ex albido perlaceo, pogonio exteriori rectricis exterioris griseo-plumbeo vel fusco.*

Hab.—Europe. North America generally. Not on the Pacific side (?). Bahamas. No West Indian or Central American record (?). Breeds variously in its North American range; winters in the United States north to 57°; passes beyond Texas (*Audubon*). (PELZELN'S record of "*wilsoni*," p. 325, Brazil, really refers to *cassini*; *fide* SCL. & SALV., P. Z. S. 1871, 565.)

Adult, summer plumage—Bill as long as the head, about equaling the tarsus and middle toe without the claw, of moderate robustness, its height at the base being contained a little more than five times in the length of its culmen. Gonys just as long as the rami, measured from the feathers on the side of the mandible to the eminentia symphysis, which latter is but slightly marked. Nasal groove moderately long and deep, a sulcus, bounded above and below by a stria, proceeding from it anteriorly to be lost at the tomia about two-thirds the way to the tip. In color it is bright coral, or light vermilion, on its basal half, or rather more than half, the remainder black, except the extreme tips of the mandibles, which are yellowish. The pileum is lustrous velvety-black, with a slight tinge of glossy-green. It extends to the lower level of the eyes, but leaves the lower lids white, and it is so broad on the lores that the white line of feathers along the side of the mandible is very narrow, and hardly reaches to the very extremity of the feathers.   The whole upper parts are grayish-blue, or rather deep pearl-blue, this color commencing insensibly on the back of the neck, deepening on the dorsum, and extending, quite undiluted, almost to the extreme apices of the tertials.   The bluish color, however, ends quite abruptly and distinctly on the rump, so that the superior caudal rectrices are pure white.   The under parts are of a considerably lighter shade of the color of the back.   On the throat, toward the chin and along the borders of the black pileum, it fades into nearly or quite pure white, as it does also on the inferior caudal tectrices and the circumanal region.   The inferior surfaces of the wings and the axillary feathers are pure white.   The shafts of all the primaries are on their superior and inferior aspects white, but deepen into blackish toward their apices.   The outer web of the first primary is black, with scarcely any hoariness.   The first four or five primaries are grayish-black, with a very strong silvery hoariness; their inner webs with a space of white along their inner margins. This space on the first primary at the base occupies the whole web, becomes narrower as it ascends, and ends, or becomes a mere line, about an inch from the apex of the quill.   On the other primaries it is of less extent, and runs up along the centre of the shaft a little further than on the edge.   On the innermost primaries, again, it is very narrow, but forms an entire margin to the inner webs, running quite to their tips. The inner primaries have scarcely any grayish-black, but are rather of the color of the mantle.   The secondaries are mostly pure white, but toward their ends have a space grayish-blue of about equal extent on both webs.   The tail is moderately elongated and forked, contained about 1¾ times in the wing; the folded wings reach one to two inches beyond it.   The central feathers are broad to their evenly rounded tips; the lateral ones successively narrower, more tapering and acute.   The under tail-coverts reach to the very tips of the central rectrices; the upper fall a little short of them.   The rectrices are on their outer webs light pearl-gray (very like the back), their inner webs nearly pure white.   The external pair, however, are on most of their inner webs, especially terminally, grayish-blue, while their outer webs are dark grayish-black.[*] Legs and feet light coral-red.

Dimensions.—Length (average), 14.50 inches; extent, about 31; wing, from the carpus, 10.50; tail, 6; depth of fork, 3.50 (average); bill, along culmen, 1.35; height at base, 0.33; from feathers on side of lower mandible to tip, 1.60; gonys, 0.80; gape, 2.10; tibiæ bare, 0.50; tarsus, 0.80 to 0.85; middle toe 0.75, its claw 0.30; outer 0.70, its claw 0.18; inner 0.48, its claw 0.14; hallux, with its claw, 0.28; whole foot, about 1.75.   Mr. Allen has given some elaborate tables of measurements, showing the following range of variation in size of adult birds from the same locality in the breeding season.   The extreme range, so far as I am aware, is as follows: length, 13 to 16; extent, 29 to 32; wing, 9.75 to 11.75; tail, 5 to 7; tarsus, 0.66 to 0.87; bill, 1.25 to 1.50. Females average a little less than the males.   Young fall under the above minima; length down to 12, wing to 9, tail to 4, bill to 1.12, &c.

Young-of-the-year in August.—Upper mandible brown, becoming blackish on the culmen toward the tip, and somewhat flesh-colored basally along the tomia.   Under mandible light yellow, darkening into brown toward the tip.   Mouth yellow; feet dull yellow, with scarcely a tinge of reddish.   Forehead grayish-white; on the vertex this gray is intermixed with large, roundish, illy-defined spots of blackish; on the occiput and nape the black is the prevailing color, the extreme tips of the feathers only being gray.   On the sides of the head, as far as the eyes, the black is also nearly pure.   The ground color of the upper parts is a rather lighter shade of the pearl-blue of the adults, but every feather is tipped with dull, light gray, and has a subterminal spot (generally a crescent or semicircle) of light brown.   These spots and tips are quite conspicuous, and give perhaps the predominating color to the upper parts; but they are not so distinctly defined, nor so dark, as in *macrura*.   The lesser wing-coverts along the edge of the fore-arm form a continuous band of nearly pure brownish-black.   The lesser and median coverts are conspicuously tipped with yellowish-gray.   The greater secondaries, however, fade into nearly pure white at their tips.   The secondaries are white, with the outer web, except at tip, and the median portion of the inner web, dark plumbeous or ashy-gray.   The primaries are colored almost exactly as in the adults.   The rump is white, with a tinge of pearl-blue.   The tail is but slightly forked, the emargination being but little more than an inch.   The inner webs of all the rectrices are nearly pure white, but the outer webs are plumbeous-gray, increasing in intensity from within outward; so that the outer pair of rectrices, which are but little tapering or elongated, have their outer webs grayish-black, deepest toward their tips.   The entire under plumage, including the under wing-coverts, is pure white, with no trace of the plumbeous wash of the adults.

I have never seen the adult winter plumage of this species, and am therefore unable

---

[*] I have seen a single undoubted specimen of this species which had the outer web of the exterior tail feathers, as well as the inner, almost pure white, both webs being of the same color as in *paradisea*.   This, however, must be very rare.

to present it. This I regret the more since it does not seem to be generally known, and even quite diverse accounts of its winter dress are given by authors. Temminck, for example, says that in winter the adults do not lose the black of the crown; " elle est seulement plus terne." Other authors ascribe to it a condition of plumage very similar to that presented by *S. forsteri* or *macrura*, and I have myself little doubt but that such is really their condition at that season. Naumann, one of the most exhaustive describers of the changes of plumage of birds, is unable to give a very satisfactory account of this plumage, for the reason, as he says, "that so long as the winter range of habitat of this species remains unknown to us, it will always be difficult to give an account of the winter plumage of the fully moulted bird." He says, however, that the forehead and cheeks are white, more or less variegated with black ; the middle of the crown white, lightly spotted or streaked with black; occiput and nape almost wholly black. In other respects, I think that the upper and under parts will both be found to be lighter than in summer, the latter especially approaching to the pure white of the young bird; the tail will be shorter and less deeply forked ; the bill and feet duller red, the former more invaded by the black of the terminal portion. Audubon says that "in winter the bill is black, with the base pale orange and the tip yellowish; the feet orange-yellow. The colors are as in the adults, the forehead white, the rest of the head dusky, the upper parts having the feathers slightly edged with lighter."

Other variations.—These consist, as usual in the subfamily, chiefly in the total size, individuals varying considerably in this respect. (See above measurements.) I scarcely find any variations in color worth noticing in specimens of equal ages at corresponding seasons. The amount of black on the bill may be increased or diminished, but I have never seen it equal in amount to that of *S. fosteri* or *longipennis*, nor yet entirely absent, as is usually the case with *S. macrura*.

Comparison with allied species.—The present being the typical species of the group, it is taken as the standard with which to compare other species; and the differences of each of them from it will be found under their respective heads.

Degland, in his Ornithologie Européenne, speaks of the occurrence of a hybrid of this species and the *S. macrura* partaking in a varying degree of the characters of either parent. Though I have never met with a specimen which I could not unhesitatingly refer to one or the other species, it is not improbable that hybrids should really occur.

Comparison of American and European bird.—Being desirous of determining definitely the relationships of our bird to that of Europe, I procured for examination an extensive series from both countries, comprising some fifty specimens. These I carefully compared in their most minute details, and in no respect could I detect the slightest discrepancy. This is contrary alike to late high authority on the subject and to my own preconceived ideas. It would be difficult to say upon what grounds the validity of *S. "wilsoni"* has been maintained, since no definite characters have ever been laid down whereby it may be separated from *S. hirundo*. The American bird was first distinguished from the European by Bonaparte, in 1838, in his Comparative List; but no diagnosis is offered. *S. "wilsoni"* is one of several species introduced by this author in the same work, for the distinguishing of which from their European representatives he seems to have relied upon some preconceived theory of geographical distribution, rather than upon any characters afforded by the birds themselves. I present the detailed measurements of five American and five European birds, taken at random from a large series. It will be noticed that in no respect do the dimensions of the birds from the two continents present greater differences than are found in the several examples from either.

A.—*S. hirundo ex Europâ.*

| Smithsonian Cat. No. | Sex. | Locality. | Wing. | Tail. | | Bill. | | Tarsus. | Middle toe and claw. |
				Outer feather.	Depth of fork.	Length.	Height at base.		
9559	♀	Europe............	10.30*	5.70	2.65	1.38	0.33	0,81	0.97
24280	♂	Holland......	9.80	5.60	2.60	1.51	0.31	0.78	0.90
21680	♂	Hungary......	10.80	6.20	2.70	1.45	0.36	0.80	0.90
23444	♀	....do	10.60	5.90	2.70	1.45	0.32	0.84	0.96
23445	♂	....do	10.80	6.50	3.00	1.35	0.31	0.80	0.90

* Inches and hundredths.

B.—*S. hirundo ex Americâ.*

Smithsonian Cat. No.	Sex.	Locality.	Wing.	Tail.		Bill.		Tarsus.	Middle toe and claw.
				Outer feather.	Depth of fork.	Length.	Height at base.		
18224	✕	Labrador............	11.00*	6.50	3.10	1.50	0.32	0.84	0.98
22287	✕	Massachusetts......	10.40	5.90	3.02	1.41	0.31	0.78	0.93
1149	♀	Cape May, N. J......	10.60	6.40	2.85.	1.36	0.31	0.78	0.93
20811	♂	Hudson's Bay.......	10.40	5.90	2.85	1.50	0.32	0.78	0.95
12474	♂	Utah..............	10.50	6.00	2.50	1.51	0.35	0.80	0.95

* Inches and hundredths.

Anatomical characters.—The mouth is only moderately large, it being exceedingly narrow anteriorly, and only widening toward the fauces, where, however, the divergence of the tomia gives it considerable breadth. The palate is concave antero-posteriorly, but is nearly flat laterally. It is soft and vascular only for about two-thirds its length, the anterior third being corneous, and being merely a deep, narrow, longitudinal depression for the reception of the closely-approximated rami of the inferior maxilla. This single depression bifurcates about three-fourths of an inch from the tip, and for the rest of the extent of the palate there is a deep depression on each side, just within the superior tomia and zygoma, for the reception of the devaricating rami of the inferior maxilla. On the median line there is a slightly marked ridge, very short, however, and quickly bifurcating to form the fissure of the posterior nares. The edges of this median elevation, on which the nares open, are beset with a single row of small obtuse papillæ. On either side of the median line is a longitudinal sulcus, which separates a lateral longitudinal ridge, which is beset posteriorly with more prominent and acutely-pointed papillæ. These various ridges and sulci all terminate in papillated extremities. Beyond them the palate is quite smooth, somewhat vaulted, still divided in two by the backward continuance of the nasal fissure. This vaulted portion is bounded posteriorly by two obliquely-placed curved rows of small acute papillæ, containing between them an oval foramen, the opening of the Eustachian tube.

The floor of the mouth has the form of an elongated, narrow isosceles triangle with concave sides. The rami are so closely approximated from the commencement of the symphysis as merely to leave room for the reception of the tongue. The floor of the mouth, though dilatable, is not so much so as in the other subfamilies, and the soft membranes terminate fully an inch from the tip. The tongue arises about opposite the termination of the feathers on the side of the mandible. It measures an inch and a quarter in length; it is exceedingly slender throughout its whole length, and tapers to a very fine and acute apex, which is not bifid. It is soft and fleshy only for a third of its length, the remainder being quite corneous. Its dorsum has a pretty well-marked longitudinal sulcus. It terminates posteriorly in an elevated, bifid, papillated extremity, the ends of the cornua being free and projecting. The rima glottidis begins about a third of an inch from the end of the tongue, and is two-tenths of an inch long. It has no papillæ along its edges, but its termination is papillate, and a row of papillæ extend transversely on either side. Near the angle of the mouth the mucous membrane is thrown up into irregular folds, the beginning of the regular longitudinal œsophageal ones. The disposition of the muscular layers of the floor of the mouth presents nothing peculiar.

The œsophagus measures about four inches in total length, including the proventriculus. It is of pretty uniform diameter throughout, but enlarges a little toward its termination; but the proventriculus is the direct continuation of it, and is not suddenly nor notably larger than the gullet itself. It is, as usual, capable of great distension. When undistended, the mucous membrane is thrown up into numerous longitudinal folds, quite straight except just at the commencement of the tube, where they are somewhat waved. The canal has evidently great contractile power, from the thickness of the two layers of muscular fibres which inclose it.

The belt of proventricular glands is about a third of an inch broad. They form an uninterrupted zone quite around the circumference of the canal, the margin of the girdle being straight and well defined. The color of the mucous membrane is here darker than elsewhere, and has also a difference of texture quite appreciable to the naked eye and to the touch. The orifices of the solvent glands may be seen as minute punctures, scattered thickly and evenly over the whole surface.

The gigerium is very small, not larger in external circumference than the proventriculus. It supervenes without any interval, and without any change of direction, directly upon the proventriculus, with which it communicates by a large orifice. It is flattened and suboval; its distal extremity a little elongated, so as to give it some-what of a cordiform contour. It is evidently not very powerful, its muscles being hardly a tenth of an inch thick. The tendinous portion of its parietes is of small extent: Its cuticular lining is dense and firm, and thrown up into somewhat irregular but chiefly longitudinal folds. Corresponding elevations and depressions are found on the inner surface of the proper parietes of the organ. There are no pyloric valves, but only corrugations of the cuticular lining at this orifice.

The intestinal canal is very short, measuring only between twelve and thirteen inches between the pylorus and anus. The duodenal fold is about one and a half inches in length. The pancreas stretches the whole length of the concavity between the two folds, and appears as if double, there being an elongated, narrow, flattened mass of the glandular substance on each side of the fold. After forming this fold the intestines become convoluted and coiled upon each other to within three or four inches of the cœca. There another regular loop or fold of the intestine occurs, nearly as large and perfect as the duodenal one itself, against which it is opposed for nearly its whole extent, and connected by reflections of the mesentery.

There are two *cœca coli*, situate about one and a half inches from the anus. They differ greatly from those of *Lestridinœ* and *Larinœ* in their extreme brevity. They measure only about two-tenths of an inch in total length, and are so closely applied and bound down to the colon that they might readily be overlooked.

The "large" intestine is exceedingly short, straight, and scarcely, if at all, larger than the small intestine. It preserves a pretty uniform width to near the anus, where it suddenly expands into a capacious globular cloaca. The cloaca is completely divided into two parts—a larger anterior and internal portion, and a smaller posterior and external. The latter is a slight pouch, or *cul-de-sac*, partially separated from the former by a projecting transverse reduplication of the lining membrane. Just above the edge of this fold, at the extremity of the inner compartment of the cloaca, there is on each side of the median line a small oval depression, surrounded by a corrugated, sphincter-like elevation of mucous membrane, in which the efferent ducts of the urinary and seminal organs terminate.

The kidneys are quite peculiar in shape. The entire renal mass is nearly as long as broad, and in shape almost perfectly rectangular. The upper lobes have but a slight convexity of contour, and are but little larger than the lower. Each kidney is divided into from four to six irregularly rectangular or polyhedral masses. These lobes are more or less completely separated from each other, but are closely coaptated, the sides and angles of each mass being adapted to those of the masses which lie about it. The ureters, formed by the union of the efferent ducts from each one of these masses, run along nearly parallel to each other on each side of the median line of the spine, at a little distance from it, converging somewhat toward their termination to open in the cloaca, as already described.

The testes lie immediately superimposed upon the superior lobes of the kidneys. Their size varies greatly with age and season. The vas deferens runs backward in close relation to the ureters, to terminate in the above-mentioned depressions on each side of the cloaca.

The other organs of this species do not differ sufficiently from those of *Larus* to require special mention.

Bibliography.—This is one of the "antique" species, though its synonyms are comparatively few. A chief point that arises is, whether the name "*hirundo*" belongs here or to the Arctic Tern (*macrura*, NAUM.). The name has been with much reason referred to the latter, where it probably belongs; but it scarcely seems necessary to make the change in this instance. The earlier diagnoses may apply to either, and, in fact, probably included both, for it will be remembered that the two were not generally distinguished until about 1820. Linnæus' *hirundo* may as well be kept for this species, with which it is commonly associated in ornithological record. *Hirundo* of Brünnich, Faber, and Fabricius, is apparently *macrura*; *hirundo* of Richardson is *forsteri*. Brisson called the bird *Sterna major*, a name of course to be disregarded in binominal nomenclature. Eyton has it *S. marina*, after a pre-Linnæan writer. "*Wilsoni*, BP.," and "*fluviatilis*, NAUM.," are the two most firmly-established synonyms; but the latter only arose upon reference of *hirundo*, LINN., to *macrura*, while, as I have shown, the former has no basis at all.

It is somewhat singular that the North American range of so common and well known a species as this should not be better made out than it is. A similar uncertainty respecting at least its winter range seems to prevail in the matter of its European distribution. In this country it is attributed to Brazil by Pelzeln, but this is the sole extralimital record I have found, except Dr. Bryant's Bahaman quotation. Messrs. Sclater and Salvin do not give it among Neotropical *Laridœ*. The truth probably is, that it does not proceed beyond the United States, as a rule at least. We have some citations from the interior, but none that I am aware of from the Pacific side. Its track appears to be mainly along the Atlantic coast from Texas to Labrador. My own experience with it is confined to this line, from the Carolinas to Labrador. I find no record north of the last-named region; the bird is obviously not so boreal as *macrura*. It appears to breed at places all along the line indicated. I found it in Labrador in summer, and Mr. Dresser speaks of its breeding in Texas. The New England breeding references are numerous and unanimous. In North Carolina the bird is very common during the migration, arriving from the south early in April, passing on during the following month, and being again abundant during September and October. The numerous specimens I observed at the latter season all retained the black cap, though even in September they had mostly completed the fall moult, being newly feathered, except on the crown, where the black was worn and faded, yet not much mixed with white, excepting, perhaps, a few specks on the forehead. The change of the pileum appears to be very gradual, and, as already intimated, it probably never progresses to a stage in which the cap is mostly white. At this season the feet were simply orange-yellow, not vermilion, and the bill was shaded with dusky throughout. Some of the year's young had nearly perfect wing and tail feathers; but the mantle showed dusky mottling, with some blackish areas on the wing-coverts. Still younger birds were beautifully variegated with gray and light brown. In all the young the feet were yellowish, more or less obscured with dusky; the bill was mostly black, with yellow or orange on the basal part of the under mandibles; the bill was invariably smaller than it is when adult, not so hard, and more obtuse at the tip.

STERNA MACRURA, Naum.

Arctic Tern.

(?) *Sterna hirundo*, BRÜNN., Orn. Bor. 1764.—FABRIC., Fn. Groenl. 1780, 105.—FABER, Prod. Isl. Orn. 1822, 68 (certainly belongs here).—LINN., Syst. Nat. i, 1766, 227.
Sterna hirundo, BP., Compt. Rend. 1856, 772.—GRAY, Hand-list, iii, 1871, 118, No. 11020.— DRESS., B. Eur. pt. xii, 1872; and of other authors who thus identify *hirundo*, LINN.
(?) *Sterna paradisea*, BRÜNN., Orn. Bor. 1764, 42 (most probably).—BLAS., J. f. O. 1866, 74, 78.
Sterna macrura, NAUM, Isis, xii, 1819, p. 1847.—BREHM., V. D. 1831, 784.—NAUM., V. D. x, 1840, 114, pl. 253.—KEYS. & BLAS., Wirb. Eur. 1840, 97.—DEGL., Orn. Eur. ii, 1849, 344.—GRAY, Gen. of B. iii, 1849, 659; List Br. B. 1863, 240.—MIDD., Sib. Reise, ii, 1853, 245.—LAWR., B. N. A. 1858, 862.—WHEAT., Ohio Agric. Rep. 1860, No. 274.—CASS., Pr. Phila. Acad. 1862, 325 (Bering Straits).—COUES, Pr. Phila. Acad. 1862, 549.—BOARDM., Pr. Bost. Soc. ix, 1862, 131 (Maine, breeding).—VERR., Pr. Bost. Soc. ix, 1862, 141 (Anticosti).—VERR., Pr. Ess. Inst. iii, 1862, 161 (Maine, breeding).—ALLEN, Pr. Ess. Inst. iv, 1864, 90 (Massachusetts).—COUES, ibid. v, 1868, 308 (New England).—RADDE, Reise, ii, 1863, 388 (Siberia).—LAWR., Ann. Lyc. N. Y. viii, 1866, 299 (New York).—MALMG., J. f. O. 1865, 200 (Spitzbergen).—NEWT., Ibis, 1865, 506.—DALL & BANN., Tr. Chic. Acad. 1869, 306 (Alaska).—ALLEN, Am. Nat. 1870, 642.—MAYN., Guide, 1870, 152 (Massachusetts, breeding).—COUES, Key, 1872, 321; Check-list, No. 567.—DALL, Pr. Cal. Acad. 1873 and 1874, p. — (Aleutian Islands).
Sterna arctica, TEMM., Man. ii, 1820, 742.—BOIE, Isis, 1822, 563.—STEPH., G. Z. xiii, 152.— FLEM., Br. B. 1828, 144.—BP., Syn. 1828, 354.—KAUP, Sk. Ent. Eur. Thierw. 1829, 26.—BREHM., V. D. 1831, 785.—LESS., Tr. Orn. 1831, 631.—SW. & RICH., F. B. A. ii, 1831, 414.—NUTT., Man. ii, 1834, 275.—JEN., Man. 1835, 267.—EYT., Cat. Br. B. 1836, 54.—AUD., Orn. Biog. iii, 1835, 366, pl. 250; Syn. 1839, 319; B. Am. vii, 1844, 107, pl. 424.—BP., List, 1838, 61.—SCHINZ, Eur. Fn. 1840, 373.— MACGIL., Man. ii, 1842, 232.—SCHL., Rev. Crit. 1844, 129.—PUTN., Pr. Ess. Inst. i, 1856, 221 (Massachusetts).—BRY., Pr. Bost. Soc. vi, 1858, 120.—TURNB., B. E. Pa. 1869, 139 (autumn and winter).

Sterna argentata, BREHM, Beitr. iii, 1822, 692; V. D. 1831, 782, pl. 38, fig. 5.
Sterna argentacea, BREHM, V. D. 1831, 783.
Sterna nitzschii, KAUP, Isis, 1824, 153.—BREHM, V. D. 1831, 786.—BP., C. R. 1856, 772.
Sterna brachytarsa, GRABA, Reise nach Faroe, 1830, 218.
Sterna brachypus, SWAINSON, B. W. Afr. ii, 1837, 252.
Sterna coccineirostris, REICH. (*fide* GRAY).—BP., Compt. Rend. 1856, 772.
Sterna pikei, LAWR., Ann. Lyc. N. Y. vi, 1853, 3; B. N. A. 1858, 853, pl. 95.—BP., Compt. Rend. 1856, 772 ("*pykii*").—COUES, Pr. Phila. Acad. 1862, 550.

DIAG. *St. rostro gracile, rubro ; pedibus brevissimis, rubris ; corpore cœrulescente-plumbeo, subtus dilutiore ; caudâ, uropygio, tectricibusque caudalibus inferioribus albis ; rectrice laterali valdè elongatâ, pogonio externo griseo-fusco.*

Hab.—Europe. Asia. Africa. North America generally, south to the Middle States, and on the Pacific side to California. Breeds from Massachusetts northward. No valid extralimital record south of the United States; compare, however, PHILLIPPI, Cat. 1869, 49 (Chili !! ?).

Adult in breeding plumage.—Bill shorter than the head, equal to the middle toe and tarsus together, slender, compressed, acute. Culmen somewhat broad and flattish toward the base, more compressed and narrower anteriorly; about straight to beyond the nostrils, declinato-convex for the rest of its length. Commissure very slightly curved. Gonys about as long as the rami; perfectly straight; the outline of the latter a little concave. Inter-crural space very narrow; about half filled with feathers. Nasal groove rather long, but becoming obsolete before it reaches the tomia. A quite prominent stria proceeds from its anterior extremity to the tomia, but little behind the tip of the bill. The bill is deep carmine, or lake red; usually without any black, but this color sometimes appears in a limited degree.

The feet are remarkably small and weak. The tibiæ are bare for a moderate distance. The tarsi are exceedingly short, being less than the middle toe without its claw, or, at least, only equal to it. The toes are rather long for the size of the feet; the outer falls but little short of the middle one, while the tip of the claw of the inner hardly reaches beyond the third articulation of the middle one. Hallux of ordinary relative length. Webs rather narrow; moderately emarginated; the inner, as usual, the most so. The feet are a lighter tint of the color of the bill, somewhat tending toward vermilion or coral-red, but are not so light as those of *hirundo*.

The wings are very long; the primaries attenuated, narrow, tapering to their roundish but slender apices. The tertials are short, and do not reach half way to the tips of the primaries in the folded wing. The shafts of all are white, with scarcely darker tips. The outer web of the first primary is grayish-black, lightening into silvery-gray at its tip; its inner web is white, with only a very narrow line of grayish-dusky along the shaft. This longitudinal dusky space is very much narrower and lighter than in *hirundo*, so much so, that it is placed as a diagnostic feature by Naumann in his "Keunzeichen der Art." The next four or five primaries are silvery-gray, darkest toward their tips; their inner webs mostly white (wholly so at their bases); but the white does not extend so far toward the tips of the feathers as on the first primary, and it runs up farther in the centre of the web than on the edge of it. The inner primaries are the color of the back, broadly tipped and margined internally with white.

The tail is exceedingly long, the exterior feather being as much lengthened, and as narrow, tapering and acute, as in *S. paradisea*. The tail feathers reach beyond the tips of the folded wings. The under coverts reach to the extremity of the broad and rounded central rectrices; the upper ones fall short of this length. The tail is pure white, the outer web of its exterior feather being grayish-black, lighter basally, and its inner web, and the outer webs of the next two rectrices, having a considerable wash of pearl-blue.

The pileum is pure, lustrous greenish-black, so broad on the cheeks as to leave only a slender line of white to extend along the edge of the feathers on the side of the upper mandible. The whole upper parts, as far as the superior caudal rectrices, and including the alar coverts, pearl-blue, of about the same shade as in *hirundo*. This color, however, fades into white at the tips of the tertials and inner secondaries. The under parts are but a little lighter shade of the color of the back, this color fading insensibly into whitish on the chin, throat, and edges of the black pileum, and ending abruptly at the under tail-coverts, which are pure white, in marked contrast to the rest of the under parts. The inferior alar rectrices and axillary feathers are also pure white.

Winter plumage of the adults.—Differs from the above-described summer plumage chiefly in the color of the feathers of the head, as usual in the subfamily. The forehead is white; the crown white, but marked with narrow shaft-lines of black, which increase from before backward until, on the nape, the black is nearly or quite pure. A lateral stripe, more or less pure and distinct, extends forward on the sides of the head over the auriculars, to just in front of the eye, leaving, however, the eyelids white. Upper parts much as in summer, but the under parts from the chin to the vent, have a much lighter wash of plumbeous. The deep carmine of the bill and feet becomes lighter and duller, but does not assume the coral-red tint of the feet of *hirundo* or *forsteri*. Otherwise generally as in summer.

Plumage of the young-of-the-year.—The bill is much smaller than in the adults, being only $1\frac{1}{2}$ inches long; brownish-black toward its tip; the gonys and the sides of the lower mandible toward the angle of the mouth dull orange-color, as are also the mouth and tongue. The feet are only orange-colored on the soles, being otherwise brownish-red. The tail is much shorter than in the adults, being only 4.75 to 5 inches long, and the outer pair of rectrices are much broader and scarcely at all tapering in form. The forehead is white, the crown streaked with narrow, longitudinal spots of white upon a black ground color, which extends as far as the eyes, and runs back over the temples and auriculars as far as the nape; whole under parts, from the chin, including the inferior caudal tectrices and under surfaces of the wings, pure white. On the back there predominates everywhere a uniform, light bluish-gray (somewhat darker than in *S. hirundo*), all the feathers tipped with yellowish-white or white, most of them with a blackish-brown streak or crescent-shaped spot near the end; these spots darkest on the tertials and inner secondaries, and aggregated into a single, broad, slate-colored streak on the least wing-coverts along the edge of the wing. The ashen-blue primaries deepen into slate color toward their tips; their shafts are white, their inner webs with a longitudinal space of white, the outer web of the first slaty-black. The inner tail feathers are white, as are their shafts; their apices white, each with a subterminal crescent-shaped spot of brownish-black.

When the young have flown for some time, the bill and feet become considerably redder, and the dark spots on the back lighter, though still not so much so as in the young *hirundo*. After their first moult, which begins while they are migrating and only ends when they have reached their winter habitat, they acquire a plumage very like that of the old birds in winter, but still distinguishable from it by the yet remaining dark tips of the tail-feathers. These, however, are gradually lost, growing lighter and lighter until, by the following spring, they differ but slightly from the adults.[*]

The brilliant color of the feet is sometimes washed off on the plumage, staining it red or salmon color.

Dimensions of the adult.—Length (extremely variable from the varying length of the tail), 14 to 17 inches; extent, 29 to 33; wing, from the carpus, 10 to 10.75; tail, usually 7 to 8, sometimes 6.50 to 8.50; depth of fork, 4 to 5; tibiæ bare, 0.45; tarsus, 0.55 to 0.65; middle toe and claw, 0.80 to 0.85; inner toe and claw, 0.55; bill, along culmen, 1.20 to 1.40; height at base, 0.30; from feathers of side of lower mandible to tip, 1.40; gape, 1.90; gonys, 0.75.

Accidental variations.—These are chiefly noticeable in dimensions, and in the intensity of the color of the under parts. The species is subject to very considerable variations in size, even among apparently equally adult examples. The bill, particularly, is sometimes very much smaller than is usual, and much more slender. Thus, *e. g.*, a female from Nova Scotia, before us, has a bill only 1.08, or less than that assigned to *Sterna pikei*; and it is quite as slender as in that species. The tail, as might be expected from its shape, varies greatly. Two adult summer birds before me differ two inches in the amount of elongation of the external rectrices; and one and a half inches is a very

---

[*] The two preceding paragraphs are compiled from Naumann's Naturgeschichte Vögel Deutschlands. Mr. Maynard gave the following description of the same stage:

"*The young-of-the-year in autumn* differs from the preceding in having the forehead quite white; a few white feathers on the back of the head; the black is not quite as intense—more brownish. The feathers of the back are edged with rufous. The shoulders are darker. The tips of the tail-feathers are rufous. The whole under parts are pure white. The white line from the base of the bill is discontinued just in front of the eye, and the portion occupied by it is *quite dusky, almost black*. The feet are dull orange. The bill is black, with the base of the lower mandible orange. * * * * Young-of-the-year are readily distinguished [from *hirundo*] by the rump of *hirundo* being ashy, the feet larger, the tarsi longer, with a smoother appearance. The bill is much the same color, but in *hirundo* it is longer. It never has the dusky appearance below the eye seen in *macrura*."

Messrs. Sharpe and Dresser give the following:

"*Young-bird-of-the-year.*—The upper plumage, though gray like the adult's, is much mottled with blackish, and has all the back-feathers conspicuously tipped with white, the wings and tail feathers being marked in the same manner; the forehead is white, and the hinder part of the head black, mixed on the forepart with a few whitish spots; the cheeks, hinder neck, and entire under surface of the body are pure white, without any admixture of gray; bill black, reddish at base of lower mandible. *Nestling:* Covered with golden-buff down, inclining to ochre, the upper surface varied with little blackish markings; the forehead and throat brownish-black; under surface of the body yellowish-white, with the flanks and lower abdomen inclining to brownish."

common amount of difference. The wing, from the flexure, differs among the several specimens before me almost or quite an inch. The usual length appears to be about ten inches, though many are half an inch longer, and some hardly over nine. The tarsus and toes, both in their relative and absolute lengths, are very constant, hardly varying appreciably in the large series before me.

The color of the bill is pretty constant, a uniform deep lake. Sometimes, however, it acquires considerable of a blackish tinge toward the tip; but the black never equals that of *S. hirundo* in extent. The shade of the color of the under parts may be lighter or darker, but in summer birds it is always darker than in *hirundo*, and extends in nearly or quite full intensity to the under tail-coverts. Its other variations in color are unimportant.

The North Pacific birds of this species are perhaps rather smaller, upon an average, with somewhat slenderer bill and shorter wings, than those of the Atlantic.

Synonymy.—The questions arising chiefly relate to the "*hirundo*" of some of the earlier authors, already considered; but, as intimated under head of the last species, it may not be absolutely necessary to make a change so likely to provoke confusion. Temminck named the bird *arctica* in 1820, but the designation must yield to *macrura*, Naumann (1819), the priority of which Temminck admits, but does not make valid claim to his name in the fact that it is the more appropriate one. *Coccineirostris* of Reichenbach is considered by both Gray and Bonaparte, who separate the North American bird from the European, to belong to the former. I have seen no authentic specimen of it, but it is quite certain that no differences subsist between the birds of the two continents. There seems to be no question whatever of the pertinence here of the names *argentata, argentacea, brachytarsa, nitzschii* and *brachypus*. In considering *pikei* of Lawrence to belong here, I am guided by a very thorough re-examination of the type-specimen, which was not readily accessible when, in the Key, I too hastily referred it to *longipennis*. Satisfied that it was not a distinct species, I followed other authority in assigning it there; but I now find nothing in *S. pikei* not nearly matched by some of the Pacific specimens of *S. macrura* I have latterly examined. What is left of the broken-off bill is rather slenderer than usual, but not noticeably more so than in some young specimens of *macrura*.

STERNA DOUGALLI, Mont.

Roseate Tern.

(??) *Sterna paradisea*, Brünn., Orn. Bor. 1764, 46 (more likely *macrura*).

Sterna paradisea, Keys. & Blas., Wirb. Eur. 1840, 97.—Schl., Rev. Crit. Ois. Eur. 1844, 130.—Degl., Orn. Eur. ii, 1849, 346.—Gray, Gen. of B. iii, 1849, 659; List Br. B. 1863, 239.—Bp., Compt. Rend. 1856, 772.—Lawr., B. N. A. 1858, 863.—(?) Wheat., Ohio Agric. Rep. 1860, No. 275.—Coues, Pr. Phila. Acad. 1862, 551.—Leót., Ois. Trinidad, 539.—Coues, Ibis, 1864, 389 (Honduras).—Salv., Ibis, 1866, 199 (the same).—Gundl., Repert. F. N. i, 392 (Cuba).—Lawr., Ann. Lyc. N. Y. viii, 1866, 299 (New York).—Allen, Pr. Ess. Inst. iv, 1864, 90 (Massachusetts, rare).—Coues, *ibid.* v, 1868, 60 (Massachusetts, common, breeding).—Coues, Pr. Bost. Soc. xii, 1868, 126 (South Carolina, in summer).—Mayn., Guide, 1870, 156 (Massachusetts, common).—Allen, Am. Nat. iii, 1870, 643 (Massachusetts, breeding).—Coues, Key, 1872, 321.

Sterna dougalli, Mont., Orn. Dict. Suppl. 1813.—Leach, Cat. 1816, 41.—Vieill., Nouv. Dict. d'Hist. Nat. xxxii, 1819, 438.—Temm., Man. ii, 1820, 738.—Boie, Isis, 1822, 363.—Steph., Gen. Zool. xiii, 1826, 153.—Flem., Br. An. 1828, 143.—Less., Tr. Orn. 1831, 691.—Brehm, V. D. 1831, 779.—Nutt., Man. ii, 1834, 278.—Jen., Man. 1835, 265.—Eyt., Cat. Br. B. 1836, 55.—Bp., List, 1838, 61.—Aud., Orn. Biog. iii, 1835, 296, pl. 240; Syn. 1839, 320; B. Am. vii, 1844, 112, pl. 437.—Naum., V. D. x. 1840, 78, pl. 251.—Gir., B. L. I. 1844, 351.—Cab., Pr. Bost. Soc. ii, 248 (Massachusetts).—Putn., Pr. Ess. Inst. i, 1856, 221 (Massachusetts).—Turnb., B. E. Pa., 1869, 38.—Sund., Ofv. K. A. Forh. 1869, 589 (St. Bartholomew).—Scl. & Salv., P. Z. S. 1871, 571 (Tropical America).

Thalassœa dougalli, Kaup., Sk. Ent. Eur. Thierw. 1829, 97.

Hydrocecropis dougalli, Boie, Isis, 1844, 179.

Sterna macdougalli, Macgil., Man. ii, 1842, 233.

Sterna douglasi, Blas., J. f. O. 1866, 80.

Sterna bicuspis et *tenuirostris*, Licht. (*Fide* Blas.)

Diag. *S. rostro tenue, nigro, ad basin rubescente, pedibus rubro-aurantiacis, caudâ longissimâ, albidâ, remigibus albo-marginatis ad apices ipsas; pallio perlaceo, gastrœo rosaceoalbo.*

Hab.—Europe. In North America, observed from Massachusetts to Florida, thence to Central America. Various West Indian Islands. Breeds apparently throughout its range. No United States record of wintering.

Adult, breeding plumage.—Bill about equal to the head, nearly as long as the tarsus, middle toe and claw, together; straight, slender, much compressed, much higher than broad at the base, the tip excessively acute, culmen very narrow and transversely very convex, even at the base; gently and equally curved from base to tip. Commissure a little sinuate toward the base, gradually declinato-convex for the rest of its length. Gonys very long, much exceeding the rami, its outline very sharp, perfectly straight. Outline of crura decidedly concave; the intercrural space very narrow, two-thirds filled with feathers; the eminentia symphysis very acute, but not prominent. Tomia of both mandibles inflected, and, from the great compression of the bill, very closely approximated for two-thirds their length. Nasal groove moderately long and wide, but so exceedingly shallow as hardly to merit the name of *sulcus.* It terminates before it reaches the tomia, and a well-defined slender ridge runs forward from its anterior extremity till it is lost in the tomia. Nostrils of ordinary size and shape. Encroachment of the feathers on the bill as usual. Wings considerably short for this genus, a little rounded; the first primary only moderately longer than the second; all rather obtuse, with rounded tips. Tertials and inner secondaries rather long and flowing. Tail exceedingly long, contained scarcely 1½ times in the wing; the central feathers short and rounded at their ends; the lateral excessively elongated, slender, tapering regularly to a very acute point.* The feet are of moderate length and stoutness. The tibiæ are bare for only a remarkably short distance. The usual scutellation and reticulation. Tarsus a little longer than the middle toe alone; a little shorter than the middle toe and claw. Lateral toes short; the outer not reaching the base of the claw of the middle; the tip of the claw of the inner falling short of the base of the claw of the middle. Webs of moderate width and amount of emargination. Claws rather short, and all remarkably arched and curved, moderately acute, the edge of the inner a little dilated.

Bill pure black; its tip *in extremo* slightly yellowish; its base for a varying distance, and the inside of the mouth, bright red. Pileum pure, lustrous, velvety black; extending far down on the nape and also very broad, reaching to the lower level of the eyes, and widening somewhat on the temples and auriculars. Under eyelid, however, white, as is also a rather broad streak which runs along the side of the upper mandible to the extremity of the feathers. Neck all round and whole under parts, including the under surfaces of the wings, pure white, with a more or less notable tinge of a delicate rosy color. On the back of the neck the white insensibly shades into the very light, delicate pearl-blue which extends over the whole upper parts, including the rump and base of the tail, where, however, it is slightly lighter than on the dorsum. The tips of the tertials and the inner vanes of the secondaries fade into pure white. The shafts of all the primaries are on both sides pure white nearly to their tips. The outer web of the first primary is deep grayish-black, lighter at the tip. All the primaries are light grayish-black, very strongly silvered over. The inner webs of all of them are pure white for more than half their breadth; this white portion being broadest on the first, toward the base of which it occupies the whole web; and on all of them continuing quite to the apices of the feathers, and even going around the tips slightly on to the outer web. The long rectrices are white, with just an appreciable shade of pearly. The legs and feet bright yellowish-red; the webs lighter, the claws black.

Adult, winter plumage.—Bill dull black; the tip for a greater distance dull yellowish; the base of the under mandible somewhat brownish. The forehead and cheeks white. The crown of the head, the occiput, nape, auricular and circumocular regions, brownish-black, almost or quite unmixed with white, except just on the vertex. There is, therefore, a greater extent and permanency of the pileum than in most other species. Neck all round and under parts white, without any roseate tinge. Lesser coverts along the edge of the fore-arm brownish, but the band narrow and not very dark colored. Something of the brownish is also to be traced along the edge of the metacarpus. Primaries and secondaries much as in summer. The tail has, however, quite lost its length, the external rectrices being so much abbreviated as to produce only one or two inches of emargination, and the tail, with its coverts, may be pearly like the back.

Young-of-the-year before the moult.—Length 10.50 to 11 inches. The bill is exceedingly small, slender, and weak; its tip obtuse; its ridges and angles poorly defined; and it is everywhere covered with skin so soft as to wrinkle in drying. It measures hardly 1.10 inches in length by 0.25 in height at the base (compare dimensions of adult); it is wholly dull greenish-black, a little lighter at the base of the lower mandible. The primaries have not fully grown out, so that the wing from the carpus measures only 7.25; the second primary is longest, third nearly equal, first short, scarcely exceeding the fourth. The primaries are colored, however, almost exactly as in the adults, as regards their pattern, the broad white inner margins extending around their tips. The shafts of all are pure white, except apically. The outer web of the first primary

---

* The external rectrices of this species are for the *Sterninæ* almost what the central rectrices of *Stercorarius buffoni* are for the *Lestridinæ,* in comparison with other species of their respective subfamilies.

is nearly pure black, lightening a little at the tip. The dark portion of the feathers grows lighter on each successively, until the inner ones are very light pearl—so light as to appear to fade insensibly into the white which broadly margins them. The secondaries are white, with the greater part of their outer and a small part of their inner webs pearl-blue. The tail is exceedingly short, measuring less than four inches, the amount of emargination being only one inch, or even less. The outer pair of rectrices are narrower than the others, but hardly longer than the next pair, and not more acutely pointed. The rectrices are pearl-blue, darkest on their outer vanes, so light as to be almost white on their inner. The outer web of the outer feather, however, is not so dark as the next. Toward the extremities of the rectrices there is a subterminal border of brownish-black extending around the tip, and for half an inch or more down on each side. External to this rim of black there is another, which ends the feather, of pure or yellowish white. The markings of the tail are abrupt and well defined. The legs and feet are dull greenish-black, like the bill, with a shade of reddish slightly apparent over some of the joints; the soles inclining to yellowish, the claws black, with whitish tips. Length of tarsus, 0.75; middle toe and claw, 0.90. The ground color of the upper parts is a very light pearl-blue, much as in the adults, and is pretty pure and uninterrupted on the rump and greater wing-coverts. But on the back, the hind neck between the shoulders, the scapulars, tertials, median coverts and inner secondaries, this color is almost completely obscured and hidden by a very beautiful, fine, delicate, continuous mottling of black and light yellowish or fawn-color. This black is disposed chiefly in narrow, irregular, zigzag transverse lines, but their continuity everywhere interrupted by the mottling of fawn-color. This appearance is very difficult to describe; it is quite unlike anything else I have seen among Terns, and rather reminds one of the delicately but inextricably blended colors of a *Scops*, a *Caprimulgus*, or perhaps of some *Scolopacinæ*. On the tertials, inner secondaries, inner longest coverts, the pattern of mottling becomes larger and more distinct, for the feathers are, toward their termination, almost wholly black, with yellowish borders. The head is as peculiar as the back. The forehead and cheeks are of a uniform, delicately blended, and soft, light grayish-brown, which on the vertex and occiput becomes resolved into small, broad, indistinct longitudinal stripes of quite deep black and dull fawn-color, the streaks again being lost on the nape in perfectly uniform dull blackish. Just before and above the eye there is a spot almost pure silvery white; the eye is encircled by nearly pure black, aggregated into a pretty well-defined semilune before it, stretching out behind it as an extensive spot, covering the auricular and temporal regions; pretty sharply defined with the white below; being insensibly blended with the color of the occiput above. The under parts are pure white; but on the sides of the breast, or quite across it, the extreme tips of the feathers are a little obscured by dusky, causing them to appear exactly as if soiled. There is the ordinary band along the edge of the fore-arm of dull black, but it is obscured by some light fawn-colored tips of the feathers.

Dimensions of the adult.—Length, 14 to a little over 15 inches; extent, about 30; wing, from carpus, 9¼ to 9¾; tail, 7¼ to 7¾; depth of fork, 3½ to 4½; bill, along culmen, 1.50; from nostrils to tip, 1.25; from feathers on side of lower mandible to tip, 1.75; height at base, 0.35; gonys, 1; rami, 0.75; tibiæ bare, 0.40; tarsus, 0.85; middle toe alone, 0.75; its claw, 0.25.

Dimensions of young-of-year.—Length, average, about 11 inches; extent, 28; wing, from carpus, 9.25; tail averaging 4 inches, with a depth of forking only 1 to 1½; length of bill, 1.35; its other dimensions, and those of the feet, correspondingly less than in the adult. (Compare also measurements given in the description of the young-of-the-year before the first moult.)

Though of about the same size as the typical species of *Sterna*, its form is more slender. The bill is relatively longer, slenderer, more acute, with a but slightly convex culmen, and the gonys longer than, instead of about equal to, the exposed portion of the rami. The wings are shorter, with less tapering and acute tip. The relative length and attenuation of the exterior rectrices surpasses that of any other species of *Sterna.* The tibiæ are bare for a considerably shorter space. The claws are remarkably arched, especially that of the outer toe. In the pattern of coloration it adheres more closely to the type, though the bill is black and the pileum of a different shape and degree of persistency in winter. No other species of *Sterna* proper has so marked a roseate tint on its under parts, it being in this respect, for its genus, what *galericulata* is for "*Thalasseus.*"

The bill of perfectly adult birds is pure black, except the extreme base, which, with the mouth, is bright red. In immature specimens of various ages it is, for a greater or less extent toward the base, light-colored, with considerable of a vermilion or rather light carmine tint during life. In others the whole bill is pure black. I have never seen it, however, so largely red as it is represented to be in Audubon's plate. The other variations, beyond those normal and constant ones of age and sea on above detailed, consist chiefly in a greater or less elongation of the tail.

It is impossible to confound this species, in mature summer plumage, with any other of North America, and consequently no comparisons need be made. The young bird-of-the-year resembles a good deal the same age of *macrura*, so much so that Naumann is at considerable pains to contradistinguish them. As the bird is then smaller than when adult, with a very short tail, flesh-colored or reddish bill; and as the *macrura* is then pure white below, they might perhaps be confounded. *S. dougalli* is, however, at once to be known by the different character of its more persistent and larger pileum ; much lighter color of the upper parts, and lighter and more obsolete and indistinct color of its spots, when young enough to have any; the lighter color of the web of its exterior tail-feather; much shorter wings and larger and longer feet, &c.

I have been unable to detect any difference between numerous examples of this species from Europe and America.

Though this species has often of late years been called "*paradisea*," yet the questionable identification of Brünnich's name had probably best give way to that one to which no doubt attaches.

STERNA PORTLANDICA, Ridgw.

Portland Tern.

Sterna portlandica, RIDGW., Am. Nat. viii, 1874, 433.

Adult(?), summer plumage.—(No. 64394, Mus. Smith. Inst., Portland, Maine, July, 1873, *F. Benner ;* type of the species, as described *l. c.*). Forehead, sides of head, neck all around, upper tail-coverts, and whole under parts, including lining of wings, pure white. Occiput, crown from opposite eyes, and space around eye, slaty-black. Mantle an average shade of pearl-gray. A slaty bar along cubital edge of wing. Primaries light-silvered dusky, with white shaft, the outer web of the first black, the inner webs of all with large and long white space, which occupies the whole width of the web at base, and on the first reaches nearly to the tip. Tail white, with light pearly shade; the outer web of the outer feather dusky. Bill and feet black, but the latter with a perceptible reddishness. Bill in size and shape identical with that of a young *dougalli*. Feet very small (just as in *macrura*); the tarsus notably shorter than the middle toe and claw. Length, about 12.50 (tail defective; size apparently of *dougalli*); wing, 9.75; tail, 5 (with perhaps an inch gone) ; the fork, 2.25 (probably over 3) ; bill, along culmen, 1.20; along gape, 1.60 ; tarsus, only 0.60 ; middle toe and claw, 0.85.

The subject of the present article differs materially from any other Tern I have seen. I cannot refer it to any species known to me. It apparently comes nearest *dougalli*, with which it is to be particularly compared. I will first observe that, though shot in July, it is by no means certain that it is an adult bird; in fact the chances are the other way. The white of the forehead is not a firm, sharp lunule, but, on the contrary, an indefinite restriction of a black cap to the vertex and occiput, the black and white shading gradually into each other. The pattern of the head is *identical* with that of a specimen of undoubted *dougalli* before me. Another strong mark of immaturity is seen in the slaty bar along the cubital border of the wing. This is also precisely as in the specimen of *dougalli* just mentioned. The pure white of the whole under parts and of the cervix, as well as the size of the white areas on the inner webs of the primaries, are exactly as in *dougalli*. The bill, in size, shape, and color, is identical with that of *dougalli*. So far we see nothing incompatible with the characters of *dougalli*. But in *dougalli* the mantle is extremely pale pearly, extending uninterrupted over the rump and tail ; in *portlandica* the mantle is about as in *hirundo*, and the rump is white. (However, a winter specimen of *dougalli* has the mantle scarcely paler than in *portlandica*.) In *dougalli* the feet are coral-red or orange, obscured in the young in winter, and the tarsi are scarcely or not shorter than in the middle toe and claw ; in *portlandica* the feet are quite blackish, and the tarsus is 0.25 shorter than the middle toe and claw. In the proportions of the feet, in fact, *portlandica* is the same as *macrura*. From *macrura*, *portlandica* is at once separated by its black bill and feet, and pure white under parts.

If it could be shown that the tarsi of *dougalli* are ever so short as this, perhaps the other differences from *dougalli* might be reconciled with the varying characters of age or season in that species; but at present the discrepancies are insurmountable. I have therefore no alternative to accepting Mr. Ridgway's name, at least for the present. On examining the type-specimen with him, I had a suspicion that the bird might be *longipennis*, and he has expressed this doubt; but on conferring with Middendorff, Schrenck, and Radde, we find that the characters of *longipennis* do not agree at all with those of our bird.*

A second specimen of *portlandica* has been taken by Mr. William Brewster in Massachusetts. It agrees exactly, except that the black cap is more restricted, the white reaching along the middle line over the vertex to the occiput (comprising my view of the instability of this character). It is slightly larger. Wing, 10.25; tail, 6.30; culmen, 1.25; tarsus, 0.65; middle toe *without* claw, the same.

This specimen was not included in the analysis of the subgenus on p. 675, and its supposed validity requires confirmation.

STERNA SUPERCILIARIS var. ANTILLARUM, Coues.

Least Tern.

a. *superciliaris.*

Sterna superciliaris, VIEILL., Nouv. Dict. xxxii, 1819, 126; E. M. 350 (*Hati ceja blanca*, Az., Apunt. iii, 377).—COUES, Ibis, 1864, 390.—BLAS., J. f. O. 1866, 74.—SCL. & SALV., P. Z. S. 1866, 200 (Ucayali); 1867, 593; 1871, 571; 1873, 310.—REINH., Vid. Med. 1870, 19 (Brazil).
Sterna maculata, VIEILL., E. M. 350 (*Hati tacheté*, AZARA).
Sterna argentea, MAXIM., Beit. iv, 871.—BURM., Syst. Uebers. iii, 542; Reise, ii, 519.— PELZ., O. B. 325 (Brazil).

b. *antillarum.*

Sterna minuta, WILS., Am. Orn. vii, 1813, 80, pl. 70, f. 2 (not of Linnæus and European writers).—BP., Syn. 1828, 355.—AUD., Orn. Biog. iv, 1838, 175, pl. 319; Syn. 1839, 321; B. Am. vii, 1844, 119, 439.—GIR., B. L. I. 1844, 350.—PUTN., Pr. Ess. Inst. i, 1856, 221 (Massachusetts).
Sterna minuta americana, SUND., Ofv. K.-A. Forh. 1869, 589 (Porto Rico).
Sterna argentea, NUTT., Man. ii, 1834, 280.—BP., List, 1838, 61.—LEÓT., Ois. Trinidad, 545.
Sternula antillarum, LESS., Descr. Mammif. et Ois. 1847, 256.
Sterna antillarum COUES, Pr. Phila. Acad. 1862, 552 (critical).—COUES, Ibis, 1864, 390 (Belize).—COUES, Ibis, 1866, 64 (coast of California) —COUES, Pr. Phila. Acad. 1866, 100 (the same).—COUES, Pr. Ess. Inst. v, 1868, 308 (New England, breeding).—COUES, Pr. Bost. Soc. xii, 1868, 126 (South Carolina).—COUES, Am. Nat. iii, 1869, 337 (biography).—COUES, Pr. Phila. Acad. 1871, 45 (North Carolina, breeding).—LAWR., Ann. Lyc. viii, 1864, 107 (Sombrero); viii, 1866, 299 (New York).—DRESS., Ibis. 1866, 44 (Texas).—GUNDL., Repert. F. N. i, 1865, 393 (Cuba).—SCL. & SALV., P. Z. S. 1871, 571 (Central America).—RIDGW., Ann. Lyc. N. Y. x, 1874, 391 (Illinois).
Sternula melanorhyncha, LESS., *op. et. loc. cit.* (*juv.*).
Sterna frenata, GAMB., Pr. Phila. Acad. iv, 1848, 128.—LAWR., B. N. A. 1858, 864.—WHEAT., Ohio Agric. Rep. 1860, No. 276.—COUES & PRENT., Smiths. Rep. 1861, 418 (Washington, D. C.).—HAYD., Rep. 1862 (Missouri region).—ALLEN, Pr. Ess. Inst. iv, 1864, 90 (Massachusetts).—TURNB., B. E. Pa. 1869, 39.—SNOW, B. Kans. 1873, 12 (rare).
Sternula frenata, BP., Compt. Rend. 1856, 773.
Sterna superciliaris, CAB., J. f. O. v, 232 (Cuba).—COUES, Key, 1872, 322 (North America).
Sterna (*Sternula*) *superciliaris*, GRAY, Hand-list, iii, 1871, 121, No. 11066 (includes both).

---

* Since writing the foregoing, I have had an opportunity of inspecting a fine example of *longipennis*, through the kind attentions of Dr. Otto Finsch, of Bremen. I fail to see how *longipennis* differs from *hirundo* (*auct.*) except in the more extensively black bill. It is of exactly the same size, proportion of parts, and general aspect. The species (if it be one) has given ornithologists some trouble, apparently; but the only question seems to me to be its distinctness from *hirundo*.

Diag. *S. minutæ similis ejusdemque staturæ; sed uropygio candáque cum pallio concoloribus, rostro breviore, graciliore, vittâ frontali angustiore; rostro flavo, apice nigro, pedibus flavis.*

Hab.—Temperate North America, especially along the Atlantic coast of the United States, but also on the larger inland waters. Up the Pacific coast to California (*Xantus, Coues*). South into the Antilles and Middle America generally. Apparently winters beyond the United States. (The typical *superciliaris* from South America; Brazil, Paraguay, &c.)

Lieutenant Warren's Expedition.—9005, Platte River; 9007, Loup Fork; 8999, Yellowstone River.

Adult, breeding plumage.—Bill about as long as the head, slightly exceeding the tarsus and middle toe together without the claw; compressed; only moderately robust; the tip very acute, but not much attenuated nor decurved. Culmen straight to the nostrils, slightly but equally decurved for the rest of its extent; commissure curved throughout; rami concave in outline, short; gonys straight, much longer than the ramus. Nasal groove tolerably wide, but very short, and not deep. Tomia slightly inflected. Wings of moderate length; first primary but very slightly longer than the second; the rest successively more and more rapidly graduated. Tertials and inner secondaries very short, reaching in the folded wing only half way to its tip. Tail rather short, and only moderately forked; the central rectrices broad, with broadly rounded tips; the external pair narrowing rapidly to a very acute tip. Tibiæ bare but a very short distance. Feet small, short, slender; tarsus equal to middle toe and half its claw; of ordinary characters as regards scutellation and reticulation. Outer toe almost or quite as long as the middle, with its claw very much shorter and weaker; inner toe short, its claw just reaching to the base of the middle claw. Unguis of hallux extremely minute. Webs moderately broad; the outer only slightly, the inner very considerably, incised.

Bill yellow, its tip for usually an eighth to a fourth of an inch black, but sometimes altogether yellow. The junction of this black with the yellow is quite straight and perpendicular, as it does not run off on the gonys, nor culmen, nor tomia. Pileum glossy greenish-black. On the forehead a *narrow* lunula of white, the posterior border of which is very concave, the narrow cornua of which extend over the eyes just to their posterior borders. This crescent extends quite to the bill, but is separated from the white of the cheeks by a narrow line of black, which runs forward as a prolongation of the pileum, through the eyes, to the extreme tip of the feathers on the side of the bill. The entire upper parts of the bird, including its rump, nape, upper tail-coverts, and the rectrices themselves, are pearl-blue, with a considerable tinge of plumbeous. This color extends undiluted quite to the black pileum, on the sides of the neck and head fading insensibly into the pure white of the under parts. The rectrices are about the color of the back, only they grow lighter toward their bases, and their under surfaces, together with the outer web of the first, are nearly white. The color of the back extends undiluted to the extreme apices of the secondaries and tertials, but the inner webs of these feathers are basally nearly white. The shafts of the first two primaries are white inferiorly, black superiorly; the webs themselves black, the inner with a considerable space white; this white space separated from the black by a tolerably distinct line of definition, not extending to the tip of the feather. The other primaries are a considerably darker shade of the color of the back, their inner webs fading into whitish along their borders, which thus become conspicuously margined with white quite to their tips. Whole under parts, including the inferior alar tectrices, pure white, without the least wash of plumbeous or tinge of rosy. Feet orange yellow, the claws black.

Toward the middle or latter part of July, the bird above described begins to change, and, until it has fully completed its autumn moult, its plumage is as follows:

Adults during the August moult.—Bill mostly black, but a greater or less degree of yellow remaining. The black pileum has already become variegated with white, the front being mostly of that color. The upper parts are as in summer, but there are indications of the dusky band that is to appear along the fore-arm. Tail scarcely at all forked, from wearing away of the central rectrices. A larger number of the primaries are blackish, without a silvery tinge, and this grayish-black extends along the radial edge of the metacarpus to the carpal joint on the feathers of the *ala spuria.*

At the finishing of the moult we have the—

Adult, winter plumage.—Bill black; legs and feet dull yellowish. Forehead and lores pure white; vertex white, with more or less numerous, narrow, longitudinal lines of black; occiput and nape wholly brownish-black, sending forward on each side over the auriculars, to just in front of the eye, a band of the same. The upper parts are as in the adults in summer, but rather darker, and the mantle does not, as in summer, extend quite up to the nape, but leaves a portion of the neck behind white, as are also the whole under parts. There is a continuous band of grayish-black along the forearm; the bend of the wing from the primaries to the carpal joint is also of this color.

The primaries are about as described last. The tail is colored much as in summer, but the lateral feathers have not the elongation that they acquire during that season.

The immature winter plumage, or that of a young bird which has just completed its first autumn moult, differs from the above as follows: It is somewhat smaller, with considerably weaker bill, the basal portions of which are still more or less dirty flesh-color. The forehead and vertex are rather grayish-white than pure white, and the brownish-black of the nape is interrupted with light grayish. The uniformity of the colors of the upper parts is interfered with by the still remaining lighter tips of most of the feathers, while some may yet retain the brownish subapical spots of the *avis hornotina.* The tail has still some traces of dark subapical spots. It is only in early winter that this particular plumage can be seen, for toward spring the birds are hardly to be distinguished from the adults.

We have yet to describe the bird-of-the-year in July and August, before its first moult; the following is the plumage of the—

Avis hornotina.—Bill nearly as stout at the base as in the adults, but shorter, more obtuse, with illy-developed symphyseal eminence; brownish-black; under mandible basally dull flesh. Frons mostly white; the vertex and occiput variegated with brownish-black and white, the former color mostly aggregated into a post-ocular patch. Dorsum and alar tectrices lightly washed with the pearl-gray of the adults, but the continuity of this color greatly interrupted by hastate or crescentic spots of brown, which mottle the whole upper parts, one or more being on each feather. Primaries grayish-black, growing lighter from without inward. Their inner webs are bordered with white, broadest on the outer primary, growing narrower and longer on the others till, on the inner ones, it goes quite around the tip of the feather on to the outer web; outer web of first primary, and shafts of all the primaries, pure black superiorly, pure white inferiorly. Tail deeply emarginate, the lateral feathers scarcely elongated; pearl-blue, deepening towards the tips of the rectrices into dusky-gray, the extreme apices again white. Whole under parts pure white. Size somewhat less than the adults.

Dimensions of the adult.—Length, about 9; extent, 20; wing, 6.60; tail 3.50, its fork 1.75; bill along culmen, 1.20; depth at base, 0.28; tarsus, 0.60; middle toe and claw, 0.72. *Young* correspondingly smaller in all dimensions: Length, about 8.50; wing, 6.35; tail, 3.25; bill down sometimes to 1.

Other variations.—As in all Terns, there is a notable variation in the length and stoutness of the bill; but the largest I have seen do not equal those of either *minuta* or *superciliaris* proper. But when we come to compare typical *superciliaris* of South America with *minuta*, we find no notable difference; so that size of the bill can only be used to distinguish the North American variety of *superciliaris* from *minuta*—not whole American form from its European representative. In color, the bill of var. *antillarum* usually presents us with a black tip one-eighth to one-fourth of an inch long; while in *superciliaris* the bill is wholly yellow. But, in enumerating the different points of *superciliaris* and *antillarum*, Messrs. Sclater and Salvin, who separate the two, have overlooked the fact, which I only lately learned myself, that in a certain percentage of *antillarum* itself the bill is wholly yellow, and that sometimes the bill of *superciliaris* is dark at the tip.* In examining a great many fresh specimens of *antillarum*,

* This is the case, for example, with No. 21082, from the Parana, South America, in which the bill is yellow, clouded with olivaceous on the under mandible, and with the tip brownish for nearly a fourth of an inch. The bill is notably longer and larger than in var. *antillarum*—almost 1.40 along culmen, and 0.30 deep at base. The bird is also larger—the wing 7.15, or about an inch longer than usual in *antillarum*.

A specimen of *S. nereis*, Gould, from New Zealand (No. 66268, Dr. J. Haast), agrees substantially with European *minuta*, in the pearly-gray not extending on the tail, and large dark-tipped bill. The bill is, however, even stouter, especially deeper at the base than in *minuta*, and the general size is notably greater; wing, 7.10; bill 1.25 along culmen, 0.32 deep at base.

S. exilis of Tschudi (Peru) I have not seen. As understood by Messrs. Sclater and Salvin (who refer to it *S. loricata*, PH. & LANDB., Wieg. Arch. 1863, 124, Bay of Arica), it appears decidedly different from the rest. Without considering the question of positive taxonomic rank, the several forms just mentioned may be thus tabulated:

A. Entirely white below.

    a. Pearly of mantle not extending on tail, which is white.

        1. Smaller; wing, under 7; bill, about 0.25 deep at base.....   *minuta.*

        2. Larger; wing, 7 or more; bill, 0.30 or more at base.......   *nereis.*

    b. Pearly of mantle extending uninterrupted on tail.

        3. Smaller; wing, under 7; bill, under 1.25, usually black tipped..   *antillarum.*

        4. Larger; wing, over 7; bill, over 1.25, seldom black tipped..   *superciliaris.*

B. "Gray" below; bill very slender, its terminal half black..............   *exilis.*

which I shot on the Carolina coast in the breeding season, I found many with the black tip reduced to a mere point, and a few without trace of black. This supposed distinction, therefore, fails as a test, though an *average* difference in this respect really holds, enough perhaps to warrant our recognition of a var. *antillarum*, coupled as this character is with the notably smaller size, especially of the bill. But I feel quite confident that I was right in uniting *antillarum* specifically with *superciliaris*, as I did in the " Key," following Hartlaub, Cabanis, and Gray.

Antillarum being referable specifically to *superciliaris*, which latter has a bill equaling in size that of *minuta* of Europe, we are reduced, in separating these two species, to the character of extent of the pearl-gray mantle of *superciliaris* over the rump and tail, which latter parts are in *minuta* pure white, like the belly. In the American bird, according to my observations, the white frontal lunula at least averages considerably narrower than that of the European, but this is not a very reliable character. I continue to separate the two specifically, though there is much to be said in favor of their merely varietal difference, as held by Sundevall.

The term *minuta*, used by earlier American writers, being preoccupied for the European bird, while *superciliaris* may perhaps be best restricted to the South American (where its synonymn *argentea* also belongs); the name *antillarum*, Lesson (1847), antedating Gambel's *frenata* of 1848, may be applied to the North and Middle American form, as I pointed out in 1862. There is no question of its pertinence here, nor that Lesson's *melanorhyncha* is the young of the same.

Although this species is more particularly abundant along the Atlantic coast, yet its distribution in the interior of the United States, along the larger water-courses, is more general than has been commonly supposed. Dr. Hayden got it in various parts of the Missouri region, and Prof. Snow has it in his list. It migrates up the Mississippi from the Gulf, though most of the individuals prefer to pass along the coast. On the Pacific side it reaches California. It breeds at various points all along, and in winter retires far south, as seen by the above quotations. The best opportunity I have had of studying its habits occurred to me on the North Carolina coast, where it is a summer resident, from early in April until October, and, except at the height of the influx of the other kinds, the most abundant Tern of all. It breeds there in great numbers. A specimen, shot May 17, had then an egg ready to be laid; but most of the eggs are deposited toward June, and during the fore part of that month. The first young birds I noticed were flying June 20; but this was early for them, the broods not being fairly on wing until the middle of July. During all of May and June, indeed, there are plenty of immature birds about; but these, it should be observed, are of the last summer's broods, rendering the conclusion obvious that at least two years are required to assume the perfect dress. These birds have the bill black, no black cap or white crescent, slaty auriculars and occiput, dark bar along the front edge of the wing, imperfectly-colored primaries, and slightly forked tail; thus not possibly to be confounded with birds of the season, which are curiously variegated with gray-brown and white, and show no pearly-blue. The yearlings were in plenty with the adults at the breeding-grounds; but whether or not they were paired and had eggs too, was plainly impossible to determine, as Terns' eggs are almost never identified as to the exact parent, when numbers of the birds are breeding together, as they were in this case. The usual number of eggs is two, not three, and often only one is laid; they do no not average over $1\frac{1}{4}$ by 1 inch. The eggs here were laid on the pebbly shingle just back of the beach, among the sand-dunes, and were deposited on the bare ground all around, in a scarcely perceptible depression, or none at all. During the season the air is filled with the shrill cries of the birds winging overhead; they are fearless in attempted defence of their charge, often dashing down within a few feet of one's head. The eggs are very difficult to find, even when numerous, as they are colored much like their surroundings. The ground color varies from clear, pale greenish-white to pale dull drab or olivaceous. The markings are numerous, and generally distributed, though they frequently tend to wreathe around the large end, especially when they are of large size; they consist of small splashes, irregular spots, and mere dots of clear brown of several shades, together with numerous pale, ill-defined lilac or gray shell-markings.

STERNA ALEUTICA, Bd.

Aleutian Tern.

Sterna aleutica, BD., Tr. Chic. Acad. i, 1869, 321, pl. 31, f. 1.—DALL & BANN., *ibid.* 307 (Kodiak).—COUES, Key, 1872, 322.
Sterna "*camtschatica*, PALL.," FINSCH, Abh. Nat. iii, 1872, 85 (Alaska).

DIAG. *S. rostro, pedibus, vertice, nuchâ, et fascia transoculari, nigris; lunulâ frontali, gulâ, genis et caudâ, albis; corpore griseo-plumbeo, subtus dilutiore, magis perlaceo; magnitudine circiter S. macruræ.*

Hab.—Aleutian Islands. (Kodiak.)

Adult.—(No. 52517, Mus. Smiths.; Kodiak, June 12, 1868. The type of the species.) The bill has the usual shape, as in *hirundo, macrura,* &c. It is entirely black. The feet are small, as in the species just named, but depart somewhat from the typical condition of this genus in having the webs more deeply incised. The emargination is not so great, however, as in the genus *Hydrochelidon*. It is much as in *Haliplana*. The tibiæ are bare to the usual extent. The wings and tail are exactly as in *Sterna* proper, the latter, in its length and depth of fork, recalling *macrura* and *forsteri*. The crown and nape are black; there is a large white frontal crescent, the horns of which reach to the posterior border of the eyes, the convexity of which extends into the nasal fossæ, the concavity of which is opposite the anterior border of the eyes. It is thus seen to be broader than in most species similarly marked. The black vertex sends through the eye a band that crosses the cheeks and reaches the bill just posterior to the point of greatest extension of the feathers on the latter. The chin, auriculars, and other parts of the head bordering this vitta below, are pure white, presently deepening insensibly into the hue of the under parts. The tail is wholly pure white; no pearly wash on either vane of any of the feathers. The upper parts at large are of a dark pearl-gray, with a dull leaden hue, different from the clear pearly of *macrura*, &c., and the smoky cast of *panayensis*, &c.; it is a tint intermediate between these, that I find difficult to name satisfactorily. The whole under parts, from the white of the chin, just noticed, to the under tail-coverts, are of a paler and more decidedly pearly tint of the same color, more nearly as in full-plumaged *macrura*, yet more grayish. Both under and upper tail-coverts are, like the tail, white. The color of the back mounts on the neck behind to the black of the nape without intervention of white. The under wing-coverts and the edge of the wing are pure white; so also are all the shafts of the primaries. The primaries are blackish lead-color, with silvery hoariness, and each with a large white space on the inner web. This white space on the first primary occupies at the base the whole width of the inner web, but grows narrower toward the tip of the feather, ending about an inch from the tip, which is wholly blackish lead-color, as just described, this color running down as a narrow margining of the inner vane for two inches or more. On the other primaries successively this white space diminishes in size, and is also less distinctly defined. The secondaries are colored much like the back, but the greater part of the inner web of all is white, and there is a narrow oblique touch of white on the outer web near its end, which forms a bar across the wing when closed.

Dimensions.—Bill along culmen, 1.40; along gape, 1.70; height at base, 0.30; length of gonys, 0.80; wing, 9.75; tail, 6.50; depth of fork, about 2.40; tarsus, 0.60; middle toe alone, 0.80; its claw, nearly 0.30.

No special comparison with any other known species is required.

This Tern, recently described (as above), is interesting in several respects. It is singular that so strongly marked a species should have remained so long unnoticed, but we find no indication of it in the names or descriptions of previous writers. It gives us a new style of coloration for North American species. At first sight it suggests species of *Haliplana*, without, however, presenting anything like the special coloration of the type of that subgenus, *fuliginosa*. It more nearly resembles the paler-colored species of the genus, as *panayensis* for example; and, again, comes nearer still to certain southern forms of what are usually rated as *Sterna* proper; for instance, S. *lunata*, Peale. The black bill and feet, white frontal lunula, dullness of the upper parts, &c., which suggest *Haliplana*, are supplemented by an approach to that genus from another direction, viz, the deep incision of the webs, which is as well marked perhaps as in *H. fuliginosa*, but which evidently falls short of the requirements of *Hydrochelidon* in this respect. With all this mimetic resemblance to several species of a different group, *S. aleutica* cannot be severed from those of *Sterna* proper. The species of *Haliplana* are white below, and have the tail more or less similarly colored with the upper parts; *S. aleutica*, like *macrura* and its allies, is strongly washed on the under parts with a diluted tint of the same color as the upper parts, the tail remaining pure white, in strong contrast.

The differences between *H. fuliginosa* and one of the typical *Sternæ*, as *hirundo* for example, are strongly marked, and were only this species to be taken into consideration, it might seem advisable to separate it generically; but investigation of intermediate forms shows the propriety of retaining *Haliplana* to be very questionable. From the extreme of form and pattern of coloration that *fuliginosa* shows, there are easy gradations toward *Sterna* proper through *panayensis*, and certain species, usually called *Sterna*, as *infuscata*, *lunata*, and perhaps other exotics with which I am not well acquainted, these being referable to either genus with equal propriety. Finally, another strong link is afforded by this *S. aleutica*, which is unquestionably a *Sterna*, yet leans in the direction of *Haliplana* in certain points both of form and coloration.

At present only the original specimen of this species is known. It is in mature, doubtless breeding plumage, having been shot in June. In winter the species may be expected to differ in wanting the pure black of the crown, which may then be largely replaced by white, obscuring the outlines of the frontal lunula. The stripe through the eye will probably be retained; so will some black upon the occiput. The general colors will be paler, the wings more canescent. Young birds will differ in imperfection of the head markings, much as just suggested; the bill and feet may be in part light colored; the under parts pure white.

Since the foregoing was penned, three more specimens have come to hand, from the same region as the type, and are exactly like it. Dr. Finsch's determination that the species is *camtschatica* of Pallas, is open to grave doubt; I cannot make such an identification, after careful examination of Pallas's description.

Subgenus HALIPLANA, *Wagl.*

< *Sterna*, GM., Syst. Nat. i, 1788, 605, *et aliq.*
= *Onychoprion*, WAGL., Isis, 1832, 277. (*Sterna serrata*, FORST.)
= *Planeis*, WAGL., Isis, 1832, 1222 (type —?).
= *Haliplana*, WAGL., Isis, 1832, 1224. (*S. fuliginosa*, GM.)
= *Haliplanes*, apud BLAS., List B. Eur. 1862, 22.
> *Anous*, LESS., Descr. Mammif. et Ois. 1847, 255, *nec* LEACH.
< *Hydrochelidon*, BP., List, 1838, 61, *partim*; *nec* BOIE.
= *Thalassipora*, BOIE (*fide* GRAY; type given as "*infuscata*, LICHT.").
= *Melanosterna*, BL. (*fide* GRAY).

GEN. CHAR. Bill as long as the head, scarcely exceeded by the tarsus and middle toe together, staight, stout at the base, where it is nearly as broad as high, but tapering; the tip rather acute. Culmen broad, especially at the base, and but slightly convex; gonys straight, ascending, making the commissure scarcely at all decurved; the rami slightly convex; the eminentia symphysis obtuse and little developed; the tomia of both mandibles inflected. Nasal groove long and deep, but rather irregularly defined, terminating beyond the middle of the bill; the nostrils more anterior than in *Sterna*, though not so much so as in *Anous*. Outline of feathers on bill as in *Sterna*. Wings exceedingly long, pointed, but the first primary scarcely longer than the second. Tail very long, very deeply forked, as in *Sterna*, but the feathers broader and stiffer, and not so regularly tapering. Feet moderately long, the tibiæ denuded for a considerable distance; toes all short, the inner extremely so; the middle, with its claw, scarcely longer than the tarsus, which is of moderate length, slender. The webs moderately broad, the outer very lightly, the inner more deeply incised. Of moderate size and slender, graceful form. Bicolor. Characters of mouth as in *Sterninæ* generally. Trachea of small calibre flattened above, but soon becoming quite cylindrical. Lower larynx very small, its muscles feeble. Bronchial half-rings very delicate, but distinct from the first, which is as usual larger and stronger. Zone of proventricular glands unusually narrow. Hepatic and cystic ducts very short. Cœca* minute,

---

* I cannot reconcile Audubon's description of the organs of digestion with the results obtained by my own scalpel. In the specimens examined the œsophagus was not "within the thorax dilated into an enormous sac," nor were its walls "extremely thin, so as to be membranous and transparent." The organ in question was of pretty uniform calibre throughout, and as muscular as in any other Tern. There must have existed in Audubon's specimen a temporary and accidental dilation, as might readily be the case. I cannot account for the difference in length of cœca as given by him, and as I have found. In my specimens the cœca, instead of being like those of the *Lestridinæ*, are exceedingly short, and strictly sternine in character.

scarcely two-tenths of an inch long. Rectum extremely short. Cloaca large and globular. Kidneys only divided into three or four lobes.

This subgenus in many respects is allied to *Anous*, apparently connecting the two sections *Sterneæ* and *Anoëæ*, though unquestionably belonging to the former. Its essential features lie in the shape of the bill, position of the nostrils, &c. In pattern of coloration there is a considerable deviation from the ordinary type. There are few noticeable anatomical points, the chief being the slenderness of the trachea, weakness of the lower larynx, and narrowness of the proventricular zone.

Three names proposed for the genus are by the same author and bear the same date. In this instance it seems to be a matter of choice which to adopt; and, although *Haliplana* is instituted several pages after *Onychoprion* and *Planetis*, I prefer to adopt it, as its type is the well-known *S. fuliginosa*, and as it is the most euphonious.

Until recently but a single species of the section was known to inhabit North America. Mr. G. N. Lawrence introduced the Central American *anosthæta* ("*discolor*") into our fauna, by virtue of specimens in his cabinet from Mr. Audubon's collection, labeled as having been taken in Florida. It appears to be a common bird of the Central American coast and islands.

The following analytical table will serve to distinguish the two North American species of the section—*H. lunata*, Peale, not an inhabitant of North America, being introduced for further comparison:

Common characters.—Bill and feet black. Under parts and a frontal lunula white.

I. Back like crown.
    1. Above, deep brownish-black.. *fuliginosa.*
II. Back not like crown; crown black.
    2. Back deep smoky-gray.. *anæstheta.*
    3. Back light pearl-gray.. *lunata.*

STERNA (HALIPLANA) FULIGINOSA, Gm.

Sooty Tern.

Sterna fuliginosa, GM., Syst. Nat. i, 1788, 605.—LATH., Ind. Orn. ii, 804 (BUFF., viii, 345; *Sooty Tern*, Arct. Zool. ii, No. 447; Gen. Syn. vi, 352, &c.).—WILS., Am. Orn. viii, 1814, 145, pl. 72, f. —.—BP., Syn. 1828, 355.—NUTT., Man. ii, 1834, 284.— AUD., Orn. Biog. iii, 1835, 263; v, 1839, 641; pl. 235; Syn. 1839, 317; B. Am. vii, 1844, 90, pl. 432.—CAB., J. f. O. v, 233 (Cuba).—LAWR., B. N. A. 1858, 861.— CASS., Orn. U. S. Ex. Exp. 1858, 386.—HARTL., Ibis, 1859, 350 (? Red Sea).—BRY., Pr. Bost. Soc. vii, 1859, 134 (Bahamas).—ALLEN, Pr. Ess. Inst. iv, 1864, 90 (Massachusetts, breeding).—DRESS., Ibis, 1866, 44 (Texas).—TAYLOR, Ibis, 1864, 172 (St. Thomas).—SUND., Öfv. Vet. Ak. Förh. 1869, 589 (St. Bartholomew).— HARTING, Br. B. 1872, 169 (Tutbury, England; MOSELEY, N. H. Tutb. 110; HARTING, *The Field*, June 26, 1869; Zool. 1869, p. 1867).
Sterna (*Onychoprion*) *fuliginosa*, GRAY, List Br. B. 1863, 242 (Tutbury, England; quotes BROWN, Zool. 1853, 3755; YARR., Br. B. 3d ed. 542).
Sterna (*Haliplanes*) *fuliginosa*, BLAS., List B. Eur. 22 (quotes Magdeburg, NAUM., v, 412).
Sterna (*Haliplana*) *fuliginosa*, COUES, Key, 1872, 322.
Onychoprion fuliginosa, WAGL., Isis, 1832, 277.—GOULD, Introd. B. Aust. 1848, 113; B. Aust. pl. 32.—SCL., P. Z. S. 1856, 144 (Ascension Island).—SCL. & SALV., P. Z. S. 1871, 572 (Middle America).
Haliplana fuliginosa, WAGL., Isis, 1832, 1224.—BP., Compt. Rend. 1856, 772.—COUES, Pr. Phila. Acad. 1862, 556 (critical).—COUES, Ibis, 1864, 392 (Honduras).—SALV., Ibis, 1866, 200 (the same).—GUNDL., Rep. F. N. i, 1865, 393 (Cuba).—COUES, Pr. Ess. Inst. v, 1868, 309 (? Massachusetts, breeding).—COUES, Pr. Phila. Acad. 1871, 46 (North Carolina).—LAWR., Ann. Lyc. N. Y. viii, 184 (Nicaragua).—ALLEN, Am. Nat. iii, 1870, 644 (occurrence in Massachusetts denied by Dr. Brewer).
Hydrochelidon fuliginosum, BP., List, 1838, 61.—GOSSE, B. Jam. 1847, 433.
Sterna serrata, FORST., Descr. An. ed. Licht. 1844, 276.
Onychoprion serrata, WAGL., Isis, 1832, 277.
Haliplana serrata, BP., Compt. Rend. 1856, 772.
Sterna guttata, FORST., Descr. An. ed. Licht. 1844, 211. (*Juv.*)
Anous l'herminieri, LESS, Descr. Mammif. et Ois. 1847, 255 (Antilles). (*Juv.*)
Sterna melanoptera, SW. (*fide* BLAS.).
Sterna gouldii, REICH. (*fide* GRAY).
Sterna luctuosa, PHIL. & LANDB., Wieg. Arch. 1866, 126 (*fide* SCL. & SALV.).
Sterna fuliginosa var. *crissalis*, BD., *apud* LAWR., Pr. Bost. Soc. 1871 (Socorro).

DIAG. *S. bicolor, corpore suprà, rostro, pedibus remigibusque nigris, infrà cum rectrice laterali nisi in apice, albis; vittâ frontali albâ, freno per lora ducto nigro. Juv. corpore toto brunneo-nigro, subtus dilutiore, dorso transversim rufo-undulato, abdomine crissoque griseo-albis, tectricibus alarum albo-terminatis.*

Hab.—Warmer parts of the world. South Sea Islands. Australia. Red Sea (?).

Casual in Europe (as above). Ascension Island (*Collingwood*, Zool. 980; *Sperling*, Ibis, 1868, 286). South America to Chili (*Phil. & Landb.*). Middle America and various West Indian islands. Pacific coast of Mexico (Socorro, *Grayson*). In North America on the South Atlantic and Gulf coast; north regularly only to the Carolinas; casually to Pennsylvania (Chester County, *Barnard, in lit., Baird*); extension to New England denied.

Adult in spring plumage.—With the form, &c., as already detailed under head of the subgenus. Bill black. Legs and feet black. Claws black. Iris dull red. On the forehead is a broad lunula of white, the cornua of which extend backward over the eye to about opposite its middle; its convex borders separated from the white of the lower part of the cheeks by a straight rather broad band of brownish-black, which extends from the eye obliquely downward and forward to the bill. The entire upper parts are black, deep and uniform, with considerable of a greenish gloss, specially noticeable on the crown. Entire under parts from chin to end 'of inferior tail-coverts, sides of the head below the eye, sides of the neck more than half way around, with inferior alar tectrices, pure white. Primaries deep brownish-black, lighter on the inner webs; their shafts superiorly light brown, inferiorly white. Secondaries like the primaries, but the greater part of their inner webs whitish. Tail glossy brownish-black above, duller below; the elongated exterior rectrices white, with white shafts, deepening into blackish toward the extremities, principally of their inner webs.

Young-of-the-year.—Smaller than the adults, the bill especially much smaller and weaker. Upper mandible black; the under dull reddish, deeper toward the tip; eyes and feet dull reddish. The entire plumage is of a nearly uniform brownish or grayish fuliginous; darker on the upper parts; still deeper on the primaries, where it is almost black; lighter on the under parts, so much so as to fade on the abdomen into grayish-white. The superior alar tectrices and the scapulars are all broadly tipped with white, which gives a very peculiar spotted aspect to the parts. The feathers of the back, rump, and upper tail-coverts, are all margined and tipped with dull rufous, which causes these parts to present a remarkable transversely-waved appearance. The tail is uniformly of much the same color as the wings, all the rectrices fading toward their apices into dull brownish. It is simply emarginate, instead of being deeply forked the lateral rectrices having but a slight elongation.

Dimensions of the adult.—Average length, about 16.50; extent of wings, 33 to 35. Wing from the carpus, 12; tail, 7 to 7.50; depth of fork, 3. to 3.50. Bill along culmen, 1.80; along commissure, 2.50; from feathers on side of lower mandible, 1.90; height at base 0.50. Tibiæ bare, 0.70; tarsus, 1; middle toe and claw, 1.20; outer ditto, 1.05; inner ditto, 0.75; hallux and its claw, 0.30.

This species is too well known, and too distinct from any other of North America, to require any further description or comparison. The plumage of the young, above detailed, is very peculiar, and interesting as being a state upon which one or two nominal species have been founded. It is very different from that of the adults. As the bird in this condition grows older the abdomen and under parts generally become lighter at the same time that the upper portions of the body deepen in color. The rufous margins of the feathers of the back and the white tips of the alar tectrices gradually disappear, and the white front begins to make its appearance. The lateral feathers of the tail acquire length and tenuity and become whitish. While the bird is undergoing these changes it has also been characterized by some authors as a distinct species.

A specimen from Socorro (No. 50861, A. J. Grayson), and another from Isabella Island, are different in some respects from any others I have seen. The under parts from the middle of the belly backward, including the tail-coverts, are distinctly washed over with clear, pale slate-gray, which appears in striking contrast to the pure white of the rest of the under parts. The line of demarcation of the two colors is evident. I have not specimens enough to say whether this is a constant feature of the birds from that locality. This is the form named var. *crissalis*, as above.

A large suite of specimens from various Pacific localities, in the Smithsonian, collected by the United States Exploring Expedition, shows me no characters by which a second species may be distinguished from *fuliginosa*.

Anatomical characters.—The mouth presents but slight variations from the ordinary type. Median ridge commences an inch and a quarter from the tip; is broad and not very prominent; small obtuse papillæ are thinly scattered over its whole surface. Lateral ridges are somewhat sinuate, and extend backward hardly beyond the termination of the median ridge. They are thickly papillate. Opening of posterior nares three-fourths of an inch long. Palate posteriorly considerably vaulted; the oval aperture at its extremity short; the oblique fringe of papillæ that proceed on either side short and slightly developed. This portion of the mouth is marked with delicate oblique striæ. There are several folds of mucous membrane at the angle of the mouth. Tongue one and a quarter inches long; very acute, corneous on its anterior two-thirds; its posterior extremity obtusely emarginate, thickly papillate. Rima glottidis one-fourth long; situate rather more than this distance from the base of the tongue; its edges smooth, terminally papillate, and these papillæ extend for some distance on either side. Œsophagus between five and six inches long, including the proventriculus; presenting the ordinary characters as to muscularity and dilatability; of pretty uniform calibre throughout. The gastric zone is very narrow, less than half an inch. The mucous membrane differs but little in color from that of the œsophagus, but is somewhat darker, with broader and more irregular rugæ, and presents the usual soft, velvety, vascular appearance. The gigerium is situate far back, and turns a little to the right from the line of the œsophagus. It measures when empty about one by one and a half inches, presenting the usual constriction at its neck. Its cuticular lining is thrown up into numerous longitudinal rugæ, except over the tendons of the musculi laterales, where there is a smooth button formed.

The duodenal fold is short, only about 1¼ inches; just at its termination the intestine receives the hepatic, cystic, and pancreatic ducts, the latter piercing the intestine between the two former. All are quite short and open near each other. The liver is of ordinary size, the right lobe nearly double the size of the left. The two are loosely connected by a fibrous band, but little if any of the glandular substance being interposed. Gall-bladder present, of ordinary size and shape. The kidneys measure one and a half long by about one in breadth. Each is divided into three or four lobes, of which the superior are strictly reniform, the inferior nearly rectangular, the median irregularly oval and elongated.

The intestines measure about sixteen inches from pylorus to anus. The cœca are extremely short, only about two-tenths in length; oval in shape. Rectum short, only about half an inch long. The cloaca large and globular. It is fully described, with the oviduct, infrà.

The trachea is about four inches long, consisting of from ninety to ninety-five rings. It is weak and thin, and of small calibre throughout. Superiorly it is very flat, but about an inch from the larynx becomes almost perfectly cylindrical, and continues so for the rest of its length. The lower larynx is extremely small and delicate, comparatively more so than in other species; its cartilage appears softer and less dense. Its anterior wall is very short, scarcely one-tenth of an inch. Its anterior inferior apex and lateral inferior angles are very prominent and acute, the edges between them concave, as is also the posterior wall. The lateral bronchial apertures are narrow. The bronchial half-rings are about twenty-six in number, delicate, but quite distinct up to the first one, which, as usual, is larger and stronger than the rest. The laryngeal and tracheal muscles are as in the other species, but small and weak.

The following description of the ovaries, oviduct, and cloaca of this species was taken from a perfect female, obtained in 1858, at Bird Keys, Florida:

The condition of the organs show that the bird was taken while these were at their period of full activity. The left ovary, the one developed, as usual, contains a large quantity of ova, the majority of which are of the size of a pin-head. Five or six, however, have attained the size of peas, and hang out from the rest of the mass upon long, slender, well-developed pedicles. Upon the largest of these the vessels are distinctly visible, ramifying over its surface, and converging toward the white zone, already well marked, which indicates the place where the envelope is to be ruptured for the exclusion of the ovum. A calyx larger than any of the others has been emptied of its contents, and hangs by a very long pedicle in a shrunken, collapsed condition. The line of rupture is quite straight and smooth, extending over somewhat less than a third of the circumference of the envelope, and is located on that part directly opposite to the pedicle. The walls are quite thick, and have a fibrous feel between the fingers, but they are delicate and easily torn. Their internal surface is soft and perfectly smooth, and studded everywhere with minute puncta. The pedicle is about an eighth of an inch long.

The oviduct measures, when outstretched, about ten inches in length. In situ, however, its length is only from the anus to the extremity of the kidneys, a distance of about two and a half inches. It is consequently much convoluted. Its two extremities are widely diverse in appearance, the upper being so delicate and attenuated that it can hardly be examined except under water, while near the cloaca it is a stout, thick, muscular tube, half an inch in diameter. For two or three inches it is simply a very delicate membrane, upon which no structure is recognizable by the naked eye beyond a few slender, muscular fasciculi, arranged chiefly in a longitudinal direction. The tube then becomes quite abruptly thicker and stouter, and its lining membrane is thrown up into well-marked longitudinal rugæ, which have a good deal the appearance of the ordinary œsophageal folds. They are, however, more irregular and convoluted, and no one fold extends the whole length of this portion of the tube, they subsiding into the level of the canal at various places, and being interrupted by numerous transverse depressions. They cannot be made entirely to disappear by stretching the membrane transversely. On this portion of the duct, which is about four inches in length, both circular and longitudinal muscular fibres are very apparent. Beyond this the tube, for a short distance, again becomes more delicate, resembling somewhat the superior portions, but with the longitudinal rugæ still distinct. It then resumes the physical characters of the second portion, until within an inch and a half of its termination, where both the mucous and muscular coats undergo a total change. The former is greatly increased in thickness, so as to give great contractile power to this portion of the duct, enabling it to expel the fully-formed egg. Simultaneously with this increase of the muscular parietes, the longitudinal rugæ become vastly augmented in size, and lose their straight character. They become highly convoluted and irregular, and in the undilated state of the parts present, on cutting into the tube, the appearance of numerous, waved, flattened folds, pressed closely together side by side. The aggregate thickness of these mucous rugæ and the muscle together, make the diameter of the tube scarcely less than half an inch. The lining of this portion of the canal is parti-colored, being variegated with irregular patches of black.

The cloaca is, as usual in the family, very capacious, and of a globular shape. The two portions into which it is divided are better marked than in any other species I have examined. The semicircular fold of mucous membrane is very distinct, and the part beyond it is deepened into a perfect pouch or bursa, the orifice of which can be closed by the apposition of the elevated fold of mucous membrane against the posterior border of the anus. Just above this fold the ureters open upon papillæ in the usual position. To the left of the left orifice, on the side of the cloaca, is the opening of the oviduct, ordinarily tightly closed by a spincter, which produces puckering and corrugation of the membrane around the orifice, similar to those caused by the spincter ani.

Synonymy.—The Atlantic references to this bird are comparatively few and definite, there being scarcely a synonym excepting *Anous l'herminieri*, Less., and this unquestionably belongs here. His bird was from the Antilles, and the description is applicable in every particular to the characters of the very young bird above described. There are, however, a considerable number of Pacific quotations which will bear discussion. We may first state that *S. serrata* of Forster (the basis of *Onychoprion*, Wagl.), is undoubtedly founded upon the adult of this species. Forster's *guttata* is also, no doubt, a synonym of the young of this species, in the curiously spotted condition of early immaturity, yet with the white front and whitish under parts appearing. The *S. oahuensis* of Bloxham is uncertain; it may have been either this or the succeeding species. I quote several other names, of which I know nothing myself, upon authority cited with each.

STERNA (HALIPLANA) ANÆSTHETA,* Scop.

Bridled Tern.

(?) *Sterna nubilosa*, SPARRM., Mus. Carls. pl. 62 (*fide* SUND.).—SUND., Öfv. Vet. Ak. Förh. 1869, 589 (St. Bartholomew.) (= *S. boysii*, var. γ, LATH.)
Sterna anosthæta, SCOP. (ex SONN., Voy. pl. 84 ; Panay).
Sterna (Haliplana) anosthæta, COUES, Key, 1872, 322.
Hydrochelidon (Haliplana) anosthætus, GRAY, Hand-list, iii, 1871, 122, No. 11080.
Sterna panayensis, GM., Syst. Nat. i, 1788, 607 (*ex L'hirondelle de mer de l'isle de Panay*, SONN., *l. c.* p. 125).
Haliplana panayensis, SALV., Ibis, 1864, 381, 392 ; *ibid.* 1866, 199 (Honduras).
Onychoprion panayensis, SCL. & SALV., P. Z. S. 1871, 572 (Middle America).
Sterna panayo, LATH., Ind. Orn. ii, 1790, 808 (same as *panayensis*, GM.).
Onychoprion panaya, GOULD, B. Aust. vii, pl. 33.
Haliplana panaya, COUES, Ibis, 1864, 391 (Honduras).
(?) *Sterna antarctica*, CUV., *fide* GRAY et BLAS. (BP. says = *fuliginosa*).
(?) *Sterna oahuensis*, BLOX., Voy. Blonde, 1826, 251, *fide* GRAY et BLAS. (CASS. says = *fuliginosa*).
Haliplana discolor, COUES, Ibis, 1864, 392 (Honduras).—LAWR., Ann. Lyc. N. Y. viii, 105 (Sombrero).—ELLIOT, B. N. Am. ii, pl. 57. (May be a fair variety.)
Sterna "*melanoptera*, Sw.," *apud* GRAY (BLAS. says = *fuliginosa*).
Sterna "*infuscata*, RÜPP. ; *fuliginosa* et *fuligula*, LICHT. ;" *apud* BLAS., J. f. O. 1866, 81.

DIAG. *S. suprà cinereo-brunnea, alis cinereo-nigris, rectricibus exterioribus duabus fere ex toto albis, pileo nigro, cervice ex albido cinerascente, lunulâ frontali albâ, angustatâ, post oculos porrectâ, freno nigro per oculos in frontem extremam extenso.*

Hab.—Warmer parts of the globe. Originally described from the Philippine Islands. Australia. Middle America. West Indies. Florida (spec. in cab. G. N. L., so labeled by Audubon). The American may be varietally distinguishable.

Description (from an adult Florida specimen, received from Mr. Audubon, in the cabinet of G. N. Lawrence) : Form typical of the genus, as already described. Bill and feet black. Crown, and a moderately broad stripe through the eyes to the nostrils,

---

* I have not seen the original, which Gray quotes as "*anosthætus* ;" but if, as I presume, the word is allied to *anæsthesia, anæsthetic,* in allusion to an apparent stolidity of temper of the bird, this spelling is evidently more nearly correct.

black. The frontal white lunula is narrower than *fuliginosa*, of about the same width as in *lunata*, and, as in that species, extends some distance behind the eye, which is not the case in *fuliginosa*. The black pileum is, on the nape, sharply defined against ashy-white, which, as it proceeds backward, gradually deepens into the cinereous-brown, which is the prevailing color of the upper parts. The wings, and especially the prima-ries, are darker than the rest of the upper parts, and have scarcely a shade of cinereous; the tail, with its coverts, however, is much lighter and more ashy, approaching the nape in color. The primaries, as in *lunata*, have well-defined, pure white spaces run-ning for a considerable distance from their bases along the inner web, while in *fuliginosa* the inner webs are simply grayish-brown, with no well-marked pictura. A large part of the inner webs of the secondaries and tertials are also white. All the under wing-coverts are pure white. The central tail feathers are, as already described, brownish-ashy, concolor with their coverts. The lateral ones have much white toward their bases, especially on the inner webs, and this increases on each feather success-ively to such an extent that the next to the outer one is wholly white except a small space at its tip, while the outermost is entirely white. In *fuliginosa* only the outer-most one is white. (Compare descriptions.) The shafts of the primaries are brownish-black above, white beneath; of the rectrices, dark along the cinereous, and white along other portions of the feathers. Below the bird is entirely pure white.

Dimensions.—Length, 14 to 15 inches; wing, from the carpus, 10.50; tail, 6 to 7;* bill, 1.40 to 1.60; height at base, 0.35 to 0.40; width, slightly less; tarsus, 0.85; middle toe the same, with the claw 1.20; outer toe and claw, 1.00; inner, 0.75. These measure-ments, it will be seen, are intermediate between those of *fuliginosa* and *lunata*.

Immature plumage.—A specimen (No. 11394, Nicaragua, Oct., 1858, *Dr. Caldwell*), probably a bird of the first year, is slightly smaller, as would have been expected, but in form is the same. The differences in the plumage are: The black of the pileum is imperfect, largely mixed with white on the vertex, so that it fades insensibly into the white of the lunula, which latter is thus obscured. The black frenum is correspond-ingly imperfect. The upper parts are paler and grayer, some of the feathers being margined with whitish. The lateral rectrices are not wholly white. The under parts are pure white, as before. This is probably not the youngest plumage (of which I have yet to see specimens, that may perhaps be all dusky, white-spotted, like *fuliginosa*), but rather represents a plumage that closely resembles, if it be not identical with, the ordinary winter plumage of the adult.

This bird scarcely requires comparison with *fuliginosa*. The light ashy-white nape and hind neck; the black cap contrasting with the color of the back, besides being separated by the whitish cervix; the wings darker than the back; the amount of white on the tail; the narrowness and length of the frontal lunule; the differently-shaped bill and the smaller size, at once distinguish it. The species in fact comes nearer *lunata*, Peale, a rather dark-colored species, in which the crown and back are also conspicu-ously different from each other in color. *S. lunata*, however, is a smaller bird, with a grayish-plumbeous mantle, more nearly as in typical *Sternæ*. It is well described and figured by Mr. Cassin in the Ornithology of the United States Exploring Expedition.

Synonymy.—In 1864 I reached, by some devious path I do not now remember, the conclusion that *panayensis*, Gm. (or *panaya*, Lath.), were rather referable to *fuliginosa* than to this species; but upon reconsideration of the subject, I see that the less said on this score the better. It was upon this erroneous consideration that I proposed the term *discolor*, not that I desired to separate the American bird from that of other regions. The names of Gmelin and Latham are current for the species, but they are based upon Sonnerat (as above), and upon the same basis appears the name "*anosthœ-tus*" (as given by Gray), which has priority. Sundevall, indeed, finds a still earlier de-signation in *nubilosa*, "Sparrm., Mus. Carls. t. 62." This I have not been able to look up, but as there seems to be some uncertainty about it, it may be best held in check. Thus Gray, in the Hand-list, gives "*nubilosa*, Sparmm., M. C. t. 63," as a synonym of No. 11082 ("*infuscata*, Licht."); while in 1863, in his List of British Birds, he has a "*nebulosa*, Sparmm., M. C. t. 63," under *Sterna cantiaca*,† Gm. Without the work before me, I can only presume that Sundevall's quotation of "t. 62" is pl. 62, and that Gray's "*nebulosa*" is a slip for *nubilosa*.

In not adopting this name *nubilosa* for the present species, I am influenced by the following considerations: There appears to be another very closely-related species, or rather variety, and it is uncertain to which one of the two *nubilosa* belongs. This species is given by Gray, No. 11082, as "*infuscata*, Licht.," and put in a different sub-genus. There are in the Smithsonian two specimens which I take to be this species: one, No. 57093, from the Schlütter collection, marked "*Sterna fuscata*, ♂, ad., Insel Candia;" and another, No. 28475, marked "Bengal," but without further labeling.

---

* But the length of the tail, as in all Terns, varies very greatly, according to the age of the elongated lateral feathers. A discrepancy of several inches is by no means unusual in this subgenus and in *Sterna*.

† Latham quotes "*nubilosa*, M. C. t. 63, *pullus*," as a synonym of his *S. boysii* var. γ.

These two are the same bird, and I presume them to be the "*infuscata*, Licht.," of Gray's Hand-list, though I have no means of satisfying myself that such is the case. These birds run extremely close to the subject of the present article (my former *discolor*)—too close to be specifically separated, though a geographical variety is indicated. The bill is much slenderer, only 0.30 high at the base. The frontal lunula reaches but little beyond the eyes, instead of nearly half an inch behind them; the loral black stripe is narrower. The black cap is separated from the smoky-gray back by a very narrow, sharp, cervical collar, instead of a more gradual change. Only the outer tail feather is mostly white, instead of the two outer. The size of equally adult specimens is noticeably less—wing about 9.75 instead of 10.50. Now there is no reasonable doubt that Gray's Nos. 11080 and 11082 are one and the same bird; *i. e.*, that there is but one of these "sooty" Terns beside *fuliginosa;* Blasius has already said so, and I entirely agree with him. The question is as to the distribution of the synonymy between the two varieties. Gmelin's and Latham's names, *panayensis* and *panaya* (both = *anœstheta*, Scop., *l. c.*), apply as well to one as to the other. As to *nubilosa*, Sparmm., Gray has it under *infuscata*, while Blasius assigns it far elsewhere—to *cantiaca;* the name is thus obviously too uncertain to be used.

Blasius recognizes but three species of *Haliplana: lunata*, Peale, *panayensis* and *fuliginosa;* and such is emphatically my own decision. To the latter, *fuliginosa*, he assigns as synonyms *infuscata*, Licht., and *melanoptera*, Sw., besides the well-known *serrata* and *guttata* of Forster, throwing upon *panayensis* all the rest of the synonymy, namely, *fuliginosa* and *fuligula*, Licht.; *infuscata*, Rupp.; *antarctica*, Cuv.; *oahuensis*, Blox.; and *discolor*, Coues. It is probably not possible to locate all these names satisfactorily, nor to reconcile the conflicting views respecting them.

To complete an account of this group of dark-colored Terns with white frontal lunula and white under parts, and black bill and feet, I append a notice of *S. lunata*, Peale.*

Genus HYDROCHELIDON, *Boie.*

× *Rallus*, sp., LINN., Syst. Nat. i, 1758 (ed. x), 153.
< *Sterna*, LINN., Syst. Nat.
= *Hydrochelidon*, BOIE, Isis, 1822, 563. (Type *S. nigra*, LINN.)
= *Viralva*, LEACH, Gen. Zool. xiii, 1826, 166. (Same type.)
= *Pelodes*, KAUP, Sk. Ent. Eur. Thierw. 1829, p. 107. (Type *S. leucopareia*, NATTERER; = *hybrida*, PALL.)

GEN. CH. Bill a little shorter than the head, longer than the middle toe and claw; *very delicate, slender, acute;* culmen and commissure decidedly declinato-convex, the amount of curvature increasing toward the tip; outline of rami and gonys both concave, the former most so; eminentia symphysis prominent and very acute. Wings exceedingly long, pointed, of same color as back, without distinct markings on either web. Primaries broad and not very tapering, not acute; the tertials very short, rounded, not slender nor flowing, reaching in the folded wing only half way to the tip of the longest primary. Tail *rather short*, contained 2¼ times in the wings, *only moderately emarginate* (much as in *Gelochelidon*), the lateral feathers but little exceeding the next, not tapering and acuminate; all the feathers broad and rounded. Feet slender and short; tarsi much abbreviated, rather less than the middle toe alone. Toes moderately long; the webs rather narrow, *and very deeply incised.* Size small, general form delicate; *colors mostly black, the wings and tail plumbeous,* in type of the genus.

The group of Terns, of which *S. lariformis* of Linnæus may be taken as the type, forms a natural assemblage very closely allied to *Sterna* proper, but differing in certain

---

* *Sterna lunata*, PEALE, U. S. Expl. Exped. 1848, No. 725; CASS., *ibid.* 1858, No. 716; FINSCH & HARTL., Fd. Central Pol. pl. 18, f. 3.—*Hydrochelidon (Haliplana) lunata*, GRAY, Hand-list, No. 11081.—*Haliplana lunata*, BLAS., J. f. O. 1866, 80. (Description from the type of the species, No. 15744, Paumotu Islands (Vincennes), Sept. 1839.) Bill and feet black. Cap black, with a long, narrow, white frontal lunule, whose horns reach behind the eyes, cutting off a black stripe through the eye to the base of the bill at the nasal fossa. Upper parts uniform dark grayish plumbeous (not smoky gray), the color extending on the wing-coverts and tail. Cubital edge of fore-arm rather darker than other upper parts. Quills fuscous, silvered with the color of the mantle, their inner webs with the usual white stripe, which, however, does not nearly reach their ends. On the longer primaries, where this stripe is sharpest, it is bordered internally with a narrow prolongation of the fuscous along the margin of the inner web. Outer tail feather white for all that portion which is overlaid by the next feather, its outer web white to the tip; next tail feather with considerable white basally on the inner webs. Entire under parts pure white. Length may have been about 13 inches; wing, 10.25; tail about 6, forked full half its length; bill along culmen, 1.60; tarsus, 0.75; middle toe and claw, rather over 1. This species is the obvious link between "*Haliplana*" and *Sterna* proper.

features. These consist principally in the extreme slenderness of the bill, and the amount of deflection of its very acute tip; in the narrow and very deeply incised interdigital membranes; in the short and not deeply forked tail. The size is small, and the pattern of coloration peculiar. In the character of the tail the genus approaches *Gelochelidon*, but there the resemblance ends. It seems, while most closely allied to the typical *Sternæ*, to form the connecting link between them and *Haliplana ;* and among the *Megaloptereæ*, to have affinity with such genera as that of which Gould's *Anous plumbeus* is typical.

North America has a single representative of this genus, the young of which was described by Wilson as *S. plumbea*, but which is apparently identical specifically with the *H. fissipes* of Europe. The European species are three—*lariformis*, Linn. (*Sterna nigra*, Briss., and of many authors); *nigra*, Linn. (*leucoptera*, Auct.); and *hybrida*, Pall. (*leucopareia*, Natt., and most authors). The second of these has lately been detected in North America, but can only be considered as a straggler.

The first distinctive name for the genus is that of Boie of 1822. Leach's *Viralva* of 1826, and Kaup's *Pelodes* of 1829, are entirely synonymous. Of the several species of this genus indicated by authors, the two occurring in North America may be distinguished from each other and from *H. hybrida*, as follows :

A. Head all around, and under parts, black; the crissum abruptly white.
　　Small.　Wing under 8.　Bill dark.
　　　a. Wings and tail above plumbeous, like the back................. *lariformis.*
　　　b. Wings whitening along fore-arm border; tail with its upper
　　　　　coverts white... *nigra.*
B. Cap alone black; body above and below, with wings and tail, dark
　　pearly plumbeous, whitening on crissum and sides of head.　Large.
　　Wing over 9; bill light .... *hybrida.**

HYDROCHELIDON LARIFORMIS, (Linn.) Coues.

Black Tern.

a. (*European references.*)

Rallus lariformis, LINN., Syst. Nat. i, ed. 10th, 1758, 153 (= *S. nævia* of ed. 12th).
Sterna fissipes, LINN., Syst. Nat. i, 1766, 228 (based primarily on *S. nigra*, BRISS., Orn. vi, 211, pl. 20, f. 1).—GM., Syst. Nat. i, 1788, 610.—LATH., Ind. Orn. ii, 1790, 810.—SCHÆFF., Mus. Orn. 1779, 65.—BRÜNN., Orn. Bor. 1764, No. 153.—DEGL., Orn. Eur. ii, 1849, 349.
Hydrochelidon fissipes, GRAY, Gen. of B. iii, 1849, 660; List Br. B. 1863, 243.—BLAS., J. f. O. 1866, 82.
Sterna nigra, BRISS., Orn. vi, 1760, 211, pl. 20, f. 1.—RETZ., Fn. Suec. 1800, 164.—MEY., Tasch. ii, 1811, 461.—TEMM., Man. 1815, 484; ii, 1820, 749.—LEACH, Cat. 1816, 41.—VIEILL., Nouv. Dict. xxxii, 1819, 170; Fn. Franc. 1828, 400.—FLEM., Br. B. 1828, 144.—NILSS., Orn. Suec. ii, 1821, 160.—LESS., Tr. Orn. 1831, 622.—JEN., Man. 1835, 268.—EYT., Cat. 1836, 55.—KEYS. & BLAS., Wirb. Eur. 1840, 98.— SCHINZ, Eur. Fn. 1840, 375.—NAUM., V. D. x, 1840, 198, pl. 256.—MACGIL., Man. Orn. ii, 1840, 233; Br. B. v, —.—SCHL., Rev. Crit. Ois. Eur. 1844, 130.
Hydrochelidon nigra, BOIE, Isis, 1822, 563.—KAUP, Sk. Ent. Eur. Thierw. 1829, 109.— BREHM, V. D. 1831, 793.—BP., List, 1838, 61.
Viralva nigra, LEACH, Gen. Zool. xiii, 1826, 167.
Sterna nævia, LINN., Syst. Nat. i, 1766, 228 (based on *S. nævia*, BRISS., vi, 217, pl. 20, f. 2, and *Rallus lariformis* of ed. x, 1758, 153).—SCHÆFF., Mus. Orn. 1779, 66.— GM., Syst. Nat. i, 1788, 609 (*Sterna boysii* var. B. of LATH., Ind. Orn. ii, 806, is the same as this).
(?) *Sterna obscura*, GM., Syst. Nat. i, 1788, 608.—LATH., Ind. Orn. ii, 1790, 810.
Hydrochelidon nigricans et *obscura*, BREHM, V. D. 1831, 794, 795.

* *Sterna hybrida*, PALL., Zoog. R. A. ii, 1811, 338.—KEYS. & BLAS., Wirb. Eur. 1840, 98.
Hydrochelidon hybrida, GRAY, Gen. of B. iii, 1849, 660; List Br. B. 1863, 242.—BLAS., J. f. O. 1866, 82.
Sterna leucopareia, NATT.—TEMM., Man. ii, 1820, 746.—NAUM., V. D. x, 1840, 168, pl. 255.
Viralva leucopareia, STEPH., Gen. Zool. xiii, 1826, 171.
Pelodes leucopareia, KAUP, Sk. Ent. Eur. Thierw. 1829, 107.
Hydrochelidon leucopareia, BOIE.—BREHM, V. D. 1831, 797, pl. 39, f. 1.
Sterna delamottei, VIEILL., Ency. Meth. 350.
"*Sterna grisea*, HORSF.; *indica*, STEPH.; *albistriata* et *similis*, GRAY; *fluviatilis*, GOULD; *delalandii*, BP." (*Fide* BLAS., J. f. O. 1866, 82.)

Since the term "*hybrida*" is obviously meaningless in such employ—in fact wholly incorrect and inapplicable—should it not be passed over, like any other glaringly inappropriate designation, in favor of the better known and well-fitting, though subsequent, appellation *leucopareia?*

b. (American references.)

Sterna surinamensis, GM., Syst. Nat. i, 1788, 604.—LATH., Ind. Orn. ii, 1790, 804 (*Surinam Tern*, Gen. Syn. vi, 352).
Hydrochelidon surinamensis, BP., Comptes Rendus, 1856, 773.
Hydrochelidon (Pelodes) surniamensis, GRAY, Hand-list, iii, 1871, 122, No. 11074.
Sterna plumbea, WILS., Am. Orn. vii, 1813, 83. pl. 60, f. — (young).—PELZ., Novara Reise, Orn. 155.
Hydrochelidon plumbea, LAWR., B. N. A. 1858, 864.—WHEAT., Ohio Agric. Rep. 1860, No. 277.—COUES & PRENT., Smiths. Rep. 1861, 418.—HAYD., Rep. 1862, 176.—CAB., J. f. O. v, 232 (Cuba).—SCL., P. Z. S. 1864, 179 (Mexico).—DRESS., Ibis, 1866, 45 (Texas).—SNOW, B. Kans. 1873. 12.
Sterna nigra, BP., Syn. 1828, 355.—SW. & RICH., F. B. A. ii, 1831, 415.—NUTT., Man. ii, 1834, 282.—AUD., Orn. Biog. iii, 1835, 593 ; v, 1839, 642 ; pl. 180 ; Syn. 1839, 320 ; B. Am. vii, 1844, 116, pl. 438.—DEKAY, N. Y. Zool. ii, 1844, 300, pl. 126, f. 278.—GIR., B. L. I. 1844, 352.—HOY, Smiths. Rep. 1864, 438.—TRIPPE, Pr. Ess. Inst. vi, 1871, 119 (Minnesota).—AIKEN, P. Bost. Soc. xv, 1872, 210 (Colorado).
Hydrochelidon nigrum, BP., List, 1838, 61.
Hydrochelidon fissipes, COUES, Pr. Phila. Acad. 1862, 554 (critical).—COUES, *ibid.* 1866, 99 (Colorado River) ; *ibid.* 1871, 46 (North Carolina, migratory).—COUES, Pr. Ess. Inst. v, 1868, 309 (New England).—COUES, Pr. Bost. Soc. xii, 1868, 127 (South Carolina, in summer).—COUES, Ibis, 1864, 391 (Honduras).—SALV., Ibis, 1864, 385 (the same).—GUNDL., Rep. F. N. i, 1865, 393 (Cuba).—LAWR., Ann. Lyc. N. Y. viii, 1866, 299 (New York).—ALLEN, Pr. Ess. Inst. iv, 1864, 91 (Massachusetts).— McILWR., *ibid.* v, 1866, 96 (Canada).—DALL & BANN., Tr. Chic. Acad. 1869, 307 (Alaska).—ALLEN, Am. Nat. iii, 1870, 644.—MAYN., Guide, 1870, 157.—SCL. & SALV., P. Z. S. 1871, 573 (Middle America).—ALLEN, Bull. M. C. Z. iii, 1872, 183 (Kansas, &c.).
Sterna fissipes, TURNB., B. E. Pa. 1869, 39.
Sterna "frenata," SALV., Ibis, 1860, 278 (error ; see Ibis. 1866, 205).

DIAG. *S. nigra, dorso, alis, caudâque plumbeis, remigibus nigro-griseis rhachidibus albis, crisso albo.*

Hab.—Europe, &c. North America generally. Alaska. Middle America. South America to Chili. Breeds at large in North America. Winters chiefly or entirely extralimital.

Adult, breeding plumage.—The culmen is throughout exceedingly narrow, and transversely very convex, even at the the base it being scarcely at all broadened or flattened. The bill is strongly compressed from the nostrils, causing the gonys as well as the culmen to be very sharp and narrow. The nasal fossa is notably short, becoming obsolete rather abruptly, and in the middle of the upper mandible. The nostrils nearly fill its whole length, are pretty large and wide, of ordinary general characteristics. The feathers on the sides of the mandible extend but little further than on the culmen, and have a broad rounded outline. Those on the submental or intercrural space nearly fill it. This space is very narrow and elongated. The tibiæ are bare for a moderate distance. The very short tarsus is quite smooth, being covered posteriorly and laterally with small, smooth, regular plates, anteriorly with equally smooth transverse scutella. The toes are very long, the middle one without its claw fully equaling the tarsus. The outer is as long as, perhaps even slightly exceeding, the middle ; the claw of the inner just reaches to the base of the middle claw. The emargination of the inner web extends to opposite the second articulation of the middle toe, that of the outer to the middle of the second phalanx of the same toe. The claws are all moderately arched, slender and compressed, acute, the inner edge of the middle one but slightly dilated. The remiges and rectrices are notable for their great breadth, and neither tapers to a very acute point, but are rather broad to near the apices, which are rounded. The inferior caudal tectrices are very long and full.

Head and neck all round, and under parts to the vent, pure black. On the back of the neck, and between the shoulders, the black becomes gradually changed into leaden-gray or plumbeous, which extends undiluted to the very apices of the tail feathers. The tertials are of the same color as the back ; the secondaries even a little darker, tending toward the color of the primaries. The shafts of all the primaries are whitish, deepening into black at the tips. The primaries are blackish or deep plumbeous-gray, darkest on the outer web of the first, the inner webs of all, but especially the outer one, fading into lighter on their margins. The superior surfaces of all the primaries have a considerable amount of the ordinary silveriness. The under surfaces of the wings are white, but considerably deepened by a plumbeous wash, this plumbeous-white extending slightly over the edge of the wing on to the lesser coverts. The long, full, under tail-coverts are pure white, in marked contrast to the black of the rest of the under parts.

Adult, in winter plumage.—Very different from the adult in summer. The forehead,

45

the sides of the head below the eyes and ear-coverts, the chin, throat, neck all round, and the whole under parts, *pure white*. The under wing-coverts retain a good deal of their plumbeous hue. The upper parts generally, and especially the primaries, are much as in summer; but the tint of the plumbeous, especially on the rump, is considerably lighter, and the feathers have faint whitish margins. The back between the shoulders is considerably lighter than in summer, but a little darker than the rump. Along the fore-arm, just beyond the whitish edge of the wing, there is a rather broad band of grayish-black, formed by several rows of the lesser coverts. Along the dorsal aspect of the arm, also, there is something of this black band, but the color is concealed by the scapular feathers. The secondaries are considerably darker than in summer, being in this respect fully equal to the primaries; and the comparative shades of their inner and outer webs are exactly as in the primaries. On the crown the white of the forehead becomes obscured and variegated with blackish or grayish-plumbeous, which grows darker on the nape, and on the sides of the head sends forward a band through the eye, to become intensified into a blacker spot just anterior to it. The feet are brownish-black, with little or no reddish; the bill pure black. The rhachides of the primaries are darker than in summer. There is no appreciable difference in the emargination of the tail, nor in the shape of its individual feathers.

While changing, in August, during the moult, the adults are in a peculiar state of plumage. The entire under parts (except the inferior caudal tectrices), and the head and neck all round, are remarkably variegated with pure white and pure black. The relative amounts of the two colors varies with almost every specimen, depending of course upon the particular stage arrived at. In general, the forehead and throat, as far as the breast, become first pretty uninterruptedly white. The crown, occiput, and nape are then equally variegated with the two colors, in small spots and lines; but the auriculars, and a spot just before the eye, are usually pretty purely black. The shoulders and edges of the wings show traces of the grayish-black that is to appear. The now old and worn-out primaries have lost most of their silvery hoariness, and the shafts are nearly pure yellowish-white, except at their extreme apices. The bird in other respects is generally as in summer.

Young-of-the-year in August.—The size is less than that of the adults; the bill is smaller, weaker, softer, without very sharply defined angles or ridges. The emargination of the tail is very slight, being only about half an inch, and the lateral rectrices want even the slight elongation and tapering which those of the adults have, being broad to their very apices, which are somewhat oblique truncated. There is an indescribable softness and general mollipilose condition to the plumage, readily recognizable, both by sight and touch, to the expert in such matters.

Bill brownish-black, the base of the lower mandible dull, dirty flesh-color, the inside of the mouth yellow. Legs and feet light brown. Forehead grayish-white, this color extending over the eyes as such, but deepening on the crown and occiput into grayish-brown. This color extends over the nape down to the back, and there obscures the general plumbeous hue of the parts. On the middle of the back, between the shoulders, this brown is quite uniform; on other parts it merely forms tips and margins for the feathers, including the superior alar and caudal tectrices, and the tertials and scapulars. The row of least upper wing-coverts is grayish-black, as in the adults in winter. The tertials have also whitish tips, in addition to their subterminal brown ones. Before the eye is a crescent of deep, pure black; behind the eye a patch of pure black extends over the auriculars and a little distance on the sides of the neck. The under parts are pure white; on each side of the breast there is a large spot of plumbeous-brown, which, however, does not meet its fellow of the opposite side. The sides under the wings are very light plumbeous, much the same hue as the inferior alar tectrices and axillary feathers. The secondaries are like those of the adults in winter; the primaries like those of the full-plumaged summer birds, only that their shafts are superiorly brown, not white.

Dimensions of the adult.—Bill above, 1.10; along commissure, 1.60; from feathers on side of lower mandible, 1.08; gonys, 0.60; height at base, 0.25; length, 9.25; extent of wings, 24 to 25; wing from carpus, 8.25; tail, 3.75; depth of forking, 0.90; tarsus, 0.68; middle toe and claw, 0.90; tibiæ bare, 0.40.

Dimensions of the young-of-the-year.—Bill above, 0.95 to 1; depth at base, 0.20; from feathers on side of lower mandible, 0.95; gonys, 45; tarsus, 0.60; middle toe and claw, 0.85; length, 7.75 to 8; extent of wings, 23.50 to 24; tail, 3; depth of emargination, 0.50.

Anatomical characters.—The mouth is narrow, its sides concave, and its tip attenuated, beyond that of any other species. The palate is soft and vascular to within half an inch of the tip. The median palatal ridge commences far forward; it is narrow, but prominent, its edges posteriorly, and the edges of the nasal aperture, slightly papillate. The sulcus between it and the lateral ridge is well marked and deep. The lateral ridges are short and sinuate, extending no further back than the median. The posterior vaulted space small but well arched, the nasal slit extending far into it. Posterior fringe of oblique papillæ well developed. Tongue exceedingly acute, narrow, longitudinally grooved along the dorsum, anteriorly corneous, its apex bifid, its posterior extremity emarginate, slightly papillate; nine-tenths long. Rima glottidis one-fourth of an inch long; sparsely papillate. The alimentary canal is exceedingly similar in all respects to that of *Sterna*. Œsophagus, proventriculus, and gigerium in a straight line, all of ordinary characters, the former $3\frac{1}{4}$ to 4 inches long. Proventricular belt 0.3 to 0.4 wide, forming a complete zone, as usual. Duodenal fold 1.40 long. Hepatic and cystic ducts short, opening into intestine at the ordinary place. Lobes of liver of nearly equal size; their anterior surface convex, their posterior slightly concave; their apices divaricating, as usual, to receive the heart between them, their inferior extremities in apposition. They are connected by glandular substance. The chief fold after the duodenal is a short distance above the cœca, and lies apposed to the posterior surface of the gizzard; after which the intestine proceeds in a slightly convoluted course to the cœca. These are the shortest throughout the subfamily measuring hardly one-eighth of an inch in length. Rectum moderately long (for this subfamily), measuring six-tenths. Cloaca large and globular; three-fourths long. Its posterior division small, but well marked. Orifices of ureters and vasa deferentia in the usual place. The kidneys, as in *Sterna*, are divided into five or six lobes by the segmentation of the middle portions. The whole renal mass measures about an inch in length by six-tenths in breadth. The trachea is about $2\frac{1}{2}$ inches long, of the usual number of rings. It is flattened superiorly; below it becomes perfectly cylindrical and narrower. The lower larynx is exceedingly small, measuring only one-tenth of an inch across its widest part. Its sides are concave, its apices acute and projecting. Bronchial apertures extremely narrow, of an oval, inclining to a crescentic, shape. The sterno-tracheales join the trachea only one-fourth of an inch above the larynx. Bronchi of ordinary length, of about twenty-two half rings.

Synonymy.—The first tenable binomial name of this species appears to be *lariformis*, Linn., 1758, in adopting which I hope not to be accused of arbitrary innovation. No valid reason appears why Linnæus should not be adopted at this date, rather than at 1766, and in spite of custom to the contrary, this view is constantly gaining ground. I myself am entirely in favor of it. The changes it requires are not many, and they are in some cases desirable ones, as, for instance, when we are furnished with *Chætura pelagica* (1758) instead of the unmeaning *C. pelasgia* of 1766. This bird is also the *S. fissipes*, Linn.; a name not commonly adopted until after Mr. Gray's rectification of the synonymy, the term *nigra* (ex Briss.) having been generally employed. But *nigra*, Linn., clearly belongs to *leucoptera*, Meisner. Other old names of this species are *nævia*, *obscura*, and *surinamensis*, all based upon immature conditions of plumage. Latham put *nævia* down as *S. boysii* var. B. Wilson renamed the species *plumbea*, doubtless in simple ignorance of the prior designations.

I must continue to disagree with several ornithological friends, for whose opinions I have great respect, in holding the American bird to be specifically identical. Nevertheless, in deference to their views, I have collated the synonymy in two sets.

In my review of the *Sterninæ*, I state that "the birds of the two continents were first formally separated by Bonaparte in his Comparative List of 1838." This is a slip of the pen. Both are there given as *Hydrochelidon nigrum;* he makes the distinction in 1856 (Tabl. Longip. C. R.), giving the American as *Hydrochelidon surinamensis*.

Lieutenant Warren's Expedition.—9023, Loup Fork of the Platte.
Later Expeditions.—54322, Wyoming.

The Black Tern migrates both coastwise and over the water-courses of the interior. On the coast of North Carolina I saw none, in spring, until the second week in May, when they became very abundant for a few days and then disappeared on their way north. These spring birds were always, so far as I ascertained, in full plumage. The Terns revisit the same region very early, in advance of most of the migrants, in the fore part of August, and proceed much more leisurely than in spring. For about two months they were constantly to be seen hovering over the marshes in airy troops, fluttering hither and thither like so many Swallows or Night-hawks, busily foraging for insects. These fall arrivals were chiefly young birds; and of the old ones, none were seen still wearing the breeding dress, which, therefore, must be early laid aside. These Terns, like the other smaller species, but just the reverse of the large kinds, are perfectly familiar, or rather heedless, at all times. In the spring, at their breeding resorts, they dash close down to an intruder, repeating with angry vehemence their shrill *crik, crik, crik;* in the fall, when nearly silent, they are equally regardless of approach, often fluttering within a few feet of one's head, and then sailing off again, in the manner of Swallows. The flight is buoyant in the extreme, and wayward, desultory, uncertain; perhaps no bird of this country has so great an expanse of wing for its weight, and certainly none fly more lightly. In hovering along on the lookout for insects, they hold the bill pointing straight downward, like others of the family. In the spring I have observed them plunging, like other Terns, into the water for food, probably small fry, but in the fall they seem to feed chiefly on winged insects, which they capture like Night-hawks, as noted above.

The Black Tern I have found breeding in various parts of the West. On the 10th of June, 1864, I passed a large colony which had settled on a marshy tract along the Arkansas River, near Fort Lyons. The birds were all in full plumage, and doubtless had eggs at the time, although, from the untoward circumstances of observation—hurried traveling by stage—I could not examine the nesting places as I wished. In June again, 1873, I found a colony breeding in a prairie slough along the Red River; shot the greater part of the whole number, and secured many eggs. The birds were breeding in company with a great number of Yellow-headed Blackbirds, some Red-wings, and Short-billed Marsh Wrens. The eggs, in every instance, were placed on masses of floating débris of last year's reeds, where the water was two or three feet deep, in the midst of the slough. They had to be closely looked after, for they were laid directly on the moist matting, without any nest in any instance, and readily eluded observation, from their similarity in color to the bed of reeds they rested on. They were two, oftener three, in number, and resembled those of some Sandpipers in size, shape, and coloration. The shape is pointedly pyriform, yet with considerable bulge at the sides; the dimensions, 1.35 by 0.95, with the usual variation either way. The ground color is brownish-olive, rather light and clear, this thickly marked with spots and blotches of every size, from mere points up to masses, but for the most part large and bold, with a tendency to aggregate at the but, or, at least, around the larger half of the egg. No part of the surface, however, is unspotted. The coloration is a rich, warm brown, of every shade, from light brown to blackish-brown, according to the quantity of pigment. With these markings are associated a few neutral tints or stone-gray spots, in the shell.

HYDROCHELIDON NIGRA, (Linn.) Gray.

White-winged Black Tern.

Sterna atricapilla, BRISS., Orn. vi, 1760, 214.
Sterna nigra, LINN., Fn. Suec. 56, No. 159; Syst. Nat. i, 1766, 227.—GM., Syst. Nat. i, 1788, 608.—LATH., Ind. Orn. ii, 1790, 810 (quotes *S. atricapilla*, BRISS., vi, 214). (Not of BRISS., nor of many authors.)
Hydrochelidon nigra, GRAY, Gen. of B. iii, 1849, 660; List Br. B. 1863, 243; Hand-list, iii, 1871, 121, No. 11070.—BLAS., J. f. O. 1866, 82.
Sterna leucoptera, MEISNER, Vög. Schweiz. 1815, 264.—TEMM., Man. ii, 1820, 747.—NAUM., V. D. x, 1840, 215, pl. 257.—KEYS. & BLAS., Wirb. Eur. 1840, 98.—SCHL., Rev. Crit. 1844, 131.—MCCOY, Ann. Mag. N. H. 1845, 271.—COUES, Check-list, 1874, No. 575 *bis* (first introduced into Fauna N. Am.; spec. in Mus. Smiths. Inst., from Wisconsin, *T. Kumlein*, through *Dr. Brewer*).
Sterna (Hydrochelidon) leucoptera, SCHRENCK, Reise, 511.—RADDE, Reisen, ii, 1863, 389.
Hydrochelidon leucoptera, BOIE, Isis, 1822, 563.—KAUP, Sk. Ent. Eur. Thierw. 1829, 109.—BREHM, V. D. 1831, 796.
Viralva leucoptera, LEACH, Steph. Gen. Zool. xiii, 1826, 170.
Sterna fissipes, PALL., Zoog. R. A. ii, 1811, 338. (Adult. Not of authors; quotations of true *fissipes*, but description unmistakably of this species.)
Sterna nævia, PALL., Zoog. R. A. ii, 337. (Young. Not of authors; identified on same grounds as the preceding.)

DIAG. *H. nigra, pallio schistaceo-nigro, caudâ crissoque albis, autibrachiis albicantibus, alis plumbeis, remigibus argentato-fuscis rhachidibus albis, rostro rubescente-nigro, pedibus rubris.*

Hab.—Europe, &c.   Accidental in North America (one instance known).

Adult, summer plumage.—(No. 66213, Mus. Smiths. Inst. ♀, Lake Koskonong, Wisconsin, July 5, 1873, *T. Kumlein.*)   Bill black, with a reddish tinge; feet red; claws black. Head and neck all around and whole under parts to the crissum pure black, shading on the back and scapulars into dark slaty-plumbeous.   Wings dark silvery-plumbeous, fading into white along the fore-arm border; the quills silvered dusky, with white shafts and a dull white area on the greater part of the inner webs of the primaries. Lining of wings sooty-blackish, varied with dull white along the border.   Tail, with its coverts, both above and below, white, abruptly contrasting with the black of the belly and the dark slate of the rump.   The tail feathers shaded with pearly-gray toward the ends.

Length (of skin), 8; wing, 7.50; tail, 2.75; the emargination under 0.50; bill along culmen, 0.90; along gape, 1.20; height at base, 1.20; tarsus, 0.75; middle toe and claw, 0.87.

The series of specimens before me does not fully illustrate the changes of plumage of this species.   It shows, however, that the various plumages are closely coincident with those of *H. lariformis*, already detailed.   Immature birds, plumbeous above and mostly white beneath, may be recognized from the same stage of *H. lariformis* by the hoary-white fore-arm border of the wing, and contrast of white upper tail-coverts with the plumbeous of the back.

As stated in the Check-list, p. 137, a specimen of White-winged Tern was taken in Wisconsin, July 5, 1873, by Mr. Thure Kumlein, and presented to the Smithsonian by Dr. T. M. Brewer.   The individual is a female, in perfect breeding dress, and was said to have contained well-formed eggs in the ovary, leading to the belief that it would have bred in the vicinity before long.   This, so far as I know, is the first and only instance of the occurrence of the species in this country.   I have carefully compared the specimen with European ones, finding it identical in every particular.

Section MEGALOPTEREÆ.

I have already presented the character of the "Noddy" group of Terns, as drawn from the leading genus, *Anous.*   Beside this principal form, with its several species, there are two others, namely, *Nænia* * and *Procelsterna*†.   The last named is cinereous, and very near *Anous;* the former is unique, in possession of long, white, curly plumes on each side of the head.   *Gygis*‡ is a peculiar intermediate genus, pure white, with a singularly shaped bill.   *Anous* alone occurs in this country.

Genus ANOUS, *Leach.*

< *Sterna*, LINN., Syst. Nat. i, 1758, *nec* 1735.
< *Gavia*, BRISS., Orn. vi, 1760, 199, *nec* MÖHR.—Sw., Classif. B. ii, 1837, 373 (*stolida*).
" *Nodinus*, RAF., 1815 ?" (*Gray*).
= *Noddi*, CUV., R. A. i, 1817, 521 (*stolida*).
= *Anous*, LEACH, Steph. Gen. Zool. xiii, 1826, 139 (*stolida*).
= *Megalopterus*, BOIE, Isis, 1826, 980 (*stolida*).
= *Stolida*, LESS., Tr. Orn. 1831, 620 (*stolida*).
= *Aganaphron*, GLOGER, 1842.   (*Gray*.)

GEN. CHAR.   Bill much longer than the tarsus, rather exceeding the middle toe and claw, about equaling the head, moderately robust, depressed, and as broad as high at

* NÆNIA, *Boie*, Isis, 1849, 189 (= *Larosterna*, BLYTH, Cat. Asiat. Soc. 1849, 293 = *Inca*, JARD., Contr. Orn. 1850, 32).
NÆNIA INCA.—*Sterna inca*, LESS., Voy. Coquille, 1826, 731, pl. 47; *Anous inca*, GRAY, Gen. of B. iii, 1849, 661; *Larosterna inca*, BLYTH, *l. c.*; *Inca mystacalis*, JARD., *l. c*
Hab.—South America (Peru and Chili).

† PROCELSTERNA, *Lafr.*, Rev. Zool. 1841, 242.   The several nominal species of this section may be reduced to two at most; I have recognized but one.   South Seas and Australia.

‡ GYGIS, *Waql.*, 1832; type *alba.*   The single species inhabits the South Seas.

the base; elsewhere depressed, tapering to an acuminate and somewhat decurved tip.
Fore end of nostrils nearly half-way to end of bill, the fossæ long and deep. No frontal
antiæ; outline of feathers on base of bill convex (reverse of *Sterna*). Wings but moderately long for this subfamily, the second primary but little shorter than the first.
Tail very long, broad, fan-shaped, double-rounded, *i. e.*, graduated laterally, yet with
central feathers shorter than the next. Tarsi very short, robust, less than the middle
toe without its claw. Lateral toes, especially the inner, unusually lengthened; hallux
well developed. Webs broad and full, not incised. Claws short, stout, little curved,
but very acute. Podotheca nearly smooth, from tendency to fusion of the plates, there
being but a single defined row of scutella in front, with delicate reticulations elsewhere; the soles of the webs are perfectly smooth. Edges of middle claw dilated and
somewhat pectinate. Plumage dark or nearly unicolor.

In addition to these external characters may be noted: Eyes small, the anterior canthus just over the angle of the mouth. Lobes of liver very unequal. Proventricular
zone narrow, with small follicles. Cæca remarkably long for this subfamily. Duodenal fold very short. Hepatic and pancreatic ducts opening close by each other.
Bronchial half-rings weak and imperfect, the upper part of the tube being almost membranous. Lobulation of the kidneys more as in *Larus* than in *Sterna*.

The generic synonyms above given all apply to *stolida* and its immediate allies, of
which there are several. Only one occurs in North America; a second, *A. tenuirostris,*[*]
is found in Middle America.

ANOUS STOLIDUS, (Linn.) Gray.

Noddy Tern.

Sterna stolida, LINN., i, 1766, 227 (Amoen. Acad. 240; *Hirundo marina major, capite albo,*
     SLOANE, Jam. i, 31, pl. 6, f. 2; CAT., Car. i, 80; *Larus gavia fusca*, BRISS., vi,
     199, pl. 18, f. 2; *Passer stultus*, RAY, 154).—GM., Syst. Nat. i, 1788, 605.—LATH.,
     Ind. Orn. ii, 1790, 805.—LESS., Voy. Coq. i, 1826, 244 (Chili).—BP., Syn. 1828,
     356.—NUTT., Man. ii, 1834, 285.—AUD., Orn. Biog. iii, 1835, 516; v, 1839, 642;
     pl. 275; Syn. 1839, 322; B. Am. vii, 1844, 153, pl, 440.—JENYNS, Man. 1835, 270
     (Ireland).— SCHL., Rev. Crit. 1844, 131 (Europe).—THOMPS., Trans. Linn. Soc.
     1835; Nat. Hist. Ireland, iii, 308 (Ireland).—KNOX, Zool. 1866, 306 (Ireland).—
     HARTING, Br. B. 1872, 170 (Ireland).—MAXIM., Beitr. iv, 874.—BURM., Syst.
     Uebers. iii, 543.
Megalopterus stolidus, BP., List, 1838, 61.—KEYS. & BLAS., Wirb. Eur. 1840, 98.—MACGIL.,
     Man. ii, 1842, 236.
Anous stolidus, GRAY, List Gen. of B. iii, 1841, 100; Gen. of B. iii, 1849, 661; List Brit.
     B. 1863, 244 (Ireland).—CAB., J. f. O. v, 234 (Cuba).—LAWR., B. N. A. 1858,
     865.—SCL., Ibis, i, 1859, 233 (Central America).—BRY., Pr. Bost. Soc. vii, 134
     (Bahamas).—BLAS., List B. Eur. 1862, 22 (quotes YARR., iii, 417).—COUES, Pr.
     Phila. Acad. 1862, 557.—COUES, Ibis, 1864, 393 (Honduras).—LAWR., Ann. Lyc.
     N. Y. viii, 1864, 106 (Sombrero).—GUNDL., Rep. F. N. i, 393 (Cuba).—SUND.,
     Öfv. K. A. V. Förh. (St. Bartholomew); P. Z. S. 1871, 125 (Galapagos).—SCL.
     & SALV., P. Z. S. 1871, 556 (Middle America, south to Brazil and Chili).—
     (?) HUTTON, B. N. Zeal. 1871, 43.—COUES, Key, 1872, 323.
Anous niger, STEPH., Gen. Zool. xiii, 140.—EYT., Cat. Br. B. 1836, 55.
Gavia leucoceps, SW., Classif. B. ii, 1837, 373 (type P. E. 997).
(?) *Anous frater*, COUES, Pr. Phila. Acad. 1862, 558 (Pacific). (Var.?)
(?) *Sterna pileata*, SCOP., Sonn. Voy. 125, pl. 85.
(?) *Sterna philippina*, LATH., Ind. Orn. ii, 1790, 805 (=*pileata*, SCOP.).
" *Anous rousseaui*, HARTL.," *fide* GRAY & BLAS.
" *Anous unicolor*, ERM., juv.," *fide* GRAY & BLAS.
" *Sterna tenuirostris*, BLYTH," *fide* BLAS. (Not of TEMM.)

DIAG. *A. fuliginosus unicolor, alis caudâque nigrescentibus, fronti et vertice albis, pedibus
     rubescente-fuscis, rostro nigro. Long.* 16.00 *poll.*; *ala* 10.00–10.50; *rostr.* 1.75; *tars.* 1.00.

Hab.—South Atlantic and Gulf coast of North America. Bahamas. Cuba. Middle
America generally, both sides. South to Brazil and Chili. Various warm seas. Australia (*Gould*); New Zealand (*Hutton*). Accidental in Europe.

---

[*] ANOUS TENUIROSTRIS (*Temm.*).
Sterna tenuirostris, TEMM., P. C. 202.
Anous tenuirostris, COUES, Ibis, 1864, 393 (Honduras).—SALV., Ibis, 1866, 200 (the
     same).—SCL. & SALV., P. Z. S. 1871, 566 (the same).
     This is readily distinguished from *A. stolidus* by its blackish instead of fuliginous
plumage, slender bill, and other characters. The discrimination, however, of the several current blackish species is difficult. Gray places *tenuirostris*, Temm., as a synonym
of *senex*, Leach, and gives the habitat as Afrcia.

Adult, breeding plumage.—Both mandibles marked with more or less distinct longitudinal striæ; their tomia inflected. Nasal sulcus deep and long, formed by the rounded culmen and a prominent ridge, which runs along the upper mandible from its base to beyond the nostrils, where it is gradually lost. Just above the base there is a small but distinct fossa, separated by an oblique ridge from the large nasal sulcus. Culmen about straight for half its length, regularly decurved toward the tip, basally broad and flat. Commissure slightly declinato-convex. Outline both of rami and gonys concave, the former most so; eminentia symphysis illy defined and not acute. Primaries unicolor, very broad almost to their tips, which are rounded; first primary scarcely surpassing the second. Tail very long and much graduated; but there is also a slight emargination, the two central rectrices being a little shorter than the next pair. Bill and claws black. Mouth black to a little beyond the angle of the jaws, the fauces yellowish. Tarsi and toes dark reddish-brown, nearly black in the dried skin. Occiput bluish-plumbeous, becoming pure white on the front. Sides of the head and neck all round with a decided wash of bluish-plumbeous. The whole body is a deep fuliginous-brown, growing almost black on the remiges and rectrices, with a very dark spot anterior to and just above the eye.

Dimensions.—Length, 16 inches; extent of wings, 31; wing from flexure, 10 to 10.50; tail, about 6; bill along culmen, 1.75; height or width at base, 0.38; tarsus, 1; middle toe and claw, 1.45; outer ditto, but slightly shorter; inner ditto, 1.20; hallux, 0.40; breadth of webs, 0.90; diameter of eye, 0.30.

Anatomical characters.—Mouth long and narrow, its lateral outlines slightly concave. Palate nearly flat behind; longitudinally arched before; soft and vascular to within an inch of the tip. A prominent central ridge, beset with obtuse papillæ, bifurcated posteriorly for 0.6, to give passage to the posterior nares. The narrow well-marked lateral ridges commencing one and a half inches from the tip of the bill, extending beyond the termination of the median ridge, smooth anteriorly, thickly papillate posteriorly. On each side, just within the tomia, is a groove for the reception of the inferior maxilla. The palate is black nearly as far as the angle of the mouth; the fauces yellowish. Posterior nares 0.9 long, anteriorly smooth, terminally papillate. Rima glottidis 0.25. The oblique converging rows of papillæ on the vaulted space at the back of the palate are but slightly developed. Tongue 1.90 long, very acute, corneous for more than two-thirds its length; its posterior extremity emarginate, papillate. Œsophagus very long, measuring with the proventriculus, 6 inches; as usual, very muscular and distensible. Proventriculus a straight continuation of the canal; its zone of gastric follicles very narrow, the glands exceedingly small. This portion of the tube does not present the marked differences from the œsophagus as regards its lining membrane that is ordinarily found. Gizzard situate very far back in the abdomen, deflected at a considerable angle toward the right; its middle about opposite the ramus of the pubis. The œsophagus is not of equal calibre throughout, but dilates a good deal toward the proventriculus, where the muscular parietes are thicker, and the longitudinal rugæ of mucous membrane more numerous than elsewhere. The intestine measures 14 inches in total length, from pylorus to anus. The duodenal fold is exceedingly short, being less than one inch. It curves round to the left beneath the gigerium. Lying below the duodenal fold, and in contact with it, is the last intestinal fold, which has its apex about three inches from the origin of the cœca. The cœca are elongated, being longer than in any other representative of the subfamily. They measure 1.40 inches. They are club-shaped, growing broader toward their extremities, after a small uniform diameter for half their length. Rectum exceedingly short, barely three-quarters of an inch. Cloaca, as usual, very capacious, globular, 0.75 long. The urinary and spermatic ducts open upon well-marked elevated papillæ, side by side, and close to the posterior median line. Posterior division of the cloaca well marked by elevated folds of mucous membrane. The pancreas is very short, scarcely an inch in length, owing to the shortness of the duodenal fold. The lobes of the liver are of very unequal dimensions, the left being so small as to appear but a mere appendage to the right. The former measures one and a half in length by one in breadth; is thick, with a rounded smooth surface. The latter is scarcely three-quarters long by one-half broad. It is of much the same shape as the right, to which it is closely connected by a short band of glandular substance. The pancreatic and hepatic ducts pierce the intestine in close proximity, about two inches below the pylorus. The kidneys are one and a quarter inches long by three-quarters broad. They are much less lobulated than in *Sterna*, and are more like those of *Larus*. Their upper lobes are smaller than their lower, having very convex borders. The lower are subquadrangular in shape; the central ones only partially divided into several small irregular masses. Heart elongated, tapering, acute; its width across the base of the ventricles seven-tenths. The trachea is short, being little more than three inches; its rings about one hundred; flattened above, becoming more cylindrical as it proceeds downward. Bronchi very short and quite wide. They are very feeble at their commencement, being almost entirely membranous, the half-rings hardly distinct enough to be counted. These number about twenty-four. Muscles as in the *Sterninæ* generally; the sterno-tracheales join the trachea only three-tenths above the lower larynx.

Considerable doubt has been expressed whether the Noddies of the *stolidus* pattern (excluding those of the blackish *tenuirostris* type) are all identical. Mr. Cassin, in 1858, remarks upon certain observable discrepancies; and later I proposed the term *frater* for the Pacific bird, upon examination of the matter in company with Mr. Cassin and Prof. Baird, who both agreed that there were recognizable peculiarities. The Pacific material in the Smithsonian shows a deeper, though not longer, and consequently differently-shaped bill; a different proportion of tarsus to toes; a much longer tail, with greater emargination and somewhat different coloration. While I would by no means now insist upon, or even concede specific validity in this case, I still think there may be a varietal difference. The case may be summed as follows, although there is little or no probability that the name *frater* is not anticipated.

Var. STOLIDUS : Wing, 10 to 10.50; tail about 6, the emargination slight; bill, 0.38 deep at base; tarsus, 1; middle toe and claw, 1.45. Occiput bluish-plumbeous, purely whitening on forehead. Sides of head and neck washed with bluish-plumbeous. Feet drying black.

Var. FRATER : Wing, 11 to 11.25; tail 7, the emargination 0.50; bill, 0.43 deep at base; tarsus 1 (as in *stolidus*), but middle toe and claw 1.60. Occiput brownish-ash, becoming ashy-white on the forehead. Sides of head and neck like rest of body. Feet drying reddish-brown.

Subfamily RHYNCHOPINÆ : *Skimmers.*

DIAG. *Laridæ hypognathæ, rostro cultrato, mandibulâ maxillâ longiore.*

Body slender and elongate. Neck of moderate length. Head large; the forehead high and broad. Upper mandible shorter than the under, its cutting edges rapidly converging to the nostrils, thence parallel and closely soldered to the tip. Mandibular rami at first widely separated and nearly parallel, then rapidly converging to the symphysis, the union then complete both of tomial and gonydeal margins. Nostrils basal, inferior, their near end behind the projection of the feathers on the culmen. Interramal space fully feathered. Tibiæ anteriorly scutellate. Remiges, 10; rectrices, 12; and other general characters of *Sterninæ.*

Upper mandible very freely movable, owing to the mobility of the fronto-maxillary suture. Mouth short, broad, of moderate gape. Palate flat; internal nares long. Tongue short, broad, fixed. Digestive and respiratory organs, in all essential respects, similar to those of *Sterninæ.*

The Skimmers are so much the Terns in general character, that no detailed account is required; but the remarkable peculiarities of the skulls merit special attention.

Skull.—The most important differences are found in the shape of the cranium; in the fronto-maxillary suture, and other elements which enter into and produce the mobility of the superior mandible; and in the shape and character of the mandibles themselves. In the terms used in the following description, reference is always had to the normal *Laridine* type, as compared with the special modification of it under consideration.

The cranium is exceedingly narrow posteriorly, at that portion which forms the encephalic cavity. The post-orbital are hardly, if at all, more widely separated than are the ante-orbital. The convexity of the vertex of the cranium antero-posteriorly is very slight indeed, and the superior curved line of the occiput rises high up and is exceedingly prominent. Its inferior extremities curve greatly forward and outward, forming very protuberent zygomatic processes overhanging the articulation of the tympanic bone. At the same time the occipital ridge is hardly appreciable as such; the dorsum of the occipital bone being very flat, or even a little concave. The crotaphyte depression between the zygomatic and post-orbital processes is very deep, from the great bulk of the muscles lodged in it. This increased volume of muscle is also indicated by the meeting on the median line of the skull of the two roughened depressions which lodge the temporalis, these depressions being only separated by a narrow longitudinal ridge, as in *Puffinus* or *Colymbus,* instead of by a wide space. The anterior division of this temporal fossa (distinctly separated from the posterior by a well-marked ridge) is also deep, and extends further toward the median line of the skull.

From the narrowness and straightness of the posterior parts of the cranium, the orbits are notably wide and shallow. Their posterior processes are very small and slightly developed, being in fact much smaller and no more widely separated from each other than the anterior processes. These latter are remarkably developed, being large, broad and heavy, and projecting backward and outward with very convex outlines. The supra-orbital ridge included between them is not nearly so deeply concave as in the other subfamilies, both on account of the closer approximation of the post-orbital processes, and of the character of the depression for the nasal gland. The convex borders of the fossæ do not nearly approach each other on the median line, but are widely separated. The fossæ themselves are narrow and imperfect, not nearly containing the whole of the glands, which consequently project greatly over the edge of the orbit. The fossæ are continued each as a well-marked groove, under the anteorbital processes, their ducts passing through a very large foramen on their way to the lining membrane of the nose. The interorbital septum is complete. The olfactory nerve runs along in a furrow so deep as to be almost a canal. From the completeness of the septum, between the orbits, the foramina of exit of the nerves at the posterior part of the orbits are more perfect and less closely approximated than in the other subfamilies. The conjointed bases of the sphenoid and ethmoid, which form the inferior border of the septum, and along which the palatal and vomerine bones slide, is much thicker and stouter than ordinary, and does not extend nearly so far forward, nor has it an acute apex nor deeply concave anterior edge.

The forehead is exceedingly broad, and slopes down from the vertex at an unusually great angle of descent. In its centre it is slightly concave laterally, owing to the development and prominence of the anteorbital processes. Anterior to these it is perfectly plane, wide, with parallel, straight sides, dipping down deeply with a square truncated base which forms, with the superior mandible, the very peculiar fronto-maxillary suture. This "articulation" admits of a far greater degree of motion than exists in the other subfamilies, and greatly exceeds that usually found among birds, excepting, of course, the *Psittaci*. The connection between the bones of the cranium and superior mandible is perfectly straight and transverse; very wide (being the whole width of the broad frontal bone), and at the same time exceedingly thin and elastic. On the superior surface of the suture there is a deep groove between the bones, a little wider at either extremity than in the middle, but the under surface is quite smooth. The osseo-cartilaginous connective substance is pliable and elastic, so much so, that in an old and dried preparation before me, the original mobility of the parts is in a great measure retained.

In the adult skull before me there are no discernible traces of any nasal bones, properly speaking; but the suture is formed entirely by the apposed terminations of the broad frontal, and equally broad mesial process of the intermaxillary. That portion of bone usually known as the "maxillary" or descending process of the nasal, exists, unusually developed, and in an unusual position. Below it is firmly anchylosed and completely consolidated with the mandibular ramus, just anterior to the malar anchylosis. From this base it extends upward and backward as a long, very slender, compressed bone, running parallel with, but not touching the sides of, the os frontis, to be received by this thin, flat, laterally expanded termination into a slight depression in the under and anterior edge of the ante-orbital process. As it participates in all the movements of the upper jaw, its union with the ante-orbital processes is a movable suture, of apparently the same general characters as the fronto-maxillary suture, of which it is to be considered as really a part.

The other elements which assist to produce the movements of the upper jaw, are all by their shape or position subservient to its increased mobility. The ossa pedicellata are long and strong, and especially remarkable for the increased development of their malar eminences, which carry the ends of the zygomata far outward and downward, and thus are enabled, with an ordinary degree of motion of the tympanic bones themselves, to impress upon the malar, and through them upon the superior maxillary bones, an increased amount of motion. They also produce a somewhat peculiar shape of the articulating surface for the inferior mandible. The orbital processes of the tympanic bones are very short, small, and exceedingly acute. The pterygoid bones present no special peculiarities of shape, but, from the narrowness of the skull, are not so widely divergent as in the other subfamilies. The palatal bones are remarkable for stoutness and width, and also for the solidity and extent of their anchylosis with the superior maxillaries. The outline of their posterior margins is very oblique, and they terminate with quite prominent processes for the pterygo-palatal articulation. Posteriorly their inferior surfaces have considerable lateral concavity from the elevation of their borders; more anteriorly they are plane and smooth, their surface being directly continuous with the plane of the maxillaries. The vomer is shorter than usual, and bifurcate to a less extent. The malar bones are perfectly straight; their axes in a line with the general inclination of the axes of the mandibular processes of the intermaxillary; but just at their union with the maxillary bones there is a considerable angle formed, from the increased divergence of the latter at that point. They are throughout laterally compressed, except just at their anterior extremities, where they become horizontally depressed and flattened, to give them the necessary mobility of elasticity in an upward and downward direction.

The intermaxillary bone is entirely peculiar in shape and general characters. It is remarkable for the preponderance in size of the mesial over the mandibular processes, and for the unusual extent to which the latter are united with the former

The consolidation is perfect for fully two-thirds of the length of the bill, causing the nasal aperture formed by the divergence of these processes to be extremely small, short, and narrow. The mandibular processes are also closely approximated to each other (only a narrow groove being left between them) for two-thirds their length, when they rather suddenly divaricate at a considerable angle. The palatal fissure thus left between them is very short, and only commences about opposite the termination of the palate bones, instead of much further forward, as in the other subfamilies. The superior or mesial process of the intermaxillary is thus almost wholly concerned in the production of the shape of the upper mandible. It is large at the base, being there as broad as the os frontis, and about half as high as broad, with inflated, very convex and bulging sides. Beyond the nostrils it becomes more compressed and deeper, and begins to present a ridge along its culmen in place of the groove which exists at its base. The sides become, as they advance, more and more compressed, and less bulging and convex, until they terminate in a very acute point. This bone is remarkable in being *hollow* throughout, from base to extreme apex, with very thin walls, and consequently very light. Its interior is partially occupied by a very light, delicate web of open cancellated structure, most marked toward the base; more anteriorly its complete hollowness is only interrupted by delicate trabeculæ of bone, which extend across, from side to side, in every direction. This peculiarity of structure calls to mind the bill of the *Rhamphastidæ*.

The bony frame-work of the under mandible, though not abnormal in structure, has yet even a more peculiar shape than that of the upper. The rami of the inferior maxilla are at first nearly parallel, and are very thin and delicate. Toward their symphysis they become stouter, and very suddenly converge toward each other with a considerable degree of convexity. At the symphysis, which is strong and firm, the tomial as well as the dorsal edges of the bone at once unite; and the rami, thus completely consolidated, extend forward as a straight, thin, sharp prolongation of bone, with flat, erect sides, and perfectly straight edges, which converge toward an acute apex. The axis of the symphysis declines downward at a considerable angle of divergence from the axis of the rami. The conjoined tomia are at their base on a level with the superior edges of the rami, but the dorsal outline is at its beginning much below the level of the inferior edge of the rami, in consequence of a marked deepening of the bone just at its symphysis. On account of the peculiar direction of the inferior maxilla, the tomial edges of the two mandibles are not usually in contact throughout in their ordinary positions. Posteriorly the upper outline of the rami dips down with a considerable angle to the articulating surface. This latter differs from the ordinary type in its width, which is great, in consequence of the development of its internal and external angular processes, and in the depth of the internal concavity. These differences correspond to the differences in shape of the face of the tympanic bone; in the prominence of its malar and pterygoid processes, and the depth of the sulcus between them. The roughened ridges and eminences about the joint for muscular attachment are all well marked. The triangular space just posterior to the articulation, for the attachment of the digastricus, does not present so much downward and forward as in the other subfamiles.

The single known genus of this subfamily is represented in North America by its type species, the long and well-known *R. nigra*.

Genus RHYNCHOPS, *Linn.*

Phalacrocorax, MOÈHR., Gen. Av. 1752.
Rynchops, LINN., Syst. Nat. i, 1758; 1766, 228 (*R. nigra*).
Rygchopsalia, BRISS., Orn. vi, 1860, 223.
Rhynchops, LATH., Ind. Orn. ii, 1790, 802.
Anisorhamphus, DUM. (*Gray*).
Psalidorhamphus, RANZ, 1823 (*Gray*).
Rhynchopsalia, GLOGER, 1842 (*Gray*).

The characters of the single genus being the same as those of the subfamily, it is unnecessary to repeat them.

Moèhring's name unquestionably belongs here, but is used in a different acceptation. *Rynchops* of Linnæus, more correctly written *Rhynchops*, may be employed instead, though I hardly know upon what grounds, for as Linnæus called the Cormorants *Pelecanus*, *Phalacrocorax*, Moèhr., does not conflict with a Linnæan name, and we date some accepted genera back to 1735. The original *Rygchopsalia* of Brisson is variously spelled by subsequent authors. I quote *Anisorhamphus* and *Psalidorhamphus* on Gray's authority, having no means of verifying or completing the references.

RHYNCHOPS NIGRA, Linn.

Black Skimmer; Cut-water.

Rhynchops nigra, LINN., Syst. Nat. i, 1766, 228.—GM., Syst. Nat. i, 1788, 611.—LATH., Ind.
Orn. ii, 1790, 802; and of authors generally.—BURM., Syst. Übers. iii, 454;
Reise, 520 (La Plata).—LEÓT., Ois. Trinidad, 534.—MAXIM., Beit. iv, 877.—
PELZ., Orn. Bras. 324.—PH. & LANDB., Cat. 50 (Chili).—GUNDL., Rep. F. N. i,
393 (Cuba).—SALV., Ibis, 1865, 193; 1866 (Guatemala).—SCL. & SALV., P. Z. S.
1858, 77 (Rio Napo); 1871, 566 (south to 45°, *Darwin*).—SCL., P. Z. S. 1867, 340
(Chili).—SCL., P. Z. S. 1864, 179 (Mexico).—DRESS., Ibis, 1866, 45 (Texas).—
LAWR., B. N. Am. 1858, 866.—LAWR., Ann. Lyc., viii, 1866, 299 (New York).—
TURNB., B. E. Pa. 1869, 39 (New Jersey, frequent).—COUES, Pr. Ess. Inst. v,
1868, 309 (? New England; quotes EMMONS, Cat. B. Mass. 1835, 6; LINSL., Am.
Journ. Sci. xliv, 1843, 249; PUTN., Pr. Ess. Inst. i, 1856, 231).—COUES & PRENT.,
Smiths. Rep. 1861, 419 (Washington, D. C.).—COUES, Pr. Bost. Soc. xii, 1868,
127 (South Carolina).—ALLEN, Bull. M. C. Z. ii, 1871, 368 (Florida, in winter).—
COUES, Pr. Phila. Acad. 1871, 46 (North Carolina).—COUES, Key, 1872, 324.
Rhynchops fulva, LINN., Syst. Nat. i, 1766, 229.—GM., Syst. Nat. i, 1788, 611.
Rhynchops cinerascens et *brevirostris*, SPIX, A. B. pls. 102, 103 (*juniores*).
Rhynchops melanurus, BOIE.—SW., An. in Men. 1838, 340 (Demarara).—CAB., Schomb.
Guian. iii, 761.—SCL. & SALV., P. Z. S. 1866, 201 (Ucayali); 1867, 593 (Mexiana);
1867, 754 (Peru).
Rhynchops borealis, SW., An. in Men. 1838, 340.

DIAG. *R. rostro rubro nigro dimidiato, notœo cum primariis 6 exterioribus nigris, pogoniis
internis primariorum 4 interiorum et apicibus albis, fronte et gastrœo albis plus minusve
rosaceis, caudâ albâ nigro dimidiatâ, pedibus rubris.*

Hab.—Warmer parts of America. South to 45° (*Darwin*). Various West Indian
Islands. In North America, Gulf and Atlantic coasts regularly to New Jersey; casually,
if at all, to New England.

Adult.—Upper mandible with its culmen curved for its whole length, sinking a little
at the base; highest just beyond the nostrils; gradually curved to the tip, which is
more acute than that of the lower mandible, but still very convex in profile; the ridge
sharp and narrow for its whole length. The sides of the upper mandible are, from the
base for half its length, very convex and bulging, so as to give to the base of the bill
a much rounded transverse outline; but the sides gradually become more and more
compressed, till they hardly project at all, but are quite perpendicular. The tomia of
the superior mandible, from the angle of the mouth, at first converge very rapidly, at
a quite obtuse angle, and at the same time are so much inflected that the sides of the
mandible just above them look almost directly downward as far as the distal extremity
of the nostrils; there the tomia are parallel, very closely approximated, with perfectly
perpendicular sides, leaving between them only a narrow groove for the reception of
the tomial symphysis of the inferior mandible. The nasal groove is short and wide,
and rather shallow, its width and shallowness being caused by the great difference in
amount of divergence of the nasal and mandibular processes of the intermaxillary bone.
The nostrils are situated at the anterior extremity of this groove, and are of ordinary
laridine shape and size. The feathers run far forward on the broad and depressed base
of the culmen, with a rather obtuse angle, and then slope backward to the angle of
the mouth with a sinuate outline, at first concave, then convex. The lower mandible
is compressed for the whole of the extent which is bare of feathers, except just at the
extreme base, where the rami are rapidly approaching the median line; very flexible,
being capable of being greatly bent in a lateral direction; its tip with a very thin,
sharp edge, and a broadly convex perpendicular profile outline. Its sides are nearly
erect and flat, bulging but slightly at the base, not at all terminally; marked with
about sixty straight, very oblique ridges and sulci, running at an angle of about
45° downward and backward; of a length equal to about half the height of the
mandible; most distinct toward the middle of the bill, more obsolete toward either
extremity. The tomial edges, of which the symphysis is complete from a point about
opposite the nostrils to the tip, are slightly convexo-declinate for their whole length;
the gonys, which is as thin and sharp as the tomium, is somewhat more decidedly con-
cavo-declinate. The outline of the inferior mandibular rami is perpendicularly very
concave, horizontally sinuate, the submental space being filled with feathers to the
very symphysis. The basal half, or a little less, of both mandibles are carmine-red,
the terminal half black.
The feet are of moderate length for this family. The tibiæ are naked for a very
considerable space, nearly half their total length. This bare portion shows a decided
tendency, most marked on its anterior face, to become transversely scutellate, like the
tarsus. The tarsus is defended anteriorly by a single row of scutella, which become

obsolete toward the joint, and have exceedingly oblique margins. Laterally and pos-teriorly there are plates, small, regular, smooth, of a polyhedral (mostly hexagonal) shape, largest and flattest on the sides of the tarsus, smaller and more roughened behind and on the joint. The toes superiorly are defended, as is the tarsus, by scutella, the webs by small reticulated plates; on the inferior surfaces of both the plates are nearly obsolete. The middle and outer toes are of much the same length, the inner much shorter, the tip of its claw reaching the base of the middle claw. The hallux is of moderate length for this family; its claw short, stout, blunt, little curved. The anterior claws are all long, slender, depressed, moderately arched, rather acute, the inner edges of all dilated, that of the middle one most so. The interdigital membranes are of the ordinary width and amount of emargination. The feet in life are carmine-red, in the dried state dull yellowish, with a tinge of pink.

The wings are excessively long and powerful. The primaries are broad, their rhachides strong, outer five or six of a somewhat falcate shape, narrowing rather sud-denly when near the tip to their only moderately acute and rather rounded apices. The secondaries are short, broad to their very tips, which are rounded, with a very slight amount of excision of the extremities of their outer webs. The superior surface of the wings is glossy black, like the back; their inferior aspect, except a narrow line along their metacarpal edge, white; this color deepening toward the ends of the pri-maries, first into grayish, and then into blackish. The first six primaries are concolor, black, pure and deep on their outer web, lighter and of a brownish tinge on their inner; their rhachides black. The inner four primaries are brown; their inner webs, and the tips of both webs, white. The secondaries are white, with a space of dark brown occupying nearly the whole of their outer and a small part of their inner webs. The amount of brown is least on the outer ones; increases on each feather suc-cessively, till the last four secondaries and the tertials are brownish-black, except a narrow apical margin.

The tail is of moderate length, being contained rather less than three times in the wing. It is moderately emarginate. The feathers are rather narrow, the central pair rounded at their tips, the lateral ones converging to a very obtuse point. The upper tail-coverts are short, being scarcely half the length of the tail; the inferior ones, how-ever, reach within a short distance of the tips of the central rectrices. The tail and its under coverts are white, the inner webs of all the rectrices more or less obscured with dark brown, deepest on the central pair. The superior coverts are black like the back, except the outer row on each side, which are white.

Crown of the head, its sides just below the eyes, the back of the neck, and whole upper parts, pure glossy black. The forehead, cheeks, sides of the head below the eye, sides of the neck, and whole under parts, pure white; tinged in life, during the nuptial season, with rosy.

Dimensions.—Length (of males), 20; extent of wings, 49; wing from flexure, 16 to 16.50; from apex of longest secondary to tip of first primary, 6; tail, 5.50 to 6; depth of fork, 1 to 1.25; upper mandible along culmen, 3; along gape, 4; height opposite middle of nostrils, 0.60; width at same place, 0.45; length of nasal fossa, 0.75; of nostrils, 0.40; under mandible along gonys, 3.75; along fused tomia, 3.60; along gape, 4.50; from feathers on its side to tip, 4.10; its depth at deepest part, just anterior to beginning of symphysis, 0.60; depth at tip, about 0.25; length of longest oblique stria, about 0.40; tibiæ bare, 1.10; tarsus, 1.45; middle toe and claw, 1.30; outer toe and claw, 1.20; inner toe and claw, 0.95; hallux and claw, 0.35.

The preceding description was taken from a large and very perfect specimen obtained in Florida. The dimensions are perhaps somewhat greater than the average of exam-ples, but not more so than is frequently found to be the case. Individuals vary greatly in size, many apparently equally adult examples being much smaller than the one whose dimensions I have just given. I believe that Audubon is quite correct in saying that the females are smaller than the males. They will not average probably more than 16 or 17 inches in length, by about 42 in extent of wings, as he has said. I have also found the bills to be much thinner, lighter, and weaker. In colors the sexes hardly differ notably.

Young-of-the-year.—Bill smaller than in the adult, thinner, weaker, its ridges less sharply defined, and the two mandibles of less unequal length. General proportions less than in adult. Bill brownish-black for three-fourths of its length, fading into dull horn-color just at its tip, lightening into more or less intense flesh color, or light red-dish, toward the base. The striæ on the sides of the lower mandible are as numerous as, but much less distinct than, in the adult. Tail shorter and less deeply emarginate. Legs and feet dull light reddish. Entire upper parts a rather light grayish-brown, deepest on the wing-coverts and tertials; each feather with a tolerably broad margin and tip of white, broadest and most conspicuous on the wing-coverts and tertials. Forehead, sides of the head below the eyes, the neck all round, the edge of the fore-arm, inferior surfaces of the wings, and whole under parts, white. Primaries almost exactly as in the adults, except that the innermost have more white, and there is a slight white terminal margin as far as the fourth or fifth. Secondaries about as in the adults, but their brown portions lighter and duller. Tail white; the greater part of the two central rectrices, and the inner webs of the others, with a tinge of dull grayish-brown, deepest on the middle pair.

I once saw a single specimen of this bird on the Potomac River, near Washington. Otherwise my personal observations are confined, up to the present time, to the coast of North Carolina, where the birds are plentiful. There I only noticed them late in the summer and during the autumn, though I presume they pass by in the spring; none breed there, to my knowledge. In September they become plentiful, and so continue until the latter part of November, some doubtless remaining later. In examining large numbers of specimens I found a great difference in size, and particularly in the bill. Some individuals are fully a third heavier than others. The bill varies over an inch in length, and especially in the length of the under mandible. Sometimes the difference between the two mandibles is hardly a third of an inch, at others over an inch. The oblique striæ on the under one are sometimes obsolete. In high condition the bill is bright red (vermilion) and black; otherwise orange and black, or even mostly dusky, only yellowish at base. The young in the fall are curiously variegated with dusky and whitish above, few specimens being exactly alike. The note of this species is instantly distinguished from that of any of our other species of this family by its deep guttural intonation, more like the croaking of some Herons than the cries of the Gulls and Terns. The bird also differs from its allies in going in true flocks, as distinguished from the gatherings, however large, in community of interest, that occur with the Gulls and Terns. The birds move synchronously, which is not the case with any of the others. They feed chiefly by night, or at any rate in the dusk of the evening, at which time, in passing over the harbor, one may hear their hoarse notes on every hand, and see the birds gliding swiftly along just over the water, either singly or in small flocks. During the daytime, when the Gulls and Terns are busy fishing, the Skimmers are generally seen reposing on the sand-bars. They never drop on their prey on the wing, like their allies. Their mode of feeding is not exactly made out, but it is believed they skim over the surface with the body inclined downward, the bill open, and the under mandible in the water, so they really take their prey in a manner analogous to the feeding of whales.

ORDER PYGOPODES: DIVING BIRDS.

Excluding the *Sphenisci*, or Penguins, which may form a group of equal value with *Pygopodes*, the latter consist of three families, readily distinguished, as follows:

Common characters.—Feet palmate or lobate. Legs feathered to the heel-joint, buried in common integument nearly to the same extent, situate far posterior, restricting terrestrial locomotion, and necessitating more or less nearly erect attitude on land. Hallux elevated, free or joined by lobe to base only of inner toe, small or altogether wanting. Bill of indeterminate shape, corneous, not lamellate or serrate, not furnished with a gular pouch. Nostrils variable in shape and position, naked or feathered. Wings short, stiff, stout, never reaching when folded to the end and often not to the base of the tail. Tail always short, sometimes rudimentary. Palate schizognathous. Carotid sometimes single (in *Podiceps* and *Mergulus*). Tibia often with a long apophysis. Sternum variable. Nature altricial or præcocial; young ptilopædic. Habit highly natatorial and urinatorial.

Colymbidæ.—Feet completely palmate, four-toed, the hallux joined by its slight flap to base of inner toe. Tarsi reticulate, extremely compressed, with smooth sharp hinder edge. Tibio-tarsal joint feathered. Claws strong, narrow, arched. Bill lengthened, tapering, acute, straight, wholly hard. Tail perfect, of many feathers. Wings with stiff inner secondaries much shorter than the primaries, the primaries not emarginate. Lores completely feathered. Nostrils linear, reached by the frontal antiæ, their upper edge lobate. Eye large. Back of adult spotted; young not striped on head; no crests or ruffs at any season. Seasonal changes of plumage slight. Sternum with long, broad xiphoid prolongation and shorter lateral apophyses. A long tibial apophysis. Carotids double. Nature præcocial. Eggs few, variegated in color. The very few species confined to the Northern hemisphere.

Podicipidæ.—Feet lobate and semipalmate, four-toed, the hallux free, with large lobe. Tarsi transversely scutellate, compressed, the hinder edge serrate, with a double row of small pointed scales. Tibio-tarsal joint naked. Claws broad, flat, obtuse. Bill usually lengthened and straight, but the tip sometimes decurved. Tail rudimentary—a mere tuft of downy feathers. Wings with long, broad inner secondaries overlying the primaries when closed; primaries eleven, several emarginate. Lores with a naked strip. Nostrils linear, oblong or oval, not lobed, not reached by the frontal feathers. Size medium and small. Back of adult not spotted; young usually with striped head; adults in breeding season usually with lengthened colored crests or ruffs or bristly feathers. Seasonal changes of plumage great. Sternum short in middle line, with long lateral apophyses. A long tibial apophysis. Carotids usually (always?) single. Nature præcocial. Eggs numerous, plainly colored. The numerous species cosmopolitan.

Alcidæ.—Feet palmate, three-toed (hallux wanting). Tarsi reticulate or partly scutellate. Tibio-tarsal joint naked. Claws ordinary. Bill of wholly indeterminate shape, often much as in *Colymbidæ* or *Podicipidæ;* often curiously shaped, with various ridges, furrows, or horny protuberances. Tail perfect, of few feathers. Lores completely feathered. Nostrils wholly variable in shape and position, naked or feathered. Legs very variable. Coloration variable; head often with curious long curly crests. No tibial apophysis. Usually (always?) an anconal sesamoid, sometimes double. Carotids usually double (single in *Mergulus*). Nature altricial. Eggs few or single, plain or variegated. The numerous species confined to the Northern hemisphere.

As stated at p. 589, the *Alcidæ*—marine species without representatives in the Missouri region—will not be presented in this work, while the *Colymbidæ* and *Podicipidæ* of North America will be treated monographically. The basis of the following account was prepared by the present writer several years ago for a report upon which he was then engaged with Dr. George Suckley.[*] It has, however, been entirely recast for the present purpose, and is altogether a different paper.

Family COLYMBIDÆ: Loons.

For diagnosis see above.

By many modern writers the Loons and Grebes are held as respectively composing the subfamilies *Colymbinæ* and *Podicipinæ*, of a single family, *Colymbidæ*. These divisions correspond with the *Colymbi pedibus palmatis* and *C. pedibus lobatis* of Gmelin, the

---

[*] An abstract of which was published in the Proceedings of the Philadelphia Academy of Natural Sciences for 1862, pp. 226-233.

genera *Colymbus* and *Podiceps* of Latham, and nearly with the *Cepphi* and *Colymbi* of Pallas. All were united under the genus *Colymbus* by Linnæus.* But the groups are sufficiently distinct to bear family rank. Temminck, indeed, separated them widely by intervention of the *Longipennes* and *Anseres*, though this seems hardly permissible. As this family contains but one genus, further characters are considered under that head.

Genus COLYMBUS, *Linn.* (*emend.*)

< *Colymbus*, LINN., Syst. Nat. 1735–1766, and of authors.   (Not of Illiger, 1811, nor of Pallas, 1811, nor of Brisson, 1760.)
< *Cepphus*, MÖHRING, Gen. Av. 1752, 69.
< *Mergus*, BRISSON, Orn. 1760.
× *Cepphus*, PALL., Zoog. R.-A. ii, 1811, 339.
= *Eudytes*, ILLIGER, Prod. 1811, 282.
= *Eudites*, KAUP, Sk. Ent. Eur. Thierw. 1829, 144.

CH. Bill long, strong, straight, acute, compressed. Culmen convex or nearly straight, commissure corresponding, gonys generally convex. Rami long separate, the gonydeal union usually denoted by a groove sometimes almost to tip, the angle always evident. Maxilla more or less striate basally. Mandible dilated along tomia, with groove just below. Nasal fossæ well marked, continued anteriorly in sulci. Nostrils long, linear, pervious, subbasal, reached by the antiæ, and having a peculiar flap hanging from the upper border. Head densely and evenly feathered, with long acute antiæ running into the nasal fossæ; no naked spaces nor bristly nor lengthened feathers about the head or neck. Ear small and inconspicuous. Eye with its anterior canthus just over the angle of the mouth. Wings moderately long (for this group), very powerful, concavo-convex, with somewhat falcate primaries, the first longest, the rest rapidly graduated, the inner secondaries short, stiff, broad, falling far short of the ends of the primaries in the closed wing. Tail short, but fully developed, rounded, with stiffish acuminate feathers, but upper and under coverts reaching nearly to the end. Legs short, very stout and powerful; tibiæ feathered on the suffrago; tarsi extremely compressed, entirely reticulated, with small polygonal scales and smooth sharp fore and hind edges. Toes lengthened, exceeding the tarsus, outer longest, inner shortest of the anterior ones, all full-webbed; hallux small, slightly lobed with a flap continuous with base of second toe. Claws strong, narrow, obtuse, convex above.

The three species which compose the genus are characteristic of the Northern hemisphere. They are heavy, powerful, and hardy birds, eminent in powers of flight and in swimming and diving, but progressing on land with difficulty. They are migratory, breeding far north, generally dispersed in winter. The voice is loud, penetrating, and raucous; the nature wild and wary. The eggs are few, generally two or three. The young betake themselves directly to the water, near which the nest is placed—a rude structure of rushes or other aquatic vegetation, built on the ground. The sexes are alike; the young are different from the old.

COLYMBUS TORQUATUS, Brünn.

Great Northern Loon, or Diver.

a. *torquatus*.

Colymbus torquatus, BRÜNN., Orn. Bor. 1764, No. 134.—KEYS. & BLAS., Wirb. Eur. 1840, 91.—LAWR., B. N. A. 1858, 888.—COOP. & SUCK., N. H. Wash. Ter. 1860, 278.—COUES, Pr. Phila. Acad. 1861, 248; 1862, 227; 1864, 21.—COUES, Mem. Bost. Soc. N. H. i, 131 (osteology and myology).—COUES, Key, 1872, 334; and of most late United States writers.
Cepphus torquatus, PALL., Zoog. R.-A. ii, 1811, 340.
Colymbus glacialis, LINN., Syst. Nat. i, 1766, 221.—GM., Syst. Nat. i, 1788, 588.—LATH., Ind. Orn. ii, 1790, 799.—FORST., Phil. Trans. lxii, 1772, 383.—TEMM., Man. Orn. 1815, 597.—STEPH., Gen. Zool. xii, 1824, 233, pl. 61.—GRAY, Gen. of B. iii, 631.—SUND., Svensk. Fögl. pl. 53.—WILS., Am. Orn. ix, 1824, 84, pl. 74.—BP., Syn. 1828, 420; List, 1838, 65.—Sw. & RICH., F. B. Am. ii, 1831, 474.—NUTT., Man. ii, 1834, 513.—AUD., Orn. Biog. iv, 1838, 43, pl. 306; Syn. 1839, 353; B. Am. vii, 1844, 282, pl. 476.—GIR., B. L. I. 1844, 378; and of most authors.
Eudytes glacialis, ILLIGER, Prodromus, 1811, 282.—NAUM., V. D. xii, 1844, 397, pl. 327.
Eudites glacialis, KAUP, Sk. Ent. Eur. Thierw. 1829, 144.

---

* Admitting the pertinence of the remarks of Sundevall (Meth. Av. Teut. Disp. 1873) and others on the question of nomenclature, we do not find it necessary to use *Eudytes* of Illiger for the Loons, to leave the name *Colymbus* for the Grebes.

Colymbus immer, LINN., Syst. Nat. i, 1766, 222.—GM., Syst. Nat. i, 1788, 588.—LATH., Ind.
Orn. ii, 1790, 800.—LEACH, Cat. 1816, 36.
Colymbus atrigularis, MEYER, Taschenb. Vög. Deutschl. ii, 449.
Colymbus maximus et *hiemalis*, BREHM, V. D. 971, 972.

b. *adamsii*.

Colymbus adamsii, GRAY, P. Z. S. 1859, 167 (Russian America).—COUES, Pr. Phila. Acad.
1862, 227 ; 1864, 21 (cranium).—ELLIOT, B. N. A. pl. 63.—DALL & BANN., Tr.
Chic. Acad. i, 1869, 308 (Alaska).—FINSCH, Abh. Nat. iii, 1872 (Alaska).
Colymbus torquatus var. *adamsii*, COUES, Key, 1872, 334.
Colymbus glacialis, var., SWINHOE.

Hab.—The Northern hemisphere. Var. *adamsii* from Alaska and interior of Arctic
America ; also, Asia. "England."

Var. TORQUATUS : *Common Loon.*

Adult.—Bill black, the tip and cutting edges sometimes yellowish. Feet black. Head
and neck deep glossy greenish-black, with lustrous purplish reflections on the front
and sides of the head. A patch of sharp white streaks on the throat, and another
larger triangular patch of the same on each side of the neck lower down, the two last
nearly or quite meeting behind, separate in front. Sides of breast striped with black
and white. Entire upper parts, wing-coverts, inner secondaries, and sides under the
wings, deep glossy bluish-green ; all except the sides thickly marked with white spots ;
those of the scapulars, tertials, and middle back, large, square, and regular ; those of
other parts smaller, oval, smallest on rump, most numerous on wing-coverts. Upper
tail-coverts greenish-black, immaculate. Wing-quills brownish-black, lighter on inner
webs. Under surface of wings, axillars, and under parts generally from the neck, pure
white ; the lower belly with a dusky band.
Young.—Bill smaller than in the adult, bluish-white, with dusky ridge. Crown and
cervix dull brownish-black ; other upper parts similar, but the feathers, especially of
the foreback, with light gray edgings. Primaries black, with brown inner webs. Tail
feathers with gray tips. Traces of lighter and darker lineation on sides of breast.
Sides of head mottled with ashy and whitish ; chin, throat, neck in front, and whole
under parts, white.
Dimensions.—Length 31 to 36 inches ; wing, 12.50 to 14.25 ; bill, 2.75 to 3 along culmen ; gape, 4 to 4.25 ; height at nostrils, about 0.80 ; width there, about 0.40 ; tarsus,
3 to 3.50 ; middle toe and claw, 4.25 to 5.

Hab.—The Northern hemisphere. In winter, generally dispersed in the United States.

The white throat-patch consists usually of five or six streaks ; in this, as in the lateral neck-stripes, the individual feathers are broadly black, with sharp white edges
toward their ends. The texture of the feathers is peculiar—the outer surface is hollowed, with raised edges of specially firm, smooth, polished character, so that these
patches may be *felt* as well as seen. The white spots on the back occur in a pair on
each feather near its end, their aggregation in any region being therefore determined
by the size of the feathers themselves.
Beginning binomial nomenclature at 1758, the name *torquatus*, Brünn. (1764), antedates *glacialis*, Linn. (1766). No synonyms require discussion.

Var. ADAMSII : *Yellow-billed Loon.*

CH. Larger than *C. torquatus*, with the bill rather larger and somewhat differently
shaped and colored. Bill about equaling head, longer than tarsus, much compressed, tip
very acute, not at all decurved, the culmen being almost perfectly straight, as the commissure also is. Gonys straight or nearly so to the angle, which is very prominent.
Frontal antiæ reaching beyond middle of nostrils. Bill fine light yellowish horn-color,
only dusky at base. Head and neck deep steel-blue, with purplish and violet reflections, glossed only on the cervix with deep green. Throat-patch of white streaks
smaller than in *torquatus*, but the individual streaks larger, as are those of the neck-
patches. White spots of upper parts larger than in *torquatus*, rectangular instead of
square on the scapulars and tertials, being somewhat longer than broad. Bill along
culmen, 3.50 to 3.75 ; along gape. 5 to 5.25 ; height at nostrils, 0.95 to 1.10 ; width, 0.40 to
0.50 ; tarsus, 3.50 ; outer toe, 4.65 to 5.10. General dimensions somewhat exceeding
those of *torquatus*, but not so much so as in the bill.
A comparative table of characters is subjoined :
Var. TORQUATUS : Culmen, 2.75 to 3 ; gape, 4 to 4.25 ; height of bill at nostrils, average, under 1. Bill along culmen shorter than tarsus. Color of bill mostly black, its

culmen convex; commissure somewhat decurved; gonys convex, with slight angle. Frontal antiæ falling short of middle of nostrils. Gloss of head and neck mostly green. White spots of back nearly square.

Var. ADAMSII: Culmen, about 3.75 ; gape, about 5 ; height of bill at nostrils, average, over 1.   Bill along culmen longer than tarsus.   Color of bill mostly yellow ; its culmen nearly straight; commissure straight; gonys straight, with prominent angle. Frontal antiæ reaching middle of nostrils.   Gloss of head and neck mostly blue.   White spots of back longer than broad.

The type of this form was from Russian America, now Alaska. Numerous specimens in breeding plumage have been received at the Smithsonian from various parts of Arctic America.   The form appears to have been also recorded in Asia, and is even quoted from England.   I have seen no United States examples ; nor have I recognized the bird in its young plumage, when, probably, it could not be distinguished with any certainty from ordinary *torquatus*.   Specimens are labeled as having the iris light reddish-brown, the feet olivaceous.

Notwithstanding the distinctions in the size, shape, and color of the bill, I am now rating this bird as a variety of *torquatus*, being satisfied that the characters intergrade with those of the latter.

COLYMBUS ARCTICUS, Linn.

Black-throated Diver.

a. *arcticus.*

Colymbus arcticus, LINN., Syst. Nat. i, 1766, 221.—GM., Syst. Nat. i, 1788, 587.—LATH., Ind. Orn. ii, 1790, 800.—BRÜNN., Orn. Bor. 1764, No. 133.—TEMM., Man. Orn. 1815, 599.—STEPH., Gen. Zool. xii, 1824, 236.—KEYS. & BLAS., Wirb. Eur. 1840, 91.—GRAY, Gen. of B. iii, 631, pl. 171.—SUND., Svensk. Fögl. pl. 53.—BP., Syn. 1828, 420 ; List, 1838, 65 —AUD., Orn. Biog. iv, 1838, 345, pl. 346 ; Syn. 1839, 354 ; B. Am. vii, 1844, 295, pl. 477.—NUTT., Man. ii, 1834, 517.—SW. & RICH., F. B. A. ii, 1831, 475.—LAWR., B. N. A. 1858, 888 ; Ann. Lyc. N. Y. viii, 1866, 300 (New York).—COUES, Pr. Phila. Acad. 1862, 228.—COUES, Pr. Ess. Inst. v, 1868, 309 (New England).—DALL & BANN., Tr. Chic. Acad. 1869, 307 (Alaska).— FINSCH, Abh. Nat. iii, 1872, 74 (Alaska).—COUES, Key, 1872, 334.—COUES, Elliott's Prybilov Islands, 1874.—RIDGW., Ann. Lyc. N. Y. x, 1874, 392 (Illinois) ; and of authors generally.
Cepphus arcticus, PALL., Zoog. R.-A. ii, 1811, 91.
Eudytes arcticus, ILL., Prod. 1811, 282.—NAUM., V. D. xii, 1844, 418, pl. 328.
Colymbus macrorhynchos, BREHM, V. D. 1831, 974.
Colymbus megarhynchos, BREHM, Naūm. v, 1855, 300 ; V. D. 974.
Colymbus balthicus, HORNSCH., Verz. Pommersch. Vög. 21.
" *Colymbus ignotus* et *leucopus,* BECHST., Naturg. iv, 782."

b. *pacificus.*

Colymbus pacificus, LAWR., B. N. A. 1858, 889.—COUES, Pr. Phila. Acad. 1862, 228.—COOP. & SUCK., N. H. Wash. Ter. 1860, 279.—COUES, Ibis, 1866, 273 (Southern California).—COUES, Pr. Phila. Acad. 1866, 100.
Colymbus arcticus var. pacificus, COUES, Key, 1872, 335.

Hab.—The Northern hemisphere.   Var. *pacificus* from the Pacific coast of North America.

This species, which was not noticed by either of the Expeditions, appears to be a more northerly bird than the last, and, according to my experience, it is rare in the United States.   Audubon, however, states that it comes as far south as Texas.   The Pacific variety is a common bird on the coast of California in winter.

Var. ARCTICUS : *Black-throated Diver.*

CHAR. Bill generally as in *torquatus*, but smaller; color black. Chin, throat, and neck in front, black, with purplish and violet reflections on the sides of the head, gradually fading into a fine, clear bluish-gray, deepest on the forehead, lightest behind, and separated from the black of the throat by a series of white streaks. A crescent of short, white streaks across upper throat ; sides of breast striped with pure white and glossy

46

black, these stripes nearly meeting in front. Entire upper parts deep, glossy greenish-black, each feather of scapulars and interscapulars with a white spot near end of each web; those of the scapulars largest, forming four patches in transverse rows. Wing-coverts thickly speckled with small ovate white spots. Inner webs of quills and tail feathers below, light grayish-brown. Sides under wings like back. Lining of wings and entire under parts from the neck, pure white, with a narrow dusky band across lower belly; under tail-coverts dusky, tipped with white.

Young.—Bill light bluish-gray, dusky along the ridge. Iris brown. Feet dusky. Upper part of head and neck dark grayish-brown; sides of head dark grayish-white, minutely streaked with brown. Upper parts with a reticulated or scaly appearance, the feathers being brownish-black with broad bluish-gray margins; the rump dull brownish-gray. Primaries and their coverts brownish-black; secondaries and tail feathers dusky, margined with gray. Forepart of neck grayish-white, minutely and faintly dotted with brown; its sides below streaked with the same. Lower parts, including under surface of wings, pure white, the sides of the body and rump, with part of the lower tail-coverts, dusky, edged with bluish-gray. (*Audubon.*)

Dimensions.—Wing, 11.75; bill along culmen, 2.45; along gape, 3.40; its height at nostrils, 0.65; its width there, 0.35; tarsus, 2.90; outer toe and claw, 3.80.

The foregoing description is taken from a fine adult European specimen, no unquestionable North American one being before me. The account of the young is derived from Audubon. I am not sure that I have recognized it from North America, the young of the *arcticus* type before me being apparently all var. *pacificus*. It may be distinguished from the young of *torquatus* by its decidedly inferior size. The questions arising from consideration of var. *pacificus* are treated under the next head.

Var. PACIFICUS : *Pacific Black-throated Diver.*

In 1858 Mr. Lawrence separated, "with some hesitation," two specimens of the *arcticus* type from that species, under the name of *pacificus*, on the ground of smaller size, and especially smaller, weaker bill. A young bird in the Philadelphia collection, "which may have come from the Pacific," being exactly like the types of *pacificus;* and the fact that young *arcticus* is described as closely resembling young *torquatus*, whereas the types of *pacificus* are quite different, strengthened the opinion that *pacificus* was distinct, and I so treated it in 1862. But now, with Mr. Lawrence's types and several fully adult specimens before me, I reduce the differences merely to a point of size, which, as is well known, is very variable in this family. The bird is evidently only a slight variety, as will be perceived by the following examination of specimens:

No. 21795, Mus. Smith. Inst., adult, Europe: Bill moderately stout, little compressed, shorter than head or tarsus, tip rather acute, culmen regularly convex throughout, commissure greatly decurved, under outline straight to the angle, gonys straight, angle well defined. Culmen, 2.45; gape, 3.40; height at nostril, 0.65; width there, 0.35; wing, 11.75.

No. 16014, adult, Fraser's River, collected by Dr. Kennerly on the Northwest Boundary Survey: Apparently pure *arcticus*. Wing, 11.75; tarsus, 2.90; outer toe, 3.80; thus fully as large. The upper mandible is shot away from the nostrils, but according to the under mandible the bill was 0.25 shorter than in the preceding; its height at base is the same.

No. 17052, intermediate in age, California: Smaller. Wing, 11.30; tarsus, 2.85; outer toe, 3.55; culmen, 2; gape, 2.90; height of bill at base, 0.48. The bill is considerably shorter and slenderer than in the European; the culmen decidedly convex; gonys convex.

No. 20229, adult, Great Slave Lake: Smaller than either of the preceding. Wing, only 11; tarsus, 2.60; outer toe, 3.60; culmen, 2.05; gape, 3.20; height of bill at base, 0.50. The bill thus differs little from the preceding.

No. 9924, young, Puget's Sound: A type of the species; about the size and proportions of 17052. Wing, 11.20; tarsus, 2.80; culmen, 2.12; gape, 3; height, 0.50. This has the bill a little larger than in 17052, the culmen considerably curved, the gonydeal angle pretty well defined. (Difference in length of culmen between this and the European specimen, about 0.30; the wing only 0.75 shorter.)

No. 20231, adult, M'Kenzie's River: Small. Wing, barely 11; tarsus, 2.50; outer toe, 3.50; *culmen only* 1.90; height of bill, 0.45. This has the smallest, straightest, and slenderest bill of all. The culmen is even a little concave at the nostrils; commissure perfectly straight; gonydeal angle slight. Were this shape and size of bill constant, a species might be predicated.

No. 11862, young, Fraser's River: Smallest of the specimens. Wing, 10.75; tarsus, 2.75; outer toe, 3.80; culmen, 2; gape, 2.85; height of bill, 0.45. The bill resembles some others of the foregoing more than it does that of 20231.

The complete graduation is established by the above series, showing that we can only recognize a var. *pacificus* as one extreme of an unbroken chain.

There is something very curious in the relationships that many birds of the families *Colymbidæ* and *Podicipidæ* bear to each other. Most of the species are, as it were, duplicated; that is, there is another scarcely differing except in the size, one being the *fratercule*, or "little brother," of the other. This fact is easily illustrated, taking our several species as examples. Our common Loon is the *fratercule* of *C. adamsii*, described by Mr. Gray, in 1859, from Russian, and lately found extensively dispersed in British America. It is larger than *torquatus*, with a relatively as well as absolutely larger bill, differently shaped, and mostly yellow instead of wholly black; there are also some differences in the coloration of the plumage. The Pacific Diver is the smaller representative of the Black-throated; it has also a disproportionately smaller and slenderer bill. It was first described by Mr. Lawrence, in 1858, from young birds taken on the Pacific coast of the United States; but since that time great numbers of the adults have been secured, my examination of which has convinced me that the only differences are those just stated. The Red-throated Loon also has its smaller race, though I am not aware that it has been formally recognized; I have seen some full-grown ones scarcely two-thirds the average size. Among the Grebes the rule is finely illustrated in the cases of *P. occidentalis* and *P. clarkii*. All the American Red-necked Grebes I have seen have been larger, and otherwise different from the European *P. griseigena*. I recognize them as varietally distinct under Reinhardt's name of *P. holbölli*. There are said to be similar races of the Horned Grebes (*P. cornutus*), but here the difference is not very evident. The American and European Eared Grebes are singularly correlated; while of the same size, they differ constantly in the amount of white on the wing, as I showed some years since, in separating our bird, under the name of *P. californicus*, from *P. auritus*. There are relations of corresponding character between the Dabchick of Europe (*Sylbeocyclus minor*) and that of Central America (*S. dominicus*); between the North and South American Dabchick (*Podilymbus podiceps* and *P. antarcticus*); while among exotic forms several geographical races or subspecies are easily recognized.

The Pacific Diver, as its name indicates, is confined to the West, and in the United States chiefly to the coast itself; but it occurs abundantly in Western British America. With us it is only known as a winter resident, at which season it reaches our extreme southern border, if not still further; in the spring it passes north, and breeds as high as explorers have penetrated. I had rare opportunities of studying these birds while I was in Southern California, in November, 1865. They were very plentiful about the bay of San Pedro. The first thing that attracted my attention was their remarkable familiarity; they were tamer than any other water-fowl I have seen. They showed no concern at the near approach of a boat, scarcely availed themselves of the powers of diving, in which the whole family excels, and I had no trouble in shooting as many as I wanted. They even came up to the wharves, and played about as unconcerned as domestic Ducks; they constantly swam around the vessels lying at anchor in the harbor, and all their motions, both on and under the clear water, could be studied to as much advantage as if the birds had been placed in artificial tanks for the purpose. Now two or three would ride lightly over the surface, with the neck gracefully curved, propelled with idle strokes of their broad paddles to this side and that, one leg after the other stretched at ease almost horizontally backward, while their flashing eyes, first directed upward with curious sidelong glance, then peering into the depths below, sought for some attractive morsel. In an instant, with the peculiar motion, impossible to describe, they would disappear beneath the surface, leaving a little foam and bubbles to mark where they went down, and I could follow their course under water; see them shoot with marvellous swiftness through the limpid element, as, urged by powerful strokes of the webbed feet and beats of the half-opened wings, they flew rather than swam; see them dart out the arrow-like bill, transfix an unlucky fish, and lightly rise to the surface again. While under water, the bubbles of air carried down with them cling to the feathers, and they seem bespangled with glittering jewels, borrowed for the time from their native element, and lightly parted with as they leave it, when they arrange their feathers with a slight shiver, shaking off the last sparkling drop.

The feathers look as dry as if the bird had never been under water; the fish is swallowed head first, with a curious jerking motion, and the bird again swims at ease, with the same graceful curve of the neck.

COLYMBUS SEPTENTRIONALIS, Linn.

Red-throated Diver.

Colymbus septentrionalis, LINN., Syst. Nat. i, 1766, 220 (adult).—LATH., Ind. Orn. ii, 1790, 801.—TEMM., Man. 1815, 602.—BOIE, Isis, 1822, 561.—STEPH., G. Z. xii, 1824, 238.—KEYS. & BLAS., Wirb. Eur. 1840, 91.—GRAY, Gen. of B. iii, 631.—SUND., Svensk. Fogl. pl. 53.—BP., Syn. 1828, 421; List, 1838, 65.—SW. & RICH., F. B. A. ii, 1831, 476.—NUTT., Man. ii, 1834, 519.—AUD., Orn. Biog. iii, 1835, 20, pl. 202; Syn. 1839, 354; B. Am. vii, 1844, 299, pl. 478.—GIR., B. L. I. 1844, 380.— LAWR., B. N. A. 1858, 890; Ann. Lyc. N. Y. viii, 1866, 300 (New York).—COUES, Pr. Phila. Acad. 1862, 228.—NEWT., Ibis, 1865, 317 (Spitzbergen).—COOP. & SUCK., N. H. Wash. Ter. 1860, 279.—DALL & BANN., Tr. Chic. Acad. i, 1869, 307 (Alaska).—FINSCH, Abh. Nat. iii, 1872, 75 (Alaska).—TURNB., B. E. Pa. 1869, 39 (rather rare).—COUES, Key, 1872, 335; and of authors generally.
Cepphus septentrionalis, PALL., Zoog. Rosso-As. ii, 1811, 342.
Eudytes septentrionalis, ILL., Prod. 1811, 282.—NAUM., Vög. Deut. xii, 1844, 435, pl. 329.
Colymbus lumme, BRÜNN., Orn. Bor. 1764, 39 (adult).
Colymbus stellatus, BRÜNN., Orn. Bor. 1764, No. 130 (young).—GM., Syst. Nat. i, 1788, 587.—LATH., Ind. Orn. ii, 1790, 800.—LEACH, Cat. 1816, 35.
Cepphus stellatus, PALL., Zoog. R.-A. ii, 1811, —.
Colymbus borealis, BRÜNN., Orn. Bor. 1764, No. 131.—LATH., Ind. Orn. ii, 1790, 801.— BREHM, V. D. 1831, 979.
Colymbus striatus, GM., Syst. Nat. i, 1788, 586 (young).—LATH., Ind. Orn. ii, 1790, 802.
Colymbus rufogularis, MEYER, Tasch. Deutsch. Vög. ii, 453.
Colymbus microrhynchus, BREHM, Naum. v, 1855, 300.

Hab.—The Northern hemisphere.

CHAR. Bill usually slenderer than in the foregoing; culmen slightly concave at the nostrils, gently convex to tip, which is rather obtuse and a little decurved. Outline of rami nearly straight; gonys slightly convex. Frontal antiæ scarcely extending beyond base of nostrils. Tarsus relatively rather longer than in foregoing species, about four-fifths the middle toe.

Adult.—Bill black, rather lighter at the tip. Crown and broad cervical stripe glossy greenish-black, the latter thickly streaked with white, which streaks, on the sides of the breast, spread so as to nearly meet in front. Throat and sides of head clear bluish-gray. A large, well-defined, triangular, chestnut-brown throat-patch. Entire upper parts and sides under the wings deep brownish-black, with greenish gloss, everywhere profusely spotted with white, the spots small, oval. Primaries blackish, paler on the inner webs. Tail narrowly tipped with white. Under parts and lining of wings white, the axillars with narrow, dusky shaft-streaks, and the lower belly, with some of the under tail-coverts, dusky.

Young.—Bill mostly light bluish-white, with dusky ridge. Crown of head and neck behind bluish-gray, the feathers of the former bordered with whitish. Entire upper parts brownish- or grayish-black, everywhere profusely marked with small oval and linear spots of white. Throat without red patch, its sides and those of the the head mottled with dusky. Other parts as in the adult.

Dimensions.—Length, about 27; wing, 11 or less; bill along culmen, 2; along gape, 3; height at nostril, 0.50; width there, 0.35; tarsus, 2.75; outer toe, 3.50.

This species varies greatly in general size, and in the size and shape of the bill. Nevertheless, it may always be recognized by the peculiar profuse spotting of the upper parts, as well as, when adult, by the red throat-patch. The spots are smallest and most numerous on the wing-coverts and upper back, where they grade into the streaks of the hind neck; largest on the tertials, scapulars, and sides under the wings, where they are rather lines than spots, and are fewest, or almost wanting, on the middle of the back. The marking results from a small spot or stripe near the end of each feather, on the edge of each web; there is occasionally a second pair nearer the base of the feather. The amount of spotting is very variable with individuals; in the young the spots are always larger and more numerous than in the adults, and usually lengthened into oblique lines, producing a regular diamond-shaped reticulation.

A specimen (No. 9923) collected by Mr. George Gibbs, on the Northwestern Bound. ry Survey, is an albino—a state I have not observed in either of the other species. The neck and upper parts are pure white, irregularly mottled with patches of light reddish-ash, of which color are the primaries, wing-coverts and flanks. The bill is slenderer and more recurved than usual, the culmen being concave throughout. The specimen measured 24 by 44 in extent, the wing 9.90.

Family PODICIPIDÆ : Grebes.

Bill of variable length, much longer or shorter than head; culmen usually about straight, sometimes a little concave, or quite convex, especially at the end. Commissure nearly straight, but more or less corresponding with the curve of the culmen, usually sinuate at base. Under outline of bill in general convex, with slight gonydeal angle or none. Sides of bill more or less striate. Nasal fossæ well marked, the nostrils near their termination. Nostrils linear and pervious (broader in *Podilymbus*), upper edge straight, not lobed. Frontal extension of feathers considerable, and usually antiæ run still further into the nasal fossa. A groove along the symphysis of the mandible extends often nearly to the tip. Eyes far forward, with a loral strip of bare skin running thence to base of upper mandible, very narrow in the typical forms, broader in *Tachybaptes* and *Podilymbus*. Head usually adorned in the breeding season with variously lengthened colored crests or ruffs; when these are wanting the frontal feathers may be bristly. Neck usually long, slender, and sinuous. Plumage thick and compact, smoothly imbricated above, below of a peculiar smooth, satiny texture. Wings short but ample, very concavo-convex; primaries *eleven*,* narrow, somewhat falcate, graduated, the three or four outer ones attenuate on one or both webs; secondaries short and broad; tertials very long, hiding the rest of the quills when the wing is closed. Bastard quills unusually long, their tips reaching over half way to the ends of the primaries. Greater coverts also very long. Tail rudimentary, represented by a tuft of downy feathers.† Characters of the feet peculiar; for in other lobe-footed birds, as Phalaropes and Coots, the lobation is of a different character. Tarsi exceedingly compressed, with only a slightly thickened tract within which the tendons pass. Front edge a single smooth row of overlapping, the hinder serrate, with a double row of pointed scales ; sides regularly transversely scutellate, as are the upper surfaces of the toes, the latter being inferiorly reticulate with an edging of pectinated scales. Toes flattened out and further widened with broad lobes, especially wide toward the end, and at base connected for a varying distance by interdigital webs. Hind toe highly elevated, broadly lobate, free. Claws short, broad, flat, obtuse, of squarish shape ; that of the hallux minute. Tarsus no longer or much shorter than the middle toe and claw ; outer toe usually rather longer than the middle ; the inner the shortest of the anterior ones.

This is a very natural group of numerous closely-related species. Extremes of form may be seen in *Podiceps occidentalis* and *Podilymbus podiceps*. There are but two strongly marked genera, though many have been instituted. These genera, one of which has several subdivisions, may be defined as follows, to include all the subgenera found in North America :

Analysis of North American genera and subgenera.

A. Bill slender or only moderately stout, paragnathous, acute. Nostrils narrow or linear. Loral bare strip narrow. Frontal feathers normal. Tarsus generally but little, if any, shorter than the middle toe—at least three-fourths as long. Semipalmation of toes moderate. Lobe of hallux broad. Usually with conspicuous crests or ruffs during the breeding season... PODICEPS.

    1. Bill longer than head, extremely slender and acute. Tarsus equal to the middle toe and claw. Crests and ruffs slight. Large .... *Æchmophorus.*

    2. Bill not longer than head, moderately stout. Tarsus shorter than middle toe and claw. Crests and ruffs decided. Size over 10 inches. .... *Podiceps.*

    3. Bill much shorter than head, not two-thirds the tarsus, quite stout. Tarsus about three-fourths the middle toe. Outer and middle toes equal. No decided crests or ruffs. Small; length 10 inches or less..................................... *Tachybaptes.*

---

* A greater number than have been shown to occur in other birds, with few exceptions. The same number is stated to occur among *Phasianidæ.*

† "The tail of the Grebes is usually described as a small tuft of feathers, but on carefully removing the coverts and downy parts the tail may be satisfactorily traced. In this species [*P. cristatus*] there are fourteen feathers ; on each side seven, arranged in a semicircular manner. The two middle feathers are separated to the distance of about one-twelfth, and the two outer or lateral approach each other below, leaving an interval of about the same space. When the feathers are broken across their bases, which they frequently are, there is thus produced an appearance of a small circular tuft. When perfect, they are about 1½ inches long, and arched, with loose barbs, downy at their extremity." (*Audubon.*)

B. Bill stout, epignathous, obtuse. Commissure decurved abruptly at end. Nostrils broadly oval. Loral bare strip broad. Frontal feathers bristly. Tarsus not three-fourths the middle toe. Semipalmation of toes extensive. Lobe of hallux moderate. No decided crests or ruffs .... PODILYMBUS.

The foregoing appears to be a natural sequence of the forms; and the analysis is nearly carried down to the species, there being but one group in North America containing two or more species. *Æchmophorus*, in its large size, slender form, very long, slender, acute bill, and long tarsi, forms one extreme. Next comes *Podiceps* proper, as illustrated by *P. cristatus*, in which the ruffs and crests reach their highest development In *P. cornutus*, *auritus*, and *griseigena*, the crests and ruffs decrease in development successively, while the bill grows stouter; in the latter, moreover, the tarsus is relatively the shortest. But these four species need not be even subgenerically distinguished. The way is directly opened to the subgenus *Tachybaptes*, very small, with short, stout bill, short tarsi, and absence of decided crests or ruffs, furnishing in some sense a link with the quite distinct genus *Podilymbus*.

Genus PODICEPS, *Lath.*

$<$ *Colymbus*, BRISS., Orn. vi, 1760, 33; not of Linnæus, nor of authors.
$=$ *Colymbus*, ILL., Prod. 1811, 281.—SUND., Meth. Av. Disp. 1873.
$=$ *Colymbus*, PALLAS, Zoog. R.-A. ii, 1811, 352.
$<$ *Podiceps*, LATH., Ind. Orn. ii, 1790, 780. (*C. cristatus*, LINN.)
$=$ *Podiceps*, AUCT. recent.
$>$ *Pedetaithya*,* KAUP, Sk. Ent. Eur. Thierw. 1829, 44. (*C. griseigena*, BODD.)
$>$ *Lophaithyia*, KAUP, *op. cit.* 72. (*C. cristatus*, LINN.)
$>$ *Lophæthyia*, AGASS.
$>$ *Dytes*, KAUP, *op. cit.* 41. (*C. cornatus*, GM.)
$>$ *Proctopus*, KAUP, *op. cit.* 49. (*C. auritus*.)
$>$ *Poliocephalus*, SELBY. (*Fide Gray;* type *nestor*, GOULD.)
$>$ *Tachybaptes*, REICH. (*C. minor*, GM.)
$>$ *Otodytes*, REICH., Handb. Sp. Orn. (*= Proctopus*, KAUP.)
$>$ *Calipareus*, BP., 1855. (*Gray*.) (*P. kalipareus*, GARN.)
$>$ *Rollandia*, BP., 1856. (*Gray*.) (*P. rollandi*, Q. & G.)
$>$ *Sylbeocylus*, "BP.," *apud* GRAY. (*Nec* BP., whose type was *C. podiceps*, LINN.)
$>$ *Æchmophorus*, COUES, Pr. Phila. Acad. 1862, 229. (*P. occidentalis*, LAWR.)
$>$ *Centropelma*, SCL. & SALV., Exot. Orn. pt. xii. (*P. micropterus*, GOULD.)

While most of the above names are purely synonymical, others may be entitled to subgeneric rank, especially *Tachybaptes*, *Æchmophorus*, and *Centropelma*. The general characters of the genus having been sufficiently elucidated, we may at once proceed to consider the North American species, under the three subgenera *Æchmophorus*, *Podiceps*, and *Tachybaptes*.

Subgenus ÆCHMOPHORUS, *Coues.*

Æchmophorus, COUES, Pr. Phila. Acad. 1862, 229.

CHAR. Bill very long, exceeding the head, straight or slightly recurved, very slender, attenuate, and acute. Culmen straight or slightly concave; commissure about straight, somewhat sinuate at base; under outline concave at base, without angle at symphysis. Bare loral strip very narrow. Wings comparatively long, with much attenuated outer primaries. Legs long; tarsus exceeding the bill, as long as the middle toe and claw. Basal webbing of toes slight. Size large; body slender; neck long. Crest and ruffs inconspicuous (not found colored in the North American species).

This section is quite well marked. A South American species, *P. leucopterus*, King, appears to belong here. Schlegel, indeed, unites all the largest American Grebes † under our specific name. They *may* be identical specifically, but I have yet to see either of our North American forms with any decided coloration about the head, though we have them in breeding plumage, as I correctly stated in 1862 (*op. cit.* 404). This statement, made with reference to var. *clarkii*, has been confirmed by Mr. Ridgway, who found numbers of *occidentalis* breeding at Pyramid Lake, Nevada, late in May. They were also seen at Great Salt Lake in June. They were all in the same dress—no colored crests or ruffs; no bright colors at all about the head and neck. It is certainly singular that this species should thus depart from the rule of seasonal changes of

---

* Found spelled, among writers, *Pedetaithyia, Podetaithyia, Pedeaithyia*, &c.
† The references are: *C. major*, BODD., P. E. 404; *= C. cayennensis*, GM.; *P. cayana*, LATH.; *P. bicornis*, LICHT.; *longirostris*, JAUB.; *leucopterus*, KING.

plumage in this family, but such is apparently the case. Under these circumstances it is obviously proper to hold Schlegel's determination in check.

There are two well-marked forms of this species, quite easy to recognize in their extreme manifestations, yet apparently not separable specifically. They may be distinguished as follows:

Var. OCCIDENTALIS: Large; length (extreme), about 29 inches; wing, about 8; bill and tarsus, each about 3. Bill equal to tarsus, straight, mostly dark olivaceous, brighter yellowish at tip and along cutting edges. Under outline of bill straight from base to the slight angle, gonys thence straight to tip. Lores ashy-gray.

Var. CLARKII: Small; length, about 22 inches; wing, about 7; bill, 2.25; tarsus, 2.75. Bill shorter than tarsus, slightly recurved, under outline almost regularly convex from base to tip, with barely appreciable angle. Lores pure white.

PODICEPS (ÆCHMOPHORUS) OCCIDENTALIS, Lawr.

Western Grebe.

a. *occidentalis.*

Podiceps occidentalis, LAWR., B. N. A. 1858, 894.—COOP. & SUCK., N. H. Wash. Ter. 1860,
    281, pl. 38.—COUES, Key, 1872, 336.
Æchmophorus occidentalis, COUES, Pr. Phila. Acad. 1862, 229.—COUES, Ibis, Apr. 1866,
    273 (Southern California).

b. *clarkii.*

Podiceps clarkii, LAWR., B. N. A. 1858, 895.
Æchmophorus clarkii, COUES, Pr. Phila. Acad. 1862, 229 ; *ibid.* 404 (breeding plumage).
Podiceps occidentalis var. *clarkii*, COUES, Key, 1872, 336.

Hab.—Both varieties occur together in the United States west of the Rocky Mountains.

Var. OCCIDENTALIS : *Western Grebe.*

Adult.—Culmen and gonys dusky olivaceous, the bill becoming yellowish toward the end and along the cutting edges. Iris orange-red with a pinkish shade, surrounded with a white ring. Hard parts of palate in life like the bill; soft parts light purplish or lavender. Insides of tarsi and soles black; outsides of tarsi and top of foot dull bluish-green, becoming yellowish in centre of the webs. Forehead and lores dark silvery-ash. A short occipital crest and indications of cheek ruffs, but neither brightly colored, agreeing with the plain dark and white colors of the parts. Top of head and line down back of neck fuliginous blackish, fading on the back and upper parts generally into a lighter, rather brownish-black, the feathers of the back with grayish margins. Primaries mostly deep chocolate-brown, basally white, their shafts whitish at base, black terminally. Secondaries mostly white, but more or fewer of the outer webs, wholly or in part, dark. Sides under the wings washed with a pale shade of the color of the back. Lining of wings and whole under parts from the bill pure silky white.

Dimensions.—Length, 24 to 29 inches ; wing, about 8 ; bill along culmen, tarsus, and middle toe with claw, each, 3 ; gape of bill, 3.60 ; its height at nostril, 0.50.

This is a remarkable Grebe, the largest of this country, and one requiring comparison with no other for its determination. It was originally described from the Pacific coast, along which it is found from Oregon and Washington Territories to Southern California, or further : while latterly it has been found breeding in Nevada and Utah by Mr. Ridgway. I observed it frequently on the California coast, at San Pedro, in November, where it was common on the waters of the harbor, with the Pacific Diver, Cormorants, and numerous other water-fowl. It is a fine-looking bird on the water, has a trim and shapely aspect, like a clipper ship, while its long sinuous neck is held in a graceful curve, or variously deflected to either side. A specimen which I opened had the stomach filled with a kind of aquatic grass. The birds were not very shy, and several were readily procured, notwithstanding their great powers of diving.

Among Dr. Kennerly's Mss. I find the following : "This species, and the *Podiceps cornutus*, are very common on Puget Sound. They are rather more rare during the summer months than in the autumn and winter. During the latter seasons they may almost always be found— two, rarely more, in company—coasting near the shore, diving rapidly in search of food. When desirous of descending beneath the water, they seem to raise themselves partially from the surface, and describing, as they descend, almost a perfect arc of a circle. Few birds are more graceful on the water than these interesting species; and it has afforded us many moments of real enjoyment to watch them gliding rapidly and smoothly over its surface, or performing in rapid succession their graceful curves as they disappear beneath its surface. They do not often take to wing, relying more on their powers of swimming and diving as a means of escape from enemies; when they do fly, they rise very awkwardly from the water, often for a long distance dragging their dangling legs before they succeed, and often, under such circumstances, abandoning the effort, they stop and suddenly disappear beneath the surface. They follow up the streams emptying into the Sound for long distances, many of them spending their summer on the lakes far inland, in the neighborhood of which they probably breed with the Large Loon (*C. torquatus*). I have often seen large flocks of them on Chiloweyuck Lake from August to September, and perhaps later."

Var. CLARKII : *Clarke's Grebe.*

Bill about as long as the head, shorter than the tarsus, slightly recurved, extremely slender and acute; the culmen a little concave, the under outline almost one unbroken curve from base to tip.

Adult in breeding plumage.—Under mandible, and tip and cutting edges of the upper, chrome-yellow, in marked contrast to the black of the culmen. Loral bare strip leaden-blue. Crown, occiput, and hind neck deep grayish-black; almost pure black on the hind head, fading gradually along the neck into the lighter blackish-gray of the upper parts generally. Lores broadly pure white, as are the entire under parts, with a sharp line of demarcation along the sides of the head and neck. A decided occipital crest, the feathers about an inch long and quite filiform, but not colored apart from the general coloration. No decided ruffs—no colored ruffs at all; but the white feathers of the sides of the head behind and across the throat are longer and fuller than elsewhere—about as in *griseigena*. Wings and general coloration (except the white lores) exactly as in var. *occidentalis*.

Winter dress not materially different from the foregoing.

Dimensions.—Length, about 22 inches; extent, 28.50; wing, 7; bill along culmen, 2.30; along gape, 2.75; height at nostrils, 0.40; tarsus, and middle toe with claw, each, about 2.75.

With only extremes before us of the two varieties, one might well consider them distinct species; but other specimens show the intergradation. Thus, Nos. 9544 and 9938, especially the latter, differ from typical *clarkii* in stouter and less recurved as well as darker-colored bill, the culmen not obviously concave, and the under outline not regularly curved. The loral space has an ashy tinge in the white. The general dimensions are those of *clarkii*. In size the two varieties inosculate at about two feet of total length.

In examining more extensive material than I formerly possessed, lack of specific distinction between the two forms becomes still more obvious. Thus we frequently find specimens as small as typical *clarkii*, and with equally slender bill, yet with the color of the bill wholly olivaceous and the lores ashy, as in typical *occidentalis*.

Subgenus PODICEPS, *Lath.*

CHAR. Bill moderately stout, usually more or less compressed, equaling or shorter than the head or tarsus. Tarsus obviously shorter than the middle toe and claw. Outer lateral toe a little longer than the middle. Head in the breeding season with lengthened colored crests or ruffs, or both. (Including, among North American representatives, *Pedetaithyia, Lophaithyia, Dytes, Otodytes*, and *Proctopus*.)

Thus restricting *Podiceps* to exclude, of American forms, the subgenera *Æchmophorus* and *Tachybaptes*, as well as the genus *Podilymbus*, we find that the four North American representatives may be thus analyzed :

A. Large; length, over 15 inches. Bill more or less nearly equaling the head or tarsus in length.

    1. Crests, and especially ruffs, long and conspicuous. Neck without red or gray in front; under parts pure silky white. Tarsus averaging equal to the middle toe without its claw......   *cristatus.*

    2. Crests moderate; ruffs inconspicuous. Neck with red or gray in front; underparts watered with dusky (sometimes but slightly). Tarsus averaging less than the middle toe and claw..*griseigena* var. *holbölli.*

B. Small; length, under 15 inches. Bill much shorter than head; little over half the tarsus.

    3. Bill compressed, higher than broad at the nostrils. Crests and ruffs very conspicuous; neck red in front...................   *cornutus.*

    4. Bill depressed, broader than high at the nostrils. Crests in form of auricular tufts; neck black in front............*auritus* var. *californicus.*

In 1862 I adopted an analysis of this section, resting primarily upon the shortness of the tarsus in *Pedataithyia* ((*griseigena*) as contrasted with its greater length relatively to the toes in *cristatus, cornutus,* and *auritus.* This holds good with typical *griseigena,* but is subject to some uncertainty of determination in its application to the American var. *holbölli* or "*cooperi,*" as I now find upon examination of further material. It is also practically difficult to establish a division upon this basis, not only because the limits of individual variability are wide, but because different methods of measuring the peculiarly-shaped feet of these birds give different results. The subject is discussed further on. Meanwhile, the foregoing is presented as a more convenient analysis, since it is probably available for determination of young as well as old birds.

PODICEPS CRISTATUS, (Linn.) Lath.

Crested Grebe.

Colymbus cristatus, LINN., Syst. Nat. i, 1766, 222.—NAUM., V. D. ix, 1838, 686, pl. 242.—GLOGER, J. f. O. 1866, 285 (albino).
Podiceps cristatus, LATH., Ind. Orn. ii, 1790, 780.—TEMM., Man. 1815, 462.—BOIE, Isis, 1822, 561.—STEPH., Gen. Zool. xiii, 1825, 3.—KEYS. & BLAS., Wirb. Eur. 1840, 90.—MACGIL., Man. ii, 202.—GRAY, Gen. of B. iii, 633.—SCHL., Mus. P.-B. livr. ix, 34.—SUND., Svensk. Fogl. pl. 54.—SW. & RICH., F. B. A. ii, 1831, 410.—NUTT., Man. ii, 1834, 250.—BP., Syn. 1828, 417; List, 1838, 65.—AUD., Orn. Biog. iii, 1835, 598, pl. 292; Syn. 1839, 356; B. Am. vii, 1844, 308, pl. 479.—GIR., B. L. I. 1844, 383.—LAWR., B. N. A. 1858, 893; Ann. Lyc. N. Y. viii, 1866, 300.—COUES, Pr. Phila. Acad. 1862, 230.—COOP. & SUCK., N. H. Wash. Ter. 1860, 280.—BOARDM., Pr. Bost. Soc. ix, 1862, 131 (Maine, breeding).—COUES, Pr. Ess. Inst. v, 1868, 310.—TURNB., B. E. Pa. 1869, 39 ("not uncommon").—COUES, Key, 1872, 336; and of authors generally.
Lophairthyia cristata, KAUP, Sk. Ent. Eur. Thierw. 1829, 72.
Colymbus urinator, LINN., Syst. Nat. i, 1766, 223.
Colymbus cornutus, PALL., Zoog. R.-A. ii, 1811, 353. (Not of *Gmelin.*)
(?) *Podiceps australis,* GOULD.—DIGGLES, Orn. Aust. pt. xx, pl. —.
Podiceps longirostris, BP.
Podiceps mitratus et *patagiatus,* BREHM, V. D. 953, 954.
(?) *Podiceps hectori,* BULLER, Ess. Orn. N. Zeal. 19.—HUTTON, B. N. Zeal. 1871, 39. (See FINSCH, Ibis, 1869, 380.)
"*Podiceps widhalmi,* GÖBEL, J. f. O. qviii, 1870, 312."

Adult, breeding plumage.—Crown and long occipital crests glossy black; terminal half of the long ruff the same, the basal part bright reddish-brown, fading gradually into pure silky-white of the throat and sides of head. Superciliary and loral line white, more or less tinged with fulvous. Neck behind and general upper parts dark brown, the feathers of the back with gray margins. Primaries deep chocolate-brown, with black shafts, the tips of the inner ones white, as are all the secondaries and long humeral feathers, excepting a little part of the outer webs of the former. Inner webs of greater wing-coverts white, outer chocolate-brown; lesser coverts wholly brown. Under parts pure silky-white, without a trace of the dusky mottling seen in *P. griseigena*; the sides of the neck and body tinged with reddish and mixed with dusky on the flanks, where also the feathers have blackish shaft-lines. "Bill in life blackish-brown, tinged with carmine; bare loral space and eyelids dusky green; iris carmine; feet greenish-black; webs grayish-blue."

Dimensions.—Length, 24; extent, 33; wing, 7; bill along culmen, 2; along gape, 2.70; height at nostrils, 0.50; tarsus 2.50; middle toe and claw, 2.65.

Hab.—North America generally. Europe, and various other parts of the Old World.

The changes of plumage of this species chiefly affect the head, in the absence of the crest and ruffs, the parts being plainly colored, corresponding to the dark of the crown and nape and white of the sides of the head and throat. In any plumage, the species may be known by its subgeneric characters; and from *P. griseigena*, the only one of *Podiceps* proper that approaches it in size, by the pure white instead of dusky-mottled under parts, more white on the wing, relatively longer tarsi, &c.

I see no difference between American and European specimens.

PODICEPS GRISEIGENA var. HOLBÖLLI, (Reinh.) Coues.

Red-necked Grebe.

a. *griseigena*.

Colymbus griseigena, BODD., Tab. Pl. Enl. 55; pl. 404, fig. 1.
Podiceps griseigena, GRAY, Gen. of B. iii, 633.—SCHL., M. P.-B. ix, 38.
Colymbus parotis, SPARRM., Mus. Carls. pl. 9.—GM., Syst. Nat. i, 1788, 592.
Colymbus subcristatus, JACQ., Beit. 1784, 37, pl. 18.—GM., Syst. Nat. i, 1788, 590.
Podiceps subcristatus, BECHST., Naturg. Deutschl. 546.—BREHM, Vög. Deutschl. 957.—
   KEYS. & BLAS., Wirb. Eur. 1840, 90.
Pedeaithyia subcristata, KAUP, Sk. Ent. Eur. Thierw. 1829, 44.
Podiceps rubricollis, LATH., Ind. Orn. ii, 1790, 783.—TEMM., Man. 1815, 465.—STEPH., G.
   Z. xiii, 1825, 8.—BREHM, V. D. 956.—MACGIL., Man. ii, 203; and of European
   authors generally.
Colymbus cucullatus et *nævias*, PALL., Zoog. R.-A. ii, 1811, 355, 356.
Podiceps canigularis, BREHM., Vög. Deutschl. 958.

b. *holbölli*.

Podiceps rubricollis, BP., Syn. 1828, 417; List, 1838, 65.—SW. & RICH., F. B. A. ii, 1831,
   411.—NUTT., Man. ii, 1834, 253.—AUD., Orn. Biog. iii, 1835, 617, pl. 298; Syn.
   1839, 357; B. Am. vii, 1844, 312, pl. 480.—GIR., B. L. I. 1844, 384.—TURNB., B. E.
   Pa. 1869, 39.
Podiceps griseigena, LAWR., B. N. A. 1858, 892; Ann. Lyc. N. Y. viii, 1866, 300.—DALL &
   BANN., Tr. Chic. Acad. i, 1869, 308 (Alaska); and of most late United States
   writers.
Podiceps holbölli, REINH., Ibis, iii, 1861, 14 (Greenland).—COUES, Pr. Phila. Acad.
   1862, 231.
Podiceps griseigena var. *holbölli*, COUES, Key, 1872, 337.—RIDGW., Ann. Lyc. N. Y. x,
   1874, 392 (Illinois).
Podiceps cooperi, LAWR., B. N. A. 1858 (in text).—COUES, Pr. Phila. Acad. 1862, 230.—
   FINSCH., Abh. Nat. iii, 1872, 75 (Alaska). (Beyond doubt!)
(?) *Podiceps affinis*, SALVAD., Atti Soc. Ital. Sc. viii, 1866.—ELLIOT, B. N. A. (Introd. No.
   98 with fig. of head).—VON MARTENS, J. f. O. 1868, 70.

Hab.—The typical form in Europe. Var. *holbölli* from Greenland and North America; with this Asiatic and Japanese specimens are stated to agree.

Adult, breeding plumage.—Crests short, and ruffs scarcely apparent. Bill black, the tomia of the upper mandible at base and most of the lower mandible yellowish. Crown and occiput glossy greenish-black; back of the neck the same, less intense, and the upper parts generally the same, with grayish edgings of the feathers. Wing-coverts and primaries uniform chocolate-brown, the shafts of the latter black. Secondaries white, mostly with black shafts and brownish tips. Lining of wings and axillars white. A broad patch of silvery-ash on the throat, extending around on sides of head, whitening along line of juncture with the black of the crown. Neck, except the dorsal line, deep brownish-red, which extends diluted some distance on the breast. Under parts silky-white, with a shade of silvery-ash, each feather having a dark shaft-line and terminal spot, producing a peculiar dappled appearance.

Winter plumage, and young.—Crests scarcely appreciable. Bill mostly yellowish, the ridge more or less dusky. Red of the neck replaced by brownish-ash of very variable shade, from quite dark to whitish. Ash of throat and sides of head replaced by pure white. Under parts ashy-white, the mottling not so conspicuous as in summer.

Dimensions.—Length, about 19; wing, 7.60; bill along culmen, 1.90; along gape, 2.40; height at nostrils, 0.55; tarsus, 2.10; middle toe and claw, 2.65.

This bird could only be confounded with *cristatus* in immature dress. It is smaller, stouter, and more thick-set, with stouter bill, with nebulated under plumage, and usually has rather shorter tarsi—only about four-fifths the middle toe and claw, instead of about equal to the middle toe alone. as in *cristatus*.

Until the appearance of my article, the present bird was considered identical with that of the Old World. Such, however, is not the case. The differences prove to be even more decided and more constant than I at first supposed; in fact, I am almost inclined to hold them as of specific value. The size is uniformly greater; the bill disproportionately larger, stouter, differently shaped and colored; the tarsus longer, both absolutely and relatively to the length of the toes; in fact, so much longer as to rather invalidate one of the distinctions I drew between *cristatus* and *rubricollis*.

Upon attentive re-examination of the types of *Podiceps cooperi*, which, in 1362, I followed Mr. Lawrence in comparing with *cristatus*, finding evident distinction from the latter, I am now satisfied that they belong to the American var. *holböllii* of *griseigena*. The types were young birds, in very poor preservation, showing little or no distinctive color-marks, while the length of the tarsus, grading into the particular proportions of tarsus and toes of *cristatus*, misled me as to their proper position. We have now numerous specimens from the northwest coast, some just like the types, others in better plumage, showing the reddish of the neck of var. *holbölli*, and all inseparable from unquestioned American *griseigena*. My suspicions were first aroused by detecting on the under parts of the type of *cooperi* traces of the peculiar dusky mottling characteristic of *griseigena* and *holbölli*, as contrasted with the pure silky-white of the under parts of *cristatus*; when further examination, and especially careful measurements of the feet, led to the above-mentioned result. I append a table of measurements, &c., of various American *holbölli*, the types of "*cooperi*," typical *griseigena* of Europe, and typical *cristatus*.

S. I. No.	Species or variety.	Locality.	Wing.	Along culmen.	Along gape.	Depth at nostrils.	Tarsus.	Middle toe and claw.	Remarks.
					Bill.				
18905	*cristatus*	Europe	6.80	2.00	2.40	0.48	2.40	2.65	Adult; perfect plumage.
21797	*griseigena* ...	Denmark	6.60	1.50	2.00	....	2.10	2.55	Do.
18906	*griseigena* ...	Russia	6.20	1.60	1.95	0.40	2.00	2.40	Do.
13115	Var. *holböllii*.	Red River........	7.00	2.00	2.60	0.48	2.60	2.80	Adult; nearly perfect plumage.
44563	Var. *holböllii*.	Great Slave Lake.	7.30	(*)	(*)	0.52	2.35	2.80	Adult; perfect plumage.
61624	Var. *holböllii*.	Unalashka	7.50	2.20	2.75	0.56	2.60	3.05	Adult; traces of red neck evident.
16017	Var. *holböllii*.	Puget Sound	7.50	1.90	....	0.50	2.50	2.85	Young; neck gray; traces of mottling on under parts.
58163	Var. *holböllii*	Kodiak, Alaska ..	7.50	2.15	2.80	0.51	2.50	2.85	Winter; neck dark gray; mottling of breast, &c., very evident.
4500	Var. *holböllii*.	Shoalwater Bay ..	7.00	2.10	2.60	0.50	2.35	2.25	A type of *cooperi*; young; neck gray; mottling barely appreciable.
4499	Var. *holböllii*.	......do	7.80	2.40	3.10	0.55	2.50	2.90	The type of *cooperi*; young; neck gray; mottling slight but evident.

* Bill broken.

NOTE.—The wing is measured with a straight-edge under the border, not over its convexity. Depth of bill at posterior extremity of nostrils. Tarsus in front, from protuberance in middle of tibio-tarsal joint to the nick on the skin over the joint of middle toe. Middle toe from the last-named point to end of the claw.

There seems to be little doubt that *P. affinis*, Salvadori, belongs here, to judge from the life-size figure of the head published by Elliot, which is exactly matched by some of the specimens of "*cooperi*" before me.

PODICEPS CORNUTUS, Lath.

Horned Grebe.

Colymbus auritus, LINN., *partim.*
Colymbus duplicatus, MÜLL., Syst. Nat. 1776, 107.
Colymbus cornutus, GM., Syst. Nat. i, 591.— NAUM., Vög. Deutschl. ix, 1838, 739, pl. 244.
Podiceps cornutus, LATH., Ind. Orn. ii, 1790, 783.—TEMM., Man. Orn. 1815, 466.—BOIE, Isis, 1822, 561.—STEPH., G. Z. xiii, 1825, 9.—KEYS. & BLAS., Wirb. Eur.—GRAY, Gen. of B. iii, 633.—SCHL., M. P.-B. ix, 36.—BP., Syn. 1828, 417; List, 1838, 65.— SW. & RICH., F. B. Am. ii, 1831, 411.—NUTT., Man. ii, 1834, 254.—AUD., Orn. Biog. iii, 1835, 429, pl. 259; Syn. 1839, 357; B. Am. vii, 1844, 316, pl. 481.— GIR., B. L. I. 1844, 381.—LAWR., B. N. A. 1858, 895.—COOP. & SUCK., N. H. Wash. Ter. 1860, 281.—COUES, Pr. Phila. Acad. 1862, 231.—DALL & BANN., Tr. Chic. Acad. 1869, 208.—FINSCH, Abh. Nat. iii, 1872, 76.—COUES, Key, 1872, 337.—SNOW, B. Kans. 1873, 12; and of authors generally.
Dytes cornutus, KAUP, Sk. Ent. Eur. Thierw. 1829, 41.

Colymbus obscurus, GM., Syst. Nat. i, 1788, 592.
Podiceps obscurus, LATH., Ind. Orn. ii, 1790, 782.—LEACH, Cat. 1816, 35.
Colymbus caspicus, S. G. GM., Reise, iv, 137.—GM., Syst. Nat. i, 1788, 593.
Podiceps caspicus, LATH., Ind. Orn. ii, 1790, 784.
Colymbus nigricans, SCOPOLI, Ann. i, No. 101 (?).
Podiceps arcticus, BOIE.
Podiceps sclavus, BP.

  Hab.—North America. Europe. Asia.

List of specimens.

19329	....	....	....	....	F. V. Hayden.	......	......	......

Adult, breeding plumage.—Bill black, tipped with yellow. A brownish-yellow stripe over eye, widening behind and deepening in color at the ends of the long crests, and being dark chestnut between eye and bill. Crown, chin, and the very full ruff glossy greenish-black. Upper parts brownish-black, with paler edges of the feathers. Primaries rather light chocolate-brown, with black shafts, except at the base. Secondaries white. Neck all round, except stripe down behind and sides of the body, rich dark brownish-red or purplish wine-red, mixed with dusky on the flanks. Under parts pure silky-white.

Winter plumage, and young.—Bill dusky, much of the under mandible bluish or yellowish-white. Indications of crests and ruff in the length and fullness of the feathers of the parts. Crown and neck behind, and sides of the body, sooty-blackish. Other upper parts and the wings as in the adult. Chin, throat, and sides of head, pure white, this color nearly encircling the nape. Neck in front and lower belly lightly washed with ashy-gray. Under parts as before.

Newly-fledged young are curiously striped on the head with rufous, dusky and white, as in *Podilymbus* and elsewhere.

Dimensions.—Length, about 14 inches ; extent, 24 ; wing, 5.75 ; tarsus, 1.75 ; middle toe and claw, 2.10 ; bill along culmen, about 0.90 ; along gape, 1.30 ; its height at the nostrils, 0.30 ; its width there, 0.25.

The bill in this species is compressed, tapering, with considerably curved culmen—quite different from the broad depressed bill with straight tip and much ascending gonys of *P. auritus*. It varies much in size, even among equally adult examples ; in the young it is always smaller and weaker than in the old. Black, yellow-tipped in the old, we find it variously lighter in the young—usually dusky on the ridge, elsewhere tinged with olivaceous, yellowish, or even orange or extensively bluish-white. In breeding plumage this bird is conspicuously different from any other ; but the young are much like those of *P. auritus*, requiring sometimes careful discrimination, as pointed out under head of the latter.

This species is much more abundant and generally dispersed in winter in the United States than either of the two larger ones, and it also nests within our limits. I found it breeding at various points in Northern Dakota, as along the Red River, in the prairie sloughs, with Coots, Phalaropes, and various Ducks, and in pools about the base of Turtle Mountain in company with *P. californicus* and the Dabchick. I took fresh eggs on the 20th of June, at Pembina, finding them scattered on a soaking bed of decayed reeds, as they had doubtless been disturbed by the hasty movements of the parents in quitting the nest ; there were only four ; probably more would have been laid. They are elliptical in shape, with little or no difference in contour at either end ; dull whitish, with a very faint shade, quite smooth, and measure about 1.70 by 1.20. On Turtle Mountain, late in July, I procured newly-hatched young, swimming with their parents in the various pools. At this early stage the neck is striped as in the common Dabchick. Later in the season, during the migration, the Horned Grebes were numerous all along the Souris or Mouse River, in company with an equal or even greater number of Eared Grebes, nearly all of both species being the young-of-the-year. In their immature plumage the two cannot be distinguished on the water, and indeed specimens sometimes occur which are with difficulty discriminated at this early age. But the smaller size, somewhat different proportions of tarsus and toes, and the flatter, comparatively broader bill of *P. auritus*, is generally characteristic.

I once noticed a singular fact connected with the power these birds have, in common with other Grebes, of sinking quietly into the water. By the respiratory process they are able to very materially reduce or enlarge their bulk, with the consequence of displacing a varying bulk of water, and so of changing their specific gravity. Once holding a wounded Grebe in my hand, I observed its whole body to swell with a labored inspiration. As the air permeated the interior, a sort of ripple or wave passed gradually along, puffing out the belly and raising the plumage as it advanced. With the expiration, the reverse change occurred from the opposite direction, and the bird visibly shrunk in dimensions, the skin fitting tightly and the feathers lying close.

PODICEPS AURITUS var. CALIFORNICUS, (Heerm.) Coues.

American Eared Grebe.

a. *auritus.*

Colymbus auritus, LINN., Syst. Nat. 1766, 222 (*partim*).—NAUM., Vög. Deutschl, ix, 1838, 768, pl. 246.
Podiceps auritus, LATH., Ind. Orn. ii, 1790, 781.—TEMM., Man. 1815, 469.—BOIE, Isis, 1822, 561.—STEPH., Gen. Zool. xiii, 1825, 12.—KEYS. & BLAS., Wirb. Eur. 1840, 90.—SCHL., Rev. Crit. 105; M. P.-B. ix, 40.—MACGIL., Man. ii, 204.—GRAY, Gen. of B. iii, 633 ; and of European authors generally.
Proctopus auritus, KAUP, Sk. Ent. Eur. Thierw. 1829, 49.
Otodytes auritus, REICHENBACH.
Podiceps et Colymbus nigricollis, SUNDEVALL.

b. *californicus.*

Podiceps auritus, NUTT., Man. ii, 1834, 256 ("will probably be found in North America").—AUD., Orn. Biog. v, 1839, 108, pl. 404 ; Syn. 1839, 358 ; B. Am. vii, 1844, 322, pl. 482 (described from species *said* to be North American).—BP., List, 1838, 64.—LAWR., B. N. A. 1858, 897.—MAXIM., J. f. O. vii, 1859, 246 (description).
Podiceps californicus, HEERM., Pr. Phila. Acad. 1854, 179 ; P. R. R. Rep. x, 1859, 76, pl. 8 (young).—NEWB., P. R. R. Rep. vi, 1857, 110.—LAWR., B. N. A. 1858, 896.—COOP. & SUCK., N. H. Wash. Ter. 1860, 282.—HAYD., Rep. 1862, 176.—STEV., U. S. Geol. Surv. Ter. 1870, 466 (North Platte).—ELLIOT, B. N. A. pl. 64.—COUES, Ibis, 1866, 273.—SCL., P. Z. S. 1864, 179 (city of Mexico, in full plumage).—DRESS, Ibis, 1866, 46 (Texas, winter).—SALV., Ibis, 1866, 200 (Guatemala).
Podiceps (Proctopus) californicus, COUES, Pr. Phila. Acad. 1862, 231, 404.—COUES, *ibid.* 1866, 100 (Arizona).
Podiceps auritus var. californicus, COUES, Key, 1872, 337.—COUES, Am. Nat. viii, 1874 (Dakota).—HENSHAW, Am. Nat. viii, 1874, 243 (breeding).—RIDGW., Ann. Lyc. N. Y. x, 1874, 392 (Illinois).—SNOW, Am. Nat. viii, 1874, 757 (Kansas).

Hab.—The typical form from Europe, Asia, and Africa. Var. *californicus* from Western North America, from Great Slave Lake to Guatemala. East to Texas, Dakota (*Coues,* Am. Nat. vii, 1873, 745), Kansas (*Snow*), and Illinois (*Ridgway*). Breeds apparently throughout its range.

Lieutenant Warren's Expedition.—5476, Fort Berthold; 5477, Snake River.
Later Expeditions.—60863, North Platte.

Adult, breeding plumage.—Bill shorter than head, rather stout at base, much depressed, broader than high at the nostrils, tip acute, not decurved, gonys straight, ascending, culmen a little concave basally, nearly straight terminally. Tarsus about equal to middle toe without its claw. Bill entirely black. Conspicuous, long auricular tufts, golden-brown or tawny, finely displayed upon a black ground. Crown, chin, and neck all round, black. All the primaries entirely chocolate-brown, with usually a wash of dull reddish-brown externally. Secondaries white, but the bases of all, and a considerable part of the two outer ones, dusky ; their shafts mostly all dusky. Sides deep purplish-brown or wine-red ; this color washed across the breast, behind the black of the neck, and also across the anal region. Under parts silky-white, the abdomen grayish.

Young.—Bill shaped generally as in the adult, but smaller, with less firm outlines, so that its distinctive shape is somewhat obscured. Little or no trace of the auricular tufts. Crown, sides of head, and neck all around, sooty-grayish, paler and more ashy on the foreneck. Upper parts rather lighter and duller colored than in the adults.

Primaries as in the adults, but without the reddish tinge; a few of the innermost ones sometimes white tipped. Sides under the wings washed with a lighter shade of the color of the back; lower belly grayish.

Dimensions.—Length, 12 to 14 inches, usually 13 or less; extent, 21.50 to 24; wing, 4.75 to 5.25; bill, 1 or less; along gape, 1.25; height at nostril, 0.22; width there, 0.26; tarsus, 1.60; middle toe and claw, 1.95.

While the breeding plumages of *P. cornutus* and the present species are widely different, there is much similarity between the young and winter dress of the two species. As a rule, *auritus* is smaller; even traces of ruffs are less appreciable; the fore-neck is scarcely lighter than the hind-neck; the back is rather deeper colored and more uniform. The shape and proportions of the bill, however, furnish the most reliable characters. The differences may be thus tabulated:

P. cornutus: Bill rather slender, much compressed, tip rather obtuse; lateral outlines concave; height at nostrils greater than width; culmen nearly straight over nostrils, very convex at the end; gonys convex, little ascending, with little appreciable angle.

P. auritus: Bill rather stout, much depressed, tip very acute; lateral outlines convex; height at nostrils less than width; culmen decidedly concave at nostrils, scarcely convex at tip; gonys straight, or even concave, much ascending, with quite an angle.

As I pointed out in 1862, the type of "*californicus*" is merely the young of the American Eared Grebe, now well known from Western United States in all its plumages. I continue to use the name as indicating a bird varietally distinct from the true *auritus* of Europe. I verify the following distinctions:

In the American bird, the primaries are all entirely dark; the first two secondaries are mostly the same, while the bases and shafts of all are for some distance dark. In European *auritus*, the inner four primaries are entirely pure white, and all the rest have more or less white, while the secondaries are all entirely white, except a few of the innermost, which have a slight dusky spot near the end. Thus the European has much more white on the wing, and this white is moreover bodily shifted, as it were, nearer the outer edge of the wing. I do not know how much the extent of the white may change with age, or what is its limit of individual variability; but the above differences hold throughout a quite extensive series of specimens examined.

The *Colymbus auritus* of Linnæus has been by many referred to *P. cornutus*, Gm., and the name *nigricollis*, after Sundevall, adopted for the present species. The case seems parallel with that of *Sterna hirundo*, Linn., and I see no necessity for the undesirable change of names, especially as Linnæus apparently included *both* species under the term *auritus*. Audubon's *auritus* may have been really based upon *auritus* proper, but he meant the American bird.

The abundance and general dispersion of this species in the West have only lately become known. The earlier authors were not aware of its existence in this country; Audubon figures and describes specimens said to be North American, and his account is copied, so late as 1858, by Mr. Lawrence, in default of specimens. In the article above quoted I showed that *P. "californicus"* was the young of the Eared Grebe, pointing out, at the same time, certain distinctions between the bird of this country and of Europe, which I considered sufficient to warrant their separation. The points mentioned appear to hold good, though I am at present disinclined to accord them more than varietal significance. In 1859 Maximilian gave a full account of the bird, and of late quotations have multiplied until its range has been determined as above given.

I first saw the species alive in Southern California, where I found it to be very common, both on the waters of the bay of San Pedro and in the sloughs back of the coast. They were of course in immature dress, the season being November. During the past year I was pleased to find the birds breeding, in pools about Turtle Mountain, with various other water-fowl. This is apparently the northeasternmost point at which the species has been observed. Visiting this locality in July, I was too late for eggs, for the young were already swimming, and, in most cases, fledged. The birds were very common, rather more so than *P. cornutus*, with which they were associated. Many specimens were secured in their full nuptial dress. The change begins in August, but it is not completed until well into the following month, as traces of the breeding plumage persist several weeks after it has grown faded and obscure. On the breeding grounds, as just said, the Eared Grebes were more plentiful than the Horned, since a majority of the latter breed further north; but upon the migration, when these come south, the proportion is reversed. Both species were to be seen together upon all the water-courses'of Northern Dakota when I left the country in the middle of October. I saw nothing notably different in their general habits.

Other observers have found the Eared Grebe in full dress, and nesting,. in various of our western Territories, demonstrating a very general breeding range. Mr. Henshaw has lately taken the eggs in Southern Colorado. He informs us that he found them, in the absence of parents, completely covered over and concealed by reedy material, so that they were discovered by mere accident. The following is his article in the American Naturalist above quoted:

" In a series of alkali lakes about thirty miles northwest of Fort Garland, Southern Colorado, I found this species common and breeding. A colony of perhaps a dozen pairs had established themselves in a small pond four or five acres in extent. In the middle of this, in a bed of reeds, were found upward of a dozen nests. These in each case merely consisted of a slightly hollowed pile of decaying weeds and rushes, four or five inches in diameter, and scarcely raised above the surface of the water upon which they floated. In a number of instances they were but a few feet distant from the nests of the Coot (*Fulica americana*), which abounded. Every Grebe's nest discovered contained three eggs, which in most instances were fresh, but in some nests were considerably advanced. These vary but little in shape, are considerably elongated, one end being slightly more pointed than the other. They vary in length from 1.70 to 1.80, and in breadth 1.18 to 1.33. The color is a faint yellowish-white, usually much stained from contact with the nest. The texture is generally quite smooth, in some instances roughened by a chalky deposit. The eggs were wholly concealed from view by a pile of weeds and other vegetable material laid across. That they were thus carefully covered merely for concealment I cannot think, since in the isolated position in which these nests are usually found the bird has no enemy against which such precaution would avail. On first approaching the locality the Grebes all congregated at the further end of the pond, and shortly betook themselves through an opening to the neighboring slough; nor, so far as I could ascertain, did they again approach the nests during my stay of three days. Is it not, then, possible that they are more or less dependent for the hatching of their eggs upon the artificial heat induced by the decaying vegetable substances of which the nests are wholly composed?"

Subgenus TACHYBAPTES, *Reich.*

Bill very short, much less than the head, scarcely over half the tarsus; stout, little compressed, rather obtuse. Lateral outlines nearly straight; culmen slightly concave at the nostrils, elsewhere convex; commissure straight, except a little sinuation at base; under outline straight to angle, gonys thence straight to tip, the angle well defined. Wings short, with considerable and abrupt attenuation of the outer primaries. Tarsus stout, little over three-fourths the middle toe and claw; outer lateral about equal to the middle toe. Size very small; body full; neck short; no decided crests or ruffs. (Type *P. minor :* these characters drawn from *P. dominicus.*)

This section in a measure connects *Podiceps* with *Podilymbus.* By G. R. Gray *Sylbeocyclus,* Bp., is given as founded on *P. minor;* but Bonaparte expressly says (Cat. Met. Ucc. 1842, 83) that this was a typographical error, he having intended the name for *C. podiceps,* Linn. Dr. Sclater has lately called attention to the point (Ibis, Jan. 1874). It may be a technical question, however, after all, whether an author must not be held to what he did say, rather than to what he meant to say.

PODICEPS (TACHYBAPTES) DOMINICUS, Linn.

St. Domingo Grebe.

Colymbus dominicus, LINN., Syst. Nat. i, 1766, 223 (*C. fluviatilis dominicensis*, BRISS., vi, 64, pl. 5, f. 2).—GM., Syst. Nat. i, 1788, 593.
Podiceps dominicus, LATH., Ind. Orn. ii, 1790, 785.—SPIX, Av. Bras. pl. 101.—BD., Mex. B. Surv. ii, 1859, pt. ii, Birds, 28; B. N. Am. 1860, pl. 99, f. 1 (no text, and not in ed. of 1858).—SCL., P. Z. S. 1857, 207.—LAWR., Ann. Lyc. N. Y. vii, 1861, 334 (Panama).—SCL. & SALV., Exot. Orn. i, 1869, 190.—REINH., Vid. Med. 1870, 17 (Brazil).
Podiceps (Sylbeocyclus) dominicus, GRAY, Hand-list, iii, 1871, 94, No. 10768.
Sylbeocyclus dominicus (BP. ?) COUES, Pr. Phila. Acad. 1862, 232.
Tachybaptes dominicus, COUES.

Hab.—Warmer parts of America. West Indies. North to the Rio Grande. California (*Gambel*).

Adult.—Form as above described under head of the subgenus. Crown and occiput deep glossy steel-blue. Sides of head and neck all around dark ashy-gray, darkest behind, where tinged with bluish. Chin varied with ashy and white. Upper parts brownish-black, with glossy-greenish reflections. Primaries chocolate-brown, the greater portion of the inner vanes of all, and nearly all of the inner four or five, together with all the secondaries, pure white. Under parts silky-white, thickly mottled with dusky. Upper mandible dusky, the lower mostly yellowish.
Dimensions.—Length, about 9.50; wing, 3.60; bill along culmen, 0.70; along gape, 1; tarsus, 1.25; middle toe, 1.75.
This small Grebe, the only North American * representative of the group, has only lately been ascertained to reach our southern border. It requires comparison with no other of our country, its small size alone being diagnostic. Without a series of specimens I cannot present the changes of plumage.

Genus PODILYMBUS, *Less.*

< *Colymbus*, LINN., Syst. Nat. i, 1766, 223 (not type).
< *Podiceps*, LATH., Ind. Orn. ii, 1790 (not type).
= *Podilymbus*, LESS., Tr. Orn. i, 1831, 595 (*P. carolinensis*, LATH.).
= *Sylbeocyclus*, BP., Saggio, 1834 (same type intended).
= *Hydroka*, NUTT., Man. ii, 1834, 259 (type *carolinensis*).

CHAR. Bill shorter than head, stoutest in the family, compressed, with obtuse and hooked tip; culmen about straight to the nostrils, thence declinato-convex; gonys regularly convex without decided angle; commissure slightly sinuate at base, then straight, then much deflected. Upper mandible covered with soft skin to the nostrils, between which are two fossæ, the anterior shallow, oblong, the other deep, triangular, separated from the bare loral space by an intervening ridge. Nostrils broadly oval, far anterior. No crests or ruffs, but shafts of frontal feathers prolonged into bristles. Eyelids peculiarly thickened. Outer three or four primaries abruptly sinuate near the end. Tarsus much abbreviated, comparatively stout, about three-fourths as long as middle toe and claw. Middle and outer toes nearly equal. Basal semipalmation of toes more extensive than in *Podiceps*. Lobe of hind toe moderate.
The essential characters of this genus lie in the stout hooked bill, broad anterior nostrils, absence of crest or ruff, bristly forehead, great emargination of primaries, and extensive semipalmation of the toes. The genus *Dasyptilus* of Swainson (Classif. B. ii, 1837, 369), which has been referred here, agrees very well as to the characters assigned, but *P. poliocephalus* is given as type. In any event the name is a synonym, being anticipated in publication. *Hydroka* is based upon *carolinensis*, but is antedated. *Sylbeocyclus*, BP., was meant for this genus, but, it seems, was by a blunder given over head of *P. minor*.
There is apparently but a single good species of this genus, although several are indicated by authors. The *P. antarcticus* of Lesson (with which *P. brevirostris*, GRAY, Gen. of B. iii, 1849, pl. 172, is synonymous), from South America, is a recognizable race which may be defined as follows:
PODILYMBUS PODICEPS var. ANTARCTICUS (*Less.*) *Coues.*
Nos. 15663, 15664, Mus. Smiths. Inst., Chili, U. S. Astron. Exped.: Size, coloration, and general appearance of *P. podiceps.* Bill not shorter than in this species, but stouter

* *P. minor* is given by Nuttall as inhabiting this country, but the evidence is altogether unsatisfactory.

toward the end, where more obtuse and less hooked ; commissure not so suddenly decurved, nor to such extent. Legs rather longer and stouter than in *P. podiceps.* Gular
patch extending further around on sides of head ; under parts more heavily mottled
with dusky.

PODILYMBUS PODICEPS, (Linn.) Lawr.

Pied-billed Grebe; Dabchick; Water-witch.

a. *podiceps.*

Colymbus podiceps, LINN., Syst. Nat. i, 1766, 223 (based on *P. minor rostro vario,* CATES.,
    91; *C. fluviatilis carolinensis,* BRISS., vi, 63).—GM., Syst. Nat. i, 1788, 594.
Podilymbus podiceps, LAWR., B. N. A. 1858, 898.—COOP. & SUCK., N. H. Wash. Ter. 1860,
    283.—COUES, Pr. Phila. Acad. 1862, 233.—COUES, Key, 1872, 338 ; and of most
    late United States writers.
Sylbeocyclus podiceps, BP.
Colymbus ludovicianus, GM., Syst. Nat, i, 1788, 592.
Podiceps ludovicianus, LATH., Ind. Orn. ii, 1790, 785.
Podiceps carolinensis, LATH., Ind. Orn. ii, 1790, 785.—BP., Syn. 1828, 418.—SW. & RICH.,
    F. B. A. ii, 1831, 412.—NUTT., Man. ii, 1834, 259.—AUD., Orn. Biog. iii, 1835, 359;
    Syn. 1839, 358 ; B. Am. vii, 1844, 324, pl. 483.—GIR., B. L. I. 1844, 382.—MAX.,
    J. f. O. vii, 1859, 248 ; and of writers generally.
Sylbeocyclus carolinensis, BP., List, 1838, 64.
Podilymbus lineatus, HEERM., Pr. Phila. Acad. 1854, 179 ; P. R. R. Rep. x, 1859, 77, pl. 9
    (very young).
Sylbeocyclus lineatus, BP.

b. *antarcticus.*

Podiceps carolinensis, SPIX, A. B. pl. 100.
Podiceps antarcticus, LESSON.
Sylbeocyclus antarcticus, BP.
Podilymbus antarcticus, GRAY, Hand-list, iii, 1871, 95, No. 10771.
Podiceps brevirostris, GRAY, Genera of Birds, iii, 1839, pl. 172.
Quid " eurytes, BP."—GRAY, Hand-list, No. 10772, *ex Montevideo?*

Hab.—North, Central, and part of South America. West Indies. (Guatemala,
breeding, SCL., Ibis, i, 1859, 234. Veragua, SALV., P. Z. S. 1870, 219. Venezuela, SCL.
& SALV., P. Z. S. 1869, 252. Brazil, PELZ., O. B. 322; REINH., V. D. Med. 1870, 18.
Cuba, CAB., J. f. O. iv, 1856, 431. Jamaica, SCL., P. Z. S. 1861, 81.) Var. *antarcticus*
from Southern South America.

Adult, breeding plumage.—Bill light dull bluish, dusky on upper mandible, encircled
with a broad black band. Frontal and coronal bristles black. Crown, occiput, and
neck behind, grayish-black, the feathers with slightly lighter edges. Sides of head and
neck brownish-gray. A broad black throat-patch, extending on sides of lower mandible. Upper parts brownish-black, the feathers with scarcely lighter edges. Primaries and secondaries chocolate-brown, the latter frequently with a white area on the
inner webs. Under parts ashy, washed over with silvery-gray, thickly, though obsoletely, mottled with dusky ; these dark spots most numerous and evident on the sides.
Lower belly nearly uniformly dusky.
Winter plumage.—Bill light dull yellowish, without a dark band, more or less dusky
on the ridge. No gular patch. Crown and occiput dusky brown. Upper parts with
more evident pale edgings of the feathers than in summer. Neck, breast, and sides,
light brown, darker posteriorly, where more or less conspicuously mottled with dusky.
Under parts otherwise pure silky-white, immaculate ; lower belly grayish.
Young-of-the-year.—White gular patch invaded by streaks of the brownish of the
head, and the latter much streaked with white. Otherwise as in the preceding.
Dimensions.—Length, about 13 ; extent, 24 ; wing, about 5 ; bill along culmen, 0.75 ;
along gape, 1.20 ; height at nostrils, 0.40 ; width, 0.25 ; tarsus, 1.50 ; middle toe and
claw, 2.15.
There is no species of this country with which the present requires comparison, as
its generic peculiarities suffice for its recognition under any circumstances of plumage.
The slight peculiarities of var. *antarcticus* have been already given.

Published December, 1874.

47

INDEX.

48

50

Additions and Corrections to Index.

NATURAL SCIENCES IN AMERICA

An Arno Press Collection

Allen, J[oel] A[saph]. **The American Bisons,** Living and Extinct. 1876

Allen, Joel Asaph. **History of the North American Pinnipeds:** A Monograph of the Walruses, Sea-Lions, Sea-Bears and Seals of North America. 1880

American Natural History Studies: The Bairdian Period. 1974

American Ornithological Bibliography. 1974

Anker, Jean. **Bird Books and Bird Art.** 1938

Audubon, John James and John Bachman. **The Quadrupeds of North America.** Three vols. 1854

Baird, Spencer F[ullerton]. **Mammals of North America.** 1859

Baird, S[pencer] F[ullerton], T[homas] M. Brewer and R[obert] Ridgway. **A History of North American Birds:** Land Birds. Three vols., 1874

Baird, Spencer F[ullerton], John Cassin and George N. Lawrence. **The Birds of North America.** 1860. Two vols. in one.

Baird, S[pencer] F[ullerton], T[homas] M. Brewer, and R[obert] Ridgway. **The Water Birds of North America.** 1884. Two vols. in one.

Barton, Benjamin Smith. **Notes on the Animals of North America.** Edited, with an Introduction by Keir B. Sterling. 1792

Bendire, Charles [Emil]. **Life Histories of North American Birds** With Special Reference to Their Breeding Habits and Eggs. 1892/1895. Two vols. in one.

Bonaparte, Charles Lucian [Jules Laurent]. **American Ornithology:** Or The Natural History of Birds Inhabiting the United States, Not Given by Wilson. 1825/1828/1833. Four vols. in one.

Cameron, Jenks. **The Bureau of Biological Survey:** Its History, Activities, and Organization. 1929

Caton, John Dean. **The Antelope and Deer of America:** A Comprehensive Scientific Treatise Upon the Natural History, Including the Characteristics, Habits, Affinities, and Capacity for Domestication of the Antilocapra and Cervidae of North America. 1877

Contributions to American Systematics. 1974

Contributions to the Bibliographical Literature of American Mammals. 1974

Contributions to the History of American Natural History. 1974

Contributions to the History of American Ornithology. 1974

Cooper, J[ames] G[raham]. **Ornithology.** Volume I, Land Birds. 1870

Cope, E[dward] D[rinker]. **The Origin of the Fittest:** Essays on Evolution and **The Primary Factors of Organic Evolution.** 1887/1896. Two vols. in one.

Coues, Elliott. **Birds of the Colorado Valley.** 1878

Coues, Elliott. **Birds of the Northwest.** 1874

Coues, Elliott. **Key To North American Birds.** Two vols. 1903

Early Nineteenth-Century Studies and Surveys. 1974

Emmons, Ebenezer. **American Geology:** Containing a Statement of the Principles of the Science. 1855. Two vols. in one.

Fauna Americana. 1825-1826

Fisher, A[lbert] K[enrick]. **The Hawks and Owls of the United States in Their Relation to Agriculture.** 1893

Godman, John D. **American Natural History:** Part I — Mastology and **Rambles of a Naturalist.** 1826-28/1833. Three vols. in one.

Gregory, William King. **Evolution Emerging:** A Survey of Changing Patterns from Primeval Life to Man. Two vols. 1951

Hay, Oliver Perry. **Bibliography and Catalogue of the Fossil Vertebrata of North America.** 1902

Heilprin, Angelo. **The Geographical and Geological Distribution of Animals.** 1887

Hitchcock, Edward. **A Report on the Sandstone of the Connecticut Valley,** Especially Its Fossil Footmarks. 1858

Hubbs, Carl L., editor. **Zoogeography.** 1958

[Kessel, Edward L., editor]. **A Century of Progress in the Natural Sciences: 1853-1953.** 1955

Leidy, Joseph. **The Extinct Mammalian Fauna of Dakota and Nebraska,** Including an Account of Some Allied Forms from Other Localities, Together with a Synopsis of the Mammalian Remains of North America. 1869

Lyon, Marcus Ward, Jr. **Mammals of Indiana.** 1936

Matthew, W[illiam] D[iller]. **Climate and Evolution.** 1915

Mayr, Ernst, editor. **The Species Problem.** 1957

Mearns, Edgar Alexander. **Mammals of the Mexican Boundary of the United States.** Part I: Families Didelphiidae to Muridae. 1907

Merriam, Clinton Hart. **The Mammals of the Adirondack Region,** Northeastern New York. 1884

Nuttall, Thomas. **A Manual of the Ornithology of the United States and of Canada.** Two vols. 1832-1834

Nuttall Ornithological Club. **Bulletin of the Nuttall Ornithological Club:** A Quarterly Journal of Ornithology. 1876-1883. Eight vols. in three.

[Pennant, Thomas]. **Arctic Zoology.** 1784-1787. Two vols. in one.

Richardson, John. **Fauna Boreali-Americana;** Or the Zoology of the Northern Parts of British America, Containing Descriptions of the Objects of Natural History Collected on the Late Northern Land Expeditions Under Command of Captain Sir John Franklin, R. N. Part I: Quadrupeds. 1829

Richardson, John and William Swainson. **Fauna Boreali-Americana:** Or the Zoology of the Northern Parts of British America, Containing Descriptions of the Objects of Natural History Collected by the Late Northern Land Expeditions Under Command of Captain Sir John Franklin, R. N. Part II: The Birds. 1831

Ridgway, Robert. **Ornithology.** 1877

Selected Works By Eighteenth-Century Naturalists and Travellers. 1974

Selected Works in Nineteenth-Century North American Paleontology. 1974

Selected Works of Clinton Hart Merriam. 1974

Selected Works of Joel Asaph Allen. 1974

Selections From the Literature of American Biogeography. 1974

Seton, Ernest Thompson. **Life-Histories of Northern Animals: An Account of the Mammals of Manitoba.** Two vols. 1909

Sterling, Keir Brooks. **Last of the Naturalists:** The Career of C. Hart Merriam. 1974

Vieillot, L. P. **Histoire Naturelle Des Oiseaux de L'Amerique Septentrionale,** Contenant Un Grand Nombre D'Especes Decrites ou Figurees Pour La Premiere Fois. 1807. Two vols. in one.

Wilson, Scott B., assisted by A. H. Evans. **Aves Hawaiienses:** The Birds of the Sandwich Islands. 1890-99

Wood, Casey A., editor. **An Introduction to the Literature of Vertebrate Zoology.** 1931

Zimmer, John Todd. **Catalogue of the Edward E. Ayer Ornithological Library.** 1926